WORLD FACTS
AND FIGURES

The planet Earth photographed from the Apollo 17 spacecraft during the sixth and last successful lunar landing mission in December 1972. (Credit: NASA.)

WORLD FACTS AND FIGURES
Third Edition

Victor Showers

WILEY

A Wiley-Interscience Publication

JOHN WILEY & SONS

New York / Chichester / Brisbane / Toronto / Singapore

Library of Congress Cataloging in Publication Data

Showers, Victor, 1910–
    World facts and figures / Victor Showers. — 3rd ed.
        p.   cm.

    "A Wiley-Interscience publication."
    Bibliography: p.
    Includes index.
    ISBN 0-471-85775-0
    1. Geography—Tables. 2. Cities and towns—Statistics.

I. Title.
G109.S52   1989   88-31698
910′.212—dc19   CIP

Printed in the United States of America

10 9 8 7 6 5 4 3 2

CONTENTS

PREFACE TO THE THIRD EDITION

The second edition of *World Facts and Figures* (1979) included tabular data for all countries on nine subjects: area, current population, density of population, evolution of population from the year 1800, birth rates, death rates, life expectancy, energy production and consumption, and gross national product. The third edition has similar data on 19 subjects, updating the original nine and adding: urbanization rates, natural increase in population, infant mortality rates, exports and imports by value, roads and motor vehicles, railroad route lengths and traffic, airline traffic, telephones and radio and television receivers, total school and college and university enrollments, and rates of illiteracy.

The number of comparative rankings of the (usually 50) leading countries in all categories has been tripled—from 15 in the second edition to 45 in the third.

By adding to the previously listed (1) cities of considerable size, (2) historically important cities, and (3) cities attractive to tourists: (1) university centers and (2) capitals of countries and their major divisions, regardless of size, the number of world cities for which data are given has been increased by 30% (from 2045 to 2664), and the number of US cities has been increased by 50% (from 426 to 637).

Even the basic and comparative tables of geographic features (seas, islands, rivers, mountains, lakes, and waterfalls) have been revised and expanded, particularly those relating to seas. In this category, the second edition listed only 65 entries and gave only the area of each, whereas the third edition lists 132 and supplies both area and greatest depth for all entries.

* * *

An overall summary of the contents of the third edition is given in the Introduction, which follows. Here instead is a diversified sampling of the many striking and unexpected facts that emerge from a study of the book's various tables, with references to the pages where the information can be derived.

Niagara Falls is the greatest waterfall with a height of at least 100 feet, as measured by the volume of water carried—but only since 1982. In that year the Sete Quedas Falls on the Parana River, which used to rank first, was submerged by the Itaipu Dam. (See p 637.)

Question: Which is the largest sea adjacent to the Atlantic Ocean, the Mediterranean or the Caribbean? Surprising answer: Neither; the Weddell Sea in the Antarctic has a greater area than either of those two. (See p 484.)

The Amazon River in South America and the Congo River in Africa have the highest average discharge rates. How do they compare in this respect? There is no real comparison, for the discharge rate of the Amazon is more than four times greater than that of the Congo. In fact, five of the ten rivers with highest discharge rates are in South America. (See pp 562–563.)

It is true, as most people realize, that Africa includes more separate countries (58) than any other continent, but Africa is a large continent in area, and Europe, with only 38 separate countries, has far more for its size. In fact, the average area of European countries is only 104,000 square miles, while the average area of African countries is 202,000 square miles. On average, South America is the continent with the largest countries in area, for its 14 average 492,000 square miles. (See pp 4, 24.)

Excluding uninhabited Antarctica, the average area of all the world's 218 countries is 240,771 square miles. The Central African Republic comes closest with 240,535. The average population of all countries in mid-1986 was estimated to be 22,475,000. In population, Morocco was the most typical, with an estimated total of 22,476,000. (See pp 24, 29, 30.)

Every one knows that China, with over a billion inhabitants, is the largest country in population. It is not generally realized, however, that India's population already exceeds three-quarters of a billion. Or that the former British India—adding Pakistan, Bangladesh, and Burma to present-day India—also has more than a billion inhabitants and is growing nearly twice as fast as China. (See pp 7, 32, 34–35.)

Excluding countries with areas under 1,000 square miles, Bangladesh ranks first in density of population, followed in turn by Taiwan, South Korea, Puerto Rico, and the Netherlands. All five of these countries have population densities more than ten times the world average, but Bangladesh is more than twenty times as crowded as the world in general. Density of population throughout the world averages 84.6 persons per square mile, and the country that comes closest to that average is the Faeroe Islands, with a density of 85. Located in the Atlantic Ocean between Iceland and Scotland, the Faeroes have a latitude comparable to that of Anchorage, Alaska, or Yakutsk, Siberia, but, like Iceland itself, they are warmed by the Gulf Stream. (See pp 5–6, 24, 36, 360.)

Which is the world's largest city? According to the latest census figures (1980), the urbanized area of New York City had a population of 15,590,000 and that of Mexico City had only 13,354,000 inhabitants. Yet, with Mexico City's population increasing at an annual rate of 4.3% and New York's actually decreasing, it is probable that Mexico surpassed New York as the largest urbanized area sometime in the year 1984. (See pp 202, 224, 404, 405.)

In keeping with its new preeminence in population, Mexico City now boasts the largest university in the world. The Universidad Nacional Autonoma de Mexico, which ranked tenth a decade ago with 120,000 students, now enrolls about 327,000. (See p 440.)

Of course, Mexico still lags far behind in the total number of its college and university students (15 per thousand inhabitants compared with 53 for the USA), but the total number of students enrolled in its schools is quite respectable (23 million, or 59% of the school-age population, compared with 54 million, or 71%, in the USA). Strangely, however, the US Virgin Islands, Puerto Rico, and even the US Trust Territory of the Pacific Islands outrank the US itself in the percentage of school-age population attending schools. (See pp 125, 126, 399.)

The Isle of Man, a dependency of the UK in the Irish Sea, is universally known for its tailless cats, called Manx after the name of the island. It can now claim another distinction, for the latest statistics indicate that it has a higher proportion of college and university students than any other country—57 per thousand inhabitants, compared with 53 for the US, which ranks second. (See p 400.)

In 1976 the three leading countries in per capita GNP (or GDP) were all oil-producing states—Kuwait, the United Arab Emirates, and Qatar. Ten years later (oil prices having plummeted), the picture is drastically altered, and Switzerland, fourth in 1976, now ranks first in this important respect, with the USA coming in second and Norway third. Incidentally, Japan, which now ranks immediately behind Norway, ranked 24th in 1976. (See pp 11, 373.)

The chasm that separates the richest from the poorest countries is nowhere better exemplified than by comparing the highest and lowest rankings in GDP. Of the 16 trillion dollars of wealth created by 214 countries in the latest reported year, the 25 countries at the top of the rankings, with only 10% of the world's population, created 55%, while the 25 countries at the bottom, with 60% of the world's population, generated a mere 3%. (See pp 12, 373.)

Meanwhile, between 1975 and 1985, Japan has supplanted four countries in north-western Europe to become the leader in life expectancy by raising its average by three full years to 77.4 years. The USA, on the other hand, dropped from tenth to 15th place, and now ranks below Greece, Spain, and even Panama in this respect. But the life expectancy of no less than 30 developed countries is at least *twice* that of the three underdeveloped countries with lowest life expectancies—Sierra Leone, the Gambia, and war-ravaged Afghanistan. (See pp 9–10, 371.)

Despite its well-publicized unfavorable balance of trade, the USA ranked first in the value of both exports and imports during the period 1981–1986. But in the final year of that period it was finally outranked in exports, not by Japan but by West Germany. Yet on a per capita basis West Germany ranked 24th among 196 countries in the value of its exports in 1986 (Japan was 40th and the US 54th). (See pp 81, 86, 89, 383, 384, 386.)

Few would guess that the Falkland Islands, with 526 passenger cars per thousand inhabitants, ranks only slightly below the USA in the ownership of automobiles. Or that tiny Andorra, with 474 per thousand, ranks far ahead of both France and Spain, its powerful neighbors. These facts become less surprising, however, when one learns that the Falklands have a per capita GDP over twice that of any other country in South America, and that Andorra has a per capita GDP of about $10,000 as compared with one of about $13,000 for France and one only slightly above $4,000 for Spain. (See pp 67–69, 97, 100, 390.)

Although Japan builds more motor vehicles than any other country and has a greater road density than any except Belgium and a few small countries (nearly five times that of the US), it ranks 44th in the number of passenger cars in use per thousand inhabitants (236 compared with 552 for the US). (See pp 93–100, 390.)

Considering its expertise in electronics, it is surprising also that Japan ranks only 29th in the number of its radio receivers per thousand inhabitants (713 compared with 2,042 for the top-ranking USA). The comparable statistics for television receivers show Japan in sixth place with 556 per thousand inhabitants compared with 790 for the USA, which also leads all countries in this respect. (See pp 111–118, 396.)

Ranking 13th in the length of its railroad routes, Japan is nonetheless second only to the USSR in the volume of its railroad passenger traffic (and of course far ahead on a per capita basis). The USA, on the other hand, ranks first in length of routes (12 times greater than Japan's) but only tenth in passenger traffic (9% of Japan's). Japan, however, carries only 0.06% as much railroad freight as the USSR and only 1.6% as much as the USA, the two runaway leaders in that category. China, incidentally, ranks third in both passenger and freight traffic and fifth in the length of its railroad routes. (See pp 391–392.)

Probably the most notable engineering project of recent times, the Seikan Tunnel, which connects the main Japanese islands of Honshu and Hokkaido, was finally opened for traffic in 1988. It is two and a half times longer than any other railroad tunnel in the world. (See p 467.)

While the USSR maintains a dominant position in railroad passenger and freight traffic, the USA has an insurmountable lead in both kinds of civil airline traffic. USA airlines have a passenger traffic volume greater than all the airlines of the next ten countries combined, and a freight traffic volume greater than the combined airlines of Japan, France, and the USSR, which rank second, third, and fourth, respectively. It is noteworthy, however, that China, though still far behind the leaders in both categories, increased its airline passenger traffic by 239% and its airline freight traffic by 233% between 1980 and 1985. (See pp 15, 393.)

Japan now leads all large countries in having a low infant mortality rate, closely followed by Sweden, Iceland, Finland, and Switzerland, all of which lose fewer than seven children per thousand live births in the first year of life. At the other extreme, it is estimated that one or more out of every ten children born live dies before reaching the age of one year in 50 of 200 countries worldwide. Of these 50 countries, 34 are in Africa, 14 in Asia, one in North America (Haiti), and one in South America (Bolivia). (See pp 8–9, 56–64.)

At least half the adult (15 years and above) inhabitants in 46 out of 203 countries are currently reported to be illiterate. Thirty-one of the 46 are in Africa, 11 in Asia, one in North America (Haiti again), and three in Oceania. Even more shocking, however, is the fact that nine of the 46 countries have an illiteracy rate of at least 80%. (See p 402.)

Alexandria, Virginia   VICTOR SHOWERS
March, 1989

WORLD FACTS AND FIGURES

INTRODUCTION

The third edition of *World Facts and Figures,* completely revised and updated, provides a wealth of significant and comparative information about all of the world's 218 countries, 2,664 of its largest and best-known cities, and 2,982 geographic and cultural features. No other known work in any language gives such information on a strictly comparable basis.

As indicated in the table of contents, the book is divided into 11 main chapters. The first of these consists of 11 separate tables providing important data on the demography, economy, transportation, communications, and educational activities of all 218 countries, arranged alphabetically by continent.

The corresponding city tables of Chapter 2 occupy more than a third of the book's pages. Listing the 2,664 cities alphabetically by continent and country, these two extensive tables give for each city its latitude and longitude, elevation, date of settlement, growth of population from 1800 to the latest possible date, alternate and former names, hydrographic features, universities with their founding dates and enrollments, principal libraries with their founding dates and number of volumes, and for the larger countries the political or regional division in which the city is located. The number of cities for which this information is given is 30% greater than in the second edition of this work, which was published in 1979 (50% greater for US cities), chiefly because the present edition includes university centers and capitals of countries and their major divisions, even if they are much smaller than other cities in the tables.

Chapters 3 and 4 of *World Facts and Figures* are devoted, respectively, to country and city comparisons, compiled principally from the preceding two chapters. Here, for example, is a table ranking the 65 countries with largest areas and populations, and a table ranking the 50 countries with largest total and largest and smallest per capita gross domestic product (GDP). Altogether, there are 17 comparative country tables with a total of 45 different rankings (the second edition had only 15 such rankings).

The comparative city tables, each ranking more than 100 world cities by population, elevation, age, average temperature (warmest and coolest), and average precipitation (wettest and driest), are similar to those in the preceding edition, but the rankings are quite different, partly because of updating but chiefly because the number of cities compared is 30% greater.

Chapter 5, which provides statistical comparisons of the largest educational institutions and the greatest engineering projects (the so-called cultural features), is a revision of the second edition's chapter entitled "Outstanding Works of Man." Here are ranked

1

according to size the 100 largest universities, the 100 largest libraries, and a total of 561 of the highest buildings, longest bridges, longest railroad and highway tunnels, and highest and largest dams standing or under construction.

The last portion of the book—Chapters 6 through 11—is devoted to 2,218 geographic features, revising and expanding the comprehensive tables in Chapters 1 through 6 of the second edition. Here the largest seas, islands, and natural lakes, the longest rivers, and the highest mountains and waterfalls are listed according to size, usually by continent.

These basic geographic tables are not simple lists, such as one might find in an encyclopedia, almanac, or atlas, giving merely the conventional name of the feature and its area, length, or height. On the contrary, they are so constructed as to give the greatest amount of useful information consistent with clarity. The basic table of rivers, for example, which lists 710 of the longest and most important streams in the world, gives the conventional, alternate, and former names of the river and of its tributaries (if any) constituting the longest watercourse, the length of that watercourse in miles and kilometers, the area of its drainage basin in square miles and square kilometers, its average discharge rate in cubic feet per second and cubic meters per second, its outflow (sea, lake, or river) and the division and country in which that is located, and the latitude and longitude at the mouth of the river. The basic table of islands, listing 422 of the largest and best known, gives conventional, alternate, and former names, latitude and longitude at the center of the island, the principal body of water, the division and country in which the island is located, its area in square miles and square kilometers, its highest elevation in feet and meters, and (if inhabited) the name and latest population of the largest settlement.

Except for seas and waterfalls, these basic geographic tables, furthermore, are supplemented by subsidiary tables listing the largest island, longest river, and so forth, in each country. Other subsidiary tables rank the 50 largest seas, islands, and lakes and the 50 longest rivers irrespective of continent, but not the 50 highest mountains, since all of these are located in Asia. Finally, there are special tables showing the 50 rivers with largest drainage basins and the 50 with highest discharge rates, the 50 deepest lakes and the 20 with greatest volume of water, and the 13 waterfalls with greatest volume of water.

Following the 11 chapters summarized above is a Selected Bibliography of 258 references, arranged by subject, and a cross-reference index of approximately 9,700 names, arranged letter by letter in accordance with the English alphabet.

In compiling the tables in this book, official data have been used whenever they were available. When unofficial figures are given, they have been verified for authenticity if possible, but they are still identified as unofficial. The date of the information supplied is given in all tables where it is appropriate. Although each table is reasonably self-explanatory, its exact contents and coverage are described at the beginning of the table.

Because Arabic numerals are now employed universally, *World Facts and Figures* can be understood without difficulty by people in all countries. To increase its usefulness in countries that have adopted the metric system, most measurement data are given in both English and metric units.

Another important characteristic of the book is the provision of latitude and longitude for every city and almost every physiographic feature listed. This has been done to facilitate their location on maps and to make possible a rapid comparison of geographic positions. Many of the features cited, and even a few of the cities, cannot be found in a number of popular world atlases, either because the maps in these atlases have too small a scale or because they are not sufficiently up to date, but supplied with latitude and longitude, the reader can still locate them with respect to better-known features and cities that are shown in these atlases.

Since the information in most of the book's tables is derived from numerous official and unofficial sources, it is impossible to cite sources for each table, but the Selected Bibliography following Chapter 11 lists the more important sources from which this information has been taken. It should be noted, however, that some of the figures supplied in the tables are not found in any of the references cited in the Bibliography. A considerable number of the foundation dates for libraries, for example, are not given in any of the library directories listed. It is precisely to uncover more information, as well as for purposes of verification, that innumerable books and periodicals of a more specialized nature—population census reports, histories and guidebooks of particular localities, meteorological and water supply bulletins, and civil engineering and architectural journals—have also been consulted in the preparation of this work.

World Facts and Figures gives striking evidence of a shrinking earth. A few decades ago the compilation of an authoritative digest of comparative statistics of this scope would have been impossible. Now, with jet aircraft flying travelers to every corner of the globe and television flashing instant pictures of important events by satellite, there is no longer a *terra incognita* anywhere. Census taking has become almost universal, meteorological data are collected in nearly every important community, and some of the most underdeveloped nations vie with the most "advanced" in the production of official statistical yearbooks.

Nor is it only that we know more about the remote regions of the world. We have simultaneously acquired far greater knowledge of our own and neighboring countries. Until 50 years ago the longest watercourse of the Mississippi River (from the source of the Red Rock to the Gulf of Mexico) was generally regarded as the longest river in the world; its length was officially stated to be 4,221 miles, or 6,793 kilometers. By 1939, however, the US Geological Survey had reduced that figure to 3,988 miles (6,418 kilometers), and ten years later it was again reduced to 3,872 miles (6,231 kilometers). Further revisions have decreased the length to 3,710 miles (5,971 kilometers), and the Mississippi is now known to rank behind the Nile, Amazon, and Yangtze as the fourth longest of the world's great rivers.

CURRENT TRENDS IN WORLD FACTS AND FIGURES

As noted in Table 1a, which estimates their latest area and population, *World Facts and Figures* (Third Edition) records important information about all conventionally recognized countries regardless of size or sovereignty.

The total number is admittedly somewhat arbitrary, since six overseas departments of France (French Guiana, Guadeloupe, Martinique, Mayotte, Reunion, and Saint-Pierre and Miquelon) are listed as separate countries, whereas the external provinces of Spain constituting the Balearic and Canary Islands and the overseas districts of Portugal known as the Azores and the Madeira Islands are considered integral parts of the mother countries. It is partly for this reason that these Spanish and Portuguese possessions are listed as separate entities in Table 1a and some of the other country tables.

In any event, the total number of separate countries listed is now 218, divided by continents as follows:

Africa—58
Asia—44
Europe—38
North America—37
Oceania—27
South America—14

Since the publication of the preceding edition of *World Facts and Figures* in 1979, seven new names have been added to the roster of world countries:

Aruba, which was detached from the Netherlands Antilles in 1986.

Burkina Faso, renamed from Upper Volta in 1984.

Central African Republic, which resumed its old name after a three-year hiatus from 1976 to 1979, during which it was known as the Central African Empire.

Kampuchea, long the official short designation for Cambodia, now accepted as a conventional name in English.

Kiribati, which was known as the Gilbert Islands until it became independent in 1979.

Vanuatu, which was called the New Hebrides until it achieved independence in 1980. Zimbabwe, which was designated Southern Rhodesia until Northern Rhodesia became Zambia in 1964, and thereafter simply Rhodesia until it became independent in 1980.

Apart from these changes in name, there have been many significant changes in world facts and figures during the past ten years. A primary purpose of this summary is to highlight some of these changes and thereby to delineate some important trends in the various fields covered by this work.

INCREASE AND DISTRIBUTION OF POPULATION

Increasing at an annual rate of approximately 1.84%, the world's population has grown by more than 800 million during the ten-year period ending in 1986. If this rate of growth were to continue throughout the next decade, the total population would reach 6 billion by the year 1997. With this figure in mind, it is indeed startling to realize that world population only reached 1 billion around 1808 and 2 billion around 1927. The 3-billion mark was attained 33 years later in 1960, the 4-billion mark 15 years after that in 1975, and the 5-billion mark after only 12 more years in 1987.

As can be seen in Table 3a, more than a third of the world's total population is concentrated in two countries—China and India. The five largest countries (China, India, the USSR, the USA, and Indonesia) account for more than half the total—51.2% to be exact, according to the best estimates for 1 July 1986. This represents no significant change from 1976, when the same five countries held 51.8% of the world's inhabitants.

POPULATION DENSITIES

Largely because the USSR covers such a vast territory (almost 15% of all land area), the five countries that have more than half the world's population do not exhibit an unusually large total density. Together occupying 31.1% of all land area, they have a total population density of 139 persons per square mile (53.8 per square kilometer), compared with a world average of 84.6/mi^2 (32.7/km^2). But population density in the USSR is only 32.4/mi^2 (12.5/km^2), and three of the other four countries have densities far higher than the average. Moreover, if one includes the next five largest countries in population, the total density is still only 138/mi^2, yet seven of the ten have densities significantly higher than the world average, as the following table shows.

Country	1986 Population (thousands)	Surface Area (mi^2)	Population Density (per mi^2)
China	1,052,838	3,691,508	285
India	766,135	1,237,071	619
USSR	280,144	8,649,539	32.4
USA	241,596	3,679,395	65.7
Indonesia	166,940	741,101	225

Country (*cont.*)	1986 Population (thousands) (*cont.*)	Surface Area (mi²) (*cont.*)	Population Density (per mi²) (*cont.*)
Brazil	138,493	3,286,488	42.1
Japan	121,492	145,834	833
Pakistan	101,653	342,762	297
Bangladesh	100,616	55,598	1,810
Nigeria	98,517	356,669	276
Total	3,068,424	22,185,965	138
World	4,899,615	57,884,030	84.6

During the last decade (1976–1986), the average density of population throughout the world has increased by 20%—from 70.6/mi² to 84.6/mi²—and the density for the ten largest countries has increased by 19%—from 116/mi² to 138/mi².

POPULATION GROWTH RATES

It is not population density, however, that most concerns the underdeveloped nations but rather the threat of overpopulation. Death rates have sharply declined everywhere, as modern sanitary practices and medical advances have spread throughout the world, but birth rates have remained intractably high except in the largely industrialized countries. Thus the underdeveloped countries, faced with mounting population pressures, have failed to increase their wealth with respect to their industrialized counterparts. With the increased demand for energy, there are now a few more rich nations than there were a few years ago, but the gap between these rich nations and those that are poor is wider than ever, and calamities, such as drought or civil war, continually threaten the latter with widespread malnutrition and actual starvation.

We have noted, for example, that world population has grown during the last decade at an annual rate of 1.84%. But this average rate masks greatly different rates of growth among the various continents and individual countries. In Africa the annual rate of increase in population from 1976 to 1986 was above 2.8%, and in South America it was above 2.4%. Both of these continents include a number of underdeveloped countries. In Asia, where several highly developed nations coexist with a number of underdeveloped ones, the average growth rate was 2.0%. But the remaining three continents, where industrialized societies predominate, showed quite different rates of population increase: North America, 1.5%; Oceania, 1.5%; and Europe, only slightly above 0.4%.

Of the 50 countries that have the highest rates of natural increase in population (i.e., the greatest excess of births over deaths), 28 are in Africa. Nineteen of those 28 countries are among the 50 poorest as measured by per capita gross domestic product (GDP). The correlation between high birth rates and poverty is even closer. Thirty-nine of the 50 countries that rank highest by birth rate are in Africa, and 28 of those 39 are among the 50 that rank lowest in per capita GDP. (See Tables 3d, 3f, and 3i for more detail.)

The 25 largest countries together account for 78% of the world's population. Fifteen of them are growing faster than the average annual growth rate of 1.84%. In order of *annual percentage* growth, these are as follows:

Country	Actual Growth Rate, 1976–86	Rate of Natural Increase, 1980–85
Ethiopia	4.59e[1]	2.65e
Pakistan	3.18	2.77e
Iran	3.14	2.88e
Bangladesh	2.85	2.73e
Philippines	2.70	2.49e
Egypt	2.65	2.72
Vietnam	2.59	2.08e
Nigeria	2.49e	3.33e
Mexico	2.47	2.84
Brazil	2.41	2.22e
Turkey	2.36	2.08e
India	2.26	2.15e
Burma	2.17	2.52e
Indonesia	2.08	1.95e
Thailand	2.06	2.00e

The other ten countries are growing more slowly, as indicated below.

Country	Actual Growth Rate, 1976–86	Rate of Natural Increase, 1980–85
China	1.68e[2]	1.23e
South Korea	1.49	1.68
USA	1.17	0.70
USSR	0.92	0.89
Spain	0.76	0.58
Japan	0.72	0.62
France	0.45	0.41
Italy	0.18	0.11
UK	0.15	0.13
West Germany	− 0.08	−0.16

[1]This figure is obviously too high. The first complete census of Ethiopia was taken in 1984, and the estimate of its population in 1976 was apparently far too low.

[2]This figure assumes constant growth between 1964 and 1982 and accuracy of the censuses taken in those two years. (See Tables 1a and 1b for the totals.)

Note. Many of the rates of natural increase are marked "e" because a deficiency of registration data makes it necessary to estimate the birth and death rates.

Seven of the 25 countries listed above are among the 50 richest countries, as measured by per capita GDP, and seven are among the 50 poorest. The first group includes the USA, Japan, West Germany, France, Italy, the UK, and the USSR. The second group includes Ethiopia, Bangladesh, Burma, China, India, Vietnam, and Pakistan. (See Table 3i for more detail.)

BIRTH AND DEATH RATES

As indicated in the preceding section, birth rates in the underdeveloped countries have remained exceptionally high. Particularly is this true in Africa, where 22 of the 25 countries with the highest birth rates were located in the period 1980–85. Ten years earlier—in 1970–75—only 17 of the 25 that ranked highest were in the African continent. In the 20 African nations that ranked highest in this respect in 1980–85, the average birth rate actually increased during the past ten years from 47.9 per thousand inhabitants to 49.9. And in the 20 African nations that ranked highest in 1970–75, the average birth rate declined insignificantly, from 49.3 to 48.8.

Among countries with the lowest birth rates, an equally high proportion is located in Europe—18 of the first 25 in 1971–75 and 22 of the first 25 in 1981–86. Moreover, the birth rates in Europe seem still to be declining. Among the 20 European countries with the highest birth rates in 1981–86, the average rate dropped from 14.8 in 1971–75 to 12.0 in 1981–86, while the 20 European nations that ranked highest in the earlier period showed a decline from 13.7 in 1971–75 to 12.5 in 1981–86.

Meanwhile, the death rate in Africa, although still far above that of the more developed areas of the world, continues to decline, thereby exacerbating the remarkably high rate of growth in population. In the 20 African nations with the highest birth rates in 1980–85, for instance, the average death rate fell from 21.8 in 1970–75 to 20.1 in 1980–85. These African figures are of course estimates, but there is no reason to doubt the trend.

In Europe, on the other hand, the death rate during the past decade has remained almost stationary. For the 20 European nations with the lowest birth rates in the period 1981–86, the average death rate was 10.4 in 1971–75 and 10.3 in 1981–86. With declining birth rates and constant death rates, five countries in that continent have already attained a negative or zero natural growth rate, and seven others have reached the stage where their annual excess of births over deaths ia approximately 0.1% or less. All but two of these had higher natural growth rates ten years ago, as shown below.

Country	Annual Percentage Rate of Natural Increase, 1971–75	Annual Percentage Rate of Natural Increase, 1981–86
Isle of Man	−0.37	−0.43
West Germany	−0.11	−0.16
Hungary	0.42	−0.14
Denmark	0.46	−0.09
Austria	0.07	0
Channel Islands	0.04	0.02
East Germany	−0.23	0.04
Sweden	0.30	0.04
Luxembourg	−0.05	0.05
Belgium	0.11	0.07
Italy	0.61	0.11
UK	0.23	0.13

Twenty-four of the 25 countries with the lowest rates of natural increase in population are located in Europe. (See Table 3f for further detail.)

The rate of infant mortality, which is defined as the number of deaths per thousand live births that occur in the first year of life, is today considered a prime criterion of the quality of life. According to the latest available data, this rate ranges from less than 4 for the two smaller countries of Andorra and Monaco to 205 for war-ravaged Afghanistan. Among countries with a total population of at least 100,000, the lowest rates of infant mortality are found in:

Rank	Country	Year	Rate
1.	Japan	1985	5.5
2.	Sweden	1986	5.9
3.	Iceland	1984	6.1
4.	Finland	1985	6.3
5.	Switzerland	1985	6.9
6.	Macao	1986	7.2
7.	Hong Kong	1985	7.5
7.	Taiwan	1984	7.5
9.	Canada	1985	7.9
9.	Denmark	1985	7.9
9.	France	1986	7.9
9.	Luxembourg	1986	7.9

The extremely high rates of infant mortality are almost invariably estimates, since few of the underdeveloped nations maintain accurate or detailed records of births and deaths, but 50 of the 200 countries worldwide for which infant deaths, estimated or not, are available now have rates in excess of 100 per thousand births. Of those 50 countries, 34 are in Africa, 14 in Asia, one in North America (Haiti), and one in South America (Bolivia). It is rather surprising to find Saudi Arabia, Oman, and Iran among the 50 highest, since all three are above average in per capita income. (See Table 3g for more detail.)

LIFE EXPECTANCY

Although the number of years people can, on average, expect to live is not ascertainable with any certainty in most of the underdeveloped world, the latest estimates indicate that in at least three countries—Sierra Leone, the Gambia, and Afghanistan—the average length of life is less than half that of at least 25 countries that rank highest in life expectancy. Those three countries have lower life expectancies than they had ten years ago.

In general, however, even the underdeveloped nations have made considerable progress in this respect during the past decade. Of 164 countries for which such estimates were available ten years or so ago, only 14 have lower life expectancies in the latest statistics. Two of these (Afghanistan and Kampuchea) are in Asia, one (Poland) is in Europe, two (Mexico and Montserrat) are in North America, and two more (Fiji and Kiribati) are in Oceania. The other seven (the Gambia, Guinea, Namibia, Sierra Leone, Somalia, the Sudan, and Uganda) are in Africa, but it is only fair to note that many of the African countries have increased their life expectancies more impressively than the highly industrialized nations. The latter have continued to inch up to higher levels, but observe these improvements among the more populous African states:

Country	Life Expectancy, 1970–75 (years)	Life Expectancy, 1980–85 (years)	% Increase
Algeria	53.2	59.9	12.6
Egypt	51.7	59.5	15.1
Ethiopia	38.0	40.9	7.6
Ghana	43.5	52.0	19.5
Kenya	49.0	57.0	16.3
Morocco	52.9	58.3	10.2
Nigeria	36.9	49.8	35.0
South Africa	51.5	63.6	23.5
Tanzania	40.4	51.0	26.2
Zaire	43.5	50.0	14.9

Meanwhile, the ten nations that ranked highest in life expectancy a decade ago have registered improvements ranging from 0.8 to 4.2% and averaging only 2.7%, as shown below.

Country	Life Expectancy, ca 1975 (years)	Life Expectancy, ca 1985 (years)	% Increase
Norway	74.9	76.2	1.7
Sweden	74.9	76.9	2.7
Iceland	74.5	76.5	2.7
Netherlands	74.5	76.3	2.4
Japan	74.4	77.4	4.0
Denmark	73.9	74.5	0.8
Switzerland	73.3	76.4	4.2
France	72.9	74.7	2.5
Canada	72.8	75.4	3.6
USA	72.6	74.7	2.9

In consequence of these changes, Japan has now moved into first place with an average life expectancy of 77.4 years, while Denmark, France, Canada, and the USA have lost their places among the first ten and have been replaced by the Faeroe Islands, Greece, Australia, and Spain. Table 3h provides a ranksd list of the 50 countries with the currently highest and lowest life expectancies.

Table 1c gives the latest available data on the respective life expectancies of men and women in 202 countries. In only five of those 202 countries can men expect to live longer than women, and all five are in Asia—Bhutan, India, Iran, the Maldives, and Nepal. In the developed world, where life expectancy is highest for both sexes, women can expect, on average, to live about six years longer than men. In the 25 countries with highest expectancies, for example, the difference was 6.2 years ca 1975 and 5.9 years ca 1985.

GROSS DOMESTIC PRODUCT (GDP)

It is technically inexact (and could be misleading) to use GDP or GNP (gross national product) data as a measure of national or per capita wealth. These data represent only the market value of the goods and services produced within a given country during a particular year. (For the distinction between GDP and GNP, see note 1 on p 65.) When converted into a common currency, such as the US dollar, however, they do permit a rough comparison of the economic output of various countries. And in conjunction with population statistics (i.e., per capita GDP), they serve as an indication of comparative personal income among the various countries. Unfortunately, the GDP or GNP figures given for the so-called "Communist countries" and for a number of smaller non-Communist countries are only estimates of no official standing and of doubtful validity, and should be regarded with skepticism.

Bearing all this in mind, we find that for the latest year of record (usually 1985 or 1986) the five nations standing highest in GDP togethsr accounted for 61.5% of the total GDP given for all 214 reporting countries, which was almost exactly $16 trillion. (See Table ld for particulars.) The same five nations ranked highest in 1976, at which time they accounted for 55.9% of the total, as the following table shows.

| | % of Total Reported GDP (GNP) | |
Country	1985–86	1976
USA	26.2	25.2
USSR	12.9	10.5
Japan	12.3	8.2
West Germany	5.6	6.8
France	4.5	5.2

Excluding countries with fewer than 100,000 inhabitants, Switzerland has the highest per capita GDP, according to the latest available figures, followed in turn by the USA, Norway, Japan, and Iceland. The ranking was very different in 1976, when the top five countries were, in order, Kuwait, the United Arab Emirates, Qatar, Switzerland, and Sweden. The United Arab Emirates still ranks sixth, but falling oil prices have plunged Kuwait and Qatar into 15th and 16th places, respectively. The following table shows the top ten countries in per capita GDP (GNP) for 1976 and for 1985 or 1986.

| | 1976 Per Capita GNP | | | 1985/1986 Per Capita GDP | |
Rank	Country	Million US Dollars	Rank	Country	Million US Dollars
1.	Kuwait	15,984	1.	Switzerland	20,820
2.	United Arab Emirates	14,428	2.	USA	17,362
3.	Qatar	14,059	3.	Norway	16,738
4.	Switzerland	8,966	4.	Japan[1]	16,155
5.	Sweden	8,671	5.	Iceland	15,955
6.	USA	7,894	6.	United Arab Emirates	15,803
7.	Canada	7,573	7.	Sweden	15,699
8.	Denmark	7,445	8.	Brunei	15,277
9.	West Germany	7,438	9.	West Germany	14,664
10.	Norway	7,432	10.	Finland	14,354

[1]In 1976 Japan ranked 24th with a per capita GNP of only $4,891 million.

The startling contrast between the 50 highest-ranked countries in per capita GDP and the 50 lowest-ranked ones is shown in Table 3i. The former range from an annual $20,820 to $6,465, the latter from a mere $81 to only $480. The highest-ranked 50 countries include 25 in Europe, 10 in North America, seven each in Asia and Oceania, and one in Africa (Libya). The lowest-ranked 50 countries, on the other hand, include 33 in Africa, 15 in Asia, and one each in North America (Haiti) and Oceania (Kiribati). Note that South America is not represented in either list.

GDP data not only provide a graphic illustration of the gulf that separates the rich nations from the poor, they also emphasize the pervasiveness of the world's poverty. The 25 countries that rank highest in per capita GDP in Table 3i, for example, had a total population of 546,958,000 in 1986 and a combined GDP of $8,767,567 million, while the 25 countries that rank lowest had a total population of 2,156,820,000 and a combined GDP of only $512,252 million. In effect, 10% of the world's inhabitants generated 55% of the total GDP, while 60% of its inhabitants created a mere 3%.

ENERGY PRODUCTION AND CONSUMPTION

In the ten years between 1975 and 1985 the world production of primary commercial energy increased by 10.8%. (Primary commercial energy includes coal and lignite, crude petroleum and natural gas liquids, natural gas, and hydro and nuclear electricity.) During the same period world consumption of energy increased by 14.4%. Both figures are considerably below the percentage increase in population but may, of course, reflect improved energy efficiency rather than a decline in living standards.

Far more interesting is the relative standing of the leading countries. In 1985 just three countries—the USSR, the USA, and China—accounted for 52.5% of the total world energy production, and the 13 leading countries accounted for 75% of the total. Ten years earlier the same three countries provided exactly 50% of the energy produced, but 75% of the total production was concentrated in only 11 countries. The rankings and proportions also changed considerably, as the USA, Saudi Arabia, Iran, Venezuela, West Germany, and Iraq went down the scale, while the USSR, Canada, the UK, Mexico, India, and Australia moved up. The following table compares the 1975 and 1985 production levels of countries supplying 75% of the world's primary commercial energy.

	1975 Energy Production				1985 Energy Production		
Rank	Country	1,000 MT[1]	% of Total	Rank	Country	1,000 MT[1]	% of Total
1.	USA	2,036,671	23.8	1.	USSR	2,167,893	22.9
2.	USSR	1,650,472	19.3	2.	USA	2,016,276	21.3
3.	China	596,812	7.0	3.	China	798,368	8.4
4.	Saudi Arabia	530,102	6.2	4.	Canada	324,770	3.4
5.	Iran	426,636	5.0	5.	UK	324,287	3.4
6.	Canada	268,424	3.1	6.	Saudi Arabia	258,115	2.7
7.	Venezuela	201,113	2.3	7.	Mexico[3]	249,542	2.6
8.	Poland	192,417	2.2	8.	India[3]	182,230	1.9

1975 Energy Production				1985 Energy Production		
Rank	Country	1,000 MT[1]	% of Total	Rank	Country	1,000 MT[1]	% of Total
9.	UK	183,988	2.1	9.	Poland	175,347	1.8
10.	West Germany	165,867	1.9	10.	Australia[3]	171,147	1.8
11.	Iraq[2]	165,620	1.9	11.	Iran	169,692	1.8
				12.	West Germany	160,727	1.7
				13.	Venezuela	156,427	1.6

[1]1,000 metric tons of coal equivalent.
[2]In 1985 Iraq ranked 20th.
[3]In 1975 Mexico ranked 20th, India 15th, and Australia 18th.

The energy consumption comparisons are far more stable, since the rankings of the first eight countries were identical in 1975 and 1985. The USA and the UK, however, used a considerably smaller share of the energy consumed in the latter year, while India and Mexico used a much larger share. A comparison of the consumption levels for the countries that used 75% of the world total follows.

1975 Energy Consumption				1985 Energy Consumption		
Rank	Country	1,000 MT[1]	% of Total	Rank	Country	1,000 MT[1]	% of Total
1.	USA	2,349,549	29.3	1.	USA	2,276,274	24.8
2.	USSR	1,410,781	17.6	2.	USSR	1,708,248	18.6
3.	China	570,467	7.1	3.	China	720,468	7.9
4.	Japan	401,884	5.0	4.	Japan	448,505	4.9
5.	West Germany	330,490	4.1	5.	West Germany	349,947	3.8
6.	UK	295,329	3.7	6.	UK	276,790	3.0
7.	Canada	225,568	2.8	7.	Canada	251,978	2.7
8.	France	208,877	2.6	8.	France	219,292	2.4
9.	Poland	170,338	2.1	9.	India	192,966	2.1
10.	Italy	168,088	2.1	10.	Italy	188,611	2.1
				11.	Poland	172,393	1.9
				12.	Mexico	132,491	1.4

[1]1,000 metric tons of coal equivalent.

EXPORTS AND IMPORTS

Measured in US currency, the average annual volume of world foreign trade from 1981 through 1986 was valued at nearly $4 trillion, and between those two years exports increased by 7.9% and imports by 9.3%. (See Table 1f for details.) For the year 1986 total exports amounted, on average, to $434 and imports to $454 for each of the 4 billion 900 million persons on earth.

During 1981–86 the USA, West Germany, and Japan alone accounted for nearly a third of all exports and imports, and two-thirds were monopolized by the 11 leading countries in each category. The two lists are remarkably similar, as the following table shows.

	Annual Value of Exports, 1981–86				Annual Value of Imports, 1981–86		
Rank	Country	Million US Dollars	% of Total	Rank	Country	Million US Dollars	% of Total
1.	USA	215,815	11.2	1.	USA	314,666	15.7
2.	West Germany	186,249	9.7	2.	West Germany	161,844	8.1
3.	Japan	165,423	8.6	3.	Japan	132,337	6.6
4.	France	99,278	5.2	4.	France	113,727	5.7
5.	UK	99,113	5.1	5.	UK	107,351	5.3
6.	USSR	87,190[1]	4.5	6.	Italy	88,791	4.4
7.	Canada	78,827	4.1	7.	USSR	78,910[1]	3.9
8.	Italy	78,574	4.1	8.	Canada	68,983	3.4
9.	Saudi Arabia	70,508[2]	3.7	9.	Netherlands	65,527	3.3
10.	Netherlands	69,236	3.6	10.	Belgium	59,356	3.0
11.	Belgium	55,725	2.9	11.	Saudi Arabia	34,484[1]	1.7

[1]1981–1985.
[2]1981–1984.

Although the relative standing for the entire six-year period of the 11 nations that predominate in world trade was almost identical for exports and imports, the trend from 1981 to 1986 was quite different. The USA, for example, lost 7% in exports and gained 42% in imports, while West Germany increased its exports by 38% and its imports by 16%, and Japan gained 38% in exports and lost 12% in imports. As a result, West Germany ranked first in exports in 1986 with 11.4% of the world total, while the USA had 10.2% and Japan 9.8%. Meanwhile, 17.4% of all imports were streaming into the USA in 1986, as compared with 13.4% in 1981.

The difference in the foreign trade figures between 1981 and 1986 for the 11 major trading nations was as follows:

Country	Exports	Imports	Country	Exports	Imports
USA	Down 7.0%	Up 41.6%	Italy	Up 30.1%	Up 9.8%
West Germany	Up 37.7%	Up 15.6%	Canada	Up 23.9%	Up 22.3%
Japan	Up 37.6%	Down 11.8%	Netherlands	Up 17.2%	Up 14.7%
France	Up 17.8%	Up 6.6%	Belgium	Up 23.6%	Up 9.9%
UK	Up 4.1%	Up 22.9%	Saudi Arabia	Down 69.4%[2]	Down 33.0%[1]
USSR	Up 10.2%[1]	Up 13.4%[1]			

[1]Between 1981 and 1985.
[2]Between 1981 and 1984.

Table 1f gives the actual export and import figures for each of the six years as well as averages for the entire period and per capita values for 1986. The balance of foreign trade can readily be determined by subtracting the import from the export figures.

On a per capita basis, many smaller countries outrank the 11 major trading nations by a wide margin, as Table 3k makes abundantly clear. Belgium ranks 11th in exports and 12th in imports, and the Netherlands is number 17 in exports and number 22 in imports, but the others rank even farther down the scale, and the USA and USSR do not even rank among the top 50 in either category.

AIRLINE PASSENGER AND FREIGHT TRAFFIC

Civil airline passenger traffic increased by 41% between 1980 and 1985, and freight traffic by 32%. In the former year US airlines accounted for 41% of the passenger traffic and 28% of the freight traffic. In 1985 the USA still maintained its dominant position, but its passenger share dropped to 36% and its share of freight traffic declined to 24%.

In fact, however, US airlines actually improved their standing in passenger traffic during that five-year period relative to the other leaders. Table 1i shows that only one of the ten top-ranked countries in 1985 exceeded the world average increase of 41%. The percentage increase in passenger traffic between 1980 and 1985 for each of the ten leaders (listed in order of traffic volume) is given below.

Country	% Increase	Country	% Increase
USA	25	France	18
USSR	17	Australia	− 1
UK	20	West Germany	16
Japan	24	Spain	30
Canada	0.5	Singapore	47

Many of the devoloping countries, on the other hand, registered large gains in airline passenger traffic, which markedly raised the world average. China was outstanding with a 239% increase between 1980 and 1985, but the following gains should also be noted: Cuba 152%, Nigeria 90%, Kuwait 79%, Thailand 71%, Algeria 65%, Indonesia 62%, Egypt 57%, and Saudi Arabia 55%.

The airline freight traffic picture is somewhat different, for among the ten top-ranked countries in 1985 in this respect no fewer than seven outpaced the average world gain of 32%. The percentage increase in freight traffic between 1980 and 1985 for each of these ten countries (again listed in order of traffic volume) is given below.

Country	% Increase	Country	% Increase
USA	13	UK	7
Japan	64	Taiwan	78
France	45	Netherlands	48
USSR	7	South Korea	59
West Germany	58	Canada	44

Again, China had a phenomenal increase of 233% in airline freight traffic, and the other developing nations cited above, except for Indonesia, registered gains far above the world average: Nigeria 438%, Egypt 238%, Saudi Arabia 176%, Kuwait 128%, Thailand 75%, Cuba 70%, Algeria 62%, and Indonesia 27%.

ABBREVIATIONS USED IN THIS WORK

AD	Anno Domini (i.e., since the birth of Christ)	km²	square kilometers
		L	lake
alt	alternate name (or names)	lag	lagoon
avg	average	lib	library
B	bay	m	meters
BC	before Christ (other dates are AD)	m³	cubic meters
		m³/sec	cubic meters per second
bef	before	mi	miles
bldg	building	mi²	square miles
c	century	mm	millimeters
C	Celsius (or centigrade)	mt	mountain (peak or massif)
ca	circa	mts	mountains (range or system)
cfs	cubic feet per second	N	north
ctry	country	ND	no date
e	estimated (other population data are from census returns)	NP	no place
		nr	near (usually, within approximately 10 mi, or 16 km)
E	east	NWT	Northwest Territories (of Canada)
ed	edition		
Ed	editor	O	ocean
elev	elevation (i.e., altitude above sea level)	off	official name (or names)
		p	page
exc	excluding	pp	pages
F	Fahrenheit	?	exact date unknown
for	former name (or names)	R	river
ft	feet	s	with adjacent suburban areas
ft²	square feet	S	south
G	gulf	sec	seconds
GDP	gross domestic product	UC	under construction
GNP	gross national product	UK	United Kingdom of Great Britain and Northern Ireland
I	island		
in	inches		
inc	including	univ	university
km	kilometers	unp	unpaged

US, USA	United States of America	•	unofficial data
USSR	Union of Soviet Socialist Republics	*	capital (of a country or a division of a country)
v	volume (or volumes)	***	used to divide tables into two
volc	active volcano		parts, the portion above
W	west		the *** representing all-
wf	waterfall		inclusive coverage and that
yd³	cubic yards		below the ***, selective
yrs	years		coverage
°	degrees (of temperature)		

GENERAL EXPLANATORY NOTES

A brief explanation of the contents and coverage of each statistical table in this work precedes the table in question. The notes in this section are of a more general nature or pertain to more than one table.

SPELLING

The spelling of geographic names accords generally with that in the various gazetteers initiated by the US Office of Geography and now published by the US Defense Mapping Agency (see reference 127 in Bibliography). Accent and other diacritical marks are omitted for simplicity.[1] Exception to this spelling rule is, of course, made when the name has been changed since publication of the relevant gazetteer or when, as evidenced by a consensus of later authorities, the spelling is manifestly outdated. The spelling of nongeographic names is that adopted officially or that approved by recognized authorities in the appropriate field.

CONVENTIONAL AND OTHER NAMES

Many cities and physiographic features have conventional names in English that differ from their official names. The difference may be substantial (as Casablanca for Dar al Baida or Florence for Firenze) or minimal (as Lyons for Lyon). In either case the conventional English name is always given in this work, and the initial citation of the city or feature is by this name if it is in general use. The official name or names, marked "off," are also given in appropriate places in the tables, and if no "off" name appears in these places, it can be assumed that the conventional name is also an official one.

Two other sorts of names appear in the tables: alternate ("alt") names and former ("for") names. If no "off" name is listed, the "alt" name or names are other official

---

[1]Readers versed in foreign languages will inevitably notice the omission of these diacritical marks. Since their primary function, however, is to indicate proper pronunciation, with which this work is not concerned, their inclusion would be of limited value at best. On the other hand, the marks are so numerous and so frequent in occurrence that their inclusion would serve to clutter the book, confuse the English-speaking reader, and raise serious problems in alphabetizing.

names or (rarely) English names infrequently used. Often these other official names are names used in another country. The Danube River, which flows through eight countries in Europe, has no fewer than six official names, none of which is Danube, the conventional English name. Sometimes, however, there is more than one official name within a single country. Helsinki and Helsingfors are both official names for the capital of Finland, since both Finnish and Swedish are official languages in that country.

Former ("for") names are, as the term implies, names that were once in general use but have become obsolete or obsolescent. Ancient (i.e., classical) names are not given in this book, but names dating from more recent historical periods are entered unless the name was used for a very brief time.

Countries are entered under their conventional short-form names in English, which have become familiar through repeated use in English-language books and periodicals. In the few instances in which common usage differs, alternate short-form names (e.g., Cambodia for Kampuchea; Western Samoa for Samoa) are given in footnotes to Table 1a and are cross-referenced in the index. Former short-form names for countries (e.g., Bechuanaland for Botswana; Friendly Islands for Tonga) are also cited in footnotes to Table 1a and cross-referenced in the index.

Most of these countries would probably prefer to be listed under the English equivalent of their more descriptive official names, such as Islamic Republic of Pakistan (rather than simply Pakistan) or Socialist Republic of the Union of Burma (rather than Burma). This nomenclature, however, would obviously be too unwieldy for use in statistical tables.

In addition to the employment of short-form names for countries to save space, three large countries are always entered under their commonly used abbreviations, as follows:

UK, for United Kingdom of Great Britain and Northern Ireland

USA, for United States of America

USSR, for Union of Soviet Socialist Republics

In the citation of foreign physiographic features, that portion of the name signifying river, mountain (or mount), lake, or the like is usually deleted, and an abbreviation for the English-language equivalent is substituted for it, unless, of course, this equivalent is a tabular heading. Thus the river known in Brazil as Rio Negro is listed simply as Negro in Tables 8a, 8c, and 8d and as Negro R (for River) in Table 2b. But note that foreign-language designations for river, and so on, used in countries where the language in question does not prevail, are not deleted. For example, Rio Grande R, not Grande R, designates the river in the southwestern USA.

In addition, when the foreign-language designation for a physiographic feature is little known, and especially when the particular feature is almost never cited in English-language works without its full name even though this makes the citation redundant, that portion of the name signifying river, and so forth, is retained but is parenthesized [e.g., (Tonle) Sap L and Kizil (Irmak) R]. Portions of conventional geographic names that are redundant or misleading but are invariably used are also retained and parenthesized [e.g., Dead (Sea)]. The Dead Sea is actually a saltwater lake.

ALPHABETIZATION

Some of the individual tables, as well as the index, are arranged alphabetically. Alphabetizing in this work is letter by letter, in accordance with the English alphabet, without regard for spaces, punctuation marks, or foreign combination letters. Thus Newark precedes New Britain, and Chile precedes Cienfuegos, even though the latter words are Spanish and in Spanish "ch" is a separate letter that follows the letter "c." Abbreviations are alphabetized as they are spelled (e.g., USA falls among the "us's," not among the "un's"). When, however, names begin with words like "Saint" that are often abbreviated in other books, these words are spelled out. And names beginning with Arabic numerals (e.g., 1600 Smith Street) are alphabetized as if the numerals were spelled out.

TRANSLATION AND TRANSLITERATION

In accordance with the practice of many educational authorities, the names of universities and libraries in countries where the more common Italic and Germanic languages prevail (i.e., most countries in western Europe) are entered in their original form (e.g., Universita degli Studi di Firenze and Deutsche Staatsbibliothek). The names of all other universities and libraries in countries where the English language does not prevail are translated into English.

Since the spelling of geographic names generally follows the pattern set by the US Defense Mapping Agency gazetteers, it follows that the systems of transliteration adopted by that agency in listing these names for countries that do not use the Roman alphabet are employed in this work. This accounts, for instance, for the spelling "Gorkiy" in preference to "Gorki," "Gorkii," or "Gorky."

The treatment of Chinese names requires a special explanation. In years past the predominant system of transliteration from Chinese to English was the so-called Wade-Giles system, which was originally followed in the gazetteers cited above and employed in the previous editions of this book. In 1979, however, the Chinese Government authorized the use of a different system of transliteration known as Pinyin, and this system is now in general use for English-language publications worldwide. In this edition, therefore, all Chinese cities and most Chinese physiographic features are initially entered under their Pinyin spellings. The only exceptions are a few seas, rivers, mountains, and lakes that are far better known by their conventional English-language names (e.g., Yangtze River). In these cases, the Pinyin spelling is also given—in parentheses after the abbreviation "off" (or "alt" if the feature is shared by another country)—in Tables 6a, 8a, 9a, and 10a. But because Pinyin spellings may still be unfamiliar to many readers, the older Wade-Giles spellings of cities and physiographic features are also given—in parentheses after the abbreviation "alt"—if they differ from Pinyin, in Tables 2b, 6a, 8a, 9a, and 10a. Also, of course, cross-reference entries can be found in the index, not only for the Wade-Giles spellings of Chinese names, but for other alternate and former names as well.

DEFINITION OF "UNIVERSITY"

For purposes of inclusion in this work, a university is defined as an educational institution that either of itself or in conjunction with constituent or affiliated institutions offers undergraduate work leading to a bachelor's degree and graduate work leading to at least a master's degree. In addition, however, so-called universities that offer work in only one specialized field (e.g., some agricultural and industrial "universities") are excluded from the listings even if they confer graduate degrees. Independent institutions that offer only graduate work are also excluded.

This definition, of course, excludes institutions that call themselves universities but confer no graduate degrees. On the other hand, a number of so-called colleges and institutes of technology have educational standards as high or higher than many of the qualifying universities. These are included if they confer doctorates, and the abbreviation "univ" is placed in parentheses after their names. Branch campuses of universities are entered in Table 2b only if they too offer work leading to both a bachelor's and a master's degree.

Because of the different standards that prevail in various countries, it is not always possible to apply this definition of "university" to the letter, but every effort has been made to adhere to it as closely as possible.

ROUNDING

Many of the statistical figures in this book are rounded. This means, for example, that a population of 151,743 is given as 152,000 (151,499 would, of course, become 151,000). Population data are usually rounded to the nearest 1,000, but when the original figure is less than 1,000 the rounding is done to the nearest 100. Other figures in the book may be rounded to the nearest 10 ft (m) (mountain elevations) or to the nearest three significant digits (island areas).[2] The extent of the rounding, when done, is described in the explanatory notes preceding individual tables.

Although the rounding of all population figures to the nearest 1,000 obviously saves space, since the word "thousands" can be inserted into the tabular heading and the figure printed as 152 instead of 152,000, the main purpose of rounding is to promote understanding—to make the statistical tables easier to read and the data they contain easier to comprehend. To one untrained in statistics, it might appear that rounding sacrifices accuracy, but this is not necessarily so. If done with discrimination, it may actually enhance statistical significance. To say that Mount Lucania is 17,147 feet high is really misleading, for mountain elevations cannot be determined with such accuracy. As for populations, they tend to grow so fast and the census techniques by which they are ascertained are so inexact that expressions of their size to the last digit are meaningless.

DIVISIONS OF COUNTRIES

No statistical data are given for political or regional divisions of countries, nor are they listed in the index. Nevertheless, such divisions are cited throughout the book for larger countries, both to facilitate the location of cities and physiographic features and for general interest. Only "great" divisions are listed (e.g., regions rather than departments for France), and these are cited by conventional or official names[3] without alternative designations. The following kinds of divisions are listed:

[2] This means, for instance, that the area of Madagascar, which is greater than 100,000 mi2 and 100,000 km2, is given as 227,000 mi2, or 587,000 km2; and that of Reunion, which is less than 1,000 mi2 and less than 10,000 km2, is given as 969 mi2, or 2,510 km2.

[3] Official names are used for the divisions of France, Italy, Spain, and West Germany because only a few of these have different conventional names in English.

Argentina—provinces
Australia—states and territories
Brazil—states and territories
Canada—provinces and territories
China—provinces and regions
Czechoslovakia—regions
France—regions
India—states and territories
Indonesia—islands
Italy—regions
Japan—islands
Libya—regions
Malaysia—divisions
Mexico—states and territories
New Zealand—islands
Philippines—islands
Saudi Arabia—regions
South Africa—provinces
Spain—regions
Tanzania—divisions
UK—divisions
USA—states
USSR—republics
West Germany—states
Yugoslavia—republics

LATITUDE AND LONGITUDE

Further to facilitate geographic location, latitude and longitude to the nearest minute are given for all cities and almost all physiographic features. Almost exclusively, the latitudes and longitudes are derived from the US Defense Mapping Agency gazetteers mentioned previously; these are based on official large-scale maps of the relevant countries and regions. They can therefore be depended upon for accuracy. For reasons of simplicity they are given in this form: 50.46N, 6.06E (this defines the geographic position of Aachen, West Germany, and means 50 degrees 46 minutes north of the equator and 6 degrees 6 minutes east of Greenwich, a section of London).

SPECIAL SYMBOLS

Every effort has been made to obtain official data for the various statistical tables. If such data are unavailable, the most reliable unofficial figures are given. In Tables 7a through 10e, unofficial data are identified by the symbol "●" placed before the name of the physiographic feature in question.

All population figures are from census returns except those for which an "e" is placed after the year of record; the "e," of course, indicates that the figure has been estimated, usually by official sources. For many cities, two sets of population figures are given. Figures without a symbol are for the city proper; those followed by an "s" are for the city and adjacent suburban areas. Preferably, the latter figures are for the urbanized area or conurbation only, but some officially reported suburban areas include rural districts.

The asterisk (*) is another special symbol used in this work. This symbol indicates that the city cited is the capital of a country or division. If the asterisk is placed before the name of the city, it is the capital of the country under which it is listed. If the asterisk is placed before the name of the division, the city cited is the capital of that division. It should be noted that some countries have more than one capital.

Finally, most of the tables that are arranged by some measurement, rather than alphabetically, are divided into two parts separated by three centered asterisks (***). When this division is made, the portion of the table that is above the centered asterisks represents all-inclusive coverage, and the portion that is below, selective coverage.

AREA AND POPULATION OF CONTINENTS AND OF THE WORLD

Contents

Conventional name of continent.

Surface area, including inland waters and adjacent islands,[1] in square miles and square kilometers, and percentage of world total.

Estimated population on 1 July 1986, in thousands, and percentage of world total.

Density of population on 1 July 1986 (estimated population divided by surface area) per square mile and per square kilometer.

Coverage

All seven continents.

Entries

8.

AREA AND POPULATION OF CONTINENTS AND OF THE WORLD

Continent	Surface Area			1986 Estimated Population		Density of Population	
	mi²	km²	%	Thousands	%	Per mi²	Per km²
Africa	11,717,589	30,348,430	20.2	570,011	11.6	48.6	18.8
Antarctica	5,395,775	13,975,000	9.3	0	0	0	0
Asia	17,089,047	44,260,448	29.5	2,937,776	60.0	172	66.4
Europe	3,953,394	10,239,247	6.8	689,556	14.1	174	67.3
North America	9,392,593	24,326,715	16.2	402,536	8.2	42.9	16.5
Oceania	3,453,274	8,943,942	6.0	27,258	0.6	7.89	3.05
South America	6,882,358	17,825,232	11.9	272,478	5.6	39.6	15.3
World	57,884,030	149,919,014	100	4,899,615	100	84.6	32.7

[1]In this work the islands of the West Indies, as well as the countries of so-called "Central America," are considered to be part of North America.

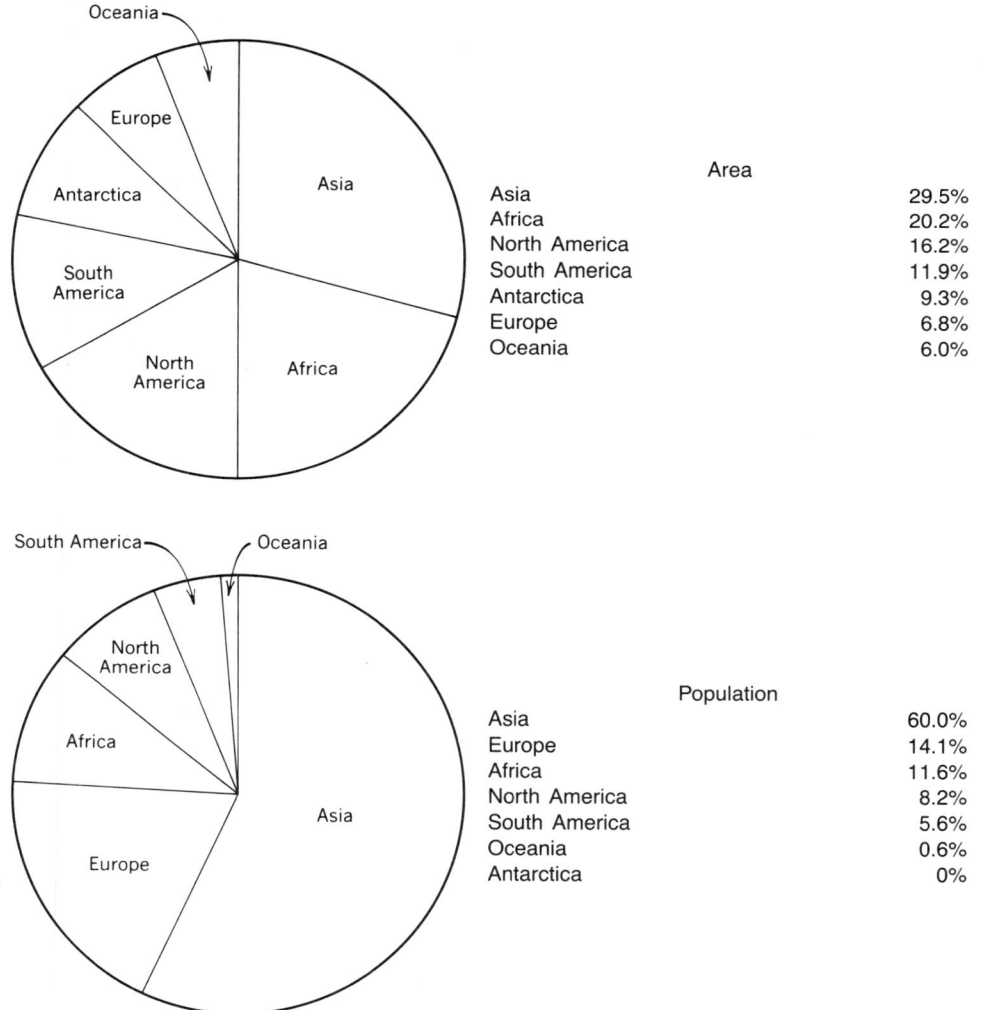

Area	
Asia	29.5%
Africa	20.2%
North America	16.2%
South America	11.9%
Antarctica	9.3%
Europe	6.8%
Oceania	6.0%

Population	
Asia	60.0%
Europe	14.1%
Africa	11.6%
North America	8.2%
South America	5.6%
Oceania	0.6%
Antarctica	0%

Figure 1. *Area and population of continents.*

1

COUNTRY TABLES, BY CONTINENT

DEMOGRAPHY

1a. Latest Area, Population, Density of Population, and Rate of Urbanization

Contents

Conventional name of country. (Alternate and former names are given in footnotes.)

Surface area of land and inland waters (lakes and rivers), in square miles and square kilometers.

Latest census population in thousands, with year of data in parentheses.

Estimated population, in thousands, on 1 July 1986. Most of the figures given here are official estimates, based either on registration data or on birth, death, and migration records. Only occasionally are they simple projections from past growth rates.

Density of population in 1986 (estimated population divided by surface area), per square mile and per square kilometer.

Percentage of population residing in urban areas at the latest date for which this information is available, with year of data in parentheses.[1]

Coverage

All countries, regardless of size or sovereignty, but excluding provinces, states, territories, and regions generally recognized as divisions of another country (e.g., Tibet, a division of China, and the Ukraine, a division of the USSR). For historical reasons, however, some states and other areas that once were separate countries are entered under the names of the countries of which they are now divisions. All countries located in more than one continent are listed under each applicable continent.

---

[1]The data in this column are not strictly comparable, since each country has its own definition of the term "urban area." The various definitions are given in the 1985 *Demographic Yearbook* of the United Nations, pp 172–175 (see reference 153 in Bibliography).

Rounding

Populations are rounded to the nearest 1,000 (to the nearest 100 if the total is less than 10,000).

Densities of population are rounded to the nearest three significant digits.

Entries

249, as follows: Africa—63

Asia—53

Europe—48

North America—40

Oceania—30

South America—15

TABLE 1a. LATEST AREA, POPULATION, DENSITY OF POPULATION, AND RATE OF URBANIZATION

Country	Surface Area		Latest Population (thousands)		Density of Population		% Urban and Year
	mi²	km²	Census and Year	1986 Estimate	Per mi²	Per km²	
AFRICA							
Algeria	919,595	2,381,741	18,250 (1977)	22,421	24.4	9.41	43.0 (1980)
Angola[1]	481,354	1,246,700	5,646 (1970)	8,981	18.7	7.20	21.0 (1982)
Benin[2]	43,484	112,622	3,331 (1979)	4,042	93.0	35.9	26.5 (1982)
Botswana[3]	231,805	600,372	941 (1981)	1,128	4.87	1.88	20.0 (1985)
British Indian Ocean Territory	23	60	0.7 (1962)	2.0	87.0	33.3	0
Burkina Faso[4]	105,869	274,200	7,747 (1985)	8,194	77.4	29.9	7.7 (1980)
Burundi[5]	10,747	27,834	4,114 (1979)	4,852	451	174	5.0 (1985)
Cameroon	183,569	475,442	7,090 (1976)	10,446	56.9	22.0	36.1 (1984)
Cape Verde	1,557	4,033	296 (1980)	342	220	84.8	22.3 (1980)
Central African Republic[6]	240,535	622,984	2,055 (1985)	2,740	11.4	4.40	35.3 (1980)
Chad	495,755	1,284,000	4,030 (1975)	5,139	10.4	4.00	23.9 (1986)
Comoros[7]	719	1,862	335 (1980)	402	559	216	23.3 (1980)
Congo[8]	132,047	342,000	1,300 (1974) 1,854 (1985)	1,900	14.4	5.56	43.3 (1980)
Djibouti[9]	8,958	23,200	81 (1960–61)	456	50.9	19.7	46.9 (1981)

[1]Inc Cabinda.
[2]For Dahomey.
[3]For Bechuanaland.
[4]For Upper Volta.
[5]For Urundi.
[6]For Ubangi-Shari.
[7]Exc Mayotte (alt Mahore), listed below, which was detached from the Comoros in 1976.
[8]For Middle Congo.
[9]For French Somaliland, French Territory of the Afars and the Issas.

(Continued)

TABLE 1a. (Continued)

Country	Surface Area		Latest Population (thousands)		1986 Estimate	Density of Population		% Urban and Year
	mi²	km²	Census and Year			Per mi²	Per km²	
Egypt	386,662	1,001,449	38,198	(1976)	49,609	128	49.5	44.6 (1985)
Equatorial Guinea[10]	10,831	28,051	304	(1983)	401	37.0	14.3	40.3 (1985)
Ethiopia[11]	471,778	1,221,900	42,169	(1984)	44,927	95.2	36.8	14.4 (1982)
Eritrea	45,328	117,400	2,615	(1984)	2,700	59.6	23.0	28.3 (1979)
French Southern and Antarctic Lands	2,922	7,567	0.2	(1970)	0.2	0.068	0.026	0
Gabon	103,347	267,667	950	(1969–70)	1,225	11.9	4.58	40.9 (1985)
Gambia	4,361	11,295	688	(1983)	760	174	67.3	18.2 (1980)
Ghana[12]	92,100	238,537	12,206	(1984)	12,840	139	53.8	31.3 (1984)
Guinea[13]	94,926	245,857	5,781	(1983)	5,970	62.9	24.3	16.2 (1980)
Guinea-Bissau[14]	13,948	36,125	768	(1979)	906	65.0	25.1	23.8 (1982)
Ivory Coast[15]	124,504	322,463	6,710	(1975)	10,165	81.6	31.5	42.5 (1983)
Kenya[16]	224,961	582,646	15,327	(1979)	21,163	94.1	36.3	17.7 (1983)
Lesotho[17]	11,720	30,355	1,217	(1976)	1,578	135	52.0	4.5 (1982)
			1,578	(1986)				
Liberia	43,000	111,369	1,503	(1974)	2,245	52.2	20.2	40.2 (1985)
			2,102	(1984)				
Libya	679,362	1,759,540	3,245	(1979)	3,805	5.60	2.16	53.9 (1981)
			3,637	(1984)				
Madagascar[18]	226,658	587,041	7,604	(1975)	10,303	45.5	17.6	17.6 (1980)
Malawi[19]	45,747	118,484	5,547	(1977)	7,279	159	61.4	11.7 (1984)
Mali[20]	478,767	1,240,000	6,395	(1976)	8,438	17.6	6.80	17.7 (1983)
Mauritania	397,956	1,030,700	1,481	(1976)	1,946	4.89	1.89	23.0 (1979)
Mauritius[21]	790	2,045	1,000	(1983)	1,029	1,303	503	41.7 (1984)
Mayotte	144	374	47	(1978)	69	479	184	23.1 (1980)
			67	(1985)				
Morocco[22]	172,414	446,550	20,450	(1982)	22,476	130	50.3	42.7 (1982)
Mozambique	309,496	801,590	11,674	(1980)	14,174	45.8	17.7	13.2 (1980)
Namibia[23]	318,261	824,292	1,033	(1981)	1,595	5.01	1.93	12.0 (1970)
Niger	489,191	1,267,000	5,098	(1977)	6,698	13.7	5.29	16.2 (1985)

Nigeria	356,669	923,769	79,759 (1973)	98,517	276	107	25.5 (1975)
Portugal: Madeira Islands	307	794	253 (1981)	269	876	339	19.1 (1981)
Reunion[24]	969	2,510	477 (1974) / 516 (1982)	560	578	223	97.7 (1982)
Rwanda	10,169	26,338	4,800 (1978)	6,275	617	238	5.2 (1981)
Saint Helena[25]	162	419	6.2 (1976)	8.0	49.4	19.1	24.0 (1976)
Sao Tome and Principe	372	964	97 (1981)	110	296	114	33.5 (1981)
Senegal	75,750	196,192	5,085 (1976)	6,614	87.3	33.7	34.3 (1976)
Seychelles	175	453	62 (1977)	66	377	146	37.1 (1977)
Sierra Leone	27,699	71,740	3,516 (1985)	3,732	135	52.0	24.5 (1982)
Somalia[26]	246,201	637,657	3,253 (1975)	4,820	19.6	7.56	20.0 (1980)
South Africa[27]	471,445	1,221,037	28,983 (1980) / 28,818 (1985)	29,000	61.5	23.8	52.6 (1980)
Spain: Canary Islands	2,796	7,242	1,445 (1981)	1,442	516	199	99.2 (1981)
Sudan[28]	967,500	2,505,813	20,564 (1983)	22,178	22.9	8.85	20.2 (1983)
Swaziland	6,704	17,363	495 (1976) / 676 (1986)	676	101	38.9	26.3 (1985)

10For Spanish Guinea.
11For Abyssinia. Inc Eritrea.
12For Gold Coast.
13For French Guinea.
14For Portuguese Guinea.
15Alt Cote d'Ivoire.
16For British East Africa.
17For Basutoland.
18For Malagasy Republic.
19For Nyasaland.
20For French Sudan.
21For Ile de France. Inc Rodrigues.
22Exc Western Sahara (for Spanish Sahara), listed below.
23Alt South-West Africa.
24For Bourbon.
25Inc the dependencies of Ascension and Tristan da Cunha.
26For British Somaliland and Italian Somaliland.
27Inc Bantu "Homelands."
28For Anglo-Egyptian Sudan.

For an explanation of symbols and abbreviations, see pages 16–17.

(Continued)

TABLE 1a. (Continued)

Country	Surface Area		Latest Population (thousands) Census and Year	1986 Estimate	Density of Population		% Urban and Year
	mi²	km²			Per mi²	Per km²	
Tanzania	364,927	945,158	17,513 (1978)	22,462	61.6	23.8	17.6 (1985)
Tanganyika[29]	364,011	942,784	17,036 (1978)	21,874	60.1	23.2	17.1 (1985)
Zanzibar[30]	917	2,374	476 (1978)	588	64.1	24.8	35.2 (1985)
Togo	21,925	56,785	2,703 (1981)	3,052	139	53.7	15.2 (1980)
Tunisia	63,170	163,610	5,572 (1975)	7,234	115	44.2	52.8 (1984)
			6,966 (1984)				
Uganda	91,134	236,036	12,631 (1980)	16,018	176	67.9	14.4 (1985)
Western Sahara	102,703	266,000	164 (1982)	180	1.75	0.677	45.1 (1974)
Zaire[31]	905,568	2,345,409	25,569 (1975)	30,850	34.1	13.2	34.2 (1980)
			29,671 (1984)				
Zambia[32]	290,586	752,614	5,662 (1980)	6,896	23.7	9.16	40.4 (1979)
Zimbabwe[33]	150,804	390,580	7,532 (1982)	8,406	55.7	21.5	23.6 (1983)
ASIA							
Afghanistan	251,825	652,225	15,551 (1979)	18,614	73.9	28.5	16.4 (1983)
Bahrain	240	622	351 (1981)	412	1,717	662	80.7 (1981)
Bangladesh[34]	55,598	143,998	87,120 (1981)	100,616	1,810	699	15.2 (1981)
Bhutan	18,147	47,000	1,035 (1969)	1,447	79.7	30.8	4.5 (1985)
Brunei	2,226	5,765	193 (1981)	244	110	42.3	63.6 (1982)
Burma	261,218	676,552	35,308 (1983)	38,438	147	56.8	23.9 (1983)
China[35]	3,691,508	9,560,961	1,008,181 (1982)	1,052,838	285	110	20.6 (1982)

29For German East Africa.
30Inc Pemba.
31For Belgian Congo.
32For Northern Rhodesia.
33For Southern Rhodesia and (after Northern Rhodesia became Zambia) Rhodesia.
34For East Pakistan.
35Exc Taiwan, listed below.
For an explanation of symbols and abbreviations, see pages 16–17.

(Continued)

Figure 2. *Busy street scene in 1987 around the high-rise International Hotel in downtown Beijing, capital of China, the largest country in population and third largest in area. (Credit: Embassy of the People's Republic of China, Washington.)*

TABLE 1a. (Continued)

Country	Surface Area		Latest Population (thousands)		Density of Population		% Urban and Year
	mi2	km2	Census and Year	1986 Estimate	Per mi2	Per km2	
Cyprus[36]	3,572	9,251	613 (1976) 643 (1982)	673	188	72.7	63.6 (1982)
Gaza Strip	146	378	356 (1967)	550	3,767	1,455	74.4 (1967)
Hong Kong	412	1,067	4,987 (1981) 5,396 (1986)	5,396	13,097	5,057	91.7 (1981)
India[37]	1,237,071	3,204,000	685,185 (1981)	766,135	619	239	25.0 (1985)
Indonesia[38]	741,101	1,919,443	147,490 (1980)	166,940	225	87.0	22.4 (1980)
in Asia	578,173	1,497,462	146,316 (1980)	165,590	286	111	
East Timor	5,743	14,874	555 (1980)	676	118	45.4	12.1 (1980)
Iran[39]	636,296	1,648,000	33,709 (1976)	45,914	72.2	27.9	51.4 (1984)
Iraq[40]	167,925	434,924	12,000 (1977)	16,450	98.0	37.8	68.0 (1982)
Israel[41]	8,302	21,501	4,038 (1983)	4,296	517	200	89.6 (1983)
Japan[42]	145,834	377,708	117,060 (1980) 121,047 (1985)	121,492	833	322	76.2 (1980)
Jordan[43]	35,467	91,860	2,148 (1979)	2,790	78.7	30.4	60.0 (1985)
Kampuchea[44]	69,898	181,035	6,682 (1981)	7,492	107	41.4	13.9 (1982)
Korea[45]							
North Korea	46,540	120,538		20,883	449	173	62.0 (1985)
South Korea	38,279	99,143	37,436 (1980) 40,467 (1985)	41,569	1,086	419	65.4 (1985)
Kuwait	6,880	17,818	1,358 (1980) 1,697 (1985)	1,791	260	101	93.7 (1985)
Laos	91,429	236,800	3,585 (1985)	3,703	40.5	15.6	15.9 (1985)
Lebanon	4,015	10,400	2,790 (1970)	2,707	674	260	83.7 (1985)
Macao[46]	5.98	15.5	298 (1981)	420	70,234	27,097	96.3 (1981)
Malaysia	127,317	329,749	13,745 (1980)	16,109	127	48.9	34.2 (1980)
Peninsular Malaysia[47]	50,807	131,590	11,427 (1980)	13,335	262	101	37.2 (1980)
Sabah[48]	28,460	73,711	1,011 (1980)	1,248	43.9	16.9	17.6 (1970)
Sarawak	48,050	124,449	1,308 (1980)	1,526	31.8	12.3	18.0 (1980)

Country	Area (mi²)	Area (km²)	Population (census)	Population	Density per mi²	Density per km²	% urban
Maldives	115	298	143 (1977); 181 (1985)	189	1,643	634	25.5 (1985)
Mongolia[49]	604,250	1,565,000	1,595 (1979)	1,940	3.21	1.24	51.7 (1985)
Nepal	56,827	147,181	15,023 (1981)	17,131	301	116	6.4 (1981)
Oman[50]	82,030	212,457		2,065	25.2	9.72	7.3 (1982)
Pakistan[51]	342,762	887,750	86,442 (1981)	101,653	297	115	28.2 (1984)
Philippines	115,831	300,000	48,098 (1980)	56,004	483	187	39.9 (1985)
Qatar	4,247	11,000	245 (1981)	335	78.9	30.5	86.1 (1982)
Saudi Arabia	830,000	2,149,690	7,013 (1974)	12,006	14.5	5.58	66.8 (1982)
Singapore	239	618	2,414 (1980)	2,586	10,820	4,184	100 (1980)
Sri Lanka[52]	25,332	65,610	14,848 (1981)	16,117	636	246	21.5 (1981)
Syria	71,498	185,180	9,053 (1981)	10,612	148	57.3	48.6 (1985)
Taiwan[53]	13,900	36,000	18,030 (1980)	19,365	1,393	538	94.1 (1981)
Thailand[54]	198,457	514,000	44,825 (1980)	52,654	265	102	19.8 (1985)
Turkey[55]	300,948	779,452	44,737 (1980); 50,664 (1985)	51,940	173	66.6	46.0 (1985)

36 Inc both the Greek zone and the Turkish (Northern Cyprus) zone.
37 Inc India-held Kashmir (Jammu and Kashmir), the relevant data for which follow. Area: 53,666 mi²,m 138,995 km²; population: 5,988 (1981), 6,815 (1986e); density of population: 127 per mi², 49.0 per km².
38 For Dutch East Indies; Netherlands Indies. Inc East Timor (for Portuguese Timor) and Irian Jaya (for Netherlands New Guinea), which is listed under OCEANIA, below.
39 For Persia.
40 For Mesopotamia.
41 Exc the Gaza Strip and West Bank, which have been occupied by Israel since 1967. Both are listed separately.
42 Inc Ryukyu Islands.
43 For Trans-Jordan. Exc the West Bank, listed below, which has been occupied by Israel since 1967.
44 Alt Cambodia.
45 For Chosen.
46 Off Macau.
47 For British Malaya; West Malaysia.
48 For British North Borneo.
49 For Outer Mongolia. Inner Mongolia is an autonomous region of China.
50 For Muscat and Oman.
51 For West Pakistan. Inc Pakistan-held Kashmir, the relevant data for which follow. Area: 32,358 mi², 83,806 km²; population: 2,188 (1981e), 2,490 (1986e); density of population: 77.0 per mi², 29.7 per km².
52 For Ceylon; Serendib.
53 For Formosa.
54 For Siam.
55 For Ottoman Empire.

For an explanation of symbols and abbreviations, see pages 16–17.

(Continued)

TABLE 1a. (Continued)

Country	Surface Area		Latest Population (thousands)		Density of Population		% Urban and Year
	mi²	km²	Census and Year	1986 Estimate	Per mi²	Per km²	
in Asia	291,773	755,688	40,412 (1980) 45,575 (1985)	46,684	160	61.8	
United Arab Emirates	32,278	83,600	1,040 (1980) 1,622 (1985)	1,770	54.8	21.2	80.9 (1980)
USSR (in Asia)	6,607,830	17,114,200	77,075 (1979)	86,703	13.1	5.07	
Vietnam	127,242	329,556	52,742 (1979)	60,919	479	185	19.8 (1982)
West Bank[56]	2,270	5,880	599 (1967)	835	368	142	24.8 (1971)
Yemen							
North Yemen[57]	75,290	195,000	7,162 (1981) 9,274 (1986)	9,274	123	47.6	10.2 (1982)
South Yemen[58]	128,560	332,968	1,590 (1973)	2,365	18.4	7.10	36.9 (1973)
EUROPE							
Albania	11,100	28,748	2,591 (1979)	3,022	272	105	33.8 (1985)
Andorra	175	453	27 (1975) 38 (1982)	47	269	194	39.3 (1982)
Austria	32,374	83,849	7,555 (1981)	7,571	234	90.3	55.1 (1981)
Belgium	11,781	30,513	9,855 (1981)	9,859	837	323	94.6 (1976)
Bulgaria	42,823	110,912	8,728 (1975) 8,948 (1985)	8,959	209	80.8	65.5 (1985)
Channel Islands[59]	75	195	131 (1981) 138 (1986)	138	1,840	708	33.2 (1976)
Czechoslovakia	49,371	127,869	15,283 (1980)	15,534	315	121	62.9 (1982)
Denmark	16,629	43,069	5,112 (1979)	5,121	308	119	84.2 (1984)
Faeroe Islands	540	1,399	42 (1977)	46	85.0	32.9	28.0 (1977)
Finland	130,559	338,145	4,785 (1980)	4,918	37.7	14.5	59.8 (1985)
France	210,026	543,965	52,656 (1975) 54,335 (1982)	55,392	264	102	73.3 (1982)

Germany									
East Germany	41,828	108,333	16,706	(1981)	16,624	397	153	76.6	(1985)
West Germany	96,030	248,717	60,651	(1970)	61,048	636	245	94.0	(1983)
Gibraltar	2.3	5.9	30	(1981)	29	12,609	4,915	100	(1981)
Greece	50,945	131,957	9,740	(1981)	9,966	196	75.5	58.1	(1981)
Hungary	35,919	93,030	10,709	(1980)	10,627	296	114	56.2	(1984)
Iceland	39,769	103,000	229	(1980)	243	6.11	2.36	89.2	(1984)
Ireland60	27,137	70,284	3,443	(1981)	3,537	130	50.3	55.6	(1981)
			3,537	(1986)					
Isle of Man	227	588	65	(1981)	64	282	109	71.5	(1981)
			64	(1986)					
Italy	116,324	301,277	56,557	(1981)	57,221	492	190	71.7	(1985)
Liechtenstein	61	157	26	(1981)	27	443	172	100	(1981)
Luxembourg	998	2,586	365	(1981)	367	368	142	81.8	(1985)
Malta61	122	316	316	(1967)	385	3,156	1,218	83.4	(1982)
Monaco	0.575	1.49	27	(1982)	27	46,957	18,121	100	(1982)
Netherlands62	16,133	41,785	13,046	(1971)	14,563	903	349	88.5	(1984)
Norway	125,050	323,878	4,091	(1980)	4,169	33.3	12.9	70.7	(1980)
Poland	120,725	312,677	35,061	(1978)	37,456	310	120	60.1	(1985)
Portugal63	35,516	91,985	9,833	(1981)	10,250	289	111	29.7	(1981)
in Europe	35,209	91,191	9,580	(1981)	9,981	283	109		
Azores	868	2,247	243	(1981)	253	291	113	13.5	(1981)
Romania	91,699	237,500	21,560	(1977)	23,174	253	97.6	49.2	(1984)
San Marino	23.5	61	21	(1982)	22	936	361	90.4	(1986)
Spain64	194,897	504,782	37,617	(1981)	38,668	198	76.6	77.4	(1985)
in Europe	192,101	497,540	36,172	(1981)	37,226	194	74.8		
Balearic Islands	1,936	5,014	685	(1981)	675	349	135	97.9	(1981)

56Alt Judea and Samaria. The latter is listed under AFRICA, above.
57For Yemen.
58For Hadhramaut; South Arabia.
59Inc Jersey, Guernsey, and dependencies.
60Alt Eire. Exc Northern Ireland, listed below under UK.
61Inc Gozo.
62Alt Holland.
63Inc Azores and Madeira Islands. The latter is listed under AFRICA, above.
64Inc Balearic Islands and Canary Islands. The latter is listed under AFRICA, above.
For an explanation of symbols and abbreviations, see pages 16–17.

(Continued)

Figure 3. With the Kremlin towers in the foreground, this panorama shows the central part of Moscow, capital of the USSR, the largest country in area and third largest in population. (Credit: Embassy of the USSR, Washington.)

TABLE 1a. (Continued)

Country	Surface Area		Latest Population (thousands)		Density of Population		% Urban and Year
	mi²	km²	Census and Year	1986 Estimate	Per mi²	Per km²	
Svalbard[65]	24,209	62,700	4.2 (1971)	4.0	0.165	0.064	0
Sweden	173,732	449,964	8,320 (1980)	8,370	48.2	18.6	83.1 (1980)
Switzerland	15,943	41,293	6,366 (1980)	6,504	408	158	60.4 (1985)
Turkey (in Europe)	9,175	23,764	4,325 (1980)	5,256	573	221	
			5,089 (1985)				
UK[66]	94,248	244,100	55,848 (1981)	56,763	602	233	75.1 (1981)
England and Wales	58,381	151,207	49,155 (1981)	50,037	857	331	76.2 (1981)
Northern Ireland	5,452	14,121	1,562 (1981)	1,585	291	112	
Scotland	30,414	78,772	5,131 (1981)	5,142	169	65.3	87.7 (1981)
USSR[67]	8,649,539	22,402,200	262,436 (1979)	280,144	32.4	12.5	65.7 (1986)
in Europe	2,041,709	5,288,000	185,361 (1979)	192,081	94.1	36.3	
Vatican City[68]	0.17	0.44	0.9 (1948)	0.7	4,118	1,591	100 (1978)
Yugoslavia[69]	98,766	255,425	22,425 (1981)	23,214	235	90.7	46.1 (1981)
NORTH AMERICA							
Anguilla[70]	37	96	6.8 (1984)	7.0	189	72.9	0
Antigua and Barbuda	170	440	66 (1970)	81	474	183	30.8 (1985)
Aruba	74.5	193	60 (1981)	70	940	363	28.3 (1981)
Bahamas	5,380	13,935	210 (1980)	236	43.9	16.9	60.0 (1980)
Barbados	166	431	249 (1980)	253	1,524	587	42.3 (1985)
Belize[71]	8,867	22,965	143 (1980)	171	19.3	7.45	51.7 (1980)

65Alt Spitsbergen.
66Alt Great Britain and Northern Ireland; United Kingdom.
67Alt Soviet Union, Union of Soviet Socialist Republics.
68Alt Holy See.
69Alt Jugoslavia.
70For Snake Island.
71For British Honduras.
For an explanation of symbols and abbreviations, see pages 16–17.

(Continued)

TABLE 1a. (Continued)

Country	Surface Area		Latest Population (thousands)		Density of Population		% Urban and Year
	mi²	km²	Census and Year	1986 Estimate	Per mi²	Per km²	
Bermuda[72]	20.6	53.3	55 (1980)	58	2,816	1,088	100 (1980)
Canada[73]	3,831,033	9,922,330	24,343 (1981) / 25,354 (1986)	25,354	6.62	2.56	75.9 (1985)
Newfoundland	156,185	404,517	568 (1981) / 568 (1986)	568	3.64	1.40	58.6 (1981)
Cayman Islands	100	259	17 (1979)	22	220	84.9	100 (1979)
Costa Rica	19,575	50,700	2,417 (1984)	2,534	129	50.0	48.4 (1984)
Cuba	42,803	110,860	9,724 (1981)	10,246	239	92.4	70.8 (1984)
Dominica	290	751	75 (1981)	85	293	113	14.1 (1981)
Dominican Republic	18,704	48,442	5,648 (1981)	6,416	343	132	52.0 (1982)
El Salvador[74]	8,124	21,041	3,555 (1971)	4,913	605	233	43.0 (1984)
Greenland[75]	840,004	2,175,600	50 (1976)	54	0.064	0.025	78.8 (1986)
Grenada	133	344	89 (1981)	93	699	270	7.3 (1983)
Guadeloupe	687	1,780	328 (1982)	333	485	187	89.9 (1982)
Guatemala	42,042	108,889	6,054 (1981)	8,195	195	75.3	39.1 (1982)
Haiti	10,714	27,750	4,584 (1975) / 5,054 (1982)	5,358	500	193	25.2 (1984)
Honduras	43,277	112,088	2,657 (1974)	4,514	104	40.3	39.7 (1985)
Jamaica	4,244	10,991	2,206 (1982)	2,355	555	214	69.3 (1980)
Martinique	425	1,100	329 (1982)	328	772	298	81.8 (1982)
Mexico	756,066	1,958,201	66,847 (1980)	79,563	105	40.6	66.7 (1982)
Montserrat	38	98	12 (1980)	12	316	122	29.0 (1980)
Netherlands Antilles[76]	309	800	172 (1981)	200	647	250	48.8 (1983)
Nicaragua	50,193	130,000	1,878 (1971)	3,385	67.4	26.0	55.2 (1982)
Panama	29,762	77,082	1,825 (1980)	2,227	74.8	28.9	51.0 (1984)
Puerto Rico	3,515	9,104	3,197 (1980)	3,300	939	362	66.8 (1980)
Saint Christopher and Nevis[77]	101	261	43 (1980)	47	465	179	35.8 (1980)
Saint Lucia	238	616	123 (1980)	142	597	231	40.5 (1978)

Saint-Pierre and Miquelon	93	242	6.0 (1982)	6.3	67.7	26.0	89.6 (1982)	
Saint Vincent and the Grenadines	150	388	98 (1980)	105	700	271	19.4 (1980)	
Trinidad and Tobago	1,981	5,130	1,080 (1980)	1,204	608	235	21.5 (1980)	
Turks and Caicos Islands	166	430	7.4 (1980)	8.0	48.2	18.6	42.8 (1975)	
USA[78]	3,679,395	9,529,589	226,546 (1980)	241,596	65.7	25.4	73.7 (1980)	
in North America	3,672,924	9,512,830	225,581 (1980)	240,534	65.5	25.3		
Alaska[79]	591,007	1,530,701	402 (1980)	534	0.904	0.349	64.3 (1980)	
Virgin Islands (UK)[80]	59	153	11 (1980)	13	220	85.0	20.6 (1980)	
Virgin Islands (USA)[81]	132	342	97 (1980)	114	864	333	39.1 (1980)	
OCEANIA								
American Samoa[82]	77	199	32 (1980)	37	481	186	17.5 (1980)	
Australia[83]	2,966,153	7,682,300	14,923 (1981)	15,974	5.39	2.08	85.7 (1981)	
Tasmania	26,178	67,800	427 (1981)	447	17.1	6.59	79.9 (1981)	
Christmas Island (Australia)	52	135	2.9 (1981)	3.2	61.5	23.7	37.5 (1983)	
Cocos Islands[84]	5.48	14.2	0.6 (1981)	0.6	109	42.3	0	
Cook Islands[85]	91	236	18 (1981)	17	187	72.0	53.7 (1981)	
			17 (1986)					

[72]For Somers Islands.
[73]Inc Newfoundland since 1949.
[74]Alt Salvador.
[75]Alt Kalaallit Nunaat.
[76]For Dutch West Indies. Exc Aruba, listed above, which was detached from the Netherlands Antilles in 1986.
[77]Alt Saint Kitts and Nevis. Exc Anguilla, listed above, which was detached from Saint Christopher in 1980.
[78]Alt United States; United States of America; US. Inc Alaska and Hawaii since 1959, the latter being listed under OCEANIA, below. The area has been adjusted to include the portion of the Great Lakes belonging to the USA.
[79]For Russian America.
[80]Off British Virgin Islands.
[81]For Danish West Indies.
[82]Alt Eastern Samoa.
[83]Inc Tasmania (for Van Diemen's Land) since 1901.
[84]Alt Keeling Islands.
[85]For Harvey Islands.

For an explanation of symbols and abbreviations, see pages 16–17.

(Continued)

TABLE 1a. (Continued)

Country	Surface Area		Latest Population (thousands)		Density of Population		% Urban and Year
	mi²	km²	Census and Year	1986 Estimate	Per mi²	Per km²	
Fiji	7,056	18,274	588 (1976) 715 (1986)	715	101	39.1	38.4 (1983)
French Polynesia[86]	1,544	4,000	137 (1977) 167 (1983)	173	112	43.2	73.4 (1985)
Guam	209	541	106 (1980)	128	612	237	39.5 (1980)
Indonesia; Irian Jaya	162,928	421,981	1,174 (1980)	1,350	8.29	3.20	16.3 (1971)
Johnston Island	0.4	1.04	0.3 (1980)	0.3	750	288	0
Kiribati[87]	328	849	56 (1978) 64 (1985)	65	198	76.6	33.4 (1985)
Midway Islands	2	5.18	0.5 (1980)	0.5	250	96.5	0
Nauru[88]	8.2	21.2	7.3 (1977) 8.0 (1983)	8.0	976	377	100 (1983)
New Caledonia	7,358	19,058	133 (1976) 145 (1983)	156	21.2	8.19	60.0 (1978)
New Zealand	103,736	268,676	3,176 (1981) 3,307 (1986)	3,307	31.9	12.3	83.7 (1985)
Niue[89]	100	259	3.3 (1981) 2.9 (1984)	2.5	25.0	9.65	29.1 (1981)
Norfolk Island	13.3	34.5	2.2 (1981) 2.4 (1986)	2.4	180	69.6	0
Pacific Islands (USA)[90]	717	1,857	133 (1980)	158	220	85.1	28.5 (1980)
Papua New Guinea[91]	178,260	461,691	3,011 (1980)	3,400	19.1	7.36	13.1 (1980)
Pitcairn Island	1.75	4.53	0.05 (1985)	0.064	36.6	14.1	100 (1983)
Samoa[92]	1,097	2,842	156 (1981) 159 (1986)	159	145	55.9	21.2 (1981)
Solomon Islands[93]	10,983	28,446	197 (1976)	277	25.2	9.74	9.1 (1976)
Tokelau[94]	3.9	10	1.6 (1981)	1.7	436	170	0
Tonga[95]	270	699	90 (1976) 96 (1984)	98	363	140	20.3 (1976)
Tuvalu[96]	9.25	24	7.3 (1979) 8.2 (1985)	8.2	886	342	34.2 (1985)

USA: Hawaii[97]	6,471	16,759	965 (1980)	1,062	164	63.4	86.5 (1980)
Vanuatu[98]	5,700	14,763	111 (1979)	140	24.6	9.48	17.8 (1979)
Wake Island	3	7.77	0.3 (1980)	0.3	100	38.6	0 (1980)
Wallis and Futuna Islands	98	255	9.2 (1976) 12 (1983)	14	143	54.9	12.9 (1976)

SOUTH AMERICA

Argentina	1,068,301	2,766,889	27,497 (1980)	31,030	29.0	11.2	83.6 (1985)
Bolivia	424,165	1,098,581	4,613 (1976)	6,547	15.4	5.96	47.7 (1985)
Brazil	3,286,488	8,511,965	119,003 (1980)	138,493	42.1	16.3	70.8 (1985)
Chile	292,258	756,945	11,330 (1982)	12,327	42.2	16.3	83.2 (1984)
Colombia[99]	440,831	1,141,748	27,867 (1985)	28,365	64.3	24.8	66.1 (1985)
Ecuador	109,484	283,561	8,139 (1982)	9,647	88.1	34.0	51.4 (1985)
Galapagos Islands[100]	3,093	8,010	6.1 (1982)	7.0	2.26	0.874	66.2 (1982)
Falkland Islands[101]	6,207	16,076	1.9 (1980)	1.9	0.306	0.118	58.9 (1980)
French Guiana	35,135	91,000	73 (1982)	84	2.39	0.923	80.7 (1982)
Guyana[102]	83,000	214,969	759 (1980)	797	9.60	3.71	31.2 (1985)
Paraguay	157,048	406,752	3,030 (1982)	3,807	24.2	9.36	42.8 (1982)
Peru	496,225	1,285,216	17,005 (1981)	20,207	40.7	15.7	68.9 (1984)
Suriname[103]	63,037	163,265	355 (1980)	398	6.31	2.44	45.2 (1985)
Uruguay[104]	68,037	176,215	2,931 (1985)	2,983	43.8	16.9	84.5 (1984)
Venezuela	352,144	912,050	14,517 (1981)	17,791	50.5	19.5	76.4 (1981)

86For French Oceania.
87For Gilbert Islands.
88For Pleasant Island.
89For Savage Island.
90Off Trust Territory of the Pacific Islands. Inc Caroline, Mariana, and Marshall Islands (except Guam in the Marianas, which is listed above).
91Inc New Guinea (Australia) and Papua.
92Alt Western Samoa. For Navigators' Islands.
93For British Solomon Islands.
94Alt Union Islands.
95For Friendly Islands.
96For Ellice Islands.
97For Sandwich Islands.
98For New Hebrides.
99For New Granada.
100Off Colon Islands.
101Alt Malvina Islands. Inc the dependency of South Georgia.
102For British Guiana.
103For Dutch Guiana; Netherlands Guiana.
104For Banda Oriental.

For an explanation of symbols and abbreviations, see pages 16–17.

1b.   Evolution of Population from 1800 to 1970

Contents

Conventional name of country.

Population, in thousands, for the years 1970, 1950, 1930, 1900, 1850, and 1800, or
for the dates nearest those years for which reliable data are available, with the
exact year given in parentheses. For countries that have taken censuses irregu-
larly, the census figures are usually given even if they are several years removed
from the desired date rather than dubious estimates for the exact year; for example, Argentina, where the 1914 census figure is entered under "ca 1930" and the
1869 census figure is entered under "ca 1850." Except where indicated otherwise
in a footnote, the population given is for the country as it existed at the time that
was determined, not for its present-day area.

Coverage

All countries listed in Table 1a.

Rounding

Populations are rounded to the nearest 1,000 (to the nearest 100 if the total is less
than 10,000).

Entries

249, as follows: Africa—63

Asia—53

Europe—48

North America—40

Oceania—30

South America—15

TABLE 1b. EVOLUTION OF POPULATION FROM 1800 TO 1970

Country	Population (thousands)					
	ca 1970	ca 1950	ca 1930	ca 1900	ca 1850	ca 1800
AFRICA						
Algeria	11,822 (66)	8,682 (48)	6,553 (31)	4,429 (96)	2,496 (56)	1,500 (00?e)
Angola	5,646 (70)	4,145 (50)	2,615 (29)	4,790 (00e)	5,387 (46e)	
Benin	2,720 (70e)	1,535 (51e)	980 (26)	749 (06)		
Botswana	574 (71)	296 (46)	266 (36)	121 (04)		
British Indian Ocean Territory	0.7 (62)					
Burkina Faso	4,400 (60–61)	3,109 (51e)	3,240 (26)			
Burundi1	3,350 (70–71)	1,902 (52)				
Cameroon	5,017 (60–65)	5,085 (50e)	3,023 (31)	3,500 (00?e)		
Cape Verde	273 (70)	148 (50)	146 (30)	147 (00)		
Central African Republic	1,203 (59–60)	1,072 (50e)	1,066 (26)	2,130 (06e)		
Chad	3,254 (63–64)	2,241 (50e)	974 (26)	885 (06e)		
Comoros	212 (66)	150 (50)	111 (36)	86 (06)	53 (67)	21 (00?e)
Congo	797 (60–61)	684 (50e)	699 (26)	259 (06e)		
Djibouti	166 (70e)	56 (51e)	70 (31)	208 (06)		
Egypt	30,076 (66)	18,967 (47)	14,178 (27)	9,794 (97)	4,476 (46)	2,460 (00e)
Equatorial Guinea	246 (60)	199 (50)	167 (32)	161 (00e)		
Ethiopia	24,069 (70e)	15,000 (50e)	5,500 (30?e)	4,500 (00?e)	3,000 (31e)	1,800 (00?e)
Eritrea	1,894 (70e)	1,104 (50e)	598 (31)	330 (99)		
French Southern and Antarctic Lands	0.2 (70)	0.1 (63e)				
Gabon	950 (69–70)	409 (50e)	389 (26)	376 (06e)		
Gambia	493 (73)	280 (51)	200 (31)	103 (01)		
Ghana	8,559 (70)	4,118 (48)	2,870 (31)	1,550 (01)	408 (71e)	

1Burundi with Rwanda: 3,406 (1935e).
2Mali with Niger: 5,059 (1906).
For an explanation of symbols and abbreviations, see pages 16–17.

(Continued)

TABLE 1b. (Continued)

Population (thousands)

Country	ca 1970	ca 1950	ca 1930	ca 1900	ca 1850	ca 1800
Guinea	5,143 (72)	2,570 (55)	2,096 (26)	1,498 (06)		
Guinea-Bissau	487 (70)	511 (50)	377 (31)	820 (00?e)		
Ivory Coast	6,710 (75)	3,100 (57–58)	1,725 (26)	889 (06)		
Kenya	10,943 (69)	5,406 (48)	3,025 (31)	3,000 (00?e)		
Lesotho	852 (66)	564 (46)	562 (36)	349 (04)	128 (75)	
Liberia	1,016 (62)	1,648 (49e)	2,500 (30?e)	2,060 (00?e)	250 (50e)	
Libya	2,052 (73)	1,089 (54)	704 (31)	1,000 (00?e)	750 (50?e)	1,000 (00?e)
Madagascar	6,200 (66)	4,149 (48)	3,759 (31)	2,664 (05)	3,000 (50?e)	4,000 (00?e)
Malawi	4,040 (66)	2,050 (45)	1,603 (31)	737 (01)		
Mali²	4,040 (60–61)	3,347 (51e)	2,635 (26)			
Mauritania	1,030 (64–65)	657 (51e)	289 (26)	223 (06)		
Mauritius	851 (72)	517 (52)	403 (31)	371 (01)	181 (51)	59 (97)
Mayotte	32 (66)	19 (50)	17 (36)	10 (06)	5.3 (49)	
Morocco	15,379 (71)	9,125 (52)	6,235 (31)	7,000 (00?e)	8,500 (50?e)	5,000 (00?e)
Mozambique	8,169 (70)	5,739 (50)	4,006 (30)	3,120 (00?e)	350 (50?e)	
Namibia	762 (70)	434 (51)	259 (26)	207 (04e)		
Niger²	3,997 (70e)	2,876 (59–60)	1,219 (26)			
Nigeria	55,670 (63)	29,731 (52–53)	19,158 (31)	17,133 (11e)		
Portugal: Madeira Islands	253 (70)	270 (50)	212 (30)	151 (00)	107 (54)	90 (00?e)
Reunion	417 (67)	242 (46)	198 (31)	173 (02)	106 (52)	65 (04)
Rwanda¹	3,573 (70)	2,144 (52)				
Saint Helena	5.4 (66)	5.0 (46)	4.2 (31)	3.3 (01)	6.3 (54)	
Sao Tome and Principe	74 (70)	60 (50)	56 (21)	42 (00)	17 (50?e)	
Senegal	3,620 (70–71)	2,093 (51e)	1,358 (26)	1,247 (11)		
Seychelles	53 (71)	34 (47)	27 (31)	19 (01)	6.8 (51)	2.1 (03)
Sierra Leone	2,735 (74)	1,858 (48)	1,768 (31)	1,403 (11)		
Somalia	2,789 (70e)	1,747 (51e)	1,027 (31)	400 (00?e)		
South Africa³	21,794 (70)	12,671 (51)	9,590 (36)	5,175 (04)	267 (56)	62 (98)
Spain: Canary Islands	1,170 (70)	793 (50)	555 (30)	359 (00)	234 (57)	174 (97)
Sudan	14,114 (73)	10,263 (55–56)	5,508 (31e)	3,000 (10e)		
Swaziland	375 (66)	188 (46)	157 (36)	86 (04)		

Tanzania	12,313 (67)					
Tanganyika	11,959 (67)	7,480 (48)	5,064 (31)	4,145 (13)		
Zanzibar	355 (67)	264 (48)	235 (31)	197 (10)	130 (46e)	200 (11e)
Togo	1,997 (70)	1,440 (58–60)	1,044 (31e)	2,250 (00?e)		
Tunisia	4,533 (66)	3,231 (46)	2,411 (31)	1,939 (11)	1,520 (81)	1,000 (00?e)
Uganda	9,549 (69)	4,959 (48)	3,554 (31)	2,843 (11)		
Western Sahara	76 (70)	37 (50e)	32 (30?e)	115 (00?e)		
Zaire	21,638 (70)	11,258 (50e)	8,764 (30e)	9,000 (10e)		
Zambia	4,057 (69)	1,930 (50–51)	1,345 (31)	497 (00?e)		
Zimbabwe	5,099 (69)	1,765 (48)	1,109 (31)	613 (04e)		
ASIA						
Afghanistan	17,086 (70e)	12,000 (50e)	7,000 (30?e)	4,550 (00?e)	4,000 (50?e)	3,000 (00?e)
Bahrain	216 (71)	110 (50)	90 (41)	70		
Bangladesh[4]	71,479 (74)	[42,063 (51)]	[35,604 (31)]	[28,928 (01)]		
Bhutan	1,035 (69)	300 (50e)	250 (30?e)	20 (64e)		
Brunei	136 (71)	41 (47)	30 (31)	22		
Burma	28,886 (73)	16,824 (41)	14,467 (31)	10,491 (01)	7,722 (91)	4,231 (26e)
China	694,582 (64)	582,603 (53)	438,933 (31e)	372,563 (10e)	429,931 (50e)	295,273 (00e)
Cyprus	632 (73)	450 (46)	348 (31)	237 (01)	186 (81)	84 (00?e)
Gaza Strip	356 (67)	198 (50e)				
Hong Kong	3,948 (71)	3,133 (61)	840 (31)	399	33 (50)	
India[5]	548,160 (71)	360,695 (51)	338,061 (31)	283,870 (01)	203,415 (67–72)	131,000 (20e)
Indonesia[6]	119,208 (71)	97,086 (61)	60,727 (30)	37,694 (00e)	19,319 (63e)	13,476 (00?e)
in Asia	118,285 (71)	96,327 (61)	60,413 (30)	37,494 (00e)	19,119 (63e)	
East Timor	611 (70)	517 (60)	442 (26)	300 (00?e)		
Iran	25,785 (66)	18,955 (56)	15,055 (33)	9,000 (97e)	5,000 (50?e)	
Iraq	8,047 (65)	4,816 (47)	3,300 (30?e)	[1,398 (10e)]		
Israel	3,148 (72)	873 (48)	1,036 (31)			
Japan	104,665 (70)	84,115 (50)	64,450 (30)	43,756 (97)	34,806 (72)	25,471 (98e)
Jordan[7]	1,706 (61)	1,329 (52)	300 (29e)			

3 Inc Bantu "Homelands."

4 Included with Pakistan in 1951 and with India in 1931 and 1901.

5 Exc Burma but inc India-held Kashmir (Jammu and Kashmir), the population of which was: 4,617 (1971), 3,254 (1951), 2,670 (1931), and 2,139 (1901). The Indian population totals derived from the census of 1867–72 and the official estimates for 1820 represent incomplete counts; the population of the entire territory is unofficially estimated to have been 255,166 in 1871 and 186,000 in 1800.

6 Exc East Timor (for Portuguese Timor).

7 Inc the West Bank, held by Israel since 1967. Its population for 1967 and 1952 is given below. For 1961 the population of the West Bank was given as 805.

For an explanation of symbols and abbreviations, see pages 16–17.

(Continued)

TABLE 1b. (Continued)

Country	Population (thousands)					
	ca 1970	ca 1950	ca 1930	ca 1900	ca 1850	ca 1800
Kampuchea	5,729 (62)	4,740 (58)	2,806 (31)	1,194 (06)	1,000 (50?e)	1,000 (00?e)
Korea			21,058 (30)	12,934 (09)	10,519 (83)	
North Korea	13,892 (70e)	9,102 (49e)				
South Korea	31,466 (70)	20,189 (49)				
Kuwait	737 (70)	206 (57)	51 (30?e)			
Laos	2,962 (70e)	1,360 (51e)	944 (31)	664 (06)	1,000 (50?e)	3,000 (00?e)
Lebanon	2,126 (70)	1,257 (50e)	629 (21–22)	[200 (00?e)]		
Macao	249 (70)	188 (50)	157 (27)	64 (99)	52 (62e)	34 (22e)
Malaysia	10,439 (70)					
Peninsular Malaysia	8,810 (47)	4,908 (47)	3,788 (31)	2,339 (11)		
Sabah	654 (70)	334 (51)	270 (31)	105 (01)		
Sarawak	976 (70)	546 (47)	440 (37e)	500 (01e)		
Maldives	123 (72)	82 (46)	79 (31)	72 (11)	175 (50?e)	
Mongolia	1,198 (69)	732 (50)	648 (18)			
Nepal	11,556 (71)	8,257 (52)	5,574 (20)	5,639 (11)	2,000 (50?e)	2,000 (20?e)
Oman	657 (70e)	550 (50e)	500 (30?e)	1,000 (00?e)		
Pakistan[8]	66,997 (72)	76,992 (51)	[21,283 (31)]	[16,577 (01)]		
Philippines	36,681 (70)	19,254 (48)	16,003 (39)	7,635 (03)	6,171 (77)	1,522 (99e)
Qatar	110 (70e)	17 (51e)	26 (30?e)			
Saudi Arabia	6,400 (62e)	6,000 (51e)	4,200 (30?e)	[3,000 (00?e)]	[4,000 (50?e)]	
Singapore	2,075 (70)	938 (47)	560 (31)	229 (01)	54 (50)	0.2 (00?e)
Sri Lanka	12,690 (71)	8,098 (53)	5,307 (31)	3,566 (01)	1,576 (50)	852 (24)
Syria	6,305 (70)	3,503 (50e)	1,506 (21–22)	[2,690 (00?e)]		
Taiwan	14,990 (70)	7,618 (50)	4,593 (30)	2,925 (01)		
Thailand	34,397 (70)	17,443 (47)	11,506 (29)	8,266 (11)	5,000 (54e)	1,900 (00?e)
Turkey	35,605 (70)	20,947 (50)	13,648 (27)	23,814 (10e)	26,636 (44–50e)	20,912 (00?e)
in Asia[9]	32,394 (70)	19,363 (50)	12,608 (27)	17,683 (10e)	16,050 (50)	11,090 (00?e)

United Arab Emirates	179 (68)	80 (49e)				
USSR (in Asia)	66,848 (70)	53,559 (59)	26,752 (26)	13,506 (97)	4,103 (56)	2,500 (95?e)
Vietnam	39,486 (70e)	25,880 (53e)	17,702 (31)	14,281 (06)	10,000 (50?e)	17,000 (00?e)
West Bank	599 (67)	[742] (52)]				
Yemen						
North Yemen	5,238 (75)	4,500 (50e)	2,000 (30?e)	[750] (10e)]		
South Yemen	1,590 (73)	750 (50e)	650 (37e)	194 (00?e)		
EUROPE						
Albania	1,626 (60)	1,219 (50)	1,003 (30)			
Andorra	14 (65)	5.7 (50)	5.2 (21)	5.2 (99)	7.0 (50?e)	
Austria	7,492 (71)	6,934 (51)	6,760 (34)	27,490 (00)	17,535 (50)	8,511 (00)
Belgium	9,651 (70)	8,512 (47)	8,092 (30)	6,694 (00)	4,337 (46)	3,008 (00)
Bulgaria	8,228 (65)	7,029 (46)	5,479 (26)	3,744 (00)	[2,008] (80)]	[1,800] (00?e)]
Channel Islands	123 (71)	103 (51)	93 (31)	96 (01)	91 (51)	49 (21)
Czechoslovakia	14,345 (70)	12,338 (50)	14,730 (30)			
Denmark	4,938 (70)	4,281 (50)	3,551 (30)	2,450 (01)	1,415 (50)	929 (01)
Faeroe Islands	39 (70)	32 (50)	24 (30)	15 (01)	8.2 (50)	5.2 (12)
Finland	4,598 (70)	4,030 (50)	3,463 (30)	2,656 (00)	1,637 (50)	833 (00)
France	49,797 (68)	42,774 (54)	41,835 (31)	38,962 (00)	35,783 (51)	27,349 (01)
Germany			66,030 (33)	56,367 (00)	33,413 (52)	22,377 (16)
East Germany	17,068 (71)	18,388 (50)				
West Germany	60,651 (70)	50,809 (50)				
Gibraltar	27 (70)	21 (51)	17 (31)	20 (01)	16 (44)	2.9 (91)
Greece	8,769 (71)	7,633 (51)	6,205 (28)	2,434 (96)	987 (48)	[753] (28)]
Hungary	10,322 (70)	9,205 (49)	8,688 (30)	19,255 (00)	13,192 (50)	8,003 (85)
Iceland	205 (70)	144 (50)	109 (30)	78 (01)	59 (50)	47 (01)

[8]Inc Pakistan-held Kashmir, the population of which is estimated to have been 1,688 in 1971 and 1,189 in 1951. The 1951 population also includes East Pakistan, now Bangladesh. For 1931 and 1901, included with India.

[9]For 1910 and earlier, the populations given for Turkey are those of the Ottoman Empire, inc (in Asia) Iraq, Lebanon, Saudi Arabia, Syria, and North Yemen.

For an explanation of symbols and abbreviations, see pages 16–17.

(Continued)

TABLE 1b. (Continued)

Population (thousands)

Country	ca 1970		ca 1950		ca 1930		ca 1900		ca 1850		ca 1800	
Ireland[10]	2,978	(71)	2,961	(51)	2,972	(26)	4,459	(01)	6,552	(51)	6,802	(21)
Isle of Man	56	(71)	55	(51)	49	(31)	55	(01)	52	(51)	28	(92)
Italy	54,137	(71)	47,151	(51)	41,652	(31)	32,965	(01)	22,212	(61)	17,237	(00e)
Liechtenstein	21	(70)	14	(50)	10	(30)	9.5	(01)	7.4	(52?)	5.0	(00e)
Luxembourg	340	(70)	291	(47)	300	(30)	235	(00)	190	(49)	134	(21)
Malta	316	(67)	306	(48)	242	(31)	185	(01)	123	(51)	114	(98)
Monaco	23	(68)	20	(51)	25	(28)	15	(97)	7.0	(50?e)	6.0	(00?e)
Netherlands	13,046	(71)	9,625	(47)	7,936	(30)	5,104	(99)	3,057	(49)	1,880	(95)
Norway	3,874	(70)	3,279	(50)	2,814	(30)	2,240	(00)	1,490	(55)	883	(01)
Poland	32,642	(70)	25,008	(50)	32,107	(31)	9,456	(97)	4,852	(54e)	2,600	(15e)
Portugal	8,663	(70)	8,510	(50)	6,826	(30)	5,423	(00)	3,844	(54)	3,115	(01e)
in Europe	8,410	(70)	8,240	(50)	6,614	(30)	5,272	(00)	3,737	(54)	3,025	(01e)
Azores	287	(70)	319	(50)	255	(30)	256	(00)	238	(54)	142	(00?e)
Romania	19,103	(66)	15,873	(48)	14,281	(30)	5,957	(99)	[3,865	(59)]	[2,200	(00?e)]
San Marino	18	(71)	12	(47)	13	(30e)	11	(06)	7.3	(64)	5.5	(00?e)
Spain	33,956	(70)	28,118	(50)	23,677	(30)	18,618	(00)	15,455	(57)	10,541	(97)
in Europe	32,786	(70)	27,325	(50)	23,122	(30)	18,259	(00)	15,220	(57)	10,367	(97)
Balearic Islands	558	(70)	422	(50)	366	(30)	312	(00)	263	(57)	187	(97)
Svalbard	4.2	(71)	1.5	(46)	0.6	(30)						
Sweden	8,077	(70)	7,042	(50)	6,142	(30)	5,136	(00)	3,483	(50)	2,347	(00)
Switzerland	6,270	(70)	4,715	(50)	4,066	(30)	3,315	(00)	2,393	(50)	1,843	(95)
Turkey (in Europe)[11]	3,211	(70)	1,584	(50)	1,041	(27)	6,130	(10e)	10,586	(44e)	9,822	(00?e)
UK[12]	55,515	(71)	50,225	(51)	46,052	(31)	37,000	(01)	20,817	(51)	10,501	(01)
England and Wales	48,750	(71)	43,758	(51)	39,952	(31)	32,528	(01)	17,928	(51)	8,893	(01)
Northern Ireland	1,536	(71)	1,371	(51)	1,257	(26)						
Scotland	5,229	(71)	5,096	(51)	4,843	(31)	4,472	(01)	2,889	(51)	1,608	(01)
USSR	241,720	(70)	208,827	(59)	147,028	(26)	116,238	(97)	64,903	(56)	33,000	(95?e)
in Europe	174,872	(70)	155,268	(59)	120,276	(26)	102,732	(97)	60,800	(56)	30,500	(95?e)

Vatican City	0.7 (70e)	0.9 (48)	0.6 (30)		3.1 (25)
Yugoslavia	20,523 (71)	15,772 (48)	13,934 (31)		36 (17)
NORTH AMERICA					
Anguilla	6.5 (74)	5.0 (46)	4.2 (21)	3.9 (01)	
Antigua and Barbuda	66 (70)	42 (46)	30 (21)	35 (01)	
Aruba	58 (72)	51 (50e)	13 (30)	9.7 (00)	0 (00)
Bahamas	170 (70)	85 (53)	60 (31)	54 (01)	14 (03)
Barbados	238 (70)	193 (46)	156 (21)	183 (91)	82 (11)
Belize	121 (70)	59 (46)	51 (31)	37 (01)	
Bermuda	53 (70)	37 (50)	28 (31)	18 (01)	10 (90)
Canada[13]	21,568 (71)	14,009 (51)	10,377 (31)	5,371 (01)	430 (14e)
Newfoundland	[522 (71)]	[361 (51)]	290 (35)	221 (01)	70 (16e)
Cayman Islands	10 (70)	7.5 (54)	5.9 (31)	4.3 (91)	0.9 (02)
Costa Rica	1,872 (73)	801 (50)	472 (27)	243 (92)	25 (78)
Cuba	8,569 (70)	5,829 (53)	3,962 (31)	1,573 (99)	272 (92)
Dominica	71 (70)	48 (46)	37 (21)	29 (01)	26 (05)
Dominican Republic	4,009 (70)	2,136 (50)	1,479 (35)	610 (00?e)	153 (85)
El Salvador	3,555 (71)	1,856 (50)	1,434 (30)	1,007 (01)	165 (07)
Greenland	47 (70)	24 (51)	17 (30)	12 (01)	20 (00?e)
Grenada	94 (70)	72 (46)	66 (21)	63 (01)	31 (11)
Guadeloupe	313 (67)	278 (46)	267 (31)	182 (01)	115 (12)
Guatemala	5,160 (73)	2,791 (50)	2,005 (21)	1,365 (93)	396 (78)
Haiti	4,330 (71)	3,097 (50)	2,291 (18)	1,294 (01)	511 (89e)
Honduras	1,885 (61)	1,369 (50)	854 (30)	544 (01)	93 (91)
Jamaica	2,657 (74)	1,237 (43)	858 (21)	639 (91)	219 (91e)
Martinique	320 (67)	262 (46)	235 (31)	208 (01)	84 (89)
Mexico	48,225 (70)	25,791 (50)	16,553 (30)	13,607 (00)	5,800 (03e)
Montserrat	12 (70)	14 (46)	12 (21)	12 (01)	11 (00?e)

10Exc Northern Ireland in 1971, 1951, and 1926.
11For 1844, inc Bulgaria and Romania; for1800, inc Bulgaria, Greece, and Romania.
12For 1901 and earlier, exc Ireland.
13For 1931 and earlier, exc Newfoundland.
For an explanation of symbols and abbreviations, see pages 16–17.

(Continued)

TABLE 1b. (Continued)

Country	Population (thousands)					
	ca 1970	ca 1950	ca 1930	ca 1900	ca 1850	ca 1800
Netherlands Antilles[14]	165 (72)	112 (50e)	59 (30)	42 (00)	25 (49–50)	21 (15–17)
Nicaragua	1,878 (71)	1,057 (50)	638 (20)	505 (06)	257 (67)	107 (78)
Panama	1,428 (70)	805 (50)	467 (30)	337 (11)		
Puerto Rico	2,712 (70)	2,211 (50)	1,544 (30)	953 (99)	448 (46)	155 (00)
Saint Christopher and Nevis	45 (70)	41 (46)	34 (21)	43 (01)	33 (50)	44 (00?e)
Saint Lucia	101 (70)	70 (46)	52 (21)	50 (01)	24 (51)	17 (03)
Saint-Pierre and Miquelon	5.2 (67)	4.6 (51)	4.3 (31)	6.5 (06)	3.1 (61)	2.0 (00?e)
Saint Vincent and the Grenadines	87 (70)	62 (46)	48 (31)	41 (91)	30 (51)	24 (12?)
Trinidad and Tobago	941 (70)	563 (46)	413 (31)	274 (01)	83 (51)	34 (02)
Turks and Caicos Islands	5.6 (70)	5.1 (54)	5.5 (21)	4.8 (91)	4.4 (61)	2.5 (03e)
USA[15]	203,302 (70)	150,697 (50)	122,775 (30)	75,995 (00)	23,192 (50)	5,308 (00)
in North America	202,532 (70)	150,697 (50)	122,775 (30)	75,995 (00)	23,192 (50)	5,308 (00)
Alaska	[303] (70)]	129 (50)	59 (29)	64 (00)	11 (56)	0.8 (00?e)
Virgin Islands (UK)	9.7 (70)	6.5 (46)	5.1 (21)	4.9 (01)	6.7 (44)	11 (05e)
Virgin Islands (USA)	62 (70)	27 (50)	22 (30)	31 (01)	40 (50)	37 (96)
OCEANIA						
American Samoa	27 (70)	19 (50)	10 (30)	5.7 (00)		
Australia[16]	12,756 (71)	7,626 (47)	6,690 (33)	3,954 (01)	407 (51)	5.2 (00e)
Tasmania	[390] (71)]	[257] (47)]	[228] (33)]	[172] (01)]	70 (51)	5.4 (20e)
Christmas Island (Australia)	2.7 (71)	0.9 (47)	1.0 (26)	0.04 (98e)		

Cocos Islands	0.6 (71)	1.8 (47)	0.2 (24)	0.6 (98)		
Cook Islands	21 (71)	15 (51)	10 (26)	8.2 (02)	16 (50?e)	
Fiji	477 (66)	260 (46)	198 (36)	120 (01)	127 (81)	120 (00?e)
French Polynesia	119 (71)	63 (51)	40 (31)	31 (06)	16 (76)	
Guam	85 (70)	59 (50)	19 (30)	9.7 (01)		
Indonesia: Irian Jaya	923 (71)	758 (61)	314 (30)	200 (00?e)	200 (65e)	
Johnston Island	1.0 (70)	0.05 (50)	0.07 (40)			
Kiribati	47 (68)	32 (47)	29 (31)	26 (11)		
Midway Islands	2.2 (70)	0.4 (50)	0.04 (30)			
Nauru	6.1 (66)	3.3 (49)	2.6 (33)			
New Caledonia	101 (69)	65 (51)	57 (31)	54 (01)	42 (50?e)	
New Zealand	2,863 (71)	1,939 (51)	1,408 (26)	816 (01)	102 (61)	100 (00?e)
Niue	5.0 (71)	4.6 (51)	3.7 (28)	4.0 (00)	1.0 (54e)	
Norfolk Island	1.7 (71)	0.9 (47)	1.2 (33)	0.8 (01)	0.5 (71)	0.9 (05)
Pacific Islands (USA)	91 (70)	55 (50)	50 (30)	49 (20)		
Papua New Guinea	2,490 (71)	1,453 (50e)	800 (33e)	460 (00?e)		
Pitcairn Island	0.09 (71)	0.1 (47)	0.2 (21)	0.2 (05)	0.2 (51)	0.03 (00)
Samoa	147 (71)	85 (51)	40 (26)	33 (00)	34 (50?e)	
Solomon Islands	161 (70)	124 (59)	94 (31)	150 (11e)		
Tokelau	1.6 (72)	1.6 (51)	1.0 (26)	0.9 (00)		
Tonga	77 (66)	57 (56)	29 (31)	21 (01)	18 (50?e)	
Tuvalu	6.3 (68)	4.5 (47)	4.1 (31)	3.1 (11)	20 (50?e)	
USA: Hawaii	[770 (70)]	500 (50)	368 (30)	154 (00)	84 (50)	200 (00?e)
Vanuatu	78 (67)	49 (50e)	60 (30e)	50 (00?e)	200 (50?e)	130 (32)
Wake Island	1.6 (70)	0.3 (50)				110 (00?e)
Wallis and Futuna Islands	8.5 (69)	10 (55e)	6.3 (31e)	6.0 (00?e)		

[14]Exc Aruba, listed above.
[15]For 1950 and earlier, exc Alaska and Hawaii. (The evolution of Hawaii's population is given under OCEANIA, below.)
[16]For 1851 and 1800, exc Tasmania and aborigines in Australia.
For an explanation of symbols and abbreviations, see pages 16–17.

(Continued)

TABLE 1b. (Continued)

Country	Population (thousands)					
	ca 1970	ca 1950	ca 1930	ca 1900	ca 1850	ca 1800
SOUTH AMERICA						
Argentina	23,390 (70)	15,894 (47)	7,885 (14)	3,993 (95)	1,767 (69)	311 (97e)
Bolivia	3,824 (60e)	3,019 (50)	2,397 (30e)	1,696 (00)	1,544 (54)	1,019 (31)
Brazil	93,139 (70)	51,976 (50)	30,636 (20)	17,438 (00)	10,112 (72)	3,200 (06e)
Chile	8,885 (70)	5,933 (52)	4,287 (30)	2,712 (95)	1,439 (54)	1,010 (35)
Colombia	22,915 (73)	11,548 (51)	8,702 (38)	4,144 (05)	2,243 (51)	1,047 (82)
Ecuador	6,522 (74)	3,203 (50)	2,702 (35e)	1,272 (92e)	870 (46e)	558 (25)
Galapagos Islands	4.0 (74)	1.3 (50)	2.0 (35e)	0.2 (00?e)	0.2 (35e)	0 (00)
Falkland Islands	2.0 (72)	2.2 (53)	2.4 (31)	2.0 (01)	0.3 (47)	16 (15e)
French Guiana	44 (67)	29 (46)	28 (31)	33 (01)	21 (41)	98 (31)
Guyana	702 (70)	376 (46)	311 (31)	278 (91)	136 (51)	
Paraguay	2,358 (72)	1,341 (50)	932 (36)	644 (99–00)	1,337 (57)	560 (00?e)
Peru	13,578 (72)	9,907 (61)	7,023 (40)	4,610 (96e)	2,001 (50)	1,076 (91–95)
Suriname	380 (72)	178 (50)	119 (21)	87 (01)	64 (51)	
Uruguay	2,788 (75)	2,596 (63)	1,599 (30e)	916 (00)	132 (52)	31 (96e)
Venezuela	10,722 (71)	5,035 (50)	3,027 (26)	2,324 (91)	1,564 (54)	660 (25)

For an explanation of symbols and abbreviations, see pages 16–17.

1c. Vital Statistics

Contents

Conventional name of country.

Period of record for birth and death rates.

Average annual number of live births per thousand inhabitants.

Average annual number of deaths per thousand inhabitants.

Percentage rate of natural increase in population (i.e., excess of births over deaths as a percentage of the total population).

Period of record for infant mortality rate.

Infant mortality rate (i.e., the number of deaths per thousand live births that occur in the first year of life).

Period of record for life expectancies.

Expectation of life at birth, in years, for men, for women, and for both (average).

Coverage

All countries listed in Table 1a for which data are available.

Entries

224.

TABLE 1c. VITAL STATISTICS

Country	Period	Birth Rate	Death Rate	Natural Increase[1]	Infant Mortality Period	Rate[2]	Life Expectancy at Birth (years) Period	Men	Women	Average
AFRICA										
Algeria	1980–85	45.1e	12.3e	3.28e	1980–85	88e	1982	58.5	61.4	59.9
Angola	1980–85	47.3e	22.2e	2.51e	1980–85	149e	1980–85	40.4e	43.6e	42.0e
Benin	1980–85	50.7e	21.2e	2.95e	1980–85	120e	1980–85	42.4e	45.6e	44.0e
Botswana	1980–85	49.9e	12.6e	3.73e	1980–85	76e	1980–81	52.7	59.3	56.0
Burkina Faso	1980–85	47.8e	20.1e	2.77e	1980–85	150e	1980–85	43.4e	45.6e	44.5e
Burundi	1980–85	47.2e	19.0e	2.82e	1980–85	124e	1980–85	45.2e	48.4e	46.8e
Cameroon	1980–85	42.9e	15.8e	2.71e	1980–85	103e	1980–85	49.2e	52.6e	50.9e
Cape Verde	1980, 83, 85	34.0	8.5	2.55	1985	76.5	1979–81	58.9	61.0	60.0
Central African Republic	1980–85	44.6e	21.8e	2.28e	1980–85	142e	1980–85	46.1e	49.4e	47.7e
Chad	1980–85	44.2e	21.4e	2.28e	1980–85	143e	1980–85	42.5e	44.6e	43.5e
Comoros-Mayotte	1980–85	46.4e	15.9e	3.05e	1980–85	88e	1980–85	48.3e	51.7e	50.0e
Congo	1980–85	44.5e	18.6e	2.59e	1980–85	81e	1980–85	44.9e	48.1e	46.5e
Djibouti	1980–85	49.2e	18.3e	3.09e	1982	63.4	1980–85	45.4e	48.7e	47.0e
Egypt	1981–85	37.0	9.8	2.72	1982	70.5	1984	58.0	61.1	59.5
Equatorial Guinea	1980–85	42.5e	21.0e	2.15e	1980–85	137e	1980–85	42.4e	45.6e	44.0e
Ethiopia	1980–85	49.7e	23.2e	2.65e	1980–85	155e	1980–85	39.3e	42.5e	40.9e
Gabon	1980–85	33.8e	18.1e	1.57e	1980–85	112e	1980–85	48.0e	51.4e	49.7e
Gambia	1980–85	48.4e	29.0e	1.94e	1980–85	174e	1980–85	33.5e	36.5e	35.0e
Ghana	1980–85	46.9e	14.6e	3.23e	1980–85	98e	1980–85	50.3e	53.8e	52.0e
Guinea	1980–85	46.8e	23.5e	2.33e	1980–85	159e	1980–85	38.7e	41.8e	40.2e
Guinea-Bissau	1980–85	40.7e	21.7e	1.90e	1980–85	143e	1980–85	41.4e	44.6e	43.0e
Ivory Coast	1980–85	46.0e	18.0e	2.80e	1980–85	110e	1980–85	48.8e	52.2e	50.5e
Kenya	1980–85	55.1e	14.0e	4.11e	1980–85	80e	1980–85	55.2e	58.9e	57.0e
Lesotho	1980–85	41.8e	16.5e	2.53e	1980–85	111e	1980–85	46.3e	52.3e	49.3e
Liberia	1980–85	48.7e	17.2e	3.15e	1980–85	132e	1980–85	52.1e	55.7e	53.9e
Libya	1980–85	45.6e	10.9e	3.47e	1980–85	97e	1980–85	56.6e	60.0e	58.3e
Madagascar	1980–85	44.4e	16.5e	2.79e	1980–85	67e	1980–85	46.5e	49.8e	48.1e
Malawi	1980–85	53.2e	21.5e	3.17e	1980–85	165e	1980–85	42.5e	45.8e	44.1e

Mali	1980–85	50.6e	22.5e	2.81e	1980–85	149e	1980–85	43.4e	46.6e	45.0e
Mauritania	1980–85	50.1e	20.9e	2.92e	1980–85	137e	1980–85	42.4e	45.6e	44.0e
Mauritius	1981–86	20.8	6.7	1.41	1986	27.2	1982–84	64.4	71.2	67.8
Morocco	1980–85	36.4e	11.3e	2.51e	1980–85	97e	1980–85	56.6e	60.0e	58.3e
Mozambique	1980–85	45.1e	19.7e	2.54e	1980–85	153e	1980–85	44.4e	46.2e	45.3e
Namibia	1980–85	45.1e	17.3e	2.78e	1980–85	116e	1980–85	46.6e	49.9e	48.2e
Niger	1980–85	51.0e	22.9e	2.81e	1980–85	146e	1980–85	40.9e	44.1e	42.5e
Nigeria	1980–85	50.4e	17.1e	3.33e	1980–85	114e	1980–85	48.1e	51.5e	49.8e
Portugal: Madeira Islands	1983–85	16.3	9.7	0.66						
Reunion	1981–85	24.0	5.9	1.81	1980–85	13e	1980–85	64.7e	68.6e	66.6e
Rwanda	1980–85	51.9e	18.9e	3.30e	1980–85	132e	1980–85	44.7e	48.0e	46.3e
Saint Helena	1981–82, 84	21.0	8.8	1.22	1986	34.5				
Sao Tome and Principe	1982, 85	36.8	9.3	2.75	1985	61.7				
Senegal	1980–85	46.4e	20.9e	2.25e	1980–85	142e	1980–85	41.7e	44.9e	43.3e
Seychelles	1981–86	26.3	7.3	1.90	1986	17.4	1978–82	66.2	73.5	69.8
Sierra Leone	1980–85	47.4e	29.7e	1.77e	1980–85	180e	1980–85	32.5e	35.5e	34.0e
Somalia	1980–85	47.9e	23.3e	2.46e	1980–85	155e	1980–85	39.3e	42.5e	40.9e
South Africa	1980–85	38.7e	13.9e	2.48e	1980–85	83e	1980–85	61.7e	65.5e	63.6e
Spain: Canary Islands	1980–83	15.7	6.0	0.97						
Sudan	1980–85	45.9e	17.4e	2.85e	1980–85	118e	1980–85	46.6e	49.0e	47.8e
Swaziland	1980–85	47.3e	17.2e	3.01e	1980–85	129e	1980–85	46.9e	50.2e	48.5e
Tanzania	1980–85	50.4e	15.3e	3.51e	1980–85	115e	1980–85	49.3e	52.7e	51.0e
Togo	1980–85	45.2e	15.7e	2.95e	1980–85	102e	1980–85	45.4e	48.7e	47.0e
Tunisia	1980–85	34.1e	10.0e	2.41e	1980–85	85e	1980–85	60.1e	61.1e	60.6e
Uganda	1980–85	50.3e	16.8e	3.35e	1980–85	112e	1980–85	47.4e	50.7e	49.0e
Western Sahara	1980–85	29.0e	4.5e	2.45e						
Zaire	1980–85	45.1e	15.8e	2.93e	1980–85	107e	1980–85	48.3e	51.7e	50.0e
Zambia	1980–85	48.1e	15.1e	3.30e	1980–85	88e	1980–85	49.6e	53.1e	51.3e
Zimbabwe	1980–85	47.1e	12.2e	3.49e	1980–85	80e	1980–85	54.0e	57.6e	55.8e
ASIA										
Afghanistan	1980–85	48.9e	27.3e	2.16e	1980–85	205e	1980–85	36.6e	37.3e	36.9e
Bahrain	1980–85	32.2e	4.5e	2.77e	1981	32e	1981	65.9	68.9	67.4

1 The difference between birth and death rates expressed as a percentage rate, representing the annual percentage growth in population without regard for migration.

2 This rate represents the number of deaths per thousand live births that occur in the first year of life.

For an explanation of symbols and abbreviations, see pages 16–17.

(Continued)

TABLE 1c. (Continued)

Country	Period	Birth Rate	Death Rate	Natural Increase1	Infant Mortality Period	Rate2	Life Expectancy at Birth (years) Period	Men	Women	Average
Bangladesh	1980–85	44.8e	17.5e	2.73e	1980–85	128e	1982	54.5	54.8	54.6
Bhutan	1980–85	38.4e	19.8e	1.86e	1980–85	139e	1980–85	46.6e	45.1e	45.8e
Brunei	1981–85	29.6	3.6	2.60	1985	12.0	1981	70.1	72.7	71.4
Burma	1980–85	37.9e	12.7e	2.52e	1980–85	70e	1980–85	55.8e	59.3e	57.5e
China	1980–85	19.0e	6.7e	1.23e	1980–85	39e	1980–85	66.7e	68.9e	67.8e
Cyprus	1980–85	20.7e	8.5e	1.22e	1980–85	17e	1978–82	72.3	77.0	74.6
Gaza Strip	1980–81, 83–84	47.3	29.1	1.82	1980–85	109e	1980–85	54.2e	57.6e	55.9e
Hong Kong	1981–85	15.5	4.8	1.07	1985	7.5	1983	72.5	78.4	75.4
India	1980–84	33.8e	12.3e	2.15e	1983	105e	1981	52.0e	50.0e	51.0e
Indonesia	1980–85	32.1e	12.6e	1.95e	1980–85	84e	1980–85	52.0e	55.2e	53.6e
East Timor	1980–85	48.0e	23.0e	2.50e	1980–85	183e	1980–85	39.2e	40.7e	39.9e
Iran	1980–85	40.8e	12.0e	2.88e	1980–85	101e	1980–85	60.4e	60.0e	60.2e
Iraq	1980–85	44.4e	8.7e	3.57e	1980–85	77e	1980–85	61.5e	63.3e	62.4e
Israel	1981–86	23.6	6.7	1.69	1986	11.4	1984	73.1	76.6	74.8
Japan	1981–86	12.4	6.2	0.62	1985	5.5	1984	74.5	80.2	77.4
Jordan	1980–85	44.7e	7.9e	3.68e	1980–85	54e	1980–85	61.6e	65.4e	63.5e
Kampuchea	1980–85	45.5e	19.7e	2.58e	1980–85	160e	1980–85	42.0e	44.9e	43.4e
Korea										
North Korea	1980–85	30.5e	6.0e	2.45e	1980–85	30e	1980–85	64.6e	71.0e	67.8e
South Korea	1980–84	23.3	6.5	1.68	1980–85	30e	1985	64.5	70.9	67.7
Kuwait	1981–85	34.8	3.0	3.18	1984	18.5	1980–85	68.9e	73.7e	71.3e
Laos	1980–85	40.8e	15.7e	2.51e	1980–85	122e	1980–85	48.3e	51.2e	49.7e
Lebanon	1980–85	29.3e	8.8e	2.05e	1980–85	48e	1980–85	63.1e	67.0e	65.0e
Macao	1981–86	17.8	4.3	1.35	1986	7.2	1980–85	65.6e	69.5e	67.5e
Malaysia	1981–85	31.3e	5.1e	2.62e	1985	18.3e	1985	65.8	69.8	67.8
Peninsular Malaysia	1981–85	30.6	5.3	2.53	1985	16.9	1982	67.7	72.5	70.1
Sabah	1981–82	41.3	4.4	3.69	1981	27.2	1970	48.8	45.4	47.1
Sarawak	1981–83	28.1	3.8	2.43	1980	23.9	1970	51.1	52.7	51.9
Maldives	1980–84, 86	45.1	10.8	3.43	1986	57.5	1982	53.4	49.5	51.5

1The difference between birth and death rates expressed as a percentage rate, representing the annual percentage growth in population without regard for migration.
2This rate represents the number of deaths per thousand live births that occur in the first year of life.

For an explanation of symbols and abbreviations, see pages 16–17.

(Continued)

Figure 4. *The Imperial Palace grounds surrounded by the high-rise buildings of central Tokyo, the largest urbanized area in Asia and capital of Japan, the country with the highest life expectancy. (Credit: Embassy of Japan, Washington.)*

59

TABLE 1c. (Continued)

Country	Period	Birth Rate	Death Rate	Natural Increase[1]	Infant Mortality Period	Rate[2]	Life Expectancy at Birth (years) Period	Men	Women	Average
Mongolia	1980–85	35.9e	8.3e	2.76e	1980–85	53e	1980–85	60.0e	64.1e	62.0e
Nepal	1980–85	41.7e	18.4e	2.33e	1980–85	139e	1981	50.9	48.1	49.5
Oman	1980–85	47.0e	14.3e	3.27e	1980–85	117e	1980–85	51.0e	53.7e	52.3e
Pakistan	1980–85	43.0e	15.3e	2.77e	1980–85	120e	1976–78	59.0	59.2	59.1
Philippines	1980–85	33.3e	8.4e	2.49e	1980–85	51e	1980–85	60.2e	63.7e	61.9e
Qatar	1980–85	38.3e	4.6e	3.37e	1980–85	38e	1980–85	65.4e	69.8e	67.6e
Saudi Arabia	1980–85	42.1e	8.9e	3.32e	1980–85	166e	1980–85	59.2e	62.7e	60.9e
Singapore	1981–86	16.4	5.2	1.12	1986	9.1	1985	69.7	75.2	72.4
Sri Lanka	1981–85	26.1	6.2	1.99	1982	30.5	1981	67.8	71.7	69.7
Syria	1980–85	46.5e	8.7e	3.78e	1980–85	59e	1984	63.3	67.0	65.1
Taiwan	1981–85	20.7	4.8	1.59	1984	7.5	1985	70.8	75.8	73.3
Thailand	1980–85	28.0e	8.0e	2.00e	1980–85	48e	1980–85	61.0e	64.8e	62.9e
Turkey	1980–85	30.2e	9.4e	2.08e	1980–85	92e	1980–85	60.6e	65.5e	63.0e
United Arab Emirates	1980–85	29.8e	4.3e	2.55e	1980–85	38e	1980–85	65.4e	69.8e	67.6e
Vietnam	1980–85	31.0e	10.2e	2.08e	1980–85	76e	1980–85	56.7e	61.1e	58.9e
West Bank	1980–81, 83–84	40.7	17.4	2.33						
Yemen										
North Yemen	1980–85	48.6e	18.4e	3.02e	1980–85	135e	1980–85	46.9e	49.9e	48.4e
South Yemen	1980–85	47.0e	17.4e	2.96e	1980–85	135e	1980–85	46.9e	49.9e	48.4e
EUROPE										
Albania	1981–85	26.8	6.0	2.08	1980–85	43e	1980–85	69.6e	73.5e	71.5e
Andorra	1980–81, 83–84, 86	13.7	4.1	0.96	1986	3.7	1980			70.0
Austria	1981–86	11.9	11.9	0	1986	10.3	1984	70.1	77.2	73.7
Belgium	1981–86	12.0	11.3	0.07	1986	9.7	1982	70.0	76.8	73.4
Bulgaria	1981–86	13.6	11.3	0.23	1986	14.5	1983	68.4	74.4	71.4
Channel Islands	1981–86	11.6	11.4	0.02	1985	8.4	1972	67.0	74.0	70.5
Czechoslovakia	1981–86	14.8	11.8	0.30	1985	14.0	1985	67.2	74.4	70.8
Denmark	1981–86	10.3	11.2	−0.09	1985	7.9	1983–84	71.5	77.5	74.5
Faeroe Islands	1981–86	16.2	7.4	0.88	1985	8.9	1976–80	73.4	78.7	76.0

Country	Period	Birth rate	Death rate	Growth %[1]	Year	Infant mortality[2]	Year	Life exp.	Life exp.	Life exp.
Finland	1981–86	13.2	9.3	0.49	1985	6.3	1984	70.4	74.6	78.8
France	1981–86	14.2	10.1	0.41	1986	7.9	1983	70.7	74.7	78.8
Germany										
East Germany	1981–86	13.9	13.5	0.04	1986	9.2	1984	69.6	72.5	75.4
West Germany	1981–86	9.9	11.5	-0.16	1985	8.9	1982–84	70.8	74.2	77.5
Gibraltar	1981–86	17.7	8.8	0.89	1976	9.8	?	71.4	73.4	75.5
Greece	1981–86	13.0	9.0	0.40	1986	12.3	1982	73.6	75.9	78.3
Hungary	1981–86	12.3	13.7	-0.14	1986	18.9	1984	65.5	69.6	73.7
Iceland	1981–86	17.3	6.9	1.04	1984	6.1	1985	73.5	76.5	79.5
Ireland	1981–86	18.9	9.3	0.96	1986	8.7	1980–82	70.1	72.9	75.6
Isle of Man	1981–86	11.0	15.3	-0.43	1986	15.5				
Italy	1981–85	10.6	9.5	0.11	1985	10.9	1980	70.6	74.0	77.4
Liechtenstein	1981–85	14.3	6.3	0.80	1984	7.4	1980–84	71.1	74.4	77.8
Luxembourg	1981–86	11.7	11.2	0.05	1986	7.9	1980–82	70.0	73.3	76.7
Malta	1981–85	15.2	8.1	0.71	1985	13.6	1984	70.7	72.9	75.0
Monaco	1981, 83–85	19.6	17.6	0.20	1983	3.8				
Netherlands	1981–86	12.2	8.3	0.39	1986	8.1	1984	73.0	76.3	79.7
Norway	1981–86	12.3	10.2	0.21	1985	8.5	1984	72.9	76.2	79.6
Poland	1981–86	18.7	9.7	0.90	1986	17.5	1984	66.8	70.9	75.0
Portugal	1981–85	14.4	9.5	0.49	1985	17.8	1985	68.6	71.9	75.3
Azores	1983–85	19.2	11.4	0.78						
Romania	1981–85	15.6	10.3	0.53	1985	25.6	1982–84	67.0	69.8	72.6
San Marino	1981–85	10.4	7.2	0.32	1985	14.5	1980–85	70.7	73.4	76.2
Spain	1980–84	13.4	7.6	0.58	1983	10.5	1980–81	72.6	75.6	78.6
Balearic Islands	1980–83	13.3	8.5	0.48						
Sweden	1981–86	11.4	11.0	0.04	1986	5.9	1984	73.8	76.9	79.9
Switzerland	1981–86	11.6	9.2	0.24	1985	6.9	1983–84	73.1	76.4	79.7
UK	1981–86	13.0	11.7	0.13	1985	9.3	1982–84	71.4	74.3	77.2
England and Wales	1981–86	12.9	11.6	0.13	1985	9.4	1982–84	71.6	74.5	77.4
Northern Ireland	1981–86	17.7	10.4	0.73	1985	9.6	1982–84	70.2	73.2	76.2
Scotland	1981–86	12.9	12.4	0.05	1986	8.8	1982–84	69.6	72.6	75.6
USSR	1981–86	19.3	10.4	0.89	1986	25.1	1980–85	64.6e	69.1e	73.7e
Yugoslavia	1981–86	16.3	9.2	0.71	1986	27.3	1982	67.8	70.7	73.7

[1]The difference between birth and death rates expressed as a percentage rate, representing the annual percentage growth in population without regard for migration.

[2]This rate represents the number of deaths per thousand live births that occur in the first year of life.

For an explanation of symbols and abbreviations, see pages 16–17.

(Continued)

TABLE 1c. (Continued)

Country	Period	Birth Rate	Death Rate	Natural Increase[1]	Infant Mortality Period	Infant Mortality Rate[2]	Life Expectancy at Birth (years) Period	Men	Women	Average
NORTH AMERICA										
Anguilla	1982, 85	25.7	9.9	1.65	1985	33.9	?	68.6	71.9	70.2
Antigua and Barbuda	1981–85	14.9	4.9	1.00	1983	7.7	1980–85	70.4e	74.2e	72.3e
Aruba	1980–83	16.5	4.8	1.17	1982	8.0	1981	71.6	76.8	74.2
Bahamas	1981–85	23.8	5.2	1.86	1985	26.4	1980–85	66.9e	70.9e	68.9e
Barbados	1980–84, 86	17.2	7.9	0.93	1986	10.8	1980–85	68.9e	74.5e	71.7e
Belize	1981–82, 84–86	38.7	4.4	3.43	1986	21.5	1980–85	63.2e	67.1e	65.1e
Bermuda	1981–85	14.6	7.2	0.74	1985	10.9	1980	68.8	76.3	72.5
Canada	1981–86	15.0	7.1	0.79	1985	7.9	1980–82	71.9	79.0	75.4
Newfoundland	1981–85	15.7	6.0	0.97	1984	9.2	1980–82	71.9	78.6	75.3
Cayman Islands	1981–86	19.2	5.9	1.33	1986	11.1	?	68.6	71.9	70.2
Costa Rica	1981–85	31.4	4.1	2.73	1984	18.9	1980–85	71.9e	75.7e	73.8e
Cuba	1981–86	16.3	6.0	1.03	1986	13.6	1983–84	72.7	76.1	74.4
Dominica	1983–84	22.5	5.1	1.74	1978	19.6	1980–85	72.2e	75.9e	74.0e
Dominican Republic	1980–85	33.1e	8.0e	2.51e	1980–85	75e	1982	70.5	74.5	72.5
El Salvador	1980–84	33.4	7.4	2.60	1984	35.1	1980–85	61.7e	65.5e	63.6e
Greenland	1981–86	20.2	8.1	1.21	1985	24.6	1976–80	59.7	67.3	63.5
Grenada	1982–83	30.1	8.3	2.18	1979	15.4	1980–85	68.5e	72.5e	70.5e
Guadeloupe	1981–85	20.2	6.7	1.35	1985	15.3	1980–85	67.8e	73.2e	70.5e
Guatemala	1981–85	39.2	9.5	2.97	1985	56.0	1980–85	58.1e	61.8e	59.9e
Haiti	1980–85	41.3e	14.2e	2.71e	1980–85	128e	1980–85	51.2e	54.4e	52.8e
Honduras	1980–85	43.9e	11.8e	3.21e	1980–85	82e	1980–85	57.9e	61.7e	59.8e
Jamaica	1980–84	26.8	5.8	2.10	1984	13.2	1980–85	70.9e	74.7e	72.8e
Martinique	1981–86	17.3	6.5	1.08	1986	10.0	1980–85	72.8e	76.5e	74.6e
Mexico	1980–83, 85	34.1	5.7	2.84	1980–85	53e	1979	62.1	66.0	64.0
Montserrat	1981–82, 85	21.1	10.5	1.06	1982	7.7	1980–85	61.2e	65.0e	63.1e
Netherlands Antilles	1980–81	17.9	5.0	1.29	1982	8.2	1981	71.1	75.7	73.4
Nicaragua	1980–85	44.2e	9.7e	3.45e	1980–85	76e	1980–85	58.7e	61.0e	59.8e
Panama	1981–85	26 6	5.4e	2.12e	1980–85	26e	1983	72.8	77.0	74.9

	Years	Birth rate	Death rate	Growth[1]	Year	Rate[2]	Years			
Puerto Rico	1981–85	20.5	6.7	1.38	1985	14.9	1981–83	70.5	77.4	74.0
Saint Christopher and Nevis	1981–85	25.1	10.4	1.47	1984	27.8	1980–85	61.2e	65.0e	63.1e
Saint Lucia	1981–85	30.4	6.1	2.43	1984	17.6	1985	68.6	75.5	72.0
Saint-Pierre and Miquelon	1980–84	17.7	6.8	1.09			?	65.8	71.6	68.7
Saint Vincent and the Grenadines	1980–84	28.6	6.6	2.20	1984	26.5	1980–85	67.5e	71.4e	69.4e
Trinidad and Tobago	1980–83	28.7	6.8	2.19	1983	12.7	1980	66.2	70.4	68.3
Turks and Caicos Islands	1980, 82–83	27.3	3.5	2.38	1982	24.5	?	68.6	71.9	70.2
USA	1981–86	15.7	8.7	0.70	1986	10.4	1985	71.2	78.2	74.7
Alaska	1980–84	24.6	4.0	2.06	1983	12.4	1979–81	68.7	76.9	72.8
Virgin Islands (UK)	1980–84	21.7	5.6	1.61	1984	12.2	?	68.6	71.9	70.2
Virgin Islands (USA)	1980–83, 85	24.3	5.0	1.93	1982	19.5	1980–85	66.7e	70.7e	68.7e
OCEANIA										
American Samoa	1980, 82–85	36.8	4.4	3.24	1985	11.1	1969–71	65.0	69.1	67.0
Australia	1981–86	15.5	7.3	0.82	1985	11.1	1984	72.6	79.1	75.8
Tasmania	1980–82	16.3	7.9	0.84	1982	7.8	1982	70.9	77.4	74.2
Christmas Island (Australia)	1980–83, 85	10.0	0.9	0.91			?	63.0	66.5	64.7
Cocos Islands	1981, 86	17.1	2.5	1.46			?	63.0	66.5	64.7
Cook Islands	1981–85	24.0	6.2	1.78	1985	8.1	1974–78	63.2	67.1	65.1
Fiji	1981–85	29.2	5.5	2.37	1985	18.5	1980–85	67.0e	71.0e	69.0e
French Polynesia	1981–85	30.6	5.7	2.49	1984	20.5	1980–85	61.3e	65.1e	63.2e
Guam	1980–83, 85	25.2	3.6	2.16	1985	12.2	1980–82	69.6	74.5	72.0
Kiribati	1980–85	34.9e	13.9e	2.10e	1971	48.9	1980–85	50.7e	53.7e	52.2e
Nauru	1981–83	29.7	8.5	2.12	1975	19.0	1976–81	49.0	62.0	55.5
New Caledonia	1980–84	25.8	6.2	1.96	1983	16.8	1980–85	64.6e	68.5e	66.5e
New Zealand	1981–86	16.0	8.1	0.79	1985	10.8	1985	71.0	76.8	73.9
Niue	1981–85	29.6	7.1	2.25			?	63.0	66.5	64.7
Norfolk Island	1981, 83–84	10.6	6.7	0.39			?	58.0	59.9	58.9

(Continued)

[1] The difference between birth and death rates expressed as a percentage rate, representing the annual percentage growth in population without regard for migration.
[2] This rate represents the number of deaths per thousand live births that occur in the first year of life.
For an explanation of symbols and abbreviations, see pages 16–17.

TABLE 1c. (Continued)

Country	Period	Birth Rate	Death Rate	Natural Increase[1]	Infant Mortality		Life Expectancy at Birth (years)			
					Period	Rate[2]	Period	Men	Women	Average
Pacific Islands (USA)	1980–83	28.7	4.3	2.44	1982	21.5	1980–85	68.8e	72.8e	70.8e
Papua New Guinea	1980–85	38.8e	13.1e	2.57e	1980–85	74e	1980–85	51.2e	52.7e	51.9e
Samoa	1982–83	31.0e	7.4e	2.36e	1982–83	33e	1980–85	63.2e	67.0e	65.1e
Solomon Islands	1980–85	43.2e	11.7e	3.15e	1980–85	86e	1980–85	55.1e	58.5e	56.8e
Tokelau	1980–83	26.6	6.5	2.01			?	63.0	66.5	64.7
Tonga	1981–85	27.8	3.2	2.46	1985	5.0	1980–85	61.0e	64.8e	62.9e
Tuvalu	1982	34.8	7.6	2.72			1979	57.0	60.0	58.5
USA: Hawaii	1980–84	18.5	5.2	1.33	1983	9.4	1979–81	74.1	80.3	77.2
Vanuatu	1980–85	39.4e	12.4e	2.70e	1980–85	98e	1980–85	52.8e	56.1e	54.4e
Wallis and Futuna Islands	1978	41.1	10.6	3.05	1978	40.5	1974–78	62.0	63.0	62.5
SOUTH AMERICA										
Argentina	1980–81, 83	24.1	8.3	1.58	1983	35.3	1980–85	66.4	73.1e	69.7e
Bolivia	1980–85	44.0e	15.9e	2.81e	1980–85	124e	1980–85	48.6e	53.0e	50.8e
Brazil	1980–85	30.6e	8.4e	2.22e	1980–85	71e	1980–85	62.2e	66.0e	64.1e
Chile	1981–85	22.7	6.2	1.65	1985	19.5	1980–85	68.1e	72.0e	70.0e
Colombia	1980–85	31.0e	7.7e	2.33e	1980–85	50e	1980–85	61.4e	66.0e	63.7e
Ecuador	1980–85	36.8e	8.1e	2.87e	1980–85	70e	1980–85	60.9e	64.7e	62.8e
Falkland Islands	1980–81	16.4	5.1	1.13						
French Guiana	1981–85	29.9	6.2	2.37	1985	20.1	1975–79	63.4	69.7	66.5
Guyana	1980–85	28.5e	5.9e	2.26e	1980–85	35e	1980–85	66.8e	70.8e	68.8e
Paraguay	1980–85	36.0e	7.2e	2.88e	1980–85	45e	1980–85	63.2e	67.0e	65.1e
Peru	1980–85	36.7e	10.7e	2.60e	1980–85	99e	1980–85	56.7e	60.4e	58.5e
Suriname	1980–85	28.8e	6.8e	2.20e	1980–85	36e	1980–85	63.2e	67.0e	65.1e
Uruguay	1980–83, 85	18.4	9.4	0.90	1985	29.5	1980–85	67.1	73.7	70.4
Venezuela	1980–85	33.0e	5.5e	2.75e	1985	26.1	1980	65.8	71.4	68.6

[1] The difference between birth and death rates expressed as a percentage rate, representing the annual percentage growth in population without regard for migration.
[2] This rate represents the number of deaths per thousand live births that occur in the first year of life.
For an explanation of symbols and abbreviations, see pages 16–17.

ECONOMY

1d. Gross Domestic Product (GDP)

Contents

Conventional name of country.

Year of data: the latest year for which dependable information is available.

Gross domestic product (GDP) preferably, or gross national product (GNP)[1] (indicated by a superscript "3"), in millions of US dollars at market prices and at the average rate of exchange for the year in question.[2]

GDP per capita, in US dollars, based on the best population estimate for 1 July of the year in question.

Coverage

All countries listed in Table 1a for which data are available.

Entries

214.

---

[1]GDP is the total market value of all goods and services produced within the borders of a country during a particular year. GNP equals GDP plus the income accruing to a country's residents from investment abroad, less the income earned in the domestic market accruing to foreigners abroad.

[2]Most of the *total* GDP figures are those of the World Bank (see reference 160 in Bibliography), based generally on official national account statistics. For countries not covered by the World Bank, most of the figures given are estimates by the US Central Intelligence Agency (see reference 163) and are designated as estimates in the table. This includes most of the so-called "Communist countries."

TABLE 1d. GROSS DOMESTIC PRODUCT (GDP)

Country	Year	Gross Domestic Product Total[1]	Per Capita[2]	Country	Year	Gross Domestic Product Total[1]	Per Capita[2]
AFRICA							
Algeria	1983	48,425	2,362	Mali	1983	2,075	276
Angola	1986	3,000e	334e	Mauritania	1984	697	380
Benin	1983	1,011	272	Mauritius	1985	1,076	1,055
Botswana	1985	807	742	Mayotte	1982	20e	345e
Burkina Faso	1984	833	111	Morocco	1985	11,892	542
Burundi	1986	1,314	271	Mozambique	1984	1,955	143
Cameroon	1984	7,312	748	Namibia	1985	1,247	805
Cape Verde	1983	110[3]	346[3]	Niger	1983	1,830	313
Central African Republic	1985	709	272	Nigeria	1984	74,213	806
				Reunion	1983	1,760	3,352
Chad	1985	406e	81e	Rwanda	1983	1,504	264
Comoros	1985	114e[3]	302e[3]	Saint Helena	1982	9.6e	1,297e
Congo	1984	2,106	1,170	Sao Tome and Principe	1982	50e	505
Djibouti	1984	339	847				
Egypt	1985	24,995	515	Senegal	1985	2,642	410
Equatorial Guinea	1983	75e[3]	247e[3]	Seychelles	1984	152	2,338
Ethiopia	1986	5,473	122	Sierra Leone	1984	1,373	399
Gabon	1984	3,331	2,897	Somalia	1983	1,140[3]	261[3]
Gambia	1985	102	139	South Africa	1986	61,957	1,865
Ghana	1985	6,367	509	Sudan	1984	7,310	347
Guinea	1984	1,600e[3]	274e[3]	Swaziland	1984	571	906
Guinea-Bissau	1983	154	181	Tanzania	1985	6,187	285
Ivory Coast	1983	6,555	714	Togo	1984	668	231
Kenya	1985	5,771	284	Tunisia	1986	8,950	1,184
Lesotho	1983	388	266	Uganda	1983	5,900e	403e
Liberia	1985	811	374	Western Sahara	1982	116e	707e
Libya	1984	26,756	7,357	Zaire	1985	2,952	97
Madagascar	1985	2,345	235	Zambia	1986	1,656	240
Malawi	1986	1,222	168	Zimbabwe	1985	5,025	600

TABLE 1d. (Continued)

Country	Gross Domestic Product			Country	Gross Domestic Product		
	Year	Total[1]	Per Capita[2]		Year	Total[1]	Per Capita[2]
ASIA				Maldives	1985	84	464
Afghanistan	1985	3,520e[3]	194e[3]	Mongolia	1985	1,675e	886e
Bahrain	1983	4,846	12,923	Nepal	1986	2,539	148
Bangladesh	1986	15,376	153	Oman	1985	10,350	5,175
Bhutan	1984	177	128	Pakistan	1986	33,125	326
Brunei	1985	3,422	15,277	Philippines	1986	30,743	549
Burma	1986	7,974	202	Qatar	1984	3,400	11,684
China	1986	262,000e[3]	249e[3]	Saudi Arabia	1986	77,415	6,448
Cyprus	1985	2,541	3,821	Singapore	1986	17,348	6,708
Gaza Strip	1983	306	621	Sri Lanka	1986	6,407	398
Hong Kong	1985	33,934	6,391	Syria	1985	20,267	1,974
India	1985	196,904	262	Taiwan	1985	59,151	3,091
Indonesia	1985	86,499	529	Thailand	1986	41,764	802
Iran	1985	168,100	3,802	Turkey	1986	74,597	1,436
Iraq	1986	35,000e[3]	2,128e[3]	United Arab Emirates	1985	25,633	15,803
Israel	1986	27,587	6,422	Vietnam	1984	18,100e[3]	310e[3]
Japan	1986	1,962,687	16,155	West Bank	1983	809	1,055
Jordan	1986	4,612	1,261	Yemen			
Kampuchea	1983	810e	116e	North Yemen	1986	3,205	345
Korea				South Yemen	1985	1,100e[3]	480e[3]
North Korea	1985	24,000e[3]	1,177e[3]				
South Korea	1986	98,145	2,361	**EUROPE**			
Kuwait	1985	19,923	11,740	Albania	1986	2,800e[3]	927e[3]
Laos	1984	765e[3]	219e[3]	Andorra	1982	364e	9,579e
Lebanon	1983	5,300e	2,011e	Austria	1986	94,393	12,468
Macao	1985	1,030e[3]	2,628e[3]				
Malaysia	1986	27,788	1,725				

[1]In millions of US dollars at market prices.
[2]In US dollars at market prices.
[3]GNP.

For an explanation of symbols and abbreviations, see pages 16–17.

(Continued)

TABLE 1d. (Continued)

Country	Gross Domestic Product		
	Year	Total[1]	Per Capita[2]
Belgium	1985	81,040	8,221
Bulgaria	1985	57,800e[3]	6,465e[3]
Channel Islands	1983	1,380[3]	10,615[3]
Czechoslovakia	1985	135,600e[3]	8,748e[3]
Denmark	1985	57,125	11,170
Faeroe Islands	1984	474	10,533
Finland	1986	70,595	14,354
France	1986	724,203	13,074
Germany			
East Germany	1985	174,700e[3]	10,496e[3]
West Germany	1986	895,234	14,664
Gibraltar	1983	130[3]	4,883[3]
Greece	1986	39,753	3,989
Hungary	1985	80,100e[3]	7,522e[3]
Iceland	1986	3,877	15,955
Ireland	1985	18,386	5,176
Isle of Man	1983	261[3]	4,078[3]
Italy	1986	599,921	10,484
Liechtenstein	1984	405e	15,000e
Luxembourg	1985	4,163	11,343
Malta	1985	1,018	2,658
Monaco	1982	289e	10,704e
Netherlands	1985	124,255	8,579
Norway	1986	69,782	16,738
Poland	1985	240,600e[3]	6,467e[3]
Portugal	1985	20,687	2,037
Romania	1985	123,700e[3]	5,374e[3]
San Marino	1982	133e	6,333e
Spain	1984	161,327	4,206
Sweden	1986	131,404	15,699
Switzerland	1986	135,416	20,820
UK	1985	455,740	8,049
USSR	1985	2,062,600e[3]	7,403e[3]
Yugoslavia	1985	129,400e[3]	5,596e[3]

Country	Gross Domestic Product		
	Year	Total[1]	Per Capita[2]
NORTH AMERICA			
Anguilla	1983	6e	857e
Antigua and Barbuda	1984	161	2,038
Aruba	1984	461e[3]	6,779e[3]
Bahamas	1984	1,655	7,227
Barbados	1985	1,230	4,862
Belize	1985	193	1,163
Bermuda	1985	1,058	18,561
Canada	1986	363,606	14,197
Cayman Islands	1983	158e	8,316e
Costa Rica	1986	4,259	1,664
Cuba	1985	29,765e	2,948e
Dominica	1984	85	1,109
Dominican Republic	1986	5,563	867
El Salvador	1986	5,344	1,088
Greenland	1983	550[3]	10,577[3]
Grenada	1985	96	1,043
Guadeloupe	1983	1,113	3,393
Guatemala	1986	8,419	1,027
Haiti	1986	2,244	419
Honduras	1986	3,738	828
Jamaica	1985	2,026	875
Martinique	1983	1,307	3,997
Mexico	1985	177,477	2,260
Montserrat	1985	37	3,083
Netherlands Antilles	1984	1,360e	6,939e
Nicaragua	1985	4,354	1,331
Panama	1985	4,881	2,239
Puerto Rico	1986	21,109	6,397
Saint Christopher and Nevis	1983	51	1,133
Saint Lucia	1984	148	1,096

TABLE 1d. (Continued)

Country	Gross Domestic Product		
	Year	Total[1]	Per Capita[2]
Saint-Pierre and Miquelon	1982	46e	7,667e
Saint Vincent and the Grenadines	1983	92	911
Trinidad and Tobago	1985	7,404	6,248
Turks and Caicos Islands	1982	15e	1,875e
USA	1986	4,194,500	17,362
Virgin Islands (UK)	1985	75	5,769
Virgin Islands (USA)	1983	890[3]	8,558[3]
OCEANIA			
American Samoa	1983	140[3]	4,118[3]
Australia	1986	166,819	10,524
Christmas Island (Australia)	1982	61e	20,333e
Cocos Islands	1982	1.8e	1,667e
Cook Islands	1983	21e	1,235e
Fiji	1985	1,163	1,661
French Polynesia	1984	886	5,121
Guam	1983	733e	6,319e
Johnston Island	1982	5e	16,667e
Kiribati	1984	25	397
Midway Islands	1982	3e	6,000e
Nauru	1984	160e[3]	20,000e[3]
New Caledonia	1983	824	5,683
New Zealand	1985	22,362	6,872
Niue	1984	3e[3]	1,000e[3]
Norfolk Island	1982	12e	5,455e

Country	Gross Domestic Product		
	Year	Total[1]	Per Capita[2]
Pacific Islands (USA)	1983	140[3]	966[3]
Papua New Guinea	1985	2,292	688
Pitcairn Island	1982	0.6e	10,000e
Samoa	1983	150e	932e
Solomon Islands	1983	155	610
Tokelau	1982	1.5e	937e
Tonga	1985	100e	1,031e
Tuvalu	1984	4e[3]	500e[3]
Vanuatu	1985	79e	603e
Wake Island	1982	2.5e	8,333e
Wallis and Futuna Islands	1985	7e	583e
SOUTH AMERICA			
Argentina	1983	64,835	2,188
Bolivia	1985	6,266	975
Brazil	1986	270,026	1,950
Chile	1986	16,882	1,370
Colombia	1986	32,983	1,163
Ecuador	1986	11,128	1,154
Falkland Islands	1982	12e	6,316e
French Guiana	1982	210[3]	2,877[3]
Guyana	1986	519	651
Paraguay	1986	5,407	1,420
Peru	1985	14,394	731
Suriname	1984	1,013	2,604
Uruguay	1986	6,218	2,084
Venezuela	1986	49,962	2,808
Total		15,998,854[4]	

[1]In millions of US dollars at market prices.
[2]In US dollars at market prices.
[3]GNP.
[4]This is not the total world GDP for any particular year, but merely the total of GDP and GNP estimates given in this table for the years cited.
For an explanation of symbols and abbreviations, see pages 16–17.

Figure 5. *Looking east to the Capitol from the top of the Washington Monument in Washington, capital of the USA, the country with the largest gross domestic product (GDP). Here the grass-covered Mall is lined on both sides by national museums and art galleries. (Credit: US National Park Service.)*

1e. Commercial Energy Production and Consumption, 1985

Contents

Conventional name of country.

Production of primary commercial energy in 1985, expressed in thousands of metric tons of coal equivalent. Primary energy includes coal and lignite, crude petroleum and natural gas liquids, natural gas, and hydro and nuclear electricity. The production estimates are those of the United Nations (see reference 161 in Bibliography) but are based generally on official statistics. The United Nations is also responsible for the conversion of each type of energy into coal equivalence.

Consumption of energy in 1985, expressed in thousands of metric tons of coal equivalent. The consumption estimates are those of the United Nations (see reference 161) and include coal and lignite, petroleum products, natural gas, and hydro and nuclear electricity. The United Nations is also responsible for the conversion of each type of energy into coal equivalence.

Consumption of energy per capita in 1985, expressed in kilograms of coal equivalent, based on the best population estimate for 1 July 1985.

Coverage

All countries listed in Table 1a for which data are available.

Entries

189.

TABLE 1e. COMMERCIAL ENERGY PRODUCTION AND CONSUMPTION, 1985

Country	Production (1,000 MT[1])	Consumption	
		Total (1,000 MT[1])	Per Capita (kg[2])
AFRICA			
Algeria	103,828	16,654	767
Angola	16,642	1,065	122
Benin	1	157	40
Burkina Faso	0	198	26
Burundi	5	92	19
Cameroon	9,841	4,417	434
Cape Verde	0	45	135
Central African Republic	9	97	37
Chad	0	102	20
Comoros-Mayotte	0	18	41
Congo	8,357	167	90
Djibouti	0	96	223
Egypt	70,543	31,032	640
Equatorial Guinea	0	37	94
Ethiopia	79	774	18
Gabon	12,016	1,338	1,109
Gambia	0	81	110
Ghana	502	1,214	97
Guinea	10	429	73
Guinea-Bissau	0	40	45
Ivory Coast	2,181	2,038	208
Kenya	248	1,711	84
Liberia	42	771	355
Libya	78,049	12,746	3,426
Madagascar	30	400	40

Country	Production (1,000 MT[1])	Consumption	
		Total (1,000 MT[1])	Per Capita (kg[2])
Malawi	60	259	37
Mali	17	216	26
Mauritania	0	294	156
Mauritius	14	303	297
Morocco	1,089	7,174	327
Mozambique	569	1,259	90
Niger	61	365	60
Nigeria	112,382	21,576	227
Reunion	69	442	807
Rwanda	21	205	34
Saint Helena	0	1	125
Sao Tome and Principe	1	17	157
Senegal	0	1,074	167
Seychelles	0	39	600
Sierra Leone	?	264	75
Somalia	0	524	113
South Africa[3]	132,251	114,172	3,069
Sudan	63	1,549	72
Tanzania	77	904	42
Togo	0	142	48
Tunisia	8,333	5,385	742
Uganda	79	388	25
Western Sahara	0	84	431
Zaire	2,495	1,940	64

[3]Inc Botswana, Lesotho, Namibia, and Swaziland.

TABLE 1e. (Continued)

Country	Production (1,000 MT[1])	Consumption Total (1,000 MT[1])	Consumption Per Capita (kg[2])	Country	Production (1,000 MT[1])	Consumption Total (1,000 MT[1])	Consumption Per Capita (kg[2])
Zambia	1,665	2,153	323	Malaysia	50,285	24,507	1,563
Zimbabwe	2,766	3,852	460	Maldives	0	13	72
				Mongolia	2,473	3,437	1,818
ASIA				Nepal	49	288	17
Afghanistan	4,055	1,697	94	Oman	50,524	16,591	8,296
Bahrain	7,996	5,528	13,820	Pakistan	15,966	25,146	261
Bangladesh	3,740	5,744	58	Philippines	3,203	15,835	291
Bhutan	1	17	12	Qatar	27,618	6,569	20,854
Brunei	24,085	2,847	12,710	Saudi Arabia	258,115	41,622	3,606
Burma	3,811	3,274	86	Singapore	0	19,685	7,695
China	798,368	720,468	693	Sri Lanka	294	1,784	113
Cyprus	0	1,287	1,935	Syria	13,750	12,904	1,257
Hong Kong	0	9,265	1,745	Taiwan	5,962	45,638	2,385
India	182,230	192,966	257	Thailand	7,999	21,436	418
Indonesia	131,260	42,510	260	Turkey	22,920	45,479	898
Iran	169,692	55,864	1,264	United Arab Emirates	94,775	9,653	5,951
Iraq	101,136	10,317	649	Vietnam	5,533	7,035	118
Israel	78	10,352	2,446	Yemen			
Japan	49,195	448,505	3,705	North Yemen	0	1,286	146
Jordan	0	3,314	1,232	South Yemen	0	2,203	960
Kampuchea	5	23	3.2				
Korea				**EUROPE**			
North Korea	49,639	54,661	2,681	Albania	6,661	3,927	1,326
South Korea	17,320	66,587	1,645	Austria	8,360	29,668	3,927
Kuwait	87,491	12,919	7,613	Belgium	11,363	49,494	5,021
Laos	160	155	43	Bulgaria	18,038	51,885	5,799
Lebanon	72	2,762	1,035	Czechoslovakia	66,804	97,078	6,263
Macao	0	300	765	Denmark	5,672	27,322	5,343

[1]1,000 metric tons of coal equivalent.
[2]Kilograms of coal equivalent.
For an explanation of symbols and abbreviations, see pages 16–17.

(Continued)

TABLE 1e. (Continued)

Country	Production (1,000 MT[1])	Consumption Total (1,000 MT[1])	Consumption Per Capita (kg[2])
Faeroe Islands	6	249	5,413
Finland	4,919	25,601	5,223
France[4]	63,799	219,292	3,973
Germany			
East Germany	100,820	130,623	7,848
West Germany	160,727	349,947	5,735
Gibraltar	0	7	241
Greece	9,225	23,032	2,319
Hungary	23,277	41,630	3,909
Iceland	496	1,228	5,095
Ireland	4,280	11,127	3,133
Italy[5]	28,518	188,611	3,300
Luxembourg	9	4,186	11,406
Malta	0	490	1,279
Netherlands	103,429	83,409	5,759
Norway[6]	104,641	26,951	6,483
Poland	175,347	172,393	4,634
Portugal	1,559	13,295	1,309
Romania	90,648	109,923	4,776
Spain	30,790	84,152	2,180
Sweden	15,967	41,430	4,962
Switzerland[7]	6,534	24,360	3,748
UK	324,287	276,790	4,889
USSR	2,167,893	1,708,248	6,131
Yugoslavia	36,581	58,349	2,523

Country	Production (1,000 MT[1])	Consumption Total (1,000 MT[1])	Consumption Per Capita (kg[2])
NORTH AMERICA			
Antigua and Barbuda	0	70	875
Bahamas	0	1,038	4,436
Barbados	167	350	1,383
Belize	0	87	524
Bermuda	0	209	3,732
Canada	324,770	251,978	9,929
Cayman Islands	0	50	2,500
Costa Rica	340	1,262	507
Cuba	1,255	14,333	1,419
Dominica	2	20	256
Dominican Republic	64	2,966	475
El Salvador	193	963	200
Greenland	0	247	4,660
Grenada	0	29	315
Guadeloupe	0	312	943
Guatemala	346	1,578	198
Haiti	32	339	64
Honduras	107	960	220
Jamaica	18	2,744	1,185
Martinique	0	279	851
Mexico	249,542	132,491	1,687
Montserrat	0	9	750
Netherlands Antilles-Aruba	0	2,848	10,667

4Inc Monaco.
5Inc San Marino.
6Inc Svalbard.
7Inc Liechtenstein.

TABLE 1e. (Continued)

Country	Production (1,000 MT[1])	Consumption Total (1,000 MT[1])	Consumption Per Capita (kg[2])
Nicaragua	69	1,006	307
Panama	237	1,442	661
Puerto Rico	18	8,489	2,587
Saint Christopher and Nevis	0	25	543
Saint Lucia	0	59	428
Saint-Pierre and Miquelon	0	20	3,333
Saint Vincent and the Grenadines	2	21	202
Trinidad and Tobago	16,882	5,984	5,050
USA	2,016,276	2,276,274	9,513
Virgin Islands (UK)	0	18	1,385
Virgin Islands (USA)	0	3,505	31,577
OCEANIA			
American Samoa	0	216	6,000
Australia8	171,147	102,949	6,532
Cook Islands	0	305	16,944
Fiji	36	285	407
French Polynesia	4	279	1,632
Guam	0	1,183	9,540
Kiribati	0	13	203
Nauru	0	59	7,375
New Caledonia	59	680	4,444
New Zealand	10,061	11,386	3,499
Niue	0	1	333
Pacific Islands (USA)	2	56	364
Papua New Guinea	52	1,052	316
Samoa	2	57	350
Solomon Islands	0	64	237
Tonga	0	22	227
Vanuatu	0	28	206
SOUTH AMERICA			
Argentina	58,338	52,046	1,703
Bolivia	4,583	1,947	303
Brazil	70,710	93,773	692
Chile	6,621	10,709	883
Colombia	27,884	24,116	865
Ecuador	21,132	5,983	638
Falkland Islands	5	11	5,789
French Guiana	0	156	1,880
Guyana	1	663	839
Paraguay	184	934	254
Peru	16,061	11,640	591
Suriname	240	590	1,482
Uruguay	792	1,822	622
Venezuela	156,427	54,545	3,150
World	9,487,084	9,175,983	1,888e

11,000 metric tons of coal equivalent.
2Kilograms of coal equivalent.
8Inc Christmas Island (Australia).
For an explanation of symbols and abbreviations, see pages 16–17.

1f. Volume of Exports and Imports, by Value

Contents

Conventional name of country.

Total volume of exports (top line) and imports (bottom line) for the years 1981 through 1986 (if available) in millions of US dollars at the average rate of exchange for the year in question.

Average annual volume of exports and imports for the period of record in millions of US dollars.

Per capita volume of exports and imports for the latest year for which total volume is given, in US dollars, based on the best population estimate for 1 July of the year in question.

Coverage

All countries listed in Table 1a for which data are available.

Rounding

Export and import figures are rounded to the nearest million US dollars.

Entries

196.

TABLE 1f. VOLUME OF EXPORTS AND IMPORTS, BY VALUE

Country	Total Volume of Exports (top line) and Imports (bottom line) (million US dollars)						Average	Per Capita Volume Latest Year (US dollars)
	1981	1982	1983	1984	1985	1986		
AFRICA								
Algeria	13,296	11,476	11,163	11,886	10,149	7,876	10,974	351
	11,269	10,738	10,395	10,289	9,841	10,162	10,449	453
Angola	1,874	1,645	1,840	2,029	2,001		1,878	215
	1,678	876	682	657	1,392		1,057	121
Benin	34	24					29	7
	542	464					503	128
Botswana	400	457	636	674	744	858	628	761
	798	688	736	707	583	684	699	606
Burkina Faso	75	56	57	79			67	11
	338	346	288	207			295	28
Burundi	71	88	80	98	110	233	113	48
	161	214	183	186	186	206	189	42
Cameroon	1,122	1,080	939	882	722	784	908	75
	1,428	1,211	1,217	1,106	1,151	1,705	1,303	163
Cape Verde	3	4	3	3			3	9
	71	71	48	42			58	129
Central African Republic	79	109	75	86	88		87	34
	95	127	85	87	109		101	42
Chad	83	58	74	138			88	28
	108	109	117	162			124	33
Comoros				7	16		11	29
				43	37		40	106
Congo	1,073	977	1,066	1,183	1,077		1,075	581
	804	807	806	618	751		757	405
Djibouti	9	13	11				11	33
	224	226	221				224	670
Egypt	3,233	3,120	3,215	3,140	3,714		3,284	77
	8,839	9,078	10,274	10,766	9,962		9,784	205

For an explanation of symbols and abbreviations, see pages 16–17.

(Continued)

TABLE 1f. (Continued)

Country	Total Volume of Exports (top line) and Imports (bottom line) (million US dollars)							Per Capita Volume Latest Year (US dollars)
	1981	1982	1983	1984	1985	1986	Average	
Equatorial Guinea	15	17					16	57
	46	48					47	160
Ethiopia	389	404	402	417	333		389	8
	739	787	876	942	996		868	23
Gabon	2,200	2,160	1,975	2,018	1,920		2,055	1,592
	841	723	853	888	976		856	809
Gambia	27	44	48	47	43		42	59
	122	97	115	98	93		105	127
Ghana	1,063	873	2,563	571	617	862	1,091	61
	1,106	705	2,534	591	731	783	1,075	56
Guinea				537			537	92
				403			403	69
Guinea-Bissau	14	12	9				12	10
	50	50	55				52	64
Ivory Coast	2,535	2,235	2,067	2,698	2,939		2,495	300
	2,384	2,090	1,808	1,511	1,742		1,907	178
Kenya	1,188	977	983	1,083	958	1,200	1,065	57
	2,069	1,613	1,358	1,547	1,437	1,613	1,606	76
Lesotho	49	36	30	28	21		33	14
	516	524	571	504	377		498	247
Liberia	529	477	428	452	436	408	455	184
	477	428	412	363	284	259	370	117
Libya	14,371	13,951	10,957	11,136	10,841		12,251	2,914
	8,382	7,175	7,467	6,800	5,422		7,049	1,458
Madagascar	316	310	296	333	274		306	27
	540	425	387	366	402		424	40
Malawi	270	246	229	313	252	243	259	33
	350	311	311	269	284	252	296	35
Mali	154	146	165	195	170	192	170	23
	385	332	345	375	410	438	381	52

Mauritania	261	232	305	297	374	349	303	179
	265	273	227	246	234	213	243	109
Mauritius	324	367	368	373	441	672	424	653
	554	464	442	472	528	675	522	656
Mayotte				4			4	61
				21			21	328
Morocco	2,320	2,059	2,062	2,172	2,165	2,640	2,236	117
	4,356	4,316	3,599	3,907	3,849	4,069	4,016	181
Mozambique	281	229	132	86			182	6
	801	836	636	482			689	35
Namibia		924	829	739			831	490
		1,010	890	754			885	500
Niger	455	332	298				362	52
	510	466	324				433	56
Nigeria	18,087	13,660	10,715	12,572	13,134		13,634	138
	20,453	15,003	9,062	5,863	6,205		11,317	65
Reunion	107	105	87	77	97	230	117	411
	786	804	837	791	841	1,138	866	2,032
Rwanda	88	93	79	83	112	118	95	19
	256	276	269	295	343	352	298	56
Sao Tome and Principe	9		9				9	90
	17	18	18				17	180
Senegal	500	548	543	534	410		509	64
	861	992	1,039	1,010	635		907	99
Seychelles	5	4	20	26	28		17	431
	93	98	88	87	99		93	1,523
Sierra Leone	153	89	92	148	112		119	32
	312	240	166	166	156		208	44
Somalia	152	199	103	45	91		118	20
	512	330	180	109	112		249	24
South Africa[1]	20,844	17,801	18,581	17,311	16,612	18,491	18,273	484
	21,077	16,971	14,528	14,956	10,319	12,057	14,985	316
Sudan	658	499	624	629	367		555	17
	1,578	1,285	1,354	1,147	757		1,224	35
Swaziland	366	322	291	256	167		280	258
	597	520	548	442	324		486	501

[1]Inc Botswana, Lesotho, Namibia, and Swaziland.
For an explanation of symbols and abbreviations, see pages 16–17.

(Continued)

TABLE 1f. (Continued)

Country	Total Volume of Exports (top line) and Imports (bottom line) (million US dollars)							Per Capita Volume Latest Year (US dollars)
	1981	1982	1983	1984	1985	1986	Average	
Tanzania	613	455	366	378	284		419	13
	1,212	1,131	822	889	1,026		1,016	47
Togo	212	177	162	197			187	69
	435	391	284	278			347	97
Tunisia	2,499	1,986	1,872	1,797	1,627	1,760	1,923	237
	3,779	3,402	3,102	3,218	2,597	2,888	3,164	388
Uganda	242	347	372	399			340	27
		458	510	509			492	34
Zaire	662	569	1,134	1,004	591	1,092	842	35
	672	480	498	659	997	884	698	29
Zambia	1,074	1,066	828	655	539		832	81
	1,062	831	703	608	698		780	105
Zimbabwe	1,406	1,273	1,128	1,003	1,053	1,020	1,147	121
	1,472	1,430	1,052	959	969	985	1,144	117
ASIA								
Afghanistan	694	708	457	808	566	537	628	29
	622	695	525	1,156	999		799	55
Bahrain	4,347	3,791	3,200	3,139	2,863	2,369	3,285	5,750
	4,124	3,614	3,342	3,530	3,159	2,427	3,366	5,891
Bangladesh	662	667	690	934	927	880	793	9
	1,813	1,737	1,587	2,052	2,170	2,703	2,009	27
Bhutan		18	14				16	10
		53	41				47	30
Brunei	4,066	3,808	3,386	3,197			3,614	14,272
	599	734	728	622			671	2,777
Burma	476	393	378	310	315	265	356	7
	373	408	268	239	283	304	312	8
China	22,007	21,913	22,150	24,871	27,343	31,050	24,889	29
	22,014	18,939	21,324	27,750	42,491	42,620	29,190	40

Cyprus	556	555	494	575	479	499	526	741
	1,165	1,215	1,219	1,364	1,247	1,279	1,248	1,900
Gaza Strip	198	190	181	115			171	225
	309	310	332	279			307	547
Hong Kong	21,737	20,985	21,951	28,317	29,927	35,439	26,393	6,405
	24,680	23,554	24,009	28,567	29,578	35,366	27,626	6,392
India	8,373	8,807	8,713	8,793	8,510	9,043	8,706	12
	15,654	14,365	13,434	13,953	15,092	14,529	14,504	19
Indonesia	25,164	22,328	21,146	21,888	18,590	14,805	20,653	89
	13,272	16,859	16,352	13,882	10,259	10,718	13,557	64
Iran	12,587	19,414	20,247	13,979	12,378		15,721	280
	12,549	11,539	18,296				14,128	435
Iraq	10,530	10,250	9,785	9,681	10,534		10,061	639
	20,735	21,534	12,166	11,078			15,209	663
Israel	5,329	4,991	4,894	5,804	6,080	6,846	5,657	1,594
	7,847	7,960	8,370	8,411	8,021	9,827	8,406	2,287
Japan	152,016	138,911	146,668	170,107	175,683	209,153	165,423	1,722
	143,288	131,932	126,392	136,522	129,480	126,408	132,337	1,040
Jordan	732	753	579	752	838	647	717	177
	3,149	3,241	3,030	2,784	2,656	2,432	2,882	665
Kampuchea								
Korea								
North Korea								
South Korea	21,254	21,853	24,445	29,245	30,283	35,776	27,143	861
	26,131	24,251	26,192	30,631	31,136	32,790	28,522	789
Kuwait	16,298	10,861	11,500	10,751	10,126		11,907	5,967
	6,969	8,283	7,312	7,699			7,566	4,738
Laos	33		26	12			24	3
	125		92	48			88	14
Lebanon	1,262	1,108	595				988	226
	3,564	3,399					3,481	1,292
Macao	686	722	763	913	903	1,028	836	2,570
	723	715	730	798	776	871	769	2,177
Malaysia	11,766	12,027	14,107	16,452	15,764	13,869	13,997	861
	11,546	12,423	13,265	14,017	12,602	10,839	12,449	673

(Continued)

For an explanation of symbols and abbreviations, see pages 16–17.

TABLE 1f. (Continued)

Country	Total Volume of Exports (top line) and Imports (bottom line) (million US dollars)						Per Capita Volume Latest Year (US dollars)
	1981	1982	1983	1984	1985	1986	Average	

Country	1981	1982	1983	1984	1985	1986	Average	Per Capita Volume Latest Year (US dollars)
Maldives	9	10	13	18	23		15	127
	31	43	57	53	53		47	293
Mongolia	436	505	533	520	566		512	299
	655	712	810	750	905		766	479
Nepal	125	88	93	127	161	142	123	8
	390	395	464	417	463	459	431	27
Oman	4,696	4,421	4,248	4,422	4,972		4,552	2,486
	2,288	2,682	2,492	2,748	3,153		2,673	1,576
Pakistan	2,880	2,395	3,074	2,614	2,719	3,306	2,831	33
	5,549	5,385	5,341	4,873	5,892	5,373	5,402	53
Philippines	5,722	5,021	5,005	5,322	4,544	4,842	5,076	86
	7,946	8,255	7,980	6,051	5,261	5,394	6,814	96
Qatar	5,844	4,507	3,297	4,513	3,541		4,340	11,241
	1,518	1,945	1,456	1,162	1,139		1,444	3,616
Saudi Arabia	120,240	79,124	45,835	36,834	23,622		70,508	3,403
	35,244	40,654	39,206	33,696	22,817	22,495	34,484	2,047
Singapore	20,967	20,788	21,833	24,108	22,817	22,495	22,168	8,699
	27,608	28,167	28,158	28,712	26,285	25,512	27,407	9,865
Sri Lanka	1,044	1,015	1,066	1,454	1,191	1,119	1,148	69
	1,849	1,771	1,787	1,845	1,874	1,827	1,825	113
Syria	2,103	2,026	1,923	1,853	1,637		1,908	159
	5,040	4,015	4,542	4,116	2,536		4,050	247
Taiwan	22,611	22,203	25,125	30,455	30,719		26,223	1,605
	21,203	18,888	20,291	21,954	20,102		20,488	1,051
Thailand	7,038	6,945	6,368	7,413	7,122	8,753	7,273	168
	9,951	8,548	10,287	10,398	9,244	9,176	9,601	176
Turkey	4,703	5,685	5,694	7,086	7,913	7,401	6,414	142
	8,932	8,923	9,348	10,822	11,394	11,145	10,094	215
United Arab Emirates	20,240	17,257	14,596	14,103	14,337		16,107	8,839
	9,646	9,419	8,356				9,140	6,144

For an explanation of symbols and abbreviations, see pages 16–17.

(Continued)

Figure 6. Waterfront at Singapore, capital of the Republic of Singapore. Excluding countries with less than a million inhabitants, Singapore ranks first in the per capita value of its foreign trade, leading in imports and placing second to the United Arab Emirates in exports. (Credit: Singapore Tourist Promotion Board, New York.)

Figure 7. Modern skyline of Abu Zaby, capital of the United Arab Emirates, which holds first place among countries with at least a million inhabitants in the per capita value of its exports. (Credit: Embassy of the United Arab Emirates, Washington.)

TABLE 1f. (Continued)

Country	Total Volume of Exports (top line) and Imports (bottom line) (million US dollars)							Per Capita Volume Latest Year (US dollars)
	1981	1982	1983	1984	1985	1986	Average	
Vietnam	424	531	596				517	10
	1,786	1,716	1,815				1,772	32
West Bank	205	201	205	184			199	234
	428	418	453	407			426	517
Yemen								
North Yemen	47	39	27	9	10		26	1
	1,758	1,521	1,593	1,539	1,289		1,540	146
South Yemen	607	795	674	645			680	290
	1,419	1,599	1,483	1,543			1,511	693
EUROPE								
Albania								
Andorra			10	10			10	238
			233	232			232	5,524
Austria	15,845	15,685	15,428	15,741	17,226	22,522	17,074	2,975
	21,048	19,557	19,364	19,631	20,937	26,843	21,230	3,546
Belgium[2]	55,705	52,364	51,939	51,779	53,688	68,873	55,725	6,735
	62,464	58,239	55,314	55,303	56,166	68,650	59,356	6,713
Bulgaria	10,689	11,428	12,130	12,850	13,348		12,089	1,490
	10,801	11,527	12,283	12,714	13,656		12,196	1,525
Czechoslovakia	14,876	15,597	16,477	17,196	17,541	20,456	17,024	1,317
	14,658	15,397	16,324	17,080	17,627	20,950	17,006	1,349
Denmark	16,236	15,595	16,047	15,959	16,699	21,201	16,956	4,140
	17,735	16,958	16,276	16,585	18,429	22,811	18,132	4,454
Faeroe Islands	160	151	172	160	179	242	177	5,261
	208	199	243	264	248	329	248	7,152
Finland	14,015	13,132	12,519	13,505	13,617	16,340	13,855	3,322
	14,202	13,387	12,856	12,443	13,233	15,325	13,574	3,116

2Inc Luxembourg.

For an explanation of symbols and abbreviations, see pages 16–17.

(Continued)

TABLE 1f. (Continued)

Country	Total Volume of Exports (top line) and Imports (bottom line) (million US dollars)							Per Capita Volume Latest Year (US dollars)
	1981	1982	1983	1984	1985	1986	Average	
France[3]	101,371	92,629	91,231	93,276	97,726	119,435	99,278	2,155
	120,872	115,645	105,395	103,807	107,809	128,836	113,727	2,325
Germany								
East Germany	19,858	21,743	23,793	24,836	25,268	27,729	23,871	1,668
	20,181	20,196	21,524	22,940	23,433	27,414	22,615	1,649
West Germany	176,043	176,428	169,425	169,784	183,406	242,411	186,249	3,971
	163,934	155,856	152,899	151,246	157,645	189,484	161,844	3,104
Gibraltar	52	42	37	35	62		46	2,138
	133	120	94	91	147		117	5,069
Greece	4,281	4,297	4,459	4,811	4,542	5,650	4,673	567
	8,885	10,023	9,632	9,434	10,139	11,349	9,910	1,139
Hungary	8,712	8,767	8,696	8,563	8,542	9,158	8,740	862
	9,128	8,814	8,503	8,091	8,228	9,583	8,724	902
Iceland	859	685	749	740	814	1,096	824	4,510
	980	942	816	839	904	1,116	933	4,593
Ireland	7,675	8,948	8,620	9,629	10,360	13,161	9,732	3,721
	10,607	9,728	9,189	9,663	10,028	12,610	10,304	3,565
Italy[4]	75,187	73,479	72,681	73,303	78,957	97,835	78,574	1,709
	91,022	86,213	80,367	84,215	90,994	99,937	88,791	1,746
Liechtenstein	476	458	454	451	484		465	17,286
	226	199	187	185			199	6,852
Malta	448	411	363	394	400	497	419	1,291
	855	789	733	717	758	887	790	2,304
Netherlands	68,732	66,288	65,678	65,881	68,282	80,555	69,236	5,531
	65,921	62,669	61,637	62,136	65,218	75,580	65,527	5,190
Norway	18,220	17,595	17,628	18,892	19,991	18,096	18,403	4,341
	15,562	15,479	13,238	13,889	15,560	20,306	15,672	4,871
Poland	13,182	11,174	10,951	11,649	11,447	11,884	11,714	317
	15,224	10,204	9,995	10,548	10,761	11,107	11,306	297
Portugal	4,180	4,171	4,599	5,208	5,711	7,205	5,179	700
	9,951	9,599	8,241	7,978	7,792	9,458	8,836	919

(Continued)

Romania	11,180	10,123	15,256	10,735			11,823	474
	10,978	8,323	12,782	7,565			9,912	334
Spain	20,351	20,283	19,794	23,587	25,112	27,158	22,714	702
	32,218	31,550	29,201	28,867	30,995	35,022	31,309	906
Sweden	28,664	26,817	27,466	29,378	30,006	37,221	30,006	4,447
	28,845	27,596	26,120	26,416	28,584	32,508	28,345	3,884
Switzerland	27,042	26,024	25,595	25,863	27,451	37,674	28,275	5,792
	30,696	28,670	29,119	29,469	30,722	41,278	31,659	6,347
UK	102,820	97,075	91,939	94,502	101,332	107,013	99,113	1,885
	102,725	99,708	100,235	105,961	109,269	126,208	107,351	2,223
USSR	79,003	86,912	91,343	91,652	87,041		87,190	312
	72,960	77,752	80,412	80,680	82,748		78,910	297
Yugoslavia	10,929	10,265	9,038	9,811	10,641	10,297	10,163	444
	15,817	13,346	11,104	11,538	12,164	11,749	12,620	506

NORTH AMERICA

Antigua and Barbuda	34	21	20	18			23	228
	111	139	109	132			123	1,671
Aruba			2,089	2,089			2,089	30,721
			2,126	2,126			2,126	31,265
Bahamas	6,189	4,534	3,970	3,393	2,728		4,163	11,658
	7,284	6,349	4,616	4,098	3,081		5,086	13,167
Barbados	194	257	321	391	352	275	298	1,087
	572	551	621	659	607	587	599	2,320
Belize	119	91	78	93	90	91	94	532
	162	128	112	130	103	123	126	719
Bermuda	29	17	23	41	23		27	411
	323	351	378	414	402		374	7,179
Canada	70,018	68,496	73,514	86,729	87,479	86,725	78,827	3,386
	66,303	55,035	61,343	73,705	76,413	81,099	68,983	3,166
Cayman Islands							3[5]	167
							101[5]	5,611
Costa Rica	1,008	871	866	978	989	1,026	956	401
	1,209	893	988	1,085	1,098	1,130	1,067	441

[3] Inc Monaco.
[4] Inc San Marino.
[5] 1980.

For an explanation of symbols and abbreviations, see pages 16–17.

TABLE 1f. (Continued)

Country	Total Volume of Exports (top line) and Imports (bottom line) (million US dollars)							Per Capita Volume Latest Year (US dollars)
	1981	1982	1983	1984	1985	1986	Average	
Cuba	5,406	5,920	6,424	6,164	8,567		6,496	848
	6,545	6,637	7,232	8,134	8,593		7,428	851
Dominica	19	24	27	26	29		25	372
	50	47	45	58	54	44	50	557
Dominican Republic	1,188	768	785	868	750		872	120
	1,450	1,256	1,279	1,257	1,247		1,298	200
El Salvador	797	699	735	607	679		703	141
	985	857	891	1,314	961		1,002	199
Greenland	203	172	185	175	172	236	190	4,370
	295	277	267	279	295	360	295	6,667
Grenada	19	19	19	18	22	28	21	304
	54	56	56	56	69	83	62	902
Guadeloupe	92	83	83	86	75		84	227
	652	624	660	599	647		636	1,955
Guatemala	1,226	1,120	1,159	1,122	1,066		1,139	134
	1,673	1,388	1,135	1,278	1,175		1,330	148
Haiti	151	163	154	179	174	170	165	32
	448	387	440	472	442		438	84
Honduras	728	668	670	746	780		718	178
	945	692	823	954	888		860	203
Jamaica	974	767	732	747	564	596	730	253
	1,473	1,381	1,530	1,146	1,110	981	1,270	416
Martinique	169	116	115	105	145	209	143	637
	776	736	735	647	683	879	743	2,680
Mexico	20,041	20,929	21,012	23,602	21,822	15,774	20,530	198
	24,161	15,041	8,201	11,280	14,015	11,995	14,115	151
Montserrat	2	3		1	3		2	242
	19	20		20	18		19	1,500
Netherlands Antilles				1,639			1,639	8,405
				1,898			1,898	9,733

	1	2	3	4	5	6	7	8
Nicaragua	500	406	429	385			430	122
	999	776	807	826			852	261
Panama	319	309	304	256	306	331	304	149
	1,392	1,407	1,412	1,423	1,391	1,275	1,383	573
Puerto Rico	7,047	8,888	8,242	9,426	11,087		8,938	3,378
	9,329	8,167	8,708	10,116	10,162		9,296	3,096
Saint Christopher and Nevis	24	19	48	48			21	432
	48	44	107	119			46	1,000
Saint Lucia	41	42			52		46	377
	129	118			144		123	1,043
Saint-Pierre and Miquelon	7	6	6	8			7	1,333
	41	42	37	44			41	7,333
Saint Vincent and the Grenadines	24	32		54	62		43	596
	58	61		77	79		69	760
Trinidad and Tobago	3,764	3,072	2,347	2,173	2,164	1,378	2,483	1,145
	3,109	3,699	2,580	1,919	1,525	1,362	2,366	1,131
Turks and Caicos Islands			3	3			3	375
			26	26			26	3,250
USA[6]	233,739	212,275	200,538	217,888	213,146	217,304	215,815	887
	273,352	254,884	269,878	341,177	361,626	387,081	314,666	1,580
Virgin Islands (UK)	2	1	3				2	273
	50	59	67				59	6,091
Virgin Islands (USA)			3,649		3,357		3,503	30,243
			4,669		3,741		4,205	33,703
OCEANIA								
American Samoa	199	187	177	212			194	6,235
	234	198	227	284			236	8,353
Australia	21,767	22,038	20,687	23,998	22,853	22,496	22,306	1,408
	23,768	24,187	19,393	23,424	23,450	23,847	23,011	1,493
Cook Islands	4	20	3	4			4	222
	25		23	21			22	1,167
Fiji	311	286	240	256	236	264	265	369
	632	515	484	450	442	422	491	590
French Polynesia	29	28	34	32	41		33	228
	546	520	533	539	549		537	3,050

6Inc Puerto Rico and Virgin Islands (USA)
For an explanation of symbols and abbreviations, see pages 16–17.

(Continued)

TABLE 1f. (Continued)

Country	Total Volume of Exports (top line) and Imports (bottom line) (million US dollars)							Per Capita Volume Latest Year (US dollars)
	1981	1982	1983	1984	1985	1986	Average	
Guam	77		39				58	333
	355		636				495	5,436
Kiribati	4	3	2	11			5	175
	23		15	21			20	333
Nauru	89						89	11,125
	17						17	2,125
New Caledonia	343	265	154	207	271		248	1,771
	408	367	304	311	348		348	2,275
New Zealand	5,563	5,539	5,284	5,358	5,736	5,944	5,571	1,797
	5,684	5,825	5,333	6,010	6,080	6,135	5,844	1,855
Niue	0.5	0.5	0.5				0.5	167
	3	3	2				3	667
Norfolk Island				2	2		2	833
				14	17		15	7,083
Pacific Islands (USA)				6	15		10	97
				176	132		154	857
Papua New Guinea	863	771	813	895	909		850	273
	1,096	1,017	982	968	873		987	262
Samoa	11	13	19	19	15	12	15	73
	56	50	56	50	51	48	52	293
Solomon Islands	66	58	61	93	70	67	69	239
	76	59	61	66	69	63	66	225
Tonga	7	4	6	9	5	5	6	51
	40	42	38	41	41	38	40	388
Tuvalu	0.04	0.04	0.07				0.05	9
	3	3	3				3	375
Vanuatu	32	23	29	44	31	14	29	121
	58	59	63	69	71	57	63	407
Wallis and Futuna Islands	7						7	636

SOUTH AMERICA

Argentina	9,143	7,626	7,835	8,107	8,396		8,221	275
	9,430	5,337	4,501	4,585	3,814		5,533	125
Bolivia	984	899	818	773	673		829	105
	917	554	532	631	765		680	119
Brazil	23,680	20,213	21,899	27,005	25,639		23,687	189
	24,079	21,069	15,428	14,935	13,168		17,736	97
Chile	3,906	3,710	3,836	3,657	3,823	4,222	3,859	343
	6,364	3,831	2,969	3,481	3,007	3,040	3,782	247
Colombia	2,956	3,095	3,081	3,483	3,552	5,058	3,538	173
	5,199	5,478	4,968	4,492	4,131	3,843	4,685	132
Ecuador	2,542	2,341	2,203	2,581	2,780	2,171	2,436	225
	2,246	2,189	1,465	1,716	1,674	1,867	1,859	194
Falkland Islands	5		3				5	2,421
	6						5	1,421
French Guiana	35	33	38	37	37		36	446
	250	250	279	249	257		257	3,096
Guyana	346	241	189	210	207		239	262
	436	280	230	252	255		291	323
Paraguay	296	330	284	386	403	275	329	72
	506	581	506	563	719	746	603	196
Peru	3,249	3,227	3,027	3,131	2,705	2,467	2,968	122
	3,803	3,080	2,147	1,870	2,048	2,160	2,518	107
Suriname	474	429	345	356	299		401	915
	568	511	446	346			434	751
Uruguay	1,215	1,023	1,045	925	854	1,087	1,025	364
	1,641	1,110	788	776	708	815	973	273
Venezuela	20,125	16,443	15,002	14,337	12,272	9,734	14,652	547
	11,813	11,670	7,851	6,676	7,559	9,235	9,134	519
World	1,970,068	1,831,611	1,805,705	1,899,638	1,922,791	2,124,719	1,925,755	434
	2,032,628	1,906,068	1,877,255	1,983,831	2,024,878	2,222,196	2,007,809	454

For an explanation of symbols and abbreviations, see pages 16–17.

TRANSPORTATION AND COMMUNICATIONS

1g. Length of Roads and Motor Vehicles in Use

Contents

Conventional name of country.

Year of data for roads.

Length of paved and unpaved roads in thousands of miles and thousands of kilometers.

Road mileage per thousand square miles of surface area.

Year of data for motor vehicles.

Thousands of passenger cars in use at end of year.

Number of passenger cars in use per thousand inhabitants.

Thousands of commercial motor vehicles (chiefly trucks and buses) in use at end of year.

Thousands of motor vehicles, excluding motorcycles and agricultural tractors, in use at end of year.

Coverage

All countries listed in Table 1a for which data are available.

Entries

226.

TABLE 1g. LENGTH OF ROADS AND MOTOR VEHICLES IN USE

Country	Year	Length of Roads			Year	Motor Vehicles[1] in Use			
		1,000 Miles	1,000 km	Per 1,000 mi²		Passenger Cars		Commercial Vehicles[2] Total (1,000)	Grand Total (1,000)
						Total (1,000)	Per 1,000 Inhabitants		
AFRICA									
Algeria	1986	48.7	78.4	53	1984	577	27	365	941
Angola	1984	44.9	72.3	93	1984	57	6.7	29	86
Benin	1985	4.6	7.4	106	1984	22	5.8	12	34
Botswana	1986	8.4	13.5	36	1986	16	14	25	41
Burkina Faso	1986	7.0	11.2	66	1983	21	2.9	7	28
Burundi	1981	3.2	5.1	298	1984	8.5	1.9	5.1	14
Cameroon	1986	32.4	52.2	177	1985	67	6.6	26	93
Cape Verde	1982	1.4	2.2	899	1984	3.0	9.5	0.7	3.7
Central African Republic	1986	12.6	20.3	52	1983	41	17	4	45
Chad	1983	24.9	40.0	50	1982	7	1.5	5	12
Comoros	1980	0.3	0.5	417	1983	3.6	9.8	2.0	5.6
Congo	1980	5.1	8.2	39	1984	38	22	22	60
Djibouti	1986	1.8	2.9	201	1984	18	44	6.7	25
Egypt	1986	19.6	31.6	51	1984	890	19	264	1,154
Equatorial Guinea	1982	1.7	2.8	157	1982	4	15	3	7
Ethiopia	1985	23.5	37.9	50	1985	41	0.9	19	60
Gabon	1984	4.7	7.5	45	1982	16	14	11	27
Gambia	1985	1.5	2.4	344	1985	5.2	7.1	0.7	5.9
Ghana	1983	13.5	21.7	147	1984	62	5.1	46	107
Guinea	1984	17.6	28.4	185	1982	12	2.1	10	22
Guinea-Bissau	1982	3.2	5.1	229	1982	3	3.5	2	5

[1]Exc motorcycles and agricultural tractors.
[2]Chiefly trucks and buses.
For an explanation of symbols and abbreviations, see pages 16–17.

(Continued)

TABLE 1g. (Continued)

| Country | Length of Roads | | | | | Motor Vehicles[1] in Use | | | |
| | | | | | | Passenger Cars | | Commercial Vehicles[2] | Grand |
	Year	1,000 Miles	1,000 km	Per 1,000 mi²	Year	Total (1,000)	Per 1,000 Inhabitants	Total (1,000)	Total (1,000)
Ivory Coast	1984	33.4	53.7	268	1984	183	19	52	235
Kenya	1984	33.9	54.6	151	1984	122	6.2	97	219
Lesotho	1985	2.6	4.2	222	1982	5.1	3.6	12	17
Liberia	1981	3.4	5.4	79	1984	26	12	23	49
Libya	1982	12.0	19.3	18	1984	426	117	324	749
Madagascar	1985	30.9	49.7	136	1985	22	2.2	20	42
Malawi	1985	7.6	12.2	166	1984	16	2.3	13	29
Mali	1986	9.8	15.7	20	1982	20	2.6	5	25
Mauritania	1985	4.5	7.3	11	1985	15	7.9	2	17
Mauritius	1986	1.1	1.8	1,392	1986	35	34	10	45
Mayotte	1980	0.1	0.2	694	1982				2.4
Morocco	1984	35.9	57.7	208	1984	491	23	233	724
Mozambique	1986	16.2	26.1	52	1984	89	6.5	24	113
Namibia	1985	28.8	46.3	90	1981	27	26	19	46
Niger	1985	11.8	19.0	24	1984	22	3.7	21	44
Nigeria	1984	76.1	124.0	213	1984	761	8.3	621	1,382
Portugal: Madeira Islands	1980	0.4	0.6	1,303	1985				14
Reunion	1981	1.6	2.5	1,651	1984	122	227	40	163
Rwanda	1986	7.5	12.1	738	1986	7.4	1.2	10	18
Saint Helena	1980	0.1	0.2	617	1982				1.1
Sao Tome and Principe	1973	0.2	0.3	538	1979	1.3	14	1.9	3.2
Senegal	1986	9.3	15.0	123	1980	79	14	32	111
Seychelles	1983	0.2	0.3	1,143	1984	3.4	52	1.2	4.6
Sierra Leone	1978	4.6	7.4	166	1984	23	6.6	10	33
Somalia	1983	13.2	21.3	54	1983	9.5	2.2	19	29
South Africa	1985	114.3	183.9	242	1986	3,130	94	1,204	4,334
Spain: Canary Islands	1984	2.7	4.3	966	1982	318	221	78	396

Sudan	1985	4.1	6.6	4.2	1985	99	4.6	18	117
Swaziland	1982	1.7	2.7	254	1983	17	28	9	26
Tanzania	1984	50.9	81.9	139	1984	42	2.0	50	92
Tanganyika					1984	42	2.0	49	91
Zanzibar					1979	0.5	1.0	0.8	1.3
Togo	1986	4.3	7.0	196	1984	24	8.4	12	36
Tunisia	1986	16.6	26.7	263	1986	271	37	155	426
Uganda	1985	17.6	28.3	193	1985	32	2.1	9	41
Western Sahara	1969	3.9	6.3	38	1980	6	37	1	7
Zaire	1985	90.1	145.0	99	1985	96	3.2	72	168
Zambia	1986	23.2	37.4	80	1983	101	16	68	169
Zimbabwe	1985	48.4	77.9	321	1985	253	30	29	282
ASIA									
Afghanistan	1982	11.8	19.0	47	1983	33	1.9	27	60
Bahrain	1984	0.1	0.2	417	1984	72	186	24	96
Bangladesh	1982	98.5	158.6	1,772	1984	37	0.4	24	61
Bhutan	1984	1.3	2.0	72	1984	1.9	1.4	0.7	2.6
Brunei	1985	1.0	1.5	449	1985	79	353	16	95
Burma	1985	14.3	23.1	55	1982	30	0.9	44	74
China	1985	584.1	940.0	158	1985	100	0.1	2,926	3,026
Cyprus	1986	7.5	12.0	2,100	1986	132	196	50	182
Gaza Strip					1984	16	31	6	22
Hong Kong	1986	0.8	1.3	1,942	1986	184	33	96	280
India	1983	965.7	1,554.2	781	1985	1,178	1.6	1,695	2,873
Indonesia	1986	136.1	219.0	184	1986	1,060	6.3	1,133	2,193
Iran	1984	84.8	136.4	133	1983	1,687	40	452	2,139
Iraq	1982	15.7	25.3	93	1983	250	17	271	522
Israel	1984	7.8	12.6	940	1985	614	145	134	748
Japan	1986	700.5	1,127.4	4,803	1986	28,654	236	19,324	47,978
Jordan	1986	3.5	5.7	99	1986	159	43	4	163
Kampuchea	1981	8.1	13.0	116	1981	0.7	0.1	1.8	2.5
Korea									
North Korea	1985	13.7	22.0	294	1982				180
South Korea	1986	33.4	53.7	873	1986	664	16	627	1,291
Kuwait	1986	2.3	3.7	334	1986	421	235	114	535

[1] Exc motorcycles and agricultural tractors.
[2] Chiefly trucks and buses.
For an explanation of symbols and abbreviations, see pages 16–17.

(Continued)

TABLE 1g. (Continued)

| Country | Length of Roads | | | | Motor Vehicles[1] in Use | | | | |
	Year	1,000 Miles	1,000 km	Per 1,000 mi²	Year	Passenger Cars Total (1,000)	Per 1,000 Inhabitants	Commercial Vehicles[2] Total (1,000)	Grand Total (1,000)
Laos	1985	8.1	13.0	89	1982	15	3.6	3	18
Lebanon	1982	4.3	7.0	1,071	1984	478	181	52	530
Macao	1982	0.06	0.09	10,033	1985	18	46	4.4	22
Malaysia	1986	32.2	51.9	253	1986	1,485	92	409	1,894
Peninsular Malaysia	1986	24.3	39.1	478	1986	1,316	99	337	1,653
Sabah	1984	4.2	6.7	148	1982	98	90	51	149
Sarawak	1984	3.8	6.1	79	1982	71	52	21	92
Maldives	1965	0.06	0.1	522	1981	0.3	1.9	0.1	0.4
Mongolia	1983	29.0	46.7	48					
Nepal	1984	3.5	5.6	62	1978	14	1.0	10	24
Oman	1984	14.0	22.6	171	1984	93	46	86	179
Pakistan	1985	64.2	103.4	207	1984	380	4.1	151	532
Philippines	1986	100.8	162.3	870	1986	357	6.4	526	883
Qatar	1981	0.8	1.3	188	1982	40	151	25	65
Saudi Arabia	1986	56.8	91.3	68	1986	2,245	187	2,023	4,268
Singapore	1985	1.6	2.6	6,695	1985	225	88	76	301
Sri Lanka	1981	94.7	152.4	3,738	1985	149	9.4	136	285
Syria	1986	17.5	28.1	245	1984	114	11	123	237
Taiwan	1984	12.0	19.3	863	1985	916	48	429	1,345
Thailand	1986	51.8	83.3	261	1985	545	11	857	1,402
Turkey	1983	188.2	302.8	625	1985	984	19	553	1,537
United Arab Emirates	1981	0.8	1.3	25	1984	218	147	127	345
Vietnam	1983	37.3	60.0	293	1976	100	2.1	200	300
West Bank					1984	30	38	16	46
Yemen									
North Yemen	1986	23.1	37.2	307	1986	121	13	176	297
South Yemen	1977	4.2	6.7	33	1980	17	8.7	16	33

EUROPE

	Year				Year				
Albania	1981	13.0	21.0	1,171	1970	3.5	1.7	11	15
Andorra	1981	0.1	0.2	571	1982	18	474	2	20
Austria	1986	67.8	109.1	2,094	1986	2,609	345	222	2,831
Belgium	1986	79.6	128.1	6,757	1986	3,379	343	297	3,676
Bulgaria	1986	23.2	37.4	542	1986	1,083	121	177	1,260
Channel Islands					1983	73	562	11	84
Czechoslovakia	1986	45.5	73.3	922	1984	2,640	171	378	3,018
Denmark	1986	43.6	70.2	2,622	1986	1,618	316	216	1,834
Faeroe Islands	1984	0.1	0.2	185	1984	12	267	2.6	14
Finland	1986	47.3	76.2	362	1986	1,620	329	196	1,816
France	1986	500.1	804.8	2,381	1986	21,250	384	3,406	24,656
Germany									
East Germany	1980	74.9	120.5	1,791	1985	3,306	199	417	3,723
West Germany	1986	305.2	491.2	3,178	1986	24,700	405	3,888	28,588
Gibraltar	1984	0.03	0.05	13,043	1986	13	448	1.0	14
Greece	1985	64.2	103.3	1,260	1985	1,264	127	621	1,885
Hungary	1986	56.4	90.7	1,570	1986	1,539	145	189	1,728
Iceland	1986	7.1	11.4	179	1986	113	465	13	126
Ireland	1986	57.4	92.3	2,115	1985	710	200	98	808
Isle of Man	1983	0.5	0.8	2,203	1984	28	431	4.1	32
Italy	1985	187.2	301.3	1,609	1985	22,398	392	1,902	24,300
Liechtenstein	1980	0.2	0.3	3,279	1985	15	536	1.6	17
Luxembourg	1986	3.2	5.2	3,206	1986	156	425	10	166
Malta	1982	0.8	1.3	6,557	1985	80	209	21	101
Monaco	1986	0.03	0.05	52,174	1986	19	704	0.6	19
Netherlands	1986	70.6	113.6	4,376	1986	4,950	340	409	5,359
Norway	1986	53.5	86.1	428	1986	1,592	382	283	1,875
Poland	1986	186.8	300.6	1,547	1986	3,962	106	913	4,875
Portugal	1981	32.2	51.9	907	1985	1,702	168	105	1,807
Azores	1980	1.4	2.3	1,613	1985				13
Romania	1985	45.2	72.8	493	1982	250	11	150	400
San Marino	1985	0.1	0.2	4,255	1985	15	682	1.7	16
Spain	1986	198.2	319.0	1,017	1986	9,762	252	1,727	11,489
Balearic Islands	1984	1.3	2.1	671	1982	247	369	35	282

1 Exc motorcycles and agricultural tractors.
2 Chiefly trucks and buses.
For an explanation of symbols and abbreviations, see pages 16–17.

(Continued)

TABLE 1g. (Continued)

| Country | Length of Roads | | | | Motor Vehicles[1] in Use | | | | |
| | | | | | | Passenger Cars | | Commercial Vehicles[2] | Grand |
	Year	1,000 Miles	1,000 km	Per 1,000 mi²	Year	Total (1,000)	Per 1,000 Inhabitants	Total (1,000)	Total (1,000)
Sweden	1986	81.3	130.8	468	1986	3,254	389	243	3,497
Switzerland	1986	43.9	70.6	2,754	1986	2,679	412	218	2,897
UK	1984	230.6	371.1	2,447	1986	17,395	306	2,952	20,347
England and Wales	1983	182.8	294.2	3,131	1984	16,497	332	572	17,069
Northern Ireland	1982	14.7	23.7	2,696	1984	444	281	39	483
Scotland	1983	30.8	49.5	1,013	1984	1,224	238	120	1,344
USSR	1983	861.8	1,387.0	100	1984	11,737	43	9,614	21,351
Yugoslavia	1985	73.1	117.7	740	1985	2,874	124	182	3,056
NORTH AMERICA									
Anguilla	1980	0.06	0.09	1,622	1982	1.0	167	0.3	1.3
Antigua and Barbuda	1984	0.3	0.5	1,765	1982	7.1	92	1.2	8.3
Aruba	1983	0.2	0.4	2,685	1983	21	313	1.8	23
Bahamas	1984	2.5	4.1	465	1984	88	379	5.6	94
Barbados	1984	1.0	1.6	6,024	1984	31	123	5.5	36
Belize	1984	1.6	2.6	180	1982	8	53	4	12
Bermuda	1982	0.2	0.4	9,709	1986	17	298	4.2	21
Canada	1981	576.8	928.3	151	1985	11,118	438	3,149	14,267
Newfoundland	1976	8.2	13.2	53	1982	129	226	56	186
Cayman Islands	1981	0.06	0.1	600	1983	7.4	389	1.8	9.2
Costa Rica	1984	18.1	29.1	925	1984	104	43	78	182
Cuba	1984	21.1	34.0	493	1984	200	20	164	365
Dominica	1984	0.5	0.8	1,724	1983	2.7	36	1.2	4.0
Dominican Republic	1982	10.8	17.4	577	1984	102	17	61	163
El Salvador	1985	7.6	12.2	935	1984	129	27	19	148
Greenland	1980	0.1	0.2	0.1	1984	1.6	30	1.3	2.9
Grenada	1981	0.6	0.9	4,511	1981	4.8	54	1.0	5.8
Guadeloupe	1986	1.3	2.1	1,892	1986	69	207	27	96
Guatemala	1979	10.7	17.3	255	1983	188	25	58	247

Haiti	1977	2.5	4.0	233	1983	34	6.6	4.3	38
Honduras	1986	8.8	14.2	203	1986	41	9.1	53	94
Jamaica	1984	10.3	16.6	2,427	1983	107	50	29	137
Martinique	1984	1.1	1.8	2,588	1984	140	428	3.7	144
Mexico	1986	140.2	225.7	185	1984	5,029	65	2,167	7,196
Montserrat	1982	0.2	0.3	5,263	1982	1.3	108	0.1	1.4
Netherlands Antilles	1983	0.5	0.8	1,618	1982	43	226	8	51
Nicaragua	1986	9.3	15.0	185	1986	46	14	31	77
Panama	1984	5.9	9.5	198	1984	121	57	45	166
Puerto Rico	1986	5.8	9.4	1,650	1986	1,175	356	210	1,385
Saint Christopher and Nevis	1983	0.1	0.2	990	1984	3.6	80	0.9	4.5
Saint Lucia	1983	0.8	1.3	3,361	1984	5.5	41	3.5	9.0
Saint-Pierre and Miquelon	1985	0.07	0.1	753	1980	1.6	267	0.5	2.1
Saint Vincent and the Grenadines	1983	0.6	1.0	4,000	1982	4.5	45	2.4	6.9
Trinidad and Tobago	1985	3.2	5.2	1,615	1985	242	204	82	324
Turks and Caicos Islands	1980	0.06	0.1	361					
USA	1985	3,861.1	6,213.9	1,049	1985	132,108	552	39,583	171,691
Alaska	1981	9.1	14.6	15	1985	220	422	133	353
Virgin Islands (UK)	1985	0.07	0.1	1,186	1985	4	308	0	4
Virgin Islands (USA)	1980	0.6	0.9	4,545	1980	27	278	4	31
OCEANIA									
American Samoa	1980	0.2	0.3	2,597	1984	3.3	97	0.3	3.6
Australia	1985	530.0	853.0	179	1985	6,843	434	2,137	8,980
Tasmania	1981	14.0	22.5	535	1984	195	447	55	250
Christmas Island (Australia)	1980	0.02	0.03	385	1980	0.8	276	0.4	1.1
Cocos Islands	1980	0.01	0.02	1,825	1980				
Cook Islands	1980	0.1	0.2	1,099	1980	1.1	61	0.3	1.4
Fiji	1982	2.7	4.3	383	1985	32	46	22	54
French Polynesia	1982	0.4	0.7	259	1984	33	195	13	46
Guam	1983	0.4	0.7	1,914	1984	62	517	17	79
Kiribati	1982	0.4	0.6	1,220	1978				0.2
Nauru	1980	0.01	0.02	1,220	1984				1.8
New Caledonia	1983	3.7	6.0	503	1984	44	295	16	60
New Zealand	1986	57.8	93.0	557	1986	1,553	470	318	1,871

[1]Exc motorcycles and agricultural tractors.
[2]Chiefly trucks and buses.

For an explanation of symbols and abbreviations, see pages 16–17.

(Continued)

TABLE 1g. (Continued)

| Country | Length of Roads | | | | Motor Vehicles[1] in Use | | | | |
| | | | | | Passenger Cars | | | Commercial Vehicles[2] | Grand Total |
	Year	1,000 Miles	1,000 km	Per 1,000 mi²	Year	Total (1,000)	Per 1,000 Inhabitants	Total (1,000)	Total (1,000)
Niue	1980	0.1	0.2	1,000	1980	0.3	91	0.06	0.3
Norfolk Island	1980	0.05	0.08	3,759	1982	1.2	545	0.1	1.3
Pacific Islands (USA)	1980	1.0	1.6	1,395	1978	4	31	2	6
Papua New Guinea	1986	12.2	19.7	68	1986	19	5.6	10	29
Pitcairn Island	1983	0.004	0.006	2,286	1986				0
Samoa	1984	1.3	2.1	1,185	1984	1.8	11	2.7	4.5
Solomon Islands	1976	0.3	0.5	27	1980	1.0	4.3	1.3	2.3
Tokelau									
Tonga	1982	0.2	0.4	741	1982	0.6	6.4	0.9	1.5
Tuvalu	1983	0.005	0.008	541					
USA: Hawaii	1981	4.1	6.6	634	1985	569	540	82	651
Vanuatu	1983	0.6	0.9	105	1984	2.3	18	1.2	3.5
Wallis and Futuna Islands	1977	0.06	0.1	612					
SOUTH AMERICA									
Argentina	1981	130.6	210.2	122	1986	3,898	126	1,335	5,233
Bolivia	1983	25.5	41.0	60	1983	107	18	43	150
Brazil	1986	990.3	1,593.7	301	1985	10,432	77	1,110	11,542
Chile	1986	49.2	79.1	168	1986	638	52	263	901
Colombia	1986	66.0	106.2	150	1986	841	29	391	1,232
Ecuador	1986	22.5	36.2	206	1986	257	27	39	296
Falkland Islands	1980	0.3	0.5	48	1982	1.0	526	0.5	1.5
French Guiana	1986	5.5	8.9	157	1986	27	321	8	35
Guyana	1984	3.4	5.5	41	1982	31	40	12	43
Paraguay	1984	9.0	14.5	57	1984	91	26	35	126
Peru	1981	40.8	65.6	82	1985	385	20	209	595
Suriname	1986	5.7	9.1	90	1986	35	86	15	50
Uruguay	1981	30.9	49.8	454	1981	281	98	50	331
Venezuela	1986	62.5	100.6	177	1986	2,300	129	1,248	3,548

[1]Exc motorcycles and agricultural tractors.
[2]Chiefly trucks and buses.
For an explanation of symbols and abbreviations, see pages 16–17.

1h. Railroad Route Lengths and Passenger and Freight Traffic

Contents

Conventional name of country.

Year of data for railroad routes.

Length of railroad routes (not tracks), in miles and kilometers.

Year of passenger traffic data.

Millions of railroad passenger-kilometers. (Passenger-kilometers are the number of passengers multiplied by the number of kilometers each passenger is carried.)

Year of freight traffic data.

Millions of metric ton-kilometers of railroad freight.

Coverage

All countries with operating railroads.

Entries

136.

TABLE 1h. RAILROAD ROUTE LENGTHS AND PASSENGER AND FREIGHT TRAFFIC

Country	Railroad Route Length			Passenger Traffic		Freight Traffic	
	Year	Miles	Kilometers	Year	Million Passenger-km	Year	Million MT-km
AFRICA							
Algeria	1984	2,337	3,761	1984	1,835	1984	2,647
Angola	1979	1,834	2,952	1979	495	1979	207
Benin	1979	360	579	1984	138	1984	177
Botswana	1984	438	705			1984	1,320
Burkina Faso	1984	367	591	1984	429	1984	265
Cameroon	1984	692	1,114	1985	463	1985	996
Congo	1984	498	802	1984	408	1984	480
Djibouti	1983	62	100				
Egypt	1984	3,144	5,060	1983	14,468	1983	2,303
Ethiopia	1983	614	988	1983	360	1983	122
Eritrea	1979	190	306				
Gabon	1983	325	523				
Ghana	1981	590	950	1983	380	1983	61
Guinea	1983	584	940	1967	50	1967	20
Ivory Coast	1984	367	591	1984	429	1984	265
Kenya	1984	1,295	2,084	1983	1,276	1984	2,246
Lesotho	1982	1	2				
Liberia	1984	304	490	1983	6	1983	2,622
Madagascar	1984	549	884	1983	225	1983	212

For an explanation of symbols and abbreviations, see pages 16–17. (Continued)

TABLE 1h. (Continued)

Country	Railroad Route Length Year	Miles	Kilometers	Passenger Traffic Year	Million Passenger- km	Freight Traffic Year	Million MT- km
Malawi	1984	506	815	1984	109	1984	120
Mali	1979	398	640	1980	156	1984	350
Mauritania	1984	416	670	1984	7	1984	6,142
Morocco	1984	1,105	1,779	1984	1,612	1984	4,575
Mozambique	1984	1,950	3,138	1984	387	1984	536
Namibia	1982	1,454	2,340				
Nigeria	1984	2,178	3,505	1983	1,950	1984	1,246
Reunion	1982	382	614				
Senegal	1984	642	1,034	1983	153	1983	356
Sierra Leone	1984	52	84				
South Africa	1984	13,316	21,430	1984	20,137[1]	1985	92,616[1]
Sudan	1982	2,974	4,786	1983	1,031	1983	3,190
Swaziland	1982	194	312			1984	107
Tanzania	1980	2,218	3,569	1982	929	1982	694
Togo	1982	326	525	1984	79	1984	10
Tunisia	1984	1,304	2,099	1985	744	1985	1,710
Uganda	1984	799	1,286				
Zaire	1984	3,209	5,165	1984	346	1984	1,863
Zambia	1983	1,302	2,095				
Zimbabwe	1984	2,109	3,394	1984	2,050	1985	6,204
ASIA							
Bangladesh	1984	1,797	2,892	1984	6,284	1984	779
Brunei	1983	12	19				
Burma	1978	1,949	3,137	1985	3,864	1985	624
China	1984	32,390	52,127	1985	241,380	1985	811,116
Hong Kong	1984	50	81	1985	1,776	1984	93
India	1984	38,143	61,385	1985	240,000	1985	196,488
Indonesia	1981	4,273	6,877	1984	6,384	1984	1,176
Iran	1984	2,838	4,567	1984	6,130	1984	7,566
Iraq	1984	1,504	2,420	1983	1,375	1984	1,299
Israel	1984	333	536	1984	220	1984	893
Japan	1984	13,105	21,091	1985	328,452	1985	22,104
Jordan	1982	384	618	1984	?	1984	870
Kampuchea	1983	403	649				
Korea							
North Korea	1981	2,734	4,400				
South Korea	1984	1,939	3,120	1984	21,884	1985	12,084
Lebanon	1984	258	415	1980	9	1980	42
Malaysia	1982	1,091	1,755	1984	1,512[2]	1984	1,080[2]
Peninsular Malaysia	1982	1,004	1,615				
Sabah	1981	87	140				
Mongolia	1984	1,056	1,700	1984	420	1984	5,121
Nepal	1984	63	101	1983	286	1983	362
Pakistan	1984	5,482	8,823	1985	17,808	1985	7,200
Philippines	1980	567	913	1985	144	1985	12
Saudi Arabia	1984	865	1,392	1984	74	1984	1,329

[1] Inc Namibia.
[2] Inc Singapore.

TABLE 1h. (Continued)

Country	Railroad Route Length			Passenger Traffic		Freight Traffic	
	Year	Miles	Kilometers	Year	Million Passenger-km	Year	Million MT-km
Singapore	1984	16	26				
Sri Lanka	1982	903	1,453	1985	2,088	1985	240
Syria	1984	1,200	1,932	1984	757	1984	966
Taiwan	1984	668	1,075	1984	8,447	1984	2,385
Thailand	1982	2,321	3,735	1985	9,144	1985	2,712
Turkey	1984	5,076	8,169	1985	6,492	1985	7,752
Vietnam	1978	1,616	2,600	1981	4,554	1983	2,245
EUROPE							
Albania	1984	210	338	1981	291	1981	127
Austria	1984	3,980	6,405	1984	7,004	1984	11,565
Belgium	1984	2,734	4,400	1985	6,552	1985	8,256
Bulgaria	1984	2,697	4,341	1985	7,788	1985	18,168
Czechoslovakia	1984	8,149	13,114	1985	19,836	1985	73,596
Denmark	1984	1,847	2,972	1984	4,421	1984	1,715
Finland	1984	3,725	5,995	1985	3,228	1985	8,064
France	1984	23,075	37,135	1985	60,780	1985	58,488
Germany							
East Germany	1984	8,839	14,225	1985	22,452	1985	58,668
West Germany	1984	18,969	30,528	1985	41,208	1985	63,876
Greece	1984	1,529	2,461	1985	1,500	1985	732
Hungary	1984	4,872	7,840	1985	10,464	1985	21,816
Ireland	1984	2,056	3,309	1984	903	1984	601
Italy	1983	12,088	19,454	1985	39,264	1985	18,192
Liechtenstein	1984	11	18				
Luxembourg	1984	168	270	1985	288	1985	648
Monaco	1984	1	2				
Netherlands	1984	1,896	3,052	1985	9,228	1985	3,216
Norway	1984	2,671	4,299	1985	2,232	1985	2,928
Poland	1984	15,132	24,353	1985	51,984	1985	120,648
Portugal	1984	2,245	3,613	1985	5,724	1985	1,308
Romania	1984	6,530	10,509	1984	28,785	1984	75,159
Spain	1984	9,704	15,617	1985	15,972	1985	11,712
Sweden	1984	7,397	11,905	1985	6,588	1985	17,592
Switzerland	1983	3,108	5,002	1985	9,408	1985	7,044
UK	1984	10,647	17,134	1984	36,400	1984	15,842
England and Wales							
Northern Ireland	1984	206	331				
Scotland							
USSR	1984	89,540	144,100	1984	363,986	1984	3,638,834
Vatican City	1984	1	1				
Yugoslavia	1984	5,766	9,279	1985	12,216	1985	28,320
NORTH AMERICA							
Canada	1982	42,797	68,875	1984	2,467	1984	360,371
Newfoundland	1977	915	1,473				
Costa Rica	1984	590	950	1976	99	1976	16
Cuba	1984	9,039	14,547	1985	2,256	1985	2,796
Dominican Republic	1984	1,388	2,234				

For an explanation of symbols and abbreviations, see pages 16–17.

(Continued)

TABLE 1h. (Continued)

Country	Railroad Route Length			Passenger Traffic		Freight Traffic	
	Year	Miles	Kilometers	Year	Million Passenger-km	Year	Million MT-km
El Salvador	1983	373	600	1984	5	1984	24
Guatemala	1984	466	750			1976	117
Haiti	1977	155	250				
Honduras	1984	571	919				
Jamaica	1984	209	337	1982	31	1982	69
Mexico	1984	12,388	19,936	1985	5,940	1985	45,444
Nicaragua	1984	178	287	1984	60	1984	5
Panama	1982	281	452				
Puerto Rico	1983	60	96				
Saint Christopher and Nevis	1983	31	50				
USA	1984	163,230	262,693	1984	29,773	1984	1,377,264
Alaska	1984	526	846	1984	25	1984	1,128
OCEANIA							
Australia	1979	24,475	39,388	1979	6,457e	1984	39,448
Tasmania	1979	537	864				
Fiji	1983	370	595				
Nauru	1980	3	5				
New Zealand	1984	2,668	4,293	1983	417	1983	3,165
USA: Hawaii	1981	6	10				
SOUTH AMERICA							
Argentina	1984	21,601	34,764	1985	10,740	1985	9,504
Bolivia	1984	2,298	3,698	1984	447	1984	400
Brazil	1984	17,982	28,940	1983	13,797	1983	74,792
Chile	1984	5,325	8,570	1985	1,524	1985	2,352
Colombia	1983	1,670	2,688	1985	228	1985	780
Ecuador	1984	600	965	1982	50	1982	14
Guyana	1984	55	88	1974	6	1974	0
Paraguay	1984	274	441	1983	2	1983	30
Peru	1983	2,326	3,743	1984	486	1984	1,014
Suriname	1984	43	70				
Uruguay	1983	1,865	3,001	1983	312	1983	218
Venezuela	1981	339	546	1984	12	1984	11
World		737,471	1,186,845				

For an explanation of symbols and abbreviations, see pages 16–17.

1i. Airline Passenger and Freight Traffic, 1980 and 1985

Contents

Conventional name of country.

Millions of civil airline passenger-kilometers[1] in 1980 and in 1985. (Passenger-kilometers are the number of passengers multiplied by the number of kilometers each passenger is carried.)

Millions of metric ton-kilometers of civil airline scheduled freight[1] in 1980 and in 1985.

Coverage

All countries with civil airlines in operation that report comparable traffic figures.

Entries

158.

[1]The traffic data given here cover all civil airlines of the country listed, including both domestic and international flights.

TABLE 1i. AIRLINE PASSENGER AND FREIGHT TRAFFIC, 1980 AND 1985

Country	Passenger Traffic (million passenger-kilometers)		Scheduled Freight Traffic (million metric ton-kilometers)	
	1980	1985	1980	1985
AFRICA				
Algeria	2,300	3,794	13	21
Angola	588	998	21	26
Benin	185	235	18	18
Botswana	15	22	0	0.1
Burkina Faso	190	246	18	18
Burundi	5	2	0.1	0
Cameroon	477	580	28	57
Cape Verde	12	32	0.2	0.4
Central African Republic	197	243	18	18
Chad	217	241	19	18
Comoros-Mayotte		16		0.1
Congo	204	302	18	20
Djibouti	53	72	0.2	0.4
Egypt	3,145	4,927	29	98
Equatorial Guinea	7	7	0.1	0.1
Ethiopia	709	1,068	25	66
Gabon	374	516	26	36
Gambia				
Ghana	324	289	2.8	9.4
Guinea	34	160	0.2	0.6
Guinea-Bissau	8	9	0.1	0.1
Ivory Coast	222	395	18	18

For an explanation of symbols and abbreviations, see pages 16–17. (Continued)

TABLE 1i. (Continued)

Country	Passenger Traffic (million passenger-kilometers)		Scheduled Freight Traffic (million metric ton-kilometers)	
	1980	1985	1980	1985
Kenya	1,018	1,151	18	30
Lesotho	11	17	0	0.1
Liberia	17	11	0.1	0.1
Libya	1,101	1,766	11	5.4
Madagascar	380	388	20	20
Malawi	107	121	0.8	0.8
Mali	97	94	0.5	0.7
Mauritania	225	294	18	14
Mauritius	185	648	2.3	15
Morocco	2,619	3,117	26	36
Mozambique	510	487	8.7	9.1
Namibia				
Niger	206	232	18	18
Nigeria	1,877	3,560	9.3	50
Reunion				
Rwanda				
Sao Tome and Principe		6.1		0
Senegal	203	253	18	18
Seychelles	2	157	0	0.4
Sierra Leone	86	115	1.3	2.2
Somalia	140	238	0.5	3.3
South Africa	8,950	8,751	251	392
Sudan	710	580	12	7.3
Swaziland	30	26	0.1	0.2
Tanzania	295	261	1.9	3.3
Togo	186	233	18	18
Tunisia	2,095	2,238	12	16
Uganda	68	76	8.5	11
Zaire	890	364	34	30
Zambia	469	662	47	25
Zimbabwe	362	664	3.2	11
ASIA				
Afghanistan	209	204	21	20
Bahrain	714	1,245	26	53
Bangladesh	1,179	1,644	20	69
Bhutan				
Brunei		247		4.4
Burma	218	229	1.5	2.3
China	3,578	12,114	121	403
Cyprus	798	1,580	19	25
Hong Kong				
India	10,796	14,938	366	490
Indonesia	6,239	10,116	122	155
Iran	2,324	5,208	20	104
Iraq	1,179	1,525	52	55
Israel	5,434	6,684	295	592
Japan	52,290	64,968	1,871	3,071
Jordan	2,630	3,579	80	152

TABLE 1i. (Continued)

Country	Passenger Traffic (million passenger-kilometers)		Scheduled Freight Traffic (million metric ton-kilometers)	
	1980	1985	1980	1985
Kampuchea	48[1]		0.5[1]	
Korea				
North Korea	90	141	2.2	2.4
South Korea	10,907	12,393	836	1,332
Kuwait	2,124	3,808	72	164
Laos	7	9	0.1	0.2
Lebanon	1,687	999	531	200
Macao				
Malaysia	4,290	6,385	110	204
Maldives	20	110	0.3	1.3
Mongolia		261[2]		5.02[2]
Nepal	234	334	2.5	6.7
Oman	714	1,245	26	33
Pakistan	5,702	7,026	235	310
Philippines	6,034	8,615	150	225
Qatar	714	1,245	26	33
Saudi Arabia	10,202	15,857	165	455
Singapore	14,792	21,802	544	981
Sri Lanka	691	2,509	9.7	68
Syria	985	985	16	16
Taiwan	8,225	11,246	1,035	1,839
Thailand	6,290	10,781	239	419
Turkey	1,811	2,996	10	24
United Arab Emirates	714	1,245	26	33
Vietnam	3	80	0.1	0.8
Yemen				
North Yemen	291	576	0.6	9.3
South Yemen	84	240	1.7	3.0
EUROPE				
Albania				
Austria	1,120	1,483	12	19
Belgium	4,852	5,664	394	565
Bulgaria	775	1,655	8.9	11
Czechoslovakia	1,774	2,122	12	17
Denmark	3,325	4,487	116	116
Finland	3,683	5,242	48	77
France	34,130	40,131	1,986	2,873
Germany				
East Germany	2,053	2,541	67	72
West Germany	21,102	24,570	1,506	2,378
Greece	5,119	7,545	61	103
Hungary	1,076	1,333	9.2[3]	8.6[3]
Iceland	1,455	2,587	23	18
Ireland	2,686	3,014	89	81
Italy	14,270	18,342	523	757

[1] 1974.
[2] 1983.
[3] 1984.

For an explanation of symbols and abbreviations, see pages 16–17.

(Continued)

TABLE 1i. (Continued)

Country	Passenger Traffic (million passenger-kilometers)		Scheduled Freight Traffic (million metric ton-kilometers)	
	1980	1985	1980	1985
Luxembourg	256	331	0.2	0.5
Malta	1,170	1,207	4.1	4.4
Monaco	1	2	0	0
Netherlands	15,448	18,952	947	1,404
Norway	5,675	6,430	120	122
Poland	2,714	2,860	14	7.9
Portugal	3,806	4,655	106	134
Romania	1,209	1,462	12	9.7
Spain	17,265	22,364	390	522
Sweden	5,431	6,403	175	172
Switzerland	10,887	12,777	421	637
UK	66,046	79,065	1,427	2,299
USSR	160,299	188,206	2,511	2,688
Yugoslavia	3,726	5,568	38	82
NORTH AMERICA				
Antigua and Barbuda	124	130	0.1	0.1
Bahamas	539	131	3.0	0.2
Barbados	330	213	0.5	2.6
Belise				
Bermuda				
Canada	40,055	40,220	689	990
Costa Rica	498	585	22	25
Cuba	961	2,417	10	17
Dominica				
Dominican Republic	550	694	11	8.5
El Salvador	290	575	17	0
Greenland		22[3]		0.06[3]
Grenada				
Guadeloupe				
Guatemala	159	156	6.4	9.0
Haiti	0	0	1.9	4.8
Honduras	391	782	3.8	1.0
Jamaica	1,647	1,496	9.4	19
Martinique				
Mexico	14,052	18,004	131	170
Netherlands Antilles	167[4]		0.6[4]	
Nicaragua	76	115	1.3	1.4
Panama	420	551	2.7	4.3
Puerto Rico				
Saint Lucia	95[5]		10[5]	
Saint Vincent and the Grenadines				
Trinidad and Tobago	1,546	2,064	18	10
USA	427,853	533,141	8,371	9,472
Virgin Islands (UK)				
Virgin Islands (USA)				

[3]1984.
[4]1981.
[5]1982.

TABLE 1i. (Continued)

Country	Passenger Traffic (million passenger-kilometers)		Scheduled Freight Traffic (million metric ton-kilometers)	
	1980	1985	1980	1985
OCEANIA				
American Samoa				
Australia	28,583	28,287	516	818
Fiji	250	420	0	3.8
French Polynesia				
Kiribati	18[4]	7.4	0.3[4]	0.1
Nauru	107	410	0.5	1.6
New Zealand	5,754	7,927	186	305
Pacific Islands (USA)	302[6]		5.6[6]	
Samoa				
Solomon Islands		11		0
Tonga		1		0
Tuvalu				
Vanuatu		25		0.1
SOUTH AMERICA				
Argentina	8,045	7,571	195	177
Bolivia	956	922	38	41
Brazil	15,822	19,018	588	909
Chile	1,933	1,825	145	112
Colombia	4,198	4,260	147	342
Ecuador	984	969	40	51
French Guiana				
Guyana	6	168	0.8	2.3
Paraguay	262	635	2.6	3.1
Peru	1,974	1,601	40	47
Suriname	245	304	3.6	11
Uruguay	178	389	0.7	1.9
Venezuela	4,422	4,667	149	92
World	1,052,100	1,484,690	30,095	39,650

[4]1981.
[6]1978.
For an explanation of symbols and abbreviations, see pages 16–17.

1j. Communications

Contents

Conventional name of country.
Year of data for telephones.
Thousands of telephones in use.
Number of telephones per thousand inhabitants.
Year of data for radio receivers.
Thousands of radio receivers in use.
Number of radio receivers per thousand inhabitants.
Year of data for television receivers.
Thousands of television receivers in use.
Number of television receivers per thousand inhabitants.

Coverage

All countries listed in Table 1a for which data are available.

Entries

208.

TABLE 1j. COMMUNICATIONS

Country	Telephones			Radio Receivers			Television Receivers		
	Year	Thou-sands	Per 1,000 Inhab-itants	Year	Thou-sands	Per 1,000 Inhab-itants	Year	Thou-sands	Per 1,000 Inhab-itants
AFRICA									
Algeria	1983	656	32	1983	4,400	214	1983	1,325	64
Angola	1981	40	5.1	1983	162	19	1983	33	4.0
Benin	1978	16	5.0	1983	290	78	1983	13	3.5
Botswana	1983	18	18	1983	120	119	1972	5	7.8
Burkina Faso	1983	14	1.9	1983	122	17	1983	35	4.8
Burundi	1983	6	1.4	1983	178	40	1979	6	1.5
Cameroon	1983	47	5.1	1983	820	89	1974	22	3.3
Cape Verde	1982	1.7	5.5	1983	47	150			
Central African Republic	1981	5.0	2.1	1983	140	57	1983	1.4	0.6
Chad	1979	6.2	1.4	1982	120	26	1979	6.0	1.4
Comoros	1981	3.2	9.3	1983	40	109	1978	2	6.5
Congo	1983	18	11	1983	100	61	1983	4.5	2.7
Djibouti	1983	7.2	22	1983	23	70	1983	11	33
Egypt	1981	534	12	1983	8,000	174	1983	2,000	44
Equatorial Guinea	1982	2.0	6.9	1983	115	378	1983	2.0	6.6
Ethiopia	1983	110	2.7	1983	3,300	80	1983	40	1.0
Gabon	1983	14	12	1983	102	91	1983	20	18
Gambia	1979	3.2	5.3	1983	90	129	1980	3.5	5.6
Ghana	1982	71	6.1	1983	2,200	185	1983	76	6.4
Guinea	1981	10	1.8	1983	160	28	1983	8	1.4
Guinea-Bissau	1981	2.6	3.2	1983	28	32			
Ivory Coast	1980	88	11	1983	1,200	129	1983	370	40
Kenya	1983	231	12	1983	640	34	1983	75	4.0

(Continued)

For an explanation of symbols and abbreviations, see pages 16–17.

TABLE 1j. (Continued)

Country	Telephones			Radio Receivers			Television Receivers		
	Year	Thou-sands	Per 1,000 Inhab-itants	Year	Thou-sands	Per 1,000 Inhab-itants	Year	Thou-sands	Per 1,000 Inhab-itants
Lesotho	1981	5.9	4.2	1983	40	28	1972	3.2	3.0
Liberia	1980	7.7	4.2	1983	380	185	1983	24	12
Libya	1977	142	46	1983	750	211	1983	220	62
Madagascar	1981	38	4.3	1983	2,000	213	1983	71	7.6
Malawi	1983	37	5.8	1983	310	48	1965	7	1.7
Mali	1982	8.5	1.1	1983	121	16	1979	14	2.0
Mauritania	1983	4.8	2.7	1983	180	101	1984	0.5	0.3
Mauritius	1983	48	48	1983	210	210	1983	85	85
Mayotte	1981	0.4	7.5	1983	14	255			
Morocco	1983	270	13	1983	3,600	172	1983	860	41
Mozambique	1982	57	4.4	1983	275	21	1983	2.1	0.2
Namibia	1982	57	49	1984	54	36	1984	22	15
Niger	1982	9.8	1.8	1983	280	49	1983	11	1.9
Nigeria	1982	708	8.2	1983	7,000	79	1983	457	5.1
Reunion	1982	72	140	1983	120	230	1983	90	173
Rwanda	1981	3.2	0.6	1983	300	52	1978	5	1.0
Saint Helena	1980	0.8	114	1983	1.8	237			
Sao Tome and Principe	1983	2.2	22	1983	25	250			
Senegal	1979	40	7.3	1983	440	70	1983	6	0.9
Seychelles	1983	9.1	142	1983	23	359	1983	0.5	7.8
Sierra Leone	1982	16	4.8	1983	700	208	1983	22	6.5
Somalia	1981	4.8	1.2	1983	134	30			
South Africa	1983	3,472	113	1983	8,700	282	1983	2,300	75
Sudan	1982	68	3.4	1983	5,000	243	1983	1,000	49
Swaziland	1981	13	23	1983	93	154	1983	2.5	4.1
Tanzania	1983	104	5.1	1983	591	29	1983	9.0	0.4
Togo	1983	12	4.4	1983	590	214	1983	13	4.7
Tunisia	1983	233	34	1983	1,124	163	1983	370	54
Uganda	1983	54	3.7	1983	320	22	1983	81	5.5

Western Sahara	1982	1.0	6.1		32		195		2.7	16
Zaire	1982	31	1.1	1983	3,000	1983	103	1983	12	0.4
Zambia	1983	72	12	1983	170	1983	27	1983	76	12
Zimbabwe	1983	247	32	1983	350	1983	45	1983	97	13
ASIA										
Afghanistan	1980	32	2.0	1983	1,350	1983	78	1983	51	3.0
Bahrain	1983	98	257	1983	160	1983	419	1983	121	317
Bangladesh	1983	140	1.5	1983	770	1983	8.1	1983	203	2.1
Bhutan	1981	15	12	1983	12	1983	8.8			
Brunei	1981	22	114	1983	49	1983	229	1983	29	136
Burma	1983	49	1.4	1983	864	1983	24	1983	6	0.2
China	1984	5,150	5.0	1983	70,000	1983	69	1983	7,000	6.9
Cyprus	1983	164	253	1983	400	1983	616	1983	91	140
Gaza Strip										
Hong Kong	1983	2,042	384	1983	2,710	1983	510	1983	1,195	225
India	1983	3,238	4.4	1983	45,000	1983	62	1983	2,096	2.9
Indonesia	1982	669	4.3	1983	22,000	1983	140	1983	3,500	22
Iran	1983	2,144	51	1983	7,500	1983	178	1983	2,300	55
Iraq	1983	631	43	1983	2,750	1983	186	1983	800	54
Israel	1984	1,595	380	1983	1,107	1983	274	1983	1,050	260
Japan	1983	61,208	513	1983	85,000	1983	713	1983	66,342	556
Jordan	1981	21	9.1	1983	620	1983	248	1983	220	88
Kampuchea	1981	7	1.0	1983	900	1983	131	1983	60	8.7
Korea										
North Korea				1984	4,100	1984	209	1984	1,050	53
South Korea	1983	5,948	149	1983	18,000	1983	451	1983	7,119	178
Kuwait	1983	258	165	1983	477	1983	306	1983	431	276
Laos	1977	6.5	2.2	1983	400	1983	114			
Lebanon	1983	150	57	1983	2,100	1983	797	1983	780	296
Macao	1983	27	79	1983	100	1983	294			
Malaysia	1983	976	66	1983	6,500	1983	439	1983	1,425	96
Maldives	1979	0.8	5.3	1983	15	1983	89	1983	1	6.0
Mongolia	1983	45	25	1983	187	1983	104	1983	71	
Nepal	1983	18	1.1	1983	390	1983	25			39

For an explanation of symbols and abbreviations, see pages 16–17.

(Continued)

TABLE 1j. (Continued)

Country	Telephones			Radio Receivers			Television Receivers		
	Year	Thou-sands	Per 1,000 Inhab-itants	Year	Thou-sands	Per 1,000 Inhab-itants	Year	Thou-sands	Per 1,000 Inhab-itants
Oman	1983	62	55	1983	700	619	1983	45	40
Pakistan	1983	474	5.2	1983	7,000	77	1983	1,116	12
Philippines	1983	78	15	1983	2,342	45	1983	1,350	26
Qatar	1983	96	342	1983	129	459	1983	130	463
Saudi Arabia	1983	1,624	152	1983	3,075	288	1983	2,650	249
Singapore	1983	923	369	1983	681	249	1983	472	189
Sri Lanka	1983	106	6.9	1983	1,800	117	1983	50	3.2
Syria	1983	513	53	1983	1,970	205	1983	423	44
Taiwan	1984	3,947	209	1983	5,000	269	1983	5,060	272
Thailand	1983	623	13	1983	7,200	146	1983	840	17
Turkey	1983	2,665	55	1983	5,800	119	1983	5,600	115
United Arab Emirates	1983	308	255	1983	280	232	1983	110	91
Vietnam	1983	103	1.8	1983	3,000	52	1983	2,000	35
West Bank									
Yemen									
North Yemen	1982	90	12	1983	125	16	1983	17	2.1
South Yemen	1982	23	11	1983	132	61	1983	39	18
EUROPE									
Albania	1981	4.8	1.8	1983	476	168	1983	196	69
Andorra	1982	18	474	1983	7.0	175	1983	5.0	125
Austria	1983	3,469	459	1983	4,000	530	1983	2,348	311
Belgium	1983	4,111	417	1983	4,617	468	1983	2,981	302
Bulgaria	1983	1,790	200	1983	2,055	230	1983	1,691	189
Channel Islands	1983	103	792						
Czechoslovakia	1983	3,402	221	1983	4,165	270	1983	4,323	280
Denmark	1983	3,590	702	1983	2,005	392	1983	1,889	369
Faeroe Islands	1983	24	533	1983	17	378			
Finland	1983	2,777	571	1983	4,800	987	1983	2,100	432

France	1983	29,374	537	1983	47,000	859	1983	20,500	375
Germany									
East Germany	1983	3,441	206	1983	6,415	384	1983	5,970	358
West Germany	1983	35,137	572	1983	24,604	401	1983	22,132	360
Gibraltar	1981	9.4	313	1983	34	1172	1983	7	241
Greece	1983	3,313	336	1983	4,000	406	1983	1,700	173
Hungary	1983	1,383	129	1983	5,770	540	1983	3,970	371
Iceland	1983	125	527	1983	139	586	1983	70	295
Ireland	1983	824	235	1983	1,600	456	1983	838	239
Isle of Man	1985	25	385				1985	21	323
Italy	1983	22,992	405	1983	14,213	250	1983	13,831	243
Liechtenstein	1982	22	846	1983	17	654	1983	8	308
Luxembourg	1984	199	544	1983	196	536	1983	93	254
Malta	1983	113	300	1983	150	398	1983	100	265
Monaco	1983	35	1296	1983	10	370	1983	18	667
Netherlands	1983	8,272	576	1983	11,385	793	1983	6,460	450
Norway	1983	2,395	579	1983	1,700	411	1983	1,316	318
Poland	1983	3,846	105	1983	9,050	247	1983	8,542	234
Portugal	1983	1,685	169	1983	1,700	171	1983	1,500	151
Romania	1981	2,077	93	1983	3,223	143	1983	3,912	173
San Marino	1981	7.7	367	1983	11	500	1983	7	318
Spain	1983	13,345	350	1983	10,900	286	1983	9,850	258
Sweden	1983	7,410	890	1983	7,150	858	1983	3,245	390
Switzerland	1983	5,113	796	1983	2,358	367	1983	2,450	382
UK	1984	29,518	523	1983	56,000	993	1983	27,000	479
USSR	1984	29,462	107	1983	140,000	514	1983	84,000	308
Yugoslavia	1983	2,795	123	1983	5,419	238	1983	4,618	203
NORTH AMERICA									
Anguilla	1983	0.9	129	1983	6.3	900	1983	19	244
Antigua and Barbuda	1980	6.7	89	1983	20	256			
Aruba	1982	10	152						
Bahamas	1983	84	368	1983	118	518	1983	36	158
Barbados	1983	75	299	1983	191	761	1983	55	219
Belize	1981	6	41	1983	79	506	1981	6	41

For an explanation of symbols and abbreviations, see pages 16–17.

(Continued)

TABLE 1j. (Continued)

Country	Telephones			Radio Receivers			Television Receivers		
	Year	Thou-sands	Per 1,000 Inhab-itants	Year	Thou-sands	Per 1,000 Inhab-itants	Year	Thou-sands	Per 1,000 Inhab-itants
Bermuda	1981	46	836	1983	65	1182	1983	39	709
Canada	1983	16,618	668	1983	18,950	761	1983	11,530	463
Cayman Islands	1981	7.3	406	1983	18	947	1983	3.5	184
Costa Rica	1983	292	123	1983	205	86	1983	181	76
Cuba	1983	493	50	1983	3,121	315	1983	1,658	168
Dominica	1981	2.9	39	1983	39	513			
Dominican Republic	1983	175	29	1983	1,200	201	1983	550	92
El Salvador	1983	116	25	1983	1,900	412	1983	330	72
Greenland	1983	17	327	1983	19	365	1983	4.4	85
Grenada	1983	5.6	62	1983	38	422			
Guadeloupe	1982	57	174	1983	39	119	1983	38	116
Guatemala	1983	97	13	1983	340	45	1983	202	27
Haiti	1980	35	7.1	1983	120	23	1983	19	3.7
Honduras	1983	35	8.6	1983	200	49	1983	52	13
Jamaica	1982	124	59	1983	890	420	1983	200	94
Martinique	1982	69	211	1983	55	168	1983	42	128
Mexico	1983	6,414	86	1983	21,800	291	1983	8,300	111
Montserrat	1983	3.0	250	1983	6	500			
Netherlands Antilles	1982	32	168	1983	1975[1]	673[1]	1983	571	219[1]
Nicaragua	1984	42	13	1983	850	278	1983	200	65
Panama	1983	220	105	1983	335	160	1983	255	122
Puerto Rico	1981	631	196	1981	2,450	750	1981	980	300
Saint Christopher and Nevis	1981	2.4	55	1983	21	467	1983	4.5	100
Saint Lucia	1980	8.2	67	1983	96	733	1983	2.0	15
Saint-Pierre and Miquelon	1982	3.2	533	1983	4.0	667	1983	3.4	567
Saint Vincent and the Grenadines	1980	5.5	56	1983	55	539	1983	8.0	78

Trinidad and Tobago	1983	109	95	1983	355	309	1983	300	261
Turks and Caicos Islands	1983	1.4	175	1983	4	500			
USA	1984	182,558	771	1983	479,000	2042	1983	185,300	790
Virgin Islands (UK)	1981	3.0	273	1983	6	462	1983	2.5	192
Virgin Islands (USA)	1982	48	471	1983	90	865	1983	56	538
OCEANIA									
American Samoa	1982	6.0	182	1983	45	1324	1983	6	176
Australia	1983	8,267	538	1983	20,000	1300	1983	6,500	423
Christmas Island (Australia)				1983	4	1250			
Cocos Islands	1982	0.1	167	1983	0.8	1333			
Cook Islands	1983	1.2	59	1983	10	588			
Fiji	1983	50	75	1983	400	597	1971	17	32
French Polynesia	1983	33	198	1983	84	503	1983	26	156
Guam	1981	28	257	1983	140	1207	1983	78	672
Kiribati	1983	0.9	15	1983	13	210			
Nauru	1979	1.6	213	1983	6	750			
New Caledonia	1983	32	221	1983	82	566	1983	30	207
New Zealand	1984	2,011	623	1983	2,850	890	1983	922	288
Niue	1982	0.2	67	1984	0.9	300			
Norfolk Island	1982	1.0	500	1983	2.0	1000			
Pacific Islands (USA)	1982	9.2	66	1975	72	626	1983	7	49
Papua New Guinea	1983	51	16	1983	215	67	1981	49	16
Pitcairn Island	1981	0.02	333						
Samoa	1983	5.9	37	1983	70	437	1983	3.5	22
Solomon Islands	1982	2.7	11	1983	24	95			
Tokelau									
Tonga	1983	3.5	37	1983	75	789			
Tuvalu	1982	0.1	13	1984	7.0	875	1984	1.0	125
Vanuatu	1983	2.4	19	1983	30	242			
Wallis and Futuna Islands	1983	0.2	17						

(Continued)

1Inc Aruba.

For an explanation of symbols and abbreviations, see pages 16–17.

TABLE 1j. (Continued)

Country	Telephones			Radio Receivers			Television Receivers		
	Year	Thou-sands	Per 1,000 Inhab-itants	Year	Thou-sands	Per 1,000 Inhab-itants	Year	Thou-sands	Per 1,000 Inhab-itants
SOUTH AMERICA									
Argentina	1983	3,108	105	1983	16,000	540	1983	5,910	199
Bolivia	1983	144	24	1983	3,500	575	1983	386	63
Brazil	1983	9,856	76	1983	50,000	386	1983	16,500	127
Chile	1983	629	54	1983	3,550	304	1983	1,350	116
Colombia	1983	1,894	73	1983	3,650	141	1983	2,700	105
Ecuador	1983	318	38	1983	2,950	356	1983	570	69
Falkland Islands	1983	0.4	211	1983	1.5	789			
French Guiana	1982	20	274	1983	60	789	1983	12	158
Guyana	1981	27	35	1983	350	450			
Paraguay	1983	78	24	1983	260	80	1983	81	25
Peru	1983	543	30	1983	3,000	164	1983	920	50
Suriname	1983	27	74	1983	220	603	1983	43	118
Uruguay	1983	337	116	1983	1,700	586	1983	376	130
Venezuela	1983	1,441	88	1983	6,650	406	1983	2,050	125

For an explanation of symbols and abbreviations, see pages 16–17.

EDUCATION

1k. School Enrollments and Rates of Illiteracy

Contents

Conventional name of country.

Year of data for total school enrollments.

Thousands of full-time and part-time students, excluding correspondence students and excluding pupils enrolled in kindergartens and nursery schools.

Percentage of school-age population (i.e., 5–24 years of age) enrolled in schools.

Year of data for college and university enrollments.

Thousands of college and university students.

Number of college and university students per thousand inhabitants.

Year of data for illiteracy rate.

Percentage of adult population (generally defined in this connection as persons aged 15 years or over) that is illiterate (i.e., unable to read and write).

Coverage

All countries listed in Table 1a for which data are available.

Entries

218.

TABLE 1k. SCHOOL ENROLLMENTS AND RATES OF ILLITERACY

Country	All Students[1]			College and University Students			Estimated Rate of Illiteracy[3]	
	Year	Total (1,000)	Per- cent[2]	Year	Total (1,000)	Per 1,000 Inhab- itants	Year	% Illit- erate
AFRICA								
Algeria	1983	4,906	49.7	1982	96	4.8	1985	50.4
Angola	1982	1,313	36.4	1982	2.7	0.3	1985	59.0
Benin	1982	559	36.1	1982	6.3	1.7	1985	74.1
Botswana	1984	236	49.6	1984	1.6	1.5	1985	29.2
Burkina Faso	1984	328	9.5	1984	3.9	0.5	1985	86.8
Burundi	1984	361	16.7	1983	2.1	0.5	1982	66.2
Cameroon	1983	1,865	45.7	1981	12	1.4	1985	43.8
Cape Verde	1982	61	41.8		0		1985	52.6
Central African Republic	1983	348	37.0	1983	2.4	1.0	1985	59.8
Chad	1984	335	16.1	1984	1.4	0.3	1985	74.7
Comoros	1980	58	37.9		0		1984	85.0
Congo	1982	622	87.2	1981	8.3	5.3	1985	37.1
Djibouti	1984	30	16.0		0		1980	88.1
Egypt	1983	9,186	44.0	1982	634	14.2	1985	55.5
Equatorial Guinea	1980	44	28.9	1981	1.1	3.1	1980	63.0
Ethiopia	1982	3,071	16.8	1983	16	0.4	1983	37.6
Gabon	1982	202	48.8	1982	3.0	2.7	1985	38.4
Gambia	1983	75	24.6	1983	0		1985	74.9
Ghana	1983	2,423	43.8	1981	16	1.4	1985	46.8
Guinea	1984	395	14.9	1982	13	2.3	1985	71.7
Guinea-Bissau	1983	83	23.5	1983	0.2	0.2	1985	68.6
Ivory Coast	1984	1,443	34.5	1984	19	2.0	1985	57.3
Kenya	1983	4,863	52.5	1983	22	1.2	1985	40.8
Lesotho	1982	310	50.2	1983	2.7	1.9	1985	26.4
Liberia	1981	307	36.3	1979	3.8	2.1	1985	65.0

Libya	1,091	1982	69.1	28	8.1	1985	33.1
Madagascar	1,520	1978	40.4	33	3.6	1985	32.5
Malawi	893	1982	32.4	2.3	0.4	1985	58.8
Mali	372	1982	12.4	5.8	0.8	1985	83.2
Mauritania	137	1982	18.4	1.6	0.9	1976	82.6
Mauritius	218	1983	49.0	0.7	0.7	1985	17.2
Mayotte	16	1984	61.5	0		1982	25.0
Morocco	3,624	1983	35.9	110	5.3	1985	66.9
Mozambique	1,285	1982	21.1	1.2	0.09	1985	62.0
Namibia	331	1985	47.2	0		1985	27.5
Niger	280	1981	11.1	2.4	0.4	1985	86.1
Nigeria	15,792	1980	42.0	177	2.1	1985	57.6
Reunion	148	1983	60.4	3.4	6.6	1982	21.3
Rwanda	837	1984	29.5	1.5	0.3	1985	53.4
Saint Helena	1.2	1983	37.5	0.04	5.6	1976	2.5
Sao Tome and Principe	22	1984	52.4	0		1981	42.6
Senegal	659	1983	24.0	12	1.9	1985	71.9
Seychelles	18	1985	57.1	1.5	23.1	1971	42.3
Sierra Leone	439	1984	31.4	2.4	0.7	1985	70.7
Somalia	289	1983	15.2	4.6	1.0	1985	88.4
South Africa	6,096	1983	44.6	248	8.1	1980	20.7
Sudan	2,068	1982	25.2	33	1.7	1980	78.4
Swaziland	160	1983	56.7	1.7	2.9	1985	32.1
Tanzania	3,640	1983	39.3	4.7	0.2	1980	52.5
Togo	563	1983	44.4	4.0	1.4	1985	59.3
Tunisia	1,663	1984	50.6	39	5.6	1985	45.8
Uganda	1,769	1982	27.7	7.3	0.5	1985	42.7
Western Sahara	10	1980	15.2	0			
Zaire	4,771	1978	38.2	32	1.1	1985	38.8
Zambia	1,240	1984	41.2	8.3	1.3	1985	24.3
Zimbabwe	2,757	1985	68.7	30	3.7	1985	26.0
ASIA							
Afghanistan	578	1982	7.5	20	1.2	1985	76.3
Bahrain	79	1984	46.7	2.7	7.7	1985	27.3

1 Exc pupils enrolled in kindergartens and nursery schools.
2 Percentage of school-age population (i.e., 5–24 years of age) enrolled in schools.
3 Illiterates are, in general, persons aged 15 years or over that are unable to read and write.

For an explanation of symbols and abbreviations, see pages 16–17.

(Continued)

TABLE 1k. (Continued)

Country	All Students[1]			College and University Students			Estimated Rate of Illiteracy[3]	
	Year	Total (1,000)	Per-cent[2]	Year	Total (1,000)	Per 1,000 Inhab-itants	Year	% Illit-erate
Bangladesh	1984	12,413	27.4	1983	387	4.1	1985	66.9
Bhutan	1984	50	8.2	1980	0.3	0.2	1977	82.0
Brunei	1982	51	55.4	1983	0.2	1.0	1981	22.2
Burma	1984	6,297	39.0	1984	174	4.8	1980	34.1
China	1984	185,427	40.8	1983	1,237	1.2	1985	30.7
Cyprus	1983	129	58.1	1983	2.2	3.4	1976	9.5
Gaza Strip	1984	153	60.0	1984	0.8	1.6		
Hong Kong	1983	1,064	54.3	1982	71	13.6	1985	11.9
India	1983	126,698	38.0	1979	5,346	8.2	1985	56.5
Indonesia	1983	37,171	51.7	1982	616	4.0	1985	25.9
Iran	1983	8,978	48.1	1983	151	3.6	1985	49.2
Iraq	1983	3,894	55.2	1983	127	8.6	1985	10.7
Israel	1983	1,014	65.6	1983	99	24.5	1985	4.9
Japan	1984	24,524	68.1	1984	2,337	19.5	1984	0
Jordan	1983	850	66.6	1983	51	20.4	1985	25.0
Kampuchea	1982	1,692	49.4	1982	5.3	0.8	1980	52.0
Korea								
North Korea	1976	4,062	53.5	1974	300	19.4	1979	10.0
South Korea	1984	10,952	61.8	1984	1,193	29.4	1981	7.3
Kuwait	1983	406	61.2	1983	19	12.2	1985	30.0
Laos	1983	586	36.6	1983	4.9	1.4	1985	16.1
Lebanon	1982	755	60.3	1982	73	27.7	1985	23.0
Macao	1982	46	26.6	1982	1.2	3.7	1981	38.7
Malaysia	1985	3,693	50.5	1982	69	4.9	1985	26.6
Peninsular Malaysia	1982	2,747	48.2	1982	67	5.5	1980	27.0
Sabah	1982	233	47.8		0		1980	42.0
Sarawak	1981	306	47.5	1978	1.5	1.2	1980	48.9
Maldives	1983	40	49.4		0		1977	17.6

Mongolia	1983	489	60.5	1983	26	14.4	1980	10.5
Nepal	1984	2,202	31.3	1984	55	3.5	1985	74.4
Oman	1984	195	38.4	1983	0.4	0.4	1985	70.4
Pakistan	1983	9,255	22.1	1983	556	6.1	1981	73.8
Philippines	1983	13,498	55.7	1983	1,576	30.3	1985	14.3
Qatar	1983	61	55.5	1983	4.6	16.4	1981	48.9
Saudi Arabia	1983	1,742	37.7	1983	82	8.0	1980	75.4
Singapore	1984	527	52.9	1984	36	14.2	1985	13.9
Sri Lanka	1984	3,591	52.5	1983	63	4.1	1981	13.9
Syria	1983	2,720	57.8	1982	141	15.2	1985	40.0
Taiwan	1984	4,620	57.9	1984	412	21.8	1982	12.9
Thailand	1983	10,517	45.3	1982	1,057	21.8	1985	9.0
Turkey	1983	9,373	42.3	1983	335	6.9	1984	25.8
United Arab Emirates	1983	185	37.6	1983	5.9	4.3	1980	32.0
Vietnam	1980	11,936	50.1	1980	115	2.1	1979	16.0
West Bank	1984	267	67.3	1984	1.6	2.0		
Yemen								
North Yemen	1983	758	20.1	1980	4.5	0.7	1985	86.3
South Yemen	1983	333	34.2	1981	3.6	1.8	1985	58.6
EUROPE								
Albania	1983	647	52.6	1983	20	7.0	1970	25.0
Andorra	1982	6.0	46.2		0		1981	0
Austria	1984	1,401	61.6	1984	152	20.1	1983	0
Belgium	1983	1,809	61.4	1983	225	22.8	1981	1.0
Bulgaria	1983	1,480	57.7	1983	99	11.1	1983	5.5
Channel Islands	1982	20	53.2		0			
Czechoslovakia	1983	2,547	54.7	1983	182	11.8	1979	0.5
Denmark	1983	1,034	68.7	1982	111	21.7	1983	0
Faeroe Islands	1984	11	65.4	1984	2.0	44.4	1982	0
Finland	1983	923	66.8	1983	120	24.7	1982	0
France	1983	10,693	64.5	1983	1,207	22.1	1980	1.2
Germany								
East Germany	1983	2,833	59.1	1982	403	24.1	1981	0
West Germany	1984	11,570	65.9	1984	1,314	21.5	1983	0

1Exc pupils enrolled in kindergartens and nursery schools.
2Percentage of school-age population (i.e., 5–24 years of age) enrolled in schools.
3Illiterates are, in general, persons aged 15 years or over that are unable to read and write.
For an explanation of symbols and abbreviations, see pages 16–17.

(Continued)

TABLE 1k. (Continued)

Country	All Students[1] Year	Total (1,000)	Per-cent[2]	College and University Students Year	Total (1,000)	Per 1,000 Inhabitants	Estimated Rate of Illiteracy[3] Year	% Illiterate
Gibraltar	1984	5.8	69.0	1982	0		1970	10.3
Greece	1982	1,800	61.7	1984	137	14.0	1985	7.7
Hungary	1984	1,706	58.1	1983	100	9.4	1980	1.1
Iceland	1983	57	65.5	1981	5.2	21.9	1983	0
Ireland	1983	945	72.2	1985	60	17.4	1980	0.5
Isle of Man	1985	14	77.8	1983	3.7	56.9		
Italy	1983	10,518	60.1	1983	1,120	19.7	1985	3.0
Liechtenstein	1983	3.6	37.9	1983	0		1981	0.3
Luxembourg	1984	51	49.0	1983	2.5	6.8	1983	0
Malta	1983	63	53.4	1983	1.3	3.4	1985	15.9
Monaco	1982	5.1	96.2	1983	0.6	22.2		
Netherlands	1983	2,986	65.8	1982	379	26.5	1984	0
Norway	1982	833	66.4	1982	89	21.6	1982	0
Poland	1984	7,012	60.5	1984	350	9.5	1978	1.2
Portugal	1982	1,768	52.4	1981	95	9.6	1985	16.0
Romania	1983	4,513	62.9	1983	174	7.7	1980	4.2
San Marino	1983	2.8	39.4	1983	0		1982	2.8
Spain	1982	8,534	66.1	1982	731	19.3	1985	5.6
Sweden	1983	1,475	66.3	1983	223	26.8	1982	0
Switzerland	1984	1,141	61.1	1984	106	16.5	1982	0.1
UK	1982	11,152	65.5	1982	1,111	19.7	1984	0.1
England and Wales	1982	9,632	65.2	1982	844	17.0		
Northern Ireland	1982	386	69.2	1982	28	17.8		
Scotland	1982	1,134	68.6	1982	239	46.2		
USSR	1983	48,020	51.5	1983	5,301	19.5	1983	0
Vatican City	1983	9.2		1983	9.2			
Yugoslavia	1983	4,205	56.2	1983	375	16.4	1985	8.8

NORTH AMERICA

	Year			Year			Year	
Anguilla	1983	2.1	54.5		0		1984	4.0
Antigua and Barbuda	1983	16	42.1		0		1977	5.0
Aruba	1982	13	53.1	1982	0.06	0.9		
Bahamas	1982	65	65.0	1983	2.0	8.8	1979	7.0
Barbados	1983	64	58.7	1983	5.1	20.3	1980	2.0
Belize	1984	45	57.7	1984	0.8	5.0	1982	10.0
Bermuda	1983	13	73.9	1982	2.7	49.1	1970	1.6
Canada	1983	5,616	68.6	1983	1,041	41.8	1975	4.4
Cayman Islands	1980	4.2	66.7		0		1970	2.5
Costa Rica	1983	531	43.8	1983	64	26.9	1985	6.4
Cuba	1983	2,499	59.1	1983	192	19.4	1981	2.2
Dominica	1983	21	56.8	1980	0.3	4.1	1970	5.9
Dominican Republic	1983	1,420	60.1	1977	59	11.7	1985	22.7
El Salvador	1984	1,043	46.2	1984	74	15.7	1985	27.9
Greenland	1982	10	46.1		0		1979	0
Grenada	1982	28	59.6	1982	0.5	5.6	1981	15.0
Guadeloupe	1982	104	68.9	1981	3.8	11.7	1982	9.9
Guatemala	1984	1,202	33.1	1982	47	6.4	1985	45.0
Haiti	1981	766	33.7	1980	5.6	1.1	1985	62.4
Honduras	1984	892	44.0	1984	32	7.6	1985	40.5
Jamaica	1983	589	56.8	1980	14	6.8	1980	11.4
Martinique	1982	91	61.5	1983	2.1	6.4	1982	7.5
Mexico	1984	22,578	59.3	1983	1,121	15.0	1985	9.6
Montserrat	1985	2.2	42.3	1985	0.06	5.0	1970	3.4
Netherlands Antilles	1982	41	52.6	1983	0.9	4.7	1980	5.0⁴
Nicaragua	1984	729	47.6	1984	33	10.4	1980	13.0
Panama	1984	576	58.4	1984	51	23.9	1985	11.8
Puerto Rico	1983	949	72.6	1983	154	47.1	1980	10.9
Saint Christopher and Nevis	1983	12	54.5	1979	0.04	0.9	1970	2.4
Saint Lucia	1983	38	63.3	1983	0.5	4.0	1970	18.3
Saint-Pierre and Miquelon	1983	1.4	60.9		0		1983	0.5

1Exc pupils enrolled in kindergartens and nursery schools.
2Percentage of school-age population (i.e., 5–24 years of age) enrolled in schools.
3Illiterates are, in general, persons aged 15 years or over that are unable to read and write.
4Inc Aruba.

For an explanation of symbols and abbreviations, see pages 16–17.

(Continued)

TABLE 1k. (Continued)

Country	All Students[1]			College and University Students			Estimated Rate of Illiteracy[3]	
	Year	Total (1,000)	Per- cent[2]	Year	Total (1,000)	Per 1,000 Inhab- itants	Year	% Illit- erate
Saint Vincent and the Grenadines	1982	31	61.4	1982	1.2	12.0	1983	15.0
Trinidad and Tobago	1982	267	52.3	1982	5.7	5.0	1985	3.9
Turks and Caicos Islands	1984	2.1	55.3		0		1970	1.9
USA	1982	53,959	71.2	1982	12,426	53.5	1980	4.5
Virgin Islands (UK)	1983	3.4	57.6		0		1970	11.7
Virgin Islands (USA)	1985	35	75.3	1985	2.8	25.5	1980	4.4
OCEANIA								
American Samoa	1983	11	68.7	1979	0.9	28.1	1980	5.5
Australia	1983	3,169	60.8	1983	349	22.7	1980	0.5
Christmas Island (Australia)	1983	0.62	80.5		0		1984	60.0
Cocos Islands	1974	0.09	39.1		0			
Cook Islands	1983	6.0	68.2	1980	0.4		1982	9.2
Fiji	1984	173	56.5	1982	2.7	4.1	1985	14.5
French Polynesia	1984	46	59.0	1982	0.07	0.4	1977	2.2
Guam	1983	32	64.0	1979	3.2	30.8	1980	3.6
Kiribati	1984	16	53.3	1983	0.3	4.8	1982	10.0
Nauru	1985	1.9	61.3		0		1979	1.0
New Caledonia	1984	53	80.3	1984	0.7	4.8	1976	8.7
New Zealand	1983	792	68.3	1983	85	26.5	1982	0
Niue	1984	0.9	60.0		0		?	3.0
Norfolk Island	1982	0.2	35.2		0		1981	0
Pacific Islands (USA)	1983	49	72.1	1982	2.0	14.4	1980	12.6
Papua New Guinea	1984	403	27.8	1982	5.6	1.8	1985	54.5

	Year			Year			Year	
Pitcairn Island					0.6		1984	3.5
Samoa	1983	54	64.3	1983	0.5	3.8	1971	2.2
Solomon Islands	1984	43	36.1	1983	0	2.0	1976	45.9
Tokelau	1983	0.76	102.8		0.8		1982	0.2
Tonga	1984	37	75.5	1984	0	8.3	1976	0.4
Tuvalu	1984	1.5	40.5		0		1979	4.5
Vanuatu	1983	25	43.9		0		1979	47.1
Wallis and Futuna Islands	1983	4.0	69.0				?	65.8
SOUTH AMERICA								
Argentina	1983	6,363	61.4	1983	581	19.6	1985	4.5
Bolivia	1983	1,361	49.6	1982	72	12.2	1985	25.8
Brazil	1983	29,240	50.1	1984	1,453	11.0	1985	22.3
Chile	1984	2,837	58.7	1983	127	10.9	1983	5.6
Colombia	1984	6,323	48.6	1983	379	14.7	1985	11.9
Ecuador	1983	2,591	66.3	1981	264	33.6	1985	17.6
Falkland Islands	1980	0.3	50.0		0		1980	2.0
French Guiana	1982	18	59.0	1982	0.2	2.7	1982	17.2
Guyana	1981	211	53.8	1983	2.1	2.7	1985	4.1
Paraguay	1982	735	52.5	1983	31	9.6	1985	11.8
Peru	1982	5,010	62.7	1982	365	20.7	1985	15.2
Suriname	1981	118	57.8	1979	1.0	2.9	1985	10.0
Uruguay	1983	598	60.6	1983	50	17.2	1983	3.7
Venezuela	1983	4,097	53.1	1983	367	22.4	1985	13.1

1Exc pupils enrolled in kindergartens and nursery schools.
2Percentage of school-age population (i.e., 5–24 years of age) enrolled in schools.
3Illiterates are, in general, persons aged 15 years or over that are unable to read and write.
For an explanation of symbols and abbreviations, see pages 16–17.

2

CITY TABLES, BY CONTINENT AND COUNTRY

2a. Cities: Location, Elevation, Date of Settlement, and Evolution of Population, 1800 to Latest Date

Contents

Latitude and longitude, in degrees and minutes.

Elevation (i.e., altitude above sea level), in feet. When available, the given elevation is that of the city center or principal business district, or is an average of elevations at several points in the city; otherwise, it is that of the meteorological station.

Conventional name of city. Other names are given in Table 2b.

Date of settlement (i.e., year or century in which the first permanent settlement within present city limits was made). A question mark following a given date usually indicates that although its exact origin is unknown, the city in question was first mentioned in historical records at that date. When the exact time of settlement cannot be ascertained but the city is known to have existed before a certain date, that date is given, preceded by the abbreviation "bef." It should be observed that the settlement date of a city bears no relation either to the date when the city was formally established or chartered or to the date when the present name was adopted.

Latest population in thousands, followed (in parentheses) by year of data. If the year is followed by the letter "e," the population has been estimated; otherwise, the figure given is from census returns. For many cities, two population figures are listed for a given year. The first figure is for the city proper, and the second, followed by the letter "s," for the city and adjacent suburban areas. Preferably, this is the population of the urbanized area or conurbation only; some officially reported surburban areas, however, include rural districts.

Similar population data for the years 1980, 1970, 1950, 1930, 1900, 1850, and 1800, or for the years nearest to those dates for which reliable figures are available, with the exact year stated. All populations are for the city as it existed at the time the population was determined, not for its present-day area. Also, census figures determined several years before or after the desired date are entered in preference to estimates for the exact year. Question marks are employed when the exact year is unknown; for example, the notation "(00?e)" below the tabular heading "ca 1900" indicates that the population preceding it was estimated about, but not necessarily during, the year 1900.

Coverage

All cities with a present population (including suburbs) of at least 100,000 in North America and Oceania and 200,000 in other continents, and all capitals (regardless of size) of countries with a present population of at least 100,000 and their major divisions. In addition, many other well-known cities almost as large are included, as well as numerous smaller cities that are university centers, are important historically, or are particularly attractive to tourists.

Rounding

Populations are rounded to the nearest 1,000 (to the nearest 100 if the total is less than 1,000).

Entries

2,664, as follows: Africa—175
Asia—753
Europe—671
North America—825
Oceania—39
South America—201

TABLE 2a. CITIES: LOCATION, ELEVATION, DATE OF SETTLEMENT, AND EVOLUTION OF POPULATION, 1800 TO LATEST DATE

Latitude and Longitude	Elev (ft)	City	Date Settled	Population (thousands)							
				Latest	ca 1980	ca 1970	ca 1950	ca 1930	ca 1900	ca 1850	ca 1800
AFRICA											
Algeria											
36.47N, 3.03E	194	*Algiers	10th c	1722 (83e)	1523 (77)	904 (66)	266 (48)	221 (31)	97 (01)	97 (49)	73 (08e)
36.54N, 7.46E	10	Annaba	7th c	348 (83e)	240 (77)	152 (66)	78 (48)	66 (31)	32 (01)	10 (47)	
36.28N, 2.50E	876	Blida	16th c	191 (83e)	138 (77)	86 (66)	30 (48)	39 (31)	29 (01)	8 (72)	
36.22N, 6.37E	1906	Constantine	3rd c BC?	449 (83e)	344 (77)	246 (66)	80 (48)	79 (31)	41 (01)	23 (49)	20 (08e)
35.42N, 0.38W	295	Oran	10th c	664 (83e)	491 (77)	326 (66)	245 (48)	154 (31)	88 (01)	25 (49)	16 (00?e)
36.12N, 5.24E	3547	Setif	1st c	187 (83e)	130 (77)	88 (66)	40 (48)	37 (31)	15 (01)	4 (72)	
Angola											
8.48S, 13.14E	140	*Luanda	1575	960 (84e)	700 (82e)	475 (70)	142 (50)	67 (40)	20 (98)	16 (70)	
Benin											
6.21N, 2.26E	43	Cotonou	bef 1868	487 (82e)	328 (79)	139 (70e)	23 (46-49e)	8 (32)	4 (11)		
6.29N, 2.37E	66	*Porto-Novo	16th c	208 (82e)	132 (79)	87 (70e)	31 (46-49e)	27 (32)	30 (00?e)		
Botswana											
24.40S, 25.54E	3329	*Gaborone	1895?	79 (84e)	60 (81)	18 (71)	12s(46)	8s(36)			
Burkina Faso											
11.12N, 4.18W	1421	Bobo Dioulasso	15th c?	231 (85)	149 (80e)	68 (67e)	38 (46-49e)	11 (31)	3 (00?e)		
12.22N, 1.31W	997	*Ouagadougou	12th c?	442 (85)	248 (80e)	110 (70e)	21 (46-49e)	11 (31)	5 (00?e)		
Burundi											
3.23S, 29.22E	2569	*Bujumbura	1897	235 (84e)	172 (79)	79 (70e)	17 (49e)				
Cameroon											
4.03N, 9.42E	43	Douala	bef 1884	763 (84e)	458 (76)	250 (70e)	125 (56)	28 (31)	23 (02e)		
3.52N, 11.31E	2494	*Yaounde	1888	522 (84e)	313 (76)	166 (69e)	30 (50e)	6 (36)			
(Canary Islands), Spain											
28.29N, 16.19W	1805	La Laguna	1496	108 (84e)	106 (81)	80 (70)	42 (50)	24 (30)	13 (00)	10 (60)	9 (1768)

(Continued)

For an explanation of symbols and abbreviations, see pages 16–17.

TABLE 2a. (Continued)

Latitude and Longitude	Elev (ft)	City	Date Settled	Population (thousands)							
				Latest	ca 1980	ca 1970	ca 1950	ca 1930	ca 1900	ca 1850	ca 1800
28.06N, 15.24W	43	*Las Palmas	1478	379 (85e)	366 (81)	287 (70)	153 (50)	78 (30)	45 (00)	16 (60)	9 (00?e)
28.27N, 16.14W	13	*Santa Cruz de Tenerife	1494	194 (85e)	191 (81)	151 (70)	103 (50)	62 (30)	38 (00)	14 (60)	7 (1768)
Cape Verde											
14.55N, 23.31W	92	*Praia	1652?	49 (85e)	38 (80)	21 (70)	10 (50)	6 (30?)	4 (00?)	2 (50?)	village
Central African Republic											
4.23N, 18.35E	1250	*Bangui	1890	474 (84e)	301 (75)	299 (68)	41 (50e)	13 (26)			
Chad											
12.07N, 15.03E	984	*Ndjamena	1900	512 (86e)	303 (79e)	157 (70e)	23 (50e)	6 (26)			
Comoros											
11.41S 43.16E	194	*Moroni	bef 1886		20 (80)	12 (66)	6 (48e)	3 (28)	2 (00?e)		
Congo											
4.16S, 15.17E	1683	*Brazzaville	1880	456 (83e)	422 (80e)	290 (74)	83 (50e)	4 (26)	5 (00?e)		
4.48S, 11.51E	56	Pointe-Noire	16th c?	214 (83e)	185 (80e)	140 (74)	22 (50)	5 (36e)	village		
Djibouti											
11.36N, 43.09E	20	*Djibouti	1888	200 (85e)	150 (81e)	62 (70e)	9 (28)	15 (00e)			
Egypt											
31.12N, 29.54E	13	Alexandria	332 BC	2821 (85e)	2318 (76)	1801 (66)	919 (47)	573 (27)	320 (97)	164 (62)	15 (00)
24.05N, 32.53E	433	Aswan	6th c BC?	183 (85e)	144 (76)	128 (66)	26 (47)	16 (27)	13 (97)	6 (82)	
27.11N, 31.11E	217	Asyut	bef 2160 BC	274 (85e)	214 (76)	154 (66)	90 (47)	57 (27)	42 (97)	26 (62)	12 (00e)
30.03N, 31.15E	79	*Cairo	641?	6205 (85e)	5074 (76)	4220 (66)	2091 (47)	1065 (27)	570 (97)	257 (62)	260 (00e)
31.02N, 30.28E	20	Damanhur	11th c?	221 (85e)	171 (76)	146 (66)	85 (47)	52 (27)	32 (97)	20 (82)	
29.19N, 30.50E	98	Fayyum	20th c BC?	218 (85e)	167 (76)	134 (66)	74 (47)	53 (27)	31 (97)	25 (82)	
30.01N, 31.13E	82	Giza	bef 2568 BC	1608 (85e)	1231 (76)	571 (66)	66 (47)	27 (27)	17 (97)	11 (72)	3 (00e)
29.51N, 31.20E	377	Hulwan	690?	346 (85e)	283 (76)	203 (66)	1 (47)				
30.35N, 32.16E	33	Ismailia	1863	192 (85e)	146 (76)	144 (66)	68 (47)	25 (27)	7 (97)	3 (72)	
25.41N, 32.39E	256	Luxor	bef 2160 BC	137 (85e)	94 (76)	77 (66)	24 (47)	13 (27)	11 (97)	4 (82)	

For an explanation of symbols and abbreviations, see pages 16–17.

(Continued)

Figure 8. *Buildings clustered around Liberation Square in Cairo, the largest urbanized area in Africa. The Nile River and part of Zamalik Island can be seen in the background. (Credit: Ministry of Culture, Arab Republic of Egypt.)*

TABLE 2a. (Continued)

Latitude and Longitude	Elev (ft)	City	Date Settled	Population (thousands)							
				Latest	ca 1980	ca 1970	ca 1950	ca 1930	ca 1900	ca 1850	ca 1800
30.58N, 31.10E		Mahalla al Kubra	985?	363 (85e)	292 (76)	225 (66)	116 (47)	46 (27)	32 (97)	28 (82)	17 (00e)
31.03N, 31.23E	23	Mansurah	1221	329 (85e)	259 (76)	191 (66)	102 (47)	64 (27)	36 (97)	16 (72)	7 (00e)
28.06N, 30.45E	141	Minya	bef 2568 BC	192 (85e)	146 (76)	113 (66)	70 (47)	48 (27)	20 (97)	16 (82)	
31.16N, 32.18E	72	Port Said	1859	374 (85e)	263 (76)	283 (66)	178 (47)	101 (27)	42 (97)	9 (72)	
30.33N, 31.01E	39	Shibin al Kawm		130 (85e)	103 (76)	66 (66)	42 (47)	27 (27)	21 (97)	12 (72)	
30.06N, 31.15E		Shubra al Khaymah		515 (85e)	394 (76)	173 (66)	15 (47)	7 (27?)	2 (97?)	2 (82)	
29.58N, 32.33E	13	Suez	15th c	254 (85e)	193 (76)	264 (66)	107 (47)	41 (27)	17 (97)	13 (72)	
30.47N, 31.00E	46	Tanta	12th c?	365 (85e)	283 (76)	230 (66)	140 (47)	90 (27)	57 (97)	19 (62)	10 (00e)
30.35N, 31.31E	36	Zagazig	1850?	267 (85e)	203 (76)	151 (66)	82 (47)	53 (27)	36 (97)	20 (82)	
Equatorial Guinea											
3.45N, 8.48E	66	*Malabo	1827		37 (83)	19 (70e)	9 (42)	8 (31)	1 (00?e)		
Ethiopia											
9.02N, 38.42E	7900	*Addis Ababa	1887	1423 (84)	1277 (80e)	796 (70)	400 (51e)	70 (28e)	30 (00e)		
15.20N, 38.56E	7789	Asmara	bef 1889	275 (84)	425 (80e)	218 (70)	117 (48e)	22 (31)	9 (05)		
9.19N, 42.07E	6089	Harar	7th c?	62 (84)	63 (80e)	45 (70e)	40 (48e)	36 (30?e)	40 (00?e)	30 (70?e)	
Gabon											
0.23N, 9.27E	10	*Libreville	1849	350 (83e)	251 (75)	105 (69–70)	10 (50e)	4 (31)	3 (03e)		
Gambia											
13.27N, 16.34W	7	*Banjul	1816		45 (83)	39 (73)	20 (51)	14 (31)	7 (01)	4 (50?e)	
Ghana											
5.31N, 0.12W	213	*Accra	16th c		965 (84) 1420s(84)	564 (70) 738s(70)	134 (48)	61 (31)	15 (01)	3 (50?e)	
5.06N, 1.15W	174	Cape Coast	1652		58 (84)	52 (70)	23 (48)	18 (31)	29 (01)	5 (50?e)	
6.43N, 1.37W	961	Kumasi	17th c		349 (84)	260 (70) 345s(70)	71 (48)	36 (31)	6 (06)	18 (50?e)	13 (17e)

Lat/Long		Elev	City	Founded	Pop	Pop	Pop	Pop	Pop	Pop	Pop	Pop
4.56N,	1.42W	30	Sekondi-Takoradi	17th c	94 (84)	92 (70) 161s(70)	44 (48)	17 (31)		17 (31)		
9.24N,	0.50W	659	Tamale		137 (84)	84 (70)	17 (48)	13 (31)		13 (31)		
Guinea												
9.31N,	13.43W	151	*Conakry	1890	705 (83)	526 (72)	38 (46–49e)	9 (31)	7 (11)			
10.23N,	9.18W	1237	Kankan	bef 1600	89 (83)	85 (72)	16 (46–49e)	11 (31)	6 (00?e)	6 (50?e)		
Guinea-Bissau												
11.51N,	15.35W	66	*Bissau	1758	109 (79)	71 (70)	18 (50)	1 (30)				
Ivory Coast												
5.19N,	4.02W	23	*Abidjan	1904	1850s(82e)	686 (75) 951s(75)	550 (70e)	56 (46–49e)	10 (31)	1 (11)		
7.41N,	5.02W	1194	Bouake	bef 1898	640s(82e)	173 (75)	120 (70e)	22 (50?e)	5 (37e)			
6.49N,	5.17W	682	Yamoussoukro	bef 1905	70 (83e)	36 (75)		0.5 (50e)				
Kenya												
0.06S,	34.45E	3725	Kisumu	1900	167 (84e)	153 (79)	32 (69)	11 (48)	5 (31?e)	5 (31?e)		
4.03S,	39.40E	52	Mombasa	8th c?	426 (84e)	341 (79)	247 (69)	85 (48)	56 (31)	27 (00?e)		
1.17S,	36.49E	5453	*Nairobi	1899	1104 (84e)	828 (79)	509 (69)	75 (48)	48 (31)	5 (07)		
Lesotho												
29.20S,	27.30E	5154	*Maseru	1869	109s(86)	15 (76) 47s(76)	14 (66) 18s(66)	3 (46e)	2 (21)	0.9 (04)		
Liberia												
6.19N,	10.49W	75	*Monrovia	1822	425 (84e)	243 (80e)	172 (74)	41 (56)	10 (30?e)	5 (97e)	2 (52e)	
Libya												
32.07N,	20.04E	82	Bengasi	6th c BC		268 (79)	219 (73)	70 (54)	31 (28)	15 (00?e)	3 (50?e)	5 (00?e)
32.54N,	13.11E	72	*Tripoli	7th c BC?		587 (79)	481 (73)	130 (54)	72 (31)	42 (00e)	15 (42e)	15 (05e)
Madagascar												
18.55S,	47.31E	4531	*Antananarivo	bef 1613	663 (85e)	551 (79e)	406 (75)	171 (48)	92 (31)	63 (11)	25 (50?e)	
(Madeira Islands), Portugal												
32.38N,	16.54W	82	*Funchal	1425		44 (81)	40 (70)	37 (50)	31 (30)	21 (00)	17 (45)	15 (00e)

For an explanation of symbols and abbreviations, see pages 16–17.

(Continued)

TABLE 2a. (Continued)

Latitude and Longitude	Elev (ft)	City	Date Settled	Population (thousands)							
				Latest	ca 1980	ca 1970	ca 1950	ca 1930	ca 1900	ca 1850	ca 1800
Malawi											
15.48S, 35.01E	3501	Blantyre	1876	355 (85e)	219 (77)	104 (66)	6 (49e)	8 (30e)	6 (00?e)		
13.59S, 33.47E	3501	*Lilongwe	1947	187 (85e)	99 (77)	19 (66)	2 (49e)				
15.23S, 35.20E	3140	Zomba	1885	53 (85e)	24 (77)	20 (66)	9 (56)	3 (32e)			
Mali											
12.39N, 8.00W	1089	*Bamako	bef 1883	802 (85e)	404 (76)	182 (68e)	60 (46–49e)	20 (31)	7 (11)	0.8(83)	
16.46N, 3.01W	978	Timbuktu	11th c		20 (76)	12 (71e)	7 (46–49e)	6 (31)	7 (11)	13 (54e)	60 (00?e)
Mauritania											
18.06N, 15.57W	16	*Nouakchott	1903	350 (84e)	135 (76)	30 (70e)	0.4 (50?e)				
Mauritius											
20.10S, 57.30E	181	*Port Louis	1735	138 (86e)	132 (83)	134 (72)	70 (52)	54 (31)	53 (01)	50 (51)	20 (00?e)
Morocco											
33.36N, 7.37W	164	Casablanca	1515		2139 (82) 2263s(82)	1506 (71) 1583s(71)	682 (52)	160 (31)	20 (00?e)	0.7 (50?e)	0.1 (00?e)
34.03N, 4.59W	1368	Fez	808		449 (82)	325 (71)	179 (52)	107 (31)	145 (00?e)	88 (50?e)	100 (00?e)
34.16N, 6.36W	39	Kenitra	bef 1913		188 (82)	139 (71)	57 (51)	19 (31)	50 (00e)		
31.37N, 8.00W	1509	Marrakesh	1062		440 (82)	333 (71)	215 (52)	192 (31)	50 (00e)	80 (50e)	30 (00?e)
33.54N, 5.33W	1831	Meknes	10th c		320 (82)	248 (71)	140 (52)	54 (31)	35 (00?e)	50 (50?e)	15 (00?e)
34.40N, 1.54W	1526	Oujda	994		260 (82)	176 (71)	81 (52)	29 (31)	8 (00?e)		
34.02N, 6.50W	213	*Rabat	1150		519 (82)	368 (71)	156 (52)	53 (31)	31 (00e)	28 (50e)	
32.18N, 9.14W	148	Safi	bef 1st c		197 (82)	129 (71)	57 (51)	26 (31)	12 (00?e)	9 (78)	
34.04N, 6.48W	328	Sale	1039?		289 (82)	156 (71)	47 (52)	26 (31)	30 (00e)	10 (50e)	
35.47N, 5.48W	246	Tangier	15th c BC?		266 (82)	186 (71)	85 (47e)	80 (26e)	35 (00e)	8 (50e)	12 (00?e)
35.34N, 5.22W	16	Tetouan	2nd c?		200 (82)	139 (71)	81 (50)	43 (30?e)	25 (00?e)	20 (50?e)	16 (00?e)
Mozambique											
19.50S, 34.52E	26	Beira	1891	270 (86e)	350 (80)	130 (70)	43 (50)	25 (30)	3 (00)		
25.58S, 32.33E	194	*Maputo	1544	883 (86e)	755 (80)	102 (70)	94 (50)	43 (30)	6 (00)	1 (67e)	

Namibia

Lat/Long	Alt	City	Founded								
22.35S, 17.05E	5428	*Windhoek	bef 1890	104 (83e)	89 (81)	61 (70)	20 (51)	8 (26)	60 (00?e)	60 (50e)	

Niger

Lat/Long	Alt	City	Founded								
13.30N, 2.08E	728	*Niamey	16th c?	399 (83e)	225 (77)	79 (68e)	9 (46–49e)	3 (31)			

Nigeria

Lat/Long	Alt	City	Founded								
5.07N, 7.22E	200	Aba	1830	216 (83e)	177 (75e)	131 (63)	58 (52)	13 (31)			
7.10N, 3.20E	220	Abeokuta	19th c?	309 (83e)	253 (75e)	187 (63)	84 (52)	46 (31)			
7.38N, 5.13E	1650	Ado-Ekiti	1300?	266 (83e)	213 (75e)	158 (63)	30 (52)	9 (31)			
6.20N, 5.38E	371	Benin City	17th c	166 (83e)	136 (75e)	101 (63)	54 (52)	17 (31)		15 (50?e)	
4.57N, 8.19E	39	Calabar	1500?	126 (83e)	105 (75e)	76 (63)	47 (53)	52 (31)	27 (11)	7 (50?e)	
7.44N, 4.26E	990	Ede	1909	222 (83e)	182 (75e)	135 (63)	45 (52)	13 (31)			
6.27N, 7.28E	466	Enugu	bef 1821	228 (83e)	187 (75e)	138 (63)	63 (53)				
7.23N, 3.53E	651	Ibadan	11th c?	1060 (83e)	847 (75e)	627 (63)	459 (52)	387 (31)	345 (11)	70 (51e)	
7.28N, 4.34E	1000	Ife	18th c?	214 (83e)	176 (75e)	130 (63)	111 (52)	24 (31)	36 (11)		
7.38N, 4.45E	1100?	Ilesha	18th c	273 (83e)	224 (75e)	166 (63)	72 (52)	22 (31)	40 (00?e)		
8.45N, 4.32E	1079	Ilorin	16th c?	344 (83e)	282 (75e)	209 (63)	41 (52)	48 (31)	36 (11)	70 (51e)	
7.38, 4.11E		Iwo		262 (83e)	214 (75e)	159 (63)	100 (52)	57 (31)	60 (00?e)		
9.55N, 8.54E	4009	Jos	1913	149 (83e)	123 (75e)	90 (63)	39 (52)	12 (31)			
10.31N, 7.26E	2113	Kaduna	12th c?	202 (83e)	202 (75e)	150 (63)	39 (52)	11 (31)		30 (51e)	35 (24e)
12.00N, 8.30E	1533	Kano	1700?	487 (83e)	399 (75e)	295 (63)	130 (52)	97 (31)	39 (11)	29 (71)	5 (89e)
6.26N, 3.23E	9	*Lagos	bef 1904	1097 (83e)	1061 (75e)	665 (63)	267 (52)	126 (31)	42 (01)		
11.51N, 13.09E	1186	Maiduguri		231 (83e)	189 (75e)	140 (63)	55 (52)	24 (31)			
6.32N, 3.22E		Mushin		241 (83e)	197 (75e)	146 (63)	32 (52)				
6.52N, 7.23E	1300	Nsukka		43 (83e)	30 (73e)	26 (63)					
8.05N, 4.11E	1200	Ogbomosho	17th c	527 (83e)	432 (75e)	320 (63)	140 (52)	87 (31)	60 (00?e)	25 (51e)	
6.10N, 6.47E	300	Onitsha	17th c	269 (83e)	220 (75e)	163 (63)	77 (53)	18 (31)	16 (00?e)		
7.50N, 4.35E	990	Oshogbo	1600?	344 (83e)	282 (75e)	209 (63)	123 (52)	50 (31)	35 (00?e)		
7.51N, 3.56E	850	Oyo	bef 1835	185 (83e)	152 (75e)	112 (63)	72 (52)	49 (31)			
4.43N, 7.05E	64	Port Harcourt	1912	296 (83e)	242 (75e)	180 (63)	72 (53)	15 (31)			
13.04N, 5.15E	1161	Sokoto	1809	148 (83e)	118 (75e)	90 (63)	48 (52)	20 (31)			
11.07N, 7.44E	2100	Zaria	1095?	274 (83e)	224 (75e)	166 (63)	54 (52)	28 (31)	45 (00?e)	50 (50?e)	

Reunion

Lat/Long	Alt	City	Founded								
20.52S, 55.28E	36	*Saint-Denis	1665		109 (82)	85 (67)	42 (54)	27 (31)	27 (02)	18 (51)	

Rwanda

Lat/Long	Alt	City	Founded								
1.57S, 30.04E	5053	*Kigali	bef 1935	157 (81e)	118 (78)	50 (70)	2 (49)				7 (04)

For an explanation of symbols and abbreviations, see pages 16–17.

(Continued)

TABLE 2a. (Continued)

Latitude and Longitude	Elev (ft)	City	Date Settled	Population (thousands)							
				Latest	ca 1980	ca 1970	ca 1950	ca 1930	ca 1900	ca 1850	ca 1800
Sao Tome and Principe											
0.20N, 6.44E	56	*Sao Tome	1493	35 (84e)	25 (78e)	17 (70)	6 (50)	3 (21)	3 (00e)	2 (50?e)	
Senegal											
14.40N, 17.26W	79	*Dakar	1857	671 (84e)	790 (76)	583 (70–71)	171 (46e)	54 (31)	18 (04)	3 (65)	
Seychelles											
4.37S, 55.27E	9	*Victoria	1768	25 (82e)	23 (77)	14 (71)	9 (47)	5 (31)			
Sierra Leone											
8.29N, 13.13W	86	*Freetown	1788	470 (85)	316 (82)	274 (74)	65 (47e)	55 (31)	34 (01)	18 (60)	5s(20)
Somalia											
9.35N, 44.04E	4377	Hargeisa	19th c	150 (82e)	90 (76e)	80 (69e)	35 (50?e)	20 (36e)	1 (00?e)		
2.04N, 45.22E	33	*Mogadishu	908?	600 (82e)	285 (76e)	173 (67)	74 (48e)	36 (31)	7 (00?e)	4 (50?e)	4 (25e)
South Africa											
33.54S, 18.38E	102	Bellville	bef 1861	100 (84e)	66 (80)	49 (70)	18 (51)	6 (36)	0.4 (11)		
26.11S, 28.19E	5419	Benoni	1887?	95 (85)	68 (80) 198s(80)	151 (70) 182s(70)	94 (51)	78 (36)	48 (21)		
29.08S, 26.13E	4678	Bloemfontein	1846	104 (85) 233s(85)	103 (80) 221s(80)	150 (70)	81 (51)	53 (36)	34 (04)	1 (65?e)	
33.55S, 18.27E	40	*Cape Town	1652	777 (85) 1912s(85)	860 (80) 1443s(80)	698 (70) 1108s(70)	441 (51) 578s(51)	296 (36) 344s(36)	78 (04) 170s(04)	26 (56)	17 (00?)
29.53S, 31.02E	22	Durban	1824	634 (85) 982s(85)	678 (80) 988s(80)	737 (70) 851s(70)	435 (51) 480s(51)	240 (36) 260s(36)	68 (04)	5 (66)	
33.02S, 27.55E	410	East London	1846	85 (85) 194s(85)	77 (80) 116s(80)	120 (70) 125s(70)	91 (51)	47 (36)	25 (04)		
26.15S, 28.10E	5450	Germiston	1887	117 (85)	113 (80) 166s(80)	222 (70)	116 (51) 168s(51)	68 (36) 79s(36)	29 (04)		
33.18S, 26.32E	1745	Grahamstown	1812		25 (80) 51s(80)	41 (70)	24 (51)	20 (36)	14 (04)	7 (65)	

(Continued)

Lat, Long	Elev	City	Founded							
26.11S, 28.03E	5709	Johannesburg	1886	632 (85)	704 (80)	654 (70)	632 (51)	475 (36)	99 (04)	
				1609s(85)	1534s(80)	1441s(70)	884s(51)	519s(36)	156s(04)	
28.48S, 24.46E	4013	Kimberley	1871	74 (85)	71 (80)	105 (70)	59 (51)	41 (36)	34 (04)	14 (77)
				150s(85)	145s(80)					
29.37S, 30.23E	2128	Pietermaritzburg	1839	104 (85)	126 (80)	115 (70)	73 (51)	47 (36)	31 (04)	
				192s(85)	192s(80)	161s(70)	92s(51)	56s(36)		
33.58S, 25.37E	176	Port Elizabeth	1820	273 (85)	282 (80)	392 (70)	169 (51)	99 (36)	33 (04)	12 (65)
				652s(85)	534s(80)	476s(70)	189s(51)	110s(36)		
25.45S, 28.12E	4375	*Pretoria	1855	443 (85)	435 (80)	545 (70)	232 (51)	108 (36)	37 (04)	
				823s(85)	785s(80)	563s(70)	285s(51)	129s(36)		
26.17S, 27.50E	5709	Soweto			869 (80)	602 (70)				
33.56S, 18.51E	322	Stellenbosch	1679		38 (80)	30 (70)	18 (51)	9 (36)	5 (04)	2 (45)
					43s(80)					
25.58S, 28.14E		Tembisa			195 (80)	84 (70)				
30.00S, 30.50E		Umlazi	1836	134 (85)	177 (80)	123 (70)	5 (60)			
					190s(80)					
26.41S, 27.56E	4725	Vereeniging	1892	61 (85)	61 (80)	173 (70)	60 (51)	20 (36)		
				540s(85)	154s(80)	310s(70)	123s(51)			

Sudan

Lat, Long	Elev	City	Founded							
4.51N, 31.37E	1503	Juba			116 (80e)	57 (73)	11 (56)			
15.36N, 32.32E	1257	*Khartoum	1823	45 (85e)	476 (83)	334 (73)	93 (56)	41 (29e)	8 (00e)	25 (50e)
					1343s(83)	784s(73)	246s(56)	134s(29e)		
15.38N, 32.33E	1280	Khartoum North			341 (83)	151 (73)	39 (56)	14 (29e)		
15.38N, 32.30E	1263	Omdurman	18th c?		526 (83)	299 (73)	114 (55)	79 (29e)	43 (09)	
19.37N, 37.14E	20	Port Sudan	1906?		207 (83)	133 (73)	48 (56)	19 (32)		
14.24N, 33.32E	1339	Wad Madani	19th c?		141 (83)	107 (73)	48 (56)	33 (29e)		

Swaziland

Lat, Long	Elev	City	Founded							
26.19S, 31.08E	3816	*Mbabane	1902	45 (85e)	23 (76)	14 (66)	3 (56)	0.2 (30?)		

Tanzania

Lat, Long	Elev	City	Founded							
6.48S, 39.17E	47	*Dar es Salaam	1862	1096 (85e)	769 (78)	273 (67)	69 (48)	23 (31)	17 (00e)	
6.10S, 35.40E	3724	Dodoma	1907?	141 (85e)	46 (78)	24 (67)	9 (48)	3 (31)		
2.31S, 32.54E	3740	Mwanza	bef 1888	189 (85e)	111 (78)	35 (67)	11 (48)	4 (31)	3 (00e)	
6.10S, 39.11E	61	Zanzibar	16th c	133 (85e)	111 (78)	68 (67)	45 (48)	45 (31)	58 (00e)	25 (50?e)

For an explanation of symbols and abbreviations, see pages 16–17.

TABLE 2a. (Continued)

Latitude and Longitude	Elev (ft)	City	Date Settled	Latest	ca 1980	ca 1970	ca 1950	ca 1930	ca 1900	ca 1850	ca 1800
Togo											
6.08N, 1.13E	66	*Lome	19th c	366 (83e)	229 (77e)	148 (70)	33 (50)	18 (31)	4 (03)	6 (50?e)	
Tunisia											
34.44N, 10.46E	69	Sfax	2nd c?	232 (84)	171 (75) / 267s(75)	73 (66) / 250s(66)	55 (46)	40 (31)	15 (00?e)	12 (50?e)	
35.49N, 10.38E	7	Sousse	7th c	84 (84)	70 (75) / 173s(75)	56 (66) / 83s(66)	37 (46)	25 (31)	12 (91)	7 (70e)	
36.48N, 10.12E	217	*Tunis	4th c BC?	597 (84)	550 (75) / 906s(75)	463 (66) / 642s(66)	365 (46)	202 (31)	228 (06)	130 (50?e)	125 (00e)
Uganda											
0.19N, 32.35E	3910	*Kampala	1890		458 (80)	331 (69)	22 (48)	5 (30e)	3 (11)		
Western Sahara											
27.10N, 13.12W	138	*Aaiun	bef 1938		50 (82e)	25 (70)	6 (60)	2 (40)			
Zaire											
2.30S, 28.52E	5296	Bukavu	1901	171 (84)	209 (76e)	135 (70)	10 (48)	2 (37e)			
5.54S, 22.25E	2215	Kananga	1884	291 (84)	704 (76e)	429 (70)	11 (48e)				
5.02S, 18.49E	1591	Kikwit		147 (84)	172 (76e)	112 (70)	8 (48e)				
4.18S, 15.18E	951	*Kinshasa	1887	2654 (84)	2444 (76e)	1323 (70)	209 (50e)	40 (32e)	5 (01e)		
0.30N, 25.12E	1362	Kisangani	1882	283 (84)	339 (76e)	230 (70)	25 (48e)	12 (30e)	0.4 (00?)		
10.59S, 26.44E	4167	Likasi	1917	194 (84)	162 (76e)	146 (70)	35 (48e)				
11.40S, 27.28E	4035	Lubumbashi	1910	543 (84)	451 (76e)	318 (70)	103 (50e)	17 (32e)	1 (01e)		
5.49S, 13.27E	285	Matadi	1879	145 (84)	162 (76e)	110 (70)	22 (48e)	10 (32e)			
6.09S, 23.36E		Mbuji-Mayi		423 (84)	383 (76e)	256 (70)	41 (58e)				

Population (thousands)

Location	Alt.	City	Founded	Pop.	Pop.	Pop.	Pop.	Pop.	Pop.	Pop.	Pop.
Zambia											
12.49S, 28.13E	4429	Kitwe	1931?		315 (80)	200 (69)	54 (50–51)	2 (31)		45 (50?e)	100 (10e)
15.25S, 28.17E	4196	*Lusaka	1910?		538 (80)	262 (69)	31 (50–51)	8 (31)		40 (53e)	200 (00?e)
12.58S, 28.38E	4137	Ndola	19th c?		282 (80)	160 (69)	28 (50–51)			58 (50e)	100 (09e)
Zimbabwe											
20.09S, 28.36E	4405	Bulawayo	1893		414 (82)	245 (69)	53 (46–48)	31 (31e)	5 (00?e)		
17.50S, 31.03E	4831	*Harare	1890		656 (82)	386 (69)	119 (51)	29 (31e)	5 (00?e)		
ASIA											
Afghanistan											
34.22N, 62.09E	3025	Herat	4th c BC?	160 (84e)	140 (79)	102 (70e)	76 (48e)	30 (30?e)	45 (00?e)		
34.30N, 69.13E	5971	*Kabul	4th c BC?	1179 (84e)	913 (79)	307 (70e)	206 (48e)	80 (30?e)	100 (00e)		
31.27N, 65.43E	3462	Kandahar	1747	311 (84e)	178 (79)	130 (70e)	77 (48e)	45 (30?e)	40 (00e)		
Bahrain											
26.13N, 50.35E	3	*Manama	1507?		109 (81)	82 (71)	40 (50)	25 (30?e)	8 (00?e)	5 (50?e)	
Bangladesh											
22.20N, 91.50E	46	Chittagong	8th c?		980 (81) / 1388s(81)	458 (74) / 890s(74)	294 (51)	53 (31)	22 (01)	21 (72)	
23.43N, 90.25E	27	*Dhaka	1608?		1850 (81) / 3459s(81)	1320 (74) / 1680s(74)	339 (51)	139 (31)	90 (01)	69 (72)	68 (38)
22.48N, 89.33E	16	Khulna	18th c?		327 (81) / 623s(81)	437s(74)	42 (51)	19 (31)	10 (01)		
24.45N, 90.24E	62	Mymensingh	1495?		108 (81) / 225s(81)	76 (74) / 182s(74)	45 (51)	30 (31)	15 (01)	11 (72)	
23.37N, 90.30E	26	Narayanganj	17th c?		196 (81) / 355s(81)	176 (74) / 271s(74)	73 (51)	34 (31)	24 (01)	11 (72)	
24.22N, 88.36E		Rajshahi	18th c		172 (81) / 254s(81)	133s(74)	40 (51)	27 (31)	22 (01)	19 (72)	6 (38)
24.54N, 91.52E	115	Sylhet	14th c		168s(81)	60s(74)	33 (51)	21 (31)	14 (01)	17 (72)	

(Continued)

For an explanation of symbols and abbreviations, see pages 16–17.

TABLE 2a. (Continued)

Latitude and Longitude	Elev (ft)	City	Date Settled	Latest	ca 1980	ca 1970	ca 1950	ca 1930	ca 1900	ca 1850	ca 1800
Bhutan											
27.32N, 89.43E	7950	*Thimphu	1581	20 (85e)	9 (77)	10 (71e)					
Brunei											
4.53N, 114.56E	10	*Bandar Seri Begawan	15th c?	55 (85e)	50 (81)	37 (71)	11 (47)	10 (31)	15 (00?e)	22 (48e)	
Burma											
16.47N, 94.44E	33	Bassein	12th c?	213 (85e)	144 (83)	126 (73)	78 (53)	46 (31)	32 (01)	21 (72)	8 (26e)
16.43N, 96.00E		Kanbe				254 (73)	21 (53)	7 (31)	village		
22.00N, 96.05E	75	Mandalay	1857	361 (85e)	533 (83)	418 (73)	186 (53)	148 (31)	184 (01)	189 (91)	
16.30N, 97.38E	72	Moulmein	bef 1826	193 (84e)	220 (83)	172 (73)	103 (53)	66 (31)	58 (01)	24 (57)	
17.20N, 96.29E		Pegu	573	197 (84e)	150 (83)	124 (73)	47 (53)	22 (31)	14 (01)	4 (72)	
16.47N, 96.10E	20	*Rangoon	585 BC		2459 (83)	1586 (73)	737 (53)	400 (31)	235 (01)	99 (72)	30 (00?e)
China											
30.31N, 117.02E	128	Anqing	13th c	213 (85e)	160 (82e)	135 (75e)	105 (53)	117 (38e)	40 (00?e)		
41.07N, 122.57E	115	Anshan	1908	1109 (85e)	1030 (82e)	1050 (75e)	549 (53)	214 (40)			
36.05N, 114.21E	220	Anyang	14th c BC?	361 (85e)	250 (82e)	175 (75e)	125 (53)	94 (38e)	60 (22e)		
45.37N, 122.49E		Baicheng	1902	193 (84e)	150 (82e)	125 (75e)	75 (53e)				
38.52N, 115.29E	72	Baoding	13th c	423 (85e)	392 (82e)	350 (75e)	197 (53)	216 (38e)	60 (07e)		
34.23N, 107.09E	2041	Baoji	3rd c BC?	286 (85e)	271 (82e)	250 (75e)	130 (53)	56 (48e)			
40.36N, 110.03E	3425	Baotou	11th c?	904 (85e)	853 (82e)	650 (75e)	149 (53)	70 (38e)	20 (00?e)		
48.16N, 126.36E		Beian	1930s	197 (84e)		80 (75e)	70 (53)	25 (40?e)			
39.56N, 116.24E	171	*Beijing	3rd c BC?	5103 (85e)	5598 (82)	5400 (75e)	2768 (53)	1574 (38e)	700 (05e)	1649 (45)	700 (00?e)
32.57N, 117.20E	66	Bengbu	bef 1912	404 (85e)	362 (82e)	400 (75e)	253 (53)	136 (38e)			
41.20N, 123.45E		Benxi	bef 1726	699 (85e)	654 (82e)	500 (75e)	449 (53)	100 (40)	3 (00?e)		
38.19N, 116.52E		Cangzhou	5th c	191 (84e)	120 (82e)	100 (75e)	75 (53e)				
43.52N, 125.21E	709	Changchun	11th c?	1474 (85e)	1340 (82e)	1300 (75e)	855 (53)	555 (40)	80 (08e)		

Population (thousands)

Coordinates		City	Founded							
29.02N,111.41E	121	Changde	2nd c BC	170 (84e)	175 (82e)	125 (75e)	95 (53)	85 (38e)	300 (05e)	
28.12N,112.58E	157	Changsha	3rd c BC?	959 (85e)	859 (82e)	840 (75e)	651 (53)	464 (38e)	230 (05e)	
31.39N,120.44E		Changshu	bef 540	281 (85e)		95 (75e)	101 (53)	94 (38e)	200 (00?e)	
36.11N,113.06E	2999	Changzhi	18th c BC	273 (85e)	265 (82e)	100 (75e)	98 (53)			
31.47N,119.58E		Changzhou	1st c?	461 (85e)	425 (82e)	300 (75e)	296 (53)	125 (38e)	200 (00?e)	
23.41N,116.38E		Chaozhou	413	265 (85e)	130 (82e)	95 (75e)	101 (53)	152 (38e)	200 (00?e)	54 (94e)
40.58N,117.53E	1050	Chengde	bef 907	227 (85e)	150 (82e)	90 (75e)	93 (53)	43 (38e)	250 (00?e)	41 (82e)
30.40N,104.04E	1634	Chengdu	3rd c BC?	1591 (85e)	1410 (82e)	1800 (75e)	857 (53)	458 (38e)	475 (00?e)	110 (27e)
42.17N,118.53E	1873	Chifeng	3rd c?	299 (85e)	99 (82e)	75 (75e)	49 (53)	40 (38e)	10 (00?e)	800 (72e)
29.34N,106.35E	639	Chongqing	250?	2080 (85e)	1940 (82e)	2900 (75e)	772 (53)	528 (38e)	620 (05e)	200(61e)
38.55N,121.39E	315	Dalian	600?	1378 (85e)	1240 (82e)	1100 (75e)	766 (53)	293 (30)	40 (00?e)	
40.08N,124.24E	20	Dandong	1896?	466 (85e)	400 (82e)	300 (75e)	360 (53)	315 (40)	20 (08)	
46.37N,124.59E		Daqing	1949	543 (85e)	493 (82e)					
40.05N,113.18E	3442	Datong	10th c BC?	704 (85e)	605 (82e)	350 (75e)	228 (53)	70 (38e)	50 (22e)	
23.02N,113.44E		Dongguan	3rd c?	255 (85e)		55 (75e)	35 (53)	64 (48e)		
26.33N,101.44E		Dukou		380 (85e)	200 (82e)	120 (75e)				
43.21N,128.13E		Dunhua	bef 1943	217 (85e)		60 (75e)	35 (53e)			
30.24N,114.50E		Ezhou	bef 1940	217 (85e)	28 (82e)			11 (40?e)		
23.02N,113.07E	50	Foshan	13th c?	243 (85e)	200 (82e)	125 (75e)	122 (53)	135 (38e)	400 (00?e)	400 (69e)
41.52N,123.53E		Fushun	1669	1100 (85e)	1040 (82e)	1150 (75e)	679 (53)	270 (40)		
42.04N,121.44E		Fuxin	1900?	572 (85e)	534 (82e)	350 (75e)	189 (53)	143 (40)		
26.05N,119.18E	289	Fuzhou	10th c BC?	784 (85e)	709 (82e)	725 (75e)	553 (53)	343 (38e)	624 (05e)	600 (47e)
25.51N,114.56E	361	Ganzhou	2nd c BC?	185 (84e)	180 (82e)	140 (75e)	99 (53)	58 (38e)		
23.23N,103.09E	5709	Gejiu	bef 1900	190 (84e)	250 (82e)	100 (75e)	160 (53)	50 (22e)	10 (00?e)	
23.07N,113.15E	59	Guangzhou	9th c BC?	2569 (85e)	2380 (82e)	2500 (75e)	1599 (53)	1022 (38e)	900 (05e)	1236 (47e)
25.17N,110.17E	548	Guilin	4th c BC?	324 (85e)	306 (82e)	250 (75e)	145 (53)	88 (38e)	150 (07e)	1500 (00?e)
26.35N,106.43E	3514	Guiyang	14th c	893 (85e)	838 (82e)	800 (75e)	271 (53)	145 (38e)	100 (00?e)	
40.52N,122.45E		Haicheng	bef 1943	211 (85e)		90 (75e)	75 (53e)			
20.03N,110.19E	46	Haikou	bef 1876	209 (85e)	190 (82e)	275 (75e)	135 (53)	15 (30?e)	12 (00?e)	
49.12N,119.42E	2218	Hailar	1734	149 (84e)	90 (82e)	85 (75e)	43 (53)	40 (40)	5 (00?e)	
36.35N,114.29E		Handan	4th c BC	736 (85e)	676 (82e)	480 (75e)	90 (53)	30 (46e)		
30.15N,120.10E	16	Hangzhou	606	1018 (85e)	927 (82e)	900 (75e)	697 (53)	575 (38e)	350 (05e)	700 (50?e)
45.45N,126.39E	476	Harbin	1896?	2252 (85e)	2150 (82e)	2400 (75e)	1163 (53)	661 (40)	20 (02e)	1000 (00?e)
31.51N,117.17E	85	Hefei	10th c BC?	625 (85e)	555 (82e)	450 (75e)	184 (53)	94 (38e)		
47.24N,130.22E		Hegang	1916	478 (85e)	325 (82e)	250 (75e)	90 (53)	20 (40)		
26.54N,112.36E	308	Hengyang	7th c BC?	419 (85e)	350 (82e)	350 (75e)	235 (53)	122 (38e)	20 (00?e)	

For an explanation of symbols and abbreviations, see pages 16–17.

(Continued)

TABLE 2a. (Continued)

Latitude and Longitude	Elev (ft)	City	Date Settled	Population (thousands)							
				Latest	ca 1980	ca 1970	ca 1950	ca 1930	ca 1900	ca 1850	ca 1800
40.47N,111.37E	3484	Hohhot	9th c	567 (85e)	515 (82e)	450 (75e)	148 (53)	94 (38e)	200 (05e)		
33.57N,116.45E		Huaibei	19th c?	252 (85e)	251 (82e)	75 (75e)	287 (53)				
32.40N,117.00E		Huainan	19th c?	619 (85e)	550 (82e)	400 (75e)	77 (53)				
33.35N,119.02E	66	Huaiyin	2nd c BC?	202 (85e)	124 (82e)	100 (75e)	110 (53)	73 (38e)			
30.13N,115.06E		Huangshi	7th c BC?	400 (85e)	200 (82e)	140 (75e)		6 (20?e)			
41.54N,126.26E		Hunjiang	bef 1956	443 (85e)	447 (82e)	50 (75e)					
30.52N,120.06E		Huzhou	2nd c BC	208 (85e)	135 (82e)	90 (75e)	63 (53)	66 (38e)	100 (00?e)		
46.50N,130.21E	266	Jiamusi	19th c?	430 (85e)	350 (82e)	300 (75e)	146 (53)	129 (40)	20 (31)		
35.15N,113.13E		Jiaozuo	12th c?	335 (85e)	318 (82e)	275 (75e)	35 (53)				
30.46N,120.45E		Jiaxing	3rd c BC	210 (85e)	175 (82e)	150 (75e)	78 (53)	92 (38e)			
43.51N,126.33E	689	Jilin	1673	906 (85e)	837 (82e)	775 (75e)	435 (53)	173 (40)	120 (09e)	135 (64e)	300 (12e)
36.40N,117.00E	180	Jinan	6th c	1159 (85e)	1040 (82e)	1125 (75e)	680 (53)	472 (38e)	100 (00?e)		
29.16N,117.11E		Jingdezhen	6th c	304 (85e)	326 (82e)	300 (75e)	92 (53)	125 (38e)	200 (05e)	1000 (50?e)	1000 (00?e)
31.02N,112.06E		Jingmen	3rd c?	227 (85e)	27 (82e)						
35.24N,116.33E		Jining	bef 1122 BC	223 (85e)	150 (82e)	130 (75e)	86 (53)	150 (36e)	150 (00?e)		
40.45N,120.50E		Jinxi	bef 1879	223 (85e)	223 (82e)	50 (75e)	75 (53e)				
41.07N,121.06E	217	Jinzhou	12th c	608 (85e)	552 (82e)	450 (75e)	352 (53)	142 (40)	14 (00?e)		
29.44N,115.59E	269	Jiujiang	3rd c?	248 (85e)	150 (82e)	100 (75e)	65 (53)	93 (38e)	36 (00?e)		
45.18N,130.58E	719	Jixi	1935?	635 (85e)	613 (82e)	325 (75e)	35 (53e)				
34.51N,114.21E	246	Kaifeng	7th c BC?	459 (85e)	439 (82e)	350 (75e)	299 (53)	303 (38e)	200 (08e)		
39.29N,75.58E	4629	Kashi	2nd c BC?	139 (84e)	150 (82e)	100 (75e)	91 (53)	80 (30?e)	65 (00?e)	30 (50?e)	
25.04N,102.41E	6211	Kunming	1st c?	991 (85e)	1020 (82e)	1225 (75e)	699 (53)	184 (38e)	45 (07)		
36.03N,103.41E	4948	Lanzhou	1st c?	1172 (85e)	1080 (82e)	950 (75e)	397 (53)	122 (38e)	337 (00e)		
29.34N,103.44E		Leshan	4th c?	307 (85e)	150 (82e)	70 (75e)	75 (53e)	32 (48e)			
29.39N, 91.06E	12,002	Lhasa	400?	84 (85e)	84 (82e)	80 (75e)	70 (53)	20 (30?e)	30 (00?e)	50 (50?e)	50 (00?e)
34.36N,119.13E	13	Lianyungang	3rd c BC?	288 (85e)	249 (82e)	250 (75e)	208 (53)	125 (46e)			
41.17N,123.11E	85	Liaoyang	15th c BC?	443 (85e)	275 (82e)	250 (75e)	147 (53)	100 (40)	60 (00?e)	80 (73e)	
42.55N,125.09E		Liaoyuan	19th c	314 (85e)	300 (82e)	250 (75e)	120 (53)	32 (38e)			
26.33N,104.52E		Liupanshui	bef 1943	363 (85e)	346 (82e)		3 (48e)				
24.19N,109.24E	322	Liuzhou	3rd c BC?	524 (85e)	375 (82e)	300 (75e)	159 (53)	60 (22e)	35 (00?e)		

Coordinates	No.	City	Founded								
34.41N,112.28E	453	Luoyang	1900 BC?	650 (85e)	582 (82e)	750 (75e)	171 (53)	73 (38e)	20 (00?e)		
28.53N,105.23E	1000	Luzhou	2nd c?	238 (85e)	201 (82e)	175 (75e)	289 (53)	68 (38e)	40 (00?e)		
31.44N,118.28E		Maanshan	1949?	259 (85e)	248 (82e)	60 (75e)					
31.28N,104.46E	1263	Mianyang	bef 1850	234 (85e)	100 (82e)	50 (75e)	35 (53e)	31 (48e)	70 (00?e)		
44.35N,129.36E	761	Mudanjiang	bef 1903	499 (85e)	400 (82e)	350 (75e)	151 (53)	178 (40)			
28.41N,115.53E	161	Nanchang	12th c?	909 (85e)	835 (82e)	700 (75e)	398 (53)	275 (38e)	233 (00e)	300 (50?e)	
30.48N,106.04E	978	Nanchong	10th c BC?	150 (84e)	228 (82e)	225 (75e)	165 (53)	55 (38e)			
32.03N,118.47E	200	Nanjing	2nd c BC?	1919 (85e)	1740 (82e)	1800 (75e)	1092 (53)	440 (38e)	270 (05e)	400 (50?e)	1000 (00?e)
22.49N,108.19E	246	Nanning	10th c BC?	599 (85e)	525 (82e)	350 (75e)	195 (53)	101 (38e)		40 (70?e)	
32.02N,102.53E	361	Nantong	1st c?	309 (85e)	300 (82e)	275 (75e)	260 (53)	155 (38e)			
33.00N,112.32E	410	Nanyang	3rd c BC?	181 (84e)	100 (82e)	60 (75e)	75 (53e)	50 (38e)			
29.35N,105.03E	1165	Neijiang	1st c?	179 (84e)	225 (82e)	225 (75e)	190 (53)	32 (48e)			
29.53N,121.33E	15	Ningbo	8th c	552 (85e)	259 (82e)	300 (75e)	238 (53)	247 (38e)	260 (05e)	280 (50e)	
41.12N,122.04E		Panjin		248 (85e)							
33.44N,113.18E		Pingdingshan	bef 1957	363 (85e)	208 (82e)	85 (75e)	70 (58e)	22 (48e)			
27.37N,113.51E		Pingxiang	bef 267	369 (85e)	150 (82e)	120 (75e)	35 (53e)		35 (07)		
36.04N,120.19E	253	Qingdao	bef 1891	1162 (85e)	1080 (82e)	1200 (75e)	917 (53)	592 (38e)	5 (05e)		
39.56N,119.37E	10	Qinhuangdao	bef 1879	307 (85e)	278 (82e)	275 (75e)	187 (53)	47 (38e)	25 (00?e)		
47.22N,123.57E	482	Qiqihar	1691	970 (85e)	920 (82e)	850 (75e)	345 (53)	133 (40)		60 (68e)	
35.36N,116.59E		Qufu	12th c BC?			30 (75e)	20 (49e)				
38.24N, 77.15E	4187	Shache	2nd C BC?	248 (85e)		50 (75e)	80 (53)		70 (00?e)		
31.14N,121.28E	15	Shanghai	bef 11th c	6871 (85e)	6321 (82)	8100 (75e)	6204 (53)	3595 (38e)		50 (50?e)	
23.22N,116.40E	14	Shantou	bef 1860	489 (85e)	400 (82e)	325 (75e)	280 (53)	196 (38e)	423 (95)	149 (65)	
24.48N,113.35E	285	Shaoguan	3rd c BC?	312 (85e)	160 (82e)	100 (75e)	82 (53)	176 (38e)	60 (05e)	45 (72e)	
30.00N,120.35E		Shaoxing	2000 BC?	149 (84e)	225 (82e)	150 (75e)	131 (53)	149 (38e)	100 (00?e)	500 (71e)	
27.15N,111.28E	817	Shaoyang	7th c BC?	219 (85e)	186 (82e)	215 (75e)	118 (53)	83 (38e)	500 (00?e)		
30.19N,112.14E		Shashi	bef 6th c BC	221 (85e)	175 (82e)	120 (75e)	86 (53)	104 (38e)	80 (05e)		
41.48N,123.27E	138	Shenyang	4th c?	3253 (85e)	3030 (82e)	3300 (75e)	2300 (53)	1134 (40)	158 (08e)	170 (64e)	
22.32N,114.08E		Shenzhen	bef 1950	190 (85e)	80 (82e)						
44.18N, 86.02E	1453	Shihezi	1950	305 (85e)	75 (82e)						
38.03N,114.29E	269	Shijiazhuang	bef 1904	932 (85e)	845 (82e)	940 (75e)	373 (53)	194 (38e)			
32.34N,110.47E		Shiyan	bef 1956	227 (85e)	210 (82e)						
39.10N,106.45E		Shizuishan	bef 1943	225 (85e)	135 (82e)						
46.40N,131.21E		Shuangyashan	1949?	361 (85e)	200 (82e)	150 (75e)	35 (53e)				
43.10N,124.20E	535	Siping	bef 1900	280 (85e)	280 (82e)	165 (75e)	126 (53)	68 (40)			
46.39N,126.59E		Suihua	bef 1943	200 (85e)	200 (82e)	70 (75e)	75 (53e)				

(Continued)

For an explanation of symbols and abbreviations, see pages 16–17.

TABLE 2a. (Continued)

Latitude and Longitude	Elev (ft)	City	Date Settled	Population (thousands)							
				Latest	ca 1980	ca 1970	ca 1950	ca 1930	ca 1900	ca 1850	ca 1800
31.18N,120.37E	52	Suzhou	525 BC?	634 (85e)	568 (82e)	750 (75e)	474 (53)	388 (38e)	500 (05e)	2000 (52e)	
36.12N,117.07E	502	Taian	8th c?	216 (85e)	125 (82e)	50 (75e)	20 (53e)	80 (34e)			
37.52N,112.33E	2566	Taiyuan	3rd c BC	1391 (85e)	1280 (82e)	1350 (75e)	721 (53)	177 (38e)	230 (00?e)	250 (66e)	
39.38N,118.11E	187	Tangshan	1878?	938 (85e)	887 (82e)	650 (75e)	693 (53)	146 (38e)			
39.08N,117.12E	11	Tianjin	bef 13th c	4202 (85e)	3920 (82e)	4500 (75e)	2694 (53)	1223 (38e)	750 (05e)	300 (50e)	
34.35N,105.43E	3714	Tianshui	bef 2nd c BC	209 (85e)	125 (82e)	85 (75e)	63 (53)	59 (38e)	150 (00?e)		
42.18N,123.49E		Tieling	13th c?	326 (85e)	159 (82e)	75 (75e)	75 (53e)	56 (40)	20 (00?e)		
35.05N,109.05E		Tongchuan	611	269 (85e)	200 (82e)	75 (75e)	35 (53e)	19 (48e)			
41.41N,125.45E	1611	Tonghua	1862?	290 (85e)	200 (82e)	175 (75e)	129 (53)	42 (38e)			
43.37N,122.16E		Tongliao	1912	184 (84e)	80 (82e)	60 (75e)	40 (53)	40 (38e)			
43.48N, 87.35E	2996	Urumqi	bef 7th c	935 (85e)	899 (82e)	400 (75e)	141 (53)	45 (38e)	40 (00e)	150 (00e)	
39.38N,122.00E		Wafangdian	bef 1900	246 (85e)		85 (75e)	75 (53e)	20 (38e)	village		
36.43N,119.06E	207	Weifang	1st c?	312 (85e)	275 (82e)	240 (75e)	149 (53)	98 (38e)	100 (00?e)	100 (69e)	
28.01N,120.39E	16	Wenzhou	4th c?	372 (85e)	325 (82e)	260 (75e)	202 (53)	237 (38e)	80 (05e)	500 (70e)	
39.47N,106.52E		Wuhai	bef 1968	236 (85e)	237 (82e)						
30.35N,114.16E	75	Wuhan	3rd c	2963 (85e)	2730 (82e)	3000 (75e)	1427 (53)	1242 (38e)	1500 (00?e)	996 (50e)	
31.21N,118.22E	43	Wuhu	3rd c?	396 (85e)	354 (82e)	325 (75e)	242 (53)	168 (38e)	137 (05e)		
31.35N,120.18E	23	Wuxi	1st c?	725 (85e)	637 (82e)	700 (75e)	582 (53)	272 (38e)	200 (00?e)		
23.29N,111.19E	390	Wuzhou	1st c BC	190 (84e)	245 (82e)	160 (75e)	111 (53)	103 (38e)	65 (05e)		
24.27N,118.05E	131	Xiamen	16th c?	344 (85e)	319 (82e)	300 (75e)	224 (53)	177 (38e)	96 (97)	275 (47e)	145 (32)
34.16N,108.54E	1352	Xian	2205 BC?	1732 (85e)	1610 (82e)	1900 (75e)	787 (53)	218 (38e)	1000 (00?e)	1000 (72e)	232 (12)
32.03N,112.05E		Xiangfan	2nd c BC?	315 (85e)	175 (82e)	110 (75e)	73 (53)		140 (00?e)		
27.51N,112.54E	640	Xiangtan	3rd c BC?	389 (85e)	350 (82e)	325 (75e)	184 (53)	103 (38e)	300 (00?e)	1000 (70e)	
34.22N,108.42E		Xianyang	bef 350 BC	286 (85e)	200 (82e)	85 (75e)	70 (53)	16 (48e)			
37.03N,114.30E		Xingtai	8th c	266 (85e)	253 (82e)	115 (75e)	75 (53e)				
36.37N,101.46E	7363	Xining	2nd c BC?	504 (85e)	400 (82e)	300 (75e)	94 (53)	59 (48e)	60 (00?e)		
35.19N,113.52E		Xinxiang	1st c?	411 (85e)	325 (82e)	250 (75e)	170 (53)				
34.16N,117.11E	112	Xuzhou	7th c BC?	727 (85e)	668 (82e)	800 (75e)	373 (53)	205 (38e)	40 (05e)		
49.17N,120.44E		Yakeshi	bef 1956	351 (85e)							
36.36N,109.28E	3400	Yanan	1st c?	150 (84e)	150 (82e)	45 (71e)	30 (50e)	30 (30e)			
33.23N,120.08E		Yancheng	3rd c?	258 (85e)		60 (75e)	50 (53)	102 (35e)			

Coordinates		City	Founded								
37.54N,113.36E	2181	Yangquan	bef 283 BC	295 (85e)	294 (82e)	275 (75e)	177 (53)	127 (38e)	100 (00?e)	360 (68e)	
32.24N,119.26E	656	Yangzhou	7th c BC?	321 (85e)	225 (82e)	175 (75e)	180 (53)	166 (38e)	82 (05e)	10 (69e)	
37.32N,121.24E	151	Yantai	bef 1862	327 (85e)	176 (82e)	150 (75e)	116 (53)	78 (38e)	50 (07e)		
28.46N,104.34E	938	Yibin	1st c?	219 (85e)	84 (82e)	250 (75e)	178 (53)	108 (31e)	45 (05e)		
30.42N,111.17E	436	Yichang	1st c?	338 (85e)	175 (82e)	120 (75e)	73 (53)				
47.42N,128.54E		Yichun	1948?	761 (85e)	748 (82e)	90 (75e)	35 (53)				
38.28N,106.19E	3645	Yinchuan	bef 2nd c BC	268 (85e)	200 (82e)	125 (75e)	84 (53)	58 (38e)	12 (00?e)	80 (64e)	
40.40N,122.17E	11	Yingkou	1836	367 (85e)	200 (82e)	175 (75e)	131 (53)	181 (40)	60 (00?e)		
29.23N,113.06E	171	Yueyang	bef 206 BC	228 (84e)	125 (82e)	60 (75e)	35 (53e)	20 (20)	20 (00?e)		
40.53N,117.34E		Zaozhuang	bef 1938	292 (85e)	150 (82e)	80 (75e)					
40.50N,114.56E	2494	Zhangjiakou	1429	493 (85e)	350 (82e)	300 (75e)	229 (53)	146 (38e)	47 (00e)	1000 (50e)	
24.31N,117.40E		Zhangzhou	10th c BC?	155 (84e)	160 (82e)	110 (75e)	81 (53)	56 (38e)	500 (05e)		
21.12N,110.23E	85	Zhanjiang	3rd c BC?	335 (85e)	300 (82e)	200 (75e)	166 (53)	245 (38e)	177 (06)		
34.45N,113.40E	358	Zhengzhou	10th c BC?	1003 (85e)	895 (82e)	1100 (75e)	595 (53)	197 (38e)	168 (05e)	137 (50e)	
32.13N,119.26E	39	Zhenjiang	12th c?	337 (85e)	250 (82e)	225 (75e)	201 (53)	213 (38e)			
22.31N,113.22E		Zhongshan	11th c	239 (85e)		90 (75e)	93 (53)	81 (38e)			
27.50N,113.09E		Zhuzhou	bef 1912	345 (85e)	264 (82e)	250 (75e)	127 (53)	7 (48e)			
36.48N,118.03E	590	Zibo	1st c?	801 (85e)	643 (82e)	160 (75e)	184 (53)	50 (20?e)	45 (00?e)		
29.24N,104.47E		Zigong	3rd c BC	362 (85e)	345 (82e)	325 (75e)	291 (53)	176 (38e)			
27.42N,106.55E	2769	Zunyi	bef 640	237 (85e)	239 (82e)	250 (75e)	97 (53)	72 (38e)			
Cyprus											
35.11N, 33.23E	508	*Nicosia	12th c?		217 (82e)	116 (73)	34 (46)	24 (31)	15 (01)	12 (81)	12 (00?e)
Gaza Strip											
31.30N, 34.28E	157	*Gaza	1468 BC?		120 (79e)	118 (67)	38 (46e)	17 (31)	21 (00e)	3 (50?e)	5 (00e)
Hong Kong											
22.17N,114.09E	109	*Hong Kong	5th c?	5396 (86)	4987 (81)	3937 (71)	3130 (61)	840 (31)	284 (01)	33 (50)	
India											
23.49N, 91.16E	4200	Agartala	1830?		132 (81)	60 (71) / 100s(71)	43 (51)	10 (31)	6 (01)	0.9 (64)	
27.11N, 78.01E	553	Agra	12th c?		694 (81) / 747s(81)	592 (71) / 635s(71)	334 (51) / 376s(51)	230 (31)	188 (01)	125 (53)	60 (13e)
23.02N, 72.37E	180	Ahmadabad	bef 1298		2060 (81) / 2548s(81)	1586 (71) / 1742s(71)	788 (51) / 794s(51)	314 (31)	186 (01)	97 (51)	100 (20e)
19.05N, 74.44E	2156	Ahmadnagar	1490		144 (81) / 181s(81)	118 (71) / 148s(71)	81 (51) / 105s(51)	42 (31) / 58s(31)	36 (01)	33 (72)	21 (28)

For an explanation of symbols and abbreviations, see pages 16–17.

(Continued)

TABLE 2a. (Continued)

Latitude and Longitude	Elev (ft)	City	Date Settled	Population (thousands)							
				Latest	ca 1980	ca 1970	ca 1950	ca 1930	ca 1900	ca 1850	ca 1800
23.45N, 92.45E	2953	Aizawl	1890		74 (81)	32 (71)	7 (51)		2 (01)		
26.27N, 74.38E	1593	Ajmer	145?		376 (81)	264 (71)	197 (51)	120 (31)	74 (01)	35 (72)	23 (37e)
20.44N, 77.00E	925	Akola	1658?		225 (81)	168 (71)	90 (51)	48 (31)	29 (01)	12 (67)	
27.53N, 78.05E	615	Aligarh	12th c?		321 (81)	252 (71)	142 (51)	84 (31)	72 (01)	59 (72)	
25.27N, 81.51E	322	Allahabad	240 BC?		616 (81) 650s(81)	491 (71) 513s(71)	312 (51) 332s(51)	184 (31)	172 (01)	72 (53)	20 (03e)
30.21N, 76.50E	892	Ambala	14th c?		105 (81) 226s(81)	186 (71)	152 (51)	85 (31)	79 (01)	51 (68)	
20.56N, 77.45E	1214	Amravati	bef 1756		261 (81)	194 (71)	103 (51)	47 (31)	34 (01)	23 (67)	
31.35N, 74.53E	768	Amritsar	1574		595 (81)	408 (71) 458s(71)	326 (51)	265 (31)	162 (01)	134 (68)	80 (00e)
23.41N, 86.59E	414	Asansol	bef 1881		183 (81) 366s(81)	156 (71) 242s(71)	76 (51) 95s(51)	31 (31)	15 (01)		
19.53N, 75.20E	1906	Aurangabad	1610		285 (81) 316s(81)	150 (71) 165s(71)	67 (51)	37 (31)	37 (01)	30 (81)	60 (25e)
12.59N, 77.35E	3021	Bangalore	1537		2629 (81) 2922s(81)	1541 (71) 1654s(71)	779 (51)	306 (31)	69 (01) 159s(01)	61 (71) 143s(71)	60 (05e)
28.21N, 79.25E	568	Bareilly	1537?		387 (81) 449s(81)	296 (71) 326s(71)	195 (51) 208s(51)	144 (31)	131 (01)	111 (53)	66 (22)
15.52N, 74.30E	2470	Belgaum	bef 1160		274 (81) 300s(81)	192 (71) 214s(71)	104 (51) 120s(51)	41 (31)	26 (01)	32 (72)	8 (20)
15.09N, 76.56E	1473	Bellary	bef 1565		202 (81)	125 (71)	70 (51)	48 (31)	58 (01)	52 (71)	30 (36)
25.15N, 87.00E	161	Bhagalpur	bef 7th c		225 (81)	172 (71)	115 (51)	84 (31)	76 (01)	70 (72)	30 (10e)
22.52N, 88.24E		Bhatpara	bef 1815		261 (81)	205 (71)	135 (51)	85 (31)	22 (01)	10 (81)	
21.46N, 72.09E	55	Bhavnagar	1723		307 (81) 309s(81)	225 (71) 226s(71)	138 (51)	76 (31)	56 (01)	36 (72)	
21.13N, 81.26E	967	Bhilainagar-Durg	10th c?		490 (81)	225 (71) 245s(71)	20 (51)	13 (31)	4 (01)	4 (81)	
23.16N, 77.24E	1716	Bhopal	11th c?		671 (81)	298 (71) 385s(71)	102 (51)	61 (31)	77 (01)	55 (81)	
20.14N, 85.50E	146	Bhubaneswar	4th c BC?		219 (81)	105 (71)	17 (51)	7 (31)	3 (01)		

Lat., Long.	No.	City	Founded							
28.01N, 73.18E	734	Bikaner	1488	253 (81) 288s(81)	189 (71) 209s(71)	117 (51)	86 (31)	53 (01)	33 (81)	162 (16)
22.05N, 82.09E	902	Bilaspur	1580?	147 (81) 187s(81)	98 (71) 131s(71)	39 (51)	31 (31)	19 (01)	5 (77)	
23.46N, 85.55E		Bokaro Steel City		224 (81) 264s(81)	94 (71) 107s(71)	10 (51)				
18.58N, 72.50E	37	Bombay	150?	8243 (81)	5971 (71)	2839 (51)	1161 (31)	776 (01)	566 (49)	162 (16)
19.19N, 84.74E	112	Brahmapur		163 (81) 167s(81)	118 (71) 121s(71)	62 (51)	38 (31)	26 (01)	22 (71)	
23.15N, 87.51E	105	Burdwan	bef 1574	167 (81)	143 (71)	75 (51) 193s(51)	40 (31)	35 (01)	39 (72)	54 (14e)
22.32N, 88.22E	21	Calcutta	1495?	3288 (81) 9194s(81)	3149 (71) 7031s(71)	2549 (51) 4578s(51)	1197 (31) 1486s(31)	848 (01) 949s(01)	413 (50) 795s(72)	230 (37)
11.15N, 75.46E	26	Calicut	7th c	394 (81)	334 (71)	159 (51)	99 (31)	77 (01)	48 (71)	
30.43N, 76.47E	1300	Chandigarh	1950	374 (81) 423s(81)	219 (71) 233s(71)	5 (51)				
9.58N, 76.14E	10	Cochin	bef 4th c	513 (81) 686s(81)	439 (71) 686s(71)	26 (51) 193s(51)	23 (31)	19 (01)	14 (71)	
11.00N, 76.58E	1341	Coimbatore	bef 1768	705 (81) 920s(81)	356 (71) 736s(71)	198 (51)	95 (31)	53 (01)	35 (71)	
20.30N, 85.50E	89	Cuttack	10th c?	270 (81) 327s(81)	194 (71) 206s(71)	103 (51)	65 (31)	51 (01)	43 (72)	40 (22e)
26.10N, 85.54E	161	Darbhanga	13th c?	176 (81)	132 (71)	85 (51)	61 (31)	66 (01)	47 (72)	
27.02N, 88.16E	7002	Darjiling	1835	58 (81)	43 (71)	34 (51)	22 (31)	17 (01)	3 (72)	
14.28N, 75.55E	1916	Davanagere	bef 1770	197 (81)	121 (71)	56 (51)	23 (31)	10 (01)	6 (81)	
30.19N, 78.02E	2238	Dehra Dun	1699	211 (81) 293s(81)	166 (71) 203s(71)	116 (51) 144s(51)	40 (31)	28 (01)	7 (72)	
28.40N, 77.13E	770	Delhi	993	4884 (81) 5729s(81)	3288 (71) 3647s(71)	915 (51) 1384s(51)	348 (31) 447s(31)	209 (01)	152 (53)	150 (20e)
23.48N, 86.27E	843	Dhanbad	bef 1860	120 (81) 678s(81)	80 (71) 434s(71)	34 (51) 74s(51)	16 (31)	12 (21)		
20.54N, 74.47E		Dhule	1804	211 (81)	137 (71)	77 (51)	40 (31)	25 (01)	12 (72)	
27.29N, 94.54E	348	Dibrugarh			80 (71)	38 (51)	19 (31)	11 (01)	4 (72)	
23.30N, 87.20E		Durgapur	1960?	312 (81)	207 (71)	42 (61)				
11.21N, 77.44E		Erode	10th c?	142 (81) 276s(81)	105 (71) 170s(71)	58 (51)	34 (31)	16 (01)	10 (71)	15 (1750?e)

(Continued)

For an explanation of symbols and abbreviations, see pages 16–17.

TABLE 2a. (Continued)

Latitude and Longitude	Elev (ft)	City	Date Settled	Population (thousands)							
				Latest	ca 1980	ca 1970	ca 1950	ca 1930	ca 1900	ca 1850	ca 1800
26.47N, 82.08E	390	Faizabad	1730		102 (81)	103 (71)	77 (51)	66 (31)	71 (01)	38 (69)	
					143s(81)	110s(71)	82s(51)				
28.26N, 77.19E		Faridabad	1607		331 (81)	86 (71)	23 (51)	5 (31)	5 (01)	8 (68)	
27.09N, 78.25E	554	Firozabad	bef 1566		202 (81)	134 (71)	65 (51)	23 (31)	17 (01)	14 (72)	
23.15N, 72.45E		Gandhinagar	1966		62 (81)	24 (71)					
27.20N, 88.37E	5381	Gangtok	12th c?		38 (81)	13 (71)	3 (51)		0.7(01)		
22.33N, 88.17E		Garden Reach	bef 1768		191 (81)	155 (71)	109 (51)	56 (31)	28 (01)	11 (72)	
26.11N, 91.44E	180	Gauhati	16th c?			124 (71)	44 (51)	22 (31)	12 (01)		
						200s(71)					
24.47N, 85.00E	381	Gaya	545 BC?		247 (81)	180 (71)	134 (51)	88 (31)	71 (01)	67 (72)	
28.40N, 77.26E	499	Ghaziabad	1740		272 (81)	119 (71)	44 (51)	19 (31)	11 (01)	5 (47)	
					287s(81)	128s(71)					
26.45N, 83.22E	254	Gorakhpur	1400?		291 (81)	231 (71)	124 (51)	59 (31)	64 (01)	55 (53)	
					308s(81)						
17.20N, 76.50E	1503	Gulbarga	bef 1345		221 (81)	146 (71)	77 (51)	41 (31)	29 (01)	23 (81)	
16.18N, 80.27E		Guntur	18th c		368 (81)	270 (71)	125 (51)	65 (31)	31 (01)	18 (71)	
26.13N, 78.10E	681	Gwalior	525?		539 (81)	385 (71)	34 (51)	22 (31)	17 (01)	65 (72)	
					556s(81)	406s(71)	242s(51)	127s(31)	139s(01)	88s(81)	
22.35N, 88.20E		Haora	17th c?		744 (81)	738 (71)	434 (51)	225 (31)	158 (01)	84 (72)	
15.21N, 75.10E	2297	Hubli-Dharwar	11th c?		527 (81)	379 (71)	196 (51)	132 (31)	91 (01)	65 (72)	
17.23N, 78.28E	1788	Hyderabad	1589		2150 (81)	1607 (71)	860 (51)	346 (31)	352 (01)	124 (81)	100 (00?e)
					2546s(81)	1796s(71)	1129s(51)	467s(31)	448s(01)	367s(81)	
24.49N, 93.57E	2566	Imphal	15th c?		157 (81)	100 (71)	100 (41)	86 (31)	72 (01)	75 (81)	
22.43N, 75.50E	1823	Indore	1715		829 (81)	543 (71)	311 (51)	127 (31)	87 (01)	55 (72)	10 (18e)
						561s(71)					
23.10N, 79.57E	1289	Jabalpur	1100?		614 (81)	426 (71)	204 (51)	124 (31)	90 (01)		
					757s(81)	535s(71)	357s(51)				
22.31N, 88.24E		Jadabpur	bef 1961		252 (81)	13 (71)	6 (61)				
26.55N, 75.49E	1431	Jaipur	1728		977 (81)	615 (71)	291 (51)	144 (31)	160 (01)	138 (70)	72 (00e)
					1015s(81)	637s(71)					
31.19N, 75.34E		Jalandhar	100?		408 (81)	296 (71)	169 (51)	89 (31)	68 (01)	50 (68)	
32.44N, 74.52E	1201	Jammu	12th c?		206 (81)	158 (71)	50 (41)	39 (31)	36 (01)	8 (44e)	150(1750?e)
					223s(81)	164s(71)					

22.28N, 70.04E	60	Jamnagar	1540	278 (81) 317s(81)	200 (71) 228s(71)	103 (51) 104s(51)	55 (31)	54 (01)	35 (72)	
22.48N, 86.11E	423	Jamshedpur	1908?	457 (81) 670s(81)	342 (71) 456s(71)	194 (51) 218s(51)	84 (31)	6 (11)		
25.26N, 78.35E	848	Jhansi	1553?	246 (81) 284s(81)	173 (71) 198s(71)	127 (51)	77 (31)	56 (01)	30 (72e)	
26.17N, 73.02E	736	Jodhpur	1459	506 (81)	318 (71)	181 (51)	95 (31)	79 (01)	63 (81)	
16.56N, 82.13E	26	Kakinada	bef 1628	226 (81)	164 (71)	100 (51)	66 (31)	48 (01)	18 (71)	
22.45N, 88.21E		Kamarhati		235 (81)	169 (71)	77 (51)	30 (31)	13 (01)	10 (81)	
26.28N, 80.21E	413	Kanpur	1778	1482 (81) 1639s(81)	1154 (71) 1275s(71)	636 (51) 705s(51)	244 (31)	197 (01)	118 (53)	
22.20N, 87.20E	144	Kharagpur		150 (81) 233s(81)	161 (71)	130 (51)	58 (31)	4 (01)		
25.40N, 94.07E	4738	Kohima	bef 1878	34 (81)	22 (71)	4 (51)	3 (31)	3 (01)		
16.42N, 74.13E	1880	Kolhapur	2nd c?	341 (81) 351s(81)	259 (71) 268s(71)	137 (51)	70 (31)	54 (01)	40 (72)	
25.11N, 75.50E	843	Kota	14th c?	358 (81)	213 (71)	65 (51)	38 (31)	34 (01)	40 (81)	
15.50N, 78.03E	922	Kurnool	12th c?	206 (81)	137 (71)	60 (51)	35 (31)	25 (01)	21 (61)	
29.59N, 76.49E	850	Kurukshetra	1500 BC?	49 (81)	30 (71)	11 (51)	5 (31)	5 (01)	6 (81)	300 (00e)
26.51N, 80.55E	364	Lucknow	bef 1478	896 (81) 1008s(81)	749 (71) 814s(71)	445 (51) 497s(51)	275 (31)	264 (01)	285 (69)	
30.54N, 75.51E	812	Ludhiana	1480	607 (81)	398 (71) 401s(71)	154 (51)	69 (31)	49 (01)	40 (68)	
13.05N, 80.17E	51	Madras	1504	3277 (81) 4289s(81)	2469 (71) 3170s(71)	1416 (51)	647 (31)	509 (01)	368(71)	300s(94e)
9.56N, 78.07E	437	Madurai	5th c BC?	821 (81) 908s(81)	549 (71) 712s(71)	362 (51)	182 (31)	106 (01)	42 (51)	20 (12)
20.33N, 74.32E	1432	Malegaon	1740	246 (81)	192 (71)	55 (51)	29 (31)	19 (01)	10 (72)	
12.52N, 74.53E	72	Mangalore	6th c?	172 (81) 194s(81)	165 (71) 215s(71)	117 (51)	67 (31)	44 (01)	30 (71)	20 (00?e)
27.30N, 77.41E	600	Mathura	600 BC?	147 (81) 159s(81)	132 (71) 140s(71)	99 (51) 106s(51)	61 (31)	60 (01)	66 (53)	
22.26N, 87.20E	148	Medinipur		86 (81)	71 (71)	45 (51)	32 (31)	33 (01)	31 (72)	
28.59N, 77.42E	733	Meerut	3rd c BC?	417 (81) 537s(81)	271 (71) 368s(71)	158 (51) 233s(51)	137 (31)	118 (01)	82 (53)	
28.50N, 78.47E	197	Moradabad	1625	330 (81) 345s(81)	259 (71) 273s(71)	154 (51) 162s(51)	111 (31)	75 (01)	57 (53)	

For an explanation of symbols and abbreviations, see pages 16–17.

(Continued)

TABLE 2a. (Continued)

Latitude and Longitude	Elev (ft)	City	Date Settled	Latest	Population (thousands)						
					ca 1980	ca 1970	ca 1950	ca 1930	ca 1900	ca 1850	ca 1800
26.07N, 85.24E	177	Muzaffarpur	18th c		190 (81)	126 (71)	74 (51)	43 (31)	46 (01)	38 (72)	
12.18N, 76.39E	2518	Mysore	10th c?		442 (81) 479s(81)	356 (71)	244 (51)	107 (31)	68 (01)	58 (71)	
21.09N, 79.06E	1017	Nagpur	1700?		1219 (81) 1302s(81)	866 (71) 930s(71)	449 (51)	215 (31)	128 (01)	111 (54)	80 (00?e)
19.09N, 77.20E	1175	Nanded	13th c?		191 (81)	127 (71)	65 (51)	27 (31)	14 (01)	14 (81)	
19.59N, 73.48E	1961	Nasik	100 BC?		262 (81) 429s(81)	176 (71) 272s(71)	97 (51)	49 (31)	21 (01)	22 (50)	30 (20e)
14.26N, 79.58E	66	Nellore	11th c?		237 (81)	134 (71)	81 (51)	46 (31)	32 (01)	30 (71)	
28.36N, 77.12E	714	*New Delhi	993		273 (81)	302 (71)	276 (51)	65 (31)	31 (21)		
18.40N, 78.07E	1250	Nizamabad	10th c?		183 (81)	116 (71)	55 (51)	19 (31)	13 (01)		
15.29N, 73.50E	197	Panaji	bef 1541		43 (81) 77s(81)	35 (71) 59s(71)	29 (50)	18 (21)	9 (01)	8 (81)	
22.42N, 88.22E		Panihati	bef 1837		206 (81)	148 (71)	50 (51)	12 (31)	11 (01)		
30.19N, 76.24E	824	Patiala	1763		205 (81) 206s(81)	149 (71) 151s(71)	98 (51)	55 (31)	54 (01)	54 (81)	
25.35N, 85.15E	173	Patna	6th c BC?		776 (81) 919s(81)	473 (71) 491s(71)	250 (51)	160 (31)	135 (01)	159 (72)	266 (22)
20.54N, 73.42E		Pimpri-Chinch-wad			221 (81)	84 (71)	20 (51)				
11.56N, 79.53E	5	Pondicherry	1st c?		163 (81) 251s(81)	91 (71) 153s(71)	52 (61)	43 (31)	47 (01)	34 (56e)	25 (16e)
18.32N, 73.52E	1834	Pune	1604?		1203 (81) 1686s(81)	856 (71) 1135s(71)	481 (51) 589s(51)	234 (31)	153 (01)	73 (51)	81 (22)
19.48N, 85.51E	20	Puri	318?		101 (81)	73 (71)	49 (51)	38 (31)	49 (01)	23 (72)	
21.14N, 81.38E	971	Raipur	750?		338 (81)	175 (71) 206s(71)	90 (51)	45 (31)	32 (01)	19 (72)	5 (18e)
16.59N, 81.47E	69	Rajahmundry	11th c?		203 (81) 268s(81)	166 (71) 189s(71)	105 (51)	64 (31)	36 (01)	20 (71)	
22.18N, 70.47E	453	Rajkot	17th c?		445 (81)	301 (71)	132 (51)	47 (31)	36 (01)	12 (72)	
28.48N, 79.04E	546	Rampur	bef 1775		205 (81)	161 (71)	134 (51)	74 (31)	79 (01)	68 (72)	
23.21N, 85.20E	2149	Ranchi	bef 1834		490 (81) 503s(81)	176 (71) 256s(71)	94 (51) 107s(51)	51 (31)	26 (01)	12 (72)	

Coordinates	Pop	City	Date							
22.16N, 85.01E		Raurkela		311 (81), 323s(81)	125 (71), 173s(71)	16 (51)				
24.32N, 81.18E	938	Rewa	11th c?	101 (81)	69 (71)	30 (51)	25 (31)	25 (01)	22 (81)	
28.54N, 76.34E	719	Rohtak	12th c?	167 (81)	125 (71)	72 (51)	35 (31)	20 (01)	15 (81)	
29.52N, 77.53E	899	Roorkee		62 (81), 79s(81)	48 (71), 62s(71)	23 (51), 33s(51)	14 (31), 17s(31)	17 (01)	16 (81)	
23.50N, 78.43E	1808	Sagar	1660	160 (81), 175s(81)	119 (71), 155s(71)	66 (51), 80s(51)	40 (31), 49s(31)	42 (01)	46 (72)	
29.58N, 77.33E	896	Saharanpur	1340?	295 (81)	225 (71)	143 (51)	79 (31)	66 (01)	32 (53)	
11.39N, 78.10E	913	Salem	16th c?	361 (81), 519s(81)	309 (71), 416s(71)	202 (51)	102 (31)	71 (01)	50 (71)	19 (43)
21.27N, 83.58E	486	Sambalpur	16th c?	110 (81), 162s(81)	74 (71), 121s(71)	24 (51)	15 (31)	13 (01)	11 (72)	
16.52N, 74.34E	1752	Sangli	10th c?	152 (81), 269s(81)	115 (71), 202s(71)	50 (51), 91s(51)	30 (31)	17 (01)	13 (72)	
27.53N, 79.55E	505	Shahjahanpur	bef 1647	185 (81), 205s(81)	136 (71), 144s(71)	99 (51), 105s(51)	79 (31), 84s(31)	76 (01)	63 (53)	
25.34N, 91.53E	4921	Shillong	bef 1864	109 (81), 175s(81)	88 (71), 123s(71)	54 (51)	21 (31)	7 (01)	1 (72)	
31.06N, 77.10E	7225	Simla	bef 1819	71 (81)	55 (71)	46 (51)	23 (31)	39 (01)	8 (68)	
17.41N, 75.55E	1570	Solapur	1345?	511 (81), 515s(81)	398 (71)	266 (51)	145 (31)	75 (01)	53 (72)	
22.37N, 88.25E	33	South Dum Dum	bef 1756	230 (81)	174 (71)	61 (51)	18 (31)	11 (01)	10 (72)	
22.30N, 88.19E		South Suburban	1495?	379 (81)	273 (71)	104 (51)	39 (31)	26 (01)		
34.05N, 74.50E	5205	Srinagar	6th c	586 (81), 606s(81)	415 (71), 423s(71)	210 (41)	174 (31)	123 (01)	133 (73)	175 (09e)
21.10N, 72.50E	39	Surat	bef 150	777 (81), 914s(81)	472 (71), 493s(71)	223 (51)	99 (31)	119 (01)	90 (51)	124 (16)
19.12N, 72.58E		Thana	11th c?	310 (81), 390s(81)	171 (71), 207s(71)	62 (51), 68s(51)	22 (31)	16 (01)	14 (72)	
10.48N, 79.09E	45	Thanjavur	10th c?	184 (81)	141 (71)	101 (51)	67 (31)	58 (01)	52 (71)	
10.49N, 78.41E	255	Tiruchirapalli	bef 200	362 (81), 610s(81)	307 (71), 465s(71)	219 (51)	143 (31)	105 (01)	77 (71)	80 (20e)
8.44N, 77.42E	213	Tirunelveli	7th c?	129 (81), 323s(81)	108 (71), 267s(71)	73 (51), 161s(51)	57 (31)	40 (01)	21 (71)	
13.39N, 79.25E	499	Tirupati	1500 BC?	115 (81), 124s(81)	66 (71), 72s(71)	25 (51)	19 (31)	15 (01)	13 (81)	

(Continued)

For an explanation of symbols and abbreviations, see pages 16–17.

TABLE 2a. (Continued)

Latitude and Longitude	Elev (ft)	City	Date Settled	Latest	Population (thousands)							
					ca 1980	ca 1970	ca 1950	ca 1930	ca 1900	ca 1850	ca 1800	
11.06N, 77.21E		Tiruppur			165 (81) 216s(81)	113 (71) 151s(71)	52 (51) 60s(51)	18 (31)	6 (01)	4 (71)		
8.29N, 76.55E	210	Trivandrum	bef 1196		483 (81) 520s(81)	410 (71)	187 (51)	96 (31)	58 (01)	38 (81)		
8.47N, 78.08E	6	Tuticorin	1540?		193 (81) 251s(81)	155 (71) 182s(71)	99 (51)	60 (31)	28 (01)	11 (71)		
24.35N, 73.41E	1910	Udaipur	1568		233 (81)	161 (71)	90 (51)	44 (31)	46 (01)	38 (81)		
23.11N, 75.46E	1680	Ujjain	bef 263 BC		278 (81) 282s(81)	203 (71) 209s(71)	130 (51)	54 (31)	40 (01)	33 (81)	100 (00?e)	
19.15N, 73.08E	46	Ulhasnagar-Kalyan	2nd c?		410 (81) 649s(81)	268 (71) 396s(71)	140 (51)	26 (31)	11 (01)	13 (72)		
22.18N, 73.12E	115	Vadodara	812?		734 (81) 745s(81)	467 (71)	211 (51)	113 (31)	104 (01)	112 (72)	100 (18e)	
25.20N, 83.00E	250	Varanasi	12th c BC?		709 (81) 797s(81)	584 (71) 607s(71)	342 (51) 356s(51)	205 (31)	209 (01)	186 (53)	168 (10?e)	
12.56N, 69.08E	702	Vellore	1274?		174 (81) 247s(81)	139 (71) 179s(71)	106 (51)	57 (31)	44 (01)	38 (71)		
16.31N, 80.37E	80	Vijayawada	17th c?		455 (81) 543s(81)	317 (71) 345s(71)	161 (51)	60 (31)	24 (01)	8 (71)		
17.42N, 83.18E	10	Visakhapatnam	14th c?		565 (81) 604s(81)	353 (71) 363s(71)	108 (51)	57 (31)	41 (01)	32 (71)	20 (00?e)	
18.18N, 79.35E	883	Warangal	12th c		335 (81)	208 (71)	133 (51)	62 (31)	5 (01)	3 (91)		
Indonesia												
3.43S, 128.12E	14	Ambon	1521		209 (80)	80 (71)	55 (61)	17 (30)	8 (95)	9 (41)	6 (00?e)	
1.17S, 116.50E	23	Balikpapan	1899?		281 (80)	137 (71)	92 (61)	30 (30)				
5.34N, 95.20E	66	Banda Aceh	bef 1292		72 (80)	54 (71)	40 (61)	11 (30)	4 (95)			
6.54S, 107.36E	2520	Bandung	1810	1567 (83e)	1463 (80)	1200 (71)	973 (61)	167 (30)	27 (95)			
3.20S, 114.36E	66	Banjarmasin	14th c	424 (83e)	381 (80)	282 (71)	214 (61)	66 (30)	45 (95)	30 (50?e)		
6.35S, 106.47E	820	Bogor	1745		247 (80)	195 (71)	154 (61)	65 (30)	25 (95)	5 (50?e)		
6.44S, 108.34E	13	Cirebon	15th c?		224 (80)	179 (71)	158 (61)	54 (30)	21 (96)	12 (50e)		
8.39S, 115.13E	131	Denpasar	16th c?		261 (80)	98 (71)	57 (61)	17 (30)				

Lat, Long	No.	City	Founded								
8.33S,125.34E	16	Dili	1769		60 (80)	29 (70)	11 (61)	3 (27)			
6.10S,106.49E	23	*Jakarta	5th c?	7873 (85e)	6503 (80)	4579 (71)	2907 (61)	435 (30)	115 (95)	54 (42)	47s(15)
1.36S,103.37E	33	Jambi	11th c?		230 (80)	158 (71)	113 (61)	23 (30)	9 (05)		3 (20e)
8.10S,113.42E	272	Jember				123 (71)	94 (61)	20 (30)	4 (95)		
7.49S,112.01E	203	Kediri	10th c?		222 (80)	179 (71)	159 (61)	49 (30)	17 (95)	6 (50?e)	
10.10S,123.35E	499	Kupang	1613		403 (80)	49 (71)	30 (61)	7 (30)	0.3(95?)		
7.59S,112.38E	1460	Malang	13th c?	547 (83e)	512 (80)	422 (71)	341 (61)	87 (30)	13 (95)		
1.29N,124.51E	13	Manado	17th c?		217 (80)	170 (71)	130 (61)	28 (30)	9 (96)	2 (50?e)	
8.35S,116.07E	49	Mataram	1849?		69 (80)	35 (71)	18 (61)		0.3(95)		
3.35N,98.40E	82	Medan	bef 1869	1805 (83e)	1379 (80)	636 (71)	479 (61)	77 (30)	13 (95)		
0.57S,100.21E	3	Padang	1637	657 (83e)	481 (80)	196 (71)	144 (61)	52 (30)	32 (95)	12 (50?e)	
0.32N,101.27E	102	Pakanbaru			186 (80)	145 (71)	71 (61)	village			
3.00S,104.46E	26	Palembang	2nd c?	874 (83e)	787 (80)	583 (71)	475 (61)	108 (30)	54 (95)	42 (55)	27 (00e)
0.53S,119.53E	20	Palu			299 (80)		17 (61)				
0.02S,109.20E	10	Pontianak	1772?	343 (83e)	305 (80)	218 (71)	150 (61)	45 (30)	17 (95)	12 (50?e)	
7.25S,109.14E		Purwokerto				94 (71)	81 (61)	33 (30)	12 (95)		
7.19S,110.30E	1916	Salatiga	16th c?		86 (80)	70 (71)	58 (61)	24 (30)	10 (95)		
0.30S,117.09E	9	Samarinda	1730		265 (80)	137 (71)	70 (61)	11 (30)	5 (05)		
6.57S,110.25E	7	Semarang	17th c?	1206 (83e)	1027 (80)	647 (71)	503 (61)	218 (30)	83 (95)	28 (50?e)	25 (00e)
7.15S,112.45E	23	Surabaya	14th c?	2224 (83e)	2028 (80)	1556 (71)	1008 (61)	342 (30)	125 (95)	85 (57)	25 (15)
7.35S,110.50E	341	Surakarta	1744	491 (83e)	470 (80)	413 (71)	368 (61)	165 (30)	105 (95)	100 (50?e)	105 (15e)
5.27S,105.16E	33	Tanjungkarang-Telukbetung	bef 1866		284 (80)	199 (71)	134 (61)	25 (30)	3 (96?)		
5.07S,119.24E	7	Ujung Pandang	15th c?	840 (83e)	709 (80)	435 (71)	384 (61)	85 (30)	17 (95)	20 (45e)	100 (00?e)
7.48S,110.22E	377	Yogyakarta	1749	421 (83e)	399 (80)	341 (71)	313 (61)	137 (30)	58 (95)	43 (50?e)	100 (15e)

Iran

Lat, Long	No.	City	Founded								
30.20N, 48.16E	10	Abadan	1047?		294 (76)	273 (66)	226 (56)	40 (33)	2 (00?e)	2 (50?e)	
31.19N, 48.42E	66	Ahwaz	12th c?	508 (85e)	334 (76)	206 (66)	120 (56)	32 (33)	7 (00?e)		
34.05N, 49.41E	5755	Arak	1808	244 (85e)	115 (76)	72 (66)	59 (56)	55 (33)			
38.15N, 48.18E	3609	Ardabil	5th c	258 (85e)	148 (76)	84 (66)	66 (56)	45 (33)	16 (00?e)	4 (50?e)	4 (25?e)
34.19N, 47.04E	4337	Bakhtaran	4th c	536 (85e)	291 (76)	188 (66)	125 (56)	70 (33)	35 (00e)	30 (50e)	9 (00?e)
27.11N, 56.17E	20	Bandar Abbas	16th c	212 (85e)	89 (76)	35 (66)	18 (56)		10 (00?e)	6 (50?e)	5 (29)
34.48N, 48.30E	5824	Hamadan	1100 BC?	262 (85e)	166 (76)	124 (66)	100 (56)	100 (33)	30 (00e)	30 (50e)	40 (00?e)
32.40N, 51.38E	5217	Isfahan	5th c BC?	1121 (85e)	662 (76)	424 (66)	255 (56)	100 (33)	86 (00e)	74 (82)	300 (00e)
35.48N, 50.59E	4350	Karaj	1800?	432 (85e)	138 (76)	44 (66)	15 (56)	village			
30.17N, 57.05E	5738	Kerman	bef 325 BC	267 (85e)	140 (76)	85 (66)	62 (56)	60 (33)	45 (00?e)	30 (50?e)	20 (00?e)

(Continued)

For an explanation of symbols and abbreviations, see pages 16–17.

TABLE 2a. (Continued)

Latitude and Longitude	Elev (ft)	City	Date Settled	Population (thousands)							
				Latest	ca 1980	ca 1970	ca 1950	ca 1930	ca 1900	ca 1850	ca 1800
33.29N, 48.21E	3806	Khorramabad	12th c?	236 (85e)	105 (76)	60 (66)	39 (56)	12 (33?)	5 (00e)	45 (50?e)	50 (00?e)
36.18N, 59.36E	3232	Meshed	817?	1103 (85e)	668 (76)	410 (66)	242 (56)	139 (33)	62 (00e)	25 (50?e)	12 (00?e)
37.33N, 45.04E	4370	Orumiyeh	1st c BC?	298 (85e)	164 (76)	111 (66)	68 (56)	50 (33)	35 (00?e)	25 (68e)	60 (09e)
36.16N, 50.00E	4272	Qazvin	250?	206 (85e)	139 (76)	88 (66)	66 (56)	60 (33)	30 (00?e)	10 (60e)	
34.39N, 50.54E	3045	Qom	7th c?	638 (85e)	247 (76)	134 (66)	96 (56)	39 (33)	23 (00e)	25 (50?e)	10 (00?e)
37.16N, 49.36E	-36	Rasht	14th c?	266 (85e)	189 (76)	144 (66)	109 (56)	90 (33)	35 (00?e)	25 (50?e)	
35.19N, 47.00E	4990	Sanandaj		207 (85e)	99 (76)	55 (66)	41 (56)	30 (40)	8 (00?e)	2 (50?e)	
29.36N, 52.32E	5049	Shiraz	693?	835 (85e)	426 (76)	270 (66)	171 (56)	120 (33)	31 (00?e)	30 (50?)	40 (00?e)
38.05N, 46.18E	4469	Tabriz	3rd c?	929 (85e)	598 (76)	403 (66)	290 (56)	220 (33)	162 (00e)	37 (50)	55 (11e)
35.40N, 51.26E	3908	*Tehran	12th c	5751 (85e)	4530 (76)	2720 (66)	1512 (56)	360 (33)	204 (00e)	70 (60)	15 (97e)
31.53N, 54.25E	4068	Yazd	5th c	223 (85e)	136 (76)	93 (66)	64 (56)	55 (33)	50 (00?e)	35 (50?e)	35 (25?e)
29.30N, 60.52E	4435	Zahedan		220 (85e)	93 (76)	40 (66)	17 (56)	5 (33)			
36.40N, 48.29E	5456	Zanjan	bef 645	206 (85e)	100 (76)	59 (66)	47 (56)	39 (41)	15 (00?e)	15 (50?e)	
Iraq											
33.21N, 44.25E	111	*Baghdad	762?	4649s (85e)	3236s (77)	1491 (65) / 1657s (65)	467 (47) / 515s (47)	145 (20e)	156 (00e)	50 (53e)	96 (00?e)
30.30N, 47.47E	8	Basra	636	617 (85e)		311 (65)	102 (47)	50 (20e)	19 (00e)	60 (50?e)	40 (00?e)
32.29N, 44.25E	89	Hillah	1102?	215 (85e)		84 (65)	51 (47)	20 (20e)	30 (00?e)	10 (50?e)	12 (00?e)
36.11N, 44.01E	1358	Irbil	bef 2000 BC	334 (85e)		91 (65)	26 (47)	10 (20?e)	12 (00?e)		
32.36N, 44.02E	85	Karbala	680?	185 (85e)		84 (65)	44 (47)	65 (20)	65 (00?e)		
35.28N, 44.28E	1086	Kirkuk	3000 BC?	571 (85e)		175 (65)	68 (47)	20 (20?e)	30 (00?e)	20 (50?e)	18 (00?e)
36.20N, 43.08E	730	Mosul	636?			264 (65)	134 (47)	65 (20e)	60 (00e)	40 (50?e)	35 (00?e)
31.59N, 44.20E	180	Najaf	8th c	243 (85e)		134 (65)	56 (47)	25 (20?e)			
35.32N, 45.27E	2799	Sulaymaniyah	1781	279 (85e)		84 (65)	41 (47)	30 (20e)	15 (00?e)		
Israel											
31.14N, 34.47E	919	Beersheba	1900		111 (83)	84 (72)	6 (46e)	3 (31)			
32.49N, 35.00E	16	Haifa	4th c?		236 (83) / 387s (83)	220 (72) / 335s (72)	147 (51e)	51 (31)	11 (00e)	3 (50?e)	
31.47N, 35.13E	2658	*Jerusalem	3000 BC?		429 (83)	314 (72)	207 (51e)	91 (31)	55 (00e)	14 (50e)	19 (97e)
32.42N, 35.18E	1312	Nazareth	1st c BC?		45 (83)	33 (72)	15 (48)	9 (31)	8 (00?e)	3 (50?e)	
32.05N, 34.49E		Ramat Gan	1922		117 (83)	117 (72)	42 (53e)	5 (39e)			

(Continued)

Lat/Long		City	Founded	328 (83) / 1555s (83)	364 (72) / 1030s (72)	345 (51e)	97 (31)	21 (00e)	5 (50e)	40 (00e)
32.05N, 34.46E	10	Tel Aviv-Jaffa	bef 1472 BC	328 (83)	364 (72)	345 (51e)	97 (31)	21 (00e)	5 (50e)	40 (00e)
Japan										
34.38N, 134.59E	20	Akashi	16th c?	263 (85)	207 (70)	66 (50)	39 (30)	21 (98)	14 (74)	
39.43N, 140.07E	30	Akita	733	296 (85)	236 (70)	126 (50)	51 (30)	29 (98)	38 (74)	
34.43N, 135.25E		Amagasaki	16th c	509 (85)	554 (70)	279 (50)	50 (30)	43 (98)	12 (74)	
40.49N, 140.45E	13	Aomori	16th c	294 (85)	240 (70)	106 (50)	77 (30)	28 (98)	11 (74)	
43.46N, 142.22E	364	Asahikawa	1893	364 (85)	288 (70)	123 (50)	83 (30)	24 (03)		
33.17N, 131.30E		Beppu		135 (85)	124 (70)	93 (50)	43 (30)	6 (98)		
35.36N, 140.07E	79	Chiba	1126	789 (85)	482 (70)	134 (50)	49 (30)	26 (98)	3 (74)	
35.39N, 139.33E		Chofu	bef 733	191 (85)	157 (70)	20 (47)		5 (98)		
35.40N, 139.29E		Fuchu	111	202 (85)	163 (70)	30 (50)				
35.09N, 138.39E		Fuji	17th c?	214 (85)	181 (70)	22 (50)				
35.21N, 139.29E		Fujisawa	14th c?	328 (85)	229 (70)	85 (50)	25 (30)	6 (98)	6 (74)	4 (43)
36.04N, 136.13E	30	Fukui	1575?	250 (85)	201 (70)	101 (50)	64 (30)	44 (98)	40 (74)	40 (00e)
33.35N, 130.24E	7	Fukuoka	bef 1281	1160 (85)	853 (70)	393 (50)	228 (30)	66 (98)	21 (74)	25 (00e)
37.45N, 140.28E	220	Fukushima	1180?	271 (85)	227 (70)	93 (50)	46 (30)	21 (98)	6 (74)	
34.29N, 133.22E	5	Fukuyama	1619	360 (85)	255 (70)	67 (50)	38 (30)	17 (98)	18 (74)	
35.42N, 139.59E		Funabashi		507 (85)	325 (70)	83 (50)	23 (30)	10 (98)	9 (74)	
35.25N, 136.45E	43	Gifu	1565?	412 (85)	386 (70)	212 (50)	90 (30)	32 (98)	11 (74)	
40.30N, 141.29E	89	Hachinohe	bef 1664	241 (85)	209 (70)	104 (50)	53 (30)	11 (98)	10 (74)	
35.39N, 139.20E		Hachioji	bef 1590	427 (85)	254 (70)	83 (50)	52 (30)	23 (98)	8 (74)	
41.45N, 140.43E	108	Hakodate	15th c?	319 (85)	242 (70)	229 (50)	197 (30)	78 (98)	113 (74)	
34.42N, 137.42E	95	Hamamatsu	1505?	514 (85)	432 (70)	152 (50)	109 (30)	12 (98)	11 (74)	6 (43)
34.39N, 135.35E		Higashiosaka		523 (85)	500 (70)	150 (50)	24 (30)			
35.15N, 136.15E	285	Hikone	1603	94 (85)	79 (70)	49 (50)	23 (35)	17 (03)		
34.49N, 134.42E	125	Himeji	10th c?	453 (85)	408 (70)	212 (50)	62 (30)	35 (98)	25 (74)	25 (00e)
34.48N, 135.38E		Hirakata		382 (85)	217 (70)	44 (50)	6 (30)	2 (98)		
35.19N, 139.21E		Hiratsuka	17th c?	230 (85)	164 (70)	52 (50)	3 (30)	1 (98)	2 (43)	
40.35N, 140.28E	131	Hirosaki	1611	176 (85)	102 (70)	44 (50)	43 (30)	35 (98)	33 (74)	
34.24N, 132.27E	95	Hiroshima	1559	1044 (85)	542 (70)	286 (50)	270 (30)	122 (98)	74 (74)	50 (04)
36.36N, 140.39E	171	Hitachi		206 (85)	193 (70)	56 (50)	28 (30)			
34.49N, 135.34E		Ibaraki	16th c?	250 (85)	164 (70)	35 (50)		3 (98)		
35.31N, 140.05E		Ichihara		238 (85)	156 (70)	5 (50)				
35.44N, 139.55E	75	Ichikawa		398 (85)	261 (70)	103 (50)	21 (30)	2 (98)	7 (74)	
35.18N, 136.48E		Ichinomiya	7th c	257 (85)	219 (70)	71 (50)	42 (30)	10 (98)		
34.29N, 136.42E	7	Ise	4 BC	105 (85)	104 (70)	69 (50)	51 (30)	28 (98)	22 (74)	10 (00e)

For an explanation of symbols and abbreviations, see pages 16–17.

TABLE 2a. (Continued)

Latitude and Longitude	Elev (ft)	City	Date Settled	Latest	ca 1980	ca 1970	ca 1950	ca 1930	ca 1900	ca 1850	ca 1800
36.57N,140.54E	10	Iwaki	14th c?	351 (85)	342 (80)	327 (70)	27 (50)	10 (30)	6 (98)	3 (74)	
31.36N,130.33E	16	Kagoshima	764?	530 (85)	505 (80)	403 (70)	229 (50)	137 (30)	53 (98)	27 (74)	72 (26)
34.46N,134.51E		Kakogawa	bef 1603	227 (85)	212 (80)	127 (70)	50 (50)		0.8 (98)		
35.19N,139.33E		Kamakura	7th c?	175 (85)	173 (80)	139 (70)	85 (50)	27 (30)	6 (98)	6 (74)	
36.34N,136.39E	89	Kanazawa	bef 1471	430 (85)	418 (80)	361 (70)	252 (50)	157 (30)	84 (98)	110 (74)	115 (95e)
35.52N,139.59E		Kashiwa	17th c?	273 (85)	239 (80)	151 (70)	21 (50)				
35.14N,136.58E		Kasugai		257 (85)	244 (80)	162 (70)	48 (50)				
35.55N,139.29E		Kawagoe	830	285 (85)	259 (80)	171 (70)	53 (50)	34 (30)	19 (98)		
35.48N,139.43E		Kawaguchi	17th c?	403 (85)	379 (80)	306 (70)	125 (50)	22 (30)	3 (98)		
35.32N,139.43E		Kawasaki	1150?	1089 (50)	1041 (80)	973 (70)	319 (50)	104 (30)	4 (98)	3 (74)	2 (43)
33.52N,130.50E	23	Kitakyushu	1318	1056 (85)	1065 (80)	1042 (70)	711 (50)	473 (30)	88 (98)		
34.41N,135.10E	190	Kobe	1160?	1411 (85)	1367 (80)	1289 (70)	765 (50)	788 (30)	216 (98)	11 (74)	
33.33N,133.33E	2	Kochi	1600?	312 (85)	301 (80)	240 (70)	162 (50)	97 (30)	37 (98)	40 (74)	25 (00e)
35.39N,138.35E	892	Kofu	13th c?	202 (85)	199 (80)	183 (70)	122 (50)	79 (30)	38 (98)	16 (74)	25 (00e)
37.24N,140.23E	837	Koriyama	17th c?	302 (85)	286 (80)	242 (70)	71 (50)	51 (30)	6 (98)	5 (74)	
35.54N,139.48E		Koshigaya		253 (85)	223 (80)	139 (70)	7 (50)		3 (98)		
32.48N,130.43E	125	Kumamoto	15th c	556 (85)	526 (80)	440 (70)	268 (50)	164 (30)	61 (98)	45 (74)	
34.35N,133.46E	10	Kurashiki	17th c?	414 (85)	404 (80)	340 (70)	53 (50)	30 (30)	7 (98)	6 (74)	
34.14N,132.34E	89	Kure	bef 1887	226 (85)	235 (80)	235 (70)	188 (50)	190 (30)	11 (98)		
33.19N,130.31E	43	Kurume	bef 1600	223 (85)	217 (80)	194 (70)	101 (50)	83 (30)	29 (98)	20 (74)	
42.58N,144.23E	108	Kushiro	17th c?	215 (85)	215 (80)	192 (70)	93 (50)	52 (30)	3 (98)		
35.00N,135.45E	135	Kyoto	8th c	1479 (85)	1473 (80)	1419 (70)	1102 (50)	765 (30)	353 (98)	239 (74)	379 (98)
35.33N,139.28E	318	Machida		321 (85)	295 (80)	203 (70)	21 (50)	7 (30)	3 (98)		
36.23N,139.04E	367	Maebashi	bef 1582	277 (85)	265 (80)	234 (70)	97 (50)	85 (30)	34 (98)	15 (74)	
35.47N,139.54E	82	Matsudo	17th c?	427 (85)	401 (80)	254 (70)	53 (50)	11 (30)	3 (98)		
35.28N,133.04E	56	Matsue	1611	140 (85)	136 (80)	118 (70)	74 (50)	45 (30)	35 (98)	38 (74)	
36.14N,137.58E	2001	Matsumoto	1504	197 (85)	192 (80)	163 (70)	86 (50)	72 (30)	31 (98)		
33.50N,132.45E	105	Matsuyama	1603	427 (85)	402 (80)	323 (70)	164 (50)	82 (30)	37 (98)	12 (74)	
36.22N,140.28E	95	Mito	12th c?	229 (85)	216 (80)	174 (70)	67 (50)	51 (30)	34 (98)		
31.54N,131.26E	23	Miyazaki		279 (85)	265 (80)	203 (70)	103 (50)	55 (30)	5 (98)	12 (74)	
39.42N,141.09E	505	Morioka	1596	235 (85)	229 (80)	196 (70)	118 (50)	62 (30)	33 (98)	21 (74)	
36.39N,138.11E	1371	Nagano	7th c	337 (85)	324 (80)	285 (70)	101 (50)	74 (30)	31 (98)	7 (74)	

Coordinates		City	Founded	(85)	(80)	(70)	(50)	(30)	(98)	(74)	
37.27N,138.51E		Nagaoka	1598?	184 (85)	180 (80)	162 (70)	67 (50)	58 (30)	16 (98)	24 (74)	15 (18e)
32.48N,129.55E	89	Nagasaki	12th c?	449 (85)	447 (80)	421 (70)	242 (50)	204 (30)	107 (98)	30 (74)	32 (89)
35.10N,136.55E	167	Nagoya	1612?	2116 (85)	2088 (80)	2036 (70)	1031 (50)	907 (30)	244 (98)	125 (74)	100 (00e)
26.13N,127.40E	89	Naha	7th c?	304 (85)	296 (80)	276 (70)	76 (50)	61 (30)	35 (98)	15 (74)	
34.41N,135.50E	345	Nara	7th c?	328 (85)	298 (80)	208 (70)	78 (50)	53 (30)	31 (98)	21 (74)	
34.46N,135.38E		Neyagawa		258 (85)	256 (80)	207 (70)	30 (50)	3 (30)			
37.55N,139.03E	7	Niigata	bef 1869	476 (85)	458 (80)	384 (70)	221 (50)	125 (30)	53 (98)	33 (74)	5 (43)
36.45N,139.37E	2001	Nikko	766	22 (85)	24 (80)	29 (70)	29 (50)	20 (30)	3 (98)	3 (74)	
34.43N,135.20E		Nishinomiya	15th c?	421 (85)	410 (80)	377 (70)	127 (50)	39 (30)	12 (98)	9 (74)	
35.06N,138.52E	23	Numazu	1579	210 (85)	204 (80)	189 (70)	102 (50)	44 (30)	12 (98)	16 (74)	
33.14N,131.36E	15	Oita	13th c?	390 (85)	360 (80)	261 (70)	94 (50)	57 (30)	9 (98)	7 (74)	
34.39N,133.55E	10	Okayama	16th c?	572 (85)	546 (80)	375 (70)	163 (50)	139 (30)	58 (98)	32 (74)	56 (1764e)
34.57N,137.10E		Okazaki	1455	285 (85)	262 (80)	211 (70)	96 (50)	66 (30)	15 (98)	13 (74)	6 (43)
35.54N,139.38E		Omiya	5th c BC?	373 (85)	354 (80)	269 (70)	100 (50)	29 (30)	2 (98)	3 (74)	
34.40N,135.30E	23	Osaka	7th c BC?	2636 (85)	2648 (80)	2980 (70)	1956 (50)	2454 (30)	821 (98)	272 (74)	376 (01)
43.13N,141.00E	79	Otaru	bef 1874	172 (85)	181 (80)	192 (70)	178 (50)	145 (30)	57 (98)	4 (74)	
35.00N,135.52E		Otsu	2nd c?	235 (85)	215 (80)	172 (70)	85 (50)	34 (30)	34 (98)		
33.15N,130.18E	13	Saga	1185?	168 (85)	164 (80)	143 (70)	67 (50)	46 (30)	33 (98)		
35.33N,139.22E		Sagamihara		483 (85)	439 (80)	278 (70)	69 (50)				
34.35N,135.28E		Sakai	bef 1336	818 (85)	810 (80)	594 (70)	214 (50)	120 (30)	50 (98)	39 (74)	45 (13)
43.03N,141.21E	56	Sapporo	1871	1543 (85)	1402 (80)	1010 (70)	314 (50)	169 (30)	37 (98)	2 (74)	
33.10N,129.43E	43	Sasebo	bef 1890	251 (85)	251 (80)	248 (70)	194 (50)	133 (30)	37 (98)	10 (90)	
38.15N,140.53E	125	Sendai	1600	700 (85)	665 (80)	545 (70)	342 (50)	190 (30)	83 (98)	52 (74)	67 (1764)
35.01N,138.29E	98	Shimizu	16th c?	242 (85)	242 (80)	235 (70)	88 (50)	56 (30)	5 (98)	4 (74)	
33.57N,130.57E	151	Shimonoseki	bef 1185	269 (85)	269 (80)	258 (70)	194 (50)	99 (30)	43 (98)	18 (74)	
34.58N,138.23E	43	Shizuoka	bef 1569	468 (85)	458 (80)	416 (70)	239 (50)	136 (30)	42 (98)	32 (74)	
35.49N,139.48E		Soka	1603?	194 (85)	187 (80)	123 (70)	15 (50)		5 (98)	5 (74)	
34.45N,135.32E		Suita		349 (85)	332 (80)	260 (70)	78 (50)	24 (30)	4 (98)	3 (74)	
34.20N,134.03E	30	Takamatsu	1335	327 (85)	317 (80)	274 (70)	125 (50)	80 (30)	34 (98)	33 (74)	
34.49N,135.21E	250	Takarazuka	1546?	194 (85)	184 (80)	127 (70)	15 (50)		0.6 (98)		
36.20N,139.01E	312	Takasaki	15th c	232 (85)	221 (80)	193 (70)	93 (50)	60 (30)	31 (98)	11 (74)	7 (01)
34.51N,135.37E		Takatsuki	16th c?	349 (85)	341 (80)	231 (70)	43 (50)	6 (30)	3 (98)		
35.47N,139.28E	233	Tokorozawa	17th c?	275 (85)	236 (80)	137 (70)	43 (50)		6 (98)		
34.04N,134.34E	4	Tokushima	bef 1585	258 (85)	249 (80)	223 (70)	121 (50)	91 (30)	62 (98)	49 (74)	40 (00e)
35.42N,139.46E	13	*Tokyo	12th c	8354 (85)	8349 (80)	8841 (70)	5385 (50)	2071 (30)	1440 (98)	596 (74)	1000 (00e)
				11828s (85)	11469s (80)	11161s (70)	6277s (50)	4971s (30)			

(Continued)

For an explanation of symbols and abbreviations, see pages 16–17.

TABLE 2a. (Continued)

Latitude and Longitude	Elev (ft)	City	Date Settled	Population (thousands)							
				Latest	ca 1980	ca 1970	ca 1950	ca 1930	ca 1900	ca 1850	ca 1800
35.30N,134.14E	56	Tottori	1550?	137 (85)	131 (80)	113 (70)	62 (50)	38 (30)	28 (98)	21 (74)	27 (41)
36.41N,137.13E	30	Toyama	1572?	314 (85)	305 (80)	269 (70)	154 (50)	75 (30)	60 (98)	45 (74)	
34.46N,137.23E	98	Toyohashi	15th c	322 (85)	304 (80)	259 (70)	146 (50)	99 (30)	22 (98)	8 (74)	
34.47N,135.28E		Toyonaka		413 (85)	403 (80)	368 (70)	86 (50)	16 (30)			
35.05N,137.09E	246	Toyota	bef 1681	308 (85)	282 (80)	197 (70)	32 (50)	14 (30)	4 (98)		
34.43N,136.31E	7	Tsu	15th c?	151 (85)	145 (80)	125 (70)	76 (50)	56 (30)	33 (98)	22 (74)	
35.51N,139.39E	66	Urawa	bef 1818	377 (85)	358 (80)	269 (70)	115 (50)	25 (30)	6 (98)	2 (74)	
36.33N,139.52E	394	Utsunomiya	12th c?	405 (85)	378 (80)	301 (70)	107 (50)	81 (30)	32 (98)	15 (74)	6 (43)
34.13N,135.11E	46	Wakayama	16th c	401 (85)	401 (80)	365 (70)	191 (50)	117 (30)	64 (98)	61 (74)	
38.15N,140.15E	495	Yamagata	764?	245 (85)	237 (80)	204 (70)	105 (50)	63 (30)	35 (98)	18 (74)	25 (00e)
34.10N,131.28E		Yamaguchi	1350	124 (85)	115 (80)	101 (70)	78 (50)	32 (30)	11 (98)	9 (74)	
34.37N,135.36E		Yao	bef 1337	276 (85)	273 (80)	228 (70)	67 (50)	11 (30)	4 (98)	3 (74)	
34.58N,136.37E	10	Yokkaichi	bef 17th c	263 (85)	255 (80)	229 (70)	124 (50)	52 (30)	25 (98)	10 (74)	7 (43)
35.27N,139.39E	128	Yokohama	bef 1854	2993 (85)	2774 (80)	2238 (70)	951 (50)	620 (30)	194 (98)	65 (74)	
35.18N,139.40E	39	Yokosuka	bef 1600	427 (85)	421 (80)	348 (70)	251 (50)	110 (30)	25 (98)	3 (74)	

Jordan

Latitude and Longitude	Elev (ft)	City	Date Settled	Latest	ca 1980	ca 1970	ca 1950	ca 1930	ca 1900	ca 1850	ca 1800
31.57N, 35.56E	2513	*Amman	1878	812 (85e)	649 (79)	330 (67)	103 (52)	12 (30e)	1 (00?e)		
32.33N, 35.51E	1919	Irbid	13th c?	141 (85e)	113 (79)	63 (67)	23 (52)	2 (30e)			
32.04N, 36.05E	2001	Zarqa	1878?	277 (85e)	216 (79)	121 (67)	3 (47e)				

Kampuchea

Latitude and Longitude	Elev (ft)	City	Date Settled	Latest	ca 1980	ca 1970	ca 1950	ca 1930	ca 1900	ca 1850	ca 1800
11.33N,104.55E	36	*Phnom-Penh	1371	700 (86e)	400 (81e)	650 (69e)	111 (48e)	96 (31)	50 (00e)	17 (66e)	

Korea: North

Latitude and Longitude	Elev (ft)	City	Date Settled	Latest	ca 1980	ca 1970	ca 1950	ca 1930	ca 1900	ca 1850	ca 1800
41.46N,129.49E	164	Chongjin			490 (80e)	265 (67e)	184 (44)	33 (30)	59 (99)		
38.02N,125.42E	259	Haeju			213 (80e)	115 (67e)	82 (44)	24 (30)			
39.54N,127.32E	108	Hamhung	15th c?		775 (80e)	300 (70e)	112 (44)	40 (30)	14 (08)		
37.58N,126.33E	197	Kaesong	bef 919		259 (80e)	238 (65e)	89 (49)	49 (30)	56 (99)		
40.41N,129.12E	13	Kimchaek			490 (80e)	265 (67e)	68 (44)	11 (30)			
38.44N,125.24E	98	Nampo	bef 1897		241 (80e)	130 (67e)	82 (44)	38 (30)			
39.01N,125.45E	95	*Pyongyang	1122 BC?		1283 (80e)	840 (67e)	343 (44)	137 (30)	74 (99)		
40.06N,124.24E	20	Sinuiju	1910?		305 (80e)	165 (67e)	118 (44)	44 (30)			
39.10N,127.26E	120	Wonsan	bef 1880		398 (80e)	350 (70e)	113 (44)	43 (30)	16 (08)		

Korea: South

Coordinates	No.	Place	Founded	(85)	(80)	(70)	(49)	(30)	(99)	earlier	earliest
37.23N,126.55E		Anyang		362 (85)	254 (80)	135 (70)	12s(49)	58 (44)	55 (99)		
37.20N,126.30E		Buchon	938?	456 (85)	221 (80)	109 (75)					
33.31N,126.32E	72	Cheju	57 BC?	203 (85)	168 (80)	106 (70)	61 (49)	38 (35)			
35.11N,128.05E	69	Chinju	10th c?	227 (85)	203 (80)	122 (70)	77 (49)	20 (30?)			
36.38N,127.30E	194	Chongju	57 BC?	350 (85)	253 (80)	141 (70)	65 (49)	38 (30)	37 (99)		
35.49N,127.09E	167	Chonju		426 (85)	367 (80)	258 (70)	101 (49)	36 (44)	15 (99)		
37.52N,127.44E	243	Chunchon	4th c?	163 (85)	155 (80)	123 (70)	55 (49)	64 (30)	27 (99)		
37.28N,126.38E	226	Inchon		1387 (85)	1084 (80)	634 (70)	266 (49)	26 (44)			
35.56N,126.57E	591	Iri		192 (85)	145 (80)	87 (70)	47 (49)	26 (30)			
35.59N,126.43E	85	Kunsan	bef 1899	186 (85)	165 (80)	112 (70)	74 (49)	26 (30)			
35.09N,126.55E	115	Kwangju	57 BC?	906 (85)	728 (80)	494 (70)	139 (49)	33 (30)	23 (99)		
34.49N,129.09E		Kwangmyong		220 (85)							
35.50N,129.13E	89	Kyongju	bef 57 BC	128 (85)	122 (80)	92 (70)	36 (49)	24 (30)	17 (99)		
35.11N,128.34E	105	Masan	13th c?	449 (85)	387 (80)	187 (70)	91 (49)	26 (30)	9 (99)		
34.47N,126.23E	20	Mokpo	bef 1897	236 (85)	222 (80)	174 (70)	111 (49)	32 (30)			
36.02N,129.22E	226	Pohang		261 (85)	201 (80)	79 (70)	51 (49)				
35.06N,129.03E	279	Pusan	bef 1443	3517 (85)	3160 (80)	1842 (70)	474 (49)	130 (30)	17 (99)	90 (50e)	
37.34N,127.00E		*Seoul	6 BC?	9646 (85)	8364 (80)	5433 (70)	1446 (49)	355 (30)	201 (99)	190 (93)	
37.25N,127.00E	121	Songnam	bef 1970	448 (85)	377 (80)	165 (73)					
37.16N,127.01E		Suwon	12th c?	431 (85)	310 (80)	167 (70)	53 (49)	14 (30?)			
35.52N,128.36E	190	Taegu	bef 8th c	2031 (85)	1605 (80)	1064 (70)	314 (49)	101 (30)	45 (99)		
36.20N,127.26E	187	Taejon		867 (85)	652 (80)	407 (70)	127 (49)	21 (30)			
35.33N,129.19E	102	Ulsan		551 (85)	418 (80)	157 (70)	24 (49)	15 (30?)			

Kuwait

Coordinates	No.	Place	Founded	(85)	(80)	(70)	(49)	(30)	(99)	earlier	earliest
29.19N, 48.02E		Hawalli	bef 1905	145 (85)	152 (80)	107 (70)	38 (61)				
29.20N, 47.59E	16	*Kuwait	17th c	44 (85)	61 (80) / 182s(80)	80 (70) / 218s(70)	80 (48e)	40 (30?e)	20 (92e)	30 (70e)	

Laos

Coordinates	No.	Place	Founded	(85)	(80)	(70)	(49)	(30)	(99)	earlier	earliest
17.58N,102.36E	558	*Vientiane	bef 1350	377 (85)	210 (81e)	177 (73)	10 (48e)	10 (31)			

Lebanon

Coordinates	No.	Place	Founded	(85)	(80)	(70)	(49)	(30)	(99)	earlier	earliest
33.53N, 35.30E	79	*Beirut	15th c BC?		702 (80e)	475 (70) / 939s(70)	201 (49e)	162 (31)	126 (00e)	12 (50?e)	7 (00?e)
34.26N, 35.51E	26	Tripoli	7th c BC		175 (80)	157 (70)	65 (49e)	37 (31)	29 (00e)	14 (50e)	16 (119e)

For an explanation of symbols and abbreviations, see pages 16–17.

Figure 9. *This prospect of downtown Seoul shows Namsan (South Mountain) with its 500-foot-high Seoul Tower in the background. Seoul, the second largest urbanized area in Asia, will surpass Tokyo in population in 1992 if current growth rates continue. (Credit: Embassy of the Republic of Korea, Washington.)*

TABLE 2a. (Continued)

Latitude and Longitude	Elev (ft)	City	Date Settled	Latest	Population (thousands)						
					ca 1980	ca 1970	ca 1950	ca 1930	ca 1900	ca 1850	ca 1800
Macao											
22.12N,113.32E	66	*Macao	1st c?	420 (86e)	298 (81)	249 (70)	188 (50)	157 (27)	64 (99)	52s(62e)	34s(22e)
Malaysia											
4.35N,101.05E	126	Ipoh	19th c		301 (80)	248 (70)	81 (47)	54 (31)	13 (01)		
1.28N,103.45E	50	Johore Baharu	1855		250 (80)	136 (70)	39 (47)	22 (31)	9 (11)		
6.08N,102.15E	16	Kota Baharu	bef 1839		171 (80)	55 (70)	23 (47)	15 (31)			
5.59N,116.04E	10	Kota Kinabalu	1899		59 (80)	41 (70)	12 (51)	5 (31)	3 (11)		
3.10N,101.42E	127	*Kuala Lumpur	1857		938 (80)	452 (70) 708s(70)	176 (47)	111 (31)	47 (11)		
5.20N,103.08E	115	Kuala Trengganu	2nd c?		187 (80)	53 (70)	27 (47)	14 (31)	14 (11)		
1.33N,110.20E	85	Kuching	1839		74 (80)	64 (70)	38 (47)	25 (30?e)	25 (00?e)		
2.12N,102.15E	23	Malacca	1402?		88 (80)	87 (70)	55 (47)	38 (31)	16 (01)	12 (32e)	12 (00?e)
5.25N,100.20E	17	Penang	1786		251 (80)	269 (70)	189 (47)	149 (31)	94 (01)	10 (50?e)	
Maldives											
4.10N, 73.30E	3	*Male	13th c?	46 (85)	30 (77)	14 (70)	8 (46)	6 (31)	2 (00?e)	2 (75?e)	
Mongolia											
47.55N,106.53E	4295	*Ulan-Bator	1649	470 (84e)	402 (79)	267 (69)	70 (51e)	30 (30?e)	34 (00e)	30 (50?e)	
Nepal											
27.42N, 85.20E	4388	*Kathmandu	723		235 (81)	150 (71)	107 (52)	109 (20)	60 (00e)	35 (50?e)	100 (00)
Oman											
23.37N, 58.35E	20	*Muscat	bef 1508		50 (81)	15 (73e)	4 (50?e)	10 (30?e)	30 (00?e)	20 (72)	15 (00?e)
Pakistan											
29.24N, 71.41E	1260	Bahawalpur	1748		180 (81)	134 (72)	42 (51)	21 (31)	19 (01)	14 (81)	
31.25N, 73.05E	605	Faisalabad	1892		1104 (81)	823 (72)	179 (51)	43 (31)	9 (01)		
32.09N, 74.11E	738	Gujranwala	630?		659 (81)	360 (72)	121 (51)	59 (31)	29 (01)	19 (68)	
25.22N, 68.22E	98	Hyderabad	bef 8th c		752 (81)	629 (72)	242 (51)	102 (31)	69 (01)	43 (72)	15 (00?e)
33.42N, 73.10E	1800	*Islamabad	1961		204 (81)	77 (72)					

For an explanation of symbols and abbreviations, see pages 16–17.

(Continued)

TABLE 2a. (Continued)

Latitude and Longitude	Elev (ft)	City	Date Settled	Population (thousands)							
				Latest	ca 1980	ca 1970	ca 1950	ca 1930	ca 1900	ca 1850	ca 1800
31.16N, 72.19E		Jhang	1462		196 (81)	132 (72)	73 (51)	36 (31)	24 (01)	20 (68)	
24.52N, 67.03E	20	Karachi	1729		5181 (81)	3515 (72)	1068 (51)	248 (31)	109 (01)	57 (72)	15 (30e)
31.35N, 74.18E	702	Lahore	1st c?		2953 (81)	2170 (72)	849 (51)	430 (31)	203 (01)	94 (55)	
30.11N, 71.29E	413	Multan	7th c?		722 (81)	539 (72)	190 (51)	119 (31)	87 (01)	46 (68)	
34.01N, 71.33E	1177	Peshawar	400?		566 (81)	273 (72)	152 (51)	122 (31)	95 (01)	53 (53)	100 (09e)
30.12N, 67.00E	5496	Quetta	11th c?		286 (81)	158 (72)	84 (51)	60 (31)	25 (01)	2 (50?e)	
33.36N, 73.04E	1676	Rawalpindi	bef 1765		795 (81)	615 (72)	237 (51)	119 (31)	88 (01)	19 (68)	
32.05N, 72.40E	614	Sargodha	1903		291 (81)	200 (72)	78 (51)	27 (31)	9 (11)		
32.30N, 74.31E	830	Sialkot	600 BC?		302 (81)	204 (72)	168 (51)	101 (31)	58 (01)	46 (81)	4 (34e)
27.42N, 68.52E	217	Sukkur	13th c?		193 (81)	159 (72)	77 (51)	65 (31)	31 (01)	13 (72)	
Philippines											
15.09N, 120.35E	466	Angeles	1796		189 (80)	135 (70)	38 (48)	26 (39)	11 (03)	10 (77)	5 (53)
10.41N, 122.56E	23	Bacolod	bef 1849		262 (80)	187 (70)	101 (48)	57 (39)	12 (03)	5 (77)	
16.25N, 120.36E	4921	Baguio	bef 1623		119 (80)	85 (70)	29 (48)	24 (39)	0.5(03)	0.7(77)	
8.29N, 124.39E	15	Cagayan de Oro	17th c		227 (80)	128 (70)	52 (48)	48 (39)	7 (03)	6 (77)	
14.38N, 121.03E	138	Caloocan	bef 1815	543 (85e)	468 (80)	274 (70)	55 (48)	39 (39)	6 (03)	8 (77)	
10.18N, 123.54E		Cebu	bef 1521		490 (80)	347 (70)	168 (48)	147 (39)	31 (03)	15 (77)	
7.13N, 124.15E	13	Cotabato	15th c		84 (80)	61 (70)	20 (48)	10 (39)	0.9(03)	0.8(77)	
16.03N, 120.20E	23	Dagupan	1590		98 (80)	84 (70)	44 (48)	33 (39)	20 (03)	16 (77)	
7.04N, 125.36E	63	Davao	1849?		610 (80)	392 (70)	111 (48)	96 (39)	9 (03)	2 (77)	
9.18N, 123.18E	10	Dumaguete	1800?		63 (80)	52 (70)	25 (48)	22 (39)	15 (03)	13 (77)	
10.42N, 122.34E	46	Iloilo	bef 1569		245 (80)	210 (70)	110 (48)	90 (39)	19 (03)	7 (77)	2 (18)
13.08N, 123.44E	20	Legaspi	1639?		100 (80)	84 (70)	79 (48)	42 (39)	9 (03)	6 (77)	
13.56N, 121.37E	26	Lucena	bef 1600		108 (80)	77 (70)	33 (48)	21 (39)	9 (03)	5 (87)	
14.34N, 121.02E		Makati	16th c?		373 (80)	265 (70)	41 (48)	34 (39)	3 (03)	4 (87)	
14.36N, 120.59E	51	*Manila	14th c?	1766 (85e) 6942s(85e)	1630 (80) 5926s(80)	1331 (70) 3967s(70)	984 (48) 1569s(48)	623 (39) 993s(39)	204 (03)	130 (70)	85 (14e)
7.59N, 124.16E	2494	Marawi	17th c?		54 (80)	56 (70)	20 (48)	11 (39)	village		
13.37N, 123.11E	20	Naga	1573		91 (80)	80 (70)	56 (48)	23 (39)	12 (03)	9 (87)	
14.33N, 121.00E		Pasay	bef 1629	332 (85e)	288 (80)	206 (70)	89 (48)	55 (39)	7 (03)	8 (77)	
14.35N, 121.05E		Pasig	bef 1582		269 (80)	156 (70)	35 (48)	28 (39)	11 (03)	16 (77)	

Lat., Long.	Elev. (ft)	City	Founded								
14.38N, 121.00E	232	Quezon City	bef 1903	1378 (85e)	1166 (80)	754 (70)	111 (48)	39 (39)	3 (03)		1 (00?e)
15.01N, 120.41E		San Fernando	1754		111 (80)	84 (70)	40 (48)	36 (39)	14 (03)		17 (77)
11.15N, 125.00E	72	Tacloban	bef 1850		103 (80)	77 (70)	45 (48)	31 (39)	12 (03)		6 (77)
9.39N, 123.51E	69	Tagbilaran	1595?		43 (80)	33 (70)	16 (48)	15 (39)	10 (03)		8 (77)
6.54N, 122.04E	15	Zamboanga	1719		344 (80)	200 (70)	103 (48)	74 (39)	21 (03)		5 (77)
Qatar											
25.17N, 51.32E	33	*Doha	1868	190 (82e)	180 (80e)	95 (71e)	10 (50?e)				
Saudi Arabia											
26.26N, 50.07E		Dammam			150 (80e)	128 (74)	25 (62–63)	village			
21.30N, 39.12E	20	*Jidda	17th c		1308 (81e)	561 (74)	148 (62–63)	40 (30?e)	25 (00e)	22 (50?e)	5 (00?e)
21.27N, 39.49E	853	Mecca	2nd c?		550 (80e)	367 (74)	159 (62–63)	130 (30?e)	60 (00e)	35 (50e)	18 (00?e)
24.28N, 39.36E	1949	Medina	135?		290 (80e)	198 (74)	72 (62–63)	30 (30?e)	44 (00e)	18 (50e)	6 (00?e)
24.38N, 46.43E	1938	*Riyadh	1824?		1000 (81e)	667 (74)	197 (62–63)	30 (30?e)	30 (00?e)	28 (62e)	
21.16N, 40.24E	5348	Taif	bef 7th c		300 (80e)	205 (74)	54 (62–63)	8 (30?e)	8 (00?e)		
Singapore											
1.17N, 103.51E	33	*Singapore	11th c?	2586 (86e)	2414 (80)	2075 (70)	680 (47) / 938s (47)	446 (31) / 560s (31)	193 (01) / 229s (01)		0.2 (00?e)
Sri Lanka											
6.56N, 79.51E	24	*Colombo	543 BC?	643 (84e)	586 (81)	562 (71)	426 (53)	284 (31)	155 (01)	100 (71)	50 (04e)
6.51N, 79.52E		Dehiwala-Mount Lavinia	1824	184 (84e)	174 (81)	154 (71)	78 (53)	34 (31)	18 (11)		
9.40N, 80.00E	10	Jaffna	bef 204 BC	133 (84e)	118 (81)	107 (71)	77 (53)	46 (31)	34 (01)	35 (71)	
6.18N, 80.38E	1572	Kandy	13th c?	120 (84e)	101 (81)	94 (71)	57 (53)	37 (31)	26 (01)	6 (50?e)	3 (19)
Syria											
36.10N, 37.10E	1243	Aleppo	bef 1000 BC	1145 (85e)	985 (81)	639 (70)	425 (60)	249 (31)	117 (00e)	100 (50?e)	200 (00?e)
33.30N, 36.18E	2320	*Damascus	bef 14th c BC	1197 (85e)	1112 (81)	837 (70)	530 (60)	229 (31)	165 (00e)	150 (50?e)	130 (00?e)
35.09N, 36.44E	919	Hama	3rd c BC?	194 (85e)	177 (81)	137 (70)	97 (60)	40 (31)	45 (00e)	40 (50?e)	85 (00?e)
34.44N, 36.43E	1667	Homs	1st c?	409 (85e)	347 (81)	215 (70)	137 (60)	53 (31)	48 (00e)	27 (50e)	25 (00?e)
35.31N, 35.47E	39	Latakia	bef 3rd c BC	230 (85e)	197 (81)	126 (70)	68 (60)	21 (29)	17 (00?e)	7 (50?e)	10 (00?e)
Taiwan											
24.05N, 120.32E	148	Changhwa	17th c	201 (85e)	181 (80)	137 (70)	85 (56)	54 (35)	16 (11)		
23.29N, 120.27E	102	Chiayi	17th c	254 (85e)	252 (80)	239 (70)	86 (50)	58 (30)	20 (01)		
25.00N, 121.29E		Chungho		325 (85e)	262 (80)	72 (70)					
24.57N, 121.13E	591	Chungli		237 (85e)	208 (80)	130 (70)	60 (56)	6 (35)			

For an explanation of symbols and abbreviations, see pages 16–17.

(Continued)

TABLE 2a. (Continued)

Latitude and Longitude	Elev (ft)	City	Date Settled	Population (thousands)							
				Latest	ca 1980	ca 1970	ca 1950	ca 1930	ca 1900	ca 1850	ca 1800
22.38N,120.21E	49	Fengshan		267 (85e)	218 (80)	102 (70)	47 (56)	11 (35)	6 (04)		
24.48N,120.58E	108	Hsinchu	bef 1731	304 (85e)	241 (80)	208 (70)	125 (50)	44 (30)	19 (01)		
25.02N,121.26E		Hsinchuang	1732	232 (85e)	178 (80)	49 (70)		6 (35)			
24.57N,121.32E		Hsintien		191 (85e)	166 (80)	95 (70)	42 (56)				
22.38N,120.17E	95	Kaohsiung	bef 1864	1303 (85e)	1220 (80)	827 (70)	268 (50)	63 (30)	14 (11)		
25.08N,121.44E	10	Keelung	1626?	352 (85e)	347 (80)	324 (70)	145 (50)	75 (30)	13 (01)		
25.01N,121.27E		Panchiao		480 (85e)	403 (80)	115 (70)	38 (55e)	5 (35)			
22.40N,120.29E		Pingtung		200 (85e)	187 (80)	165 (70)	103 (56)	46 (35)			
25.04N,121.29E		Shanchung		354 (85e)	327 (80)	236 (70)	66 (55e)				
24.09N,120.41E	253	Taichung	18th c	675 (85e)	607 (80)	448 (70)	200 (50)	54 (30)	8 (05)		
23.00N,120.12E	43	Tainan	1590	640 (85e)	582 (80)	475 (70)	221 (50)	95 (30)	48 (01)	90 (69e)	
25.03N,121.30E	26	*Taipei	1708	2508 (85e)	2268 (80)	1772 (70)	503 (50)	230 (30)	79 (01)		
24.59N,121.19E	157	Taoyuan		205 (85e)	179 (80)	106 (70)	53 (56)	8 (35)			
25.01N,121.31E	49	Yungho		233 (85e)	205 (80)	89 (70)	39 (60)				
Thailand											
13.45N,100.31E	26	*Bangkok	1782	5018 (83e)	4697 (80)	1867 (70)	605 (47)	685 (29)	587 (11)	160 (49)	35 (00?e)
18.47N,98.59E	1099	Chiang Mai	7th c?	105 (83e)	102 (80)	84 (70)	38 (47)	20 (29?)	20 (00?e)		
16.26N,102.50E	515	Khon Kaen	bef 1809	108 (83e)	86 (80)	29 (70)	10 (47)				
7.12N,100.36E	13	Songkhla	1390?	78 (83e)	68 (80)	41 (70)	18 (47)				
Turkey											
37.01N, 35.18E	66	Adana	8th c BC?	776 (85)	575 (80)	347 (70)	118 (50)	73 (27)	47 (00e)	20 (50?e)	30 (00?e)
40.46N, 30.24E	102	Adapazari	1540	155 (85)	131 (80)	101 (70)	36 (50)	23 (27)	18 (00?e)		
39.56N, 32.52E	2933	*Ankara	17th c BC?	2252 (85)	1878 (80)	1236 (70)	289 (50)	75 (27)	32 (00e)	20 (50?e)	20 (00?e)
36.53N, 30.42E	138	Antalya	150 BC?	258 (85)	174 (80)	96 (70)	28 (50)	17 (27)	25 (00e)	10 (50?e)	8 (00?e)
36.14N, 36.07E	328	Antioch	300 BC?	109 (85)	95 (80)	67 (70)	30 (50)	19 (27)	28 (00e)	20 (50e)	18 (00?e)
40.11N, 29.04E	328	Bursa	3rd c BC	614 (85)	445 (80)	276 (70)	104 (50)	62 (27)	76 (00e)	65 (50?e)	60 (02e)
37.55N, 40.14E	2165	Diyarbakir	bef 230	305 (85)	236 (80)	150 (70)	45 (50)	32 (27)	36 (00e)	27 (56)	38 (10e)
38.41N, 39.14E	3347	Elazig	1834	182 (85)	143 (80)	107 (70)	29 (50)	20 (27)	5 (00?e)		
39.55N, 41.17E	6132	Erzurum	420?	253 (85)	190 (80)	133 (70)	53 (50)	31 (27)	43 (00e)	40 (44e)	24 (00e)
39.46N, 30.32E	2625	Eskisehir	3rd c?	367 (85)	309 (80)	216 (70)	90 (50)	32 (27)	19 (00?e)	village	
37.05N, 37.22E	2805	Gaziantep	3650 BC?	466 (85)	374 (80)	228 (70)	72 (50)	40 (27)	43 (00?e)	20 (50?e)	20 (00?e)

Lat/Long	Elev	Name	Founded								
38.25N, 27.09E	82	Izmir	11th c BC?	1490 (85)	758 (80)	521 (70)	228 (50)	154 (27)	196 (00e)	140 (51e)	120 (14e)
40.46N, 29.55E	253	Izmit	264 BC	236 (85)	190 (80)	121 (70)	36 (50)	15 (27)	22 (00e)	15 (73e)	
37.36N, 36.55E	2362	Kahramanmaras	12th c BC?	212 (85)	179 (80)	111 (70)	35 (50)	26 (27)	35 (00?e)	10 (70?e)	25 (00?e)
38.43N, 35.30E	3504	Kayseri	4th c	378 (85)	281 (80)	161 (70)	65 (50)	39 (27)	72 (00e)	18 (49)	30 (00?e)
37.52N, 32.31E	3373	Konya	2600 BC?	439 (85)	329 (80)	200 (70)	64 (50)	48 (27)	44 (00e)	25 (50?e)	
38.21N, 38.19E	3274	Malatya	1113 BC?	251 (85)	179 (80)	129 (70)	49 (50)	21 (27)	30 (00e)	13 (79e)	
36.48N, 34.38E	20	Mersin	50 BC?	314 (85)	216 (80)	113 (70)	36 (50)	21 (27)	12 (00e)		2 (00e)
41.17N, 36.20E	144	Samsun	6th c BC	280 (85)	199 (80)	134 (70)	44 (50)	30 (27)	11 (00e)	2 (50?e)	20 (00?e)
37.08N, 38.46E	1772	Sanliurfa	3rd c BC	207 (85)	148 (80)	101 (70)	39 (50)	29 (27)	55 (00?e)	40 (50?e)	
39.45N, 37.02E	4183	Sivas	3rd c?	197 (85)	173 (80)	134 (70)	52 (50)	28 (27)	43 (00?e)	31 (50?e)	15 (00?e)
41.00N, 39.43E	98	Trebizond	756 BC?	156 (85)	108 (80)	81 (70)	34 (50)	25 (27)	35 (05e)	27 (50?e)	50 (00?e)
38.30N, 43.23E	5659	Van	8th c BC?	121 (85)	93 (80)	47 (70)	14 (50)	7 (27)	28 (00?e)	18 (50?e)	

United Arab Emirates

Lat/Long	Elev	Name	Founded								
24.28N, 54.22E		*Abu Zaby	1761		243 (80)	22 (68)	6 (50?e)	5 (30?e)	6 (00?e)		
25.18N, 55.18E	49	Dubayy	1799?		266 (80)	57 (68)	20 (50?e)		8 (00?e)		

USSR

Lat/Long	Elev	Name	Founded								
50.17N, 57.10E	719	Aktyubinsk	1869	231 (85e)	191 (79)	150 (70)	97 (59)	21 (26)	3 (97)		
43.15N, 76.57E	2779	Alma-Ata	1854	1068 (85e)	910 (79)	730 (70)	456 (59)	45 (26)	23 (97)	10 (67)	150 (32e)
40.45N, 72.22E	1565	Andizhan	9th c	275 (85e)	230 (79)	188 (70)	131 (59)	73 (26)	48 (97)		2 (11)
52.34N,103.54E	1368	Angarsk	1948	256 (85e)	239 (79)	203 (70)	135 (59)	10 (51e)			
37.57N, 58.23E	745	Ashkhabad	1881	356 (85e)	312 (79)	253 (70)	170 (59)	52 (26)	19 (97)		
53.22N, 83.45E	518	Barnaul	1738	578 (85e)	533 (79)	439 (70)	303 (59)	74 (26)	21 (97)	11 (56)	
52.34N, 85.15E	745	Biysk	1709	226 (85e)	212 (79)	186 (70)	146 (59)	46 (26)	17 (97)	3 (56)	7 (82)
50.16N,127.32E	427	Blagoveshchensk	1856	195 (85e)	186 (79)	128 (70)	94 (59)	61 (26)	33 (97)	3 (67)	2 (11)
56.21N,101.55E	1243	Bratsk	1631	240 (85e)	214 (79)	155 (70)	43 (59)	2 (56e)			
39.48N, 64.25E	738	Bukhara	630?	209 (85e)	185 (79)	112 (70)	69 (59)	47 (26)	65 (00e)	70 (66e)	
55.10N, 61.24E	758	Chelyabinsk	1736	1096 (85e)	1030 (79)	875 (70)	689 (59)	59 (26)	20 (97)	4 (56)	
42.18N, 69.36E	1782	Chimkent	8th c?	369 (85e)	322 (79)	247 (70)	153 (59)	21 (26)	11 (97)	4 (67)	
52.03N,113.30E	2202	Chita	1653	336 (85e)	303 (79)	241 (70)	172 (59)	62 (26)	12 (97)	0.9(56)	
38.33N, 68.48E	2697	Dushanbe	bef 1922	552 (85e)	494 (79)	374 (70)	227 (59)	6 (26)			
42.54N, 71.22E	2106	Dzhambul	18th c	303 (85e)	264 (79)	187 (70)	113 (59)	25 (26)	12 (97)	1 (67)	
40.23N, 71.46E	1903	Fergana	1877	195 (85e)	176 (79)	111 (70)	72 (59)	14 (26)	9 (97)		
42.54N, 74.36E	2480	Frunze	1825	604 (85e)	533 (79)	431 (70)	220 (59)	37 (26)	7 (97)		
52.16N,104.20E	1536	Irkutsk	1669	597 (85e)	550 (79)	451 (70)	366 (59)	99 (26)	51 (97)	24 (56)	
56.25N, 61.54E		Kamensk-Uralskiy	1682	200 (85e)	187 (79)	169 (70)	141 (59)	5 (26)	6 (97)	5 (67?e)	13 (11)

(Continued)

For an explanation of symbols and abbreviations, see pages 16–17.

TABLE 2a. (Continued)

Latitude and Longitude	City	Elev (ft)	Date Settled	Population (thousands)							
				Latest	ca 1980	ca 1970	ca 1950	ca 1930	ca 1900	ca 1850	ca 1800
49.50N, 73.10E	Karaganda	1804	1857	617 (85e)	572 (79)	523 (70)	383 (59)	0.1(26)			
55.20N, 86.05E	Kemerovo	505	1720	507 (85e)	471 (79)	385 (70)	289 (59)	22 (26)	6 (20)	0.3(60?)	
48.30N,135.06E	Khabarovsk	285	1858	576 (85e)	528 (79)	436 (70)	323 (59)	50 (26)	15 (97)	1 (67?e)	
40.30N, 70.57E	Kokand	1339	10th c?	166 (85e)	153 (79)	133 (70)	105 (59)	69 (26)	81 (97)	45 (50e)	60 (00?e)
50.35N,137.02E	Komsomolsk-na-Amure	66	1858	300 (85e)	264 (79)	218 (70)	177 (59)	71 (39)	village		
56.01N, 92.50E	Krasnoyarsk	637	1628	872 (85e)	796 (79)	648 (70)	412 (59)	72 (26)	27 (97)	6 (56)	3 (11)
55.26N, 65.18E	Kurgan	259	1553	343 (85e)	310 (79)	244 (70)	146 (59)	28 (26)	10 (97)	3 (56)	0.7(11)
53.10N, 63.35E	Kustanay	558	1883	199 (85e)	165 (79)	124 (70)	86 (59)	25 (26)	14 (97)		
44.48N, 65.28E	Kzyl-Orda	1362	1820?	183 (85e)	156 (79)	122 (70)	66 (59)	23 (26)	5 (97)	3 (75?)	
53.27N, 59.04E	Magnitogorsk	1263	1929	422 (85e)	406 (79)	364 (70)	311 (59)	146 (39)			
41.00N, 71.40E	Namangan	1555	1610	275 (85e)	227 (79)	175 (70)	123 (59)	74 (26)	62 (97)		
60.56N, 76.38E	Nizhnevartovsk		1965?	190 (85e)	109 (79)	16 (70)					
57.55N, 59.57E	Nizhniy Tagil	732	1725	419 (85e)	398 (79)	378 (70)	338 (59)	39 (26)	31 (97)	2 (63)	
69.20N, 88.06E	Norilsk	217	1935	180 (85e)	180 (79)	135 (70)	118 (59)	14 (39)			
53.45N, 87.06E	Novokuznetsk	771	1617	577 (85e)	541 (79)	499 (70)	382 (59)	4 (26)	3 (97)	2 (56)	
55.02N, 82.55E	Novosibirsk	446	1893	1393 (85e)	1312 (79)	1161 (70)	885 (59)	121 (26)	8 (97)		
42.29N, 59.38E	Nukus	256	1860s	139 (85e)	109 (79)	74 (70)	39 (59)	10 (39)	village		
55.00N, 73.24E	Omsk	410	1716	1108 (85e)	1014 (79)	821 (70)	581 (59)	162 (26)	37 (97)	16 (56)	5 (11)
40.32N, 72.48E	Osh	3324	9th c?	199 (85e)	169 (79)	120 (70)	65 (59)	31 (26)	34 (97)		
52.18N, 76.57E	Pavlodar	387	1720	315 (85e)	273 (79)	187 (70)	90 (59)	18 (26)	8 (97)	0.2(63)	
54.52N, 69.06E	Petropavlovsk	440	1752	226 (85e)	207 (79)	173 (70)	131 (59)	47 (26)	20 (97)	7 (56)	
53.01N,158.39E	Petropavlovsk-Kamchatskiy	105	1740	245 (85e)	215 (79)	154 (70)	86 (59)	2 (26)	0.4(97)	2 (56)	
53.53N, 86.45E	Prokopyevsk	715	18th c	274 (85e)	266 (79)	274 (70)	282 (59)	11 (26)			
51.30N, 81.15E	Rubtsovsk		1888	165 (85e)	157 (79)	145 (70)	111 (59)	16 (26)			
39.40N, 66.58E	Samarkand	2382	4th c BC?	371 (85e)	477 (79)	267 (70)	196 (59)	105 (26)	55 (97)	18 (50e)	
50.28N, 80.13E	Semipalatinsk	663	1718	317 (85e)	283 (79)	236 (70)	156 (59)	57 (26)	26 (97)	7 (56)	3 (11)
61.13N, 73.20E	Surgut	141	1593	203 (85e)	107 (79)	34 (70)	6 (59)	2 (48e)	village		
56.51N, 60.36E	Sverdlovsk	925	1721	1300 (85e)	1211 (79)	1025 (70)	779 (59)	136 (26)	43 (97)	17 (56)	4 (11)
41.20N, 69.18E	Tashkent	1565	7th c	2030 (85e)	1780 (79)	1385 (70)	927 (59)	324 (26)	156 (97)	64 (67)	30 (00?e)

(Continued)

Population figures are given in thousands, with the year of the figure in parentheses.

Coordinates	Elev.	Place	Founded	Pop.	Pop.	Pop.	Pop.	Pop.	Pop.	Pop.	Pop.
50.05N, 72.56E		Temirtau	1930	225 (85e)	213 (79)	166 (70)	77 (59)	5 (39)			
56.30N, 84.58E	456	Tomsk	1604	475 (85e)	421 (79)	338 (70)	249 (59)	92 (26)	52 (97)	20 (56)	9 (11)
51.10N, 71.30E	1139	Tselinograd	1830	262 (85e)	234 (79)	180 (70)	99 (59)	13 (26)	10 (97)	5 (62)	
57.09N, 65.26E	249	Tyumen	1586	425 (85e)	359 (79)	269 (70)	150 (59)	50 (26)	30 (97)	11 (56)	9 (11)
51.50N, 107.37E	1686	Ulan-Ude	1666	335 (85e)	300 (79)	254 (70)	174 (59)	29 (26)	8 (97)	3 (56)	
51.14N, 51.22E	115	Uralsk	1617?	192 (85e)	167 (79)	134 (70)	99 (59)	36 (26)	36 (97)	11 (56)	2 (11)
49.58N, 82.40E	932	Ust-Kamenogorsk	1720	307 (85e)	274 (79)	230 (70)	150 (59)	14 (26)	9 (97)	2 (56)	
43.08N, 131.54E	364	Vladivostok	1860	600 (85e)	550 (79)	441 (70)	291 (59)	108 (26)	29 (97)	0.5 (73)	2 (82)
62.00N, 129.40E	338	Yakutsk	1632	180 (85e)	152 (79)	108 (70)	74 (59)	11 (26)	7 (91)	6 (63)	3 (00?e)
46.57N, 142.44E	72	Yuzhno-Sakhalinsk	1881	158 (85e)	140 (79)	106 (70)	86 (59)	25 (30)			
55.10N, 59.40E	1503	Zlatoust	1754	204 (85e)	198 (79)	180 (70)	161 (59)	48 (26)	21 (97)	10 (61)	
Vietnam											
10.57N, 106.49E	36	Bien Hoa	1680?		190 (79)	178 (71e)	21 (52e)	17 (36)	19 (01?)	70 (50?e)	40 (00?e)
10.02N, 105.47E	10	Can Tho	18th c?		183 (79)	154 (71e)	71 (52e)	17 (36)	14 (01?)	110 (50e)	35 (00?e)
16.04N, 108.13E	20	Da Nang	17th c?		319 (79)	428 (70e)	51 (43)	6 (26)	7 (11)	60 (50?e)	30 (22e)
20.52N, 106.41E	381	Haiphong	bef 1882		331 (79) / 1279s (79)	200 (66e) / 650s (71e)	143 (48e)	70 (36)	16 (00)		
21.02N, 105.51E	56	*Hanoi	599		820 (79) / 2571s (79)	415 (60) / 644s (60)	237 (48e)	149 (36)	103 (00)		
10.45N, 106.40E	30	Ho Chi Minh City	bef 17th c		2441 (79) / 3420s (79)	1761 (70e)	1179 (58e)	256 (36)	160 (00)		
16.28N, 107.36E	49	Hue	200 BC?		166 (79)	209 (69e)	96 (53e)	61 (21)	50 (00)		
12.15N, 109.11E	20	Nha Trang	3rd c?		173 (79)	103 (69e)	25 (53e)	15 (36)			
West Bank											
31.43N, 35.12E	2250	Bethlehem	bef 1000 BC	22 (84e)	22 (80e)	16 (67)	9 (46e)	7 (31)	6 (00?)	5 (50?e)	
31.32N, 35.06E	2040	Hebron	18th c BC?	75 (84e)		38 (67)	36 (52)	18 (31)	15 (00?e)		
31.52N, 35.27E	-905	Jericho	1st c BC?		13 (80e)	7 (67)	10 (61)	0.3 (30?e)	village		
32.13N, 35.16E	1903	Nabulus	19th c BC?	80 (84e)		44 (67)	42 (52)	17 (31)	25 (00?e)	8 (50?e)	
Yemen: North											
14.48N, 42.57E	39	Hudaydah	bef 1822		126 (81)	92 (73e)	26 (48e)	35 (30?e)	45 (00?e)		
15.23N, 44.12E	7260	*Sana	bef 530		278 (81)	89 (72)	28 (48e)	22 (30?e)	59 (00e)	40 (50?e)	
Yemen: South											
12.46N, 45.01E	12	*Aden	3rd c BC?		365 (81e)	264 (73)	57 (46)	32 (31)	23 (01e)	16 (42)	

For an explanation of symbols and abbreviations, see pages 16–17.

TABLE 2a. (Continued)

Latitude and Longitude	Elev (ft)	City	Date Settled	Latest	ca 1980	ca 1970	ca 1950	ca 1930	ca 1900	ca 1850	ca 1800
							Population (thousands)				
EUROPE											
Albania											
41.20N, 19.50E	416	*Tirane	1604	211 (84)	190 (79)	171 (70e)	60 (45)	31 (30)	12 (05e)	10 (50?e)	2 (00?e)
Austria											
47.04N, 15.27E	1237	Graz	881?	243 (81)	248 (71)	226 (51)	153 (34)	138 (00)	55 (51)	30 (10)	54 (00)
47.16N, 11.24E	1909	Innsbruck	1170	117 (81)	115 (71)	95 (51)	61 (34)	27 (00)	13 (51)	9 (08e)	31 (96)
46.38N, 14.20E	1463	Klagenfurt	1193?	86 (81)	74 (71)	63 (51)	30 (34)	24 (00)	14 (51)	11 (00?e)	66 (00)
48.18N, 14.18E	853	Linz	1st c	200 (81)	203 (71)	185 (51)	109 (34)	59 (00)	27 (51)	16 (1784)	70s(00)
47.48N, 13.02E	1427	Salzburg	7th c?	139 (81)	129 (71)	103 (51)	40 (34)	33 (00)	17 (51)	13 (11)	4(00?)
48.12N, 16.22E	663	*Vienna	4th c BC?	1531 (81)	1615 (81)	1766 (51)	1875 (34)	1675 (00)	431 (51)	231 (00)	
Belgium											
51.13N, 4.25E	16	Antwerp	660?	488 (84e)	186 (81)	225 (70)	270 (47)	291 (30)	283 (00)	88 (46)	54 (00)
						671s(70)	597s(47)	582s(30)	406s(00)		
51.13N, 3.14E	39	Bruges	865	118 (84e)	118 (81)	117 (70)	53 (47)	51 (30)	52 (00)	49 (46)	31 (96)
50.50N, 4.20E	328	*Brussels	6th c?	137 (84e)	140 (81)	161 (70)	185 (47)	200 (30)	219 (00)	124 (46)	66 (00)
				982s(84e)	997s(81)	1075s(70)	956s(47)	892s(30)	626s(00)	212s(46)	70s(00)
50.25N, 4.26E	341	Charleroi	bef 1665	213 (84e)	222 (81)	24 (70)	26 (47)	29 (30)	24 (00)	7 (46)	4(00?)
						214s(70)	209s(47)				
51.03N, 3.43E	23	Ghent	7th c	235 (84e)	239 (81)	149 (70)	166 (47)	170 (30)	160 (00)	103 (46)	55 (00)
						225s(70)	228s(47)	226s(30)	203s(00)		
50.38N, 5.34E	377	Liege	558?	203 (84e)	214 (81)	146 (70)	156 (47)	166 (30)	158 (00)	76 (46)	43 (00)
						441s(70)	425s(47)	427s(30)	355s(00)		
50.53N, 4.42E	80	Louvain	9th c	85 (84e)	85 (81)	31 (70)	37 (47)	39 (30)	42 (00)	30 (46)	19 (00)
51.02N, 4.28E	23	Mechelen	bef 1333	77 (84e)	77 (81)	65 (70)	60 (47)	60 (30)	56 (00)	30 (46)	16 (01?)
50.27N, 3.56E	220	Mons	642?	91 (84e)	96 (81)	28 (70)	26 (47)	28 (30)	27 (00)	24 (46)	18 (02)
50.28N, 4.52E	482	Namur	7th c?	102 (84e)	102 (81)	32 (70)	31 (47)	31 (30)	31 (00)	22 (46)	15 (02)
51.13N, 2.55E	13	Ostend	4th c	69 (84e)	70 (81)	71 (70)	50 (47)	47 (30)	39 (00)	14 (46)	10 (02)
Bulgaria											
42.30N, 27.28E	16	Burgas	18th c	183 (85)	144 (75)	106 (65)	44 (46)	31 (26)	12 (00)	6 (50?e)	19 (00)
42.09N, 24.45E	525	Plovdiv	341 BC?	342 (85)	300 (75)	223 (65)	125 (46)	85 (26)	43 (00)	30 (50?e)	30 (17e)

Coordinates	No.	Name	Founded								
43.50N, 25.57E	151	Ruse	17th c	184 (85)	160 (75)	129 (65)	54 (46)	46 (26)	33 (00)	30 (50?e)	24 (00?e)
42.41N, 23.19E	1850	*Sofia	100?	1115 (85)	966 (75) 1065s(75)	801 (65) 894s(65)	435 (46)	213 (26)	68 (00)	43 (62e)	46 (00?e)
42.25N, 25.38E	768	Stara Zagora	6th c BC?	151 (85)	122 (75)	89 (65)	37 (46)	29 (26)	20 (00)	20 (60?e)	20 (00?e)
43.13N, 27.55E	157	Varna	6th c BC	302 (85)	252 (75)	180 (65)	78 (46)	61 (26)	33 (00)	18 (50?e)	16 (00?e)
43.04N, 25.39E	735	Veliko Turnovo	bef 1186	70 (85)	48 (75)	37 (65)	16 (46)	13 (26)	12 (05)	12 (50?e)	6 (00?e)
Channel Islands											
49.11N, 2.06W	30	Saint Helier	11th c?		25 (81)	28 (71)	25 (51)	26 (31)	28 (01)	29 (51)	6 (06)
49.27N, 2.32W	60	Saint Peter Port	13th c?		16 (76)	16 (71)	17 (51)	17 (31)	18 (01)	17 (51)	11 (21)
Czechoslovakia											
48.09N, 17.07E	538	Bratislava	892?	409 (85e)	381 (80)	284 (70)	193 (50)	124 (30)	62 (00)	42 (51)	21 (05)
49.11N, 16.37E	745	Brno	9th c	383 (85e)	371 (80)	336 (70)	285 (50)	264 (30)	109 (00)	47 (51)	23 (04)
50.14N, 12.53E	1263	Karlovy Vary	1349	59 (85e)	61 (80)	44 (70)	36 (50)	24 (30)	15 (00)	3 (51)	2 (02)
48.44N, 21.15E	676	Kosice	1235	218 (85e)	203 (80)	145 (70)	63 (50)	70 (30)	36 (00)	13 (51)	12 (00?e)
49.05N, 18.55E	1309	Martin	13th c	61 (85e)	56 (80)	43 (70)	24 (50)	18 (30)	10 (00)	5 (69)	
49.36N, 17.16E	722	Olomouc	11th c	106 (85e)	102 (80)	80 (70)	64 (50)	66 (30)	22 (00)	13 (45)	9 (08)
49.51N, 18.18E	712	Ostrava	1267	325 (85e)	322 (80)	279 (70)	189 (50)	125 (30)	30 (00)	4 (57)	0.8(00?e)
49.45N, 13.25E	1161	Plzen	976?	175 (85e)	171 (80)	148 (70)	124 (50)	114 (30)	68 (00)	11 (51)	5 (01)
50.04N, 14.27E	633	*Prague	9th c?	1190 (85e)	1182 (80)	1078 (70)	932 (50)	848 (30)	202 (00)	118 (51)	77 (00)
Denmark											
57.03N, 9.56E	10	Alborg	11th c?	114 (84e) 146s(84e)	115 (79) 145s(79)	100 (70) 143s(70)	80 (50) 88s(50)	44 (30)	31 (01)	10 (60)	6 (01)
56.09N, 10.13E	161	Arhus	10th c?	194 (84e) 241s(84e)	183 (79) 232s(79)	199 (70) 224s(70)	116 (50) 151s(50)	81 (30)	52 (01)	8 (50)	4 (01)
55.40N, 12.35E	16	*Copenhagen	1043?	483 (84e) 1366s(84e)	506 (79) 1396s(79)	623 (70) 1380s(70)	768 (50) 1168s(50)	617 (30) 771s(30)	378 (01) 477s(01)	130 (50)	101 (01)
55.24N, 10.23E	49	Odense	10th c	137 (84e) 163s(84e)	136 (79) 159s(79)	137 (70) 155s(70)	101 (50)	57 (30)	40 (01)	11 (51)	6 (01)
Faeroe Islands											
62.01N, 6.46W	79	*Torshavn	16th c?	13 (84e)	12 (77)	10 (70)	6 (50)	3 (30)	2 (01)	0.7 (51?)	0.6 (00?e)

For an explanation of symbols and abbreviations, see pages 16–17.

(Continued)

TABLE 2a. (Continued)

City	Latitude and Longitude	Elev (ft)	Date Settled	Latest	ca 1980	ca 1970	ca 1950	ca 1930	ca 1900	ca 1850	ca 1800
Finland											
*Helsinki	60.10N, 24.58E	39	1550	484 (84e) / 938s(84e)	483 (80) / 901s(80)	510 (70) / 827s(70)	369 (50) / 414s(50)	244 (30)	91 (00)	21 (50)	9 (00)
Joensuu	62.36N, 29.45E	394	1848	46 (84e)	45 (80)	36 (70)	8 (50)	5 (30)	4 (00)	0.1 (50)	
Jyvaskyla	62.14N, 25.44E	282	1837	65 (84e)	64 (80)	57 (70)	31 (50)	8 (30)	3 (00)	0.6 (50)	
Kuopio	62.54N, 27.41E	390	1782	77 (84e)	75 (80)	64 (70)	33 (50)	24 (30)	12 (00)	3 (50)	1 (15)
Oulu	65.01N, 25.28E	33	1375?	97 (84e)	94 (80)	85 (70)	38 (50)	24 (30)	15 (00)	6 (50)	3 (00)
Tampere	61.30N, 23.45E	312	1779	168 (84e) / 251s(84e)	166 (80) / 244s(80)	155 (70)	101 (50)	56 (30)	36 (00)	3 (50)	0.5 (00)
Turku	60.27N, 22.17E	52	12th c?	162 (84e) / 257s(84e)	164 (80) / 241s(80)	152 (70)	102 (50)	67 (30)	38 (00)	17 (50)	10 (00)
Vaasa	63.06N, 21.36E	13	1606	54 (84e)	54 (80)	48 (70)	35 (50)	24 (30)	15 (00)	4 (50)	3 (15)
France											
Aix-en-Provence	43.32N, 5.26E	705	123 BC	121 (82) / 127s(82)	111 (75)	90 (68)	54 (54)	38 (31)	29 (01)	27 (51)	24 (01)
Ajaccio	41.55N, 8.44E	125	7th c	54 (82)	51 (75)	42 (68)	33 (54)	24 (31)	22 (01)	12 (51)	6 (01)
Amiens	49.54N, 2.18E	118	54 BC?	131 (82) / 154s(82)	131 (75) / 153s(75)	118 (68) / 137s(68)	93 (54) / 94s(54)	90 (31)	91 (01)	52 (51)	40 (01)
Angers	47.28N, 0.33W	154	3rd c?	136 (82) / 196s(82)	138 (75) / 181s(75)	129 (68) / 163s(68)	102 (54)	86 (31)	82 (01)	47 (51)	33 (01)
Avignon	43.57N, 4.49E	180	2nd c BC?	89 (82) / 174s(82)	91 (75) / 154s(75)	86 (68) / 139s(68)	63 (54)	57 (31)	47 (01)	36 (51)	21 (01)
Besancon	47.15N, 6.02E	1207	6th c BC?	113 (82) / 121s(82)	120 (75) / 124s(75)	113 (68) / 116s(68)	73 (54)	60 (31)	55 (01)	41 (51)	30 (01)
Bethune	50.32N, 2.38E	92	11th c	26 (82) / 258s(82)	27 (75) / 145s(75)	27 (68) / 145s(68)	22 (54)	20 (31)	12 (01)	8 (51)	5 (01)
Biarritz	43.29N, 1.34W	226	12th c	27 (82)	28 (75)	27 (68)	23 (54)	23 (31)	11 (01)	2 (51)	
Bordeaux	44.50N, 0.34W	23	3rd c BC	208 (82) / 640s(82)	223 (75) / 594s(75)	267 (68) / 555s(68)	258 (54) / 416s(54)	263 (31)	257 (01)	131 (51)	91 (01)
Brest	48.24N, 4.29W	322	3rd c?	156 (82) / 201s(82)	167 (75) / 190s(75)	154 (68) / 169s(68)	111 (54)	70 (31)	84 (01)	61 (51)	27 (01)
Caen	49.11N, 0.21W	85	9th c?	114 (82) / 184s(82)	119 (75) / 183s(75)	110 (68) / 152s(68)	68 (54) / 75s(54)	58 (31)	45 (01)	45 (51)	31 (01)
Calais	50.57N, 1.50E	7	7th c	77 (82) / 101s(82)	79 (75) / 100s(75)	75 (68) / 94s(68)	60 (54)	70 (31)	60 (01)	11 (51)	7 (01?)

					(82)	(75)	(68)	(54)	(31)	(01)	(51)	(01)
43.33N,	7.01E	10	Cannes	8th c BC?	72 (82) / 296s(82)	71 (75) / 255s(75)	67 (68) / 213s(68)	50 (54) / 62s(54)	47 (31)	30 (01)	6 (51)	3 (01)
45.34N,	5.56E	883	Chambery	1016?	53 (82) / 96s(82)	57 (75) / 88s(75)	51 (68) / 75s(68)	32 (54)	25 (31)	21 (01)	16 (48)	10 (01)
48.27N,	1.30E	518	Chartres	6th c BC?	37 (82)	39 (75)	34 (68)	29 (54)	25 (31)	19 (01)	18 (51)	10 (89)
49.39N,	1.39W	43	Cherbourg	1st c BC?	28 (82) / 85s(82)	33 (75) / 83s(75)	38 (68) / 79s(68)	38 (54)	37 (31)	43 (01)	28 (51)	11 (89)
45.47N,	3.05E	1335	Clermont-Ferrand	20 BC?	147 (82) / 256s(82)	157 (75) / 229s(75)	149 (68) / 205s(68)	113 (54) / 138s(54)	103 (31)	53 (01)	34 (51)	24 (01)
47.19N,	5.01E	1109	Dijon	bef 273	141 (82) / 216s(82)	152 (75) / 208s(75)	145 (68) / 184s(68)	113 (54) / 117s(54)	91 (31)	71 (01)	32 (51)	21 (01)
50.22N,	3.04E	79	Douai	7th c?	43 (82) / 202s(82)	45 (75) / 203s(75)	49 (68) / 205s(68)	43 (54) / 47s(54)	42 (31)	34 (01)	21 (51)	18 (01)
51.03N,	2.22E	26	Dunkerque	7th c?	74 (82) / 196s(82)	83 (75) / 165s(75)	28 (68) / 143s(68)	21 (54) / 88s(54)	32 (31)	39 (01)	29 (51)	21 (01)
45.10N,	5.43E	810	Grenoble	1st c BC?	157 (82) / 392s(82)	166 (75) / 392s(75)	162 (68) / 332s(68)	116 (54) / 147s(54)	91 (31)	69 (01)	31 (51)	23 (01)
46.10N,	1.09W	26	La Rochelle	1023?	76 (82) / 102s(82)	75 (75) / 95s(75)	73 (68) / 88s(68)	59 (54)	45 (31)	26 (01)	17 (51)	18 (01)
49.30N,	0.08E	16	Le Havre	1517	199 (82) / 255s(82)	218 (75) / 265s(75)	200 (68) / 247s(68)	140 (54) / 173s(54)	165 (31)	130 (01)	29 (51)	16 (01)
48.00N,	0.12E	253	Le Mans	5th c BC?	148 (82) / 191s(82)	152 (75) / 188s(75)	143 (68) / 166s(68)	112 (54) / 113s(54)	77 (31)	63 (01)	27 (51)	17 (01)
50.26N,	2.50E	131	Lens	1096?	38 (82) / 327s(82)	40 (75) / 313s(75)	42 (68) / 326s(68)	41 (54)	34 (31)	24 (01)	10 (51)	2 (01)
50.38N,	3.04E	79	Lille	1030?	168 (82) / 936s(82)	172 (75) / 931s(75)	191 (68) / 881s(68)	195 (54) / 359s(54)	202 (31)	211 (01)	76 (51)	55 (01)
45.51N,	1.15E	942	Limoges	bef 52 BC	140 (82) / 172s(82)	144 (75) / 165s(75)	133 (68) / 148s(68)	106 (54)	93 (31)	84 (01)	42 (51)	21 (01)
43.06N,	0.03W	1322	Lourdes	1170?	17 (82)	18 (75)	18 (68)	16 (54)	11 (31)	8 (01)	4 (51)	3 (01?)
45.45N,	4.51E	738	Lyons	43 BC	413 (82) / 1221s(82)	457 (75) / 1159s(75)	528 (68) / 1075s(68)	471 (54) / 650s(54)	580 (31)	459 (01)	177 (51)	109 (01)
48.59N,	1.43E	112	Mantes-la-Jolie	865?	44 (82) / 170s(82)	42 (75) / 153s(75)	26 (68) / 58s(68)	15 (54)	14 (31)	8 (01)	4 (51)	2 (89)
43.18N,	5.24E	532	Marseilles	600 BC?	874 (82) / 1111s(82)	909 (75) / 1011s(75)	889 (68) / 954s(68)	661 (54)	801 (31)	491 (01)	195 (51)	111 (01)
49.08N,	6.10E	860	Metz	1000 BC?	114 (82) / 186s(82)	112 (75) / 181s(75)	108 (68) / 166s(68)	86 (54) / 112s(54)	79 (31)	58 (00)	43 (51)	32 (01)
43.36N,	3.53E	144	Montpellier	8th c?	197 (82) / 221s(82)	191 (75) / 210s(75)	162 (68) / 171s(68)	98 (54)	87 (31)	76 (01)	46 (51)	34 (01)

For an explanation of symbols and abbreviations, see pages 16–17.

(Continued)

TABLE 2a. (Continued)

Latitude and Longitude	Elev (ft)	City	Date Settled	Population (thousands)							
				Latest	ca 1980	ca 1970	ca 1950	ca 1930	ca 1900	ca 1850	ca 1800
47.45N, 7.20E	787	Mulhouse	717?	112 (82) 221s(82)	117 (75) 219s(75)	116 (68) 199s(68)	99 (54) 111s(54)	100 (31)	89 (00)	30 (51)	9 (06)
48.41N, 6.12E	915	Nancy	947?	96 (82) 307s(82)	108 (75) 279s(75)	123 (68) 258s(68)	125 (54) 176s(54)	121 (31)	103 (01)	45 (51)	30 (01)
47.13N, 1.33W	62	Nantes	1st c BC?	241 (82) 465s(82)	257 (75) 440s(75)	260 (68) 394s(68)	223 (54) 242s(54)	187 (31)	133 (01)	96 (51)	74 (01)
43.42N, 7.15E	151	Nice	5th c BC?	337 (82) 449s(82)	344 (75) 441s(75)	322 (68) 393s(68)	244 (54)	220 (31)	105 (01)	34 (48)	18 (01)
43.50N, 4.21E	374	Nimes	2nd c BC?	124 (82) 132s(82)	128 (75) 130s(75)	123 (68) 125s(68)	89 (54)	89 (31)	81 (01)	54 (51)	39 (01)
47.55N, 1.54E	381	Orleans	273	103 (82) 220s(82)	106 (75) 205s(75)	96 (68) 168s(68)	76 (54) 96s(54)	72 (31)	67 (01)	47 (51)	36 (01)
48.52N, 2.20E	197	*Paris	3rd c BC?	2176 (82) 8707s(82)	2300 (75) 8450s(75)	2591 (68) 8197s(68)	2850 (54) 6436s(54)	2891 (31)	2714 (01)	1053 (51) 1227s(51)	548 (01)
43.18N, 0.22W	679	Pau	12th c?	84 (82) 131s(82)	83 (75) 126s(75)	74 (68) 110s(68)	48 (54)	39 (31)	34 (01)	16 (51)	9 (01)
42.41N, 2.53E	197	Perpignan	10th c	112 (82) 138s(82)	106 (75) 114s(75)	102 (68) 107s(68)	70 (54)	74 (31)	36 (01)	22 (51)	11 (01)
46.35N, 0.20E	387	Poitiers	3rd c?	79 (82) 103s(82)	81 (75) 93s(75)	71 (68) 80s(68)	53 (54)	42 (31)	40 (01)	29 (51)	18 (01)
48.05N, 1.41W	177	Rennes	1st c BC?	195 (82) 234s(82)	198 (75) 222s(75)	181 (68) 193s(68)	124 (54)	89 (31)	75 (01)	40 (51)	26 (01)
49.15N, 4.02E	282	Rheims	300 BC?	177 (82) 199s(82)	178 (75) 202s(75)	153 (68) 168s(68)	121 (54) 126s(54)	113 (31)	108 (01)	46 (51)	20 (01)
49.26N, 1.05E	72	Rouen	bef 4th c	102 (82) 380s(82)	115 (75) 389s(75)	120 (68) 370s(68)	117 (54) 246s(54)	123 (31)	116 (01)	100 (51)	87 (01)
45.26N, 4.24E	1772	Saint-Etienne	1195?	205 (82) 317s(82)	220 (75) 337s(75)	213 (68) 331s(68)	182 (54) 185s(54)	191 (31)	147 (01)	56 (51)	16 (01)
47.17N, 2.12W	26	Saint-Nazaire	1st c BC?	68 (82) 130s(82)	69 (75) 119s(75)	63 (68) 111s(68)	39 (54)	40 (31)	36 (01)	5 (51)	3 (01)
48.35N, 7.45E	932	Strasbourg	12 BC	249 (82) 373s(82)	253 (75) 359s(75)	249 (68) 335s(68)	201 (54) 239s(54)	181 (31)	151 (00)	76 (51)	49 (01)
49.22N, 6.10E	656	Thionville	870?	41 (82) 138s(82)	43 (75) 142s(75)	37 (68) 136s(68)	23 (54)	17 (31)	10 (00)	5 (51)	5 (01)
43.07N, 5.56E	92	Toulon	9th c BC	179 (82) 410s(82)	182 (75) 382s(75)	175 (68) 340s(68)	141 (54)	133 (31)	102 (01)	69 (51)	20 (01)

For an explanation of symbols and abbreviations, see pages 16–17.

(Continued)

Figure 10. Aerial view of Paris, the largest urbanized area in Europe, showing the Eiffel Tower and the Palais de Chaillot. (Credit: French Government Tourist Office.)

TABLE 2a. (Continued)

Latitude and Longitude	Elev (ft)	City	Date Settled	Population (thousands)							
				Latest	ca 1980	ca 1970	ca 1950	ca 1930	ca 1900	ca 1850	ca 1800
43.36N, 1.26E	456	Toulouse	300 BC?	348 (82)	374 (75)	371 (68)	269 (54)	195 (31)	150 (01)	93 (51)	50 (01)
				541s(82)	504s(75)	440s(68)					
47.23N, 0.41E	180	Tours	2nd c?	132 (82)	141 (75)	128 (68)	84 (54)	79 (31)	65 (01)	11 (51)	22 (01)
				263s(82)	235s(75)	202s(68)	117s(54)			33 (56)	
48.18N, 4.05E	361	Troyes	1st c BC?	64 (82)	72 (75)	75 (68)	59 (54)	59 (31)	53 (01)	27 (51)	24 (01)
				125s(82)	128s(75)	114s(68)	84s(54)				
50.21N, 3.32E	98	Valenciennes	693?	40 (82)	42 (75)	47 (68)	43 (54)	42 (31)	31 (01)	23 (51)	17 (01)
				350s(82)	224s(75)	224s(68)	65s(54)				
48.48N, 2.08E	604	Versailles	1682	91 (82)	94 (75)	91 (68)	84 (54)	67 (31)	55 (01)	37 (51)	25 (01)
46.07N, 3.25E	853	Vichy	52 BC?	31 (82)	32 (75)	34 (68)	30 (54)	22 (31)	14 (01)	2 (51)	2 (01?)
				64s(82)	59s(75)	57s(68)					

Germany: East

*Berlin (see under Germany: West)

Latitude and Longitude	Elev (ft)	City	Date Settled	Latest	ca 1980	ca 1970	ca 1950	ca 1930	ca 1900	ca 1850	ca 1800
52.25N, 12.33E	102	Brandenburg	928	95 (85e)	95 (81)	94 (71)	82 (50)	64 (33)	49 (00)	18 (49)	13 (00)
51.03N, 13.45E	371	Dresden	1206?	520 (85e)	524 (81)	502 (71)	494 (50)	642 (33)	396 (00)	94 (49)	62 (00)
50.59N, 11.02E	656	Erfurt	741?	216 (85e)	212 (81)	197 (71)	189 (50)	145 (33)	85 (00)	32 (49)	17 (02)
50.55N, 13.22E	1378	Freiberg	1168?	50 (85e)	51 (81)	50 (71)	44 (50)	36 (33)	30 (00)	15 (52)	10 (00)
50.57N, 10.43E	1011	Gotha	775?	58 (85e)	58 (81)	57 (71)	57 (50)	48 (33)	35 (00)	15 (52)	11 (02)
54.06N, 13.23E	23	Greifswald	1241	65 (85e)	61 (81)	47 (71)	44 (50)	29 (33)	23 (00)	13 (52)	6 (00)
51.30N, 12.00E	328	Halle	806	235 (85e)	234 (81)	257 (71)	289 (50)	209 (33)	157 (00)	34 (49)	15 (00)
50.56N, 11.35E	476	Jena	9th c?	107 (85e)	105 (81)	88 (71)	80 (50)	58 (33)	21 (00)	7 (52)	4 (18)
50.50N, 12.55E	1014	Karl-Marx-Stadt	1136	315 (85e)	319 (81)	299 (71)	293 (50)	351 (33)	207 (00)	31 (49)	11 (06)
51.18N, 12.20E	387	Leipzig	10th c?	554 (85e)	560 (81)	584 (71)	618 (50)	713 (33)	456 (00)	62 (49)	31 (00)
52.10N, 11.40E	164	Magdeburg	805?	289 (85e)	289 (81)	272 (71)	260 (50)	307 (33)	230 (00)	56 (49)	23 (00)
52.24N, 13.04E	105	Potsdam	10th c?	139 (85e)	133 (81)	111 (71)	118 (50)	74 (33)	60 (00)	40 (49)	18 (01)
54.05N, 12.08E	43	Rostock	1160?	244 (85e)	236 (81)	199 (71)	133 (50)	90 (33)	44 (00)	23 (50)	14 (03)
51.52N, 12.39E	233	Wittenberg	1180?	54 (85e)	54 (81)	47 (71)	50 (50)	24 (33)	18 (00)	10 (50)	7 (00)

Germany: West

Latitude and Longitude	Elev (ft)	City	Date Settled	Latest	ca 1980	ca 1970	ca 1950	ca 1930	ca 1900	ca 1850	ca 1800
50.46N, 6.06E	568	Aachen	1st c?	239 (85e)	243 (80e)	173 (70)	130 (50)	163 (33)	135 (00)	51 (49)	24 (99)
48.22N, 10.53E	1608	Augsburg	11 BC	244 (85e)	247 (80e)	212 (70)	185 (50)	177 (33)	89 (00)	38 (49)	29 (07)
48.45N, 8.15E	594	Baden-Baden	214?	49 (85e)	49 (80e)	37 (70)	37 (50)	30 (33)	16 (00)	8 (61)	2 (04)
49.52N, 10.52E	860	Bamberg	902?	70 (85e)	72 (80e)	71 (70)	76 (50)	54 (33)	42 (00)	19 (52)	18 (11)
49.57N, 11.35E	1132	Bayreuth	1194	72 (85e)	70 (80e)	64 (70)	59 (50)	37 (33)	29 (00)	14 (52)	11 (09)
52.33N, 13.22E	112	Berlin	1230?	3069 (85e)	3065 (80-81)	3208 (70-71)	3336 (50)	4243 (33)	1889 (00)	424 (49)	172 (00)
		East Berlin		1216 (85e)	1166 (81)	1086 (71)	1189 (50)				
		West Berlin		1853 (85e)	1899 (80e)	2122 (70)	2147 (50)				

Lat	Long	No.	City	Date	(85e)	(80e)	(70)	(50)	(33)	(00)	(49)	
52.02N,	8.32E	387	Bielefeld	1015?	301 (85e)	313 (80e)	169 (70)	154 (50)	121 (33)	63 (00)	10 (49)	3 (89)
51.29N,	7.13E	328	Bochum	900?	383 (85e)	402 (80e)	344 (70)	290 (50)	315 (33)	66 (00)	5 (49)	2 (00)
50.44N,	7.06E	197	*Bonn	10 BC?	293 (85e)	287 (80e)	274 (70)	115 (50)	99 (33)	51 (00)	18 (49)	9 (01)
53.05N,	8.48E	10	Bremen	787?	529 (85e)	556 (80e)	582 (70)	445 (50)	323 (33)	163 (00)	53 (49)	36 (12)
52.16N,	10.32E	230	Brunswick	861	251 (85e)	261 (80e)	224 (70)	224 (50)	157 (33)	128 (00)	39 (49)	28 (11)
50.56N,	6.57E	174	Cologne	38 BC?	919 (85e)	977 (80e)	848 (70)	595 (50)	757 (33)	373 (00)	95 (49)	44 (00)
47.40N,	9.11E	1329	Constance	3rd c BC?	69 (85e)	68 (80e)	61 (70)	43 (50)	33 (33)	21 (00)	6 (46)	4 (10)
49.52N,	8.39E	472	Darmstadt	11th c?	135 (85e)	138 (80e)	141 (70)	95 (50)	93 (33)	72 (00)	30 (52)	9 (03)
51.31N,	7.27E	249	Dortmund	885?	575 (85e)	609 (80e)	640 (70)	507 (50)	541 (33)	143 (00)	11 (49)	4 (09)
51.26N,	6.45E	85	Duisburg	8th c	520 (85e)	559 (80e)	455 (70)	411 (50)	440 (33)	93 (00)	9 (49)	4 (00)
51.13N,	6.46E	118	Dusseldorf	1159	563 (85e)	592 (80e)	664 (70)	501 (50)	499 (33)	214 (00)	26 (49)	20 (00)
49.36N,	11.01E	919	Erlangen	1002	100 (85e)	101 (80e)	84 (70)	50 (50)	32 (33)	23 (00)	11 (52)	9 (08)
51.27N,	7.01E	249	Essen	852	622 (85e)	650 (80e)	698 (70)	605 (50)	654 (33)	119 (00)	9 (49)	4 (00)
54.47N,	9.26E	66	Flensburg	12th c	87 (85e)	88 (80e)	95 (70)	103 (50)	67 (33)	49 (00)	16 (47)	11 (03)
50.07N,	8.41E	322	Frankfurt am Main	1st c?	598 (85e)	629 (80e)	670 (70)	532 (50)	556 (33)	289 (00)	59 (49)	40 (11)
48.00N,	7.51E	912	Freiburg im Breisgau	1120	182 (85e)	174 (80e)	162 (70)	110 (50)	99 (33)	62 (00)	15 (46)	8 (00?e)
51.31N,	7.06E	171	Gelsenkirchen	1150?	286 (85e)	306 (80e)	348 (70)	315 (50)	333 (33)	37 (00)	0.8 (52)	0.3 (98)
50.35N,	8.39E	522	Giessen	1197?	71 (85e)	76 (80e)	76 (70)	47 (50)	36 (33)	25 (00)	9 (50)	5 (04)
51.32N,	9.56E	492	Gottingen	953?	132 (85e)	128 (80e)	110 (70)	79 (50)	47 (33)	30 (00)	11 (52)	9 (07)
51.21N,	7.28E	348	Hagen	14th c	207 (85e)	220 (80e)	201 (70)	146 (50)	148 (33)	51 (00)	5 (49)	2 (97)
53.33N,	10.00E	20	Hamburg	811?	1586 (85e)	1649 (80e)	1794 (70)	1606 (50)	1129 (33)	706 (00)	133 (50)	95 (11)
51.41N,	7.48E	207	Hamm	1226	166 (85e)	172 (80e)	85 (70)	60 (50)	54 (33)	31 (00)	7 (43)	3 (98)
52.22N,	9.43E	180	Hannover	1163?	511 (85e)	535 (80e)	524 (70)	444 (50)	444 (33)	236 (00)	50 (52)	23 (10)
49.25N,	8.42E	374	Heidelberg	1196?	134 (85e)	132 (80e)	121 (70)	116 (50)	85 (33)	40 (00)	15 (52)	16 (18)
51.33N,	7.13E	194	Herne	8th c?	172 (85e)	183 (80e)	104 (70)	112 (50)	99 (33)	28 (00)	1 (47)	0.6 (09)
52.09N,	9.58E	262	Hildesheim	8th c?	101 (85e)	103 (80e)	94 (70)	72 (50)	63 (33)	43 (00)	16 (52)	11 (02)
49.27N,	7.45E	787	Kaiserslautern	882?	98 (85e)	99 (80e)	100 (70)	63 (50)	63 (33)	48 (00)	10 (49)	3 (02)
49.01N,	8.24E	377	Karlsruhe	1715	268 (85e)	271 (80e)	259 (70)	199 (50)	155 (33)	97 (00)	23 (49)	8 (00)
51.19N,	9.30E	548	Kassel	913?	184 (85e)	195 (80e)	214 (70)	162 (50)	175 (33)	106 (00)	36 (49)	18 (95)
54.20N,	10.08E	46	Kiel	10th c?	245 (85e)	250 (80e)	272 (70)	254 (50)	218 (33)	108 (00)	12 (50)	7 (03)
50.21N,	7.36E	230	Koblenz	9 BC	111 (85e)	114 (80e)	119 (70)	66 (50)	65 (33)	45 (00)	25 (49)	8 (00)
51.20N,	6.34E	125	Krefeld	1105?	217 (85e)	223 (80e)	222 (70)	172 (50)	165 (33)	107 (00)	36 (49)	8 (04)
51.01N,	6.59E	144	Leverkusen	1107?	155 (85e)	161 (80e)	107 (70)	66 (50)	44 (33)	14 (00)	7 (61)	3 (97)
53.52N,	10.42E	43	Lubeck	1143	211 (85e)	221 (80e)	239 (70)	238 (50)	129 (33)	82 (00)	26 (51)	25 (07)
49.29N,	8.27E	312	Ludwigshafen	17th c	154 (85e)	160 (80e)	176 (70)	124 (50)	107 (33)	62 (00)	2 (53)	0.1 (43)
50.00N,	8.15E	269	Mainz	5th c BC?	188 (85e)	187 (80e)	172 (70)	88 (50)	143 (33)	84 (00)	41 (52)	21 (00)
49.29N,	8.28E	318	Mannheim	766?	295 (85e)	304 (80e)	332 (70)	246 (50)	275 (33)	141 (00)	24 (52)	28 (18)
50.49N,	8.46E	610	Marburg	1122	76 (85e)	75 (80e)	47 (70)	40 (50)	28 (33)	18 (00)	8 (52)	6 (91)

For an explanation of symbols and abbreviations, see pages 16–17.

(Continued)

TABLE 2a. (Continued)

Latitude and Longitude	Elev (ft)	City	Date Settled	Population (thousands)							
				Latest	ca 1980	ca 1970	ca 1950	ca 1930	ca 1900	ca 1850	ca 1800
51.12N, 6.26E	197	Monchengladbach	972	255 (85e)	258 (80e)	151 (70)	125 (50)	127 (33)	58 (00)	4 (49)	1 (98)
51.26N, 6.53E	131	Mulheim an der Ruhr	11th c?	173 (85e)	182 (80e)	191 (70)	150 (50)	133 (33)	38 (00)	11 (49)	5 (07)
48.09N, 11.35E	1706	Munich	1158	1266 (85e)	1299 (80e)	1294 (70)	832 (50)	735 (33)	500 (00)	94 (52)	40 (01)
51.58N, 7.38E	197	Munster	800?	273 (85e)	268 (80e)	198 (70)	118 (50)	122 (33)	64 (00)	25 (49)	14 (95)
49.27N, 11.05E	1014	Nuremberg	1040?	466 (85e)	484 (80e)	474 (70)	362 (50)	410 (33)	261 (00)	51 (49)	25 (06)
47.36N, 11.04E	2756	Oberammergau	9th c	5 (84e)	5 (79e)	5 (70)	5 (50)	2 (33)	2 (00)	0.9 (25?)	0.2 (19?)
51.28N, 6.51E	131	Oberhausen	1315?	223 (85e)	229 (80e)	247 (70)	203 (50)	192 (33)	42 (00)	6 (62)	4 (00)
53.10N, 8.12E	16	Oldenburg in Oldenburg	12th c?	138 (85e)	136 (80e)	131 (70)	123 (50)	67 (33)	27 (00)	7 (52)	4 (00)
52.16N, 8.03E	210	Osnabruck	772	153 (85e)	158 (80e)	144 (70)	110 (50)	94 (33)	52 (00)	14 (52)	8 (05e)
51.43N, 8.46E	361	Paderborn	777	110 (85e)	110 (80e)	67 (70)	40 (50)	37 (33)	24 (00)	9 (46)	5 (10)
48.35N, 13.29E	860	Passau	1st c?	52 (85e)	50 (80e)	31 (70)	34 (50)	25 (33)	18 (00)	9 (52)	7 (11)
49.01N, 12.06E	1112	Regensburg	5th c BC?	126 (85e)	132 (80e)	130 (70)	117 (50)	81 (33)	45 (00)	26 (52)	23 (02e)
49.14N, 7.00E	623	Saarbrucken	999?	188 (85e)	194 (80e)	128 (70)	90 (46)	129 (30)	23 (00)	9 (49)	3 (02)
50.52N, 8.02E	919	Siegen	9th c?	107 (85e)	112 (80e)	57 (70)	39 (50)	33 (33)	22 (00)	6 (43)	4 (07)
51.11N, 7.05E	725	Solingen	965?	158 (85e)	167 (80e)	176 (70)	148 (50)	140 (33)	45 (00)	7 (49)	3 (04)
48.46N, 9.11E	804	Stuttgart	1150?	561 (85e)	582 (80e)	633 (70)	498 (50)	415 (33)	177 (00)	48 (49)	18 (98)
49.45N, 6.38E	410	Trier	15 BC	94 (85e)	95 (80e)	104 (70)	76 (50)	77 (33)	43 (00)	19 (49)	9 (02)
48.32N, 9.03E	1119	Tubingen	1078?	75 (85e)	72 (80e)	55 (70)	38 (50)	23 (33)	15 (00)	9 (49)	6 (03)
48.24N, 10.00E	1568	Ulm	854?	99 (85e)	101 (80e)	93 (70)	71 (50)	62 (33)	43 (00)	21 (49)	13 (95)
50.05N, 8.15E	381	Wiesbaden	3rd c BC	267 (85e)	274 (80e)	250 (70)	221 (50)	160 (33)	86 (00)	14 (50)	2 (00)
53.31N, 8.08E	13	Wilhelmshaven	bef 1852	97 (85e)	99 (80e)	103 (70)	101 (50)	28 (33)	23 (00)	0.2 (55)	
51.16N, 7.11E	525	Wuppertal	1070?	378 (85e)	394 (80e)	418 (70)	363 (50)	409 (33)	299 (00)	75 (49)	35 (10)
49.48N, 9.56E	594	Wurzburg	7th c	129 (85e)	128 (80e)	117 (70)	78 (50)	101 (33)	75 (00)	23 (49)	16 (05)
Gibraltar											
36.06N, 5.21W	11	*Gibraltar	711		30 (81)	27 (70)	23 (51)	17 (31)	20 (01)	16 (44)	3 (87)
Greece											
37.58N, 23.43E	453	*Athens	bef 13th c BC		886 (81) 3027s(81)	867 (71) 2540s(71)	555 (51) 1379s(51)	396 (28) 802s(28)	129 (96)	26 (48)	12 (00e)
39.40N, 20.50E	1588	Ioannina	7th c?		45 (81)	40 (71)	32 (51)	20 (28)	17 (13)	30 (73e)	35 (20e)
35.20N, 25.09E	98	Iraklion	832?		102 (81) 111s(81)	78 (71) 85s(71)	51 (51) 58s(51)	33 (28)	23 (00)	15 (50?e)	13 (00?e)

Coordinates	No.	City	Founded								
39.38N, 22.25E	243	Larissa	bef 6th c BC		102 (81)	72 (71)	41 (51)	26 (28)	15 (96)	20 (50?e)	20 (00?e)
38.15N, 21.44E	15	Patras	5th c BC?		142 (81) 155s(81)	112 (71) 121s(71)	79 (51) 88s(51)	61 (28)	50 (96)	15 (48)	6 (00?e)
37.57N, 23.38E	30	Piraeus	5th c BC		196 (81)	187 (71)	186 (51)	193 (28)	51 (96)	5 (48)	6 (00?e)
36.26N, 28.13E	121	Rhodes	407 BC		40 (81)	32 (71)	24 (51)	25 (29e)	10 (00e)	10 (50?e)	6 (00?e)
40.38N, 22.56E	200	Salonika	315 BC		406 (81) 706s(81)	346 (71) 557s(71)	217 (51) 297s(51)	237 (28) 251s(28)	115 (00e)	70 (50?e)	70 (00?e)
39.22N, 22.57E	23	Volos	1425 BC?		71 (81) 107s(81)	51 (71) 88s(71)	51 (51) 74s(51)	42 (28)	17 (96)	5 (81)	5 (00?e)
Hungary											
47.30N, 19.05E	377	*Budapest	bef 19 AD	2076(86e)	2059 (80)	1945 (70)	1058 (49) 1571s(49)	1006 (30)	716 (00)	156 (51)	47 (87)
47.32N, 21.38E	404	Debrecen	1211	212 (86e)	198 (80)	157 (70)	120 (49)	117 (30)	72 (00)	31 (51)	29 (87)
48.06N, 20.47E	394	Miskolc	13th c	212 (86e)	208 (80)	172 (70)	104 (49)	64 (30)	41 (00)	16 (51)	14 (87)
46.05N, 18.14E	830	Pecs	1st c BC?	177 (86e)	169 (80)	145 (70)	78 (49)	62 (30)	42 (00)	16 (51)	9 (87)
46.15N, 20.10E	269	Szeged	1138?	182 (86e)	171 (80)	119 (70)	133 (49)	135 (30)	100 (00)	51 (51)	22 (87)
Iceland											
64.09N, 21.57W	92	*Reykjavik	874	89 (84e) 130s(84e)	84 (80)	82 (70) 95s(70)	56 (50) 59s(50)	28 (30) 29s(30)	7 (01) 7s(01)	1 (50) 2s(50)	0.3 (01) 0.9s(01)
Ireland											
51.54N, 8.28W	56	Cork	7th c	133 (86)	136 (81) 150s(81)	129 (71) 135s(71)	75 (51) 107s(51)	78 (26)	76 (01)	88 (51)	101 (21)
53.20N, 6.15W	51	*Dublin	836?	502 (86) 921s(86)	525 (81) 915s(81)	568 (71) 801s(71)	522 (51) 570s(51)	317 (26) 419s(26)	291 (01)	262 (51)	182 (98)
53.17N, 9.03W	59	Galway	1124	47 (86)	38 (81)	29 (71)	21 (51)	14 (26)	13 (01)	20 (51)	25 (13)
52.40N, 8.37W	59	Limerick	812?	56 (86)	61 (81)	57 (71)	51 (51)	39 (26)	38 (01)	53 (51)	39 (00?e)
Isle of Man											
54.09N, 4.29W	285	*Douglas	1250?	20 (86)	20 (81)	19 (71)	20 (51)	19 (31)	19 (01)	10 (51)	6 (21)
Italy											
44.54N, 8.37E	312	Alessandria	1168	98 (85e)	101 (81)	102 (71)	82 (51)	80 (31)	72 (01)	42 (48)	19 (1774)
43.38N, 13.30E	52	Ancona	390 BC?	105 (85e)	106 (81)	110 (71)	86 (51)	83 (31)	55 (01)	23 (46)	17 (00?)
43.25N, 11.53E	971	Arezzo	4th c BC?	92 (85e)	92 (81)	87 (71)	67 (51)	57 (31)	44 (01)	37 (61)	8 (00?e)
41.08N, 16.51E	16	Bari	180 BC?	368 (85e)	371 (81)	357 (71)	268 (51)	170 (31)	78 (01)	34 (61)	18 (94)
45.41N, 9.43E	817	Bergamo	5th c BC?	120 (85e)	122 (81)	127 (71)	103 (51)	79 (31)	47 (01)	34 (51)	36 (85)
44.29N, 11.20E	180	Bologna	510 BC?	442 (85e)	459 (81)	491 (71)	341 (51)	239 (31)	148 (01)	97 (53)	67 (00)

For an explanation of symbols and abbreviations, see pages 16–17.

(Continued)

TABLE 2a. (Continued)

Latitude and Longitude	Elev (ft)	City	Date Settled	Population (thousands)							
				Latest	ca 1980	ca 1970	ca 1950	ca 1930	ca 1900	ca 1850	ca 1800
46.31N, 11.22E	860	Bolzano	14 BC?	103 (85e)	105 (81)	106 (71)	71 (51)	37 (31)	14 (01)	8 (57)	8 (00?e)
45.33N, 10.15E	489	Brescia	6th c BC	202 (85e)	207 (81)	210 (71)	142 (51)	115 (31)	69 (01)	34 (51)	28 (85)
40.38N, 17.56E	33	Brindisi	5th c BC?	92 (85e)	90 (81)	82 (71)	58 (51)	40 (31)	23 (01)	9 (61)	6 (93e)
39.13N, 9.07E	13	Cagliari	540 BC	224 (85e)	234 (81)	223 (71)	139 (51)	101 (31)	53 (01)	27 (48)	19 (83)
37.30N, 15.06E	33	Catania	8th c BC	378 (85e)	380 (81)	400 (71)	300 (51)	225 (31)	147 (01)	57 (50)	45 (98)
45.47N, 9.05E	659	Como	bef 196 BC	94 (85e)	96 (81)	98 (71)	70 (51)	51 (31)	38 (01)	18 (51)	15 (00)
39.18N, 16.15E	778	Cosenza	bef 331 BC	106 (85e)	107 (81)	102 (71)	57 (51)	35 (31)	21 (01)	17 (61)	9 (94)
45.07N, 10.02E	148	Cremona	218 BC	78 (85e)	81 (81)	82 (71)	69 (51)	62 (31)	37 (01)	28 (51)	21 (00)
44.50N, 11.35E	30	Ferrara	753?	146 (85e)	149 (81)	154 (71)	134 (51)	116 (31)	87 (01)	68 (53)	26 (97)
43.46N, 11.15E	164	Florence	59 BC?	436 (85e)	448 (81)	458 (71)	375 (51)	305 (31)	198 (01)	106 (49)	78 (00)
41.27N, 15.34E	249	Foggia	1069?	158 (85e)	156 (81)	142 (71)	98 (51)	56 (31)	53 (01)	32 (61)	13 (94)
44.13N, 12.03E	112	Forli	188 BC?	111 (85e)	111 (81)	105 (71)	78 (51)	60 (31)	43 (01)	37 (61)	16 (06)
44.25N, 8.57E	62	Genoa	5th c BC?	738 (85e)	763 (81)	817 (71)	688 (51)	591 (31)	220 (01)	125 (48)	91 (99)
44.07N, 9.50E	10	La Spezia	12th c?	111 (85e)	115 (81)	125 (71)	112 (51)	115 (31)	66 (01)	12 (61)	4 (06)
40.23N, 18.11E	167	Lecce	6th c?	95 (85e)	91 (81)	83 (71)	67 (51)	47 (31)	33 (01)	21 (61)	20 (93)
43.33N, 10.19E	10	Leghorn	807?	176 (85e)	176 (81)	175 (71)	142 (51)	120 (31)	96 (01)	80 (55)	53 (00)
43.50N, 10.29E	56	Lucca	718 BC?	89 (85e)	91 (81)	91 (71)	88 (51)	80 (31)	73 (01)	66 (61)	17 (06)
45.09N, 10.48E	59	Mantua	5th c BC?	59 (85e)	61 (81)	66 (71)	54 (51)	42 (31)	30 (01)	30 (51)	22 (02)
38.11N, 15.34E	10	Messina	8th c BC	266 (85e)	260 (81)	251 (71)	221 (51)	180 (31)	147 (01)	97 (50)	44 (98)
45.28N, 9.12E	397	Milan	4th c BC	1536 (85e)	1605 (81)	1732 (71)	1274 (51)	962 (31)	490 (01)	193 (51)	135 (00)
44.40N, 10.55E	112	Modena	5th c BC?	178 (85e)	180 (81)	171 (71)	111 (51)	90 (31)	63 (01)	53 (61)	27 (05)
45.35N, 9.16E	532	Monza	5th c BC?	122 (85e)	122 (81)	114 (71)	73 (51)	60 (31)	42 (01)	19 (51)	11 (05)
40.50N, 14.15E	33	Naples	600 BC?	1207 (85e)	1212 (81)	1227 (71)	1011 (51)	832 (31)	548 (01)	416 (50)	427 (96)
45.25N, 11.53E	39	Padua	302 BC?	229 (85e)	235 (81)	232 (71)	168 (51)	127 (31)	81 (01)	54 (51)	32 (02)
38.07N, 13.22E	46	Palermo	8th c BC	716 (85e)	702 (81)	643 (71)	491 (51)	380 (31)	306 (01)	179 (50)	141 (98)
44.48N, 10.20E	187	Parma	183 BC	177 (85e)	179 (81)	175 (71)	123 (51)	69 (31)	49 (01)	41 (54)	34 (99)
45.10N, 9.10E	253	Pavia	3rd c BC?	83 (85e)	85 (81)	87 (71)	64 (51)	49 (31)	34 (01)	26 (51)	24 (00)
43.08N, 12.22E	1618	Perugia	6th c BC?	145 (85e)	142 (81)	130 (71)	95 (51)	77 (31)	61 (01)	43 (61)	16 (00?e)
43.54N, 12.55E	46	Pesaro	544		90 (81)	85 (71)	54 (51)	42 (31)	25 (01)	20 (61)	10 (00?e)
42.28N, 14.13E	13	Pescara	48 AD?	132 (85e)	131 (81)	122 (71)	65 (51)	44 (31)	7 (01)	4 (61)	
45.01N, 9.40E	200	Piacenza	218 BC	107 (85e)	109 (81)	107 (71)	73 (51)	64 (31)	36 (01)	32 (61)	28 (20)
43.43N, 10.23E	16	Pisa	11th c BC?	104 (85e)	105 (81)	103 (71)	78 (51)	71 (31)	60 (01)	49 (61)	17 (00?e)

Coordinates		City	Founded	(85e)	(81)	(71)	(51)	(31)	(01)		
43.55N, 10.54E	213	Pistoia	bef 62 BC	91 (85e)	92 (81)	93 (71)	78 (51)	73 (31)	65 (01)	12 (61)	10 (00?e)
40.38N, 15.48E	2700	Potenza	1273?	66 (85e)	65 (81)	57 (71)	33 (51)	16 (31)	12 (01)	13 (61)	8 (00)
43.53N, 11.06E	207	Prato	10th c	164 (85e)	159 (81)	143 (71)	78 (51)	67 (31)	51 (01)	35 (61)	10 (00?e)
44.25N, 12.12E	13	Ravenna	8th c BC	137 (85e)	138 (81)	132 (71)	92 (51)	77 (31)	63 (01)	54 (53)	26 (05)
38.06N, 15.39E	49	Reggio di Calabria	8th c BC	177 (85e)	173 (81)	166 (71)	141 (51)	124 (31)	45 (01)	27 (61)	18 (94)
44.43N, 10.36E	190	Reggio nell'Emilia	2nd c BC	130 (85e)	130 (81)	129 (71)	107 (51)	90 (31)	59 (01)	47 (61)	15 (05)
44.04N, 12.34E	23	Rimini	400 BC?	130 (85e)	127 (81)	118 (71)	77 (51)	63 (31)	44 (01)	33 (61)	17 (05)
41.54N, 12.29E	66	*Rome	1000 BC?	2827 (85e)	2840 (81)	2782 (71)	1652 (51)	937 (31)	425 (01)	176 (53)	153 (00)
40.41N, 14.47E	13	Salerno	197 BC	156 (85e)	157 (81)	155 (71)	91 (51)	61 (31)	42 (01)	19 (50)	9 (89)
43.49N, 7.46E	30	San Remo	1124?	61 (85e)	61 (81)	62 (71)	39 (51)	28 (31)	20 (01)	10 (61)	
40.43N, 8.34E	738	Sassari	bef 12th c	120 (85e)	120 (81)	107 (71)	70 (51)	52 (31)	38 (01)	26 (61)	16 (83)
43.19N, 11.21E	1056	Siena	5th c BC?	61 (85e)	62 (81)	66 (71)	53 (51)	46 (31)	27 (01)	20 (43)	16 (84)
37.04N, 15.18E	56	Syracuse	734 BC	119 (85e)	118 (81)	109 (71)	71 (51)	49 (31)	32 (01)	20 (61)	16 (98)
40.28N, 17.14E	49	Taranto	708 BC?	244 (85e)	244 (81)	227 (71)	169 (51)	112 (31)	60 (01)	28 (61)	18 (00?e)
46.04N, 11.08E	637	Trent	4th c BC?	100 (85e)	99 (81)	92 (71)	62 (51)	54 (31)	25 (01)	9 (51)	7 (00?e)
45.40N, 12.15E	49	Treviso	3rd c BC?	86 (85e)	88 (81)	90 (71)	63 (51)	52 (31)	33 (01)	18 (51)	11 (80)
45.40N, 13.46E	7	Trieste	181 BC?	244 (85e)	252 (81)	272 (71)	273 (51)	250 (31)	133 (00)	64 (51)	24 (01)
45.03N, 7.40E	784	Turin	4th c BC?	1050 (85e)	1117 (81)	1168 (71)	719 (51)	591 (31)	330 (01)	143 (48)	78 (00)
46.03N, 13.14E	371	Udine	983?	101 (85e)	102 (81)	101 (71)	73 (51)	64 (31)	37 (01)	23 (51)	15 (15)
43.43N, 12.38E	1480	Urbino	5th c BC?	16 (85e)	16 (81)	16 (71)	23 (51)	20 (31)	18 (01)	15 (61)	8 (00?e)
45.27N, 12.21E	3	Venice	6th c	338 (85e)	346 (81)	363 (71)	317 (51)	250 (31)	148 (01)	123 (51)	134 (02)
45.27N, 11.00E	194	Verona	bef 89 BC	261 (85e)	266 (81)	266 (71)	179 (51)	152 (31)	74 (01)	51 (51)	41 (95)
45.33N, 11.33E	128	Vicenza	1st c BC?	112 (85e)	115 (81)	117 (71)	80 (51)	64 (31)	44 (01)	30 (51)	29 (02)
Liechtenstein											
47.08N, 9.32E	1526	*Vaduz	1150?	5 (85e)	5 (80)	4 (70)	3 (50)	2 (30)	1 (01)	0.9 (52?)	0.6 (00?e)
Luxembourg											
49.36N, 6.07E	984	*Luxembourg	963	76 (86e)	79 (81)	76 (70)	62 (47)	54 (30)	21 (00)	12 (40)	9 (00e)
Malta											
35.54N, 14.32E	233	*Valletta	1566	14 (84e)	14 (80e)	16 (67)	19 (48)	23 (31)	23 (01)	25 (51)	24 (98)
Monaco											
43.44N, 7.25E	180	*Monaco	6th c BC?	27 (86e)	27 (82)	23 (68)	20 (51)	25 (28)	15 (97)	8 (57)	6 (00?e)

For an explanation of symbols and abbreviations, see pages 16–17.

(Continued)

TABLE 2a. (Continued)

Latitude and Longitude	Elev (ft)	City	Date Settled	Population (thousands)							
				Latest	ca 1980	ca 1970	ca 1950	ca 1930	ca 1900	ca 1850	ca 1800
Netherlands											
52.23N, 4.54E	5	*Amsterdam	1275?	676 (85e)	717 (80e)	783 (71)	804 (47)	757 (30)	511 (99)	224 (49)	217 (95)
				998s(85e)	1015s(80e)	873s(71)	838s(47)				
52.00N, 5.53E		Arnhem	893?	128 (85e)	128 (80e)	127 (71)	97 (47)	78 (30)	57 (99)	19 (49)	10 (95)
				293s(85e)	287s(80e)	162s(71)	114s(47)				
51.35N, 4.46E	23	Breda	1198?	119 (85e)	117 (80e)	117 (71)	82 (47)	45 (30)	26 (99)	15 (49)	8 (95)
				154s(85e)	151s(80e)	121s(71)	85s(47)				
52.00N, 4.22E	10	Delft	1075?	87 (85e)	84 (80e)	84 (71)	62 (47)	51 (30)	32 (99)	18 (49)	14 (95)
51.48N, 4.40E	13	Dordrecht	1018	107 (85e)	107 (80e)	87 (71)	68 (47)	56 (30)	38 (99)	21 (49)	18 (95)
				200s(85e)	196s(80e)	119s(71)					
51.26N, 5.30E	66	Eindhoven	1232?	192 (85e)	194 (80e)	185 (71)	135 (47)	95 (30)	5 (99)	3 (49)	3 (30)
				375s(85e)	369s(80e)	189s(71)	137s(47)				
52.13N, 6.55E	95	Enschede	1118?	145 (85e)	143 (80e)	124 (71)	80 (47)	52 (30)	24 (99)	4 (49)	3 (30)
				248s(85e)	244s(80e)	141s(71)					
53.13N, 6.34E	16	Groningen	1006?	168 (85e)	161 (80e)	156 (71)	132 (47)	105 (30)	67 (99)	34 (49)	24 (95)
				207s(85e)	200s(80e)	169s(71)	143s(47)				
52.20N, 4.36E	10	Haarlem	960?	151 (85e)	158 (80e)	169 (71)	157 (47)	120 (30)	64 (99)	26 (49)	21 (95)
				215s(85e)	225s(80e)	226s(71)	201s(47)				
52.04N, 4.19E	12	*Hague	1242?	443 (85e)	457 (80e)	526 (71)	533 (47)	438 (30)	206 (99)	72 (49)	38 (95)
				672s(85e)	675s(80e)	644s(71)	592s(47)				
50.53N, 5.59E	377	Heerlen	2nd c?	94 (85e)	71 (80e)	40 (71)	57 (47)	47 (30)	6 (99)	5 (49)	3 (01)
				267s(85e)	267s(80e)	74s(71)					
52.14N, 5.10E	16	Hilversum	13th c	87 (85e)	93 (80e)	96 (71)	85 (47)	57 (30)	19 (99)	5 (49)	3 (95)
				104s(85e)	110s(80e)	97s(71)					
52.10N, 4.30E	10	Leiden	9th c?	105 (85e)	103 (80e)	97 (71)	87 (47)	71 (30)	54 (99)	36 (49)	31 (95)
				177s(85e)	173s(80e)	130s(71)	102s(47)				
50.51N, 5.42E	161	Maastricht	50 AD?	114 (85e)	109 (80e)	91 (71)	74 (47)	61 (30)	34 (99)	25 (49)	18 (95)
				158s(85e)	145s(80e)	103s(71)					
51.50N, 5.52E	82	Nijmegen	70 AD?	146 (85e)	148 (80e)	146 (71)	107 (47)	82 (30)	43 (99)	21 (49)	13 (95)
				236s(85e)	218s(80e)	153s(71)					
51.55N, 4.29E	12	Rotterdam	9th c?	571 (85e)	579 (80e)	630 (71)	646 (47)	587 (30)	319 (99)	90 (49)	53 (95)
				1021s(85e)	1018s(80e)	776s(71)	716s(47)				

Lat	Long	No.	City	Founded								
51.41N	5.19E	26	's Hertogen-bosch	1134?	89 (85e); 188s(85e)	88 (80e); 184s(80e)	82 (71)	53 (47)	42 (30)	31 (99)	22 (49)	13 (95)
51.34N	5.05E	59	Tilburg	709?	154 (85e); 222s(85e)	152 (80e); 217s(80e)	150 (71); 152s(71)	114 (47)	79 (30)	34 (99)	15 (49)	9 (95)
52.07N	5.05E	10	Utrecht	630?	230 (85e); 504s(85e)	237 (80e); 482s(80e)	270 (71); 273s(71)	185 (47); 223s(47)	155 (30)	102 (99)	48 (49)	32 (95)
52.27N	4.49E	10	Zaanstad	1398?	128 (85e); 140s(85e)	129 (80e); 141s(80e)	65 (71); 116s(71)	42 (47)	33 (30)	21 (99)	11 (49)	10 (95)
Norway												
60.23N	5.20E	144	Bergen	1070	208 (86e)	181 (80)	182 (70)	113 (50); 144s(50)	98 (30); 118s(30)	72 (00)	22 (45)	17 (01)
59.55N	10.45E	315	*Oslo	1048	449 (86e); 703s(85e)	452 (80); 643s(80)	475 (70); 645s(70)	434 (50); 506s(50)	253 (30); 395s(30)	229 (00)	33 (45)	10 (01)
58.58N	5.45E	26	Stavanger	9th c?	95 (86e)	91 (80)	79 (70)	51 (50); 75s(50)	47 (30); 61s(30)	30 (00)	9 (45)	2 (01)
69.40N	18.58E	328	Tromso	13th c?	48 (86e)	36 (80)	29 (70)	11 (50); 16s(50)	10 (30)	7 (00)	0.9(45)	
63.25N	10.25E	417	Trondheim	997	134 (86e)	128 (80)	112 (70)	57 (50); 78s(50)	54 (30); 66s(30)	39 (00)	15 (45)	9 (01)
Poland												
53.09N	23.10E	456	Bialystok	1310	245 (85e)	212 (78)	167 (70)	69 (50)	91 (31)	64 (97)	14 (58)	6 (11)
49.50N	19.00E	1014	Bielsko-Biala	13th c	174 (85e)	156 (78)	106 (70)	57 (50)	45 (31)	25 (00)	12 (51)	6 (00?)
53.16N	17.33E	230	Bydgoszcz	13th c	361 (85e)	338 (78)	280 (70)	163 (50)	117 (31)	47 (00)	13 (49)	4 (00?)
50.22N	18.53E	935	Bytom	9th c?	239 (85e)	231 (78)	187 (70)	174 (50)	101 (33)	51 (00)	6 (49)	2 (04)
50.19N	18.56E	925	Chorzow	1136?	144 (85e)	150 (78)	151 (70)	129 (50)	81 (31)	58 (00)	4 (52)	
50.49N	19.07E	856	Czestochowa	1220?	247 (85e)	229 (78)	188 (70)	112 (50)	118 (31)	45 (97)	3 (50?e)	2 (00)
50.20N	19.12E	984	Dabrowa Gornicza	1796?	137 (85e)	134 (78)	62 (70)	32 (50)	37 (31)	4 (00)		
54.20N	18.40E	43	Gdansk	980?	467 (85e)	442 (78)	364 (70)	195 (50)	256 (29)	141 (00)	64 (49)	41 (00)
54.31N	18.30E	7	Gdynia	1253?	243 (85e)	226 (78)	190 (70)	103 (50)	30 (31)	0.9 (10)		
50.20N	18.40E	728	Gliwice	1276?	212 (85e)	194 (78)	171 (70)	133 (50)	111 (33)	52 (00)	9 (49)	3 (00)
50.15N	18.59E	932	Katowice	1598?	363 (85e)	350 (78)	303 (70)	176 (50)	126 (31)	32 (00)	8 (71)	3 (06)
50.51N	20.39E	879	Kielce	1084?	200 (85e)	164 (78)	126 (70)	61 (50)	58 (31)	23 (97)	5 (50?e)	2 (00?e)
50.05N	19.55E	778	Krakow	700?	740 (85e)	693 (78)	583 (70)	344 (50)	219 (31)	91 (00)	50 (51)	25 (98)
51.46N	19.25E	614	Lodz	1423	849 (85e)	825 (78)	762 (70)	620 (50)	605 (31)	314 (97)	16 (50)	0.8 (06)

For an explanation of symbols and abbreviations, see pages 16–17.

(Continued)

TABLE 2a. (Continued)

Latitude and Longitude	Elev (ft)	City	Date Settled	Population (thousands)							
				Latest	ca 1980	ca 1970	ca 1950	ca 1930	ca 1900	ca 1850	ca 1800
51.20N, 22.30E	561	Lublin	10th c?	324 (85e)	291 (78)	236 (70)	117 (50)	112 (31)	50 (97)	18 (58)	9 (87)
53.47N, 20.29E	377	Olsztyn	1348	147 (85e)	127 (78)	94 (70)	44 (50)	43 (33)	24 (00)	4 (49)	2 (02)
52.25N, 16.58E	282	Poznan	9th c	574 (85e)	536 (78)	469 (70)	321 (50)	245 (31)	117 (00)	44 (49)	12 (97)
51.26N, 21.10E	584	Radom	1154?	213 (85e)	184 (78)	159 (70)	80 (50)	78 (31)	29 (97)	6 (50?e)	2 (00?)
50.18N, 18.51E	938	Ruda Slaska	1303?	165 (85e)	156 (78)	142 (70)	110 (50)	24 (29)	12 (00)	0.4(50?)	
50.03N, 22.00E	656	Rzeszow	12th c?	138 (85e)	112 (78)	82 (70)	28 (50)	27 (31)	13 (00)	6 (51)	3 (00?e)
50.16N, 19.07E	820	Sosnowiec	1279?	255 (85e)	229 (78)	145 (70)	96 (50)	109 (31)	57 (00)	12 (90)	
53.26N, 14.34E	3	Szczecin	9th c	391 (85e)	385 (78)	337 (70)	179 (50)	271 (33)	211 (00)	47 (49)	18 (00)
53.01N, 18.35E	226	Torun	1231	186 (85e)	166 (78)	129 (70)	81 (50)	54 (31)	30 (00)	13 (49)	8 (02)
50.08N, 18.59E	919	Tychy	bef 1629	182 (85e)	154 (78)	71 (70)	13 (50)	6 (31)	5 (00)	3 (71)	
52.15N, 21.00E	348	*Warsaw	10th c	1649 (85e)	1552 (78)	1308 (70)	804 (50)	1172 (31)	684 (97)	164 (51)	63 (01)
51.07N, 17.02E	394	Wroclaw	980?	636 (85e)	598 (78)	523 (70)	309 (50)	625 (33)	423 (00)	111 (49)	65 (00)
50.18N, 18.47E	820	Zabrze	13th c	198 (85e)	195 (78)	197 (70)	172 (50)	130 (33)	20 (00)	6 (71)	0.9 (19?)
Portugal											
41.33N, 8.26W	623	Braga	296 BC?		63 (81)	50 (70)	33 (50)	27 (30)	24 (00)	20 (63)	12 (00?)
40.12N, 8.25W	463	Coimbra	2nd c BC?		75 (81)	57 (70)	43 (50)	27 (30)	18 (00)	18 (65)	12 (00?)
38.34N, 7.54W	755	Evora	2nd c?		35 (81)	24 (70)	26 (50)	22 (30)	16 (00)	12 (65)	12 (00?)
38.43N, 9.08W	312	*Lisbon	2000 BC?		807 (81)	769 (70)	790 (50)	594 (30)	356 (00)	251 (58)	230 (02e)
					2069s(81)	1061s(70)					
37.44N, 25.40W	115	Ponta Delgada	1439?		21 (81)	21 (70)	23 (50)	15 (30)	18 (00)	17 (78)	8 (00?e)
41.09N, 8.37W	328	Porto	2000 BC?		327 (81)	306 (70)	285 (50)	232 (30)	168 (00)	81 (58)	74 (02e)
					1562s(81)	480s(70)					
Romania											
46.11N, 21.19E	331	Arad	11th c	171 (84e)	171 (77)	126 (66)	87 (48)	77 (30)	54 (00)	20 (51)	8 (87)
46.34N, 26.54E	597	Bacau	1408?	162 (84e)	127 (77)	73 (66)	34 (48)	31 (30)	16 (99)	15 (73)	
45.16N, 27.59E	49	Braila	1368?	217 (84e)	196 (77)	139 (66)	96 (48)	68 (30)	56 (99)	9 (50?e)	30 (00?e)
45.38N, 25.35E	1941	Brasov	1225	296 (84e)	256 (77)	163 (66)	83 (48)	59 (30)	35 (00)	24 (51)	18 (89)
44.26N, 26.06E	269	*Bucharest	630?	1853 (84e)	1807 (77)	1367 (66)	886 (48)	639 (30)	276 (99)	122 (59)	32 (98)
				1961s(84e)	1934s(77)	1512s(66)	1042s(48)				
46.46N, 23.36E	1027	Cluj-Napoca	12th c	275 (84e)	263 (77)	186 (66)	118 (48)	101 (30)	47 (00)	19 (51)	15 (97)
44.11N, 28.39E	105	Constanta	7th c BC?	291 (84e)	257 (77)	150 (66)	79 (48)	59 (30)	15 (99)	5 (50?e)	

44.19N, 23.48E	345	Craiova	15th c	248 (84e)	221 (77)	149 (66)	85 (48)	63 (30)	46 (99)	8 (50?e)	2 (00?e)
45.27N, 28.03E	98	Galati	1418?	258 (84e)	238 (77)	151 (66)	80 (48)	101 (30)	63 (99)	36 (39?e)	5 (00?e)
47.10N, 27.36E	335	Iasi	1408?	271 (84e)	265 (77)	161 (66)	94 (48)	103 (30)	78 (99)	66 (59)	15 (90)
47.04N, 21.56E	449	Oradea	1080	202 (84e)	171 (77)	123 (66)	82 (48)	83 (30)	47 (00)	21 (51)	5 (87)
44.51N, 24.52E	1004	Pitesti	16th c?	145 (84e)	124 (77)	60 (66)	29 (48)	20 (30)	16 (99)	7 (59)	
44.57N, 26.01E	505	Ploiesti	16th c	218 (84e)	200 (77)	147 (66)	96 (48)	79 (30)	45 (99)	27 (59)	3 (25?e)
45.48N, 24.09E	1365	Sibiu	12th c	161 (84e)	151 (77)	110 (66)	61 (48)	49 (30)	26 (00)	16 (51)	14 (86)
45.45N, 21.13E	295	Timisoara	1212	263 (84e)	269 (77)	174 (66)	112 (48)	92 (30)	50 (00)	21 (51)	9 (87)
46.33N, 24.34E	1014	Tirgu Mures	1332?	149 (84e)	130 (77)	86 (66)	47 (48)	39 (30)	18 (00)	9 (51)	5 (87)
Spain											
40.29N, 3.22W	1929	Alcala de Henares	1038	149 (85e)	137 (81)	60 (70)	19 (50)	13 (30)	11 (00)	9 (57)	6 (00?)
40.21N, 3.50W	2356	Alcorcon	11th c?	144 (85e)	141 (81)	46 (70)	0.8 (50)	0.8 (30)	0.7 (00)	0.5 (57)	
36.08N, 5.30W	59	Algeciras	711	95 (85e)	85 (81)	82 (70)	53 (50)	21 (30)	13 (00)	14 (57)	10 (20?)
38.21N, 0.29W	10	Alicante	713?	256 (85e)	251 (81)	185 (70)	104 (50)	73 (30)	50 (00)	17 (57)	13 (04)
36.50N, 2.27W	56	Almeria	238 BC?	152 (85e)	141 (81)	115 (70)	76 (50)	54 (30)	47 (00)	23 (57)	7 (00?e)
38.53N, 6.58W	604	Badajoz	3rd c BC?	119 (85e)	114 (81)	102 (70)	79 (50)	44 (30)	31 (00)	22 (57)	10 (00?e)
41.27N, 2.15E	75	Badalona	3rd c BC?	231 (85e)	230 (81)	163 (70)	62 (50)	44 (30)	19 (00)	10 (57)	2 (16)
41.23N, 2.11E	39	Barcelona	200 BC?	1769 (85e)	1755 (81)	1745 (70)	1280 (50)	1006 (30)	533 (00)	160 (57)	115 (97)
43.15N, 2.58W	10	Bilbao	1300?	397 (85e)	433 (81)	410 (70)	229 (50)	162 (30)	83 (00)	18 (57)	11 (02)
42.21N, 3.42W	2808	Burgos	884	158 (85e)	156 (81)	120 (70)	74 (50)	40 (30)	30 (00)	26 (57)	12 (22)
36.32N, 6.18W	16	Cadiz	1100 BC?	161 (85e)	158 (81)	136 (70)	100 (50)	76 (30)	69 (00)	62 (57)	66 (87)
37.36N, 0.59W	20	Cartagena	225 BC?	176 (85e)	168 (81)	147 (70)	113 (50)	103 (30)	100 (00)	22 (57)	25 (00?e)
37.53N, 4.46W	328	Cordova	bef 8th c BC	295 (85e)	285 (81)	236 (70)	165 (50)	103 (30)	58 (00)	36 (57)	25 (00e)
38.15N, 0.42W	266	Elche	3rd c BC?	177 (85e)	165 (81)	123 (70)	56 (50)	38 (30)	27 (00)	20 (57)	17 (00?e)
41.59N, 2.49E	322	Gerona	5th c BC?	68 (85e)	88 (81)	50 (70)	29 (50)	22 (30)	16 (00)	14 (57)	14 (08e)
43.32N, 5.40W	30	Gijon	1st c BC	264 (85e)	256 (81)	188 (70)	111 (50)	78 (30)	48 (00)	10 (57)	3 (00?e)
37.13N, 3.41W	2261	Granada	5th c BC?	260 (85e)	262 (81)	190 (70)	154 (50)	118 (30)	76 (00)	62 (57)	70 (97)
41.22N, 2.08E	26	Hospitalet	987?	288 (85e)	285 (81)	242 (70)	72 (50)	38 (30)	5 (00)	3 (57)	
37.16N, 6.57W	13	Huelva	7th c BC?	139 (85e)	128 (81)	97 (70)	64 (50)	45 (30)	21 (00)	8 (57)	5 (00?e)
37.46N, 3.47W	1883	Jaen	bef 207 BC	104 (85e)	96 (81)	78 (70)	62 (50)	40 (30)	26 (00)	20 (57)	17 (92)
36.41N, 6.08W	161	Jerez de la Frontera	7th c BC?	186 (85e)	176 (81)	150 (70)	108 (50)	72 (30)	63 (00)	39 (57)	8 (00?e)
43.22N, 8.23W	79	La Coruna	bef 12th c BC	243 (85e)	232 (81)	190 (70)	134 (50)	74 (30)	44 (00)	27 (57)	4 (00?e)
40.19N, 3.45W	2188	Leganes	1280	169 (85e)	164 (81)	58 (70)	6 (50)	5 (30)	4 (00)	3 (57)	2 (20?)
42.36N, 5.34W	2697	Leon	70 AD	135 (85e)	131 (81)	105 (70)	60 (50)	29 (30)	16 (00)	10 (57)	6 (86?)

For an explanation of symbols and abbreviations, see pages 16–17.

(Continued)

TABLE 2a. (Continued)

Latitude and Longitude		Elev (ft)	City	Date Settled	Population (thousands)							
					Latest	ca 1980	ca 1970	ca 1950	ca 1930	ca 1900	ca 1850	ca 1800
41.37N,	0.37E	728	Lerida	5th c BC?	111 (85e)	110 (81)	91 (70)	53 (50)	39 (30)	21 (00)	20 (57)	17 (00?e)
40.24N,	3.41W	2100	*Madrid	931?	3209 (85e)	3188 (81)	3146 (70)	1618 (50)	953 (30)	540 (00)	271 (57)	168 (97)
36.43N,	4.25W	33	Malaga	12th c BC	548 (85e)	503 (81)	374 (70)	276 (50)	188 (30)	130 (00)	93 (57)	52 (05)
40.19N,	3.51W	2169	Mostoles	10th c?	169 (85e)	150 (81)	18 (70)	2 (50)	2 (30)	1 (00)	1 (57)	1 (20?)
37.59N,	1.07W	141	Murcia	825	309 (85e)	289 (81)	244 (70)	218 (50)	159 (30)	112 (00)	27 (57)	40 (07)
43.22N,	5.50W	705	Oviedo	761	191 (85e)	190 (81)	154 (70)	106 (50)	75 (30)	48 (00)	14 (57)	7 (00?)
39.34N,	2.39E	108	Palma	123 BC	316 (85e)	304 (81)	234 (70)	137 (50)	88 (30)	64 (00)	40 (57)	30 (87)
42.49N,	1.38W	1476	Pamplona	1st c BC?	182 (85e)	183 (81)	147 (70)	72 (50)	42 (30)	29 (00)	23 (57)	14 (00?)
41.33N,	2.06E	617	Sabadell	13th c	190 (85e)	186 (81)	159 (70)	59 (50)	46 (30)	23 (00)	14 (57)	5 (25?e)
40.58N,	5.39W	2553	Salamanca	5th c BC?	160 (85e)	167 (81)	125 (70)	80 (50)	47 (30)	26 (00)	15 (57)	15 (00?e)
43.19N,	1.59W	26	San Sabastian	1014?	180 (85e)	176 (81)	166 (70)	114 (50)	78 (30)	38 (00)	9 (57)	5 (00?)
43.28N,	3.48W	13	Santander	1068?	190 (85e)	180 (81)	150 (70)	102 (50)	85 (30)	55 (00)	25 (57)	4 (00?e)
42.53N,	8.33W	866	Santiago de Compostela	813?	86 (85e)	82 (81)	71 (70)	56 (50)	38 (30)	24 (00)	27 (57)	21 (00?)
37.23N,	5.59W	20	Seville	7th c BC?	678 (85e)	654 (81)	548 (70)	377 (50)	229 (30)	148 (00)	82 (57)	96 (87)
41.07N,	1.15E	226	Tarragona	6th c BC?	114 (85e)	112 (81)	78 (70)	39 (50)	31 (30)	23 (00)	18 (57)	7 (00?e)
39.52N,	4.01W	1729	Toledo	193 BC?	58 (85e)	58 (81)	44 (70)	40 (50)	27 (30)	23 (00)	15 (57)	22 (00?e)
39.28N,	0.22W	10	Valencia	137 BC	787 (85e)	752 (81)	654 (70)	509 (50)	320 (30)	214 (00)	87 (57)	61 (00)
41.39N,	4.43W	2270	Valladolid	1074?	333 (85e)	330 (81)	236 (70)	124 (50)	91 (30)	69 (00)	40 (57)	20 (00?e)
42.14N,	8.43W	66	Vigo	7th c BC?	282 (85e)	261 (81)	197 (70)	138 (50)	65 (30)	23 (00)	8 (57)	5 (00?e)
42.51N,	2.40W	1719	Vitoria	581	202 (85e)	193 (81)	137 (70)	52 (50)	41 (30)	31 (00)	19 (57)	6 (00?e)
41.38N,	0.53W	656	Zaragoza	bef 25 BC	605 (85e)	591 (81)	480 (70)	264 (50)	174 (30)	99 (00)	56 (57)	43 (87)
Sweden												
57.43N,	11.58E	102	Goteborg	1619	425 (85e) 704s(85e)	431 (80) 693s(80)	452 (70) 618s(70)	354 (50) 380s(50)	244 (30)	131 (00)	26 (50)	13 (00)
58.25N,	15.37E	210	Linkoping	12th c	117 (85e)	113 (80)	105 (70)	55 (50)	30 (30)	15 (00)	5 (50)	3 (00)
55.42N,	13.11E	24	Lund	1000?	82 (85e)	78 (80)	56 (70)	34 (50)	25 (30)	17 (00)	7 (50)	3 (00)
55.36N,	13.00E	10	Malmo	1150?	230 (85e) 458s(85e)	234 (80) 453s(80)	266 (70) 445s(70)	192 (50) 196s(50)	128 (30)	61 (00)	13 (50)	4 (00)
59.17N,	15.13E	118	Orebro	13th c	118 (85e)	117 (80)	116 (70)	67 (50)	38 (30)	22 (00)	5 (50)	3 (00)
59.20N,	18.03E	144	*Stockholm	1255	659 (85e) 1435s(85e)	647 (80) 1387s(80)	740 (70) 1345s(70)	744 (50) 928s(50)	502 (30)	301 (00)	93 (50)	76 (00)

Coordinates	No.	City	Founded	(85e)	(80)	(70)	(50)	(30)	(00)	(50)	(00)
63.50N, 20.15E	46	Umea	1588	85 (85e)	81 (80)	56 (70)	17 (50)	11 (30)	4 (00)	2 (50)	1 (00)
59.52N, 17.38E	79	Uppsala	9th c?	155 (85e)	146 (80)	127 (70)	63 (50)	30 (30)	23 (00)	7 (50)	5 (00)
59.37N, 16.33E	59	Vasteras	1120?	118 (85e)	117 (80)	117 (70)	60 (50)	30 (30)	12 (00)	4 (50)	3 (00)
Switzerland											
47.34N, 7.36E	1040	Basel	374?	176 (85e)	182 (80)	213 (70)	184 (50)	148 (30)	109 (00)	27 (50)	16 (95)
				363s (85e)	365s (80)	373s (70)	258s (50)				
46.57N, 7.28E	1877	*Bern	1191	141 (85e)	145 (80)	162 (70)	146 (50)	112 (30)	64 (00)	28 (50)	11 (98)
				301s (85e)	287s (80)	259s (70)	195s (50)				
46.48N, 7.09E	1929	Freiburg	1157	35 (85e)	37 (80)	40 (70)	29 (50)	22 (30)	16 (00)	9 (50)	6 (00?)
				56s (85e)	56s (80)	51s (70)					
46.12N, 6.10E	1411	Geneva	58 BC?	160 (85e)	157 (80)	174 (70)	145 (50)	124 (30)	105 (00)	29 (50)	23 (02)
				376s (85e)	335s (80)	321s (70)	195s (50)				
46.32N, 6.39E	1831	Lausanne	3rd c?	126 (85e)	127 (80)	137 (70)	107 (50)	76 (30)	47 (00)	17 (50)	10 (00?)
				257s (85e)	226s (80)	219s (70)	137s (50)				
47.03N, 8.17E	1634	Luzern	8th c	61 (85e)	63 (80)	70 (70)	61 (50)	47 (30)	29 (00)	10 (50)	4 (99)
				158s (85e)	157s (80)	149s (70)	98s (50)				
47.00N, 6.58E	1437	Neuchatel	1011?	33 (85e)	34 (80)	39 (70)	28 (50)	23 (30)	21 (00)	8 (50)	5 (00?e)
				65s (85e)	66s (80)	62s (70)					
47.28N, 9.24E	2178	Saint-Gall	614	73 (85e)	76 (80)	81 (70)	68 (50)	64 (30)	54 (00)	18 (50)	8 (08)
				124s (85e)	88s (80)						
46.30N, 9.50E	5978	Sankt Moritz	1139?		6 (80)	6 (70)	2 (50)	4 (30)	2 (00)		
47.22N, 8.31E	1539	Zurich	3000 BC?	355 (85e)	370 (80)	423 (70)	390 (50)	250 (30)	151 (00)	17 (50)	10 (90)
				835s (85e)	706s (80)	675s (70)	495s (50)				
Turkey											
41.40N, 26.34E	157	Edirne	125?	106 (85)	72 (80)	54 (70)	30 (50)	35 (27)	80 (05e)	130 (50e)	100 (00?e)
41.01N, 28.58E	128	Istanbul	658 BC	5495 (85)	2773 (80)	2132 (70)	983 (50)	691 (27)	874 (00?e)	900 (50?e)	400 (00?e)
UK											
57.08N, 2.06W	79	Aberdeen	700?		190 (81)	182 (71)	183 (51)	167 (31)	154 (01)	72 (51)	27 (01)
51.34N, 0.25E	95	Basildon	bef 1510		152 (81)	129 (71)	43 (51)	40 (31)	18 (01)	2 (51)	2 (01)
51.23N, 2.22W	67	Bath	bef 1st c		80 (81)	85 (71)	79 (51)	69 (31)	50 (01)	54 (51)	32 (01)
52.08N, 0.27W	118	Bedford	571?		74 (81)	73 (71)	53 (51)	43 (31)	35 (01)	12 (51)	4 (01)
54.36N, 5.56W	66	Belfast	1177		298 (81)	360 (71)	444 (51)	415 (26)	349 (01)	100 (51)	18 (98)
53.24N, 3.02W	60	Birkenhead	1150?		124 (81)	138 (71)	143 (51)	148 (31)	111 (01)	24 (51)	0.1s (01)
52.29N, 1.53W	425	Birmingham	11th c		920 (81)	1015 (71)	1113 (51)	1003 (31)	522 (01)	233 (51)	61 (01)
					2244s (81)	2372s (71)					

For an explanation of symbols and abbreviations, see pages 16–17.

(Continued)

TABLE 2a. (Continued)

Latitude and Longitude	Elev (ft)	City	Date Settled	Latest	Population (thousands)						
					ca 1980	ca 1970	ca 1950	ca 1930	ca 1900	ca 1850	ca 1800
53.45N, 2.29W	610	Blackburn	6th c?		88 (81)	102 (71)	111 (51)	123 (31)	128 (01)	47 (51)	12 (01)
53.50N, 3.03W	65	Blackpool	16th c?		148 (81)	152 (71)	147 (51)	102 (31)	47 (01)	2 (51)	0.5s(01)
53.35N, 2.26W	342	Bolton	11th c?		147 (81)	154 (71)	167 (51)	177 (31)	168 (01)	61 (51)	13 (01)
50.43N, 1.54W	139	Bournemouth	18th c		145 (81)	154 (71)	145 (51)	117 (31)	47 (01)	6 (71)	
53.48N, 1.45W	439	Bradford	1066?		281 (81)	294 (71)	292 (51)	299 (31)	280 (01)	104 (51)	6 (01)
50.49N, 0.08W	32	Brighton	1086?		146 (81)	161 (71)	156 (51)	147 (31)	123 (01)	70 (51)	7s (01)
51.27N, 2.35W	386	Bristol	6th c BC		388 (81)	427 (71)	443 (51)	404 (31)	329 (01)	137 (51)	41 (01)
52.12N, 0.07E	41	Cambridge	730?		90 (81)	99 (71)	81 (51)	70 (31)	38 (01)	28 (51)	10 (01)
51.17N, 1.05E	135	Canterbury	43 AD?		34 (81)	33 (71)	28 (51)	25 (31)	25 (01)	18 (51)	9 (01)
51.29N, 3.10W	203	Cardiff	1st c		274 (81)	279 (71)	244 (51)	227 (31)	164 (01)	18 (51)	2 (01)
54.53N, 2.56W	85	Carlisle	bef 1st c		72 (81)	72 (71)	68 (51)	57 (31)	45 (01)	26 (51)	10 (01)
51.44N, 0.29E	134	Chelmsford	bef 1086		58 (81)	58 (71)	38 (51)	27 (31)	13 (01)	6 (51)	4 (01)
51.54N, 2.05W	214	Cheltenham	773?		73 (81)	74 (71)	63 (51)	49 (31)	49 (01)	35 (51)	3s(01)
53.12N, 2.55W	66	Chester	48 AD?		58 (81)	63 (71)	48 (51)	41 (31)	46 (01)	28 (51)	15 (01)
50.50N, 0.47W	40	Chichester	bef 1st c		24 (81)	21 (71)	19 (51)	14 (31)	12 (01)	9 (51)	5 (01)
51.53N, 0.54E	89	Colchester	bef 43 AD		82 (81)	77 (71)	57 (51)	49 (31)	38 (01)	19 (51)	12 (01)
52.25N, 1.30W	241	Coventry	1043?		314 (81)	335 (71)	258 (51)	178 (31)	70 (01)	36 (51)	16 (01)
54.32N, 1.34W	174	Darlington	11th c?		85 (81)	86 (71)	85 (51)	72 (31)	45 (01)	11 (51)	5 (01)
52.55N, 1.28W	211	Derby	51 AD?		216 (81)	220 (71)	141 (51)	142 (31)	106 (01)	41 (51)	11 (01)
53.32N, 1.07W	41	Doncaster	70 AD?		82 (81)	83 (71)	82 (51)	63 (31)	29 (01)	12 (51)	7 (01)
51.06N, 1.18E	20	Dover	bef 43 AD		33 (81)	34 (71)	35 (51)	41 (31)	42 (01)	22 (51)	15 (01)
52.30N, 2.05W	745	Dudley	8th c?		187 (81)	186 (71)	64 (51)	60 (31)	49 (01)	38 (51)	10 (01)
56.27N, 2.58W	147	Dundee	12th c?		175 (81)	182 (71)	177 (51)	176 (31)	161 (01)	79 (51)	26 (01)
54.46N, 1.34W	336	Durham	11th c?		26 (81)	25 (71)	19 (51)	16 (31)	15 (01)	13 (51)	8 (01)
55.57N, 3.12W	441	Edinburgh	617?		419 (81)	454 (71)	467 (51)	439 (31)	317 (01)	161 (51)	67 (01)
52.24N, 0.16E	13	Ely	7th c		10 (81)	10 (71)	10 (51)	8 (31)	8 (01)	6 (51)	4s(01)
50.43N, 3.31W	110	Exeter	200 BC?		96 (81)	96 (71)	76 (51)	66 (31)	53 (01)	33 (51)	17 (01)
51.05N, 1.11E	128	Folkestone	630?		44 (81)	44 (71)	45 (51)	46 (31)	31 (01)	7 (51)	3 (01)
55.51N, 4.16W	180	Glasgow	1202?		762 (81) 1713s(81)	897 (71) 1903s(71)	1090 (51)	1088 (31)	762 (01)	345 (51)	81 (01)
51.53N, 2.14W	33	Gloucester	bef 49 AD		92 (81)	90 (71)	67 (51)	53 (31)	48 (01)	18 (51)	8 (01)
51.13N, 0.34W	184	Guildford	9th c?		57 (81)	57 (71)	48 (51)	31 (31)	16 (01)	7 (51)	3 (01)

Latitude	Longitude	No.	City	Founded							
53.59N,	1.32W	478	Harrogate	74 AD?	66 (81)	62 (71)	50 (51)	40 (31)	28 (01)	4 (51)	1s(01)
52.03N,	2.43W	292	Hereford	7th c	48 (81)	47 (71)	33 (51)	24 (31)	21 (01)	12 (51)	7 (01)
53.39N,	1.47W	762	Huddersfield	1086?	124 (81)	131 (71)	129 (51)	113 (31)	95 (01)	31 (51)	7 (01)
53.45N,	0.20W	8	Hull	13th c	268 (81)	286 (71)	299 (51)	314 (31)	240 (01)	85 (51)	22 (01)
52.04N,	1.10E	190	Ipswich	991?	120 (81)	123 (71)	107 (51)	88 (31)	67 (01)	33 (51)	11 (01)
54.04N,	2.50W	23	Lancaster	1st c?	46 (81)	50 (71)	52 (51)	43 (31)	40 (01)	15 (51)	9 (01)
53.48N,	1.32W	307	Leeds	bef 1080	449 (81)	496 (71)	505 (51)	483 (31)	429 (01)	172 (51)	53 (01)
					1676s(81)	1728s(71)					
52.38N,	1.07W	237	Leicester	bef 43 AD	280 (81)	284 (71)	285 (51)	258 (31)	212 (01)	61 (51)	17 (01)
52.41N,	1.49W	259	Lichfield	7th c	26 (81)	23 (71)	11 (51)	9 (31)	8 (01)	7 (51)	5 (01)
53.14N,	0.32W	25	Lincoln	bef 70 AD	77 (81)	74 (71)	70 (51)	66 (31)	49 (01)	18 (51)	7 (01)
53.23N,	3.00W	198	Liverpool	1190?	510 (81)	610 (71)	789 (51)	856 (31)	685 (01)	376 (51)	78 (01)
					1127s(81)	1267s(71)					
51.31N,	0.05W	149	*London	43 AD?	2497 (81)	2772 (71)	3348 (51)	4397 (31)	4537 (01)	2362 (51)	865 (01)
					6696s(81)	7452s(71)	8348s(51)	8216s(31)	6581s(01)		
55.00N,	7.20W	325	Londonderry	546	63 (81)	52 (71)	50 (51)	45 (26)	40 (01)	20 (51)	14 (31)
52.46N,	1.12W	269	Loughborough	11th c?	48 (81)	46 (71)	35 (51)	27 (31)	22 (01)	11 (51)	5s(01)
51.53N,	0.25W	381	Luton	1st c?	164 (81)	161 (71)	110 (51)	69 (31)	36 (01)	11 (51)	3s(01)
51.16N,	0.31E	36	Maidstone	1st c?	72 (81)	71 (71)	54 (51)	42 (31)	34 (01)	21 (51)	8 (01)
53.28N,	2.14W	125	Manchester	80 AD	449 (81)	544 (71)	703 (51)	766 (31)	544 (01)	303 (51)	70 (01)
					2245s(81)	2393s(71)					
54.35N,	1.14W	30	Middlesbrough	1086?	150 (81)	157 (71)	147 (51)	139 (31)	91 (01)	7 (51)	0.2s(01)
53.00N,	2.14W	587	Newcastle-under-Lyme	12th c	73 (81)	77 (71)	70 (51)	23 (31)	20 (01)	11 (51)	5 (01)
54.58N,	1.37W	255	Newcastle upon Tyne	1080	192 (81)	222 (71)	292 (51)	286 (31)	215 (01)	88 (51)	28 (01)
					731s(81)	805s(71)					
51.35N,	3.00W	265	Newport	1126?	105 (81)	112 (71)	106 (51)	89 (31)	67 (01)	19 (51)	1 (01)
52.14N,	0.54W	258	Northampton	6th c?	157 (81)	127 (71)	104 (51)	92 (31)	87 (01)	27 (51)	7 (01)
52.38N,	1.18E	110	Norwich	570?	122 (81)	122 (71)	121 (51)	126 (31)	112 (01)	68 (51)	37 (01)
52.51N,	1.08W	192	Nottingham	9th c	271 (81)	301 (71)	306 (51)	276 (31)	240 (01)	57 (51)	29 (01)
51.45N,	1.15W	208	Oxford	912?	97 (81)	109 (71)	99 (51)	81 (31)	49 (01)	28 (51)	12 (01)
55.50N,	4.26W	106	Paisley	1163	85 (81)	95 (71)	94 (51)	86 (31)	79 (01)	32 (51)	17 (01)
56.24N,	3.26W	77	Perth	84 AD?	42 (81)	43 (71)	41 (51)	35 (31)	30 (01)	24 (51)	15 (01)
52.35N,	0.15W	9	Peterborough	bef 655	115 (81)	70 (71)	53 (51)	44 (31)	31 (01)	9 (51)	3 (01)
50.23N,	4.06W	117	Plymouth	11th c?	244 (81)	239 (71)	208 (51)	213 (31)	108 (01)	52 (51)	16 (01)
50.43N,	1.59W	18	Poole	1224?	119 (81)	107 (71)	83 (51)	57 (31)	19 (01)	9 (51)	5 (01)

For an explanation of symbols and abbreviations, see pages 16–17.

(Continued)

TABLE 2a. (Continued)

Latitude and Longitude	Elev (ft)	City	Date Settled	Latest	Population (thousands)						
					ca 1980	ca 1970	ca 1950	ca 1930	ca 1900	ca 1850	ca 1800
50.48N, 1.06W	7	Portsmouth	12th c		179 (81)	197 (71)	234 (51)	252 (31)	188 (01)	72 (51)	32 (01)
53.46N, 2.42W	110	Preston	1094?		144 (81)	98 (71)	121 (51)	119 (31)	113 (01)	70 (51)	12 (01)
51.28N, 0.59W	152	Reading	871		124 (81)	133 (71)	114 (51)	97 (31)	72 (01)	21 (51)	10 (01)
51.40N, 3.30W	1220	Rhondda	951?		82 (81)	89 (71)	111 (51)	141 (31)	114 (01)	2s (51)	0.5s (01)
53.38N, 2.09W	360	Rochdale	1st c?		93 (81)	91 (71)	88 (51)	90 (31)	83 (01)	29 (51)	6 (01)
52.22N, 1.15W	390	Rugby	1086?		60 (81)	59 (71)	45 (51)	24 (31)	17 (01)	6 (51)	1 (01)
51.45N, 0.20W	272	Saint Albans	15 BC?		51 (81)	52 (71)	44 (51)	29 (31)	16 (01)	7 (51)	3 (01)
53.28N, 2.44W	160	Saint Helens	12th c?		99 (81)	104 (71)	113 (51)	107 (31)	84 (01)	15 (51)	3s (01)
53.30N, 2.16W	70	Salford	1086?		98 (81)	131 (71)	178 (51)	223 (31)	221 (01)	64 (51)	14 (01)
51.04N, 1.47W	249	Salisbury	1220		35 (81)	35 (71)	33 (51)	26 (31)	17 (01)	12 (51)	8 (01)
54.17N, 0.26W	118	Scarborough	bef 1066		43 (81)	44 (71)	45 (51)	42 (31)	38 (01)	13 (51)	6 (01)
53.23N, 1.28W	428	Sheffield	1086?		477 (81)	520 (71)	513 (51)	518 (31)	381 (01)	135 (51)	31 (01)
52.43N, 2.44W	184	Shrewsbury	5th c?		60 (81)	56 (71)	45 (51)	37 (31)	28 (01)	20 (51)	15 (01)
50.54N, 1.23W	65	Southampton	755?		204 (81)	215 (71)	178 (51)	176 (31)	105 (01)	35 (51)	8 (01)
51.33N, 0.43E	90	Southend-on-Sea	1121		157 (81)	163 (71)	152 (51)	120 (31)	29 (01)	1 (51)	0.1 (09)
53.40N, 3.00W	16	Southport	1797		90 (81)	85 (71)	84 (51)	79 (31)	48 (01)	5 (51)	
52.49N, 2.06W	247	Stafford	bef 913		55 (81)	55 (71)	40 (51)	29 (31)	21 (01)	12 (51)	4 (01)
56.07N, 3.57W	125	Stirling	bef 1124		39 (81)	30 (71)	27 (51)	23 (31)	19 (01)	10 (51)	5 (01)
53.25N, 2.10W	135	Stockport	12th c?		136 (81)	140 (71)	142 (51)	125 (31)	79 (01)	54 (51)	15 (01)
54.35N, 1.25W	62	Stockton-on-Tees	12th c?		149 (81)	148 (71)	74 (51)	68 (31)	51 (01)	10 (51)	5s (01)
53.00N, 2.11W	390	Stoke-on-Trent	1086?		252 (81)	265 (71)	275 (51)	277 (31)	268 (01)	84 (51)	23s (01)
52.11N, 1.42W	161	Stratford-on-Avon	693?		21 (81)	19 (71)	15 (51)	12 (31)	8 (01)	3 (51)	2 (01)
54.55N, 1.22W	216	Sunderland	674		196 (81)	217 (71)	182 (51)	186 (31)	146 (01)	64 (51)	12 (01)
51.37N, 3.56W	32	Swansea	1099?		168 (81)	173 (71)	161 (51)	165 (31)	95 (01)	31 (51)	6 (01)
50.28N, 3.30W	27	Torbay	12th c?		116 (81)	109 (71)	53 (51)	46 (31)	34 (01)	8 (51)	0.8s (01)
51.08N, 0.17E	351	Tunbridge Wells	1606		45 (81)	45 (71)	38 (51)	35 (31)	33 (01)	11 (51)	4s (01)
53.42N, 1.29W	115	Wakefield	7th c?		61 (81)	60 (71)	60 (51)	59 (31)	41 (01)	22 (51)	8 (01)
52.35N, 1.58W	455	Walsall	996?		179 (81)	185 (71)	115 (51)	103 (31)	86 (01)	26 (51)	5 (01)
52.30N, 1.58W	610	Warley	1086?		152 (81)	164 (71)	179 (51)	161 (31)	115 (01)	8 (51)	1 (01)
53.23N, 2.36W	43	Warrington	79 AD?		136 (81)	68 (71)	81 (51)	79 (31)	64 (01)	23 (51)	11 (01)

(Continued)

Coordinates	No.	Name	Founded								
52.31N, 1.59W	543	West Bromwich	1086?		155 (81)	167 (71)	88 (51)	81 (31)	65 (01)	35s(51)	6s(01)
51.01N, 1.19W	120	Winchester	50 BC?		31 (81)	31 (71)	26 (51)	23 (31)	21 (01)	14 (51)	6 (01)
51.29N, 0.36W	69	Windsor	1110		28 (81)	30 (71)	23 (51)	20 (31)	14 (01)	10 (51)	3 (01)
52.36N, 2.08W	430	Wolverhampton	985?		252 (81)	269 (71)	163 (51)	133 (31)	94 (01)	50 (51)	13 (01)
52.12N, 2.12W	94	Worcester	bef 1st c		75 (81)	73 (71)	62 (51)	51 (31)	47 (01)	28 (51)	11 (01)
53.57N, 1.05W	57	York	71 AD?		100 (81)	105 (71)	105 (51)	94 (31)	78 (01)	36 (51)	16 (01)
USSR											
58.03N, 38.50E	341	Andropov	1137?	251 (85e)	239 (79)	218 (70)	182 (59)	55 (26)	25 (97)	9 (56)	3 (11)
64.34N, 40.32E	10	Archangel	1553	408 (85e)	385 (79)	343 (70)	258 (59)	73 (26)	21 (97)	15 (56)	11 (11)
45.00N, 41.08E	518	Armavir	1848	168 (85e)	162 (79)	145 (70)	111 (59)	75 (26)	18 (97)	10 (51)	
46.21N, 48.03E	-72	Astrakhan	13th c	493 (85e)	461 (79)	410 (70)	305 (59)	177 (26)	113 (97)	35 (56)	38 (11)
40.23N, 49.51E	7	Baku	5th c?	1104 (85e)	1022 (79)	852 (70)	643 (59)	453 (26)	112 (97)	8 (56)	
				1693s(85e)		1266s(70)	968s(59)				
52.02N, 47.47E	105	Balakovo	1762	180 (85e)	152 (79)	103 (70)	36 (59)	19 (26)	19 (97)	3 (60)	
49.47N, 30.07E	604	Belaya Tserkov	1155?	181 (85e)	151 (79)	109 (70)	71 (59)	43 (26)	35 (97)	15 (56)	
50.36N, 36.34E	410	Belgorod	1237?	280 (85e)	240 (79)	151 (70)	72 (59)	31 (26)	27 (97)	13 (56)	8 (11)
59.24N, 56.46E	525	Berezniki	1883	195 (85e)	185 (79)	146 (70)	106 (59)	11 (26)			
53.09N, 29.14E	472	Bobruysk	16th c	223 (85e)	192 (79)	138 (70)	98 (59)	51 (26)	34 (97)	17 (56)	2 (11)
52.06N, 23.42E	528	Brest	1017?	222 (85e)	177 (79)	122 (70)	74 (59)	51 (31)	47 (97)	17 (56)	4 (11)
53.15N, 34.22E	607	Bryansk	1146	430 (85e)	394 (79)	318 (70)	207 (59)	27 (26)	25 (97)	11 (56)	5 (11)
56.09N, 47.15E	413	Cheboksary	1371?	389 (85e)	308 (79)	216 (70)	104 (59)	9 (26)	5 (97)	5 (56)	4 (11)
59.08N, 37.54E	308	Cherepovets	14th c	299 (85e)	266 (79)	188 (70)	92 (59)	22 (26)	7 (97)	3 (56)	1 (11)
49.26N, 32.04E	443	Cherkassy	14th c	273 (85e)	228 (79)	158 (70)	85 (59)	40 (26)	30 (97)	12 (56)	5 (11)
51.30N, 31.18E	1148	Chernigov	7th c?	278 (85e)	238 (79)	159 (70)	90 (59)	35 (26)	28 (97)	4 (56)	5 (11)
48.18N, 25.56E	322	Chernovtsy	1407?	244 (85e)	219 (79)	187 (70)	152 (59)	112 (30)	70 (00)	21 (51)	5 (00?e)
48.30N, 34.37E	659	Dneprodzerzhinsk	1750?	271 (85e)	250 (79)	227 (70)	194 (59)	34 (26)	17 (97)	3 (61)	
48.27N, 34.59E		Dnepropetrovsk	1783	1153 (85e)	1066 (79)	862 (70)	661 (59)	233 (26)	113 (97)	13 (56)	9 (11)
48.00N, 37.48E		Donetsk	1869	1073 (85e)	1021 (79)	879 (70)	708 (59)	106 (26)	28 (97)		
56.15N, 43.24E		Dzerzhinsk	bef 1917	274 (85e)	257 (79)	221 (70)	164 (59)	9 (26)	1 (20)		
46.16N, 44.14E		Elista	1865	81 (85e)	70 (79)	50 (70)	23 (59)	4 (23)	village		
51.30N, 46.07E	66	Engels	1747	177 (85e)	161 (79)	130 (70)	91 (59)	34 (26)	22 (97)	13 (67?e)	
52.25N, 31.00E	453	Gomel	1142??	465 (85e)	383 (79)	272 (70)	168 (59)	86 (26)	37 (97)	10 (56)	
56.20N, 44.00E	532	Gorkiy	1221	1399 (85e)	1344 (79)	1170 (70)	941 (59)	185 (26)	90 (97)	36 (56)	14 (11)
48.18N, 38.03E	423	Gorlovka	1867	342 (85e)	336 (79)	335 (70)	308 (59)	23 (26)	2 (97)		
53.41N, 23.50E	404	Grodno	bef 1128	247 (85e)	195 (79)	132 (70)	73 (59)	50 (31)	47 (97)	15 (56)	11 (11)
43.20N, 45.42E		Groznyy	1818	393 (85e)	375 (79)	341 (70)	250 (59)	71 (26)	16 (97)	3 (67)	

For an explanation of symbols and abbreviations, see pages 16–17.

TABLE 2a. (Continued)

Latitude and Longitude	Elev (ft)	City	Date Settled	Population (thousands) Latest	ca 1980	ca 1970	ca 1950	ca 1930	ca 1900	ca 1850	ca 1800
48.56N, 24.43E	801	Ivano-Frankovsk	1662	210 (85e)	150 (79)	105 (70)	66 (59)	61 (31)	30 (00)	13 (57)	6 (20?)
57.00N, 40.59E	420	Ivanovo	16th c	474 (85e)	465 (79)	420 (70)	335 (59)	111 (26)	54 (97)	6 (61)	
56.51N, 53.14E	479	Izhevsk	1760	611 (85e)	549 (79)	422 (70)	285 (59)	63 (26)	41 (97)	21 (59)	17 (11)
56.52N, 35.55E	446	Kalinin	1135	438 (85e)	412 (79)	345 (70)	261 (59)	108 (26)	54 (97)	13 (56)	
54.43N, 20.30E	20	Kaliningrad	1255	385 (85e)	355 (79)	297 (70)	204 (59)	316 (33)	189 (00)	75 (49)	55 (02)
54.31N, 36.16E	663	Kaluga	1389?	297 (85e)	265 (79)	211 (70)	134 (59)	52 (23)	50 (97)	31 (56)	23 (11)
54.54N, 23.54E	246	Kaunas	1030	405 (85e)	370 (79)	305 (70)	219 (59)	92 (23)	71 (97)	20 (56)	2 (11)
55.45N, 49.08E	276	Kazan	1437	1047 (85e)	993 (79)	869 (70)	667 (59)	179 (26)	130 (97)	56 (56)	54 (11)
45.21N, 36.28E	13	Kerch	6th c BC	168 (85e)	157 (79)	128 (70)	98 (59)	35 (26)	33 (97)	13 (56)	1 (11)
50.00N, 36.15E	410	Kharkov	1656	1554 (85e)	1444 (79)	1223 (70)	953 (59)	417 (26)	174 (97)	31 (56)	10 (11)
46.38N, 32.36E	59	Kherson	1778	346 (85e)	319 (79)	261 (70)	158 (59)	59 (26)	59 (97)	34 (56)	9 (11)
49.25N, 27.00E		Khmelnitskiy	1493?	217 (85e)	172 (79)	113 (70)	62 (59)	32 (26)	23 (97)		2 (11)
50.26N, 30.31E	440	Kiev	430?	2448 (85e)	2144 (79)	1632 (70)	1110 (59)	514 (26)	248 (97)	62 (56)	23 (11)
58.33N, 49.42E	545	Kirov	1174	411 (85e)	390 (79)	333 (70)	252 (59)	62 (26)	25 (97)	15 (56)	4 (11)
40.41N, 46.22E	1024	Kirovabad	12th c?	261 (85e)	232 (79)	190 (70)	136 (59)	57 (26)	34 (97)	11 (56)	
40.48N, 44.30E	4429	Kirovakan	bef 1826	165 (85e)	146 (79)	107 (70)	49 (59)	14 (34)	9 (97)		
48.30N, 32.18E	427	Kirovograd	1754	263 (85e)	237 (79)	189 (70)	132 (59)	66 (26)	61 (97)	13 (56)	5 (11)
47.00N, 28.50E	295	Kishinev	1420?	624 (85e)	503 (79)	356 (70)	216 (59)	115 (30)	108 (97)	63 (56)	7 (12e)
55.43N, 21.07E	26	Klaypeda	1252	195 (85e)	176 (79)	140 (70)	90 (59)	37 (31)	21 (05)	11 (49)	5 (02)
57.46N, 40.55E	456	Kostroma	1152	269 (85e)	255 (79)	223 (70)	172 (59)	74 (26)	41 (97)	6 (56)	10 (11)
48.43N, 37.32E		Kramatorsk	1897	192 (85e)	178 (79)	150 (70)	115 (59)	12 (26)			
45.02N, 39.00E	95	Krasnodar	1794	609 (85e)	560 (79)	464 (70)	313 (59)	163 (26)	66 (97)	9 (56)	4 (25)
49.04N, 33.25E		Kremenchug	1571	224 (85e)	210 (79)	148 (70)	87 (59)	59 (26)	63 (97)	20 (56)	8 (11)
47.55N, 33.21E	325	Krivoy Rog	17th c	684 (85e)	650 (79)	573 (70)	401 (59)	31 (26)	15 (97)	3 (67?e)	
51.42N, 36.12E	738	Kursk	9th c	420 (85e)	375 (79)	284 (70)	205 (59)	99 (26)	76 (97)	41 (56)	23 (11)
42.15N, 42.40E	374	Kutaisi	6th c BC	214 (85e)	194 (79)	161 (70)	128 (59)	48 (26)	32 (97)	8 (67)	
53.12N, 50.09E	446	Kuybyshev	1586	1257 (85e)	1216 (79)	1045 (70)	806 (59)	176 (26)	90 (97)	24 (56)	4 (11)
40.48N, 43.50E	5105	Leninakan	773	223 (85e)	207 (79)	165 (70)	108 (59)	42 (26)	31 (97)	12 (56)	
59.55N, 30.15E	7	Leningrad	1703	4329 (85e)	4073 (79)	3513 (70)	2985 (59)	1614 (26)	1265 (97)	491 (56)	271 (05)
				4867s(85e)	4588s(79)	3950s(70)	3321s(59)				
52.37N, 39.35E	541	Lipetsk	13th c	447 (85e)	396 (79)	289 (70)	157 (59)	21 (26)	21 (97)	11 (56)	5 (11)
50.45N, 25.20E	643	Lutsk	1085?	172 (85e)	137 (79)	94 (70)	56 (59)	36 (31)	16 (97)	7 (56)	2 (11)

Coordinates	Elev	Town	Founded								
49.50N, 24.00E	984	Lvov	1250?	742 (85e)	667 (79)	553 (70)	411 (59)	316 (31)	160 (00)	68 (51)	39 (95)
48.02N, 37.58E	623	Makeyevka	1899	451 (85e)	436 (79)	392 (70)	371 (59)	51 (26)			
42.58N, 47.30E	-69	Makhachkala	1844	301 (85e)	251 (79)	186 (70)	119 (59)	32 (26)	10 (97)	4 (67)	
46.50N, 35.22E	46	Melitopol	18th c	170 (85e)	161 (79)	137 (70)	95 (59)	25 (26)	15 (97)	4 (56)	
53.54N, 27.34E	732	Minsk	1067?	1472 (85e)	1262 (79)	907 (70)	509 (59)	132 (26)	91 (97)	26 (56)	11 (11)
53.54N, 30.21E	499	Mogilev	1267	343 (85e)	290 (79)	202 (70)	122 (59)	50 (26)	43 (97)	23 (56)	6 (11)
55.45N, 37.35E	548	*Moscow	1147?	8408 (85e)	7831 (79)	6942 (70)	6009 (59)	2026 (26)	1039 (97)	369 (56)	270 (11)
				8642s (85e)	8011s (79)	7077s (70)	6044s (59)				
68.58N, 33.05E	187	Murmansk	1915	419 (85e)	381 (79)	309 (70)	222 (59)	9 (26)			
55.42N, 52.19E	249	Naberezhnyye Chelny	bef 1898	437 (85e)	301 (79)	38 (70)	16 (59)	5 (32)	3 (00?e)	1 (67?e)	
43.29N, 43.37E	1447	Nalchik	1818	227 (85e)	207 (79)	146 (70)	88 (59)	13 (26)	5 (97)		
46.58N, 32.00E	98	Nikolayev	1788	486 (85e)	440 (79)	331 (70)	235 (59)	105 (26)	92 (97)	44 (56)	4 (11)
55.36N, 51.47E		Nizhnekamsk	1966?	170 (85e)	134 (79)	49 (70)					
58.31N, 31.17E	79	Novgorod	859?	220 (85e)	186 (79)	128 (70)	61 (59)	33 (26)	26 (97)	13 (56)	6 (11)
47.25N, 37.47E	341	Novocherkassk	1805	186 (85e)	183 (79)	162 (70)	123 (59)	62 (26)	52 (97)	18 (56)	6 (11)
44.43N, 37.47E	121	Novorossiysk	1838	175 (85e)	159 (79)	133 (70)	93 (59)	68 (26)	17 (97)		
46.28N, 30.44E	138	Odessa	14th c	1126 (85e)	1046 (79)	892 (70)	664 (59)	421 (26)	404 (97)	101 (56)	11 (11)
43.00N, 44.40E	2192	Ordzhonikidze	1784	303 (85e)	279 (79)	236 (70)	164 (59)	78 (26)	44 (97)	6 (63)	25 (11)
52.55N, 36.05E	666	Orel	1566	328 (85e)	305 (79)	232 (70)	150 (59)	78 (26)	70 (97)	35 (56)	5 (11)
51.45N, 55.06E	358	Orenburg	1743	519 (85e)	459 (79)	344 (70)	267 (59)	123 (26)	72 (97)	14 (56)	2 (00?e)
51.12N, 58.34E	673	Orsk	1735	266 (85e)	247 (79)	225 (70)	176 (59)	14 (26)	14 (97)	2 (63)	15 (11)
53.13N, 45.00E	764	Penza	1666	527 (85e)	483 (79)	374 (70)	255 (59)	92 (26)	60 (97)	24 (56)	3 (11)
58.00N, 56.15E	535	Perm	1568	1056 (85e)	999 (79)	850 (70)	629 (59)	85 (26)	45 (97)	9 (56)	5 (11)
61.49N, 34.20E	361	Petrozavodsk	1703	255 (85e)	234 (79)	184 (70)	135 (59)	27 (26)	13 (97)	10 (56)	0.9 (11)
55.26N, 37.33E	525	Podolsk	bef 1781	208 (85e)	202 (79)	169 (70)	129 (59)	20 (26)	4 (97)	4 (56)	
49.35N, 34.34E	138	Poltava	1174?	302 (85e)	279 (79)	220 (70)	143 (59)	92 (26)	54 (97)	21 (56)	10 (11)
57.50N, 28.20E	138	Pskov	903?	194 (85e)	176 (79)	127 (70)	81 (59)	44 (26)	30 (97)	16 (56)	9 (11)
56.57N, 24.06E	30	Riga	1201?	883 (85e)	835 (79)	732 (70)	580 (59)	378 (30)	282 (97)	70 (56)	32 (11)
47.14N, 39.42E	217	Rostov-na-Donu	1761	986 (85e)	934 (79)	789 (70)	600 (59)	308 (26)	119 (97)	13 (56)	4 (11)
50.37N, 26.15E	768	Rovno	1282?	221 (85e)	179 (79)	116 (70)	56 (59)	42 (31)	25 (97)	5 (56)	3 (11)
54.38N, 39.44E	512	Ryazan	1095?	494 (85e)	453 (79)	350 (70)	214 (59)	51 (26)	46 (97)	21 (56)	8 (11)
54.11N, 45.11E	230	Saransk	1641	307 (85e)	263 (79)	191 (70)	91 (59)	15 (26)	15 (97)	5 (56)	9 (11)
51.34N, 46.02E	492	Saratov	1590	899 (85e)	856 (79)	757 (70)	579 (59)	215 (26)	137 (97)	62 (56)	27 (11)
44.36N, 33.32E	23	Sevastopol	16th c	341 (85e)	301 (79)	229 (70)	144 (59)	75 (26)	54 (97)	6 (56)	2 (82)
64.34N, 39.50E	3	Severodvinsk	1918?	230 (85e)	197 (79)	145 (70)	79 (59)	21 (39)			

(Continued)

For an explanation of symbols and abbreviations, see pages 16–17.

TABLE 2a. (Continued)

Latitude and Longitude	Elev (ft)	City	Date Settled	Population (thousands)							
				Latest	ca 1980	ca 1970	ca 1950	ca 1930	ca 1900	ca 1850	ca 1800
47.42N, 40.13E	384	Shakhty	1839	221 (85e)	209 (79)	205 (70)	196 (59)	33 (26)	16 (97)	4 (63)	0.8 (11)
44.57N, 34.06E	669	Simferopol	16th c?	331 (85e)	302 (79)	249 (70)	186 (59)	88 (26)	49 (97)	26 (56)	2 (11)
54.47N, 32.03E	764	Smolensk	865	331 (85e)	299 (79)	211 (70)	147 (59)	79 (26)	47 (97)	9 (56)	12 (11)
43.35N, 39.45E	39	Sochi	1896	310 (85e)	287 (79)	224 (70)	127 (59)	10 (26)	0.4 (97)		
45.03N, 41.58E	1552	Stavropol	1777	293 (85e)	258 (79)	198 (70)	141 (59)	59 (26)	42 (97)	17 (56)	
53.37N, 55.58E	423	Sterlitamak	1766	240 (85e)	220 (79)	185 (70)	112 (59)	25 (26)	16 (97)	6 (56)	2 (11)
40.36N, 49.38E	-66	Sumgait	bef 1882	223 (85e)	190 (79)	124 (70)	51 (59)	6 (39)			
50.54N, 34.48E	449	Sumy	1658	256 (85e)	228 (79)	159 (70)	98 (59)	44 (26)	28 (97)	12 (56)	9 (11)
61.40N, 50.48E	427	Syktyvkar	16th c	213 (85e)	171 (79)	125 (70)	69 (59)	5 (26)	4 (97)	3 (56)	2 (11)
53.11N, 48.27E	187	Syzran	1683	173 (85e)	166 (79)	173 (70)	148 (59)	50 (26)	32 (97)	18 (56)	7 (11)
47.12N, 38.56E	46	Taganrog	1698	289 (85e)	276 (79)	254 (70)	202 (59)	86 (26)	51 (97)	19 (56)	7 (11)
59.25N, 24.45E	39	Tallin	1154	464 (85e)	430 (79)	363 (70)	282 (59)	125 (27)	65 (97)	20 (56)	18 (11)
52.43N, 41.27E	459	Tambov	1636	296 (85e)	270 (79)	230 (70)	172 (59)	76 (26)	48 (97)	22 (56)	17 (11)
58.23N, 26.43E	217	Tartu	1030	111 (85e)	105 (79)	90 (70)	74 (59)	60 (27)	41 (97)	13 (56)	6 (11)
41.42N, 44.45E	1322	Tbilisi	4th c?	1158 (85e)	1066 (79)	889 (70)	703 (59)	294 (26)	160 (97)	38 (56)	22 (97e)
49.33N, 25.35E	1063	Ternopol	1540	182 (85e)	144 (79)	85 (70)	53 (59)	36 (31)	30 (00)	17 (57)	7 (20?)
46.50N, 29.37E	62	Tiraspol	1792	162 (85e)	139 (79)	105 (70)	63 (59)	18 (26)	32 (97)	6 (50?)	
53.31N, 49.20E	151	Tolyatti	1738	594 (85e)	502 (79)	251 (70)	72 (59)	6 (26)	6 (97)	4 (56)	2 (11)
54.12N, 37.37E	541	Tula	1146?	532 (85e)	514 (79)	462 (70)	351 (59)	153 (26)	115 (97)	51 (56)	52 (11)
54.44N, 55.56E	568	Ufa	1586	1064 (85e)	969 (79)	771 (70)	547 (59)	99 (26)	49 (97)	13 (56)	9 (11)
54.20N, 48.24E	558	Ulyanovsk	1648	544 (85e)	464 (79)	351 (70)	206 (59)	72 (26)	42 (97)	27 (56)	13 (11)
48.37N, 22.18E	397	Uzhgorod	903?	107 (85e)	91 (79)	65 (70)	47 (59)	27 (31)	15 (01)	9 (57)	3 (00?e)
54.41N, 25.19E	486	Vilnyus	10th c	544 (85e)	481 (79)	372 (70)	236 (59)	196 (31)	155 (97)	46 (56)	25 (00)
49.14N, 28.29E	791	Vinnitsa	14th c	367 (85e)	314 (79)	212 (70)	122 (59)	58 (26)	31 (97)	9 (56)	3 (11)
55.12N, 30.11E	545	Vitebsk	1021?	335 (85e)	297 (79)	231 (70)	148 (59)	99 (26)	66 (97)	21 (56)	17 (11)
56.10N, 40.25E	551	Vladimir	1108?	331 (85e)	296 (79)	234 (70)	154 (59)	40 (26)	28 (97)	13 (56)	6 (11)
47.32N, 42.09E		Volgodonsk	bef 1956	165 (85e)	91 (79)	28 (70)	16 (59)				
48.45N, 44.25E	75	Volgograd	1589	974 (85e)	929 (79)	818 (70)	591 (59)	148 (26)	55 (97)	7 (56)	4 (11)
59.13N, 39.54E	430	Vologda	1147?	269 (85e)	237 (79)	178 (70)	139 (59)	58 (26)	28 (97)	14 (56)	10 (11)
48.49N, 44.44E		Volzhskiy	1951	245 (85e)	209 (79)	142 (70)	67 (59)				

Coordinates	No.	City	Founded								
51.38N, 39.12E	482	Voronezh	1586	850 (85e)	783 (79)	660 (70)	447 (59)	120 (26)	81 (97)	38 (56)	22 (11)
48.34N, 39.20E	194	Voroshilovgrad	18th c	497 (85e)	463 (79)	383 (70)	275 (59)	72 (26)	20 (97)	7 (61)	0.8 (82)
44.30N, 34.10E	13	Yalta	2nd c	86 (85e)	80 (79)	62 (70)	44 (59)	29 (26)	13 (97)	1 (63)	
57.37N, 39.52E	322	Yaroslavl	1024	626 (85e)	597 (79)	517 (70)	407 (59)	114 (26)	72 (97)	27 (56)	24 (11)
40.11N, 44.30E	2986	Yerevan	607?	1133 (85e)	1019 (79)	767 (70)	493 (59)	65 (26)	29 (97)	13 (56)	15 (00?e)
56.40N, 47.55E	328	Yoshkar-Ola	1578	231 (85e)	201 (79)	166 (70)	89 (59)	4 (26)	2 (97)	1 (67?e)	1 (11)
47.49N, 35.11E	161	Zaporozhye	1770	852 (85e)	781 (79)	658 (70)	449 (59)	56 (26)	19 (97)	3 (56)	
47.06N, 37.33E	10	Zhdanov	1779	522 (85e)	503 (79)	417 (70)	284 (59)	41 (26)	31 (97)	7 (56)	3 (11)
50.15N, 28.40E	597	Zhitomir	1240?	275 (85e)	244 (79)	161 (70)	106 (59)	77 (26)	66 (97)	31 (56)	8 (11)
Yugoslavia											
44.46N, 17.10E	535	Banja Luka	1295?		124 (81)	91 (71)	30 (48)	22 (31)	15 (95)	15 (50?e)	15 (00?e)
44.50N, 20.30E	433	*Belgrade	3rd c BC		1088 (81); 1470s(81)	746 (71); 775s(71)	368 (48)	266 (31)	70 (00)	15 (50)	25 (89e)
41.02N, 21.20E	2034	Bitola	1014?		79 (81)	65 (71)	31 (48)	33 (31)	50 (00?e)	40 (58e)	15 (00?e)
42.39N, 18.07E	161	Dubrovnik	7th c		44 (81)	31 (71)	17 (48)	19 (31)	13 (00)	5 (51)	7 (08)
44.01N, 20.55E	600	Kragujevac	1565?		88 (81)	71 (71)	33 (48)	27 (31)	16 (00)	6 (66)	
46.02N, 14.30E	981	Ljubljana	34 BC		225 (81)	174 (71); 213s(71)	98 (48)	60 (31)	37 (00)	17 (51)	11 (00?e)
46.33N, 15.39E	902	Maribor	1147?		106 (81)	97 (71)	63 (48)	33 (31)	25 (00)	7 (51)	5 (00?e)
43.21N, 17.49E	194	Mostar	1452?		63 (81)	48 (71)	22 (48)	20 (31)	17 (95)	10 (50?e)	9 (00?e)
43.19N, 21.54E	663	Nis	140?		161 (81)	128 (71)	49 (48)	35 (31)	25 (00)	4 (50?e)	4 (00?e)
45.15N, 19.50E	433	Novi Sad	1687		170 (81)	141 (71); 163s(71); 271s(71)	69 (48)	64 (31)	29 (00)	10 (51)	13 (08)
45.33N, 18.42E	292	Osijek	8 AD?		105 (81)	95 (71)	50 (48)	40 (31)	25 (00)	13 (51)	9 (00?e)
42.40N, 21.10E	2169	Pristina	12th c?		108 (81)	70 (71)	20 (48)	16 (31)	15 (00?e)	12 (50?e)	
45.21N, 14.24E	341	Rijeka	28 AD		159 (81)	132 (71)	69 (48)	53 (31)	38 (00)	11 (51)	9 (10)
43.50N, 18.25E	2067	Sarajevo	1262		319 (81)	244 (71)	99 (48)	78 (31)	42 (95)	50 (50e)	40 (00?e)
42.00N, 21.29E	787	Skopje	2nd c?		408 (81)	313 (71)	92 (48)	65 (31)	20 (00?e)	10 (50?e)	8 (00?e)
43.31N, 16.26E	400	Split	305		169 (81)	153 (71)	64 (48)	35 (31)	27 (00)	11 (51)	7 (00?)
46.06N, 19.40E	361	Subotica	1391?		101 (81)	89 (71)	63 (48)	100 (31)	82 (01)	48 (51)	28 (08?e)
42.26N, 19.16E	184	Titograd	1326?		96 (81)	55 (71)	11 (48)	11 (31)	7 (96)	6 (50?e)	
44.33N, 18.41E	761	Tuzla	12th c?		65 (81)	54 (71)	21 (48)	17 (31)	11 (95)	14 (51)	
45.48N, 16.00E	515	Zagreb	7th c?		650 (81)	566 (71)	280 (48)	186 (31)	58 (00)	14 (51)	13 (00e)

For an explanation of symbols and abbreviations, see pages 16–17.

(Continued)

TABLE 2a. (Continued)

Latitude and Longitude	Elev (ft)	City	Date Settled	Population (thousands)							
				Latest	ca 1980	ca 1970	ca 1950	ca 1930	ca 1900	ca 1850	ca 1800
NORTH AMERICA											
Antigua and Barbuda											
17.06N, 61.51W	20	*Saint John's	1681?	36 (83e)	25 (79e)	22 (70)	11 (46)	10 (31)	9 (01)		
Aruba											
12.31N, 70.02W	52	*Oranjestad	1820		17 (80e)	16 (68e)					
Bahamas											
25.05N, 77.21W	18	*Nassau	1729		135s(80)	102s(70)	46s(53)	20s(31)	13s(01)	8s(51)	6s(00?)
Barbados											
13.06N, 59.37W	181	*Bridgetown	1628		8 (80) 90s(80)	9 (70) 115s(70)	13 (46) 69s(46)	13 (21)	21 (91)	20 (51)	17 (00?e)
Belize											
17.30N, 88.12W	16	Belize	1638?	47 (85e)	40 (80)	39 (70)	22 (46)	17 (31)	9 (01)	4 (55e)	1 (00?e)
17.15N, 88.47W		*Belmopan	1966	4 (85e)	3 (80)	0.3 (70)					
Bermuda											
32.17N, 64.46W	158	*Hamilton	1790		2 (80) 15s(80)	3 (70) 14s(70)	2 (50)	3 (31)	2 (01)		1 (00?e)
Canada											
43.41N, 79.46W	722	Brampton	1830	188 (86)	149 (81)	41 (71)	8 (51)	6 (31)	3 (01)	2 (71)	
43.08N, 80.16W	706	Brantford	1784	76 (86) 91s(86)	74 (81) 88s(81)	64 (71) 80s(71)	37 (51)	30 (31)	17 (01)	4 (52)	
43.19N, 79.47W	281	Burlington	1810	117 (86)	115 (81)	87 (71)	6 (51)	3 (31)	1 (01)		
51.03N,114.05W	3428	Calgary	1875	636 (86) 667s(86)	593 (81) 593s(81)	403 (71) 403s(71)	129 (51) 139s(51)	84 (31)	4 (01)	0.4 (84)	
46.14N, 63.08W	8	Charlottetown	1768	16 (86)	15 (81) 45s(81)	19 (71)	16 (51)	13 (31)	12 (01)	5 (48)	2 (28)
48.26N, 71.06W	19	Chicoutimi	1676	61 (86) 157s(86)	60 (81) 135s(81)	34 (71) 134s(71)	23 (51)	12 (31)	4 (01)	1 (71)	
44.40N, 63.34W	14	Dartmouth	1750	65 (86)	62 (81)	65 (71)	15 (51)	9 (31)	5 (01)	3 (61)	

(Continued)

Coordinates	No.	City	Founded	(86)	(81)	(71)	(51)	(31)	(01)		
53.33N,113.28W	2188	Edmonton	1819?	574 (86), 780s(86)	532 (81), 657s(81)	438 (71), 496s(71)	160 (51), 173s(51)	79 (31)	3 (01)		
45.57N, 66.38W	29	Fredericton	1785	44 (86)	44 (81), 64s(81)	24 (71)	16 (51)	9 (31)	7 (01)	6 (71)	
43.33N, 80.15W	1063	Guelph	1827	78 (86), 86s(86)	71 (81), 78s(81)	60 (71), 63s(71)	27 (51)	21 (31)	11 (01)	2 (52)	
44.39N, 63.36W	57	Halifax	1749	114 (86), 296s(86)	115 (81), 278s(81)	122 (71), 223s(71)	86 (51), 134s(51)	59 (31)	41 (01)	26 (52)	5 (91)
43.15N, 79.51W	306	Hamilton	1813	307 (86), 557s(86)	306 (81), 542s(81)	309 (71), 499s(71)	208 (51), 260s(51)	156 (31)	53 (01)	14 (52)	3 (36)
45.26N, 75.44W	191	Hull	1800	59 (86)	56 (81)	64 (71)	43 (51)	29 (31)	14 (01)	4 (61)	
48.25N, 71.15W	484	Jonquiere	1847	58 (86)	60 (81)	28 (71)	22 (51)	9 (31)	2 (11)		
50.40N,120.20W	1159	Kamloops	1812	62 (86)	64 (81), 65s(81)	26 (71)	8 (51)	6 (31)	2 (01)		
49.54N,119.29W	1160	Kelowna	1859	61 (86), 90s(86)	59 (81), 77s(81)	19 (71)	9 (51)	5 (31)	2 (11)		
44.14N, 76.29W	264	Kingston	1783	55 (86), 122s(86)	53 (81), 115s(81)	59 (71), 86s(71)	33 (51)	23 (31)	18 (01)	12 (52)	0.3 (94)
43.27N, 80.29W	1100	Kitchener	1806	151 (86), 311s(86)	140 (81), 288s(81)	112 (71), 227s(71)	45 (51), 63s(51)	31 (31)	10 (01)	2 (61)	
45.25N, 73.39W	131	La Salle	1668	76 (86)	76 (81)	73 (71)	12 (51)	2 (31)	6 (01)	1 (51)	
45.33N, 73.43W	130	Laval	1699	284 (86)	268 (81)	228 (71)	38s(51)	16s(31)	10s(01)	10s(52)	
49.42N,112.50W	2993	Lethbridge	1870	59 (86)	54 (81)	41 (71)	23 (51)	13 (31)	2 (01)		
42.59N, 81.14W	809	London	1826	269 (86), 342s(86)	254 (81), 284s(81)	223 (71), 286s(71)	95 (51), 122s(51)	71 (31)	38 (01)	7 (52)	
45.32N, 73.31W	55	Longueuil	1657	125 (86)	124 (81)	98 (71)	11 (51)	5 (31)	3 (01)	1s(52)	
45.52N, 79.16W	640	Markham	1792	115 (86)	77 (81)	37 (71)	2 (51)	1 (31)	1 (01)	1 (81)	
43.34N, 79.37W	391	Mississauga	bef 1852	374 (86)	315 (81)	156 (71)	299s(51)	10s(31)	5s(01)	8s(52)	
46.05N, 64.46W	33	Moncton	1763	55 (86)	55 (81), 98s(81)	48 (71), 70s(71)	27 (51)	21 (31)	9 (01)	1 (61)	
45.30N, 73.35W	104	Montreal	1642	1015 (86), 2897s(86)	980 (81), 2828s(81)	1214 (71), 2743s(71)	1022 (51), 1395s(51)	819 (31), 1010s(31)	268 (01)	58 (52)	16 (16)
45.36N, 73.38W	69	Montreal-Nord	bef 1915	90 (86)	95 (81)	89 (71)	14 (51)	5 (31)	1 (21)		
45.16N, 75.46W	372	Nepean	1811	95 (86)	84 (81)	65 (71)	4s(51)	11s(31)	6s(01)		
43.06N, 79.04W	584	Niagara Falls	1776	72 (86)	71 (81)	67 (71)	23 (51)	19 (31)	4 (01)	2 (71)	
46.18N, 79.27W	662	North Bay	1882	51 (86), 57s(86)	51 (81), 57s(81)	49 (71), 51s(71)	18 (51)	16 (31)	3 (01)	2 (91)	

For an explanation of symbols and abbreviations, see pages 16–17.

TABLE 2a. (Continued)

Latitude and Longitude	Elev (ft)	City	Date Settled	Population (thousands)							
				Latest	ca 1980	ca 1970	ca 1950	ca 1930	ca 1900	ca 1850	ca 1800
43.44N, 79.26W	576	North York	1816?	556 (86)	560 (81)	504 (71)	86 (51)	13 (31)			
43.26N, 79.40W	328	Oakville	1805	87 (86)	76 (81)	61 (71)	7 (51)	4 (31)	2 (01)	2 (71)	
43.54N, 78.51W	325	Oshawa	1791	124 (86)	118 (81)	92 (71)	42 (51)	23 (31)	4 (01)	1 (52)	
				204s(86)	154s(81)	120s(71)	52s(51)				
45.25N, 75.42W	284	*Ottawa	1826	301 (86)	295 (81)	302 (71)	202 (51)	127 (31)	60 (01)	8 (52)	1 (30)
				819s(86)	718s(81)	603s(71)	282s(51)	166s(31)			
44.18N, 78.20W	632	Peterborough	1821	61 (86)	61 (81)	58 (71)	38 (51)	22 (31)	11 (01)	2 (51)	
				87s(86)	86s(81)	64s(71)					
53.55N, 122.46W	1867	Prince George	1807	68 (86)	68 (81)	33 (71)	5 (51)	2 (31)	2 (21)		
					68s(81)						
46.49N, 71.13W	130	Quebec	1608	165 (86)	166 (81)	186 (71)	164 (51)	131 (31)	69 (01)	42 (52)	12 (00e)
				598s(86)	576s(81)	481s(71)	275s(51)	165s(31)			
50.25N, 104.39W	1885	Regina	1882	175 (86)	163 (81)	139 (71)	71 (51)	53 (31)	2 (01)		
				185s(86)	164s(81)	141s(71)					
43.10N, 79.15W	347	Saint Catharines	1792	123 (86)	124 (81)	110 (71)	38 (51)	25 (31)	10 (01)	4s(52)	
				343s(86)	304s(81)	303s(71)	67s(51)				
45.16N, 66.03W	42	Saint John	1783?	76 (86)	81 (81)	89 (71)	51 (51)	48 (31)	41 (01)	23 (52)	9 (21e)
				120s(86)	114s(81)	107s(71)	78s(51)				
47.33N, 52.43W	200	Saint John's	1583?	96 (86)	84 (81)	88 (71)	53 (51)	40 (35)	30 (01)	21 (52)	3 (02)
				161s(86)	155s(81)	132s(71)	68s(51)				
45.35N, 73.39W	69	Saint-Leonard	bef 1886	76 (86)	79 (81)	52 (71)	0.7 (51)	0.5 (31)	0.5 (21)		
42.58N, 82.24W	625	Sarnia	1833	49 (86)	51 (81)	58 (71)	35 (51)	18 (31)	8 (01)	3 (71)	
				86s(86)	84s(81)	78s(71)					
52.07N, 106.38W	1574	Saskatoon	1883	178 (86)	154 (81)	126 (71)	53 (51)	43 (31)	0.1 (01)		
				199s(86)	154s(81)	126s(71)					
46.30N, 84.20W	634	Sault Sainte Marie	1814	81 (86)	83 (81)	80 (71)	32 (51)	23 (31)	7 (01)	0.9 (71)	
				85s(86)	87s(81)	81s(71)					
45.24N, 71.54W	521	Sherbrooke	1794	74 (86)	74 (81)	81 (71)	51 (51)	29 (31)	12 (01)	3 (52)	
					117s(81)	85s(71)	56s(51)				
46.30N, 81.00W	857	Sudbury	1887	89 (86)	92 (81)	91 (71)	42 (51)	19 (31)	2 (01)		
				149s(86)	150s(81)	155s(71)	71s(51)				

(Continued)

Location	Elev.	Station	Year	(86e)	(81)	(71)	(51)	(31)	(01)		
46.09N, 60.11W	42	Sydney	1784	28 (86)	29 (81)	33 (71)	31 (51)	23 (31)	10 (01)	2 (61)	
				119s(86)	87s(81)	91s(71)	104s(51)				
48.25N, 89.14W	615	Thunder Bay	1678	112 (86)	112 (81)	108 (71)	66 (51)	46 (31)	7 (01)	2 (81)	
				122s(86)	121s(81)	112s(71)	71s(51)				
43.39N, 79.23W	273	Toronto	1793	612 (86)	599 (81)	713 (71)	676 (51)	631 (31)	208 (01)	31 (52)	1 (17)
				3427s(86)	2999s(81)	2628s(71)	1117s(51)	665s(31)			
46.21N, 72.34W	51	Trois-Rivieres	1634	50 (86)	50 (81)	56 (71)	46 (51)	35 (31)	10 (01)	5 (52)	2 (00?e)
					111s(81)	98s(71)	68s(51)				
49.17N,123.07W	38	Vancouver	1870?	431 (86)	414 (81)	426 (71)	345 (51)	247 (31)	26 (01)		
				1381s(86)	1268s(81)	1082s(71)	531s(51)	273s(31)			
48.25N,123.22W	55	Victoria	1851?	66 (86)	64 (81)	62 (71)	51 (51)	39 (31)	21 (01)	0.2 (54)	
				256s(86)	233s(81)	196s(71)	104s(51)				
43.28N, 80.32W	1076	Waterloo	1806	59 (86)	49 (81)	36 (71)	12 (51)	8 (31)	4 (01)	1 (61)	
60.43N,135.03W	2307	Whitehorse	1897	15 (86)	15 (81)	11 (71)	3 (51)	0.5 (31)	0.3 (21)	0.1 (52)	
42.18N, 83.01W	602	Windsor	1745?	193 (86)	192 (81)	203 (71)	120 (51)	63 (31)	12 (01)	0.2 (71)	
				254s(86)	246s(81)	259s(71)	158s(51)	106s(31)			
49.53N, 97.09W	757	Winnipeg	1812	595 (86)	564 (81)	246 (71)	236 (51)	219 (31)	42 (01)		
				625s(86)	585s(81)	540s(71)	354s(51)	239s(31)			
62.27N,114.21W	673	Yellowknife	1935	12 (86)	9 (81)	6 (71)	3 (51)				
Costa Rica											
9.56N, 84.05W	3845	*San Jose	1736		241 (84)	215 (73)	87 (50)	51 (27)	35 (03)	6 (44)	8 (23)
						406s(73)	140s(50)	63s(27)			
Cuba											
20.23N, 76.39W		Bayamo	1513	122 (85e)	101 (81)	71 (70)	26 (53)	12 (31)	3 (99)	5 (46)	7 (27)
21.23N, 77.55W	397	Camaguey	1528	267 (85e)	245 (81)	198 (70)	110 (53)	62 (31)	25 (99)	19 (46)	49 (27)
22.09N, 80.27W	98	Cienfuegos	1738?	117 (85e)	102 (81)	81 (70)	58 (53)	50 (31)	30 (99)	4 (46)	
20.08N, 75.12W	75	Guantanamo	1819	195 (85e)	167 (81)	129 (70)	65 (53)	28 (31)	7 (99)	0.9 (46)	
23.08N, 82.22W	161	*Havana	1519	2015 (85e)	1925 (81)	1751 (70)	785 (53)	521 (31)	236 (99)	107 (46)	51 (91)
							1218s(53)				
20.53N, 76.15W	361	Holguin	1754	211 (85e)	186 (81)	132 (70)	59 (53)	24 (31)	6 (99)	3 (46)	9 (27)
20.58N, 76.57W		Las Tunas	1759	104 (85e)	85 (81)	54 (70)	20 (53)	8 (31)	0.7(99)	1 (46)	2 (27)
20.21N, 77.07W	164	Manzanillo	1784	104 (85e)	95 (81)	78 (70)	42 (53)	30 (31)	14 (99)	3 (41)	
23.03N, 81.35W		Matanzas	1693	111 (85e)	99 (81)	87 (70)	64 (53)	50 (31)	36 (99)	18 (46)	11 (27)
22.25N, 83.42W	180	Pinar del Rio	1571	116 (85e)	95 (81)	75 (70)	39 (53)	20 (31)	9 (99)	1 (46)	
22.24N, 79.58W	377	Santa Clara	1689	186 (85e)	172 (81)	130 (70)	77 (53)	38 (31)	14 (99)	6 (46)	9 (27)

For an explanation of symbols and abbreviations, see pages 16–17.

TABLE 2a. (Continued)

Latitude and Longitude	Elev (ft)	City	Date Settled	Population (thousands)							
				Latest	ca 1980	ca 1970	ca 1950	ca 1930	ca 1900	ca 1850	ca 1800
20.01N, 75.49W	115	Santiago de Cuba	1514	396 (85e)	345 (81)	278 (70)	163 (53)	102 (31)	43 (99)	24 (46)	27 (27)
Dominica											
15.18N, 61.24W	26	*Roseau	17th c		8 (81)	10 (70)	10 (46)	7 (30)	6 (01)	5 (50?e)	
Dominican Republic											
18.25N, 68.58W	16	La Romana	late 19th c		92 (81)	37 (70)	14 (50)	11 (35)	6 (20		
18.27N, 69.18W	13	San Pedro de Macoris	1880		79 (81)	44 (70)	20 (50)	19 (35)	7 (00?e)		
19.27N, 70.42W	728	Santiago de los Caballeros	1504		279 (81)	155 (70)	57 (50)	34 (35)	12 (00?e)	12 (50?e)	12 (00?e)
18.28N, 69.54W	46	*Santo Domingo	1496		1313 (81)	669 (70)	182 (50)	71 (35)	22 (00e)	12 (50?e)	12 (00?e)
El Salvador											
13.43N, 89.12W	2067	Mejicanos	bef 1740	89 (84e)	79 (80e)	56 (71)	9 (50)	6 (30)			
13.28N, 88.12W	345	San Miguel	1530	87 (84e)	80 (80e)	62 (71)	27 (50)	18 (30)	25 (01)	6 (50?e)	
13.42N, 89.12W	2290	*San Salvador	1525	455 (84e)	423 (80e)	336 (71)	162 (50)	89 (30)	60 (01)	25 (50)	12 (07)
13.59N, 89.34W	2116	Santa Ana	1576?	135 (84e)	119 (80e)	98 (71)	52 (50)	41 (30)	48 (01)	10 (50?e)	
Greenland											
64.11N, 51.45W	82	*Godthab	1721	11 (85e)	9 (76)	8 (70)	1 (51)	0.4(28)	0.9(01)		
Grenada											
12.03N, 61.45W	302	*Saint George's	1650		7 (81e)	7 (70)	6 (46)	5 (21)	5 (01)	4 (44)	
Guadeloupe											
16.00N, 61.43W	66	*Basse-Terre	1643		14 (82)	15 (67)	12 (54)	9 (31)	7 (01)	9 (50?e)	5 (22)
16.16N, 61.31W	23	Les Abymes	bef 1828		56 (82)	36 (67)	18 (54)	11 (31)	8 (06)	5 (72)	
16.14N, 61.32W	23	Pointe-a-Pitre	1759		121s(82) 25 (82)	30 (67)	26 (54)	30 (31)	19 (01)	18 (46)	15 (00?3)
Guatemala											
14.38N, 90.31W	4928	*Guatemala	1776		754 (81)	701 (73)	284 (50)	164 (40)	62 (93)	37 (50e)	24 (95)

Haiti

Coordinates	Elev.	City	Founded								
19.45N, 72.12W	49	Cap-Haitien	1670	64 (82)	55 (75)	46 (71)	25 (50)	20 (27e)	15 (00?e)	12 (50?e)	15 (90e)
18.32N, 72.20W	135	*Port-au-Prince	1749	450 (82)	459 (75)	306 (71)	134 (50)	80 (29)	60 (00?e)	25 (50?e)	

Honduras

Coordinates	Elev.	City	Founded								
15.27N, 88.02W	233	San Pedro Sula	1536	344 (83e)	276 (80e)	151 (74)	21 (50)	13 (30)	7 (01)		
14.06N, 87.13W	3304	*Tegucigalpa	1578	532 (83e)	445 (80e)	274 (74)	72 (50)	17 (30)	24 (01)	8 (50?e)	

Jamaica

Coordinates	Elev.	City	Founded								
18.00N, 76.48W	110	*Kingston	1692		104 (82) / 509s(82)	112 (70) / 476s(70)	110 (43)	64 (21)	49 (91)	33 (44)	26 (88e)
18.28N, 77.55W	98	Montego Bay	bef 1733		60 (82)	44 (70)	12 (43)	7 (21)	5 (91)	4 (50?e)	
17.59N, 76.57W	95	Spanish Town	1534		81 (82)	41 (70)	12 (43)	9 (21)	5 (91)	6 (50?e)	5 (00?e)

Martinique

Coordinates	Elev.	City	Founded								
14.36N, 61.05W	13	*Fort-de-France	1672		100 (82)	97 (67)	61 (54)	48 (31)	22 (01)	13 (67?)	10 (00?e)

Mexico

Coordinates	Elev.	City	Founded								
16.50N, 99.55W	13	Acapulco	1550		302 (80)	174 (70)	28 (50)	7 (30)	5 (00)	4 (50e)	5 (93)
21.53N,102.18W	6195	Aguascalientes	1575		293 (80)	181 (70)	93 (50)	62 (30)	35 (00)	23 (62)	8 (94)
19.51N, 90.32W	16	Campeche	bef 1517		128 (80)	70 (70)	31 (50)	20 (30)	17 (00)	16 (61)	6 (00?e)
20.31N,100.49W	5932	Celaya	1570		142 (80)	80 (70)	34 (50)	24 (30)	26 (00)	7 (50?e)	
18.30N, 88.18W	20	Chetumal	1899		57 (80)	24 (70)	7 (50)	2 (30)	2 (21)		
28.38N,106.05W	4692	Chihuahua	1639		386 (80)	257 (70)	87 (50)	46 (30)	30 (00)	11 (31)	12 (03e)
17.33N, 99.30W	4462	Chilpancingo	1591		67 (80)	36 (70)	13 (50)	8 (30)	7 (00)	3 (50?e)	
31.44N,106.29W	3734	Ciudad Juarez	1662		544 (80)	407 (70)	123 (50)	40 (30)	8 (00)	2 (50?e)	
19.33N, 99.15W	7507	Ciudad Lopez Mateos			188 (80)	6 (70)	2 (50)	1 (30)	2 (00)		
22.16N, 97.50W	377	Ciudad Madero	bef 1910		132 (80)	91 (70)	41 (50)	22 (30)	15 (21)		
27.29N,109.56W	131	Ciudad Obregon	1907		166 (80)	114 (70)	31 (50)	8 (30)	0.2(21)		
23.44N, 99.08W	1053	Ciudad Victoria	1750		140 (80)	84 (70)	32 (50)	18 (30)	10 (00)	6 (52e)	4 (21e)
18.09N, 94.25W	7	Coatzacoalcos	1580		127 (80)	70 (70)	20 (50)	8 (30)	3 (00)		
19.14N,103.43W	1503	Colima	1522		86 (80)	58 (70)	29 (50)	21 (30)	21 (00)	32 (46)	9 (90)
18.53N, 96.56W	3032	Cordoba	1617		100 (80)	78 (70)	33 (50)	16 (30)	8 (00)	6 (50?e)	
18.55N, 99.15W	5059	Cuernavaca	bef 1521		193 (80)	134 (70)	31 (50)	9 (30)	10 (00)	2 (50)	
24.48N,107.24W	276	Culiacan	1533		305 (80)	168 (70)	49 (50)	18 (30)	10 (00)	11 (58)	
24.02N,104.40W	6198	Durango	1563		258 (80)	151 (70)	59 (50)	36 (30)	31 (00)	15 (49)	11 (03e)
19.35N, 99.04W	7497	Ecatepec	bef 1815		742 (80)	12 (70)	2 (50)	1 (30)	1 (00)		11 (90)

For an explanation of symbols and abbreviations, see pages 16–17.

(Continued)

TABLE 2a. (Continued)

Latitude and Longitude	Elev (ft)	City	Date Settled	Latest	ca 1980	ca 1970	ca 1950	ca 1930	ca 1900	ca 1850	ca 1800
31.52N,116.37W	43	Ensenada	1870		120 (80)	78 (70)	18 (50)	3 (30)	2 (00)		
25.40N,100.24W	2231	Garza Garcia	1882?		82 (80)	21 (70)	4 (50)	1 (30)	1 (00)		
25.39N,103.30W	3727	Gomez Palacio	1886		117 (80)	80 (70)	46 (50)	24 (30)	8 (00)		
20.40N,103.20W	5141	Guadalajara	1542		1626 (80) 2193s(80)	1194 (70) 1491s(70)	377 (50) 441s(50)	180 (30)	101 (00)	63 (52e)	24 (92)
25.11N,99.19W	673	Guadalupe	1715		371 (80)	52 (70)	10 (50)	2 (30)	1 (00)		
21.01N,101.15W	6726	Guanajuato	bef 1400		49 (80)	37 (70)	23 (50)	18 (30)	41 (00)	40 (54e)	32 (90)
29.04N,110.58W	778	Hermosillo	1750		297 (80)	177 (70)	44 (50)	20 (30)	11 (00)	4 (50)	8 (17e)
20.41N,101.28W	5656	Irapuato	1547		170 (80)	117 (70)	49 (50)	29 (30)	20 (00)		8 (93)
19.32N,96.55W	4682	Jalapa	1313?		205 (80)	122 (70)	51 (50)	37 (30)	20 (00)	17 (50?e)	6 (91)
24.10N,110.18W	33	La Paz	1720		91 (80)	46 (70)	13 (50)	8 (30)	5 (00)	1 (57e)	
21.07N,101.40W	6185	Leon	1576		593 (80)	365 (70)	123 (50)	69 (30)	63 (00)	6 (60?e)	
25.45N,108.57W	50	Los Mochis	1903		123 (80)	68 (70)	21 (50)	10 (30)	7 (21)		
25.53N,97.30W	26	Matamoros	1748		189 (80)	138 (70)	46 (50)	10 (30)	6 (00)	20 (50?e)	
23.13N,106.25W	256	Mazatlan	bef 1541		200 (80)	120 (70)	41 (50)	29 (30)	18 (00)	11 (50?e)	
20.58N,89.37W	30	Merida	bef 1528		400 (80)	212 (70)	143 (50)	95 (30)	44 (00)	24 (57e)	28 (93)
32.40N,115.29W	0	Mexicali	1901		342 (80)	267(70)	65 (50)	15 (30)	7 (21)		
19.24N,99.09W	7546	*Mexico	1325		8831 (80) 13,354s(80)	2903 (70) 8800s(70)	2235 (50) 3138s(50)	1029 (30)	345 (00)	210 (62)	105 (90)
17.59N,94.31W	210	Minatitlan	1822		107 (80)	68 (70)	22 (50)	12 (30)	1 (00)		
26.54N,101.25W	1923	Monclova	1699		116 (80)	78 (70)	19 (50)	7 (30)	7 (00)		
25.40N,100.19W	1765	Monterrey	1579?		1085 (80) 1913s(80)	858 (70) 1246s(70)	333 (50) 375s(50)	133 (30)	62 (00)	14 (49)	11 (03e)
19.42N,101.07W	6368	Morelia	1541		298 (80)	161 (70)	63 (50)	40 (30)	37 (00)	25 (52e)	17 (90)
19.28N,99.14W	7438	Naucalpan	bef 1874		724 (80)	9 (70)	4 (50)	1 (30)	1 (00)		
19.36N,99.00W	7474	Netzahualcoyotl	16th c?		1341 (80)	580 (70)	0.6(50)				
27.30N,99.31W	561	Nuevo Laredo	1755		202 (80)	149 (70)	58 (50)	22 (30)	7 (00)		
17.03N,96.43W	5086	Oaxaca	1486		154 (80)	100 (70)	47 (50)	33 (30)	35 (00)	25 (50)	18 (92)
18.51N,97.06W	4213	Orizaba	1457		115 (80)	93 (70)	56 (50)	43 (30)	32 (00)	16 (68e)	9 (93)
20.07N,98.44W	7960	Pachuca de Soto	1534		110 (80)	84 (70)	59 (50)	43 (30)	37 (00)	5 (52e)	1 (88e)
20.33N,97.27W	197	Poza Rica	1939?		167 (80)	120 (70)	15 (50)	4 (40)			

For an explanation of symbols and abbreviations, see pages 16–17.

(Continued)

Figure 11. *Monumento a la Independencia, popularly known as El Angel, on the Paseo de la Reforma in Mexico City, the second largest urbanized area in North America and the world according to the latest census figures, which, because of its current annual growth rate of 4.3%, probably surpassed New York City in population in 1984. (Credit: Mexican Government Tourism Office.)*

TABLE 2a. (Continued)

Latitude and Longitude	Elev (ft)	City	Date Settled	Latest	ca 1980	ca 1970	ca 1950	ca 1930	ca 1900	ca 1850	ca 1800
							Population (thousands)				
19.03N, 98.12W	7094	Puebla	1532		773 (80)	402 (70)	211 (50)	115 (30)	94 (00)	72 (48)	57 (93)
20.37N,105.15W	7	Puerto Vallarta	bef 1918		39 (80)	24 (70)	5 (50)	3 (30)	3 (21)		
20.36N,100.23W	5528	Queretaro	1440		216 (80)	113 (70)	49 (50)	33 (30)	33 (00)	27 (54e)	20 (92)
26.07N, 98.18W	125	Reynosa	bef 1870		195 (80)	137 (70)	34 (50)	5 (30)	2 (00)		
20.34N,101.12W	5765	Salamanca	1603		97 (80)	61 (70)	21 (50)	12 (30)	14 (00)	15 (50?e)	6 (03e)
25.25N,101.00W	5246	Saltillo	1575		285 (80)	161 (70)	70 (50)	45 (30)	24 (00)	20 (49)	
22.09N,100.59W	6158	San Luis Potosi	1576		362 (80)	230 (70)	126 (50)	74 (30)	61 (00)	11 (57e)	9 (93)
25.45N,100.18W	1765	San Nicolas de los Garza	1835?		281 (80)	29 (70)	7 (50)	2 (30)	2 (00)		
25.41N,100.28W	2231	Santa Catarina	1597		88 (80)	14 (70)	2 (50)	1 (30)	2 (00)		
22.13N, 97.51W	39	Tampico	1823		268 (80)	180 (70)	94 (50)	68 (30)	16 (00)	7 (50?e)	
18.33N, 99.36W	5840	Taxco	1529		36 (80)	27 (70)	10 (50)	4 (30)	4 (00)	1 (30?e)	
18.27N, 97.23W	5499	Tehuacan	1540		80 (80)	47 (70)	23 (50)	11 (30)	7 (00)	6 (50?e)	
21.30N,104.54W	3002	Tepic	bef 1524		146 (80)	88 (70)	25 (50)	15 (30)	15 (00)	10 (50?e)	
32.32N,117.01W	95	Tijuana	1830?		429 (80)	277 (70)	60 (50)	8 (30)	0.2(00)		
19.33N, 99.12W	7382	Tlalnepantla	15th c		778 (80)	46 (70)	10 (50)	3 (30)	2 (00)		
20.39N,103.19W	5227	Tlaquepaque	15th c?		133 (80)	60 (70)	21 (50)	8 (30)	4 (00)		
19.19N, 98.14W	7389	Tlaxcala	1120?		18 (80)	10 (70)	5 (50)	2 (30)	2 (00)		
19.17N, 99.40W	8793	Toluca			200 (80)	114 (70)	53 (50)	41 (30)	26 (00)	3 (57e)	
25.33N,103.26W	3708	Torreon	1893		328 (80)	223 (70)	129 (50)	66 (30)	14 (00)	12 (57e)	7 (93)
16.45N, 93.07W	1732	Tuxtla Gutierrez	1829		131 (80)	67 (70)	28 (50)	15 (30)	9 (00)		
19.25N,101.58W	5361	Uruapan del Progreso	1536		123 (80)	83 (70)	31 (50)	17 (30)	10 (00)	7 (70e)	6 (28e)
19.12N, 96.08W	10	Veracruz	1599		285 (80)	214 (70)	101 (50)	68 (30)	29 (00)	8 (52e)	16 (90)
17.59N, 92.55W	33	Villahermosa	1596		158 (80)	100 (70)	34 (50)	15 (30)	11 (00)	4 (57e)	
22.47N,102.35W	8189	Zacatecas	1548		80 (80)	50 (70)	24 (50)	19 (30)	33 (00)	31 (68)	22 (90)
19.59N,102.16W	5141	Zamora	1540		87 (80)	58 (70)	23 (50)	13 (30)	13 (00)		
20.43N,103.24W	5243	Zapopan	1541		345 (80)	45 (70)	6 (50)	3 (30)	2 (00)		
Netherlands Antilles											
12.06N, 68.57W	75	*Willemstad	1527		100 (80e)	50 (70e)	41 (48e)	19 (31)	14 (05)	8 (50?e)	

Nicaragua											
12.26N, 86.54W	325	Leon	1610	101 (85e)	82 (78e)	56 (71)	31 (50)	24 (26e)	34 (00?e)	30 (47e)	
12.09N, 86.17W	184	*Managua	bef 1521	682 (85e)	553 (78e)	396 (71)	109 (50)	28 (20)	30 (05e)	12 (50?e)	
Panama											
9.22N, 79.54W	36	Colon	1850		60 (80)	68 (70)	52 (50)	30 (30)	18 (11)	18 (60)	17s(22)
8.57N, 79.32W	118	*Panama	1673	435 (86e)	386 (80)	349 (70)	128 (50)	74 (30)	38 (11)		
9.02N, 79.30W		San Miguelito		222 (86e)	156 (80)	49 (70)	13s(60)				
Puerto Rico											
18.24N, 66.09W	54	Bayamon	1750		185 (80)	148 (70)	20 (50)	13 (30)	2 (99)		2 (76)
18.14N, 66.02W	240	Caguas	1700?		87 (80)	63 (70)	34 (50)	20 (30)	5 (99)		
					157s(80)	66s(70)					
18.23N, 65.57W	39	Carolina	bef 1851		148 (80)	94 (70)	5 (50)	4 (30)	2 (99)		2 (76)
18.12N, 67.09W	79	Mayaguez	1760		98s(80)	70s(70)					
					83 (80)	69 (70)	59 (50)	37 (30)	15 (99)		
18.01N, 66.37W	53	Ponce	1680		162 (80)	128 (70)	99 (50)	53 (30)	28 (99)	30 (60)	6 (76)
					168s(80)	128s(70)					
18.28N, 66.07W	57	*San Juan	1521		425 (80)	453 (70)	225 (50)	115 (30)	32 (99)	18 (60)	8 (76)
					1081s(80)	820s(70)					
Saint Lucia											
14.01N, 61.00W	69	*Castries	1768	51s(84e)	49s(80e)	4 (70)	7 (46)	6 (21)	8 (01)	5 (50?e)	
						39s(70)	17s(46)				
Saint Vincent and the Grenadines											
13.09N, 61.14W	79	*Kingstown	1763		24 (80)	17 (70)	5 (46)	4 (31)	5 (91)	6 (48)	
Trinidad and Tobago											
10.39N, 61.31W	67	*Port of Spain	bef 1595		58 (80)	68 (70)	93 (46)	70 (31)	54 (01)	18 (51)	10 (00?e)
USA											
45.28N, 98.29W	1229	Aberdeen	1881	26 (86e)	26 (80)	26 (70)	21 (50)	16 (30)	4 (00)	3 (90)	
32.28N, 99.43W	1719	Abilene	1881	112 (86e)	98 (80)	90 (70)	46 (50)	23 (30)	3 (00)	3 (90)	
					100s(80)	91s(70)					
41.05N, 81.31W	874	Akron	1807	222 (86e)	237 (80)	275 (70)	275 (50)	255 (30)	43 (00)	3 (50)	2 (40)
					516s(80)	543s(70)	367s(50)				
37.46N,122.15W	25	Alameda	1850?	73 (86e)	64 (80)	71 (70)	64 (50)	35 (30)	16 (00)	0.5(60)	
31.34N, 84.09W	184	Albany (Georgia)	1836	85 (86e)	74 (80)	73 (70)	31 (50)	15 (30)	5 (00)	2 (60)	
					89s(80)	77s(70)					

(Continued)

For an explanation of symbols and abbreviations, see pages 16–17.

TABLE 2a. (Continued)

Latitude and Longitude	Elev (ft)	City	Date Settled	Population (thousands)							
				Latest	ca 1980	ca 1970	ca 1950	ca 1930	ca 1900	ca 1850	ca 1800
42.39N, 73.45W	20	Albany (New York)	1624	97 (86e)	102 (80) 490s(80)	116 (70) 487s(70)	135 (50) 292s(50)	127 (30)	94 (00)	51 (50)	5 (00)
35.05N,106.39W	4950	Albuquerque	1706	367 (86e)	332 (80) 418s(80)	245 (70) 297s(70)	97 (50)	27 (30)	6 (00)	6 (50e)	5 (99e)
31.18N, 92.27W	79	Alexandria (Louisiana)	1805	51 (86e)	52 (80) 93s(80)	42 (70) 78s(70)	35 (50)	23 (30)	6 (00)	0.7(50)	
38.48N, 77.03W	47	Alexandria (Virginia)	1713?	108 (86e)	103 (80)	111 (70)	62 (50)	24 (30)	15 (00)	9 (50)	5 (00)
34.08N,118.06W	450	Alhambra	1874	72 (86e)	65 (80)	62 (70)	51 (50)	29 (30)	5 (10)	0.6(70)	
40.36N, 75.28W	255	Allentown	1762	104 (86e)	104 (80)	110 (70)	107 (50)	93 (30)	35 (00)	4 (50)	1 (00)
38.53N, 90.10W	488	Alton	1783	33 (86e)	34 (80) 382s(80)	40 (70) 364s(70)	33 (50) 226s(50)	30 (30)	14 (00)	4 (50)	2 (40)
40.31N, 78.24W	1180	Altoona	1849	53 (86e)	57 (80) 89s(80)	63 (70) 96s(70)	77 (50) 87s(50)	82 (30)	39 (00)	4 (60)	
35.12N,101.50W	3676	Amarillo	1887	166 (86e)	149 (80) 149s(80)	127 (70) 127s(70)	74 (50) 74s(50)	43 (30)	1 (00)		
42.02N, 93.37W	926	Ames	1864	44 (86e)	46 (80)	40 (70)	23 (50)	10 (30)	2 (00)		
42.23N, 72.31W	356	Amherst	1703	32 (86e)	18 (80)	18 (70)	8 (50)	6 (30)	5 (00)	3 (50)	1 (00)
33.50N,117.55W	165	Anaheim	1857	241 (86e)	219 (80)	166 (70)	15 (50)	11 (30)	1 (00)	0.9(70)	
61.13N,149.53W	118	Anchorage	1914	235 (86e)	174 (80) 170s(80)	48 (70) 111s(70)	11 (50)	2 (30)	2 (20)		
40.10N, 85.41W	874	Anderson	1823	61 (86e)	65 (80) 79s(80)	71 (70) 81s(70)	47 (50)	40 (30)	20 (00)	0.4(50)	
38.59N, 76.30W	20	Annapolis	1649	33 (86e)	32 (80) 64s(80)	30 (70)	10 (50)	10 (30)	8 (00)	3 (50)	2 (20)
42.17N, 83.45W	880	Ann Arbor	1824	108 (86e)	108 (80) 209s(80)	100 (70) 179s(70)	48 (50)	27 (30)	15 (00)	5 (50)	
33.39N, 85.50W	710	Anniston	1872	29 (86e)	29 (80) 76s(80)	32 (70) 59s(70)	31 (50)	22 (30)	10 (00)	0.9(80)	

Coordinates		Place	Founded	1986(e)	1980	1970	1950	1930	1900		
38.01N,121.48W	25	Antioch	1849	50 (86e)	43 (80)	28 (70)	11 (50)	4 (30)	0.7 (00)	0.6 (80)	
44.16N, 88.25W	723	Appleton	1835	64 (86e)	59 (80) / 86s (80)	56 (70) / 60s (70)	34 (50) / 58s (50)	25 (30)	15 (00)	2 (60)	
38.36N,121.25W	60	Arden‑Arcade	bef 1890		88 (80) / 142s (80)	82 (70) / 130s (70)	73 (60)				
32.44N, 97.07W	616	Arlington (Texas)	1876	250 (86e)	160 (80)	90 (70)	8 (50)	4 (30)	1 (00)	0.7 (90)	
38.53N, 77.07W	200	Arlington (Virginia)	1700?	159 (86e)	153 (80)	174 (70)	135 (50)	27 (30)	3s (00)		
42.05N, 87.59W	704	Arlington Heights	1836	70 (86e)	66 (80)	65 (70)	9 (50)	5 (30)	1 (00)		
39.48N,105.05W	5300	Arvada	1859	91 (86e)	85 (80)	50 (70)	2 (50)	1 (30)	0.8 (10)		
35.36N, 82.33W	1985	Asheville	1794	60 (86e)	54 (80) / 63s (80)	58 (70) / 72s (70)	53 (50)	50 (30)	15 (00)	0.5 (50)	0.04 (00)
46.11N,123.50W	12	Astoria	1843	10 (86e)	10 (80)	10 (70)	12 (50)	10 (30)	8 (00)	0.3 (50)	
33.57N, 83.23W	771	Athens (Georgia)	1801	43 (86e)	43 (80) / 63s (80)	44 (70)	28 (50)	18 (30)	10 (00)	2 (50)	
39.20N, 82.06W	720	Athens (Ohio)	1800	21 (86e)	20 (80)	24 (70)	12 (50)	7 (30)	3 (00)	2 (50)	
33.45N, 84.24W	1050	Atlanta	1837	422 (86e)	425 (80) / 1613s (80)	495 (70) / 1173s (70)	331 (50) / 508s (50)	270 (30)	90 (00)	3 (50)	
39.22N, 74.26W	10	Atlantic City	1790?	36 (86e)	40 (80) / 146s (80)	48 (70) / 134s (70)	62 (50) / 105s (50)	66 (30)	28 (00)	0.7 (60)	
32.36N, 85.29W	698	Auburn	1836	30 (86e)	28 (80) / 52s (80)	23 (70)	13 (50)	3 (30)	1 (00)	1 (70)	
33.28N, 81.58W	143	Augusta (Georgia)	1735	45 (86e)	48 (80) / 251s (80)	60 (70) / 149s (70)	72 (50) / 88s (50)	60 (30)	39 (00)	12 (52)	1 (91e)
44.19N, 69.47W	120	Augusta (Maine)	1762	21 (86e)	22 (80)	22 (70)	21 (50)	17 (30)	12 (00)	8 (50)	1 (00)
39.44N,104.52W	5342	Aurora (Colorado)	1890	218 (86e)	159 (80)	75 (70)	11 (50)	2 (30)	0.2 (00)		
41.45N, 88.19W	638	Aurora (Illinois)	bef 1834	85 (86e)	81 (80) / 159s (80)	74 (70) / 233s (70)	51 (50)	47 (30)	24 (00)	6 (60)	
30.16N, 97.45W	505	Austin	1839	467 (86e)	346 (80) / 380s (80)	254 (70) / 264s (70)	132 (50) / 136s (50)	53 (30)	22 (00)	0.6 (50)	
34.08N,117.51W	611	Azusa	1887	36 (86e)	29 (80)	25 (70)	11 (50)	5 (30)	0.9 (00)		
35.22N,119.01W	420	Bakersfield	1868	150 (86e)	106 (80) / 222s (80)	70 (70) / 176s (70)	35 (50)	26 (30)	5 (00)	0.8 (80)	
39.17N, 76.37W	20	Baltimore	1730	753 (86e)	787 (80) / 1755s (80)	906 (70) / 1580s (70)	950 (50) / 1162s (50)	805 (30)	509 (00)	169 (50)	27 (00)

For an explanation of symbols and abbreviations, see pages 16–17.

(Continued)

TABLE 2a. (Continued)

Latitude and Longitude	Elev (ft)	City	Date Settled	Population (thousands)							
				Latest	ca 1980	ca 1970	ca 1950	ca 1930	ca 1900	ca 1850	ca 1800
44.48N, 68.46W	20	Bangor	1769	30 (86e)	32 (80) 60s(80)	33 (70)	32 (50)	29 (30)	22 (00)	14 (50)	0.3(00)
30.27N, 91.11W	57	Baton Rouge	1719	241 (86e)	220 (80) 351s(80)	166 (70) 249s(70)	126 (50) 139s(50)	31 (30)	11 (00)	4 (50)	4 (10)
42.19N, 85.11W	885	Battle Creek	1831	54 (86e)	36 (80) 78s(80)	39 (70) 78s(70)	49 (50)	44 (30)	19 (00)	1 (50)	
43.36N, 83.53W	595	Bay City	1831	40 (86e)	42 (80) 78s(80)	49 (70) 78s(70)	53 (50)	47 (30)	28 (00)	2 (60)	
40.40N, 74.07W	40	Bayonne	1656	63 (86e)	65 (80)	73 (70)	77 (50)	89 (30)	33 (00)	4 (70)	
30.05N, 94.06W	20	Beaumont	1835	120 (86e)	118 (80) 124s(80)	118 (70) 116s(70)	94 (50) 94s(50)	58 (30)	9 (00)	0.1(50?)	
47.37N, 122.12W	200	Bellevue	1882	81 (86e)	74 (80)	61 (70)	13 (60)	1s(40)	0.6s(10)		
48.46N, 122.29W	68	Bellingham	1852	45 (86e)	46 (80) 51s(80)	39 (70)	34 (50)	31 (30)			
37.52N, 122.16W	40	Berkeley	1853	104 (86e)	103 (80)	114 (70)	114 (50)	82 (30)	13 (00)	5 (90)	
38.59N, 77.05W	340	Bethesda	1820?		63 (80)	72 (70)	46s(50)	12s(30)	2s(00)	1s(80)	
40.37N, 75.23W	237	Bethlehem	1741	70 (86e)	70 (80)	73 (70)	66 (50)	58 (30)	7 (00)	2 (50)	0.5(00)
34.04N, 118.25W	292	Beverly Hills	1906	34 (86e)	32 (80)	33 (70)	29 (50)	17 (30)	0.7(20)		
45.47N, 108.30W	3117	Billings	1882	80 (86e)	67 (80) 84s(80)	62 (70) 71s(70)	32 (50)	16 (30)	3 (00)	0.8(90)	
30.24N, 88.53W	22	Biloxi	1719	48 (86e)	49 (80) 179s(80)	48 (70) 128s(70)	37 (50)	15 (30)	5 (00)	1 (70)	0.4(01e)
42.06N, 75.55W	865	Binghamton	1787	53 (86e)	56 (80) 161s(80)	64 (70) 167s(70)	81 (50) 144s(50)	77 (30)	40 (00)	5 (50)	0.3(12e)
33.31N, 86.49W	600	Birmingham	1871	278 (86e)	284 (80) 606s(80)	301 (70) 558s(70)	326 (50) 445s(50)	260 (30)	38 (00)	3 (80)	
46.48N, 100.47W	1670	Bismarck	1872	48 (86e)	44 (80) 61s(80)	35 (70)	19 (50)	11 (30)	3 (00)	2 (80)	
37.14N, 80.25W	2170	Blacksburg	1772	30 (86e)	31 (80)	9 (70)	3 (50)	1 (30)	0.8(00)		
40.29N, 89.00W	830	Bloomington (Illinois)	1822	46 (86e)	44 (80) 82s(80)	40 (70) 69s(70)	34 (50)	31 (30)	23 (00)	2 (50)	

Coordinates	Elev.	City	Year	(86e)	(80)	(70)	(50)	(30)	(00)		
39.10N, 86.32W	752	Bloomington (Indiana)	1815	52 (86e)	52 (80)	43 (70)	28 (50)	18 (30)	6 (00)	1 (50)	
44.49N, 93.16W	830	Bloomington (Minnesota)	1843	86 (86e)	82 (80) 64s(80)	82 (70)	10 (50)	3s(30)	1s(00)	0.4s(50)	
26.21N, 80.05W	17	Boca Raton	1897	59 (86e)	50 (80)	29 (70)	1 (50)	0.4(30)	6 (00)	1 (70)	
43.37N,116.12W	2704	Boise City	1863	108 (86e)	102 (80) 135s(80)	75 (70) 85s(70)	34 (50)	22 (30)	6 (00)		
42.21N, 71.03W	21	Boston	1630	574 (86e)	563 (80) 2679s(80)	641 (70) 2653s(70)	801 (50) 2233s(50)	781 (30)	561 (00)	137 (50)	25 (00)
40.01N,105.17W	5430	Boulder	1859	76 (86e)	77 (80) 81s(80)	67 (70) 69s(70)	20 (50)	11 (30)	6 (00)	0.3(70)	
36.59N, 86.27W	469	Bowling Green (Kentucky)	1790?	41 (86e)	40 (80)	37 (70)	18 (50)	12 (30)	8 (00)	5 (70)	
41.22N, 83.39W	700	Bowling Green (Ohio)	1833	25 (86e)	26 (80) 65s(80)	22 (70)	12 (50)	7 (30)	5 (00)	2 (50)	
45.41N,111.02W	4754	Bozeman	1864	23 (86e)	22 (80)	19 (70)	11 (50)	7 (30)	3 (00)	0.2(70)	
47.34N,122.38W	12	Bremerton	1891	34 (86e)	36 (80)	35 (70)	28 (50)	10 (30)	3 (10)		
41.11N, 73.11W	10	Bridgeport	1639	142 (86e)	143 (80) 411s(80)	157 (70) 413s(70)	159 (50) 237s(50)	147 (30)	71 (00)	6 (50)	0.6(10)
41.40N, 72.57W	240	Bristol	1727	59 (86e)	57 (80) 84s(80)	55 (70) 72s(70)	36 (50)	28 (30)	6 (00)	3 (50)	3 (00)
42.05N, 71.01W	130	Brockton	1700	94 (86e)	95 (80) 178s(80)	89 (70) 149s(70)	63 (50) 92s(50)	64 (30)	40 (00)	4 (50)	2 (30)
44.19N, 96.48W	1636	Brookings	1857	15 (86e)	15 (80)	14 (70)	8 (50)	4 (30)	2 (00)	2 (90)	
42.20N, 71.07W	40	Brookline	1638?	52 (86e)	55 (80)	59 (70)	58 (50)	47 (30)	20 (00)	3 (50)	
25.54N, 97.30W	57	Brownsville	1846	102 (86e)	85 (80) 92s(80)	53 (70) 53s(70)	36 (50)	22 (30)	6 (00)	3 (60)	0.6(00)
30.40N, 96.22W	367	Bryan	1859	62 (86e)	44 (80) 83s(80)	34 (70) 51s(70)	18 (50)	8 (30)	4 (00)	3 (90)	
42.53N, 78.52W	585	Buffalo	1803	325 (86e)	358 (80) 1002s(80)	463 (70) 1087s(70)	580 (50) 798s(50)	573 (30)	352 (00)	42 (50)	2 (10)
34.11N,118.19W	560	Burbank	1887	89 (86e)	85 (80)	89 (70)	79 (50)	17 (30)	0.3(00e)		
36.06N, 79.26W	658	Burlington (North Carolina)	1855	37 (86e)	37 (80) 67s(80)	36 (70) 60s(70)	25 (50)	10 (30)	4 (00)	0.8(80)	

For an explanation of symbols and abbreviations, see pages 16–17.

(Continued)

TABLE 2a. (Continued)

Latitude and Longitude	Elev (ft)	City	Date Settled	Population (thousands)							
				Latest	ca 1980	ca 1970	ca 1950	ca 1930	ca 1900	ca 1850	ca 1800
44.29N, 73.13W	110	Burlington (Vermont)	1773	38 (86e)	38 (80) 77s(80)	39 (70)	33 (50)	25 (30)	19 (00)	6 (50)	0.8(00)
46.00N, 112.32W	5755	Butte	1864	33 (86e)	37 (80)	23 (70)	33 (50)	40 (30)	30 (00)	3 (80)	2 (00)
42.22N, 71.06W	20	Cambridge	1630	91 (86e)	95 (80)	100 (70)	121 (50)	114 (30)	92 (00)	15 (50)	
39.57N, 75.07W	30	Camden	1681	83 (86e)	85 (80)	103 (70)	125 (50)	119 (30)	76 (00)	9 (50)	1 (28)
40.48N, 81.23W	1030	Canton	1805	87 (86e)	93 (80) 245s(80)	110 (70) 244s(70)	117 (50) 174s(50)	105 (30)	31 (00)	3 (50)	0.8(10)
37.19N, 89.32W	347	Cape Girardeau	1792	34 (86e)	34 (80)	31 (70)	22 (50)	16 (30)	5 (00)	3 (60)	
37.44N, 89.13W	416	Carbondale	1852	24 (86e)	26 (80)	23 (70)	11 (50)	8 (30)	3 (00)	2 (80)	
33.48N, 118.17W	40	Carson	bef 1954	88 (86e)	81 (80)	71 (70)	38 (60)				
39.10N, 119.46W	4660	Carson City	1858	37 (86e)	32 (80)	15 (70)	3 (50)	2 (30)	2 (00)	4 (80)	
42.51N, 106.19W	5123	Casper	1888	47 (86e)	51 (80) 59s(80)	39 (70)	24 (50)	17 (30)	0.9(00)	0.5(90)	
42.31N, 92.27W	854	Cedar Falls	1845	33 (86e)	36 (80)	30 (70)	14 (50)	7 (30)	5 (00)	2 (60)	
41.58N, 91.40W	730	Cedar Rapids	1838	108 (86e)	110 (80) 136s(80)	111 (70) 132s(70)	72 (50) 78s(50)	56 (30)	26 (00)	2 (60)	
40.07N, 88.15W	740	Champaign	1854	59 (86e)	58 (80) 109s(80)	57 (70) 100s(70)	40 (50)	20 (30)	9 (00)	2 (60)	
35.55N, 79.04W	501	Chapel Hill	1793	34 (86e)	32 (80)	26 (70)	9 (50)	3 (30)	1 (00)	0.8(80)	
32.47N, 79.56W	9	Charleston (South Carolina)	1670	69 (86e)	70 (80) 329s(80)	67 (70) 228s(70)	70 (50) 120s(50)	62 (30)	56 (00)	43 (50)	19 (00)
38.21N, 81.38W	601	Charleston (West Virginia)	1788	58 (86e)	64 (80) 154s(80)	72 (70) 158s(70)	74 (50) 131s(50)	60 (30)	11 (00)	1 (50)	0.6(00)
35.13N, 80.51W	720	Charlotte	1748	352 (86e)	315 (80) 351s(80)	241 (70) 279s(70)	134 (50) 141s(50)	83 (30)	18 (00)	1 (50)	0.1(00)
38.02N, 78.30W	480	Charlottesville	1762	41 (86e)	40 (80) 59s(80)	39 (70)	26 (50)	15 (30)	6 (00)	3 (70)	
35.03N, 85.19W	675	Chattanooga	1815	162 (86e)	170 (80) 302s(80)	120 (70) 224s(70)	131 (50) 168s(50)	120 (30)	30 (00)	3 (53)	
42.54N, 78.45W	630	Cheektowaga	1809	103 (86e)	92 (80)	94 (70)	39 (50)	15s(30)	4s(00)	3s(50)	
39.56N, 75.02W	59	Cherry Hill	1685?	72 (86e)	69 (80)	64 (70)	10s(50)	6s(30)	2s(00)	1s(80)	

Coordinates		City	Founded								
36.49N, 76.17W	20	Chesapeake	1620?	134 (86e)	114 (80)	90 (70)	10 (50)	8 (30)	8 (20)	2 (50)	0.7(20)
39.51N, 75.22W	23	Chester	1644	44 (86e)	46 (80)	56 (70)	66 (50)	59 (30)	34 (00)	1 (70)	
41.08N,104.49W	6062	Cheyenne	1867	54 (86e)	47 (80) / 58s(80)	41 (70)	32 (50)	17 (30)	14 (00)		
41.52N, 87.38W	595	Chicago	1803	3012 (86e)	3005 (80) / 6780s(80) / 52s(80)	3369 (70) / 6715s(70)	3621 (50) / 4921s(50)	3376 (30)	1699 (00)	30 (50)	4 (40)
39.44N,121.50W	193	Chico	1860	33 (86e)	27 (80)	20 (70)	12 (50)	8 (30)	3 (00)	2 (70e)	
42.09N, 72.37W	92	Chicopee	1652	57 (86e)	55 (80)	67 (70)	49 (50)	44 (30)	19 (00)	8 (50)	
32.39N,117.05W	74	Chula Vista	1888	119 (86e)	84 (80)	68 (70)	16 (50)	4 (30)	2 (20)	1 (60)	
41.51N, 87.45W	610	Cicero	bef 1857	62 (86e)	61 (80)	67 (70)	68 (50)	67 (30)	16 (00)		
39.06N, 84.31W	550	Cincinnati	1789	370 (86e)	385 (80) / 1123s(80)	454 (70) / 1111s(70)	504 (50) / 813s(50)	451 (30)	326 (00)	115 (50)	0.7(00)
38.42N,121.17W	160	Citrus Heights	bef 1964		86 (80)	22 (70)					
34.06N,117.43W	1155	Claremont	1887	35 (86e)	31 (80)	24 (70)	6 (50)	3 (30)	1 (10)		
36.32N, 87.21W	444	Clarksville	1784	61 (86e)	55 (80) / 78s(80)	32 (70) / 58s(70)	16 (50)	9 (30)	9 (00)	3 (70)	
27.58N, 82.48W	29	Clearwater	1841	98 (86e)	86 (80)	52 (70)	16 (50)	8 (30)	0.3(00)		
41.30N, 81.42W	660	Cleveland	1796	536 (86e)	574 (80) / 1752s(80)	751 (70) / 1960s(70)	915 (50) / 1384s(50)	900 (30)	382 (00)	17 (50)	0.5(10)
40.53N, 74.09W	70	Clifton	1685	76 (86e)	74 (80)	82 (70)	65 (50)	47 (30)	26 (20)		
38.59N, 76.56W	60	College Park	1798	22 (86e)	24 (80)	26 (70)	11 (50)	0.3(30)			
30.37N, 96.21W	308	College Station	1876	46 (86e)	37 (80)	18 (70)	8 (50)	2 (40)			
38.50N,104.49W	6012	Colorado Springs	1859	273 (86e)	215 (80) / 277s(80)	136 (70) / 205s(70)	45 (50)	33 (30)	21 (00)	4 (80)	
39.14N, 76.50W	402	Columbia (Maryland)	1769		53 (80)	9 (70)					
38.57N, 92.20W	748	Columbia (Missouri)	1819	63 (86e)	62 (80) / 65s(80)	59 (70) / 59s(70)	32 (50)	15 (30)	6 (00)	0.7(50)	
34.00N, 81.02W	190	Columbia (South Carolina)	1786	93 (86e)	101 (80) / 312s(80)	114 (70) / 242s(70)	87 (50) / 121s(50)	52 (30)	21 (00)	6 (50)	2 (16)
32.28N, 84.59W	265	Columbus (Georgia)	1828	180 (86e)	169 (80) / 215s(80)	155 (70) / 209s(70)	80 (50) / 118s(50)	43 (30)	18 (00)	6 (50)	3 (40)
33.30N, 88.25W	250	Columbus (Mississippi)	1817	28 (86e)	28 (80)	26 (70)	17 (50)	11 (30)	6 (00)	3 (50)	
39.58N, 83.00W	780	Columbus (Ohio)	1797	566 (86e)	565 (80) / 834s(80)	540 (70) / 790s(70)	376 (50) / 438s(50)	291 (30)	126 (00)	18 (50)	2 (30)

For an explanation of symbols and abbreviations, see pages 16–17.

(Continued)

TABLE 2a. (Continued)

Latitude and Longitude	Elev (ft)	City	Date Settled	ca 1800	ca 1850	ca 1900	ca 1930	ca 1950	ca 1970	ca 1980	Latest
33.54N, 118.13W	66	Compton	1867			0.9(10)	13 (30)	48 (50)	79 (70)	81 (80)	94 (86e)
37.58N, 122.02W	65	Concord (California)	1868			0.7(10)	1 (30)	7 (50)	85 (70)	104 (80)	106 (86e)
43.12N, 71.32W	288	Concord (New Hampshire)	1726	2 (00)	9 (50)	20 (00)	25 (30)	28 (50)	30 (70)	30 (80)	33 (86e)
35.05N, 92.26W	321	Conway	1871		1 (80)	2 (00)	6 (30)	9 (50)	16 (70)	20 (80)	23 (86e)
36.10N, 85.30W	1050	Cookeville	1854		0.2(70)	2 (10)	4 (30)	7 (50)	14 (70)	21 (80)	24 (86e)
25.45N, 80.16W	11	Coral Gables	1921				6 (30)	20 (50)	42 (70)	43 (80)	42 (86e)
27.48N, 97.24W	35	Corpus Christi	1839		0.5(50)	5 (00)	28 (30)	108 (50) 123s(50)	205 (70) 213s(70)	231 (80) 246s(80)	264 (86e)
44.34N, 123.16W	227	Corvallis	1845		1 (60)	2 (00)	8 (30)	16 (50)	35 (70)	41 (80)	40 (86e)
33.38N, 117.55W	100	Costa Mesa	1910					12 (50)	73 (70)	83 (80)	88 (86e)
41.16N, 95.52W	984	Council Bluffs	1827		2 (60)	26 (00)	42 (30)	45 (50)	60 (70)	56 (80)	57 (86e)
39.05N, 84.31W	513	Covington	1815	0.7(30)	9 (50)	43 (00)	65 (30)	64 (50)	53 (70)	50 (80)	46 (86e)
41.47N, 71.26W	60	Cranston	1638	2 (00)	4 (50)	13 (00)	43 (30)	55 (50)	74 (70)	72 (80)	74 (86e)
39.39N, 78.46W	641	Cumberland	1750		6 (50)	17 (00)	38 (30)	38 (50)	30 (70)	26 (80) 59s(80)	23 (86e)
32.47N, 96.48W	435	Dallas	1842		0.2(50)	43 (00)	260 (30)	434 (50) 539s(50)	844 (70) 1339s(70)	904 (80) 2451s(80)	1004 (86e)
37.42N, 122.28W	190	Daly City	1866?			4 (20)	8 (30)	15 (50)	67 (70)	78 (80)	83 (86e)
41.24N, 73.28W	375	Danbury	1684	3 (00)	6 (50)	17 (00)	22 (30)	22 (50)	51 (70) 67s(70)	60 (80) 95s(80)	65 (86e)
40.08N, 87.37W	611	Danville (Illinois)	1827	0.5(40)	0.7(50)	16 (00)	37 (30)	38 (50)	43 (70)	39 (80) 52s(80)	57 (86e)
36.35N, 79.23W	408	Danville (Virginia)	1793		2 (50)	17 (00)	22 (30)	35 (50)	46 (70)	46 (80) 55s(80)	45 (86e)
41.31N, 90.35W	590	Davenport	1836		2 (50)	35 (00)	61 (30)	75 (50) 195s(50)	98 (70) 266s(70)	103 (80) 285s(80)	99 (86e)
38.33N, 121.44W	54	Davis	1856?		0.4(80)	0.7(91e)	1 (30)	4 (50)	23 (70)	37 (80)	41 (86e)
39.46N, 84.12W	745	Dayton	1796		11 (50)	85 (00)	201 (30)	244 (50) 347s(50)	243 (70) 686s(70)	194 (80) 595s(80)	179 (86e)
29.13N, 81.01W	7	Daytona Beach	1870	0.4(10)		0.3(10)	17 (30)	30 (50)	45 (70) 115s(70)	54 (80) 171s(80)	58 (86e)

Lat / Long	Elev	Name	Founded	(86e)	(80)	(70)	(50)	(30)	(00)		
42.19N, 83.10W	604	Dearborn	1795?	86 (86e)	91 (80)	104 (70)	95 (50)	50 (30)	0.8(00)	1 (50)	
42.19N, 83.17W	625	Dearborn Heights	1796?	62 (86e)	68 (80)	80 (70)	20s(50)	1s(30)			
39.51N, 88.57W	682	Decatur	1829	90 (86e)	94 (80)	90 (70)	66 (50)	58 (30)	21 (00)	4 (60)	
					108s(80)	100s(70)	74s(50)				
41.56N, 88.46W	886	De Kalb	1838	32 (86e)	33 (80)	33 (70)	12 (50)	9 (30)	6 (00)	0.9(60)	
33.13N, 97.08W	620	Denton	1857	55 (86e)	48 (80)	40 (70)	21 (50)	10 (30)	4 (00)	0.4(70)	
39.45N, 104.59W	5280	Denver	1858	505 (86e)	492 (80)	515 (70)	416 (50)	288 (30)	134 (00)	5 (60)	
					1352s(80)	1047s(70)	499s(50)				
41.35N, 93.37W	805	Des Moines	1843	192 (86e)	191 (80)	201 (70)	178 (50)	143 (30)	62 (00)	1 (50)	
					267s(80)	256s(70)	200s(50)				
42.20N, 83.03W	585	Detroit	1701	1086 (86e)	1203 (80)	1514 (70)	1850 (50)	1569 (30)	286 (00)	21 (50)	0.8(10)
					3809s(80)	3971s(70)	2659s(50)				
31.13N, 85.24W	355	Dothan	1858	54 (86e)	49 (80)	37 (70)	22 (50)	16 (30)	3 (00)	0.2(90)	
					52s(80)						
39.10N, 75.32W	20	Dover	1683	23 (86e)	24 (80)	17 (70)	6 (50)	5 (30)	3 (00)	4s(50)	
33.56N, 118.07W	118	Downey	1873	85 (86e)	83 (80)	89 (70)	83 (60)	9 (40)	1 (00e)		2s(00)
42.30N, 90.40W	612	Dubuque	1837	60 (86e)	62 (80)	62 (70)	50 (50)	42 (30)	36 (00)	3 (50)	
					68s(80)	66s(70)					
46.47N, 92.06W	610	Duluth	1852	82 (86e)	93 (80)	101 (70)	105 (50)	101 (30)	53 (00)	0.1(60)	
					133s(80)	138s(70)	143s(50)				
39.16N, 76.31W	20	Dundalk	1750?		71 (80)	85 (70)	39 (50)	2 (30?)			
36.00N, 78.55W	405	Durham	1822?	114 (86e)	101 (80)	95 (70)	71 (50)	52 (30)	7 (00)	0.3(70)	
					157s(80)	101s(70)	73s(50)				
42.44N, 84.29W	840	East Lansing	1849	48 (86e)	51 (80)	48 (70)	20 (50)	4 (30)	0.8(10)		
34.01N, 118.09W	280	East Los Angeles	1874?	77 (86e)	110 (80)	105 (70)	104 (60)	42 (40)			
40.46N, 74.13W	170	East Orange	1678	49 (86e)	78 (80)	75 (70)	79 (50)	68 (30)	22 (00)	4s(70)	
38.37N, 90.09W	418	East Saint Louis	1797	55 (86e)	55 (80)	70 (70)	82 (50)	74 (30)	30 (00)	6 (70)	
44.49N, 91.30W	880	Eau Claire	1847	55 (86e)	52 (80)	45 (70)	36 (50)	26 (30)	18 (00)	2 (70)	
					72s(80)						
26.18N, 98.10W	91	Edinburg	1908	32 (86e)	24 (80)	17 (70)	12 (50)	5 (30)	1 (20)	4s(80)	
40.31N, 74.25W	93	Edison	1668	82 (86e)	70 (80)	67 (70)	16s(50)	10s(30)	3s(00)		
35.39N, 97.29W	1200	Edmond	1887	51 (86e)	34 (80)	16 (70)	6 (50)	4 (30)	1 (00)	0.3(90)	
32.48N, 116.58W	450	El Cajon	1869?	84 (86e)	74 (80)	52 (70)	6 (50)	1 (30)	0.5(20)		
42.02N, 88.17W	717	Elgin	1835	72 (86e)	64 (80)	56 (70)	44 (50)	36 (30)	22 (00)	3 (60)	
					107s(80)						
40.40N, 74.13W	21	Elizabeth	1664	107 (86e)	106 (80)	113 (70)	113 (50)	115 (30)	52 (00)	6 (50)	3 (10)

(Continued)

For an explanation of symbols and abbreviations, see pages 16–17.

TABLE 2a. (Continued)

Latitude and Longitude	Elev (ft)	City	Date Settled	Latest	ca 1980	ca 1970	ca 1950	ca 1930	ca 1900	ca 1850	ca 1800
41.41N, 85.58W	753	Elkhart	1832	44 (86e)	41 (80) 84s(80)	43 (70)	36 (50)	33 (30)	15 (00)	1 (60)	
42.06N, 76.48W	860	Elmira	1788	32 (86e)	35 (80) 68s(80)	40 (70) 74s(70)	50 (50)	47 (30)	36 (00)	8 (50)	
34.04N, 118.01W	280	El Monte	1852	97 (86e)	79 (80)	70 (70)	8 (50)	3 (30)			
31.46N, 106.29W	3762	El Paso	1827	492 (86e)	425 (80) 454s(80)	322 (70) 337s(70)	130 (50) 137s(50)	102 (30)	16 (00)	0.4(60)	
41.22N, 82.07W	730	Elyria	1817	57 (86e)	58 (80)	53 (70)	30 (50)	26 (30)	9 (00)	1 (50)	
38.24N, 96.11W	1133	Emporia	1857	25 (86e)	25 (80)	23 (70)	16 (50)	14 (30)	8 (00)	0.8(60)	
36.24N, 97.52W	1246	Enid	1893	50 (86e)	50 (80) 51s(80)	45 (70)	36 (50)	26 (30)	3 (00)		
42.07N, 80.05W	685	Erie	1795	115 (86e)	119 (80) 178s(80)	129 (70) 175s(70)	131 (50) 152s(50)	116 (30)	53 (00)	6 (50)	0.1(00)
33.07N, 117.05W	650	Escondido	1885	84 (86e)	64 (80)	37 (70)	7 (50)	3 (30)	0.8(00)	0.5(90)	
41.34N, 81.32W	648	Euclid	1798	57 (86e)	60 (80)	72 (70)	41 (50)	13 (30)	2 (10)	0.1(50?e)	
44.03N, 123.05W	422	Eugene	1851	105 (86e)	106 (80) 182s(80)	79 (70) 139s(70)	36 (50)	19 (30)	3 (00)	0.9(70)	
42.03N, 87.41W	601	Evanston	1826	72 (86e)	74 (80)	80 (70)	74 (50)	63 (30)	19 (00)	0.8(60)	
37.58N, 87.34W	385	Evansville	1812	129 (86e)	130 (80) 180s(80)	139 (70) 142s(70)	129 (50) 138s(50)	102 (30)	59 (00)	3 (50)	
47.59N, 122.12W	30	Everett	1862	60 (86e)	54 (80)	54 (70)	34 (50)	31 (30)	8 (00)	3 (91e)	
64.51N, 147.43W	448	Fairbanks	1901	28 (86e)	23 (80)	15 (70)	6 (50)	2 (30)	4 (10)		
38.15N, 122.02W	12	Fairfield (California)	1859	69 (86e)	58 (80) 69s(80)	44 (70) 85s(70)	3 (50)	1 (30)	0.8(10)		
41.08N, 73.16W	10	Fairfield (Connecticut)	1639	53 (86e)	55 (80)	56 (70)	30 (50)	17 (30)	4 (00)	4 (50)	4 (00)
41.42N, 71.09W	40	Fall River	1656	90 (86e)	93 (80) 142s(80)	97 (70) 139s(70)	112 (50) 118s(50)	115 (30)	105 (00)	12 (50)	1 (10)
46.52N, 96.47W	900	Fargo	1871	68 (86e)	61 (80) 105s(80)	53 (70) 85s(70)	38 (50)	29 (30)	10 (00)	3 (80)	
36.04N, 94.10W	1427	Fayetteville (Arkansas)	1828	40 (86e)	37 (80) 63s(80)	31 (70)	17 (50)	7 (30)	4 (00)	0.6(50)	

Coordinates	Pop	Name	Founded	(86e)	(80)	(70)	(50)	(30)	(00)	(50)	(00)
35.03N, 78.53W	100	Fayetteville (North Carolina)	1729?	76 (86e)	60 (80) 216s(80)	54 (70) 161s(70)	35 (50)	13 (30)	5 (00)	5 (50)	2 (00)
42.35N, 71.48W	458	Fitchburg	1730?	39 (86e)	40 (80) 77s(80)	43 (70) 78s(70)	43 (50)	41 (30)	32 (00)	5 (50)	1 (00)
35.12N, 111.39W	6907	Flagstaff	1881	39 (86e)	35 (80)	26 (70)	8 (50)	4 (30)	1 (00)	1 (90)	
43.01N, 83.42W	715	Flint	1819	146 (86e)	160 (80) 332s(80)	193 (70) 330s(70)	163 (50) 198s(50)	156 (30)	13 (00)	2 (50)	
34.48N, 87.40W	541	Florence (Alabama)	1818	36 (86e)	37 (80) 73s(80)	34 (70) 63s(70)	24 (50)	12 (30)	6 (00)	0.8(50)	
34.12N, 79.46W	136	Florence (South Carolina)	1859	32 (86e)	30 (80) 56s(80)	26 (70)	23 (50)	15 (30)	5 (00)	2 (80)	
40.35N, 105.05W	4984	Fort Collins	1864	74 (86e)	65 (80) 78s(80)	43 (70)	15 (50)	11 (30)	3 (00)	1 (80)	
26.07N, 80.08W	7	Fort Lauderdale	1838	149 (86e)	153 (80) 1009s(80)	140 (70) 614s(70)	36 (50)	9 (30)	0.1(00)		
26.38N, 81.52W	9	Fort Myers	1839	40 (86e)	37 (80) 141s(80)	27 (70) 69s(7)	13 (50)	9 (30)	0.9(00)	0.6(90)	
27.27N, 80.20W	24	Fort Pierce	1838	37 (86e)	34 (80) 70s(80)	30 (70)	14 (50)	5 (30)	1 (10)		
35.23N, 94.25W	423	Fort Smith	1817	74 (86e)	72 (80) 90s(80)	63 (70) 76s(70)	48 (50) 56s(50)	31 (30)	12 (00)	1 (50)	
30.25N, 86.36W	23	Fort Walton Beach	bef 1500	23 (86e)	21 (80) 85s(80)	20 (70)	2 (50)				
41.04N, 85.08W	790	Fort Wayne	bef 1685	173 (86e)	172 (80) 236s(80)	178 (70) 225s(70)	134 (50) 140s(50)	115 (30)	45 (00)	4 (50)	2 (40)
32.45N, 97.20W	670	Fort Worth	1843	430 (86e)	385[1](80)	393 (70) 677s(70)	279 (50) 316s(50)	163 (30)	27 (00)	7 (80)	
42.17N, 71.25W	189	Framingham	1650	64 (86e)	65 (80)	64 (70)	28 (50)	22 (30)	11 (00)	4 (50)	2 (00)
38.12N, 84.52W	504	Frankfort	1774	27 (86e)	26 (80)	22 (70)	12 (50)	12 (30)	9 (00)	3 (50)	0.6(00)
37.32N, 121.57W	50	Fremont	1797	154 (86e)	132 (80)	101 (70)	5 (50)	6 (40e)	2 (00e)		
36.44N, 119.47W	285	Fresno	1872	285 (86e)	217 (80) 332s(80)	166 (70) 263s(70)	92 (50) 131s(50)	53 (30)	12 (00)	1 (80)	
33.52N, 117.55W	161	Fullerton	1887	109 (86e)	102 (80)	86 (70)	14 (50)	11 (30)	2 (10)		

1Urbanized area population for 1980 included in Dallas urbanized area.

For an explanation of symbols and abbreviations, see pages 16–17.

(Continued)

TABLE 2a. (Continued)

Latitude and Longitude	Elev (ft)	City	Date Settled	Population (thousands)							
				Latest	ca 1980	ca 1970	ca 1950	ca 1930	ca 1900	ca 1850	ca 1800
34.01N, 86.01W	555	Gadsden	1836?	45 (86e)	48 (80) 75s(80)	54 (70)	56 (50)	24 (30)	4 (00)	2 (80)	
29.40N, 82.20W	185	Gainesville	1830	85 (86e)	81 (80) 104s(80)	65 (70) 69s(70)	27 (50)	10 (30)	4 (00)	0.3(60)	
29.18N, 94.48W	5	Galveston	1816	60 (86e)	62 (80) 61s(80)	62 (70) 62s(70)	67 (50) 72s(50)	53 (30)	38 (00)	4 (50)	
33.46N, 117.55W	93	Garden Grove	1876	135 (86e)	123 (80)	121 (70)	4 (50)	2 (40?e)	0.1(00e)		
32.54N, 96.38W	541	Garland	1886	177 (86e)	139 (80)	81 (70)	11 (50)	2 (30)	0.8(00)	0.5(90)	
41.36N, 81.20W	590	Gary	1906	137 (86e)	152 (80)	175 (70)	134 (50)	100 (30)	17 (10)		
35.16N, 81.11W	825	Gastonia	bef 1877	53 (86e)	47 (80) 107s(80)	47 (70) 95s(70)	23 (50)	17 (30)	5 (00)	0.2(80)	
33.32N, 112.11W	1100	Glendale (Arizona)	1892	126 (86e)	97 (80)	36 (70)	8 (50)	4 (30)	3 (20)		
34.08N, 118.15W	573	Glendale (California)	1886	154 (86e)	139 (80)	133 (70)	96 (50)	63 (30)	3 (10)		
42.37N, 70.40W	57	Gloucester	1623	28 (86e)	28 (80)	28 (70)	25 (50)	24 (30)	26 (00)	8 (50)	5 (00)
35.23N, 77.59W	111	Goldsboro	1838	35 (86e)	32 (80) 58s(80)	27 (70)	21 (50)	15 (30)	6 (00)	0.9(60)	
47.55N, 97.03W	830	Grand Forks	1871	45 (86e)	44 (80) 52s(80)	39 (70)	27 (50)	17 (30)	8 (00)	2 (80)	
40.55N, 98.21W	1861	Grand Island	1866	39 (86e)	33 (80)	32 (70)	23 (50)	18 (30)	8 (00)	3 (80)	
39.04N, 108.33W	4596	Grand Junction	1881	32 (86e)	28 (80) 57s(80)	20 (70)	15 (50)	10 (30)	4 (00)	2 (90)	
32.45N, 97.00W	528	Grand Prairie	1852	96 (86e)	71 (80) 66s(80)	51 (70)	15 (50)	2 (30)	1 (10)		
42.58N, 85.40W	610	Grand Rapids	1824?	187 (86e)	182 (80) 375s(80)	198 (70) 353s(70)	177 (50) 227s(50)	169 (30)	88 (00)	3 (50)	
47.30N, 111.17W	3330	Great Falls	1883	57 (86e)	57 (80) 66s(80)	60 (70) 71s(70)	39 (50)	29 (30)	15 (00)	4 (90)	
40.25N, 104.42W	4663	Greeley	1870	57 (86e)	53 (80) 62s(80)	39 (70)	20 (50)	12 (30)	3 (00)	0.5(70)	
44.31N, 88.01W	590	Green Bay	bef 1669	93 (86e)	88 (80) 143s(80)	88 (70) 129s(70)	53 (50)	37 (30)	19 (00)	2 (50)	0.5(20e)

(Continued)

Coordinates	Elev.	Name	Founded	(86e)	(80)	(70)	(50)	(30)	(00)	(70)	early
36.04N, 79.47W	839	Greensboro	1749	177 (86e)	156 (80)	144 (70)	74 (50)	54 (30)	10 (00)	0.5(70)	0.4(29)
					170s(80)	152s(70)	83s(50)				
33.24N, 91.04W	125	Greenville (Mississippi)	1866	40 (86e)	41 (80)	40 (70)	30 (50)	15 (30)	8 (00)	0.9(70)	
35.36N, 77.23W	71	Greenville (North Carolina)	1786	39 (86e)	36 (80)	29 (70)	17 (50)	9 (30)	3 (00)	2 (50)	0.2(00)
34.51N, 82.24W	966	Greenville (South Carolina)	1797	58 (86e)	58 (80)	61 (70)	58 (50)	29 (30)	12 (00)	1 (50)	0.2(10)
					229s(80)	157s(70)					
41.02N, 73.37W	60	Greenwich	1640	58 (86e)	60 (80)	60 (70)	41 (50)	33 (30)	12 (00)	5 (50)	3 (00)
30.22N, 89.05W	19	Gulfport	1887	43 (86e)	40 (80)	41 (70)	23 (50)	13 (30)	1 (00)		
30.39N, 77.43W	560	Hagerstown	1737	34 (86e)	34 (80)	36 (70)	36 (50)	31 (30)	14 (00)	4 (50)	3 (30)
39.24N, 84.34W	600	Hamilton	1791	65 (86e)	63 (80)	68 (70)	58 (50)	52 (30)	24 (00)	3 (50)	0.3(10)
					66s(80)	91s(70)	63s(50)				
41.38N, 87.30W	590	Hammond	1851	86 (86e)	94 (80)	108 (70)	88 (50)	65 (30)	12 (00)	0.7(80)	
					105s(80)						
37.01N, 76.20W	3	Hampton	1610	126 (86e)	123 (80)	121 (70)	6 (50)	6 (30)	3 (00)	1 (53?e)	
43.42N, 72.17W	530	Hanover	1765	10 (86e)	7 (80)	6 (70)	5 (50)	2 (40e)			
26.11N, 97.42W	36	Harlingen	1905	55 (86e)	44 (80)	34 (70)	23 (50)	12 (30)	2 (20)		
					67s(80)	50s(70)					
40.16N, 76.53W	365	Harrisburg	1785	52 (86e)	53 (80)	68 (70)	90 (50)	80 (30)	50 (00)	8 (50)	1 (00)
					278s(80)	241s(70)	170s(50)				
38.27N, 78.52W	1937	Harrisonburg	1739	27 (86e)	20 (80)	15 (70)	11 (50)	7 (30)	4 (00)	1 (60)	
41.46N, 72.41W	40	Hartford	1635	138 (86e)	136 (80)	158 (70)	177 (50)	164 (30)	80 (00)	14 (50)	5 (00)
					510s(80)	465s(70)	301s(50)				
31.20N, 89.17W	143	Hattiesburg	1881	41 (86e)	41 (80)	38 (70)	29 (50)	19 (30)	4 (00)	1 (90)	
37.40N, 122.05W	116	Hayward	1854	102 (86e)	94 (80)	93 (70)	14 (50)	6 (30)	2 (00)	0.5(70)	
					57s(80)						
46.36N, 112.02W	4124	Helena	1864	25 (86e)	24 (80)	23 (70)	18 (50)	12 (30)	11 (00)	3 (70)	
40.42N, 73.37W	65	Hempstead	1644	43 (86e)	40 (80)	39 (70)	29 (50)	13 (30)	4 (00)	2 (70)	
25.50N, 80.17W	8	Hialeah	1921	162 (86e)	145 (80)	102 (70)	20 (50)	3 (30)			
35.57N, 80.00W	940	High Point	1853	67 (86e)	64 (80)	63 (70)	40 (50)	37 (30)	4 (00)	1 (80)	
					100s(80)	93s(70)					
40.44N, 74.02W	5	Hoboken	1630?	42 (86e)	42 (80)	45 (70)	51 (50)	59 (30)	59 (00)	3 (50)	
26.01N, 80.09W	10	Hollywood	1921	121 (86e)	121 (80)	107 (70)	14 (50)	3 (30)			
42.12N, 72.36W	152	Holyoke	1745	42 (86e)	45 (80)	50 (70)	55 (50)	57 (30)	46 (00)	3 (50)	
34.30N, 93.03W	599	Hot Springs	1807	37 (86e)	36 (80)	36 (70)	29 (50)	20 (30)	10 (00)	0.2(60)	

For an explanation of symbols and abbreviations, see pages 16–17.

TABLE 2a. (Continued)

Latitude and Longitude	Elev (ft)	City	Date Settled	Population (thousands)							
				Latest	ca 1980	ca 1970	ca 1950	ca 1930	ca 1900	ca 1850	ca 1800
29.36N, 90.43W	12	Houma	1765	35 (86e)	33 (80) 66s(80)	31 (70)	12 (50)	7 (30)	3 (00)	0.4(60)	
29.45N, 95.22W	40	Houston	1836	1729 (86e)	1595 (80) 2412s(80)	1234 (70) 1678s(70)	596 (50) 701s(50)	292 (30)	45 (00)	2 (50)	
38.25N, 82.27W	565	Huntington	1871	59 (86e)	64 (80) 180s(80)	74 (70) 168s(70)	86 (50) 156s(50)	76 (30)	12 (00)	3 (80)	
33.40N, 118.05W	35	Huntington Beach	bef 1904	184 (86e)	171 (80)	116 (70)	5 (50)	4 (30)	0.8(10)		
34.44N, 86.35W	636	Huntsville (Alabama)	1807	163 (86e)	143 (80) 154s(80)	139 (70) 147s(70)	16 (50)	12 (30)	8 (00)	3 (50)	
30.43N, 95.33W	401	Huntsville (Texas)	1836	33 (86e)	24 (80)	18 (70)	10 (50)	5 (30)	2 (00)	0.9(60)	
43.29N, 112.02W	4709	Idaho Falls	1865	43 (86e)	40 (80)	36 (70)	19 (50)	9 (30)	1 (00)		
39.06N, 94.25W	1051	Independence	1825	113 (86e)	112 (80)	112 (70)	37 (50)	15 (30)	7 (00)	3 (60)	
39.46N, 86.10W	710	Indianapolis	1820	720 (86e)	701 (80) 836s(80)	737 (70) 820s(70)	427 (50) 502s(50)	364 (30)	169 (00)	8 (50)	3 (40)
33.58N, 118.21W	140	Inglewood	1887	103 (86e)	94 (80)	90 (70)	46 (50)	19 (30)	2 (10)		
41.40N, 91.32W	685	Iowa City	1839	50 (86e)	51 (80) 59s(80)	47 (70) 79s(70)	27 (50)	15 (30)	8 (00)	1 (50)	
33.40N, 117.46W	208	Irvine	1870?	88 (86e)	62 (80)	7 (70)	0.8(60e)	0.2(40e)			
32.49N, 96.56W	470	Irving	1902	129 (86e)	110 (80)	97 (70)	3 (50)	0.7(30)	0.4(20)		
40.44N, 74.13W	185	Irvington	1692?	62 (86e)	61 (80)	60 (70)	59 (50)	57 (30)	5 (00)	2 (80)	
42.26N, 76.30W	900	Ithaca	1788	26 (86e)	29 (80)	26 (70)	29 (50)	21 (30)	13 (00)	5 (50)	
42.15N, 84.24W	940	Jackson (Michigan)	1829	37 (86e)	40 (80) 81s(80)	45 (70) 79s(70)	51 (50)	55 (30)	25 (00)	2 (50)	
32.18N, 90.11W	298	Jackson (Mississippi)	bef 1800	208 (86e)	203 (80) 265s(80)	154 (70) 190s(70)	98 (50) 100s(50)	48 (30)	8 (00)	3 (60)	
30.20N, 81.40W	20	Jacksonville	1816	610 (86e)	541 (80) 598s(80)	504 (70) 530s(70)	205 (50) 243s(50)	130 (30)	28 (00)	1 (50)	
42.41N, 89.01W	801	Janesville	1835	52 (86e)	51 (80) 52s(80)	46 (70)	25 (50)	22 (30)	13 (00)	3 (50)	

Coordinates	No.	City	Year								
38.34N, 92.10W	557	Jefferson City	1821	36 (86e)	34 (80)	32 (70)	25 (50)	22 (30)	10 (00)	3 (60)	1 (40)
40.44N, 74.04W	20	Jersey City	1629?	219 (86e)	224 (80)	260 (70)	299 (50)	317 (30)	206 (00)	7 (50)	1 (20)
36.19N, 82.21W	1717	Johnson City	1777	45 (86e)	40 (80) 78s(80)	34 (70)	28 (50)	25 (30)	5 (00)	0.7(80)	
40.20N, 78.55W	1185	Johnstown	1800	32 (86e)	35 (80) 90s(80)	42 (70) 96s(70)	63 (50) 93s(50)	67 (30)	36 (00)	1 (50)	0.9(40)
41.32N, 88.05W	607	Joliet	1831	76 (86e)	78 (80) 167s(80)	79 (70) 155s(70)	52 (50)	43 (30)	29 (00)	3 (50)	
35.50N, 90.42W	344	Jonesboro	1859	30 (86e)	32 (80)	27 (70)	16 (50)	10 (30)	5 (00)	0.2(70)	
37.06N, 94.31W	1009	Joplin	1838	40 (86e)	39 (80) 58s(80)	39 (70)	39 (50)	33 (30)	26 (00)	7 (80)	
58.18N, 134.24W	100	Juneau	1880	25 (86e)	20 (80)	6 (70)	4 (50)	4 (30)	2 (00)	1 (90)	
42.17N, 85.35W	755	Kalamazoo	1829	77 (86e)	80 (80) 155s(80)	86 (70) 152s(70)	58 (50) 83s(50)	55 (30)	24 (00)	3 (50)	
39.07N, 94.38W	750	Kansas City (Kansas)	1843	162 (86e)	161 (80)	168 (70)	130 (50)	122 (30)	51 (00)	3 (80)	
39.05N, 94.35W	750	Kansas City (Missouri)	1821	441 (86e)	448 (80) 1098s(80)	507 (70) 1102s(70)	457 (50) 698s(50)	400 (30)	164 (00)	4 (60)	
42.56N, 72.17W	485	Keene	1750	22 (86e)	21 (80)	20 (70)	16 (50)	14 (30)	9 (00)	3 (50)	2 (00)
46.12N, 119.07W	355	Kennewick	1892	39 (86e)	34 (80)	15 (70)	10 (50)	2 (30)	1 (10)		
42.36N, 87.50W	610	Kenosha	1835	75 (86e)	78 (80) 86s(80)	79 (70) 84s(70)	54 (50)	50 (30)	12 (00)	3 (50)	0.3(40)
41.09N, 81.22W	1071	Kent	1805?	28 (86e)	26 (80)	28 (70)	12 (50)	8 (30)	5 (00)	3 (80)	
39.41N, 84.10W	1008	Kettering	1796	60 (86e)	61 (80)	72 (70)	22s(50)	11s(30)	3s(00)	1s(50)	
24.33N, 81.48W	7	Key West	1822	25 (86e)	24 (80)	29 (70)	26 (50)	13 (30)	17 (00)	2 (50)	0.7(40)
31.07N, 97.43W	833	Killeen	1882	60 (86e)	46 (80) 88s(80)	36 (70) 74s(70)	7 (50)	1 (30)	0.8(00)	0.3(90)	
36.33N, 82.33W	1284	Kingsport	1774?	31 (86e)	32 (80) 90s(80)	32 (70) 70s(70)	20 (50)	12 (30)	6 (20)	0.3(50)	
27.31N, 97.52W	66	Kingsville	1902	29 (86e)	29 (80)	29 (70)	17 (50)	7 (30)	5 (20)		
35.58N, 83.55W	890	Knoxville	1786	173 (86e)	175 (80) 285s(80)	175 (70) 191s(70)	125 (50) 148s(50)	106 (30)	33 (00)	2 (50)	0.4(00)
40.29N, 86.08W	828	Kokomo	1842	46 (86e)	48 (80) 61s(80)	44 (70)	39 (50)	33 (30)	11 (00)	1 (60)	
43.48N, 91.15W	649	La Crosse	1841	48 (86e)	48 (80) 68s(80)	50 (70) 63s(70)	48 (50)	40 (30)	29 (00)	4 (60)	

For an explanation of symbols and abbreviations, see pages 16–17.

(Continued)

TABLE 2a. (Continued)

Latitude and Longitude	Elev (ft)	City	Date Settled	Population (thousands)							
				Latest	ca 1980	ca 1970	ca 1950	ca 1930	ca 1900	ca 1850	ca 1800
40.25N, 86.54W	550	Lafayette (Indiana)	1825	44 (86e)	43 (80) 91s(80)	45 (70) 79s(70)	36 (50)	26 (30)	18 (00)	6 (50)	
30.13N, 92.01W	40	Lafayette (Louisiana)	1770?	90 (86e)	82 (80) 114s(80)	69 (70) 79s(70)	34 (50)	15 (30)	3 (00)	2 (90)	
30.14N, 93.13W	16	Lake Charles	1803?	73 (86e)	75 (80) 124s(80)	78 (70) 88s(70)	41 (50)	16 (30)	7 (00)	0.4(60)	
28.03N, 81.57W	206	Lakeland	1881	62 (86e)	47 (80) 114s(80)	43 (70) 67s(70)	31 (50)	19 (30)	1 (00)	0.6(90)	
33.51N, 118.08W	50	Lakewood (California)	1934	76 (86e)	75 (80)	83 (70)	67 (60)	2 (40)			
39.44N, 105.05W	5355	Lakewood (Colorado)	1872	122 (86e)	114 (80)	93 (70)	4 (50)	1 (30)	0.5(00)		
41.29N, 81.48W	685	Lakewood (Ohio)	1808	60 (86e)	62 (80)	70 (70)	68 (50)	71 (30)	3 (00)	1s(50)	
33.51N, 118.02W	115	La Mirada	1953	42 (86e)	41 (80)	31 (70)	22 (60)				
39.43N, 82.36W	898	Lancaster (Ohio)	1800	35 (86e)	35 (80)	33 (70)	24 (50)	19 (30)	9 (00)	3 (50)	2 (30)
40.02N, 76.18W	355	Lancaster (Pennsylvania)	1709?	57 (86e)	55 (80) 157s(80)	58 (70) 117s(70)	64 (50) 76s(50)	60 (30)	41 (00)	12 (50)	4 (00)
42.44N, 84.33W	830	Lansing	1843	129 (86e)	130 (80) 255s(80)	131 (70) 230s(70)	92 (50) 134s(50)	78 (30)	16 (00)	1 (50)	
41.19N, 105.35W	7145	Laramie	1868	25 (86e)	24 (80)	23 (70)	16 (50)	9 (30)	8 (00)	3 (80)	
27.30N, 99.30W	440	Laredo	1755	117 (86e)	91 (80) 95s(80)	69 (70) 70s(70)	52 (50)	33 (30)	13 (00)	1 (60)	1 (23)
32.19N, 106.47W	3895	Las Cruces	1848	54 (86e)	45 (80) 55s(80)	38 (70)	12 (50)	6 (30)	4 (10)	1s(70)	
36.10N, 115.09W	2030	Las Vegas	1905	192 (86e)	165 (80) 433s(80)	126 (70) 237s(70)	25 (50)	5 (30)	2 (20)		
38.48N, 95.14W	840	Lawrence (Kansas)	1854	56 (86e)	53 (80) 53s(80)	46 (70)	23 (50)	14 (30)	11 (00)	2 (60)	
42.42N, 71.10W	65	Lawrence (Massachusetts)	1655	63 (86e)	63 (80) 211s(80)	67 (70) 200s(70)	81 (50) 112s(50)	85 (30)	63 (00)	8 (50)	
34.37N, 98.25W	1111	Lawton	1901	83 (86e)	80 (80) 96s(80)	74 (70) 96s(70)	35 (50)	12 (30)	6 (07)		

Coordinates		City		(86e)	(80)	(70)	(50)	(30)	(00)	(50)	(00)
44.06N, 70.13W	196	Lewiston	1770	39 (86e)	40 (80) / 70s(80)	42 (70) / 65s(70)	41 (50)	35 (30)	24 (00)	4 (50)	0.9(00)
38.03N, 84.30W	955	Lexington	1779	213 (86e)	204 (80) / 194s(80)	108 (70) / 160s(70)	56 (50)	46 (30)	26 (00)	9 (50)	2 (00)
40.45N, 84.06W	865	Lima	1831	46 (86e)	48 (80) / 70s(80)	54 (70) / 70s(70)	50 (50)	42 (30)	22 (00)	0.8(50)	
40.49N, 96.42W	1150	Lincoln	1864	183 (86e)	172 (80) / 174s(80)	150 (70) / 153s(70)	99 (50) / 100s(50)	76 (30)	40 (00)	13 (80)	
34.45N, 92.17W	300	Little Rock	1820	181 (86e)	159 (80) / 295s(80)	132 (70) / 223s(70)	102 (50) / 154s(50)	82 (30)	38 (00)	2 (50)	
42.23N, 83.22W	663	Livonia	1832	101 (86e)	105 (80)	110 (70)	18 (50)	3s(30)	1s(00)		
41.44N,111.50W	4535	Logan	1859	29 (86e)	27 (80)	22 (70)	17 (50)	10 (30)	5 (00)	2 (70)	
33.46N,118.11W	35	Long Beach	1881	396 (86e)	361 (80)	359 (70)	251 (50)	142 (30)	2 (00)		
32.29N, 94.44W	339	Longview (Texas)	1865	74 (86e)	63 (80) / 70s(80)	46 (70)	25 (50)	5 (30)	4 (00)	2 (80)	
46.08N,122.56W	13	Longview (Washington)	1922	29 (86e)	31 (80) / 55s(80)	28 (70)	20 (50)	11 (30)			
41.28N, 82.11W	610	Lorain	1807	72 (86e)	75 (80) / 225s(80)	78 (70) / 192s(70)	51 (50)	45 (30)	16 (00)	2 (80)	
34.03N,118.14W	340	Los Angeles	1781	3259 (86e)	2969 (80) / 9480s(80)	2812 (70) / 8351s(70)	1970 (50) / 3997s(50)	1238 (30)	102 (00)	2 (50)	0.3(00)
38.15N, 85.46W	450	Louisville	1778	286 (86e)	299 (80) / 761s(80)	362 (70) / 739s(70)	369 (50) / 473s(50)	308 (30)	205 (00)	43 (50)	0.4(00)
42.38N, 71.19W	100	Lowell	1653	93 (86e)	92 (80) / 157s(80)	94 (70) / 183s(70)	97 (50) / 107s(50)	100 (30)	95 (00)	33 (50)	6 (30)
33.35N,101.51W	3241	Lubbock	1891	186 (86e)	174 (80) / 175s(80)	149 (70) / 150s(70)	72 (50)	21 (30)	2 (10)		
37.25N, 79.09W	517	Lynchburg	1787?	68 (86e)	67 (80) / 94s(80)	54 (70) / 71s(70)	48 (50)	41 (30)	19 (00)	8 (50)	5 (30)
42.28N, 70.57W	34	Lynn	1629	79 (86e)	78 (80)	90 (70)	100 (50)	102 (30)	69 (00)	14 (50)	3 (00)
32.50N, 83.38W	335	Macon	1806	118 (86e)	117 (80) / 131s(80)	122 (70) / 128s(70)	70 (50) / 93s(50)	54 (30)	23 (00)	6 (50)	3 (30)
43.04N, 89.23W	860	Madison	1837	176 (86e)	171 (80) / 214s(80)	172 (70) / 205s(70)	96 (50) / 110s(50)	58 (30)	19 (00)	2 (50)	
34.02N,118.41W	25	Malibu	1928		16 (80)	4 (70e)		0.4(30)			0.6(00)
42.59N, 71.28W	175	Manchester	1722	97 (86e)	91 (80) / 103s(80)	88 (70) / 95s(70)	83 (50) / 85s(50)	77 (30)	57 (00)	14 (50)	0.6(00)

For an explanation of symbols and abbreviations, see pages 16–17.

(Continued)

TABLE 2a. (Continued)

Latitude and Longitude	Elev (ft)	City	Date Settled	Population (thousands)								
				Latest	ca 1980	ca 1970	ca 1950	ca 1930	ca 1900	ca 1850	ca 1800	
39.11N, 96.34W	1012	Manhattan	1854	34 (86e)	33 (80)	28 (70)	19 (50)	10 (30)	3 (00)	1 (70)		
44.10N, 94.00W	785	Mankato	1852	30 (86e)	29 (80)	31 (70)	19 (50)	14 (30)	11 (00)	2 (60)		
40.45N, 82.31W	1154	Mansfield	1808?	51 (86e)	54 (80) 79s(80)	55 (70) 78s(70)	44 (50)	34 (30)	18 (00)	4 (50)		
46.33N, 87.24W	602	Marquette	1849	21 (86e)	23 (80)	22 (70)	17 (50)	15 (30)	10 (00)	4 (70)		
26.12N, 98.14W	122	McAllen	1904	83 (86e)	66 (80) 157s(80)	38 (70) 91s(70)	20 (50)	9 (30)	5 (20)			
42.25N, 71.07W	12	Medford (Massachusetts)	1630	57 (86e)	58 (80)	64 (70)	66 (50)	60 (30)	18 (00)	4 (50)	1 (00)	
42.19N, 122.52W	1377	Medford (Oregon)	1883	44 (86e)	40 (80) 52s(80)	29 (70)	17 (50)	11 (30)	2 (00)	1 (90)		
28.05N, 80.36W	22	Melbourne	1878	57 (86e)	47 (80) 213s(80)	40 (70) 179s(70)	4 (50)	3 (30)	0.1(00)	0.1(90)		
35.09N, 90.03W	275	Memphis	1819	653 (86e)	646 (80) 775s(80)	624 (70) 664s(70)	396 (50) 406s(50)	253 (30)	102 (00)	9 (50)	0.7(30)	
41.32N, 72.47W	150	Meriden	1661	58 (86e)	57 (80) 57s(80)	56 (70) 98s(70)	44 (50)	38 (30)	24 (00)	4 (50)	1 (10)	
32.22N, 88.42W	341	Meridian	1831	43 (86e)	47 (80)	45 (70)	42 (50)	32 (30)	14 (00)	3 (70)		
33.25N, 111.50W	1161	Mesa	1878	251 (86e)	152 (80)	63 (70)	17 (50)	4 (30)	0.7(00)			
32.46N, 96.36W	491	Mesquite	1872	89 (86e)	67 (80)	55 (70)	2 (50)	0.7(30)	0.4(00)	0.1(90)		
29.58N, 90.09W	5	Metairie	1730s		164 (80)	136 (70)	73 (60)	3 (40)				
25.47N, 80.12W	10	Miami	1870	374 (86e)	347 (80) 1608s(80)	335 (70) 1220s(70)	249 (50) 459s(50)	111 (30)	2 (00)			
25.47N, 80.08W	6	Miami Beach	1913	95 (86e)	96 (80)	87 (70)	46 (50)	6 (30)	0.6(20)			
41.34N, 72.39W	50	Middletown (Connecticut)	1650	39 (86e)	39 (80)	37 (70)	30 (50)	25 (30)	10 (00)	4 (50)	2 (10)	
39.31N, 84.24W	666	Middletown (Ohio)	1802	46 (86e)	44 (80) 92s(80)	49 (70)	34 (50)	30 (30)	9 (00)	1 (50)		
32.00N, 102.05W	2779	Midland	1885	98 (86e)	71 (80) 72s(80)	59 (70) 60s(70)	22 (50)	5 (30)	2 (10)			
43.02N, 87.54W	635	Milwaukee	1818	605 (86e)	636 (80) 1207s(80)	717 (70) 1252s(70)	637 (50) 829s(50)	578 (30)	285 (00)	20 (50)	2 (40)	

(Continued)

Coordinates		Name	Year	(86e)	(80)	(70)	(50)	(30)	(00)		
44.59N, 93.16W	815	Minneapolis	1847	357 (86e)	371 (80) / 1788s(80)	434 (70) / 1701s(70)	522 (50) / 985s(50)	464 (30)	203 (00)	3 (60)	1 (13)
48.14N,101.18W	1557	Minot	1886	36 (86e)	33 (80)	32 (70)	22 (50)	16 (30)	1 (00)	0.6(90)	
46.52N,114.00W	3223	Missoula	1864	34 (86e)	33 (80) / 58s(80)	29 (70)	22 (50)	15 (30)	4 (00)	3 (90)	
30.42N, 88.03W	5	Mobile	1711	203 (86e)	200 (80) / 295s(80)	190 (70) / 258s(70)	129 (50) / 183s(50)	68 (30)	38 (00)	21 (50)	
37.39N,121.00W	88	Modesto	1870	133 (86e)	107 (80) / 160s(80)	62 (70) / 106s(70)	17 (50)	14 (30)	2 (00)	2 (80)	
41.30N, 90.30W	580	Moline	1829	44 (86e)	46 (80)	46 (70)	37 (50)	32 (30)	17 (00)	2 (60)	
32.30N, 92.07W	77	Monroe	1785	56 (86e)	58 (80) / 113s(80)	56 (70) / 91s(70)	39 (50)	26 (30)	5 (00)	0.4(50)	
36.37N,121.55W	40	Monterey	1770	30 (86e)	28 (80)	26 (70)	16 (50)	9 (30)	2 (00)	1 (50)	
32.23N, 86.19W	160	Montgomery	1817	194 (86e)	178 (80) / 197s(80)	133 (70) / 139s(70)	107 (50) / 109s(50)	66 (30)	30 (00)	5 (50)	2 (40)
44.16N, 72.35W	523	Montpelier	1788	8 (86e)	8 (80)	9 (70)	9 (50)	8 (30)	6 (00)	2 (50)	0.9(00)
46.53N, 96.45W	929	Moorhead	1871	28 (86e)	30 (80)	30 (70)	15 (50)	8 (30)	4 (00)	2 (90)	
39.38N, 79.57W	892	Morgantown	1767	27 (86e)	28 (80)	29 (70)	26 (50)	16 (30)	2 (00)	0.9(50)	
46.44N,117.00W	2564	Moscow	1871	18 (86e)	17 (80)	14 (70)	11 (50)	4 (30)	2 (00)		
43.36N, 84.46W	765	Mount Pleasant	1850s	22 (86e)	24 (80)	21 (70)	11 (50)	5 (30)	4 (00)	1 (80)	
40.55N, 73.49W	100	Mount Vernon	1664	68 (86e)	67 (80)	73 (70)	72 (50)	61 (30)	21 (00)	3 (70)	
40.11N, 85.23W	950	Muncie	1827	73 (86e)	77 (80) / 91s(80)	69 (70) / 90s(70)	58 (50)	47 (30)	21 (00)	0.7(50)	
35.51N, 86.23W	616	Murfreesboro	1811	41 (86e)	33 (80)	26 (70)	13 (50)	8 (30)	4 (00)	2 (50)	
43.14N, 86.16W	625	Muskegon	1812	40 (86e)	41 (80) / 106s(80)	45 (70) / 106s(70)	48 (50) / 85s(50)	41 (30)	21 (00)	0.5(50)	
35.45N, 95.22W	617	Muskogee	1872	42 (86e)	40 (80)	37 (70)	37 (50)	32 (30)	4 (00)	2 (89)	
31.36N, 94.39W	283	Nacogdoches	1779	28 (86e)	27 (80)	23 (70)	12 (50)	6 (30)	2 (00)	0.5(50)	0.7(99)
38.18N,122.17W	20	Napa	1840	57 (86e)	51 (80) / 59s(80)	36 (70)	14 (50)	6 (30)	4 (00)	0.2(50)	
26.08N, 81.48W	9	Naples	1887	19 (86e)	18 (80) / 54s(80)	12 (70)	1 (50)	0.4(30)			
42.45N, 71.28W	152	Nashua	1656	77 (86e)	68 (80) / 75s(80)	56 (70) / 61s(70)	35 (50)	31 (30)	24 (00)	6 (50)	0.9(00)
36.10N, 86.47W	450	Nashville	1780	474 (86e)	456 (80) / 518s(80)	426 (70) / 448s(70)	174 (50) / 259s(50)	154 (30)	81 (00)	10 (50)	0.3(00)

For an explanation of symbols and abbreviations, see pages 16–17.

TABLE 2a. (Continued)

Latitude and Longitude	Elev (ft)	City	Date Settled	Population (thousands)							
				Latest	ca 1980	ca 1970	ca 1950	ca 1930	ca 1900	ca 1850	ca 1800
31.34N, 91.23W	202	Natchez	1716	22 (86e)	22 (80)	20 (70)	23 (50)	13 (30)	12 (00)	4 (50)	2 (10)
38.18N, 85.49W	459	New Albany	1813	37 (86e)	37 (80)	38 (70)	29 (50)	26 (30)	21 (00)	8 (50)	2 (30)
39.41N, 75.45W	135	Newark (Delaware)	1747?	24 (86e)	25 (80)	21 (70)	7 (50)	4 (30)	1 (00)	0.8(60)	0.9(00)
40.44N, 74.10W	55	Newark (New Jersey)	1666	316 (86e)	329 (80)	382 (70)	439 (50)	442 (30)	246 (00)	39 (50)	7 (10)
41.38N, 70.56W	15	New Bedford	1640	96 (86e)	98 (80)	102 (70)	109 (50)	113 (30)	62 (00)	16 (50)	4 (00)
					133s(80)	134s(70)	125s(50)				
41.40N, 72.47W	200	New Britain	1686	72 (86e)	74 (80)	83 (70)	74 (50)	68 (30)	26 (00)	3 (50)	0.9(00)
					136s(80)	131s(70)	123s(50)				
40.30N, 74.27W	42	New Brunswick	1681	40 (86e)	41 (80)	42 (70)	39 (50)	35 (30)	20 (00)	10 (50)	5 (29)
41.18N, 72.55W	40	New Haven	1638	123 (86e)	126 (80)	138 (70)	164 (50)	163 (30)	108 (00)	20 (50)	4 (00)
					368s(80)	348s(70)	245s(50)				
41.22N, 72.06W	40	New London	1646	29 (86e)	29 (80)	32 (70)	31 (50)	30 (30)	18 (00)	9 (50)	5 (00)
29.57N, 90.04W	5	New Orleans	1718	554 (86e)	558 (80)	593 (70)	570 (50)	459 (30)	287 (00)	116 (50)	8 (97)
					1078s(80)	962s(70)	660s(50)				
41.29N, 71.19W	10	Newport	1639	29 (86e)	29 (80)	35 (70)	38 (50)	28 (30)	22 (00)	10 (50)	7 (00)
					51s(80)						
33.37N, 117.56W	10	Newport Beach	1892	67 (86e)	64 (80)	50 (70)	12 (50)	2 (30)	0.4(10)		
36.59N, 76.25W	22	Newport News	1621	162 (86e)	145 (80)	138 (70)	42 (50)	34 (30)	20 (00)	0.8(70)	
					329s(80)	268s(70)					
40.54N, 73.47W	72	New Rochelle	1688	69 (86e)	71 (80)	75 (70)	60 (50)	54 (30)	15 (00)	0.3(70)	1s(10)
42.21N, 71.12W	33	Newton	1639	82 (86e)	84 (80)	91 (70)	82 (50)	65 (30)	34 (00)	5 (50)	1 (00)
40.45N, 74.00W	55	New York	1624	7263 (86e)	7072 (80)	7896 (70)	7892 (50)	6930 (30)	3437 (00)	516 (50)	60 (00)
					15,590s(80)	16,207s(70)	12,296s(50)				
43.06N, 79.03W	570	Niagara Falls	1807	65 (86e)	71 (80)	86 (70)	91 (50)	75 (30)	19 (00)	3 (70)	0.5(20)
36.51N, 76.17W	10	Norfolk	1682	275 (86e)	267 (80)	308 (70)	214 (50)	130 (30)	47 (00)	14 (50)	7 (00)
					771s(80)	668s(70)	385s(50)				
40.30N, 88.59W	829	Normal	1831	37 (86e)	36 (80)	26 (70)	10 (50)	7 (30)	4 (00)	0.8(60)	
35.13N, 97.26W	1160	Norman	1889	78 (86e)	68 (80)	52 (70)	27 (50)	10 (30)	2 (00)	0.8(90)	
42.19N, 72.38W	130	Northampton	1654	28 (86e)	29 (80)	30 (70)	29 (50)	24 (30)	19 (00)	5 (50)	2 (00)
32.53N, 80.00W	25	North Charleston	17th c	61 (86e)	63 (80)	21 (70)	13s(50)	3s(30)	2s(00)	5s(50)	5s(00)

(Continued)

For an explanation of symbols and abbreviations, see pages 16–17.

Figure 12. Skyscrapers of midtown New York as seen from the East River, with the United Nations Secretariat Building in the foreground and, in the background from left to right, the Empire State, Chrysler, and Pan Am buildings. New York is the largest urbanized area in North America and the world according to the latest censuses but probably now ranks second to Mexico City. (Credit: New York Convention and Visitors Bureau, Inc.)

TABLE 2a. (Continued)

Latitude and Longitude	Elev (ft)	City	Date Settled	Population (thousands)							
				Latest	ca 1980	ca 1970	ca 1950	ca 1930	ca 1900	ca 1850	ca 1800
33.54N,118.05W	93	Norwalk (California)	1874	90 (86e)	85 (80)	90 (70)	89 (60)	4 (40)	0.5(13e)		
41.07N, 73.22W	60	Norwalk (Connecticut)	1649	77 (86e)	78 (80) 108s(80)	79 (70) 107s(70)	49 (50) 55s(50)	36 (30)	6 (00)	5 (50)	5 (00)
41.31N, 72.05W	35	Norwich	1659	38 (86e)	38 (80) 149s(80)	42 (70) 139s(70)	23 (50)	23 (30)	17 (00)	6 (50)	3 (00)
37.48N,122.16W	25	Oakland	1848	357 (86e)	339 (80)	362 (70)	385 (50)	284 (30)	67 (00)	2 (60)	
41.53N, 87.46W	630	Oak Park	1833	54 (86e)	55 (80)	63 (70)	64 (50)	64 (30)	19 (10)		
33.12N,117.23W	45	Oceanside	1883	99 (86e)	77 (80)	40 (70)	13 (50)	4 (30)	0.3(00)		
31.51N,102.22W	2890	Odessa	1881	101 (86e)	90 (80) 102s(80)	78 (70) 82s(70)	29 (50)	2 (30)			
41.14N,111.58W	4299	Ogden	1845?	67 (86e)	64 (80) 206s(80)	69 (70) 150s(70)	57 (50)	40 (30)	16 (00)	1 (60)	
35.28N, 97.31W	1195	Oklahoma City	1889	446 (86e)	403 (80) 674s(80)	368 (70) 580s(70)	244 (50) 275s(50)	185 (30)	10 (00)	4 (90)	
47.03N,122.53W	71	Olympia	1848	30 (86e)	27 (80) 69s(80)	23 (70)	16 (50)	12 (30)	4 (00)	1 (70)	
41.16N, 95.56W	1040	Omaha	1854	349 (86e)	314 (80) 512s(80)	347 (70) 492s(70)	251 (50) 310s(50)	214 (30)	103 (00)	2 (60)	
34.04N,117.39W	980	Ontario	1882	114 (86e)	89 (80)	64 (70)	23 (50)	14 (30)	0.7(00)	0.7(90)	
33.47N,117.51W	176	Orange	1868	101 (86e)	91 (80)	77 (70)	10 (50)	8 (30)	1 (00)	0.7(80)	
40.19N,111.42W	4756	Orem	1861	62 (86e)	52 (80)	26 (70)	8 (50)	2 (30)			
28.33N, 81.23W	70	Orlando	1837	146 (86e)	128 (80) 577s(80)	99 (70) 305s(70)	52 (50) 73s(50)	27 (30)	2 (00)		
44.01N, 88.33W	761	Oshkosh	1836	51 (86e)	50 (80) 53s(80)	53 (70) 55s(70)	41 (50)	40 (30)	28 (00)	2 (53)	
38.58N, 94.40W	950	Overland Park	1906	97 (86e)	82 (80)	78 (70)	21 (60)	3 (40)			
37.46N, 87.07W	765	Owensboro	1800?	56 (86e)	54 (80) 58s(80)	50 (70) 53s(70)	34 (50)	23 (30)	13 (00)	1 (50)	0.2(30)
34.22N, 89.31W	458	Oxford (Mississippi)	1835	9 (86e)	10 (80)	9 (70)	4 (50)	3 (30)	2 (00)	1 (53)	

Coordinates		City	Date	(86e)	(80)	(70)	(50)	(30)	(00)	earlier
39.31N, 84.45W	952	Oxford (Ohio)	1810	17 (86e)	18 (80)	16 (70)	7 (50)	3 (30)	2 (00)	1 (50) · 0.7(30)
34.12N,119.10W	50	Oxnard	1898	127 (86e)	108 (80) · 378s(80)	71 (70) · 245s(70)	22 (50)	6 (30)	3 (10)	
26.43N, 80.02W	10	Palm Beach	1872	11 (86e)	10 (80)	9 (70)	4 (50)	2 (30)	0.3(95)	
33.50N,116.33W	430	Palm Springs	1876	31 (86e)	32 (80) · 66s(80)	21 (70)	8 (50)	3 (40)	0.05(00?e)	
37.26N,122.10W	63	Palo Alto	1876	56 (86e)	55 (80)	56 (70)	25 (50)	14 (30)	2 (00)	
30.10N, 85.40W	29	Panama City	1765?	36 (86e)	33 (80) · 79s(80)	32 (70)	26 (50)	5 (30)	0.4(10)	
36.09N,115.10W	4520	Paradise	bef 1970		85 (80)	24 (70)				
39.16N, 81.33W	615	Parkersburg	1785	39 (86e)	40 (80) · 63s(80)	44 (70) · 65s(70)	30 (50)	30 (30)	12 (00)	1 (50)
41.23N, 81.43W	846	Parma	1826?	89 (86e)	93 (80)	100 (70)	29 (50)	14 (30)	1 (00)	1 (50)
34.09N,118.09W	830	Pasadena (California)	1874	130 (86e)	118 (80)	113 (70)	105 (50)	76 (30)	9 (00)	0.4(80) · 0.3(10)
29.43N, 95.13W	34	Pasadena (Texas)	1895	118 (86e)	113 (80)	90 (70)	22 (50)	2 (30)		1 (30)
30.21N, 88.33W	15	Pascagoula	1718	31 (86e)	29 (80) · 65s(80)	27 (70)	11 (50)	4 (30)	0.7(00)	0.6(02)
40.51N, 74.07W	70	Passaic	1678	54 (86e)	52 (80)	55 (70)	58 (50)	63 (30)	28 (00)	7 (80)
40.55N, 74.10W	100	Paterson	1679	139 (86e)	138 (80)	145 (70)	139 (50)	139 (30)	105 (00)	11 (50)
41.53N, 71.23W	25	Pawtucket	1671	73 (86e)	71 (80)	77 (70)	81 (50)	77 (30)	39 (00)	4 (50)
30.25N, 87.13W	15	Pensacola	1698	64 (86e)	58 (80) · 216s(80)	60 (70) · 167s(70)	43 (50)	32 (30)	18 (00)	2 (50)
40.42N, 89.36W	470	Peoria	1691?	110 (86e)	124 (80) · 261s(80)	127 (70) · 247s(70)	112 (50) · 155s(50)	105 (30)	56 (00)	5 (50) · 1 (40)
37.14N, 77.24W	87	Petersburg	1646	40 (86e)	41 (80) · 107s(80)	36 (70) · 101s(70)	35 (50)	29 (30)	22 (00)	14 (50) · 4 (00)
39.57N, 75.09W	100	Philadelphia	1677?	1643 (86e)	1688 (80) · 4113s(80)	1950 (70) · 4021s(70)	2072 (50) · 2922s(50)	1951 (30)	1294 (00)	121 (50) · 340s(50) · 41 (00) · 69s(00)
33.27N,112.04W	1090	Phoenix	1867	894 (86e)	790 (80) · 1409s(80)	584 (70) · 863s(70)	107 (50) · 216s(50)	48 (30)	6 (00)	2 (80)
44.22N,100.21W	1442	Pierre	1880	13 (86e)	12 (80)	10 (70)	6 (50)	4 (30)	2 (00)	3 (90)
34.13N, 92.01W	221	Pine Bluff	1819	61 (86e)	57 (80) · 63s(80)	57 (70) · 61s(70)	37 (50)	21 (30)	11 (00)	0.5(50)
40.26N, 80.00W	745	Pittsburgh	1758?	387 (86e)	424 (80) · 1810s(80)	520 (70) · 1846s(70)	677 (50) · 1533s(50)	670 (30)	322 (00)	47 (50) · 2 (00)

(Continued)

For an explanation of symbols and abbreviations, see pages 16–17.

TABLE 2a. (Continued)

Latitude and Longitude	Elev (ft)	City	Date Settled	Population (thousands)							
				Latest	ca 1980	ca 1970	ca 1950	ca 1930	ca 1900	ca 1850	ca 1800
42.27N, 73.15W	1015	Pittsfield	1752	50 (86e)	52 (80) 58s(80)	57 (70) 63s(70)	53 (50)	50 (30)	22 (00)	6 (50)	2 (00)
40.37N, 74.25W	100	Plainfield	1684	46 (86e)	46 (80)	47 (70)	42 (50)	34 (30)	15 (00)	5 (70)	
33.01N, 96.42W	655	Plano	1848	111 (86e)	72 (80)	18 (70)	2 (50)	2 (30)	1 (00)	0.8(90)	
44.42N, 73.28W	140	Plattsburgh	1784	21 (86e)	21 (80)	19 (70)	18 (50)	13 (30)	8 (00)	3 (60)	1s(00)
41.57N, 70.40W	29	Plymouth	1620		7 (80)	7 (70)	11 (50)	13s(30)	10s(00)	6s(50)	4s(00)
42.52N, 112.27W	4464	Pocatello	1882	44 (86e)	46 (80) 53s(80)	40 (70)	26 (50)	16 (30)	4 (00)		
34.04N, 117.45W	861	Pomona	1875	116 (86e)	93 (80)	87 (70)	35 (50)	21 (30)	6 (00)	4 (90)	
26.14N, 80.07W	15	Pompano Beach	1884	67 (86e)	53 (80)	39 (70)	6 (50)	3 (30)	0.3(10)		
42.38N, 83.17W	932	Pontiac	1818	71 (86e)	77 (80)	85 (70)	74 (50)	65 (30)	10 (00)	2 (50)	2 (40)
29.54N, 93.56W	10	Port Arthur	1895	62 (86e)	61 (80) 119s(80)	57 (70) 116s(70)	58 (50) 82s(50)	51 (30)	0.9(00)		
42.58N, 82.26W	599	Port Huron	1790	34 (86e)	34 (80) 60s(80)	36 (70)	36 (50)	31 (30)	19 (00)	2 (50)	
43.40N, 70.15W	25	Portland (Maine)	1716	63 (86e)	62 (80) 107s(80)	65 (70) 107s(70)	78 (50) 113s(50)	71 (30)	50 (00)	21 (50)	4 (00)
45.31N, 122.41W	77	Portland (Oregon)	1845	388 (86e)	366 (80) 1026s(80)	380 (70) 825s(70)	374 (50) 513s(50)	302 (30)	90 (00)	0.8(50)	
43.04N, 70.45W	30	Portsmouth (New Hampshire)	1624	26 (86e)	26 (80) 104s(80)	26 (70)	19 (50)	14 (30)	11 (00)	10 (50)	5 (00)
36.50N, 76.18W	10	Portsmouth (Virginia)	1752	111 (86e)	105 (80)	111 (70)	80 (50)	46 (30)	17 (00)	9 (50)	2 (90)
41.42N, 73.56W	175	Poughkeepsie	1687	30 (86e)	30 (80) 137s(80)	32 (70) 103s(70)	41 (50)	40 (30)	24 (00)	14s(50)	3s(00)
40.21N, 74.39W	215	Princeton	1681	12 (86e)	12 (80)	12 (70)	12 (50)	7 (30)	4 (00)	3 (70)	
41.50N, 71.25W	80	Providence	1636	157 (86e)	157 (80) 796s(80)	179 (70) 795s(70)	249 (50) 583s(50)	253 (30)	176 (00)	42 (50)	8 (00)
40.14N, 111.39W	4549	Provo	1849	77 (86e)	74 (80) 170s(80)	53 (70) 104s(70)	29 (50)	15 (30)	6 (00)	2 (60)	
38.16N, 104.37W	4695	Pueblo	1842	101 (86e)	102 (80) 109s(80)	98 (70) 103s(70)	64 (50) 73s(50)	50 (30)	28 (00)	3 (80)	

Lat/Long	No.	Place	Founded	(86e)	(80)	(70)	(50)	(30)	(00)		
46.44N, 117.10W	2345	Pullman	1882	23 (86e)	24 (80)	21 (70)	12 (50)	3 (30)	1 (00)	0.9 (90)	1 (00)
42.15N, 71.00W	42	Quincy	1625	83 (86e)	85 (80)	88 (70)	84 (50)	72 (30)	24 (00)	5 (50)	
42.44N, 87.47W	630	Racine	1834	82 (86e)	86 (80)	95 (70)	71 (50)	68 (30)	29 (00)	5 (50)	
					119s (80)	117s (70)	77s (50)				
35.47N, 78.38W	365	Raleigh	1760?	180 (86e)	150 (80)	123 (70)	66 (50)	37 (30)	14 (00)	5 (50)	0.7 (00)
					207s (80)	152s (70)	69s (50)				
44.05N, 103.14W	3231	Rapid City	1876	52 (86e)	46 (80)	44 (70)	25 (50)	10 (30)	1 (00)	0.3 (80)	
					51s (80)						
40.20N, 75.56W	265	Reading	1733	78 (86e)	79 (80)	88 (70)	109 (50)	111 (30)	79 (00)	16 (50)	2 (00)
					173s (80)	168s (70)	155s (50)				
34.03N, 117.11W	1351	Redlands	1887	53 (86e)	44 (80)	36 (70)	18 (50)	14 (30)	5 (00)	2 (90)	
39.31N, 119.49W	4491	Reno	1868	110 (86e)	101 (80)	73 (70)	32 (50)	19 (30)	4 (00)	1 (70)	
					162s (80)	100s (70)					
32.57N, 96.43W	630	Richardson	1873	78 (86e)	72 (80)	48 (70)	1 (50)	0.6 (30)	0.7s (10)		
46.17N, 119.17W	390	Richland	1892	33 (86e)	34¹ (80)	26 (70)	22 (50)	0.2 (30)			
						71s (70)					
37.56N, 122.21W	12	Richmond (California)	1899	78 (86e)	75 (80)	79 (70)	100 (50)	20 (30)	7 (10)		0.1 (00)
37.45N, 84.18W	926	Richmond (Kentucky)	1784	23 (86e)	22 (80)	17 (70)	10 (50)	6 (30)	5 (00)	0.4 (50)	6 (00)
37.32N, 77.26W	160	Richmond (Virginia)	1737	218 (86e)	219 (80)	249 (70)	230 (50)	183 (30)	85 (00)	28 (50)	
					492s (80)	417s (70)	258s (50)				
33.59N, 117.22W	851	Riverside	1870	197 (86e)	171 (80)	140 (70)	47 (50)	30 (30)	8 (00)	5 (90)	
					705s (80)	584s (70)					
37.16N, 79.57W	905	Roanoke	1834	102 (86e)	100 (80)	92 (70)	92 (50)	69 (30)	21 (00)	0.7 (80)	
					177s (80)	157s (70)	107s (50)				
44.01N, 92.28W	988	Rochester (Minnesota)	1854	58 (86e)	58 (80)	54 (70)	30 (50)	21 (30)	7 (00)	1 (60)	
					60s (80)	57s (70)					
43.10N, 77.36W	515	Rochester (New York)	1812	236 (86e)	242 (80)	295 (70)	332 (50)	328 (30)	163 (00)	36 (50)	9 (30)
					606s (80)	601s (70)	409s (50)				
42.17N, 89.06W	715	Rockford	1834	136 (86e)	140 (80)	147 (70)	93 (50)	86 (30)	31 (00)	2 (50)	
					204s (80)	206s (70)	122s (50)				
34.56N, 81.01W	680	Rock Hill	1851	42 (86e)	35 (80)	34 (70)	25 (50)	11 (30)	5 (00)	0.8 (80)	
					51s (80)						
41.29N, 90.34W	563	Rock Island	1816	44 (86e)	47 (80)	50 (70)	49 (50)	38 (30)	19 (00)	2 (50)	
39.05N, 77.09W	421	Rockville	1769?	47 (86e)	44 (80)	43 (70)	7 (50)	1 (30)	1 (00)	0.4 (60)	

¹Urbanized area population for 1980 included in Kennewick urbanized area.

For an explanation of symbols and abbreviations, see pages 16–17.

(Continued)

TABLE 2a. (Continued)

Latitude and Longitude	Elev (ft)	City	Date Settled	Population (thousands)							
				Latest	ca 1980	ca 1970	ca 1950	ca 1930	ca 1900	ca 1850	ca 1800
34.15N, 85.10W	614	Rome (Georgia)	1834	31 (86e)	30 (80)	31 (70)	30 (50)	22 (30)	7 (00)	3 (50)	
					51s(80)						
43.13N, 75.27W	440	Rome (New York)	1786	42 (86e)	44 (80)	50 (70)	42 (50)	32 (30)	15 (00)	4 (60)	1 (00?e)
33.24N,104.32W	3600	Roswell	1869	44 (86e)	40 (80)	34 (70)	26 (50)	11 (30)	2 (00)	0.3(90)	
42.30N, 83.09W	693	Royal Oak	1822	66 (86e)	71 (80)	86 (70)	47 (50)	23 (30)	0.5(00)		
32.31N, 92.38W	319	Ruston	1883	21 (86e)	21 (80)	17 (70)	10 (50)	4 (30)	1 (00)	0.8(90)	
43.36N, 72.58W	560	Rutland	1770	18 (86e)	18 (80)	19 (70)	18 (50)	17 (30)	11 (00)	4 (50)	2 (00)
38.35N,121.30W	30	Sacramento	1839	324 (86e)	276 (80)	257 (70)	138 (50)	94 (30)	29 (00)	7 (50)	
					796s(80)	641s(70)	212s(50)				
43.26N, 83.56W	595	Saginaw	1816	72 (86e)	78 (80)	92 (70)	93 (50)	81 (30)	42 (00)	1 (50)	
					147s(80)	148s(70)	106s(50)				
29.53N, 81.19W	7	Saint Augustine	1565	12 (86e)	12 (80)	12 (70)	14 (50)	12 (30)	4 (00)	2 (50)	5 (00e)
42.30N, 82.53W	586	Saint Clair Shores	1818?	72 (86e)	76 (80)	88 (70)	20 (50)	7 (30)			
45.34N, 94.10W	1032	Saint Cloud	1853	43 (86e)	43 (80)	40 (70)	28 (50)	21 (30)	9 (00)	2 (70)	
					58s(80)	52s(70)					
39.46N, 94.51W	850	Saint Joseph	1826	74 (86e)	77 (80)	73 (70)	79 (50)	81 (30)	103 (00)	9 (60)	0.9(46)
					80s(80)	77s(70)	82s(50)				
38.38N, 90.12W	455	Saint Louis	1764	426 (86e)	453 (80)	622 (70)	857 (50)	822 (30)	575 (00)	78 (50)	2 (10)
					1849s(80)	1883s(70)	1400s(50)				
44.57N, 93.06W	780	Saint Paul	1838	264 (86e)	270 (80)	310 (70)	311 (50)	272 (30)	163 (00)	1 (50)	
27.46N, 82.38W	20	Saint Petersburg	1856	239 (86e)	239 (80)	216 (70)	97 (50)	40 (30)	2 (00)	0.3(90)	
					833s(80)	495s(70)	115s(50)				
42.31N, 70.53W	13	Salem (Massachusetts)	1626	38 (86e)	38 (80)	41 (70)	42 (50)	43 (30)	36 (00)	20 (50)	9 (00)
44.56N,123.02W	163	Salem (Oregon)	1841	94 (86e)	89 (80)	69 (70)	43 (50)	26 (30)	4 (00)	1 (70)	
					136s(80)	93s(70)					
36.40N,121.39W	44	Salinas	1856	97 (86e)	80 (80)	59 (70)	14 (50)	10 (30)	3 (00)	0.6(70)	
					83s(80)	62s(70)					
40.45N,111.53W	4266	Salt Lake City	1847	158 (86e)	163 (80)	176 (70)	182 (50)	140 (30)	54 (00)	10 (53)	
					674s(80)	479s(70)	227s(50)				
31.28N,100.26W	1847	San Angelo	1882	86 (86e)	73 (80)	64 (70)	52 (50)	25 (30)	10 (10)		
					74s(80)	64s(70)					

Coordinates	No.	City	Founded								
29.26N, 98.29W	650	San Antonio	1718	914 (86e)	786 (80) / 945s(80)	654 (70) / 773s(70)	408 (50) / 450s(50)	232 (30)	53 (00)	3 (50)	2 (10?e)
34.06N,117.17W	1080	San Bernardino	1851	139 (86e)	119¹ (80)	107¹ (70)	63 (50) / 136s(50)	37 (30)	6 (00)	2 (80)	
32.43N,117.09W	20	San Diego	1769	1015 (86e)	876 (80) / 1704s(80)	697 (70) / 1198s(70)	334 (50) / 433s(50)	148 (30)	18 (00)	3 (52)	2 (02)
37.47N,122.25W	65	San Francisco	1776	749 (86e)	679 (80) / 3191s(80)	716 (70) / 2988s(70)	775 (50) / 2022s(50)	634 (30)	343 (00)	35 (52)	0.8(03e)
37.20N,121.53W	90	San Jose	1777	712 (86e)	630 (80) / 1244s(80)	460 (70) / 1025s(70)	95 (50) / 176s(50)	58 (30)	21 (00)	3 (52)	0.2(00e)
35.17N,120.40W	201	San Luis Obispo	1772	37 (86e)	34 (80)	28 (70)	14 (50)	8 (30)	3 (00)	0.3(50)	
29.53N, 97.56W	581	San Marcos	1845	29 (86e)	23 (80)	19 (70)	10 (50)	5 (30)	2 (00)	0.7(70)	
37.34N,122.19W	22	San Mateo	1851	81 (86e)	78 (80)	79 (70)	42 (50)	13 (30)	2 (00)		
33.46N,117.52W	133	Santa Ana	1869	237 (86e)	204 (80) / 150s(80)	156 (70) / 130s(70)	46 (50)	30 (30)	5 (00)	0.7(80)	
34.25N,119.42W	100	Santa Barbara	1782	79 (86e)	74 (80)	70 (70)	45 (50)	34 (30)	7 (00)	3 (80)	1 (03e)
37.21N,121.57W	94	Santa Clara	1777	89 (86e)	88 (80)	86 (70)	12 (50)	6 (30)	4 (00)	2 (80)	
36.58N,122.01W	15	Santa Cruz	1791	46 (86e)	41 (80) / 123s(80)	32 (70) / 74s(70)	22 (50)	14 (30)	6 (00)	0.9(60)	
35.41N,105.56W	6950	Santa Fe	1609	56 (86e)	49 (80) / 52s(80)	41 (70)	28 (50)	11 (30)	6 (00)	5 (50e)	5 (99e)
34.01N,118.29W	100	Santa Monica	1875	93 (86e)	88 (80)	88 (70)	72 (50)	37 (30)	3 (00)	0.4(80)	
38.26N,122.43W	150	Santa Rosa	1833	98 (86e)	83 (80) / 137s(80)	50 (70) / 75s(70)	18 (50)	11 (30)	7 (00)	0.4(60)	
27.20N, 82.32W	18	Sarasota	1885	51 (86e)	49 (80) / 305s(80)	40 (70) / 167s(70)	19 (50)	8 (30)	0.8(10)		
43.05N, 73.47W	330	Saratoga Springs	1789	24 (86e)	24 (80)	19 (70)	15 (50)	13 (30)	12 (00)	5 (50)	2 (20)
32.05N, 81.06W	20	Savannah	1733	147 (86e)	142 (80) / 187s(80)	118 (70) / 164s(70)	120 (50) / 128s(50)	85 (30)	54 (00)	15 (50)	5 (00)
42.49N, 73.57W	220	Schenectady	1662	67 (86e)	68 (80)	78 (70)	92 (50)	96 (30)	32 (00)	9 (50)	5 (00)
33.29N,111.56W	1250	Scottsdale	1882	111 (86e)	89 (80)	68 (70)	2 (50)	3s(30)	1s(20)		
41.25N, 75.40W	725	Scranton	1771?	82 (86e)	88 (80) / 407s(80)	103 (70) / 204s(70)	126 (50) / 236s(50)	143 (30)	102 (00)	2 (50)	
36.37N,121.50W	20	Seaside	1900	37 (86e)	37 (80) / 115s(80)	37 (70) / 93s(70)	10 (50)	2 (40)		2 (50)	

¹Urbanized area population for 1970 and 1980 included in Riverside urbanized area.

For an explanation of symbols and abbreviations, see pages 16–17.

(Continued)

TABLE 2a. (Continued)

Latitude and Longitude	Elev (ft)	City	Date Settled	Latest	ca 1980	ca 1970	ca 1950	ca 1930	ca 1900	ca 1850	ca 1800
47.37N,122.20W	10	Seattle	1851	486 (86e)	494 (80) / 1392s(80)	531 (70) / 1238s(70)	468 (50) / 622s(50)	366 (30)	81 (00)	1 (70)	
43.46N, 87.45W	589	Sheboygan	1843	47 (86e)	48 (80) / 59s(80)	48 (70)	42 (50)	39 (30)	23 (00)	4 (60)	
32.31N, 93.45W	204	Shreveport	1837	220 (86e)	206 (80) / 264s(80)	182 (70) / 235s(70)	127 (50) / 150s(50)	77 (30)	16 (00)	2 (50)	
38.59N, 77.02W	340	Silver Spring	1842?		73 (80) / 80s(80)	77 (70) / 57s(70)	65 (50e)	7 (30?e)		0.05(70?e)	
34.16N,118.47W	690	Simi Valley	1850	90 (86e)	77 (80)	60 (70)	0.3(50?e)	0.2(30?e)	0.06(00?e)		
42.30N, 96.24W	1110	Sioux City	1848	80 (86e)	82 (80) / 97s(80)	86 (70) / 96s(70)	84 (50) / 90s(50)	79 (30)	33 (00)	0.8(60)	
43.33N, 96.44W	1395	Sioux Falls	1865	98 (86e)	81 (80) / 86s(80)	72 (70) / 75s(70)	53 (50)	33 (30)	10 (00)	2 (80)	
42.03N, 87.45W	625	Skokie	1834	59 (86e)	60 (80)	68 (70)	15 (50)	5 (30)	0.5(00)		
42.23N, 71.06W	41	Somerville	1630	72 (86e)	77 (80)	89 (70)	102 (50)	104 (30)	62 (00)	4 (50)	
41.41N, 86.15W	710	South Bend	1820	107 (86e)	110 (80) / 226s(80)	126 (70) / 289s(70)	116 (50) / 168s(50)	104 (30)	36 (00)	2 (50)	
42.28N, 83.17W	675	Southfield	1829	73 (86e)	76 (80)	69 (70)	18s(50)	3s(30)	1s(00)	2s(50)	
33.57N,118.12W	120	South Gate	1918	81 (86e)	67 (80)	57 (70)	51 (50)	20 (30)	11 (00)	1 (50)	
34.56N, 81.57W	875	Spartanburg	bef 1785	44 (86e)	44 (80) / 101s(80)	45 (70) / 74s(70)	37 (50)	29 (30)		0.3(80)	
47.40N,117.26W	1890	Spokane	1872	173 (86e)	171 (80) / 267s(80)	171 (70) / 230s(70)	162 (50) / 176s(50)	116 (30)	37 (00)		
39.48N, 89.39W	610	Springfield (Illinois)	1818	100 (86e)	100 (80) / 123s(80)	92 (70) / 121s(70)	82 (50) / 97s(50)	72 (30)	34 (00)	5 (50)	3 (40)
42.06N, 72.36W	85	Springfield (Massachusetts)	1636	149 (86e)	152 (80) / 506s(80)	164 (70) / 514s(70)	162 (50) / 357s(50)	150 (30)	62 (00)	12 (50)	2 (00)
37.13N, 93.18W	1300	Springfield (Missouri)	1830	139 (86e)	133 (80) / 139s(80)	120 (70) / 121s(70)	67 (50) / 76s(50)	58 (30)	23 (00)	0.4(50)	
39.56N, 83.48W	980	Springfield (Ohio)	1799	69 (86e)	73 (80) / 87s(80)	82 (70) / 94s(70)	79 (50) / 82s(50)	69 (30)	38 (00)	5 (50)	2 (20)

Coordinates	Elev.	City	Founded	(86e)	(80)	(70)	(50)	(30)	(00)	(50)	(00)
41.03N, 73.32W	35	Stamford	1641	101 (86e)	102 (80)	109 (70)	74 (50)	46 (30)	16 (00)	5 (50)	4 (00)
					183s(80)	185s(70)	118s(50)				
33.28N, 88.49W	362	Starkville	1834	17 (86e)	15 (80)	11 (70)	7 (50)	4 (30)	2 (00)	0.5(70)	
40.47N, 77.52W	1191	State College	1859	34 (86e)	36 (80)	33 (70)	17 (50)	4 (30)	0.9(00)		
					51s(80)						
42.33N, 83.02W	645	Sterling Heights	bef 1835	112 (86e)	109 (80)	61 (70)	7s(50)	2s(30)	2s(00)	0.9s(50)	
40.22N, 80.37W	660	Steubenville	1786	24 (86e)	26 (80)	31 (70)	36 (50)	35 (30)	14 (00)	6 (50)	3 (30)
					78s(80)	81s(70)					
44.31N, 89.34W	1085	Stevens Point	1839	22 (86e)	23 (80)	23 (70)	17 (50)	14 (30)	10 (00)	0.1(60)	
36.07N, 97.04W	985	Stillwater	1889	37 (86e)	38 (80)	31 (70)	20 (50)	7 (30)	2 (00)	0.5(90)	
37.57N,121.17W	20	Stockton	1844	183 (86e)	150 (80)	110 (70)	71 (50)	48 (30)	18 (00)	3 (52)	
					197s(80)	160s(70)	113s(50)				
41.49N, 72.15W	640	Storrs	1692?		11 (80)	11 (70)	6 (60)	0.2(40e)			
37.23N,122.02W	130	Sunnyvale	bef 1901	112 (86e)	107 (80)	96 (70)	10 (50)	3 (30)	2 (20)		
46.44N, 92.06W	629	Superior	1853	27 (86e)	30 (80)	32 (70)	35 (50)	36 (30)	31 (00)	0.5(60)	3 (30)
43.03N, 76.09W	400	Syracuse	1797	161 (86e)	170 (80)	197 (70)	221 (50)	209 (30)	108 (00)	22 (50)	
					379s(80)	376s(70)	265s(50)				
47.15N,122.26W	110	Tacoma	1864?	159 (86e)	159 (80)	154 (70)	144 (50)	107 (30)	38 (00)	1 (80)	
					402s(80)	333s(70)	168s(50)				
30.27N, 84.17W	216	Tallahassee	bef 1539	119 (86e)	82 (80)	73 (70)	27 (50)	11 (30)	3 (00)	2 (60)	0.9(30)
					119s(80)	78s(70)					
27.57N, 82.27W	15	Tampa	1823	278 (86e)	272 (80)	278 (70)	125 (50)	101 (30)	16 (00)	1 (50)	
					521s(80)	369s(70)	179s(50)				
41.54N, 71.06W	37	Taunton	1638	46 (86e)	45 (80)	44 (70)	40 (50)	37 (30)	31 (00)	10 (50)	4 (00)
					52s(80)						
42.13N, 83.16W	612	Taylor	1847	72 (86e)	78 (80)	70 (70)	8 (50)	2s(30)	1s(00)	0.3s(50)	
33.25N,111.56W	1150	Tempe	1870	136 (86e)	107 (80)	64 (70)	8 (50)	2 (30)	0.9(00)		
39.28N, 87.24W	496	Terre Haute	1811	58 (86e)	61 (80)	70 (70)	64 (50)	63 (30)	37 (00)	4 (50)	
					75s(80)	81s(70)	78s(50)				
29.24N, 94.54W	12	Texas City	1893	42 (86e)	41 (80)	39 (70)	17 (50)	4 (30)	3 (20)		
					109s(80)	84s(70)					
34.10N,118.50W	800	Thousand Oaks	1881?	96 (86e)	77 (80)	36 (70)	1 (50)	0.2(30?)			
41.39N, 83.33W	585	Toledo	1817	341 (86e)	355 (80)	383 (70)	304 (50)	291 (30)	132 (00)	4 (50)	1 (40)
					485s(80)	488s(70)	364s(50)				
43.01N, 78.52W	575	Tonawanda	1805	84 (86e)	73 (80)	86 (70)	35 (50)	9 (30)	7 (00)	2 (50)	
39.03N, 95.40W	930	Topeka	1854	119 (86e)	115 (80)	125 (70)	79 (50)	64 (30)	34 (00)	0.8(60)	
					126s(80)	132s(70)	89s(50)				

For an explanation of symbols and abbreviations, see pages 16–17.

(Continued)

TABLE 2a. (Continued)

Latitude and Longitude	Elev (ft)	City	Date Settled	Population (thousands)							
				Latest	ca 1980	ca 1970	ca 1950	ca 1930	ca 1900	ca 1850	ca 1800
33.49N,118.18W	75	Torrance	1911	136 (86e)	130 (80)	135 (70)	22 (50)	7 (30)			
39.24N,76.36W	465	Towson	1768		51 (80)	78 (70)	19 (60)	11 (40)	1 (00?e)	1 (70?e)	
40.13N,74.46W	35	Trenton	1679	91 (86e)	92 (80)	105 (70)	128 (50)	123 (30)	73 (00)	6 (50)	3 (10)
					261s(80)	274s(70)	189s(50)				
42.37N,83.09W	670	Troy (Michigan)	1825?	67 (86e)	67 (80)	39 (70)	19 (60)				
42.44N,73.41W	34	Troy (New York)	1786	54 (86e)	57 (80)	63 (70)	72 (50)	73 (30)	61 (00)	29 (50)	5 (00)
32.13N,110.58W	2390	Tucson	1776	359 (86e)	331 (80)	263 (70)	45 (50)	33 (30)	8 (00)	3 (70)	
					450s(80)	294s(70)					
36.09N,96.00W	804	Tulsa	1832?	374 (86e)	361 (80)	330 (70)	183 (50)	141 (30)	1 (00)	0.3 (57)	
					443s(80)	371s(70)	206s(50)				
33.12N,87.34W	172	Tuscaloosa	1816	74 (86e)	75 (80)	66 (70)	46 (50)	21 (30)	5 (00)	4 (60)	2 (40)
					100s(80)	86s(70)					
32.21N,95.18W	558	Tyler	1846	75 (86e)	71 (80)	58 (70)	39 (50)	17 (30)	8 (00)	1 (60)	
					73s(80)	60s(70)					
39.58N,75.16W	100	Upper Darby	1683	86 (86e)	84 (80)	96 (70)	85 (50)	47 (30)	4 (00)	2 (50)	0.9 (00)
40.07N,88.12W	727	Urbana	1822	36 (86e)	36 (80)	34 (70)	23 (50)	13 (30)	6 (00)	0.2 (50)	
43.06N,75.14W	415	Utica	1786?	69 (86e)	76 (80)	91 (70)	102 (50)	102 (30)	56 (00)	18 (50)	3 (10)
					155s(80)	180s(70)	117s(50)				
38.07N,122.15W	10	Vallejo	1850	93 (86e)	80 (80)	72 (70)	26 (50)	16 (30)	8 (00)	6 (80)	
45.37N,122.40W	115	Vancouver	1824	44 (86e)	43 (80)	42 (70)	42 (50)	16 (30)	3 (00)	2 (80)	
34.17N,119.18W	48	Ventura	1782	86 (86e)	74 (80)	58 (70)	17 (50)	12 (30)	2 (00)	1 (80)	
42.47N,96.56W	1131	Vermillion	1859	9 (86e)	10 (80)	9 (70)	5 (50)	3 (30)	2 (00)	0.7 (80)	
32.21N,90.53W	206	Vicksburg	1790	26 (86e)	25 (80)	25 (70)	28 (50)	23 (30)	15 (00)	4 (50)	
39.29N,75.02W	110	Vineland	1861	54 (86e)	54 (80)	47 (70)	8 (50)	8 (30)	4 (00)	3 (87)	
					89s(80)	72s(70)					
36.51N,75.58W	13	Virginia Beach	1887	333 (86e)	262 (80)	172 (70)	5 (50)	2 (30)	0.2 (00e)		
31.33N,97.08W	405	Waco	1849	105 (86e)	101 (80)	95 (70)	85 (50)	53 (30)	21 (00)	3 (70)	
					134s(80)	119s(70)	93s(50)				
46.04N,118.20W	954	Walla Walla	1855	25 (86e)	26 (80)	24 (70)	24 (50)	16 (30)	10 (00)	1 (70)	
42.23N,71.14W	48	Waltham	1634	57 (86e)	58 (80)	62 (70)	47 (50)	39 (30)	23 (00)	4 (50)	0.9 (00)
42.30N,83.02W	619	Warren (Michigan)	1837?	150 (86e)	161 (80)	179 (70)	0.7 (50)	0.5 (30)	0.3 (00)	0.7 (50)	

Coordinates	Pop	City	Founded	(86e)	(80)	(70)	(50)	(30)	(00)	(50)	
41.14N, 80.48W	904	Warren (Ohio)	1798	53	57	63	50	41	9	2 (60)	2 (40)
41.42N, 71.27W	174	Warwick	1642	87	87	84	43	23	21	8 (50)	3 (00)
38.54N, 77.01W	25	*Washington	1665?	626	638	757	802	487	279	40 (50)	3 (00)
					2763s	2481s	1287s				
41.33N, 73.03W	260	Waterbury	1674	102	103	108	104	100	46	5 (50)	3 (00)
					160s	157s	132s				
42.30N, 92.20W	850	Waterloo	1845	70	76	76	65	46	13	1 (60)	
					120s	113s	84s				
42.21N, 87.50W	669	Waukegan	1835	74	68	65	39	33	9	3 (60)	
43.01N, 88.14W	821	Waukesha	bef 1833	53	50	40	21	17	7	1 (60)	
43.00N, 88.00W	723	West Allis	1827	64	64	72	43	35	7 (10)		
34.04N, 117.54W	390	West Covina	bef 1923	97	81	68	4	0.8(30)			
41.45N, 72.44W	100	West Hartford	1679	58	61	68	44	25	3	1 (60)	
41.17N, 72.57W	10	West Haven	1648	53	53	53	32	26	5	2 (70)	
40.27N, 86.55W	545	West Lafayette	1845	21	21	19	12	5	2	0.7(80)	
42.18N, 83.23W	650	Westland	1839	81	85	87	17s	10s	2s	2s(50)	
33.46N, 118.00W	30	Westminster	1872	73	71	60	3				
26.43N, 80.03W	16	West Palm Beach	1880	69	63	57	43	27	0.6(00)		
					487s	288s					
40.42N, 111.58W	4255	West Valley City	1849	91	72	9					
40.04N, 80.43W	650	Wheeling	1769	40	43	48	59	62	39	11 (50)	0.5(00e)
					101s	93s	107s				
41.02N, 73.46W	467	White Plains	1683	45	47	50	43	36	8	1 (50)	0.6(00)
33.58N, 118.02W	250	Whittier	1887	73	69	73	23	15	2	0.6(90)	
37.41N, 97.20W	1290	Wichita	1864	289	280	277	168	111	25	5 (80)	
					306s	302s	194s				
33.55N, 98.29W	945	Wichita Falls	1876	100	94	96	68	44	2	2 (90)	
					95s	98s					
41.15N, 75.53W	640	Wilkes-Barre	1769	48	52[1]	59	77	87	52	3 (50)	0.8(00)
							223s	272s			
37.16N, 76.42W	81	Williamsburg	1633	11	10	9	7	4	2	0.9(50)	1 (82)
41.15N, 77.00W	524	Williamsport	1795	32	33	38	45	46	29	2 (50)	0.4(00)
					59s	64s					
39.45N, 75.33W	135	Wilmington (Delaware)	1638	70	70	80	110	107	77	14 (50)	4 (10)
					406s	371s	187s				

[1]Urbanized area population for 1980 included in Scranton urbanized area.

For an explanation of symbols and abbreviations, see pages 16–17.

(Continued)

TABLE 2a. (Continued)

Latitude and Longitude	Elev (ft)	City	Date Settled	Population (thousands)							
				Latest	ca 1980	ca 1970	ca 1950	ca 1930	ca 1900	ca 1850	ca 1800
34.14N, 77.55W	32	Wilmington (North Carolina)	1732	54 (86e)	44 (80)	46 (70) 58s(70)	45 (50)	32 (30)	21 (00)	7 (50)	2 (00)
44.03N, 91.38W	664	Winona	1851	24 (86e)	25 (80)	26 (70)	25 (50)	21 (30)	20 (00)	2 (60)	
36.06N, 80.15W	860	Winston-Salem	1766	148 (86e)	132 (80) 172s(80)	134 (70) 143s(70)	88 (50) 92s(50)	75 (30)	14 (00)	1 (53)	0.2(00)
28.01N, 81.44W	175	Winter Haven	1883	24 (86e)	21 (80) 73s(80)	16 (70)	9 (50)	7 (30)	0.4(05)		
40.34N, 74.17W	16	Woodbridge	1665	94 (86e)	90 (80)	99 (70)	36 (50)	25 (30)	8 (00)	5 (50)	4 (10)
42.16N, 71.48W	475	Worcester	1713	158 (86e)	162 (80) 276s(80)	177 (70) 247s(70)	203 (50) 219s(50)	195 (30)	118 (00)	17 (50)	2 (00)
46.36N,120.31W	1075	Yakima	1858	49 (86e)	50 (80) 81s(80)	46 (70) 65s(70)	38 (50)	22 (30)	3 (00)	2 (90)	
40.56N, 73.54W	10	Yonkers	bef 1639	186 (86e)	195 (80)	204 (70)	153 (50)	135 (30)	48 (00)	4 (50)	1 (00)
39.58N, 76.44W	370	York	1741	44 (86e)	45 (80) 129s(80)	50 (70) 123s(70)	60 (50) 79s(50)	55 (30)	34 (00)	7 (50)	3 (00)
41.06N, 80.39W	840	Youngstown	1797	105 (86e)	115 (80) 383s(80)	140 (70) 396s(70)	168 (50) 298s(50)	170 (30)	45 (00)	3 (50)	1 (10)
42.14N, 83.37W	713	Ypsilanti	1823	23 (86e)	24 (80)	30 (70)	18 (50)	10 (30)	7 (00)	3 (50)	
32.43N,114.37W	160	Yuma	1854	47 (86e)	42 (80) 55s(80)	29 (70)	9 (50)	5 (30)	2 (00)	1 (70)	
39.56N, 82.00W	720	Zanesville	1797	28 (86e)	29 (80)	33 (70)	41 (50)	36 (30)	24 (00)	8 (50)	2 (20)
Virgin Islands (USA)											
18.21N, 64.56W	15	*Charlotte Amalie	1666		12 (80)	12 (70)	11 (50)	7 (30)	9 (01)	11 (50)	11 (35)
OCEANIA											
American Samoa											
14.16S,170.42W	16	*Pago Pago	bef 1872		3 (80)	2 (70)	2 (50)	0.6(30)			
Australia											
34.56S,138.36E	140	Adelaide	1836	993s(86e)	953s(81)	809s(71)	382s(47)	313s(33)	163s(01)	18 (61)	7 (46)
27.30S,153.01E	134	Brisbane	1824	1171s(86e)	1096s(81)	818s(71)	402s(47)	300s(33)	119s(01)	6 (61)	

(Continued)

Coordinates		Place	Founded								
35.20S,149.10E	1906	*Canberra	1824?	286s(86e)	246s(81)	156s(71)	15s(47)	7(33)			4(41)
12.28S,130.50E	89	Darwin	1869	68(85e)	56(81)	36(71)	3(47)	2(33)	0.9(11)		
38.09S,144.21E	57	Geelong	1837	148s(86e)	142s(81)	115s(71)	45s(47)	39s(33)	23s(01)	17(61)	
27.59S,153.22E	22	Gold Coast	1874	219s(86e)	164s(81)	74s(71)	14s(47)	6(33)	1(01)	19(61)	
42.55S,147.20E	177	Hobart	1804	180s(86e)	171s(81)	130s(71)	77s(47)	60s(33)	34s(01)		
37.50S,145.00E	114	Melbourne	1835	2942s(86e)	2806s(81)	2394s(71)	1226s(47)	992s(33)	502s(01)	140s(61)	
32.55S,151.45E	106	Newcastle	1804	429s(86e)	403s(81)	250s(71)	127s(47)	104s(33)	55s(01)	4s(61)	
31.56S,115.50E	210	Perth	1829	1025s(86e)	922s(81)	642s(71)	273s(47)	207s(33)	36(01)	3(61)	
33.53S,151.12E	138	Sydney	1788	3431s(86e)	3279s(81)	2725s(71)	1484s(47)	1235s(33)	488s(01)	93s(61)	3(00)
19.15S,146.48E	20	Townsville	1864	104s(86e)	86s(81)	69s(71)	34(47)	26(33)	16(01)	1(71)	
34.25S,150.54E	150	Wollongong	1815	238s(86e)	231s(81)	186s(71)	18(47)	11(33)	4(01)	1(61)	
Fiji											
18.08S,178.25E	30	*Suva	bef 1877	69(86)	64(76)	54(66)	11(46)	13(31e)			
French Polynesia											
17.32S,149.34W	7	*Papeete	1840?	23(83)	23(77)	25(71)	12(46)	7(31)	4(97)	3(65)	
				79s(83)	66s(77)	65s(71)					
Guam											
13.28N,144.45E	256	*Agana	bef 1668		0.9(80)	2(70)	2(50)	9(30)	6(00?e)	3(50?e)	3(16)
(Hawaii), USA											
19.43N,155.05W	60	Hilo	bef 1778		35(80)	26(70)	27(50)	19(30)	7(10)	4(72)	
21.19N,157.52W	21	*Honolulu	bef 1794	372(86e)	365(80)	325(70)	248(50)	138(30)	39(00)	14(66)	
					582s(80)	442s(70)					
21.24N,157.44W	10	Kailua	1924?		36(80)	34(70)	0.3(50)	2s(40)			
					106s(80)						
(Irian Jaya), Indonesia											
2.32S,140.42E	10	*Jayapura	bef 1869		150(80)	46(71)	14(61e)	6s(30?)			
Kiribati											
1.25N,173.00E	7	*Tarawa	bef 1788	21(85)	18(78)	8(73)	4(47)	3(33e)			
New Caledonia											
22.16S,166.27E	10	*Noumea	1854	60(83)	56(76)	47(69)	10(46)	10(26)	2(00?e)	7(98)	1(86e)
New Zealand											
36.51S,174.45E	160	Auckland	1841	149(86)	145(81)	152(71)	127(51)	88(26)	34s(01)	5(47)	
				821s(86)	770s(81)	650s(71)	329s(51)	193s(26)	67s(01)		

For an explanation of symbols and abbreviations, see pages 16–17.

Figure 13. Aerial view of Sydney, the largest urbanized area in Oceania, with the famous Sydney Harbour steel arch bridge in the center of the picture. (Credit: Australian Overseas Information Service.)

TABLE 2a. (Continued)

Latitude and Longitude	Elev (ft)	City	Date Settled	Population (thousands)							
				Latest	ca 1980	ca 1970	ca 1950	ca 1930	ca 1900	ca 1850	ca 1800
43.35S,172.36E	22	Christchurch	1850	168 (86) 299s(86)	165 (81) 290s(81)	166 (71) 276s(71)	124 (51) 174s(51)	83 (26) 119s(26)	18 (01) 57s(01)	1 (58)	
45.52S,170.30E	5	Dunedin	1845	77 (86) 114s(86)	77 (81) 107s(81)	82 (71) 111s(71)	69 (51) 95s(51)	68 (26) 85s(26)	25 (01) 52s(01)	0.4(49)	
37.47S,175.17E	131	Hamilton	1864	95 (86) 168s(86)	91 (81) 98s(81)	75 (71) 81s(71)	30 (51) 33s(51)	14 (26) 17s(26)	1 (01)	0.7(74)	
36.58S,174.48E	40	Manukau	bef 1853	177 (86)	159 (81)	104 (71)	16s(51)	7s(26)	12s(01)	9s(78)	
39.29S,176.55E	5	Napier	1844?	49 (86) 115s(86)	48 (81) 112s(81)	40 (71) 97s(71)	20 (51) 25s(51)	15 (26) 18s(26)	9 (01)	2 (67)	
40.21S,175.37E	146	Palmerston North	1866	61 (86) 93s(86)	60 (81) 67s(81)	52 (71) 57s(71)	31 (51)	18 (26)	6 (01)	0.9(78)	
41.28S,174.51E	415	*Wellington	1840	137 (86) 326s(86)	136 (81) 321s(81)	137 (71) 308s(71)	120 (51) 133s(51)	99 (26) 122s(26)	44 (01) 49s(01)	3 (48)	
Pacific Islands (USA)											
15.12N,145.45E	10	*Saipan	bef 1521		15 (80)	13 (73)	5 (46)	6 (25)	1 (00)	0.9(87)	
Papua New Guinea											
6.43S,147.01E	26	Lae	1927		62 (80)	39 (71)	1 (57)				
9.29S,147.08E	92	*Port Moresby	1873	150 (85e)	124 (80)	77 (71)	14 (56)	2 (30?e)			
4.12S,152.11E	13	Rabaul	1907	16 (84e)	15 (80)	25 (71)	10 (50?e)	2 (31)			
Samoa											
13.50S,171.44W	7	*Apia	bef 1850	23 (84e)	33 (81)	30 (71)	12 (51)	5 (36)	1 (00?e)		
Solomon Islands											
9.27S,159.57E	180	*Honiara	1942	28 (84)	21 (81)	11 (70)	4 (59)				
Tonga											
21.08S,175.12W	7	*Nukualofa	bef 1862	28 (84)	18 (76)	16 (66)	7 (56)				
Vanuatu											
17.44S,168.19E	66	*Vila	bef 1863	14 (85e)	15 (79)	8 (67)	2 (44e)	2 (31e)	3 (98e)	3 (75e)	

For an explanation of symbols and abbreviations, see pages 16–17.

(Continued)

TABLE 2a. (Continued)

Latitude and Longitude	Elev (ft)	City	Date Settled	Population (thousands)							
				Latest	ca 1980	ca 1970	ca 1950	ca 1930	ca 1900	ca 1850	ca 1800
SOUTH AMERICA											
Argentina											
38.43S, 62.17W	66	Bahia Blanca	1828		211 (80) 221s(80)	174 (70) 182s(70)	113 (47)	44 (14)	9 (95)	1 (69)	
34.36S, 58.27W	82	*Buenos Aires	1580		2923 (80) 9766s(80)	2972 (70) 8462s(70)	2981 (47) 4722s(47)	1561 (14) 2034s(14)	663 (95) 781s(95)	178 (69)	40 (97e)
28.28S, 65.47W	1424	Catamarca	1683		88 (80)	64 (70)	30 (47)	13 (14)	7 (95)	6 (69)	
45.52S, 67.30W	200	Comodoro Rivadavia	1901		97 (80)	73 (70)	25 (47)	2 (14)			
32.29S, 58.14W	59	Concepcion del Uruguay	1783		46 (80)	39 (70)	31 (47)	14 (14)	10 (95)	7 (69)	
31.24S, 64.11W	1450	Cordoba	1573		969 (80) 982s(80)	782 (70) 793s(70)	370 (47)	105 (14)	48 (95)	29 (69)	11 (13)
27.28S, 58.50W	180	Corrientes	1588		180 (80)	137 (70)	57 (47)	29 (14)	16 (95)	11 (69)	4 (97e)
26.11S, 58.11W	213	Formosa	1879		95 (80)	61 (70)	17 (47)	4 (14)	2 (95)		
24.11S, 65.18W	4215	Jujuy	1593		124 (80)	83 (70)	31 (47)	8 (14)	4 (95)	3 (69)	
34.55S, 57.57W	59	La Plata	1800		206 (80) 560s(80)	391 (70) 486s(70)	207 (47)	90 (14)	45 (95)	0.6(69)	
29.26S, 66.51W	1411	La Rioja	1591		67 (80)	46 (70)	23 (47)	8 (14)	6 (95)	4 (69)	
38.00S, 57.33W	79	Mar del Plata	1862		407 (80)	302 (70)	115 (47)	28 (14)	5 (95)		
32.53S, 68.49W	2523	Mendoza	1561		118 (80) 597s(80)	119 (70) 478s(70)	97 (47)	59 (14)	29 (95)	8 (69)	5 (12)
38.57S, 68.04W	869	Neuquen	1904		90 (80)	43 (70)	7 (47)	2 (14)			
31.44S, 60.32W	243	Parana	1730		160 (80)	128 (70)	84 (47)	36 (14)	24 (95)	10 (69)	
27.23S, 55.53W	364	Posadas	1869		140 (80)	98 (70)	38 (47)	10 (14)	4 (95)		
43.18S, 65.06W	23	Rawson	1865		13 (80)	7 (70)	2 (47)	1 (14)	1 (95)		
27.27S, 58.59W	171	Resistencia	1750		173 (80) 218s(80)	119 (70) 143s(70)	52 (47)	8 (14)	1 (95)		
33.08S, 64.21W	1434	Rio Cuarto	1794		110 (80)	89 (70)	49 (47)	18 (14)	12 (95)	2 (50?e)	
51.38S, 69.13W	85	Rio Gallegos	1885		43 (80)	28 (70)	6 (47)	2 (14)	0.1(95)		

For an explanation of symbols and abbreviations, see pages 16–17.

(Continued)

Figure 14. *Avenida Nueve de Julio in the center of Buenos Aires, looking toward the Plaza de la Republica with its 221-foot-high Obelisk. Buenos Aires is the largest urbanized area in South America by the latest censuses but probably now ranks second to Sao Paulo. (Credit: Organization of American States.)*

TABLE 2a. (Continued)

Latitude and Longitude	Elev (ft)	City	Date Settled	Population (thousands)							
				ca 1800	ca 1850	ca 1900	ca 1930	ca 1950	ca 1970	ca 1980	Latest
32.57S, 60.40W	85	Rosario	1725	5 (16)	23 (69)	94 (95)	223 (14)	468 (47)	750 (70) 813s(70)	792 (80) 955s(80)	
24.47S, 65.25W	3878	Salta	1582	5 (01e)	12 (69)	17 (95)	28 (14)	67 (47)	176 (70)	260 (80)	
31.32S, 68.31W	2110	San Juan	1562	6 (77)	8 (69)	10 (95)	17 (14)	82 (47)	113 (70) 223s(70)	118 (80) 290s(80)	
33.18S, 66.21W	2428	San Luis	1594		4 (69)	10 (95)	15 (14)	26 (47)	51 (70)	71 (80)	
31.38S, 60.42W	121	Santa Fe	1573	7 (17)	11 (69)	22 (95)	60 (14)	169 (47)	245 (70)	287 (80)	
36.37S, 64.17W	620	Santa Rosa	1892				5 (14)	15 (47)	34 (70)	52 (80)	
27.47S, 64.16W	617	Santiago del Estero	1553	2 (00?e)	8 (69)	10 (95)	23 (14)	60 (47)	105 (70)	148 (80)	
37.19S, 59.09W	584	Tandil	1823		2 (69)	7 (95)	16 (14)	39 (47)	66 (70)	79 (80)	
26.49S, 65.13W	1385	Tucuman	1685	4 (12)	17 (69)	34 (95)	91 (14)	194 (47)	312 (70) 366s(70)	393 (80) 497s(80)	
54.48S, 68.18W	23	Ushuaia	1862			0.2(95)	1 (14)	2 (47)	5 (70)	11 (80)	
40.48S, 63.00W	23	Viedma	1779			1 (95)	3 (14)	5 (47)	13 (70)	24 (80)	
Bolivia											
17.24S, 66.09W	8390	Cochabamba	1574	22 (88)	41 (58)	22 (00)	36 (29e)	75 (50)	153 (70e)	205 (76)	317 (85e)
16.30S, 68.09W	11,910	*La Paz	bef 1548	21 (96)	43 (45)	53 (00)	147 (29e)	267 (50)	538 (70e)	635 (76)	993 (85e)
17.59S, 67.09W	12,146	Oruro	1595		8 (58)	16 (00)	41 (29e)	63 (50)	99 (70e)	124 (76)	178 (85e)
19.35S, 65.45W	13,045	Potosi	1545	23 (79)	23 (58)	21 (00)	34 (29e)	43 (50)	69 (70e)	77 (76)	110 (84e)
17.48S, 63.10W	1365	Santa Cruz	1595	6 (00?e)	10 (58)	16 (00)	30 (29e)	41 (50)	116 (70e)	255 (76)	442 (85e)
19.02S, 65.17W	9331	*Sucre	bef 1538	18 (26e)	24 (58)	21 (00)	35 (29e)	38 (50)	51 (70e)	64 (76)	85 (84e)
Brazil											
16.20S, 48.58W	3183	Anapolis	1879				8 (40) 16s(20)	18 (50) 50s(50)	89 (70) 105s(70)	161 (80) 180s(80)	227s(85e)
10.55S, 37.04W	16	Aracaju	1855		6 (72) 10s(72)	16 (90) 21s(00)	37 (20) 37s(20)	68 (50) 78s(50)	179 (70) 184s(70)	288 (80) 293s(80)	362s(85e)
22.19S, 49.04W	1637	Bauru	1889				18 (20) 20s(20)	52 (50) 65s(50)	120 (70) 132s(70)	180 (80) 187s(80)	221s(85e)
1.27S, 48.29W	46	Belem	1616	12 (00?e)	12 (33) 62s(72)	8s(00) 97s(00)	145 (20) 236s(20)	225 (50) 255s(50)	565 (70) 634s(70)	756 (80) 933s(80)	1121s(85e)

(Continued)

Coordinates	No.	City	Founded	Population (census-year codes; s = agglomeration)
19.55S, 43.56W	2723	Belo Horizonte	1701	1442 (80) · 1107 (70) · 339 (50) · 56 (20) · 13s (00) · 8 (64e) / 2122s (85e) · 1781s (80) · 1235s (70) · 353s (50) · 56s (20)
26.56S, 49.03W	46	Blumenau	1850	145 (80) · 86 (70) · 23 (50) · 24 (20) · 25 (90) · 3 (70) / 193s (85e) · 157s (80) · 100s (70) · 48s (50) · 72s (20) · 35s (00)
2.49S, 60.40W	295	Boa Vista	18th c	42 (80) · 17 (70) · 5 (50) · 7 (20) · 3 (90) / 66s (85e) · 67s (80) · 36s (70) · 17s (50) · 14s (20)
15.47S, 47.55W	3809	*Brasília	1957	411 (80) · 282 (70) · 90 (60) / 1577s (85e) · 1177s (80) · 538s (70) · 142s (60)
7.13S, 35.53W	1804	Campina Grande	1697	222 (80) · 163 (70) · 72 (50) · 42 (20) · 21 (90) · 15 (72) / 281s (85e) · 248s (80) · 196s (70) · 173s (50) · 71s (20) · 38s (00) · 15s (72)
22.54S, 47.05W	2274	Campinas	1773	567 (80) · 328 (70) · 99 (50) · 78 (40) · 20 (90) · 6 (50?e) / 845s (85e) · 664s (80) · 376s (70) · 137s (50) · 116s (20) · 68s (00) · 31s (72)
20.27S, 54.37W	1772	Campo Grande	1875	283 (80) · 131 (70) · 32 (50) · 23 (40) · 8s (90) / 387s (85e) · 292s (80) · 140s (70) · 57s (50) · 21s (20)
21.45S, 41.18W	46	Campos	1634	174 (80) · 153 (70) · 62 (50) · 48 (20) · 23 (90) · 20 (72) / 367s (85e) · 349s (80) · 319s (70) · 238s (50) · 176s (20) · 91s (00) · 89s (72)
29.56S, 51.11W	72	Canoas	1839	214 (80) · 150 (70) · 19 (50) · 11 (40) / 262s (85e) · 221s (80) · 154s (70) · 40s (50) · 18s (40)
23.31S, 46.50W	2352	Carapicuiba	1842?	186 (80) · 55 (70) · 6 (50) / 268s (85e) · 186s (80) · 55s (70)
20.16S, 40.25W	118	Cariacica	1837?	5 (70) · 2 (50) · 1 (40) · 8s (90) · 5s (72) / 244s (85e) · 189s (80) · 101s (70) · 22s (50) · 12s (20)
8.17S, 35.58W	1805	Caruaru	bef 1848	101 (70) · 44 (50) · 25 (40) · 12s (72) / 191s (85e) · 138 (80) · 119s (70) · 103s (50) · 62s (20)
24.57S, 53.28W	2625	Cascavel	1930	100 (80) · 34 (70) · 0.4 (50) · 1s (40) · 35s (00) / 201s (85e) · 163s (80) · 89s (70)
29.10S, 51.11W	2494	Caxias do Sul	1875	199 (80) · 107 (70) · 32 (50) · 17 (40) · 19s (90) / 268s (85e) · 221s (80) · 144s (70) · 59s (50) · 40s (40)
19.55S, 44.06W	2710	Contagem	1714	112 (80) · 28 (70) · 2 (50) / 386s (85e) · 281s (80) · 111s (70) · 6s (50)
15.35S, 56.05W	541	Cuiaba	1719	168 (80) · 86 (70) · 24 (50) · 14 (20) · 18s (90) · 11 (72) / 283s (85e) · 213s (80) · 101s (70) · 56s (50) · 34s (20) · 36s (72)
25.25S, 49.15W	3117	Curitiba	1654	843 (80) · 484 (70) · 138 (50) · 57 (20) · 23 (90) · 13 (72) / 1285s (85e) · 1025s (80) · 608s (70) · 181s (50) · 79s (20) · 50s (00) · 13s (72)
23.42S, 46.37W	2500	Diadema	1830	229 (80) · 69 (70) · 1 (50) · 18s (97e) · 11s (20) / 322s (85e) · 229s (80) · 79s (70) · 3s (50)

For an explanation of symbols and abbreviations, see pages 16–17.

TABLE 2a. (Continued)

Latitude and Longitude	Elev (ft)	City	Date Settled	Population (thousands)							
				Latest	ca 1980	ca 1970	ca 1950	ca 1930	ca 1900	ca 1850	ca 1800
22.47S, 43.18W	13	Duque de Caxias	1669		306 (80)	257 (70)	74 (50)	24 (40)			
				666s(85e)	576s(80)	431s(70)	92s(50)				
12.15S, 38.57W	820	Feira de Santana	bef 1696		225 (80)	127 (70)	27 (50)	14 (20)	11 (90)	8 (72)	
				357s(85e)	289s(80)	187s(70)	107s(50)	78s(20)	63s(00)	52s(72)	
27.35S, 48.34W	7	Florianopolis	1700		154 (80)	116 (70)	48 (50)	20 (20)	11 (90)	9 (72)	
				219s(85e)	188s(80)	139s(70)	68s(50)	41s(20)	32s(00)	26s(72)	
3.43S, 38.30W	82	Fortaleza	1609		648 (80)	520 (70)	205 (50)	68 (20)		21 (72)	
				1589s(85e)	1308s(80)	859s(70)	270s(50)	79s(20)	48s(00)	42s(72)	12s(10)
25.33S, 54.35W	394	Foz do Iguacu	1889		94 (80)	19 (70)	3 (50)	1 (40)			
				183s(85e)	136s(80)	34s(70)	16s(50)	8s(40)			
16.40S, 49.16W	2493	Goiania	1935		703 (80)	362 (70)	40 (50)	15 (40)			
				928s(85e)	718s(80)	381s(70)	52s(50)	48s(40)			
18.51S, 41.56W	545	Governador Valadares	1808		174 (80)	134 (70)	20 (50)	6 (40)	1 (90)		
				217s(85e)	196s(80)	162s(70)	61s(50)	38s(40)			
23.29S, 46.31W	2493	Guarulhos	1560		395 (80)	222 (70)	16 (50)	6 (20)		3 (72)	
				718s(85e)	533s(80)	237s(70)	35s(50)	6s(20)	3s(00)		
5.32S, 47.29W	312	Imperatriz	1852		112 (80)	35 (70)	1 (50)				
				237s(85e)	220s(80)	81s(70)	14s(50)	9s(20)	4s(90)		
19.30S, 42.32W	787	Ipatinga			105 (80)	36 (70)	0.2(50)				
				214s(85e)	150s(80)	48s(70)	5s(50)				
22.52S, 43.47W	13	Itaguai	1818			11 (70)	3 (50)	7 (20)	6 (90)	6 (72)	
				106s(85e)	90s(80)	45s(70)	30s(50)	16s(20)			4s(50?e)
20.04S, 44.35W	2654	Itauna	bef 1901		49 (80)	33 (70)	9 (50)	12 (20)			
				62s(85e)	53s(80)	38s(70)	19s(50)	31s(20)	14s(90)	14s(72)	
8.07S, 35.01W	148	Jaboatao	1648		67 (80)	52 (70)	34 (50)	14 (20)	9 (90)	12 (72)	
				411s(85e)	331s(80)	201s(70)	57s(50)	48s(20)	23s(00)		
7.07S, 34.53W	148	Joao Pessoa	1585		290 (80)	197 (70)	96 (50)	39 (20)			
				398s(85e)	330s(80)	221s(70)	119s(50)	53s(20)	29s(00)	25s(72)	
26.18S, 48.50W	20	Joinville	1849		217 (80)	78 (70)	21 (50)	17 (40)		8 (72)	
				304s(85e)	236s(80)	126s(70)	43s(50)	46s(40)	14s(90)	8s(72)	

Lat/Long	Elev	City	Founded	1872	1890	1900	1920/40	1950	1970	1980	1985e
21.45S, 43.20W	2218	Juiz de Fora	1850?	19 (72)	23 (90)		51 (20)	85 (50)	219 (70)	300 (80)	
				38s(72)		91s(00)	118s(20)	127s(50)	239s(70)	308s(80)	351s(85e)
23.11S, 46.52W	2461	Jundiai	1600?	5 (59e)	12 (90)		25 (20)	39 (50)	146 (70)	210 (80)	
						15s(00)	44s(20)	69s(50)	169s(70)	259s(80)	315s(85e)
23.18S, 51.09W	1969	Londrina	1929				11 (40)	33 (50)	156 (70)	258 (80)	
							75s(40)	71s(50)	229s(70)	302s(80)	348s(85e)
0.02N, 51.03W	49	Macapa	1687	0.9 (72)	5 (90)		9 (20)	10 (50)	51 (70)	89 (80)	
				0.9s(72)	5s(90)		18s(20)	21s(50)	86s(70)	137s(80)	170s(85e)
9.40S, 35.43W	16	Maceio	1815				39 (20)	99 (50)	243 (70)	376 (80)	
				28s(72)		36s(00)	74s(20)	121s(50)	264s(70)	400s(80)	484s(85e)
22.39S, 43.02W	13	Mage	1696		5 (90)		5 (40)	7 (50)	20 (70)		
				6s(72)		16s(00)	19s(20)	37s(50)	113s(70)	167s(80)	200s(85e)
30.08S, 60.01W	197	Manaus	1669	18 (72)			44 (20)	90 (50)	284 (70)	613 (80)	
						65s(00)	76s(20)	108s(50)	312s(70)	635s(80)	835s(85e)
23.25S, 51.55W	555	Maringa	bef 1947					7 (50)	52 (70)	158 (80)	
				29s(72)			3 (40)	39s(50)	121s(70)	168s(80)	198s(85e)
23.40S, 46.27W	2507	Maua						5 (50)	102 (70)	206 (80)	
								9s(50)	102s(70)	206s(80)	271s(85e)
23.31S, 46.11W	2494	Mogi das Cruzes	1560	11 (72)	11 (90)		14 (40)	31 (50)	91 (70)	122 (80)	
				17s(72)	19s(90)		48s(40)	62s(50)	139s(70)	198s(80)	235s(85e)
16.43S, 43.52W	2093	Montes Claros	1769	10 (72)	15 (90)		14 (40)	20 (50)	82 (70)	152 (80)	
				40s(72)	62s(90)		20s(20)	72s(50)	116s(70)	177s(80)	215s(85e)
5.11S, 37.20W	66	Mossoro	bef 1852	8 (72)			13 (40)	21 (50)	77 (70)	118 (80)	
							31s(20)	41s(50)	97s(70)	146s(80)	159s(85e)
5.47S, 35.13W	10	Natal	1669	9 (72)	10 (90)	1 (00?e)	25 (20)	95 (50)	251 (70)	377 (80)	
				20s(72)		13s(00)	86s(20)	98s(50)	265s(70)	417s(80)	512s(85e)
22.53S, 43.07W	8	Niteroi	1565	21 (72)			21 (40)	171 (50)	292 (70)	386 (80)	
						16s(00)	141s(40)	186s(50)	324s(70)	400s(80)	443s(85e)
22.45S, 43.27W	85	Nova Iguacu	1567?				16 (20)	59 (50)	331 (70)	492 (80)	
				48s(72)		31s(00)	52s(20)	146s(50)	728s(70)	1095s(80)	1325s(85e)
8.01S, 34.51W	98	Olinda	1535	8 (45e)			15 (40)	38 (50)	187 (70)	266 (80)	
				13s(72)				62s(50)	196s(70)	282s(80)	336s(85e)
23.32S, 46.46W	2366	Osasco	1890?				5 (20)	43 (50)	283 (70)	474 (80)	
						19s(00)	52s(20)		283s(70)	474s(80)	594s(85e)
20.23S, 43.30W	3481	Ouro Preto	1698	10 (50?e)	11 (90)	20 (00?e)	5 (20)	9 (50)	24 (70)	28 (80)	
				48s(72)	59s(90)		51s(20)	33s(50)	46s(70)	53s(80)	62s(85e)

For an explanation of symbols and abbreviations, see pages 16–17.

(Continued)

TABLE 2a. (Continued)

Latitude and Longitude	Elev (ft)	City	Date Settled	Population (thousands)							
				ca 1800	ca 1850	ca 1900	ca 1930	ca 1950	ca 1970	ca 1980	Latest
28.15S, 52.24W	2326	Passo Fundo	1857		8 (72)	18 (90)	13 (20)	24 (50)	69 (70)	103 (80)	
						21s(00)	75s(20)	36s(50)	94s(70)	121s(80)	138s(85e)
31.46S, 52.20W	23	Pelotas	1780			23 (90)	48 (20)	78 (50)	150 (70)	197 (80)	
					17s(72)	45s(00)	82s(20)	128s(50)	208s(70)	260s(80)	278s(85e)
22.31S, 43.10W	2667	Petropolis	1814		15 (72)		38 (20)	61 (50)	116 (70)	149 (80)	
					21s(72)	40s(00)	68s(20)	108s(50)	189s(70)	242s(80)	275s(85e)
22.43S, 47.38W	1772	Piracicaba	1767		7 (72)	14 (90)	32 (20)	46 (50)	128 (70)	179 (80)	
					7s(72)	28s(90)	76s(40)	88s(50)	153s(70)	214s(80)	253s(85e)
25.05S, 50.09W	2930	Ponta Grossa	1812		9 (72)	5 (90)	16 (20)	43 (50)	92 (70)	172 (80)	
						8s(00)	20s(20)	54s(50)	127s(70)	187s(80)	224s(85e)
30.04S, 51.11W	13	Porto Alegre	1740	4 (03)	25 (72)		154 (20)	375 (50)	870 (70)	1115 (80)	
					44s(72)	74s(00)	179s(20)	394s(50)	886s(70)	1125s(80)	1275s(85e)
8.46S, 63.54W	322	Porto Velho	1907				4 (20)	10 (50)	41 (70)	101 (80)	
							5s(20)	27s(50)	84s(70)	134s(80)	202s(85e)
8.03S, 34.54W	180	Recife	1535?	25 (10e)	74 (45)		328 (40)	512 (50)	1061 (70)	1183 (80)	
					117s(72)	113s(00)	239s(20)	525s(50)	1061s(70)	1204s(80)	1290s(85e)
21.10S, 47.48W	1700	Ribeirao Preto	1856		6 (72)	12 (90)	62 (20)	63 (50)	191 (70)	301 (80)	
					6s(72)	59s(00)	69s(20)	92s(50)	212s(70)	318s(80)	385s(85e)
9.58S, 67.48W	322	Rio Branco	1902				4 (40)	9 (50)	34 (70)	87 (80)	
							20s(20)	28s(50)	84s(70)	117s(80)	146s(85e)
22.54S, 43.14W	102	Rio de Janeiro	1565	43 (99)			1564 (40)	2303 (50)	4252 (70)	5091 (80)	
					266s(49)	811s(06)	1158s(20)	2377s(50)	4252s(70)	5091s(80)	5615s(85e)
32.02S, 52.05W	16	Rio Grande	1745		14 (72)	20 (90)	43 (20)	63 (50)	99 (70)	130 (80)	
					21s(72)	29s(00)	54s(20)	78s(50)	116s(70)	146s(80)	165s(85e)
12.59S, 38.31W	28	Salvador	1549	46 (05)			293 (40)	389 (50)	1007 (70)	1492 (80)	
				100s(03e)	129s(72)	206s(00)	283s(20)	417s(50)	1008s(70)	1502s(80)	1811s(85e)
29.41S, 53.48W	502	Santa Maria	1797		8 (72)	18 (90)	17 (20)	45 (50)	121 (70)	151 (80)	
						30s(00)	57s(20)	83s(50)	157s(70)	182s(80)	197s(85e)
2.26S, 54.42W	118	Santarem	1661		9 (72)	12 (90)	8 (40)	14 (50)	51 (70)	102 (80)	
							48s(40)	60s(50)	136s(70)	192s(80)	227s(85e)
23.40S, 46.31W	2438	Santo Andre	1551				7 (20)	97 (50)	415 (70)	549 (80)	
					9s(72)	14s(90)	91s(40)	107s(50)	419s(70)	553s(80)	637s(85e)

Lat/Long	No.	Name	Founded	(85e)	(80)	(70)	(50)	(20)/(40)	(90)/(00)	(72)	(00?e)/(36)
23.57S, 46.20W	13	Santos	1536	461s(85e)	411(80) 417s(80)	341(70) 346s(70)	198(50) 204s(50)	103(20) 103s(20)	13(90) 50s(00)	9(72)	6(00?e)
23.42S, 46.33W	2507	Sao Bernardo do Campo	1552	566s(85e)	381(80) 426s(80)	188(70) 201s(70)	20(50) 29s(50)	6(20) 25s(20)	7(90) 10s(00)	9s(72)	
22.01S, 47.54W	2903	Sao Carlos	bef 1865	141s(85e)	109(80) 120s(80)	75(70) 85s(70)	32(50) 48s(50)	42(20) 54s(20)	13(90) 56s(00)	3(72)	
22.51S, 43.04W	43	Sao Goncalo	1647	731s(85e)	221(80) 615s(80)	161(70) 430s(70)	21(50) 127s(50)	31(20) 47s(20)	9(90) 19s(00)	7(72)	
22.48S, 43.22W	233	Sao Joao de Meriti	1645	459s(85e)	211(80) 399s(80)	164(70) 303s(70)	44(50) 76s(50)	39(40)	3(90)	3(72)	
20.48S, 49.23W	1558	Sao Jose do Rio Preto	1852	230s(85e)	172(80) 189s(80)	108(70) 122s(70)	37(50) 66s(50)	24(40) 14s(20)	3(90)	3(72)	
23.11S, 45.53W	2110	Sao Jose dos Campos	1611	375s(85e)	268(80) 288s(80)	132(70) 148s(70)	26(50) 45s(50)	13(40) 36s(40)	19s(90)	13(72)	
29.46S, 51.09W	85	Sao Leopoldo	1824	114s(85e)	95(80) 99s(80)	63(70) 64s(70)	18(50) 76s(50)	10(20) 48s(20)	8(90) 29s(00)	15s(72)	
2.31S, 44.16W	13	Sao Luis	1612	564s(85e)	182(80) 450s(80)	168(70) 266s(70)	80(50) 104s(50)	59(40) 53s(20)	29s(00)	7(72) 31s(72)	12(00?e)
23.32S, 46.37W	2690	Sao Paulo	1554	10,099s(85e)	7033(80) 8493s(80)	5922(70) 5922s(70)	2017(50) 2198s(50)	1269(40) 579s(20)	240s(00)	31s(72) 32s(72)	9(36)
23.58S, 46.23W	15	Sao Vicente	1510?	241s(85e)	193(80) 193s(80)	116(70) 117s(70)	28(50) 32s(50)	13(40) 17s(40)	3s(90)	2(72) 2s(72)	22s(36)
23.29S, 47.27W	1805	Sorocaba	1589	329s(85e)	255(80) 270s(80)	166(70) 176s(70)	69(50) 94s(50)	40(20) 43s(20)	17(90) 19s(90)	14(72) 14s(72)	
23.02S, 45.33W	1818	Taubate	1645	206s(85e)	155(80) 169s(80)	99(70) 111s(70)	36(50) 53s(50)	28(40) 45s(20)	21(90) 37s(00)	19(72) 21s(72)	
5.05S, 42.49W	213	Teresina	1851	476s(85e)	339(80) 378s(80)	181(70) 221s(70)	51(50) 91s(50)	57(20) 57s(20)	45s(00)	22s(72)	
19.45S, 47.55W	2576	Uberaba	bef 1811	246s(85e)	180(80) 199s(80)	109(70) 125s(70)	42(50) 69s(50)	31(40) 59s(40)	12(90) 27s(90)	11(72)	
18.56S, 48.18W	2802	Uberlandia	1846	314s(85e)	230(80) 241s(80)	110(70) 125s(70)	35(50) 55s(50)	22(40) 42s(40)	8(90)	20s(72)	
20.45S, 42.53W	2129	Vicosa	bef 1832	45s(85e)	29(80) 39s(80)	16(70) 26s(70)	6(50) 18s(50)	9(20) 56s(20)	3(00?)	4(72)	
20.20S, 40.17W	10	Vila Velha	1535	253s(85e)	74(80) 203s(80)	43(70) 124s(70)	10(50) 23s(50)	6(40) 17s(40)	2s(90)	2(72) 2s(72)	

For an explanation of symbols and abbreviations, see pages 16–17.

(Continued)

Figure 15.   *Aerial view of the skyline of Sao Paulo, the second largest urbanized area in South America by the latest census figures, which, because of its current high growth rate, probably surpassed Buenos Aires in population in 1987. (Credit: Varig Brazilian Airlines.)*

TABLE 2a. (Continued)

Latitude and Longitude	Elev (ft)	City	Date Settled	Population (thousands)							
				Latest	ca 1980	ca 1970	ca 1950	ca 1930	ca 1900	ca 1850	ca 1800
20.19S, 40.21W	10	Vitoria	1535		144 (80)	122 (70)	50 (50)	19 (20)	7 (90)	4 (72)	
				254s(85e)	208s(80)	133s(70)	51s(50)	22s(20)	12s(00)	16s(72)	
14.51S, 40.51W	3412	Vitoria da Conquista	1752		126 (80)	82 (70)	18 (50)	8 (40)			
				199s(85e)	171s(80)	126s(70)	97s(50)	75s(40)	29s(00)	19s(72)	
22.32S, 44.07W	1247	Volta Redonda	1864		178 (80)	122 (70)	32 (50)	1 (40)			
				220s(85e)	184s(80)	125s(70)	36s(50)				
Chile											
23.39S, 70.24W	400	Antofagasta	1866	175 (85e)	161 (82)	138 (70)	62 (52)	58 (30)	14 (95)	6 (75)	
18.29S, 70.20W	138	Arica	1545	128 (85e)	139 (82)	88 (70)	19 (52)	13 (30)	3 (95)	3 (76)	29 (25?)
36.50S, 73.03W	43	Concepcion	1550	218 (85e)	199 (82)	196 (70)	120 (52)	78 (30)	40 (95)	14 (65)	10 (00?e)
					519s(82)						
29.54S, 71.16W	26	La Serena	1552		87 (82)	62 (70)	34 (52)	21 (30)	16 (95)	7 (65)	
53.09S, 70.55W	26	Punta Arenas	1847		99 (82)	62 (70)	35 (52)	24 (30)	3 (95)	0.2 (65)	
33.27S, 70.40W	1706	*Santiago	1541	4318s(85e)	3853 (82)	2662s(70)	1350s(52)	696s(30)	256 (95)	115 (65)	46 (00?e)
					4108s(82)						
35.26S, 71.40W	295	Talca	1742	145 (85e)	126 (82)	94 (70)	55 (52)	45 (30)	33 (95)	18 (65)	
36.43S, 73.07W	276	Talcahuano	1769	221 (85e)	217 (82)	135 (70)	55 (52)	28 (30)	11 (95)	2 (65)	
38.44S, 72.36W	361	Temuco	1881	172 (85e)	157 (82)	110 (70)	56 (52)	36 (30)	7 (95)		
39.48S, 73.14W	39	Valdivia	1552	120 (85e)	103 (82)	82 (70)	47 (52)	34 (30)	8 (95)	3 (65)	
33.02S, 71.38W	135	Valparaiso	1544?	267 (85e)	226 (82)	293 (70)	219 (52)	193 (30)	122 (95)	70 (65)	2 (00?e)
					620s(82)						
33.02S, 71.34W	16	Vina del Mar	1586?	316 (85e)	273 (82)	153 (70)	85 (52)	49 (30)	11 (95)		6 (00?e)
Colombia											
4.31N, 75.41W	4866	Armenia	1889	180 (85)	180 (80e)	146 (73)	57 (51)	30 (38)	14 (12)		
10.59N, 74.48W	16	Barranquilla	1629	889 (85)	886 (80e)	693 (73)	276 (51)	150 (38)	49 (12)	6 (51)	
6.20N, 75.33W	4987	Bello	bef 1538	198 (85)	165 (80e)	116 (73)	28 (51)	8 (38)			
4.36N, 74.05W	8675	*Bogota	bef 1538	3957 (85)	4294 (80e)	2804 (73)	639 (51)	326 (38)	121 (12)	30 (51)	24 (00)
7.08N, 73.09W	3035	Bucaramanga	1622	342 (85)	417 (80e)	309 (73)	103 (51)	42 (38)	20 (12)	10 (51)	
3.53N, 77.04W	39	Buenaventura	1821	158 (85)	183 (80e)	109 (73)	35 (51)	15 (38)	6 (12)	2 (51)	
3.27N, 76.31W	3432	Cali	1536	1318 (85)	1380 (80e)	961 (73)	241 (51)	88 (38)	28 (12)	12 (51)	6 (97)

For an explanation of symbols and abbreviations, see pages 16–17.

(Continued)

TABLE 2a. (Continued)

Latitude and Longitude	Elev (ft)	City	Date Settled	Latest	ca 1980	ca 1970	ca 1950	ca 1930	ca 1900	ca 1850	ca 1800
10.25N, 75.32W	0	Cartagena	1533	528 (85)	452 (80e)	307 (73)	111 (51)	73 (38)	37 (12)	10 (51)	24 (00?e)
7.54N, 72.31W	965	Cucuta	1733	346 (85)	396 (80e)	227 (73)	70 (51)	37 (38)	20 (12)	6 (51)	4 (93)
4.27N, 75.14W	4098	Ibague	1551	266 (85)	197 (80e)	199 (73)	54 (51)	27 (38)	25 (12)	7 (51)	2 (00?e)
5.04N, 75.37W	7021	Manizales	1849	275 (85)	250 (80e)	201 (73)	89 (51)	51 (38)	35 (12)	3 (51)	
6.15N, 75.35W	5056	Medellin	1616	1422 (85)	1574 (80e)	1100 (73)	328 (51)	144 (38)	71 (12)	14 (51)	6 (26e)
8.46N, 75.53W	59	Monteria	1774	158 (85)	218 (80e)	102 (73)	24 (51)	13 (38)	22 (12)	2 (51)	
2.56N, 75.18W	1480	Neiva	1612	185 (85)	161 (80e)	106 (73)	33 (51)	15 (38)	22 (12)	7 (50?e)	
3.32N, 76.16W	3301	Palmira	1680	174 (85)	231 (80e)	140 (73)	54 (51)	21 (38)	24 (12)	1 (51)	
1.13N, 77.17W	8291	Pasto	1539	197 (85)	206 (80e)	126 (73)	49 (51)	28 (38)	28 (12)	8 (51)	7 (00?e)
4.49N, 75.43W	4672	Pereira	1863	232 (85)	262 (80e)	182 (73)	76 (51)	31 (38)	18 (12)	0.6 (70)	
2.27N, 76.36W	5774	Popayan	1536	150 (85)	93 (80e)	75 (73)	32 (51)	18 (38)	19 (12)	7 (50?e)	25 (25?e)
11.15N, 74.13W	20	Santa Marta	1525	193 (85)	201 (80e)	107 (73)	37 (51)	25 (38)	8 (12)	4 (51)	
5.31N, 73.22W	9252	Tunja	bef 1539	83 (85)	66 (80e)	52 (73)	23 (51)	17 (38)	9 (12)	7 (50?e)	
10.29N, 73.15W	554	Valledupar	1550	140 (85)	277 (80e)	96 (73)	9 (51)	3 (38)	7 (12)		
4.09N, 73.37W	1532	Villavicencio	1840	160 (85)	116 (80e)	85 (73)	17 (51)	6 (38)	5 (12)		
Ecuador											
1.15S, 78.37W	8389	Ambato	1698?	122 (86e)	100 (82)	72 (74)	34 (50)	14 (31e)	10 (97e)	8 (67e)	
2.53S, 78.59W	8468	Cuenca	bef 1534	193 (86e)	152 (82)	105 (74)	46 (50)	40 (31e)	30 (97e)	20 (50?e)	20 (00?e)
2.10S, 79.50W	10	Guayaquil	1537	1509 (86e)	1199 (82)	823 (74)	259 (50)	92 (19)	45 (90)	28 (50?e)	14 (05)
4.00S, 79.13W	7005	Loja	1548		72 (82)	47 (74)	18 (50)	10 (31e)	10 (00e)	10 (50?e)	10 (00?e)
3.16S, 79.58W	20	Machala		105 (86e)	106 (82)	68 (74)	7 (50)	6 (31e)	3 (00e)		
1.03S, 80.27W	144	Portoviejo	1628	134 (86e)	103 (82)	59 (74)	18 (50)	8 (31e)	5 (00e)	4 (25?e)	
0.13S, 78.30W	9249	*Quito	1000?	1093 (86e)	866 (82)	560 (74)	219 (50)	81 (22)	52 (06)	36 (57)	28 (80)
French Guiana											
4.56N, 52.20W	30	*Cayenne	1664		38 (82)	30 (74)	11 (46)	14 (26)	13 (01)	5 (36)	1 (00?e)
Guyana											
6.49N, 58.10W	7	*Georgetown	1625	188s(83e)	72 (80)	66 (70) 167s(70)	74 (46) 94s(46)	63 (31)	49 (91) 55s(91)	26 (51)	8 (00?e)
Paraguay											
25.16S, 57.40W	210	*Asuncion	1537		457 (82)	389 (72)	203 (50)	77 (28)	52 (00)	10 (50?e)	7 (93)

Coordinates	Elev.	Name	Founded	Pop.	Pop.	Pop.	Pop.	Pop.	Pop.	Pop.	Pop.
Peru											
16.24S, 71.33W	7559	Arequipa	bef 1425	532s(85e)	108 (81)	96 (72)	83 (61)	77 (40)	35 (96e)	29 (76)	28 (04)
12.04S, 77.09W	20	Callao	1537		262 (81)	191 (72)	156 (61)	82 (40)	29 (98)	34 (76)	5 (00?e)
6.46S, 79.51W	89	Chiclayo	1720	515s(85e)	448s(81)	321s(72)	214s(61)	32 (40)	13 (89)	12 (76)	
9.05S, 78.36W	10	Chimbote	1822	348s(85e)	196 (81)	147 (72)	96 (61)	4 (40)		0.6 (76)	
13.31S, 71.59W	11,152	Cuzco	11th c	253s(85e)	211 (81)	160 (72)	60 (61)	41 (40)	19 (06)	18 (76)	32 (94)
12.04S, 75.14W	10,660	Huancayo	bef 1571	226s(85e)	85 (81)	64 (72)	60 (61)	27 (40)		4 (76)	
14.04S, 75.42W	1306	Ica	1664?	187s(85e)	78 (81)	67 (72)	46 (61)	21 (40)	6 (06e)	7 (76)	6 (25?e)
3.46S, 73.15W	348	Iquitos	16th c	215s(85e)	80 (81)	63 (72)	49 (61)	32 (40)	3 (90)	1 (76)	
12.03S, 77.03W	505	*Lima	bef 1532	5008s(85e)	3969 (81)	2834 (72)	1488 (61)	541 (40)	130 (03)	101 (76)	53 (91)
					4154s(81)	2981s(72)	1632s(61)				
5.12S, 80.38W	95	Piura	1588	256s(85e)	142 (81)	81 (72)	43 (61)	28 (40)	11 (96e)	7 (76)	6 (00?e)
8.07S, 79.02W	108	Trujillo	1534	439s(85e)	194 (81)	126 (72)	100 (61)	37 (40)	6 (06e)	8 (76)	
Suriname											
5.50N, 55.13W	12	*Paramaribo	1540?		68 (80)	102 (71)	74 (50)	48 (31)	32 (01)	18 (60)	20 (00?e)
Uruguay											
34.53S, 56.11W	72	*Montevideo	1726	1304 (85)	1180 (75)	1164 (63)	784 (49e)	482 (31)	268 (00)	34 (52)	14 (03)
Venezuela											
10.08N, 64.42W	16	Barcelona	1671	198 (85e)	156 (81)	78 (71)	25 (50)	11 (26)	14 (91)		15 (07e)
10.04N, 69.19W	1857	Barquisimeto	1552	621 (85e)	498 (81)	331 (71)	105 (50)	23 (26)	27 (91)	26 (73)	15 (07)
10.26N, 66.53W	2887	Baruta	1591?	240 (85e)	200 (81)	121 (71)	7 (50)	4s(26)			8 (00?e)
10.23N, 71.28W	3	Cabimas	bef 1926	159 (85e)	140 (81)	118 (71)	48 (50)	12 (26)			31 (02)
10.30N, 66.55W	3025	*Caracas	1567	1218 (85e)	1045 (81)	1035 (71)	495 (50)	135 (26)	72 (91)	49 (73)	
				2426s(85e)	2071s(81)	2184s(71)	694s(50)	168s(26)	98s(91)	68s(73)	
8.08N, 63.33W	177	Ciudad Bolivar	1764	223 (85e)	182 (81)	104 (71)	31 (50)	23 (26)	18 (91)	8 (73)	5 (25?e)
8.17N, 62.44W	256	Ciudad Guayana	1595	410 (85e)	314 (81)	144 (71)	4 (50)	1s(26)	1s(91)	0.7s(73)	
10.28N, 64.10W	52	Cumana	1523	209 (85e)	180 (81)	120 (71)	46 (50)	23 (26)	11 (91)	9 (73)	18 (00?e)
10.40N, 71.37W	20	Maracaibo	1571	1070 (85e)	891 (81)	652 (71)	236 (50)	75 (26)	35 (91)	26 (73)	22 (01e)
10.15N, 67.36W	1460	Maracay	17th c	468 (85e)	388 (81)	255 (71)	65 (50)	11 (26)	6 (91)	5 (73)	8 (00?e)
9.45N, 63.11W	243	Maturin	1710	190 (85e)	155 (81)	98 (71)	25 (50)	15 (26)	16 (91)	13 (73)	
8.36N, 71.08W	5384	Merida	1558	178 (85e)	143 (81)	74 (71)	25 (50)	14 (26)	13 (91)	10 (73)	11 (00?e)
10.29N, 66.49W	2769	Petare	1704	467 (85e)	396 (81)	228 (71)	21 (50)	10s(26)	2 (91)	6s(73)	
7.46N, 72.14W	2707	San Cristobal	1561	227 (85e)	199 (81)	152 (71)	54 (50)	28 (26)	17 (91)	12 (73)	
10.11N, 68.00W	1568	Valencia	1555	792 (85e)	616 (81)	367 (71)	89 (50)	37 (26)	54 (91)	29 (73)	7 (00)

For an explanation of symbols and abbreviations, see pages 16–17.

2b. Cities: Supplemental Information

Contents

Conventional name of city.

[a]Division of country in which city is located. (This information is given for cities in the larger countries; see General Explanatory Notes for details.) Also, island (if any) on which city is located.

[b]Alternate, former, and official names of city. (See General Explanatory Notes for details.) In addition, important formerly separate cities that have been incorporated into the city cited and certain well-known sections of the city sometimes regarded as separate cities (e.g., Hollywood, a section of Los Angeles) are listed after the abbreviation "inc." If a date is given in conjunction with the "inc" listing, this is related to the populations entered in Table 2a. Thus, the notation under New York that reads "inc Brooklyn since 1898" means that the populations given for New York before 1898 exclude Brooklyn.

[c]Hydrographic features within present city limits. These are listed in the following order: seas (including oceans, gulfs, bays, straits, etc) by size; rivers by length, except that main rivers are listed before their tributaries; and natural lakes by size. Creeks and other small streams are cited only if there is no river. When there is no sea, river, or lake within the city limits, the nearest hydrographic feature within approximately 10 miles (16 kilometers) is given, preceded by the abbreviation "nr." Unconventional names of rivers and lakes are not entered here if the river or lake in question is listed in Table 8a or 10a, and thus in the Index.

[d]Universities, with date of foundation (in parentheses), student enrollment (i.e., thousands of full-time and part-time students, excluding correspondence students, enrolled in the university and its affiliated institutions),[1] and academic staff (i.e., number of full-time and part-time teachers). Wherever possible, however, the figures for students and teachers exclude those at branches and campuses where no graduate degrees are conferred. Universities are listed in order of student enrollment.

Except as noted in footnotes, all universities, as defined in the General Explanatory Notes, within approximately 10 miles (16 kilometers) of the city are entered, provided, of course, that the university in question is not located in another city listed in this table. Those outside the city limits, however, are described like this example under Visakhapatnam, India: "Andhra University (at Waltair, nr Visakhapatnam)." If a university was founded other than at its present location, the notation reads as in this example under Macon, USA: "Mercer University (1833 at Penfield, relocated 1871)."

The date given for the foundation of a university is the year in which the institution itself or (preferably) its oldest constituent college or the educational institution from which it directly evolved, was established or chartered. This date may precede by several years the date when instruction was first given. Also, it bears no necessary relation to the length of time during which the university has

---

[1]In India most universities include as affiliates numerous educational institutions of lower level, such as preparatory or other secondary schools; thus the size of these universities is usually exaggerated with respect to that of universities in other countries, where only college-level students are included in the enrollment statistics.

been operative, since many universities have been closed for periods of years or even decades.

If no university exists at or near a given city, the notation "none" appears after d.

[e]Largest libraries, with date of foundation (in parentheses) and size of collection (i.e., thousands of volumes of books and pamphlets, usually including bound volumes of periodicals).[2]

Although only the largest libraries are listed for each city, if the city has a public library of any importance, it is listed along with all other libraries that are larger. The names of libraries are usually given in full, but to save space, the name of the city is omitted fron the name of each city (or municipal) public library, and the names of universities already entered under d are not repeated when a university library is listed unless it is impossible without the name to determine to which university the library belongs; instead, the library is entered simply as ". . . University Library" or "University . . . Library," depending on whether the university in question is called, for example, New York University or University of New York. Memorial names (e.g., Bodleian, for University of Oxford, Library) are also omitted from university library entries because these names are generally applicable only to the main or central library, and the size of collection figures given here include whenever possible the collections of branch and departmental libraries belonging to the university in the same city.

As with universities, large libraries located within approximately 10 miles (16 kilometers) of the city are also listed, but are identified as being "nr" the city in question. Again, as with universities, those founded elsewhere and subsequently moved to the city under which they are cited are entered as in this example under Miskolc, Hungary: ". . . University Library (1763 at Banska Stiavnica, Czechoslovakia; relocated 1949)."

The date of foundation given for libraries is preferably the year in which the library was opened on a permanent basis, that is, the one since which it has been continuously operative. By "library," however, is meant the nucleus of the present book collection, not necessarily the institution under its present name.

[f]Supplemental population data. These most often include populations at various dates of the cities listed after "inc" in section b of this table. All data are in thousands, followed by the year of record in parentheses.

Coverage

All cities listed in Table 2a.

Rounding

University student enrollments are rounded to the nearest 1,000 (to the nearest 100 if the total is less than 1,000).

Library collections are rounded to the nearest 1,000 volumes.

Entries

2,664, as follows: Africa—175

Asia—753

[2]See note 1 on p 445.

Europe—671
North America—825
Oceania—39
South America—201

TABLE 2b. CITIES: SUPPLEMENTAL INFORMATION

AFRICA

Algeria

*Algiers: [b]alt Alger; off Jazair. [c]B of Algiers of Mediterranean Sea. [d]Universite d'Alger (1859) 17 – 1530; Universite des Sciences et de la Technologie Houari Boumedienne (1974) 13 – 1300. [e]Bibliotheque Nationale (1835) 950; Bibliotheque de l'Universite d'Alger (1880) 700; Bibliotheque Centrale Municipale (1951) 75.

Annaba: [b]for Bone. [c]Mediterranean Sea. [d]Universite d'Annaba (1971) 9 – 967. [e]Bibliotheque de l'Universite . . . (1975) 80; Bibliotheque du Centre Culturel Francais (1954) 29; Bibliotheque Municipale (1885) 15.

Blida: [b]none. [c]Kebir R. [d]none.

Constantine: [b]off Qusantina. [c]Rummel R. [d]Universite de Constantine (1961) 12 – 1023. [e]Bibliotheque de l'Universite . . . (1970) 300; Bibliotheque Municipale (1882) 32.

Oran: [b]off Ouahran. [c]Mediterranean Sea. [d]Universite d'Oran (1961) 9 – 1000; Universite des Sciences et de la Technologie (1975) ? – ? [e]Bibliotheque de l'Universite d'Oran (1965) 70; Bibliotheque du Centre Culturel Francais (1964) 48; Bibliotheque Municipale (1860) 26.

Setif: [b]none. [c]nr Bou Sellam R. [d]Universite de Setif (1978) 6 – 480. [e]Bibliotheque de l'Universite . . . (1978?) 35.

Angola

*Luanda: [b]for Loanda, Sao Paulo de Loanda. [c]Atlantic O. [d]Universidade de Angola (1963) 3 – 293. [e]Biblioteca da Universidade . . . (1963?) 75; Biblioteca Nacional de Angola (1938) 30; Biblioteca Municipal (?) 15.

Benin

Cotonou: [b]for Kotonu. [c]Bight of Benin of G of Guinea. [d]Universite Nationale du Benin (1962) 5 – 709. [e]Bibliotheque de l'Universite . . . (1970) 27; Bibliotheque du Centre Culturel Francais (1963) 17.

*Porto-Novo: [b]none. [c]Porto-Novo Lagoon. [d]none. [e]Bibliotheque Nationale (1961) 35.

Botswana

*Gaborone: [b]for Gaberones. [c]nr Notwani R. [d]University of Botswana (1972) 2 – 166. [e]Botswana National Library Service (1967) 190; Public Library (1967) 160; University . . . Library (1971) 80.

Burkina Faso

Bobo Dioulasso: [b]for Sia. [c]none. [d]none.

*Ouagadougou: [b]for Wagadugu. [c]nr Ouadmana R. [d]Universite de Ouagadougou (1965) 3 – 240. [e]Bibliotheque de l'Universite . . . (1974) 73; Bibliotheque Nationale (?) ?

Burundi

*Bujumbura: [b]for Usumbura. [c]Tanganyika L. [d]Universite du Burundi (1958) 2 – 277. [e]Bibliotheque de l'Universite . . . (1960) 110; Bibliotheque Publique (?) 27.

Cameroon

Douala: [b]alt Duala. [c]Wouri R. [d]none. [e]Bibliotheque du Centre Culturel Francais (1964) 15.

*Yaounde: [b]alt Yaunde. [c]none. [d]Universite de Yaounde (1961) 13 – 562. [e]Bibliotheque de l'Universite . . . (1967) 85; Bibliotheque du Centre Culturel Francais (1961) 19; Bibliotheque Nationale du Cameroun (?) 10.

(Canary Islands), Spain

La Laguna: [a]Tenerife I. [b]none. [c]nr Atlantic O. [d]Universidad de La Laguna (1701) 15 – 648. [e]Biblioteca de la Universidad . . . (1701) 70.

TABLE 2b. (Continued)

*Las Palmas: [a]Gran Canaria I. [b]alt Las Palmas de Gran Canaria, Palmas. [c]Atlantic O. [d]Universidad Politecnica de Las Palmas (1980) 3 – 368. [e]Biblioteca del Museo Canario (1879) 45.

*Santa Cruz de Tenerife: [a]Tenerife I. [b]none. [c]Atlantic O. [d]none. [e]Biblioteca Publica Municipal (1888) 60.

Cape Verde

*Praia: [a]Sao Tiago I. [b]none. [c]Atlantic O. [d]none.

Central African Republic

*Bangui: [b]none. [c]Ubangi R. [d]Universite de Bangui (1919) 2 – 270. [e]Bibliotheque de l'Universite . . . (1919?) 19; Bibliotheque du Centre Culturel Francais (?) 18.

Chad

*Ndjamena: [b]for Fort-Lamy. [c]Shari R; Logone R. [d]Universite du Tchad (1971) 1 – 93. [e]Bibliotheque de l'Universite . . . (1962) 12; Bibliotheque du Centre Culturel Francais (1968) 12.

Comoros

*Moroni: [a]Njazidja I. [b]for Maroni. [c]Mozambique Channel. [d]none.

Congo

*Brazzaville: [b]none. [c]Congo R. [d]Universite Marien-Ngouabi (1959) 9 – 565. [e]Bibliotheque Universitaire (1960) 80; Bibliotheque du Centre Culturel Francais (1961) 33; Bibliotheque Publique (1950) 15.

Pointe-Noire: [b]none. [c]Atlantic O. [d]none. [e]Bibliotheque du Centre Culturel Francais (?) 8.

Djibouti

*Djibouti: [b]alt Jibuti. [c]G of Aden. [d]none. [e]Arab Maritime Academy Library (?) 8.

Egypt

Alexandria: [b]off Iskandariyah. [c]Mediterranean Sea; Mareotis (off Maryut) L. [d]Alexandria University (1942) 92 – 3610. [e] . . . University Library (1942) 1000; Municipal Library (1892) 62.

Aswan: [b]alt Assuan. [c]Nile R. [d]none.

Asyut: [b]alt Assiut; for Siut. [c]Nile R. [d]Asyut University (1949) 43 – 2110. [e] . . . University Library (1957) 250.

*Cairo: [b]off Qahirah. [c]Nile R. [d]Ain Shams University (1950) 122 – 4220; Al-Azhar University (970) 90 – 3604; American University in Cairo (1919) 2 – 278. [e]Egyptian National Library (1870) 1500; American University in Cairo Library (1919) 185; Bibliotheque de l'Institut d'Egypte (1859) 160.

Damanhur: [b]none. [c]nr Rosetta (off Rashid) R (Nile R distributary). [d]none. [e]Municipal Library (?) 13.

Fayyum: [b]alt Faiyum, Fayum. [c]Yousouf R. [d]none. [e]Municipal Library (?) 6.

Giza: [b]alt Gizeh; off Jizah. [c]Nile R; [d]Cairo University (1908) 114 – 5830. [e] . . . University Library (1908) 1460.

Hulwan: [b]alt Helwan. [c]Nile R. [d]Hulwan University (bef 1975) 33 – 2350. [e] . . . University Library (bef 1975) 435.

Ismailia: [b]off Ismailiyah. [c]Timsah L. [d]Suez Canal University (1976) 18 – 863.

Luxor: [b]off Uqsur. [c]Nile R. [d]none.

Mahalla al Kubra: [b]for Mehallet el Kebir. [c]nr Damietta (off Dumyat) R (Nile R distributary). [d]none.

Mansurah: [b]alt Mansura. [c]Damietta (off Dumyat) R (Nile R distributary). [d]Mansurah University (1960) 45 – 1820. [e]Polytechnic Institute Library (1959) 23; Municipal Library (?) 18; . . . University Library (1960?) ?

Minya: [b]none. [c]Nile R. [d]Minya University (1976) 16 – 770. [e] . . . University Library (1976?) 89.

Port Said: [b]off Bur Said. [c]Mediterranean Sea; Manzala Lagoon. [d]none.

Shibin al Kawm: [b]alt Shibin el-Kom. [c]Shibin R. [d]Menoufia University (1976) 18 – 863. [e] . . . University Library (1976?) ?

Shubra al Khaymah: [b]alt Shubra el-Kheima [c]Nile R. [d]none.

Suez: [b]off Suways. [c]G of Suez of Red Sea. [d]none.

Tanta: [b]none. [c]nr Rosetta (off Rashid) R (Nile R distributary). [d]Tanta University (1963) 36 – 1470. [e]Municipal Library (?) 23; . . . University Library (1963?) ?

Zagazig: [b]off Zaqaziq. [c]none. [d]Zagazig University (1973) 71 – 3080. [e]Sharkia Provincial Council Library (?) 12; . . . University Library (1973?) ?

Equatorial Guinea

*Malabo: [a]Bioko I. [b]for Santa Isabel. [c]Bight of Bonny of G of Guinea. [d]none.

For an explanation of symbols and abbreviations, see pages 16–17.

(Continued)

TABLE 2b. (Continued)

Ethiopia

*Addis Ababa: [b]off Adis Abeba. [c]nr Akaki R. [d]Addis Ababa University (1950) 18 – 863. [e] . . . University Library (1950) 600; National Library of Ethiopia (1944) 100.

Asmara: [a]*Eritrea. [b]off Asmera. [c]nr Anseba R. [d]Asmara University (1958) 4 – 174. [e] . . . University Library (1969) 65; Public Library (1955) 14.

Harar: [b]off Harer. [c]Errer R. [d]none. [e]National Military Academy Library (1950) 6.

Gabon

*Libreville: [b]none. [c]G of Guinea; Gabon (for Gabun) R. [d]Universite Omar Bongo (1970) 3 – 385. [e]Bibliotheque de l'Universite . . . (1976) 70; Bibliotheque du Centre Culturel Francais (?) 18.

Gambia

*Banjul: [b]for Bathurst. [c]Atlantic O; Gambia R. [d]none. [e]National Library (1946) 59.

Ghana

*Accra: [b]for Akkra. [c]G of Guinea. [d]University of Ghana (at Legon, nr Accra) (1927) 3 – 419. [e]Ghana Library Board (1950) 1339; University . . . Library (at Legon) (1948) 312; Central Library (1950) ?

Cape Coast: [b]none. [c]G of Guinea. [d]University of Cape Coast (1962) 2 – 200. [e]University . . . Library (1962) 134.

Kumasi: [b]for Coomassie. [c]none. [d]University of Science and Technology (1951) 3 – 453. [e]University . . . Library (1952) 130; Ashanti Regional Library (1954) 50.

Sekondi-Takoradi: [b]none. [c]G of Guinea. [d]none. [e]Regional Library (?) ?

Tamale: [b]none. [c]Jolo R. [d]none.

Guinea

*Conakry: [b]for Konakry. [c]Atlantic O. [d]none. [e]Bibliotheque Nationale (1958) 40; Bibliotheque de l'Institut Polytechnique de Conakry (1963) 15.

Kankan: [b]none. [c]Milo R. [d]none.

Guinea-Bissau

*Bissau: [a]Bissau I. [b]none. [c]Atlantic O: Geba R. [d]none. [e]Biblioteca Nacional da Guine-Bissau (1970) 25.

Ivory Coast

*Abidjan: [b]none. [c]Ebrie Lagoon. [d]Universite Nationale de Cote d'Ivoire (1959) 13 – 696. [e]Bibliotheque de l'Universite . . . (1963) 95; Bibliotheque Nationale (1968) 70; Bibliotheque Municipale (1952) 50.

Bouake: [b]none. [c]nr Kan R. [d]none.

Yamoussoukro: [b]none. [c]nr Bandama R. [d]none.

Kenya

Kisumu: [b]for Port Florence. [c]Kavirondo G of Victoria L. [d]none. [e]Kisumu Area Library (1971) 32.

Mombasa: [b]alt Mvita. [c]Indian O. [d]none. [e]Seif Bin Salim Public Library (1903) 20.

*Nairobi: [b]none. [c]Nairobi R; Mathari R. [d]University of Nairobi (1954) 6 – 825. [e]University . . . Library (1956) 340; McMillan Memorial Library (1931) 165.

Lesotho

*Maseru: [b]none. [c]Caledon R. [d]National University of Lesotho (at Roma, nr Maseru) (1945) 1 – 161. [e] . . . University Library (at Roma) (1966) 150; Lesotho National Library Service (?) ?

Liberia

*Monrovia: [b]none. [c]Atlantic O. [d]University of Liberia (1851) 3 – 249. [e]University . . . Library (1862) 107; Cuttington University College Library (1889) 92; National Library (1926) 20.

Libya

Bengasi: [a]*Cyrenaica. [b]alt Benghazi; off Banghazi. [c]Mediterranean Sea. [d]University of Garyounis (1955) 9 – 510. [e]University . . . Library (1955) 295; National Library (?) 35; Public Library (1955) 14.

*Tripoli, [a]*Tripolitania. [b]off Tarabulus. [c]Mediterranean Sea. [d]University of Al Fateh (1955) 7 – 830. [e]University . . . Library (1972) 135; Public Library (1917) 37; National Library (?) ?

TABLE 2b. (Continued)

Madagascar

*Antananarivo: ^{a}Madagascar I. ^{b}for Tananarive. ^{c}Ikopa R; Anosy L. ^{d}Universite de Madagascar (1896) 37 – 943. ^{e}Bibliotheque Universitaire (1960) 180; Bibliotheque Nationale (1961) 165; Bibliotheque Municipale (1961) 23.

(Madeira Islands), Portugal

*Funchal: ^{a}Madeira I. ^{b}none. ^{c}Atlantic O. ^{d}none. ^{e}Biblioteca Municipal (1838) 36.

Malawi

Blantyre: ^{b}none. ^{c}Mudi R. ^{d}University of Malawi, Blantyre campus (1964) 0.5 – 67. ^{e}Blantyre Campus Library of the University . . . (1966) 41.

*Lilongwe: ^{b}none. ^{c}Lilongwe R. ^{d}University of Malawi, Lilongwe campus (1964) 0.6 – 81. ^{e}National Library Service (1968) 130.

Zomba: ^{b}none. ^{c}none. ^{d}University of Malawi (1964) 2 – 302. ^{e}University . . . Main Library (1965) 168.

Mali

*Bamako: ^{b}none. ^{c}Niger R. ^{d}none. ^{e}Bibliotheque du Centre Culturel Francais (1962) 30; Bibliotheque Nationale (1913) 15; Bibliotheque Municipale (1949) ?

Timbuktu: ^{b}off Tombouctou. ^{c}nr Niger R. ^{d}none. ^{e}Bibliotheque du Centre de Documentation Ahmed Baba (1966) ?

Mauritania

*Nouakchott: ^{b}none. ^{c}nr Atlantic O. ^{d}Universite de Nouakchott (1983) 1 – ? ^{e}Bibliotheque du Centre Culturel Saint-Exupery (?) 20; Bibliotheque Nationale (1965) 10; Bibliotheque Publique Centrale (?) ?

Mauritius

*Port Louis: ^{b}none. ^{c}Indian O. ^{d}University of Mauritius (at Reduit, nr Port Louis (1965) 0.4 – 64. ^{e}City Library (1851) 80; University . . . Library (at Reduit) (1965) 75; Mauritius Institute Public Library (1902) 52.

Morocco

Casablanca: ^{b}off Dar al Baida. ^{c}Atlantic O. ^{d}Universite Hassan II (1975) 21 – 448. ^{e}Bibliotheque Municipale (1917) 318.

Fez: ^{b}alt Fes; off Fas. ^{c}Fez (alt Fes; off Fas) R. ^{d}Universite Mohammed Ben Abdalla (1974) 9 – 245; Universite Qarawiyine (859) 5 – 90. ^{e}Bibliotheque de l'Universite Mohammed Ben Abdalla (1974?) 72; Bibliotheque de l'Universite Qarawiyine (1963?) 31.

Kenitra: ^{b}for Port-Lyautey. ^{c}Sebou R. ^{d}none. ^{e}Bibliotheque de la Ville (?) 6.

Marrakesh: ^{b}alt Marrakech; for Morocco; off Marrakush. ^{c}Issil R. ^{d}Universite Qadi Iyad (1979) 7 – 310. ^{e}Bibliotheque de l'Universite . . . (1979?) 15; Bibliotheque Municipale (1923) 13.

Meknes: ^{b}for Mequinez; off Miknasa. ^{c}Boufekrane R. ^{d}none. ^{e}Bibliotheque Municipale (?) 57.

Oujda: ^{b}none. ^{c}nr Isly R. ^{d}Universite Mohammed I (1979) 7 – 351. ^{e}Bibliotheque du Centre Culturel Ibn Khaldoun (?) 30; Bibliotheque Municipale (1964) 18.

*Rabat: ^{b}none. ^{c}Atlantic O; Bou Regreg R. ^{d}Universite Mohammed V (1912) 27 – 1883. ^{e}Bibliotheque Generale (1920) 600; Bibliotheque de l'Universite . . . (1945) 370.

Safi: ^{b}for Asfi. ^{c}Atlantic O. ^{d}none. ^{e}Bibliotheque Municipale (1930) 4.

Sale: ^{b}for Sallee; off Sla. ^{c}Atlantic O; Bou Regreg R. ^{d}none.

Tangier: ^{b}alt Tanger; off Tanjah. ^{c}Strait of Gibraltar. ^{d}none. ^{e}Biblioteca Publica Espanola (1941) 41.

Tetouan: ^{b}for Tetuan. ^{c}(Oued) Martin R. ^{d}none. ^{e}Bibliotheque Generale (1939) 60.

Mozambique

Beira: ^{b}none. ^{c}Mozambique Channel; Pungue R; Buzi R. ^{d}none.

*Maputo: ^{b}for Lourenco Marques. ^{c}Delagoa B of Indian O. ^{d}Universidade Eduardo Mondlane (1962) 0.8 – 224. ^{e}Biblioteca Nacional de Mocambique (1961) 110; Biblioteca da Universidade . . . (1963) 68; Biblioteca Municipal (?) 8.

Namibia

*Windhoek: ^{b}for Aigams, Windhuk. ^{c}none. ^{d}none. ^{e}Public Library (1924) 72; Administration Library (1926) 38.

For an explanation of symbols and abbreviations, see pages 16–17.   (Continued)

TABLE 2b. (Continued)

Niger

*Niamey: [b]none. [c]Niger R. [d]Universite de Niamey (1971) 2 – 288. [e]Bibliotheque de l'Ecole Nationale d'Administration (1963) 18; Bibliotheque Universitaire (1971?) 15.

Nigeria

Aba: [b]none. [c]Aba R. [d]none.

Abeokuta: [b]none. [c]Ogun R. [d]none. [e]Ogun State Library (1976) 22.

Ado-Ekiti: [b]none. [c]nr Ogbesse R. [d]Ondo State University (1982) 0.6 – 25. [e]Federal Polytechnic Library (1978?) 22.

Benin City: [b]none. [c]Gwato Creek. [d]University of Benin (1970) 9 – 600. [e]Bendel State Library (1970) 405; University . . . Library (1970?) 100.

Calabar: [b]for Old Calabar. [c]Calabar R. [d]University of Calabar (1975) 5 – 408. [e]University . . . Library (1975?) 69; Polytechnic Library (1973) 22; Cross River State Library (?) ?

Ede: [b]none. [c]Oshun R. [d]none.

Enugu: [b]none. [c]Asata R; Aria R. [d]none. [e]Anambra State Library (1955) 140.

Ibadan: [b]none. [c]Ogunpa R. [d]University of Ibadan (1948) 14 – 1068. [e]University . . . Library (1948) 900; Oyo State Library (1956) 94.

Ife: [b]for Ile-Ife. [c]nr Shasha R. [d]University of Ife (1961) 12 – 1113. [e]University . . . Library (1961) 450.

Ilesha: [b]none. [c]nr Shasha R. [d]none.

Ilorin: [b]none. [c]Awun R. [d]University of Ilorin (1975) 5 – 376. [e]University . . . Library (1976) 34; Kwara State Library (1968) 21.

Iwo: [b]none. [c]nr Oba R. [d]none.

Jos: [b]none. [c]Delimi R. [d]University of Jos (1972) 5 – 404. [e]University . . . Library (1972) 94; Plateau State Library (1968) 40.

Kaduna: [b]none. [c]Kaduna R. [d]none. [e]Kaduna State Library (1953) 162.

Kano: [b]none. [c]Jakara R. [d]Bayero University (1960) 4 – 358. [e]Kano State Library (1967) 150; . . . University Library (1964) 121.

*Lagos : [b]none. [c]Bight of Benin of G of Guinea; Lagos (for Cradu) Lagoon. [d]University of Lagos (1962) 15 – 600. [e]University . . . Library (1962), 250; City Council Library (1946) 243; National Library of Nigeria (1962) 158.

Maiduguri: [b]for Yerwa-Maiduguri. [c]Ngadda R. [d]University of Maiduguri (1975) 5 – 457. [e]University . . . Library (1975) 86; Borno State Library (1968) 52.

Mushin: [b]none. [c]nr Ogun R. [d]none.

Nsukka: [b]none. [c]none. [d]University of Nigeria (1960) 14 – 921. [e]University . . . Library (1960) 411.

Ogbomosho: [b]none. [c]nr Oba R. [d]none.

Onitsha: [b]none. [c]Niger R. [d]none.

Oshogbo: [b]none. [c]Oshun R. [d]none.

Oyo: [b]for Agaw Ojja. [c]none. [d]none.

Port Harcourt: [b]none. [c]Bonny R (Niger R distributary). [d]University of Port Harcourt (1975) 4 – 337; Rivers State University of Science and Technology (1971) 3 – 310. [e] . . . University Library (1971) 75; Rivers State Central Library (1962) 44; University . . . Library (1976) 38.

Sokoto: [b]none. [c]Sokoto R; Kebbi R. [d]University of Sokoto (1975) 3 – 361, [e]University . . . Library (1977) 50; Sokoto State Library (?) ?

Zaria: [b]none. [c]Galma R. [d]Ahmadu Bello University (1946) 19 – 1900. [e] . . . University Library (1931) 275.

Reunion

*Saint-Denis: [b]none. [c]Indian O; Saint-Denis R. [d]Universite de la Reunion (1950) 3 – 74. [e]Bibliotheque Centrale de Pret (1956) 150; Bibliotheque Departementale (1855) 95; Bibliotheque Universitaire (1971) 60.

Rwanda

*Kigali: [b]none. [c]nr Nyabarongo R. [d]none. [e]Bibliotheque Publique (?) 10.

Sao Tome and Principe

*Sao Tome: [a]Sao Tome I. [b]for Sao Thome. [c]Ana de Chaves B of G of Guinea. [d]none.

TABLE 2b. (Continued)

Senegal

*Dakar: ^{b}none. ^{c}Atlantic O. ^{d}Universite de Dakar (1918) 11 – 722. ^{e}Bibliotheque Universitaire (1952) 400; Bibliotheque de l'Institut Fondamental d'Afrique Noire (1938) 60.

Seychelles

*Victoria: ^{a}Mahe I. ^{b}alt Port Victoria; for Mahe. ^{c}Indian O. ^{d}none.

Sierra Leone

*Freetown: ^{b}none. ^{c}Atlantic O. ^{d}University of Sierra Leone (1827) 2 – 259. ^{e}University . . . Library (1827) 170; Sierra Leone Library Board (1959) 157; J. J. Thomas Library (?) 20.

Somalia

Hargeisa: ^{b}off Hargeysa. ^{c}nr (Wadi) Merodi R. ^{d}none. ^{e}Local Government Council Library (1958) 3.

*Mogadishu: ^{b}alt Mogadiscio, Muqdisho; off Hamar. ^{c}Indian O. ^{d}Universita Nazionale della Somalia (1954) 5 – 549. ^{e}National Library of Higher Education and Culture (1934) 9; Biblioteca dell'Universita . . . (1954) 8; National Library Service (?) 8.

South Africa

Bellville: ^{a}Cape of Good Hope. ^{b}none. ^{c}Kuils R; Diep R. ^{d}University of the Western Cape (1960) 6 – 301. ^{e}University . . . Library (1960) 100; Public Library 1918) 50.

Benoni: ^{a}Transvaal. ^{b}none. ^{c}nr Bleskop (Spruit) Creek. ^{d}none. ^{e}Public Library (1923) 140.

Bloemfontein: ^{a*}Orange Free State. ^{b}none. ^{c}Bloem(spruit) Creek. ^{d}University of the Orange Free State (1855) 8 – 533. ^{e}Orange Free State Provincial Library Service (1948) 2431; Bloemfontein Regional Library (1950) 500; University . . . Library (1906) 385; Public Library (1875) 300.

*Cape Town: ^{a*}Cape of Good Hope. ^{b}alt Kaapstad. ^{c}Table B of Atlantic O. ^{d}University of Cape Town (1829) 12 – 1260. ^{e}Cape Provincial Library Service (1945) 5652; City Library (1952) 1124; University . . . Library (1829) 1092; South African Library (1818) 600.

Durban: ^{a}Natal. ^{b}none. ^{c}Natal B of Indian O. ^{d}University of Natal (at Durban and Pietermaritzburg) (1909) 11 – 3077 [Durban campus: (1922) ? – ?]; University of Durban-Westville (1961) 7 – 597. ^{e}Municipal Library (1853) 711; Durban Campus Library of the University of Natal (1922) 360.

East London: ^{a}Cape of Good Hope. ^{b}alt Oos-Londen. ^{c}Indian O; Buffalo R. ^{d}none. ^{e}Municipal Library (1976) 201.

Germiston: ^{a}Transvaal. ^{b}none. ^{c}Germiston L. ^{d}none. ^{e}Public Library (1909) 133.

Grahamstown: ^{a}Cape of Good Hope. ^{b}alt Grahamstad. ^{c}Kowie R. ^{d}Rhodes University (1904) 3 – 298. ^{e} . . . University Library (1904) 305; Public Library (1842) 72.

Johannesburg: ^{a}Transvaal. ^{b}none. ^{c}none. ^{d}University of the Witwatersrand (1896 at Kimberley, relocated 1904) 17 – 1313; Rand Afrikaans University (1906) 6 – 323. ^{e}Public Library (1889) 1441; University . . . Library (1922) 823.

Kimberley: ^{a}Cape of Good Hope. ^{b}none. ^{c}nr Vaal R. ^{d}none. ^{e}Public Library (1882) 145.

Pietermaritzburg: ^{a*}Natal. ^{b}none. ^{c}Umsindusi R. ^{d}University of Natal (at Durban and Pietermaritzburg) (1909) 11 – 3077 [Pietermaritzburg campus: (1909) ? – ?]. ^{e}Natal Provincial Library Service (1952) 1672; Natal Society Library (1851) 355; Pietermaritzburg Campus Library of the University . . . (1912) 250.

Port Elizabeth: ^{a}Cape of Good Hope. ^{b}none. ^{c}Algoa B of Indian O. ^{d}University of Port Elizabeth (1964) 11 – 395. ^{e}City Library (1848) 426; University . . . Library (1965) 285.

*Pretoria: ^{a*}Transvaal ^{b}none. ^{c}Apies R. ^{d}University of Pretoria (1908) 17 – 1299. ^{e}Transvaal Provincial Library Service (1943) 4359; University of South Africa Library (1947) 990; State Library (1887) 890; Public Library (1964) 802; University of Pretoria Library (1908) 700.

Soweto: ^{a}Transvaal. ^{b}none. ^{c}none. ^{d}none.

Stellenbosch: ^{a}Cape of Good Hope. ^{b}none. ^{c}Eerste R. ^{d}University of Stellenbosch (1918) 12 – 774. ^{e}University . . . Library (1900) 643; Public Library (1940) 35.

Tembisa: ^{a}Transvaal. ^{b}none. ^{c}none. ^{d}none.

Umlazi: ^{a}Natal. ^{b}none. ^{c}Umlazi R. ^{d}none.

Vereeniging: ^{a}Transvaal. ^{b}none. ^{c}Vaal R. ^{d}none. ^{e}Public Library (1912) 90.

For an explanation of symbols and abbreviations, see pages 16–17.

(Continued)

TABLE 2b. (Continued)

Sudan

Juba: [b]none. [c]Jabal (alt Mountain Nile) R. [d]University of Juba (1975) 0.6 – 130.

*Khartoum: [b]off Khurtum. [c]Nile R; Blue Nile R. [d]Cairo University, Khartoum Branch (1955) 20 – 120; University of Khartoum (1902) 14 – 675. [e]University . . . Library (1924) 350.

Khartoum North: [b]off Khurtum Bahri. [c]Blue Nile R. [d]none. [e]Shambat Library of the University of Khartoum (1938) 60.

Omdurman: [b]off Umm Durman. [c]Nile R; Blue Nile R. [d]Islamic University of Omdurman (1912) 2 – 192. [e] . . . University Library (1912) 90; Central Public Library (1951) 18.

Port Sudan: [b]off Bur Sudan. [c]Red Sea. [d]none. [e]Public Library (?) 2.

Wad Madani: [b]alt Wad Medani. [c]Blue Nile R. [d]University of Gezira (1975) 0.8 – 148. [e]British Council Library (1960) 8; University . . . Library (1975?) 7; Municipal Council Library (1946) 6.

Swaziland

*Mbabane: [b]none. [c]Mbabane R. [d]none. [e]Swaziland College of Technology Library (1968?) 10.

Tanzania

*Dar es Salaam: [a]*Tanganyika. [b]none. [c]Indian O. [d]University of Dar es Salaam (1961) 4 – 884. [e]Tanzania Library Service (1963) 1000; University . . . Library (1961) 350.

Dodoma: [a]Tanganyika. [b]none. [c]none. [d]none. [e]Geology and Mines Division Library (1923) 6.

Mwanza: [a]Tanganyika. [b]none. [c]Victoria L. [d]none. [e]Public Library (?) 27.

Zanzibar: [a]*Zanzibar; Zanzibar I. [b]alt Unguja. [c]Zanzibar Channel. [d]none. [e]Government Museum Library (1934) 5.

Togo

*Lome: [b]none. [c]Bight of Benin of G of Guinea. [d]Universite du Benin (1962) 4 – 398. [e]Bibliotheque Universitaire (1970) 50; Bibliotheque du Centre Culturel Francais (1962) 20; Bibliotheque Nationale (1960) 15.

Tunisia

Sfax: [b]off Safaqis. [c]Mediterranean Sea. [d]none. [e]Bibliotheque Publique (?) ?

Sousse: [b]off Susah. [c]G of Hammamet of Mediterranean Sea. [d]none. [e]Bibliotheque Publique (?)?

*Tunis: [b]none. [c]Tunis Lagoon. [d]Universite de Tunis (1945) 30 – 5557. [e]Bibliotheque Nationale (1883) 800; Bibliotheque Universitaire (1962) 210; Bibliotheque Centrale (1852) 150.

Uganda

*Kampala: [b]none. [c]nr Victoria L. [d]Makerere University (1922) 5 – 512. [e] . . . University Library (1922) 400; Public Library Board (1964) 110.

Western Sahara

*Aaiun: [b]alt Aiun. [c](Saguia el) Hamra R. [d]none.

Zaire

Bukavu: [b]for Costermansville. [c]Kivu L. [d]none. [e]Bibliotheque de l'Institut pour la Recherche Scientifique en Afrique Centrale (1953) 145; Bibliotheque Publique (?) 16.

Kananga: [b]for Luluabourg. [c]Lulua R. [d]none. [e]Bibliotheque Publique (1896) 19.

Kikwit: [b]none. [c]Kwilu R. [d]none. [e]Bibliotheque Publique (?) 20.

*Kinshasa: [b]for Leopoldville. [c]Congo R. [d]Universite de Kinshasa (1925) 6 – 536. [e]Bibliotheque Nationale (1949) 1200; Bibliotheque de l'Universite . . . (1953) 367; Bibliotheque Publique (1932) 24.

Kisangani: [b]for Stanleyville. [c]Congo R; Tshope R. [d]Universite de Kisangani (1963) 1 – 216. [e]Bibliotheque de l'Universite . . . (1963) 58; Bibliotheque Publique (1930) 25.

Likasi: [b]for Jadotville. [c]Likasi R. [d]none.

Lubumbashi: [b]for Elisabethville. [c]Lubumbashi R. [d]Universite de Lubumbashi (1955) 4 – 403. [e]Bibliotheque de l'Universite . . . (1956) 115; Bibliotheque Publique (?) 35.

Matadi: [b]none. [c]Congo R. [d]none. [e]Bibliotheque Publique (?) 14.

Mbuji-Mayi: [b]for Bakwanga. [c]Bushimaie R. [d]none. [e]Bibliotheque de l'Institut Superieur Pedagogique (1968) 7; Bibliotheque Publique (?) 2.

TABLE 2b. (Continued)

Zambia

Kitwe: *b*none. *c*nr Kafue R. *d*none. *e*Hammarskjold Memorial Library (1963) 35; Public Library (1954) 33; Zambia Institute of Technology Library (1972) 22.

*Lusaka: *b*none. *c*none. *d*University of Zambia (1965) 4 – 526. *e*Zambia Library Service (1962) 500; University . . . Library (1965) 327; City Library (1943) 145.

Ndola: *b*none. *c*none. *d*none. *e*Public Library (1934) 72.

Zimbabwe

Bulawayo: *b*none. *c*Matsheumhlope R. *d*none. *e*Public Library (1896) 85; National Free Library of Zimbabwe (1944) 84.

*Harare: *b*for Salisbury. *c*Makabusi R. *d*University of Zimbabwe (1953) 5 – 392. *e*University . . . Library (1956) 360; Library of Parliament (1899) 110; City Library (1902) 100.

ASIA

Afghanistan

Herat: *b*none. *c*Hari (Rud) R. *d*none.

*Kabul: *b*for Cabul. *c*Kabul (for Cabul) R. *d*Kabul University (1931) 6 – 569. *e* . . . University Library (1931) 120; Public Library (1920) 65.

Kandahar: *b*alt Qandahar. *c*Arghandab R. *d*none.

Bahrain

*Manama: *a*Bahrain I. *b*off Manamah. *c*Persian G. *d*none. *e*Central Library (1946) 127; University College of Arts, Science, and Education Library (1978?) 60.

Bangladesh

Chittagong: *b*for Islamabad, Porto Grande. *c*Karnaphuli R. *d*University of Chittagong (1966) 37 – 434. *e*University . . . Library (1869) 122; Public Library (1904) 40.

*Dhaka: *b*alt Dacca; for Jahangirnagar. *c*Burhi Ganga R (Brahmaputra R distributary). *d*University of Dhaka (1910) 84 – 950; Bangladesh University of Engineering and Technology (1961) 3 – 275; Jahangirnagar University (1970) 2 – 153. *e*Central Public Library (1958) 1000; University . . . Library (1921) 440.

Khulna: *b*none. *c*Bhairab R (Ganges R distributary). *d*none. *e*Public Library (1964) 33.

Mymensingh: *b*for Nasirabad. *c*Brahmaputra R. *d*none. *e*Bangladesh Agricultural University Library (1961) 115; Muslim Institute Public Lbrary (1931) 8.

Narayanganj: *b*none. *c*Dhaleswari R (Brahmaputra R distributary); Lakhya R (Brahmaputra R distributary). *d*none. *e*Rahmatullah Muslim Institute Library (?) 4; Municipal Public Library (?) ?

Rajshahi: *b*for Rampur Boalia. *c*Padma R. *d*University of Rajshahi (1953) 12 – 369. *e*University . . . Library (1955) 206; Public Library (1884) 13.

Sylhet: *b*none. *c*Surma R. *d*none. *e*Central Sahitya Sangsad Library (1941) 24.

Bhutan

*Thimphu: *b*alt Thimbu; off Tashi Chho (Dzong). *c*Wong R. *d*none.

Brunei

*Bandar Seri Begawan: *a*Borneo I. *b*for Borneo, Brunei, Brunei Town. *c*Brunei (for Borneo) R. *d*none. *e*Language and Literature Bureau Library (1967) 75.

Burma

Bassein: *b*off Puthein. *c*Bassein (off Puthein) R. *d*none. *e*Bassein College Library (1964) 19; State Library (1963) 1.

Kanbe: *b*none. *c*nr Rangoon (off Yangon) R. *d*none.

Mandalay: *b*off Mandale. *c*Irrawaddy R. *d*University of Mandalay (1923) 7 – 430. *e*University . . . Library (1958) 144; State Library (1955) 7.

Moulmein: *b*off Mawlamyaing. *c*G of Martaban of Andaman Sea; Salween R; Ataran R; Gyaing R. *d*none. *e*Moulmein College Library (1964) 43; State Library (1955) 13.

For an explanation of symbols and abbreviations, see pages 16–17.

(Continued)

TABLE 2b. (Continued)

Pegu: [b]none. [c]Pegu R. [d]none. [e]Thahaya Yuwa Library (?) ? [f]150 (1600e).

*Rangoon: [b]off Yangon. [c]Rangoon (off Yangon) R; Pegu R; Myitmaka R. [d]University of Rangoon (1885) 12 – 560. [e]Universities' Central Library (1929) 250; Sarpay Beikman Public Library (1956) 74; National Library (1952) 49.

China

Anqing: [a]Anhui. [b]alt Anching; for Huaining. [c]Yangtze R. [d]none.

Anshan: [a]Liaoning. [b]for Shaho. [c]nr Taizi (alt Taitzu) R. [d]none. [e]City Library (1948) 860.

Anyang: [a]Henan. [b]alt Changte, Zhangde. [c]Anyang R. [d]none.

Baicheng: [a]Jilin. [b]alt Paicheng, Taoan; for Tsingan. [c]nr Taoer (alt Taoerh) R. [d]none.

Baoding: [a]Hebei. [b]alt Paoting; for Tsingyuan. [c]Fu R. [d]Hebei University (1960) ? – ? [e] . . . University Library (1921) 1150.

Baoji: [a]Shaanxi. [b]alt Paochi. [c]Wei R. [d]none.

Baotou: [a]Inner Mongolia (off Nei Monggol). [b]alt Paotou. [c]Huang R. [d]none.

Beian: [a]Heilongjiang. [b]alt Peian. [c]none. [d]none.

*Beijing: [a](independent city). [b]alt Peiching, Peking; for Peiping. [c]Bei (alt Pei) L; Zhong (alt Chung) L; Nan L. [d]Beijing University (1898) 12 – 2890; Qinghua (alt Tsinghua) University (1911) 11 – 3300; People's University of China (1950) 5 – 1307. [e]National Library of China (1910) 11,000; Central Library of the Chinese Academy of Sciences (1951) 5200; Beijing University Library (1902) 3500; Beijing Normal University Library (1917) 2100; Qinghua University Library (1911) 2000; Shondu Public Library (?) 1950; People's University of China Library (1950) 1830.

Bengbu: [a]Anhui. [b]alt Pangpu; for Pangfou. [c]Huai R. [d]none.

Benxi: [a]Liaoning. [b]alt Penhsi; for Penchihu. [c]Taizi (alt Taitzu) R. [d]none.

Cangzhou: [a]Hebei. [b]alt Tsangchou; for Tsanghsien. [c]Jiedijian (alt Chiehtichien) R. [d]none.

Changchun: [a,*]Jilin. [b]for Hsinking. [c]Yitong (alt Itung) R. [d]Jilin University (1946) 5 – 1427. [e]Jilin Provincial Library (1960) 2230; . . . University Library (1948) 1300; City Library (?) 1000.

Changde: [a]Hunan. [b]alt Changte. [c]Yuan R. [d]none.

Changsha: [a,*]Hunan. [b]none. [c]Xiang R. [d]Hunan University (1959) ? – ? [e]Hunan Provincial Library (1904) 2600; Hunan Teachers College Library (1953) 1090; . . . University Library (1926) 710.

Changshu: [a]Jiangsu. [b]none. [c]nr Yangtze R. [d]none.

Changzhi: [a]Shanxi. [b]alt Changchih; for Luan. [c]nr Zhuozhang (alt Chochang) R. [d]none.

Changzhou: [a]Jiangsu. [b]alt Changchou: for Wutsin. [c]nr He (alt Ho) L. [d]none. [e]City Library (1906) 557.

Chaozhou: [a]Guangdong. [b]alt Chaoan, Chaochou. [c]Han R. [d]none.

Chengde: [a]Hebei. [b]alt Chengte; for Jehol. [c]Wulie (alt Wulieh; for Je) R. [d]none.

Chengdu: [a,*]Sichuan. [b]alt Chengtu. [c]Min R. [d]Sichuan University (1931) 4 – ? [e]Sichuan Provincial Library (1912) 1775; Sichuan Normal College Library (1951) 890; City Library (?) 740; Chengdu University of Science and Technology Library (1954) 593; Sichuan University Library (1931) ?

Chifeng: [a]Inner Mongolia (off Nei Monggol). [b]alt Chihfeng. [c]Yingjin (alt Yingchin) R. [d]none.

Chongqing: [a]Sichuan. [b]alt Chungching, Chungking, Yuchou, Yuzhou; for Pahsien. [c]Yangtze R; Jialing R. [d]Chongqing University (1929) 6 – 1500; [e]City Library (1950) 2200; Southwest China Teachers College Library (1950) 855; . . . University Library (1930) 710.

Dalian: [a]Liaoning. [b]alt Talien; for Dairen, Dalny. [c]Korea B of Yellow Sea. [d]none. [e]City Library (1950) 1398; Dalian Institute of Technology Library (1949) 1200.

Dandong: [a]Liaoning. [b]alt Tantung; for Antung. [c]Yalu R. [d]none.

Daqing: [a]Heilongjiang. [b]alt Taching. [c]none. [d]none.

Datong: [a]Shanxi. [b]alt Tatung. [c]Yu R. [d]none.

Dongguan: [a]Guangdong. [b]alt Tunguan. [c]Dong (alt Tung, East) R. [d]none.

Dukou: [a]Sichuan. [b]alt Tukou. [c]Yangtze R: Yalong R. [d]none.

Dunhua: [a]Jilin. [b]alt Tunhua. [c]Mudan (alt Mutan) R. [d]none.

Ezhou: [a]Hubei. [b]alt Echou; for Echeng, Ocheng. [c]Yangtze R. [d]none.

Foshan: [a]Guangdong. [b]alt Fatshan: for Namhoi, Nanhai. [c]Fen R. [d]none.

Fushun: [a]Liaoning. [b]none. [c]Hun (alt Shen) R. [d]none.

Fuxin: [a]Liaoning. [b]alt Fuhsin. [c]Xi R. [d]none.

Fuzhou: [a,*]Fujian. [b]alt Foochow, Fuchou; for Minhou. [c]Min R. [d]Fuzhou University (?)? – ? [e]Fujian Provincial Library (1908) 1616; Fujian Teachers University Library (1951) 1250; Fuzhou University Library (?) ?

TABLE 2b. (Continued)

Ganzhou: [a]Jiangxi. [b]alt Kanchou; for Kanhsien. [c]Gan R; Gong (alt Kong) (Shui) R; Zhang (alt Chang) (Shui) R. [d]none.

Gejiu: [a]Yunnan. [b]alt Kochiu; for Kokiuchang. [c]nr Xiao (alt Hsiao) R. [d]none.

Guangzhou: [a*]Guangdong. [b]alt Canton, Kuangchou. [c]Zhu R. [d]Zhongshan (alt Sun Yat-Sen) University (1924) 6 – 1700. [e]Zhongshan Library of Guangdong Province (1910) 2600; . . . University Library (1924) 1355; South China Teachers College Library (1951) 1139.

Guilin: [a]Guangxi. [b]alt Kueilin. [c]Gui (alt Kuei) R. [d]none. [e]First Library of Guangxi Province (alt City Library) (1909) 812.

Guiyang: [a*]Guizhou. [b]alt Kueiyang; for Kueichu. [c]Nanming R; Niulu R. [d]Guizhou University (1958) ? – ? [e]Guizhou Provincial Library (1937) 1270: Guiyang Teachers College Library (1941) 716: People's Library of Guiyang (?) 250; . . . University Library (?)?

Haicheng: [a]Liaoning. [b]none. [c]Hun R tributary. [d]none.

Haikou: [a]Guangdong; Hainan I. [b]alt Hoihow. [c]Hainan Strait; Nandu (alt Nantu) R. [d]none.

Hailar: [a]Inner Mongolia (off Nei Monggol). [b]alt Hailaerh; for Hulun. [c]Argun R. [d]none.

Handan: [a]Hebei. [b]alt Hantan. [c]Fuyang R. [d]none.

Hangzhou: [a*]Zhejiang. [b]alt Hangchou, Hangchow. [c]Qiantang R; Xi (alt Hsi) L. [d]Zhejiang University (1897) 7 – 1700; Hangzhou University (1952) 5 – 2304. [e]Zhejiang Provincial Library (1872) 2250; Hangzhou University Library (1959) 1000; Zhejiang University Library (1928) 820.

Harbin: [a*]Heilongjiang. [b]alt Haerhpin; for Pinchiang. [c]Sungari R. [d]Heilongjiang Univsersity (?) ? – ? [e]Heilongjiang Provincial Library (1962) 1220; Harbin Normal University Library (1951) 824; City Library (1950) 780; Harbin Polytechnic University Library (1921) 700.

Hefei: [a*]Anhui. [b]alt Hofei: for Luchou. [c]Nanfei R. [d]Anhui University (1958) ? – ? [e]Anhui Provincial Library (1953) 1351;. . . University Library (1958) 800; University of Science and Technology of China Library (1958) 750.

Hegang: [a]Heilongjiang. [b]alt Hokang; for Haoli. [c]Alingta R. [d]none.

Hengyang: [a]Hunan. [b]for Hengchou. [c]Xiang R; Lei (Shui) R; Zheng (alt Cheng) (Shui) R. [d]none.

Hohhot: [a*]Inner Mongolia (off Nei Monggol). [b]alt Huhehot, Huhohaote, Kuku-Khoto; for Kweisui. [c]Dahei (alt Tahei) R. [d]Inner Mongolia University (1957) ? – ? [e]Inner Mongolia Regional Library (1950) 1150; Inner Mongolia Normal College Library (1952) 931; . . . University Library (1957)?

Huaibei: [a]Anhui. [b]alt Huaipei. [c]Sui R. [d]none.

Huainan: [a]Anhui. [b]for Tienchiaan. [c]Huai R. [d]none.

Huaiyin: [a]Jiangsu. [b]for Qingjiang, Chingchiang. [c]Yan (alt Yen) R; Xinhuai (alt Hsinhuai) R. [d]none.

Huangshi: [a]Hubei. [b]alt Huangshih, Huangshihchiang. [c]Yangtze R. [d]none.

Hunjiang: [a]Jilin. [b]alt Hunchiang. [c]Hun R. [d]none.

Huzhou: [a]Zhejiang. [b]alt Huchou, Wuxing, Wuhsing. [c]Dongtiao (alt Tungtiao) R. [d]none.

Jiamusi: [a]Heilongjiang. [b]alt Chiamussu, Kiamusze. [c]Sungari R. [d]none.

Jiaozuo: [a]Henan. [b]alt Chiaotso, Tsiaotso. [c]Yunliang R. [d]none.

Jiaxing: [a]Zhejiang. [b]alt Chiahsing, Kashing. [c]Dayun (alt Tayun) R. [d]none.

Jilin: [a]Jilin. [b]alt Chilin, Kirin; for Yungchi. [c]Sungari R. [d]none. [e]City Library (1909) 1219.

Jinan: [a*]Shandong. [b]alt Chinan, Tsinan; for Licheng. [c]Xiaoqing (alt Hsiaoching) R. Daming (alt Taming) L. [d]Shandong University (1926) ? – ? [e]Shandong Provincial Library (1908) 3200; . . . University Library (1922) 1000; Shandong Normal College Library (1949) 830; City Library (1953) 646.

Jingdezhen: [a]Jiangxi. [b]alt Chingtechen, Kingtehchen; for Fouliang. [c]Chang R. [d]none.

Jingmen: [a]Hubei. [b]alt Chingmen, Kingmen. [c]Han (Shui) R tributary. [d]none.

Jining: [a]Shandong. [b]alt Chining, Tsining. [c]Dayun (alt Tayun) R. [d]none.

Jinxi: [a]Liaoning. [b]alt Chinhsi; for Lienshan. [c]G of Liaodong (alt Liaotung) of Yellow Sea. [d]none.

Jinzhou: [a]Liaoning. [b]alt Chinchou. [c]Daling (alt Taling) R. [d]none.

Jiujiang: [a]Jiangxi. [b]alt Chiuchiang, Kiukiang. [c]Yangtze R. [d]none.

Jixi: [a]Heilongjiang. [b]alt Chihsi, Kisi. [c]Muleng R. [d]none.

Kaifeng: [a]Henan. [b]none. [c]nr Huang R. [d]none.

Kashi: [a]Xinjiang. [b]alt Kashgar, Koshih; for Shufu. [c]Kaxgar R. [d]none.

Kunming: [a*]Yunnan. [b]for Yunnan. [c]Dian L. [d]Yunnan University (1923)? – ? [e]Yunnan Provincial Library (1909) 1450; Kunming Teachers College Library (1946) 743; . . . University Library (1923) 709.

Lanzhou: [a*]Gansu. [b]alt Lanchou; for Kaolan. [c]Huang R. [d]Lanzhou University (1946) 2 – ? [e]Gansu Provincial Library (1916) 1857; . . . University Library (1946) 785; City Library (1957) 241.

For an explanation of symbols and abbreviations, see pages 16–17. (Continued)

TABLE 2b. (Continued)

Leshan: [a]Sichuan. [b]for Kiating, Chiating, Loshan. [c]Min R; Dadu (alt Tatu) R. [d]none.

Lhasa: [a]*Tibet (off Xizang). [b]alt Lasa. [c]Lhasa (alt Lasa) R. [d]none.

Lianyungang: [a]Jiangsu. [b]alt Lienyunkang; for Hsinhailien, Sinhailien. [c]Yellow Sea; Yan (alt Yen) R. [d]none.

Liaoyang: [a]Liaoning. [b]none. [c]Taizi (alt Taitzu) R. [d]none.

Liaoyuan: [a]Jilin. [b]alt Dongliao, Tungliao. [c]Dongliao (alt Tungliao) R. [d]none.

Liupanshui: [a]Guizhou. [b]for Shuicheng. [c]Wu R. [d]none.

Liuzhou: [a]Guangxi. [b]alt Liuchou; for Maping. [c] Liu R. [d]none.

Luoyang: [a]Henan. [b]alt Loyang; for Honan. [c]Luo (alt Lo) R. [d]none.

Luzhou: [a]Sichuan. [b]alt Luchou; for Luhsien. [c]Yangtze R; Tuo (alt To) R. [d]none.

Maanshan: [a]Anhui. [b]none. [c]Yangtze R. [d]none.

Mianyang: [a]Sichuan. [b]alt Mienyang; for Mienchou. [c]Fu R. [d]none.

Mudanjiang: [a]Heilongjiang. [b]alt Mutanchiang. [c]Mudan (alt Mutan) R. [d]none.

Nanchang: [a]*Jiangxi. [b]none. [c]Gan (alt Kan) R; Fu R. [d]Jiangxi University (1958) ? – ? [e]Jiangxi Provincial Library (1920) 1700; Jiangxi Normal College Library (1940) 836; . . . University Library (1958) 510.

Nanchong: [a]Sichuan. [b]alt Nanchung; for Shunching. [c]Jialing R. [d]none. [e]Nanchong Teachers College Library (1956) 523.

Nanjing: [a]*Jiangsu. [b]alt Nanching, Nanking; for Chiangning. [c]Yangtze R; Qinhuai (alt Chinhuai) R. [d]Nanjing University (1902) ? – ? [e]Nanjing Library (1908) 5400; . . . University Library (1902) 1850.

Nanning: [a]*Guangxi. [b]for Yungning. [c]Yong (alt Yung) R. [d]Guangxi University (1958) ? – ? [e]Second Library of Guangxi Province (alt Guangxi Regional Library) (1953) 873.

Nantong: [a]Jiangsu. [b]alt Nantung; for Tungchou. [c]Yangtze R. [d]none.

Nanyang: [a]Henan. [b]none. [c]Bai (alt Pai) R. [d]none.

Neijiang: [a]Sichuan. [b]alt Neichiang. [c]Tuo (alt To) R. [d]none.

Ningbo: [a]Zhejiang. [b]alt Ningpo; for Ninghsien. [c]Yong (alt Yung) R; Fenghua R; Yuyao R. [d]none.

Panjin: [a]Liaoning. [b]alt Panchin; for Panshan, Shuangtaitzu. [c]Liao R. [d]none.

Pingdingshan: [a]Henan. [b]alt Pingtingshan. [c]Sha R. [d]none.

Pingxiang: [a]Jiangxi. [b]alt Pinghsiang. [c]Lu (Shui) R. [d]none.

Qingdao: [a]Shandong. [b]alt Chingtao, Tsingtao. [c]Yellow Sea. [d]none. [e]Qingdao Library (1949) 748; Shandong College of Oceanology Library (1959) 550.

Qinhuangdao: [a]Hebei. [b]alt Chinhuangtao. [c]G of Liaodong (alt Liaotung) of Yellow Sea. [d]none.

Qiqihar: [a]Heilongjiang. [b]alt Chichihaerh, Tsitsihar; for Lungchiang, Pukwei. [c]Nen R. [d]none.

Qufu: [a]Shandong. [b]alt Chufu. [c]Si (alt Ssu) R. [d]none. [e]Qufu Normal School Library (1955) 782.

Shache: [a]Xinjiang. [b]alt Yarkand, Yarkant; for Soche. [c]Yarkant R. [d]none.

Shanghai: [a](independent city). [b]none. [c]East China Sea; Yangtze R; Huangpu (alt Whangpoo) R; Wusong (alt Wusung) R. [d]Fudan University (1905) 7 – 2300; Jiaotong University (1896) 7 – ?; Tongji University (1908) 6 – ? [e]Shanghai Library (1952) 7000; Fudan University Library (1918) 1836; East China Normal University Library (1951) 1575; Jiaotong University Library (1896?) ? [f]48 (1730?).

Shantou: [a]Guangdong. [b]alt Swatow [c]South China Sea; Han R. [d]none.

Shaoguan: [a]Guangdong. [b]alt Shaokuan, Shiukwan; for Chuchiang, Kukong, Shaochou, Shiuchow. [c]Bei (alt Pei) R; Wu (Shui) R; Zhen (alt Chen) (Shui) R. [d]none.

Shaoxing: [a]Zhejiang. [b]alt Shaohsing. [c]nr Hangzhou (alt Hangchou) B of East China Sea. [d]none.

Shaoyang: [a]Hunan. [b]alt Baoqing, Paoching. [c]Fuyi (alt Fui) (Shui) R. [d]none.

Shashi: [a]Hubei. [b]alt Shashih. [c]Yangtze R. [d]none.

Shenyang: [a]*Liaoning. [b]alt Mukden; for Fengtien. [c]Hun R; Xinkai (alt Hsinkai) R. [d]Liaoning University (1958) ? – ? [e]Liaoning Provincial Library (1948) 2000; City Library (1908) 1460; . . . University Library (1958) 937.

Shenzhen: [a]Guangdong. [b]alt Shenchen; for Paoan, Shenchuan. [c]Zhu R. [d]none.

Shihezi: [a]Xinjiang. [b]alt Shihhotzu. [c]nr Manasi (alt Manassu) R. [d]none.

Shijiazhuang: [a]*Hebei. [b]alt Shihchiachuang; for Shihmen. [c]nr Hutuo (alt Huto) R. [d]none. [e]Hebei Normal University Library (1956) 661; City Library (1958) 637; Hebei Provincial Library (?) 180.

Shiyan: [a]Hubei. [b]alt Shihyen. [c]Han (Shui) R tributary. [d]none.

Shizuishan: [a]Ningxia. [b]alt Shihtsuishan. [c]Huang R. [d]none.

Shuangyashan: [a]Heilongjiang. [b]none. [c]none. [d]none.

Siping: [a]Jilin. [b]alt Ssuping, Szeping; for Ssupingchien, Szepingkai. [c]Diaozi (alt Tiaotzu) R. [d]none.

TABLE 2b. (Continued)

Suihua: [a]Heilongjiang. [b]alt Suihwa; for Peilintzu. [c]nr Hulan R. [d]none.

Suzhou: [a]Jiangsu. [b]alt Soochow, Suchou; for Wuhsien. [c]nr Yangcheng L; nr Dushu (alt Tushu) L. [d]none. [e]Jiangsu Teachers College Library (1952) 179.

Taian: [a]Shandong. [b]none. [c]Wen (Shui) R. [d]none. [e]Shandong Agricultural College Library (1949) 350.

Taiyuan: [a]*Shanxi. [b]for Yangchu. [c]Fen R. [d]Shanxi University (1902) ? – ? [e] Shanxi Provincial Library (1918) 1067; . . . University Library (1902) 910; Taiyuan Polytechnic College Library (1953) 900.

Tangshan: [a]Hebei. [b]none. [c]Dong (alt Tung) R. [d]none.

Tianjin: [a](independent city). [b]alt Tienching, Tientsin. [c]Hai R; Jinzhong (alt Chinchung) R; Xinkai (alt Hsinkai) R; Ziya (alt Tzuya) R; Weijing (alt Weiching) R; Yun R. [d]Tianjin University (1895) 8 – 2500; Nankai University (1914) 6 – 1617 [e]Peoples Library of Tianjin (1907) 2500; Nankai University Library (1919) 1500; Tianjin University Library (1952) 963.

Tianshui: [a]Gansu. [b]alt Tienshui; for Tsinchou. [c]Wei R. [d]none.

Tieling: [a]Liaoning. [b]alt Tiehling. [c]Liao R. [d]none.

Tongchuan: [a]Shaanxi. [b]alt Tungchuan. [c]Huang R. [d]none.

Tonghua: [a]Jilin. [b]alt Kuaidamao, Kuaitamao, Tunghua. [c]nr Hun R. [d]none.

Tongliao: [a]Inner Mongolia (off Nei Monggol). [b]alt Tungliao. [c]Xiliao (alt Hsiliao) R. [d]none.

Urumqi: [a]*Xinjiang. [b]alt Urumchi, Urumtsi, Wulumuchi, Wulumuqi; for Tihua. [c]Wulumuqi (alt Wulumuchi) R. [d]Xinjiang University (1960) 2 – ? [e] . . . University Library (1944) 731; Xinjiang Regional Library (1946) 547.

Wafangdian: [a]Liaoning. [b]alt Wafangtien; for Fuxian, Fuhsien. [c]nr Fuzhou (alt Fuchou) R. [d]none.

Weifang: [a]Shandong. [b]for Weihsien. [c]Bailang (alt Pailang) R. [d]none.

Wenzhou: [a]Zhejiang. [b]alt Wenchou; for Yungchia. [c]Ou R. [d]none.

Wuhai: [a]Inner Mongolia (off Nei Monggol). [b]for Haipowan. [c]Huang R. [d]none.

Wuhan: [a]*Hubei. [b]inc Hankou, Hanyang, Wuchang. [c]Yangtze R; Han (Shui) R; Dong (alt Tung) L. [d]Wuhan University (1913) 6 – 1800. [e]Hubei Provincial Library (1904) 2200; . . . University Library (1917) 1438; Wuhan Library (1953) 1400; Central China Teachers College Library (1951) 1253; Central China University of Science and Technology Library (1953) 1180. [f]Hankou: 850 (1900?e), 690 (1850e); Hanyang: 100 (1900?e), 100 (1850e); Wuchang: 550 (1900?e), 206 (1850e).

Wuhu: [a]Anhui. [b]none. [c]Yangtze R; Qingyi (alt Chingi) R; Suiyang R. [d]none. [e]Anhui Normal University Library (?) 1500.

Wuxi: [a]Jiangsu. [b]alt Wuhsi. [c]nr Tai L. [d]none.

Wuzhou: [a]Guangxi. [b]alt Wuchou; for Tsangwu. [c]Xi R; Gui (alt Kuei) R. [d]none.

Xiamen: [a]Fujian. [b]alt Amoy, Hsiamen; for Ssuming, Szeming. [c]Formosa (alt Taiwan) Strait; Jiulong (alt Chiulung, Kiulung) R. [d]Xiamen University (1921) 4 – 1243. [e] . . . University Library (1921) 1368; City Library (?) 680.

Xian: [a]*Shaanxi. [b]alt Hsian, Sian; for Changan, Siking, Singan. [c]nr Wei R. [d]Xian Jiaotong University (1884) 8 – 1630; Northwestern University (1937) 3 – 900. [e]Shaanxi Provincial Library (1909) 1830; Shaanxi Normal University Library (1953) 1275; Northwestern University Library (1937) 1004; Xian Jiaotong University Library (1896) 1000.

Xiangfan: [a]Hubei. [b]alt Hsiangfan; inc Fancheng, Hsiangyang. [c]Han (Shui) R. [d]none. [f]Fancheng: 100 (1900?e); Hsiangyang: 40 (1900?e).

Xiangtan: [a]Hunan. [b]alt Hsiangtan, Siangtan. [c]Xiang R. [d]Xiangtan University (1974) ? – ? [e] . . . University Library (1974) 558.

Xianyang: [a]Shaanxi. [b]alt Hsienyang. [c]Wei R. [d]none.

Xingtai: [a]Hebei. [b]alt Hsingtai; for Shunteh. [c]Ziwa (alt Tzuya) R. [d]none.

Xining: [a]*Qinghai. [b]alt Hsining, Sining. [c]Huang (Shui) R. [d]none. [e]Qinghai Provincial Library (1935) 1250.

Xinxiang: [a]Henan. [b]alt Hsinhsiang, Sinsiang. [c]Wei R. [d]none.

Xuzhou: [a]Jiangsu. [b]alt Hsuchou, Suchow, Tongshan, Tungshan. [c]nr Weishan L. [d]none.

Yakeshi: [a]Inner Mongolia (off Nei Monggol). [b]alt Yakoshi. [c]Liduer (alt Lituerh) R. [d]none.

Yanan: [a]Shaanxi. [b]alt Yenan; for Fushih. [c]Yan (alt Yen) R. [d]none.

Yancheng: [a]Jiangsu. [b]alt Yencheng. [c]Chuanchang R; Xinyang (alt Hsinyang) R. [d]none.

Yangquan: [a]Shanxi. [b]alt Yangchuan. [c]Mian (alt Mien) (Shui) R. [d]none.

Yangzhou: [a]Jiangsu. [b]alt Yangchou; for Chiangtu. [c]nr Yangtze R. [d]none.

Yantai: [a]Shandong. [b]alt Chefoo, Yentai. [c]G of Chihli (alt Bo G, Po G) of Yellow Sea. [d]none.

Yibin: [a]Sichuan. [b]alt Ipin; for Hsuchou, Suifu. [c]Yangtze R; Min R. [d]none.

For an explanation of symbols and abbreviations, see pages 16–17.

(Continued)

TABLE 2b. (Continued)

Yichang: [a]Hubei. [b]alt Ichang. [c]Yangtze R. [d]none.

Yichun: [a]Heilongjiang. [b]alt Ichun. [c]Tangwang R. [d]none.

Yinchuan: [a]*Ningxia. [b]for Ningxia, Ningsia. [c]nr Huang R. [d]Ningxia University (1962) 1 – ? [e]Ningxia Regional Library (1958) 1100; . . . University Library (1962) ?

Yingkou: [a]Liaoning. [b]for Yingtze. [c]G of Liaodong (alt Liaotung) of Yellow Sea; Liao R. [d]none.

Yueyang: [a]Hunan. [b]alt Yuehyang; for Yochow, Yoyang, Yuehchou. [c]Dongting L. [d]none.

Zaozhuang: [a]Shandong. [b]alt Tsaochuang. [c]none. [d]none.

Zhangjiakou: [a]Hebei. [b]alt Changchiakou, Kalgan; for Wanchuan. [c]Qingshui (alt Chingshui) R. [d]none.

Zhangzhou: [a]Fujian. [b]alt Changchou; for Lungchi. [c]Jiulong (alt Chiulung) R. [d]none.

Zhanjiang: [a]Guangdong. [b]alt Chanchiang, Tsamkong; for Fort-Bayard, Siying. [c] Zhanjiang (alt Chanchiang) B of South China Sea. [d]none.

Zhengzhou: [a]*Henan. [b]alt Chengchou; for Chenghsien. [c]Jialu (alt Chialu, Kialu) R. [d]Zhengzhou University (1956) ? – ? [e]Henan Provincial Library (1909) 1530; . . . University Library (1956) 735.

Zhenjiang: [a]Jiangsu. [b]alt Chenchiang, Chinkiang. [c]Yangtze R. [d]none.

Zhongshan: [a]Guangdong. [b]alt Chungshan; for Shihchichen, Shiqizhen. [c]Zhu R. [d]none.

Zhuzhou: [a]Hunan. [b]alt Chuchou. [c]Xiang R. [d]none.

Zibo: [a]Shandong. [b]alt Changtien, Tzepo, Tzupo, Zhangdian. [c]Chenghuang R. [d]none.

Zigong: [a]Sichuan. [b]alt Tzekung, Tzukung. [c]Qing (alt Ching) R. [d]none.

Zunyi: [a]Guizhou. b alt Nanbai, Nanpai, Tsuni. [c]Zunyi (alt Tsuni) R. [d]none.

Cyprus

*Nicosia: [b]off Levkosia. [c]Pedias R. [d]none. [e]Library of Phaneromeni (1934) 45; Pan-Cyprian Gymnasium Library (1927) 35.

Gaza Strip

*Gaza: [b]alt Azzah; off Ghazzah. [c]Mediterranean Sea. [d]none.

Hong Kong

*Hong Kong: [b]alt Xiangjiang, Hsiangchiang, Hsiangkang; inc Kowloon, New Kowloon, Victoria. [c]South China Sea; Zhu R. [d]University of Hong Kong (1887) 8 – 664; Chinese University of Hong Kong (1949) 7 – 900. [e]Urban Council Public Library (1962) 1200; . . . University Library (1949) 831; University . . . Library (1912) 740. [f]Kowloon: 799 (1981), 716 (1971), 725 (1961), 232 (1931); New Kowloon: 1651 (1981). 1479 (1971), 853 (1961), 23 (1931); Victoria: 1184 (1981), 996 (1971), 1005 (1961), 411 (1931).

India

Agartala: [a]*Tripura. [b]none. [c]Haora R. [d]none.

Agra: [a]Uttar Pradesh. [b]none. [c]Yamuna R. [d]Agra University (1927) 44 – ? [e] . . . University Library (1927) 190; District Central Library (1957) 9.

Ahmadabad: [a]Gujarat. [b]alt Ahmedabad; for Asawal. [c]Sabarmati R. [d]Gujarat University (1949) 94 – ? [e]Gujarat Vidyapith Library (1920) 335; Gujarat University Library (1949) 277; Gujarat State Central Library (1933) 178.

Ahmadnagar: [a]Maharashtra. [b]none. [c]Sina R. [d]none. [e]Mahatma Phule Agricultural University Library (1967?) 52.

Aizawl: [a]*Mizoram. [b]for Aijal. [c]nr Dhaleswari R; nr Tuirial R. [d]none.

Ajmer: [a]Rajasthan. [b]none. [c]Ana L. [d]none. [e]Municipal Public Library (1899) 35.

Akola: [a]Maharashtra. [b]none. [c]Murna R. [d]none. [e]Punjabrao Agricultural University Library (1969) 96.

Aligarh: [a]Uttar Pradesh. [b]none. [c]none. [d]Aligarh Muslim University (1875) 11 – 880. [e] . . . University Library (1921) 579; Lytton Library (1880) ?

Allahabad: [a]Uttar Pradesh. [b]none. [c]Ganges R; Yamuna R. [d]University of Allahabad (1887) 31 – ? [e]University . . . Library (1900) 523; Public Library (1864) 66.

Ambala: [a]Haryana. [b]for Umballa. [c]nr Ghaggar R. [d]none. [e]D. A. V. College Library (1886) 24; S. A. Jain College Library (?) 14.

Amravati: [a]Maharashtra. [b]alt Amraoti. [c]nr Pedhi R. [d]Amravati University (1983) 12 – ? [e]District Central Library (1923) 40; . . . University Library (1983?) ?

Amritsar: [a]Punjab. [b]none. [c]none. [d]Guru Nanak Dev University (1969) 59 – 2712. [e] . . . University Library (1969) 224; Municipal Public Library (1900) 42.

TABLE 2b. (Continued)

Asansol: [a]West Bengal. [b]none. [c]nr Damodar R; nr Barakar R. [d]none. [e]Burdwan District Library (1959) 5.

Aurangabad: [a]Maharashtra. [b]none. [c]Kaum R. [d]Marathwada University (1958) 36 – 2751. [e] . . . University Library (1958) 247.

Bangalore: [a*]Karnataka. [b]none. [c]nr Pinikini R. [d]Bangalore University (1858) 75 – 4415. [e]Indian Institute of Science Library (1909) 262; . . . University Library (1865) 238; Karnataka State Central Library (1914) 140.

Bareilly: [a]Uttar Pradesh. [b]for Bareli. [c]Jooah R; Sunkra R. [d]Rohilkhand University (1975) 31 – 902. [e] . . . University Library (1837) 33; District Central Library (1957) 7.

Belgaum: [a]Karnataka. [b]none. [c]Markandeya R. [d]none. [e]General Library (1848) ?

Bellary: [a]Karnataka. [b]none. [c]nr Hagari R. [d]none.

Bhagalpur: [a]Bihar. [b]for Boglipore, Sujanganj. [c]Ganges R. [d]Bhagalpur University (1887) 57 – 900. [e] . . . University Library (1960) 88.

Bhatpara: [a]West Bengal. [b]none. [c]Hooghly R (Ganges R distributary). [d]none. [e]Bhatpara Literary Association Library (?) ?

Bhavnagar: [a]Gujarat. [b]alt Bhaunagar. [c]G of Cambay of Arabian Sea. [d]Bhavnagar University (1978) 5 – 200. [e] . . . University Library (1978?) 48; District Central Library (1959) 30.

Bhilainagar-Durg: [a]Madhya Pradesh. [b]inc Bhilainagar (for Bhilai), Durg (for Drug). [c]nr Seonath R. [d]none. [f]Bhilainagar: 290 (1981), 157 (1971), 86 (1961); Durg: 115 (1981), 68 (1971), 47 (1961), 20 (1951), 13 (1931), 4 (1901), 4 (1881).

Bhopal: [a*]Madhya Pradesh. [b]none. [c]Bess R; Patra R; Pukhta-Pul Talao L. [d]Bhopal University (1946) 40 – 782. [e] . . . University Library (1970) 356; Maulana Azad Central Library (?) 60.

Bhubaneswar: [a*]Orissa. [b]none. [c]Kuakhai R. [d]Utkal University (1943) 102 – 3000. [e]Utkal University Library (1943) 189; Orissa University of Agriculture and Technology Library (1962) 102.

Bikaner: [a]Rajasthan. [b]none. [c]none. [d]none. [e]Rajasthan State Divisional Library (1937) 43.

Bilaspur: [a]Madhya Pradesh. [b]none. [c]Arpa R. [d]Guru Ghasidas University (1983) 35 – ? [e] . . . University Library (1983?) ?

Bokaro Steel City: [a]Bihar. [b]none. [c]Bokaro R. [d]none.

Bombay: [a*]Maharashtra. [b]none. [c]Arabian Sea. [d]University of Bombay (1832) 125 – ?; Shreemati Nathibai Damodar Thackersey Women's University (1916) 16 – 1004; Indian Institute of Technology, Bombay (univ) (1958) 3 – 399. [e]University . . . Library (1869) 517; . . . Institute Library (1958) 302; Asiatic Society of Bombay Library (1804) 205.

Brahmapur: [a]Orissa. [b]for Berhampur. [c]nr B of Bengal. [d]Brahmapur University (1967) 22 – 1490. [e] . . . University Library (1967?) 29.

Burdwan: [a]West Bengal. [b]alt Barddhaman. [c]Banka R. [d]University of Burdwan (1960) 64 – 2587. [e]University . . . Library (1960) 145.

Calcutta: [a*]West Bengal. [b]none. [c]Hooghly R (Ganges R distributary). [d]University of Calcutta (1817) 141 – ?; Jadavpur University (1906) 6 – 500; Rabindra Bharati University (1962) 5 – 300. [e]National Library (1836) 1800; University of Calcutta Library (1857) 577; Jadavpur University Library (1956) 350.

Calicut: [a]Kerala. [b]alt Kozhikode. [c]Arabian Sea; Kallayi R. [d]University of Calicut (1968) 111 – 4169. [e]University . . . Library (1968?) 53; City Library (?) ?

Chandigarh: [a*]Chandigarh; *Haryana; *Punjab. [b]none. [c]Ghaggar R. [d]Panjab University (1947 at Simla, relocated 1957) 87 – ? [e] . . . University Library (1947) 541; Central State Library (?) 65.

Cochin: [a]Kerala. [b]inc Ernakulam. [c]Arabian Sea; Vembanad Lagoon. [d]University of Cochin (1971) 0.9 – 125. [e]University . . . Library (1971) 136; Public Library (?) ? [f]Ernakulam: 62 (1951), 37 (1931), 22 (1901), 14 (1875).

Coimbatore: [a]Tamil Nadu. [b]none. [c]Noyil R. [d]Bharathiar University (1982) 11 – 1900. [e]Tamil Nadu Agricultural University Library (1876) 240; District Central Library (1952) 20.

Cuttack: [a]Orissa. [b]none. [c]Mahanadi R. [d]none. [e]Ravenshaw College Library (1919) 67.

Darbhanga: [a]Bihar. [b]none. [c]Little Baghmati R. [d]Lalit Narayan Mithila University (1938) 110 – 1251; Kameshwara Singh Darbhanga Sanskrit University (1961) 23 – ? [e]Lalit Narayan Mithila University Library (1972) 168; Kameshwara Singh Darbhanga Sanskrit University Library (1961) 90.

Darjiling: [a]West Bengal. [b]alt Darjeeling. [c]Great Rangit R. [d]University of North Bengal (1962) 25 – ? [e]University . . . Library (1962?) 84.

Davanagere: [a]Karnataka. [b]none. [c]nr Tungabhadra R. [d]none.

Dehra Dun: [a]Uttar Pradesh. [b]for Dehra. [c]Rispana R; Bindal R. [d]none. [e]Forest Research Institute Library (1906) 75; Mahatma Kushiram Public Library (1921)?

For an explanation of symbols and abbreviations, see pages 16–17.   (Continued)

TABLE 2b. (Continued)

Delhi: [a]*Delhi. [b]none. [c]Yamuna R. [d]University of Delhi (1881) 89 – ? [e]University . . . Library (1922) 972; Public Library (1951) 706.

Dhanbad: [a]Bihar. [b]none. [c]nr Damodar R. [d]none. [e]Indian School of Mines Library (1926) 60; District Central Library (1956) 11.

Dhule: [a]Maharashtra. [b]for Dhulia. [c]Panjhra R. [d]none.

Dibrugarh: [a]Assam. [b]none. [c]Brahmaputra R. [d]Dibrugarh University (1965) 65 – ? [e] . . . University Library (1965) 110.

Durgapur: [a]West Bengal. [b]none. [c]Damodar R. [d]none. [e]Central Mechanical Engineering Institute Library (1958) 26.

Erode: [a]Tamil Nadu. [b]none. [c]Kaveri R. [d]none.

Faizabad: [a]Uttar Pradesh. [b]for Fyzabad. [c]Ghaghara R. [d]Avadh University (1975) 21 – ? [e] . . . University Library (1975?)?

Faridabad: [a]Haryana. [b]none. [c]nr Yamuna R. [d]none.

Firozabad: [a]Uttar Pradesh. [b]none. [c]nr Yamuna R. [d]none.

Gandhinagar: [a]*Gujarat. [b]none. [c]Sabarmati R. [d]none.

Gangtok: [a]*Sikkim. [b]none. [c]Rongni R; Roro R. [d]none.

Garden Reach: [a]West Bengal. [b]none. [c]Hooghly R (Ganges R distributary). [d]none.

Gauhati: [a]*Assam. [b]none. [c]Brahmaputra R. [d]Gauhati University (1914) 115 – ? [e] . . . University Library (1948) 188; District Central Library (?) 39.

Gaya: [a]Bihar. [b]none. [c]Phalgu R. [d]Magadh University (at Bodh Gaya, nr Gaya) (1944) 63 – 3000. [e] . . . University Library (at Bodh Gaya) (1962?) 219; District Central Library (1855) 14; Mannulal Library (1911)?

Ghaziabad: [a]Uttar Pradesh. [b]none. [c]Hindan R. [d]none.

Gorakhpur: [a]Uttar Pradesh. [b]none. [c]Rapti R. [d]University of Gorakhpur (1933) 143 – ? [e]University . . . Library (1957) 223; District Central Library (1957) 9.

Gulbarga: [a]Karnataka. [b]none. [c]nr Benithora R. [d]Gulbarga University (1980) 22 – ? [e] . . . University Library (1980?) 42.

Guntur: [a]Andhra Pradesh. [b]for Guntoor. [c]none. [d]none. [e]District Central Library (1918) 31.

Gwalior: [a]Madhya Pradesh. [b]inc Lashkar since 1951. [c]Sonrekha (Nadi) Creek. [d]Jiwaji University (1887) 32 – ? [e]Government Central Library (1928) 77; . . . University Library (1964) 66. [f]Lashkar: 151 (1951), 79 (1931), 89 (1901), 88 (1881).

Haora: [a]West Bengal. [b]alt Howrah; inc Bally (alt Baly) since 1969. [c]Hooghly R (Ganges R distributary). [d]none. [e]Sibpur Public Library (?) 21; Bally Public Library (?) 20. [f]Bally: 63 (1951), 30 (1931), 19 (1901), 14 (1872).

Hubli-Dharwar: [a]Karnataka. [b]inc Dharwar, Hubli. [c]nr Bedti R. [d]Karnatak University (1917) 51 – 3506. [e] . . . University Library (1950) 282; City Central Library (1948) 50. [f]Dharwar: 66 (1951), 42 (1931), 31 (1901), 27 (1872); Hubli: 130 (1951), 90 (1931), 60 (1901), 38 (1872).

Hyderabad: [a]*Andhra Pradesh. [b]for Bhagnagar, Haidarabad; inc Secunderabad since 1951. [c]Musi R; Hussain L. [d]Osmania University (1887) 78 – ?; Jawaharlal Nehru Technological University (1946) 4 – 399; University of Hyderabad (1974) 0.7 – 100. [e]Osmania University Library (1918) 389; Andhra Pradesh State Central Library (1891) 248. [f]Secunderabad: 225 (1951), 121 (1931), 96 (1901).

Imphal: [a]*Manipur. [b]none. [c]Manipur R. [d]Manipur University (1980) 10 – 900. [e] . . . University Library (1980?) 28.

Indore: [a]Madhya Pradesh. [b]none. [c]Katki R. [d]Devi Ahilya University (1884) 24 – 932. [e] . . . University Library (1964) 101; General Library (1854) ?

Jabalpur: [a]Madhya Pradesh. [b]for Jubbulpore. [c]nr Narmada R. [d]Rani Durgavati University (1933) 38 – 950. [e]Rani Durgavati University Library (1957) 250; Jawaharlal Nehru Agricultural University Library (1966) 84; Government Central Library (1956) 45.

Jadabpur: [a]West Bengal. [b]none. [c]nr Hooghly R (Ganges R distributary). [d]none.

Jaipur: [a]*Rajasthan. [b]none. [c]nr Dhund (Nadi) Creek. [d]University of Rajasthan (1873) 134 – ? [e]University . . . Library (1947) 328; Public Library (1866) 90.

Jalandhar: [a]Punjab. [b]alt Jullundur. [c]nr East Bein (alt White Bein) R. [d]none. [e]District Central Library (1955) 20.

Jammu: [a]*Jammu and Kashmir. [b]none. [c]Tawi R. [d]University of Jammu (1969) 11 – 210. [e]University . . . Library (1969) 219; Shri Rambir Library (1879) ?

Jamnagar: [a]Gujarat. [b]for Navanagar. [c]G of Cutch of Arabian Sea. [d]Gujarat Ayurved University (1946) 1 – ? [e]District Central Library (1956) 34; . . . University Library (1966) 29.

Jamshedpur: [a]Bihar. [b]none. [c]Subarnarekha R. [d]none. [e]National Metallurgical Laboratory Library (1950) 32.

TABLE 2b. (Continued)

Jhansi: [a]Uttar Pradesh. [b]none. [c]nr Betwa R. [d]Bundelkhand University (1975) 49 – ? [e] . . . University Library (1975?) 9; District Central Library (1957) 7.

Jodhpur: [a]Rajasthan. [b]none. [c]nr Umed L. [d]University of Jodhpur (1892) 9 – 585. [e]University . . . Library (1962) 271; Sumer Public Library (1915) 38.

Kakinada: [a]Andhra Pradesh. [b]for Cocanada. [c]B of Bengal. [d]none.

Kamarhati: [a]West Bengal. [b]none. [c]Hooghly R (Ganges R distributary). [d]none.

Kanpur: [a]Uttar Pradesh. [b]for Cawnpore. [c]Ganges R. [d]Kanpur University (1955) 115 – ?; Indian Institute of Technology, Kanpur (univ) (1960) 2 – 285. [e] . . . Institute Library (1960?) 232; Government Agricultural Library (1904) 62; . . . University Library (1966) 40; District Central Library (1957) 7.

Kharagpur: [a]West Bengal. [b]none. [c]nr Kasai R. [d]Indian Institute of Technology, Kharagpur (univ) (1951) 3 – 462. [e] . . . Institute Library (1950) 234.

Kohima: [a]*Nagaland. [b]none. [c]nr Dzucharu R; nr Dzuna R; nr Dzuza R; nr Pheru R. [d]none.

Kolhapur: [a]Maharashtra. [b]none. [c]Panchaganga R. [d]Shivaji University (1962) 52 – 3122. [e] . . . University Library (1962) 172; District Central Library (1850) 37.

Kota: [a]Rajasthan, [b]alt Kotah. [c]Chambal R. [d]none. [e]Herbert College Library (?)?

Kurnool: [a]Andhra Pradesh. [b]none. [c]Tungabhadra R; Hindri R. [d]none.

Kurukshetra: [a]Haryana. [b]alt Thanesar. [c]Saraswati R. [d]Kurukshetra University (1956) 61 – 1949. [e] . . . University Library (1957) 204.

Lucknow: [a]*Uttar Pradesh. [b]none. [c]Gumti R. [d]University of Lucknow (1911) 33— 600. [e]University . . . Library (1921) 366; Uttar Pradesh Legislative Library (1931) 160; Uttar Pradesh State Central Library (1910) 75.

Ludhiana: [a]Punjab. [b]none. [c]none. [d]none. [e]Punjab Agricultural University Library (1962) 213; Panjab University Extension Library (1960) 109.

Madras: [a]*Tamil Nadu. [b]none. [c]B of Bengal; Cooum R; Adyar R. [d]University of Madras (1794) 203 – ?; Anna University (1978) 5 – 385; Indian Institute of Technology, Madras (univ) (1959) 2 – 345. [e]University . . . Library (1857) 428; Connemara Public Library (1896) 372; . . . Institute Library (1959) 209.

Madurai: [a]Tamil Nadu. [b]alt Madura. [c]Vaigai R. [d]Madurai-Kamaraj University (1958) 119 – ? [e] . . . University Library (1958) 170; District Central Library (1952) 14.

Malegaon: [a]Maharashtra. [b]none. [c]Girna R. [d]none.

Mangalore: [a]Karnataka. [b]none. [c]Arabian Sea; Netravati R; Gurpur R. [d]Mangalore University (1980) 33 – ? [e]South Kanara District Central Library (1950) 74; . . . University Library (1980?) 48.

Mathura: [a]Uttar Pradesh. [b]for Muttra. [c]Yamuna R. [d]none. [e]Uttar Pradesh College of Veterinary Science and Animal Husbandry Library (?) 10.

Medinipur: [a]West Bengal. [b]for Midnapore. [c]Kasai R. [d]Vidyasagar University (1981) ? – ?

Meerut: [a]Uttar Pradesh. [b]none. [c]nr Kali (Nadi) Creek. [d]Meerut University (1965) 59 – 1942. [e]Meerut College Library (1892) 85; . . . University Library (1966) 72; Tialk Library (1886) 30; District Central Library (1957) 7.

Moradabad: [a]Uttar Pradesh. [b]none. [c]Ramganga R. [d]none. [e]K. G. K. College Library (1940?) 19; Hindu College Library (1949) 9.

Muzaffarpur: [a]Bihar. [b]none. [c]nr Burhi Gandak R. [d]University of Bihar (1952) 70 – ? [e]University . . . Library (1952?) 91.

Mysore: [a]Karnataka. [b]none. [c]nr Kaveri R. [d]University of Mysore (1833) 55 – ? [e]University . . . Library (1916) 492; Oriental Research Institute Library (1891) 48; City Central Library (1915)?

Nagpur: [a]Maharashtra. [b]none. [c]Nag R; Chamar R. [d]Nagpur University (1923) 45 – 2738. [e] . . . University Library (1923) 317; District Central Library (1955) 71.

Nanded: [a]Maharashtra. [b]for Nander. [c]Godavari R. [d]none.

Nasik: [a]Maharashtra. [b]alt Nashik. [c]Godavari R. [d]none. [e]District Central Library (1840) 35; Hansraj Pragji Thackersey College Library (1924) 27.

Nellore: [a]Andhra Pradesh. [b]none. [c]Penner R. [d]none. [e]V. R. College Library (?) 15.

*New Delhi: [a]Delhi. [b]none. [c]Yamuna R. [d]Indian Institute of Technology, Delhi (univ) (1961) 3 – 410; Jawaharlal Nehru University (1969) 2 – 305. [e]Central Secretariat Library (1900) 700; Indian Agricultural Research Institute Library (1905) 300; . . . University Library (1969) 281; . . . Institute Library (1961?) 198.

Nizamabad: [a]Andhra Pradesh. [b]for Indur. [c]Phulong R; Borgaon R. [d]none.

Panaji: [a]*Goa, Daman, and Diu. [b]for Nova Goa, Panjim. [c]Mandovi R. [d]none.

Panihati: [a]West Bengal. [b]none. [c]Hooghly R (Ganges R distributary). [d]none.

Patiala: [a]Punjab. [b]none. [c]Patiala R. [d]Punjabi University (1962) 41 – ? [e] . . . University Library (1962) 217; Central State Library (1955) 68.

For an explanation of symbols and abbreviations, see pages 16–17.

(Continued)

TABLE 2b. (Continued)

Patna: [a]*Bihar. [b]none. [c]Ganges R. [d]Patna University (1863) 19 – 735. [e] . . . University Library (1917) 219; Bihar State Central Library (1924) 127.

Pimpri-Chinchwad: [a]Maharashtra. [b]none. [c]none. [d]none.

Pondicherry: [a]*Pondicherry. [b]for Pondichery. [c]B of Bengal. [d]none.

Pune: [a]Maharashtra. [b]alt Poona. [c]Mutha Mula R; Mutha R; Mula R. [d]University of Pune (1885) 95 – ? [e]University . . . Library (1949) 309; Gokhale Institute of Politics and Economics Library (1930) 207; District Central Library (1947) 80.

Puri: [a]Orissa. [b]none. [c]B of Bengal. [d]Jagannath Sanskrit University (1981) 5 – ? [e]Samanta Chandra Sekhar College Library (?) 18; . . . University Library (1981?) 2.

Raipur: [a]Madhya Pradesh. [b]none. [c]Karun R. [d]Ravishankar University (1948) 40 – ? [e] . . . University Library (1948) 62.

Rajahmundry: [a]Andhra Pradesh. [b]none. [c]Godavari R. [d]none. [e]Gauthami Library (1898) 48.

Rajkot: [a]Gujarat. [b]none. [c]Aji R. [d]Saurashtra University (1965) 33 – 1436. [e] . . . University Library (1967) 89; Sir Lakhajiraj Library (1868) 40; District Central Library (1956) 34.

Rampur: [a]Uttar Pradesh. [b]none. [c]Kosi R. [d]none.

Ranchi: [a]Bihar. [b]none. [c]Subarnarekha R. [d]Ranchi University (1899) 66 – 2000. [e]Birsa Agricultural University Library (1980?) 70; Ranchi University Library (1960) 61; District Central Library (1953) 13.

Raurkela: [a]Orissa. [b]for Rourkela. [c]nr Brahmani R. [d]none.

Rewa: [a]Madhya Pradesh. [b]none. [c]none. [d]Awadhesh Pratap Singh University (1968) 55 – ? [e] . . . University Library (1968) 128.

Rohtak: [a]Haryana. [b]for Rohtasgarh. [c]none. [d]Maharshi Dayanand University (1976) 37 – ? [e] . . . University Library (1976?) 129.

Roorkee: [a]Uttar Pradesh. [b]none. [c]Solani R. [d]University of Roorkee (1847) 3 – 500. [e]University . . . Library (1847) 204.

Sagar: [a]Madhya Pradesh. [b]for Saugor. [c]Hindi L. [d]Doctor Harisingh Gour University (1946) 33 – ? [e] . . . University Library (1946) 229.

Saharanpur: [a]Uttar Pradesh. [b]none. [c]Dhamola R. [d]none. [e]City Library (?)?

Salem: [a]Tamil Nadu. [b]none. [c]Tirumanimutar (alt Salem) R. [d]none. [e]District Central Library (1953) 10.

Sambalpur: [a]Orissa. [b]none. [c]Mahanadi R. [d]Sambalpur University (1967) 50 – 1537. [e] . . . University Library (1967) 61.

Sangli: [a]Maharashtra. [b]none. [c]Krishna R. [d]none.

Shahjahanpur: [a]Uttar Pradesh. [b]none. [c]Deoha (alt Garra) R. [d]none. [e]Gandhi Faizam College Library (?) 12.

Shillong: [a]*Meghalaya. [b]none. [c]Umkhrah R; Umshirpi R. [d]North-Eastern Hill University (1973) 25 – ? [e]Meghalaya State Central Library (?) 160; . . . University Library (1973?) 96.

Simla: [a]*Himachal Pradesh. [b]alt Shimla. [c]nr Sutlej R. [d]Himachal Pradesh University (1962) 25 – 228. [e] . . . University Library (1965) 107; Indian Institute of Advanced Study Library (1965) 70; Dwarka Dass Library (?) 30.

Solapur: [a]Maharashtra. [b]alt Sholapur. [c]nr Ekruk L. [d]none. [e]Dayanand College Library (1940?) 33; District Central Library (1857) 26.

South Dum Dum: [a]West Bengal. [b]none. [c]nr Hooghly R (Ganges R distributary). [d]none.

South Suburban: [a]West Bengal. [b]inc Behala. [c]nr Hooghly R (Ganges R distributary). [d]none. [e]Behala Library (?)?

Srinagar: [a]*Jammu and Kashmir. [b]for Cashmere. [c]Jhelum R. [d]University of Kashmir (1948) 12 – 842. [e]University . . . Library (1948) 254.

Surat: [a]Gujarat. [b]none. [c]Tapti R. [d]South Gujarat University (1965) 27 – 1000. [e] . . . University Library (1967) 96; District Central Library (1850) 15.

Thana: [a]Maharashtra. [b]alt Thane. [c]Thana (Nadi) Creek. [d]none.

Thanjavur: [a]Tamil Nadu. [b]for Tanjore. [c]Kaveri R. [d]Tamil University (1981) 0.04 – 35. [e] . . . University Library (1981?) 30.

Tiruchirapalli: [a]Tamil Nadu. [b]for Trichinopoly. [c]Kaveri R. [d]Bharathidasan University (1982) 37 – 3000. [e] . . . University Library (1982?) 22; District Central Library (1952) 7.

Tirunelveli: [a]Tamil Nadu. [b]for Tinnevelly. [c]Tambraparni R. [d]none. [e]District Central Library (1952) 23.

Tirupati: [a]Andhra Pradesh. [b]none. [c]nr Swarnamukhi R. [d]Sri Venkateswara University (1954) 51 – 3000. [e] . . . University Library (1930) 264.

Tiruppur: [a]Tamil Nadu. [b]none. [c]Noyil R. [d]none.

TABLE 2b. (Continued)

Trivandrum: [a]*Kerala. [b]none. [c]Arabian Sea. [d]University of Kerala (1937) 102 – ? [e]University . . . Library (1937) 382; Kerala State Central Library (1851) 185.

Tuticorin: [a]Tamil Nadu. [b]none. [c]G of Mannar of Indian O. [d]none.

Udaipur: [a]Rajasthan. [b]none. [c]Pichola L. [d]Mohan Lal Sukhadia University (1962) 14 – 498. [e] . . . University Library (1956) 320.

Ujjain: [a]Madhya Pradesh. [b]none. [c]Sipra R. [d]Vikram University (1896) 36 – ? [e] . . . University Library (1957) 99; Yuvraj General Library (1913) ?

Ulhasnagar-Kalyan: [a]Maharashtra. [b]inc Kalyan, Ulhasnagar. [c]Ulhas R. [d]none. [f]Kalyan: 136 (1981), 100 (1971), 59 (1951), 26 (1931), 11 (1901), 13 (1872); Ulhasnagar: 274 (1981), 168 (1971), 81 (1951).

Vadodara: [a]Gujarat. [b]for Baroda. [c]Vishvamitri R. [d]Maharaja Sayajirao University of Vadodara (1881) 24 – 1050. [e] . . . University Library (1950) 323; District Central Library (1910) 234.

Varanasi: [a]Uttar Pradesh. [b]alt Banaras; for Benares. [c]Ganges R. [d]Sampurnanand Sanskrit University (1958) 97 – ?; Banaras Hindu University (1898) 14 – 1483.; Kashi Vidyapith (1921) 5 – ? [e]Banaras Hindu University Library (1916) 668; Sampurnanand Sanskrit University Library (1958) 262; Carmichael Library (1872) 60; District Central Library (1957) 6.

Vellore: [a]Tamil Nadu. [b]none. [c]Palar R. [d]none. [e]Christian Medical College Library (1942?) 14.

Vijayawada: [a]Andhra Pradesh. [b]alt Vijayavada; for Bezwada. [c]Krishna R. [d]none. [e]Ram Mohan Free Library (1911) 31.

Visakhapatnam: [a]Andhra Pradesh. [b]Vishakhapatnam; for Vizagapatam. [c]B of Bengal. [d]Andhra University (at Waltair, nr Visakhapatnam) (1926) 69 – 800. [e] . . . University Library (at Waltair) (1926) 317.

Warangal: [a]Andhra Pradesh. [b]alt Hanamkonda. [c]none. [d]Kakatiya University (1976) 11 – ? [e] . . . University Library (1976?) 56; District Central Library (1958) 8.

Indonesia

Ambon: [a]Ambon I. [b]alt Amboina. [c]Ambon B of Banda Sea. [d]Pattimura University (1956) 5 – 234. [e]Province of the Mollucas Provincial Library (1956) 45; . . . University Library (1956?) 12.

Balikpapan: [a]Borneo I. [b]none. [c]Makassar Strait. [d]none.

Banda Aceh: [a]Sumatra I. [b]for Banda Atjeh, Kutaradja. [c]Achin R. [d]Syiah Kuala University (1959) 13 – 423. [e] . . . University Library (1959) ?; Public Library (?) ?

Bandung: [a]Java I. [b]for Bandoeng. [c](Ci)kapundung R. [d]Pajajaran University (1952) 12 – 1326; Bandung Institute of Technology (univ) (1920) 8 – 739; Parahyangan Catholic University (1955) 7 – 1160; Nusantara Islamic University (1959) 5 – 275. [e]West Java Provincial Public Library (1953) 200; . . . Institute Library (1920) 155; Pajajaran University Library (1957) 140; Parahyangan Catholic University Library (1955?) 90.

Banjarmasin: [a]Borneo I. [b]for Bandjermasin. [c]Barito R; Martapura R. [d]Lambung Mangkurat University (1958) 6 – 268. [e] . . . University Library (1960) ?; Public Library (?)?

Bogor: [a]Java I. [b]for Buitenzorg. [c](Ci)liwung R. [d]Bogor Pertanian Institute (univ) (1941) 6 – 700; Ibnu Chaldun University (1958) 0.8 – 80; Pakuan University (1958) 0.3 – 60. [e]Bibliotheca Bogoriensis (1842) 350; Bogor Agricultural University Library (1963) 75.

Cirebon: [a]Java I. [b]for Cheribon, Tjirebon. [c]Java Sea. [d]Indonesian Islamic University (?)? – ? [e] . . . University Library (?)?

Denpasar: [a]Bali I. [b]none. [c]Badung (for Badoeng) R. [d]Udayana University (1950) 3 – 570. [e] . . . University Library (1950?) 12.

Dili: [a]*East Timor; Timor I. [b]for Dilly. [c]Ombai Strait. [d]none.

*Jakarta: [a]Java I. [b]for Batavia, Djakarta. [c]Java Sea; (Ci)liwung R. [d1]Jayabaya University (1958) 15 – 782; University of Indonesia (1920) 13 – 2816; Trisakti University (1966) 10 – 1165; Indonesian Christian University (1953) 6 – 760. [e]National Library (1778) 600; Library of the Indonesian Parliament (1950) 200; University of Indonesia Library (1940) 150.

Jambi: [a]Sumatra I. [b]alt Telanaipura; for Djambi. [c]Hari (for Djambi) R. [d]Jambi University (1963) 3 – 250. [e] . . . University Library (1963) 16; Public Library (?)?

Jember: [a]Java I. [b]for Djember. [c]none. [d]Jember University (1957) 8 – 342. [e] . . . University Library (1957) 61.

Kediri: [a]Java I. [b]none. [c]Brantas R. [d]nore.

Kupang: [a]Timor I. [b]for Koepang. [c]Savu Sea. [d]Nusa Cendana University (1962) 1 – 230. [e] . . . University Library (1962?) 7; Public Library (?) ?

Malang: [a]Java I. [b]for Singasari. [c]Brantas R. [d]Brawijaya University (1957) 7 – 383; Merdeka University (1962)

---

[1]Universities with 5,000 or more students.

For an explanation of symbols and abbreviations, see pages 16–17.

(Continued)

TABLE 2b. (Continued)

0.8 – 180. [e]Malang Institute of Teacher Training and Education Library (1958) 87; Brawijaya University Library (1957?) ?

Manado: [a]Celebes I. [b]alt Menado. [c]Celebes Sea; Manado (alt Menado) R. [d]Sam Ratulangi University (1961) 3 – 946. [e] . . . University Library (1961?) 9; State General Research Public Library (1961) ?

Mataram: [a]Lombok I. [b]for Karangasem. [c]Jangkok R. [d]Mataram University (1963) 0.8 – 68. [e]Public Library (?) ?

Medan: [a]Sumatra I. [b]none. [c]Deli R. [d]University of North Sumatra (1952) 14 – 992; HKBP Nommensen University (1954) 8 – 300; North Sumatra Islamic University (1952) 5 – 543. [e]Sumatra Planters Association Research Institute Library (1918) 20; HKBP Nommensen University Library (1954?) ?; North Sumatra Islamic University Library (1952?) ?; Public Library (?) ?; University of North Sumatra Library (1952?) ?

Padang: [a]Sumatra I. [b]none. [c]Indian O; Padang R. [d]Andalas University (1956) 6 – 582. [e] . . . University Library (1956?) ?; Public Library (1959) ?

Pakanbaru: [a]Sumatra I. [b]alt Pekanbaru. [c]Siak R. [d]Riau University (1962) 5 – 575. [e] . . . University Library (1962?) ?

Palembang: [a]Sumatra I. [b]none. [c]Musi R. [d]Sriwijaya University (1953) 8 – 1157. [e] . . . University Library (1953?) 12; Public Library (?) ?

Palu: [a]Celebes I. [b]for Paloe. [c]Palu B of Makassar Strait; Palu R. [d]none.

Pontianak: [a]Borneo I. [b]none. [c]Kapuas-Kecil R (Kapuas R distributary); Landak R. [d]Tanjungpura University (1959) 4 – 656. [e] . . . University Library (1959?) ?

Purwokerto: [a]Java I. [b]for Poerwakerto. [c]none. [d]General Sudirman University (1963) 2 – 293. [e] . . . University Library (1963?) ?

Salatiga: [a]Java I. [b]none. [c]none. [d]Satya Wacana Christian University (1956) 3 – 143. [e] . . . University Library (1956?) 53.

Samarinda: [a]Borneo I. [b]none. [c]Mahakam R. [d]Mulawarman University (1962) 5 – 224. [e] . . . University Library (1962?) ?; Public Library (?) ?

Semarang: [a]Java I. [b]alt Samarang. [c]Java Sea; Semarang (alt Samarang) R. [d]Diponegoro University (1956) 12 – 1402; Sultan Agung Islamic University (1962) 0.9 – 260. [e]Public Library (?) 21; Diponegoro University Library (1960) 15.

Surabaya: [a]Java I. [b]for Soerabaja, Surabaja. [c]Surabaya Strait; Mas R. [d]Airlangga University (1954) 7 – 1038; Surabaya 10th of November Institute of Technology (univ) (1957) 6 – 360; Peter Christian University (1961) 2 – 226. [e] . . . Institute Library (1960) 50; Airlangga University Library (1954) 25; Public Library (1959)?

Surakarta: [a]Java I. [b]alt Solo; for Soerakarta. [c]Solo R; Pepe R. [d]Sebelas Maret University (1976) 12 – 765; Cokroaminoto University (1955) 4 – 100. [e]Sebelas Maret University Library (1976?) 84.

Tanjungkarang-Telukbetung: [a]Sumatra I. [b]alt Bandar Lampung; inc Tanjungkarang, Telukbetung; Tanjungkarang: for Tandjoengkarang; Telukbetung: for Teloekbetoeng. [c]Lampung B of Sunda Strait. [d]Lampung University (1961) 5 – 193. [e] . . . University Library (1961?) ?

Ujung Pandang: [a]Celebes I. [b]for Macassar, Makasar, Makassar. [c]Makassar Strait. [d]Hasanuddin University (1949) 8 – 688; Veteran University (1959) 2 – 220. [e]Hasanuddin University Library (1949) 72; Public Library (1969) 17.

Yogyakarta: [a]Java I. [b]for Djokjakarta, Jogjakarta. [c]Codeh (for Tjodeh) R. [d]Gajah Mada University (1949) 20 – 1483; Indonesian Islamic University (1945) 8 – 505. [e]Gajah Mada University Library (1947) 130; Islamic Library (1942) 74; Provincial State Library (1949) 65.

Iran

Abadan: [b]none. [c](Shatt al) Arab R. [d]none. [e]Abadan Institute of Technology Library (1939) 31.

Ahwaz: [b]alt Ahvaz. [c]Karun R. [d]Shahid Chamran University (1955) 5 – 415. [e] . . . University Library (1955) 76.

Arak: [b]for Sultanabad. [c]nr Namak-e Mighan (for Tuzlu) L. [d]none.

Ardabil: [b]for Erdebil. [c]none. [d]none.

Bakhtaran: [b]for Kermanshah. [c]nr Qareh (Su) [alt Qara (Chai)] R. [d]Razi University (1974) 2 – 115. [e]Public Library (bef 1969) ?

Bandar Abbas: [b]for Gombroon. [c]Strait of Hormuz. [d]none.

Hamadan: [b]none. [c]Qareh (Su) [alt Qara (Chai)] R. [d]Bou-Ali Sina University (1974) 0.1 – 80. [e] . . . University Library (1974?)?

Isfahan: [b]alt Ispahan; off Esfahan. [c]Zayandeh R. [d]University of Isfahan (1946) 10 – 480. [e]University . . . Library (1950) 180; Municipal Library (?) 31.

Karaj: [b]none. [c]Karaj R. [d]none. [e]Institute of Standards and Industrial Research Library (1971) 6; Razi Institute Library (?) 5.

TABLE 2b. (Continued)

Kerman: [b]alt Kirman. [c]none. [d]University of Kerman (1970) 2 – 113. [e]University . . . Library (1970?) 35.

Khorramabad: [b]alt Khurramabad. [c]Khorramabad (alt Khurramabad) R. [d]none.

Meshed: [b]off Mashhad. [c]nr Kashaf R. [d]Meshed University (1937) 6 – 450; Islamic Sciences University (1984) 2 – ? [e]Meshed University Library (1956) 200; Astaneh Qods Central Library (15th c) 120.

Orumiyeh: [b]for Rezaiyeh, Urmia. [c]nr Orumiyeh L. [d]none.

Qazvin: [b]alt Kazvin; for Casbin. [c]none. [d]none.

Qom: [b]alt Ghom, Qum; for Kum. [c]Qom (alt Ghom, Qum; for Kum) R. [d]none.

Rasht: [b]alt Resht. [c]Siah R. [d]Rasht University (1977) ? – ? [e] . . . University Library (1977?)?

Sanandaj: [b]for Sinneh. [c]none. [d]none.

Shiraz: [b]none. [c]Khoshk R. [d]University of Shiraz (1945) 5 – 520. [e]University . . . Library (1946) 205; Fars National Library (?) 12.

Tabriz: [b]none. [c]Talkheh (alt Aji) R. [d]University of Tabriz (1946) 6 – 494. [e]University . . . Library (1947) 240; Tarbiat Library (?) 20; Public Library (?) 13.

*Tehran: [b]alt Teheran. [c]none. [d]University of Tehran (1934) 21 – 1760; Shaheed Beheshty University (1960) 11 – 628; University of Science and Technology (1928) 5 – 285; University Complex of Engineering and Technology (1980) 3 – 78; Art University Complex (1980) 0.8 – 93. [e]University of Tehran Library (1932) 750; National Library (1935) 200; Parliament Library (1924) 120.

Yazd: [b]alt Yezd. [c]Mehriz R. [d]none.

Zahedan: [b]alt Zahidan; for Duzdab. [c]none. [d]University of Sistan and Baluchistan (1975) 0.7 – 45. [e]University . . . Library (1975?) ?

Zanjan: [b]alt Zenjan. [c]Zanjan (alt Zenjan) R. [d]none.

Iraq

*Baghdad: [b]alt Bagdad. [c]Tigris R. [d]University of Baghdad (1908) 19 – 1500; Al-Mustansiriyah University (1963) 11 – 328; University of Technology (1960) 7 – 429. [e]University of Baghdad Library (1952) 270; National Library (1920) 140; Al-Mustansiriyah University Library (1963) 120; Iraqi Museum Library (1934) 100; Iraqi Academy Library (1947) 60; Al-Awqaf Library (1928) 30.

Basra: [b]off Basrah. [c](Shatt al) Arab R [d]University of Basra (1964) 11 – 554. [e]University . . . Library (1964) 370; Public Library (?) ?

Hillah: [b]alt Hilla. [c]Euphrates R. [d]none. [e]Public Library (?) 30.

Irbil: [b]alt Arbil, Erbil. [c]none. [d]University of Salahaddin (1968) 6 – 404. [e]University . . . Library (1968?) 100; Public Library (?) ?

Karbala: [b]alt Kerbela. [c]Jadwal R. [d]none. [e]Public Library (?) ?

Kirkuk: [b]alt Kerkuk; for Zor. [c]Qada (alt Qadha) (Chai) R. [d]none. [e]Public Library (?) ?

Mosul: [b]off Mawsil. [c]Tigris R. [d]University of Mosul (1967) 16 – 915. [e]University . . . Library (1965) 148; Public Library (1930) 66.

Najaf: [b]alt Nedjef. [c]Najaf L. [d]none. [e]Public Library (?) ?

Sulaymaniyah: [b]alt Sulaimaniya. [c]Tanjero R. [d]University of Sulaymaniyah (1968) 6 – 404. [e]University . . . Library (1968?) 100.

Israel

Beersheba: [b]off Beer Sheva. [c]Beer Sheva R. [d]Ben Gurion University of the Negev (1964) 5 – 960. [e] . . . University Library (1966) 275.

Haifa: [b]off Hefa. [c]B of Acre of Mediterranean Sea; Kishon R. [d]Technion—Israel Institute of Technology (univ) (1912) 8 – 1100; University of Haifa (1963) 6 – 375. [e]University . . . Library (1951) 600; . . . Institute Library (1925) 510; Pevsner Public Library (1930) 200; Borochov Library (1921) 100.

*Jerusalem: [b]alt Quds ash Sharif; off Yerushalayim. [c]nr Dead (Sea) L. [d]Hebrew University of Jerusalem (1918) 15 – 2492. [e]Jewish National and University Library (1884) 2500; City Library (1961) 750.

Nazareth: [b]off Nazerat. [c]none. [d]none.

Ramat Gan: [b]none. [c]Yarqon R. [d]Bar-Ilan University (1953) 10 – 1100. [e] . . . University Library (1954) 600; Dvir Bialik Public Library (1945) 250.

Tel Aviv-Jaffa: [b]inc Jaffa, Tel Aviv; Jaffa: off Yafo. [c]Mediterranean Sea; Yarqon R. [d]Tel Aviv University (1953) 18 – 1894. [e] . . . University Library (1953) 1240; Shaar Zion Central Public Library (1886) 720. [f]Jaffa: 51 (1931), 21 (1900e), 5 (1850e).

For an explanation of symbols and abbreviations, see pages 16–17.

(Continued)

TABLE 2b. (Continued)

Japan

Akashi: [a]Honshu I. [b]none. [c]Akashi Channel. [d]none. [e]Hyogo Prefectural Agricultural Experiment Station Library (?) 64.

Akita: [a]Honshu I. [b]none. [c]Sea of Japan; Omono R. [d]Akita University (1875) 4 – 886. [e]Akita Prefectural Library (1899) 382; . . . University Library (1911) 260

Amagasaki: [a]Honshu I. [b]none. [c]Osaka B of Inland (alt Seto) Sea; Yodo R. [d]none. [e]Municipal Library (1919) 68; Eichi University Library (1963?) 54.

Aomori: [a]Honshu I. [b]none. [c]Aomori B of Tsugaru Strait. [d]none. [e]Aomori Prefectural Library (1928) 85.

Asahikawa: [a]Hokkaido I. [b]alt Asahigawa. [c]Ishikari R. [d]none. [e]Asahikawa Medical College Library (1973) 81.

Beppu: [a]Kyushu I. [b]none. [c]Beppu B of Inland (alt Seto) Sea. [d]none. [e]Beppu University Library (1946?) 50; Municipal Library (1922) ?

Chiba: [a]Honshu I. [b]none. [c]Tokyo B of Pacific O. [d]Chiba University (1872) 11 – 2190. [e] . . . University Library (1949) 728; Chiba Prefectural Library (1924) 268.

Chofu: [a]Honshu I. [b]none. [c]Tama R. [d]none.

Fuchu: [a]Honshu I. [b]none. [c]nr Tama R. [d]none.

Fuji: [a]Honshu I. [b]inc Yoshiwara since 1966. [c]Fuji R. [d]none. [f]Yoshiwara: 33 (1950), 3 (1898).

Fujisawa: [a]Honshu I. [b]none. [c]Sagami B of Pacific O. [d]none.

Fukui: [a]Honshu I. [b]none. [c]Asuwa R. [d]none. [e]Fukui University Library (1923?) 128; Fukui Prefectural Library (1909) 65.

Fukuoka: [a]Kyushu I. [b]inc Hakata. [c]Hakata B of East China Sea; Naka R. [d]Fukuoka University (1934) 21 – 766; Kyushu University (1903) 12 – 2872. [e]Kyushu University Library (1911) 2517; Fukuoka University Library (1934?) 760; Fukuoka Prefectural Library (1918) 203.

Fukushima: [a]Honshu I. [b]none. [c]Abukuma R. [d]Fukushima University (1921) 2 – 145 [e]Fukushima Prefectural Library (1929) 120; Fukushima Medical College Library (1944) 98.

Fukuyama: [a]Honshu I. [b]none. [c]Inland (alt Seto) Sea; Ashida R. [d]none. [e]Yoshikura Library (1910) ?

Funabashi: [a]Honshu I. [b]none. [c]Tokyo B of Pacific O. [d]none.

Gifu: [a]Honshu I. [b]for Imaizumi. [c]Nagara R. [d]Gifu University (1875) 5 – 1103. [e] . . . University Library (1875?) 547; Gifu Prefectural Library (1909) 174.

Hachinohe: [a]Honshu I. [b]none. [c]Mabechi R. [d]none. [e]Hachinohe Institute of Technology Library (1972?) 35; Municipal Library (1913) ?

Hachioji: [a]Honshu I. [b]none. [c]Asa R; Kawaguchi R. [d]Chuo University (1885) 32 – 1382. [e] . . . University Library (1885?) ?; Tokyo Metropolitan Hachioji Library (1911)?

Hakodate: [a]Hokkaido I. [b]none. [c]Tsugaru Strait. [d]none. [e]Municipal Library (1926) 122.

Hamamatsu: [a]Honshu I. [b]none. [c]Pacific O. [d]none. [e]Hamamatsu Technical College Library (1924) ?; Municipal Library (1920) ?

Higashiosaka: [a]Honshu I. [b]for Fuse. [c]nr Yodo R. [d]Kinki University (1925) 24 – 530. [e] . . . University Library (1925?) 212.

Hikone: [a]Honshu I. [b]none. [c]Biwa L. [d]Shiga University (1922) 3 – 397. [e] . . . University Library (1922?) 362.

Himeji: [a]Honshu I. [b]none. [c]Ichi R. [d]none. [e]Himeji Institute of Technology Library (1944?) 122; Municipal Library (1912) ?

Hirakata: [a]Honshu I. [b]none. [c]Yodo R. [d]none.

Hiratsuka: [a]Honshu I. [b]none. [c]Sagami B of Pacific O. [d]none. [e]Tokai University Library (1943?) 308.

Hirosaki: [a]Honshu I. [b]none. [c]nr Iwaki R; nr Aseishi R. [d]Hirosaki University (1920) 6 – 1040. [e] . . . University Library (1920?) 496.

Hiroshima: [a]Honshu I. [b]none. [c]Hiroshima B of Inland (alt Seto) Sea. [d]Hiroshima University (1902) 13 – 2098; Hiroshima Shudo University (1952) 5 – 256. [e]Hiroshima University Library (1949) 2093; Hiroshima Prefectural Library (?) 100.

Hitachi: [a]Honshu I. [b]none. [c]Pacific O. [d]none.

Ibaraki: [a]Honshu I. [b]none. [c]nr Yodo R. [d]none.

Ichihara: [a]Honshu I. [b]none. [c]Tokyo B of Pacific O. [d]none.

Ichikawa: [a]Honshu I. [b]none. [c]Edo R. [d]none.

Ichinomiya: [a]Honshu I. [b]none. [c]nr Kiso R. [d]none. [e]Municipal Library (1915)?

Ise: [a]Honshu I. [b]for Uji-Yamada. [c]Ise B of Pacific O. [d]none. [e]Mie Shinto Library (1928) 195; Kogakukan University Library (1882?) 50.

TABLE 2b. (Continued)

Iwaki: [a]Honshu I. [b]for Onahama; inc Taira since 1965. [c]Pacific O; Kamata R. [d]none. [f]Taira: 43 (1950), 25 (1930), 11 (1898), 4 (1874)

Kagoshima: [a]Kyushu I. [b]none. [c]Kagoshima B of East China Sea. [d]Kagoshima University (1901) 8 – 1334. [e] . . . University Library (1949) 793; Kagoshima Prefectural Library (1912) 292.

Kakogawa: [a]Honshu I. [b]none. [c]Kako R. [d]none.

Kamakura: [a]Honshu I. [b]none. [c]Sagami B of Pacific O. [d]none. [e]Nomura Research Institute of Technology and Economics Library (?) 120; Municipal Library (1911) ?

Kanazawa: [a]Honshu I. [b]none. [c]Sea of Japan; Ono R. [d]Kanazawa University (1923) 8 – 1301. [e] . . . University Library (1949) 1043; Ishikawa Prefectural Library (1912) 165; Municipal Library (1929) 157.

Kashiwa: [a]Honshu I. [b]none. [c]nr Tone R. [d]none.

Kasugai: [a]Honshu I. [b]none. [c]Shonai R. [d]none. [e]Chubu University Library (1938?) 130.

Kawagoe: [a]Honshu I. [b]none. [c]Shingashi R. [d]none. [e]International College of Commerce and Economics Library (1965?) 119; Municipal Library (1915) ?

Kawaguchi: [a]Honshu I. [b]none. [c]Ara R. [d]none.

Kawasaki: [a]Honshu I. [b]none. [c]Tokyo B of Pacific O. [d]none. [e]Kanagawa Prefectural Library (1958) 148.

Kitakyushu: [a]Kyushu I. [b]inc Kokura, Moji, Tobata, Wakamatsu, Yahata (alt Yawata). [c]Kammon Strait. [d]Kitakyushu University (1946) 4 – 228. [e] . . . University Library (1946?) 268. [f]Kokura: 199 (1950), 88 (1930), 28 (1898), 7 (1874); Moji: 124 (1950), 108 (1930), 25 (1898); Tobata: 88 (1950), 52 (1930), 3 (1898); Wakamatsu: 90 (1950), 57 (1930), 29 (1898); Yahata: 210 (1950), 168 (1930), 3 (1898).

Kobe: [a]Honshu I. [b]inc Hyogo (alt Hiogo) since 1878. [c]Osaka B of Inland (alt Seto) Sea; Minato R. [d]Kobe University (1902) 11 – 1679; Konan University (1919) 8 – 380; Kobe Gakuin University (1966) 6 – 319. [e]Kobe University Library (1903) 1778; Konan University Library (1919?) 561; Municipal Library (1911) 240. [f]Hyogo: 30 (1877), 22 (1796).

Kochi: [a]Shikoku I. [b]none. [c]Tosa B of Pacific O; Kagami R. [d]Kochi University (1874) 3 – 290. [e]Municipal Library (1949) 292; . . . University Library (1925) 291; Kochi Prefectural Library (1915) 142.

Kofu: [a]Honshu I. [b]none. [c]Ara R. [d]Yamanashi University (1924) 3 – 456. [e] . . . University Library (1924?) 363; Yamanashi Prefectural Library (1931) 138.

Koriyama: [a]Honshu I. [b]none. [c]Abukuma R. [d]none. [e]Koriyama Women's College Library (1950?) 70; Municipal Library (1944) ?

Koshigaya: [a]Honshu I. [b]none. [c]Moto-Ara R. [d]none.

Kumamoto: [a]Kyushu I. [b]none. [c]Shira R. [d]Kumamoto University (1874) 7 – 1273. [e] . . . University Library (1949) 800.

Kurashiki: a Honshu I. [b]none. [c]Kurashiki R. [d]none. [e]Okayama University Institute for Agricultural and Biological Sciences Library (1921) 142; Kawasaki Medical College Library (1970?) 80.

Kure: [a]Honshu I. [b]none. [c]Hiroshima B of Inland (alt Seto) Sea. [d]none. [e]Municipal Library (1924) ?

Kurume: [a]Kyushu I. [b]none. [c]Chikugo R. [d]Kurume University (1928) 5 – 920. [e] . . . University Library (1928) 314; Municipal Library (1938) ?

Kushiro: [a]Hokkaido I. [b]none. [c]Pacific O; Kushiro R. [d]none. [e]Municipal Popular Library (1925)?

Kyoto: [a]Honshu I. [b]alt Kioto; for Miyako. [c]Kamo R. [d1]Ritsumeikan University (1900) 21 – 903; Doshisha University (1875) 20 – 945; Kyoto University (1897) 15 – 7208; Ryukoku University (1639) 8 – 651; University of Buddhism (1887) 4 – 200. [e]Kyoto University Library (1897) 4259; Doshisha University Library (1875) 1000; Ryukoku University Library (1639) 791; Ritsumeikan University Library (1900?) 432; Kyoto Prefectural Library (1899) 400.

Machida: [a]Honshu I. [b]none. [c]Sakai R. [d]none. [e]Tamagawa University Library (1929) 336.

Maebashi: [a]Honshu I. [b]for Umayabashi. [c]Tone R. [d]Gumma University (1876) 6 – 704 [e] . . . University Library (1949) 222; Municipal Library (1915) 92.

Matsudo: [a]Honshu I. [b]none. [c]Edo R. [d]none.

Matsue: [a]Honshu I. [b]none. [c]Ohashi R; Nakaumi Lagoon; Shinji L. [d]Shimane University (1920) 4 – 326. [e] . . . University Library (1949?) 514.

Matsumoto: [a]Honshu I. [b]for Fukashi. [c]Narai R. [d]Shinshu University (1910) 7 – 1210. [e] . . . University Library (1920) 609; Municipal Library (1921) 74.

Matsuyama: [a]Shikoku I. [b]none. [c]nr Inland (alt Seto) Sea. [d]Ehime University (1896) 6 – 800. [e]Ehime University Library (1949) 530; Matsuyama University of Commerce Library (1923) 317; Ehime Prefectural Library (1935) 82.

---

[1]Universities with 4,000 or more students.

For an explanation of symbols and abbreviations, see pages 16–17.

(Continued)

TABLE 2b. (Continued)

Mito: [a]Honshu I. [b]none. [c]Naka R. [d]Ibaraki University (1920) 5 – 830, [e] . . . University Library (1920?) 350; Ibaraki Prefectural Library (1903) 95.

Miyazaki: [a]Kyushu I. [b]none. [c]Oyodo R. [d]Miyazaki University (1923) 3 – 400. [e] . . . University Library (1926) 169; Miyazaki Prefectural Library (1902) 78.

Morioka: [a]Honshu I. [b]none. [c]Kitakami R. [d]Iwate University (1902) 6 – 440. [e] . . . University Library (1902) 440; Iwate Prefectural Library (1922) 132.

Nagano: [a]Honshu I. [b]for Zenkoji. [c]Sai R. [d]none. [e]Nagano Prefectural Library (1929) 174.

Nagaoka: [a]Honshu I. [b]none. [c]Shinano R. [d]none. [e]Nagaoka University of Technology Library (1976?) 34.

Nagasaki: [a]Kyushu I. [b]none. [c]East China Sea. [d]Nagasaki University (1857) 6 – 825. [e]Nagasaki Prefectural Library (1912) 780; . . . University Library (1949) 468.

Nagoya: [a]Honshu I. [b]none. [c]Ise B of Pacific O; Shonai R; Yata R. [d1]Meijo University (1924) 18 – 470; Aichi Gakuin University (1876) 11 – 402; Nagoya University (1871) 10 – 3198; Nanzan University (1932) 5 – 385. [e]Nagoya University Library (1939) 1795; Municipal Library (1923) 410; Meijo University Library (1950) 362; Aichi Prefectural Library (?) 170.

Naha: [a]Okinawa I. [b]alt Nawa. [c]East China Sea; Kokuba R. [d]Ryukyus University (1950) 6 – 770. [e] . . . University Library (1950) 430; Ryukyu Islands Central Library (1950) 46.

Nara: [a]Honshu I. [b]none. [c]Saho R; Noto R. [d]Nara Women's University (1908) 12 – 372. [e]Tenri Central Library (at Tenri, nr Nara) (1926) 1244; . . . University Library (1909) 200; Nara Prefectural Library (1908) 164.

Neyagawa: [a]Honshu I. [b]alt Neyakawa. [c]nr Yodo R. [d]none. [e]Osaka Electro-Communication University Library (?) 42.

Niigata: [a]Honshu I. [b]for Kambaratsu. [c]Sea of Japan; Shinano R. [d]Niigata University (1910) 9 – 1426. [e] . . . University Library (1949) 846; Niigata Prefectural Library (1915) 219.

Nikko: [a]Honshu I. [b]none. [c]Daiya R. [d]none. [e]Nikko Bunko Library (1924) ?

Nishinomiya: [a]Honshu I. [b]none. [c]Osaka B of Inland (alt Seto) Sea. [d]Kwansei Gakuin University (1889) 14 – 848; Mukogawa Women's University (1939) 10 – 610. [e]Kwansei Gakuin University Library (1889) 580.

Numazu: [a]Honshu I. [b]none. [c]Suruga B of Pacific O; Kano R. [d]none. [e]Numazu Bunko Library (1898) ?

Oita: [a]Kyushu I. [b]for Funai. [c]Beppu B of Inland (alt Seto) Sea; Oita R. [d]Oita University (1875) 4 – 352, [e] . . . University Library (1922) 347; Oita Prefectural Library (1902) 65.

Okayama: [a]Honshu I. [b]none. [c]Asahi R. [d]Okayama University (1874) 9 – 3660. [e] . . . University Library (1949) 1126.

Okazaki: [a]Honshu I. [b]none [c]Yahagi R. [d]none. [e]Aichi Gakugei College Library (1945?) 125; Municipal Library (1922) ?

Omiya: [a]Honshu I. [b]none. [c]nr Shiba R. [d]none. [e]Municipal Library (1921) ?

Osaka: [a]Honshu I. [b]none. [c]Osaka B of Inland (alt Seto) Sea; Yodo R. [d1]Osaka Gakuin University (1962) 8 – 270; Osaka Municipal University (1928) 7 – 1297. [e]Osaka Municipal University Library (1928) 1392; Osaka Gakuin University Library (1962?) 1000; Osaka Prefectural Library (1903) 960.

Otaru: [a]Hokkaido I. [b]none. [c]Ishikari (alt Otaru) B of Sea of Japan [d]none. [e]Otaru University of Commerce Library (1911) 232.

Otsu: [a]Honshu I. [b]none. [c]Biwa L. [d]none. [e]Shiga Prefectural Library (1943) 52.

Saga: [a]Kyushu I. [b]none. [c]Chikugo R. [d]Saga University (1949) 3 – 420. [e] . . . University Library (1949?) 379.

Sagamihara: [a]Honshu I. [b]inc Kami-Mizo, Ono. [c]Sakai R. [d]none. [e]Azabu Veterinary College Library (1949) 400.

Sakai: [a]Honshu I. [b]none. [c]Osaka B of Inland (alt Seto) Sea; Yamato R. [d]University of Osaka Prefecture (1939) 4 – 640. [e]University . . . Library (1939?) 468; Municipal Library (1872) 62.

Sapporo: [a]Hokkaido I. [b]none. [c]Toyohira R. [d]Hokkaido University (1872) 13 – 2007. [e] . . . University Library (1876) 2034; Hokkaido Prefectural Library (1924) 407.

Sasebo; [a]Kyushu I. [b]none. [c]East China Sea. [d]none. [e]Nagasaki Prefectural College of International Economics Library (1951) 64; Municipal Library (1918) ?

Sendai: [a]Honshu I. [b]none. [c]Hirose R. [d]Tohoku Gakuin University (1886) 13 – 350; Tohoku University (1907) 12 – 3324. [e]Tohoku University Library (1911) 2443; Tohoku Gakuin University Library (1890) 152; Miyagi Prefectural Library (1881) 110.

Shimizu: [a]Honshu I. [b]none. [c]Suruga B of Pacific O. [d]none. [e]Municipal Library (1931) ?; Nautical College Library (1943)?

Shimonoseki: [a]Honshu I. [b]for Akamagaseki, Bakwan. [c]Kammon Strait. [d]none. [e]Shimonoseki Municipal College Library (1956?) 40; Municipal Library (1882) ?

---

[1]Universities with 5,000 or more students.

TABLE 2b. (Continued)

Shizuoka: [a]Honshu I. [b]for Fuchu, Shunpei, Sumpu. [c]Suruga B of Pacific O. [d]Shizuoka University (1875) 7 – 660. [e]Shizuoka Prefectural Library (1922) 229; . . . University Library (1949) 201.

Soka: [a]Honshu I. [b]none. [c]nr Ara R. [d]Dokkyo University (1964) 9 – 378. [e] . . . University Library (1964?) 320.

Suita: [a]Honshu I. [b]none. [c]Yodo R. [d]Kansai University (1886) 22 – 890. [e] . . . University Library (1886) 1136.

Takamatsu: [a]Shikoku I. [b]none. [c]Inland (alt Seto) Sea. [d]Kagawa University (1923) 4 – 600. [e] . . . University Library (1924) 501; Kagawa Prefectural Library (1934) ?

Takarazuka: [a]Honshu I. [b]for Kohama. [c]Muko R. [d]none.

Takasaki: [a]Honshu I. [b]none. [c]Karasu R. [d]none. [e]Takasaki Municipal College of Economics Library (1952) 71; Municipal Library (1910) ?

Takatsuki: [a]Honshu I. [b]none. [c]Yodo R. [d]none.

Tokorozawa: [a]Honshu I. [b]none. [c]nr Iruma R. [d]none.

Tokushima: [a]Shikoku I. [b]none. [c]Kii Channel; Yoshino R. [d]Tokushima University (1922) 4 – 749. [e] . . . University Library (1949) 257: Tokushima Prefectural Library (1916) 88.

*Tokyo: [a]Honshu I. [b]alt Tokio; for Edo, Yedo. [c]Tokyo B of Pacific O; Sumida R; Ara R. [d][1]Nihon University (1889) 81 – 6016; Waseda University (1882) 43 – 2889; Meiji University (1881) 33 – 1446; Tokai University (1943) 31 – 1790; Hosei University (1880) 27 – 1410; Keio University (1858) 25 – 2945; Senshu University (1880) 19 – 591; Toyo University (1887) 19 – 922; University of Tokyo (1789?) 19 – 3727; Aoyama Gakuin University (1874) 18 – 905; Komazawa University (1759) 18 – 790; Kokushikan University (1917) 17 – 510; Tokyo University of Science (1881) 16 – 954. [e]National Diet Library (1872) 8466; University of Tokyo Library (1886) 5015; Nihon University Library (1889) 3249; Keio University Library (1912) 1310; Metropolitan Central Library (1908) 1207; Waseda University Library (1882) 1186.

Tottori: [a]Honshu I. [b]none. [c]Sea of Japan; Sendai R. [d]Tottori University (1920) 4 – 677. [e] . . . University Library (1920?) 384.

Toyama: [a]Honshu I. [b]none. [c]Jintsu R. [d]Toyama University (1894) 5 – 590. [e] . . . University Library (1949) 426; Toyama Prefectural Library (1940) 165.

Toyohashi: [a]Honshu I. [b]for Yoshida. [c]Atsumi B of Pacific O. [d]Aichi University (1946) 11 – 465. [e] . . . University Library (1946?) 482; Municipal Library (1912) 78.

Toyonaka: [a]Honshu I. [b]none. [c]Yodo R. [d]Osaka University (1843) 13 – 2624. [e] . . . University Library (1931) 1742.

Toyota: [a]Honshu I. [b]for Koromo. [c]Yahagi R. [d]none. [e]Toyota Motor Company Library (1936) 62; Toyota Branch Library of Chukyo University (?) 61.

Tsu: [a]Honshu I. [b]for Anotsu. [c]Ise B of Pacific O; Ano R. [d]Mie University (1875) 5 – 712. [e] . . . University Library (1875?) 535.

Urawa: [a]Honshu I. [b]none. [c]Ara R. [d]Saitama University (1921) 6 – 847. [e] . . . University Library (1924) 323; Saitama Prefectural Library (1924) 57.

Utsunomiya: [a]Honshu I. [b]none. [c]Ta R. [d]Utsunomiya University (1922) 4 – 450. [e] . . . University Library (1922) 263; Tochigi Prefectural Library (?) 197.

Wakayama: [a]Honshu I. [b]none. [c]Kitan Strait; Kino R. [d]Wakayama University (1871) 3 – 210; Koyasan University (1886) 0.8 – 90. [e]Wakayama University Library (1923) 510; Wakayama Prefectural Library (1908) 68.

Yamagata: [a]Honshu I. [b]none. [c]nr Mogami R. [d]Yamagata University (1920) 7 – 1100. [e] . . . University Library (1949) 602; Yamagata Prefectural Library (1910) 108.

Yamaguchi: [a]Honshu I. [b]none. [c]Fushino R. [d]Yamaguchi University (1853) 8 – 820. [e] . . . University Library (1949) 1058; Yamaguchi Prefectural Library (1903) 389.

Yao: [a]Honshu I. [b]none. [c]nr Yamato R. [d]none.

Yokkaichi: [a]Honshu I. [b]none. [c]Ise B of Pacific O. [d]none. [e]Municipal Library (1908) 52.

Yokohama: [a]Honshu I. [b]none. [c]Tokyo B of Pacific O. [d]Kanagawa University (1929) 9 – 340; Kanto Gakuin University (1884) 8 – 491; Yokohama National University (1876) 7 – 1170; Yokohama Municipal University (1928) 3 – 410. [e]Yokohama National University Library (1949) 542; Kanagawa Prefectural Library (1930) 475; Yokohama Municipal University Library (1949) 317; Municipal Library (1925) 184.

Yokosuka: [a]Honshu I. [b]none. [c]Tokyo B of Pacific 0. [d]none. [e]Kanagawa Dental College Library (1964?) 59.

Jordan

*Amman: [b]none. [c](Wadi) Amman R. [d]University of Jordan (1962) 11 – 580. [e]University . . . Library (1962) 380; Public Library (1958) 95; Royal Scientific Society Library (1970) 40.

[1]Universities with 15,000 or more students.

For an explanation of symbols and abbreviations, see pages 16–17.   (Continued)

TABLE 2b. (Continued)

Irbid: [b]none. [c]none. [d]Yarmouk University (1976) 11 – 394. [e] . . . University Library (1975) 96; Public Library (1957) 30.

Zarqa: [b]alt Zerka, Zerqa. [c]Zarqa (alt Zerka, Zerqa) R. [d]none.

Kampuchea

*Phnom-Penh: [b]none. [c]Mekong R; Bassac R; Tonle Sap R. [d]Universite de Phnom-Penh (1946) 1 – ? [e]Bibliotheque de l'Institut Bouddhique (1923) 40; Bibliotheque de l'Universite . . . (1960) 36; Bibliotheque Nationale (1921) 33.

Korea: North

Chongjin: [b]for Seishin. [c]Sea of Japan. [d]none. [e]City Library (?) 23; North Hamgyong Provincial Library (?) ?

Haeju: [b]for Kaishu. [c]Haeju B of Yellow Sea. [d]none. [e]South Hwanghae Provincial Library (?) 33.

Hamhung: [b]for Kanko; inc Hungnam (for Konan) since 1960. [c]Sea of Japan; Tongsong R. [d]none. [e]South Hamgyong Provincial Library (?) 40; City Library (?) ? [f]Hungnam: 144 (1944), 23 (1930).

Kaesong: [b]for Kaijo. Songdo. [c]nr Han R. nr Yesong R. [d]none. [e]City Library (?) 28.

Kimchaek: [b]for Joshin, Songjin. [c]Sea of Japan; Susong R. [d]none.

Nampo: [b]for Chinnampo. [c]Taedong R. [d]none.

*Pyongyang: [b]for Heijo. [c]Taedong R. [d]Kim Il Sung University (1946) 16 – 3000. [e]Academy of Sciences Library (1952?) 2000; State Central Library (1964) 1500; . . . University Library (1946) 60; South Pyongan Provincial Library (?) ?

Sinuiju: [b]for Shingishu. [c]Yalu R. [d]none. [e]North Pyongan Provincial Library (?) ?

Wonsan: [b]for Gensan. [c]Sea of Japan. [d]none. [e]Kangwon Provincial Library (?) ?

Korea: South

Anyang: [b]none. [c]nr Han R. [d]none.

Buchon: [b]alt Bucheon, Puchon. [c]Yellow Sea. [d]none.

Cheju: [a]Cheju I. [b]alt Jeju; for Chyei Chyu, Saishu. [c]Cheju Strait. [d]Cheju National University (1955) 0.6 – 60. [e] . . . University Library (1952) 12.

Chinju: [b]alt Jinju; for Shinshu. [c]Namchon R. [d]Gyeong Sang National University (1948) 6 – 306. [e] . . . University Library (1948?) 57.

Chongju: [b]alt Cheongju; for Seishu. [c]Musim R. [d]Chung Buk National University (1951) 11 – 439; Cheongju University (1946) 1 – 50. [e]Chung Buk National University Library (1952) 125.

Chonju: [b]alt Jeonju; for Zenshu. [c]Chonju (alt Jeonju) R. [d]Jeonbug National University (1951) 10 – 377. [e] . . . University Library (1952) 150.

Chunchon: [b]alt Chuncheon; for Shunsen. [c]Pukhan R. [d]Kangweon National University (1947) 6 – 490. [e] . . . University Library (1947?) 200.

Inchon: [b]alt Incheon; for Chemulpo. Zinsen. [c]Yellow Sea. [d]In Ha University (1952) 13 – 260. [e] . . . University Library (1955) 195; Public Library (1921) ?

Iri: [b]for Riri. [c]none. [d]Won Kwang University (1946) 15 – 292. [e] . . . University Library (1946) ?

Kunsan: [b]for Gunzan. [c]Yellow Sea; Kum R. [d]none.

Kwangju: [b]alt Gwangju; for Koshu. [c]nr Yongsan R. [d]Chosun University (1946) 23 – 493; Chonnam National University (1952) 6 – 321. [e]Chosun University Library (1950) 371; Chonnam National University Library (1952) 158.

Kwangmyong: [b]none. [c]Korea Strait. [d]none.

Kyongju: [b]for Keishu. Sorabol. [c]Puk R; Nam R; So R. [d]none.

Masan: [b]for Masampo. [c]Chinhae B of Korea Strait. [d]Kyung Nam University (1947) ? – ? [e] . . . University Library (1947?) ?

Mokpo: [b]alt Mogpo; for Moppo. [c]Yellow Sea. [d]none.

Pohang: [b]for Hoko. [c]Yongil B of Sea of Japan. [d]none.

Pusan: [b]alt Busan; for Fusan. [c]Korea Strait. [d]Pusan National University (1946) 22 – 810; Dong-A University (1947) 21 – 352. [e]Dong-A University Library (1947) 260; Pusan National University Library (1946) 230.

*Seoul: [b]alt Kyongsong; for Hanyang. Keijo; off Soul. [c]Han R. [d1]Hanyang University (1939) 27 – 1287; Yonsei University (1885) 27 – 750; Kyung Hee University (1949) 25 – 700; Seoul National University (1946) 25 – 1883; Korea University (1905) 24 – 1456; Chungang University (1918) 20 – 1243; Kon Kuk University (1946) 18 – 492; Dongguk University (1906) 16 – 500; Sung Kyun Kwan University (992) 15 – 270. [e]Seoul

---

[1]Universities with 15,000 or more students.

TABLE 2b. (Continued)

National University Library (1946) 1150; National Central Library (1923) 853; Yonsei University Library (1915) 681; Kyung Hee University Library (1950) 532; Korea University Library (1937) 473.

Songnam: [b]alt Seongnam. [c]nr Han R. [d]none.

Suwon: [b]alt Suweon; for Suigen. [c]none. [d]Ajou University (1972) 4 – 94. [e] . . . University Library (1972?) 53.

Taegu: [b]alt Daegu; for Taikyu. [c]Tae R. [d]Kyungpook National University (1946) 21 – 907; Yeungnam University (1947) 20 – 454; Keimyung University (1954) 6 – 225; Daegu University (?) ? – ? [e]Yeungnam University Library (1947?) 320; Kyungpook National University Library (1952) 262; Keimyung University Library (1954?) 250.

Taejon: [b]alt Daejeon; for Taiden. [c]Taejon (alt Daejeon) R. [d]Chung Nam National University (1952) 14 – 436. [e] . . . University Library (1952) 60.

Ulsan: [b]for Urusan. [c]Ulsan B of Korea Strait, Ulsan R. [d]none.

Kuwait

Hawalli: [b]none. [c]Persian G. [d]none.

*Kuwait: [b]alt Kuweit; off Kuwayt. [c]Persian G. [d]Kuwait University (1962) 17 – 608. [e] . . . University Library (1966) 348; Central Library (1936) 297.

Laos

*Vientiane: [b]none. [c]Mekong R. [d]Universite Sisavangvong (1928) 2 – 150. [e]Bibliotheque Nationale (1957) 50; Bibliotheque de l'Universite . . . (1928?) 15.

Lebanon

*Beirut: [b]for Beyrouth; off Bayrut. [c]Mediterranean Sea. [d]Beirut Arab University (1960) 27 – 217; Universite Libanaise (1951) 27 – 1602; Universite Saint-Joseph (1846) 6 – 911; American University of Beirut (1866) 5 – 486; Universite Saint-Esprit de Kaslik (at Jounie, nr Beirut) (1950) 3 – 410. [e]American University of Beirut Library (1866) 435; Bibliotheque de l'Universite Saint-Joseph (1875) 320; Beirut Arab University Library (1960) 200; Bibliotheque de l'Universite Saint-Esprit de Kaslik (at Jounie) (1950?) 135; Bibliotheque Nationale du Liban (1921) 100.

Tripoli: [b]off Tarabulus. [c]Mediterranean Sea. [d]none. [e]Bibliotheque de l'Institut Culturel (1959) 4.

Macao

*Macao: [b]alt Aomen; off Macau. [c]South China Sea; Zhu R. [d]Universidade da Asia Oriental (1981) 0.9 – 15. [e]Biblioteca Nacional de Macau (1929) 60; Biblioteca Municipal (?) 18.

Malaysia

Ipoh: [a]Peninsular Malaysia. [b]none. [c]Kinta R. [d]none. [e]Tun Razak Library (1931) 164.

Johore Baharu: [a]Peninsular Malaysia. [b]alt Johore Bahru. [c]Johore Strait. [d]none. [e]Sultan Ismail Library (1964) 106.

Kota Baharu: [a]Peninsular Malaysia. [b]alt Kota Bharu. [c]Kelantan R. [d]none. [e]Teachers' Training College Library (1954) 20; Kelantan Public Library (1938) 15.

Kota Kinabalu: [a]*Sabah; Borneo I. [b]for Jesselton. [c]Gaya B of South China Sea. [d]none. [e]Sabah State Library (1953) 543.

*Kuala Lumpur: [a]Peninsular Malaysia. [b]none. [c]Klang R. [d]University of Malaya (1905) 10 – 1280; National University of Malaysia (at Bangi, nr Kuala Lumpur) (1970) 8 – 908; University of Technology. Malaysia (1954) 5 – 580. [e]University of Malaya Library (1957) 900; Selangor Public Library (1971) 574; National University of Malaysia Library (at Bangi) (1970) 409.

Kuala Trengganu: [a]Peninsular Malaysia. [b]alt Kuala Terengganu. [c]South China Sea; Trengganu (alt Terengganu) R. [d]none [e]Trengganu Public Library (1974) 85.

Kuching: [a]*Sarawak; Borneo I. [b]none. [c]Sarawak R. [d]none. [e]Sarawak State Library (1950) 400; Kuching Municipal Council Library (1970) 52.

Malacca: [a]Peninsular Malaysia. [b]off Melaka. [c]Strait of Malacca; Malacca (off Melaka) R. [d]none. [e]Public Library (1881) 30.

Penang: [a]Peninsular Malaysia; Penang (off Pinang) I. [b]alt George Town; off Pinang. [c]Strait of Malacca. [d]University of Science, Malaysia (1969) 6 – 697. [e]University . . . Library (1969) 380; Public Library (1817) 115.

Maldives

*Male: [a]Male (alt King's) I. [b]none. [c]Indian O. [d]none.

For an explanation of symbols and abbreviations, see pages 16–17.

(Continued)

TABLE 2b. (Continued)

Mongolia

*Ulan-Bator: [b]for Kulun, Urga; off Ulaanbaatar. [c]Tuul R. [d]Mongolian State University (1942) 4 – 240. [e]State Public Library (1921) 3000; . . . University Library (1942) 400; Academy of Sciences Library (1921) ?

Nepal

*Kathmandu: [b]alt Katmandu. [c]Baghmati R. [d]Tribhuvan University (1958) 34 – 3290. [e] . . . University Library (1959) 67; Nepal-Bharat Sanskritik Kendra Library (1952) 41; National Library (?) 20.

Oman

*Muscat: [b]off Masqat. [c]Muscat B of Arabian Sea. [d]none. [e]British Council Library (at Matrah, nr Muscat) (1973) 8; Directorate of the Omani Heritage Library (1973) 3.

Pakistan

Bahawalpur: [b]none. [c]nr Sutlej R. [d]Islamia University of Bahawalpur (1975) 1 – 111. [e]Central Library (1948) 92; . . . University Library (1975?) 58.

Faisalabad: [b]for Lyallpur. [c]none. [d]none. [e]University of Agriculture Library (1909) 70.

Gujranwala: [b]none. [c]none. [d]none. [e]Islamia College Library (?) 11; Municipal Public Library (?) 6.

Hyderabad: [b]for Nerankot. [c]Indus R. [d]University of Sind (1947 at Karachi, relocated 1951) 6 – 488; Mehran University of Engineering and Technology (1963) 2 – 150. [e]University . . . Library (1947) 183; . . . University Library (1963?) 50; Hayat-e-Adab Library (?) 34.

*Islamabad: [b]none. [c]Soan R; Rawal L; Lohi Shir L. [d]Quaid-i-Azam University (1965) 1 – 160; International Islamic University (1980) 0.7 – 82. [e]Quaid-i-Azam University Library (1965) 110; Ministry of Law and Parliamentary Affairs Library (1947 at Karachi, relocated 1970?) 40; National Library of Pakistan (?) 27.

Jhang: [b]for Jhang Maghiana. [c]nr Chenab R. [d]none. [e]Government College Library (?) 7.

Karachi: [b]none. [c]Arabian Sea; Layari R. [d]University of Karachi (1951) 10 – 425; NED University of Engineering and Technology (1922) 3 – 116. [e]University . . . Library (1952) 400; Liaquat Memorial Library (1950) 100.

Lahore: [b]none. [c]Ravi R. [d]University of the Punjab (1858) 8 – 353; University of Engineering and Technology (1923) 4 – 212. [e]University of the Punjab Library (1882) 312; Punjab Public Library (1884) 200; University of Engineering and Technology Library (1923) 110.

Multan: [b]none. [c]nr Chenab R. [d]Bahauddin Zakariya University (1971) 1 – 101. [e] . . . University Library (1971?) 35; Public Library (?) 10.

Peshawar: [b]none. [c]nr Bara R. [d]University of Peshawar (1913) 9 – 575. [e]University . . . Library (1913) 113.

Quetta: [b]none. [c]Sariab (Lora) R. [d]University of Baluchistan (1970) 2 – 180. [e]University . . . Library (1970) 57; Sandeman Library (1886) 21.

Rawalpindi: [b]none. [c]Leh R. [d]none. [e]Gordon College Library (1893?) 28; Rawalpindi Polytechnic Institute Library (1958) 22.

Sargodha: [b]none. [c]none. [d]none. [e]De Montmorency College Library (1934?) 12.

Sialkot: [b]for Sealkote. [c]Aik (Nala) Creek. [d]none. [e]Murray College Library (1889?) 26; Municipal Library (?) 5.

Sukkur: [b]none. [c]Indus R. [d]none

Philippines

Angeles: [a]Luzon I. [b]none. [c]Pasig R. [d]Angeles University (1962) 10 – 358. [e] . . . University Library (1962) 50.

Bacolod: [a]Negros I. [b]none. [c]Guimaras Strait; Lupit R. [d]University of Negros Occidental-Recoletos (1941) 11 – 344. [e]University . . . Library (1941) 32.

Baguio: [a]Luzon I. [b]none. [c]none. [d]Saint Louis University (1910) 19 – 438; University of Baguio (1948) 11 – 235; Baguio Central University (?) ? – ? [e]Saint Louis University Library (1910) 228; University of Baguio Library (1948) 53.

Cagayan de Oro: [a]Mindanao I. [b]none. [c]Cagayan R. [d]Xavier University (1933) 5 – 238. [e] . . . University Library (1933) 85.

Caloocan: [a]Luzon I. [b]none. [c]Manila B of South China Sea. [d]Gregorio Araneta University (at Malabon, nr Caloocan) (1946) 6 – 262. [e] . . . University Library (at Malabon) (1946) 133.

Cebu: [a]Cebu I. [b]for Zebu. [c]Bohol Strait. [d]University of the Visayas (1919) 20 – 500; University of San Carlos (1595) 19 – 568; Southwestern University (1946) 14 – 450; University of Southern Philippines (1927) 7 – 197. [e]University of San Carlos Library (1947) 192; Southwestern University Library (1960) 60.

Cotabato: [a]Mindanao I. [b]none. [c]Mindanao R. [d]Notre Dame University (1949) 6 – 183. [e] . . . University Library (1948) 57.

TABLE 2b. (Continued)

Dagupan: [a]Luzon I. [b]none. [c]Dagupan R. [d]University of Pangasinan (1925) 11 – 333. [e]University . . . Library (1948) 78.

Davao: [a]Mindanao I. [b]none. [c]Davao G of Pacific O; Davao R. [d]University of Mindanao (1946) 18 – 350; International Harvardian University (1951) 6 – 89; Ateneo de Davao University (1951) 3 – 103; University of Southeastern Philippines (1979) ? – ? [e]University of Mindanao Library (1946) 53; City Library (1952) 19.

Dumaguete: [a]Negros I. [b]none. [c]Mindanao Sea. [d]Silliman University (1901) 7 – 321; Foundation University (1949) 4 – 153. [e]Silliman University Library (1906) 127; Foundation University Library (1949) 44.

Iloilo: [a]Panay I. [b]none. [c]Iloilo Strait; Iloilo R. [d]University of San Agustin (1904) 12 – 405; Central Philippine University (1905) 10 – 265; University of Iloilo (at Rizal, nr Iloilo) (1947) ? – ? [e]University of San Agustin Library (1904) 80; Central Philippine University Library (1905) 77.

Legaspi: [a]Luzon I. [b]alt Legazpi. [c]Albay G of Philippine Sea. [d]Bicol University (1969) 11 – 400; Aquinas University (1948) 4 – 162. [e]Bicol University Library (1969) 51; Aquinas University Library (1948) 50.

Lucena: [a]Luzon I. [b]for Buenavista, Oroquieta. [c]Tayabas B of Sibuyan Sea. [d]Luzonian University (1947) 13 – 170. [e] . . . University Library (1947) 35; Quezon Provincial Library (1929) 26.

Makati: [a]Luzon I. [b]for San Pedro Macati. [c]Pasig R. [d]none. [e]International School Library (?) 42; Estrella Public Library (?) ?

*Manila: [a]Luzon I. [b]none. [c]Manila B of South China Sea; Pasig R. [d1]University of the East (1946) 64 – 1534; University of Santo Tomas (1611) 43 – 1650; Far Eastern University (1928) 40 – 1150; Feati University (1946) 30 – 850; Manuel L. Quezon University (1947) 23 – 564; Polytechnic University of the Philippines (1904) 21 – 861; Adamson University (1932) 19 – 534; Philippine Women's University (1919) 15 – 600; University of Manila (1913) 12 – 220; Ateneo de Manila University (1859) 11 – 534; Centro Escolar University (1907) 11 – 492; Arellano University (1938) 10 – 335; Philippine Christian University (1946) 10 – 96. [e]National Library (1901) 1297: University of Santo Tomas Library (1605) 823; University of the East Library (1946) 279; Ateneo de Manila University Library (1859) 200; Far Eastern University Library (1934) 161; City Library (1946) 77.

Marawi: [a]Mindanao I. [b]for Dansalan. [c]Lanao L. [d]Mindanao State University (1955) 9 – 596. [e] . . . University Library (1961) 100.

Naga: [a]Luzon I. [b]for Nueva Caceres. [c]Bicol R. [d]University of Nueva Caceres (1948) 7 – 248. [e]University . . . Library (1948) 60.

Pasay: [a]Luzon I. [b]for Pineda, Rizal. [c]Manila B of South China Sea. [d]none. [e]Lopez Memorial Museum and Library (1960) 14; City Library (1950) 9.

Pasig: [a]Luzon I. [b]none. [c]Pasig R; Marikina R. [d]none. [e]Rizal Provincial Library (1951) 6.

Quezon City: [a]Luzon I. [b]none. [c]Marikina R; Dario R. [d]University of the Philippines (1908 at Manila, relocated 1948) 30 – 2740. [e]University . . . Library (1911 at Manila, relocated 1948) 737.

San Fernando: [a]Luzon I. [b]none. [c]Betis R. [d]University of the Assumption (1963) 7 – ? [e]University . . . Library (1963?) ?

Tacloban: [a]Leyte I. [b]none. [c]San Pedro B of Philippine Sea. [d]Divine Word University (1929) 9 – 323. [e] . . . University Library (1929?) 65; Leyte Provincial Branch Library (?) 61.

Tagbilaran: [a]Bohol I. [b]none. [c]Bohol Strait. [d]University of Bohol (1946) 10 – 152. [e]University . . . Library (1946?) 50; Bohol Provincial Library (1925) 9.

Zamboanga: [a]Mindanao I. [b]for Samboangan. [c]Basilan Strait. [d]Western Mindanao State University (1918) 6 – 211. [e] . . . University Library (1918?) 26; City Library (1924) 9.

Qatar

*Doha: [b]off Dawhah. [c]Persian G. [d]University of Qatar (1973) 5 – 395. [e]Qatar National Library (1963) 125; University . . . Library (1973) 30.

Saudi Arabia

Dammam: [a]Nejd. [b]none. [c]Persian G. [d]King Faisal University (1974) 1 – 500. [e] . . . University Library (1974?) ?

*Jidda: [a]Hejaz. [b]alt Jedda; off Juddah. [c]Red Sea. [d]King Abdul Aziz University (1962) 15 – 1411. [e] . . . University Library (1967) 435.

Mecca: [a]*Hejaz. [b]alt Mekka; off Makkah. [c]nr (Wadi) Shayi R. [d]Umm al-Qura University (1979) ? – ? [e] . . . University Library (1979) 224; Abbas Kattan Library (?) 8; Library of Alharam (?) 7.

Medina: [a]Hejaz. [b]off Madinah. [c](Wadi) Buthan R. [d]Islamic University (1961) 3 – 350. [e] . . . University Library (1961) 292; General Library (?) 10.

---

[1]Universities with 10,000 or more students.

For an explanation of symbols and abbreviations, see pages 16–17.

(Continued)

TABLE 2b. (Continued)

*Riyadh: [a]*Nejd. [b]off Riyad. [c](Wadi) Hanifah R. [d]King Saud University (1951) 23 – 2000; Islamic University of Imam Muhammad Ibn Saud (1950) 11 – 1113. [e]King Saud University Library (1957) 1000; Institute of Public Administration Library (1962) 114; Islamic University Library (1974) 30; National Library (1968) 16.

Taif: [a]Hejaz. [b]none. [c]none. [d]none. [e]Taif Campus Library of Umm al-Qura University (1981) 50.

Singapore

*Singapore: [b]alt Singapura. [c]Singapore Strait; Johore Strait; Singapore R. [d]National University of Singapore (1905) 13 – 1200. [e]National Library (1823) 1771; . . . University Library (1905) 1415.

Sri Lanka

*Colombo: [b]none. [c]Indian O; Colombo L. [d]University of Colombo (1921) 3 – 275; University of Kelaniya (at Kelaniya, nr Colombo) (1959) 3 – 185; University of Sri Jayewardenepura (at Nugegoda, nr Colombo) (1959) 3 – 195; University of Moratuwa (at Moratuwa, nr Colombo) (1966) 2 – 232; Buddhist and Pali University of Sri Lanka (1982) 0.2 – 60. [e]Colombo National Museum Library (1877) 600; Public Library (1925) 195; University of Colombo Library (1967) 155; University of Sri Jayewardenepura Library (at Nugegoda) (1959) 92.

Dehiwala-Mount Lavinia: [b]inc Dehiwala, Mount Lavinia. [c]Indian O. [d]none.

Jaffna: [b]none. [c]Jaffna Lagoon. [d]University of Jaffna (1974) 2 – 191. [e]University . . . Library (1974?) 96; Public Library (?) 29.

Kandy: [b]for Candy. [c]Mahaweli Ganga R; Kandy L. [d]University of Peradeniya (at Peradeniya, nr Kandy) (1870) 5 – 440. [e]University . . . Library (at Peradeniya) (1921) 410; Public Library (?) ?

Syria

Aleppo: [b]off Halab. [c]Quwayq (alt Kuweik) R. [d]University of Aleppo (1946) 36 – 429. [e]University . . . Library (1960) 36; National Library (1924) ?

*Damascus: [b]off Dimashq. [c]Barada R. [d]University of Damascus (1903) 56 – 955. [e]University . . . Library (1919) 150; Public Library (1880) 120; Assad National Library (1880) 100.

Hama: [b]off Hamah. [c]Orontes R. [d]none. [e]Library of the Cultural Center (?) ?

Homs: [b]alt Hums; for Lebda; off Hims. [c]nr Orontes R. [d]Al-Baath University (1979) 9 – 67. [e] . . . University Library (1979?) 11; National Library (?) ?

Latakia: [b]alt Lattakia; off Ladhiqiyah. [c]Mediterranean Sea. [d]University of October (1971) 12 – 114. [e]National Library (1944) 12; University . . . Library (1971?) 4.

Taiwan

Changhwa: [b]for Shoka. [c]nr Taito R. [d]none. [e]Changhwa County Library (1936) 59.

Chiayi: [b]alt Chiai, Kiayi; for Kagi. [c]Pachang R. [d]none. [e]National Chiayi Institute of Agriculture Library (1919) 30; Chiayi County Library (1946) 25.

Chungho: [b]none. [c]nr Hsintien (alt Sintien) R. [d]none.

Chungli: [b]for Churekei. [c]nr Tanshui (for Tamsui) R. [d]Chungyuan Christian University (1955) 8 – 690; National Central University (1915 at Nanjing, China; relocated 1962) 2 – 296. [e]Chungyuan Christian University Library (1955) 120.

Fengshan: [b]for Hozan. [c]none. [d]none.

Hsinchu: [b]alt Sinchu; for Chuchien, Shinchiku. [c]Formosa (alt Taiwan) Strait. [d]National Chiaotung University (1896) 3 – 342; National Tsinghua University (1911 at Beijing, China; relocated 1956) 3 – 377. [e]National Chiaotung University Library (1896?) 100; National Tsinghua University Library (1967) 77.

Hsinchuang: [b]alt Sinchwang; for Shinsho. [c]Tanshui (for Tamsui) R. [d]Fujen Catholic University (1923 at Beijing, China; relocated 1963) 13 – 1220. [e] . . . University Library (1963) 332.

Hsintien: [b]alt Sintien; for Shinten. [c]Hsintien (alt Sintien) R. [d]none.

Kaohsiung: [b]for Takao; inc Kigo. [c]Formosa (alt Taiwan) Strait; Kaohsiung (alt Ai) R. [d]National Chungshan University (1980) 0.6 – 154. [e]National Kaohsiung Teachers' College Library (1909?) 106; City Library (1945) 81. [f]Kigo: 7 (1911).

Keelung: [b]alt Chilung; for Kiirun. [c]East China Sea; Keelung (alt Chilung) R. [d]none. [e]National Taiwan College of Marine Science and Technology (1953) 83; City Library (1932) 20.

Panchiao: [b]alt Panchiau; for Itahashi, Taipeihsien. [c]nr Tanshui (for Tamsui) R. [d]none. [e]National Taiwan Academy of Arts Library (1956?) 53; Taipei County Library (1948) 27.

Pingtung: [b]for Ako, Akow, Heito. [c]nr Hsiatanshui R. [d]none. [e]National Pingtung Institute of Agriculture Library (1955) 59; Pingtung County Library (1947) 30.

TABLE 2b. (Continued)

Shanchung: [b]alt Sanchung. [c]Tanshui (for Tamsui) R. [d]none.

Taichung: [b]for Taichu. [c]Yanagi R; Midori R. [d]Fengchia University (1961) 15 – 1335; National Chunghsin University (1919 at Taipei, relocated 1942) 10 – 1429; Tunghai University (1955) 8 – 844. [e]National Chunghsin University Library (1961) 337; Fengchia University Library (1961?) 300; Providence College Library (1949) 255; Tunghai University Library (1958) 192; Provincial Taichung Library (1947) 110.

Tainan: [b]for Taiwan. [c]Formosa (alt Taiwan) Strait. [d]National Chengkung University (1927) 11 – 1154. [e] . . . University Library (1946) 303; City Library (1919) 63.

*Taipei: [b]for Taihoku; inc Daitotei, Moko (alt Banka, Manka). [c]Tanshui (for Tamsui) R; Keelung (alt Chilung) R. [d]Tamkang University (at Taipeihsien, nr Taipei) (1950) 17 – 1237; University of Chinese Culture (1963) 17 – 2044; National Taiwan University (1928) 14 – 1895; Soochow University (1900 at Suzhou, China; relocated 1954) 10 – 1144; National Chengchi University (1927 at Nanjing, China; relocated 1954) 6 – 737. [e]National Taiwan University Library (1899) 1500; National Central Library (1933 at Nanjing, China; relocated 1954) 1286; National Chengchi University Library (1952) 869; National Taiwan Normal University Library (1946) 513; City Library (1952) 125. [f]Daitotei: 50 (1901); Moko: 29 (1901), 50 (1864e).

Taoyuan: [b]for Toen. [c]Tanshui (for Tamsui) R. [d]none. [e]Chungcheng Institute of Technology Library (1960) 80; Taoyuan County Library (1923) 23.

Yungho: [b]none. [c]Hsintien (alt Sintien) R. [d]none.

Thailand

*Bangkok: [b]inc Thon Buri bef 1937 and since 1971; off Krungthep Mahanakhon. [c]Chao Phraya R. [d]Sri Nakharinwirot University (1954) 24 – 1352; Chulalongkorn University (1902) 17 – 2355; Kasetsart University (1904) 11 – 1338; Thammasat University (1933) 10 – 567; Mahidol University (1880) 9 – 1953. [e]National Library of Thailand (1905) 902; Thammasat University Library (1934) 445; Chulalongkorn University Library (1910) 412. [f]Thon Buri: 628 (1970), 177 (1947).

Chiang Mai: [b]alt Chiengmai. [c]Ping R. [d]Chiang Mai University (1964) 10 – 1259. [e] . . . University Library (1960) 140.

Khon Kaen: [b]none. [c]nr Chi R. [d]Khon Kaen University (1964) 6 – 1010. [e] . . . University Library (1964?) 211.

Songkhla: [b]alt Singora. [c]G of Thailand. [d]Prince of Songkhla University (1964) 5 – 992. [e] . . . University Library (1964) 72.

Turkey

Adana: [b]for Seyhan. [c]Seyhan R. [d]Cukurova University (1973) 11 – 715. [e] . . . University Library (1973) 25.

Adapazari: [b]alt Sakarya; for Adabazar. [c]nr Sakarya R. [d]none.

*Ankara: [b]for Angora. [c]Ankara R; Cubuk R. [d]Gazi University (1982) 34 – 1521; Ankara University (1925) 26 – 2044; Hacettepe University (1206 at Kayseri, relocated 1967) 21 – 3300; Middle East Technical University (1956) 15 – 1300. [e]National Library (1946) 687; Ankara University Library (1925?) 635; Middle East Technical University Library (1956) 297; Hacettepe University Library (1967) 190; Grand National Assembly Library (1920) 175; Public Library (1922) 32.

Antalya: [b]for Adalia. [c]G of Antalya of Mediterranean Sea. [d]Mediterranean Sea University (1982) 5 – 268. [e] . . . University Library (1982?) ?

Antioch: [b]for Hatay; off Antakya. [c]Orontes R. [d]none.

Bursa: [b]alt Brusa. [c]Gok R. [d]Uludag University (1975) 9 – 666. [e]Public Library (?) 33; . . . University Library (1975) 23.

Diyarbakir: [b]alt Diyarbekir. [c]Tigris R. [d]Tigris University (1966) 6 – 349. [e]Public Library (?) 14; . . . University Library (1973) 11.

Elazig: [b]for Mezre, Yeni Harput. [c]nr Murat R. [d]Euphrates University (1975) 2 – 286. [e] . . . University Library (1975?) ?

Erzurum: [b]none. [c]nr Araks R. [d]Ataturk University (1958) 18 – 850. [e] . . . University Library (1957) 200.

Eskisehir: [b]alt Eskishehir. [c]Porsuk R. [d]Anatolian University (1973) 11 – 724. [e]Public Library (?) 14; . . . University Library (1973) ?

Gaziantep: [b]for Aintab, Antep. [c]Kavalik Creek; Ainleben Creek. [d]none. [e]Public Library (?) 9.

Izmir: [b]for Smyrna. [c]G of Izmir of Aegean Sea. [d]Ninth of September University (1982) 24 – 938; Aegean University (1955) 13 – 1424. [e]Ninth of September University Library (1982?) 135; Aegean University Library (1955) 125; General Library (1912) 96.

Izmit: [b]alt Kocaeli; for Ismid. [c]G of Izmit of Sea of Marmara. [d]none.

Kahramanmaras: [b]for Maras. [c]nr Aksu R. [d]none.

For an explanation of symbols and abbreviations, see pages 16–17.

(Continued)

TABLE 2b. (Continued)

Kayseri: [b]for Caesarea. [c]Kizil (Irmak) R. [d]Erciyes University (1978) 3 – 188. [e]Public Library (?) 15; . . . University Library (1978?) ?

Konya: [b]alt Konia. [c]none. [d]Selcuk University (1975) 8 – 497. [e]Public Library (1947) 20; . . . University Library (1975?) ?

Malatya: [b]none. [c]nr Sultan R. [d]Inonu University (1975) 1 – 110. [e] . . . University Library (1975?) ?

Mersin: [b]alt Icel. [c]Mediterranean Sea. [d]none.

Samsun: [b]none. [c]Black Sea. [d]Nineteenth of May University (1975) 6 – 397. [e]Public Library (?) 16; . . . University Library (1975) 3.

Sanliurfa: [b]for Edessa, Urfa. [c]none. [d]none.

Sivas: [b]none. [c]Kizil (Irmak) R. [d]Republican University (1974) 3 – 370. [e] . . . University Library (1973) ?

Trebizond: [b]off Trabzon. [c]Black Sea. [d]Black Sea University (1963) 8 – 539. [e] . . . University Library (1963) 60.

Van: [b]none. [c]Van L. [d]Centennial University (1982) 0.5 – 26. [e] . . . University Library (1982?) ?

United Arab Emirates

*Abu Zaby: [a]*Abu Dhabi; Abu Zaby (alt Abu Dhabi) I. [b]alt Abu Dhabi. [c]Persian G. [d]United Arab Emirates University (1976) 4 – 275. [e] . . . University Library (1976?) 50; Public Library (?) ?

Dubayy: [a]*Dubai. [b]alt Dubai; for Dibai. [c]Persian G. [d]none. [e]Public Library (?) 15; British Council Library (1970) 11.

USSR

Aktyubinsk: [a]Kazakhstan. [b]none. [c]Ilek R. [d]none. [e]Medical Institute Library (1953) 196; Scientific-Technical Library (1965) 196; Aktyubinsk District Library (1932) 105.

Alma-Ata: [a]*Kazakhstan. [b]for Vernyy. [c]Bolshaya Almatinka R. [d]S. M. Kirov Kazakh State University (1934) 12 – 920. [e]Scientific-Technical Library (1960) 5150; A. S. Pushkin State Library of the Kazakh SSR (1931) 3459; Central Scientific Library of the Kazakh Academy of Sciences (1933) 3088; . . . University Library (1934) 1275.

Andizhan: [a]Uzbekistan. [b]none. [c]Andizhan(-Say) R. [d]none. [e]Z. M. Babur Andizhan District Library (1906) 333.

Angarsk: [a]Russia in Asia. [b]none. [c]Angara R. [d]none. [e]City Library (1951) 83.

Ashkhabad: [a]*Turkmenia. [b]for Poltoratsk. [c]Geami R. [d]A. M. Gorkiy Turkmen State University (1950) 11 – ? [e]Karl Marx State Public Library of the Turkmen SSR (1895) 4000; Central Scientific Library of the Turkmen Academy of Sciences (1941) 800; . . . University Library (1950) 542.

Barnaul: [a]Russia in Asia. [b]none. [c]Ob R; Barnaulka R. [d]Altay State University (1973) 1 – ? [e]Scientific-Technical Library (1942) 653; Altay Regional Library (1888) 628; Altay Polytechnic Institute Library (1942) 400.

Biysk: [a]Russia in Asia. [b]alt Biisk, Bisk. [c]Biya R. [d]none. [e]Pedagogic Institute Library (1931) 205; Central City Library (1899) 111.

Blagoveshchensk: [a]Russia in Asia. [b]none. [c]Amur R; Zeya R. [d]none. [e]Amur District Library (1937) 311.

Bratsk: [a]Russia in Asia. [b]none. [c]Angara R. [d]none. [e]City Library (1957) 24.

Bukhara: [a]Uzbekistan. [b]alt Bokhara. [c]nr Zeravshan R. [d]none. [e]Pedagogic Institute Library (1930) 515; Ibn Sina Bukhara District Library (1921) 204.

Chelyabinsk: [a]Russia in Asia. [b]none. [c]Miass R. [d]Chelyabinsk State University (1975) ? – ? [e]Fiftieth Anniversary of Great October Chelyabinsk District Library (1898) 1380; Polytechnic Institute Library (1943) 835.

Chimkent: [a]Kazakhstan. [b]none. [c]Badam R. [d]none. [e]Scientific-Technical Library (1965) 547; Institute of Chemical Technology Library (1943) 259; A. S. Pushkin Chimkent District Library (1815) 157.

Chita: [a]Russia in Asia. [b]none. [c]Ingoda R. [d]none. [e]A. S. Pushkin Chita District Library (1895) 471; Scientific-Technical Library (1958) 300.

Dushanbe: [a]*Tadzhikistan. [b]for Dyushambe, Stalinabad. [c]Kafirnigan R; Dushanbinka R. [d]V. I. Lenin Tadzhik State University (1948) 9 – 750. [e]A. Firdousi State Library of the Tadzhik SSR (1933) 2716; Central Scientific Library of the Tadzhik Academy of Sciences (1933) 753; . . . University Library (1948) 640.

Dzhambul: [a]Kazakhstan. [b]for Auliye-Ata. [c]Talas R. [d]none. [e]Technological Institute of the Light and Food Industries Library (1963) 188; C. Valikhanov Dzhambul District Library (1898) 135.

Fergana: [a]Uzbekistan. [b]for Novyy Margelan, Skobelev. [c]Skakhimardan R. [d]none. [e]Pedagogic Institute Library (1930) 295; Fergana District Library (1899) 191.

Frunze: [a]*Kirgizia. [b]for Pishpek. [c]Alamedin R; Alarcha R; Dzhirgozar R. [d]Kirgiz State University (1951) 12 – 600. [e]N. G. Chernyshevskiy State Library of the Kirgiz SSR (1934) 3515; . . . University Library (1932) 931; Central Scientific Library of the Kirgiz Academy of Sciences (1943) 815.

TABLE 2b. (Continued)

Irkutsk: [a]Russia in Asia. [b]none. [c]Angara R; Irkut R. [d]A. A. Zhdanov Irkutsk State University (1918) 9 – 500. [e] . . . University Library (1918) 3200; Polytechnic Institute Library (1930) 950; I. I. Molchanov-Sibirskiy Irkutsk District Library (1861) 772.

Kamensk-Uralskiy: [a]Russia in Asia. [b]for Kamensk. [c]Iset R; Kamenka R. [d]none. [e]Technical Library of the Ural Aluminum Works (1936) 70.

Karaganda: [a]Kazakhstan. [b]none. [c]nr Nura R. [d]Karaganda State University (1972) 3 – ? [e] . . . University Library (1972) 400; Polytechnic Institute Library (1953) 344; N. V. Gogol Karaganda District Library (1938) 223.

Kemerovo: [a]Russia in Asia. [b]for Shcheglovsk. [c]Tom R. [d]Kemerovo State University (1974) 3 – 380. [e]Kemerovo District Scientific Library (1920) 895; Scientific-Technical Library (1957) 488; . . . University Library (1974?) 350; Polytechnic Institute Library (1950) 350.

Khabarovsk: [a]Russia in Asia. [b]none. [c]Amur R. [d]none. [e]Scientific-Technical Library (1960) 2621; Khabarovsk Regional Scientific Library (1894) 1328.

Kokand: [a]Uzbekistan. [b]alt Khokand. [c]Sokh R. [d]none. [e]Pedagogic Institute Library (1930) 165.

Komsomolsk-na-Amure: [a]Russia in Asia. [b]for Permskoye. [c]Amur R. [d]none. [e]Pedagogic Institute Library (1954) 135; Polytechnic Institute Library (1955) 125; Central City Library (1934) 82.

Krasnoyarsk: [a]Russia in Asia. [b]none. [c]Yenisey R. [d]Krasnoyarsk State University (1970) 2 – ? [e]A. S. Pushkin Krasnoyarsk Regional Library (1935) 1173; Scientific-Technical Library (1958) 742.

Kurgan: [a]Russia in Asia. [b]none. [c]Tobol R. [d]none. [e]Kurgan District Library (1943) 672.

Kustanay: [a]Kazakhstan. [b]none. [c]Tobol R. [d]none. [e]L. N. Tolstoy Kustanay District Library (1919) 297.

Kzyl-Orda: [a]Kazakhstan. [b]for Ak-Mechet, Perovsk. [c]Syr (Darya) R. [d]none. [e]M. Gorkiy Kzyl-Orda District Library (1937) 290; Pedagogic Institute Library (1937) 276.

Magnitogorsk: [a]Russia in Asia. [b]none. [c]Ural R. [d]none. [e]Institute of Ore Mining and Metallurgy Library (1932) 440; Metallurgical Combine Scientific-Technical Library (1931) 308; Pedagogic Institute Library (1932) 193; Central City Library (1929) 78.

Namangan: [a]Uzbekistan. [b]none. [c]nr Naryn R. [d]none. [e]Namangan District Library (1918) 143; Pedagogic Institute Library (1946) 127.

Nizhnevartovsk: [a]Russia in Asia. [b]none. [c]Ob R. [d]none.

Nizhniy Tagil: [a]Russia in Asia. [b]alt Nizhni Tagil. [c]Tagil R. [d]none. [e]Pedagogic Institute Library (1939) 215.

Norilsk: [a]Russia in Asia. [b]none. [c]nr Norilskaya R. [d]none. [e]Mining and Metallurgical Combine Technical Library (1938) 508; Institute for Education in Industry Library (1962) 195.

Novokuznetsk: [a]Russia in Asia. [b]for Stalinsk. [c]Tom R; Kondoma R; Aba R. [d]none. [e]Kuznetsk Metallurgical Combine Scientific-Technical Library (1927) 1014; Siberian Metallurgical Institute Scientific-Technical Library (1930) 416; Pedagogic Institute Library (1939) 206; Central City Library (1929) 125.

Novosibirsk: [a]Russia in Asia. [b]for Novonikolayevsk. [c]Ob R; Inya R; Yeltsovka R. [d]Novosibirsk State University (1959) 4 – 628. [e]State Public Scientific-Technical Library of the Siberian Department of the USSR Academy of Sciences (1918) 9974; Scientific-Technical Library (1934) 1138; Novosibirsk District Library (1929) 1013.

Nukus: [a]Uzbekistan; *Kara-Kalpak ASSR. [b]none. [c]Amu (Darya) R. [d]Nukus State University (1979) ? – ? [e]Pedagogic Institute Library (1934) 187; State Library of the Kara-Kalpak ASSR (1937) 145.

Omsk: [a]Russia in Asia. [b]none. [c]Irtysh R; Om R. [d]Omsk State University (1974) 1 – ? [e]A. S. Pushkin Omsk District Library (1899) 1126.

Osh: [a]Kirgizia. [b]none. [c]Akbura R. [d]none. [e]Pedagogic Institute Library (1947) 343; Osh District Library (1949) 281.

Pavlodar: [a]Kazakhstan. [b]none. [c]Irtysh R. [d]none. [e]Industrial Institute Library (1960) 220; N. Ostrovskiy Pavlodar District Library (1919) 144.

Petropavlovsk: [a]Kazakhstan. [b]none. [c]Ishim R. [d]none. [e]Pedagogic Institute Library (1937) 289; North Kazakhstan District Library (1919) 155.

Petropavlovsk-Kamchatskiy: [a]Russia in Asia. [b]for Petropavlovsk. [c]Avacha B of Pacific O. [d]none. [e]Kamchatka District Library (1914) 198.

Prokopyevsk: [a]Russia in Asia. [b]alt Prokopevsk. [c]Aba R. [d]none. [e]Mining Institute Technical Library (1945) 102.

Rubtsovsk: [a]Russia in Asia. [b]none. [c]Aley R. [d]none. [e]Altay Tractor Works Scientific-Technical Library (1942) 109; City Library (1929) 52.

Samarkand: [a]Uzbekistan. [b]none. [c]nr Zeravshan R. [d]Alisher Navoi Samarkand State University (1927) 10 – 600. [e] . . . University Library (1927) 1632; A. S. Pushkin Samarkand District Library (1911) 226.

For an explanation of symbols and abbreviations, see pages 16–17.   (Continued)

TABLE 2b. (Continued)

Semipalatinsk: [a]Kazakhstan. [b]none. [c]Irtysh R. [d]none. [e]N. V. Gogol Semipalatinsk District Library (1883) 252; Pedagogic Institute Library (1935) 190.

Surgut: [a]Russia in Asia. [b]none. [c]Ob R. [d]none.

Sverdlovsk: [a]Russia in Asia. [b]for Ekaterinburg, Yekaterinburg. [c]Iset R. [d]A. M. Gorkiy Ural State University (1920) 10 – 1000. [e]V. G. Belinskiy State Public Library (1899) 1962; Ural Polytechnic Institute Library (1920) 1615; . . . University Library (1920) 1000.

Tashkent: [a]*Uzbekistan. [b]alt Tashkend. [c]Chirchik R. [d]V. I. Lenin Tashkent State University (1920) 18 – 1480. [e]Alisher Navoi State Library of the Uzbek SSR (1870) 4157; . . . University Library (1918) 2460; Central Library of the Uzbek Academy of Sciences (1933) 1650.

Temirtau: [a]Kazakhstan. [b]for Samarkandskiy. [c]Nura R. [d]none. [e]Karaganda Metallurgical Plant Library (1963) 88.

Tomsk: [a]Russia in Asia. [b]none. [c]Tom R. [d]V. V. Kuybyshev Tomsk State University (1888) 8 – 700. [e] . . . University Library (1888) 3320; Polytechnic Institute Library (1900) 1115; A. S. Pushkin Tomsk District Library (1899) 380.

Tselinograd: [a]Kazakhstan. [b]for Akmolinsk. [c]Ishim R. [d]none. [e]Saken Seyfullin Tselinograd District Library (1941) 412; Scientific-Technical Library (1965) 364.

Tyumen: [a]Russia in Asia. [b]alt Tiumen. [c]Tura R. [d]Tyumen State University (1973) 3 – ? [e]Tyumen District Library (1875) 581; . . . University Library (1973) 382.

Ulan-Ude: [a]Russia in Asia; *Buryat ASSR. [b]for Udinskoye, Verkhne-Udinsk. [c]Selenga R; Uda R. [d]none. [e]M. Gorkiy State Library of the Buryat ASSR (1881) 574.

Uralsk: [a]Kazakhstan. [b]for Yaitskiy Gorodok. [c]Ural R. [d]none. [e]Pedagogic Institute Library (1932) 396; N. K. Krupskaya Uralsk District Library (1871) 131.

Ust-Kamenogorsk: [a]Kazakhstan. [b]for Zashchita. [c]Irtysh R; Ulba R. [d]none. [e]Scientific-Technical Library (1964) 544; A. S. Pushkin East Kazakhstan District Library (1896) 175.

Vladivostok: [a]Russia in Asia. [b]none. [c]Sea of Japan. [d]Far Eastern State University (1899) 8 – 560. [e] . . . University Library (1956) 700; A. M. Gorkiy Maritime Regional Library (1887) 563.

Yakutsk: [a]Russia in Asia; *Yakutsk ASSR. [b]none. [c]Lena R. [d]Yakutsk State University (1934) 8 – 400. [e]A. S. Pushkin State Library of the Yakutsk ASSR (1925) 1027; . . . University Library (1934) 429.

Yuzhno-Sakhalinsk: [a]Russia in Asia; Sakhalin I. [b]for Toyohara, Vladimirovka. [c]Susuya R. [d]none. [e]Sakhalin District Library (1946) 719.

Zlatoust: [a]Russia in Asia. [b]none. [c]Ay R. [d]none. [e]Zlatoust Metallurgical Works Library (1933) 122.

Vietnam

Bien Hoa: [b]none. [c]Dong Nai R. [d]none.

Can Tho: [b]none. [c]Bassac (off Hau Giang) R. [d]none. [e]Can Tho College Library (?) ?

Da Nang: [b]for Tourane. [c]South China Sea; Da Nang R. [d]none.

Haiphong: [b]none. [c](Cua) Cam R; Kinh Thay R; Tram Bac (alt Tambac) R. [d]none.

*Hanoi: [b]for Kecho. [c]Red R; Tay L; Truc Bach L. [d]Technical University of Hanoi (1956) 5 – 882; University of Hanoi (1904) 3 – 800. [e]National Library (1918) 1200; . . . University Library (1956?) 600; Central Social Sciences Library (1975) 300; Central Library of Science and Technology (1960) 255; University . . . Library (1904?) 150.

Ho Chi Minh City: [b]for Saigon; inc Cholon. [c]Sai Gon R; (Arroyo) Chinois Creek. [d]University of Ho Chi Minh City (1917 at Hanoi, relocated 1954) 25 – 700; Technical University of Ho Chi Minh City (1957) 3 – 529. [e]General Scientific Library (1976) 600; . . . University Library (1957?) 200; University . . . Library (1955) 40.

Hue: [b]none. [c]Huong (alt Parfums) R. [d]University of Hue (1957) 6 – 470. [e]University . . . Library (1957) 30.

Nha Trang: [b]for Kanh Hoa. [c]South China Sea; Cai R. [d]none. [e]Oceanographic Institute Library (1922) 55.

West Bank

Bethlehem: [b]off Bayt Lahm. [c]nr (Wadi) Mushash R. [d]Bethlehem University (1893) 1 – 115. [e] . . . University Library (1973) 100.

Hebron: [b]off Khalil. [c]none. [d]Hebron University (1971) 1 – 45. [e]Public Library (?) 20; . . . University Library (1971?) 10.

Jericho: [b]alt Ariha. [c]nr Jordan R; nr Dead (Sea) L. [d]none.

Nabulus: [b]alt Nablus. [c]none. [d]Al-Najah National University (1918) 3 – 216. [e] . . . University Library (1918?) 75; Public Library (1960) 39.

TABLE 2b. (Continued)

Yemen: North

Hudaydah: ^{b}alt Hodeida. ^{c}Red Sea. ^{d}none.

*Sana: ^{b}alt Sanaa. ^{c}(Wadi) Alaf R; (Wadi) Shaub R. ^{d}Sana University (1970) 11 – 332. ^{e} . . . University Library (1970?) 37; Great Mosque Library (1925) 10; British Council Library (1974) 9.

Yemen: South

*Aden: ^{b}off Adan. ^{c}G of Aden. ^{d}University of Aden (1970) 5 – 464. ^{e}Miswat Library (1951) 40; University . . . Library (1975?) ?

EUROPE

Albania

*Tirane: ^{b}alt Tirana. ^{c}nr Ishm R. ^{d}Enver Hoxha University of Tirane (1957) 9 – 820. ^{e}National Library (1922) 850; . . . University Library (1957) 600.

Austria

Graz: ^{b}none. ^{c}Mur R. ^{d}Karl-Franzens-Universitat (1586) 18 – 2080; Technische Universitat Graz (1811) 6 – 490. ^{e}Universitatsbibliothek (1573) 1890; Steiermarkische Landesbibliothek (1811) 540.

Innsbruck: ^{b}none. ^{c}Inn R; Sill R. ^{d}Leopold-Franzens-Universitat (1669) 16 – 1000. ^{e}Universitatsbibliothek (1745) 1825.

Klagenfurt: ^{b}none. ^{c}Glan R. ^{d}Universitat fur Bildungswissenschaften (1970) 2 – 100. ^{e}Bundesstaatliche Studienbibliothek (1775) 400; Universitatsbibliothek (1776) 372.

Linz: ^{b}none. ^{c}Danube R. ^{d}Johannes-Kepler-Universitat (1962) 6 – 294. ^{e}Universitatsbibliothek (1965) 306; Bundesstaatliche Studienbibliothek (1774) 223; Bucherei der Stadt (?) 200.

Salzburg: ^{b}none. ^{c}Salzach R. ^{d}Universitat Salzburg (1617) 9 – 750. ^{e}Universitatsbibliothek (1623) 1169; Benediktiner-Erzabtei Sankt Peter Bibliothek (700) 120; Stadtbucherei (1941) 65.

*Vienna: ^{b}off Wien. ^{c}Danube R. ^{d}Universitat Wien (1365) 48 – 3995; Technische Universitat Wien (1815) 11 – 1665; Wirtschaftsuniversitat Wien (1898) 10 – 350; Universitat fur Bodenkultur (1872) 4 – 295. ^{e}Universitatsbibliothek (1365) 4315; Osterreichische Nationalbibliothek (1526) 2400; Osterreichischer Gewerkschaftsbund Bibliothek (?) 1200; Stadtische Bucherei (1936) 900.

Belgium

Antwerp: ^{b}off Antwerpen, Anvers. ^{c}Scheldt R. ^{d}none. ^{e}Stadsbibliotheek (1470) 750; Bibliotheek der Universitaire Faculteiten Sint-Ignatius (1852) 434.

Bruges: ^{b}alt Brugge. ^{c}Rei (alt Reye, Roye) R. ^{d}none. ^{e}Bibliotheek Sint-Andriesabdij (1902) 110; Stedelijke Openbare Bibliotheek (1789) 109; Bibliotheque du Grand Seminaire (1833) 103; Europa-College Bibliotheek (1951) 100.

*Brussels: ^{b}off Brussel, Bruxelles. ^{c}Senne (alt Zenne) R. ^{d}Universite Libre de Bruxelles (1834) 14 – 1800; Vrije Universiteit Brussel (1834) 6 – 400. ^{e}Bibliotheque du Parlement (1831) 3000; Bibliotheque Royale Albert Ier (1559) 2839; Bibliotheque de l'Universite . . . (1846) 1492.

Charleroi: ^{b}none. ^{c}Sambre R. ^{d}none. ^{e}Bibliotheque Alfred Langlois (1903) 88; Bibliotheque Publique Communale (1863) 59.

Ghent: ^{b}off Gand, Gent. ^{c}Scheldt R; Lys R. ^{d}Rijksuniversiteit te Gent (1817) 14 – 412. ^{e}Bibliotheek van de Rijksuniversiteit . . . (1797) 2100; Bibliotheque Publique Municipale (1945) 94.

Liege: ^{b}alt Luik. ^{c}Meuse R; Ourthe R. ^{d}Universite de l'Etat a Liege (1816) 10 – 389. ^{e}Bibliotheque de l'Universite . . . (1817) 1700; Bibliotheque Publique Centrale (1907) 450.

Louvain: ^{b}alt Leuven. ^{c}Dijle (alt Dyle) R. ^{d}Katholieke Universiteit Leuven (1425) 22 – 823; Universite Catholique de Louvain (1425) 18 – 963. ^{e}Universiteitsbibliotheek (1425) 2000; Bibliotheque de l'Universite . . . (1425) 1700; Stedelijke Openbare Bibliotheek (1866) 50.

Mechelen: ^{b}alt Malines. ^{c}Dijle (alt Dyle) R. ^{d}none. ^{e}Stadsbibliotheek (1684) 79.

Mons: ^{b}alt Bergen. ^{c}nr Haine R; nr Trouille R. ^{d}Universite de l'Etat a Mons (1899) 2 – 218. ^{e}Bibliotheque de l'Universite . . . (1797) 590.

Namur: ^{b}alt Namen. ^{c}Meuse R; Sambre R. ^{d}none. ^{e}Bibliotheque Universitaire Moretus Plantin (1921) 800.

Ostend: ^{b}off Oostende, Ostende. ^{c}North Sea. ^{d}none. ^{e}Stedelijke Openbare Bibliotheek (1861) 66.

For an explanation of symbols and abbreviations, see pages 16–17.   (Continued)

TABLE 2b. (Continued)

Bulgaria

Burgas: [b]none. [c]G of Burgas of Black Sea. [d]none. [e]Regional Library (1890) 436.

Plovdiv: [b]for Philippopolis. [c]Maritsa R. [d]Paisij Hilendarski University of Plovdiv (1961) 3 – 282. [e]Ivan Vazov National Library (1879) 1127.

Ruse: [b]for Ruschuk. [c]Danube R. [d]none. [e]L. Karavelov Regional Library (1888) 599.

*Sofia: [b]off Sofiya. [c]Bogana R. [d]Saint Clement of Ohrid University of Sofia (1888) 10 – 1016. [e]Cyril and Methodius National Library (1878) 2543; . . . University Library (1888) 1620; Central Library of the Bulgarian Academy of Sciences (1869) 1536; City Library (1928) 663.

Stara Zagora: [b]for Eski Zagra. [c]nr Syuyutliyka R. [d]none. [e]Regional Library (1955) 361.

Varna: [b]for Stalin. [c]Black Sea; Varna L. [d]none. [e]Regional Library (1883) 599.

Veliko Turnovo: [b]for Tirnovo, Turnovo. [c]Yantra R. [d]Cyril and Methodius University of Veliko Turnovo (1963) 3 –. 273. [e]P. R. Slavejkov Regional Library (1921) 484; . . . University Library (1963) 170.

Channel Islands

Saint Helier: [a]*Jersey I. [b]none. [c]Saint Aubin's Bay of English Channel. [d]none. [e]States of Jersey Library Service (1743) 170.

Saint Peter Port: [a]*Guernsey I. [b]none. [c]English Channel. [d]none. [e]Priaulx Library (1889) 35.

Czechoslovakia

Bratislava: [a]Slovakia. [b]for Pozsony, Pressburg. [c]Danube R. [d]Comenius University (1919) 18 – 2032. [e]Slovak Technical Library (1938) 2777; . . . University Library (1919) 1848; Central Library of the Slovak Academy of Sciences (1942) 516; Central Economic Library (1940) 436; City Library (1900) 266.

Brno: [a]Moravia. [b]for Brunn. [c]Svratka R; Svitava R. [d]Purkyne University (1919) 11 – 911. [e]State Scientific Library-University Library (1770) 4404; J. Mahen Library (1921) 534.

Karlovy Vary: [a]Bohemia. [b]alt Carlsbad; for Karlsbad. [c]Ohre (alt Eger) R; Tepla (alt Tepl) R. [d]none. [e]Regional Library (1948) 232.

Kosice: [a]Slovakia. [b]for Kaschau, Kassa. [c]Hornad R. [d]Safarik University (1948) 5 – 915. [e]State Scientific Library (1657) 2323; Regional Library (1657) 500.

Martin: [a]Slovakia. [b]alt Turciansky Svaty-Martin; for Sankt Martin, Turocszentmarton. [c]Turiec R. [d]none. [e]Slovak National Library (1863) 4621.

Olomouc: [a]Moravia. [b]for Olmutz. [c]Morava (for March) R; Bystrice R. [d]Palacky University (1573) 7 – 900. [e]State Scientific Library (1566) 1379; . . . University Library (1946) 490; Regional Library (1888) 190.

Ostrava: [a]Moravia. [b]for Mahrisch-Ostrau, Moravska Ostrava. [c]Oder R; Ostravice R. [d]none. [e]State Scientific Library (1951) 688; State College of Mining and Metallurgy Library (1716) 530; City Library (1928) 187.

Plzen: [a]Bohemia. [b]for Pilsen. [c]Berounka R; Mze R; Radbuza R; Uhlava R; Uslava R. [d]none. [e]State Scientific Library (1950) 1944; City Library (1876) 266.

*Prague: [a]Bohemia. [b]for Prag; off Praha. [c]Vltava R. [d]Charles University (1348) 24 – 2889. [e]State Library of the Czech Socialist Republic (1366?) 5355; National Museum Library (1818) 3000; . . . University Library (1366) 2745; City Library (1891) 2608.

Denmark

Alborg: [b]alt Aalborg. [c]Lim Fjord of Kattegat. [d]Alborg Universitetscenter (1971) 4 – 340. [e]Nordjyske Landsbibliotek (1895) 1000; Universitetsbibliotek (1975) 324.

Arhus: [b]alt Aarhus. [c]Kattegat. [d]Arhus Universitet (1928) 13 – 1298. [e]Statsbiblioteket (1902) 1740; Kommunes Biblioteker (1934) 1700.

*Copenhagen: [a]Zealand I. [b]off Kobenhavn. [c]Oresund. [d]Kobenhavns Universitet (1479) 24 – 1610. [e]Kommunes Biblioteker (1885) 2521; Kongelige Bibliotek (1661) 2500; Universitetsbiblioteket (1482) 1800.

Odense: [a]Fyn I. [b]none. [c]Odense R. [d]Odense Universitet (1964) 5 – 575. [e]Universitetsbibliotek (1965) 715; Centralbibliotek (1924) 535.

Faeroe Islands

*Torshavn: [a]Streymoy I. [b]alt Thorshavn. [c]Norwegian Sea. [d]none. [e]National Library (1828) 90; Public Library (1969) 57.

Finland

*Helsinki: [b]alt Helsingfors. [c]G of Finland of Baltic Sea; Vantaan (alt Vanda) R. [d]Helsinki University (1640 at Turku, relocated 1828) 25 – 2786. [e] . . . University Library (1640 at Turku, relocated 1828) 5500; City Library (1860) 1833.

TABLE 2b. (Continued)

Joensuu: [b]none. [c]Pielis R; Pyhaselka L. [d]Joensuu University (1969) 4 – 279. [e]City Library (1862) 280; . . . University Library (1970) 225.

Jyvaskyla: [b]none. [c]Paijanne L. [d]Jyvaskyla University (1863) 8 – 540. [e] . . . University Library (1912) 700; City Library (1863) 152.

Kuopio: [b]none. [c]Kalla L. [d]Kuopio University (1966) 2 – 240. [e]City Library (1872) 416; . . . University Library (1972) 45.

Oulu: [b]alt Uleaborg. [c]G of Bothnia; Oulu (alt Ule) R. [d]Oulu University (1958) 7 – 650. [e] . . . University Library (1959) 954; City-County Library (1866) 333.

Tampere: [b]alt Tammerfors. [c]Tammer Rapids; Nasi L; Pyha L. [d]Tampere University (1925) 11 – 553. [e]City-County Library (1861) 835; . . . University Library (1925) 750.

Turku: [b]alt Abo. [c]G of Bothnia; Aura R. [d]Turku University (1920) 10 – 1050; Abo Academy (univ) (1918) 4 – 229. [e] . . . University Library (1919) 1300; . . . Academy Library (1918) 1250; City-County Library (1863) 916.

Vaasa: [b]alt Vasa. [c]G of Bothnia. [d]Vaasa University (1966) 2 – 98. [e]City Library (1863) 313; . . . University Library (1968) 74.

France

Aix-en-Provence: [a]Provence-Cote d'Azur. [b]alt Aix. [c]nr Arc R. [d]Universite d'Aix-Marseille (at Aix-en-Provence and Marseilles) (1413) 53 – 3172 [Aix-en-Provence campus: (1413) 14 – 1358]. [e]Bibliotheque Interuniversitaire, Aix-en-Provence campus (1879) 447; Bibliotheque Municipale (1810) 350.

Ajaccio: [a]Corse; Corsica I. [b]none. [c]Mediterranean Sea. [d]none. [e]Bibliotheque Municipale (1801) 62.

Amiens: [a]Picardie. [b]none. [c]Somme R. [d]Universite de Picardie (1750) 9 – 670. [e]Bibliotheque de l'Universite . . . (1965) 500; Bibliotheque Municipale (1791) 160.

Angers: [a]Pays de la Loire. [b]none. [c]Maine R. [d]Universite d'Angers (1364) 7 – 355; Universite Catholique de l'Ouest (1876) 4 – 197. [e]Bibliotheque Municipale (1848) 350; Bibliotheque de l'Universite Catholique de l'Ouest (1875) 300.

Avignon: [a]Provence-Cote d'Azur. [b]none. [c]Rhone R. [d]Centre Universitaire d'Avignon (1972) 2 – 106. [e]Bibliotheque Municipale Calvet (1810) 300.

Besancon: [a]Franche-Comte. [b]none. [c]Doubs R. [d]Universite de Franche-Comte (1423 at Dole, relocated 1691) 12 – 730. [e]Bibliotheque de l'Universite . . . (1880) 300; Bibliotheque Municipale (1694) 300.

Bethune: [a]Nord. [b]none. [c]Lawe R. [d]none. [e]Bibliotheque Municipale (1931) 13.

Biarritz: [a]Aquitaine. [b]none. [c]B of Biscay. [d]none. [e]Bibliotheque du Centre d'Etudes et de Recherches Scientifiques de Biarritz (1955) 7; Bibliotheque Municipale (?) ?

Bordeaux: [a]Aquitaine. [b]none. [c]Garonne R. [d]Universite de Bordeaux (at Bordeaux and Talence, nr Bordeaux) (1441) 38 – 1806. [e]Bibliotheque Interuniversitaire (1870) 1100; Bibliotheque Municipale (1740) 807.

Brest: [a]Bretagne. [b]none. [c]Alantic O. [d]Universite de Bretagne Occidentale (1970) 8 – 537. [e]Bibliotheque de l'Universite . . . (1970?) 102; Bibliotheque Municipale (1853) 86.

Caen: [a]Basse-Normandie. [b]none. [c]Orne R; Odon R. [d]Universite de Caen (1432) 12 – 760. [e]Bibliotheque de l'Universite . . . (1432) 600; Bibliotheque de la Ville (1809) 460.

Calais: [a]Nord. [b]none. [c]Strait of Dover. [d]none. [e]Bibliotheque Municipale (1790) 52.

Cannes: [a]Provence-Cote d'Azur. [b]none. [c]Mediterranean Sea. [d]none. [e]Bibliotheque Municipale (1868) 90.

Chambery: [a]Rhone-Alpes. [b]none. [c]Leysse R; Albane R. [d]Universite de Chambery (1970) 3 – 130. [e]Bibliotheque Municipale (1783) 142; Bibliotheque de l'Universite . . . (1962) 123.

Chartres: [a]Centre. [b]none. [c]Eure R. [d]none. [e]Bibliotheque Municipale (18th c) 70.

Cherbourg: [a]Basse-Normandie. [b]none. [c]English Channel; Givette R. [d]none. [e]Bibliotheque Municipale (18th c) 65.

Clermont-Ferrand: [a]Auvergne. [b]none. [c]nr Sioule R. [d]Universite de Clermont-Ferrand (1810) 15 – 1468. [e]Bibliotheque Municipale et Interuniversitaire (18th c) 560.

Dijon: [a]Bourgogne. [b]none. [c]Ouche R; Suzon R. [d]Universite de Dijon (1722) 13 – 699. [e]Bibliotheque de l'Universite . . . (1840) 460; Bibliotheque Municipale (1701) 300.

Douai: [a]Nord. [b]for Douay. [c]Scarpe R. [d]none. [e]Bibliotheque Municipale (1767) 150.

Dunkerque: [a]Nord. [b]alt Dunkirk. [c]North Sea. [d]none. [e]Bibliotheque Municipale (18th c) 57.

Grenoble: [a]Rhone-Alpes. [b]none. [c]Isere R. [d]Universite de Grenoble (1339) 28 – 1536; Institut Nationale Polytechnique (univ) (1971) 2 – 160. [e]Bibliotheque Interuniversitaire (1879) 900; Bibliotheque Municipale (1772) 564.

La Rochelle: [a]Poitou-Charentes. [b]alt Rochelle. [c]B of Biscay. [d]none. [e]Bibliotheque Municipale (1750) 230.

For an explanation of symbols and abbreviations, see pages 16–17.

(Continued)

TABLE 2b. (Continued)

Le Havre: [a]Haute-Normandie. [b]alt Havre. [c]English Channel; Seine R. [d]none. [e]Bibliotheque Municipale (1800) 250.

Le Mans: [a]Pays de la Loire. [b]alt Mans. [c]Maine R; Sarthe R; Huisne R. [d]Universite du Maine (1970) 4 – 219. [e]Bibliotheque Municipale (1790) 250.

Lens: [a]Nord. [b]none. [c]Deule R. [d]none.

Lille: [a]Nord. [b]none. [c]Deule R. [d]Universite de Lille (at Lille and Villeneuve d'Ascq, nr Lille) (1560 at Douai, relocated 1887) 40 – 1714; Federation Universitaire et Polytechnique (univ) (1875) 9 – 742. [e]Bibliotheque Interuniversitaire (1880 at Douai, relocated 1887) 1080; Bibliotheque Municipale (1726) 600; Bibliotheque de la Federation . . . (1877) 450.

Limoges: [a]Limousin. [b]none. [c]Vienne R. [d]Universite de Limoges (1626) 9 – 450. [e]Bibliotheque Municipale (1804) 300; Bibliotheque de l'Universite . . . (1962) 100.

Lourdes: [a]Midi-Pyrenees. [b]none. [c](Gave de) Pau Torrent. [d]none. [e]Bibliotheque du Musee Pyreneen (1921) ?

Lyons: [a]Rhone-Alpes. [b]off Lyon. [c]Rhone R; Saone R. [d]Universite de Lyon (1809) 48 – 2549; Facultes Catholiques (univ) (1875) 4 – 318. [e]Bibliotheque Interuniversitaire (1809?) 1130; Bibliotheque Municipale (1693) 1000.

Mantes-la-Jolie: [a]Region Parisienne. [b]for Mantes-Gassicourt. [c]Seine R. [d]none. [e]Bibliotheque Municipale (1966) 50.

Marseilles: [a]Provence-Cote d'Azur. [b]off Marseille. [c]G of Lions of Mediterranean Sea. [d]Universite d'Aix-Marseille (at Aix-en-Provence and Marseilles) (1413) 53 – 3172 [Marseilles campus: (1854) 39 – 1814]. [e]Bibliotheque Interuniversitaire, Marseilles campus (1880) 600; Bibliotheque Municipale (1799) 400.

Metz: [a]Lorraine. [b]none. [c]Moselle R; Seille R. [d]Universite de Metz (1970) 5 – 261. [e]Bibliotheque Municipale (1811) 351.

Montpellier: [a]Languedoc-Roussillon. [b]none. [c]Lez R. [d]Universite de Montpellier (1220) 35 – 1795. [e]Bibliotheque Interuniversitaire (1767) 1210; Bibliotheque de la Ville (1800) 580.

Mulhouse: [a]Alsace. [b]for Mulhausen. [c]Ill R. [d]Universite de Haute-Alsace (1970) 3 – 188. [e]Bibliotheque Municipale (1840) 362.

Nancy: [a]Lorraine. [b]none. [c]Meurthe R. [d]Universite de Nancy (1572) 22 – 1272; Institut Nationale Polytechnique de Lorraine (univ) (1970) 2 – 170. [e]Bibliotheque Interuniversitaire (1855) 930; Bibliotheque Municipale (1750) 500.

Nantes: [a]Pays de la Loire. [b]none. [c]Loire R; Sevre Nantaise R; Erdre R. [d]Universite de Nantes (1460) 16 – 1010. [e]Bibliotheque Municipale (1753) 350; Bibliotheque de l'Universite . . . (1962) 166.

Nice: [a]Provence-Cote d'Azur. [b]for Nizza. [c]Mediterranean Sea; Paillon R. [d]Universite de Nice (1965) 17 – 859. [e]Bibliotheque Municipale d'Etudes (1802) 482; Bibliotheque de l'Universite . . . (1965) 160.

Nimes: [a]Languedoc-Roussillon. [b]none. [c]nr Gard R. [d]none. [e]Bibliotheque Municipale (1794) 255.

Orleans: [a]Centre. [b]none. [c]Loire R. [d]Universite d'Orleans (1306) 7 – 385. [e]Bibliotheque Municipale (1714) 400; Bibliotheque de l'Universite . . . (1965) 165.

*Paris: [a]Region Parisienne. [b]none. [c]Seine R. [d]Universite de Paris (1200) 289 – 17,560; Institut Catholique (univ) (1875) 15 – 802. [e]Bibliotheque Nationale (1368) 12,300; Bibliotheque de l'Universite . . . (1624) 10,350, inc Bibliotheque de la Sorbonne (1763) 3000, and Bibliotheque Sainte-Genevieve (1624) 1550; Bibliotheque de l'Institut de France (1795) 1500; Bibliotheque Pedagogique (1879) 1200.

Pau: [a]Aquitaine. [b]none. [c](Gave de) Pau Torrent. [d]Universite de Pau et des Pays de l'Adour (1970) 6 – 248. [e]Bibliotheque Municipale (1744) 310; Bibliotheque de l'Universite . . . (1947) 150.

Perpignan: [a]Languedoc-Roussillon. [b]none. [c]Tet R. [d]Universite de Perpignan (1970) 3 – 190. [e]Bibliotheque Municipale (1349) 85.

Poitiers: [a]Poitou-Charentes. [b]none. [c]Clain R; Boivre R. [d]Universite de Poitiers (1431) 14 – 1185. [e]Bibliotheque de l'Universite . . . (1879) 460; Bibliotheque Municipale (1793) 350.

Rennes: [a]Bretagne. [b]none. [c]Vilaine R; Ille R. [d]Universite de Rennes (1461 at Nantes, relocated 1735) 29 – 1226. [e]Bibliotheque Interuniversitaire (1855) 1020; Bibliotheque Municipale (1790) 400.

Rheims: [a]Champagne. [b]off Reims. [c]Vesle R. [d]Universite de Reims (1548) 14 – 700. [e]Bibliotheque Municipale (1809) 348; Bibliotheque de l'Universite . . . (1950) 200.

Rouen: [a]Haute-Normandie. [b]none. [c]Seine R. [d]Universite de Rouen-Haute Normandie (at Mont-Saint-Aignan, nr Rouen) (1828) 13 – 700. [e]Bibliotheque Municipale (1791) 525.

Saint-Etienne: [a]Rhone-Alpes. [b]none. [c]Furens R. [d]Universite de Saint-Etienne (1970) 7 – 344. [e]Bibliotheque Municipale (1843) 295.

Saint-Nazaire: [a]Pays de la Loire. [b]none. [c]B of Biscay; Loire R. [d]none. [e]Bibliotheque Municipale (1889) 65.

Strasbourg: [a]Alsace. [b]for Strassburg. [c]Ill R. [d]Universite de Strasbourg (1537) 29 – 1691. [e]Bibliotheque Nationale et Universitaire (1872) 3000; Bibliotheque Municipale (1765) 360.

TABLE 2b. (Continued)

Thionville: [a]Lorraine. [b]for Diedenhofen. [c]Moselle R. [d]none. [b]Bibliotheque Municipale (1842) 12.

Toulon: [a]Provence-Cote d'Azur. [b]none. [c]Mediterranean Sea. [d]Universite de Toulon et du Var (at La Garde, nr Toulon) (1970) 3 – 117. [e]Bibliotheque Municipale (1791) 180.

Toulouse: [a]Midi-Pyrenees. [b]none. [c]Garonne R. [d]Universite de Toulouse (1229) 47 – 1819; Institut Catholique (univ) (1877) 2 – 239; Institut Nationale Polytechnique (univ) (1970) 2 – 189. [e]Bibliotheque Interuniversitaire (1823) 900; Bibliotheque Municipale (1772) 600.

Tours: [a]Centre. [b]none. [c]Loire R; Cher R. [d]Universite Francois-Rabelais de Tours (1948) 13 – 647. [e]Bibliotheque Municipale (1791) 530; Bibliotheque de l'Universite . . . (1957) 130.

Troyes: [a]Champagne. [b]none. [c]Seine R. [d]none. [e]Bibliotheque Municipale (1651) 320.

Valenciennes: [a]Nord. [b]none. [c]Scheldt R; Rhonelle R. [d]Universite de Valenciennes et du Hainaut-Cambresis (1970) 3 – 174. [e]Bibliotheque Municipale (1765) 152.

Versailles: [a]Region Parisienne. [b]none. [c]nr Seine R. [d]none. [e]Bibliotheque Municipale (1803) 526.

Vichy: [a]Auvergne. [b]none. [c]Allier R. [d]none. [e]Bibliotheque de la Societe des Sciences Medicales de Vichy (1884) 10.

Germany: East

*Berlin (see under Germany: West)

Brandenburg: [b]alt Brandenburg an der Havel. [c]Havel R. [d]none. [e]Stadtbibliothek (1892) 205.

Dresden: [b]none. [c]Elbe R; Weisseritz R. [d]Technische Universitat Dresden (1828) 11 – 2300. [e]Universitatsbibliothek (1828) 1275; Sachsische Landesbibliothek (1556) 1221; Stadt- und Bezirksbibliothek (1910) 726.

Erfurt: [b]none. [c]Gera R. [d]none. [e]Wissenschaftliche Allgemeinbibliothek (1392) 730.

Freiberg: [b]none. [c]Freiberge Mulde R. [d]Bergakademie Freiberg (univ) (1765) 3 – 833. [e]Bibliothek der Bergakademie . . . (1765) 482; Stadt- und Kreisbibliothek (1876) 92.

Gotha: [b]none. [c]nr Horsel R; nr Nesse R. [d]none. [e]Forschungsbibliothek Gotha (1647) 522; Stadt- und Kreisbibliothek Heinrich Heine (1950) 121.

Greifswald: [b]none. [c]Ryck R. [d]Ernst-Moritz-Arndt Universitat Greifswald (1456) 3 – 140. [e]Universitatsbibliothek (1604) 2015.

Halle: [b]none. [c]Saale R. [d]Martin-Luther-Universitat Halle-Wittenberg [1502 at Wittenberg, united with Universitat Halle (1694) in 1817] 9 – 2283. [e]Universitats- und Landesbibliothek Sachsen-Anhalt (1696) 3640; Stadt- und Bezirksbibliothek (1874) 461.

Jena: [b]none. [c]Saale R. [d]Friedrich-Schiller-Universitat Jena (1548) 6 – 2151. [e]Universitatsbibliothek (1558) 2528; Ernst-Abbe Bucherei (1896) 142.

Karl-Marx-Stadt: [b]for Chemnitz. [c]Chemnitz R. [d]Technische Hochschule Karl-Marx-Stadt (univ) (1836) 5 – 1527. [b]Stadt- und Bezirksbibliothek (1869) 880; Hochschulbibliothek (1836) 587.

Leipzig: [b]none. [c]White Elster (off Weisse Elster) R; Pleisse R; Parthe R. [d]Karl-Marx-Universitat Leipzig (1409) 13 – 3380. [e]Deutsche Bucherei (1912) 7379; Universitatsbibliothek (1543) 3284; Stadt- und Bezirksbibliothek (1677) 1170.

Magdeburg: [b]none. [c]Elbe R. [d]Technische Hochschule Otto von Guericke (univ) (1953) 3 – 767. [e]Stadt- und Bezirksbibliothek (1525) 632; Hochschulbibliothek (1953) 217.

Potsdam: [b]none. [c]Havel R; Templiner L; Jungfern L; Heiliger L. [d]Akademie fur Staats- und Rechtswissenschaft der DDR (univ) (1948) 2 – 440. [e]Wissenschaftliche Allgemeinbibliothek (1874) 725; Bibliothek der Akademie . . . (1948) 360.

Rostock: [b]none. [c]Warnow R. [d]Wilhelm-Pieck Universitat Rostock (1419) 6 – 1845. [e]Universitatsbibliothek (1419) 1860; Stadt- und Bezirksbibliothek (1894) 399.

Wittenberg: [b]none. [c]Elbe R. [d]none. [e]Stadt- und Kreisbibliothek (1872) 145.

Germany: West

Aachen: [a]Nordrhein-Westfalen. [b]for Aix-la-Chapelle. [c]Wurm(bach) Creek. [d]Rheinisch-Westfalische Technische Hochschule (univ) (1870) 35 – 8137. [e]Hochschulbibliothek (1870) 850; Offentliche Bibliothek der Stadt (1829) 406.

Augsburg: [a]Bayern. [b]none. [c]Lech R. [d]Universitat Augsburg (1970) 7 – 520. [e]Universitatsbibliothek (1970) 1129; Staats- und Stadtbibliothek (1537) 379; Stadtbucherei (1920) 173.

Baden-Baden: [a]Baden-Wurttemberg. [b]alt Baden. [c]Oos(bach) Creek. [d]none. [e]Stadtbucherei (1901) 70.

Bamberg: [a]Bayern. [b]none. [c]Regnitz R. [d]Universitat Bamberg (1648) 4 – 300. [e]Universitatsbibliothek (1972) 505; Staatsbibliothek (1803) 328.

Bayreuth: [a]Bayern. [b]none. [c]Roter Main R. [d]Universitat Bayreuth (1972) 4 – 463. [e]Universitatsbibliothek (1974) 560; Stadtbibliothek (1921) 87.

For an explanation of symbols and abbreviations, see pages 16–17.

(Continued)

TABLE 2b. (Continued)

Berlin: [a]West Berlin: *West-Berlin. [b]inc Charlottenburg since 1920, East Berlin (off Ost-Berlin), West Berlin (off West-Berlin). [c]Havel R; Spree R. [d]East Berlin: Humboldt-Universitat zu Berlin (1810) 19 – 5000; Hochschule fur Okonomie Bruno Leuschner (univ) (1950) 3 – 550; West Berlin: Freie Universitat Berlin (1948) 51 – 4340; Technische Universitat Berlin (1799) 25 – 2000. [e]East Berlin: Deutsche Staatsbibliothek (1661) 6896; Universitatsbibliothek (of Humboldt-Universitat . . .) (1831) 4140; Stadtbibliothek (1901) 1153; West Berlin: Universitatsbibliothek (of Freie Universitat . . .) (1948) 4930; Staatsbibliothek Preussischer Kulturbesitz (1661) 3334; Universitatsbibliothek (of Technische Universitat . . .) (1879) 1300. [f]Charlottenburg: 189 (1900), 9 (1849), 3 (1800).

Bielefeld: [a]Nordrhein-Westfalen. [b]none. [c]Lutter(bach) Creek. [d]Universitat Bielefeld (1967) 13 – 878. [e]Universitatsbibliothek (1968) 1275; Stadtbibliothek (1905) 529.

Bochum: [a]Nordrhein-Westfalen. [b]none. [c]nr Ruhr R. [d]Ruhr-Universitat Bochum (1961) 30 – 1810. [e]Universitatsbibliothek (1962) 2590; Stadtbucherei (1905) 544.

*Bonn: [a]Nordrhein-Westfalen. [b]inc Bad Godesberg (alt Godesberg) since 1968. [c]Rhine R. [d]Rheinische Friedrich-Wilhelms-Universitat Bonn (1777) 39 – 930. [e]Universitatsbibliothek (1818) 3930; Bibliothek des Deutschen Bundestages (1949) 745; Stadtbucherei (1943) 450.[f]Bad Godesberg: 65 (1961), 45 (1950), 24 (1933), 9 (1900), 0.9 (1845), 0.8 (1794).

Bremen: [a]*Bremen. [b]none. [c]Weser R. [d]Universitat Bremen (1964) 9 – 350. [e]Staats- und Universitatsbibliothek (1660) 2283; Stadtbibliothek (1901) 1000.

Brunswick: [a]Niedersachsen. [b]off Braunschweig. [c]Oker R. [d]Technische Universitat Carolo-Wilhelmina Braunschweig (1745) 14 – 681. [e]Universitatsbibliothek (1748) 921; Offentliche Bucherei (1910) 287; Stadtbibliothek (1861) 251.

Cologne: [a]Nordrhein-Westfalen. [b]off Koln, [c]Rhine R. [d]Universitat zu Koln (1388) 45 – 2070. [e]Universitats- und Stadtbibliothek (1602) 5250; Stadtbucherei (1878) 369.

Constance: [a]Baden-Wurttemberg. [b]off Konstanz. [c]Rhine R; Constance L. [d]Universitat Konstanz (1966) 6 – 546. [b]Bibliothek der Universitat . . . (1964) 1035.

Darmstadt: [a]Hessen. [b]none. [c]nr Gersprenz R. [d]Technische Hochschule Darmstadt (univ) (1836) 14 – 1005. [e]Hessische Landes- und Hochschulbibliothek (1567) 1475; Stadtbibliothek (1879) 165.

Dortmund: [a]Nordrhein-Westfalen. [b]none. [c]Emscher R. [d]Universitat Dortmund (1965) 18 – 600. [e]Universitatsbibliothek (1946) 1157; Stadtbucherei (1896) 509; Stadt- und Landesbibliothek (1907) 464.

Duisburg: [a]Nordrhein-Westfalen. [b]inc Hamborn since 1929. [c]Rhine R; Ruhr R. [d]Universitat-Gesamthochschule Duisburg (1972) 11 – 831. [e]Stadtbibliothek (1901) 956; Universitatsbibliothek (1972?) 560. [f]Hamborn: 127 (1925), 33 (1900), 1 (1871).

Dusseldorf: [a]*Nordrhein-Westfalen. [b]none. [c]Rhine R; Dussel R. [d]Universitat Dusseldorf (1708) 15 – 1510. [e]Universitatsbibliothek (1770) 1895; Stadtbucherei (1886) 757.

Erlangen: [a]Bayern. [b]none. [c]Regnitz R. [d]Friedrich-Alexander-Universitat Erlangen-Nurnberg (1743) 24 – 1810. [e]Universitatsibibliothek (1743) 2990; Stadtbucherei (1921) 109.

Essen: [a]Nordrhein-Westfalen. [b]none. [c]Ruhr R; Emscher R; Baldeney L. [d]Universitat-Gesamthochschule Essen (1972) 17 – 1190. [e]Stadtbibliothek (1902) 929; Gesamthochschulbibliothek (1972) 711.

Flensburg: [a]Schleswig-Holstein. [b]for Flensborg. [c]Flensburger (Forde) Inlet of Baltic Sea. [d]none. [e]Dansk Centralbibliotek for Sydslesvig (1920) 160; Stadtbucherei (1904) 100; Landeszentralbibliothek Schleswig-Holstein (1925) 50.

Frankfurt am Main: [a]Hessen. [b]alt Frankfort, Frankfurt. [c]Main R. [d]Johann Wolfgang Goethe-Universitat Frankfurt (1914) 29 – 6986. [e]Stadt- und Universitatsbibliothek (1484) 5010; Deutsche Bibliothek (1946) 3058; Stadtbucherei (1945) 845.

Freiburg im Breisgau: [a]Baden-Wurttemberg. [b]alt Freiburg. [c]Dreisam R. [d]Albert-Ludwigs-Universitat Freiburg (1457) 22 – 3220. [e]Universitatsbibliothek (1457) 2840; Stadtbibliothek (1893) 200.

Gelsenkirchen: [a]Nordrhein-Westfalen. [b]none. [c]Emscher R. [d]none. [e]Stadtbucherei (1910) 405.

Giessen: [a]Hessen. [b]none. [c]Lahn R. [d]Justus Liebig-Universitat Giessen (1607) 16 – 740. [e]Universitatsbibliothek (1612) 1770; Stadtbibliothek (1965) 52.

Gottingen: [a]Niedersachsen. [b]none. [c]Leine R. [d]Georg-August-Universitat Gottingen (1737) 28 – 910. [e]Niedersachsische Staats- und Universitatsbibliothek (1734) 4770; Stadtbibliothek (1897) 138.

Hagen: [a]Nordrhein-Westfalen. [b]none. [c]Ennepe R; Volme R. [d]none. [e]Stadtbucherei (1899) 270; Hochschulbibliothek (1974) 267.

Hamburg: [a]*Hamburg. [b]inc Altona since 1933. [c]Elbe R. [d]Universitat Hamburg (1919) 41 – 3317; Technische Universitat Hamburg-Harburg (?) 0.2 – ? [e]Staats- und Universitatsbibliothek (1479) 4180; Offentliche Bucherhallen (1899) 2025. [f]Altona: 242 (1933), 162 (1900), 41 (1855), 23 (1803).

Hamm: [a]Nordrhein-Westfalen. [b]none. [c]Lippe R. [d]none. [e]Stadtbucherei (1895) 196.

TABLE 2b. (Continued)

Hannover: [a]*Niedersachsen. [b]alt Hanover. [c]Leine R. [d]Universitat Hannover (1831) 25 – 1379. [e]Universitatsbibliothek (1831) 2070; Niedersachsische Landesbibliothek (1665) 1378; Stadtbibliothek (1440) 492.

Heidelberg: [a]Baden-Wurttemberg. [b]none. [c]Neckar R. [d]Ruprecht-Karls-Universitat Heidelberg (1386) 26 – 2223. [e]Universitatsbibliothek (1386) 3980; Bibliothek des Max-Planck-Instituts (1924) 298; Stadtbucherei (1906) 135.

Herne: [a]Nordrhein-Westfalen. [b]inc Wanne-Eickel since 1974; Wanne: for Bickern. [c]nr Emscher R. [d]none. [e]Stadtbucherei (1906) 301. [f]Eickel: 17 (1900), 0.6 (1843), 0.5 (1818); Wanne: 24 (1900), 0.4 (1843), 0.3 (1818); Wanne-Eickel: 99 (1970), 107 (1961), 92 (1933).

Hildesheim; [a]Niedersachsen. [b]none. [c]Innerste R. [d]Hochschule Hildesheim (univ) (1978) 2 – 113. [e]Hochschulbibliothek (1946) 173; Stadtbibliothek (1630) 170.

Kaiserslautern: [a]Rheinland-Pfalz. [b]none. [c]Lauter R. [d]Universitat Kaiserslautern (1970) 6 – 1300. [e]Universitatsbibliothek (1970) 610; Stadtbibliothek (1853) 127.

Karlsruhe: [a]Baden-Wurttemberg. [b]for Carlsruhe. [c]nr Rhine R. [d]Universitat Fridericiana Karlsruhe (1825) 16 – 1019. [e]Badische Landesbibliothek (1500 at Pforzheim, relocated 1765) 831; Universitatsbibliothek (1832) 720; Stadtbibliothek (1921) 271.

Kassel: [a]Hessen. [b]for Cassel. [c]Fulda R. [d]Universitat-Gesamthochschule Kassel (1970) 9 – 505. [e]Gesamthochschulbibliothek, Landesbibliothek und Murhardsche Bibliothek der Stadt (1580) 845; Stadtbucherei (1876) 268.

Kiel: [a]*Schleswig-Holstein. [b]none. [c]Baltic Sea. [d]Christian-Albrechts-Universitat Kiel (1665) 17 – 1739. [e]Universitatsbibliothek (1665) 2200; Bibliothek des Instituts fur Weltwirtschaft (1914) 1538; Stadtbucherei (1874) 360; Schleswig-Holsteinische Landesbibliothek (1873) 149.

Koblenz: [a]Rheinland-Pfalz. [b]alt Coblenz. [c]Rhine R; Moselle R. [d]none. [e]Stadtbibliothek (1827) 368.

Krefeld: [a]Nordrhein-Westfalen. [b]for Crefeld. [c]Rhine R. [d]none. [e]Stadtbucherei (1900) 209.

Leverkusen: [a]Nordrhein-Westfalen. [b]inc Wiesdorf since 1930. [c]Rhine R; Wupper R. [d]none. [e]Kekule-Bibliothek (1897) 523; Stadtbibliothek (1926) 219. [f]Wiesdorf: 22 (1920), 6 (1900), 1 (1861), 0.7 (1797).

Lubeck: [a]Schleswig-Holstein. [b]none. [c]Trave R; Wakenitz R. [d]none. [e]Bibliothek der Hansestadt Lubeck (1620) 930.

Ludwigshafen: [a]Rheinland-Pfalz. [b]alt Ludwigshafen am Rhein. [c]Rhine R. [d]none. [e]Stadtbibliothek (1875) 278.

Mainz: [a]*Rheinland-Pfalz. [b]for Mayence. [c]Rhine R; Main R. [d]Johannes Gutenberg-Universitat Mainz (1476) 26 – 1208. [e]Universitatsbibliothek (1946) 2150; Stadtbibliothek (1477) 464.

Mannheim: [a]Baden-Wurttemberg. [b]none. [c]Rhine R; Neckar R. [d]Universitat Mannheim (1907) 10 – 600. [e]Universitatsbibliothek (1907) 1090; Stadtbucherei (1895) 600.

Marburg: [a]Hessen. [b]alt Marburg an der Lahn. [c]Lahn R. [d]Philipps-Universitat Marburg (1527) 15 – 615. [e]Universitatsbibliothek (1527) 2970; Bibliothek des J. G. Herder-Instituts (1950) 209.

Monchengladbach: [a]Nordrhein-Westfalen. [b]for Munchen-Gladbach; inc Rheydt since 1974. [c]Niers R. [d]none. [e]Stadtbibliothek (1904) 447. [f]Rheydt: 100 (1970), 78 (1950), 77 (1933), 34 (1900), 8 (1849), 3 (1803).

Mulheim an der Ruhr: [a]Nordrhein-Westfalen. [b]alt Mulheim. [c]Ruhr R. [d]none. [e]Stadtbucherei (1883) 302.

Munich: [a]*Bayern. [b]off Munchen. [c]Isar R. [d]Ludwig-Maximilians-Universitat Munchen (1472) 54 – 10,100; Technische Universitat Munchen (1827) 21 – 2730; Ukrainische Freie Universitat (1921) 0.5 – 82. [e]Bayerische Staatsbibliothek (1558) 4850; Universitatsbibliothek (1473) 4610; Stadtische Bibliothek (1841) 2200; Universitatsbibliothek der Technische Universitat . . . (1868) 1040.

Munster: [a]Nordrhein-Westfalen. [b]none. [c]Aa R. [d]Westfalische Wilhelms-Universitat Munster (1780) 44 – 2253. [e]Universitatsbibliothek (1773) 2475; Stadtbucherei (1933) 211.

Nuremberg: [a]Bayern. [b]off Nurnberg. [c]Pegnitz R. [d]none. [e]Stadtbibliothek (1370) 753; Bibliothek des Germanischen Nationalmuseums (1852) 429.

Oberammergau: [a]Bayern. [b]none. [c]Ammer R. [d]none.

Oberhausen: [a]Nordrhein-Westfalen. [b]none. [c]nr Emscher R. [d]none. [e]Stadtbucherei (1907) 174.

Oldenburg in Oldenburg: [a]Niedersachsen. [b]alt Oldenburg. [c]Hunte R. [d]Universitat Oldenburg (1970) 9 – 399. [e]Bibliothek der Universitat . . . (1974) 560; Landesbibliothek (1792) 364.

Osnabruck: [a]Niedersachsen. [b]none. [c]Haase R. [d]Universitat Osnabruck (1970) 7 – 500. [e]Universitatsbibliothek (1953) 455; Stadtbibliothek (1902) 273.

Paderborn: [a]Nordrhein-Westfalen. [b]none. [c]Pader R. [d]Universitat-Gesamthochschule Paderborn (1972) 12 – 530. [e]Universitatsbibliothek (1972) 655; Erzbischofliche Akademische Bibliothek (1887) 219; Stadtbibliothek (1974) 117.

Passau: [a]Bayern. [b]none. [c]Danube R; Inn R; Ilz R. [d]Universitat Passau (1973) 4 – 158. [e]Universitatsbibliothek (1976) 495; Staatliche Bibliothek (1612) 184; Europa-Bucherei der Stadt (1954) 45.

For an explanation of symbols and abbreviations, see pages 16–17.   (Continued)

TABLE 2b. (Continued)

Regensburg: [a]Bayern. [b]alt Ratisbon. [c]Danube R. [d]Universitat Regensburg (1962) 12 – 1020. [e]Universitatsbibliothek (1964) 1833; Furst Thorn und Taxis Hofbibliothek (1770) 212; Bischofliche Zentralbibliothek (1962) 203; Staatliche Bibliothek (1816) 187.

Saarbrucken: [a*]Saarland. [b]for Sarrebruck. [c]Saar (alt Sarre) R; Sulz R. [d]Universitat des Saarlandes (1947) 17 – 1138. [e]Universitatsbibliothek (1950) 1950; Stadtbucherei (1924) 282.

Siegen: [a]Nordrhein-Westfalen. [b]none. [c]Sieg R. [d]Universitat-Gesamthochschule Siegen (1972) 8 – 739. [e]Universitatsbibliothek (1972) 675; Stadtbucherei (1947) 125.

Solingen: [a]Nordrhein-Westfalen. [b]none. [c]Wupper R. [d]none. [e]Stadtbucherei (1926) 191.

Stuttgart: [a*]Baden-Wurttemberg. [b]none. [c]Neckar R. [d]Universitat Stuttgart (1829) 17 – 3170; Universitat Hohenheim (1818) 5 – 600. [e]Wurttembergische Landesbibliothek (1765) 1739; Universitatsbibliothek (of Universitat Stuttgart) (1829) 1135; Stadtbucherei (1897) 860.

Trier: [a]Rheinland-Pfalz. [b]for Treves. [c]Moselle R. [d]Universitat Trier (1970) 7 – 398. [e]Universitatsbibliothek (1970) 733; Stadtbibliothek (1775) 324.

Tubingen: [a]Baden-Wurttemberg. [b]none. [c]Neckar R; Ammer R. [d]Eberhard-Karls-Universitat Tubingen (1477) 22 – 1954. [e]Universitatsbibliothek (1477) 3100; Stadtbucherei (?) 87.

Ulm: [a]Baden-Wurttemberg. [b]none. [c]Danube R. [d]Universitat Ulm (1967) 4 – 326. [e]Universitatsbibliothek (1964) 468; Stadtbibliothek (1516) 198.

Wiesbaden: [a*]Hessen. [b]none. [c]Rhine R. [d]none. [e]Hessische Landesbibliothek (1813) 529: Stadtbibliothek (1872) 350.

Wilhelmshaven: [a]Niedersachsen. [b]none. [c]Jade B of North Sea. [d]none. [e]Stadtbucherei (1872) 118.

Wuppertal: [a]Nordrhein-Westfalen. [b]inc Barmen, Elberfeld. [c]Wupper R. [d]Universitat-Gesamthochschule Wuppertal (1972) 12 – 1280. [e]Stadtbibliothek (1852) 697; Hochschulbibliothek (1972) 641. [f]Barmen: 142 (1900), 36 (1849), 16 (1810); Elberfeld: 157 (1900), 39 (1849), 19 (1810).

Wurzburg: [a]Bayern. [b]none. [c]Main R. [d]Bayerische Julius-Maximilians-Universitat Wurzburg (1402) 17 – 1193. [e]Universitatsbibliothek (1619) 2250; Stadtbucherei (1872) 168.

Gibraltar

*Gibraltar: [b]none. [c]Strait of Gibraltar. [d]none. [e]Gibraltar Garrison Library (1793) 45.

Greece

*Athens: [b]off Athinai. [c]Kifisos R; Ilissos R. [d]National and Capodistrian University of Athens (1837) 49 – 1738; National Technical University of Athens (1836) 6 – 657. [e]National Library (1828) 2000; Library of Parliament (1844) 1500.

Ioannina: [b]alt Yannina. [c]Ioannina L. [d]University of Ioannina (1964) 5 – 232. [e]University . . . Library (1970?) 240.

Iraklion: [a]Crete I. [b]alt Herakleion; for Candia. [c]Sea of Crete. [d]University of Crete (at Rethymnon, nr Iraklion) (1973) 1 – 107. [e]University . . . Library (at Rethymnon) (1973?) 125; Vikelaia Municipal Library (?) 35.

Larissa: [b]for Yeni-Shehr; off Larisa. [c]Pinios Potamos R. [d]none.

Patras: [b]off Patrai. [c]G of Patras of Ionian Sea. [d]University of Patras (1964) 7 – 458. [e]Municipal Library (?) ?; University . . . Library (1964?) ?

Piraeus: [b]off Piraievs. [c]Saronic G of Aegean Sea. [d]none. [e]Piraeus School of Business Studies Library (1938) 10; Municipal Library (1926) ?

Rhodes: [a]Rhodes (off Rodhos) I. [b]off Rodhos; for Rodi. [c]Aegean Sea. [d]none. [e]Archaeological Museum Library (1936) 16.

Salonika: [b]alt Salonica; off Thessaloniki. [c]G of Salonika of Aegean Sea. [d]Aristotelian University of Salonika (1925) 32 – 2522. [e] . . . University Library (1927) 1000.

Volos: [b]for Gholos, Volo. [c]G of Volos of Aegean Sea. [d]none. [e]Library of the Three Hierarchs (1907) 20.

Hungary

*Budapest: [b]inc Buda (for Ofen), Pest. [c]Danube R. [d]Technical University of Budapest (1782) 10 – 2888; Lorand Eotvos University (1561) 8 – 1520. [e]Ervin Szabo Municipal Library (1904) 4289; Lorand Eotvos University Library (1635) 2343; National Szechenyi Library (1802) 2256; Hungarian Academy of Sciences Library (1826) 1039. [f]Buda: 50 (1851), 25 (1787); Pest: 106 (1851), 22 (1787).

Debrecen: [b]for Debreczin. [c]nr Berettyo R. [d]Lajos Kossuth University (1538) 2 – 470. [e] . . . University Library (1912) 1600; Transtibiscan Reformed Church Library (1538) 551; Hajdu-Bihar District Library (1952) 149.

Miskolc: [b]none. [c]Szvinva R. [d]Nehezipari Technical University (1763 at Banska Stiavnica, Czechoslovakia; relocated 1949) 2 – 466. [e] . . . University Library (1763 at Banska Stiavnica, Czechoslovakia; relocated 1949) 510; Ferenc Rakoczi II District Library (1952) 265.

TABLE 2b. (Continued)

Pecs: [b]for Funfkirchen. [c]Pecsi (Viz) Creek. [d]Janus Pannonius University of Pecs (1367) 4 – 365.
[e] . . . University Library (1774) 740; Baranya District Library (1943) 160.

Szeged: [b]for Szegedin. [c]Tisza R; Maros R. [d]Attila Jozsef University of Szeged (1872 at Cluj, Romania; relocated 1921) 3 – 526. [e] . . . University Library (1921) 750; Somogyi City Library (1881) 700.

Iceland

*Reykjavik: [a]Iceland I. [b]none. [c]Faxa B of Atlantic O. [d]University of Iceland (1911) 4 – 400. [e]National Library of Iceland (1818) 372; City Library (1923) 317; University . . . Library (1940) 253.

Ireland

Cork: [b]alt Corcaigh. [c]Lee R; Mahon L. [d]University College, Cork (of National University of Ireland) (1849) 5 – 407. [e]Cork County Library (1925) 553; University College, Cork, Library (1849) 350; City Public Library (1790) 250.

*Dublin: [b]alt Baile Atha Cliath. [c]Dublin B of Irish Sea; Liffey R. [d]National University of Ireland (1845) 20 – 1706 [University College, Dublin (1851) 10 – 1052]; Trinity College, University of Dublin (1592) 7 – 495. [e]Trinity College Library (1591) 2500; Public Library (1884) 2400; University College, Dublin, Library (1854) 750; National Library of Ireland (1877) 500.

Galway: [b]none. [c]Galway B of Atlantic O; Corrib L. [d]University College, Galway (of National University of Ireland) (1845) 5 – 247. [e]Galway County Library (1925) 247; University College, Galway, Library (1849) 180.

Limerick: [b]alt Luimneach. [c]Shannon R. [d]none. [e]Limerick County Library (1935) 300; City Public Library (1893) 47.

Isle of Man

*Douglas: [a](Isle of) Man I. [b]none. [c]Irish Sea. [d]none. [e]Public Library (?) 40.

Italy

Alessandria: [a]Piemonte. [b]none. [c]Tanaro R. [d]none. [e]Biblioteca Civica (1806) 123.

Ancona: [a]Marche. [b]none. [c]Adriatic Sea. [d]Universita degli Studi di Ancona (1969) 7 – 250. [e]Biblioteca Comunale Luciano Benincasa (1669) 112.

Arezzo: [a]Toscana. [b]none. [c]nr Arno R. [d]none. [e]Biblioteca Consorziale della Citta (1603) 120.

Bari: [a]Puglia. [b]alt Bari delle Puglie. [c]Adriatic Sea. [d]Universita degli Studi di Bari (1924) 42 – 2236. [e]Biblioteca Universitaria (1874) 450; Biblioteca Nazionale Sagarriga Visconti-Volpi (1865) 250.

Bergamo: [a]Lombardia. [b]none. [c]Serio R; Brembo R. [d]none. [e]Biblioteca Civica Angelo Mai (1760) 570.

Bologna: [a]Emilia-Romagna. [b]none. [c]mr Reno R; nr Savena R. [d]Universita degli Studi di Bologna (1088?) 63 – 2560. [e]Biblioteca Universitaria (1712) 1670; Biblioteca Comunale dell'Archiginnasio (1801) 800.

Bolzano: [a]Trentino-Alto Adige. [b]for Bozen. [c]Isarco R. [d]none. [e]Biblioteca Civica Cesare Battisti (1928) 98.

Brescia: [a]Lombardia. [b]none. [c]Garza R. [d]none. [e]Biblioteca Civica Queriniana (1750) 430.

Brindisi: [a]Puglia. [b]none. [c]Adriatic Sea. [d]none. [e]Biblioteca Provinciale (1935) 30.

Cagliari: [a]Sardegna; Sardinia I. [b]none. [c]G of Cagliari of Mediterranean Sea. [d]Universita degli Studi di Cagliari (1606) 18 – 1280. [e]Biblioteca Universitaria (1606) 680; Biblioteca Comunale (1873) 50.

Catania: [a]Sicilia; Sicily I. [b]none. [c]G of Catania of Mediterranean Sea. [d]Universita degli Studi di Catania (1434) 32 – 1660. [e]Biblioteca Regionale Universitaria (1755) 480; Biblioteca Riunite Civica e Antonio Ursino Recupero (1693) 180.

Como: [a]Lombardia. [b]none. [c]Como L. [d]none. [e]Biblioteca Comunale (1663) 280.

Cosenza: [a]Calabria. [b]none. [c]Crati R; Busente R. [d]Universita degli Studi di Calabria (at Rende, nr Cosenza) (1972) 6 – 500. [e]Biblioteca Civica (1507) 203; Biblioteca Universitaria (at Rende) (1972) ?

Cremona: [a]Lombardia. [b]none. [c]Po R. [d]none. [e]Biblioteca Statale (1607) 600.

Ferrara: [a]Emilia-Romagna. [b]none. [c]Po di Volano R. [d]Universita degli Studi di Ferrara (1391) 6 – 591. [e]Biblioteca Comunale Ariostea (1753) 155; Biblioteca Universitaria (1945) 60.

Florence: [a]Toscana. [b]off Firenze. [c]Arno R. [d]Universita degli Studi di Firenze (1321) 44 – 1631. [e]Biblioteca Nazionale Centrale (1747) 4500; Biblioteca Universitaria (1859) 2575; Biblioteca Marucelliana (1752) 521; . . . ; Biblioteca Medicea-Laurenziana (1571) 74; Biblioteca Riccardiana (1816) 70.

Foggia: [a]Puglia. [b]none. [c]nr Celone R. [d]none. [e]Biblioteca Provinciale (1936) 180.

Forli: [a]Emilia-Romagna. [b]none. [c]Montone R. [d]none. [e]Biblioteca Comunale Aurelio Saffi (1750) 265.

Genoa: [a]Liguria. [b]off Genova. [c]G of Genoa of Ligurian Sea. [d]Universita degli Studi di Genova (1471) 26 – 1900. [e]Biblioteca Universitaria (1773) 940; Biblioteca Civica Berio (1775) 210.

For an explanation of symbols and abbreviations, see pages 16–17.   (Continued)

TABLE 2b. (Continued)

La Spezia: [a]Liguria. [b]alt Spezia. [c]G of Spezia of Ligurian Sea. [d]none. [e]Biblioteca Civica Ubaldo Mazzini (1898) 110.

Lecce: [a]Puglia. [b]none. [c]nr Adriatic Sea. [d]Universita degli Studi di Lecce (1967) 6 – 313. [e]Biblioteca Universitaria (1956) 114; Biblioteca Provinciale N. Bernardini (1863) 87.

Leghorn: [a]Toscana. [b]off Livorno. [c]Ligurian Sea. [d]none. [e]Biblioteca Comunale Labronica Francesco Domenico Guerrazzi (1816) 320.

Lucca: [a]Toscana. [b]none. [c]Serchio R. [d]none. [e]Biblioteca Statale (1794) 402.

Mantua: [a]Lombardia. [b]off Mantova. [c]Mincio R. [d]none. [e]Biblioteca Comunale (1780) 400.

Messina: [a]Sicilia; Sicily I. [b]none. [c]Strait of Messina. [d]Universita degli Studi di Messina (1548) 15 – 1591. [e]Biblioteca Universitaria Regionale (1548) 440.

Milan: [a]Lombardia. [b]for Mailand; off Milano. [c]Olona R. [d]Universita degli Studi di Milano (1923) 64 – 2210; Politecnico di Milano (univ) (1863) 21 – 735; Universita Cattolica del Sacro Cuore (1920) 21 – 2060; Libera Universita di Economia e Commercio Luigi Bocconi (1902) 5 – 340. [e]Biblioteca dell'Universita Cattolica . . . (1921) 1300; Biblioteca Comunale (1890) 1200; Biblioteca Nazionale Braidense (1786) 1040; Biblioteca dell'Universita degli Studi . . . (1808) 935; Biblioteca Ambrosiana (1609) 850.

Modena: [a]Emilia-Romagna. [b]none. [c]nr Secchia R. [d]Universita degli Studi di Modena (1175) 9 – 860. [e]Biblioteca Estense e Universitaria (14th c at Ferrara, relocated 1598) 710.

Monza: [a]Lombardia. [b]none. [c]Lambro R. [d]none. [e]Biblioteca Civica (1870) 100.

Naples: [a]Campania. [b]off Napoli. [c]B of Naples of Tyrrhenian Sea. [d]Universita degli Studi di Napoli (1224) 129 – 3430. [e]Biblioteca Nazionale Vittorio Emanuele III (1804) 1550; Biblioteca Universitaria (1465) 1550.

Padua: [a]Veneto. [b]off Padova. [c]Bacchiglione R. [d]Universita degli Studi di Padova (1222) 62 – 4340. [e]Biblioteca Universitaria (1629) 1400; Biblioteca Civica (1839) 405.

Palermo: [a]Sicilia; Sicily I. [b]none. [c]G of Palermo of Tyrrhenian Sea. [d]Universita degli Studi di Palermo (1779) 19 – 1300. [e]Biblioteca Universitaria (1777) 530; Biblioteca Comunale (1760) 500; Biblioteca Centrale della Regione Siciliana (1782) 489.

Parma: [a]Emilia-Romagna. [b]none. [c]Parma R. [d]Universita degli Studi di Parma (1064) 20 – 1600. [e]Biblioteca Palatina (1762) 620; Biblioteca Universitaria (1860) 210.

Pavia: [a]Lombardia. [b]none. [c]Ticino R. [d]Universita degli Studi di Pavia (825) 18 – 1779. [e]Biblioteca Universitaria (1763) 920; Biblioteca Civica Bonetta (1833) 105.

Perugia: [a]Umbria. [b]none. [c]nr Tiber R. [d]Universita degli Studi di Perugia (1200) 20 – 1143; Universita Italiana per Stranieri (1921) 9 – 126. [e]Biblioteca Universitaria (1848) 345; Biblioteca Augusta del Comune (1623) 250.

Pesaro: [a]Marche. [b]none. [c]Adriatic Sea; Foglia R. [d]none. [e]Biblioteca Oliveriana (1795) 250.

Pescara: [a]Abruzzi e Molise. [b]none. [c]Adriatic Sea; Pescara R. [d]Libera Universita Abruzzese degli Studi Gabriele d'Annunzio (at Chieti, nr Pescara) (1961) 16 – 600. [e]Biblioteca Provinciale Gabriele d'Annunzio (1929) 150.

Piacenza: [a]Emilia-Romagna. [b]none. [c]Po R. [d]none. [e]Biblioteca Comunale Passerini Landi (1791) 200.

Pisa: [a]Toscana. [b]none. [c]Arno R. [d]Universita degli Studi di Pisa (1343) 28 – 2062. [e]Biblioteca Universitaria (1742) 890.

Pistoia: [a]Toscana. [b]none. [c]Ombrone R. [d]none. [e]Biblioteca Comunale Forteguerriana (1473) 300.

Potenza: [a]Basilicata. [b]none. [c]Basento R. [d]Universita degli Studi della Basilicata (1982) ? – ? [b]Biblioteca Provinciale (1900) 67.

Prato: [a]Toscana. [b]none. [c]Bisenzio R. [d]none. [e]Biblioteca Lazzariniana Comunale e Biblioteca Roncioniana (1676) 55.

Ravenna: [a]Emilia-Romagna. [b]none. [c]nr Adriatic Sea. [d]none. [e]Biblioteca Comunale Classense (1707) 650.

Reggio di Calabria: [a]Calabria. [b]none. [c]Strait of Messina. [d]Universita degli Studi di Reggio di Calabria (1982) ? – ? [e]Biblioteca Sandicci (1957) 100; Biblioteca Comunale (1819) 56.

Reggio nell'Emilia: [a]Emiliia-Romagna. [b]none. [c]Crostolo R. [d]none. [e]Biblioteca Municipale Antonio Panizzi (1473) 300.

Rimini: [a]Emilia-Romagna. [b]none. [c]Adriatic Sea; Marecchia R. [d]none. [e]Biblioteca Civica Gambalunga (1619) 167.

*Rome: [a]Lazio. [b]off Roma. [c]Tiber R. [d1]Universita degli Studi di Roma (1303) 155 – 6366; Libera Universita Internazionale degli Studi Sociali (1945) 2 – 130; Pontificia Universitas Gregoriana[2] (1553) 2 – 303; Pontificia Universita Santo Tommaso d'Aquino[2] (1577) 1 – 126; Pontificia Universitas Lateranensis[2] (1773) 1 – 260. [e]Biblioteca Nazionale Centrale Vittorio Emanuele II (1876) 2810; Bibliotca Universitaria (1661)

---

[1]Universities with 1,000 or more students.
[2]At Vatican City, nr Rome.

TABLE 2b. (Continued)

2800; Library of the Food and Agriculture Organization of the United Nations (1909) 1000; Biblioteca Apostolica Vaticana[2] (1475) 900; Biblioteca della Pontificia Universitas Gregoriana[2] (1551) 800; . . . ; Biblioteca dell'Accademia Nazionale dei Lincei (1730) 474; Biblioteca Casanatense (1700) 415.

Salerno: [a]Campania. [b]none. [c]G of Salerno of Tyrrhenian Sea. [d]Universita degli Studi di Salerno (1944) 18 – 398. [e]Biblioteca Provinciale (1845) 200.

San Remo: [a]Liguria. [b]none. [c]Mediterranean Sea. [d]none. [e]Biblioteca Comunale Francesco Corradi (1615) 89.

Sassari: [a]Sardegna; Sardinia I. [b]none. [c]nr G of Asinara of Mediterranean Sea. [d]Universita degli Studi di Sassari (1562) 7 – 300. [e]Biblioteca Universitaria (1556) 250; Biblioteca Comunale (1934) 70.

Siena: [a]Toscana. [b]none. [c]nr Arbia R. [d]Universita degli Studi di Siena (1240) 9 – 579. [e]Biblioteca Universitaria (1240) 465; Biblioteca Comunale degli Intronati (1758) 350.

Syracuse: [a]Sicilia; Sicily I. [b]off Siracusa. [c]Ionian Sea. [d]none. [e]Biblioteca Comunale (1857) 50.

Taranto: [a]Puglia. [b]none. [c]G of Taranto of Ionian Sea. [d]none. [e]Biblioteca Civica Pietro Acclavio (1893) 90.

Trent: [a]Trentino-Alto Adige. [b]for Trient; off Trento. [c]Adige R. [d]Universita degli Studi di Trento (1962) 3 – 200. [e]Biblioteca Comunale (1856) 200; Biblioteca Universitaria (1962?) 150.

Treviso: [a]Veneto. [b]none. [c]Sile R. [d]none. [e]Biblioteca Comunale (1770) 350.

Trieste: [a]Friuli-Venezia Giulia. [b]for Triest. [c]G of Trieste of Adriatic Sea. [d]Universita degli Studi di Trieste (1877) 13 – 1119. [e]Biblioteca Universitaria (1924) 1250; Biblioteca Civica Attilio Hortis (1793 at Gorizia, relocated 1820) 400.

Turin: [a]Piemonte. [b]off Torino. [c]Po R; Dora Riparia R. [d]Universita degli Studi di Torino (1404) 42 – 2000; Politecnico di Torino (univ) (1859) 12 – 630. [e]Biblioteca Nazionale Universitaria (1720) 2100; Biblioteche Civiche e Raccolte Storiche (1869) 430.

Udine: [a]Friuli-Venezia Giulia. [b]none. [c]Torre R. [d]Universita degli Studi di Udine (1978) 2 – 176. [e]Biblioteca Comunale V. Joppi (1866) 370.

Urbino: [a]Marche. [b]none. [c]nr Metauro R; nr Foglia R. [d]Universita degli Studi di Urbino (1506) 12 – 629. [e]Biblioteca Universitaria (1720) 437.

Venice: [a]Veneto. [b]for Venedig; off Venezia. [c]Venice Lagoon. [d]Universita degli Studi di Venezia (1868) 11 – 521. [e]Biblioteca Nazionale Marciana (1468) 800; Biblioteca Universitaria (1868) 350; Biblioteca Querini Stampalia (1869) 290.

Verona: [a]Veneto. [b]none. [c]Adige R. [d]Universita degli Studi di Verona (?) ? – ? [e]Biblioteca Civica (1792) 540.

Vicenza: [a]Veneto. [b]none. [c]Bacchiglione R; Retrone R; Astichello R. [d]none. [e]Biblioteca Civica Bertoliana (1696) 376.

Liechtenstein

*Vaduz: [b]none. [c]nr Rhine R. [d]none. [e]Liechtenstein'sche Fideikommissbibliothek (?) 57; Liechtensteinische Landesbibliothek (1961) 55.

Luxembourg

*Luxembourg: [b]alt Lutzelburg, Luxemburg. [c]Alzette R. [d]Centre Universitaire de Luxembourg (1848) 0.7 – 151. [e]Bibliotheque Nationale (1798) 700; Bibliotheque du Centre Universitaire . . . (1958) 160; Bibliotheque du Parlement Europeen (1953) 60; Bibliotheque Municipale (1968) 27.

Malta

*Valletta: [a]Malta I. [b]alt Valetta. [c]Mediterranean Sea. [d]University of Malta (at Msida, nr Valletta) (1592 at Valletta, relocated from 1967) 1 – 150. [e]National Library of Malta (1555) 348; University . . . Library (at Msida) (1769 at Valletta, relocated 1967?) 244; Beltissebh Central Public Library (at Beltissebh, nr Valletta) (1974) 100.

Monaco

*Monaco: [b]inc Monte-Carlo. [c]Mediterranean Sea. [d]none. [e]Bibliotheque Louis-Notari (1909) 150.

Netherlands

*Amsterdam: [b]none. [c]Amstel R; IJssel(meer) L. [d]Universiteit van Amsterdam (1632) 26 – 3622; Vrije Universiteit, Amsterdam (1880) 13 – 1024. [e]Universiteitsbibliotheek (1578) 3400; Bibliotheek der Vrije Universiteit . . . (1880) 1000; Openbare Bibliotheek (1919) 880.

Arnhem: [b]for Arnheim. [c]Nederrijn R (Rhine R distributary). [d]none. [e]Stichting Arnhemse Openbare en Gelderse Wetenschappelijke Bibliotheek (1856) 475.

Breda: [b]none. [c]Mark R; Aa of Weerijs R. [d]none. [e]Koninklijke Militaire Academie Bibliotheek (1828) 125; Openbare Bibliotheek (1970) ?

For an explanation of symbols and abbreviations, see pages 16–17.   (Continued)

TABLE 2b. (Continued)

Delft: [b]none. [c]Schie R. [d]Technische Hogeschool te Delft (univ) (1842) 11 – 1984. [e]Bibliotheek der . . . Hogeschool (1842) 820; Stichting Samenverkende Openbare Bibliotheek (1917) 68.

Dordrecht: [b]alt Dort. [c]Lower Merwede (off Beneden Merwede) R. [d]none. [e]Verenigde Openbare Bibliotheek (1899) 200.

Eindhoven: [b]none. [c]Dommel R; Gender R. [d]Technische Hogeschool te Eindhoven (univ) (1956) 5 – 766. [e]Gemeenschappelijke Openbare Bibliotheek (1916) 830; Bibliotheek der . . . Hogeschool (1956) 350.

Enschede: [b]none. [c]nr Almeloosche R. [d]Technische Hogeschool Twente (univ) (1961) 8 – 489. [e]Openbare Bibliotheek (1862) 380; Bibliotheek der . . . Hogeschool (1964) 160.

Groningen: [b]none. [c]Drentse A (Riviertje) Creek; Hunze (Riviertje) Creek. [d]Rijksuniversiteit te Groningen (1614) 17 – 1660. [e]Bibliotheek der Rijksuniversiteit . . . (1615) 1674; Provinciale Bibliotheekcentrale (1961) 722; Stichting Openbare Bibliotheek (1903) 436.

Haarlem: [b]none. [c]Spaarne R. [d]none. [e]Openbare Bibliotheek (1596) 540.

*Hague: [b]alt The Hague; off 's Gravenhage. [c]North Sea. [d]none. [e]Koninklijke Bibliotheek (1798) 1500; Openbare Bibliotheek (1906) 1282; Bibliotheek van het Vredespaleis (1913) 1050.

Heerlen: [b]none. [c]Geleen R. [d]none. [e]Openbare Leeszaal en Bibliotheek (1913) 125.

Hilversum: [b]none. [c]nr IJssel(meer) L. [d]none. [e]Stichting Openbare Bibliotheek (1909) 210.

Leiden: [b]alt Leyden. [c]Rhine R. [d]Rijksuniversiteit te Leiden (1575) 18 – 2078. [e]Bibliotheek der Rijksuniversiteit . . . (1575) 2200; Openbare Bibliotheek (1910) 130.

Maastricht: [b]for Maestricht. [c]Meuse R; Geer R. [d]Rijksuniversiteit Limburg (1974) 3 – 449. [e]Stadsbibliotheek (1662) 325; Bibliotheek der Rijksuniversiteit . . . (1976) 250.

Nijmegen: [b]alt Nimeguen, Nimwegen. [c]Waal R (Rhine R distributary). [d]Katholieke Universiteit Nijmegen (1923) 15 – 1829. [e]Bibliotheek van de . . . Universiteit (1923) 1000; Gemeenschappelijke Openbare Bibliotheek (1916) 140.

Rotterdam: [b]none. [c]Nieuwe Maas R (Rhine R distributary). [d]Erasmus Universiteit Rotterdam (1913) 11 – 874. [e]Gemeentebibliotheek (1604) 1335; Universiteitsbibliotheek (1913) 777.

's Hertogenbosch: [b]for Bois-le-Duc. [c]Dieze R; Dommel R; Aa R. [d]none. [e]Stichting Openbare Bibliotheek (1915) 208.

Tilburg: [b]none. [c]Leij R. [d]Hogeschool te Tilburg (univ) (1927) 6 – 600. [e]Bibliotheek der Hogeschool . . . (1927) 660; Openbare Bibliotheek (1845) 460.

Utrecht: [b]none. [c]Rhine R. [d]Rijksuniversiteit te Utrecht (1636) 25 – 2340. [e]Universiteitsbibliotheek (1581) 2750; Openbare Bibliotheek (1892) 650.

Zaanstad: [b]for Zaandam. [c]Zaan R. [d]none. [e]Gemeenschappelijke Openbare Bibliotheek (1913) 292.

Norway

Bergen: [b]none. [c]North Sea. [d]Universitetet i Bergen (1948) 8 – 1653. [e]Universitetsbiblioteket (1825) 1200; Offentlige Bibliotek (1874) 548.

*Oslo: [b]for Christiania, Kristiania. [c]Oslo Fjord of Skagerrak. [d]Universitetet i Oslo (1811) 20 – 3604. [e]Universitetsbiblioteket (1811) 4650; Deichmanske Bibliotek (1785) 1327.

Stavanger: [b]none. [c]Bokn Fjord of North Sea. [d]none. [e]Stavanger Bibliotek (1885) 330.

Tromso: [a]Tromsoy I. [b]none. [c]Tromso Sound of Norwegian Sea. [d]Universitetet i Tromso (1968) 2 – 311. [e]Universitetsbiblioteket (1872) 350; Tromso Bibliotek (1871) 210.

Trondheim: [b]for Nidaros, Trondhjem. [c]Trondheim Fjord of Norwegian Sea. [d]Universitetet i Trondheim (1900) 9 – 996. [e]Universitetsbiblioteket (1760) 1600; Folkebibliotek (1980?) 292.

Poland

Bialystok: [b]for Belostok. [c]Suprasl (alt Biala) R. [d]Bialystok Technical University (1951) 2 – ? [e]Juliana Medical Academy Library (1950) 319; District Public Library (1919) 100; . . . University Library (1951?) ?

Bielsko-Biala: [b]inc Biala, Bielsko; Bielsko: for Bielitz. [c]Biala R. [d]none. [e]Regional Public Library (1945) 105; City Public Library (1947) 75; District Public Library (?) ? [f]Biala: 23 (1931), 8 (1900), 5 (1851), 3 (1800?); Bielsko: 22 (1931), 17 (1900), 7 (1851), 3 (1800?).

Bydgoszcz: [b]for Bromberg. [c]Brda R. [d]none. [e]District and City Public Library (1903) 940; Regional Public Library (1946) 100.

Bytom: [b]for Beuthen; inc Rossberg since 1927. [c]Bytomka R. [d]none. [e]City Public Library (1946) 187. [f]Rossberg: 23 (1925), 14 (1900), 3 (1871).

Chorzow: [b]for Konigshutte, Krolewska Huta. [c]Rawa R. [d]none. [e]City Public Library (1945) 149.

Czestochowa: [b]for Chenstokhov. [c]Warta R; Stradomka R. [d]Czestochowa Technical University (1949) 2 – 450.

TABLE 2b. (Continued)

[e] . . . University Library (1950) 490; District and City Public Library (1917) 214; Regional Public Library (1946) 105.

Dabrowa Gornicza: [b]for Dombrau, Dombrova. [c]Czarna Przemsza R. [d]none. [e]City Public Library (1906) 40.

Gdansk: [b]for Danzig. [c]G of Danzig of Baltic Sea; Vistula R. [d]Gdansk University (1970) 12 – 1240; Gdansk Technical University (1904) 6 – 1264. [e]Gdansk Technical University Library (1945) 787; Gdansk Library of the Polish Academy of Sciences (1596) 605; Medical Academy Library (1945) 429; Gdansk University Library (1970) 370; District Public Library (1945) 132.

Gdynia: [b]none. [c]G of Danzig of Baltic Sea. [d]none. [e]City Public Library (1950) 355.

Gliwice: [b]for Gleiwitz. [c]Klodnica R. [d]Silesian Technical University (1945) 10 – 1810. [e] . . . University Library (1945) 840; City Public Library (1946) 173.

Katowice: [b]for Kattowitz, Stalinogrod. [c]Rawa R. [d]Silesian University (1968) 11 – 1388. [e]Silesian Library (1922) 1133; . . . University Library (1968) 715; Silesian Medical Academy Library (1945) 429; District and City Public Library (1945) 231.

Kielce: [b]for Keltsy. [c]nr Czarna Nida R. [d]Swietokrzyska Technical University (1951) 2 – 353. [e]District Public Library (1909) 160; Regional Public Library (1945) 160; . . . Technical University Library (1951?) 86.

Krakow: [b]alt Cracow; for Krakau. [c]Vistula R. [d]Jagiellonian University (1364) 12 – 1726; Krakow Technical University (1835) 6 – 1085. [e]Jagiellonian Library (1364) 3340; Academy of Mining and Metallurgy Library (1919) 1514; City Public Library (1946) 1328; Krakow Technical University Library (1945) 647.

Lodz: [b]none. [c]Lodka R. [d]Lodz University (1945) 12 – 1350; Lodz Technical University (1945) 7 – 1390. [e]Lodz University Library (1945) 1972; L. Warynski City Public Library (1917) 484.

Lublin: [b]for Lyublin. [c]Bystrzyca R. [d]Marie Curie-Sklodowska University (1944) 9 – 1435; Catholic University of Lublin (1918) 3 – 390; Lublin Technical University (1953) ? – ? [e]Marie Curie-Sklodowska University Library (1944) 1778; Catholic University of Lublin Library (1918) 1219; H. Lopacinski District and City Public Library (1907) 628.

Olsztyn: [b]for Allenstein. [c]Lyna R. [d]none. [e]Academy of Agriculture and Technology Library (1950) 370; District Public Library (1946) 105.

Poznan: [b]for Posen. [c]Warta R; Cybina R. [d]Adam Mickiewicz University of Poznan (1919) 12 – 1733; Poznan Technical University (1907) 5 – 993. [e]Adam Mickiewicz University . . . Library (1902) 3662; E. Raczynski City Public Library (1829) 1267; . . . Technical University Library (1918) 421.

Radom: [b]none. [c]Mieczna R. [d]none. [e]District Public Library (1922) 150; Regional Public Library (1945) 100.

Ruda Slaska: [b]for Ruda. [c]Bytomka R. [d]none. [e]City Public Library (1949) 138.

Rzeszow: [b]none. [c]Wislok R. [d]I. Lukasiewicz Technical University of Rzeszow (1951) 4 – 380. [e]District Public Library (1945) 120; . . . University Library (1963) 95.

Sosnowiec: [b]for Sosnovets. [c]Czarna Przemsza R. [d]none. [e]City Public Library (1922) 177.

Szczecin: [b]for Stettin. [c]Oder R. [d]Szczecin Technical University (1946) 5 – 850. [e]District and City Public Library (1902) 1153; . . . University Library (1946) 461.

Torun: [b]for Thorn. [c]Vistula R. [d]Nicholas Copernicus University of Torun (1945) 7 – 981. [e] . . . University Library (1945) 2247; N. Copernicus District and City Public Library (1923) 725.

Tychy: [b]for Tichau. [c]nr Gostynka R. [d]none. [e]Regional Public Library (1955) 95; City Public Library (1956) 30.

*Warsaw: [b]off Warszawa. [c]Vistula R. [d]Warsaw University (1808) 22 – 2519; Warsaw Technical University (1826) 13 – 2860. [e]Warsaw University Library (1817) 5030; National Library (1928) 4131; Public Library (1907) 4040.

Wroclaw: [b]for Breslau. [c]Oder R; Olawa R; Sleza R. [d]Boleslaw Bierut University of Wroclaw (1505) 11 – 1519; Wroclaw Technical University (1910) 8 – 2152. [e]Boleslaw Bierut University . . . Library (1811) 2400; Ossolineum Library of the Polish Academy of Sciences (1817 at Lvov, USSR; relocated 1946) 1000; Wroclaw Technical University Library (1946) 898; District and City Public Library (1947) 108.

Zabrze: [b]for Hindenburg, Kunzendorf. [c]Bytomka R. [d]none. [e]City Public Library (1945) 238.

Portugal

Braga: [b]none. [c]nr Este R. [d]Universidade do Minho (1973) 2 – 322. [e]Biblioteca da Universidade . . . (1841) 440; Biblioteca Municipal Veiga de Macedo (1841) 300.

Coimbra: [b]none. [c]Mondego R. [d]Universidade de Coimbra (1290 at Lisbon, relocated 1537) 12 – 814. [e]Biblioteca da Universidade . . . (1716) 2600; Biblioteca Municipal (1923) 400.

Evora: [b]none. [c]nr Dejebe R; nr Xarrama R. [d]Universidade de Evora (1974) 2 – 180. [e]Biblioteca Publica (1805) 471.

*Lisbon: [b]off Lisboa. [c]Tagus R. [d]Universidade de Lisboa (1825) 19 – 1396; Universidade Tecnica de Lisboa (1759) 13 – 1569; Universidade Catolica Portuguesa (1967) 5 – 230; Universidade Nova de Lisboa (1973)

For an explanation of symbols and abbreviations, see pages 16–17.

(Continued)

TABLE 2b. (Continued)

5 – 800; Universidade Livre de Lisboa (1977) 2 – 75. [e]Biblioteca Nacional (1796) 2000; Biblioteca da Universidade de Lisboa (1781) 800; Biblioteca da Academia das Ciencias de Lisboa (1779) 400; Biblioteca Municipal Central (1931) 317.

Ponta Delgada: [a]Azores; Sao Miguel I. [b]none. [c]Atlantic O. [d]Universidade dos Acores (1976) 0.7 – 136. [e]Biblioteca Publica (1845) 243; Biblioteca da Universidade . . . (1976?) 89.

Porto: [b]alt Oporto. [c]Douro R. [d]Universidade do Porto (1762) 14 – 1700; Universidade Livre do Porto (1977) 2 – 75. [e]Biblioteca Publica Municipal (1833) 1325; Biblioteca da Universidade do Porto (1762) 340.

Romania

Arad: [b]none. [c]Maros R. [d]none. [e]Arad County Library (1888) 387.

Bacau: [b]none. [c]Bistrita R. [d]none. [e]Bacau County Library (1950) 285.

Braila: [b]for Ibraila. [c]Danube R. [d]none. [e]Braila County Library (1881) 278.

Brasov: [b]for Brasso, Kronstadt, Orasul Stalin, Stalin. [c]Timis R. [d]University of Brasov (1948) 10 – 489. [e]University . . . Library (1948) 856; Brasov County Library (1926) 473.

*Bucharest: [b]off Bucuresti. [c]Dimbovita R; Colentina R. [d]Gheorghe Gheorghiu-Dej Polytechnic Institute (univ) (1819) 26 – 3133; University of Bucharest (1694) 14 – 975. [e]Academy of the Romanian Socialist Republic Library (1867) 8794; Central State Library (1955) 7930; University . . . Library (1857) 5200; Academy of Economic Studies Library (1913) 1897; Mihail Sadoveanu Municipal Library (1935) 1460; . . . Institute Library (1868) 1350.

Cluj-Napoca: [b]for Klausenburg, Kolozsvar. [c]Somesul Mic R; Nadasul R. [d]Babes-Bolyai University (1872) 9 – 889; Cluj-Napoca Polytechnic Institute (univ) (1948) 8 – 616. [e] . . . University Library (1872) 3348; Cluj-Napoca Branch Library of the Academy of the Romanian Socialist Republic (1950) 636; . . . Institute Library (1948) 583; Cluj County Library (1945) 338.

Constanta: [b]alt Constantsa; for Kustendje. [c]Black Sea. [d]none. [e]Constanta County Library (1935) 334.

Craiova: [b]none. [c]Jiu R. [d]University of Craiova (1966) 9 – 647. [e]University . . . Library (1966) 650; Dolj County Library (1908) 311.

Galati: [b]for Galatz. [c]Danube R; Brates L. [d]University of Galati (1948) 5 – 327. [e]V. A. Urechia Galati County Library (1890) 501; University . . . Library (1951) 420.

Iasi: [b]for Jassy. [c]Bahlui R. [d]Gheorghe Asachi Polytechnic Institute (univ) (1912) 17 – 1270; Alexandru Ioan Cuza University (1860) 6 – 592. [e] . . . University Library (1640) 2300; . . . Institute Library (1937) 719; Gheorghe Asachi Iasi County Library (1920) 400.

Oradea: [b]alt Oradea Mare; for Grosswardein, Nagy-Varad. [c]Sebes-Koros (alt Crisul-Repede) R. [d]none. [e]Bihor County Library (1882) 486.

Pitesti: [b]none. [c]Arges (alt Argesul) R. [d]none. [e]Arges County Library (1950) 267.

Ploiesti: [b]alt Ploesti. [c]Teleajen R. [d]none. [e]Petroleum and Gas Institute Library (1948) 350; N. Iorga Ploiesti County Library (1921) 281.

Sibiu: [b]for Hermannstadt, Nagyszeben. [c]Cibin R. [d]none. [e]Astra Sibiu County Library (1861) 650; Brukenthal Museum Library (1815) 268.

Timisoara: [b]for Temesvar. [c]Bega R. [d]Traian Vuia Polytechnic Institute (univ) (1920) 13 – 955; University of Timisoara (1948) 5 – 430. [e]University . . . Library (1945) 1105; Timis County Library (1904) 641; . . . Institute Library (1920) 514.

Tirgu Mures: [b]alt Targu Mures; for Maros-Vasarhely. [c]Maros R. [d]none. [e]Mures County Library (1913) 838.

Spain

Alcala de Henares: [a]Castilla la Nueva. [b]none. [c]Henares R. [d]Universidad de Alcala de Henares (1977) 3 – 651. [e]Biblioteca del Instituto Nacional de Administracion Publica (1957) 30; Biblioteca de la Universidad . . . (1977?) 20.

Alcorcon: [a]Castilla la Nueva. [b]none. [c]nr Guadarrama R. [d]none.

Algeciras: [a]Andalucia. [b]none. [c]Algeciras B of Mediterranean Sea; Miel R. [d]none.

Alicante: [a]Valencia. [b]none. [c]Mediterranean Sea. [d]Universidad de Alicante (1979) 7 – 395. [e]Biblioteca Publica Provincial (?) 24; Biblioteca de la Universidad . . . (1969) 20.

Almeria: [a]Andalucia. [b]none. [c]G of Almeria of Mediterranean Sea. [d]none. [e]Biblioteca Publica Provincial (?) 22.

Badajoz: [a]Extremadura. [b]none. [c]Guadiana R. [d]Universidad de Extremadura (at Badajoz and Caceres) (1973) 10 – 545. [e]Biblioteca de la Universidad . . . (1973?) 87; Biblioteca Publica Provincial (?) 21.

Badalona: [a]Cataluna. [b]none. [c]Mediterranean Sea. [d]none.

Barcelona: [a]Cataluna. [b]none. [c]Mediterranean Sea; Besos R. [d]Universidad de Barcelona (1430) 57 – 4120;

TABLE 2b. (Continued)

Universidad Autonoma de Barcelona (1968) 22 – 1249; Universidad Politecnica de Barcelona (1851) 16 – 1665. [e]Biblioteca Publica i Universitaria (1835) 1725; Biblioteca de Catalunya (1914) 740.

Bilbao: [a]Vascongadas y Navarra. [b]none. [c]Nervion R. [d]Universidad del Pais Vasco (at Lejona, nr Bilbao) (1968) 35 – 1746; Universidad de Deusto (1886) 11 – 569. [e]Biblioteca de la Universidad de Deusto (1916) 309; Biblioteca de la Universidad del Pais Vasco (at Lejona) (1968) 69; Biblioteca Municipal (?) ?; Biblioteca Provincial (?) ?

Burgos: [a]Castilla la Vieja. [b]none. [c]Arlanzon R. [d]none. [e]Biblioteca del Colegio Maximo de San Francisco (1880) 100; Biblioteca del Facultad Teologica del Norte de Espana (1897) 82; Biblioteca Publica Provincial (1871) 60.

Cadiz: [a]Andalucia. [b]none. [c]G of Cadiz of Atlantic O. [d]Universidad de Cadiz (1979) 8 – 635. [e]Biblioteca Publica Provincial (1851) 45; Biblioteca Popular (?) 40; Biblioteca de la Universidad . . . (?) ?

Cartagena: [a]Murcia. [b]none. [c]Mediterranean Sea. [d]none. [e]Biblioteca Popular (?) 30; Biblioteca Publica Municipal (1943) 18.

Cordova: [a]Andalucia. [b]off Cordoba. [c]Guadalquivir R. [d]Universidad de Cordoba (1847) 10 – 800. [e]Biblioteca Publica Provincial (?) 27; Biblioteca de la Universidad . . . (1848) 20.

Elche: [a]Valencia. [b]none. [c]Vinalapo R. [d]none.

Gerona: [a]Cataluna. [b]none. [c]Ter R; Onar R. [d]none. [e]Biblioteca Publica (1848) 100.

Gijon: [a]Asturias. [b]none. [c]B of Biscay. [d]none. [e]Biblioteca de la Universidad Laboral (1955) 40.

Granada: [a]Andalucia. [b]none. [c]Genil R. [d]Universidad de Granada (1531) 35 – 1700. [e]Biblioteca de la Universidad . . . (1526) 600; Biblioteca Publica del Estado (1931) 43.

Hospitalet: [a]Cataluna. [b]none. [c]nr Llobregat R. [d]none.

Huelva: [a]Andalucia. [b]none. [c]Odiel R; Tinto R. [d]none. [e]Biblioteca Publica Provincial (?) 18.

Jaen: [a]Andalucia. [b]none. [c]nr Guadalbullon R. [d]none. [e]Biblioteca Publica Provincial (1896) 38.

Jerez de la Frontera: [a]Andalucia. [b]alt Jerez; for Xeres. [c]Guadalete R. [d]none. [e]Biblioteca Municipal (1873) 29.

La Coruna: [a]Galicia. [b]alt Coruna, Corunna. [c]Atlantic O. [d]none. [e]Biblioteca de la Real Academia Gallega (1905) 22; Biblioteca Publica Provincial (?) 18.

Leganes: [a]Castilla la Nueva. [b]none. [c]nr Manzanares R. [d]none.

Leon: [a]Leon. [b]none. [c]Bernesga R; Torio R. [d]Universidad de Leon (1979) 7 – 390. [e]Biblioteca Publica del Estado (1839) 79; Biblioteca de la Universidad . . . (?) ?

Lerida: [a]Cataluna. [b]none. [c]Segre R. [d]none. [e]Biblioteca Publica Provincial (?) 33.

*Madrid: [a]Castilla la Nueva. [b]none. [c]Manzanares R. [d]Universidad Complutense de Madrid (1508 at Alcala de Henares, relocated 1836) 97 – 8260; Universidad Politecnica de Madrid (1971) 39 – 3000; Universidad Autonoma de Madrid (1968) 26 – 1700; Universidad Pontificia Comillas (1892 at Comillas, relocated 1960) 5 – 355. [e]Biblioteca Nacional (1712) 3500; Biblioteca de la Universidad Complutense de Madrid (1498 at Alcala de Henares, relocated 1841) 1940; Biblioteca Popular (1915) 450.

Malaga: [a]Andalucia. [b]none. [c]Mediterranean Sea. [d]Universidad de Malaga (1972) 12 – 695. [e]Biblioteca de la Universidad . . . (1965) 120; Biblioteca Publica (1933) 27.

Mostoles: [a]Castilla la Nueva. [b]none. [c]nr Guadarrama R. [d]none.

Murcia: [a]Murcia. [b]none. [c]Segura R. [d]Universidad de Murcia (1915) 14 – 800. [e]Biblioteca de la Universidad . . . (1915) 80; Biblioteca Publica Provincial (19th c) 20.

Oviedo: [a]Asturias. [b]none. [c]nr Nalon R; nr Nora R. [d]Universidad de Oviedo (1604) 23 – 901. [e]Biblioteca de la Universidad . . . (1608) 420.

Palma: [a]Baleares; Majorca I. [b]alt Palma de Mallorca. [c]Mediterranean Sea. [d]Universidad de Palma de Mallorca (1978) 4 – 273. [e]Biblioteca Publica Provincial (?) 104; Biblioteca de la Universidad . . . (?) ?

Pamplona: [a]Vascongadas y Navarra. [b]for Pampeluna. [c]Arga R. [d]Universidad de Navarra (1952) 9 – 862. [e]Biblioteca de la Universidad . . . (1952) 391.

Sabadell: [a]Cataluna. [b]none. [c]Ripoll R. [d]none. [e]Biblioteca de la Caixa d'Estalvis de Sabadell (1928) 78.

Salamanca: [a]Leon. [b]none. [c]Tormes R. [d]Universidad de Salamanca (1218) 15 – 1158; Universidad Pontificia de Salamanca (1134) 3 – 380. [e]Biblioteca de la Universidad de Salamanca (1218) 505; Biblioteca de la Universidad Pontificia de Salamanca (1940) 120; Biblioteca Publica Provincial (?) 11.

San Sebastian: [a]Vascongadas y Navarra. [b]none. [c]B of Biscay; Urumea R. [d]none. [e]Biblioteca de los Estudios Universitarios y Tecnicos de Guipuzcoa (1956) 40.

Santander: [a]Castilla la Vieja. [b]none. [c]B of Biscay. [d]Universidad de Santander (1967) 6 – 510. [e]Biblioteca de Menendez Pelayo, Biblioteca Municipal, y Biblioteca Publica del Estado (1908) 165.

Santiago de Compostela: [a]Galicia. [b]alt Santiago. [c]Sar R; Sarela R. [d]Universidad de Santiago de Compostela (1495) 33 – 1550. [e]Biblioteca de la Universidad . . . (16th c) 185; Biblioteca Publica Provincial (?) 7.

For an explanation of symbols and abbreviations, see pages 16–17.

(Continued)

TABLE 2b. (Continued)

Seville: [a]Andalucia. [b]off Sevilla. [c]Guadalquivir R. [d]Universidad de Sevilla (1502) 32 – 1553. [e]Biblioteca de la Universidad . . . (1502) 245; Biblioteca Capitular Colombina (1450) 92; Biblioteca Publica (1954) 35.

Tarragona: [a]Cataluna. [b]none. [c]Mediterranean Sea; Francoli R. [d]none. [e]Biblioteca Publica Provincial (?) 65.

Toledo: [a]Castilla la Nueva. [b]none. [c]Tagus R. [d]none. [e]Biblioteca Provincial (1775) 98.

Valencia: [a]Valencia. [b]none. [c]Turia R. [d]Universidad de Valencia (1500) 24 – 1070; Universidad Politecnica de Valencia (1969) 11 – 1622. [e]Biblioteca de la Universidad de Valencia (1500) 270; Biblioteca Publica Provincial (?) 12.

Valladolid: [a]Castilla la Vieja. [b]none. [c]Pisuerga R; Esgueva R. [d]Universidad de Valladolid (1346) 20 – 753. [e]Biblioteca de la Universidad . . . (1346) 135; Biblioteca Publica Provincial (?) 10; Biblioteca Popular (?) 7.

Vigo: [a]Galicia. [b]none. [c]Vigo B of Atlantic O. [d]none. [e]Biblioteca Publica Municipal (?) 8.

Vitoria: [a]Vascongadas y Navarra. [b]none. [c]Zapardiel R. [d]none. [e]Biblioteca Publica Provincial (?) 85.

Zaragoza: [a]Aragon. [b]alt Saragossa. [c]Ebro R; Huerva R. [d]Universidad de Zaragoza (1474) 30 – 1500. [e]Biblioteca de la Universidad . . . (1483) 600; Biblioteca Publica (1920) 60.

Sweden

Goteborg: [b]alt Gothenburg. [c]Kattegat; Gota R. [d]Goteborgs Universitet (1891) 22 – 1000; Chalmers Tekniska Hogskola (univ) (1829) 5 – 894. [e]Universitetsbibliotek (1861) 2000; Stadsbibliotek (1861) 1550.

Linkoping: [b]none. [c]Stangan R. [d]Universitetet i Linkoping (1967) 8 – 800. [e]Stifts- och Landsbiblioteket (1926) 723; Universitetsbibliotek (1970) 250.

Lund: [b]none. [c]nr Oresund. [d]Lunds Universitet (1668) 23 – 1900. [e]Universitetsbibliotek (1671) 3600; Stadsbibliotek (1864) 425.

Malmo: [b]none. [c]Oresund. [d]none. [e]Stadsbibliotek (1905) 1153.

Orebro: [b]none. [c]Svartan R. [d]Hogskolan i Orebro (univ) (1967) 5 – 190. [e]Stadsbibliotek (1862) 610.

*Stockholm: [b]none. [c]Baltic Sea; Malaren L. [d]Stockholms Universitet (1877) 30 – 1760; Kungliga Tekniska Hogskolan (univ) (1827) 7 – 1500. [e]Universitetsbibliotek (1739?) 2700; Kungliga Biblioteket (1661) 2000; Stadsbibliotek (1927) 1927.

Umea: [b]none. [c]Ume R. [d]Umea Universitet (1956) 8 – 1376. [e]Stadsbibliotek (1903) 666; Universitetsbibliotek (1964) 500.

Uppsala: [b]alt Upsala. [c]Fyris R. [d]Uppsala Universitet (1477) 18 – 900; Sveriges Lantbruksuniversitet (1775) 2 – 277. [e]Universitetsbibliotek (1620) 2500; Stadsbibliotek (1906) 679.

Vasteras: [b]for Vesteras. [c]Svart R; Malaren L. [d]none. [e]Stadsbibliotek (1952) 720.

Switzerland

Basel: [b]alt Bale, Basilea. [c]Rhine R; Birs R; Wiese R. [d]Universitat Basel (1460) 6 – 783. [e]Universitatsbibliothek (1460) 2441; Schweizerische Wirtschaftsarchiv (1910) 438; Allgemeine Bibliotheken (1807) 150.

*Bern: [b]alt Berna, Berne. [c]Aar R. [d]Universitat Bern (1528) 8 – 767. [e]Schweizerische Landesbibliothek (1895) 1454; Stadt- und Universitatsbibliothek (1528) 1451; Schweizerische Volksbibliothek (1920) 354.

Freiburg: [b]alt Fribourg. [c]Saane (alt Sarine) R. [d]Universite de Fribourg (1889) 5 – 431. [e]Bibliotheque Cantonale et Universitaire (1848) 1469.

Geneva: [b]off Geneve, Genf, Ginevra. [c]Rhone R; Geneva L. [d]Universite de Geneve (1559) 11 – 2193. [e]Bibliotheque Publique et Universitaire (1562) 1651; Bibliotheque des Nations Unies (alt Library of the United Nations) (1919) 1000; International Labour Office Library (1919) 1000; Bibliotheque Municipale (1931) 267.

Lausanne: [b]alt Losanna. [b]Geneva L. [d]Universite de Lausanne (1537) 6 – 560 ; Ecole Polytechnique Federale de Lausanne (univ) (1853) 3 – 230. [e]Bibliotheque Cantonale et Universitaire (1537) 1096; Bibliotheque de l'Ecole . . . (1950) 262; Bibliotheque Municipale (1933) 177.

Luzern: [b]alt Lucerna, Lucerne. [c]Reuss R; Lucerne L. [d]none. [e]Zentralbibliothek (1812) 526.

Neuchatel: [b]alt Neuenburg. [c]Seyon R; Neuchatel L. [d]Universite de Neuchatel (1838) 2 – 240. [c]Bibliotheque Publique et Universitaire (1788) 419.

Saint-Gall: [b]alt San Gallo, Sankt Gallen. [c]nr Constance L. [d]none. [e]Kantonsbibliothek Vadiana (1551) 432; Kantonsbibliothek (1845) 110; Stiftsbibliothek Sankt Gallen (720) 94.

Sankt Moritz: [b]alt Saint-Moritz. [c]Inn R; Sankt Moritz (alt Saint-Moritz) L. [d]none.

Zurich: [b]alt Zurigo. [c]Limmat R; Sihl R; Zurich(see) L. [d]Universitat Zurich (1523) 17 – 1730; Eidgenossische Technische Hochschule Zurich (univ) (1855) 9 – 1478. [e]Bibliothek der . . . Hochschule (1855) 3326; Zentralbibliothek (1629) 2052.

TABLE 2b. (Continued)

Turkey

Edirne: [b]for Adrianople. [c]Maritsa R. [d]Thracian University (1982) 3 – 198. [e]Selimiye Library (1575) 30.

Istanbul: [b]for Constantinople. [c]Sea of Marmara; Bosporus Strait. [d1]Istanbul University (1453) 32 – 2457; Technical University of Istanbul (1773) 14 – 1194; Marmara University (1883) 13 – 816; Yildiz University (1911) 13 – 549; University of the Bosporus (1863) 5 – 416. [e]Istanbul University Library (1453?) 740; Beyazit State Library (1882) 467; Technical University of Istanbul Library (1795) 250; University of the Bosporus Library (1863) 180.

UK

Aberdeen: [a]Scotland. [b]none. [c]North Sea; Dee R; Don R. [d]University of Aberdeen (1495) 6 – 1091. [e]University . . . Library (1495) 1000; Public Library (1885) 467.

Basildon: [a]England. [b]for Billericay. [c]nr Thames R. [d]none. [e]Basildon Branch of Essex County Library (?) ?

Bath: [a]England. [b]none. [c]Avon R. [d]University of Bath (1856) 4 – 370. [e]Bath Branch of Avon County Library (1900) 219; University . . . Library (1960) 215.

Bedford: [a]England. [b]none. [c]Ouse R. [d]none. [e]Bedfordshire County Library (1925) 1150.

Belfast: [a]*Northern Ireland. [b]none. [c]Belfast (Lough) Inlet of North Channel; Lagan R. [d]Queen's University of Belfast (1845) 8 – 847. [e]Public Library (1888) 1730; . . . University Library (1848) 1030.

Birkenhead: [a]England. [b]none. [c]Mersey R. [d]none. [e]Wirral District Public Library (1856) 775.

Birmingham: [a]England. [b] none. [c]Tame R; Rea R. [d]University of Birmingham (1880) 10 – 1409; University of Aston in Birmingham (1895) 5 – 310. [e]Public Library (1861) 3900; University of Birmingham Library (1880) 1415.

Blackburn: [a]England. [b]none. [c]Darwen R. [d]none. [e]Blackburn Branch of Lancashire County Library (1862) 248.

Blackpool: [a]England. [b]none. [c]Irish Sea. [d]none. [e]Blackpool Branch of Lancashire County Library (1880) 220.

Bolton: [a]England. [b]none. [c]Croal R. [d]none. [e]Public Library (1853) 700.

Bournemouth: [a]England. [b]none. [c]English Channel. [d]none. [e]Bournemouth Branch of Dorset County Library (1895) 287.

Bradford: [a]England. [b]none. [c]Bradford (Beck) Creek. [d]University of Bradford (1882) 5 – 400. [e]Public Library (1872) 978; University . . . Library (1966) 390.

Brighton: [a]England. [b]none. [c]English Channel. [d]University of Sussex (1961) 5 – 450. [e]East Sussex County Library (1873) 1320; University . . . Library (1961) 640.

Bristol: [a]England. [b]none. [c]Avon R; Frome R. [d]University of Bristol (1876) 7 – 2000. [e]Avon County Library (1876) 1784; University . . . Library (1923) 900.

Cambridge: [a]England. [b]none. [c]Cam R. [d]University of Cambridge (1209?) 13 – 1500. [e]University . . . Library (1400) 4150; Cambridge Branch of Cambridgeshire County Library (1855) 245.

Canterbury: [a]England. [b]none. [c]Stour R. [d]University of Kent at Canterbury (1964) 5 – 362. [e]University . . . Library (1964) 477; Canterbury Branch of Kent County Library (1847) 113.

Cardiff: [a]*Wales. [b]alt Caerdydd. [c]Bristol Channel; Taff R. [d]University of Wales (1822) 20 – 2001 [Cardiff campus: (1866) 9 – 1000]. [e]University . . . Library (1822) 2020 [Cardiff campus: (1883) 700]; South Glamorgan County Library (1862) 1070.

Carlisle: [a]England. [b]none. [c]Eden R. [d]none. [e]Cumbria County Library (1893) 971.

Chelmsford: [a]England. [b]none. [c]Chelmer R; Cann R. [d]none. [e]Essex County Library (1906) 2597.

Cheltenham: [a]England. [b]none. [c]Chelt R. [d]none. [e]Cheltenham Branch of Gloucestershire County Library (1884) 190.

Chester: [a]England. [b]none. [c]Dee R. [d]none. [e]Cheshire County Library (1877) 1906.

Chichester: [a]England. [b]none. [c]Rother R. [d]none. [e]West Sussex County Library (1925) 1189.

Colchester: [a]England. [b]none. [c]Colne R. [d]University of Essex (1961) 3 – 271. [e]University . . . Library (1963) 350; Colchester Branch of Essex County Library (1892) 157.

Coventry: [a]England. [b]none. [c]Sherbourne R. [d]University of Warwick (1965) 6 – 500. [e]Warwickshire County Library (at Warwick, nr Coventry) (1920) 918; University . . . Library (1963) 600; Coventry Branch of Warwickshire County Library (1868) 480.

Darlington: [a]England. [b]none. [c]Skerne R. [d]none. [e]Darlington Branch of Durham County Library (1885) 219.

Derby: [a]England. [b]none. [c]Derwent R. [d]none. [e]Derbyshire County Library (1871) 1635.

Doncaster: [a]England. [b]none. [c]Don R. [d]none. [e]Public Library (1869) 785.

[1]Universities with 5,000 or more students.

For an explanation of symbols and abbreviations, see pages 16–17.

(Continued)

TABLE 2b. (Continued)

Dover: [a]England. [b]none. [c]Strait of Dover; Dour R. [d]none. [e]Dover Branch of Kent County Library (1935) 73.

Dudley: [a]England. [b]none. [c]nr Stour R. [d]none. [e]Public Library (1884) 807.

Dundee: [a]Scotland. [b]none. [c]Tay R. [d]University of Dundee (1881) 4 – 345; University of Saint Andrews (at Saint Andrews, nr Dundee) (1411) 4 – 324. [e]University of Saint Andrews Library (at Saint Andrews) (1411) 750; Public Library (1869) 574; University of Dundee Library (1883) 440.

Durham: [a]England. [b]none. [c]Wear R. [d]University of Durham (1832) 5 – 467. [e]Durham County Library (1924) 1422; University . . . Library (1833) 631.

Edinburgh: [a]*Scotland. [b]none. [c]Forth R. [d]University of Edinburgh (1583) 11 – 1159; Heriot-Watt University (1821) 4 – 325. [e]National Library of Scotland (1682) 5000; University . . . Library (1580) 1250; Public Library (1890) 998.

Ely: [a]England. [b]none. [c]Ouse (alt Great Ouse) R. [d]none.

Exeter: [a]England. [b]none. [c]Exe R. [d]University of Exeter (1855) 6 – 452. [e]Devon County Library (1870) 2212; University . . . Library (1937) 1075.

Folkestone: [a]England. [b]none. [c]Strait of Dover. [d]none. [e]Folkestone Branch of Kent County Library (1879) 105.

Glasgow: [a]Scotland. [b]none. [c]Clyde R; Kelvin R. [d]University of Glasgow (1451) 12 – 1056; University of Strathclyde (1796) 8 – 744. [e]Public Library (1877) 2770; University of Glasgow Library (1451) 1400.

Gloucester: [a]England. [b]none. [c]Severn R. [d]none. [e]Gloucestershire County Library (1897) 1427.

Guildford: [a]England. [b]none. [c]Wey R. [d]University of Surrey (1891) 4 – 347. [e]University . . . Library (1894) 250; Guildford Branch of Surrey County Library (1924) 130.

Harrogate: [a]England. [b]none. [c]Ure R. [d]none. [e]Harrogate Branch of North Yorkshire County Library (1887) 119.

Hereford: [a]England. [b]none. [c]Wye R. [d]none. [e]Hereford Branch of Hereford and Worcester County Library (1871) 90.

Huddersfield: [a]England. [b]none. [c]Colne R. [d]none. [e]Kirklees District Public Library (1889) 1018.

Hull: [a]England. [b]off Kingston upon Hull. [c]Humber R; Hull R. [d]University of Hull (1927) 6 – 480. [e]Humberside County Library (1893) 2626; University . . . Library (1929) 600.

Ipswich: [a]England. [b]none. [c]Orwell R; Gipping R. [d]none. [e]Suffolk County Library (1853) 892.

Lancaster: [a]England. [b]none. [c]Lune R. [d]University of Lancaster (1964) 5 – 450. [e]University . . . Library (1963) 600; Lancaster Branch of Lancashire County Library (1893) 109.

Leeds: [a]England. [b]none. [c]Aire R. [d]University of Leeds (1831) 11 – 1155. [e]Public Library (1870) 2017; University . . . Library (1875) 1499.

Leicester: [a]England. [b]none. [c]Soar R. [d]University of Leicester (1918) 5 – 520. [e]Leicestershire County Library (1871) 1966; University . . . Library (1921) 700.

Lichfield: [a]England. [b]none. [c]nr Trent R. [d]none. [e]Lichfield Branch of Staffordshire County Library (1859) 50.

Lincoln: [a]England. [b]none. [c]Witham R; Till R. [d]none. [e]Lincolnshire County Library (1895) 1429.

Liverpool: [a]England. [b]none. [c]Mersey R. [d]University of Liverpool (1881) 8 – 845. [e]Public Library (1852) 2455; University . . . Library (1881) 1000.

*London: [a]*England. [b]none. [c]Thames R; Lea R. [d]University of London (13th c) 104 – 6630; Brunel University (1957) 4 – 260; City University (1891) 3 – 286. [e]British Library (1753) 14,800; University . . . Library (1673) 6800; Westminster Public Library (1857) 1169.

Londonderry: [a]Northern Ireland. [b]alt Derry. [c]Foyle R. [d]University of Ulster (1965) 8 – ? [e]University . . . Library (1965) 526; Londonderry Branch of Western Education and Library Board (1923) 185.

Loughborough: [a]England. [b]none. [c]Soar R. [d]Loughborough University of Technology (1952) 6 – 500. [e] . . . University Library (1952) 600; Loughborough Branch of Leicestershire County Library (1886) 98.

Luton: [a]England. [b]none. [c]Lea R. [d]none. [e]Luton Branch of Bedfordshire County Library (1883) 375.

Maidstone: [a]England. [b]none. [c]Medway R. [d]none. [e]Kent County Library (1858) 3639.

Manchester: [a]England. [b]none. [c]Irwell R. [d]Victoria University of Manchester (1851) 18 – 1258. [e] . . . University Library (1851) 3350; Public Library (1852) 2148.

Middlesbrough: [a]England. [b]none. [c]Tees R. [d]none. [e]Cleveland County Library (1871) 1618.

Newcastle-under-Lyme: [a]England. [b]none. [c]Lyme Brook. [d]University of Keele (at Keele, nr Newcastle-under-Lyme) (1949) 3 – 269. [e]University . . . Library (at Keele) (1949) 547; Newcastle-under-Lyme Branch of Staffordshire County Library (1891) 161.

Newcastle upon Tyne: [a]England. [b]alt Newcastle. [c]Tyne R. [d]University of Newcastle upon Tyne (1834) 8 – 836. [e]Public Library (1880) 1192; University . . . Library (1871) 700.

Newport: [a]Wales. [b]alt Casnewydd-ar-Wysg. [c]Usk (alt Wysg) R. [d]none. [e]Gwent County Library (1870) 941.

TABLE 2b. **(Continued)**

Northampton: [a]England. [b]none. [c]Nene R. [d]none. [e]Northamptonshire County Library (1876) 1408.

Norwich: [a]England. [b]none. [c]Wensum R. [d]University of East Anglia (1961) 5 – 401. [e]Norfolk County Library (1857) 1546; University . . . Library (1962) 500.

Nottingham: [a]England. [b]none. [c]Trent R. [d]University of Nottingham (1881) 7 – 680. [e]Nottinghamshire County Library (1868) 2311; University . . . Library (1881) 800.

Oxford: [a]England. [b]none. [c]Thames R; Cherwell R. [d]University of Oxford (1200?) 12 – 1500. [e]University . . . Library (1602) 6000; Oxfordshire County Library (1854) 968.

Paisley: [a]Scotland. [b]none. [c]White Cart R. [d]none. [e]Renfrew District Public Library (1870) 585.

Perth: [a]Scotland. [b]for Saint Johnstoun. [c]Tay R. [d]none. [e]Perth and Kinross District Public Library (1898) 431.

Peterborough: [a]England. [b]none. [c]Nene R. [d]none. [e]Peterborough Branch of Cambridgeshire County Library (1892) 145.

Plymouth: [a]England. [b]none. [c]Plymouth Sound of English Channel; Tamar R; Plym R. [d]none. [e]Plymouth Branch of Devon County Library (1876) 502.

Poole: [a]England. [b]none. [c]English Channel. [d]none. [e]Poole Branch of Dorset County Library (1886) 204.

Portsmouth: [a]England; Portsea I. [b]none. [c]English Channel; Portsmouth Harbour of English Channel. [d]none. [e]Portsmouth Polytechnic Library (1953) 400; Portsmouth Branch of Hampshire County Library (1883) 361.

Preston: [a]England. [b]none. [c]Ribble R. [d]none. [e]Lancashire County Library (1879) 3572.

Reading: [a]England. [b]none. [c]Thames R; Kennet R. [d]University of Reading (1892) 6 – 650. [e]Berkshire County Library (1883) 1076; University . . . Library (1893) 500.

Rhondda: [a]Wales. [b]for Ystradyfodwg. [c]Rhondda Fawr R; Rhondda Fach R. [d]none. [e]Public Library (1939) 223.

Rochdale: [a]England. [b]none. [c]Roch R. [d]none. [e]Public Library (1872) 416.

Rugby: [a]England. [b]none. [c]Avon R. [d]none. [e]Rugby Branch of Warwickshire County Library (1891) 98.

Saint Albans: [a]England. [b]none. [c]Ver R. [d]none. [e]Saint Albans Branch of Hertfordshire County Library (1882) 113.

Saint Helens: [a]England. [b]none. [c]Sankey Brook. [d]none. [e]Public Library (1872) 660.

Salford: [a]England. [b]none. [c]Irwell R. [d]University of Salford (1896) 4 – 350. [e]Public Library (1850) 579; University . . . Library (1957) 300.

Salisbury: [a]England. [b]off New Sarum. [c]Avon R; Wiley R. [d]none. [e]Salisbury Branch of Wiltshire County Library (1890) 69.

Scarborough: [a]England. [b]none. [c]North Sea; Esk R. [d]none. [e]Scarborough Branch of North Yorkshire County Library (1930) 80.

Sheffield: [a]England. [b]none. [c]Don R. [d]University of Sheffield (1828) 8 – 920. [e]Public Library (1856) 1431; University . . . Library (1897) 870.

Shrewsbury: [a]England. [b]none. [c]Severn R. [d]none. [e]Shropshire County Library (1885) 641.

Southampton: [a]England. [b]none. [c]English Channel; Test R; Itchen R. [d]University of Southampton (1862) 7 – 645. [e]University . . . Library (1862) 700; Southampton Branch of Hampshire County Library (1889) 464.

Southend-on-Sea: [a]England. [b]alt Southend. [c]North Sea; Thames R. [d]none. [e]Southend-on-Sea Branch of Essex County Library (1906) 316.

Southport: [a]England. [b]none. [c]Irish Sea. [d]none. [e]Sefton District Public Library (1876) 630.

Stafford: [a]England. [b]none. [c]Trent R; Sow R. [d]none. [e]Staffordshire County Library (1882) 3445.

Stirling: [a]Scotland. [b]none. [c]Forth R. [d]University of Stirling (1967) 3 – 253. [e]Public Library (1904) 393; University . . . Library (1967) 360.

Stockport: [a]England. [b]none. [c]Mersey R; Tame R; Goyt R. [d]none. [e]Public Library (1875) 528; National Library for the Blind (1882) 380.

Stockton-on-Tees: [a]England. [b]alt Stockton. [c]Tees R. [d]none. [e]Stockton-on-Tees Branch of Cleveland County Library (1877) 136.

Stoke-on-Trent: [a]England. [b]none. [c]Trent R. [d]none. [e]Stoke-on-Trent Branch of Staffordshire County Library (1869) 395.

Stratford-on-Avon: [a]England. [b]none. [c]Avon R. [d]none. [e]Stratford-on-Avon Branch of Warwickshire County Library (1905) 62; Shakespeare Centre Library (1862) 30.

Sunderland: [a]England. [b]none. [c]Wear R. [d]none. [e]Public Library (1859) 632.

Swansea: [a]Wales. [b]alt Abertawe. [c]Swansea B of Bristol Channel; Tawe R. [d]University College of Swansea (of University of Wales) (1920) 4 – 445. [e]West Glamorgan County Library (1875) 831; University College of Swansea Library (1921) 500.

For an explanation of symbols and abbreviations, see pages 16–17.   (Continued)

TABLE 2b. (Continued)

Torbay: [a]England. [b]for Torquay. [c]English Channel. [d]none. [e]Torbay Branch of Devon County Library (1907) 231.

Tunbridge Wells: [a]England. [b]off Royal Tunbridge Wells. [c]nr Medway R. [d]none. [e]Tunbridge Wells Branch of Kent County Library (1921) 101.

Wakefield: [a]England. [b]none. [c]Aire R; Calder R. [d]none. [e]Public Library (1906) 765.

Walsall: [a]England. [b]none. [c]nr Tame R. [d]none. [e]Public Library (1859) 546.

Warley: [a]England. [b]inc Oldbury, Rowley Regis, Smethwick. [c]nr Tame R. [d]none. [e]Warley Branch of Sandwell District Public Library (1877) 333. [f]Oldbury: 54 (1951), 36 (1931), 25 (1901); Rowley Regis: 49 (1951), 41 (1931), 35 (1901); Smethwick: 76 (1951), 84 (1931), 55 (1901), 8 (1851), 1 (1801).

Warrington: [a]England. [b]none. [c]Mersey R. [d]none. [e]Warrington Branch of Cheshire County Library (1848) 147.

West Bromwich: [a]England. [b]none. [c]Tame R. [d]none. [e]Sandwell District Public Library (1874) 909.

Winchester: [a]England. [b]none. [c]Itchen R. [d]none. [e]Hampshire County Library (1851) 3216.

Windsor: [a]England. [b]off New Windsor. [c]Thames R. [d]none. [e]Windsor and Maidenhead Branch of Berkshire County Library (1904) 88; Eton College Library (1440) 31.

Wolverhampton: [a]England. [b]none. [c]nr Smestow R. [d]none. [e]Public Library (1869) 604.

Worcester: [a]England. [b]none. [c]Severn R. [d]none. [e]Hereford and Worcester County Library (1881) 1262.

York: [a]England. [b]none. [c]Ouse R; Foss R. [d]University of York (1963) 4 – 320. [e]University . . . Library (1962) 350; York Branch of North Yorkshire County Library (1893) 229.

USSR

Andropov: [a]Russia in Europe. [b]for Rybinsk, Shcherbakov. [c]Volga R; Cheremukha R; Sheksna R. [d]none. [e]Central City Library (1919) 115.

Archangel: [a]Russia in Europe. [b]off Arkhangelsk. [c]Northern Dvina R. [d]none. [e]N. A. Dobrolyubov Archangel District Library (1833) 780.

Armavir: [a]Russia in Europe. [b]none. [c]Kuban R; Urup R. [d]none. [e]Pedagogic Institute Library (1948) 140.

Astrakhan: [a]Russia in Europe. [b]none. [c]Volga R. [d]none. [e]N. K. Krupskaya Astrakhan District Scientific Library (1838) 566.

Baku: [a*]Azerbaijan. [b]none. [c]Caspian (Sea) L. [d]S. M. Kirov Azerbaijan State University (1920) 11 – 700. [e]M. F. Akhundov State Library of the Azerbaijan SSR (1923) 3122; Central Library of the Azerbaijan Academy of Sciences (1925) 2500; State Scientific Library (1930) 2164; . . . University Library (1919) 1700.

Balakovo: [a]Russia in Europe. [b]none. [c]Volga R. [d]none.

Belaya Tserkov: [a]Ukraine. [b]none. [c]Ros R. [d]none. [e]Institute of Agriculture Library (1920) 252.

Belgorod: [a]Russia in Europe. [b]none. [c]Donets R. [d]none. [e]Scientific-Technical Library (1961) 310; Belgorod District Library (1955) 268; Pedagogic Institute Library (1944) 209.

Berezniki: [a]Russia in Europe. [b]none. [c]Kama R. [d]none. [e]Soda Production Plant Technical Library (1940) 71.

Bobruysk: [a]White Russia. [b]alt Bobruisk. [c]Berezina R. [d]none.

Brest: [a]White Russia. [b]for Brest-Litovsk, Brzesc-Litewski. [c]Bug R. [d]none. [e]Gorkiy Brest District Library (1940) 400; Pedagogic Institute Library (1945) 274.

Bryansk: [a]Russia in Europe. [b]alt Briansk. [c]Desna R. [d]none. [e]Bryansk District Library (1944) 615.

Cheboksary: [a]Russia in Europe; *Chuvash ASSR. [b]none. [c]Volga R. [d]I. N. Ulyanov Chuvash State University (1967) 8–300. [e] . . . University Library (1961) 712; M.Gorkiy State Library of the Chuvash ASSR (1871) 583.

Cherepovets: [a]Russia in Europe. [b]none. [c]Sheksna R. [d]none. [e]Pedagogic Insitute Library (1875) 140.

Cherkassy: [a]Ukraine. [b]none. [c]Dnieper R. [d]none. [e]V. V. Mayakovskiy Cherkassy District Library (1954) 400; Pedagogic Institute Library (1930) 334.

Chernigov: [a]Ukraine. [b]none. [c]Desna R. [d]none. [e]V. G. Korolenko Chernigov District Library (1877) 453.

Chernovtsy: [a]Ukraine. [b]for Cernauti, Czernowitz. [c]Prut R. [d]Chernovtsky State University (1875) 10 – 500. [e] . . . University Library (1875) 1722; Chernovtsy District Library (1940) 403.

Dneprodzerzhinsk: [a]Ukraine. [b]for Kamenskoye. [c]Dnieper R. [d]none. [e]Industrial Research Institute Library (1920) 207; Palace of Culture Library (?)?

Dnepropetrovsk: [a]Ukraine. [b]for Ekaterinoslav, Yekaterinoslav. [c]Dnieper R; Samara R. [d]Dnepropetrovsk State University (1919) 13 – 700. [e] . . . University Library (1918) 1200; October Revolution Dnepropetrovsk District Library (1889) 1145.

Donetsk: [a]Ukraine. [b]for Stalino, Yuzovka, Yuzovo. [c]Kalmius R. [d]Donetsk State University (1965) 12–? [e]N. K. Krupskaya Donetsk District Library (1926) 1250; Polytechnic Institute Library (1921) 1117; . . . University Library (1937) 782.

TABLE 2b. (Continued)

Dzerzhinsk: [a]Russia in Europe. [b]for Chernorechye, Rastyapino. [c]Oka R. [d]none. [e]Dzerzhinsk Chemical Works Scientific-Technical Library (1929) 106; N.K. Krupskaya City Library (1927) 52.

Elista: [a]Russia in Europe; *Kalmyk ASSR. [b]for Stepnoy. [c]Dzhurak-Sal R. [d]Kalmyk State University (1970) 2–? [e] . . . University Library (1964) 350; A. M. Amur-Sanana State Library of the Kalmyk ASSR (1959) 139.

Engels: [a]Russia in Europe. [b]for Pokrovsk, Pokrovskaya Sloboda. [c]Volga R. [d]none. [e]Central City Library (1918) 228.

Gomel: [a]White Russia. [b]none. [c]Sozh R. [d]Gomel State University (1970) 7 – 500. [e] . . . University Library (1930) 700; V.I. Lenin Gomel District Library (1938) 464.

Gorkiy: [a]Russia in Europe. [b]alt Gorki, Gorky; for Nizhniy Novgorod. [c]Volga R; Oka R. [d]N. I. Lobachevskiy Gorkiy State University (1918) 10 – 800. [e]Scientific-Technical Library (1934) 4755; V.I. Lenin Gorkiy District Library (1930) 2600; . . . University Library (1931) 1250.

Gorlovka: [a]Ukraine. [b]none. [c]nr Lugan R. [d]none. [e]Foreign-Language Pedagogic Institute Library (1949) 121.

Grodno: [a]White Russia. [b]none. [c]Neman R. [d]Grodno State University (1978) ?–? [e]E. F. Karskiy Grodno District Library (1830) 280; Pedagogic Institute Library (1945) 241.

Groznyy: [a]Russia in Europe; *Chechen-Ingush ASSR. [b]alt Grozny. [c]Sunzha R. [d]Chechen-Ingush State University (1972) 3–? [e]A. P. Chekhov State Library of the Chechen-Ingush ASSR (1905) 902; . . . University Library (1938) 460.

Ivano-Frankovsk: [a]Ukraine. [b]for Stanislav. [c]Solotvinskaya R. [d]none. [e]Ivano-Frankovsk District Library (1939) 549.

Ivanovo: [a]Russia in Europe. [b]for Ivanovo-Voznesensk. [c]Uvod R. [d]Ivanovo State University (1974) 5–? [e]Ivanovo District Library (1919) 1105.

Izhevsk: [a]Russia in Europe; *Udmurt ASSR. [b]for Izhevskiy Zavod, Ustinov. [c]Izh R. [d]Udmurt State University (1972) 3 – ? [e]V.I. Lenin State Library of the Udmurt ASSR (1919) 732; Engineering Institute Library (1952) 420; . . . University Library (1972) 402.

Kalinin: [a]Russia in Europe. [b]for Tver. [c]Volga R; Tvertsa R; Tmaka R. [d]Kalinin State University (1971) 5–? [e]A. M. Gorkiy Kalinin District Library (1860) 1120; . . . University Library (1971) 506.

Kaliningrad: [a]Russia in Europe. [b]for Konigsberg. [c]Pregolya (for Pregel) R. [d]Kaliningrad State University (1544) 4 – 200. [e]Kaliningrad District Library (1946) 570; Scientific-Technical Library (1961) 392; . . . University Library (1949) 364.

Kaluga: [a]Russia in Europe. [b]none. [c]Oka R. [d]none. [e]V. G. Belinskiy Kaluga District Library (1944) 344.

Kaunas: [a]Lithuania. [b]alt Kovno. [c]Neman R; Viliya R. [d]none. [e]Polytechnic Institute Library (1923) 1189; Public Library (1919) 1000.

Kazan: [a]Russia in Europe; *Tatar ASSR. [b]for Kasan. [c]Kazanka R. [d]V. I. Lenin Kazan State University (1804) 11 – 700. [e] . . . University Library (1798) 4120; V. I.Lenin State Library of the Tatar ASSR (1865) 1186.

Kerch: [a]Ukraine. [b]none. [c]Kerch Strait. [d]none. [e]Scientific-Technical Library of the Azov-Black Sea Scientific Research Institute of Fisheries and Oceanography (1921) 30.

Kharkov: [a]Ukraine. [b]none. [c]Kharkov R; Lopan R; Netetcha R; Gnilopiat R; Udi R. [d]A. M.Gorkiy Kharkov State University (1805) 12 – 1020. [e]V. G. Korolenko State Scientific Library (1886) 4096; . . . University Library (1805) 3000; Center for the Dissemination of Scientific and Technical Information (1897) 1774.

Kherson: [a]Ukraine. [b]none. [c]Dnieper R. [d]none. [e]A. M.Gorkiy Kherson District Library (1872) 650.

Khmelnitskiy: [a]Ukraine. [b]for Proskurow, Proskurov. [c]Southern Bug R. [d]none. [e]N. Ostrovskiy Khmelnitskiy District Library (1901) 313.

Kiev: [a*]Ukraine. [b]off Kiyev. [c]Dnieper R. [d]T. G. Shevchenko Kiev State University (1834) 20 – 1700. [e]Central Scientific Library of the Ukrainian Academy of Sciences (1919) 7756; . . . University Library (1834) 2708; CPSU State Library of the Ukrainian SSR (1866) 2071; Polytechnic Institute Library (1898) 1550.

Kirov: [a]Russia in Europe. [b]for Khlynov, Viatka, Vyatka. [c]Vyatka R. [d]none. [e]A. I. Herzen Kirov District Library (1837) 1614.

Kirovabad: [a]Azerbaijan. [b]for Elisavetpol, Gandzha, Yelisavetpol. [c]Gyandzhachay R. [d]none. [e]Pedagogic Institute Library (1943) 247.

Kirovakan: [a]Armenia. [b]for Karaklis. [c]Pambak R; Tandzut R; Vanadzoriget R. [d]none.

Kirovograd: [a]Ukraine. [b]for Elisavetgrad, Yelisavetgrad, Zinovyevsk. [c]Ingul R. [d]none. [e]N. K. Krupskaya Kirovograd District Library (1898) 753.

Kishinev: [a*]Moldavia. [b]for Chisinau. [c]Byk R. [d]V. I. Lenin Kishinev State Unversity (1946) 13 – 848. [e]N. K. Krupskaya State Library of the Moldavian SSR (1832) 3000; . . . University Library (1946) 1385.

Klaypeda: [a]Lithuania. [b]alt Klaipeda; for Memel. [c]Baltic Sea; Neman R. [d]none. [e]Klaypeda Branch of the State Library of the Lithuanian SSR (1959) 163.

For an explanation of symbols and abbreviations, see pages 16–17.

(Continued)

TABLE 2b. (Continued)

Kostroma: [a]Russia in Europe. [b]none. [c]Volga R; Kostroma R. [d]none. [e]N.K. Krupskaya Kostroma District Library (1918) 778.

Kramatorsk: [d]Ukraine. [d]for Kramatorskaya. [d]Kazennnyy Torets R. [d]none. [d]Industrial Research Institute Library (1953) 291.

Krasnodar: [a]Russia in Europe. [b]for Ekaterinodar, Yekaterinodar. [c]Kuban R. [d]Kuban State University (1970) 10–? [e]A. S. Pushkin Krasnodar Regional Library (1900) 1045; . . . University Library (1920) 950.

Kremenchug: [a]Ukraine. [b]alt Kremenchuk. [c]Dnieper R. [d]none.

Krivoy Rog: [a]Ukraine. [b]alt Krivoi Rog. [c]Ingulets R; Saksagan R. [d]none. [e]Institute of Mining Library (1929) 470.

Kursk: [a]Russia in Europe. [b]none. [c]Tuskor R; Kur R. [d]none. [e]N. N. Aseyev Kursk District Library (1935) 633.

Kütaisi: [a]Georgia. [b]for Kutais. [c]Rioni R. [d]none. [e]Pedagogic Institute Library (1933) 345.

Kuybyshev: [a]Russia in Europe. [b]alt Kuibyshev; for Samara. [c]Volga R; Samara R. [d]Kuybyshev State University (1970) 2–? [e]V. I. Lenin Kuybyshev District Library (1860) 1784; Scientific-Technical Library (1958) 795; Polytechnic Institute Library (1939) 680.

Leninakan: [a]Armenia. [b]for Aleksandropol, Gyumri. [c]Akhuryan [alt Arpa (Cayi)] R. [d]none. [e]Pedagogic Institute Library (1934) 79.

Leningrad: [a]Russia in Europe. [b]for Petrograd, Saint Petersburg. [c]G of Finland of Baltic Sea; Neva R. [d]A. A. Zhdanov Leningrad State University (1819) 20 – 1700. [e]M. E. Saltykov-Shchedrin State Public Library (1795) 21,500; USSR Academy of Sciences Library (1714) 12,789; . . . University Library (1819) 5100; Polytechnic Institute Library (1903) 1900.

Lipetsk: [a]Russia in Europe. [b]none. [c]Voronezh R. [d]none. [e]Lipetsk District Library (1955) 586.

Lutsk: [a]Ukraine. [b]for Luck. [c]Styr R. [d]none. [e]Volynsk District Library (1939) 294; Pedagogic Institute Library (1946) 212.

Lvov: [a]Ukraine. [b]for Lemberg, Lwow. [c]Peltev R. [d]Ivan Franko Lvov State University (1661) 13 – 700. [e]V. Stefanik State Scientific Library of the Ukrainian Academy of Sciences (1940) 4500; . . . University Library (1608) 2500; Polytechnic Institute Library (1844) 1373; Scientific-Technical Library (1967) 1103; Yaroslav Galan Lvov District Library (1940) 648.

Makeyevka: [a]Ukraine. [b]alt Makeevka; for Dmitriyevsk. [c]Gruzskaya R. [d]none. [e]Library of the Institute for Labor Safety in the Mining Industry (1927) 137.

Makhachkala: [a]Russia in Europe; *Daghestan ASSR. [b]for Petrovsk. [c]Caspian (Sea) L. [d]V. I. Lenin Daghestan State University (1957) 8 – 450. [e] . . . University Library (1957) 780; A. S. Pushkin State Library of the Daghestan ASSR (1900) 403; Scientific-Technical Library (1958) 395.

Melitopol: [a]Ukraine. [b]for Novo-Aleksandrovka. [c]Molochnaya R. [d]none. [e]Institute for the Mechanization of Agriculture Library (1932) 209; Pedagogic Institute Library (1930) 141.

Minsk: [a]* White Russia. [b]none. [c]Svisloch R. [d]V. I. Lenin White Russian State University (1921) 19 – 1370. [e]V. I. Lenin State Library of the White Russian SSR (1922) 6000; Yakub Kolas Library of the White Russian Academy of Sciences (1925) 2000; . . . University Library (1921) 1377; Polytechnic Institute Library (1933) 1003.

Mogilev: [a]White Russia. [b]none. [c]Dnieper R. [d]none. [e]V. I. Lenin Mogilev District Library (1935) 435.

*Moscow: [a]Russia in Europe; *Russia. [b]off Moskva. [c]Moscow R; Yauza R. [d]M. V. Lomonosov Moscow State University (1755) 28 – 8000; Patrice Lumumba People's Friendship University (1960) 8 – 2000. [e]V. I. Lenin State Library of the USSR (1828 at Leningrad, relocated 1862) 28,745; Library for Natural Sciences of the USSR Academy of Sciences (1934) 13,541; State Public Scientific-Technical Library of the USSR (1958) 10,420; Institute of Social Sciences Library of the USSR Academy of Sciences (1918) 10,144; M.V. Lomonosov Moscow State University Library (1756) 7200; All-Union State Library of Foreign Literature (1921) 4138; Central Scientific Library of the All-Union Agricultural Academy (1930) 4000; State Central Polytechnic Library (1964) 3083; State Central Scientific Medical Library (1919) 3000; State Public Historical Library of the RSFSR (1938) 2852.

Murmansk: [a]Russia in Europe. [b]none. [c]Barents Sea. [d]none. [e]Murmansk District Library (1938) 741.

Naberezhnyye Chelny: [a]Russia in Europe; Tatar ASSR. [b]for Brezhnev, Chelny. [c]Kama R. [d]none.

Nalchik: [a]Russia in Europe; *Kabardino-Balkar ASSR. [b]none. [c]Nalchik R. [d]Kabardino-Balkar State University (1932) 9 – 500. [e]N. K. Krupskaya State Scientific Library of the Kabardino-Balkar ASSR (1921) 993; . . . University Library (1932) 738.

Nikolayev: [a]Ukraine. [b]alt Nikolaev; for Vernoleninsk. [c]Southern Bug R; Ingul R. [d]none. [e]Aleksey Gmyrev Nikolayev District Library (1881) 869.

Nizhnekamsk: [a]Russia in Europe; Tatar ASSR. [b]none. [c]Kama R. [d]none.

Novgorod: [a]Russia in Europe. [b]none. [c]Volkhoy R. [d]none. [e]Novgorod District Library (1919) 450.

Novocherkassk: [a]Russia in Europe. [b]none. [c]Ak(say) R. [d]none. [e]Polytechnic Institute Library (1907) 1580; A. S. Pushkin Central City Library (1869) 212.

TABLE 2b. (Continued)

Novorossiysk: [a]Russia in Europe. [b]alt Novorossiisk. [c]Black Sea; Tsemes R. [d]none. [a]A. M. Gorkiy Central City Library (1943) 102.

Odessa: [a]Ukraine. [b]none. [c]Black Sea. [d]I. I. Mechnikov Odessa State University (1807) 12 – 800. [e]A. M. Gorkiy State Scientific Library (1830) 3253; . . . University Library (1817) 2790; Scientific-Technical Library (1962) 1968.

Ordzhonikidze: [a]Russia in Europe; *North Ossetian ASSR. [b]for Dzaudzhikau,Vladikavkaz. [c]Terek R. [d]K. L. Khetagurov North Ossetian State University (1970) 3 – 400. [e] . . . University Library (1920) 760; S. M. Kirov State Scientific Library of the North Ossetian ASSR (1895) 508.

Orel: [a]Russia in Europe. [b]none. [c]Oka R; Orlik R. [d]none. [e]N. K. Krupskaya Orel District Library (1919) 632.

Orenburg: [a]Russia in Europe. [b]for Chkalov. [c]Ural R; Sakmara R. [d]none. [e]N. K. Krupskaya Orenburg District Library (1896) 680.

Orsk: [a]Russia in Europe. [b]none. [c]Ural R; Or R. [d]none. [e]Pedagogic Institute Library (1949) 140.

Penza: [a]Russia in Europe. [b]none. [c]Sura R; Penza R. [d]none. [e]M. Y. Lermontov Penza District Library (1892) 717.

Perm: [a]Russia in Europe. [b]for Molotov, Yegozhikhinskiy Zavod. [c]Kama R. [d]A. M. Gorkiy Perm State University (1916) 13 – 700. [e]Scientific-Technical Library (1941) 2600; M. Gorkiy Perm District Library (1831) 1389; . . . University Library (1916) 1140.

Petrozavodsk: [a]Russia in Europe; *Karelian ASSR. [b]for Kalininsk. [c]Onega L. [d]O. V. Kuusinen Petrozavodsk State University (1940) 7 – 450. [c]State Public Library of the Karelian ASSR (1860) 1577; . . . University Library (1940) 627.

Podolsk: [a]Russia in Europe. [b]none. [c]Pakhra R. [d]none. [e]Podolsk Mechanical Works Scientific-Technical Library (1932) 115.

Poltava: [a]Ukraine. [b]none. [c]Vorskla R; Kolomak R. [d]none. [e]I. P. Kotlyarevskiy Poltava District Library (1894) 357.

Pskov: [a]Russia in Europe. [b]none. [c]Velikaya R. [d]none. [e]Pskov District Library (1944) 749.

Riga: [a]*Latvia. [b]none. [c]G of Riga of Baltic Sea; Western Dvina R. [d]Pyetr Stuchka Latvian State University (1861) 11 – 721. [e]Vilis Lacis State Library of the Latvian SSR (1919) 4467; Central Library of the Latvian Academy of Sciences (1524) 2201; . . . University Library (1862) 1900.

Rostov-na-Donu: [a]Russia in Europe. [b]alt Rostov, Rostov-on-Don. [c]Don R. [d]Mikhail Souslov Rostov-na-Donu State University (1869 at Warsaw, Poland; relocated 1915) 10–? [e]North Caucasus Central Scientific-Technical Library (1933) 3210; Karl Marx Rostov-na-Donu State Scientific Library (1920) 1850; . . . University Library (1915) 1570.

Rovno: [a]Ukraine. [b]for Rowne. [c]Ustye R. [d]none. [e]Rovno District Library (1940) 317.

Ryazan: [a]Russia in Europe. [b]alt Riazan. [c]Oka R; Trobezh R. [d]none. [e]A. M. Gorkiy Ryazan District Library (1858) 857.

Saransk: [a]Russia in Europe; *Mordvinian ASSR. [b]none. [c]Insar R. [d]N. P. Ogorev Mordvinian State University (1957) 16–? [e] . . . University Library (1931) 927; A. S. Pushkin State Library of the Mordvinian ASSR (1899) 467.

Saratov: [a]Russia in Europe. [b]none. [c]Volga R. [d]N. G. Chernyshevskiy Saratov State University (1909) 10 – 700. [e] . . . University Library (1909) 2580; Saratov District Library (1831) 1012.

Sevastopol: [a]Ukraine. [b]for Sebastopol. [c]Black Sea. [d]none. [e]Instrument-Making Institute Library (1960) 285; L.N.Tolstoy Central City Library (?) ?

Severodvinsk: [a]Russia in Europe. [b]for Molotovsk, Sudostroy. [c]G of Dvina of White Sea; Northern Dvina R. [d]none.

Shakhty: [a]Russia in Europe. [b]for Aleksandrovsk-Grushevskiy. [c]Grushevka R. [d]none. [e]A. S. Pushkin Central City Library (1915) 257.

Simferopol: [a]Ukraine. [b]none. [c]Salgir R. [d]M. V. Frunze Simferopol State University (1972) 6–? [e] . . . University Library (1973) 776; I. Y. Franko Crimean District Library (1890) 600.

Smolensk: [a]Russia in Europe. [b]none. [c]Dnieper R. [d]none. [e]V. I. Lenin Smolensk District Library (1920) 789.

Sochi: [a]Russia in Europe. [b]none. [c]Black Sea; Sochi R. [d]none. [e]Central City Library (1894) 60.

Stavropol: [a]Russia in Europe. [b]for Voroshilovsk. [c]Tashla R. [d]none. [e]M. Y. Lermontov Stavropol Regional Library (1853) 817; Scientific-Technical Library (1959) 531.

Sterlitamak: [a]Russia in Europe; Bashkir ASSR. [b]none. [c]Belaya R; Sterlya R. [d]none. [e]Pedagogic Institute Library (1944) 108.

Sumgait: [a]Azerbaijan. [b]none. [c]Sumgait R; Caspian (Sea) L. [d]none.

Sumy: [a]Ukraine. [b]none. [c]Psel R. [d]none. [e]N. K. Krupskaya Sumy District Library (1939) 242; Pedagogic Institute Library (1930) 194.

For an explanation of symbols and abbreviations, see pages 16–17.

(Continued)

TABLE 2b. (Continued)

Syktyvkar: [a]Russia in Europe; *Komi ASSR. [b]for Ust-Sysolsk. [c]Vychegda R; Sysola R. [d]Syktyvkar State University (1972) 3 – 170. [e]V. I.Lenin State Library of the Komi ASSR (1902) 825; . . . University Library (1972) 205.

Syzran: [a]Russia in Europe. [b]none. [c]Volga R; Syzran R. [d]none.

Taganrog: [a]Russia in Europe. [b]none. [c]G of Taganrog of Sea of Azov. [d]none. [e]Institute of Radio Engineering Library (1952) 510; A. P. Chekhov City Library (1876) 173.

Tallin: [a]*Estonia. [b]alt Tallinn; for Reval, Revel. [c] G of Finland of Baltic Sea. [d]none. [e]F. R. Kreutzwald State Library of the Estonian SSR (1918) 3359; Scientific Library of the Estonian Academy of Sciences (1947) 3081.

Tambov: [a]Russia in Europe. [b]none. [c]Tsna R. [d]none. [e]A. S. Pushkin Tambov District Library (1830) 713.

Tartu: [a]Estonia. [b]for Derpt, Dorpat, Yurev. [c]Ema R. [d]Tartu State University (1802) 8 – 690. [e] . . . University Library (1802) 3400.

Tbilisi: [a]*Georgia. [b]alt Tiflis. [c]Kura R. [d]Tbilisi State University (1918) 16 – 1659. [e] Karl Marx State Library of the Georgian SSR (1846) 8000; Scientific-Technical Library of the Georgian SSR (1965) 3145; . . . University Library (1918) 3000; Central Scientific Library of the Georgian Academy of Sciences (1941) 2279.

Ternopol: [a]Ukraine. [b]for Tarnopol. [c]Siret R. [d]none. [e]V. P. Zatonskiy Ternopol District Library (1939) 395.

Tiraspol: [a]Moldavia. [b]none. [c]Dniester R. [d]none. [e]Pedagogic Institute Library (1930) 443.

Tolyatti: [a]Russia in Europe. [b]alt Togliatti; for Stavropol. [c]Volga R. [d]none. [e]Library of the Institute of Nonmetallic Building Materials and Hydromechanics (1958) 630.

Tula: [a]Russia in Europe. [b]none. [c]Upa R; Tulitsa R. [d]none. [e]Polytechnic Institute Library (1930) 775; V. I. Lenin Tula District Library (1919) 769.

Ufa: [a]Russia in Europe; *Bashkir ASSR. [b]none. [c]Belaya R; Ufa R. [d]Bashkir State University (1957) 8 – 300. [e]N. K. Krupskaya State Library of the Bashkir ASSR (1921) 1080; . . . University Library (1908) 780; Bashkir Central Scientific-Technical Library (1954) 600.

Ulyanovsk: [a]Russia in Europe. [b]alt Ulianovsk; for Simbirsk. [c]Volga R; Sviyaga R. [d]none. [e]Ulyanovsk District Library-V. I. Lenin Book Palace (1848) 1026.

Uzhgorod: [a]Ukraine. [b]for Ungvar, Uzhorod. [c]Uzh R. [d]Uzhgorod State University (1945) 10–? [e] . . . University Library (1945) 1160; Transcarpathian District Library (1945) 405.

Vilnyus: [a]*Lithuania. [b]alt Vilna, Vilnis; for Wilno. [c]Viliya R; Vilnia R. [d]V. Kapsukas Vilnyus State University (1579) 17 – 1170. [e]Library of the Lithuanian Institute of Technical Information and Research (1957) 6000; State Library of the Lithuanian SSR (1919) 4000; . . . University Library (1570) 4000; Central Library of the Lithuanian Academy of Sciences (1557) 2000.

Vinnitsa: [a]Ukraine. [b]none. [c]Southern Bug R. [d]none. [e]K.A. Timiryazev Vinnitsa District Library (1907) 568; Pedagogic Institute Library (1944) 381.

Vitebsk: [a]White Russia. [b]none. [c]Western Dvina R; Luchesa R. [d]none. [e]V. I. Lenin Vitebsk District Library (1925) 380.

Vladimir: [a]Russia in Europe. [b]none. [c]Klyazma R; Lybed R. [d]none. [e]M. Gorkiy Vladimir District Library (1896) 630; Scientific-Technical Library (1958) 406.

Volgodonsk: [a]Russia in Europe. [b]none. [c]Don R. [d]none. [e]Volgodonsk Branch Library of the All-Union Research Institute of Synthetic Oil Substitutes (1963) 30.

Volgograd: [a]Russia in Europe. [b]for Stalingrad,Tsaritsyn. [c]Volga R; Tsaritsa R. [d]Volgograd State University (1978) 1–? [e]M. Gorkiy Volgograd District Library (1900) 801; Scientific-Technical Library (1948) 622; Pedagogic Institute Library (1945) 305; . . . University Library (1978)?

Vologda: [a]Russia in Europe. [b]none. [c]Vologda R. [d]none. [e]I. V. Babushkin Vologda District Library (1919) 459.

Volzhskiy: [a]Russia in Europe. [b]none. [c]Volga R. [d]none. [e]Volgograd Hydroelectric Technical Library (1950) 183.

Voronezh: [a]Russia in Europe. [b]none. [c]Voronezh R. [d]Voronezh State University (1919) 12 – 800. [e] . . . University Library (1918) 1470; Scientific-Technical Library (1957) 1196; I. S. Nikitin Voronezh District Library (1864) 1008.

Voroshilovgrad: [a]Ukraine. [b]for Lugansk. [c]Lugan R. [d]none. [e]Library of the Voroshilovgrad Center for Scientific and Technical Information (1954) 3000; A. M. Gorkiy Voroshilovgrad District Library (1898) 766.

Yalta: [a]Ukraine. [b]none. [c]Black Sea. [d]none. [e]State Botanical Garden Library (1812) 127.

Yaroslavl: [a]Russia in Europe. [b]none. [c]Volga R; Kotorosl R. [d]Yaroslavl State University (1970) 2–? [e]Scientific-Technical Library (1960) 2243; N. A. Nekrasov Yaroslavl District Library (1902) 960.

Yerevan: [a]*Armenia. [b]alt Erevan; for Erivan. [c]Zanga R. [d]Yerevan State University (1920) 8 – 791. [e]A. F.

TABLE 2b. (Continued)

Myashnikyan State Library of the Armenian SSR (1832) 6400; Central Library of the Armenian Academy of Sciences (1935) 2200; . . . University Library (1921) 1500.

Yoshkar-Ola: [a]Russia in Europe;*Mari ASSR. [b]alt Ioshkar-Ola; for Krasnokokshaysk, Tsarevokokshaysk. [c]Malaya Kokshaga R. [d]Mari State University (1972) 2–? [e]State Scientific Library of the Mari ASSR (1922) 628.

Zaporozhye: [a]Ukraine. [b]alt Zaporozhe; for Aleksandrovsk. [c]Dnieper R. [d]Zaporozhye State University (1985) ?– ? [e]Library of the Zaporozhye Center for Scientific and Technical Information (1961) 1270; A. M. Gorkiy Zaporozhye District Library (1905) 937.

Zhdanov: [a]Ukraine. [b]for Mariupol. [c]Sea of Azov; Kalmius R. [d]none. [e]Metallurgical Institute Library (1933) 302; Gorkiy Library (?) ?; Korolenko Library (?) ?; Krupskaya Library (?) ?

Zhitomir: [a]Ukraine. [b]none. [c]Teterev R; Kamenka R. [d]none. [e]October Revolution Zhitomir District Library (1866) 379; Pedagogic Institute Library (1920) 302.

Yugoslavia

Banja Luka: [a]Bosnia and Herzegovina. [b]none. [c]Vrbas R. [d]Duro Pucar-Stari University of Banja Luka (1975) 10 – 420. [e]Petar Kocic Public Library (1946) 55.

*Belgrade: [a]*Serbia. [b]off Beograd. [c]Danube R; Sava R. [d]University of Belgrade (1808) 57 – 3702. [e]University . . . Library (1844) 2320; Library of the Serbian Academy of Arts and Sciences (1842) 1000; National Library of Serbia (1832) 964; City Library (1931) 400.

Bitola: [a]Macedonia. [b]for Bitol, Bitolj, Monastir. [c]Dragor R. [d]University of Bitola (1935) 9 – 149. [e]University . . . Library (1935?) 160; Public Library (1945) 27.

Dubrovnik: [a]Croatia. [b]for Ragusa. [c]Adriatic Sea. [d]none. [e]Research Library (1941) 203.

Kragujevac: [a]Serbia. [b]none. [c]Lepenica R; Zdraljica R. [d]Svetozar Markovic University of Kragujevac (1976) 16 – 280. [e]Vuk Karadzic Public Library (1866) 60; . . . University Library (1976?)?

Ljubljana: [a]* Slovenia. [b]for Laibach. [c]Ljubljanica R. [d]Edvard Kardelj University of Ljubljana (1595) 17 – 2167. [e]National and University Library (1774) 2880; Library of the Slovene Academy of Sciences (1938) 335.

Maribor: [a]Slovenia. [b]for Marburg. [c]Drava R. [d]University of Maribor (1959) 5 – 490. [e]University . . . Library (1903) 475; City Library (1949) 236.

Mostar: [a]Bosnia and Herzegovina. [b]none. [c]Neretva R. [d]Dzemal Bijedic University of Mostar (1977) 5 – 169. [e]Public Library (1945) 40; . . . University Library (1977?) ?

Nis: [a]Serbia. [b]alt Nish; for Nissa. [c]Nisava R. [d]University of Nis (1965) 30 – 938. [e]Public Library (1904) 95; University . . . Library (1948) 50.

Novi Sad: [a]Serbia. [b]for Neusatz, Ujvidek. [c]Danube R. [d]University of Novi Sad (1954) 36 – 2103. [e]Serbian National Library (1826 at Budapest, Hungary; relocated 1864) 686; University . . . Library (1938) 336.

Osijek: [a]Croatia. [b]for Esseg, Eszek. [c]Drava R. [d]University of Osijek (1975) 7 – 610. [e]University . . . Library (1975?) 56; Public Library (1946) 40.

Pristina: [a]Serbia. [b]alt Prishtina. [c]Pristevka R; Maticki R. [d]University of Kosovo in Pristina (1971) 26 – 1052. [e]National and University Library of Kosovo (1944) 600.

Rijeka: [a]Croatia. [b]for Fiume. [c]Kvarner G of Adriatic Sea. [d]University of Rijeka (1973) 13 – 720. [e]Research Library (1627) 400; University . . . Library (1973?) 305.

Sarajevo: [a]*Bosnia and Herzegovina. [b]alt Serajevo. [c]Miljacka R. [d]University of Sarajevo (1946) 33 – 1844. [e]National and University Library of Bosnia and Herzegovina (1945) 1000.

Skopje: [a]*Macedonia. [b]alt Skoplje; for Uskub. [c]Vardar R. [d]Cyril and Methodius University of Skopje (1946) 43 – 1850. [e]Clement of Ohrid National and University Library (1944) 1500; Braka Miladinovci Public Library (1935) 120.

Split: [a]Croatia. [b]for Spalato, Spalatro. [c]Adriatic Sea. [d]University of Split (1974) 12 – 618. [e]Research Library (1903) 400; Public Library (1950) 49.

Subotica: [a]Serbia. [b]for Maria-Theresiopel, Szabadka. [c]nr Koros (alt Zuti Potok) R; nr Palicsko L. [d]none. [e]Public Library (?) 145.

Titograd: [a]*Montenegro. [b]for Podgorica. [c]Moraca R; Ribnica R. [d]Veljko Vlahovic University of Titograd (1974) 10 – 950. [e]Montenegro Historical Institute Library (1948) 38; . . . University Library (1974?)?

Tuzla: [a]Bosnia and Herzegovina. [b]none. [c]Jala R; Spreca R. [d]University of Tuzla (1976) 15 – 465. [e]University . . . Library (1976?)?

Zagreb: [a]*Croatia. [b]for Agram, Zagrab. [c]Sava R. [d]University of Zagreb (1669) 42 – 3644. [e]National and University Library (1607) 1559; Library of the Yugoslav Academy of Arts and Sciences (1868) 225; City Library (1907) 205.

For an explanation of symbols and abbreviations, see pages 16–17.

(Continued)

TABLE 2b. (Continued)

NORTH AMERICA

Antigua and Barbuda

*Saint John's: [a]Antigua I. [b]none. [c]Caribbean Sea. [d]none. [e]Public Library (1854) 50.

Aruba

*Oranjestad: [a]Aruba I. [b]none. [c]Caribbean Sea. [d]Universidat di Aruba (1970) 0.2 – 20. [e]Openbare Leeszaal en Boekerij (1949) 140.

Bahamas

*Nassau: [a]New Providence I. [b]none. [c]Northeast Providence Channel. [d]none. [e]College of the Bahamas Library (1974) 66; Public Library (1847) 50.

Barbados

*Bridgetown: [a]Barbados I. [b]none. [c]Carlisle B of Atlantic O. [d]University of the West Indies, Cave Hill Campus (at Bridgetown) (1963) 2 – 278. [e]Public Library (1847) 191; Cave Hill Campus Library of the University . . . (1963) 95.

Belize

Belize: [b]none. [c]G of Honduras of Caribbean Sea; Belize R. [d]none. [e]National Library Service (1935) 100; Jubilee Public Library (1935) 32.

*Belmopan: [b]none. [c]Belize R. [d]none. [e]Belmopan Comprehensive School Library (?) ?

Bermuda

*Hamilton: [a]Bermuda I. [b]none. [c]Atlantic O. [d]none. [e]Bermuda Library (1839) 150.

Canada

Brampton: [a]Ontario. [b]none. [c]Etobicoke Creek. [d]none. [e]Public Library (1895) 300.

Brantford: [a]Ontario. [b]none. [c]Grand R. [d]none. [e]Public Library (1884) 173.

Burlington: [a]Ontario. [b]for Wellington Square. [c]Ontario L. [d]none. [e]Public Library (1872) 231.

Calgary: [a]Alberta. [b]none. [c]Bow R; Elbow R. [d]University of Calgary (1945) 19 – 1219. [e]University . . . Library (1945) 1406; Public Library (1911) 667.

Charlottetown: [a]*Prince Edward Island; Prince Edward I. [b]none. [c]Hillsborough B of Northumberland Strait; Hillsborough R; Yorke R. [d]University of Prince Edward Island (1834) 2 – 112. [e]University . . . Library (1917?) 338; Prince Edward Island Provincial Library (1933) 180.

Chicoutimi: [a]Quebec. [b]none. [c]Saguenay R; Chicoutimi R. [d]none. [e]Bibliotheque de l'Universite du Quebec a Chicoutimi (1969) 184; Bibliotheque Municipale (1950) 62.

Dartmouth: [a]Nova Scotia. [b]none. [c]Atlantic O. [d]none. [e]Dartmouth Regional Library (1963) 111.

Edmonton: [a]*Alberta. [b]none. [c]North Saskatchewan R. [d]University of Alberta (1906) 26 – 2092. [e]University . . . Library (1909) 2500; Public Library (1913) 1505.

Fredericton: [a]* New Brunswick. [b]none. [c]Saint John R. [d]University of New Brunswick (1785) 8 – 595. [e]University . . . Library (1829) 990; York Regional Library (1958) 288.

Guelph: [a]Ontario. [b]none. [c]Speed R. [d]University of Guelph (1862) 12 – 704. [e]University . . . Library (1964) 1900; Public Library (1883) 106.

Halifax: [a]*Nova Scotia. [b]none. [c]Atlantic O. [d]Dalhousie University (1818) 11 – 855; Saint Mary's University (1802) 5 – 183; Mount Saint Vincent University (1814) 4 – 108; Technical University of Nova Scotia (1907) 1 – 110. [e]Dalhousie University Library (1867) 1138; City Regional Library (1873) 331; Saint Mary's University Library (1802) 223.

Hamilton: [a]Ontario. [b]none. [c]Ontario L. [d]McMaster University (1887) 15 – 900. [e] . . . University Library (1887) 1352; Public Library (1889) 819.

Hull: [a]Quebec. [b]none. [c]Ottawa R; Gatineau R. [d]none. [e]Bibliotheque Municipale (1954) 173.

Jonquiere: [a]Quebec. [b]none. [c]Sable R. [d]none. [e]Bibliotheque Municipale (1944) 84.

Kamloops: [a]British Columbia. [b]none. [c]Thompson R; North Thompson R; South Thompson R. [d]none. [e]Cariboo Thompson Nicola Library (1974) 306.

Kelowna: [a]British Columbia. [b]none. [c]Okanagan L. [d]none. [e]Okanagan Regional Library (1936) 328.

Kingston: [a]Ontario. [b]none. [c]Saint Lawrence R; Ontario L. [d]Queen's University (1841) 15 – 819. [e] . . . University Library (1841) 2130; Royal Military College of Canada Library (1877) 249; Public Library (1834) 219.

TABLE 2b. (Continued)

Kitchener: [a]Ontario. [b]for Berlin. [c]Grand R. [d]none. [e]Public Library (1884) 428.

La Salle: [a]Quebec; Montreal I. [b]for Lachine. [c]Saint Lawrence R. [d]none. [e]L'Octogone Centre de la Culture (1958) 105.

Laval: [a]Quebec; Jesus I. [b]none. [c]Prairies R; Mille-Iles R. [d]none. [e]Laval Institute Library (1945) 14.

Lethbridge: [a]Alberta. [b]none. [c]Oldman R. [d]University of Lethbridge (1967) 2 – 160. [e]University . . . Library (1967) 210; Public Library (1919) 150.

London: [a]Ontario. [b]none. [c]Thames R. [d]University of Western Ontario (1878) 27 – 1366. [e]University . . . Library (1908) 2375; Public Library (1894) 617.

Longueuil: [a]Quebec. [b]inc Jacques-Cartier since 1970. [c]Saint Lawrence R. [d]none. [e]Bibliotheque Municipale (1967) 168. [f]Jacques-Cartier: 41 (1961), 22 (1951).

Markham: [a]Ontario. [b]none. [c]Rouge R. [d]none. [e]Crowntek Library (1972) 6.

Mississauga: [a]Ontario. [b]inc Cooksville. [c]Cooksville Creek. [d]none. [e]Public Library (1957) 613.

Moncton: [a]New Brunswick. [b]none. [c]Petitcodiac R. [d]Universite de Moncton (1864) 11 – 322. [e]Bibliotheque de l'Universite . . . (1940) 430; Albert-Westmoreland-Kent Regional Library (1957) 310.

Montreal: [a]Quebec; Montreal I. [b]for Ville-Marie. [c]Saint Lawrence R; Ottawa R. [d]Universite de Montreal (1876) 44 – 1811; Concordia University (1848) 25 – 785; McGill University (1821) 21 – 1596. [e]Bibliotheque de l'Universite . . . (1878) 2396; McGill University Library (1821) 2237; Concordia University Library (1899) 1720; Bibliotheque de la Ville (1902) 1704.

Montreal-Nord: [a]Quebec; Montreal I. [b]alt Montreal North. [c]Prairies R. [d]none. [e]Bibliotheque Municipale (1970) 116.

Nepean: [a]Ontario. [b]none. [c]Ottawa R. [d]none. [e]Public Library (1957) 238.

Niagara Falls: [a]Ontario. [b]none. [c]Niagara R. [d]none. [e]Public Library (1878) 207.

North Bay: [a]Ontario. [b]none. [c]Nipissing L. [d]none. [e]Public Library (1895) 132.

North York: [a]Ontario. [b]none. [c]Humber R. [d]York University (1959) 36 – 1023. [e] . . . University Library (1959) 1688; Public Library (1955) 1465.

Oakville: [a]Ontario. [b]none. [c]Ontario L. [d]none. [e]Public Library (1895) 185.

Oshawa: [a]Ontario. [b]none. [c]Ontario L. [d]none. [e]Public Library (1864) 350.

*Ottawa: [a]Ontario. [b]for Bytown. [c]Ottawa R; Rideau R. [d]University of Ottawa (1848) 20 – 999; Carleton University (1942) 16 – 630. [e]Library of the Canada Institute for Scientific and Technical Information (1924) 1849; University . . . Library (1903) 1574; National Library of Canada (1953) 1213; . . . University Library (1942) 1171; Agriculture Canada Library (1910) 1000; Public Library (1906) 711.

Peterborough: [a]Ontario. [b]none. [c]Otonabee R. [d]Trent University (1963) 4 – 182. [e] . . . University Library (1963) 424; Public Library (1910) 104.

Prince George: [a]British Columbia. [b]for Fort George. [c]Fraser R; Nechako R. [d]none. [e]Public Library (?) 119.

Quebec: [a]*Quebec. [b]none. [c]Saint Lawrence R; Saint-Charles R. [d]Universite du Quebec (1968) 66 – 1728 (no campus at Quebec); Universite Laval (1663) 29 – 1049. [e]Bibliotheque de l'Universite Laval (1852) 1865; Bibliotheque de Quebec (1848) 379; Bibliotheque de l'Assemblee Nationale du Quebec (1792) 300.

Regina: [a]*Saskatchewan. [b]none. [c]Waskana Creek. [d]University of Regina (1911) 9 – 377. [e]University . . . Library (1910) 681; Public Library (1909) 367; Saskatchewan Provincial Library (1953) 268.

Saint Catharines: [a]Ontario. [b]none. [c]Twelve Mile Creek. [d]Brook University (1962) 8 – 247. [e] . . . University Library (1964) 347; Public Library (1883) 299.

Saint John: [a]New Brunswick. [b]none. [c]B of Fundy of Atlantic O; Saint John R. [d]none. [e]Saint John Regional Library (1883) 255.

Saint John's: [a]*Newfoundland; Newfoundland I. [b]none. [c]Atlantic O. [d]Memorial University of Newfoundland (1925) 13 – 850. [e] . . . University Library (1925) 2305; Newfoundland Public Library Services (1935) 940.

Saint-Leonard: [a]Quebec; Montreal I. [b]none. [c]Prairies R. [d]none. [e]Bibliotheque Municipale (1966) 147.

Sarnia: [a]Ontario. [b]for Port Sarnia. [c]Saint Clair R; Huron L. [d]none. [e]Public Library (1903) 204.

Saskatoon: [a]Saskatchewan. [b]none. [c]South Saskatchewan R. [d]University of Saskatchewan (1907) 16 – 1106. [e]University . . . Library (1912) 1168; Public Library (1913) 374; Wheatland Regional Library (1967) 254.

Sault Sainte Marie: [a]Ontario. [b]none. [c]Saint Marys R. [d]none. [e]Public Library (1895) 190.

Sherbrooke: [a]Quebec. [b]none. [c]Saint-Francois R; Magog R. [d]Universite de Sherbrooke (1954) 10 – 570; Bishop's University (at Lennoxville, nr Sherbrooke) (1843) 2 – 85. [e]Bibliotheque de l'Universite . . . (1961) 800; . . . University Library (at Lennoxville) (1843) 201; Bibliotheque Municipale (1954) 120.

Sudbury: [a]Ontario. [b]none. [c]Junction Creek; Ramsey L. [d]Laurentian University (1913) 8 – 328. [e] . . . University Library (1960) 700; Public Library (1896) 210; Ontario Library Service-Voyageur (1960) 200.

For an explanation of symbols and abbreviations, see pages 16–17.

(Continued)

TABLE 2b. (Continued)

Sydney: [a]Nova Scotia; Cape Breton I. [b]none. [c]Atlantic O. [d]none. [e]University College of Cape Breton Library (1951) 155; Cape Breton Regional Library (bef 1925) 148.

Thunder Bay: [a]Ontario. [b]inc Fort William; Port Arthur. [c]Kaministikwia R; Thunder B of Superior L. [d]Lakehead University (1946) 5 – 245. [e] . . . University Library (1948) 450; Public Library (1881) 291. [f]Fort William: 35 (1951), 26 (1931), 4 (1901), 0.7 (1881); Port Arthur: 31 (1951), 20 (1931),3 (1901), 1 (1881).

Toronto: [a]*Ontario. [b]for York. [c]Humber R; Ontario L. [d]University of Toronto (1827) 52 – 2900. [e]University . . . Library (1827) 6150; Public Library (1883) 1429; Metropolitan Toronto Library (1909) 1027.

Trois-Rivieres: [a]Quebec. [b]alt Thee Rivers. [c]Saint Lawrence R; Saint-Maurice R; Sainte-Marguerite R. [d]none. [e]Bibliotheque Centrale de Pret de la Mauricie (1961) 344; Bibliotheque de l'Universite du Quebec a Trois-Rivieres (1969) 256; Bibliotheque Municipale (1946) 130.

Vancouver: [a]British Columbia. [b]none. [c]Burrard Inlet of Strait of Georgia; Fraser R. [d]University of British Columbia (1908) 28 – 1994; Simon Fraser University (1963) 15 – 490. [e]University . . . Library (1912) 3400; Public Library (1887) 978; . . . University Library (1964) 787.

Victoria: [a]*British Columbia; Vancouver I. [b]none. [c]Juan de Fuca Strait. [d]University of Victoria (1902) 11 – 498. [e]University . . . Library (1902) 1300; Public Library (1864) 485; British Columbia Provincial Library (1863) 300.

Waterloo: [a]Ontario. [b]none. [c]Grand R. [d]University of Waterloo (1957) 25 – 770; Wilfrid Laurier University (1911) 7 – 220. [e]University . . . Library (1958) 2200; . . . University Library (1911) 410; Public Library (1897) 117; Waterloo Regional Library (1966) 72.

Whitehorse: [a]*Yukon Territory. [b]none. [c]Yukon R. [d]none. [e]Government of Yukon Library (1962) 179.

Windsor: [a]Ontario. [b]none. [c]Detroit R. [d]University of Windsor (1857) 18 – 525. [e]University . . . Library (1857) 1392; Public Library (1894) 514.

Winnipeg: [a]*Manitoba. [b]none. [c]Red R; Assiniboine R. [d]University of Manitoba (1877) 24 – 1282; University of Winnipeg (1871) 7 – 203. [e]University of Manitoba Library (1885) 1386; City Library (1905) 1074; University of Winnipeg Library (1871) 398.

Yellowknife: [a]*Northwest Territories. [b]none. [c]Great Slave L. [d]none. [e]Government of the Northwest Territories Library (1973) 20; Public Library (?) 18.

Costa Rica

*San Jose: [b]none. [c]Torres R. [d]Universidad de Costa Rica (at San Pedro, nr San Jose) (1814) 28 – 2897; Universidad Nacional (at Heredia, nr San Jose) (1973) 12 – 1036; Universidad Autonoma de Centro America (1976) 8 – 550. [e]Biblioteca de la Universidad de Costa Rica (at San Pedro) (1946) 300; Biblioteca Nacional (1888) 175.

Cuba

Bayamo: [b]none. [c]Bayamo R. [d]none. [e]Biblioteca "1868" (?) ?

Camaguey: [b]for Puerto Principe. [c]Jatibonico R; Tinima R. [d]Universidad de Camaguey (1967) 5–? [e]Biblioteca de la Universidad . . . (1967?) ?; Biblioteca Municipal (1938)?

Cienfuegos: [b]none. [c]Cienfuegos B of Caribbean Sea. [d]none. [e]Biblioteca Publica Municipal (1931) 1; Biblioteca Roberto Garcia Valdes (?) ?

Guantanamo: [b]none. [c]Guaso R. [d]none. [e]Biblioteca Popular (1938)?

*Havana: [b]alt Habana; inc Marianao, San Miguel del Padron since 1969; off La Habana. [c]G of Mexico. [d]Universidad de La Habana (1728) 16 – 1433. [e]Biblioteca Nacional Jose Marti (1901) 1469; Biblioteca de la Universidad . . . (1728) 570; Biblioteca de la Sociedad Economica de Amigos del Pais (1928) 300; Biblioteca Publica Jose A. Echevarria (1959) 90. [f]Marianao: 219 (1953), 71 (1931),5 (1899), 3 (1861); San Miguel del Padron; 61 (1953), 3 (1931), 2 (1899).

Holguin: [b]none. [c]nr Maranon R. [d]none. [e]Biblioteca del Centro Universitario de Holguin; (1973?) 30.

Las Tunas: [b]alt Tunas; off Victoria de las Tunas. [c]nr Corinto R. [d]none. [e]Biblioteca Jose Marti (?) ?

Manzanillo: [b]none. [c]G of Guacanayabo of Caribbean Sea. [d]none.

Matanzas: [b]none. [c]Matanzas B of G of Mexico; San Juan R; Yumuri R. [d]none. [e]Biblioteca Publica (1835) 40.

Pinar del Rio: [b]none. [c]Guama R. [d]none. [e]Biblioteca del Centro Universitario de Pinar del Rio (1972) 10; Biblioteca Ramon Gonzalez Coro (?)?

Santa Clara: [b]for Villa Clara. [c]Monte R; Sabana R. [d]Universidad Central de Las Villas (1948) 8 – 400. [e]Biblioteca de la Universidad . . . (1953) 160; Biblioteca Provincial (1927) 9.

Santiago de Cuba: [b]alt Santiago. [c]Caribbean Sea. [d]Universidad de Oriente (1947) 12 – 800. [e]Biblioteca de la Universidad . . . (1947) 312; Biblioteca Provincial Elvira Cape (1899) 115.

TABLE 2b. (Continued)

Dominica

*Roseau: [a]Dominica I. [b]for Charlotte's Town. [c]Caribbean Sea; Roseau R. [d]none. [e]Free Library (1902) 19.

Dominican Republic

La Romana: [a]Hispaniola I. [b]alt Romana. [c]Caribbean Sea. [d]none.

San Pedro de Macoris: [a]Hispaniola I. [b]none. [c]Caribbean Sea; Macoris R. [d]Universidad Central del Este (1970) 30 – 650. [e]Biblioteca de la Universidad . . . (1970) 150.

Santiago de los Caballeros: [a]Hispaniola I. [b]alt Santiago. [c]Yaque del Norte R. [d]Universidad Catolica Madre y Maestra (1962) 7 – 465; Universidad Tecnologica de Santiago (1974) 4 – 90. [e]Biblioteca de la Universidad Catolica . . . (1962) 52; Biblioteca de la Sociedad Amantes de la Luz (1874) 18.

*Santo Domingo: [a]Hispaniola I. [b]for Ciudad Trujillo, Trujillo. [c]Caribbean Sea; Ozama R. [d]Universidad Autonoma de Santo Domingo (1538) 51 – 1178; Universidad Nacional Pedro Henriquez Urena (1966) 9 – 688. [e]Biblioteca de la Universidad Autonoma . . . (1538) 260; Biblioteca Nacional (1971) 154; Biblioteca de la Universidad Nacional . . . (1966?) 40; Biblioteca Municipal (1914) 35.

El Salvador

Mejicanos: [b]none. [c]Chacahuasta R. [d]none.

San Miguel: [b]none. [c]Grande de San Miguel R. [d]none.

*San Salvador: [b]none. [c]Acelhuate R; Urbina R; Aseseco R. [d]Universidad de El Salvador (1841) 47 – 1728; Universidad Centroamericana Jose Simeon Canas (1965) 6 – 260. [e]Biblioteca Nacional (1870) 150; Biblioteca de la Universidad de El Salvador (1847) 91; Biblioteca de la Universidad Centroamericana . . . (1965) 55.

Santa Ana: [b]none. [c](Quebrada) Santa Lucia Creek. [d]Universidad Catolica de Occidente (1982) 0.3 – 36. [e]Biblioteca Municipal (1896) 5; Biblioteca de la Universidad . . . (1982?)?

Greenland

*Godthab: [b]alt Nuk, Nuuk. [c]Godthab Fjord of Davis Strait. [d]none. [e]Central Library of Greenland (?) 267.

Grenada

*Saint George's: [a]Grenada I. [b]for Fort-Royal. [c]Caribbean Sea. [d]none. [e]Grenada Public Library (1846) 14.

Guadeloupe

*Basse-Terre: [a]Basse-Terre I. [b]none. [c]Caribbean Sea. [d]none. [e]Archives Departementales (1951) 4.

Les Abymes: [a]Grande-Terre I. [b]alt Abymes. [c]nr (Riviere) Salee Channel. [d]none.

Pointe-a-Pitre: [a]Grande-Terre I. [b]none. [c](Riviere) Salee Channel. [d]Universite Antilles-Guyane (1850) 5 – 260 [Pointe-a-Pitre campus: (1850) 3–?]. [e]Bibliotheque Universitaire, Section Guadeloupe (1970) 18.

Guatemala

*Guatemala: [b]alt Guatemala City. [c]Barranquila R; Barranca R. [d]Universidad de San Carlos de Guatemala (1676 at Antigua, relocated 1776) 48 – 3007; Universidad Rafael Landivar (1961) 7 – 763. [e]Biblioteca de la Universidad de San Carlos . . . (1676? at Antigua, relocated 1776?) 200; Biblioteca del Instituto de Nutricion de Centro America y Panama (1949) 70; Biblioteca Nacional de Guatemala (1879) 50.

Haiti

Cap-Haitien: [a]Hispaniola I. [b]for Cap-Francais. [c]Atlantic O. [d]none. [e]Bibliotheque de l'Ecole de Droit (1867?) ?

*Port-au-Prince: [a]Hispaniola I. [b]none. [c]G of Gonaives of Caribbean Sea. [d]Universite d'Etat d'Haiti (1920) 4 – 325. [e]Bibliotheque de l'Institut Francais (1945) 30; Bibliotheque Nationale d'Haiti (1940) 19; Bibliotheque de l'Universite . . . (1920) 7.

Honduras

San Pedro Sula: [b]none. [c]Piedras R. [d]none.

*Tegucigalpa: [b]none. [c]Choluteca R; Chiquito R. [d]Universidad Nacional Autonoma de Honduras (1845) 27 – 1518. [e]Biblioteca de la Universidad . . . (1847) 112; Biblioteca Nacional de Honduras (1880) 55; Biblioteca Romulo E. Duron (?) 20.

For an explanation of symbols and abbreviations, see pages 16–17.

(Continued)

TABLE 2b.   (Continued)

Jamaica

*Kingston: ^bnone. ^cCaribbean Sea. ^dUniversity of the West Indies (1948) 11 – 1408 [Mona campus (at Kingston) (1948) 5 – 850]. ^eJamaica Library Service (1948) 1220; Mona Campus Library of the University . . . (1948) 364; National Library of Jamaica (1979) 34.

Montego Bay: ^bnone. ^cMontego B of Caribbean Sea; Montego R. ^dnone.

Spanish Town: ^bfor Santiago de la Vega. ^cCobre R. ^dnone.

Martinique

*Fort-de-France: ^bfor Fort-Royal. ^cCaribbean Sea; Madame R. ^dUniversite Antilles-Guyane, Fort-de-France campus (1949) 2–? ^eBibliotheque Schoelcher (1883) 130; Bibliotheque Universitaire, Section Martinique (1972) 37.

Mexico

Acapulco: ^aGuerrero. ^boff Acapulco de Juarez. ^cPacific O. ^dnone. ^eBiblioteca de America (1971) 15.

Aguascalientes: ^a*Aguascalientes. ^bnone. ^cnr San Pedro (alt Aguascalientes, Verde) R. ^dUniversidad Autonoma de Aguascalientes (1867) 6 – 601. ^eBiblioteca de la Universidad . . . (1964) 24.

Campeche: ^a*Campeche. ^bnone. ^cB of Campeche of G of Mexico. ^dUniversidad del Sudeste (1756) 2 – 178. ^eBiblioteca de la Universidad . . . (1965) 11.

Celaya: ^aGuanajuato. ^bnone. ^cLaja R. ^dnone. ^eBiblioteca del Instituto Tecnologico de Celaya (1958) 15.

Chetumal: ^a*Quintana Roo. ^bfor Payo Obispo. ^cChetumal B of Caribbean Sea; Hondo R. ^dnone. ^eBiblioteca del Instituto Tecnologico de Chetumal (1972) 5.

Chihuahua: ^a*Chihuahua. ^bnone. ^cChuviscar R. ^dUniversidad Autonoma de Chihuahua (1954) 12 – 1269. ^eBiblioteca de la Universidad . . . (1869) 42; Biblioteca Municipal Miguel de Cervantes Saavedra (1943) 11.

Chilpancingo: ^a*Guerrero. ^bfor Ciudad de los Bravos. ^cHuacapa R. ^dUniversidad Autonoma de Guerrero (1869) ?–? ^eBiblioteca de la Universidad . . . (1946) 38.

Ciudad Juarez: ^aChihuahua. ^balt Juarez; for Paso del Norte. ^cRio Grande R. ^dUniversidad Autonoma de Ciudad Juarez (1973) 4 – 380. ^eBiblioteca Publica Municipal (1945) 24.

Ciudad Lopez Mateos: ^aMexico. ^balt Lopez Mateos; for Atizapan de Zaragoza. ^cnone. ^dnone. ^eBiblioteca del Instituto de Zaragoza (1966) 3.

Ciudad Madero: ^aTamaulipas. ^balt Madero; for Dona Cecilia, Villa de Cecilia. ^cPanuco R. ^dnone. ^eBiblioteca del Instituto Tecnologico de Ciudad Madero (1954) 15.

Ciudad Obregon: ^aSonora. ^balt Obregon; for Cajeme. ^cnr Yaqui R. ^dnone. ^eBiblioteca del Instituto Tecnologico de Sonora (1955) 11; Biblioteca Publica Municipal (1973) 11.

Ciudad Victoria: ^a*Tamaulipas. ^balt Victoria; for Nuevo Santander. ^cSan Marcos R. ^dUniversidad Autonoma de Tamaulipas (1950) 14 – 1033. ^eBiblioteca Publica Presidente Adolfo Ruiz Cortines (1962) 12; Biblioteca de la Universidad . . . (1950) 11.

Coatzacoalcos: ^aVeracruz. ^bfor Puerto Mexico. ^cB of Campeche of G of Mexico; Coatzacoalcos R. ^dnone. ^eBiblioteca Publica Municipal (1961) 4.

Colima: ^a*Colima. ^bnone. ^cColima R. ^dUniversidad de Colima (1867) 14 – 560. ^eBiblioteca de la Universidad . . . (1965) 9.

Cordoba: ^aVeracruz. ^bnone. ^cBlanco R. ^dnone. ^eBiblioteca de la Escuela Secundaria (1871) 5.

Cuernavaca: ^a*Morelos. ^bnone. ^cCuernavaca R; Amatitlan R. ^dUniversidad Autonoma del Estado de Morelos (1872) 11 – 598. ^eBiblioteca de la Universidad . . . (1887) 210; Biblioteca Municipal (1971) 6.

Culiacan: ^a*Sinaloa. ^bnone. ^cCuliacan R. ^dUniversidad Autonoma de Sinaloa (1873) 6 – 403. ^eBiblioteca de la Universidad . . . (1873) 16; Biblioteca Publica del Estado de Sinaloa (1940) 9.

Durango: ^a*Durango. ^bfor Ciudad de Victoria, Victoria; off Victoria de Durango. ^cTunal R. ^dUniversidad Juarez del Estado de Durango (1856) 8 – 740. ^eBiblioteca de la Universidad . . . (1955) 25; Biblioteca Publica del Estado de Durango (1853) 20.

Ecatepec: ^aMexico. ^bfor San Cristobal Ecatepec; off Ecatepec de Morelos. ^cnone. ^dnone.

Ensenada: ^aBaja California. ^bnone. ^cTodos Santos B of Pacific O; Ensenada R. ^dnone. ^eBiblioteca de la Escuela Superior de Ciencias Marinas (1965) 5.

Garza Garcia: ^aNuevo Leon. ^bnone. ^cSanta Catarina R. ^dnone. ^eAmerican School Library (1946) 11.

Gomez Palacio: ^aDurango. ^bnone. ^cNazas R. ^dnone. ^eBiblioteca Profesor Jose Santos Valdes (1977) 3.

Guadalajara: ^a*Jalisco. ^bnone. ^cSan Juan de Dios R; Agua Azul L. ^dUniversidad de Guadalajara (1791) 212 – 7436; Universidad Autonoma de Guadalajara (1935) 22 – 1470. ^eBiblioteca Publica del Estado de Jalisco (1861) 452; Biblioteca de la Universidad de Guadalajara (1925) 450; Biblioteca de la Universidad Autonoma de Guadalajara (1935) 80.

TABLE 2b. (Continued)

Guadalupe: [a]Nuevo Leon. [b]none. [c]Santa Catarina R. [d]none.

Guanajuato: [a]*Guanajuato. [b]none. [c]Guanajuato R. [d]Universidad de Guanajuato (1732) 14 – 1330. [e]Biblioteca de la Universidad . . . (1732) 200.

Hermosillo: [a]*Sonora. [b]none. [c]Sonora R. [d]Universidad de Sonora (1938) 18 – 1025. [e]Biblioteca de la Universidad . . . (1938) 125.

Irapuato: [a]Guanajuato. [b]none. [c]Irapuato R. [d]none. [e]Biblioteca de la Universidad de Guanajuato en Irapuato (1952) 6; Biblioteca Benito Juarez (1964) 3.

Jalapa: [a]*Veracruz. [b]alt Xalapa; off Jalapa Enriquez. [c](Arroyo de) Santiago Creek. [d]Universidad Veracruzana (1846) 40 – 2520. [e]Biblioteca de la Universidad . . . (1944) 100; Biblioteca Juan Diaz Covarrubias (1943) 8.

La Paz: [a]*Baja California Sur. [b]alt Paz. [c]La Paz B of G of California. [d]Universidad Autonoma de Baja California Sur (1975) 0.5 – 70. [e]Biblioteca John F. Kennedy (1960) 10.

Leon: [a]Guanajuato. [b]alt Leon de los Aldamas. [c]Turbio R. [d]none. [e]Biblioteca del Colegio La Salle (1953) 10; Biblioteca Efren Hernandez (1968) 6.

Los Mochis: [a]Sinaloa. [b]alt Mochis. [c]nr B of Tupolobampo of G of California. [d]Universidad de Occidente (1980) ? – ? [e]Biblioteca Municipal Licenciado Clemente Carrillo (1965) 4.

Matamoros: [a]Tamaulipas. [b]for Nueva Santander. [c]Rio Grande R. [d]none. [e]Biblioteca Profesor Juan B. Tijerina (1958) 8.

Mazatlan: [a]Sinaloa. [b]none. [c]Pacific O. [d]none. [e]Biblioteca de la Universidad Autonoma de Sinaloa en Mazatlan (1930) 9; Biblioteca Benjamin Franklin (1962) 6.

Merida: [a]*Yucatan. [b]for T'ho. [c]none. [d]Universidad de Yucatan (1624) 10 – 890. [e]Biblioteca de la Universidad . . . (1890) 55; Biblioteca Publica Manuel Cepeda Peraza (1867) 16.

Mexicali: [a]*Baja California. [b]none. [c]Nuevo R. [d]Universidad Autonoma de Baja California (1957) 23 – 1387. [e]Biblioteca de la Universidad . . . (1957) 60 Biblioteca Publica del Estado de Baja California (?) 3.

*Mexico: [a]*Distrito Federal. [b]alt Mexico City; for Tenochtitlan; inc Guadalupe Hidalgo (for Gustavo A. Madero) since 1973. [c]Piedad R; Tacubaya R. [d1]Universidad Nacional Autonoma de Mexico (1551) 327 – 27,515; Instituto Politecnico Nacional (univ) (1931) 161 – 17,405; Universidad Autonoma Metropolitana (1973) 30 – 2727; Universidad del Valle de Mexico (1960) 14 – 1200. [e]Biblioteca de la Universidad Nacional Autonoma de Mexico (1878?) 3000; Biblioteca Nacional de Mexico (1833) 1300; Biblioteca del Instituto Politecnico Nacional (1936) 520; Biblioteca Nacional de Antropologia e Historia (1831) 500; Biblioteca Publica Miguel Lerdo de Tejada (1928) 300. [f]Guadalupe Hidalgo: 103 (1960), 60 (1950), 11 (1921), 6 (1900).

Minatitlan: [a]Veracruz. [b]none. [c]Coatzacoalcos R. [d]none. [e]Biblioteca del Instituto Tecnologico de Minatitlan (1972) 6.

Monclova: [a]Coahuila. [b]none. [c]Monclova R. [d]none. [e]Biblioteca Publica (1956) 4.

Monterrey: [a]*Nuevo Leon. [b]none. [c]Santa Catarina R; Silla R. [d]Instituto Tecnologico y de Estudios Superiores (univ) (1943) 34 – 1250; Universidad Regiomontana (1951) 9 – 1069; Universidad de Monterrey (1969) 3 – 477. [e]Biblioteca del Instituto . . . (1944) 120; Biblioteca de la Universidad de Monterrey (1969) 23.

Morelia: [a]*Michoacan. [b]for Valladolid. [c]Grande R; Chiquito R. [d]Universidad Michoacana de San Nicolas de Hidalgo (1541 at Patzcuaro, relocated 1580) 45 – 1748. [e]Biblioteca de la Universidad . . . (1840) 150.

Naucalpan: [a]Mexico. [b]for San Bartolo Naucalpan; off Naucalpan de Juarez. [c]Hondo R. [d]none. [e]Biblioteca de la Universidad Nacional Autonoma de Mexico, Plantel Naucalpan (1970) 35.

Netzahualcoyotl: [a]Mexico. [b]alt Nezahualcoyotl. [c]nr Ixtapan R. [d]none. [e]Biblioteca de la Escuela Preparatoria (1972) 4.

Nuevo Laredo: [a]Tamaulipas. [b]none. [c]Rio Grande R. [d]none. [e]Biblioteca del Instituto Tecnologico de Nuevo Laredo (1964) 12; Biblioteca Publica Federal (1972) 3.

Oaxaca: [a]*Oaxaca. [b]off Oaxaca de Juarez. [c]Jalatlaco R. [d]Universidad Autonoma Benito Juarez de Oaxaca (1827) 15 – 980. [e]Biblioteca de la Universidad . . . (1827) 77.

Orizaba: [a]Veracruz. [b]none. [c]Blanco R. [d]none. [e]Biblioteca Benito Juarez (1962) 7; Biblioteca del Instituto Tecnologico de Orizaba (1957) 3.

Pachuca de Soto: [a]*Hidalgo. [b]none. [c]Avenida de Pachuca R. [d]Universidad Autonoma de Hidalgo (1869) 10 – 718. [e]Biblioteca de la Universidad . . . (1877) 45; Biblioteca Publica del Estado de Hidalgo (1933) 3.

Poza Rica: [a]Veracruz. [b]alt Poza Rica de Hidalgo. [c]Cazones R. [d]none. [e]Biblioteca Petroleos Mexicanos (1958) 10.

Puebla: [a]*Puebla. [b]off Puebla de Zaragoza. [c]Atoyac R; Alseseca R; San Francisco R. [d]Universidad Autonoma de Puebla (1578) 77 – 2650; Universidad de las Americas (1940 at Mexico, relocated 1970?) 4 – 253; Universidad Popular Autonoma del Estado de Puebla (1973) 4 – 500. [e]Biblioteca de la Universidad de las

[1]Universities with 10,000 or more students.

For an explanation of symbols and abbreviations, see pages 16–17.

(Continued)

TABLE 2b. (Continued)

Americas (1940 at Mexico, relocated 1970?) 130; Biblioteca de la Universidad Autonoma de Puebla (1874) 110;

Puerto Vallarta: ^aJalisco. ^bfor Las Penas. ^cBanderas B of Pacific O; Cuale R. ^dnone. ^eBiblioteca Agustin Flores (1963) 4.

Queretaro: ^a*Queretaro. ^bnone. ^cQueretaro R. ^dUniversidad Autonoma de Queretaro (1625) 9 – 198. ^eBiblioteca de la Universidad . . . (1963) 21; Biblioteca Josefa Ortiz de Dominguez (1963) 9.

Reynosa: ^aTamaulipas. ^balt Reinosa. ^cRio Grande R. ^dnone. ^eBiblioteca Municipal Amalia C. de Castillo Ledon (1955) 10.

Salamanca: ^aGuanajuato. ^bnone. ^cLerma R. ^dnone. ^eBiblioteca Bartolome Sanchez Torrado (1964) 4.

Saltillo: ^a*Coahuila. ^bnone. ^c(Arroyo) Barranca Creek; (Arroyo) Tortola Creek. ^dUniversidad Autonoma de Coahuila (1867) 23 – 1020; Universidad Autonoma del Noreste (1974) 4 – 480. ^eBiblioteca de la Universidad Autonoma de Coahuila (1867) 86; Biblioteca Manuel Mozquiz Blanco (1942) 10.

San Luis Potosi: ^a*San Luis Potosi. ^bnone. ^cSantiago R. ^dUniversidad Autonoma de San Luis Potosi (1624) 12 – 1100. ^eBiblioteca de la Universidad . . . (1878) 68; Biblioteca Publica Municipal (1969) 5.

San Nicolas de los Garza: ^aNuevo Leon. ^bnone. ^cnone. ^dUniversidad Autonoma de Nuevo Leon (1826 at Monterrey, relocated bef 1981) 89 – 5374. ^eBiblioteca de la Universidad . . . (1933) 170.

Santa Catarina: ^aNuevo Leon. ^bnone. ^cSanta Catarina R. ^dnone.

Tampico: ^aTamaulipas. ^bnone. ^cPanuco R. ^dUniversidad del Golfo (1972) 1 – 60. ^eBiblioteca del Centro Universitario de la Universidad Antonoma de Tamaulipas (1950) 17; Biblioteca Publica Municipal (1941) 10.

Taxco: ^aGuerrero. ^boff Taxco de Alarcon. ^cnr Amacuzac R. ^dnone. ^eBiblioteca Amigos de Taxco (1964) 3.

Tehuacan: ^aPuebla. ^bnone. ^cTehuacan R. ^dnone. ^eBiblioteca Municipal Joaquin Paredes Colin (1898) 6.

Tepic: ^a*Nayarit. ^bnone. ^cMololoa R. ^dUniversidad Autonoma de Nayarit (1925) 2 – 230. ^eBiblioteca Municipal Francisco I. Madero (1925) 3.

Tijuana: ^aBaja California. ^bnone. ^cTijuana R. ^dnone. ^eBiblioteca Publica Federal (1968) 8.

Tlalnepantla: ^aMexico. ^boff Tlalnepantla de Comonfort. ^cTlalnepantla R. ^dnone. ^eBiblioteca de la Universidad Nacional Autonoma de Mexico, Plantel Tlalnepantla (1975) 9.

Tlaquepaque: ^aJalisco. ^bfor San Pedro Tlaquepaque. ^cnone. ^dnone. ^eBiblioteca Municipal (1976) 3.

Tlaxcala: ^a*Tlaxcala. ^balt Tlaxcala de Xicotencatl. ^cZahuapan R. ^dUniversidad Autonoma de Tlaxcala (1976) 7 – 400. ^eBiblioteca Publica del Estado de Tlaxcala (1906) 6; Biblioteca de la Universidad . . . (1966) ?

Toluca: ^a*Mexico. ^boff Toluca de Lerdo. ^cXicualtenco R. ^dUniversidad Autonoma del Estado de Mexico (1828) 15 – 1338. ^eBiblioteca de la Universidad . . . (1956) 85; Biblioteca Publica del Estado de Mexico (1827) 40.

Torreon: ^aCoahuila. ^bnone. ^cNazas R. ^dnone. ^eBiblioteca del Instituto Tecnologico de La Laguna (1973) 10; Biblioteca Jose Garcia Letona (1945) 9.

Tuxtla Gutierrez: ^a*Chiapas. ^bnone. ^cGrijalva R. ^dUniversidad Autonoma de Chiapas (1975) 7 – 466. ^eBiblioteca Publica del Estado de Chiapas (1910) 45; Biblioteca de la Universidad . . . (1968) 5.

Uruapan del Progreso: ^aMichoacan. ^balt Uruapan. ^cCupatitzio R. ^dnone. ^eBiblioteca de la Universidad Michoacana de San Nicolas de Hidalgo en Uruapan del Progreso (1959) 3; Biblioteca Municipal (1969) 3.

Veracruz: ^aVeracruz. ^boff Veracruz Llave. ^cG of Mexico. ^dnone. ^eBiblioteca de la Universidad Veracruzana en Veracruz (1953) 17; Biblioteca Municipal Venustiano Carranza (1872) 15.

Villahermosa: ^a*Tabasco. ^bfor San Juan Bautista. ^cGrijalva R. ^dUniversidad Juarez Autonoma de Tabasco (1879) 4 – 440. ^eBiblioteca de la Universidad . . . (1944) 23.

Zacatecas: ^a*Zacatecas. ^bnone. ^cnone. ^dUniversidad Autonoma de Zacatecas (1834) 10 – 688. ^eBiblioteca de la Universidad . . . (1832) 42; Biblioteca Publica del Estado de Zacatecas (1826) 23.

Zamora: ^aMichoacan. ^bnone. ^cDuero R. ^dnone. ^eBiblioteca de la Escuela Normal Superior (1960) 9; Biblioteca Manuel Martinez de Nafarrete (1960) 8.

Zapopan: ^aJalisco. ^bnone. ^cnone. ^dnone.

Netherlands Antilles

*Willemstad: ^aCuracao I. ^bnone. ^cCaribbean Sea. ^dUniversiteit van de Nederlandse Antillen (1972) 0.7 – 93. ^eOpenbare Bibliotheek (1922) 105; Bibliotheek der Universiteit . . . (1979) 100.

Nicaragua

Leon: ^bnone. ^cLeon R. ^dUniversidad Nacional Autonoma de Nicaragua (1812) 24 – 1665. ^eBiblioteca de la Universidad . . . (1816) 120; Biblioteca Municipal (1921) 32.

*Managua: ^bnone. ^cManagua L. ^dUniversidad Centroamericana (1960) 4 – 318; Universidad Politecnica de Nicaragua (1968) 2 – 140. ^eBiblioteca Nacional (1881) 70.

TABLE 2b. (Continued)

Panama

Colon: [a]Manzanillo I. [b]for Aspinwall. [c]Caribbean Sea. [d]none. [e]Biblioteca Municipal (1908) ?

*Panama: [b]alt Panama City. [c]B of Panama of Pacific O. [d]Universidad de Panama (1935) 37 – 1684; Universidad Santa Maria la Antigua (1965) 4 – 301. [e]Biblioteca de la Universidad de Panama (1935) 262; Biblioteca Nacional (1892) 200.

San Miguelito: [b]none. [c]nr B of Panama of Pacific O. [d]none.

Puerto Rico

Bayamon: [b]none. [c]Bayamon R. [d]Universidad Central de Bayamon (1970) 3 – 121. e Biblioteca de la Universidad . . . (1961) 49; Bayamon Technological University College Library (1971) 38.

Caguas: [b]none. [c]Grande de Loiza R. [d]Universidad del Turabo (1972) 6 – 190. [e]Biblioteca de la Universidad . . . (1969) 43.

Carolina: [b]none. [c]Grande de Loiza R. [d]none.

Mayaguez: [b]none. [c]Mona Passage. [d]Universidad de Puerto Rico en Mayaguez . . . (1911) 9 – 553. [e]Biblioteca de la Universidad . . . (1911) 360; Biblioteca de la Universidad Catolica de Puerto Rico en Mayaguez (?) 127.

Ponce: [b]none. [c]Caribbean Sea. [d]Universidad Catolica de Puerto Rico (1948) 13 – 541 [en Ponce: (1948) 10 – 403]. [e]Biblioteca de la Universidad . . . (1948) 279; Biblioteca Publica (1890) 19.

*San Juan: [b]inc Rio Piedras since 1950. [c]Atlantic O. [d]Universidad de Puerto Rico (1903) 48 – 2996 [en San Juan: (1903) 22 – 1773]; Inter American University of Puerto Rico (1912 at San German, relocated 1960) 32 – 1595 [at San Juan: (1960) 13 – 866]. [e]Biblioteca de la Universidad . . . en San Juan (1903) 1645; . . . University Library (1912 at San German, relocated 1960) 206; Biblioteca de la Universidad del Sagrado Corazon (1936) 147; Caribbean Regional Library (1946) 119; Biblioteca General de Puerto Rico (1967) 70; Biblioteca Publica Carnegie (1916) 44. [f]Rio Piedras: 132 (1950), 13 (1930), 2 (1899).

Saint Lucia

*Castries: [a]Saint Lucia I. [b]for Fort-Castries. [c]Caribbean Sea. [d]none. [e]Central Library of Saint Lucia (1847) 38.

Saint Vincent and the Grenadines

*Kingstown: [a]Saint Vincent I. [b]none. [c]Kingstown B of Caribbean Sea. [d]none. [e] Public Library (1888) ?

Trinidad and Tobago

*Port of Spain: [a]Trinidad I. [b]none. [c]G of Paria of Caribbean Sea. [d]University of the West Indies, Saint Augustine campus (at Saint Augustine, nr Port of Spain) (1960) 3 – 280. [e]Central Library of Trinidad and Tobago (1945) 429; Saint Augustine Campus Library of the University . . . (1926) 249; Trinidad Public Library (1851) 68.

USA

Aberdeen: [a]South Dakota. [b]none. [c]Moccasin Creek. [d]none. [e]Northern State College Library (1902) 233; Alexander Mitchell Library (1884) 117.

Abilene: [a]Texas. [b]none. [c]Catclaw Creek; Kirby L; Lytle L. [d]Abilene Christian University (1906) 5 – 251; Hardin-Simmons University (1891) 2 – 120. [e]Hardin-Simmons University Library (1892) 301; Abilene Christian University Library (1906) 253; Public Library (1909) 246.

Akron: [a]Ohio. [b]none. [c]Cuyahoga R; Little Cuyahoga R. [d]University of Akron (1870) 27 – 1488. [e]Akron-Summit County Public Library (1874) 1147; University . . . Library (1872) 873.

Alameda: [a]California. [b]none. [c]San Francisco B of Pacific O; San Leandro B of Pacific O. [d]none. [e]Free Library (1879) 163.

Albany: [a]Georgia. [b]none. [c]Flint R. [d]none. [e]Dougherty County Public Library (1904) 163; Albany State College Library (1903) 143.

Albany: [a]*New York. [b]for Fort Orange. [c]Hudson R. [d]State University of New York (1844) 156 – 10,078 [Albany campus: (1844) 16 – 915]. [e]New York State Library (1818) 1927; Albany Campus Library of the . . . University (1844) 1180; Public Library (1792) 362.

Albuquerque: [a]New Mexico. [b]none. [c]Rio Grande R. [d]University of New Mexico (1889) 24 – 1118. [e]University . . . Library (1892) 1537; Public Library (1891) 405.

Alexandria: [a]Louisiana. [b]none. [c]Red R. [d]none. [e]Rapides Parish Library (1907) 257; Alexandria Campus Library of Louisiana State University (1960) 121.

Alexandria: [a]Virginia. [b]none. [c]Potomac R. [d]none. [e]Fairfax County Public Library (at Springfield, nr Alexandria) (1939) 1406; Alexandria Library (1794) 352

For an explanation of symbols and abbreviations, see pages 16–17.

(Continued)

TABLE 2b. (Continued)

Alhambra: [a]California. [b]none. [c]nr Los Angeles R. [d]none. [e]Public Library (1906) 165.

Allentown: [a]Pennsylvania. [b]for Northampton. [c]Lehigh R. [d]none. [e]Public Library (1912) 216; Muhlenberg College Library (1867) 173.

Alton: [a]Illinois. [b]none. [c]Mississippi R. [d]Southern Illinois University, Edwardsville campus (at Edwardsville, nr Alton) (1957) 10 – 650. [e]Edwardsville Campus Library of . . . University (at Edwardsville) (1957) 869; Hayner Public Library (1891) 73.

Altoona: [a]Pennsylvania. [b]none. [c]Little Juniata R. [d]none. [e]Altoona Area Public Library (1860) 152.

Amarillo: [a]Texas. [b]none. [c]Amarillo L. [d]none. [e]Public Library (1902) 424.

Ames: [a]Iowa. [b]none. [c]Skunk R. [d]Iowa State University (1858) 26 – 2063. [e] . . . University Library (1870) 1625; Public Library (1903) 115.

Amherst: [a]Massachusetts. [b]none. [c]nr Connecticut R. [d]University of Massachusetts (1863) 38 – 2059 [Amherst campus: (1863) 26 – 1465]. [e]Amherst Campus Library of the University . . . (1865) 2002; Amherst College Library (1821) 644; Jones Library (1919) 118.

Anaheim: [a]California. [b]none. [c]Santa Ana R. [d]none. [e]Public Library (1901) 374.

Anchorage: [a]Alaska. [b]none. [c]Cook Inlet of Pacific O. [d]University of Alaska, Anchorage campus (1954) 4 – 230. [e]Municipal Library (1945) 331; Anchorage Campus Library of the University . . . (1973) 315.

Anderson: [a]Indiana. [b]none. [c]West Fork of White R. [d]none. [e]Public Library (1890) 307.

Annapolis: [a]*Maryland. [b]none. [c]Severn R. [d]none. [e]Public Library of Annapolis and Anne Arundel County (bef 1923) 1476; United States Naval Academy Library (1845) 517; Maryland State Law Library (1826) 222.

Ann Arbor: [a]Michigan. [b]none. [c]Huron R. [d]University of Michigan (1817 at Detroit, relocated 1837) 45 – 3315 [Ann Arbor campus: (1837) 34 – 2768]. [e]Ann Arbor Campus Library of the University . . . (1838) 6688; Public Library (1856) 342.

Anniston: [a]Alabama. [b]none. [c]nr Choccolocco Creek. [d]Jacksonville State University (at Jacksonville, nr Anniston) (1883) 6 – 529. [e] . . . University Library (at Jacksonville) (1898) 440; Public Library of Anniston and Calhoun County (1918) 187.

Antioch: [a]California. [b]none. [c]San Joaquin R. [d]none. [e]Antioch Branch of Contra Costa County Library (bef 1954) 33.

Appleton: [a]Wisconsin. [b]none. [c]Fox R. [d]none. [e]Lawrence University Library (1850) 280; Public Library (1872) 206.

Arden-Arcade: [a]California. [b]none. [c]American R. [d]none. [e]Arcade Branch of Sacramento Public Library (bef 1954) 47; Arden Branch of Sacramento Public Library (bef 1954) 39.

Arlington: [a]Texas. [b]none. [c]West Fork of Trinity R. [d]University of Texas, Arlington campus (1895) 23 – 1269. [e]Arlington Campus Library of the University .. (1895) 1687; Public Library (1922) 214.

Arlington: [a]Virginia. [b]none. [c]Potomac R. [d]George Mason University (at Fairfax, nr Arlington) (1948) 16 – 760. [e]Arlington County Public Library (1937) 516; . . . University Library (at Fairfax) (1957) 419.

Arlington Heights: [a]Illinois. [b]none. [c]nr Des Plaines R. [d]none. [e]Arlington Heights Memorial Library (1896) 454.

Arvada: [a]Colorado. [b]none. [c]Ralston Creek. [d]none. [e]Arvada Branch of Jefferson County Public Library (bef 1954) ?

Asheville: [a]North Carolina. [b]none. [c]French Broad R. Swannanoa R. [d]none. [e]Asheville-Buncombe Library (1879) 280.

Astoria: [a]Oregon. [b]none. [c]Columbia R. [d]none. [e]Public Library (1892) 56.

Athens: [a]Georgia. [b]none. [c]Oconee R. [d]University of Georgia (1785) 25 – 1895. [e]University . . . Library (1831) 2306; Athens Regional Library (1888) 191.

Athens: [a]Ohio. [b]none. [c]Hocking R. [d]Ohio University (1804) 21 – 1107 [Athens campus: (1804) 15 – 778]. [e]Athens Campus Library of . . . University (1804) 1386.

Atlanta: [a]*Georgia. [b]none. [c]Chattahoochee R. [d]Georgia State University (1913) 21 – 996; Georgia Institute of Technology (univ) (1885) 11 – 526; Emory University (1836) 9 – 1397; Mercer University, Atlanta campus (1964) 2 – 101; Oglethorpe University (1835 at Milledgeville, relocated 1870) 1 – 55. [e]Emory University Library (1836) 2563; . . . Institute Library (1901) 1800; Atlanta-Fulton Public Library (1867) 1642; Georgia State University Library (1931) 879.

Atlantic City: [a]New Jersey. [b]none. [c]Atlantic O. [d]none. [e]Atlantic City Free Public Library (1900) 84; Ocean City Free Public Library (at Ocean City, nr Atlantic City) (1925) 73.

Auburn: [a]Alabama. [b]none. [c]nr Chewacla L. [d]Auburn University (1856) 24 – 1480 [Auburn campus: (1856) 19 – 1130]. [e]Auburn Campus Library of . . . University (1856) 1274; Hollifield Memorial Library (1960) 14.

Augusta: [a]Georgia. [b]none. [c]Savannah R. [d]none. [e]Augusta Regional Library (1848) 429; Augusta College Library (1957) 364.

Augusta: [a]*Maine. [b]none. [c]Kennebec R. [d]none. [e]Maine State Library (1839) 450; Lithgow Public Library (1882) 58.

TABLE 2b. (Continued)

Aurora: [a]Colorado. [b]none. [c]nr South Platte R. [d]none. [e]Public Library (1929) 255.

Aurora: [a]Illinois. [b]none. [c]Fox R. [d]none. [e]Public Library (1881) 217.

Austin: [a]*Texas. [b]none. [c]Colorado R. [d]University of Texas (1881) 119 – 7183 [Austin campus: (1881) 48 – 2337]; Saint Edward's University (1885) 3 – 141. [e]Austin Campus Library of the University . . . (1883) 6563; Texas State Library (1891) 1370; Public Library (1925) 821.

Azusa: [a]California. [b]none. [c]nr San Gabriel R. [d]Azusa Pacific University (1899) 3 – 156. [e]City Library (1909) 93; . . . University Library (1899) 85.

Bakersfield: [a]California. [b]none. [c]Kern R. [d]none. [e]Kern County Library (1900) 830; California State College at Bakersfield Library (1970) 264.

Baltimore: [a]Maryland. [b]none. [c]Patapsco R. [d]University of Maryland, Baltimore County campus (at Catonsville, nr Baltimore) (1963) 8 – 503; University of Baltimore (1925) 5 – 266; Morgan State University (1867) 4 – 295; Johns Hopkins University (1867) 3 – 398. [e]Johns Hopkins University Library (1876) 2486; Enoch Pratt Free Library (1886) 1893; Baltimore Campus Library of the University of Maryland (1813) 655.

Bangor: [a]Maine. [b]none. [c]Penobscot R. [d]University of Maine (at Orono, nr Bangor) (1865) 28 – 1660 [Orono campus (at Orono): (1865) 11 – 510]. [e]Orono Campus Library of the University . . . (at Orono) (1865) 623; Public Library (1883) 512.

Baton Rouge: [a]*Louisiana. [b]none. [c]Mississippi R. [d]Louisiana State University (1855 at Alexandria, relocated 1869) 44 – 2899 [Baton Rouge campus: (1869) 29 – 1282]; Southern University (1880 at New Orleans, relocated 1914) 16 – 666 [Baton Rouge campus: (1914) 13 – 486]. [e]Baton Rouge Campus Library of Louisiana State University (1860 at Alexandria, relocated 1869?) 1914; Baton Rouge Campus Library of Southern University (1928) 627; East Baton Rouge Parish Library (1889) 467; Louisiana State Library (1925) 358.

Battle Creek: [a]Michigan. [b]none. [c]Kalamazoo R. [d]none. [e]Willard Library (1870) 164.

Bay City: [a]Michigan. [b]none. [c]Saginaw R. [d]none. [e]Bay County Library (1869) 330.

Bayonne: [a]New Jersey. [b]none. [c]New York B of Atlantic O; Newark B of Atlantic O; Kill van Kull. [d]none. [e]Free Public Library (1893) 251.

Beaumont: [a]Texas. [b]none. [c]Neches R; Brakes Bayou. [d]Lamar University (1923) 16 – 571. [e] . . . University Library (1923) 439; Public Library (1926) 213.

Bellevue: [a]Washington. [b]none. [c]Washington L. [d]City University (1973) 3 – 220. [e]Bellevue Community College Library (1966) 37.

Bellingham: [a]Washington. [b]none. [c]Bellingham B of Strait of Georgia. [d]Western Washington University (1893) 9 – 527. [e] . . . University Library (1899) 456; Public Library (1904) 170; Whatcom County Public Library (1945) 142.

Berkeley: [a]California. [b]none. [c]San Francisco B of Pacific 0. [d]University of California (1855 at Oakland, relocated 1873) 143 – 14,879 [Berkeley campus: (1873) 30 – 3800]; John F. Kennedy University (at Orinda, nr Berkeley) (1864 at Martinez, relocated 1875?) 2 – 262. [e]Berkeley Campus Library of the University . . . (1868 at Oakland, relocated 1873) 7700; Public Library (1893) 459.

Bethesda: [a]Maryland. [b]none. [c]Potomac R. [d]none. [e]National Library of Medicine (1836 at Washington, relocated 1962) 1739; National Institutes of Health Library (1903) 263; Bethesda Branch of Montgomery County Public Library (1951?) 236.

Bethlehem: [a]Pennsylvania. [b]none. [c]Lehigh R. [d]Lehigh University (1865) 6 – 422. [e] . . . University Library (1877) 985; Lafayette College Library (at Easton, nr Bethlehem) (1832) 382; Moravian College Library (1807) 176; Public Library (1901) 165; Easton Area Public Library (at Easton) (1811) 165.

Beverly Hills: [a]California. [b]none. [c]nr Santa Monica B of Pacific O. [d]none. [e]Public Library (1929) 184.

Billings: [a]Montana. [b]none. [c]Yellowstone R. [d]none. [e]Parmly Billings Library (1901) 280; Eastern Montana College Library (1927) 162.

Biloxi: [a]Mississippi. [b]none. [c]Mississippi Sound of G of Mexico; B of Biloxi of G of Mexico. [d]none. [e]Public Library (bef 1918) 69.

Binghamton: [a]New York. [b]none. [c]Susquehanna R; Chenango R. [d]State University of New York, Binghamton campus (1946) 11 – 686. [e]Binghamton Campus Library of the . . . University (1946) 1122; Broome County Public Library (1904) 264.

Birmingham: [a]Alabama. [b]none. [c]Village Creek. [d]University of Alabama, Birmingham campus (1966) 14 – 1648; Samford University (1841) 4 – 291. [e]Birmingham Public and Jefferson County Free Library (1886) 1043; Birmingham Campus Library of the University . . . (1966) 831.

Bismarck: [a]*North Dakota. [b]none. [c]Missouri R. [d]none. [e]North Dakota State Library (1907) 110; Veterans Memorial Public Library (1917) 107.

Blacksburg: [a]Virginia. [b]none. [c]nr Roanoke R; nr New R. [d]Virginia Polytechnic Institute and State University

For an explanation of symbols and abbreviations, see pages 16–17.   (Continued)

TABLE 2b. (Continued)

(1872) 21 – 1942; Radford University (at Radford, nr Blacksburg) (1910) 7 – 341. *e* . . . Institute and State University Library (1872) 1132; Radford University Library (at Radford) (1913) 300; Montgomery-Floyd Regional Library (at Christiansburg, nr Blacksburg) (1942) 106.

Bloomington: *a*Illinois. *b*none. *c*Sugar Creek. *d*none. *e*Illinois Wesleyan University Library (1850) 172; Public Library (1857) 117.

Bloomington: *a*Indiana. *b*none. *c*nr Salt Creek. *d*Indiana University (1820) 68 – 3930 [Bloomington campus: (1820) 33 – 1581]. *e*Bloomington Campus Library of . . . University (1824) 6032; Monroe County Public Library (1821) 175.

Bloomington: *a*Minnesota. *b*none. *c*Minnesota R. *d*none. *e*Bloomington Branch of Hennepin County Library (1922?) 115.

Boca Raton: *a*Florida. *b*none. *c*Atlantic O. *d*Florida Atlantic University (1961) 8 – 593. *e* . . . University Library (1961) 425; Public Library (1938) 76.

Boise City: *a**Idaho. *b*alt Boise. *c*Boise R. *d*Boise State University (1932) 11 – 453. *e* . . . University Library (1932) 296; Public Library (1894) 227; Idaho State Library (1901) 130.

Boston: *a**Massachusetts. *b*none. *c*Massachusetts B of Atlantic O; Charles R. *d*Northeastern University (1898) 36 – 2785; Boston University (1839 at Newbury, Vermont; relocated 1867) 28 – 2600; University of Massachusetts, Boston campus (1965) 12 – 594; Suffolk University (1906) 6 – 282; Simmons College (univ) (1899) 3 – 276. *e*Public Library (1854) 5189; Boston University Library (1870) 1852; State Library of Massachusetts (1826) 822; Boston Athenaeum (1807) 650; Northeastern University Library (1898) 618.

Boulder: *a*Colorado. *b*none. *c*Boulder Creek. *d*University of Colorado (1861) 39 – 1835 [Boulder campus: (1861) 22 – 1151]. *e*Boulder Campus Library of the University . . . (1876) 2860; Public Library (1882) 196.

Bowling Green: *a*Kentucky. *b*none. *c*Barren R. *d*Western Kentucky University (1906) 12 – 631. *e* . . . University Library (1907) 1008; Public Library (1909) 80.

Bowling Green: *a*Ohio. *b*none. *c*nr Maumee R. *d*Bowling Green State University (1910) 17 – 839. *e* . . . University Library (1913) 768; Wood County District Public Library (1928) 126.

Bozeman: *a*Montana. *b*none. *c*nr Gallatin R. *d*Montana State University (1893) 11 – 661. *e* . . . University Library (1893) 477; Public Library (1885) 45.

Bremerton: *a*Washington. *b*none. *c*Puget Sound of Pacific O. *d*none. *e*Kitsap Regional Library (1908) 282.

Bridgeport: *a*Connecticut. *b*none. *c*Long Island Sound of Atlantic O; Pequonnock R. *d*Sacred Heart University (1963) 6 – 333; University of Bridgeport (1927) 6 – 523. *e*Public Library (1881) 508; University . . . Library (1927) 354.

Bristol: *a*Connecticut. *b*none. *c*Pequabuck R. *d*none. *e*Public Library (1892) 149.

Brockton: *a*Massachusetts. *b*none. *c*Salisbury Plain R. *d*none. *e*Public Library (1867) 281; Bridgewater State College Library (at Bridgewater, nr Brockton) (1840) 218.

Brookings: *a*South Dakota. *b*none. *c*nr Big Sioux R. *d*South Dakota State University (1881) 7 – 401. *e* . . . University Library (1884) 356; Public Library (1914) 64.

Brookline: *a*Massachusetts. *b*none. *c*Charles R. *d*none. *e*Public Library (1857) 347.

Brownsville: *a*Texas. *b*none. *c*Rio Grande R. *d*none. *e*Arnulfo L. Oliveira Memorial Library (1926) 109.

Bryan: *a*Texas. *b*none. *c*nr Brazos R. *d*none. *e*Public Library (1903) 132.

Buffalo: *a*New York. *b*none. *c*Niagara R; Erie L. *d*State University of New York, Buffalo campus (1846) 38 – 2399. *e*Buffalo and Erie County Public Library (1836) 3605; Buffalo Campus Library of the . . . University (1846) 2745.

Burbank: *a*California. *b*none. *c*Los Angeles R. *d*none. *e*Public Library (1938) 301.

Burlington: *a*North Carolina. *b*none. *c*nr Haw R. *d*none. *e*Central North Carolina Regional Library (1920) 136.

Burlington: *a*Vermont. *b*none. *c*Winooski R; Champlain L. *d*University of Vermont (1791) 9 – 877. *e*University . . . Library (1800) 929; Saint Michael's College Library (at Winooski, nr Burlington) (1904) 127; Fletcher Free Library (1873) 79.

Butte: *a*Montana. *b*off Butte-Silver Bow. *c*Clark Fork R. *d*none. *e*Montana College of Mineral Science and Technology Library (1900) 71; Butte-Silver Bow Public Library (1890) 70.

Cambridge: *a*Massachusetts. *b*none. *c*Charles R. *d*Harvard University (1636) 16 – 1934; Massachusetts Institute of Technology (univ) (1861) 10 – 1700. *e* . . . University Library (1638) 11,300; . . . Institute Library (1862) 1947; Public Library (1849) 415.

Camden: *a*New Jersey. *b*none. *c*Delaware R. *d*Rutgers University, Camden campus (1927) 5 – 214. *e*Camden Campus Library of . . . University (1926) 477; Camden County Library (at Voorhees, nr Camden) (1922 at Haddonfield, relocated 1971?) 345; Free Public Library (1898) 134.

Canton: *a*Ohio. *b*none. *c*Nimishillen Creek. *d*none. *e*Stark County District Library (1884) 623.

TABLE 2b. (Continued)

Cape Girardeau: [a]Missouri. [b]none. [c]Mississippi R. [d]Southeast Missouri State University (1873) 9 – 475. [e] . . . University Library (1873) 614; Public Library (1922) 105.

Carbondale: [a]Illinois. [b]none. [c]nr Crab Orchard L; nr Cedar L. [d]Southern Illinois University (1869) 34 – 2128 [Carbondale campus: (1869) 23 – 1478]. [e]Carbondale Campus Library of . . . University (1869) 1762; Public Library (1923) 55.

Carson: [a]California. [b]none. [c]nr Los Angeles R. [d]California State University, Dominguez Hills (1960) 8 – 489. [e]. . . .University Library (1963) 324; Carson Branch of Los Angeles County Public Library (bef 1954) 181.

Carson City: [a]*Nevada. [b]none. [c]Carson R; Tahoe L. [d]none. [e]Ormsby Public Library (1966) 72; Nevada State Supreme Court Library (1973) 61; Nevada State Library (1859) 60.

Casper: [a]Wyoming. [b]none. [c]North Platte R. [d]none. [e]Natrona County Public Library (1910) 113; Casper College Library (1945) 70.

Cedar Falls: [a]Iowa. [b]none. [c]Cedar R. [d]University of Northern Iowa (1876) 11 – 720. [e]University . . . Library (1876) 584; Public Library (1859) 75.

Cedar Rapids: [a]Iowa. [b]none. [c]Cedar R; Cedar L. [d]none. [e]Public Library (1897) 183; Coe College Library (1900) 152.

Champaign: [a]Illinois. [b]none. [c]nr Kaskaskia R; nr Embarrass (alt Embarras) R. [d]University of Illinois (at Urbana and Champaign) (1867) 59 – 3799 [Urbana-Champaign campus: (1867) 35 – 2561]. [e]Champaign Campus Library of the University . . . (1897) 446; Public Library (1876) 139.

Chapel Hill: [a]North Carolina. [b]none. [c]nr Jordan L. [d]University of North Carolina at Chapel Hill (1789) 22 – 2301. [e]University . . . Library (1795) 4079; Public Library (1958) 58.

Charleston: [a]South Carolina. [b]none. [c]Atlantic O; Ashley R; Cooper R. [d]none. [e]Charleston County Library (1930) 350; College of Charleston Library (1790) 199; Citadel Library (1842) 186.

Charleston: [a]*West Virginia. [b]none. [c]Kanawha R; Elk R. [d]University of Charleston (1888) 1 – 133. [e]Kanawha County Public Library (1909) 544; West Virginia Library Commission Science and Culture Center (1929) 530.

Charlotte: [a]North Carolina. [b]none. [c]Little Sugar Creek; Irwin Creek. [d]University of North Carolina at Charlotte (1946) 10 – 689. [e]Public Library of Charlotte and Mecklenburg County (1891) 836; University. . . . Library (1946) 362.

Charlottesville: [a]Virginia. [b]none. [c]Rivanna R. [d]University of Virginia (1819) 16 – 1579. [e]University . . . Library (1819) 3769; Jefferson-Madison Regional Library (1921) 247.

Chattanooga: [a]Tennessee. [b]none. [c]Tennessee R. [d]University of Tennessee, Chattanooga campus (1886) 7 – 415; Tennessee Temple University (1946) 2 – 143. [e]Chattanooga-Hamilton County Bicentennial Library (1905) 383; Chattanooga Campus Library of the University . . . (1872) 333.

Cheektowaga: [a]New York. [b]none. [c]Cayuga Creek. [d]none. [e]Public Library (1938) 115.

Cherry Hill: [a]New Jersey. [b]none. [c]nr Delaware R. [d]none. [e]Free Public Library (1957) 152.

Chesapeake: [a]Virginia. [b]inc South Norfolk. [c]Hampton Roads; Elizabeth R. [d]none. [e]Public Library (1963) 245. [f]South Norfolk: 22 (1960), 10 (1950), 8 (1930).

Chester: [a]Pennsylvania. [b]none. [c]Delaware R. [d]West Chester University (at West Chester, nr Chester) (1871) 10 – 534; Widener University (1821) 9 – 341 [Chester campus: (1821) 6 – 202]. [e]Swarthmore College Library (at Swarthmore, nr Chester) (1864) 700; West Chester University Library (at West Chester) (1871) 428; Chester Campus Library of Widener University (1821) 153; West Chester Public Library (at West Chester) (1872) 49; Lewis Crozer Library (1894) 48.

Cheyenne: [a]*Wyoming. [b]none. [c]Crow Creek. [d]none. [e]Wyoming State Library (1871) 154; Laramie County Library (1872) 140.

Chicago: [a]Illinois. [b]none. [c]Chicago R; Calumet (alt Grand Calumet) R; Michigan L. [d1]University of Illinois, Chicago campus (1881) 24 – 1238; Loyola University of Chicago (1870) 14 – 1322; De Paul University (1898) 12 – 868; Northeastern Illinois University (1961) 10 – 465; University of Chicago (1857) 8 – 1121; Chicago State University (1867) 7 – 430; Roosevelt University (1945) 6 – 481; Illinois Institute of Technology (univ) (1892) 5 – 485. [e]University of Chicago Library (1891) 5981; Public Library (1873) 4588; Center for Research Library (1949) 3465; Chicago Campus Library of the University of Illinois (1947) 2960; Loyola University Library (1870) 1977; Newberry Library (1887) 1372.

Chico: [a]California. [b]none. [c]nr Sacramento R. [d]California State University, Chico (1887) 14 – 877. [e] . . . University Library (1887) 614.

[1]Universities with 5,000 or more students.

For an explanation of symbols and abbreviations, see pages 16–17.

(Continued)

TABLE 2b. (Continued)

Chicopee: [a]Massachusetts. [b]none. [c]Connecticut R; Chicopee R. [d]none. [e]Public Library (1853) 100.

Chula Vista: [a]California. [b]none. [c]San Diego B of Pacific O. [d]none. [e]Public Library (1912) 195.

Cicero: [a]Illinois. [b]none. [c]Des Plaines R. [d]none. [e]Public Library (1921) 92.

Cincinnati: [a]Ohio. [b]none. [c]Ohio R. [d]University of Cincinnati (1819) 35 – 2850; Xavier University (1831) 7 – 343. [e]Public Library of Cincinnati and Hamilton County (1856) 3568; University . . . Library (1819) 1338.

Citrus Heights: [a]California. [b]none. [c]nr American R. [d]none. [e]Citrus Heights Branch of Sacramento Public Library (bef 1964) 57.

Claremont: [a]California. [b]none. [c]Thompson Creek. [d]Claremont Colleges (univ) (1925) 5 – 558; University of La Verne (at La Verne, nr Claremont) (1891) 2 – 439. [e]Claremont Colleges Library (1952) 1166; University of La Verne Library (at La Verne) (1891) 127; Claremont Branch of Los Angeles County Public Library (bef 1940) 90.

Clarksville: [a]Tennessee. [b]none. [c]Cumberland R; Red R. [d]Austin Peay State University (1927) 5 – 257. [e] . . . University Library (1927) 271; Clarksville-Montgomery County Public Library (1897) 50.

Clearwater: [a]Florida. [b]none. [c]Clearwater B of G of Mexico; Old Tampa B of G of Mexico. [d]none. [e]Public Library (1911) 215.

Cleveland: [a]Ohio. [b]none. [c]Cuyahoga R; Erie L. [d]Cleveland State University (1881) 18 – 763; Case Western Reserve University (1826) 9 – 1535; John Carroll University (at University Heights, nr Cleveland) (1886) 4 – 223. [e]Public Library (1869) 2795; Case Western Reserve University Library (1856) 2095; Cuyahoga County Public Library (1923) 1832; Cleveland State University Library (1897) 880.

Clifton: [a]New Jersey. [b]none. [c]Passaic R. [d]none. [e]Montclair State College Library (at Montclair, nr Clifton) (1908) 369; Montclair Free Public Library (at Montclair) (1893) 281; Clifton Public Library (1920) 167.

College Park: [a]Maryland. [b]none. [c]nr Anacostia R. [d]University of Maryland (1807 at Baltimore, relocated 1856) 64 – 4841 [College Park campus: (1856) 50 – 3021]. [e]College Park Campus Library of the University . . . (1813 at Baltimore, relocated 1856) 1694; National Agricultural Library (at Beltsville, nr College Park) (1862 at Washington, relocated 1969) 1800.

College Station: [a]Texas. [b]none. [c]nr Brazos R. [d]Texas A & M University (1876) 37 – 2283 [College Station campus: (1876) 37 – 2218]. [e]College Station Campus Library of . . . University (1876) 1496.

Colorado Springs: [a]Colorado. [b]none. [c]Fountain R. [d]University of Colorado, Colorado Springs campus (1955) 5 – 335. [e]United States Air Force Academy Library (1955) 443; Penrose Public Library (1885) 438; Colorado College Library (1878) 370.

Columbia: [a]Maryland. [b]none. [c]Middle Patuxent R. [d]none. [e]Howard County Library (bef 1930 at Ellicott City, relocated bef 1972) 300.

Columbia: [a]Missouri. [b]none. [c]nr Missouri R. [d]University of Missouri (1839) 53 – 4520 [Columbia campus: (1839) 23 – 2485]. [e]Columbia Campus Library of the University . . . (1841) 2693; State Historical Society of Missouri Library (1898) 432; Daniel Boone Regional Library (1900) 225; Stephens College Library (1833) 131.

Columbia: [a]*South Carolina. [b]none. [c]Congaree R; Saluda R; Broad R. [d]University of South Carolina (1801) 30 – 1739 [Columbia campus: (1801) 23 – 1247]. [e]Columbia Campus Library of the University . . . (1801) 2060; Richland County Public Library (1896) 407; South Carolina State Library (1943) 175.

Columbus: [a]Georgia. [b]none. [c]Chattahoochee R. [d]none. [e]Chattahoochee Valley Regional Library (1880) 433; Columbus College Library (1961) 195.

Columbus: [a]Mississippi. [b]none. [c]Tombigbee R; Luxapalila R. [d]Mississippi University for Women (1884) 2 – 144. [e] . . . University Library (1884) 295; Lowndes County Library (1940) 103.

Columbus: [a]*Ohio. [b]none. [c]Scioto R; Olentangy R. [d]Ohio State University (1870) 56 – 3384 [Columbus campus: (1870) 52 – 3262]; Capital University (1850) 3 – 192. [e]Columbus Campus Library of Ohio State University (1873) 5720; State Library of Ohio (1817) 1538; Public Library of Columbus and Franklin County (1872) 1291.

Compton: [a]California. [b]none. [c]Los Angeles R. [d]none. [e]Compton Branch of Los Angeles County Public Library (bef 1940) 119.

Concord: [a]California. [b]none. [c]nr Sacramento R. [d]none. [e]Contra Costa County Library (at Pleasant Hill, nr Concord) (1913 at Martinez, relocated 1961?) 1027.

Concord: [a]*New Hampshire. [b]none. [c]Merrimack R. [d]none. [e]New Hampshire State Library (1818) 796; Public Library (1855) 135.

Conway: [a]Arkansas. [b]none. [c]nr Arkansas R. [d]University of Central Arkansas (1907) 7 – 290. [e]University . . . Library, (1907) 351; Hendrix College Library (1884) 107; Faulkner-Van Buren Regional Library (1938) 56.

Cookeville: [a]Tennessee. [b]none. [c]nr Falling Water R. [d]Tennessee Technological University (1915) 7 – 400. [e] . . . University Library (1915) 235; Putnam County Library (1939) 40.

TABLE 2b. (Continued)

Coral Gables: [a]Florida. [b]none. [c]Biscayne B of Atlantic O. [d]University of Miami (1925) 14 – 1640. [e]University . . . Library (1926) 1725; Coral Gables Branch of Miami-Dade Public Library (bef 1935) 101.

Corpus Christi: [a]Texas. [b]none. [c]G of Mexico. [d]Corpus Christi State University (1971) 4 – 154. [e]Public Library (1909) 293; . . . University Library (1973) 237.

Corvallis: [a]Oregon. [b]none. [c]Willamette R. [d]Oregon State University (1850) 16 – 1623. [e] . . . University Library (1887) 986; Public Library (1899) 151.

Costa Mesa: [a]California. [b]none. [c]Santa Ana R. [d]none. [e]Orange Coast College Library (1948) 97; Southern California College Library (1920) 90; Costa Mesa Branch of Orange County Public Library (bef 1954) 87.

Council Bluffs: [a]Iowa. [b]for Kanesville. [c]Missouri R. [d]none. [e]Free Public Library (1866) 172.

Covington: [a]Kentucky. [b]none. [c]Ohio R. [d]Northern Kentucky University (at Highland Heights, nr Covington) (1873) 9 – 480. [e] . . . University Library (at Highland Heights) (1949) 411; Kenton County Public Library (1900) 207.

Cranston: [a]Rhode Island. [b]none. [c]Providence R; Pawtuxet R. [d]none. [e]Public Library (bef 1927) 143.

Cumberland: [a]Maryland. [b]none. [c]Potomac R. [d]none. [e]Allegany County Library (1924) 166.

Dallas: [a]Texas. [b]none. [c]Trinity R. [d]Southern Methodist University (1911) 9 – 637. [e]Public Library (1901) 2084; . . . University Library (1915) 2067.

Daly City: [a]California. [b]none. [c]nr Pacific O; nr San Francisco B of Pacific O. [d]none. [e]Public Library (1911) 146.

Danbury: [a]Connecticut. [b]none. [c]Still R. [d]Western Connecticut State University (1903) 6 – 220. [e] . . . University Library (1905) 153; Public Library (1869) 130.

Danville: [a]Illinois. [b]none. [c]Vermilion R. [d]none. [e]Public Library (1883) 133.

Danville: [a]Virginia. [b]none. [c]Dan R. [d]none. [e]Averett College Library (1859) 91; Public Library (1928) 90.

Davenport: [a]Iowa. [b]none. [c]Mississippi R. [d]none. [e]Public Library (1874) 326.

Davis: [a]California. [b]for Davisville. [c]nr Sacramento R. [d]University of California, Davis campus (1905) 20 – 1474. [e]Davis Campus Library of the University . . . (1908) 2100; Davis Branch of Yolo County Library (bef 1967) 85.

Dayton: [a]Ohio. [b]none. [c]Miami (alt Great Miami) R; Stillwater R; Mad R. [d]Wright State University (1964) 16 – 875; University of Dayton (1850) 11 – 678. [e]Dayton and Montgomery County Public Library (1847) 1345; University . . . Library (1928) 657; . . . University Library (1964) 411; Wright Memorial Public Library (1913) 136.

Daytona Beach: [a]Florida. [b]for Daytona. [c]Atlantic O; Halifax R. [d]none. [e]Volusia County Public Library (bef 1927) 504.

Dearborn: [a]Michigan. [b]none. [c]Rouge R. [d]University of Michigan, Dearborn campus (1959) 6 – 311. [e]Henry Ford Centennial Library (1921) 252; Dearborn Campus Library of the University . . . (1959) 236.

Dearborn Heights: [a]Michigan. [b]none. [c]Middle Rouge R. [d]none. [e]Caroline Kennedy Library (1961) 78; John F. Kennedy, Jr, Library (1965?) 35.

Decatur: [a]Illinois. [b]none. [c]Sangamon R. [d]none. [e]Public Library (1868) 199; Millikin University Library (1903) 160.

De Kalb: [a]Illinois. [b]for Buena Vista. [c]South Branch of Kishwaukee R. [d]Northern Illinois University (1895) 24 – 1230. [e] . . . University Library (1899) 1878; Public Library (1893) 101.

Denton: [a]Texas. [b]none. [c]none. [d]North Texas State University (1890) 21 – 830; Texas Woman's University (1901) 8 – 673. [e]North Texas State University Library (1890) 1528; Texas Woman's University Library (1901) 693; Public Library (1937) 88.

Denver; [a*]Colorado. [b]none. [c]South Platte R. [d]University of Colorado, Denver campus (1883) 11 – 349; University of Denver (1864) 8 – 486. [e]Public Library (1859) 1917; University of Denver Library (1862) 1333.

Des Moines: [a*]Iowa. [b]none. [c]Des Moines R; Raccoon R. [d]Drake University (1881) 6 – 343. [e] . . . University Library (1881) 669; Public Library (1866) 526; State Library of Iowa (1838) 295.

Detroit: [a]Michigan. [b]none. [c]Detroit R. [d]Wayne State University (1868) 29 – 2148; University of Detroit (1877) 6 – 425. [e] . . . University Library (1923) 4514; Public Library (1865) 2446; University . . . Library (1877) 631.

Dothan: [a]Alabama. [b]for Poplar Head. [c]nr Choctawhatchee R. [d]Troy State University, Dothan campus (1962) 1 – 76. [e]Houston Love Memorial Library (1900) 134.

Dover: [a*]Delaware. [b]none. [c]Saint Jones R. [d]none. [e]Delaware State College Library (1891) 128; Public Library (1885) 78.

Downey: [a]California. [b]none. [c]San Gabriel R; Hondo R. [d]none. [e]Los Angeles County Public Library (1912 at Los Angeles, relocated 1983?) 5825; City Library (1958) 106.

Dubuque: [a]Iowa. [b]none. [c]Mississippi R. [d]University of Dubuque (1852) 1 – 77. [e]Loras College Library (1839) 218; School of Theology in Dubuque Library (1852) 156; Carnegie-Stout Public Library (1902) 141.

For an explanation of symbols and abbreviations, see pages 16–17.   (Continued)

TABLE 2b. (Continued)

Duluth: [a]Minnesota. [b]none. [c]Saint Louis R; Superior B of Superior L. [d]University of Minnesota, Duluth campus (1895) 7 – 426. [e]Public Library (1869) 340; Duluth Campus Library of the University . . . (1902) 299.

Dundalk: [a]Maryland. [b]none. [c]Patapsco R; Back R. [d]none. [e]Dundalk Community College Library (1970?) 30; Dundalk Branch of Baltimore County Public Library (bef 1954) 16.

Durham: [a]North Carolina. [b]none. [c]Ellerbe Creek. [d]Duke University (1838 at High Point, relocated 1892) 9 – 1442; North Carolina Central University (1909) 5 – 379. [e]Duke University Library (1838 at High Point, relocated 1892?) 3885; North Carolina Central University Library (1910) 611; Durham County Library (1897) 279.

East Lansing: [a]Michigan. [b]none. [c]Red Cedar R. [d]Michigan State University (1855) 40 – 2494. [e] . . . University Library (1855) 3365: Public Library (1923) 118.

East Los Angeles: [a]California. [b]none. [c]nr Hondo R. [d]none. [e]East Los Angeles Branch of Los Angeles County Public Library (bef 1954) 71.

East Orange: [a]New Jersey. [b]none. [c]nr Passaic R. [d]Seton Hall University (at South Orange, nr East Orange) (1856) 8 – 801; Fairleigh Dickinson University, Madison campus (at Madison, nr East Orange) (1958) 4 – 231; Drew University (at Madison) (1866) 2 – 210. [e]Drew University Library (at Madison) (1867) 428; Public Library (1903) 348; Seton Hall University Library (at South Orange) (1856) 300.

East Saint Louis: [a]Illinois. [b]for Illinois Town. [c]Mississippi R. [d]none. [e]Public Library (1874) 125.

Eau Claire: [a]Wisconsin. [b]none. [c]Chippewa R; Eau Claire R. [d]University of Wisconsin, Eau Claire campus (1916) 11 – 572. [e]Eau Claire Campus Library of the University . . . (1916) 491; L. E. Phillips Memorial Public Library (1875) 174.

Edinburg: [a]Texas. [b]none. [c]none. [d]Pan American University (1927) 10 – 415. [e] . . . University Library (1927) 252; Public Library (1913) 44.

Edison: [a]New Jersey. [b]none. [c]nr Raritan R. [d]none. [e]Free Public Library (1928) 169.

Edmond: [a]Oklahoma. [b]none. [c]nr North Canadian R. [d]Central State University (1890) 13 – 448. [e] . . . University Library (1890) 233; Edmond Branch of Metropolitan Library System in Oklahoma County (1967?) ?

El Cajon: [a]California. [b]none. [c]nr San Diego R. [d]none. [e]El Cajon Branch of San Diego County Library (bef 1954) 113; Grossmont College Library (1961) 98.

Elgin: [a]Illinois. [b]none. [c]Fox R. [d]none. [e]Gail Borden Public Library (1873) 234.

Elizabeth: [a]New Jersey. [b]none. [c]Newark B of Atlantic O; Arthur Kill. [d]none. [e]Public Library (1857) 377; Kean College of New Jersey Library (at Union, nr Elizabeth) (1914) 279; Union Township Public Library (at Union) (1891) 265.

Elkhart: [a]Indiana. [b]none. [c]Saint Joseph R; Elkhart R. [d]none. [e]Public Library (1903) 145.

Elmira: [a]New York. [b]none. [c]Chemung R. [d]none. [e]Steele Memorial Library (1899) 455; Elmira College Library (1855) 262.

El Monte: [a]California. [b]none. [c]San Gabriel R. [d]none. [e]El Monte Branch of Los Angeles County Public Library (bef 1940) 82.

El Paso: [a]Texas. [b]for Franklin. [c]Rio Grande R. [d]University of Texas, El Paso campus (1913) 15 – 640. [e]El Paso Campus Library of the University . . . (1913) 761; Public Library (1896) 695.

Elyria: [a]Ohio. [b]none. [c]Black R. [d]none. [e]Oberlin College Library (at Oberlin, nr Elyria) (1833) 1005; Elyria Public Library (1870) 118; Oberlin Public Library (at Oberlin) (1908) 75.

Emporia: [a]Kansas. [b]none [c]Neosho R; Cottonwood R. [d]Emporia State University (1863) 5 – 284. [e] . . . University Library (1863) 724; Public Library (1869) 74.

Enid: [a]Oklahoma. [b]none. [c]nr Black Bear Creek. [d]Phillips University (1906) 1 – 105. [e] . . . University Library (1906) 280; Public Library of Enid and Garfield County (1908) 143.

Erie: [a]Pennsylvania. [b]none. [c]Erie L. [d]Gannon University (1933) 4 – 251; Pennsylvania State University, Behrend College (univ) (1926) 2 – 124. [e]Erie County Library (1899) 402.

Escondido: [a]California. [b]none. [c]Escondido Creek. [d]none. [e]Public Library (1894) 128.

Euclid: [a]Ohio. [b]none. [c]Erie L. [d]none. [e]Public Library (1935) 332.

Eugene: [a]Oregon. [b]none. [c]Willamette R. [d]University of Oregon (1872) 16 – 1287. [e]University . . . Library (1881) 2049; Public Library (1895) 240.

Evanston: [a]Illinois. [b]none. [c]Michigan L. [d]Northwestern University (1851) 16 – 1629. [e] . . . University Library (1856) 2831; Public Library (1871) 349.

Evansville: [a]Indiana. [b]none. [c]Ohio R. [d]University of Evansville (1854) 4 – 262. [e]Evansville-Vanderburgh County Public Library (1875) 619; University . . . Library (1872) 190.

Everett: [a]Washington. [b]none. [c]Puget Sound of Pacific O; Snohomish R. [d]none. [e]Public Library (1894) 143.

Fairbanks: [a]Alaska. [b]none. [c]Chena R. [d]University of Alaska (1917) 11 – 790 [Fairbanks campus: (1917) 5 –

TABLE 2b. (Continued)

429]. [e]Fairbanks Campus Library of the University . . . (1917) 630; Fairbanks North Star Borough Public Library (1909) 145.

Fairfield: [a]California. [b]none. [c]nr Suisun Channel. [d]none. [e]Solano County Library (1914) 519.

Fairfield: [a]Connecticut. [b]none. [c]Long Island Sound of Atlantic O. [d]Fairfield University (1942) 5 – 355. [e]Public Library (1877) 186; . . . University Library (1947) 184.

Fall River: [a]Massachusetts. [b]none. [c]Mount Hope B of Atlantic O; Taunton R; Fall R. [d]none. [e]Public Library (1861) 323.

Fargo: [a]North Dakota. [b]none. [c]Red R. [d]North Dakota State University (1890) 9 – 510. [e] . . . University Library (1889) 375; Public Library (1900) 140.

Fayetteville: [a]Arkansas. [b]none. [c]nr White R. [d]University of Arkansas (1871) 30 – 2379 [Fayetteville campus: (1871) 14 – 843]. [e]Fayetteville Campus Library of the University . . . (1872) 1370; Ozarks Regional Library (1948) 250.

Fayetteville: [a]North Carolina. [b]none. [c]Cape Fear R. [d]Fayetteville State University (1867) 3 – 175. [e]Cumberland County Public Library (1907) 228; . . . University Library (1937) 149.

Fitchburg: [a]Massachusetts. [b]none. [c]North Nashua R. [d]none. [e]Fitchburg State College Library (1895) 179; Public Library (1859) 164.

Flagstaff: [a]Arizona. [b]none. [c]San Francisco Wash. [d]Northern Arizona University (1899) 12 – 489. [e] . . . University Library (1912) 465; City-Coconino County Public Library (1894) 125.

Flint: [a]Michigan. [b]none. [c]Flint R. [d]University of Michigan, Flint campus (1956) 6 – 236. [e]Genesee District Library (1942) 474; Public Library (1851) 416.

Florence: [a]Alabama. [b]none. [c]Tennessee R. [d]University of North Alabama (1854) 5 – 225. [e]University . . . Library (1872) 197; Florence-Lauderdale Public Library (1949) 47.

Florence: [a]South Carolina. [b]none. [c]nr Pee Dee R. [d]none. [e]Francis Marion College Library (1970) 206; Florence County Library (1925) 136.

Fort Collins: [a]Colorado. [b]none. [c]Cache la Poudre R. [d]Colorado State University (1870) 18 – 1158. [e] . . . University Library (1870) 1400; Public Library (1900) 165.

Fort Lauderdale: [a]Florida. [b]none. [c]Atlantic O. [d]Nova University (1964) 6 – 403. [e]Broward County Library (1913) 1001.

Fort Myers: [a]Florida. [b]none. [c]Caloosahatchee R. [d]none. [e]Edison Community College-University of South Florida Library (1962) 94; Fort Myers-Lee County Library (1900) 52.

Fort Pierce: [a]Florida. [b]none. [c]Indian River Lagoon. [d]none. [e]Saint Lucie County Library (1953) 114.

Fort Smith: [a]Arkansas. [b]none. [c]Arkansas R. [d]none. [e]Public Library (1888) 70.

Fort Walton Beach: [a]Florida. [b]none. [c]G of Mexico. [d]none. [e]Public Library (1955) 39.

Fort Wayne: [a]Indiana. [b]none. [c]Maumee R; Saint Mary's R; Saint Joseph R. [d]Indiana University-Purdue University, Fort Wayne campus (1917) 10 – 594. [e]Allen County Public Library (1894) 1770; Fort Wayne Campus Library of . . . University (1964) 322.

Fort Worth: [a]Texas. [b]none. [c]West Fork of Trinity R. [d]Texas Christian University (1873) 7 – 519. [e] . . . University Library (1910) 992; Public Library (1901) 884.

Framingham: [a]Massachusetts. [b]none. [c]Sudbury R. [d]none. [e]Public Library (1855) 206; Framingham State College Library (1969) 140.

Frankfort: [a]*Kentucky. [b]none. [c]Kentucky R. [d]Kentucky State University (1886) 2 – 140. [e] . . . University Library (1886) 203; Kentucky State Law Library (1954) 173; Kentucky State Library (1834) 105; Paul Sawyer Public Library (1908) 60.

Fremont: [a]California. [b]none. [c]Alameda Creek. [d]none. [e]Fremont Branch of Alameda County Library (1947?) 269.

Fresno: [a]California. [b]none. [c]nr San Joaquin R. [d]California State University, Fresno (1911) 16 – 1083. [e]Fresno County Free Library (1892) 899; . . . University Library (1911) 679.

Fullerton: [a]California. [b]none. [c]nr Santa Ana R. [d]California State University, Fullerton (1957) 23 – 1388. [e] . . . University Library (1959) 599; Public Library (1907) 196.

Gadsden: [a]Alabama. [b]none. [c]Coosa R. [d]none. [e]Gadsden-Etowah County Library (1906) 161.

Gainesville: [a]Florida. [b]none. [c]nr Newnan L. [d]University of Florida (1853) 35 – 3405. [e]University . . . Library (1889) 2469; Santa Fe Regional Library (1917) 191.

Galveston: [a]Texas; Galveston I. [b]none. [c]G of Mexico; Galveston B of G of Mexico; Galveston Channel. [d]none. [e]Galveston Campus Library of the University of Texas (1891) 334; Rosenberg Library (1882) 259.

Garden Grove: [a]California. [b]none. [c]Santa Ana R. [d]none. [e]Garden Grove Branch of Orange County Public Library (1921?) 190.

For an explanation of symbols and abbreviations, see pages 16–17.

(Continued)

TABLE 2b. (Continued)

Garland: [a]Texas. [b]none. [c]Duck Creek. [d]none. [e]Nicholson Memorial Library (1933) 196.

Gary: [a]Indiana. [b]none. [c]Calumet (alt Grand Calumet) R; Little Calumet R; Michigan L. [d]Indiana University, Northwest campus (1922) 5 – 269. [e]Public Library (1908) 440.

Gastonia: [a]North Carolina. [b]none. [c]nr Catawba R. [d]none. [e]Gaston County Public Library (1905) 314.

Glendale: [a]Arizona. [b]none. [c]nr Salt R. [d]none. [e]Velma Teague Library (1895) 83.

Glendale: [a]California. [b]none. [c]Los Angeles R. [d]none. [e]Public Library (1906) 477.

Gloucester: [a]Massachusetts. [b]none. [c]Massachusetts B of Atlantic O. [d]none. [e]Gloucester Lyceum and Sawyer Free Library (1830) 100.

Goldsboro: [a]North Carolina. [b]none. [c]Neuse R. [d]none. [e]Wayne County Public Library (1907) 62.

Grand Forks: [a]North Dakota. [b]none. [c]Red R. [d]University of North Dakota (1883) 11 – 650. [e]University . . . Library (1883) 642; Public City-County Library (1900) 128.

Grand Island: [a]Nebraska. [b]none. [c]Wood R. [d]none. [e]Edith Abbott Memorial Library (1884) 78.

Grand Junction: [a]Colorado. [b]none. [c]Colorado R; Gunnison R. [d]none. [e]Mesa County Public Library (1896) 220.

Grand Prairie: [a]Texas. [b]none. [c]West Fork of Trinity R. [d]none. [e]Grand Prairie Memorial Library (1937) 83.

Grand Rapids: [a]Michigan. [b]none. [c]Grand R. [d]none. [e]Public Library (1871) 611; Kent County Library (1936) 450.

Great Falls: [a]Montana. [b]none. [c]Missouri R; Sun R. [d]none. [e]Public Library (1889) 205.

Greeley: [a]Colorado. [b]none. [c]Cache la Poudre R. [d]University of Northern Colorado (1889) 9 – 550. [e]University . . . Library (1890) 695; Public Library (1877) 123.

Green Bay: [a]Wisconsin. [b]none. [c]Fox R; Green B of Michigan L. [d]University of Wisconsin, Green Bay campus (1965) 5 – 247. [e]Brown County Library (1889) 356; Green Bay Campus Library of the University . . . (1967) 277.

Greensboro: [a]North Carolina. [b]none. [c]Buffalo Creek. [d]University of North Carolina at Greensboro (1891) 10 – 627; North Carolina Agricultural and Technical State University (1891) 5 – 386. [e]University . . . Library (1892) 957; Public Library (1902) 613; . . . University Library (1892) 361.

Greenville: [a]Mississippi. [b]none. [c]Mississippi R. [d]none. [e]Washington County Library (1913) 174.

Greenville: [a]North Carolina. [b]none. [c]Tar R. [d]East Carolina University (1907) 14 – 902. [e] . . . University Library (1907) 853; Sheppard Memorial Library (1904) 125.

Greenville: [a]South Carolina. [b]for Pleasantburg. [c]Reedy R. [d]Bob Jones University (1927) 4 – 332; Furman University (1825 at Edgefield, relocated 1851) 3 – 163. [e]Greenville County Library (1921) 552; Furman University Library (1826 at Edgefield, relocated 1851?) 284; Bob Jones University Library (1927) 194.

Greenwich: [a]Connecticut. [b]none. [c]Long Island Sound. [d]none. [e]Greenwich Library (1878) 277.

Gulfport: [a]Mississippi. [b]none. [c]Mississippi Sound of G of Mexico. [d]none. [e]Gulfport-Harrison County Library (bef 1923) 123.

Hagerstown: [a]Maryland. [b]none. [c]Antietam Creek. [d]none. [e]Washington County Free Library (1898) 246.

Hamilton: [a]Ohio. [b]none. [c]Miami (alt Great Miami) R. [d]none. [e]Lane Public Library (1866) 231.

Hammond: [a]Indiana. [b]none. [c]Calumet (alt Grand Calumet) R; Wolf L. [d]Purdue University, Calumet campus (1946) 7 – 389. [e]Public Library (1902) 329; Calumet Campus Library of . . . University (1947) 169.

Hampton: [a]Virginia. [b]none. [c]Chesapeake B of Atlantic O; Hampton Roads; Back R. [d]Hampton University (1868) 4 – 297. [e] . . . University Library (1903) 314; Charles H. Taylor Memorial Library (1926) 241.

Hanover: [a]New Hampshire. [b]none. [c]Connecticut R. [d]Dartmouth College (univ) (1769) 5 – 1324. [e] . . . College Library (1769) 1975; Howe Library (1900) 47.

Harlingen: [a]Texas. [b]none. [c]Arroyo Colorado. [d]none. [e]Public Library (1920) 78.

Harrisburg: [a]*Pennsylvania. [b]none. [c]Susquehanna R. [d]Pennsylvania State University, Capitol campus (at Middletown, nr Harrisburg) (1966) 3 – 149. [e]State Library of Pennsylvania (1745 at Philadelphia, relocated 1812?) 958; Dauphin County Library (1889) 265; Capitol Campus Library of . . . University (at Middletown (1965) 210.

Harrisonburg: [a]Virginia. [b]none. [c]Linville Creek. [d]James Madison University (1908) 9 – 542. [e] . . . University Library (1909) 326; Eastern Mennonite College Library (1917) 120; Rockingham Public Library (1928) 106.

Hartford: [a]*Connecticut. [b]none. [c]Connecticut R. [d]none. [e]Connecticut State Library (1854) 749; Trinity College Library (1823) 707; Public Library (1774) 499.

Hattiesburg: [a]Mississippi. [b]none. [c]Leaf R. [d]University of Southern Mississippi (1910) 11 – 646. [e]University . . . Library (1910) 773; Public Library (1916) 85.

Hayward: [a]California. [b]none. [c]nr San Francisco B of Pacific O. [d]California State University, Hayward (1957) 12 – 615. [e]Alameda County Library (1910 at Oakland, relocated bef 1958) 741; . . . University Library (1959) 642; Public Library (1898) 90.

TABLE 2b. (Continued)

Helena: [a]*Montana. [b]none. [c]nr Missouri R; nr Helena L. [d]none. [e]Montana State Library (1946) 142; Lewis and Clark Library (1886) 99; Carroll College Library (1928) 92.

Hempstead: [a]New York; Long I. [b]none. [c]nr Long Island Sound of Atlantic O; nr Atlantic O. [d]Adelphi University (at Garden City, nr Hempstead) (1863) 11 – 835; Hofstra University (1935) 11 – 731. [e]Hofstra University Library (1935) 1186; Adelphi University Library (at Garden City) (1896) 446; Public Library (1889) 150.

Hialeah: [a]Florida. [b]none. [c]nr Biscayne B of Atlantic O. [d]none. [e]Hialeah John F. Kennedy Library (bef 1949) 165.

High Point: [a]North Carolina. [b]none. [c]nr Uwharrie (alt Uharie) R. [d]none. [e]Public Library (1926) 225; High Point College Library (1924) 139.

Hoboken: [a]New Jersey. [b]none. [c]Hudson R. [d]Stevens Institute of Technology (univ) (1870) 3 – 240. [e] . . . Institute Library (1907) 105; Public Library (1890) 94.

Hollywood: [a]Florida. [b]none. [c]Atlantic O. [d]none. [e]Hollywood Branch of Broward County Library (1943) 166.

Holyoke: [a]Massachusetts. [b]none. [c]Connecticut R. [d]none. [e]Mount Holyoke College Library (at South Hadley, nr Holyoke) (1837) 528; Public Library (1870) 144.

Hot Springs: [a]Arkansas. [b]none. [c]nr Ouachita R. [d]none. [e]Tri-Lakes Regional Library (bef 1928) 134.

Houma: [a]Louisiana. [b]none. [c]Bayou Terrebonne. [d]none. [e]Terrebonne Parish Library (1939) 157.

Houston: [a]Texas. [b]none. [c]Buffalo Bayou. [d]University of Houston (1927) 46 – 3246; Texas Southern University (1947) 9 – 600; Rice University (1891) 4 – 421; Houston Baptist University (1960) 3 – 154; University of Saint Thomas (1947) 2 – 197. [e]Public Library (1848) 3044; University of Houston Library (1927) 1509; Rice University Library (1912) 1189; Harris County Public Library (1921) 569.

Huntington: [a]West Virginia. [b]none. [c]Ohio R. [d]Marshall University (1837) 11 – 514. [e] . . . University Library (1837) 361; Cabell County Public Library (1902) 263.

Huntington Beach: [a]California. [b]none. [c]Pacific O. [d]none. [e]Huntington Beach Library (1908) 304.

Huntsville: [a]Alabama. [b]none. [c]Indian Creek. [d]University of Alabama, Huntsville campus (1950) 6 – 431; Alabama Agricultural and Mechanical University (1875) 4 – 500. [e]Redstone Scientific Information Center (1949) 260; Huntsville-Madison County Public Library (1817) 240; Huntsville Campus Library of the University . . . (1964) 180; . . . University Library (1904) 150.

Huntsville: [a]Texas. [b]none. [c]none. [d]Sam Houston State University (1879) 10 – 428. [e] . . . University Library (1879) 1077; Public Library (1967) 36.

Idaho Falls: [a]Idaho. [b]none. [c]Snake R. [d]none. [e]Public Library (1909) 106.

Independence: [a]Missouri. [b]none. [c]Missouri R. [d]none. [e]Mid-Continent Public Library (1894) 1283.

Indianapolis: [a]*Indiana. [b]none. [c]White R. [d]Indiana University-Purdue University, Indianapolis campus (1908) 24 – 1922; Butler University (1850) 4 – 340; Indiana Central University (1902) 3 – 212. [e]Indianapolis-Marion County Public Library (1873) 1516; Indianapolis Campus Library of . . . University (1908) 789; Indiana State Library (1825) 735; Butler University Library (1855) 376.

Inglewood: [a]California. [b]none. [c]Santa Monica B of Pacific O. [d]Northrop University (1942) 2 – 175. [e]Public Library (1917) 308.

Iowa City: [a]Iowa. [b]none. [c]Iowa R. [d]University of Iowa (1847) 30 – 1634. [e]University . . . Library (1855) 3590; Public Library (1898) 157.

Irvine: [a]California. [b]none. [c]nr Pacific O. [d]University of California, Irvine campus (1961) 13 – 805. [e]Irvine Campus Library of the University . . . (1965) 1297; Irvine Branch of Orange County Public Library (bef 1976) 63.

Irving: [a]Texas. [b]none. [c]West Fork of Trinity R. [d]University of Dallas (1955) 2 – 166. [e]Public Library (1961) 254; University . . . Library (1956) 172.

Irvington: [a]New Jersey. [b]none. [c]nr Passaic R. [d]none. [e]Public Library (1915) 203.

Ithaca: [a]New York. [b]none. [c]Cayuga L; Beebe L. [d]Cornell University (1865) 18 – 1534. [e] . . . University Library (1868) 4769; Ithaca College Library (1932) 287; Tompkins County Library (1864) 81.

Jackson: [a]Michigan. [b]none. [c]Grand R. [d]none. [e]Jackson District Library (1883) 223.

Jackson: [a]*Mississippi. [b]none. [c]Pearl R. [d]Jackson State University (1877) 6 – 353. [e]Jackson Metropolitan Library (1914) 979; . . . University Library (1877) 424; Mississippi State Library (1926) 362.

Jacksonville: [a]Florida. [b]none. [c]Saint Johns R; Trout R. [d]University of North Florida (1965) 6 – 200; Jacksonville University (1934) 2 – 173. [e]Public Library (1905) 1057.

Janesville: [a]Wisconsin. [b]none. [c]Rock R. [d]none. [e]Public Library (1865) 154.

Jefferson City: [a]*Missouri. [b]none. [c]Missouri R. [d]Lincoln University (1866) 3 – 169. [e]Missouri State Library (1829) 322; Thomas Jefferson Library (1900) 210; . . . University Library (1866) 150.

Jersey City: [a]New Jersey. [b]none. [c]Hudson R; Hackensack R. [d]none. [e]Public Library (1891) 723; Jersey City State College Library (1927) 249.

For an explanation of symbols and abbreviations, see pages 16–17.   (Continued)

TABLE 2b. (Continued)

Johnson City: [a]Tennessee. [b]none. [c]nr Watauga Creek; nr Brush Creek. [d]East Tennessee State University (1909) 10 – 568. [e] . . . University Library (1911) 677; Public Library (1893) 57.

Johnstown: [a]Pennsylvania. [b]none. [c]Conemaugh R. [d]none. [e]Cambria County Library (1870) 133; Johnstown Campus Library of the University of Pittsburgh (1927) 101.

Joliet: [a]Illinois. [b]for Juliet. [c]Des Plaines R. [d]Lewis University (at Romeoville, nr Joliet) (1930) 3 – 174. [e]College of Saint Francis Library (1930) 148; Public Library (1875) 145.

Jonesboro: [a]Arkansas. [b]none. [c]nr Cache R. [d]Arkansas State University (1909) 8 – 326. [e] . . . University Library (1909) 462; Crowley Ridge Regional Library (1917) 141.

Joplin: [a]Missouri. [b]none. [c]Joplin Creek. [d]none. [e]Missouri Southern State College Library (1937) 166; Public Library (1902) 80.

Juneau: [a]*Alaska. [b]none. [c]Gastineau Channel. [d]University of Alaska, Juneau campus (1956) 2 – 131. [e]Alaska State Library (1957) 98; Juneau Campus Library of the University . . . (1956) 68; Juneau Memorial Library (1913) 45.

Kalamazoo: [a]Michigan. [b]none. [c]Kalamazoo R. [d]Western Michigan University (1903) 20 – 1160. [e] . . . University Library (1903) 1484; Public Library (1872) 289; Kalamazoo College Library (1850) 272.

Kansas City: [a]Kansas. [b]none. [c]Missouri R; Kansas R. [d]none. [e]Public Library (1890) 333.

Kansas City: [a]Missouri. [b]none. [c]Missouri R. [d]University of Missouri, Kansas City campus (1881) 11 – 1033. [e]Public Library (1873) 1370; Kansas City Campus Library of the University . . . (1933) 1044; Linda Hall Library (1946) 565.

Keene: [a]New Hampshire. [b]none. [c]Ashuelot R. [d]University of New Hampshire, Keene State College (univ) (1909) 3 – 194. [e] . . . College Library (1909) 176; Public Library (1857) 75.

Kennewick: [a]Washington. [b]none. [c]Columbia R. [d]none. [e]Mid-Columbia Library (1911) 225.

Kenosha: [a]Wisconsin. [b]none. [c]Michigan L. [d]University of Wisconsin, Parkside Campus (1965) 6 – 280. [e]Parkside Campus Library of the University . . . (1967) 271; Public Library (1897) 184.

Kent: [a]Ohio. [b]none. [c]Cuyahoga R. [d]Kent State University (1910) 20 – 1035. [e] . . . University Library (1913) 1571; Free Library (1892) 83.

Kettering: [a]Ohio. [b]none. [c]nr Miami (alt Great Miami) R. [d]none. [e]Kettering Branch of Dayton and Montgomery County Public Library (bef 1960) 94.

Key West: [a]Florida; Key West I. [b]none. [c]Atlantic O; G of Mexico. [d]none. [e]Monroe County Public Library (1892) 135.

Killeen: [a]Texas. [b]none. [c]South Nolan Creek. [d]none. [e]Public Library (1959) 67; Central Texas College Library (1967) 65.

Kingsport: [a]Tennessee. [b]none. [c]Holston R. [d]none. [e]Public Library (1921) 115.

Kingsville: [a]Texas. [b]none. [c]San Fernando Creek. [d]Texas A & I University (1925) 6 – 226. [e] . . . University Library (1925) 426; Robert J. Kleberg Public Library (1927) 81.

Knoxville: [a]Tennessee. [b]none. [c]Tennessee R; Holston R. [d]University of Tennessee (1794) 40 – 2858 [Knoxville campus: (1794) 25 – 1502]. [e]Knoxville Campus Library of the University . . . (1838) 1751; Knox County Public Library (1879) 630.

Kokomo: [a]Indiana. [b]none. [c]Wildcat Creek. [d]Indiana University, Kokomo campus (1945) 2 – 173. [e]Public Library (1885) 177; Kokomo Campus Library of . . . University (1945) 90.

La Crosse: [a]Wisconsin. [b]none. [c]Mississippi R; La Crosse R. [d]University of Wisconsin, La Crosse campus (1909) 10 – 380. [e]La Crosse Campus Library of the University . . . (1909) 246; Public Library (1888) 165; La Crosse County Library (1898) 101.

Lafayette: [a]Indiana. [b]none. [c]Wabash R. [d]none. [e]Tippecanoe County Public Library (1883) 143.

Lafayette: [a]Louisiana. [b]none. [c]Vermilion R. [d]University of Southwestern Louisiana (1898) 16 – 667. [e]University . . . Library (1901) 662; Lafayette Parish Public Library (bef 1939) 185.

Lake Charles: [a]Louisiana. [b]none. [c]Calcasieu R. [d]McNeese State University (1939) 8 – 331. [e] . . . University Library (1939) 273; Calcasieu Parish Public Library (bef 1903) 234.

Lakeland: [a]Florida. [b]none. [c]Parker L; Hollingsworth L; Hunter L; Morton L; Wire L; Mirror L. [d]none. [e]Florida Southern College Library (1885) 180; Public Library (1926) 116.

Lakewood: [a]California. [b]none. [c]San Gabriel R. [d]none. [e]Lakewood Branch of Los Angeles County Public Library (bef 1954) 138.

Lakewood: [a]Colorado. [b]none. [c]nr South Platte R. [d]Colorado School of Mines (univ) (at Golden, nr Lakewood) (1869) 3 – 210. [e]Jefferson County Public Library (1953) 458; . . . School Library (at Golden) (1874) 354.

Lakewood: [a]Ohio. [b]for East Rockport. [c]Rocky R; Erie L. [d]none. [e]Public Library (1916) 250.

La Mirada: [a]California. [b]none. [c]La Mirada Creek. [d]Biola University (1908) 3 – 253. [e] . . . University Library (1908) 179; La Mirada Branch of Los Angeles County Public Library (bef 1960) 53.

TABLE 2b. (Continued)

Lancaster: [a]Ohio. [b]none. [c]Hocking R. [d]Ohio University, Lancaster campus (1968) 2 – 113. [e]Fairfield County District Library (1878) 178; Lancaster Campus Library of . . . University (1956) 63.

Lancaster: [a]Pennsylvania. [b]none. [c]Conestoga R. [d]Millersville University (at Millersville, nr Lancaster) (1855) 7 – 338. [e] . . . University Library (at Millersville) (1855) 386; Lancaster County Library (1763) 374; Franklin and Marshall College Library (1787) 256.

Lansing: [a]*Michigan. [b]none. [c]Grand R; Red Cedar R. [d]none. [e]Library of Michigan (1828) 1824; Public Library (1882) 253.

Laramie: [a]Wyoming. [b]none. [c]Laramie R. [d]University of Wyoming (1886) 10 – 868. [e]University . . . Library (1887) 884; Albany County Public Library (1906) 110.

Laredo: [a]Texas. [b]none. [c]Rio Grande R. [d]Laredo State University (1969) 0.9 – 57 [e] . . . University Library (1968) 82; Laredo Junior College Library (1947) 70; Public Library (1900) 50.

Las Cruces: [a]New Mexico. [b]none. [c]nr Rio Grande R. [d]New Mexico State University (1888) 13 – 712. [e] . . . University Library (1888) 727; Thomas Branigan Memorial Library (bef 1930) 118.

Las Vegas: [a]Nevada. [b]alt Vegas. [c]Las Vegas Wash. [d]University of Nevada, Las Vegas campus (1951) 11 – 451. [e]Clark County Library (bef 1928) 511; Las Vegas Campus Library of the University . . . (1957) 459.

Lawrence: [a]Kansas. [b]none. [c]Kansas R. [d]University of Kansas (1855) 27 – 1692 [Lawrence campus: (1855) 24 – 1143]. [e]Lawrence Campus Library of the University . . . (1866) 3125; Public Library (1865) 161.

Lawrence: [a]Massachusetts. [b]none. [c]Merrimack R. [d]none. [e]Public Library (1847) 250.

Lawton: [a]Oklahoma. [b]none. [c]Cache Creek; Wolf Creek. [d]none. [e]Cameron University Library (1908) 184; Public Library (1903) 105.

Lewiston: [a]Maine. [b]none. [c]Androscoggin R. [d]none. [e]Bates College Library (1863) 415; Public Library (1861) 152.

Lexington: [a]Kentucky. [b]off Lexington-Fayette. [c]Town Branch Creek. [d]University of Kentucky (1865) 21 – 1842. [e]University . . . Library (1909) 2119; Public Library (1795) 263.

Lima: [a]Ohio. [b]none. [c]Ottawa R. [d]none. [e]Public Library (1901) 257.

Lincoln: [a]*Nebraska. [b]none. [c]Salt Creek; Antelope Creek. [d]University of Nebraska (1869) 41 – 2129 [Lincoln campus: (1869) 24 – 1025]. [e]Lincoln Campus Library of the University . . . (1869) 1740; City Library (1876) 458.

Little Rock: [a]*Arkansas. [b]none. [c]Arkansas R. [d]University of Arkansas, Little Rock campus (1879) 10 – 643. [e]Central Arkansas Library (1910) 488; Little Rock Campus Library of the University . . . (1879) 438; Arkansas State Library (1935) 160.

Livonia: [a]Michigan. [b]none. [c]Middle Rouge R. [d]none. [e]Public Library (1958) 164.

Logan: [a]Utah. [b]none. [c]Logan R. [d]Utah State University (1888) 12 – 504. [e] . . . University Library (1922) 1102; Logan Library (1916) 55.

Long Beach: [a]California. [b]none. [c]San Pedro B of Pacific O; Los Angeles R. [d]California State University at Long Beach (1949) 31 – 1739. [e] . . . University Library (1949) 849; Public Library (1896) 821.

Longview: [a]Texas. [b]none. [c]nr Sabine R. [d]none. [e]LeTourneau College Library (1945) 94; Nicholson Memorial Public Library (1932) 60.

Longview: [a]Washington. [b]none. [c]Columbia R; Cowlitz R. [d]none. [e]Public Library (1926) 117.

Lorain: [a]Ohio. [b]for Charleston. [c]Black R; Erie L. [d]none. [e]Public Library (1900) 307.

Los Angeles: [a]California. [b]inc Hollywood. [c]San Pedro B of Pacific O; Los Angeles R. [d1]University of California, Los Angeles campus (1881) 35 – 3200; California State University, Northridge (1956) 28 – 1554; University of Southern California (1880) 27 – 2441; California State University, Los Angeles (1947) 21 – 1150; Loyola Marymount University (1865) 6 – 359. [e]Los Angeles Campus Library of the University of California (1919) 7300; Public Library (1872) 5107; University of Southern California Library (1880) 2476.

Louisville: [a]Kentucky. [b]none. [c]Ohio R. [d]University of Louisville (1798) 20 – 1363; Spalding University (1814) 1 – 101. [e]University . . . Library (1798) 1267; Free Public Library (1816) 1116.

Lowell: [a]Massachusetts. [b]none. [c]Merrimack R; Concord R. [d]University of Lowell (1894) 16 – 782. [e]Pollard Memorial Library (1845) 341; University . . . Library (1894) 325.

Lubbock: [a]Texas. [b]none. [c]Double Mountain Fork of Brazos R. [d]Texas Tech University (1923) 23 – 1647. [e] . . . University Library (1925) 1868; City-County Library (1923) 306.

Lynchburg: [a]Virginia. [b]none. [c]James R. [d]none. [e]Randolph-Macon Woman's College Library (1896) 176; Lynchburg College Library (1903) 136; Public Library (1966) 110; Jones Memorial Library (1907) 70.

Lynn: [a]Massachusetts. [b]none. [c]Massachusetts B of Atlantic O. [d]none. [e]Public Library (1815) 257.

Macon: [a]Georgia. [b]none. [c]Ocmulgee R. [d]Mercer University (1833) at Penfield, relocated 1871) 4 – 229 [Macon campus: (1871) 2 – 128]. [e]Middle Georgia Regional Library (1874) 408; Macon Campus Library of . . . University (1833 at Penfield, relocated 1871?) 400.

1Universities with 5,000 or more students.

For an explanation of symbols and abbreviations, see pages 16–17.

(Continued)

TABLE 2b. (Continued)

Madison: [a]*Wisconsin. [b]none. [c]Yahara R; Mendota L; Monona L; Waubesa L. [d]University of Wisconsin (1848) 153 – 7836 [Madison campus: (1848) 44 – 2269]. [e]Madison Campus Library of the University . . . (1849) 5805; Public Library (1875) 566; State Historical Society of Wisconsin Library (1853) 219.

Malibu: [a]California. [b]none. [c]Santa Monica B of Pacific O. [d]Pepperdine University (1937 at Los Angeles, relocated 1973?) 3 – 243. [e] . . . University Library (1937 at Los Angeles, relocated 1973?) 304; J. Paul Getty Center Library (1974) 200; Malibu Branch of Los Angeles County Public Library (bef 1972) 44.

Manchester: [a]New Hampshire. [b]for Derryfield. [c]Merrimack R. [d]none. [e]City Library (1854) 275; Saint Anselm College Library (1929) 156.

Manhattan: [a]Kansas. [b]none. [c]Kansas R; Big Blue R. [d]Kansas State University (1858) 18 – 1544. [e] . . . University Library (1863) 957; Public Library (1904) 178.

Mankato: [a]Minnesota. [b]none. [c]Minnesota R; Blue Earth R. [d]Mankato State University (1866) 12 – 620. [e] . . . University Library (1868) 687; Minnesota Valley Regional Library (1894) 212.

Mansfield: [a]Ohio. [b]none. [c]Rocky Fork of Mohican R. [d]none. [e]Mansfield-Richland County Public Library (1887) 262.

Marquette: [a]Michigan. [b]none. [c]Superior L. [d]Northern Michigan University (1899) 8 – 309. [e] . . . University Library (1899) 395; Peter White Public Library (1891) 114.

McAllen: [a]Texas. [b]none. [c]nr Rio Grande R. [d]none. [e]McAllen Memorial Library (1932) 155.

Medford: [a]Massachusetts. [b]none. [c]Mystic R. [d]Tufts University (1852) 7 – 445. [e] . . . University Library (1854) 529; Public Library (1825) 125.

Medford: [a]Oregon. [b]none. [c]Bear Creek. [d]none. [e]Jackson County Library (1908) 278.

Melbourne: [a]Florida. [b]none. [c]Indian River Lagoon. [d]Florida Institute of Technology (univ) (1958) 6 – 613. [e] . . . Institute Library (1958) 160; Melbourne Public Library (1918) 94; Eau Gallie Public Library (1939) 58.

Memphis: [a]Tennessee. [b]none. [c]Mississippi R; Wolf R. [d]Memphis State University (1912) 21 – 922. [e]Memphis-Shelby County Public Library (1888) 1513; . . . University Library (1914) 1020.

Meriden: [a]Connecticut. [b]none. [c]Quinnipiac R. [d]none. [e]Public Library (1889) 152.

Meridian: [a]Mississippi. [b]none. [c]Sowashee Creek. [d]none. [e]Public Library (1913) 141.

Mesa: [a]Arizona. [b]none. [c]Salt R. [d]none. [e]Public Library (1925) 288.

Mesquite: [a]Texas. [b]none. [c]nr East Fork of Trinity R. [d]none. [e]Public Library (1963) 112.

Metairie: [a]Louisiana. [b]none. [c]Pontchartrain L. [d]none. [e]Jefferson Parish Library (1949) 630.

Miami: [a]Florida. [b]none. [c]Biscayne B of Atlantic O. [d]Florida International University (1965) 12 – 868; Barry University (at Miami Shores, nr Miami) (1940) 4 – 205. [e]Miami-Dade Public Library (1900) 2098; Florida International University Library (1972) 501.

Miami Beach: [a]Florida. [b]none. [c]Atlantic O; Biscayne B of Atlantic O. [d]none. [e]Public Library (1927) 170.

Middletown: [a]Connecticut. [b]none. [c]Connecticut R. [d]Wesleyan University (1831) 3 – 314. [e] . . . University Library (1831) 1134; Russell Library (1875) 110.

Middletown: [a]Ohio. [b]none. [c]Miami (alt Great Miami) R. [d]none. [e]Public Library (1911) 200.

Midland: [a]Texas. [b]none. [c]Midland Draw. [d]none. [e]Midland County Public Library (1903) 151.

Milwaukee: [a]Wisconsin. [b]none. [c]Milwaukee R; Menomonee R; Michigan L. [d]University of Wisconsin, Milwaukee campus (1956) 26 – 1258; Marquette University (1857) 12 – 929. [e]Public Library (1847) 2109; Milwaukee Campus Library of the University . . . (1956) 1945; . . . University Library (1881) 846.

Minneapolis: [a]Minnesota. [b]none. [c]Mississippi R. [d]University of Minnesota (1851) 54 – 6356 [Minneapolis campus: (1851) 45 – 5800]. [e]Minneapolis Campus Library of the University . . . (1851) 4080; Public Library (1860) 1783; Hennepin County Library (at Minnetonka, nr Minneapolis) (1922 at Minneapolis, relocated 1983?) 1232.

Minot: [a]North Dakota. [b]none. [c]Souris R. [d]none. [e]Minot State College Library (1913) 140; Public Library (1908) 84; Ward County Public Library (1960) 32.

Missoula: [a]Montana. [b]none. [c]Clark Fork R; Bitterroot R. [d]University of Montana (1893) 9 – 487. [e]University . . . Library (1895) 638; City-County Library (1894) 165.

Mobile: [a]Alabama. [b]none. [c]Mobile B of G of Mexico; Mobile R. [d]University of South Alabama (1963) 9 – 587. [e]Public Library (1874) 377; University . . . Library (1964) 218.

Modesto: [a]California. [b]none. [c]Tuolumne R. [d]none. [e]Stanislaus County Free Library (1907) 603.

Moline: [a]Illinois. [b]none. [c]Mississippi R; Rock R. [d]none. [e]Public Library (1873) 142.

Monroe: [a]Louisiana. [b]none. [c]Ouachita R. [d]Northeast Louisiana University (1931) 12 – 444. [e] . . . University Library (1931) 439; Ouachita Parish Public Library (1916) 240.

Monterey: [a]California. [b]none. [c]Monterey B of Pacific O. [d]none. [e]Naval Postgraduate School Library (1946) 419; Public Library (1906) 115.

TABLE 2b. (Continued)

Montgomery: [a]*Alabama. [b]none. [c]Alabama R. [d]Auburn University, Montgomery campus (1967) 5 – 350; Alabama State University (1873) 4 – 251; Troy State University, Montgomery campus (1957) 2 – 142. [e]City-County Public Library (1899) 400; Alabama Department of Archives and History Library (1901) 250; Alabama State University Library (1921) 221.

Montpelier: [a]*Vermont. [b]none. [c]Winooski, R. [d]Norwich University (at Northfield, nr Montpelier, and Montpelier (1819) 2 – 218. [e]Vermont State Library (1825) 558; . . . University Library (at Northfield) (1819) 331; Kellogg-Hubbard Library (1894) 40.

Moorhead: [a]Minnesota. [b]none. [c]Red R. [d]Moorhead State University (1885) 7 – 337. [e] . . . University Library (1887) 341; Concordia College Library (1891) 268; Lake Agassiz Regional Library (1904) 220.

Morgantown: [a]West Virginia. [b]none. [c]Monongahela R. [d]West Virginia University (1867) 19 – 2346. [e] . . . University Library (1867) 1403; Public Library (1929) 64.

Moscow: [a]Idaho. [b]none. [c]Paradise Creek. [d]University of Idaho (1889) 9 – 589. [e]University . . . Library (1889) 588; Moscow-Latah County Library (1901) 65.

Mount Pleasant: [a]Michigan. [b]none. [c]Chippewa R. [d]Central Michigan University (1892) 16 – 740. [e] . . . University Library (1892) 684; Veterans Memorial Library (1909) 65.

Mount Vernon: [a]New York. [b]none. [c]Bronx R. [d]none. [e]Public Library (1854) 412.

Muncie: [a]Indiana. [b]none. [c]West Fork of White R. [d]Ball State University (1898) 18 – 920. [e] . . . University Library (1918) 710; Muncie-Center Township Public Library (1874) 310.

Murfreesboro: [a]Tennessee. [b]none. [c]West Fork of Stones R. [d]Middle Tennessee State University (1909) 11 – 520. [e] . . . University Library (1911) 540; Rutherford County Library (bef 1935) 99.

Muskegon: [a]Michigan. [b]none. [c]Muskegon R: Michigan L; Muskegon L. [d]none. [e]Hackley Public Library (1889) 157; Muskegon County Library (1938) 152.

Muskogee: [a]Oklahoma. [b]none. [c]nr Arkansas R; nr Neosho R; nr Verdigris R. [d]none. [e]Public Library (1909) 186.

Nacogdoches: [a]Texas. [b]none. [c]nr Angelina R. [d]Stephen F. Austin State University (1921) 13 – 517. [e] . . . University Library (1923) 413; Public Library (1913) 40.

Napa: [a]California. [b]none. [c]Napa R. [d]none. [e]City-County Library (1963) 214.

Naples: [a]Florida. [b]none. [c]G of Mexico. [d]none. [e]Collier County Public Library (1957) 120.

Nashua: [a]New Hampshire. [b]for Dunstable. [c]Merrimack R; Nashua R. [d]none. [e]Public Library (1840) 184; Rivier College Library (1933) 106.

Nashville: [a]*Tennessee. [b]off Nashville-Davidson. [b]Cumberland R. [d]Vanderbilt University (1872) 9 – 1995; Tennessee State University (1909) 8 – 479; Fisk University (1865) 0.6 – 77. [e]Vanderbilt University Library (1873) 1650; Public Library of Nashville and Davidson County (1904) 602; Tennessee State University Library (1912) 396; Tennessee State Library and Archives (1854) 269.

Natchez: [a]Mississippi. [b]none. [c]Mississippi R. [d]none. [e]Homochitto Valley Library (1883) 93.

New Albany: [a]Indiana. [b]none. [c]Ohio R. [d]Indiana University, Southeast campus (1941) 4 – 250. [e]Southeast Campus Library of . . . University (1941) 303: New Albany-Floyd County Public Library (1884) 145.

Newark: [a]Delaware. [b]none. [c]nr Delaware R. [d]University of Delaware (1743 at New London, Pennsylvania; relocated 1765) 16 – 920. [e]University . . . Library (1834) 1615; Free Library (1897) 84.

Newark: [a]New Jersey. [b]none. [c]Newark B of Atlantic O; Passaic R. [d]Rutgers University, Newark campus (1892) 9 – 337; New Jersey Institute of Technology (univ) (1881) 7 – 421. [e]Public Library (1888) 1314; Newark Campus Library of . . . University (1927) 561.

New Bedford: [a]Massachusetts. [b]none. [c]Buzzards B of Atlantic O; Acushnet R. [d]Southeastern Massachusetts University (at North Dartmouth, nr New Bedford) (1895) 6 – 365. [e]Free Public Library (1852) 410; . . . University Library (at North Dartmouth) (1960) 290.

New Britain: [a]Connecticut. [b]none. [c]nr Quinnipiac R; nr Mattabessett R. [d]Central Connecticut State University (1849) 13 – 641. [e] . . . University Library (1850) 412; Public Library (1853) 234.

New Brunswick: [a]New Jersey. [b]none. [c]Raritan R. [d]Rutgers University (1766) 47 – 1796 [New Brunswick campus: (1766) 33 – 1245.] [e]New Brunswick Campus Library of . . . University (1766) 2141; Free Public Library (1883) 116.

New Haven: [a]Connecticut. [b]none. [c]Long Island Sound of Atlantic O; Quinnipiac R; Mill R; West R. [d]Yale University (1701) 11 – 1766; Southern Connecticut State University (1893) 10 – 657. [e]Yale University Library (1701) 11,200; Free Public Library (1887) 591.

New London: [a]Connecticut. [b]none. [c]Long Island Sound of Atlantic O; Thames R. [d]none. [e]Connecticut College Library (1911) 394; United States Coast Guard Academy Library (1876) 137; Public Library (1882) 73.

New Orleans: [a]Louisiana. [b]none. [c]Mississippi R; Pontchartrain L; Borgne R. [d]University of New Orleans (1956) 17 – 689; Tulane University (1834) 10 – 1177; Loyola University (1847) 5 – 309; Xavier University of

For an explanation of symbols and abbreviations, see pages 16–17.   (Continued)

TABLE 2b. (Continued)

Louisiana (1915) 2 – 159. [e]Tulane University Library (1834) 2027; Public Library (1843) 884; University . . . Library (1958) 799.

Newport: [a]Rhode Island. [b]none. [c]Atlantic O; Narragansett B of Atlantic O. [d]University of Rhode Island (at Kingston, nr Newport) (1888) 11 – 738. [e]University . . . Library (at Kingston) (1892) 740; United States Naval War College Library (1885) 158; Redwood Library and Athenaeum (1747) 145; Public Library (1868) 75.

Newport Beach: [a]California. [b]none. [c]Pacific O; Newport B of Pacific O. [d]none. [e]Public Library (1929) 155.

Newport News: [a]Virginia. [b]none. [c]Hampton Roads; James R. [d]none. [e]Public Library (1908) 274.

New Rochelle: [a]New York. [b]none. [c]Long Island Sound of Atlantic O. [d]none. [e]Iona College Library (1940) 217; Public Library (1894) 165; College of New Rochelle Library (1904) 161.

Newton: [a]Massachusetts. [b]none. [c]Charles R. [d]Boston College (univ) (1863) 14 – 704. [e] . . . College Library (1863) 946; Free Library (1870) 392.

New York: [a]New York. [b]alt New York City; for New Amsterdam; inc Brooklyn since 1898. [c]Long Island Sound of Atlantic O; New York B of Atlantic O; Raritan B of Atlantic O; Jamaica B of Atlantic O; Hudson R; East R; Bronx R.; Arthur Kill, Harlem R; Kill van Kull. [d1]City University of New York (1847) 123 – 8603; New York University (1831) 33 – 5422; Columbia University (1754) 22 – 1695; Long Island University (at Greenvale, nr New York) (1886 at New York, relocated 1948) 20 – 1223 [Greenvale campus: (1948) 12 – 705] [New York campus: (1886) 6 – 406]; Saint John's University (1870) 19 – 930; Pace University (1906) 18 – 1165 [New York campus: (1906) 10 – 588]; New York Institute of Technology (at Old Westbury, nr New York) (1955 at New York, relocated 1964) 13 – 1064; Fordham University (1841) 12 – 1828. [e]New York Public Library (1854) 12,450; Columbia University Library (1761) 5940; Queens Borough Public Library (1896) 4261; Brooklyn Public Library (1869) 4169; New York University Library (1835) 2932; City University of New York Library (1849) 2195; Fordham University Library (1841) 2073; . . . ; Pierpont Morgan Library (1924) 80. [f]Brooklyn: 806 (1890), 97 (1850), 4 (1800).

Niagara Falls: [a]New York. [b]none. [c]Niagara R. [d]Niagara University (at Niagara, nr Niagara Falls) (1856) 4 – 232. [e] . . . University Library (at Niagara) (1856) 207; Public Library (1838) 185.

Norfolk: [a]Virginia. [b]none. [c]Chesapeake Bay of Atlantic O; Hampton Roads; Elizabeth R. [d]Old Dominion University (1919) 15 – 717; Norfolk State University (1935) 7 – 410. [e]Public Library (1870) 760; Old Dominion University Library (1930) 519; Norfolk State University Library (1935) 298.

Normal: [a]Illinois. [b]for North Bloomington. [c]Sugar Creek. [d]Illinois State University (1857) 20 – 1064. [e] . . . University Library (1890) 771; Public Library (1939) 70.

Norman: [a]Oklahoma. [b]none. [c]Canadian R. [d]University of Oklahoma (1890) 23 – 1572 [Norman campus: (1890) 20 – 882]. [e]University . . . Library (1895) 2040; Pioneer Multi-County Library (1957) 194.

Northampton: [a]Massachusetts. [b]none. [c]Connecticut R. [d]Smith College (univ) (1871) 3 – 284. [e] . . . College Library (1909) 936; Forbes Library (1894) 327.

North Charleston: [a]South Carolina. [b]none. [c]Cooper R. [d]none. [e]Cooper River Branch of Charleston County Library (bef 1948) 34.

Norwalk: [a]California. [b]none. [c]nr San Gabriel R. [d]none. [e]Norwalk Branch of Los Angeles County Public Library (1913) 186.

Norwalk: [a]Connecticut. [b]none. [c]Long Island Sound of Atlantic O; Norwalk R. [d]none. [e]Public Library (1879) 129.

Norwich: [a]Connecticut. [b]none. [c]Thames R; Shetucket R; Yantic R. [d]none. [e]Otis Library (1850) 91.

Oakland: [a]California. [b]none. [c]San Francisco B of Pacific O. [d]none. [e]Public Library (1868) 848.

Oak Park: [a]Illinois. [b]none. [c]nr Des Plaines R. [d]none. [e]Public Library (1883) 238.

Oceanside: [a]California. [b]none. [c]Pacific O; San Luis Rey R. [d]none. [e]Public Library (1905) 168.

Odessa: [a]Texas. [b]none. [c]nr Johnson Draw. [d]University of Texas, Permian Basin campus (1969) 2 – 102. [e]Permian Basin Campus Library of the University . . . (1973) 203; Ector County Library (1938) 176.

Ogden: [a]Utah. [b]none. [c]Weber R; Ogden R. [d]none. [e]Weber State College Library (1888) 285; Weber County Library (1903) 257.

Oklahoma City: [a•]Oklahoma. [b]none. [c]Canadian R; North Canadian R: Hefner L. [d]Oklahoma City University (1904) 3 – 201. [e]Metropolitan Library in Oklahoma County (1901) 597; . . . University Library (1904) 279; Oklahoma State Library (1890) 275.

Olympia: [a•]Washington. [b]none. [c]Puget Sound of Pacific O; Deschutes R. [d]none. [e]Timberland Regional Library (1914) 608; Washington State Library (1853) 380; Washington State Law Library (1889) 245.

Omaha: [a]Nebraska. [b]none. [c]Missouri R. [d]University of Nebraska, Omaha campus (1908) 17 – 1104; Creighton University (1878) 6 – 991. [e]Omaha Campus Library of the University . . . (1902) 722; Public Library (1872) 579; . . . University Library (1878) 527.

[1]Universities with 10,000 or more students.

TABLE 2b. (Continued)

Ontario: [a]California. [b]none. [c]nr Santa Ana R. [d]none. [e]City Library (1885) 208.

Orange: [a]California. [b]none. [c]Santa Ana R. [d]none. [e]Orange County Public Library (1921 at Santa Ana, relocated 1961?) 1494; Orange Public Library (1885) 303.

Orem: [a]Utah. [b]for Provo Bench. [c]nr Provo R; nr Utah L. [d]none. [e]Public Library (1940) 95.

Orlando: [a]Florida. [b]none. [c]Clear L; Holden L; Ivanhoe L; Sue L; Concord L; Lancaster L. [d]University of Central Florida (1963) 16 – 658. [e]Orange County Library (1923) 645; University . . . Library (1966) 402; Rollins College Library (at Winter Park, nr Orlando) (1885) 205.

Oshkosh: [a]Wisconsin. [b]none. [c]Fox R; Winnebago L. [d]University of Wisconsin, Oshkosh campus (1871) 11 – 600. [e]Oshkosh Campus Library of the University . . . (1871) 343; Public Library (1896) 270.

Overland Park: [a]Kansas. [b]none. [c]nr Kansas R. [d]none. [e]Johnson County Library (at Merriam, nr Overland Park) (1955) 520.

Owensboro: [a]Kentucky. [b]for Rossborough. [c]Ohio R. [d]none. [e]Owensboro-Daviess County Public Library (1909) 113; Brescia College Library (1950) 86; Kentucky Wesleyan College Library (1866) 86.

Oxford: [a]Mississippi. [b]none. [c]nr Tallahatchie R; nr Yocona R. [d]University of Mississippi (1844) 10 – 1103 [Oxford campus: (1844) 9 – 574]. [e]Oxford Campus Library of the University . . . (1848) 700; Oxford Branch of First Regional Library (bef 1939)?

Oxford: [a]Ohio. [b]none. [c]Fourmile (alt Tallawanda) Creek. [d]Miami University (1809) 15 – 803. [e] . . . University Library (1824) 1006.

Oxnard: [a]California. [b]none. [c]nr Santa Clara R. [d]none. [e]Public Library (1906) 138.

Palm Beach: [a] Florida. [b]none. [c]Atlantic O; Worth Lagoon. [d]none. [e]Society of the Four Arts Library (1948) 32.

Palm Springs: [a]California. [b]none. [c]none. [d]none. [e]Public Library (1940) 103.

Palo Alto: [a]California. [b]none. [c]San Francisco B of Pacific O. [d]Stanford University (at Stanford, nr Palo Alto) (1885) 13 – 1263. [e] . . . University Library (at Stanford) (1892) 7755; City Library (1897) 220.

Panama City: [a]Florida. [b]none. [c]Saint Andrews B of G of Mexico. [d]none. [e]Bay County Public Library (1942) 157.

Paradise: [a]Nevada. [b]none. [c]Duck Creek. [d]none.

Parkersburg: [a]West Virginia. [b]none. [c]Ohio R; Little Kanawha R. [d]none. [e]Parkersburg and Wood County Public Library (1891) 98.

Parma: [a]Ohio. [b]none. [c]nr Cuyahoga R. [d]none. [e]Parma Branch of Cuyahoga County Public Library (bef 1964) 266; Baldwin-Wallace College Library (at Berea, nr Parma) (1845) 225.

Pasadena: [a]California. [b]none. [c]Arroyo Seco Creek. [d]California Institute of Technology (univ) (1891) 2 – 283. [e]Public Library (1882) 524; . . . Institute Library (1891) 416.

Pasadena: [a]Texas. [b]none. [c]Buffalo Bayou. [d]none. [e]Public Library (1953) 195; San Jacinto College Library (1961) 102.

Pascagoula: [a]Mississippi. [b]none. [c]Mississippi Sound of G of Mexico; Pascagoula R. [d]none. [e]Jackson-George Regional Library (1940) 153.

Passaic: [a]New Jersey. [b]none. [c]Passaic R. [d]Fairleigh Dickinson University (at Rutherford, nr Passaic) (1942) 14 – 1133 [Rutherford campus: (1942) 3 – 203] [Teaneck campus (at Teaneck, nr Passaic): (1954) 7 – 699]. [e]Teaneck Campus Library of . . . University (at Teaneck) (1954) 266; Teaneck Public Library (at Teaneck) (1921) 179; Passaic Public Library (1887) 174; Rutherford Campus Library of . . . University (at Rutherford) (1941) 168; Rutherford Free Public Library (at Rutherford) (1894) 108.

Paterson: [a]New Jersey. [b]none. [c]Passaic R. [d]none. [e]Paterson Free Public Library (1885) 337; William Paterson College Library (at Wayne, nr Paterson) (1924) 303; Wayne Public Library (at Wayne) (1922) 223.

Pawtucket: [a]Rhode Island. [b]none. [c]Blackstone (alt Seekonk) R. [d]none. [e]Public Library (1852) 180.

Pensacola: [a]Florida. [b]none. [c]Pensacola B of G of Mexico. [d]University of West Florida (1963) 6 – 342. [e]University . . . Library (1966) 387; West Florida Regional Library (1937) 325.

Peoria: [a]Illinois. [b]none. [c]Illinois R; Peoria L. [d]Bradley University (1896) 5 – 438. [e]Public Library (1855) 489; . . . University Library (1897) 392.

Petersburg: [a]Virginia. [b]none. [c]Appomattox R. [d]Virginia State University (1882) 3 – 263. [e]Chesterfield County Free Public Library (at Chester, nr Petersburg) (1965) 285; . . . University Library (1882) 218; Public Library (1924) 99.

Philadelphia: [a]Pennsylvania. [b]none. [c]Delaware R; Schuylkill R. [d][1]Temple University (1884) 35 – 2911 [Philadelphia campus: (1884) 31 – 2564] [Ambler campus (at Ambler, nr Philadelphia): (1910) 4 – 347]; University of Pennsylvania (1740) 22 – 2500; Drexel University (1891) 13 – 679; Villanova University (at Villanova, nr Philadelphia) (1842) 11 – 572; La Salle University (1863) 7 – 294; Saint Joseph's University (1851) 6 – 191. [e]Free Library (1821) 4318; University . . . Library (1750) 4316; Philadelphia Campus

[1]Universities with 5,000 or more students.

For an explanation of symbols and abbreviations, see pages 16–17.

(Continued)

TABLE 2b. (Continued)

Library of Temple University (1892) 1983; Villanova University Library (at Villanova) (1842) 785; Bryn Mawr College Library (at Bryn Mawr, nr Philadelphia (1885) 728.

Phoenix: [a]*Arizona. [b]none. [c]Salt R. [d]Western International University (1978) 0.7 – 50. [e]Public Library (1901) 1233; Arizona State Library (1864 at Prescott, relocated 1889?) 1100.

Pierre: [a]*South Dakota. [b]none. [c]Missouri R. [d]none. [e]South Dakota State Library (1913) 133; Rawlins Municipal Library (1905) 41.

Pine Bluff: [a]Arkansas. [b]none. [c]Arkansas R. [d]none. [e]Pine Bluff Campus Library of the University of Arkansas (1938) 190; Pine Bluff and Jefferson County Library (1913) 141.

Pittsburgh: [a]Pennsylvania. [b]for Pittsburg; inc Allegheny since 1906. [c]Ohio R; Allegheny R; Monongahela R. [d]University of Pittsburgh (1787) 35 – 3014 [Pittsburgh campus: (1787) 29 – 2765]; Duquesne University (1878) 7 – 492; Carnegie-Mellon University (1900) 6 – 506. [e]Pittsburgh Campus Library of the University . . . (1873) 2992; Carnegie Library (1895) 1917; Carnegie-Mellon University Library (1920) 650; Duquesne University Library (1928) 569. [f]Allegheny: 130 (1900) , 21 (1850), 3 (1830).

Pittsfield: [a]Massachusetts. [b]none. [c]Housatonic R. [d]none. [e]Berkshire Athenaeum (1871) 180.

Plainfield: [a]New Jersey. [b]for Milltown. [c]Green Brook. [d]none. [e]Public Library (1881) 183.

Plano: [a]Texas. [b]none. [c]Spring Creek. [d]none. [e]Public Library (1965) 126.

Plattsburgh: [a]New York. [b]for Plattsburg. [c]Saranac R; Champlain L. [d]State University of New York, Plattsburgh campus (1889) 6 – 370. [e]Plattsburgh Campus Library of the . . . University (1857) 293; Public Library (1894) 70.

Plymouth: [a]Massachusetts. [b]none. [c]Plymouth B of Atlantic O. [d]none. [e]Public Library (1856) 82.

Pocatello: [a]Idaho. [b]none. [c]Portneuf R. [d]Idaho State University (1901) 6 – 505. [e] . . . University Library (1902) 325; Public Library (1906) 108.

Pomona: [a]California. [b]none. [c]Chino Creek. [d]California State Polytechnic University (1938) 17 – 992. [e] . . . University Library (1938) 525; Public Library (1883) 276.

Pompano Beach: [a]Florida. [b]for Pompano. [c]Atlantic O. [d]none. [e]City Library (1940) 101.

Pontiac: [a]Michigan. [b]none. [c]Clinton R. [d]Oakland University (at Rochester, nr Pontiac) (1957) 12 – 575. [e] . . . University Library (at Rochester) (1959) 273; Public Library (1882) 129.

Port Arthur: [a]Texas. [b]none. [c]Sabine L. [d]none. [e]Public Library (1918) 115.

Port Huron: [a]Michigan. [b]none. [c]Saint Clair R; Black R; Huron L. [d]none. [e]Saint Clair County Library (1895) 356.

Portland: [a]Maine. [b]none. [c]Casco B of Atlantic O; Presumpscot R. [d]University of Southern Maine (1878) 9 – 607. [e]University . . . Library (1878) 370; Public Library (1867) 307.

Portland: [a]Oregon. [b]none. [c]Willamette R. [d]Portland State University (1946) 14 – 679; University of Portland (1901) 3 – 176. [e]Multnomah County Library (1864) 1273; . . . University Library (1946) 779.

Portsmouth: [a]New Hampshire. [b]none. [c]Atlantic O; Piscataqua R. [d]University of New Hampshire (at Durham, nr Portsmouth) (1866) 17 – 1022 [Durham campus: (1866) 10 – 639]. [e]Durham Campus Library of the University . . . (at Durham) (1868) 854; Public Library (1881) 65.

Portsmouth: [a]Virginia. [b]none. [c]Hampton Roads; Elizabeth R. [d]none. [e]Public Library (1914) 319.

Poughkeepsie: [a]New York. [b]none. [c]Hudson R. [d]State University of New York, New Paltz campus (at New Paltz, nr Poughkeepsie) (1828) 7 – 391. [e]Vassar College Library (1865) 590; New Paltz Campus Library of . . . University (at New Paltz) (1886) 345; Adriance Memorial Library (1840) 113.

Princeton: [a]New Jersey. [b]none. [c]Stony Brook. [d]Princeton University (1746) 6 – 738. [e] . . . University Library (1746) 4170; Princeton Theological Seminary Library (1812) 355; Institute for Advanced Study Library (1940) 130; Public Library (1909) 115.

Providence: [a]*Rhode Island. [b]none. [c]Providence R; Seekonk R. [d]Brown University (1764) 6 – 525; Providence College (univ) (1917) 6 – 245. [e] . . . University Library (1767) 1921; Public Library (1878) 963.

Provo: [a]Utah. [b]none. [c]Provo R; Utah L. [d]Brigham Young University (1875) 27 – 1536. [e] . . . University Library (1876) 2000; City Public Library (1904) 81.

Pueblo: [a]Colorado. [b]none. [c]Arkansas R. [d]University of Southern Colorado (1933) 5 – 264. [e]University . . . Library (1933) 193; McClelland Public Library (1873) 181.

Pullman: [a]Washington. [b]none. [c]South Fork of Palouse R. [d]Washington State University (1890) 16 – 1017. [e] . . . University Library (1892) 1384; Neill Public Library (1921) 37.

Quincy: [a]Massachusetts. [b]none. [c]Massachusetts B of Atlantic O; Neponset R; Fore R. [d]none. [e]Thomas Crane Public Library (1871) 215.

Racine: [a]Wisconsin. [b]none. [c]Root R; Michigan L. [d]none. [e]Public Library (1897) 250.

Raleigh: [a]*North Carolina. [b]none. [c]Crabtree Creek. [d]North Carolina State University (1887) 24 – 1606. [e] . . . University Library (1889) 1049; Wake County Public Library (1900) 387; North Carolina State Library (1812) 258.

TABLE 2b. (Continued)

Rapid City: [a]South Dakota. [b]none. [c]Rapid Creek. [d]South Dakota School of Mines and Technology (univ) (1885) 3 – 132. [e]Public Library (1903) 100; . . . School Library (1885) 100.

Reading: [a]Pennsylvania. [b]none. [c]Schuylkill R. [d]none. [e]Public Library (1808) 340.

Redlands: [a]California. [b]none. [c]Santa Ana R. [d]University of Redlands (1907) 1 – 184. [e]University . . . Library (1909) 272; A. K. Smiley Public Library (1894) 91.

Reno: [a]Nevada.[b]none. [c]Truckee R. [d]University of Nevada (1864 at Elko, relocated 1886) 20 – 881 [Reno campus: (1886) 9 – 430]. [e]Reno Campus Library of the University . . . (1886) 924; Washoe County Library (1904) 354.

Richardson: [a]Texas. [b]none. [c]Duck Creek; Cottonwood Creek. [d]University of Texas, Dallas campus (1969) 7 – 393. [e]Dallas Campus Library of the University . . . (1964) 298; Public Library (1959) 143.

Richland: [a]Washington. [b]none. [c]Columbia R; Yakima R. [d]none. [e]Public Library (1951) 108.

Richmond: [a]California. [b]none. [c]San Francisco B of Pacific O. [d]none. [e]Marin County Free Library (at San Rafael, nr Richmond) (1927) 425; Public Library (1907) 264.

Richmond: [a]Kentucky. [b]none. [c]nr Kentucky R. [d]Eastern Kentucky University (1906) 12 – 630. [e] . . . University Library (1907) 823; George Coon Public Library (1913) 50.

Richmond: [a]*Virginia. [b]none. [c]James R. [d]Virginia Commonwealth University (1838) 20 – 1876, University of Richmond (1830) 4 – 364; Virginia Union University (1865) 1 – 102. [e]Public Library (1891) 688; Virginia Commonwealth University Library (1913) 673; Virginia State Library (1823) 616; County of Henrico Public Library (1966) 423; University of Richmond Library (1832) 387.

Riverside: [a]California. [b]none. [c]Santa Ana R. [d]Loma Linda University (1905) 5 – 1870; University of California, Riverside campus (1907) 5 – 375. [e]Riverside Campus Library of the University . . . (1954) 1400; City and County Public Library (1876) 536.

Roanoke: [a]Virginia. [b]for Big Lick. [c]Roanoke R. [d]none. [e]City Public Library (1921) 376; Hollins College Library (at Hollins, nr Roanoke) (1855) 226; Roanoke County Public Library (1945) 209.

Rochester: [a]Minnesota. [b]none. [c]South Branch of Zumbro R. [d]none. [e]Mayo Foundation Library (1907) 305; Public Library (1883) 167.

Rochester: [a] New York. [b]none. [c]Genesee R; Ontario L. [d]University of Rochester (1850) 8 – 660. [e]University . . . Library (1850) 1697; Public Library (1886) 935.

Rockford: [a]Illinois. [b]none. [c]Rock R. [d]none. [e]Public Library (1872) 335.

Rock Hill: [a]South Carolina. [b]none. [c]nr Catawba R. [d]none. [e]Winthrop College Library (1895) 366; York County Library (1884) 143.

Rock Island: [a]Illinois. [b]none. [c]Mississippi R; Rock R. [d]none. [e]Augustana College Library (1860) 233; Public Library (1872) 161.

Rockville: [a]Maryland. [b]none. [c]nr Potomac R. [d]none. [e]Montgomery County Public Library (1951) 1140; National Oceanic and Atmospheric Administration Library (1809 at Washington, relocated 1975?) 600.

Rome: [a]Georgia. [b]none. [c]Coosa R; Etowah R; Oostanaula R. [d]none. [e]Sara Hightower Regional Library (1911) 280.

Rome: [a]New York. [b]none. [c]Mohawk R. [d]none. [e]Jervis Public Library (1894) 105.

Roswell: [a]New Mexico. [b]none. [c]Rio Hondo R. [d]none. [e]New Mexico Military Institute Library (1902) 65; Public Library (1906) 65.

Royal Oak: [a]Michigan. [b]none. [c]nr Rouge R. [d]none. [e]Public Library (1915) 124.

Ruston: [a]Louisiana. [b]none. [c]nr Cypress Creek. [d]Louisiana Tech University (1894) 11 – 487; Grambling State University (at Grambling, nr Ruston) (1901) 5 – 200. [e]Louisiana Tech University Library (1895) 296; Grambling State University Library (at Grambling) (1935) 256; Lincoln Parish Library (1962) 66.

Rutland: [a]Vermont. [b]none.[c]Otter Creek. [d]none. [e]Free Library (1886) 81.

Sacramento: [a]*California. [b]none. [c]Sacramento R; American R. [d]California State University, Sacramento (1947) 22 – 1163. [e]Public Library (1857) 1266; . . . University Library (1947) 1005; California State Library (1850) 626.

Saginaw: [a]Michigan. [b]none. [c]Saginaw R. [d]none. [e]Public Library (1855) 334.

Saint Augustine: [a]Florida. [b]none. [c]Matanzas B of Atlantic O; San Sebastian R. [d]none. [e]Flagler College Library (1968) 70; Saint Johns County Public Library (1874) 61.

Saint Clair Shores: [a]Michigan. [b]none. [c]Saint Clair L. [d]none. [e]Public Library (1935) 147.

Saint Cloud: [a]Minnesota. [b]none. [c]Mississippi R; Sauk R. [d]Saint Cloud State University (1869) 11 – 658; Saint John's University (at Collegeville, nr Saint Cloud) (1856) 2 – 158. [e]Saint Cloud State University Library (1869) 491; Great River Regional Library (1889) 371; Saint John's University Library (at Collegeville) (1856) 294.

Saint Joseph: [a]Missouri. [b]none. [c]Missouri R. [d]none. [e]Public Library (1890) 209.

For an explanation of symbols and abbreviations, see pages 16–17.　　　　　　　　　　　(Continued)

TABLE 2b. (Continued)

Saint Louis: [a]Missouri. [b]none. [c]Mississippi R. [d]University of Missouri, Saint Louis campus (1960) 11 – 669; Washington University (1853) 11 – 2590; Saint Louis University (1818) 10 – 2504; Webster University (1915) 6 – 231. [e]Washington University Library (1853) 3073; Saint Louis County Library (1946) 1823; Public Library (1865) 1333; Saint Louis University Library (1818) 1149.

Saint Paul: [a]*Minnesota. [b]none. [c]Mississippi R. [d]Metropolitan State University (1971) 4 – 481; Hamline University (1854 at Red Wing, relocated 1880) 2 – 128. [e]Public Library (1857) 688; Minnesota Historical Society Library (1849) 404; Macalester College Library (1874) 339.

Saint Petersburg: [a]Florida. [b]none. [c]Tampa B of G of Mexico; Boca Ciega B of G of Mexico. [d]none. [e]Public Library (1909) 468.

Salem: [a]Massachusetts. [b]none. [c]Atlantic O. [d]none. [e]Essex Institute Library (1821) 300; Salem State College Library (1854) 207; Public Library (1888) 178.

Salem: [a]*Oregon. [b]none. [c]Willamette R. [d]Willamette University (1842) 2 – 191. [e]Oregon State Library (1848) 368; Public Library (1904) 210; Western Oregon State College Library (at Monmouth, nr Salem) (1882) 182; . . . University Library (1844) 168.

Salinas: [a]California. [b]none. [c]Salinas R. [d]none. [e]Monterey County Library (1912) 386; Public Library (1900) 347.

Salt Lake City: [a]*Utah. [b]for Great Salt Lake City. [c]Jordan R. [d]University of Utah (1850) 25 – 2734. [e]University . . . Library (1850) 2473; Salt Lake County Library (1938) 927; Public Library (1898) 524; Utah State Library (1957) 94.

San Angelo: [a]Texas. [b]none. [c]Concho R. [d]Angelo State University (1928) 6 – 227. [e] . . . University Library (1928) 209; Tom Green County Library (1923) 199.

San Antonio: [a]Texas. [b]none. [c]San Antonio R; San Pedro R: Acequia R. [d]University of Texas, San Antonio campus (1969) 13 – 579; Saint Mary's University (1852) 3 – 193; Trinity University (1869) 3 – 283; Our Lady of the Lake University (1896) 2 – 95. [e]Public Library (1892) 1433; Saint Mary's University Library (1852) 488; San Antonio Campus Library of the University . . . (1968) 485; Trinity University Library (1869) 480.

San Bernardino: [a]California. [b]none. [c]Santa Ana R. [d]California State University, San Bernardino (1960) 6 – 272. [e]San Bernardino County Library (1914) 1000; . . . University Library (1963) 444; Public Library (1891) 246.

San Diego: [a]California. [b]inc La Jolla. [c]San Diego B of Pacific O; San Diego R. [d]San Diego State University (1897) 34 – 1935; University of California, San Diego campus (1903) 14 – 947; National University (1971) 9 – 782; University of San Diego (1949) 5 – 326; United States International University (1952) 4 – 323. [e]San Diego Campus Library of the University of California (1913) 2195; San Diego Public Library (1882) 1954; San Diego State University Library (1898) 1056; San Diego County Library (1907) 798.

San Francisco: [a]California. [b]none. [c]Pacific O; San Francisco B of Pacific O; Merced L. [d]San Francisco State University (1899) 24 – 1907; Golden Gate University (1901) 10 – 765; University of San Francisco (1855) 5 – 326; University of California, San Francisco campus (1864) 4 – 2538. [e]Public Library (1878) 1951; San Francisco Campus Library of the University of California (1864) 991; San Francisco State University Library (1899) 665.

San Jose: [a]California. [b]none. [c]Guadalupe R; Coyote R. [d]San Jose State University (1857 at San Francisco, relocated 1871) 25 – 1674. [e]Public Library (1872) 1284; Santa Clara County Free Library (1912) 962; . . . University Library (1872) 833.

San Luis Obispo: [a]California. [b]none. [c]nr San Luis Obispo B of Pacific O. [d]California Polytechnic State University (1901) 16 – 1062. [e] . . . University Library (1901) 716; City-County Library (1894) 250.

San Marcos: [a]Texas. [b]none. [c]San Marcos R. [d]Southwest Texas State University (1899) 19 – 843. [e] . . . University Library (1903) 691; Public Library (1920) 34.

San Mateo: [a]California. [b]none. [c]San Francisco B of Pacific O. [d]none. [e]San Mateo County Library (at Belmont, nr San Mateo) (1915) 617; San Mateo Public Library (1884) 305.

Santa Ana: [a]California. [b]none. [c]Santa Ana R. [d]none. [e]Public Library (1878) 350.

Santa Barbara: [a]California. [b]none. [c]Santa Barbara Channel. [d]University of California, Santa Barbara campus (1891) 17 – 1100. [e]Santa Barbara Campus Library of the University . . . (1909) 1584; Public Library (1882) 312.

Santa Clara: [a]California. [b]none. [c]Guadalupe R. [d]University of Santa Clara (1851) 7 – 457. [e]University . . . Library (1851) 428; City Library (1904) 250.

Santa Cruz: [a]California. [b]none. [c]Monterey B of Pacific O; San Lorenzo R. [d]University of California, Santa Cruz campus (1961) 7 – 640. [e]Santa Cruz Campus Library of the University . . . (1965) 904; Public Library (1868) 308.

Santa Fe: [a]*New Mexico. [b]none. [c]Santa Fe R. [d]none. [e]New Mexico State Library (1929) 200; Public Library

TABLE 2b. (Continued)

(1896) 181; New Mexico State Supreme Court Law Library (1853) 155; College of Santa Fe Library (1874) 95.

Santa Monica: [a]California. [b]none. [c]Santa Monica B of Pacific O. [d]none. [e]Public Library (1890) 325.

Santa Rosa: [a]California. [b]none. [c]nr Russian R. [d]Sonoma State University (at Rohnert Park, nr Santa Rosa) (1960) 5 – 373. [e]Sonoma County Library (1869) 649; . . . University Library (at Rohnert Park) (1961) 346.

Sarasota: [a]Florida. [b]none. [c]Sarasota B of G of Mexico. [d]none. [e]Sarasota Campus Library of the University of South Florida (1962) 187; Selby Public Library (1907) 141.

Saratoga Springs: [a]New York. [b]none. [c]nr Saratoga L. [d]State University of New York, Saratoga Springs campus (1971) 5 – 269. [e]Skidmore College Library (1911) 313; Public Library (1867) 61.

Savannah: [a]Georiga. [b]none. [c]Savannah R. [d]none. [e]Chatham-Effingham-Liberty Regional Library (1809) 423.

Schenectady: [a]New York. [b]none. [c]Mohawk R. [d]Union College (univ) (1795) 3 – 197. [e]Schenectady County Public Library (1895) 360; . . . College Library (1795) 214.

Scottsdale: [a]Arizona. [b]none. [c]nr Salt R. [d]none. [e]Public Library (1955) 183.

Scranton: [a]Pennsylvania. [b]none. [c]Lackawanna R; Scranton L. [d]University of Scranton (1888) 5 – 287. [e]Public Library (1892) 200; University . . . Library (1926) 196; Marywood College Library (1915) 172.

Seaside: [a]California. [b]none. [c]Monterey B of Pacific O. [d]none. [e]Seaside Branch of Monterey County Library (bef 1954) 56.

Seattle: [a]Washington. [b]none. [c]Puget Sound of Pacific O; Washington L; Union L; Green L. [d]University of Washington (1861) 26 – 2600; Seattle University (1891) 5 – 306; Seattle Pacific University (1891) 3 – 188. [e]University . . . Library (1862) 4292; Public Library (1873) 1566; King County Library (1943) 1343.

Sheboygan: [a]Wisconsin. [b]none. [c]Sheboygan R; Michigan L. [d]none. [e]Mead Public Library (1897) 281.

Shreveport: [a]Louisiana. [b]none. [c]Red R; Cross L. [d]none. [e]Shreveport Campus Library of Southern University (1966) 374; Shreve Memorial Library (1923) 330.

Silver Spring: [a]Maryland. [b]none. [c]Sligo Creek. [d]none. [e]Prince George's County Memorial Library (at Hyattsville, nr Silver Spring) (1946) 1134; Silver Spring Branch of Montgomery County Public Library (bef 1935) 119.

Simi Valley: [a]California. [b]for Simi. [c]Arroyo Simi Creek. [d]none. [e]Simi Valley Branch of Ventura County Library (bef 1954) 98.

Sioux City: [a]Iowa. [b]none. [c]Missouri R; Big Sioux R; Floyd R. [d]none. [e]Public Library (1870) 161; Morningside College Library (1889) 123.

Sioux Falls: [a]South Dakota. [b]none. [c]Big Sioux R. [d]none. [e]Augustana College Library (1860 at Chicago, relocated 1918?) 292; Public Library (1886) 169.

Skokie: [a]Illinois. [b]for Niles Center. [c]nr Chicago R; nr Michigan L. [d]none. [e]Public Library (1941) 330.

Somerville: [a]Massachusetts. [b]none. [c]Mystic R. [d]none. [e]Public Library (1873) 209.

South Bend: [a]Indiana. [b]none. [c]Saint Joseph R. [d]University of Notre Dame (1842) 9 – 820; Indiana University, South Bend campus (1922) 5 – 294. [e]University . . . Library (1873) 1721; Public Library (1888) 383; South Bend Campus Library of . . . University (1940) 293.

Southfield: [a]Michigan. [b]none. [c]Rouge R. [d]none. [e]Public Library (1960) 180.

South Gate: [a]California. [b]none. [c]Los Angeles R. [d]none. [e]South Gate Branch of Los Angeles County Public Library (bef 1926) 104.

Spartanburg: [a]South Carolina. [b]none. [c]Fairforest Creek. [d]none. [e]Spartanburg County Public Library (1892) 270; Wofford College Library (1854) 187; Converse College Library (1889) 139.

Spokane: [a]Washington. [b]for Spokane Falls. [c]Spokane R. [d]Eastern Washington University (at Cheney, nr Spokane) (1890) 8 – 390; Gonzaga University (1887) 3 – 280. [e]Gonzaga University Library (1887) 550; Spokane Public Library (1884) 453; Eastern Washington University Library (at Cheney) (1890) 353; Spokane County Library (1943) 239.

Springfield: [a]*Illinois. [b]none. [c]Spring Creek; Sugar Creek; Springfield L. [d]Sangamon State University (1969) 3 – 194. [e]Illinois State Library (1839) 1874; Lincoln Library (1867) 326; . . . University Library (1970) 303.

Springfield: [a]Massachusetts. [b]none. [c]Connecticut R; Chicopee R. [d]Western New England College (univ) (1919) 5 – 200; American International College (univ) (1885) 2 – 123; Springfield College (univ) (1885) 2 – 175. [e]City Library (1857) 703.

Springfield: [a]Missouri. [b]none. [c]nr James R. [d]Southwest Missouri State University (1906) 15 – 697. [e] . . . University Library (1907) 397; Springfield-Greene County Library (1903) 365.

Springfield: [a]Ohio. [b]none. [c]Mad R. [d]Antioch University (at Yellow Springs, nr Springfield) (1852) 0.6 – 67.

For an explanation of symbols and abbreviations, see pages 16–17.   (Continued)

TABLE 2b. (Continued)

[e]Wittenberg University Library (1845) 337; Warder Public Library (1872) 312; Antioch University Library (at Yellow Springs) (1852) 289.

Stamford: [a]Connecticut. [b]none. [c]Long Island Sound of Atlantic O; Rippowam R. [d]University of Connecticut, Stamford campus (1951) 1 – ? [e]Public Library (1880) 400.

Starkville: [a]Mississippi. [b]none. [c]nr Noxubee R. [d]Mississippi State University (1878) 12 – 864. [e] . . . University Library (1881) 682; Oktibbeha County Library (1929?) 30.

State College: [a]Pennsylvania. [b]none. [c]Slab Cabin Run. [d]Pennsylvania State University (1855) 40 – 2396 [State College campus: (1855) 34 – 1782]. [e]State College Campus Library of . . . University (1857) 1925; Schlow Memorial Library (1920) 74.

Sterling Heights: [a]Michigan. [b]none. [c]Clinton R. [d]none. [e]Macomb County Library (at Mount Clemens, nr Sterling Heights) (1946) 200; Mount Clemens Public Library (at Mount Clemens) (1865) 110; Sterling Heights Public Library (1971) 82.

Steubenville: [a]Ohio. [b]none. [c]Ohio R. [d]University of Steubenville (1946) 0.9 – 66. [e]University . . . Library (1946) 202; Public Library of Steubenville and Jefferson County (1902) 147.

Stevens Point: [a]Wisconsin. [b]none. [c]Wisconsin R. [d]University of Wisconsin, Stevens Point Campus (1893) 9 – 544. [e]Stevens Point Campus Library of the University . . . (1894) 302; Portage County Public Library (1895) 102.

Stillwater: [a]Oklahoma. [b]none. [c]Stillwater Creek. [d]Oklahoma State University (1890) 22 – 1071. [e] . . . University Library (1894) 1347; Public Library (1923) 69.

Stockton: [a]California. [b]none. [c]San Joaquin R; Calaveras R. [d]University of the Pacific (1851 at San Jose, relocated 1924) 6 – 331. [e]Stockton-San Joaquin County Public Library (1880) 571; University . . . Library (1852 at San Jose, relocated 1924?) 415.

Storrs: [a]Connecticut. [b]none. [c]Willimantic R. [d]University of Connecticut (1881) 20 – 1344 [Storrs campus: (1881) 17 – 1244].. [e]Storrs Campus Library of the University . . . (1881) 1532.

Sunnyvale: [a]California. [b]none. [c]nr San Francisco B of Pacific O. [d]none. [e]Public Library (bef 1923) 242.

Superior: [a]Wisconsin. [b]none. [c]Saint Louis R; Superior B of Superior L. [d]University of Wisconsin, Superior campus (1893) 2 – 144. [e]Superior Campus Library of the University . . . (1896) 303; Public Library (1888) 122.

Syracuse: [a]New York. [b]none. [c]Onondaga Creek; Onondaga L. [d]Syracuse University (1870) 23 – 1408 [Syracuse campus: (1870) 21 – 1233]. [e] . . . University Library (1871) 2317; Onondaga County Public Library (1852) 633.

Tacoma: [a]Washington. [b]none. [c]Puget Sound of Pacific O; Puyallup R. [d]Pacific Lutheran University (1890) 4 – 291; University of Puget Sound (1888) 3 – 183. [e]Public Library (1886) 628.

Tallahassee: [a]*Florida. [b]none. [c]nr Ochlockonee R; nr Jackson L. [d]Florida State University (1851) 20 – 1489; Florida Agricultural and Mechanical University (1887) 5 – 327. [e]Florida State University Library (1853) 1718; Florida Agricultural and Mechanical University Library (1909) 453; Florida State Library (1845) 389; Leon County Public Library (1906) 174.

Tampa: [a]Florida. [b]none. [c]Tampa B of G of Mexico; Old Tampa B of G of Mexico; Hillsborough B of G of Mexico; Hillsborough R. [d]University of South Florida (1956) 28 – 1138; University of Tampa (1930) 2 – 173. [e]University of South Florida Library (1960) 763; Tampa-Hillsborough County Public Library (1917) 714.

Taunton: [a]Massachusetts. [b]none. [c]Taunton R. [d]none. [e]Public Library (1866) 244.

Taylor: [a]Michigan. [b]none. [c]South Branch of Ecorse R. [d]none. [e]Public Library (bef 1954) 78.

Tempe: [a]Arizona. [b]none. [c]Salt R. [d]Arizona State University (1885) 41 – 2248. [e] . . . University Library (1891) 1928; Public Library (1935) 200.

Terre Haute: [a]Indiana. [b]none. [c]Wabash R. [d]Indiana State University (1865) 15 – 887 [Terre Haute campus: (1865) 12 – 713]. [e]Terre Haute Campus Library of . . . University (1870) 1013; Vigo County Public Library (1882) 242.

Texas City: [a]Texas. [b]none. [c]Galveston B of G of Mexico; Dickinson Bayou; Moses L. [d]none. [e]Moore Memorial Public Library (1928) 82; College of the Mainland Library (1967) 46.

Thousand Oaks: [a]California. [b]none. [c]Conejo Creek. [d]none. [e]Public Library (bef 1964) 141; California Lutheran College Library (1961) 101.

Toledo: [a]Ohio. [b]none. [c]Maumee R; Erie L. [d]University of Toledo (1872) 21 – 1194. [e]Toledo-Lucas County Public Library (1873) 1403; University . . . Library (1917) 769.

Tonawanda: [a]New York. [b]none. [c]Niagara R. [d]none. [e]Public Library (1893) 30.

Topeka: [a]*Kansas. [b]none. [c]Kansas R. [d]Washburn University of Topeka (1865) 7 – 258. [e] . . . University Library (1865) 386; Public Library (1871) 291; Kansas State Historical Society Library (1875) 171.

Torrance: [a]California. [b]none. [c]Pacific O. [d]none. [e]Public Library (1913) 407.

TABLE 2b. (Continued)

Towson: [a]Maryland. [b]none. [c]Herring Run. [d]Towson State University (1866) 15 – 866. [e]Baltimore County Public Library (1948) 1502; . . . University Library (1866) 484; Goucher College Library (1885) 221.

Trenton: [a]*New Jersey. [b]none. [c]Delaware R. [d]none. [e]New Jersey State Library (1796) 527; Trenton State College Library (1855) 460; Free Public Library (1852) 333; Mercer County Library (1929) 309; Rider College Library (at Lawrenceville, nr Trenton) (1934 at Trenton, relocated 1956?) 282.

Troy: [a]Michigan. [b]none. [c]Plum Brook. [d]none. [e]Public Library (1962) 170.

Troy: [a]New York. [b]none. [c]Hudson R. [d]Rensselaer Polytechnic Institute (univ) (1824) 7 – 638. [e] . . . Institute Library (1824) 334; Russell Sage College Library (1916) 169; Public Library (1835) 113.

Tucson: [a]Arizona. [b]none. [c]Santa Cruz R. [d]University of Arizona (1885) 30 – 1652. [e]University . . . Library (1891) 2854; Public Library (1879) 735.

Tulsa: [a]Oklahoma. [b]none. [c]Arkansas R. [d]Oral Roberts University (1963) 5 – 385; University of Tulsa (1894 at Muskogee, relocated 1907?) 5 – 473. [e]University . . . Library (1894 at Muskogee, relocated 1907?) 2059; City-County Library (1912) 635; . . . University Library (1965) 578.

Tuscaloosa: [a]Alabama. [b]none. [c]Black Warrior R. [d]University of Alabama (1820) 35 – 2998 [Tuscaloosa campus: (1820) 15 – 919] [e]Tuscaloosa Campus Library of the University . . . (1831) 1744; Public Library (1918) 132.

Tyler: [a]Texas. [b]none. [c]nr Neches R. [d]University of Texas, Tyler campus (1971) 4 – 212. [e]Tyler Campus Library of the University . . . (1973) 178; Public Library (1899) 117; Texas College Library (1894) 111.

Upper Darby: [a]Pennsylvania. [b]none. [c]Cobbs Creek. [d]Cheyney University (at Cheyney, nr Upper Darby) (1837) 2 – 153. [e] . . . University Library (at Cheyney) (1853) 167; Upper Darby Township and Sellers Free Public Library (1932) 86.

Urbana: [a]Illinois. [b]none. [c]nr Embarrass (alt Embarras) R. [d]University of Illinois (at Urbana and Champaign) (1867) 59 – 3799 [Urbana-Champaign campus: (1867) 35 – 2561]. [e]Urbana Campus Library of the University . . . (1868) 6616; Free Library (1874) 127.

Utica: [a]New York. [b]none. [c]Mohawk R. [d]none. [e]Utica College of Syracuse University Library (1946) 158; Public Library (1842) 151.

Vallejo: [a]California. [b]none. [c]San Pablo B of Pacific O; Napa R. [d]none. [e]Vallejo Branch of Solano County Library (1884) 145.

Vancouver: [a]Washington. [b]for Fort Vancouver. [c]Columbia R. [d]none. [e]Fort Vancouver Regional Library (1890) 313.

Ventura: [a]California. [b]off San Buenaventura. [c]Santa Barbara Channel. [d]none. [e]Ventura County Library (1873) 483.

Vermillion: [a]South Dakota. [b]none. [c]Missouri R; Vermillion R. [d]University of South Dakota (1862) 6 – 380. [e]University . . . Library (1882) 550; Public Library (1903) 28.

Vicksburg: [a]Mississippi. [b]none. [c]Mississippi R; Yazoo R. [d]none. [e]Engineer Waterways Experiment Station Library (1930) 340; Warren County Public Library (1915) 100.

Vineland: [a]New Jersey. [b]none. [c]nr Maurice R. [d]none. [e]Free Public Library (1901) 87; Cumberland County College Library (1966) 50.

Virginia Beach: [a]Virginia. [b]none. [c]Atlantic O; Chesapeake B of Atlantic O. [d]CBN University (1977) 0.7 – ? [e]Public Library (1959) 349.

Waco: [a]Texas. [b]none. [c]Brazos R. [d]Baylor University (1845 at Independence, relocated 1887) 11 – 596. [e] . . . University Library (1901) 1366; Waco-McLennan County Library (1899) 250.

Walla Walla: [a]Washington. [b]none. [c]Walla Walla R. [d]none. [e]Whitman College Library (1882) 336; Public Library (1897) 75.

Waltham: [a]Massachusetts. [b]none. [c]Charles R. [d]Brandeis University (1947) 3 – 452. [e] . . . University Library (1948) 774; Public Library (1865) 135; Bentley College Library (1959) 120.

Warren: [a]Michigan. [b]none. [c]nr Clinton R. [d]none. [e]Public Library (bef 1940) 280.

Warren: [a]Ohio. [b]none. [c]Mahoning R. [d]none. [e]Warren-Trumbull County Public Library (1848) 164.

Warwick: [a]Rhode Island. [b]none. [c]Narrangansett B of Atlantic O; Greenwich B of Atlantic O; Providence R; Pawtuxet R. [d]none. [e]Public Library (1886) 176.

*Washington: [a]*District of Columbia. [b]none. [c]Potomac R; Anacostia R. [d1]George Washington University (1821) 15 – 1679; University of the District of Columbia (1851) 13 – 905; Georgetown University (1789) 12 – 1555; Howard University (1867) 11 – 1968; American University (1893) 9 – 1069; Catholic University of America (1887) 7 – 708. [e]Library of Congress (1800) 19,768; Howard University Library (1867) 1849; Georgetown

[1]Universities with 5,000 or more students.

For an explanation of symbols and abbreviations, see pages 16–17.

(Continued)

TABLE 2b. (Continued)

University Library (1789) 1389; George Washington University Library (1821) 1378; Public Library of the District of Columbia (1896) 1355; Catholic University of America Library (1889) 1345; . . . ; Smithsonian Institution Library (1846) 963; Folger Shakespeare Library (1932) 234.

Waterbury: [a]Connecticut. [b]none. [c]Naugatuck R; Mad R. [d]none. [e]Silas Bronson Library (1869) 161.

Waterloo: [a]Iowa. [b]none. [c]Cedar R. [d]none. [e]Public Library (1896) 187.

Waukegan: [a]Illinois. [b]none. [c]Michigan L. [d]none. [e]Public Library (1898) 273.

Waukesha: [a]Wisconsin. [b]none. [c]Fox R. [d]none. [e]Carroll College Library (1851) 160; Public Library (1896) 144.

West Allis: [a]Wisconsin. [b]none. [c]nr Milwaukee R. [d]none. [e]Public Library (1898) 156.

West Covina: [a]California. [b]none. [c]nr San Gabriel R. [d]none. [e]West Covina Branch of Los Angeles County Public Library (bef 1940) 204.

West Hartford: [a]Connecticut. [b]none. [c]nr Connecticut R. [d]University of Hartford (1877) 8 – 620. [e]Saint Joseph College Library (1921) 478; University . . . Library (1938) 408; Public Library (1883) 259.

West Haven: [a]Connecticut. [b]none. [c]Long Island Sound of Atlantic O; West R. [d]University of New Haven (1920) 7 – 430. [e]University . . . Library (1937) 250; Public Library (1909) 118.

West Lafayette: [a]Indiana. [b]for Chauncey, Kingston. [c]Wabash R. [d]Purdue University (1865) 58 – 4898 [West Lafayette campus: (1865) 31 – 3100]. [e]West Lafayette Campus Library of . . . University (1874) 2169; Public Library (1922) 53.

Westland: [a]Michigan. [b]none. [c]Lower Rouge R. [d]none. [e]Wayne County Library (at Wayne, nr Westland) (1920) 811; Wayne-Westland Public Library (at Wayne) (1924) 58.

Westminster: [a]California. [b]none. [c]nr Pacific O;nr Santa Ana R. [d]none. [e]Westminster Branch of Orange County Public Library (bef 1954) 94.

West Palm Beach: [a]Florida. [b]none. [c]Worth Lagoon. [d]none. [e]Palm Beach County Public Library (1967) 268; West Palm Beach Public Library (1895) 108.

West Valley City: [a]Utah. [b]inc Granger, Hunter. [c]Jordan R. [d]none. [e]West Valley City Branch of Salt Lake County Library (bef 1976)?

Wheeling: [a]West Virginia. [b]none. [c]Ohio R. [d]none. [e]Wheeling College Library (1955) 125; Ohio County Public Library (1859) 122.

White Plains: [a]New York. [b]none. [c]nr Bronx R. [d]Pace University, Pleasantville campus (at Pleasantville, nr White Plains) (1963) 4 – 418; Pace University, White Plains campus (1923) 4 – 159; State University of New York, Purchase campus (at Harrison, nr White Plains) (1967) 2 – 179. [e]Manhattanville College Library (at Harrison) (1841) 318; White Plains Public Library (1899) 240; Pleasantville Campus Library of Pace University (at Pleasantville) (1963) 223; Purchase Campus Library of the State University of New York (at Harrison) (1967) 197.

Whittier: [a]California. [b]none. [c]San Gabriel R. [d]none. [c]Public Library (1900) 219; Whittier College Library (1901) 175.

Wichita: [a]Kansas. [b]none. [c]Arkansas R; Little Arkansas R. [d]Wichita State University (1887) 17 – 703. [e] . . . University Library (1895) 729; Public Library (1891) 498.

Wichita Falls: [a]Texas. [b]none. [c]Wichita R. [d]Midwestern State University (1922) 5 – 186. [e] . . . University Library (1924) 322; Kemp Public Library (1917) 115.

Wilkes-Barre: [a]Pennsylvania. [b]none. [c]Susquehanna R. [d]none. [e]Osterhout Free Library (1889) 187; Wilkes College Library (1933) 183; King's College Library (1946) 152.

Williamsburg: [a]Virginia. [b]none. [c]nr James R; nr York R. [d]College of Wiliam and Mary (univ) (1693) 7 – 504. [e]College . . . Library (1693) 919; Williamsburg Regional Library (1910) 76; Colonial Williamsburg Foundation Library (1929) 56.

Williamsport: [a]Pennsylvania. [b]none. [c]West Branch of Susquehanna R. [d]none. [e]Lycoming College Library (1812) 146; James V. Brown Library of Williamsport and Lycoming County (1905) 91.

Wilmington: [a]Delaware. [b]none. [c]Delaware R; Christina R. [d]none. [e]Wilmington Institute Library (1788) 349.

Wilmington: [a]North Carolina. [b]none. [c]Cape Fear R. [d]University of North Carolina at Wilmington (1947) 6 – 315. [e]Wilmington Campus Library of the University . . . (1947) 260; New Hanover County Public Library (1906) 172.

Winona: [a]Minnesota. [b]none. [c]Mississippi r. [d]Winona State University (1858) 5 – 270. [e] . . . University Library (1860) 188; College of Saint Teresa Library (1907) 160; Saint Mary's College Library (1925) 155; Public Library (1857) 93.

Winston-Salem: [a]North Carolina. [b]inc Salem, Winston. [c]Salem Creek. [d]Wake Forest University (1833 at Wake Forest, relocated 1956) 5 – 1160. [e] . . . University Library (1879 at Wake Forest, relocated 1956?) 1055; Forsyth County Public Library (1903) 351.

TABLE 2b. (Continued)

Winter Haven: [a]Florida. [b]none. [c]Cannon L; Shipp L. [d]none. [e]Polk Community College Library (1965) 86; Public Library (1917) 48.

Woodbridge: [a]New Jersey. [b]none. [c]Arthur Kill. [d]none. [e]Free Public Library (1879) 345.

Worcester: [a]Massachusetts. [b]none. [c]Blackstone R; Quinsigamond L; Indian L. [d]Worcester Polytechnic Institute (univ) (1865) 4 – 323; Clark University (1887) 3 – 256. [e]American Antiquarian Society Library (1812) 655; Public Library (1859) 602; . . . University Library (1889) 467; College of the Holy Cross Library (1927) 458.

Yakima: [a]Washington. [b]for North Yakima. [c]Yakima R. [d]none. [e]Yakima Valley Regional Library (1907) 314.

Yonkers: [a]New York. [b]none. [c]Hudson R; Bronx R. [d]none. [e]Public Library (1893) 227; Sarah Lawrence College Library (at Bronxville, nr Yonkers) (1928) 183.

York: [a]Pennsylvania. [b]none. [c]Codorus Creek. [d]none. [e]York College Library (1968) 120; Martin Memorial Library (1885) 112.

Youngstown: [a]Ohio. [b]none. [c]Mahoning R. [d]Youngstown State University (1908) 15 – 798. [e]Public Library of Youngstown and Mahoning County (1878) 751; . . . University Library (1931) 503.

Ypsilanti: [a]Michigan. [b]none. [c]Huron R. [d]Eastern Michigan University (1849) 20 – 833. [e] . . . University Library (1849) 524; Ypsilanti District Library (1868) 67.

Yuma: [a]Arizona. [b]none. [c]Colorado R; Gila R. [d]none. [e]City-County Library (1921) 158.

Zanesville: [a]Ohio. [b]none. [c]Muskingum R; Licking R. [d]none. [e]John McIntire Public Library (1903) 219.

Virgin Islands (USA)

*Charlotte Amalie: [a]Saint Thomas I. [b]for Saint Thomas. [c]Caribbean Sea. [d]none. [e]Division of Libraries (1920) 83; College of the Virgin Islands Library (1962) 67; Enid M. Baa Library (1920) 40.

OCEANIA

American Samoa

*Pago Pago: [a]Tutuila I. [b]for Pango Pango. [c]Pacific O. [d]none. [e]American Samoa Library Service (1913) 120.

Australia

Adelaide: [a]*South Australia. [b]none. [c]Saint Vincent G of Indian O; Torrrens R; Sturt R. [d]University of Adelaide (1874) 9 – 638; Flinders University of South Australia (1963) 4 – 301. [e]University . . . Library (1876) 1226; State Library of South Australia (1884) 864; . . . University Library (1963) 561.

Brisbane: [a]*Queensland. [b]none. [c]Brisbane R. [d]University of Queensland (1910) 16 – 1110; Griffith University (1971) 3 – 206. [e]University . . . Library (1911) 1260; State Library of Queensland (1896) 752.

*Canberra: [a]*Australian Capital Territory. [b]none. [c]Molonglo R. [d]Australian National University (1929) 6 – 598. [e]National Library of Australia (1901 at Melbourne, relocated 1927) 2168; . . . University Library (1948) 1219.

Darwin: [a]*Northern Territory. [b]for Palmerston, Port Darwin. [c]Clarence Strait. [d]none. [e]Darwin Community College Library (1973?) 110; Public Library (1952) 71; State Library of the Northern Territory (1980) 35.

Geelong: [a]Victoria. [b]none. [c]Port Phillip B of Bass Strait; Barwon R. [d]Deakin University (1974) 2 – 258. [e] . . . University Library (1974?) 200; Regional Library Service (?) 65.

Gold Coast: [a]Queensland. [b]inc Coolangatta, Southport. [c]Pacific O; Tweed R; Nerang R. [d]none.

Hobart: [a]*Tasmania; Tasmania I. [b]none. [c]Derwent R. [d]University of Tasmania (1890) 5 – 375. [e]State Library of Tasmania (1849) 1376; University . . . Library (1889) 609.

Melbourne: [a]*Victoria. [b]none. [c]Port Phillip B of Bass Strait; Yarra R. [d]University of Melbourne (1853) 16 – 1153; Monash University (1958) 14 – 1000; La Trobe University (1964) 9 – 560. [e]University . . . Library (1855) 1356; Monash University Library (1961) 1180; State Library of Victoria (1853) 1128.

Newcastle: [a]New South Wales. [b]none. [c]Pacific O; Hunter R. [d]University of Newcastle (1951) 4 – 320. [e]University . . . Library (1951) 500; Regional Public Library (1948) 353.

Perth: [a]*Western Australia. [b]none. [c]Swan R. [d]University of Western Australia (1911) 10 – 602; Murdoch University (1973) 2 – 181. [e]University . . . Library (1913) 926; State Reference Library of Western Australia (1887) 364.

Sydney: [a]*New South Wales. [b]none. [c]Pacific O; Parramatta R. [d]University of New South Wales (1949) 18 – 1321; University of Sydney (1850) 18 – 1240; Macquarie University (1964) 11 – 540. [e]University of Sydney Library (1851) 3068; State Library of New South Wales (1826) 2000; University of New South Wales Library (1949) 1170; Macquarie University Library (1965) 657; Public Library (1909) 350.

For an explanation of symbols and abbreviations, see pages 16–17.

(Continued)

TABLE 2b. (Continued)

Townsville: [a]Queensland. [b]none. [c]Cleveland B of Coral Sea. [d]James Cook University of North Queensland (1961) 3 – 266. [e] . . . University Library (1961) 366.

Wollongong: [a]New South Wales. [b]none. [c]Pacific O; Nepean R. [d]University of Wollongong (1961) 5 – 282. [e]City Library (1946) 430; University . . . Library (1961?) 300.

Fiji:

*Suva: [a]Viti Levu I. [b]none. [c]Pacific O. [d]University of the South Pacific (1968) 2 – 268. [e]University . . . Library (1968) 253; City Library (1909) 46.

French Polynesia

*Papeete: [a]Tahiti I. [b]none. [c]Pacific O. [d]none. [e]Bibliotheque de l'Office Territorial d'Action Culturelle (1981) 18.

Guam

*Agana: [a]Guam I. [b]none. [c]Agana B of Philippine Sea; Agana R. [d]University of Guam (at Mangilao, nr Agana) (1952) 3 – 168. [e]Nieves M. Flores Memorial Library (1949) 173; University ...Library (at Mangilao) (1952) 101.

(Hawaii), USA

Hilo: [a]Hawaii I. [b]none. [c]Hilo B of Pacific O; Wailuku R. [d]none. [e]Hilo Campus Library of the University of Hawaii (1947) 180; Hilo Branch of Hawaii State Library (1899) 149.

*Honolulu: [a]Oahu I. [b]none. [c]Pacific O. [d]University of Hawaii (1907) 24 – 1891 [Manoa campus:(1970) 20 – 1615]; Chaminade University of Honolulu (1955) 2 – 76. [e]Hawaii State Library (1852) 2214 (at Honolulu: 893); Manoa Campus Library of the University . . . (1907) 2104.

Kailua: [a]Oahu I. [b]none. [c]Kailua B of Pacific O. [d]none. [e]Kailua Branch of Hawaii State Library (bef 1954) 59.

(Irian Jaya), Indonesia

*Jayapura: [a]New Guinea I. [b]alt Kotabaru; for Djajapura, Hollandia. [c]Jos Sudarso (for Humboldt) B of Pacific O. [d]Cenderawasih University (1962) 1 – 75. [e] . . . University Library (1962) 40.

Kiribati

*Tarawa: [a]Tarawa I. [b]none. [c]Pacific O. [d]none. [e]National Library (1979) 25.

New Caledonia

*Noumea: [a]New Caledonia I. [b]for Port-de-France. [c]Pacific O. [d]none. [e]Bibliotheque Bernheim (1905) 60; South Pacific Commission Library (1947) 60.

New Zealand:

Auckland: [a]North I. [b]none. [c]Tasman Sea; Hauraki G of Pacific O. [d]University of Auckland (1882) 13 – 750. [e]Public Library (1880) 1120; University . . . Library (1884) 1050.

Christchurch: [a]South I. [b]none. [c]Avon R. [d]University of Canterbury (1873) 10 – 590. [e]University . . . Library (1873) 1000; Canterbury Public Library (1859) 400.

Dunedin: [a]South I. [b]none. [c]Pacific O. [d]University of Otago (1869) 7 – 462. [e]University . . . Library (1870) 965; Public Library (1908) 398.

Hamilton: [a]North I. [b]none. [c]Waikato R. [d]University of Waikato (1964) 4 – 200. [e]University . . . Library (1960) 400; Public Library (1960) 330.

Manukau: [a]North I. [b]none. [c]Tasman Sea. [d]none.

Napier: [a]North I. [b]none. [c]Hawke B of Pacific O. [d]none. [e]Public Library (?) 46.

Palmerston North: [a]North I. [b]none. [c]Manawatu R. [d]Massey University (1926) 6 – 560. [e] . . . University Library (1928) 450; Public Library (1876) 200.

*Wellington: [a]North I. [b]none. [c]Cook Strait. [d]Victoria University of Wellington (1897) 7 – 410. [e]National Library of New Zealand (1856) 1347; . . . University Library (1897) 625; Public Library (1841) 455.

Pacific Islands (USA)

*Saipan: [a]Saipan I. [b]none. [c]Philippine Sea. [d]none.

Papua New Guinea

Lae: [a]New Guinea I. [b]none. [c]Huon G of Solomon Sea; Markham R. [d]Papua New Guinea University of Technology (1965) 1 – 145. [e] . . . University Library (1965) 53.

TABLE 2b. (Continued)

*Port Moresby: [a]New Guinea I. [b]none. [c]G of Papua of Coral Sea. [d]University of Papua New Guinea (1965) 2 – 363. [e]University . . . Library (1965) 320; Administrative College of Papua New Guinea Library (1962) 75; National Library Service (1978) 45.

Rabaul: [a]New Britain I. [b]none. [c]Blanche B of Pacific O. [d]none.

Samoa

*Apia: [a]Upolu I. [b]none. [c]Pacific O; Vaisigano R. [d]none. [e]Nelson Memorial Public Library (1959) 61.

Solomon Islands

*Honiara: [a]Guadalcanal I. [b]none. [c]Pacific O. [d]none. [e]Solomon Islands National Library (1974) 22.

Tonga

*Nukualofa: [a]Tongatapu I. [b]none. [c]Pacific O. [d]none. [e]Teacher Training College Library (1944) 5.

Vanuatu

*Vila: [a]Efate I. [b]alt Port-Vila; for Franceville. [c]Mele B of Pacific O. [d]none. [e]Cultural Centre Library (1962) 14.

SOUTH AMERICA

Argentina

Bahia Blanca: [a]Buenos Aires. [b]none. [c]Naposta Grande R. [d]Universidad Nacional del Sur (1948) 5 – 1098. [e]Biblioteca de la Universidad . . . (1948) 145; Biblioteca Popular Bernardino Rivadavia (1882) 115.

*Buenos Aires: [a]*Distrito Federal. [b]for Buenos Ayres. [c]Plata R; Riachuelo R. [d][1]Universidad de Buenos Aires (1821) 105 – 16,600; Universidad Tecnologica Nacional (1953) 29 – 2124; Universidad de Moron (1960) 13 – 1350; Universidad de Belgrano (1964) 12 – 1350; Pontificia Universidad Catolica Argentina Santa Maria de los Buenos Aires (1922) 11 – 2900. [e]Biblioteca de la Universidad de Buenos Aires (1853) 2150; Biblioteca Nacional (1810) 1850; Biblioteca del Congreso de la Nacion (1859) 1400; Biblioteca Municipal (1928) 350.

Catamarca: [a]*Catamarca. [b]none. [c](Rio del) Valle R. [d]Universidad Nacional de Catamarca (1972) 2 – 304. [e]Biblioteca Popular Domingo Faustino Sarmiento (1894) 40; Biblioteca de la Universidad . . . (1973) 6.

Comodoro Rivadavia: [a]Chubut. [b]none. [c]G of San Jorge of Atlantic O. [d]Universidad Nacional de la Patagonia San Juan Bosco (1959) 2 – 680. [e]Biblioteca Publica Municipal (1946) 25; Biblioteca de la Universidad . . . (1959) 12.

Concepcion del Uruguay: [a]Entre Rios. [b]none. [c]Uruguay R. [d]Universidad Nacional de Entre Rios (1973) 3 – 485; Universidad de Concepcion del Uruguay La Fraternidad (1971) ? – ? [e]Biblioteca Popular El Porvenir (1872) 21; Biblioteca de la Universidad Nacional de Entre Rios (1962)?

Cordoba: [a]*Cordoba. [b]none. [c]Primero R. [d]Universidad Nacional de Cordoba (1613) 36 – 5172; Universidad Catolica de Cordoba (1956) 4 – 750. [e]Biblioteca de la Universidad Nacional de Cordoba (1614) 420.

Corrientes: [a]*Corrientes. [b]none. [c]Parana R. [d]Universidad Nacional del Nordeste (1957) 25 – 2332. [e]Biblioteca de la Universidad . . . (1920) 72; Biblioteca Popular (?) 20.

Formosa: [a]*Formosa. [b]none. [c]Paraguay R. [d]none.

Jujuy: [a]*Jujuy. [b]alt San Salvador de Jujuy. [c]Grande de Jujuy R. [d]Universidad Nacional de Jujuy (1959) 1 – 253. [e]Biblioteca Popular (1899) 28; Biblioteca de la Universidad ...(1946) 18.

La Plata: [a]*Buenos Aires. [b]alt Plata; for Eva Peron. [c]Plata R. [d]Universidad Nacional de La Plata (1884) 30 – 4327; Universidad Catolica de La Plata (1968) 7 – 600. [e]Biblioteca de la Universidad Nacional de La Plata (1884) 1150; Biblioteca del Museo de La Plata (1884) 180.

La Rioja: [a]*La Rioja. [b]none. [c]Rioja R. [d]Universidad Provincial de La Rioja (1960) 0.4 – 102. [e]Biblioteca de la Universidad . . . (1960?) 20.

Mar del Plata: [a]Buenos Aires. [b]for General Pueyrredon, Pueyrredon. [c]Atlantic O. [d]Universidad Nacional de Mar del Plata (1961) 5 – 1600. [e]Biblioteca Municipal Publica (?) 30; Biblioteca de la Universidad . . . (1963) 14.

Mendoza: [a]*Mendoza. [b]none. [c]Tulumaya R. [d]Universidad Nacional de Cuyo (1939) 8 – 963; Universidad de Mendoza (1960) 2 – 262; Universidad del Aconcagua (1968) 0.9 – 251; Universidad Juan Agustin Maza (1960) 0.9 – 260. [e]Biblioteca de la Universidad Nacional de Cuyo (1939) 320; Biblioteca Publica General San Martin (1822) 100.

Neuquen: [a]*Neuquen. [b]none. [c]Negro R; Neuquen R; Limay R. [d]Universidad Nacional del Comahue (1965) 3 – 698. [e]Biblioteca de la Universidad . . . (1965?) 18.

---

[1]Universities with 10,000 or more students.

For an explanation of symbols and abbreviations, see pages 16–17.

(Continued)

TABLE 2b. (Continued)

Parana: [a]*Entre Rios. [b]for Bajada de Santa Fe. [c]Parana R. [d]none. [e]Biblioteca Popular (?) 51.

Posadas: [a]*Misiones. [b]none. [c]Parana R. [d]Universidad Nacional de Misiones (1973) 2 – 664. [e]Biblioteca de la Universidad . . . (1974) 17.

Rawson: [a]*Chubut. [b]none. [c]Chubut R. [d]none. [e]Biblioteca Ex-Legislatura (1958) 23; Biblioteca Publica Provincial (1964) 4.

Resistencia: [a]*Chaco. [b]none. [c]Parana R. [d]none.

Rio Cuarto: [a]Cordoba. [b]for Concepcion. [c]Cuarto R. [d]Universidad Nacional de Rio Cuarto (1962) 5 – 936. [e]Biblioteca de la Universidad ...(1972) 19.

Rio Gallegos: [a]*Santa Cruz. [b]none. [c]Gallegos R. [d]none. [e]Biblioteca Publica Provincial (1961) 14.

Rosario: [a]Santa Fe. [b]none. [c]Parana R. [d]Universidad Nacional de Rosario (1889) 29 – 3542. [e]Biblioteca Argentina Doctor Juan Alvarez (1910) 160; Biblioteca Publica Estanislao S. Zeballos (1905) 104; Biblioteca de la Universidad . . . (1910) 103.

Salta: [a]*Salta. [b]for Lerma. [c]Arias R. [d]Universiad Nacional de Salta (1967) 4 – 830; Universidad Catolica de Salta (1963) 0.7 – 90. [e]Biblioteca de la Universiad Nacional de Salta (1962) 27; Biblioteca de la Universidad Catolica de Salta (1967) 18; Biblioteca Popular Bartolome Mitre (1917) 5.

San Juan: [a]*San Juan. [b]none. [c]San Juan R. [d]Universidad Nacional de San Juan (1964) 6 – 518; Universidad Catolica de San Juan (1953) 1 – 340. [e]Biblioteca Popular Franklin (1866) 51; Biblioteca de la Universidad Nacional de San Juan (1939) 31.

San Luis: [a]*San Luis. [b]none. [c]Chorrillo R. [d]Universidad Nacional de San Luis (1973) ? – ? [e]Biblioteca de la Universidad . . . (1973?) 35.

Santa Fe: [a]*Santa Fe. [b]none. [c]Salado R. [d]Universidad Nacional del Litoral (1889) 8 – 1328; Universidad Catolica de Santa Fe (1957) 2 – 600. [e]Biblioteca de la Universidad Nacional del Litoral (1905) 180; Biblioteca Municipal Bernardino Rivadavia (1945) 20.

Santa Rosa: [a]*La Pampa. [b]for Santa Rosa de Toay. [c]nr Tunuyan R. [d]Universidad Nacional de La Pampa (1958) 2 – 632. [e]Biblioteca de la Universidad . . . (1958) 11.

Santiago del Estero: [a]*Santiago del Estero. [b]none. [c]Dulce R. [d]Universidad Catolica de Santiago del Estero (1960) 2 – 219; Universidad Nacional de Santiago del Estero (1973) 2 – 400. [e]Biblioteca de la Universidad Nacional de Santiago del Estero (1958) 20.

Tandil: [a]Buenos Aires. [b]none. [c]nr Quenquen Grande R. [d]Universidad Nacional del Centro de la Provincia de Buenos Aires (1964) 3 – 675. [e]Biblioteca de la Universidad . . . (1975) 10.

Tucuman: [a]*Tucuman. [b]off San Miguel de Tucuman. [c]Dulce R. [d]Universidad Nacional de Tucuman (1912) 20 – 2560; Universidad del Norte Santo Tomas de Aquino (1958) 2 – 516. [e]Biblioteca de la Universidad Nacional de Tucuman (1917) 310; Biblioteca Popular Alberdi (1903) 44.

Ushuaia: [a]*Tierra del Fuego; Grande de Tierra del Fuego I. [b]none. [c]Beagle Channel. [d]none. [e]Biblioteca Popular Sarmiento (1921) 5.

Viedma: [a]*Rio Negro. [b]none. [c]Negro R. [d]none. [e]Biblioteca Popular Bartolome Mitre (1906) 10.

Bolivia

Cochabamba: [b]for Oropeza. [c]Rocha R. [d]Universidad Boliviana Mayor de San Simon (1826) 10 – 523. [e]Biblioteca de la Universidad . . . (1832) 48; Biblioteca Municipal (1831) 25.

*La Paz: [b]alt Paz; for Choqueyapu; off La Paz de Ayacucho. [c]Choqueyapo R. [d]Universidad Boliviana Mayor de San Andres (1830) 17 – 872; Universidad Catolica Boliviana (1966) 2 – 110. [e]Biblioteca de la Universidad Boliviana Mayor de San Andres (1830) 160; Biblioteca de la Direccion General de Cultura (1832) 140; Biblioteca Municipal Mariscal Andres de Santa Cruz (1836) 80.

Oruro: [b]for San Felipe de Austria. [c]nr Desaguadero R. [d]Universidad Tecnica de Oruro (1892) 13 – 705. [e]Biblioteca de la Universidad . . . (1906) 55; Biblioteca Municipal (?) 15.

Potosi: [b]none. [c]Potosi R. [d]Universidad Boliviana Mayor y Autonoma Tomas Frias (1892) 4 – 228. [e]Biblioteca de la Universidad . . . (1942) 41; Biblioteca Municipal Ricardo Jaime Freires (1920) 30.

Santa Cruz: [b]off Santa Cruz de la Sierra. [c]Piray R. [d]Universidad Boliviana Gabriel Rene Moreno (1879) 7 – 358. [e]Biblioteca de la Universidad . . . (1880) 90; Biblioteca Municipal (?)?

*Sucre: [b]for Charcas, Chuquisaca. [c]Quirpinchaca R. [d]Universidad Boliviana Mayor, Real y Pontificia de San Francisco Xavier de Chuquisaca (1624) 10 – 1345. [e]Biblioteca y Archivo Nacional de Bolivia (1836) 150; Biblioteca de la Universidad . . . (1624) 80.

Brazil

Anapolis: [a]Goias. [b]none. [c]Corumba R. [d]none. [e]Biblioteca Publica Municipal (1968) 9.

Aracaju: [a]*Sergipe. [b]none. [c]Cotinguiba R. [d]Universidade Federal de Sergipe (1948) 5 – 534. [e]Biblioteca Publica do Estado de Sergipe (1851) 160; Biblioteca da Universidade . . . (1950) 57.

TABLE 2b. (Continued)

Bauru: [a]Sao Paulo. [b]for Divino Espirito da Fortaleza. [c]Agua Funda R. [d]none. [e]Biblioteca Central Coracao de Jesus (1954) 36; Biblioteca Municipal (1973) 12.

Belem: [a]*Para. [b]for Para. [c]Para R; Guama R; Guajara R. [d]Universidade Federal do Para (1902) 12 – 1485. [e]Biblioteca Publica do Para (1871) 66; Biblioteca de Universidade . . . (1951) 65.

Belo Horizonte: [a]*Minas Gerais. [b]for Curral d'El-Rei. [c]Arrudas R. [d]Universidade Federal de Minas Gerais (1892) 24 – 2194; Universidade Catolica de Minas Gerais (1943) 13 – 674. [e]Biblioteca da Universidade Federal de Minas Gerais (1892) 530; Biblioteca Publica de Minas Gerais (1898) 204.

Blumenau: [a]Santa Catarina. [b]none. [c]Itajai R. [d]Universidade Regional de Blumenau (1968) 4 – 242. [e]Biblioteca Publica Municipal Doutor Fritz Muller (1939) 54.

Boa Vista: [a]*Roraima. [b]none. [c]Branco R. [d]none. [e]Biblioteca Publica (1945) 11.

*Brasilia: [a]*Distrito Federal. [b]none. [c]Torto R; Fundo R. [d]Universidade de Brasilia (1962) 10 – 744. [e]Biblioteca da Universidade . . . (1962) 450; Biblioteca do Ministerio das Relacoes Exteriores (1906 at Rio de Janeiro, relocated 1960?) 270; Biblioteca da Camara dos Deputados (1866 at Rio de Janeiro, relocated 1960?) 235.

Campina Grande: [a]Paraiba. [b]none. [c]nr Mamanguape R. [d]Universidade Regional do Nordeste (1966) 7 – 450. [e]Biblioteca da Universidade . . . (1966) 60; Biblioteca Publica Municipal (1938) 3.

Campinas: [a]Sao Paulo. [b]for Sao Carlos. [c]Atibaia R. [d]Pontificia Universidade Catolica de Campinas (1941) 21 – 1328; Universidade Estadual de Campinas (1962) 13 – 1537. [e]Biblioteca da Universidade . . . (1963) 300; Biblioteca da . . . Universidade (1941) 200; Biblioteca Publica Municipal (1976) 44.

Campo Grande: [a]*Mato Grosso do Sul. [b]none. [c]Anhandui R. [d]Universidade Federal de Mato Grosso do Sul (1963) 3 – 330. [e]Biblioteca Dom Bosco (1930) 104; Biblioteca da Universidade . . . (1962) 24; Biblioteca Publica Municipal (1940) 5.

Campos: [a]Rio de Janeiro. [b]for Sao Salvador. [c]Paraiba R. [d]none. [e]Biblioteca Publica Municipal (1872) 12.

Canoas: [a]Rio Grande do Sul. [b]none. [c]nr Sinos R. [d]none. [e]Biblioteca Doutor Antonio Ronna (1973) 40; Biblioteca Publica Municipal (1966) 13.

Carapicuiba: [a]Sao Paulo. [b]none. [c]Tiete R; Cotia R. [d]none. [e]Biblioteca Municipal (1968) 4.

Cariacica: [a]Espirito Santo. [b]none. [c]Cariacica R. [d]none. [e]Biblioteca Jose Maria Meira Quadros (1971) 1.

Caruaru: [a]Pernambuco. [b]none. [c]Ipojuca R. [d]none. [e]Biblioteca Publica Municipal (1948) 16.

Cascavel: [a]Parana. [b]none. [c]nr Sao Francisco R. [d]none. [e]Biblioteca Publica Municipal (1954) 7.

Caxias do Sul: [a]Rio Grande do Sul. [b]for Caxias. [c]nr Cai R; nr Antas R. [d]Universidade de Caxias do Sul (1967) 9 – 497. [e]Biblioteca da Universidade . . . (1967) 33; Biblioteca Publica Municipal (1947) 14.

Contagem: [a]Minas Gerais. [b]none. [c]Riachinho R. [d]none. [e]Biblioteca Publica Municipal (1968) 9.

Cuiaba: [a]*Mato Grosso. [b]none. [c]Cuiaba R. [d]Universidade Federal de Mato Grosso (1934) 6 – 1004. [e]Biblioteca da Universidade . . . (1972) 27; Biblioteca Publica Estadual (1912) 21.

Curitiba: [a]*Parana. [b]for Corityba. [c]nr Iguacu R. [d]Universidade Federal do Parana (1912) 15 – 2014; Universidade Catolica do Parana (1937) 7 – 489. [e]Biblioteca da Universidade Federal do Parana (1912) 350; Biblioteca Publica do Parana (1857) 210.

Diadema: [a]Sao Paulo. [b]none. [c](Ribeirao) Taboao R. [d]none. [e]Biblioteca Publica Municipal (1967) 14.

Duque de Caxias: [a]Rio de Janeiro. [b]for Caxias. [c]Guanabara B of Atlantic O. [d]none. [e]Biblioteca Castro Alves (1974) 15; Biblioteca Publica Municipal (1967) 6.

Feira de Santana: [a]Bahia. [b]for Feira de Sant'Anna. [c]Jacuipe R. [d]Universidade Estadual de Feira de Santana (1970) 3 – 291. [e]Biblioteca da Universidade . . . (1968) 28; Biblioteca Publica Municipal (1890) 20.

Florianopolis: [a]*Santa Catarina. [b]for Desterro. [c]Norte B of Atlantic O; Sul B of Atlantic O. [d]Universidade Federal de Santa Catarina (1932) 14 – 1694; Universidade para o Desenvolvimento do Estado de Santa Catarina (1965) 3 – 300. [e]Biblioteca da Universidade Federal de Santa Catarina (1932) 213; Biblioteca Publica do Estado de Santa Catarina (1855) 34.

Fortaleza: [a]*Ceara. [b]for Ceara. [c]Atlantic O. [d]Universidade Federal do Ceara (1903) 15 – 1250; Universidade de Fortaleza (1973) 10 – 464; Universidade Estadual do Ceara (1975) 9 – 658. [e]Biblioteca da Universidade Federal do Ceara (1918) 160; Biblioteca da Universidade Estadual do Ceara (1947) 50; Biblioteca Publica do Estado do Ceara (1865) 30.

Foz do Iguacu: [a]Parana. [b]none. [c]Parana R; Iguacu R. [d]none. [e]Biblioteca Publica Municipal (1966) 7.

Goiania: [a]*Goias. [b]none. [c]nr Meia Ponte R. [d]Universidade Federal de Goias (1947) 15 – 1153; Universidade Catolica de Goias (1898 at Goias, relocated 1948) 9 – 505. [e]Biblioteca da Universidade Federal de Goias (1948) 63; Biblioteca da Universidade Catolica de Goias (1971) 40; Biblioteca Publica Estadual de Goias (1936) 13; Biblioteca Publica Municipal (1942) 10.

Governador Valadares: [a]Minas Gerais. [b]for Figueira. [c]Doce R. [d]Universidade Santos Dumont (1968) 5 – 250. [e]Biblioteca da Universidade . . . (1968) 56; Biblioteca Publica Municipal Professor Paulo Zappi (1954) 40.

For an explanation of symbols and abbreviations, see pages 16–17.   (Continued)

TABLE 2b. (Continued)

Guarulhos: [a]Sao Paulo. [b]none. [c]Tiete R. [d]none. [e]Biblioteca Cerqueira Cesar (1970) 29; Biblioteca Publica Municipal (1940) 28.

Imperatriz: [a]Maranhao. [b]none. [c]Tocantins R. [d]none. [e]Biblioteca da Faculdade (1975) 5; Biblioteca Publica Municipal (1975) 1.

Ipatinga: [a]Minas Gerais. [b]none. [c]nr Doce R. [d]none. [e]Biblioteca Publica Municipal (1966) 7.

Itaguai: [a]Rio de Janeiro. [b]none. [c]nr Itaguai R. [d]Universidade Federal Rural do Rio de Janeiro (1943) 4 – 611. [e]Biblioteca da Universidade . . . (1943) 71.

Itauna: [a]Minas Gerais. [b]none. [c]Sao Joao R. [d]Universidade de Itauna (1965) 2 – 200. [e]Biblioteca da Universidade . . . (1966) 16; Biblioteca Publica Municipal (1975) 5.

Jaboatao: [a]Pernambuco. [b]none. [c]Jaboatao R. [d]none. [e]Biblioteca Publica Municipal (1952) 4.

Joao Pessoa: [a]*Paraiba. [b]for Parahyba. [c]Paraiba do Norte (alt Paraiba) R. [d]Universidade Federal da Paraiba (1947) 22 – 3028. [e]Biblioteca da Universidade . . . (1955) 144; Biblioteca Publica do Estado da Paraiba (1857) 19.

Joinville: [a]Santa Catarina. [b]none. [c]Sao Francisco B of Atlantic O; Cachoeira R. [d]none. [e]Biblioteca Publica Municipal (1945) 46.

Juiz de Fora: [a]Minas Gerais. [b]for Parahybuna. [c]Paraibuna R. [d]Universidade Federal de Juiz de Fora (1915) 7 – 781. [e]Biblioteca da Universidade . . . (1914) 70; Biblioteca do Seminario Maior Redentorista (1945) 30; Biblioteca Publica Municipal (1934) 17.

Jundiai: [a]Sao Paulo. [b]for Jundiahy. [c]Jundiai (for Jundiahy) R. [d]none. [e]Biblioteca das Escolas Faculdades Padre Anchieta (1942) 28; Biblioteca do Gabinete de Leitura Ruy Barbosa (1908) 22; Biblioteca Publica Municipal (1971) 14.

Londrina: [a]Parana. [b]none. [c]nr Tibagi R. [d]Universidade Estadual de Londrina (1957) 11 – 993. [e]Biblioteca da Universidade . . . (1956) 43; Biblioteca Publica Municipal Professor Pedro Viriato Parigot de Souza (1940) 20.

Macapa: [a]*Amapa. [b]none. [c]Amazon R. [d]none. [e]Biblioteca Publica (1945) 11.

Maceio: [a]*Alagoas. [b]none. [c]Atlantic O; Mundau R. [d]Universidade Federal de Alagoas (1931) 6 – 907. [e]Biblioteca da Universidade . . . (1955) 55; Biblioteca Publica Estadual de Alagoas (1865) 17.

Mage: [a]Rio de Janeiro. [b]none. [c]Mage R. [d]none. [e]Biblioteca Alcindo Guanabara (1974) 2.

Manaus: [a]*Amazonas. [b]alt Manaos. [c]Negro R. [d]Universidade do Amazonas (1909) 17 – 810. [e]Biblioteca Publica do Estado do Amazonas (1870) 156; Biblioteca da Universidade . . . (1909) 75.

Maringa: [a]Parana. [b]none. [c]nr Pirapo R. [d]Universidade Estadual de Maringa (1970) 7 – 733. [e]Biblioteca da Universidade . . . (1972) 69; Biblioteca Publica Municipal (1963) 22.

Maua: [a]Sao Paulo. [b]none. [c]Tamanduatei R. [d]none. [e]Biblioteca Publica Municipal (1972) 5.

Mogi das Cruzes: [a]Sao Paulo. [b]none. [c]Tiete R. [d]Universidade de Mogi das Cruzes (1964) 14 – 849. [e]Biblioteca da Federacao das Faculdades Braz Cubas (1964) 35; Biblioteca da Universidade . . . (1963) 32; Biblioteca Publica Municipal (1948) 17.

Montes Claros: [a]Minas Gerais. [b]for Formigas. [c]Verde Grande R. [d]none. [e]Biblioteca Publica Municipal (1947) 4.

Mossoro: [a]Rio Grande do Norte. [b]none. [c]Apodi (alt Mossoro) R. [d]Universidade Regional do Rio Grande do Norte (1968) 2 – 120. [e]Biblioteca Publica Municipal (1947) 9.

Natal: [a]*Rio Grande do Norte. [b]none. [c]Atlantic O; Potengi R. [d]Universidade Federal do Rio Grande do Norte (1948) 14 – 2263. [e]Biblioteca da Universidade . . . (1955) 180; Biblioteca Publica Camara Cascudo (1948) 17.

Niteroi: [a]*Rio de Janeiro. [b]for Nictheroy, Praia Grande. [c]Guanabara B of Atlantic O. [d]Universidade Federal Fluminense (1912) 21 – 2517. [e]Biblioteca Publica Estadual do Rio de Janeiro. (1927) 100; Biblioteca da Universidade . . . (1940) 65.

Nova Iguacu: [a]Rio de Janeiro. [b]for Maxambomba. [c]nr Sarapui R. [d]none. [e]Biblioteca Desembargador Acacio Aragao (1959) 13; Biblioteca Public Municipal (1973) 3.

Olinda: [a]Pernambuco. [b]none. [c]Atlantic O. [d]none. [e]Biblioteca do Mosteiro de Sao Bento (1917) 30.

Osasco: [a]Sao Paulo. [b]none. [c]Tiete R. [d]none. [e]Biblioteca da Fundacao Instituto de Ensino (1969) 15; Biblioteca Publica Monteiro Lobato (1965) 15.

Ouro Preto: [a]Minas Gerais. [b]for Vila Rica. [c]Funil R. [d]Universidade Federal de Ouro Preto (1839) 1 – 178. [e]Biblioteca da Universidade . . . (1875) 65.

Passo Fundo: [a]Rio Grande do Sul. [b]none. [c]Passo Fundo R. [d]Universidade de Passo Fundo (1956) 8 – 558. [e]Biblioteca da Universidade . . . (1957) 35; Biblioteca Publica Municipal (1940) 12.

Pelotas: [a]Rio Grande do Sul. [b]none. [c]Sao Goncalo Channel. [d]Universidade Catolica de Pelotas (1939) 5 – 408; Universidade Federal de Pelotas (1883) 5 – 885. [e]Biblioteca Publica Pelotense (1875) 128; Biblioteca da Universidade Federal de Pelotas (1916) 70.

TABLE 2b. (Continued)

Petropolis: [a]Rio de Janeiro. [b]none. [c]Piabanha R; Quitandinha R; Palatinado R. [d]Universidade Catolica de Petropolis (1954) 3 – 281. [e]Biblioteca Municipal (1876) 98; Biblioteca da Universidade . . . (1954) 69.

Piracicaba: [a]Sao Paulo. [b]none. [c]Piracicaba R. [d]Universidade Metodista de Piracicaba (1881) 7 – 600. [e]Biblioteca da Universidade . . . (1881) 42; Biblioteca Publica Municipal (1939) 21.

Ponta Grossa: [a]Parana. [b]for Estrela. [c]nr Tibagi R. [d]Universidade Estadual de Ponta Grossa (1970) 4 – 313. [e]Biblioteca da Universidade . . . (1950) 42; Biblioteca Publica Municipal Professor Bruno Enei (1940) 19.

Porto Alegre: [a*]Rio Grande do Sul. [b]none. [c]Guaiba R; Patos Lagoon. [d]Pontificia Universidade Catolica do Rio Grande do Sul (1931) 23 – 1525; Universidade Federal do Rio Grande do Sul (1896) 17 – 2451. [e]Biblioteca da Universidade . . . (1898) 843; Biblioteca da . . . Universidade (1941) 195; Biblioteca Publica do Estado do Rio Grande do Sul (1871) 115.

Porto Velho: [a*]Rondonia. [b]none. [c]Madeira R. [d]Universidade Federal de Rondonia (1982) 1 – ? [e]Biblioteca Publica Doutor Jose Pontes Pinto (1969) 7; Biblioteca Publica Municipal Francisco Meirelles (1975) 5.

Recife: [a*]Pernambuco. [b]for Pernambuco. [c]Atlantic O; Capiberibe R; Beberibe R. [d]Universidade Federal de Pernambuco (1827) 18 – 2277; Universidade Catolica de Pernambuco (1912) 11 – 539; Universidade Federal Rural de Pernambuco (1912) 4 – 364. [e]Biblioteca da Universidade Federal de Pernambuco (1830) 418; Biblioteca Publica Estadual Presidente Castelo Branco (1852) 80; Biblioteca da Universidade Catolica de Pernambuco (1943) 65.

Ribeirao Preto: [a]Sao Paulo. [b]none. [c]Preto R. [d]none. [e]Biblioteca do Campus de Ribeirao Preto (?) 27; Biblioteca Moura Lacerda (1923) 25.

Rio Branco: [a*]Acre. [b]for Artigas. [c]Acre R; Branco R. [d]Universidade Federal do Acre (1971) 1 – 253. [e]Biblioteca da Universidade . . . (1971) 11; Biblioteca Publica Estadual do Acre (1948) 10.

Rio de Janeiro: [a]Rio de Janeiro. [b]off Sao Sebastiao do Rio de Janeiro. [c]Atlantic O; Guanabara B of Atlantic O; Rodrigo de Freitas Lagoon. [d]Universidade Federal do Rio de Janeiro (1808) 31 – 3573; Universidade Gama Filho (1972) 20 – 1423; Universidade do Estado do Rio de Janeiro (1950) 13 – 1754; Universidade Santa Ursula (1939) 12 – 875; Pontificia Universidade Catolica do Rio de Janeiro (1937) 9 – 813; Universidade do Rio de Janeiro (1980) 2 – 497. [e]Biblioteca Nacional (1810) 3500; Biblioteca da Universidade Federal do Rio de Janeiro (1833) 896; Biblioteca do Instituto Historico e Geografico Brasileiro (1838) 350; Biblioteca Estadual do Rio de Janeiro (1874) 181.

Rio Grande: [a]Rio Grande do Sul. [b]none. [c]Grande R; Patos Lagoon. [d]Universidade do Rio Grande (1956) 3 – 490. [e]Biblioteca Publica Rio Grandense (1846) 187; Biblioteca da Universidade . . . (1969) 40.

Salvador: [a*]Bahia. [b]for Bahia, Sao Salvador da Bahia. [c]Todos os Santos B of Atlantic O. [d]Universidade Federal da Bahia (1808) 15 – 1642; Universidade Catolica do Salvador (1961) 11 – 550. [e]Biblioteca da Universidade Federal da Bahia (1836) 351; Biblioteca Central do Estado da Bahia (1811) 300.

Santa Maria: [a]Rio Grande do Sul. [b]none. [c]nr Jacui R. [d]Universidade Federal de Santa Maria (1931) 10 – 1362. [e]Biblioteca da Universidade . . . (1954) 68; Biblioteca Publica Municipal Henrique Bastide (1938) 33.

Santarem: [a]Para. [b]none. [c]Amazon R; Tapajos R. [d]none. [e]Biblioteca Publica Municipal Paulo Rodrigues dos Santos (1927) 3.

Santo Andre: [a]Sao Paulo. [b]none. [c]Tamanduatei R. [d]none. [e]Biblioteca Publica Municipal (1954) 43.

Santos: [a]Sao Paulo: Sao Vicente I. [b]none. [c]Santos R. [d]none. [e]Biblioteca da Faculdade de Filosofia, Ciencias e Letras de Santos (1955) 26; Biblioteca Publica Municipal (1943) 11.

Sao Bernardo do Campo: [a]Sao Paulo. [b]none. [c]nr Grande R. [d]none. [e]Biblioteca Publica Municipal Monteiro Lobato (1958) 78.

Sao Carlos: [a]Sao Paulo. [b]none. [c](Correjo) Monjolinho Creek. [d]Universidade Federal de Sao Carlos (1960) 2 – 468. [e]Biblioteca da Universidade . . . (1969) 40; Biblioteca Publica Municipal Amadeu Amaral (1942) 14.

Sao Goncalo: [a]Rio de Janeiro. [b]none. [c](Riacho) Imbuacu Creek. [d]none. [e]Biblioteca Municipal Genebaldo Rosas (1967) 5.

Sao Joao de Meriti: [a]Rio de Janeiro. [b]for Mirity. [c]Sao Joao de Meriti R. [d]none. [e]Biblioteca Publica Municipal Guimaraes Rosa (1971) 7.

Sao Jose do Rio Preto: [a]Sao Paulo. [b]none. [c]Preto R. [d]none. [e]Biblioteca do Instituto de Biociencias, Letras e Ciencias Exatas (1957) 43; Biblioteca Publica Municipal (1943) 12.

Sao Jose dos Campos: [a]Sao Paulo. [b]none. [c]Paraiba do Sul R. [d]none. [e]Biblioteca do Centro Tecnico Aerospacial (1950) 73; Biblioteca Publica Cassiano Ricardo (1968) 27.

Sao Leopoldo: [a]Rio Grande do Sul. [b]none. [c]Sinos R. [d]Universidade do Vale do Rio dos Sinos (1951) 24 – 700. [e]Biblioteca da Universidade . . . (1860) 140; Biblioteca do Colegio Cristo Rei (1942) 65; Biblioteca Publica Municipal (1941) 15.

Sao Luis: [a*]Maranhao; Sao Luis I. [b]for Maranhao; Sao Luiz. [c]Sao Marcos B of Atlantic O. [d]Universidade

For an explanation of symbols and abbreviations, see pages 16–17.

(Continued)

TABLE 2b. (Continued)

Federal do Maranhao (1945) 8 – 904. [e]Biblioteca Publica do Estado do Maranhao (1831) 100; Biblioteca da Universidade . . . (1914) 80.

Sao Paulo: [a]*Sao Paulo. [b]none. [c]Tiete R. [d]Universidade de Sao Paulo (1827) 44 – 4461; Pontificia Universidade Catolica de Sao Paulo (1908) 16 – 1526; Universidade Mackenzie (1870) 14 – 899; Universiade Estadual Paulista Julio de Mesquita Filho (1923) 9 – 2324. [e]Biblioteca da Universidade de Sao Paulo (1827) 1730; Biblioteca Municipal Mario de Andrade (1926) 1267.

Sao Vicente: [a]Sao Paulo; Sao Vicente I. [b]none. [c]Atlantic O. [d]none. [e]Biblioteca do Instituto Historico e Geografico de Sao Vicente (1960) 22.

Sorocaba: [a]Sao Paulo. [b]none. [c]Sorocaba R. [d]none. [e]Biblioteca Municipal (1978) 15.

Taubate: [a]Sao Paulo. [b]none. [c]Paraiba do Sul R. [d]Universidade de Taubate (1961) 10 – 512. [e]Biblioteca da Universidade . . . (1940) 50; Biblioteca Publica Municipal (1973) 11.

Teresina: [a]*Piaui. [b]for Therezina. [c]Parnaiba R; Poti R. [d]Universidade Federal do Piaui (1958) 9 – 1045. [e]Biblioteca da Universidade . . . (1973) 81; Biblioteca Publica Desembargador Cromwell Carvalho do Estado do Piaui (1910) 25.

Uberaba: [a]Minas Gerais. [b]none. [c]nr Uberaba R. [d]none. [e]Biblioteca Publica Municipal Bernardo Guimaraes (1948) 6.

Uberlandia: [a]Minas Gerais. [b]for Uberabinha. [c]Bom Jardim R. [d]Universidade Federal de Uberlandia (1969) 7 – 821. [e]Biblioteca da Universidade . . . (1961) 80; Biblioteca Publica Municipal (1940) 9.

Vicosa: [a]Minas Gerais. [b]none. [c]Turvo R. [d]Universidade Federal de Vicosa (1920) 6 – 682. [e]Biblioteca da Universidade . . . (1927) 91.

Vila Velha: [a]Espirito Santo. [b]for Espirito Santo. [c]Vitoria B of Atlantic O. [d]none. [e]Biblioteca Padre Champagnat (1962) 6.

Vitoria: [a]*Espirito Santo; Vitoria I. [b]for Victoria. [c]Vitoria B of Atlantic O; Santa Maria da Vitoria R. [d]Universiade Federal do Espirito Santo (1954) 9 – 1390. [e]Biblioteca da Universidade . . . (1933) 76; Biblioteca Publica Estadual da Fundacao Cultural (1855) 42.

Vitoria da Conquista: [a]Bahia. [b]for Victoria da Conquista. [c]nr Pardo R. [d]none. [e]Biblioteca Municipal (1964) 4.

Volta Redonda: [a]Rio de Janeiro. [b]none. [c]Paraiba do Sul R. [d]none. [e]Biblioteca Publica Municipal Raul de Leoni (1969) 13.

Chile

Antofagasta: [b]none. [c]Moreno B of Pacific O. [d]Universidad de Antofagasta (1981) 4 – 500; Universidad del Norte (1956) 3 – 217. [e]Biblioteca de la Universidad del Norte (1958) 65; Biblioteca de la Universidad de Antofagasta (1966) 25.

Arica: [b]none. [c]Pacific O. [d]Universidad de Tarapaca (1981) 5 – 590. [e]Biblioteca de la Universidad . . . (1953) 70.

Concepcion: [b]none. [c]Bio-Bio R. [d]Universidad de Concepcion (1919) 10 – 1350; Universidad del Bio-Bio (1981) 4 – 239. [e]Biblioteca de la Universidad de Concepcion (1919) 320.

La Serena: [b]for Coquimbo. [c]Coquimbo B of Pacific O; Elqui R. [d]Universidad de La Serena (1981) 4 – 331. [e]Biblioteca de la Universidad . . . (1961) 38.

Punta Arenas: [b]for Magallanes. [c]Strait of Magellan. [d]Universidad de Magallanes (1961) 0.8 – 136. [e]Biblioteca de la Universidad . . . (1961?) 10.

*Santiago: [b]alt Santiago de Chile. [c]Mapocho R. [d]Universidad de Chile (1738) 19 – 4663; Pontificia Universidad Catolica de Chile (1888) 16 – 2396; Universidad de Santiago de Chile (1849) 12 – 1640. [e]Biblioteca de la Universidad de Chile (1843) 1400; Biblioteca Nacional (1813) 1200; Biblioteca del Congreso Nacional (1883) 800; Biblioteca de la Pontificia Universidad Catolica de Chile (1895) 432.

Talca: [b]none. [c]nr Maule R. [d]Universidad de Talca (1981) 4 – 301. [e]Biblioteca de la Universidad . . . (1981?) 12.

Talcahuano: [b]none. [c]Concepcion B of Pacific O. [d]none.

Temuco: [b]none. [c]Cautin R. [d]Universidad de La Frontera (1981) 5 – 435. [e]Biblioteca de la Universidad . . . (1959) 25.

Valdivia: [b]none. [c]Valdivia R; Calle-Calle R; Cruces R. [d]Universidad Australe de Chile (1955) 5 – 608. [e]Biblioteca de la Universidad . . . (1962) 103.

Valparaiso: [b]none. [c]Pacific O. [d]Universidad Catolica de Valparaiso (1928) 7 – 872; Universidad de Valparaiso (1972) 3 – 909; Universidad Tecnica Federico Santa Maria (1926) 2 – 353. [e]Biblioteca de la Universidad Catolica de Valparaiso (1928) 162; Biblioteca Severin (1873) 101.

Vina del Mar: [b]none. [c]Pacific O; Marga Marga R. [d]none. [e]Biblioteca de la Universidad de Valparaiso, Sede Vina del Mar (1941) 20.

TABLE 2b. (Continued)

Colombia

Armenia: ^{b}none. ^{c}nr Quindio R. ^{d}Universidad del Quindio (1960) 4 – 219. ^{e}Biblioteca de la Universidad . . . (1962) 12.

Barranquilla: ^{b}none. ^{c}Magdalena R. ^{d}Universidad del Atlantico (1941) 9 – 592; Universidad del Norte (1966) 4 – 434. ^{e}Biblioteca Publica Departamental (1923) 32; Biblioteca de la Universidad del Atlantico (1941) 22.

Bello: ^{b}none. ^{c}Porce R. ^{d}none. ^{e}Biblioteca del Marco Fidel Suarez (?) ?

*Bogota: ^{b}for Santa Fe de Bogota, Teusaquillo. ^{c}San Agustin R; San Francisco R. ^{d1}Universidad Nacional de Colombia (1563) 20 – 3476; Pontificia Universidad Javeriana (1623) 13 – 1881; Universidad Pedagogica Nacional (1936) 9 – 746; Universidad Santo Tomas (1580) 9 – 850; Universidad La Gran Colombia (1951) 8 – 650; Universidad Social Catolica de La Salle (1964) 8 – 300. ^{e}Biblioteca Nacional de Colombia (1777) 550; Biblioteca Luis Angel Arango del Banco de la Republica (1958) 250; Biblioteca de la Universidad Nacional de Colombia (1867) 180; Biblioteca de la Pontificia Universidad Javeriana (1623?) 150.

Bucaramanga: ^{b}none. ^{c}nr Oro R; nr Surata R. ^{d}Universidad Industrial de Santander (1940) 6 – 458; Universidad Autonoma de Bucaramanga (1955) 3 – 251. ^{e}Biblioteca de la Universidad Industrial de Santander (1947) 60; Biblioteca Departamental (1898) 28.

Buenaventura: ^{a}Cascajal I. ^{b}none. ^{c}Buenaventura B of Pacific O. ^{d}none.

Cali: ^{b}none. ^{c}Cali R. ^{d}Universidad del Valle (1945) 9 – 1029. ^{e}Biblioteca de la Universidad . . . (1946) 160; Biblioteca Municipal del Centenario (1910) 22.

Cartagena: ^{b}none. ^{c}B of Cartagena of Caribbean Sea. ^{d}Universidad de Cartagena (1774) 4 – 702. ^{e}Biblioteca de la Universidad . . . (1827) 50.

Cucuta: ^{b}off San Jose de Cucuta. ^{c}Pamplonita R. ^{d}Universidad Francisco de Paula Santander (1962) 4 – 180. ^{e}Biblioteca de la Universidad . . . (1962) 11.

Ibague: ^{b}off San Bonifacio de Ibague. ^{c}nr Chipalo R; nr Combeima R. ^{d}Universidad del Tolima (1945) 4 – 342. ^{e}Biblioteca de la Universidad . . . (1945) 18.

Manizales: ^{b}none. ^{c}nr Chinchina R. ^{d}Universidad de Caldas (1937) 4 – 402. ^{e}Biblioteca de la Universidad . . . (1943) 140; Biblioteca Departamental de Caldas (1954) 15.

Medellin: ^{b}none. ^{c}Porce R. ^{d}Universidad de Antioquia (1801) 19 – 1500; Universidad de Medellin (1950) 5 – 449; Universidad Pontificia Bolivariana (1936) 5 – 658; Universidad Autonoma Latinoamericana (1966) 2 – 260. ^{e}Biblioteca de la Universidad de Antioquia (1935) 200; Biblioteca Publica Piloto de Medellin (1954) 58.

Monteria: ^{b}none. ^{c}Sinu R. ^{d}Universidad de Cordoba (1964) 3 – 280. ^{e}Biblioteca de la Universidad . . . (1965) 12.

Neiva: ^{b}none. ^{c}Magdalena R. ^{d}Universidad Surcolombiana (1968) 2 – 280. ^{e}Biblioteca de la Universidad . . . (1968?) 11.

Palmira: ^{b}none. ^{c}Amaime R. ^{d}none. ^{e}Biblioteca del Centro Internacional de Agricultura Tropical (?) 30.

Pasto: ^{b}none. ^{c}Pasto R. ^{d}Universidad de Narino (1827) 4 – 700. ^{e}Biblioteca de la Universidad . . . (1904) 30.

Pereira: ^{b}none. ^{c}Otun R. ^{d}Universidad Tecnologica de Pereira (1958) 3 – 414. ^{e}Biblioteca de la Universidad . . . (1962) 16.

Popayan: ^{b}none. ^{c}Cauca R. ^{d}Universidad del Cauca (1827) 3 – 455. ^{e}Biblioteca de la Universidad . . . (1827) 55; Biblioteca Guillermo Valencia (?) 20.

Santa Marta: ^{b}none. ^{c}Caribbean Sea. ^{d}none. ^{e}Biblioteca de la Universidad Tecnologica de Magdalena (1966) 12.

Tunja: ^{b}for Hunza. ^{c}Chulo R. ^{d}Universidad Pedagogica y Technologica de Colombia (1872) 6 – 600. ^{e}Biblioteca de la Universidad . . . (1932) 68.

Valledupar: ^{b}none. ^{c}Guatapuri R. ^{d}none. ^{e}Biblioteca de la Universidad Popular del Cesar (1972?) 10.

Villavicencio: ^{b}none. ^{c}Guatiquia R. ^{d}none.

Ecuador

Ambato: ^{b}none. ^{c}Ambato R. ^{d}Universidad Tecnica de Ambato (1959) 10 – 385. ^{e}Biblioteca de la Universidad . . . (1959?) 35.

Cuenca: ^{b}for Tomebamba. ^{c}Machangara R. ^{d}Universidad de Cuenca (1868) 20 – 592; Universidad Catolica de Cuenca (1970) 3 – 346. ^{e}Biblioteca de la Universidad de Cuenca (1868) 120; Biblioteca Hispano-Americana (1934) 55; Biblioteca Publica Municipal (1927) 50.

1Universities with 8,000 or more students.

For an explanation of symbols and abbreviations, see pages 16–17.

(Continued)

TABLE 2b. (Continued)

Guayaquil: [b]for Santiago de Guayaquil. [c]Guayas R. [d]Universidad de Guayaquil (1867) 60 – 3080; Universidad Laica Vicente Rocafuerte de Guayaquil (1847) 8 – 256; Universidad Catolica de Santiago de Guayaquil (1962) 5 – 508. [e]Biblioteca Municipal Pedro Carbo (1862) 120; Biblioteca de la Universidad de Guayaquil (1901) 50.

Loja: [b]none. [c]none. [d]Universidad Nacional de Loja (1869) 8 – 245; Universidad Tecnica Particular de Loja (1971) 8 – 266. [e]Biblioteca de la Universidad Nacional de Loja (1869) 15.

Machala: [b]none. [c]nr G of Guayaquil of Pacific O. [d]Universidad Tecnica de Machala (1969) 5 – 230. [e]Biblioteca de la Universidad . . . (1969) 3.

Portoviejo: [b]none. [c]Portoviejo R. [d]Universidad Tecnica de Manabi (1952) 10 – 380. [e]Biblioteca de la Universidad . . . (1952) 6.

*Quito: [b]none. [c]Machangara R. [d]Universidad Central del Ecuador (1586) 60 – 2500; Pontificia Universidad Catolica del Ecuador (1946) 15 – 1050. [e]Biblioteca de la Universidad . . . (1586) 175; Biblioteca Ecuatoriana Aurelio Espinosa Polit (1928) 120; Biblioteca de la . . . Universidad (1946) 60; Biblioteca Nacional (1792) 60.

French Guiana

*Cayenne: [a]Cayenne I. [b]none. [c]Atlantic O; Cayenne R. [d]Universite Antilles-Guyane, Cayenne campus (?) 0.2 – ? [e]Bibliotheque Franconie (1904) 18.

Guyana

*Georgetown: [b]none. [c]Atlantic O; Demerara R. [d]University of Guyana (1963) 2 – 232. [e]National Library (1909) 195; University . . . Library (1963) 123; Public Free Library (1909) 100.

Paraguay

*Asuncion: [b]for Nuestra Senora de La Asuncion. [c]Paraguay R. [d]Universidad Catolica Nuestra Senora de La Asuncion (1960) 9 – 659; Universidad Nacional de Asuncion (1883) 8 – 500. [e]Biblioteca y Archivo Nacionales (1869) 44; Biblioteca de la Universidad Catolica Nuestra Senora de La Asuncion (1960) 25; Biblioteca de la Universidad Nacional de Asuncion (1890?)?

Peru

Arequipa: [b]none. [c]Chili R. [d]Universidad Nacional de San Agustin (1821) 13 – 764; Universidad Catolica de Santa Maria (1961) 6 – 264. [e]Biblioteca de la Universidad Nacional de San Agustin (1828) 127; Biblioteca Publica Municipal (1821) 28.

Callao: [b]none. [c]Pacific O. [d]Universidad Nacional Tecnica del Callao (1966) 7 – 252. [e]Biblioteca del Instituto del Mar del Peru (1960) 65; Biblioteca Publica Municipal Piloto (1936) 48.

Chiclayo: [b]none. [c]Reque R. [d]Universidad Nacional Pedro Ruiz Gallo (at Lambayeque, nr Chiclayo) (1962) 5 – 261. [e]Biblioteca de la Universidad . . . (at Lambayeque) (1970) 16; Biblioteca Municipal (bef 1942) ?

Chimbote: [b]none. [c]Chimbote B of Pacific O. [d]none.

Cuzco: [b]for Cusco. [c]Chunchulnayu R; Huatanay R; Tullamayo R. [d]Universidad Nacional de San Antonio Abad (1598) 15 – 425. [e]Biblioteca de la Universidad . . . (1696) 52.

Huancayo: [b]none. [c]Mantaro R. [d]Universidad Nacional del Centro del Peru (1959) 8 – 346. [e]Biblioteca de la Universidad . . . (1962) 4.

Ica: [b]none. [c]Ica R. [d]Universidad Nacional San Luis Gonzaga (1955) 6 – 459. [e]Biblioteca del Museo Cabrera (1966) 100.

Iquitos: [b]none. [c]Amazon R. [d]Universidad Nacional de la Amazonia Peruana (1961) 4 – 195. [e]Biblioteca de la Universidad . . . (1962) ?

*Lima: [b]for Rimac. [c]Pacific O; Rimac R. [d1]Universidad Nacional Mayor de San Marcos (1551) 34 – 3150; Universidad Nacional Federico Villarreal (1963) 25 – 2000; Universidad Ricardo Palma (1969) 12 – 550; Universidad San Martin de Porres (1962) 10 – 256; Pontificia Universidad Catolica del Peru (1917) 9 – 873; Universidad de Lima (1962) 8 – 550; Universidad Inca Garcilaso de La Vega (1964) 7 – 240. [e]Biblioteca Nacional (1821) 707; Biblioteca de la Universidad Nacional Mayor de San Marcos (1551) 500; Biblioteca de la Pontificia Universidad Catolica del Peru (1917) 250.

Piura: [b]none. [c]Piura R. [d]Universidad Nacional Tecnica de Piura (1961) 5 – 250. [e]Biblioteca de la Universidad . . . (1962) 18.

Trujillo: [b]none. [c]Moche R. [d]Universidad Nacional de Trujillo (1824) 11 – 635. [e]Biblioteca de la Universidad . . . (1837) 24.

TABLE 2b. (Continued)

Suriname

*Paramaribo: [b]none. [c]Suriname R. [d]Universiteit van Suriname (1882) 0.5 – 34. [e]Stichting Cultureel Centrum Suriname Bibliotheek (1947) 225.

Uruguay

*Montevideo: [b]none. [c]Plata R. [d]Universidad de la Republica (1833) 35 – 6886. [e]Biblioteca Nacional del Uruguay (1816) 900; Biblioteca de la Universidad . . . (1849) 800; Biblioteca del Palacio Legislativo (1929) 322.

Venezuela

Barcelona: [b]none. [c]Neveri R. [d]none.

Barquisimeto: [b]none. [c]Cojedes R. [d]Universidad Centro-Occidental Lisandro Alvaredo (1963) 13 – 904. [e]Biblioteca de la Universidad . . . (1963) 26; Biblioteca Publica Pio Tamayo (1911) 22.

Baruta: [b]none. [c](Quebrada) Baruta Brook. [d]none.

Cabimas: [d]none. [c]Maracaibo L. [d]none.

*Caracas: [b]for Santiago de Leon de Caracas. [c]Guaire R. [d1]Universidad Central de Venezuela (1696) 52 – 6987; Universidad Catolica Andres Bello (1953) 10 – 600; Universidad Simon Bolivar (1967) 6 – 801. [e]Biblioteca Nacional (1833) 800; Biblioteca de la Universidad Central de Venezuela (1850) 560; Biblioteca Marcel Roche del Instituto Venezolano de Investigaciones Cientificas (1955) 400.

Ciudad Bolivar: [b]for Angostura. [c]Orinoco R. [d]none.

Ciudad Guayana: [b]alt Guayana. San Felix de Guayana; for Santo Tome de Guayana. [c]Orinoco R; Caroni R. [d]none. [e]Biblioteca Publica Caroni (1963) 3.

Cumana: [b]for Nueva Toledo. [c]Manzanares R. [d]Universidad de Oriente (1958) 21 – 1256. [e]Biblioteca de la Universidad . . . (1960) 60.

Maracaibo: [b]none. [c]Maracaibo L. [d]Universidad del Zulia (1891) 64 – 3362; Universidad Rafael Urdaneta (1973) 3 – 326. [e]Biblioteca de la Universidad del Zulia (1946) 170; Biblioteca Baralt (1962) 50.

Maracay: [b]none. [c]nr Valencia L. [d]none. [e]Biblioteca del Centro Nacional de Investigaciones Agropecuarias (1937) 200.

Maturin: [b]none. [c]Guarapiche R. [d]none.

Merida: [b]none. [c]Chama R. [d]Universidad de los Andes (1785) 35 – 2379. [e]Biblioteca de la Universidad . . . (1889) 227.

Petare: [b]none. [c]Guaire R. [d]none.

San Cristobal: [b]none. [c]Torbes R. [d]Universidad Nacional Experimental del Tachira (1974) 3 – 298. [e]Biblioteca de la Universidad . . . (1974) 72.

Valencia: [b]none. [c]Cabriales R. [d]Universidad de Carabobo (1833) 41 – 2429; Universidad Tecnologica del Centro (1981) ? – ? [e]Biblioteca de la Universidad de Carabobo (1852) 160; Biblioteca Publica del Estado (1876) 4.

[1]Universities with 5,000 or more students.

For an explanation of symbols and abbreviations, see pages 16–17.

3

COUNTRY COMPARISONS

3a. Largest Countries in Area and in Population, 1986

Contents

Rank in area.
Conventional name of country.
Surface area, including inland waters, in square miles and square kilometers.
Percentage of world land area represented by the given area.
Rank in population.
Conventional name of country.
Estimated population, in thousands, on 1 July 1986.
Percentage of estimated world population represented by the given population.

Coverage

65 largest countries in area and in population.

Entries

130.

TABLE 3a. LARGEST COUNTRIES IN AREA AND IN POPULATION, 1986

		Surface Area		% of World Land Area			Population (thousands)	% of World Population
Rank	Country	mi2	km2		Rank	Country		
1.	USSR	8,649,539	22,402,200	14.9	1.	China	1,052,838	21.5
2.	Canada	3,831,033	9,922,330	6.6	2.	India	766,135	15.6
3.	China	3,691,508	9,560,961	6.4	3.	USSR	280,144	5.7
4.	USA	3,679,395	9,529,589	6.4	4.	USA	241,596	4.9
5.	Brazil	3,286,488	8,511,965	5.7	5.	Indonesia	166,940	3.4
6.	Australia	2,966,153	7,682,300	5.1	6.	Brazil	138,493	2.8
7.	India	1,237,071	3,204,000	2.1	7.	Japan	121,492	2.5
8.	Argentina	1,068,301	2,766,889	1.8	8.	Pakistan	101,653	2.1
9.	Sudan	967,500	2,505,813	1.7	9.	Bangladesh	100,616	2.1
10.	Algeria	919,595	2,381,741	1.6	10.	Nigeria	98,517	2.0
11.	Zaire	905,568	2,345,409	1.6	11.	Mexico	79,563	1.6
12.	Greenland	840,004	2,175,600	1.5	12.	West Germany	61,048	1.2
13.	Saudi Arabia	830,000	2,149,690	1.4	13.	Vietnam	60,919	1.2
14.	Mexico	756,066	1,958,201	1.3	14.	Italy	57,221	1.2
15.	Indonesia	741,101	1,919,443	1.3	15.	UK	56,763	1.2
16.	Libya	679,362	1,759,540	1.2	16.	Philippines	56,004	1.1
17.	Iran	636,296	1,648,000	1.1	17.	France	55,392	1.1
18.	Mongolia	604,250	1,565,000	1.0	18.	Thailand	52,654	1.1
19.	Peru	496,225	1,285,216	0.86	19.	Turkey	51,940	1.1
20.	Chad	495,755	1,284,000	0.86	20.	Egypt	49,609	1.0
21.	Niger	489,191	1,267,000	0.85	21.	Iran	45,914	0.94
22.	Angola	481,354	1,246,700	0.83	22.	Ethiopia	44,927	0.92
23.	Mali	478,767	1,240,000	0.83	23.	South Korea	41,569	0.85
24.	Ethiopia	471,778	1,221,900	0.82	24.	Spain	38,668	0.79
25.	South Africa	471,445	1,221,037	0.81	25.	Burma	38,438	0.78
26.	Colombia	440,831	1,141,748	0.76	26.	Poland	37,456	0.76
27.	Bolivia	424,165	1,098,581	0.73	27.	Argentina	31,030	0.63
28.	Mauritania	397,956	1,030,700	0.69	28.	Zaire	30,850	0.63
29.	Egypt	386,662	1,001,449	0.67	29.	South Africa	29,000	0.59

For an explanation of symbols and abbreviations, see pages 16–17.

(Continued)

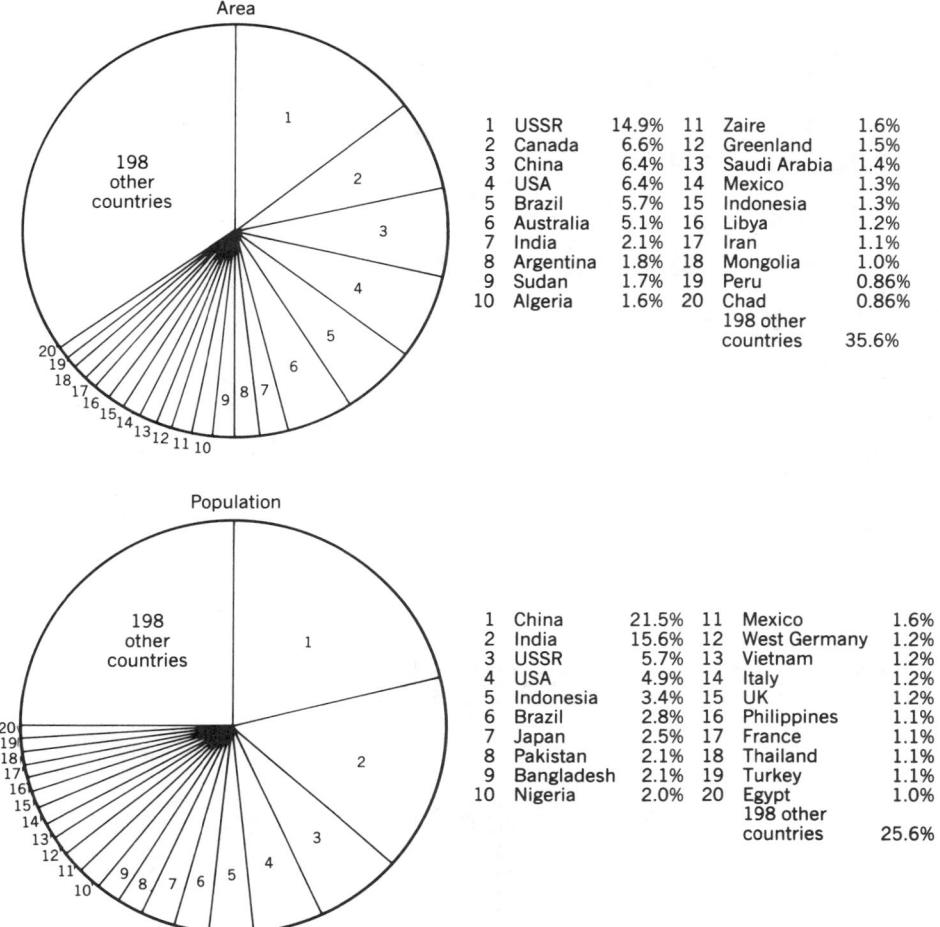

	Area				
1	USSR	14.9%	11	Zaire	1.6%
2	Canada	6.6%	12	Greenland	1.5%
3	China	6.4%	13	Saudi Arabia	1.4%
4	USA	6.4%	14	Mexico	1.3%
5	Brazil	5.7%	15	Indonesia	1.3%
6	Australia	5.1%	16	Libya	1.2%
7	India	2.1%	17	Iran	1.1%
8	Argentina	1.8%	18	Mongolia	1.0%
9	Sudan	1.7%	19	Peru	0.86%
10	Algeria	1.6%	20	Chad	0.86%
				198 other countries	35.6%

	Population				
1	China	21.5%	11	Mexico	1.6%
2	India	15.6%	12	West Germany	1.2%
3	USSR	5.7%	13	Vietnam	1.2%
4	USA	4.9%	14	Italy	1.2%
5	Indonesia	3.4%	15	UK	1.2%
6	Brazil	2.8%	16	Philippines	1.1%
7	Japan	2.5%	17	France	1.1%
8	Pakistan	2.1%	18	Thailand	1.1%
9	Bangladesh	2.1%	19	Turkey	1.1%
10	Nigeria	2.0%	20	Egypt	1.0%
				198 other countries	25.6%

Figure 16. *Area and population of countries as percentage of world land area and population.*

TABLE 3a. (Continued)

Rank	Country	Surface Area mi²	Surface Area km²	% of World Land Area	Rank	Country	Population (thousands)	% of World Population
30.	Tanzania	364,927	945,158	0.63	30.	Colombia	28,365	0.58
31.	Nigeria	356,669	923,769	0.62	31.	Canada	25,354	0.52
32.	Venezuela	352,144	912,050	0.61	32.	Yugoslavia	23,214	0.47
33.	Pakistan	342,762	887,750	0.59	33.	Romania	23,174	0.47
34.	Namibia	318,261	824,292	0.55	34.	Morocco	22,476	0.46
35.	Mozambique	309,496	801,590	0.53	35.	Tanzania	22,462	0.46
36.	Turkey	300,948	779,452	0.52	36.	Algeria	22,421	0.46
37.	Chile	292,258	756,945	0.50	37.	Sudan	22,178	0.45
38.	Zambia	290,586	752,614	0.50	38.	Kenya	21,163	0.43
39.	Burma	261,218	676,552	0.45	39.	North Korea	20,883	0.43
40.	Afghanistan	251,825	652,225	0.44	40.	Peru	20,207	0.41
41.	Somalia	246,201	637,657	0.43	41.	Taiwan	19,365	0.40
42.	Central African Republic	240,535	622,984	0.42	42.	Afghanistan	18,614	0.38
43.	Botswana	231,805	600,372	0.40	43.	Venezuela	17,791	0.36
44.	Madagascar	226,658	587,041	0.39	44.	Nepal	17,131	0.35
45.	Kenya	224,961	582,646	0.39	45.	East Germany	16,624	0.34
46.	France	210,026	543,965	0.36	46.	Iraq	16,450	0.34
47.	Thailand	198,457	514,000	0.34	47.	Sri Lanka	16,117	0.33
48.	Spain	194,897	504,782	0.34	48.	Malaysia	16,109	0.33
49.	Cameroon	183,569	475,442	0.32	49.	Uganda	16,018	0.33
50.	Papua New Guinea	178,260	461,691	0.31	50.	Australia	15,974	0.33
51.	Sweden	173,732	449,964	0.30	51.	Czechoslovakia	15,534	0.32
52.	Morocco	172,414	446,550	0.30	52.	Netherlands	14,563	0.30
53.	Iraq	167,925	434,924	0.29	53.	Mozambique	14,174	0.29
54.	Paraguay	157,048	406,752	0.27	54.	Ghana	12,840	0.26
55.	Zimbabwe	150,804	390,580	0.26	55.	Chile	12,327	0.25
56.	Japan	145,834	377,708	0.25	56.	Saudi Arabia	12,006	0.25

57.	Congo	132,047	0.23	57.	Hungary	10,627	0.22
58.	Finland	130,559	0.23	58.	Syria	10,612	0.22
59.	South Yemen	128,560	0.22	59.	Cameroon	10,446	0.21
60.	Malaysia	127,317	0.22	60.	Madagascar	10,303	0.21
61.	Vietnam	127,242	0.22	61.	Portugal	10,250	0.21
62.	Norway	125,050	0.22	62.	Cuba	10,246	0.21
63.	Ivory Coast	124,504	0.22	63.	Ivory Coast	10,165	0.21
64.	Poland	120,725	0.21	64.	Greece	9,966	0.20
65.	Italy	116,324	0.20	65.	Belgium	9,859	0.20

For an explanation of symbols and abbreviations, see pages 16–17.

3b. Countries with Highest and Lowest Densities of Population, 1986

Contents

High-density rank.

Conventional name of country.

Estimated density of population on 1 July 1986 (number of inhabitants per square mile and per square kilometer).

Low-density rank.

Conventional name of country.

Estimated density of population on 1 July 1986 (number of inhabitants per square mile and per square kilometer).

Coverage

50 most densely populated countries and 50 least densely populated countries.

Entries

100.

TABLE 3b. COUNTRIES WITH HIGHEST AND LOWEST DENSITIES OF POPULATION, 1986

		Highest Population Density				Lowest Population Density	
Rank	Country	Per mi²	Per km²	Rank	Country	Per mi²	Per km²
1.	Macao	70,234	27,097	1.	Greenland	0.064	0.025
2.	Monaco	46,957	18,121	2.	French Southern and	0.068	0.026
3.	Hong Kong	13,097	5,057		Antarctic Lands		
4.	Gibraltar	12,609	4,915	3.	Svalbard	0.165	0.064
5.	Singapore	10,820	4,184	4.	Falkland Islands	0.306	0.118
6.	Vatican City	4,118	1,591	5.	Western Sahara	1.75	0.677
7.	Gaza Strip	3,767	1,455	6.	French Guiana	2.39	0.923
8.	Malta	3,156	1,218	7.	Mongolia	3.21	1.24
9.	Bermuda	2,816	1,088	8.	Botswana	4.87	1.88
10.	Channel Islands	1,840	708	9.	Mauritania	4.89	1.89
11.	Bangladesh	1,810	699	10.	Namibia	5.01	1.93
12.	Bahrain	1,717	662	11.	Australia	5.39	2.08
13.	Maldives	1,643	634	12.	Libya	5.60	2.16
14.	Barbados	1,524	587	13.	Iceland	6.11	2.36
15.	Taiwan	1,393	538	14.	Suriname	6.31	2.44
16.	Mauritius	1,303	503	15.	Canada	6.62	2.56
17.	South Korea	1,086	419	16.	Guyana	9.60	3.71
18.	Nauru	976	377	17.	Chad	10.4	4.00
19.	Aruba	940	363	18.	Central African Republic	11.4	4.40
20.	Puerto Rico	939	362	19.	Gabon	11.9	4.58
21.	San Marino	936	361	20.	Niger	13.7	5.29
22.	Netherlands	903	349	21.	Congo	14.4	5.56
23.	Tuvalu	886	342	22.	Saudi Arabia	14.5	5.58
24.	Virgina Islands (USA)	864	333	23.	Bolivia	15.4	5.96
				24.	Mali	17.6	6.80
25.	Belgium	837	323	25.	South Yemen	18.4	7.10
26.	Japan	833	322	26.	Angola	18.7	7.20

For an explanation of symbols and abbreviations, see pages 16–17. (Continued)

Figure 17. *Motijheel commercial area of Dhaka, capital of Bangladesh, the most densely populated country with an area of at least 1,000 square miles (2,590 square kilometers). (Credit: Embassy of Bangladesh, Washington.)*

TABLE 3b. (Continued)

Rank	Country	Highest Population Density		Rank	Country	Lowest Population Density	
		Per mi²	Per km²			Per mi²	Per km²
27.	Martinique	772	298	27.	Papua New Guinea	19.1	7.36
28.	Johnston Island	750	288	28.	Belize	19.3	7.45
29.	Saint Vincent and the Grenadines	700	271	29.	Somalia	19.6	7.56
30.	Grenada	699	270	30.	New Caledonia	21.2	8.19
31.	Lebanon	674	260	31.	Sudan	22.9	8.85
32.	Netherlands Antilles	647	250	32.	Zambia	23.7	9.16
33.	Sri Lanka	636	246	33.	Paraguay	24.2	9.36
34.	West Germany	636	245	34.	Algeria	24.4	9.41
35.	India	619	239	35.	Vanuatu	24.6	9.48
36.	Rwanda	617	238	36.	Niue	25.0	9.65
37.	Guam	612	237	37.	Oman	25.2	9.72
38.	Trinidad and Tobago	608	235	38.	Solomon Islands	25.2	9.74
39.	El Salvador	605	233	39.	Argentina	29.0	11.2
40.	UK	602	233	40.	New Zealand	31.9	12.3
41.	Saint Lucia	597	231	41.	USSR	32.4	12.5
42.	Reunion	578	223	42.	Norway	33.3	12.9
43.	Comoros	559	216	43.	Zaire	34.1	13.2
44.	Jamaica	555	214	44.	Pitcairn Island	36.6	14.1
45.	Israel	517	200	45.	Equatorial Guinea	37.0	14.3
46.	Haiti	500	193	46.	Finland	37.7	14.5
47.	Italy	492	190	47.	Laos	40.5	15.6
48.	Guadeloupe	485	187	48.	Peru	40.7	15.7
49.	Philippines	483	187	49.	Brazil	42.1	16.3
50.	American Samoa	481	186	50.	Chile	42.2	16.3

For an explanation of symbols and abbreviations, see pages 16–17.

3c. Countries with Highest and Lowest Rates of Urbanization

Contents

High urbanization-rate rank.

Conventional name of country.

Year of urbanization data.

Percentage of population residing in urban areas.[1]

Low urbanization-rate rank.

Conventional name of country.

Year of urbanization data.

Percentage of population residing in urban areas.[1]

Coverage

55 countries with highest urbanization rates and 51 countries with lowest urbanization rates.

Entries

106.

[1]See note 1 on p 27.

TABLE 3c. COUNTRIES WITH HIGHEST AND LOWEST RATES OF URBANIZATION

	Highest				Lowest		
Rank	Country	Year	% Urban	Rank	Country	Year	% Urban
1.	Bermuda	1980	100	1.	Anguilla		0
1.	Cayman Islands	1979	100	1.	British Indian Ocean		0
1.	Gibraltar	1981	100		Territory		
1.	Liechtenstein	1981	100	1.	Cocos Islands		0
1.	Monaco	1982	100	1.	French Southern and		0
1.	Nauru	1983	100		Antarctic Lands		
1.	Pitcairn Island	1983	100	1.	Johnston Island		0
1.	Singapore	1980	100	1.	Midway Islands		0
1.	Vatican City	1978	100	1.	Norfolk Island		0
10.	Reunion	1982	97.7	1.	Svalbard		0
11.	Macao	1981	96.3	1.	Tokelau		0
12.	Belgium	1976	94.6	1.	Wake Island		0
13.	Taiwan	1981	94.1	11.	Bhutan	1985	4.5
14.	West Germany	1983	94.0	11.	Lesotho	1982	4.5
15.	Kuwait	1985	93.7	13.	Burundi	1985	5.0
16.	Hong Kong	1981	91.7	14.	Rwanda	1981	5.2
17.	San Marino	1986	90.4	15.	Nepal	1981	6.4
18.	Guadeloupe	1982	89.9	16.	Grenada	1983	7.3
19.	Israel	1983	89.6	16.	Oman	1982	7.3
19.	Saint-Pierre and	1982	89.6	18.	Burkina Faso	1980	7.7
	Miquelon			19.	Solomon Islands	1976	9.1
21.	Iceland	1984	89.2	20.	North Yemen	1982	10.2
22.	Netherlands	1984	88.5	21.	Malawi	1984	11.7
23.	Qatar	1982	86.1	22.	Namibia	1970	12.0
24.	Australia	1981	85.7	23.	Wallis and Futuna	1976	12.9
25.	Uruguay	1984	84.5		Islands		
26.	Denmark	1984	84.2	24.	Papua New Guinea	1980	13.1
27.	Lebanon	1985	83.7	25.	Mozambique	1980	13.2
27.	New Zealand	1985	83.7	26.	Kampuchea	1982	13.9
29.	Argentina	1985	83.6	27.	Dominica	1981	14.1
30.	Malta	1982	83.4	28.	Ethiopia	1982	14.4
31.	Chile	1984	83.2	28.	Uganda	1985	14.4
32.	Sweden	1980	83.1	30.	Bangladesh	1981	15.2
33.	Luxembourg	1985	81.8	30.	Togo	1980	15.2
33.	Martinique	1982	81.8	32.	Laos	1985	15.9
35.	United Arab Emirates	1980	80.9	33.	Guinea	1980	16.2
36.	Bahrain	1981	80.7	33.	Niger	1985	16.2
36.	French Guiana	1982	80.7	35.	Afghanistan	1983	16.4
38.	Greenland	1986	78.8	36.	American Samoa	1980	17.5
39.	Spain	1985	77.4	37.	Madagascar	1980	17.6
40.	East Germany	1985	76.6	37.	Tanzania	1985	17.6
41.	Venezuela	1981	76.4	39.	Kenya	1983	17.7
42.	Japan	1980	76.2	39.	Mali	1983	17.7
43.	Canada	1985	75.9	41.	Vanuatu	1979	17.8
44.	UK	1981	75.1	42.	Gambia	1980	18.2
45.	Gaza Strip	1967	74.4	43.	Saint Vincent and the	1980	19.4
46.	USA	1980	73.7		Grenadines		
				44.	Thailand	1985	19.8
				44.	Vietnam	1982	19.8
				46.	Botswana	1985	20.0

For an explanation of symbols and abbreviations, see pages 16–17.

(Continued)

TABLE 3c. (Continued)

	Highest				Lowest		
Rank	Country	Year	% Urban	Rank	Country	Year	% Urban
47.	French Polynesia	1985	73.4	46.	Somalia	1980	20.0
48.	France	1982	73.3	48.	Sudan	1983	20.2
49.	Italy	1985	71.7	49.	Tonga	1976	20.3
50.	Isle of Man	1981	71.5	50.	China	1982	20.6
51.	Brazil	1985	70.8	50.	Virgin Islands (UK)	1980	20.6
51.	Cuba	1984	70.8				
53.	Norway	1980	70.7				
54.	Jamaica	1980	69.3				
55.	Peru	1984	68.9				

For an explanation of symbols and abbreviations, see pages 16–17.

3d. Countries with Highest and Lowest Birth Rates

Contents

High birth-rate rank.

Conventional name of country.

Period of record for birth rate.

Average annual number of live births per thousand inhabitants.

Low birth-rate rank.

Conventional name of country.

Period of record for birth rate.

Average annual number of live births per thousand inhabitants.

Coverage

25 countries with highest birth rates and 25 countries with lowest birth rates.

Entries

50.

TABLE 3d. COUNTRIES WITH HIGHEST AND LOWEST BIRTH RATES

	Highest		Birth Rate		Lowest		Birth Rate
Rank	Country	Period		Rank	Country	Period	
1.	Kenya	1980–85	55.1e	1.	West Germany	1981–86	9.9
2.	Malawi	1980–85	53.2e	2.	Christmas Island, (Australia)	1980–83, 85	10.0
3.	Rwanda	1980–85	51.9e	3.	Denmark	1981–86	10.3
4.	Niger	1980–85	51.0e	4.	San Marino	1981–85	10.4
5.	Benin	1980–85	50.7e	5.	Italy	1981–85	10.6
6.	Mali	1980–85	50.6e	5.	Norfolk Island	1981,	10.6
7.	Nigeria	1980–85	50.4e				

TABLE 3d. (Continued)

Rank	Highest Country	Period	Birth Rate	Rank	Lowest Country	Period	Birth Rate
7.	Tanzania	1980–85	50.4e			83–84	
9.	Uganda	1980–85	50.3e	7.	Isle of Man	1981–86	11.0
10.	Mauritania	1980–85	50.1e	8.	Sweden	1981–86	11.4
11.	Botswana	1980–85	49.9e	9.	Channel Islands	1981–86	11.6
12.	Ethiopia	1980–85	49.7e	9.	Switzerland	1981–86	11.6
13.	Djibouti	1980–85	49.2e	11.	Luxembourg	1981–86	11.7
14.	Afghanistan	1980–85	48.9e	12.	Austria	1981–86	11.9
15.	Liberia	1980–85	48.7e	13.	Belgium	1981–86	12.0
16.	North Yemen	1980–85	48.6e	14.	Netherlands	1981–86	12.2
17.	Gambia	1980–85	48.4e	15.	Hungary	1981–86	12.3
18.	Zambia	1980–85	48.1e	15.	Norway	1981–86	12.3
19.	Somalia	1980–85	47.9e	17.	Japan	1981–86	12.4
20.	Burkina Faso	1980–85	47.8e	18.	Greece	1981–86	13.0
21.	Sierra Leone	1980–85	47.4e	18.	UK	1981–86	13.0
22.	Angola	1980–85	47.3e	20.	Finland	1981–86	13.2
22.	Gaza Strip	1980–81, 83–84	47.3	21.	Spain	1980–84	13.4
				22.	Bulgaria	1981–86	13.6
22.	Swaziland	1980–85	47.3e	23.	Andorra	1980–81, 83–84, 86	13.7
25.	Burundi	1980–85	47.2e				
				24.	East Germany	1981–86	13.9
				25.	France	1981–86	14.2

Note. Among countries with lowest birth rates, Canada ranks 31st, Australia 33rd, and USA 35th. See Table 1c.

For an explanation of symbols and abbreviations, see pages 16–17.

3e. Countries with Highest and Lowest Death Rates

Contents

High death-rate rank.

Conventional name of country.

Period of record for death rate.

Average annual number of deaths per thousand inhabitants.

Low death-rate rank.

Conventional name of country.

Period of record for death rate.

Average annual number of deaths per thousand inhabitants.

Coverage

25 countries with highest death rates and 26 countries with lowest death rates.

Entries

51.

TABLE 3e. COUNTRIES WITH HIGHEST AND LOWEST DEATH RATES

	Highest		Death Rate		Lowest		Death Rate
Rank	Country	Period		Rank	Country	Period	
1.	Sierra Leone	1980–85	29.7e	1.	Christmas Island	1980–83,	0.9
2.	Gaza Strip	1980–81,	29.1		(Australia)	85	
		83–84					
3.	Gambia	1980–85	29.0e	2.	Cocos Islands	1981, 86	2.5
4.	Afghanistan	1980–85	27.3e	3.	Kuwait	1981–85	3.0
5.	Guinea	1980–85	23.5e	4.	Tonga	1981–85	3.2
6.	Somalia	1980–85	23.3e	5.	Turks and Caicos	1980,	3.5
7.	Ethiopia	1980–85	23.2e		Islands	82–83	
8.	Niger	1980–85	22.9e	6.	Brunei	1981–85	3.6
9.	Mali	1980–85	22.5e	6.	Guam	1980–83,	3.6
10.	Angola	1980–85	22.2e			85	
11.	Central African	1980–85	21.8e	8.	Andorra	1980–81,	4.1
	Republic					83–84,	
12.	Guinea–Bissau	1980–85	21.7e			86	
13.	Malawi	1980–85	21.5e	8.	Costa Rica	1981–85	4.1
14.	Chad	1980–85	21.4e	10.	Macao	1981–86	4.3
15.	Benin	1980–85	21.2e	10.	Pacific Islands (USA)	1980–83	4.3
16.	Equatorial	1980–85	21.0e	10.	United Arab Emirates	1980–85	4.3e
	Guinea			13.	American Samoa	1980,	4.4
17.	Mauritania	1980–85	20.9e			82–85	
17.	Senegal	1980–85	20.9e	13.	Belize	1981–82,	4.4
19.	Burkina Faso	1980–85	20.1e			84–86	
20.	Bhutan	1980–85	19.8e	15.	Bahrain	1980–85	4.5e
21.	Kampuchea	1980–85	19.7e	15.	Western Sahara	1980–85	4.5e
21.	Mozambique	1980–85	19.7e	17.	Qatar	1980–85	4.6e
23.	Burundi	1980–85	19.0e	18.	Aruba	1980–83	4.8
24.	Rwanda	1980–85	18.9e	18.	Hong Kong	1981–85	4.8
25.	Congo	1980–85	18.6e	18.	Taiwan	1981–85	4.8
				21.	Antigua and Barbuda	1981–85	4.9
				22.	Netherlands Antilles	1980–81	5.0
				22.	Virgin Islands (USA)	1980–83,	5.0
						85	
				24.	Dominica	1983–84	5.1
				24.	Falkland Islands	1980–81	5.1
				24.	Malaysia	1981–85	5.1e

For an explanation of symbols and abbreviations, see pages 16–17.

3f. Countries with Highest and Lowest Rates of Natural Increase in Population

Contents

High natural-increase rate rank.

Conventional name of country.

Period of record.

Average annual percentage rate of natural increase in population (i.e., the difference between birth and death rates expressed as a percentage rate, representing the annual percentage growth in population without regard for migration).

Low natural-increase rate rank.

Conventional name of country.

Period of record.

Average annual percentage rate of natural inorease in population.

Coverage

52 countries with highest rates of natural increase in population and 50 countries with lowest rates of natural increase in population.

Entries

102.

TABLE 3f. COUNTRIES WITH HIGHEST AND LOWEST RATES OF NATURAL INCREASE IN POPULATION

	Highest		Annual Rate (%)		Lowest		Annual Rate (%)
Rank	Country	Period		Rank	Country	Period	
1.	Kenya	1980–85	4.11e	1.	Isle of Man	1981–86	−0.43
2.	Syria	1980–85	3.78e	2.	West Germany	1981–86	−0.16
3.	Botswana	1980–85	3.73e	3.	Hungary	1981–86	−0.14
4.	Jordan	1980–85	3.68e	4.	Denmark	1981–86	−0.09
5.	Iraq	1980–85	3.57e	5.	Austria	1981–86	0
6.	Tanzania	1980–85	3.51e	6.	Channel Islands	1981–86	0.02
7.	Zimbabwe	1980–85	3.49e	7.	East Germany	1981–86	0.04
8.	Libya	1980–85	3.47e	7.	Sweden	1981–86	0.04
9.	Nicaragua	1980–85	3.45e	9.	Luxembourg	1981–86	0.05
10.	Belize	1981–82, 84–86	3.43	10.	Belgium	1981–86	0.07
				11.	Italy	1981–85	0.11
10.	Maldives	1980–84, 86	3.43	12.	UK	1981–86	0.13
				13.	Monaco	1981, 83–85	0.20
12.	Qatar	1980–85	3.37e				
13.	Uganda	1980–85	3.35e	14.	Norway	1981–86	0.21
14.	Nigeria	1980–85	3.33e	15.	Bulgaria	1981–86	0.23
15.	Saudi Arabia	1980–85	3.32e	16.	Switzerland	1981–86	0.24
16.	Rwanda	1980–85	3.30e	17.	Czechoslovakia	1981–86	0.30
16.	Zambia	1980–85	3.30e	18.	San Marino	1981–85	0.32
18.	Algeria	1980–85	3.28e	19.	Netherlands	1981–86	0.39
19.	Oman	1980–85	3.27e	19.	Norfolk Island	1981, 83–84	0.39
20.	American Samoa	1980, 82–85	3.24				
				21.	Greece	1981–86	0.40
21.	Ghana	1980–85	3.23e	22.	France	1981–86	0.41
22.	Honduras	1980–85	3.21e	23.	Finland	1981–86	0.49
23.	Kuwait	1981–85	3.18	23.	Portugal	1981–85	0.49
24.	Malawi	1980–85	3.17e	25.	Romania	1981–85	0.53
25.	Liberia	1980–85	3.15e	26.	Spain	1980–84	0.58
25.	Solomon Islands	1980–85	3.15e	27.	Japan	1981–86	0.62
27.	Djibouti	1980–85	3.09e	28.	USA	1981–86	0.70
28.	Comoros–Mayotte	1980–85	3.05e	29.	Malta	1981–85	0.71
28.	Wallis and Futuna Islands	1978	3.05	29.	Yugoslavia	1981–86	0.71
				31.	Bermuda	1981–85	0.74
30.	North Yemen	1980–85	3.02e	32.	Canada	1981–86	0.79

For an explanation of symbols and abbreviations, see pages 16–17.   (Continued)

Figure 18. Skyline of Nairobi, capital of Kenya, the country with the highest birth rate and the highest rate of natural increase in population. (Credit: Kenya Tourist Office, Beverly Hills, California, USA.)

TABLE 3f. (Continued)

	Highest		Annual Rate (%)		Lowest		Annual Rate (%)
Rank	Country	Period		Rank	Country	Period	
31.	Swaziland	1980–85	3.01e	32.	New Zealand	1981–86	0.79
32.	Guatemala	1981–85	2.97	34.	Liechtenstein	1981–85	0.80
33.	South Yemen	1980–85	2.96e	35.	Australia	1981–86	0.82
34.	Benin	1980–85	2.95e	36.	Faeroe Islands	1981–86	0.88
34.	Togo	1980–85	2.95e	37.	Gibraltar	1981–86	0.89
36.	Zaire	1980–85	2.93e	37.	USSR	1981–86	0.89
37.	Mauritania	1980–85	2.92e	39.	Poland	1981–86	0.90
38.	Iran	1980–85	2.88e	39.	Uruguay	1980–83, 85	0.90
38.	Paraguay	1980–85	2.88e				
40.	Ecuador	1980–85	2.87e	41.	Christmas Island (Australia)	1980–83, 85	0.91
41.	Sudan	1980–85	2.85e				
42.	Mexico	1980–83, 85	2.84	42.	Barbados	1980–84, 86	0.93
43.	Burundi	1980–85	2.82e				
44.	Bolivia	1980–85	2.81e	43.	Andorra	1980–81, 83–84, 86	0.96
44.	Mali	1980–85	2.81e				
44.	Niger	1980–85	2.81e				
47.	Ivory Coast	1980–85	2.80e	43.	Ireland	1981–86	0.96
48.	Madagascar	1980–85	2.79e	45.	Antigua and Barbuda	1981–85	1.00
49.	Namibia	1980–85	2.78e				
50.	Bahrain	1980–85	2.77e	46.	Cuba	1981–86	1.03
50.	Burkina Faso	1980–85	2.77e	47.	Iceland	1981–86	1.04
50.	Pakistan	1980–85	2.77e	48.	Montserrat	1981–82, 85	1.06
				49.	Hong Kong	1981–85	1.07
				50.	Martinique	1981–86	1.08

For an explanation of symbols and abbreviations, see pages 16–17.

3g. Countries with Highest and Lowest Rates of Infant Mortality

Contents

High infant-mortality rate rank.

Conventional name of country.

Period of record.

Average annual infant-mortality rate (i.e., the number of deaths per thousand live births that occur in the first year of life).

Low infant-mortality rate rank.

Conventional name of country.

Year of data.

Infant mortality rate.

Coverage

26 countries with highest infant-mortality rates and 25 countries with lowest infant-mortality rates.

Entries

51.

TABLE 3g. COUNTRIES WITH HIGHEST AND LOWEST RATES OF INFANT MORTALITY

	Highest				Lowest		
Rank	Country	Period	Rate[1]	Rank	Country	Period	Rate[1]
1.	Afghanistan	1980–85	205e	1.	Andorra	1986	3.7
2.	Sierra Leone	1980–85	180e	2.	Monaco	1983	3.8
3.	Gambia	1980–85	174e	3.	Tonga	1985	5.0
4.	Saudi Arabia	1980–85	166e	4.	Japan	1985	5.5
5.	Malawi	1980–85	165e	5.	Sweden	1986	5.9
6.	Kampuchea	1980–85	160e	6.	Iceland	1984	6.1
7.	Guinea	1980–85	159e	7.	Finland	1985	6.3
8.	Ethiopia	1980–85	155e	8.	Switzerland	1985	6.9
8.	Somalia	1980–85	155e	9.	Macao	1986	7.2
10.	Mozambique	1980–85	153e	10.	Liechtenstein	1984	7.4
11.	Burkina Faso	1980–85	150e	11.	Hong Kong	1985	7.5
12.	Angola	1980–85	149e	11.	Taiwan	1984	7.5
12.	Mali	1980–85	149e	13.	Antigua and Barbuda	1983	7.7
14.	Niger	1980–85	146e	13.	Montserrat	1982	7.7
15.	Chad	1980–85	143e	15.	Canada	1985	7.9
15.	Guinea–Bissau	1980–85	143e	15.	Denmark	1985	7.9
				15.	France	1986	7.9
17.	Central African Republic	1980–85	142e	15.	Luxembourg	1986	7.9
				19.	Aruba	1982	8.0
17.	Senegal	1980–85	142e	20.	Cook Islands	1985	8.1
19.	Bhutan	1980–85	139e	20.	Netherlands	1986	8.1
19.	Nepal	1980–85	139e	22.	Netherlands Antilles	1982	8.2
21.	Equatorial Guinea	1980–85	137e	23.	Channel Islands	1985	8.4
				24.	Norway	1985	8.5
21.	Mauritania	1980–85	137e	25.	Ireland	1986	8.7
23.	North Yemen	1980–85	135e				
23.	South Yemen	1980–85	135e				
25.	Liberia	1980–85	132e				
25.	Rwanda	1980–85	132e				

[1]This rate represents the number of deaths per thousand live births that occur in the first year of life.
Note. Among countries with lowest rates of infant mortality, West Germany ranks 26th, East Germany 29th, UK 30th, USA 35th, and Spain 36th. See Table 1c.
For an explanation of symbols and abbreviations, see pages 16–17.

3h. Countries with Highest and Lowest Life Expectancies at Birth

Contents

I. Highest expectancies

Rank.

Conventional name of country.

Period of record.

Expectation of life at birth, in years (average of expectation for both sexes).

II. Lowest expectancies

Rank.

Conventional name of country.

Period of record.

Expectation of life at birth, in years (average of expectation for both sexes).

Coverage

50 countries with highest life expectancies and 50 countries with lowest life expectancies.

Entries

100.

TABLE 3h. COUNTRIES WITH HIGHEST AND LOWEST LIFE EXPECTANCIES AT BIRTH

I. Highest Expectancies

Rank	Country	Period	Years	Rank	Country	Period	Years
1.	Japan	1984	77.4	26.	Puerto Rico	1981–83	74.0
2.	Sweden	1984	76.9	29.	New Zealand	1985	73.9
3.	Iceland	1985	76.5	30.	Costa Rica	1980–85	73.8e
4.	Switzerland	1983–84	76.4	31.	Austria	1984	73.7
5.	Netherlands	1984	76.3	32.	Belgium	1982	73.4
6.	Norway	1984	76.2	32.	Gibraltar	?	73.4
7.	Faeroe Islands	1976–80	76.0	32.	Netherlands Antilles	1981	73.4
8.	Greece	1982	75.9	32.	San Marino	1980–85	73.4
9.	Australia	1984	75.8	36.	Luxembourg	1980–82	73.3
10.	Spain	1980–81	75.6	36.	Taiwan	1985	73.3
11.	Canada	1980–82	75.4	38.	Ireland	1980–82	72.9
11.	Hong Kong	1983	75.4	38.	Malta	1984	72.9
13.	Panama	1983	74.9	40.	Jamaica	1980–85	72.8e
14.	Israel	1984	74.8	41.	Bermuda	1980	72.5
15.	France	1983	74.7	41.	Dominican Republic	1982	72.5
15.	USA	1985	74.7	41.	East Germany	1984	72.5
17.	Cyprus	1978–82	74.6	44.	Singapore	1985	72.4
17.	Finland	1984	74.6	45.	Antigua and Barbuda	1980–85	72.3e
17.	Martinique	1980–85	74.6e	46.	Guam	1980–82	72.0
20.	Denmark	1983–84	74.5	46.	Saint Lucia	1985	72.0
21.	Cuba	1983–84	74.4	48.	Portugal	1985	71.9
21.	Liechtenstein	1980–84	74.4	49.	Barbados	1980–85	71.7e
23.	UK	1982–84	74.3	50.	Albania	1980–85	71.5e
24.	Aruba	1981	74.2				
24.	West Germany	1982–84	74.2				
26.	Dominica	1980–85	74.0e				
26.	Italy	1980	74.0				

II. Lowest Expectancies

Rank	Country	Period	Years	Rank	Country	Period	Years
1.	Sierra Leone	1980–85	34.0e	10.	Senegal	1980–85	43.3e
2.	Gambia	1980–85	35.0e	11.	Kampuchea	1980–85	43.4e
3.	Afghanistan	1980–85	36.9e	12.	Chad	1980–85	43.5e
4.	Guinea	1980–85	40.2e	13.	Benin	1980–85	44.0e
5.	Ethiopia	1980–85	40.9e	13.	Equatorial Guinea	1980–85	44.0e
5.	Somalia	1980–85	40.9e	13.	Mauritania	1980–85	44.0e
7.	Angola	1980–85	42.0e	16.	Malawi	1980–85	44.1e
8.	Niger	1980–85	42.5e	17.	Burkina Faso	1980–85	44.5e
9.	Guinea-Bissau	1980–85	43.0e	18.	Mali	1980–85	45.0e

For an explanation of symbols and abbreviations, see pages 16–17. (Continued)

TABLE 3h. (Continued)

II. Lowest Expectancies

Rank	Country	Period	Years	Rank	Country	Period	Years
19.	Mozambique	1980–85	45.3e	35.	Nepal	1981	49.5
20.	Bhutan	1980–85	45.8e	36.	Gabon	1980–85	49.7e
21.	Rwanda	1980–85	46.3e	36.	Laos	1980–85	49-7e
22.	Congo	1980–85	46.5e	38.	Nigeria	1980–85	49.8e
23.	Burundi	1980–85	46.8e	39.	Comoros-Mayotte	1980–85	50.0e
24.	Djibouti	1980–85	47.0e	39.	Zaire	1980–85	50.0e
24.	Togo	1980–85	47.0e	41.	Ivory Coast	1980–85	50.5e
26.	Central African	1980–85	47.7e	42.	Bolivia	1980–85	50.8e
	Republic			43.	Cameroon	1980–85	50.9e
27.	Sudan	1980–85	47.8e	44.	India	1981	51.0e
28.	Madagascar	1980–85	48.1e	44.	Tanzania	1980–85	51.0e
29.	Namibia	1980–85	48.2e	46.	Zambia	1980–85	51.3e
30.	North Yemen	1980–85	48.4e	47.	Maldives	1982	51.5
30.	South Yemen	1980–85	48.4e	48.	Papua New Guinea	1980–85	51.9e
32.	Swaziland	1980–85	48.5e	49.	Ghana	1980–85	52.0e
33.	Uganda	1980–85	49.0e	50.	Kiribati	1980–85	52.2e
34.	Lesotho	1980–85	49.3e				

For an explanation of symbols and abbreviations, see pages 16–17.

3i. Countries with Largest Total and Largest and Smallest per Capita Gross Domestic Product (GDP)

Contents

Rank for total GDP.

Conventional name of country.

Year of data.

Total GDP or GNP (gross national product), in millions of US dollars at market prices and at the average rate of exchange for the year in question.[1]

Rank for high per capita GDP.

Conventional name of country.

Year of data.

Per capita GDP or GNP, in US dollars, based on the best population estimate for 1 July of the year in question.

Rank for low per capita GDP.

Conventional name of country.

Year of data.

Per capita GDP or GNP, in US dollars, based on the best population estimate for 1 July of the year in question.

Coverage

50 countries each with largest total and smallest per capita GDP; 55 countries with largest per capita GDP.

Entries

155.

[1]See notes 1 and 2 on p 65.

TABLE 3i. COUNTRIES WITH LARGEST TOTAL AND LARGEST AND SMALLEST PER CAPITA GROSS DOMESTIC PRODUCT (GDP)

Rank	Country	Year	Total GDP[1]	Rank	Country	Year	Per Capita GDP[2]	Rank	Country	Year	Per Capita GDP[2]
1.	USA	1986	4,194,500	1.	Switzerland	1986	20,820	1.	Chad	1985	81e
2.	USSR	1985	2,062,600e[3]	2.	Christmas Island (Australia)	1982	20,333e	2.	Zaire	1985	97
3.	Japan	1986	1,962,687	3.	Nauru	1984	20,000e[3]	3.	Burkina Faso	1984	111
4.	West Germany	1986	895,234	4.	Bermuda	1985	18,561	4.	Kampuchea	1983	116e
5.	France	1986	724,203	5.	USA	1986	17,362	5.	Ethiopia	1986	122
6.	Italy	1986	599,921	6.	Norway	1986	16,738	6.	Bhutan	1984	128
7.	UK	1985	455,740	7.	Johnston Island	1982	16,667e	7.	Gambia	1985	139
8.	Canada	1986	363,606	8.	Japan	1986	16,155	8.	Mozambique	1984	143
9.	Brazil	1986	270,026	9.	Iceland	1986	15,955	9.	Nepal	1986	148
10.	China	1986	262,000e[3]	10.	United Arab Emirates	1985	15,803	10.	Bangladesh	1986	153
11.	Poland	1985	240,600e[3]	11.	Sweden	1986	15,699	11.	Malawi	1986	168
12.	India	1985	196,904	12.	Brunei	1985	15,277	12.	Guinea-Bissau	1983	181
13.	Mexico	1985	177,477	13.	Liechtenstein	1984	15,000e	13.	Afghanistan	1985	194e[3]
14.	East Germany	1985	174,700e[3]	14.	West Germany	1986	14,664	14.	Burma	1986	202
15.	Iran	1985	168,100	15.	Finland	1986	14,354	15.	Laos	1984	219e[3]
16.	Australia	1986	166,819	16.	Canada	1986	14,197	16.	Togo	1984	231
17.	Spain	1984	161,327	17.	France	1986	13,074	17.	Madagascar	1985	235
18.	Czechoslovakia	1985	135,600e[3]	18.	Bahrain	1983	12,923	18.	Zambia	1986	240
19.	Switzerland	1986	135,416	19.	Austria	1986	12,468	19.	Equatorial Guinea	1983	247e[3]
20.	Sweden	1986	131,404	20.	Kuwait	1985	11,740	20.	China	1986	249e[3]
21.	Yugoslavia	1985	129,400e[3]	21.	Qatar	1984	11,684	21.	Somalia	1983	261[3]
22.	Netherlands	1985	124,255	22.	Luxembourg	1985	11,343	22.	India	1985	262
23.	Romania	1985	123,700e[3]	23.	Denmark	1985	11,170	23.	Rwanda	1983	264
24.	South Korea	1986	98,145	24.	Monaco	1982	10,704e	24.	Lesotho	1983	266
25.	Austria	1986	94,393					25.	Burundi	1986	271
26.	Indonesia	1985	86,499					26.	Benin	1983	272
27.	Belgium	1985	81,040					26.	Central African Republic	1985	272
28.	Hungary	1985	80,100e[3]								

For an explanation of symbols and abbreviations, see pages 16–17.

(Continued)

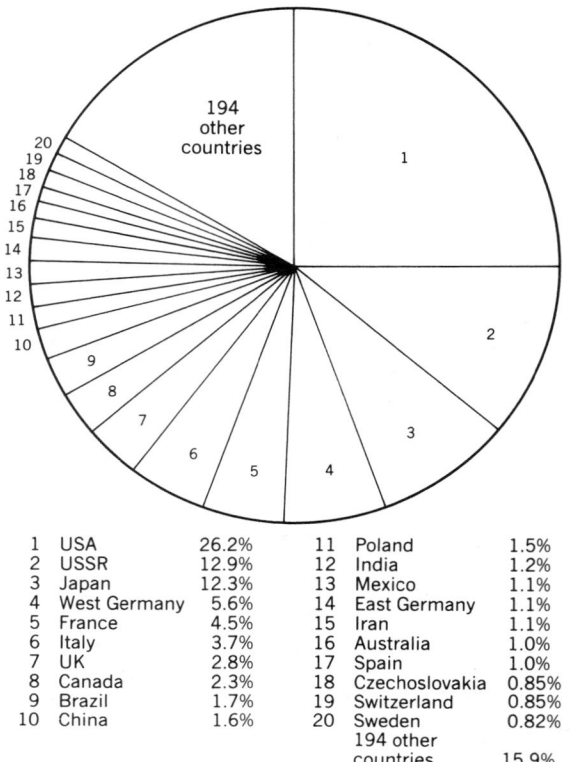

1	USA	26.2%	11	Poland	1.5%
2	USSR	12.9%	12	India	1.2%
3	Japan	12.3%	13	Mexico	1.1%
4	West Germany	5.6%	14	East Germany	1.1%
5	France	4.5%	15	Iran	1.1%
6	Italy	3.7%	16	Australia	1.0%
7	UK	2.8%	17	Spain	1.0%
8	Canada	2.3%	18	Czechoslovakia	0.85%
9	Brazil	1.7%	19	Switzerland	0.85%
10	China	1.6%	20	Sweden	0.82%
				194 other countries	15.9%

Figure 19. *Gross domestic product of countries as percentage of world total of GDP's.*

Figure 20. *Looking over the sturdy buildings and ornate roofs visible from the Cathedral tower at Bern, capital of Switzerland, the country with the largest per capita gross domestic product (GDP). (Credit: Swiss National Tourist Office.)*

TABLE 3i. (Continued)

Rank	Country	Year	Total GDP[1]	Rank	Country	Year	Per Capita GDP[2]	Rank	Country	Year	Per Capita GDP[2]
29.	Saudi Arabia	1986	77,415	25.	Channel Islands	1983	10,615[3]	28.	Guinea	1984	274e[3]
30.	Turkey	1986	74,597	26.	Greenland	1983	10,577[3]	29.	Mali	1983	276
31.	Nigeria	1984	74,213	27.	Faeroe Islands	1984	10,533	30.	Kenya	1985	284
32.	Finland	1986	70,595	28.	Australia	1986	10,524	31.	Tanzania	1985	285
33.	Norway	1986	69,782	29.	East Germany	1985	10,496e[3]	32.	Comoros	1985	302e[3]
34.	Argentina	1983	64,835	30.	Italy	1986	10,484	33.	Vietnam	1984	310e[3]
35.	South Africa	1986	61,957	31.	Pitcairn Island	1982	10,000e	34.	Niger	1983	313
36.	Taiwan	1985	59,151	32.	Andorra	1982	9,579e	35.	Pakistan	1986	326
37.	Bulgaria	1985	57,800e[3]	33.	Czechoslovakia	1985	8,748e[3]	36.	Angola	1986	334e
38.	Denmark	1985	57,125	34.	Netherlands	1985	8,579	37.	Mayotte	1982	345e
39.	Venezuela	1986	49,962	35.	Virgin Islands (USA)	1983	8,558[3]	37.	North Yemen	1986	345
40.	Algeria	1983	48,425	36.	Wake Island	1982	8,333e	39.	Cape Verde	1983	346[3]
41.	Thailand	1986	41,764	37.	Cayman Islands	1983	8,316e	40.	Sudan	1984	347
42.	Greece	1986	39,753	38.	Belgium	1985	8,221	41.	Liberia	1985	374
43.	Iraq	1986	35,000e[3]	39.	UK	1985	8,049	42.	Mauritania	1984	380
44.	Hong Kong	1985	33,934					43.	Kiribati	1984	397
45.	Pakistan	1986	33,125					44.	Sri Lanka	1986	398
46.	Colombia	1986	32,983								

	Country	Year	
47.	Philippines	1986	30,743
48.	Cuba	1985	29,765e
49.	Malaysia	1986	27,788
50.	Israel	1986	27,587

	Country	Year	
40.	Saint-Pierre and Miquelon	1982	7,667e
41.	Hungary	1985	7,522e[3]
42.	USSR	1985	7,403e[3]
43.	Libya	1984	7,357
44.	Bahamas	1984	7,227
45.	Netherlands Antilles	1984	6,939e
46.	New Zealand	1985	6,872
47.	Aruba	1984	6,779e[3]
48.	Singapore	1986	6,708
49.	Poland	1985	6,467e[3]
50.	Bulgaria	1985	6,465e[3]
51.	Saudi Arabia	1986	6,448
52.	Israel	1986	6,422
53.	Puerto Rico	1986	6,397
54.	Hong Kong	1985	6,391
55.	San Marino	1982	6,333e

	Country	Year	
45.	Sierra Leone	1984	399
46.	Uganda	1983	403e
47.	Senegal	1985	410
48.	Haiti	1986	419
49.	Maldives	1985	464
50.	South Yemen	1985	480e[3]

[1]In millions of US dollars at market prices.
[2]In US dollars at market prices.
[3]Gross national product (GNP).

For an explanation of symbols and abbreviations, see pages 16–17.

3j. Countries with Greatest Energy Production and Consumption, 1985

Contents

Energy production rank.

Conventional name of country.

Production of primary commercial energy in 1985, expressed in thousands of metric tons of coal equivalent.[1]

Percentage of world total.

Energy consumption rank.

Conventional name of country.

Consumption of energy in 1985, expressed in thousands of metric tons of coal equivalent.[1]

Percentage of world total.

Per capita energy consumption rank.

Conventional name of country.

Consumption of energy per capita, expressed in kilograms of coal equivalent, based on the best population estimate for 1 July 1985.

Coverage

50 countries each with highest energy production, highest energy consumption, and highest per capita energy consumption in 1985.

Entries

150.

[1]See p 71.

TABLE 3j. COUNTRIES WITH GREATEST ENERGY PRODUCTION AND CONSUMPTION, 1985

Production				Consumption				Per Capita Consumption		
Rank	Country	1,000 MT[1]	% of World Total	Rank	Country	1,000 MT[1]	% of World Total	Rank	Country	Kilograms[2]
1.	USSR	2,167,893	22.9	1.	USA	2,276,274	24.8	1.	Virgin Islands (USA)	31,577
2.	USA	2,016,276	21.3	2.	USSR	1,708,248	18.6	2.	Qatar	20,854
3.	China	798,368	8.4	3.	China	720,468	7.9	3.	Cook Islands	16,944
4.	Canada	324,770	3.4	4.	Japan	448,505	4.9	4.	Bahrain	13,820
5.	UK	324,287	3.4	5.	West Germany	349,947	3.8	5.	Brunei	12,710
6.	Saudi Arabia	258,115	2.7	6.	UK	276,790	3.0	6.	Luxembourg	11,406
7.	Mexico	249,542	2.6	7.	Canada	251,978	2.7	7.	Netherlands Antilles-Aruba	10,667
8.	India	182,230	1.9	8.	France	219,292	2.4			
9.	Poland	175,347	1.8	9.	India	192,966	2.1	8.	Canada	9,929
10.	Australia	171,147	1.8	10.	Italy	188,611	2.1	9.	Guam	9,540
11.	Iran	169,692	1.8	11.	Poland	172,393	1.9	10.	USA	9,513
12.	West Germany	160,727	1.7	12.	Mexico	132,491	1.4	11.	Oman	8,296
13.	Venezuela	156,427	1.6	13.	East Germany	130,623	1.4	12.	East Germany	7,848
14.	South Africa[3]	132,251	1.4	14.	South Africa[3]	114,172	1.2	13.	Singapore	7,695
15.	Indonesia	131,260	1.4	15.	Romania	109,923	1.2	14.	Kuwait	7,613
16.	Nigeria	112,382	1.2	16.	Australia	102,949	1.1	15.	Nauru	7,375
17.	Norway	104,641	1.1	17.	Czechoslovakia	97,078	1.1	16.	Australia	6,532
18.	Algeria	103,828	1.1	18.	Brazil	93,773	1.0	17.	Norway	6,483
19.	Netherlands	103,429	1.1	19.	Spain	84,152	0.9	18.	Czechoslovakia	6,263
20.	Iraq	101,136	1.1	20.	Netherlands	83,409	0.9	19.	USSR	6,131
21.	East Germany	100,820	1.1	21.	South Korea	66,587	0.7	20.	American Samoa	6,000
22.	United Arab Emirates	94,775	1.0	22.	Yugoslavia	58,349	0.6	21.	United Arab Emirates	5,951
23.	Romania	90,648	1.0	23.	Iran	55,864	0.6			
24.	Kuwait	87,491	0.9	24.	North Korea	54,661	0.6	22.	Bulgaria	5,799
25.	Libya	78,049	0.8	25.	Venezuela	54,545	0.6	23.	Falkland Islands	5,789
26.	Brazil	70,710	0.7	26.	Argentina	52,046	0.6	24.	Netherlands	5,759
				27.	Bulgaria	51,885	0.6			(Continued)

For an explanation of symbols and abbreviations, see pages 16–17.

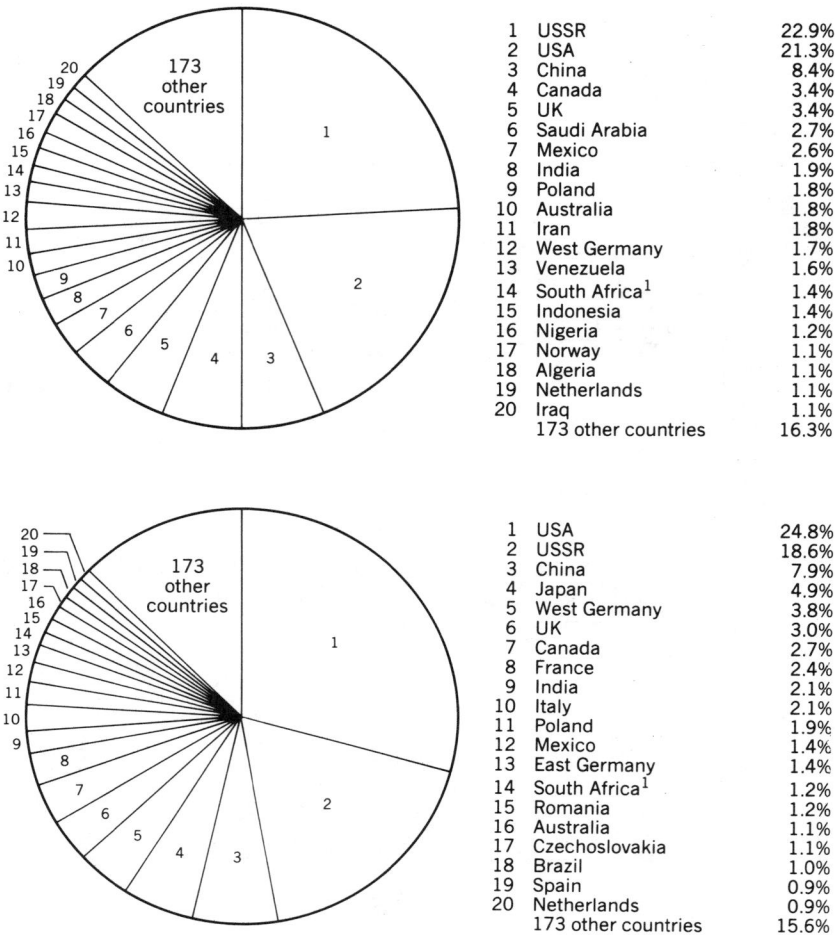

1	USSR	22.9%
2	USA	21.3%
3	China	8.4%
4	Canada	3.4%
5	UK	3.4%
6	Saudi Arabia	2.7%
7	Mexico	2.6%
8	India	1.9%
9	Poland	1.8%
10	Australia	1.8%
11	Iran	1.8%
12	West Germany	1.7%
13	Venezuela	1.6%
14	South Africa[1]	1.4%
15	Indonesia	1.4%
16	Nigeria	1.2%
17	Norway	1.1%
18	Algeria	1.1%
19	Netherlands	1.1%
20	Iraq	1.1%
	173 other countries	16.3%

1	USA	24.8%
2	USSR	18.6%
3	China	7.9%
4	Japan	4.9%
5	West Germany	3.8%
6	UK	3.0%
7	Canada	2.7%
8	France	2.4%
9	India	2.1%
10	Italy	2.1%
11	Poland	1.9%
12	Mexico	1.4%
13	East Germany	1.4%
14	South Africa[1]	1.2%
15	Romania	1.2%
16	Australia	1.1%
17	Czechoslovakia	1.1%
18	Brazil	1.0%
19	Spain	0.9%
20	Netherlands	0.9%
	173 other countries	15.6%

Figure 21. *Energy production and consumption of countries as percentage of world energy production and consumption.*

[1]Inc Botswana, Lesotho, Namibia, and Swaziland.

TABLE 3j. (Continued)

	Production				Consumption				Per Capita Consumption	
Rank	Country	1,000 MT[1]	% of World Total	Rank	Country	1,000 MT[1]	% of World Total	Rank	Country	Kilograms[2]
27.	Egypt	70,543	0.7	28.	Belgium	49,494	0.5	25.	West Germany	5,735
28.	Czechoslovakia	66,804	0.7	29.	Taiwan	45,638	0.5	26.	Faeroe Islands	5,413
29.	France	63,799	0.7	30.	Turkey	45,479	0.5	27.	Denmark	5,343
30.	Argentina	58,338	0.6	31.	Indonesia	42,510	0.5	28.	Finland	5,223
31.	Oman	50,524	0.5	32.	Hungary	41,630	0.5	29.	Iceland	5,095
32.	Malaysia	50,285	0.5	33.	Saudi Arabia	41,622	0.5	30.	Trinidad and Tobago	5,050
33.	North Korea	49,639	0.5	34.	Sweden	41,430	0.5			
34.	Japan	49,195	0.5	35.	Egypt	31,032	0.3	31.	Belgium	5,021
35.	Yugoslavia	36,581	0.4	36.	Austria	29,668	0.3	32.	Sweden	4,962
36.	Spain	30,790	0.3	37.	Denmark	27,322	0.3	33.	UK	4,889
37.	Italy	28,518	0.3	38.	Norway	26,951	0.3	34.	Romania	4,776
38.	Colombia	27,884	0.3	39.	Finland	25,601	0.3	35.	Greenland	4,660
39.	Qatar	27,618	0.3	40.	Pakistan	25,146	0.3	36.	Poland	4,634
40.	Brunei	24,085	0.3	41.	Malaysia	24,507	0.3	37.	New Caledonia	4,444
41.	Hungary	23,277	0.2	42.	Switzerland	24,360	0.3	38.	Bahamas	4,436
42.	Turkey	22,920	0.2	43.	Colombia	24,116	0.3	39.	France	3,973
43.	Ecuador	21,132	0.2	44.	Greece	23,032	0.3	40.	Austria	3,927
44.	Bulgaria	18,038	0.2	45.	Nigeria	21,576	0.2	41.	Hungary	3,909
45.	South Korea	17,320	0.2	46.	Thailand	21,436	0.2	42.	Switzerland	3,748
46.	Trinidad and Tobago	16,882	0.2	47.	Singapore	19,685	0.2	43.	Bermuda	3,732
47.	Angola	16,642	0.2	48.	Algeria	16,654	0.2	44.	Japan	3,705
48.	Peru	16,061	0.2	49.	Oman	16,591	0.2	45.	Saudi Arabia	3,606
49.	Sweden	15,967	0.2	50.	Philippines	15,835	0.2	46.	New Zealand	3,499
50.	Pakistan	15,966	0.2					47.	Libya	3,426
								48.	Saint-Pierre and Miquelon	3,333
								49.	Italy	3,300
								50.	Venezuela	3,150

[1]1,000 metric tons of coal equivalent.
[2]Kilograms of coal equivalent.
[3]Inc Botswana, Lesotho, Namibia, and Swaziland.

For an explanation of symbols and abbreviations, see pages 16–17.

3k. Countries with Greatest Total and per Capita Volume of Exports and Imports, by Value

Contents

I. Total volume (average annual value)

Rank for exports.
Conventional name of country.
Period of record.
Average annual value in millions of US dollars.
Percentage of world total.
Rank for imports.
Conventional name of country.
Period of record.
Average annual value in millions of US dollars.
Percentage of world total.

II. Per capita volume (value for latest available year)

Rank for exports.
Conventional name of country.
Year of record.
Per capita value in US dollars, based on the best population estimate for 1 July of the year in question.
Rank for imports.
Conventional name of country.
Year of record.
Per capita value in US dollars.

Coverage

50 leading countries in each of the four categories.

Entries

200.

TABLE 3k. COUNTRIES WITH GREATEST TOTAL AND PER CAPITA VOLUME OF EXPORTS AND IMPORTS, BY VALUE

I. Total Volume (Average Annual Value for All Years Reported in Table 1f)

	Exports						Imports		
Rank	Country	Period	Million US Dollars	% of World Total	Rank	Country	Period	Million US Dollars	% of World Total
1.	USA	1981–86	215,815	11.2	1.	USA	1981–86	314,666	15.7
2.	West Germany	1981–86	186,249	9.7	2.	West Germany	1981–86	161,844	8.1
3.	Japan	1981–86	165,423	8.6	3.	Japan	1981–86	132,337	6.6
4.	France	1981–86	99,278	5.2	4.	France	1981–86	113,727	5.7
5.	UK	1981–86	99,113	5.1	5.	UK	1981–86	107,351	5.3
6.	USSR	1981–85	87,190	4.5	6.	Italy	1981–86	88,791	4.4
7.	Canada	1981–86	78,827	4.1	7.	USSR	1981–85	78,910	3.9
8.	Italy	1981–86	78,574	4.1	8.	Canada	1981–86	68,983	3.4
9.	Saudi Arabia	1981–84	70,508	3.7	9.	Netherlands	1981–86	65,527	3.3
10.	Netherlands	1981–86	69,236	3.6	10.	Belgium	1981–86	59,356	3.0
11.	Belgium	1981–86	55,725	2.9	11.	Saudi Arabia	1981–85	34,484	1.7
12.	Sweden	1981–86	30,006	1.6	12.	Switzerland	1981–86	31,659	1.6
13.	Switzerland	1981–86	28,275	1.5	13.	Spain	1981–86	31,309	1.6
14.	South Korea	1981–86	27,143	1.4	14.	China	1981–86	29,190	1.5
15.	Hong Kong	1981–86	26,393	1.4	15.	South Korea	1981–86	28,522	1.4
16.	Taiwan	1981–85	26,223	1.4	16.	Sweden	1981–86	28,345	1.4
17.	China	1981–86	24,889	1.3	17.	Hong Kong	1981–86	27,626	1.4
18.	East Germany	1981–86	23,871	1.2	18.	Singapore	1981–86	27,407	1.4
19.	Brazil	1981–85	23,687	1.2	19.	Australia	1981–86	23,011	1.1
20.	Spain	1981–86	22,714	1.2	20.	East Germany	1981–86	22,615	1.1
21.	Australia	1981–86	22,306	1.2	21.	Austria	1981–86	21,230	1.1
22.	Singapore	1981–86	22,168	1.2	22.	Taiwan	1981–85	20,488	1.0
23.	Indonesia	1981–86	20,653	1.1	23.	Denmark	1981–86	18,132	0.9
24.	Mexico	1981–86	20,530	1.1	24.	Brazil	1981–85	17,736	0.9
25.	Norway	1981–86	18,403	1.0	25.	Czechoslovakia	1981–86	17,006	0.8
26.	South Africa	1981–86	18,273	0.9	26.	Norway	1981–86	15,672	0.8
27.	Austria	1981–86	17,074	0.9	27.	Iraq	1981–85	15,209	0.8
28.	Czechoslovakia	1981–86	17,024	0.9	28.	South Africa	1981–86	14,985	0.7
29.	Denmark	1981–86	16,956	0.9	29.	India	1981–86	14,504	0.7
30.	United Arab Emirates	1981–85	16,107	0.8	30.	Iran	1981–83	14,128	0.7
31.	Iran	1981–85	15,721	0.8	31.	Mexico	1981–86	14,115	0.7
32.	Venezuela	1981–86	14,652	0.8	32.	Finland	1981–86	13,574	0.7
33.	Malaysia	1981–86	13,997	0.7	33.	Indonesia	1981–86	13,557	0.7
34.	Finland	1981–86	13,855	0.7	34.	Yugoslavia	1981–86	12,620	0.6
35.	Nigeria	1981–85	13,634	0.7	35.	Malaysia	1981–86	12,449	0.6
36.	Libya	1981–85	12,251	0.6	36.	Bulgaria	1981–85	12,196	0.6
37.	Bulgaria	1981–85	12,089	0.6	37.	Nigeria	1981–85	11,317	0.6
38.	Kuwait	1981–85	11,907	0.6	38.	Poland	1981–86	11,306	0.6
39.	Romania	1981–84	11,823	0.6	39.	Algeria	1981–86	10,449	0.5
40.	Poland	1981–86	11,714	0.6	40.	Ireland	1981–86	10,304	0.5
41.	Algeria	1981–86	10,974	0.6	41.	Turkey	1981–86	10,094	0.5
42.	Yugoslavia	1981–86	10,163	0.5	42.	Romania	1981–84	9,912	0.5
43.	Iraq	1981–84	10,061	0.5	43.	Greece	1981–86	9,910	0.5
44.	Ireland	1981–86	9,732	0.5	44.	Egypt	1981–85	9,784	0.5
45.	Puerto Rico	1981–85	8,938	0.5	45.	Thailand	1981–86	9,601	0.5

For an explanation of symbols and abbreviations, see pages 16–17.   (Continued)

TABLE 3k. COUNTRIES WITH GREATEST TOTAL AND PER CAPITA VOLUME OF EXPORTS AND IMPORTS, BY VALUE

I. Total Volume (Average Annual Value for All Years Reported in Table 1f)

	Exports					Imports			
Rank	Country	Period	Million US Dollars	% of World Total	Rank	Country	Period	Million US Dollars	% of World Total
46.	Hungary	1981–86	8,740	0.5	46.	Puerto Rico	1981–85	9,296	0.5
47.	India	1981–86	8,706	0.5	47.	United Arab Emirates	1981–83	9,140	0.5
48.	Argentina	1981–85	8,221	0.4	48.	Venezuela	1981–86	9,134	0.5
49.	Thailand	1981–86	7,273	0.4	49.	Portugal	1981–86	8,836	0.4
50.	Cuba	1981–85	6,496	0.3	50.	Hungary	1981–86	8,724	0.4

II. Per Capita Volume (Value for Latest Year Reported in Table 1f)

	Exports				Imports		
Rank	Country	Year	US Dollars	Rank	Country	Year	US Dollars
1.	Aruba	1984	30,721	1.	Virgin Islands (USA)	1985	33,703
2.	Virgin Islands (USA)	1985	30,243	2.	Aruba	1984	31,265
3.	Liechtenstein	1985	17,286	3.	Bahamas	1985	13,167
4.	Brunei	1984	14,272	4.	Singapore	1986	9,865
5.	Bahamas	1985	11,658	5.	Netherlands Antilles	1984	9,733
6.	Qatar	1985	11,241	6.	American Samoa	1984	8,353
7.	Nauru	1981	11,125	7.	Saint-Pierre and Miquelon	1984	7,333
8.	United Arab Emirates	1985	8,839	8.	Bermuda	1985	7,179
9.	Singapore	1986	8,699	9.	Faeroe Islands	1986	7,152
10.	Netherlands Antilles	1984	8,405	10.	Norfolk Island	1985	7,083
11.	Belgium	1986	6,735	11.	Liechtenstein	1984	6,852
12.	Hong Kong	1986	6,405	12.	Belgium	1986	6,713
13.	American Samoa	1984	6,235	13.	Greenland	1986	6,667
14.	Kuwait	1985	5,967	14.	Hong Kong	1986	6,392
15.	Switzerland	1986	5,792	15.	Switzerland	1986	6,347
16.	Bahrain	1986	5,750	16.	United Arab Emirates	1983	6,144
17.	Netherlands	1986	5,531	17.	Virgin Islands (UK)	1983	6,091
18.	Faeroe Islands	1986	5,261	18.	Bahrain	1986	5,891
19.	Iceland	1986	4,510	19.	Cayman Islands	1980	5,611
20.	Sweden	1986	4,447	20.	Andorra	1984	5,524
21.	Greenland	1986	4,370	21.	Guam	1983	5,436
22.	Norway	1986	4,341	22.	Netherlands	1986	5,190
23.	Denmark	1986	4,140	23.	Gibraltar	1985	5,069
24.	West Germany	1986	3,971	24.	Norway	1986	4,871
25.	Ireland	1986	3,721	25.	Kuwait	1984	4,738
26.	Saudi Arabia	1984	3,403	26.	Iceland	1986	4,593
27.	Canada	1986	3,386	27.	Denmark	1986	4,454
28.	Puerto Rico	1985	3,378	28.	Sweden	1986	3,884
29.	Finland	1986	3,322	29.	Qatar	1985	3,616
30.	Austria	1986	2,975	30.	Ireland	1986	3,565
31.	Libya	1985	2,914	31.	Austria	1986	3,546
32.	Macao	1986	2,570	32.	Turks and Caicos Islands	1984	3,250

For an explanation of symbols and abbreviations, see pages 16–17.

(Continued)

Figure 22. *View of the waterfront at Charlotte Amalie, capital of the US Virgin Islands, which ranks first in the per capita value of its imports and second in the per capita value of its exports among all countries. (Credit: US Virgin Islands Division of Tourism, Washington.)*

TABLE 3k. (Continued)

II. Per Capita Volume (Value for Latest Year Reported in Table 1f)

	Exports				Imports		
Rank	Country	Year	US Dollars	Rank	Country	Year	US Dollars
33.	Oman	1985	2,486	33.	Canada	1986	3,166
34.	Falkland Islands	1981	2,421	34.	Finland	1986	3,116
35.	France	1986	2,155	35.	West Germany	1986	3,104
36.	Gibraltar	1985	2,138	36.	French Guiana	1985	3,096
37.	UK	1986	1,885	36.	Puerto Rico	1985	3,096
38.	New Zealand	1986	1,797	38.	French Polynesia	1985	3,050
39.	New Caledonia	1985	1,771	39.	Brunei	1984	2,777
40.	Japan	1986	1,722	40.	Martinique	1986	2,680
41.	Italy	1986	1,709	41.	France	1986	2,325
42.	East Germany	1986	1,668	42.	Barbados	1986	2,320
43.	Taiwan	1985	1,605	43.	Malta	1986	2,304
44.	Israel	1986	1,594	44.	Israel	1986	2,287
45.	Gabon	1985	1,592	45.	New Caledonia	1985	2,275
46.	Bulgaria	1985	1,490	46.	UK	1986	2,223
47.	Australia	1986	1,408	47.	Macao	1986	2,177
48.	Saint-Pierre and Miquelon	1984	1,333	48.	Nauru	1981	2,125
49.	Czechoslovakia	1986	1,317	49.	Saudi Arabia	1985	2,047
50.	Malta	1986	1,291	50.	Reunion	1986	2,032

For an explanation of symbols and abbreviations, see pages 16–17.

3l. Countries with Greatest Road Lengths and Largest Number of Motor Vehicles in Use

Contents

   I. Length of roads and road density

     Rank.

     Conventional name of country.

     Year of data.

     Length of paved and unpaved roads in thousands of miles and thousands of kilometers.

     Road mileage per thousand square miles of surface area.

   II. Motor vehicles in use

     Total vehicle rank.

     Conventional name of country.

     Year of data.

     Thousands of motor vehicles, excluding motorcycles and agricultural tractors, in use at end of year.

     Per capita passenger car rank.

     Conventional name of country.

Year of data.

Number of passenger cars per thousand inhabitants in use at end of year.

Coverage

50 countries with greatest road lengths and 25 countries each with largest number of motor vehicles in use and largest number of passenger cars per thousand inhabitants.

Entries

100.

TABLE 3I. COUNTRIES WITH GREATEST ROAD LENGTHS AND LARGEST NUMBER OF MOTOR VEHICLES IN USE

I. Length of Roads and Road Density

Rank	Country	Year	1,000 Miles	1,000 km	Per 1,000 mi²
1.	USA	1985	3,861.1	6,213.9	1049
2.	Brazil	1986	990.3	1,593.7	301
3.	India	1983	965.7	1,554.2	781
4.	USSR	1983	861.8	1,387.0	100
5.	Japan	1986	700.5	1,127.4	4803
6.	China	1985	584.1	940.0	158
7.	Canada	1981	576.8	928.3	151
8.	Australia	1985	530.0	853.0	179
9.	France	1986	500.1	804.8	2381
10.	West Germany	1986	305.2	491.3	3178
11.	UK	1984	230.6	371.1	2447
12.	Spain	1986	198.2	319.0	1017
13.	Turkey	1983	188.2	302.8	625
14.	Italy	1985	187.2	301.3	1609
15.	Poland	1986	186.8	300.6	1547
16.	Mexico	1986	140.2	225.7	185
17.	Indonesia	1986	136.1	219.0	184
18.	Argentina	1981	130.6	210.2	122
19.	South Africa	1985	114.3	183.9	242
20.	Philippines	1986	100.8	162.3	870
21.	Bangladesh	1982	98.5	158.6	1772
22.	Sri Lanka	1981	94.7	152.4	3738
23.	Zaire	1985	90.1	145.0	99
24.	Iran	1984	84.8	136.4	133
25.	Sweden	1986	81.3	130.8	468
26.	Belgium	1986	79.6	128.1	6757
27.	Nigeria	1984	76.1	124.0	213
28.	East Germany	1980	74.9	120.5	1791
29.	Yugoslavia	1985	73.1	117.7	740
30.	Netherlands	1986	70.6	113.6	4376
31.	Austria	1986	67.8	109.1	2094
32.	Colombia	1986	66.0	106.2	150
33.	Pakistan	1985	64.2	103.4	207
34.	Greece	1985	64.2	103.3	1260
35.	Venezuela	1986	62.5	100.6	177
36.	New Zealand	1986	57.8	93.0	557
37.	Ireland	1986	57.4	92.3	2115
38.	Saudi Arabia	1986	56.8	91.3	68
39.	Hungary	1986	56.4	90.7	1570
40.	Norway	1986	53.5	86.1	428
41.	Thailand	1986	51.8	83.3	261
42.	Tanzania	1984	50.9	81.9	139
43.	Chile	1986	49.2	79.1	168
44.	Algeria	1986	48.7	78.4	53
45.	Zimbabwe	1985	48.4	77.9	321
46.	Finland	1986	47.3	76.2	362
47.	Czechoslovakia	1986	45.5	73.3	922
48.	Romania	1985	45.2	72.8	493
49.	Angola	1984	44.9	72.3	93
50.	Switzerland	1986	43.9	70.6	2754

For an explanation of symbols and abbreviations, see pages 16–17.

(Continued)

Figure 23. The princely palace in Monaco, the country with the largest number of passenger cars and telephones per thousand inhabitants. (Credit: Monaco Government Tourist Office.)

TABLE 3l. (Continued)

II. Motor Vehicles in Use

Rank	Country	Year	Total Number (1,000)	Rank	Country	Year	Passenger Cars per 1,000 Inhabitants
1.	USA	1985	171,691	1.	Monaco	1986	704
2.	Japan	1986	47,978	2.	San Marino	1985	682
3.	West Germany	1986	28,588	3.	Channel Islands	1983	562
4.	France	1986	24,656	4.	USA	1985	552
5.	Italy	1985	24,300	5.	Norfolk Island	1982	545
6.	USSR	1984	21,351	6.	Liechtenstein	1985	536
7.	UK	1986	20,347	7.	Falkland Islands	1982	526
8.	Canada	1985	14,267	8.	Guam	1984	517
9.	Brazil	1985	11,542	9.	Andorra	1982	474
10.	Spain	1986	11,489	10.	New Zealand	1986	470
11.	Australia	1985	8,980	11.	Iceland	1986	465
12.	Mexico	1984	7,196	12.	Gibraltar	1986	448
13.	Netherlands	1986	5,359	13.	Canada	1985	438
14.	Argentina	1986	5,233	14.	Australia	1985	434
15.	Poland	1986	4,875	15.	Isle of Man	1984	431
16.	South Africa	1986	4,334	16.	Martinique	1984	428
17.	Saudi Arabia	1986	4,268	17.	Luxembourg	1986	425
18.	East Germany	1985	3,723	18.	Switzerland	1986	412
19.	Belgium	1986	3,676	19.	West Germany	1986	405
20.	Venezuela	1986	3,548	20.	Italy	1985	392
21.	Sweden	1986	3,497	21.	Cayman Islands	1983	389
22.	Yugoslavia	1985	3,056	21.	Sweden	1986	389
23.	China	1985	3,026	23.	France	1986	384
24.	Czechoslovakia	1984	3,018	24.	Norway	1986	382
25.	Switzerland	1986	2,897	25.	Bahamas	1984	379

Note. The UK ranks 36th and Japan 44th in number of passenger cars per 1,000 inhabitants. See Table 1g.
For an explanation of symbols and abbreviations, see pages 16–17.

3m. Countries with Greatest Railroad Route Lengths and Greatest Volume of Passenger and Freight Traffic

Contents

I. Length of railroad routes

Rank.
Conventional name of country.
Year of data.
Length of railroad routes (not tracks), in miles and kilometers.
Percentage of world total.

II. Passenger and freight traffic

Passenger traffic rank.
Conventional name of country.

Year of data.

Millions of railroad passenger-kilometers. (Passenger-kilometers are the number of passengers multiplied by the number of kilometers each passenger is carried.)

Freight traffic rank.

Conventional name of country.

Year of data.

Millions of metric ton-kilometers of railroad freight.

Coverage

25 countries each with greatest railroad route lengths and greatest volume of passenger and freight traffic.

Entries

75.

TABLE 3m. COUNTRIES WITH GREATEST RAILROAD ROUTE LENGTHS AND GREATEST VOLUME OF PASSENGER AND FREIGHT TRAFFIC

I. Length of Railroad Routes

Rank	Country	Year	Miles	Kilometers	% of World Total
1.	USA	1984	163,230	262,693	22.1
2.	USSR	1984	89,540	144,100	12.1
3.	Canada	1982	42,797	68,875	5.8
4.	India	1984	38,143	61,385	5.2
5.	China	1984	32,390	52,127	4.4
6.	Australia	1979	24,475	39,388	3.3
7.	France	1984	23,075	37,135	3.1
8.	Argentina	1984	21,601	34,764	2.9
9.	West Germany	1984	18,969	30,528	2.6
10.	Brazil	1984	17,982	28,940	2.4
11.	Poland	1984	15,132	24,353	2.1
12.	South Africa	1984	13,316	21,430	1.8
13.	Japan	1984	13,105	21,091	1.8
14.	Mexico	1984	12,388	19,936	1.7
15.	Italy	1983	12,088	19,454	1.6
16.	UK	1984	10,647	17,134	1.4
17.	Spain	1984	9,704	15,617	1.3
18.	Cuba	1984	9,039	14,547	1.2
19.	East Germany	1984	8,839	14,225	1.2
20.	Czechoslovakia	1984	8,149	13,114	1.1
21.	Sweden	1984	7,397	11,905	1.0
22.	Romania	1984	6,530	10,509	0.9
23.	Yugoslavia	1984	5,766	9,279	0.8
24.	Pakistan	1984	5,482	8,823	0.7
25.	Turkey	1984	5,076	8,169	0.7

For an explanation of symbols and abbreviations, see pages 16–17.   (Continued)

TABLE 3m. (Continued)

II. Passenger and Freight Traffic

Passenger Traffic				Freight Traffic			
Rank	Country	Year	Million Passenger-Kilometers	Rank	Country	Year	Million MT-km
1.	USSR	1984	363,986	1.	USSR	1984	3,638,834
2.	Japan	1985	328,452	2.	USA	1984	1,377,264
3.	China	1985	241,380	3.	China	1985	811,116
4.	India	1985	240,000	4.	Canada	1984	360,371
5.	France	1985	60,780	5.	India	1985	196,488
6.	Poland	1985	51,984	6.	Poland	1985	120,648
7.	West Germany	1985	41,208	7.	South Africa	1985	92,616
8.	Italy	1985	39,264	8.	Romania	1984	75,159
9.	UK	1984	36,400	9.	Brazil	1983	74,792
10.	USA	1984	29,773	10.	Czechoslovakia	1985	73,596
11.	Romania	1984	28,785	11.	West Germany	1985	63,876
12.	East Germany	1985	22,452	12.	East Germany	1985	58,668
13.	South Korea	1984	21,884	13.	France	1985	58,488
14.	South Africa	1984	20,137	14.	Mexico	1985	45,444
15.	Czechoslovakia	1985	19,836	15.	Australia	1984	39,448
16.	Pakistan	1985	17,808	16.	Yugoslavia	1985	28,320
17.	Spain	1985	15,972	17.	Japan	1985	22,104
18.	Egypt	1983	14,468	18.	Hungary	1985	21,816
19.	Brazil	1983	13,797	19.	Italy	1985	18,192
20.	Yugoslavia	1985	12,216	20.	Bulgaria	1985	18,168
21.	Argentina	1985	10,740	21.	Sweden	1985	17,592
22.	Hungary	1985	10,464	22.	UK	1984	15,842
23.	Switzerland	1985	9,408	23.	South Korea	1985	12,084
24.	Netherlands	1985	9,228	24.	Spain	1985	11,712
25.	Thailand	1985	9,144	25.	Austria	1984	11,565

For an explanation of symbols and abbreviations, see pages 16–17.

3n. Countries with Greatest Volume of Airline Passenger and Freight Traffic, 1985

Contents

Passenger traffic rank.

Conventional name of country.

Millions of civil airline passenger-kilometers in 1985. (Passenger-kilometers are the number of passengers multiplied by the number of kilometers each passenger is carried.)

Percentage of world total.

Freight traffic rank.

Conventional name of country.

Millions of metric ton-kilometers of civil airline scheduled freight in 1985.

Percentage of world total.

Coverage

25 countries each with greatest volume of civil airline passenger and freight traffic.

Entries

50.

TABLE 3n. COUNTRIES WITH GREATEST VOLUME OF AIRLINE PASSENGER AND FREIGHT TRAFFIC, 1985

	Passenger Traffic				Scheduled Freight Traffic		
Rank	Country	Million Passenger-Kilometers	% of World Total	Rank	Country	Million Metric Ton-Kilometers	% of World Total
1.	USA	533,141	35.9	1.	USA	9,472	23.9
2.	USSR	188,206	12.7	2.	Japan	3,071	7.7
3.	UK	79,065	5.3	3.	France	2,873	7.2
4.	Japan	64,968	4.4	4.	USSR	2,688	6.8
5.	Canada	40,220	2.7	5.	West Germany	2,378	6.0
6.	France	40,131	2.7	6.	UK	2,299	5.8
7.	Australia	28,287	1.9	7.	Taiwan	1,839	4.6
8.	West Germany	24,570	1.7	8.	Netherlands	1,404	3.5
9.	Spain	22,364	1.5	9.	South Korea	1,332	3.4
10.	Singapore	21,802	1.5	10.	Canada	990	2.5
11.	Brazil	19,018	1.3	11.	Singapore	981	2.5
12.	Netherlands	18,952	1.3	12.	Brazil	909	2.3
13.	Italy	18,342	1.2	13.	Australia	818	2.1
14.	Mexico	18,004	1.2	14.	Italy	757	1.9
15.	Saudi Arabia	15,857	1.1	15.	Switzerland	637	1.6
16.	India	14,938	1.0	16.	Israel	592	1.5
17.	Switzerland	12,777	0.9	17.	Belgium	565	1.4
18.	South Korea	12,393	0.8	18.	Spain	522	1.3
19.	China	12,114	0.8	19.	India	490	1.2
20.	Taiwan	11,246	0.8	20.	Saudi Arabia	455	1.1
21.	Thailand	10,781	0.7	21.	Thailand	419	1.1
22.	Indonesia	10,116	0.7	22.	China	403	1.0
23.	South Africa	8,751	0.6	23.	South Africa	392	1.0
24.	Philippines	8,615	0.6	24.	Colombia	342	0.9
25.	New Zealand	7,927	0.5	25.	Pakistan	310	0.8

For an explanation of symbols and abbreviations, see pages 16–17.

3o. Countries with Largest Number of Telephones and Radio and Television Receivers

Contents

I. Telephones

Rank for total number.

Conventional name of country.

Year of data.

Thousands of telephones in use.

Per capita rank.

Conventional name of country.

Year of data.

Number of telephones per thousand inhabitants.

II. Radio and television receivers, 1983

Rank for total number of radio receivers.

Conventional name of country.

Thousands of radio receivers in use in 1983.

Per capita rank for radio receivers.

Conventional name of country.

Number of radio receivers per thousand inhabitants in 1983.

Rank for total number of television receivers.

Conventional name of country.

Thousands of television receivers in use in 1983.

Per capita rank for television receivers.

Conventional name of country.

Number of television receivers per thousand inhabitants in 1983.

Coverage

25 countries each with largest number of (a) telephones, (b) telephones per thousand inhabitants, (c) radio receivers, (d) radio receivers per thousand inhabitants, (e) television receivers, and (f) television receivers per thousand inhabitants.

Entries

151.

TABLE 3o. COUNTRIES WITH LARGEST NUMBER OF TELEPHONES AND RADIO AND TELEVISION RECEIVERS

I. Telephones

Rank	Country	Year	Number (1,000)	Rank	Country	Year	Per 1,000 Inhabitants
1.	USA	1984	182,558	1.	Monaco	1983	1,296
2.	Japan	1983	61,208	2.	Sweden	1983	890
3.	West Germany	1983	35,137	3.	Liechtenstein	1982	846
4.	UK	1984	29,518	4.	Bermuda	1981	836
5.	USSR	1984	29,462	5.	Switzerland	1983	796
6.	France	1983	29,374	6.	Channel Islands	1983	792
7.	Italy	1983	22,992	7.	USA	1984	771
8.	Canada	1983	16,618	8.	Denmark	1983	702
9.	Spain	1983	13,345	9.	Canada	1983	668
10.	Brazil	1983	9,856	10.	New Zealand	1984	623
11.	Netherlands	1983	8,272	11.	Norway	1983	579
12.	Australia	1983	8,267	12.	Netherlands	1983	576
13.	Sweden	1983	7,410	13.	West Germany	1983	572
14.	Mexico	1983	6,414	14.	Finland	1983	571
15.	South Korea	1983	5,948	15.	Luxembourg	1984	544
16.	China	1984	5,150	16.	Australia	1983	538
17.	Switzerland	1983	5,113	17.	France	1983	537
18.	Belgium	1983	4,111	18.	Faeroe Islands	1983	533
19.	Taiwan	1984	3,947	18.	Saint-Pierre and Miquelon	1982	533
20.	Poland	1983	3,846	20.	Iceland	1983	527
21.	Denmark	1983	3,590	21.	UK	1984	523
22.	South Africa	1983	3,472	22.	Japan	1983	513
23.	Austria	1983	3,469	23.	Norfolk Island	1982	500
24.	East Germany	1983	3,441	24.	Andorra	1982	474
25.	Czechoslovakia	1983	3,402	25.	Virgin Islands (USA)	1982	471

For an explanation of symbols and abbreviations, see pages 16–17. (Continued)

TABLE 3o. (Continued)

II. Radio and Television Receivers, 1983

Radio Receivers

Rank	Country	Number (1,000)	Rank	Country	Per 1,000 Inhabitants
1.	USA	479,000	1.	USA	2,042
2.	USSR	136,000	2.	Cocos Islands	1,333
3.	Japan	85,000	3.	American Samoa	1,324
4.	China	70,000	4.	Australia	1,300
5.	UK	56,000	5.	Christmas Island (Australia)	1,250
6.	Brazil	50,000	6.	Guam	1,207
7.	France	47,000	7.	Bermuda	1,182
8.	India	45,000	8.	Gibraltar	1,172
9.	West Germany	24,604	9.	Norfolk Island	1,000
10.	Indonesia	22,000	10.	UK	993
11.	Mexico	21,800	11.	Finland	987
12.	Australia	20,000	12.	Cayman Islands	947
13.	Canada	18,950	13.	Anguilla	900
14.	South Korea	18,000	14.	New Zealand	890
15.	Argentina	16,000	15.	Tuvalu	875[1]
16.	Italy	14,213	16.	Virgin Islands (USA)	865
17.	Netherlands	11,385	17.	France	859
18.	Spain	10,900	18.	Sweden	858
19.	Poland	9,050			

Television Receivers

Rank	Country	Number (1,000)	Rank	Country	Per 1,000 Inhabitants
1.	USA	185,300	1.	USA	790
2.	USSR	140,000	2.	Bermuda	709
3.	Japan	66,342	3.	Guam	672
4.	UK	27,000	4.	Monaco	667
5.	West Germany	22,132	5.	Saint-Pierre and Miquelon	567
6.	France	20,500	6.	Japan	556
7.	Brazil	16,500	7.	Virgin Islands (USA)	538
8.	Italy	13,831	8.	UK	479
9.	Canada	11,530	9.	Canada	463
10.	Spain	9,850	9.	Qatar	463
11.	Poland	8,542	11.	Netherlands	450
12.	Mexico	8,300	12.	Finland	432
13.	South Korea	7,119	13.	Australia	423
14.	China	7,000	14.	Sweden	390
15.	Australia	6,500	15.	Switzerland	382
16.	Netherlands	6,460	16.	France	375
17.	East Germany	5,970	17.	Hungary	371
18.	Argentina	5,910	18.	Denmark	369
19.	Turkey	5,600			

20.	South Africa	8,700
21.	Egypt	8,000
22.	Iran	7,500
23.	Thailand	7,200
24.	Sweden	7,150
25.	Nigeria	7,000
25.	Pakistan	7,000

19.	Lebanon	797
20.	Netherlands	793
21.	Falkland Islands	789
21.	French Guiana	789
21.	Tonga	789
24.	Barbados	761
24.	Canada	761

20.	Taiwan	5,060
21.	Yugoslavia	4,618
22.	Czechoslovakia	4,323
23.	Hungary	3,970
24.	Romania	3,912
25.	Indonesia	3,500

19.	West Germany	360
20.	East Germany	358
21.	Isle of Man	323[2]
22.	Norway	318
22.	San Marino	318
24.	Bahrain	317
25.	Austria	311

[1]1984.
[2]1985.
For an explanation of symbols and abbreviations, see pages 16–17.

3p. Countries with Largest Number of Students

Contents

   I. All students

      Rank for total number of students.

      Conventional name of country.

      Year of data.

      Thousands of full-time and part-time students, excluding correspondence students and excluding pupils enrolled in kindergartens and nursery schools.

      Rank for percentage of school-age population enrolled in schools.

      Conventional name of country.

      Year of data.

      Percentage of school-age population (i.e., 5–24 years of age) enrolled in schools.

   II. College and university students

      Rank for total number of college and university students.

      Conventional name of country.

      Year of data.

      Thousands of college and university students.

      Rank for number of college and university students per capita.

      Conventional name of country.

      Year of data.

      Number of college and university students per thousand inhabitants.

Coverage

50 countries each with largest number of students, highest percentage of school-age population enrolled in schools, largest number of college and university students, and largest number of college and university students per thousand inhabitants.

Entries

201.

TABLE 3p. COUNTRIES WITH LARGEST NUMBER OF STUDENTS

I. All Students (Total Number and by Percentage of School-Age Population)

Rank	Country	Year	Students (1,000)	Rank	Country	Year	% of Population Aged 5–24
1.	China	1984	185,427	1.	Tokelau	1983	102.8
2.	India	1983	126,698	2.	Monaco	1982	96.2
3.	USA	1982	53,959	3.	Congo	1982	87.2
4.	USSR	1983	48,020	4.	Christmas Island (Australia)	1983	80.5
5.	Indonesia	1983	37,171				
6.	Brazil	1983	29,240	5.	New Caledonia	1984	80.3
7.	Japan	1984	24,524	6.	Isle of Man	1985	77.8
8.	Mexico	1984	22,578	7.	Tonga	1984	75.5
9.	Nigeria	1980	15,792	8.	Virgin Islands (USA)	1985	75.3
10.	Philippines	1983	13,498				
11.	Bangladesh	1984	12,413	9.	Bermuda	1983	73.9
12.	Vietnam	1980	11,936	10.	Puerto Rico	1983	72.6
13.	West Germany	1984	11,570	11.	Ireland	1983	72.2
14.	UK	1982	11,152	12.	Pacific Islands (USA)	1983	72.1
15.	South Korea	1984	10,952				
16.	France	1983	10,693	13.	USA	1982	71.2
17.	Italy	1983	10,518	14.	Libya	1982	69.1
18.	Thailand	1983	10,517	15.	Gibraltar	1984	69.0
19.	Turkey	1983	9,373	15.	Wallis and Futuna Islands	1983	69.0
20.	Pakistan	1983	9,255				
21.	Egypt	1983	9,186	17.	Guadeloupe	1982	68.9
22.	Iran	1983	8,978	18.	American Samoa	1983	68.7
23.	Spain	1982	8,534	18.	Denmark	1983	68.7
24.	Poland	1984	7,012	18.	Zimbabwe	1985	68.7
25.	Argentina	1983	6,363	21.	Canada	1983	68.6
26.	Colombia	1984	6,323	22.	New Zealand	1983	68.3
27.	Burma	1984	6,297	23.	Cook Islands	1983	68.2
28.	South Africa	1983	6,096	24.	Japan	1984	68.1
29.	Canada	1983	5,616	25.	West Bank	1984	67.3
30.	Peru	1982	5,010	26.	Finland	1983	66.8
31.	Algeria	1983	4,906	27.	Cayman Islands	1980	66.7
32.	Kenya	1983	4,863	28.	Jordan	1983	66.6
33.	Zaire	1978	4,771	29.	Norway	1982	66.4
34.	Taiwan	1984	4,620	30.	Ecuador	1983	66.3
35.	Romania	1983	4,513	30.	Sweden	1983	66.3
36.	Yugoslavia	1983	4,205	32.	Spain	1982	66.1
37.	Venezuela	1983	4,097	33.	West Germany	1984	65.9
38.	North Korea	1976	4,062	34.	Netherlands	1983	65.8
39.	Iraq	1983	3,894	35.	Israel	1983	65.6
40.	Malaysia	1985	3,693	36.	Iceland	1983	65.5
41.	Tanzania	1983	3,640	36.	UK	1982	65.5
42.	Morocco	1983	3,624	38.	Faeroe Islands	1984	65.4
43.	Sri Lanka	1984	3,591	39.	Bahamas	1982	65.0
44.	Australia	1983	3,169	40.	France	1983	64.5
45.	Ethiopia	1982	3,071	41.	Samoa	1983	64.3
46.	Netherlands	1983	2,986	42.	Guam	1983	64.0
47.	Chile	1984	2,837	43.	Saint Lucia	1983	63.3
48.	East Germany	1983	2,833	44.	Romania	1983	62.9
49.	Zimbabwe	1985	2,757	45.	Peru	1982	62.7
50.	Syria	1983	2,720	46.	South Korea	1984	61.8
				47.	Greece	1982	61.7
				48.	Austria	1984	61.6
				49.	Martinique	1982	61.5
				49.	Mayotte	1984	61.5

For an explanation of symbols and abbreviations, see pages 16–17.

(Continued)

TABLE 3p. (Continued)

II. College and University Students (Total Number and per Thousand Inhabitants)

Rank	Country	Year	Students (1,000)	Rank	Country	Year	Per 1,000 Inhabitants
1.	USA	1982	12,426	1.	Isle of Man	1985	56.9
2.	India	1979	5,346	2.	USA	1982	53.5
3.	USSR	1983	5,301	3.	Bermuda	1982	49.1
4.	Japan	1984	2,337	4.	Puerto Rico	1983	47.1
5.	Philippines	1983	1,576	5.	Faeroe Islands	1984	44.4
6.	Brazil	1984	1,453	6.	Canada	1983	41.8
7.	West Germany	1984	1,314	7.	Ecuador	1981	33.6
8.	China	1983	1,237	8.	Guam	1979	30.8
9.	France	1983	1,207	9.	Philippines	1983	30.3
10.	South Korea	1984	1,193	10.	South Korea	1984	29.4
11.	Mexico	1983	1,121	11.	American Samoa	1979	28.1
12.	Italy	1983	1,120	12.	Lebanon	1982	27.7
13.	UK	1982	1,111	13.	Costa Rica	1983	26.9
14.	Thailand	1982	1,057	14.	Sweden	1983	26.8
15.	Canada	1983	1,041	15.	Netherlands	1982	26.5
16.	Spain	1982	731	15.	New Zealand	1983	26.5
17.	Egypt	1982	634	17.	Virgin Islands (USA)	1985	25.5
18.	Indonesia	1982	616				
19.	Argentina	1983	581	18.	Finland	1983	24.7
20.	Pakistan	1983	556	19.	Israel	1983	24.5
21.	Taiwan	1984	412	20.	East Germany	1982	24.1
22.	East Germany	1982	403	21.	Panama	1984	23.9
23.	Bangladesh	1983	387	22.	Seychelles	1985	23.1
24.	Colombia	1983	379	23.	Belgium	1983	22.8
24.	Netherlands	1982	379	24.	Australia	1983	22.7
26.	Yugoslavia	1983	375	25.	Venezuela	1983	22.4
27.	Venezuela	1983	367	26.	Cook Islands	1980	22.2
28.	Peru	1982	365	26.	Monaco	1983	22.2
29.	Poland	1984	350	28.	France	1983	22.1
30.	Australia	1983	349	29.	Iceland	1983	21.9
31.	Turkey	1983	335	30.	Taiwan	1984	21.8
32.	North Korea	1974	300	30.	Thailand	1982	21.8
33.	Ecuador	1981	264	32.	Denmark	1982	21.7
34.	South Africa	1983	248	33.	Norway	1982	21.6
35.	Belgium	1983	225	34.	West Germany	1984	21.5
36.	Sweden	1983	223	35.	Peru	1982	20.7
37.	Cuba	1983	192	36.	Jordan	1983	20.4
38.	Czechoslovakia	1983	182	37.	Barbados	1983	20.3
39.	Nigeria	1981	177	38.	Austria	1984	20.1
40.	Burma	1984	174	39.	Italy	1983	19.7
40.	Romania	1983	174	39.	UK	1982	19.7
42.	Puerto Rico	1983	154	41.	Argentina	1983	19.6
43.	Austria	1984	152	42.	Japan	1984	19.5
44.	Iran	1983	151	42.	USSR	1983	19.5
45.	Syria	1982	141	44.	Cuba	1983	19.4
46.	Greece	1982	137	44.	North Korea	1974	19.4
47.	Chile	1983	127	46.	Spain	1982	19.3
47.	Iraq	1983	127	47.	Ireland	1981	17.4
49.	Finland	1983	120	48.	Uruguay	1983	17.2
50.	Vietnam	1980	115	49.	Switzerland	1984	16.5
				50.	Qatar	1983	16.4
				50.	Yugoslavia	1983	16.4

Figure 24. *Waterfront at Douglas, capital of the Isle of Man, a British dependency in the Irish Sea, which apparently has a higher proportion of college and university students than any other country. (Credit: British Information Services.)*

3q. Countries with Highest Rates of Illiteracy

Contents

Rank.

Conventional name of country.

Year of data.

Percentage of adult population (generally defined in this connection as persons aged 15 years or over) that is illiterate (i.e., unable to read and write).

Coverage

50 countries with highest rates of illiteracy.

Entries

50.

TABLE 3q. COUNTRIES WITH HIGHEST RATES OF ILLITERACY

Rank	Country	Year	% Illiterate	Rank	Country	Year	% Illiterate
1.	Somalia	1985	88.4	27.	Liberia	1985	65.0
2.	Djibouti	1980	88.1	28.	Equatorial Guinea	1980	63.0
3.	Burkina Faso	1985	86.8	29.	Haiti	1985	62.4
4.	North Yemen	1985	86.3	30.	Mozambique	1985	62.0
5.	Niger	1985	86.1	31.	Christmas Island	1984	60.0
6.	Comoros	1984	85.0		(Australia)		
7.	Mali	1985	83.2	32.	Central African	1985	59.8
8.	Mauritania	1976	82.6		Republic		
9.	Bhutan	1977	82.0	33.	Togo	1985	59.3
10.	Sudan	1980	78.4	34.	Angola	1985	59.0
11.	Afghanistan	1985	76.3	35.	Malawi	1985	58.8
12.	Saudi Arabia	1980	75.4	36.	South Yemen	1985	58.6
13.	Gambia	1985	74.9	37.	Nigeria	1985	57.6
14.	Chad	1985	74.7	38.	Ivory Coast	1985	57.3
15.	Nepal	1985	74.4	39.	India	1985	56.5
16.	Benin	1985	74.1	40.	Egypt	1985	55.5
17.	Pakistan	1981	73.8	41.	Papua New Guinea	1985	54.5
18.	Senegal	1985	71.9	42.	Rwanda	1985	53.4
19.	Guinea	1985	71.7	43.	Cape Verde	1985	52.6
20.	Sierra Leone	1985	70.7	44.	Tanzania	1980	52.5
21.	Oman	1985	70.4	45.	Kampuchea	1980	52.0
22.	Guinea-Bissau	1985	68.6	46.	Algeria	1985	50.4
23.	Bangladesh	1985	66.9	47.	Iran	1985	49.2
23.	Morocco	1985	66.9	48.	Qatar	1981	48.9
25.	Burundi	1982	66.2	49.	Vanuatu	1979	47.1
26.	Wallis and Futuna Islands	?	65.8	50.	Ghana	1985	46.8

For an explanation of symbols and abbreviations, see pages 16–17.

4

CITY COMPARISONS

4a. Largest Cities, Including Adjacent Suburban Areas

Contents

Rank.

Conventional name of city, and division and country in which located.

Year of data. If the year is followed by the letter "e," the population has been estimated; otherwise, the figure given is from census returns.

Latest population, in thousands, of city and adjacent suburban areas. Preferably, this is the population of the urbanized area or conurbation only, but some officially reported suburban areas include rural districts. When population data are not officially supplied for the suburbs of a city, the latest population of the city proper is given (and the letter "s" is omitted). In many instances, however, these cities have already annexed a number of suburban areas.

Coverage

All cities with a population of at least 1,500,000, including adjacent suburban areas.

Rounding

Populations are rounded to the nearest 1,000.

Entries

120.

TABLE 4a. LARGEST CITIES, INCLUDING ADJACENT SUBURBAN AREAS[1]

Rank	City and Location	Population (thousands)	Year	Rank	City and Location	Year	Population (thousands)
1.	New York, New York, USA	15,590s	1980	38.	Toronto, Ontario, Canada	1986	3,427s
2.	Mexico, Distrito Federal, Mexico	13,354s	1980	39.	Ho Chi Minh City, Vietnam	1979	3,420s
3.	Tokyo, Honshu I, Japan	11,828s	1985	40.	Shenyang, Liaoning, China	1985e	3,253
4.	Sao Paulo, Sao Paulo, Brazil	10,099s	1985e	41.	Madrid, Castilla la Nueva, Spain	1985e	3,209
5.	Buenos Aires, Distrito Federal, Argentina	9,766s	1980	42.	San Francisco, California, USA	1980	3,191s
6.	Seoul, South Korea	9,646	1985	43.	Berlin, East and West Germany	1985e	3,069
7.	Los Angeles, California, USA	9,480s	1980		East Berlin, East Germany	1985e	1,216
8.	Calcutta, West Bengal, India	9,194s	1981		West Berlin, West Berlin, West Germany	1985e	1,853
9.	Paris, Region Parisienne, France	8,707s	1982	44.	Athens, Greece	1981	3,027s
10.	Moscow, Russia in Europe, USSR	8,642s	1985e	45.	Yokohama, Honshu I, Japan	1985	2,993
11.	Bombay, Maharashtra, India	8,243	1981	46.	Wuhan, Hubei, China	1985e	2,963
12.	Jakarta, Java I, Indonesia	7,873	1985e	47.	Lahore, Pakistan	1981	2,953
13.	Manila, Luzon I, Philippines	6,942s	1985e	48.	Melbourne, Victoria, Australia	1986e	2,942s
14.	Shanghai, China	6,871	1986e	49.	Bangalore, Karnataka, India	1981	2,922s
15.	Chicago, Illinois, USA	6,780s	1980	50.	Montreal, Quebec, Canada	1986	2,897s
16.	London, England, UK	6,696s	1981	51.	Rome, Lazio, Italy	1985e	2,827
17.	Cairo, Egypt	6,205	1985e	52.	Alexandria, Egypt	1985e	2,821
18.	Tehran, Iran	5,751	1985e	53.	Washington, District of Columbia, USA	1980	2,763s
19.	Delhi, Delhi, India	5,729s	1981	54.	Boston, Massachusetts, USA	1980	2,679s
20.	Rio de Janeiro, Rio de Janeiro, Brazil	5,615e	1985e	55.	Kinshasa, Zaire	1984	2,654
21.	Istanbul, Turkey	5,495	1985	56.	Osaka, Honshu I, Japan	1985	2,636
22.	Hong Kong, Hong Kong	5,396	1986	57.	Singapore, Singapore	1986e	2,586
23.	Karachi, Pakistan	5,181	1981	58.	Hanoi, Vietnam	1979	2,571s
24.	Beijing, China	5,103	1985e	59.	Guangzhou, Guangdong, China	1985e	2,569
25.	Bangkok, Thailand	5,018	1983e	60.	Ahmadabad, Gujarat, India	1981	2,548s
26.	Lima, Peru	5,008s	1985e	61.	Hyderabad, Andhra Pradesh, India	1981	2,546s
27.	Leningrad, Russia in Europe, USSR	4,867s	1985e	62.	Taipei, Taiwan	1985e	2,508
28.	Baghdad, Iraq	4,649s	1985e	63.	Rangoon, Burma	1983	2,459
29.	Santiago, Chile	4,318s	1985e	64.	Dallas, Texas, USA	1980	2,451s
30.	Madras, Tamil Nadu, India	4,289s	1981	65.	Kiev, Ukraine, USSR	1985e	2,448
31.	Tianjin, China	4,202	1985e	66.	Caracas, Venezuela	1980	2,426s
32.	Philadelphia, Pennsylvania, USA	4,113s	1980	67.	Houston, Texas, USA	1985	2,412s
33.	Bogota, Colombia	3,957	1985	68.	Casablanca, Morocco	1980	2,263s
34.	Detroit, Michigan, USA	3,809s	1980	69.	Ankara, Turkey	1982	2,252
35.	Pusan, South Korea	3,517	1985	70.	Harbin, Heilongjiang, China	1985	2,252
36.	Dhaka, Bangladesh	3,459s	1981	71.	Manchester, England, UK	1985e	2,245s
37.	Sydney, New South Wales, Australia	3,431s	1986e				

Rank	City	Year	Population
72.	Birmingham, England, UK	1981	2,244s
73.	Surabaya, Java I, Indonesia	1983e	2,224
74.	Guadalajara, Jalisco, Mexico	1980	2,193s
75.	Belo Horizonte, Minas Gerais, Brazil	1985e	2,122s
76.	Nagoya, Honshu I, Japan	1985	2,116
77.	Chongqing, Sichuan, China	1985e	2,080
78.	Budapest, Hungary	1986e	2,076
79.	Lisbon, Portugal	1981	2,069s
80.	Taegu, South Korea	1985	2,031
81.	Tashkent, Uzbekistan, USSR	1985e	2,030
82.	Havana, Cuba	1985e	2,015
83.	Bucharest, Romania	1984e	1,961s
84.	Nanjing, Jiangsu, China	1985e	1,919
85.	Monterrey, Nuevo Leon, Mexico	1980	1,913s
86.	Cape Town, Cape of Good Hope, South Africa	1985	1,912s
87.	Abidjan, Ivory Coast	1982e	1,850s
88.	Saint Louis, Missouri, USA	1980	1,849s
89.	Salvador, Bahia, Brazil	1985e	1,811s
90.	Pittsburgh, Pennsylvania, USA	1980	1,810s
91.	Medan, Sumatra I, Indonesia	1983e	1,805
92.	Minneapolis, Minnesota, USA	1980	1,788s
93.	Barcelona, Cataluna, Spain	1985e	1,769
94.	Baltimore, Maryland, USA	1980	1,755s
95.	Cleveland, Ohio, USA	1980	1,752s
96.	Xian, Shaanxi, China	1985e	1,732
97.	Algiers, Algeria	1983e	1,722
98.	Glasgow, Scotland, UK	1981	1,713s
99.	San Diego, California, USA	1980	1,704s
100.	Baku, Azerbaijan, USSR	1985e	1,693s
101.	Pune, Maharashtra, India	1981	1,686s
102.	Leeds, England, UK	1981	1,676s
103.	Warsaw, Poland	1985e	1,649
104.	Kanpur, Uttar Pradesh, India	1981	1,639s
105.	Atlanta, Georgia, USA	1980	1,613s
106.	Johannesburg, Tranvaal, South Africa	1985	1,609s
107.	Giza, Egypt	1985e	1,608
107.	Miami, Florida, USA	1980	1,608s
109.	Chengdu, Sichuan, China	1985e	1,591
110.	Fortaleza, Ceara, Brazil	1985	1,589s
111.	Hamburg, Hamburg, West Germany	1985e	1,586
112.	Brasilia, Distrito Federal, Brazil	1985e	1,577s
113.	Bandung, Java I, Indonesia	1983e	1,567
114.	Porto, Portugal	1981	1,562s
115.	Tel Aviv-Jaffa, Israel	1983	1,555s
116.	Kharkov, Ukraine, USSR	1985e	1,554
117.	Sapporo, Hokkaido I, Japan	1985	1,543
118.	Milan, Lombardia, Italy	1985e	1,536
119.	Vienna, Austria	1981	1,531
120.	Guayaquil, Ecuador	1986e	1,509s

Rank	City	Annual Growth Rate	Projected Population, Mid-1990	Rank	City	Annual Growth Rate	Projected Population, Mid-1990
1.	Mexico	4.3%	20,345,000s	7.	Seoul	3.4%	11,401,000
2.	New York	-0.4%	14,978,000s	8.	Buenos Aires	1.4%	11,223,000s
3.	Tokyo	0.2%	11,947,000s	9.	Los Angeles	1.3%	10,787,000s
4.	Sao Paulo	3.4%	11,937,000s	10.	Jakarta	3.9%	9,533,000
5.	Calcutta	2.7%	11,685,000s	11.	Moscow	1.2%	9,173,000s
6.	Bombay	3.3%	11,405,000	12.	Paris	0.4%	8,990,000s

[1]Population projections are unscientific and apt to be grossly misleading because of the many indeterminate factors involved. For this reason *World Facts and Figures* generally excludes them. Because of the great interest in the relative size of the world's largest cities, however, we have projected the population of the 12 largest cities, including adjacent suburban areas, to the year 1990, based solely on the current growth rates indicated in Table 2a, as follows:

For an explanation of symbols and abbreviations, see pages 16–17.

4b. Highest Cities

Contents

Rank.

Conventional name of city, and division and country in which located.

Elevation (i.e., altitude above sea level), in feet and meters. When available, the
given elevation is that of the city center or principal business district, or is an
average of elevations at several points in the city; otherwise, it is that of the
meteorological station.

Coverage

All cities listed in Table 2a with an elevation of at least 4,000 ft (1,219 m).

Entries

158.

TABLE 4b. HIGHEST CITIES

Rank	City and Location	Elevation ft	Elevation m	Rank	City and Location	Elevation ft	Elevation m
1.	Potosi, Bolivia	13,045	3976	34.	Manizales, Colombia	7,021	2140
2.	Oruro, Bolivia	12,146	3702	35.	Loja, Ecuador	7,005	2135
3.	Lhasa, Tibet, China	12,002	3658	36.	Darjiling, West Bengal, India	7,002	2134
4.	La Paz, Bolivia	11,910	3630	37.	Santa Fe, New Mexico, USA	6,950	2118
5.	Cuzco, Peru	11,152	3399	38.	Flagstaff, Arizona, USA	6,907	2105
6.	Huancayo, Peru	10,660	3249	39.	Guanajuato, Guanajuato, Mexico	6,726	2050
7.	Sucre, Bolivia	9,331	2844	40.	Morelia, Michoacan, Mexico	6,368	1941
8.	Tunja, Colombia	9,252	2820	41.	Kunming, Yunnan, China	6,211	1893
9.	Quito, Ecuador	9,249	2819	42.	Durango, Durango, Mexico	6,198	1889
10.	Toluca, Mexico, Mexico	8,793	2680	43.	Aguascalientes, Aguascalientes, Mexico	6,195	1888
11.	Bogota, Colombia	8,675	2644	44.	Leon, Guanajuato, Mexico	6,185	1885
12.	Cuenca, Ecuador	8,468	2581	45.	San Luis Potosi, San Luis Potosi, Mexico	6,158	1877
13.	Cochabamba, Bolivia	8,390	2557	46.	Erzurum, Turkey	6,132	1869
14.	Ambato, Ecuador	8,389	2557	47.	Harar, Ethiopia	6,089	1856
15.	Pasto, Colombia	8,291	2527	48.	Cheyenne, Wyoming, USA	6,062	1848
16.	Zacatecas, Zacatecas, Mexico	8,189	2496	49.	Colorado Springs, Colorado, USA	6,012	1832
17.	Pachuca de Soto, Hildalgo, Mexico	7,960	2426	50.	Sankt Moritz, Switzerland	5,978	1822
18.	Thimphu, Bhutan	7,950	2423	51.	Kabul, Afghanistan	5,971	1820
19.	Addis Ababa, Ethiopia	7,900	2408	52.	Celaya, Guanajuato, Mexico	5,932	1808
20.	Asmara, Ethiopia	7,789	2374	53.	Taxco, Guerrero, Mexico	5,840	1780
21.	Arequipa, Peru	7,559	2304	54.	Hamadan, Iran	5,824	1775
22.	Mexico, Distrito Federal, Mexico	7,546	2300	55.	Popayan, Colombia	5,774	1760
23.	Ciudad Lopez Mateos, Mexico, Mexico	7,507	2288	56.	Salamanca, Guanajuato, Mexico	5,765	1757
24.	Ecatepec, Mexico, Mexico	7,497	2285	57.	Arak, Iran	5,755	1754
25.	Netzahualcoyotl, Mexico, Mexico	7,474	2278	57.	Butte, Montana, USA	5,755	1754
26.	Naucalpan, Mexico, Mexico	7,438	2267	59.	Kerman, Iran	5,738	1749
27.	Tlaxcala, Tlaxcala, Mexico	7,389	2250	60.	Gejiu, Yunnan, China	5,709	1740
28.	Tlalnepantla, Mexico, Mexico	7,382	2250	60.	Johannesburg, Transvaal, South Africa	5,709	1740
29.	Xining, Qinghai, China	7,363	2244	60.	Soweto, Transvaal, South Africa	5,709	1740
30.	Sana, North Yemen	7,260	2213	63.	Van, Turkey	5,659	1725
31.	Simla, Himachal Pradesh, India	7,225	2202	64.	Irapuato, Guanajuato, Mexico	5,656	1724
32.	Laramie, Wyoming, USA	7,145	2178	65.	Queretaro, Queretaro, Mexico	5,528	1685
33.	Puebla, Puebla, Mexico	7,094	2162				

For an explanation of symbols and abbreviations, see pages 16–17.

(Continued)

Figure 25. Panorama of Potosi, Bolivia, the world's highest city, with Cerro Rico, celebrated for its silver lode, in the background. (Credit: Bolivian Institute of Tourism.)

TABLE 4b. (Continued)

Rank	City and Location	ft	m	Rank	City and Location	ft	m
66.	Tehuacan, Puebla, Mexico	5,499	1676	98.	Sanandaj, Iran	4,990	1521
67.	Quetta, Pakistan	5,496	1675	99.	Bello, Colombia	4,987	1520
68.	Zanjan, Iran	5,456	1663	100.	Fort Collins, Colorado, USA	4,984	1519
69.	Nairobi, Kenya	5,453	1662	101.	Albuquerque, New Mexico, USA	4,950	1509
70.	Germiston, Transvaal, South Africa	5,450	1661	102.	Lanzhou, Gansu, China	4,948	1508
71.	Boulder, Colorado, USA	5,430	1655	103.	Guatemala, Guatemala	4,928	1502
72.	Windhoek, Namibia	5,428	1654	104.	Baguio, Luzon I, Philippines	4,921	1500
73.	Benoni, Transvaal, South Africa	5,419	1652	104.	Shillong, Meghalaya, India	4,921	1500
74.	Merida, Venezuela	5,384	1641	106.	Armenia, Colombia	4,866	1483
75.	Gangtok, Sikkim, India	5,381	1640	107.	Harare, Zimbabwe	4,831	1472
76.	Uruapan del Progreso, Michoacan, Mexico	5,361	1634	108.	Orem, Utah, USA	4,756	1450
77.	Lakewood, Colorado, USA	5,355	1632	109.	Bozeman, Montana, USA	4,754	1449
78.	Taif, Hejaz, Saudi Arabia	5,348	1630	110.	Kohima, Nagaland, India	4,738	1444
79.	Aurora, Colorado, USA	5,342	1628	111.	Vereeniging, Transvaal, South Africa	4,725	1440
80.	Arvada, Colorado, USA	5,300	1615				
81.	Bukavu, Zaire	5,296	1614	112.	Idaho Falls, Idaho, USA	4,709	1435
82.	Denver, Colorado, USA	5,280	1609	113.	Pueblo, Colorado, USA	4,695	1431
83.	Saltillo, Coahuila, Mexico	5,246	1599	114.	Chihuahua, Chihuahua, Mexico	4,692	1430
84.	Zapopan, Jalisco, Mexico	5,243	1598	115.	Jalapa, Veracruz, Mexico	4,682	1427
85.	Tlaquepaque, Jalisco, Mexico	5,227	1593	116.	Bloemfontein, Orange Free State, South Africa	4,678	1426
86.	Isfahan, Iran	5,217	1590				
87.	Srinagar, Jammu and Kashmir, India	5,205	1586	117.	Pereira, Colombia	4,672	1424
88.	Maseru, Lesotho	5,154	1571	118.	Greeley, Colorado, USA	4,663	1421
89.	Guadalajara, Jalisco, Mexico	5,141	1567	119.	Carson City, Nevada, USA	4,660	1420
89.	Zamora, Michoacan, Mexico	5,141	1567	120.	Kashi, Xinjiang, China	4,629	1411
91.	Casper, Wyoming, USA	5,123	1561	121.	Grand Junction, Colorado, USA	4,596	1401
92.	Leninakan, Armenia, USSR	5,105	1556	122.	Provo, Utah, USA	4,549	1387
93.	Oaxaca, Oaxaca, Mexico	5,086	1550	123.	Logan, Utah, USA	4,535	1382
94.	Cuernavaca, Morelos, Mexico	5,059	1542	124.	Antananarivo, Madagascar	4,531	1381
95.	Medellin, Colombia	5,056	1541	125.	Paradise, Nevada, USA	4,520	1378
96.	Kigali, Rwanda	5,053	1540	126.	Reno, Nevada, USA	4,491	1369
97.	Shiraz, Iran	5,049	1539	127.	Tabriz, Iran	4,469	1362

For an explanation of symbols and abbreviations, see pages 16–17.

(Continued)

TABLE 4b. (Continued)

Rank	City and Location	Elevation ft	m	Rank	City and Location	Elevation ft	m
128.	Pocatello, Idaho, USA	4,464	1361	144.	West Valley City, Utah, USA	4,255	1297
129.	Chilpancingo, Guerrero, Mexico	4,462	1360	145.	Jujuy, Jujuy, Argentina	4,215	1285
130.	Zahedan, Iran	4,435	1352	146.	Orizaba, Veracruz, Mexico	4,213	1284
131.	Kirovakan, Armenia, USSR	4,429	1350	147.	Agartala, Tripura, India	4,200	1280
131.	Kitwe, Zambia	4,429	1350	148.	Lusaka, Zambia	4,196	1279
133.	Bulawayo, Zimbabwe	4,405	1343	149.	Shache, Xinjiang, China	4,187	1276
134.	Kathmandu, Nepal	4,388	1337	150.	Sivas, Turkey	4,183	1275
135.	Hargeisa, Somalia	4,377	1334	151.	Likasi, Zaire	4,167	1270
136.	Pretoria, Transvaal, South Africa	4,375	1333	152.	Ndola, Zambia	4,137	1261
137.	Orumiyeh, Iran	4,370	1332	153.	Helena, Montana, USA	4,124	1257
138.	Karaj, Iran	4,350	1326	154.	Ibague, Colombia	4,098	1249
139.	Bakhtaran, Iran	4,337	1322	155.	Yazd, Iran	4,068	1240
140.	Ogden, Utah, USA	4,299	1310	156.	Lubumbashi, Zaire	4,035	1230
141.	Ulan-Bator Mongolia	4,295	1309	157.	Kimberley, Cape of Good Hope, South Africa	4,013	1223
142.	Qazvin, Iran	4,272	1302	158.	Jos, Nigeria	4,009	1222
143.	Salt Lake City, Utah, USA	4,266	1300				

For an explanation of symbols and abbreviations, see pages 16–17.

4c. Oldest Cities, by Continent

Contents

Rank.

Conventional name of city, and division and country in which located.

Year or century in which the first permanent settlement within present city limits was made. A question mark following a given date usually indicates that although its exact origin is unknown, the city in question was first mentioned in historical records at that date. When the exact time of settlement cannot be ascertained but the city is known to have existed before a certain date, that date is given, preceded by the abbreviation "bef." It should be observed that the settlement date of a city bears no relation either to the date when the city was formally established or chartered or to the date when the present name was adopted.

Coverage

All cities listed in Table 2a that were settled as early as the following dates:

Africa—1600 AD
Asia—500 BC
Europe—300 BC
North America—1640 AD
Oceania—1850 AD
South America—1640 AD

Entries

407, as follows: Africa—61
Asia—58
Europe—76
North America—105
Oceania—22
South America—85

TABLE 4c. OLDEST CITIES, BY CONTINENT

AFRICA

Rank	City and Location	Date Settled	Rank	City and Location	Date Settled
1.	Giza, Egypt	bef 2568 BC	31.	Ife, Nigeria	11th c?
1.	Minya, Egypt	bef 2568 BC	31.	Timbuktu, Mali	11th c
3.	Asyut, Egypt	bef 2160 BC	34.	Marrakesh, Morocco	1062
3.	Luxor, Egypt	bef 2160 BC	35.	Zaria, Nigeria	1095?
5.	Fayyum, Egypt	20th c BC?	36.	Kano, Nigeria	12th c?
6.	Tangier, Morocco	15th c BC?	36.	Ouagadougou, Burkina Faso	12th c?
7.	Tripoli, Tripolitania, Libya	7th c BC?	36.	Rabat, Morocco	1150
8.	Aswan, Egypt	6th c BC?	36.	Tanta, Egypt	12th c?
8.	Bengasi, Cyrenaica, Libya	6th c BC?	40.	Mansurah, Egypt	1221
10.	Tunis, Tunisia	4th c BC?	41.	Benin City, Nigeria	1300?
11.	Alexandria, Egypt	332 BC	42.	Funchal, (Madeira Islands), Portugal	1425
12.	Constantine, Algeria	3rd c BC?	43.	Bobo Dioulasso, Burkina Faso	15th c?
13.	Safi, Morocco	bef 1st c AD	43.	Suez, Egypt	15th c
14.	Setif, Algeria	1st c	45.	Las Palmas, (Canary Islands), Spain	1478
15.	Sfax, Tunisia	2nd c?	46.	Sao Tome, Sao Tome and Principe	1493
15.	Tetouan, Morocco	2nd c?	47.	Santa Cruz de Tenerife, (Canary Islands), Spain	1494
17.	Cairo, Egypt	641?	48.	La Laguna, (Canary Islands), Spain	1496
18.	Annaba, Algeria	7th c	49.	Ede, Nigeria	1500?
18.	Harar, Ethiopia	7th c?	50.	Casablanca, Morocco	1515
18.	Sousse, Tunisia	7th c	51.	Maputo, Mozambique	1544
21.	Hulwan, Egypt	690?	52.	Accra, Ghana	16th c
22.	Mombasa, Kenya	8th c?	52.	Blida, Algeria	16th c
23.	Fez, Morocco	808	52.	Iwo, Nigeria	16th c
24.	Mogadishu, Somalia	908?	52.	Niamey, Niger	16th c?
25.	Algiers, Algeria	10th c	52.	Pointe-Noire, Congo	16th c?
25.	Meknes, Morocco	10th c	52.	Porto-Novo, Benin	16th c?
25.	Oran, Algeria	10th c	52.	Zanzibar, Zanzibar, Tanzania	16th c
28.	Mahalla al Kubra, Egypt	985?	59.	Luanda, Angola	1575
29.	Oujda, Morocco	994	60.	Kankan, Guinea	bef 1600
30.	Sale, Morocco	1039?	61.	Oshogbo, Nigeria	1600?
31.	Damanhur, Egypt	11th c?			

TABLE 4c. (Continued)

Rank	City and Location	Date Settled		Rank	City and Location	Date Settled
ASIA						
1.	Gaziantep, Turkey	3650 BC?		31.	Fuzhou, Fujian, China	10th c BC?
2.	Jerusalem, Israel	3000 BC?		31.	Hefei, Anhui, China	10th c BC?
2.	Kirkuk, Iraq	3000 BC?		31.	Nanchong, Sichuan, China	10th c BC?
4.	Konya, Turkey	2600 BC?		31.	Nanning, Guangxi, China	10th c BC?
5.	Xian, Shaanxi, China	2205 BC?		31.	Zhangshou, Fujian, China	10th c BC?
6.	Irbil, Iraq	bef 2000 BC		31.	Zhengzhou, Henan, China	10th c BC?
7.	Shaoxing, Zhejiang, China	2000 BC?		38.	Guangzhou, Guangdong, China	9th c BC?
8.	Luoyang, Henan, China	1900 BC?		39.	Trebizond, Turkey	756 BC?
9.	Nabulus, West Bank	19th c BC?		40.	Adana, Turkey	8th c BC?
10.	Changzhi, Shanxi, China	18th c BC		40.	Van, Turkey	8th c BC?
10.	Hebron, West Bank	18th c BC?		42.	Hengyang, Hunan, China	7th c BC?
12.	Ankara, Turkey	17th c BC?		42.	Huangshi, Hubei, China	7th c BC?
13.	Kurukshetra, Haryana, India	1500 BC?		42.	Kaifeng, Henan, China	7th c BC?
13.	Tirupati, Andhra Pradesh, India	1500 BC?		42.	Osaka, Honshu I, Japan	7th c BC?
15.	Tel Aviv-Jaffa, Israel	bef 1472 BC		42.	Shaoyang, Hunan, China	7th c BC?
16.	Gaza, Gaza Strip	1468 BC?		42.	Tripoli, Lebanon	7th c BC
17.	Beirut, Lebanon	15th c BC?		42.	Xuzhou, Jiangsu, China	7th c BC?
17.	Liaoyang, Liaoning, China	15th c BC?		42.	Yangzhou, Jiangsu, China	7th c BC?
19.	Damascus, Syria	bef 14th c BC		50.	Shashi, Hubei, China	bef 6th c BC
20.	Anyang, Henan, China	14th c BC?		51.	Mathura, Uttar Pradesh, India	600 BC?
21.	Kahramanmaras, Turkey	12th c BC?		51.	Sialkot, Pakistan	600 BC?
21.	Qufu, Shandong, China	12th c BC?		53.	Rangoon, Burma	585 BC
21.	Varanasi, Uttar Pradesh, India	12th c BC?		54.	Patna, Bihar, India	6th c BC?
24.	Jining, Shandong, China	bef 1122 BC		54.	Samsun, Turkey	6th c BC
25.	Pyongyang, North Korea	1122 BC		56.	Gaya, Bihar, India	545 BC?
26.	Malatya, Turkey	1113 BC?		57.	Colombo, Sri Lanka	543 BC?
27.	Hamadan, Iran	1100 BC?		58.	Suzhou, Jiangsu, China	525 BC?
28.	Izmir, Turkey	11th c BC?				
29.	Aleppo, Syria	bef 1000 BC		**EUROPE**		
29.	Bethlehem, West Bank	bef 1000 BC		1.	Zurich, Switzerland	3000 BC?
31.	Datong, Shanxi, China	10th c BC?		2.	Lisbon, Portugal	2000 BC?
						(Continued)

For an explanation of symbols and abbreviations, see pages 16–17.

Figure 26. *Vista of Gaziantep, Turkey, probably the oldest continuously populated city in the world, which was settled more than 5,600 years ago. (Credit: Turkish Tourism and Information Office.)*

TABLE 4c. (Continued)

Rank	City and Location	Date Settled	Rank	City and Location	Date Settled
2.	Porto, Portugal	2000 BC?	32.	Chartres, Centre, France	6th c BC?
4.	Volos, Greece	1425 BC?	32.	Kerch, Ukraine, USSR	6th c BC
5.	Athens, Greece	bef 13th c BC	32.	Kutaisi, Georgia, USSR	6th c BC
6.	La Coruna, Galicia, Spain	bef 12th c BC	32.	Monaco, Monaco	6th c BC?
7.	Malaga, Andalucia, Spain	12th c BC	32.	Perugia, Umbria, Italy	6th c BC?
8.	Cadiz, Andalucia, Spain	1100 BC	32.	Stara Zagora, Bulgaria	6th c BC?
9.	Pisa, Toscana, Italy	11th c BC?	32.	Tarragona, Cataluna, Spain	6th c BC?
10.	Metz, Lorraine, France	1000 BC?	32.	Varna, Bulgaria	6th c BC
10.	Rome, Lazio, Italy	1000 BC?	43.	Cagliari, Sardegna, Italy	540 BC
12.	Toulon, Provence-Cote d'Azur, France	9th c BC	44.	Bologna, Emilia-Romagna, Italy	510 BC?
13.	Cordova, Andalucia, Spain	bef 8th c BC	45.	Bergamo, Lombardia, Italy	5th c BC?
14.	Cannes, Provence-Cote d'Azur, France	8th c BC?	45.	Brindisi, Puglia, Italy	5th c BC?
14.	Catania, Sicilia, Italy	8th c BC	45.	Genoa, Liguria, Italy	5th c BC?
14.	Messina, Sicilia, Italy	8th c BC	45.	Gerona, Cataluna, Spain	5th c BC?
14.	Palermo, Sicilia, Italy	8th c BC	45.	Granada, Andalucia, Spain	5th c BC?
14.	Ravenna, Emilia-Romagna, Italy	8th c BC	45.	Le Mans, Pays de la Loire, France	5th c BC?
14.	Reggio di Calabria, Calabria, Italy	8th c BC	45.	Lerida, Cataluna, Spain	5th c BC
20.	Syracuse, Sicilia, Italy	734 BC	45.	Mainz, Rheinland-Pfalz, West Germany	5th c BC?
21.	Lucca, Toscana, Italy	718 BC?	45.	Mantua, Lombardia, Italy	5th c BC?
22.	Taranto, Puglia, Italy	708 BC?	45.	Modena, Emilia-Romagna, Italy	5th c BC?
23.	Istanbul, Turkey	658 BC	45.	Monza, Lombardia, Italy	5th c BC
24.	Constanta, Romania	7th c BC?	45.	Nice, Provence-Cote d'Azur, France	5th c BC?
24.	Huelva, Andalucia, Spain	7th c BC?	45.	Patras, Greece	5th c BC?
24.	Jerez de la Frontera, Andalucia, Spain	7th c BC?	45.	Piraeus, Greece	5th c BC
24.	Seville, Andalucia, Spain	7th c BC?	45.	Regensburg, Bayern, West Germany	5th c BC?
24.	Vigo, Galicia, Spain	7th c BC?	45.	Salamanca, Leon, Spain	5th c BC?
29.	Larissa, Greece	bef 6th c BC	45.	Siena, Toscana, Italy	5th c BC?
30.	Marseilles, Provence-Cote d'Azur, France	600 BC?	45.	Urbino, Marche, Italy	5th c BC?
30.	Naples, Campania, Italy	600 BC?	63.	Rhodes, Greece	407 BC
32.	Besancon, Franche-Comte, France	6th c BC?	64.	Rimini, Emilia-Romagna, Italy	400 BC?
32.	Brescia, Lombardia, Italy	6th c BC	65.	Ancona, Marche, Italy	390 BC?
32.	Bristol, England, UK	6th c BC	66.	Arezzo, Toscana, Italy	4th c BC?

For an explanation of symbols and abbreviations, see pages 16–17.

(Continued)

TABLE 4c. (Continued)

Rank	City and Location	Date Settled
66.	Milan, Lombardia, Italy	4th c BC
66.	Trent, Trentino-Alto Adige, Italy	4th c BC?
66.	Turin, Piemonte, Italy	4th c BC?
66.	Vienna, Austria	4th c BC?
71.	Plovdiv, Bulgaria	341 BC?
72.	Cosenza, Calabria, Italy	bef 331 BC
73.	Salonika, Greece	315 BC
74.	Padua, Veneto, Italy	302 BC?
75.	Rheims, Champagne, France	300 BC?
75.	Toulouse, Midi-Pyrenees, France	300 BC?

NORTH AMERICA

Rank	City and Location	Date Settled
1.	Toluca, Mexico, Mexico	1120 AD?
2.	Jalapa, Veracruz, Mexico	1313?
3.	Mexico, Distrito Federal, Mexico	1325
4.	Guanajuato, Guanajuato, Mexico	bef 1400
5.	Queretaro, Queretaro, Mexico	1440
6.	Tlalnepantla, Mexico, Mexico	15th c
6.	Tlaxcala, Tlaxcala, Mexico	15th c?
8.	Orizaba, Veracruz, Mexico	1457
9.	Oaxaca, Oaxaca, Mexico	1486
10.	Santo Domingo, Dominican Republic	1496
11.	Fort Walton Beach, Florida, USA	bef 1500
12.	Santiago de los Caballeros, Dominican Republic	1504
13.	Bayamo, Cuba	1513
14.	Santiago de Cuba, Cuba	1514
15.	Campeche, Campeche, Mexico	bef 1517
16.	Havana, Cuba	1519
17.	Cuernavaca, Morelos, Mexico	bef 1521
17.	Managua, Nicaragua	bef 1521
19.	San Juan, Puerto Rico	1521
20.	Colima, Colima, Mexico	1522
21.	Tepic, Nayarit, Mexico	bef 1524
22.	San Salvador, El Salvador	1525
23.	Willemstad, Netherlands Antilles	1527
24.	Merida, Yucatan, Mexico	bef 1528
25.	Camaguey, Cuba	1528
26.	Taxco, Guerrero, Mexico	1529
27.	San Miguel, El Salvador	1530
28.	Puebla, Puebla, Mexico	1532
29.	Culiacan, Sinaloa, Mexico	1533
30.	Pachuca de Soto, Hidalgo, Mexico	1534
30.	Spanish Town, Jamaica	1534
32.	San Pedro Sula, Honduras	1536
32.	Uruapan del Progreso, Michoacan, Mexico	1536
34.	Tallahassee, Florida, USA	bef 1539
35.	Tehuacan, Puebla, Mexico	1540
35.	Zamora, Michoacan, Mexico	1540
37.	Mazatlan, Sinaloa, Mexico	bef 1541
38.	Morelia, Michoacan, Mexico	1541
38.	Zapopan, Jalisco, Mexico	1541
40.	Guadalajara, Jalisco, Mexico	1542
41.	Irapuato, Guanajuato, Mexico	1547
42.	Zacatecas, Zacatecas, Mexico	1548
43.	Acapulco, Guerrero, Mexico	1550
43.	Netzahualcoyotl, Mexico, Mexico	16th c?
45.	Durango, Durango, Mexico	1563
46.	Saint Augustine, Florida, USA	1565
47.	Celaya, Guanajuato, Mexico	1570
48.	Pinar del Rio, Cuba	1571
49.	Aguascalientes, Aguascalientes, Mexico	1575
49.	Saltillo, Coahuila, Mexico	1575
51.	Leon, Guanajuato, Mexico	1576
51.	San Luis Potosi, San Luis Potosi, Mexico	1576
51.	Santa Ana, El Salvador	1576?

TABLE 4c. (Continued)

Rank	City and Location	Date Settled
54.	Tegucigalpa, Honduras	1578
55.	Monterrey, Nuevo Leon, Mexico	1579?
56.	Coatzacoalcos, Veracruz, Mexico	1580
57.	Saint John's, Newfoundland, Canada	1583?
58.	Chilpancingo, Guerrero, Mexico	1591
59.	Port of Spain, Trinidad and Tobago	bef 1595
60.	Villahermosa, Tabasco, Mexico	1596
61.	Santa Catarina, Nuevo Leon, Mexico	1597
62.	Veracruz, Veracruz, Mexico	1599
63.	Salamanca, Guanajuato, Mexico	1603
64.	Quebec, Quebec, Canada	1608
65.	Santa Fe, New Mexico, USA	1609
66.	Hampton, Virginia, USA	1610
66.	Leon, Nicaragua	1610
68.	Cordoba, Veracruz, Mexico	1617
69.	Chesapeake, Virginia, USA	1620?
69.	Plymouth, Massachusetts, USA	1620
71.	Newport News, Virginia, USA	1621
72.	Gloucester, Massachusetts, USA	1623
73.	Albany, New York, USA	1624
73.	New York, New York, USA	1624
73.	Portsmouth, New Hampshire, USA	1624
76.	Quincy, Massachusetts, USA	1625
77.	Salem, Massachusetts, USA	1626
78.	Bridgetown, Barbados	1628
79.	Jersey City, New Jersey, USA	1629?
79.	Lynn, Massachusetts, USA	1629
81.	Boston, Massachusetts, USA	1630
81.	Cambridge, Massachusetts, USA	1630
81.	Hoboken, New Jersey, USA	1630?
81.	Medford, Massachusetts, USA	1630
81.	Somerville, Massachusetts, USA	1630
86.	Williamsburg, Virginia, USA	1633
87.	Trois-Rivieres, Quebec, Canada	1634
87.	Waltham, Massachusetts, USA	1634
89.	Hartford, Connecticut, USA	1635
90.	Providence, Rhode Island, USA	1636
90.	Springfield, Massachusetts, USA	1636
92.	Belize, Belize	1638?
92.	Brookline, Massachusetts, USA	1638?
92.	Cranston, Rhode Island, USA	1638
92.	New Haven, Connecticut, USA	1638
92.	Taunton, Massachusetts, USA	1638
92.	Wilmington, Delaware, USA	1638
98.	Yonkers, New York, USA	bef 1639
99.	Bridgeport, Connecticut, USA	1639
99.	Chihuahua, Chihuahua, Mexico	1639
99.	Fairfield, Connecticut, USA	1639
99.	Newport, Rhode Island, USA	1639
99.	Newton, Massachusetts, USA	1639
104.	Greenwich, Connecticut, USA	1640
104.	New Bedford, Massachusetts, USA	1640

OCEANIA

Rank	City and Location	Date Settled
1.	Saipan, Pacific Islands (USA)	bef 1521 AD
2.	Agana, Guam	bef 1668
3.	Hilo, Hawaii, USA	bef 1778
4.	Tarawa, Kiribati	bef 1788
5.	Sydney, New South Wales, Australia	1788
6.	Honolulu, Hawaii, USA	bef 1794
7.	Hobart, Tasmania, Australia	1804
7.	Newcastle, New South Wales, Australia	1804
9.	Wollongong, New South Wales, Australia	1815

(Continued)

For an explanation of symbols and abbreviations, see pages 16–17.

TABLE 4c. (Continued)

Rank	City and Location	Date Settled
10.	Brisbane, Queensland, Australia	1824
10.	Canberra, Australian Capital Territory, Australia	1824?
12.	Perth, Western Australia, Australia	1829
13.	Melbourne, Victoria, Australia	1835
14.	Adelaide, South Australia, Australia	1836
15.	Geelong, Victoria, Australia	1837
16.	Papeete, French Polynesia	1840?
16.	Wellington, North I, New Zealand	1840
18.	Auckland, North I, New Zealand	1841
19.	Napier, North I, New Zealand	1844?
20.	Dunedin, South I, New Zealand	1845
21.	Apia, Samoa	bef 1850
22.	Christchurch, South I, New Zealand	1850

SOUTH AMERICA

Rank	City and Location	Date Settled
1.	Quito, Ecuador	1000 AD?
2.	Cuzco, Peru	11th c
3.	Arequipa, Peru	bef 1425
4.	Sao Vicente, Sao Paulo, Brazil	1510?
5.	Cumana, Venezuela	1523
6.	Santa Marta, Colombia	1525
7.	Lima, Peru	bef 1532
8.	Cartagena, Colombia	1533
9.	Cuenca, Ecuador	bef 1534
10.	Trujillo, Peru	1534
11.	Olinda, Pernambuco, Brazil	1535
11.	Recife, Pernambuco, Brazil	1535?
11.	Vila Velha, Espirito Santo, Brazil	1535
11.	Vitoria, Espirito Santo, Brazil	1535
15.	Cali, Colombia	1536
15.	Popayan, Colombia	1536
15.	Santos, Sao Paulo, Brazil	1536

Rank	City and Location	Date Settled
18.	Asuncion, Paraguay	1537
18.	Callao, Peru	1537
18.	Guayaquil, Ecuador	1537
21.	Bogota, Colombia	bef 1538
21.	Sucre, Bolivia	bef 1538
23.	Tunja, Colombia	bef 1539
24.	Pasto, Colombia	1539
25.	Paramaribo, Suriname	1540?
26.	Santiago, Chile	1541
27.	Valparaiso, Chile	1544?
28.	Arica, Chile	1545
28.	Potosi, Bolivia	1545
30.	La Paz, Bolivia	bef 1548
31.	Loja, Ecuador	1548
32.	Salvador, Bahia, Brazil	1549
33.	Concepcion, Chile	1550
33.	Iquitos, Peru	16th c
33.	Valledupar, Colombia	1550
36.	Ibague, Colombia	1551
36.	Santo Andre, Sao Paulo, Brazil	1551
38.	Barquisimeto, Venezuela	1552
38.	La Serena, Chile	1552
38.	Sao Bernardo do Campo, Sao Paulo, Brazil	1552
38.	Valdivia, Chile	1552
42.	Santiago del Estero, Santiago del Estero, Argentina	1553
43.	Sao Paulo, Sao Paulo, Brazil	1554
44.	Valencia, Venezuela	1555
45.	Merida, Venezuela	1558
46.	Guarulhos, Sao Paulo, Brazil	1560
46.	Mogi das Cruzes, Sao Paulo, Brazil	1560
48.	Mendoza, Mendoza, Argentina	1561

For an explanation of symbols and abbreviations, see pages 16–17.

(Continued)

Figure 27. The famous Church of San Francisco (completed in 1605) at Quito, probably the oldest city in the Western Hemisphere. (Credit: Ecuadorian Foundation for the Promotion of Tourism, Miami, Florida, USA.)

TABLE 4c. (Continued)

Rank	City and Location	Date Settled	Rank	City and Location	Date Settled
48.	San Cristobal, Venezuela	1561	67.	La Rioja, La Rioja, Argentina	1591
50.	San Juan, San Juan, Argentina	1562	69.	Jujuy, Jujuy, Argentina	1593
51.	Niteroi, Rio de Janeiro, Brazil	1565	70.	San Luis, San Luis, Argentina	1594
51.	Rio de Janeiro, Rio de Janeiro, Brazil	1565	71.	Ciudad Guayana, Venezuela	1595
53.	Caracas, Venezuela	1567	71.	Oruro, Bolivia	1595
53.	Nova Iguacu, Rio de Janeiro, Brazil	1567?	71.	Santa Cruz, Bolivia	1595
55.	Huancayo, Peru	bef 1571	74.	Jundiai, Sao Paulo, Brazil	1600?
56.	Maracaibo, Venezuela	1571	75.	Fortaleza, Ceara, Brazil	1609
57.	Cordoba, Cordoba, Argentina	1573	76.	Sao Jose dos Campos, Sao Paulo, Brazil	1611
57.	Santa Fe, Santa Fe, Argentina	1573	77.	Neiva, Colombia	1612
59.	Cochabamba, Bolivia	1574	77.	Sao Luis, Maranhao, Brazil	1612
60.	Buenos Aires, Distrito Federal, Argentina	1580	79.	Belem, Para, Brazil	1616
61.	Salta, Salta, Argentina	1582	79.	Medellin, Colombia	1616
62.	Joao Pessoa, Paraiba, Brazil	1585	81.	Bucaramanga, Colombia	1622
63.	Vina del Mar, Chile	1586?	82.	Georgetown, Guyana	1625
64.	Corrientes, Corrientes, Argentina	1588	83.	Portoviejo, Ecuador	1628
64.	Piura, Peru	1588	84.	Barranquilla, Colombia	1629
66.	Sorocaba, Sao Paulo, Brazil	1589	85.	Campos, Rio de Janeiro, Brazil	1634
67.	Baruta, Venezuela	1591?			

For an explanation of symbols and abbreviations, see pages 16–17.

4d. Warmest Cities

Contents

Rank.

Conventional name of city, and division and country in which located.

Average temperature throughout the year, in degrees Fahrenheit and in degrees Celsius (centigrade).

Period of time on which the average temperature is based.

Coverage

All cities listed in Table 2a with an average temperature of at least 81° F (27.2°C). For a few cities whose average temperature is unavailable, the temperature given is that of a nearby city of fairly similar elevation; the city so chosen is cited in a footnote.

Entries

103.

Note. More detailed climatic tables, giving temperature and precipitation data for all important cities, can be found on pp 484–578 of the previous edition of *World Facts and Figures*.

TABLE 4d. WARMEST CITIES

Rank	City and Location	Avg Temperature		Period of Record
		°F	°C	
1.	Djibouti, Djibouti	86.0	30.0	1912–14, 1939–60
2.	Timbuktu, Mali	84.7	29.3	1951–60
2.	Tirunelveli, Tamil Nadu, India	84.7[1]	29.3[1]	1951–60
2.	Tuticorin, Tamil Nadu, India	84.7[1]	29.3[1]	1951–60
5.	Nellore, Andhra Pradesh, India	84.6	29.2	1931–60
5.	Santa Marta, Colombia	84.6	29.2	1940–42, 1944
7.	Aden, South Yemen	84.0	28.9	1926–60
7.	Madurai, Tamil Nadu, India	84.0	28.9	1931–60
7.	Niamey, Niger	84.0	28.9	1945–60
10.	Hudaydah, North Yemen	83.8	28.8	? yrs bef 1971
10.	Ouagadougou, Burkina Faso	83.8	28.8	25 yrs bef 1960
10.	Thanjavur, Tamil Nadu, India	83.8[2]	28.8[2]	1931–60
10.	Tiruchirapalli, Tamil Nadu, India	83.8	28.8	1931–60
14.	Khartoum, Sudan	83.7	28.7	1931–60
14.	Khartoum North, Sudan	83.7[3]	28.7[3]	1931–60
14.	Omdurman, Sudan	83.7[3]	28.7[3]	1931–60
17.	Madras, Tamil Nadu, India	83.5	28.6	1931–60
17.	Port Sudan, Sudan	83.5	28.6	1943-60
19.	Jidda, Hejaz, Saudi Arabia	83.3	28.5	1951–60
20.	Tamale, Ghana	83.1	28.4	18 yrs bef 1961

[1]Data for Palayamcottai, nr Tirunelveli and Tuticorin.
[2]Data for Tiruchirapalli, nr Thanjavur.
[3]Data for Khartoum, nr Khartoum North and Omdurman.
For an explanation of symbols and abbreviations, see pages 16–17.

(Continued)

Figure 28. *Minaret of the Great Mosque at Djibouti in northeastern Africa, whose average daily temperature of 86° F (30° C) qualifies it as the world's warmest city. (Credit: Press and Information Division, Embassy of France, Washington.)*

TABLE 4d. WARMEST CITIES

Rank	City and Location	Avg Temperature		Period of Record
		°F	°C	
21.	Saint George's, Grenada	82.9	28.3	1951–60
21.	Sokoto, Nigeria	82.9	28.3	1931–48, 1951–60
23.	Bamako, Mali	82.6	28.1	1941–60
23.	Bangkok, Thailand	82.6	28.1	1931–60
23.	Pondicherry, Pondicherry, India	82.6[4]	28.1[4]	1931–60
23.	Tarawa, Kiribati	82.6	28.1	1951–70
27.	Kurnool, Andhra Pradesh, India	82.5	28.0	1931–60
27.	Male, Maldives	82.5	28.0	4 yrs bef 1948
29.	Ciudad Bolivar, Venezuela	82.4	28.0	1970–82
29.	Ciudad Guayana, Venezuela	82.4[5]	28.0[5]	1970–82
29.	Dagupan, Luzon I, Philippines	82.4	28.0	1951–70
29.	Erode, Tamil Nadu, India	82.4[6]	28.0[6]	1931–60
29.	Ndjamena, Chad	82.4	28.0	1951–60
29.	Salem, Tamil Nadu, India	82.4	28.0	1931–60
35.	Leon, Nicaragua	82.2	27.9	1965–73
35.	Muscat, Oman	82.2	27.9	1893–1960
35.	Phnom–Penh, Kampuchea	82.2	27.9	42 yrs bef 1961
35.	Valledupar, Colombia	82.2	27.9	1954–58
35.	Vellore, Tamil Nadu, India	82.2	27.9	1931–60
40.	Barranquilla, Colombia	82.0	27.8	1942–53, 1957–61
40.	Guntur, Andhra Pradesh, India	82.0[7]	27.8[7]	1931–60
40.	Jaffna, Sri Lanka	82.0	27.8	26 yrs bef 1930
40.	Oranjestad, Aruba	82.0	27.8	1961–72
40.	Penang, Peninsular Malaysia, Malaysia	82.0	27.8	49 yrs bef 1939
40.	Vijayawada, Andhra Pradesh, India	82.0[7]	27.8[7]	1931–60
40.	Wad Madani, Sudan	82.0	27.8	23 yrs bef 1934
47.	Cuttack, Orissa, India	81.9	27.7	1931–60
47.	Kakinada, Andhra Pradesh, India	81.9	27.7	1931–60
47.	Mandalay, Burma	81.9	27.7	1891–1961
47.	Rajahmundry, Andhra Pradesh, India	81.9[8]	27.7[8]	1931–60
47.	Surat, Gujarat, India	81.9	27.7	1931–60
47.	Warangal, Andhra Pradesh, India	81.9	27.7	1931–60
53.	Acapulco, Guerrero, Mexico	81.7	27.6	1921–60
53.	Ho Chi Minh City, Vietnam	81.7	27.6	1897–1944, 1947–60
53.	Ipoh, Peninsular Malaysia, Malaysia	81.7	27.6	? yrs bef 1963
53.	Songkhla, Thailand	81.7	27.6	1951–60
57.	Cabimas, Venezuela	81.6[9]	27.6[9]	28 yrs bef 1979
57.	Maracaibo, Venezuela	81.6	27.6	28 yrs bef 1979
59.	Bellary, Karnataka, India	81.6	27.5	1931–60
60.	Bandar Seri Begawan, Brunei	81.5	27.5	5 yrs bef 1967
60.	Boa Vista, Roraima, Brazil	81.5	27.5	? yrs bef 1975
60.	Cirebon, Java I, Indonesia	81.5	27.5	5 yrs bef 1980
60.	Dammam, Nejd, Saudi Arabia	81.5[10]	27.5[10]	1951–60
60.	Doha, Qatar	81.5[10]	27.5[10]	1951–60

[4]Data for Cuddalore, nr Pondicherry.
[5]Data for Ciudad Bolivar, nr Ciudad Guayana.
[6]Data for Salem, nr Erode.
[7]Data for Masulipatnam, nr Guntur and Vijayawada.
[8]Data for Kakinada, nr Rajahmundry.
[9]Data for Maracaibo, nr Cabimas.
[10]Data for Dhahran, Saudi Arabia, nr Dammam and Doha.

For an explanation of symbols and abbreviations, see pages 16–17.

(Continued)

TABLE 4d. WARMEST CITIES

Rank	City and Location	°F	°C	Period of Record
		Avg Temperature		
60.	Hyderabad, Pakistan	81.5	27.5	1931–60
60.	Willemstad, Netherlands Antilles	81.5	27.5	1948–70
67.	Bhubaneswar, Orissa, India	81.4	27.4	1952–58
68.	Cebu, Cebu I, Philippines	81.3	27.4	52 yrs bef 1961
68.	Cotonou, Berin	81.3	27.4	1952–60
68.	Denpasar, Bali I, Indonesia	81.3	27.4	12 yrs bef 1971
68.	Kanbe, Burma	81.3[11]	27.4[11]	1881–1940, 1949–60
68.	Pegu, Burma	81.3[11]	27.4[11]	1881–1940, 1949–60
68.	Porto–Novo, Berin	81.3	27.4	1941–70
68.	Rangoon, Burma	81.3	27.4	1881–1940, 1949–60
68.	Teresina, Piaui, Brazil	81.3	27.4	1931–60
76.	Ahmadabad, Gujarat, India	81.1	27.3	1931–60
76.	Bandar Abbas, Iran	81.1	27.3	1951–69
76.	Bilaspur, Madhya Pradesh, India	81.1[12]	27.3[12]	1951–60
76.	Bombay, Maharashtra, India	81.1	27.3	1931–60
76.	Calicut, Kerala, India	81.1	27.3	1931–60
76.	Cucuta, Colombia	81.1	27.3	1942–54, 1958–61
76.	Darwin, Northern Territory, Australia	81.1	27.3	1941–70
76.	Enugu, Nigeria	81.1	27.3	1951–60
76.	Medina, Hejaz, Saudi Arabia	81.1	27.3	1957–60
76.	Monteria, Colombia	81.1	27.3	1951–61
76.	Paramaribo, Suriname	81.1	27.3	1931–60
76.	Semarang, Java I, Indonesia	81.1	27.3	1961–70
76.	Tacloban, Leyte I, Philippines	81.1	27.3	1951–70
76.	Thana, Maharashtra, India	81.1[13]	27.3[13]	1931–60
76.	Ulhasnagar–Kalyan, Maharashtra, India	81.1[13]	27.3[13]	1931–60
91.	Agana, Guam	81.0	27.2	1951–70
91.	Akola, Maharashtra, India	81.0	27.2	1931–60
91.	Amravati, Maharashtra, India	81.0	27.2	1931–60
91.	Bhavnagar, Gujarat, India	81.0	27.2	1931–60
91.	Bobo Dioulasso, Burkina Faso	81.0	27.2	29 yrs bef 1956
91.	Gulbarga, Karnataka, India	81.0	27.2	1931–60
91.	Kuala Trengganu, Peninsular Malaysia, Malaysia	81.0	27.2	1924–36
91.	Kupang, Timor I, Indonesia	81.0	27.2	13 yrs bef 1971
91.	Mogadishu, Somalia	81.0	27.2	1931–60
91.	Peshawar, Pakistan	81.0	27.2	1931–60
91.	Sukkur, Pakistan	81.0[14]	27.2[14]	1929–61
91.	Surabaya, Java I, Indonesia	81.0	27.2	12 yrs bef 1971
91.	Visakhapatnam, Andhra Pradesh, India	81.0	27.2	1931–60

[11]Data for Rangoon, nr Kanbe and Pegu.
[12]Data for Champa, nr Bilaspur.
[13]Data for Bombay, nr Thana and Ulhasnagar–Kalyan.
[14]Data for Jacobabad, nr Sukkur.
For an explanation of symbols and abbreviations, see pages 16–17.

4e. Coolest Cities

Contents

Rank.

Conventional name of city, and division and country in which located.

Average temperature throughout the year, in degrees Fahrenheit and in degrees Celsius (centigrade).

Period of time on which the average temperature is based.

Coverage

All cities listed in Table 2a with an average temperature of 40°F (4.4°C) or lower. For a few cities whose average temperature is unavailable, the temperature given is that of a nearby city of fairly similar elevation; the city so chosen is cited in a footnote.

Entries

131.

Note. More detailed climatic tables, giving temperature and precipitation data for all important cities, can be found on pp 484–578 of the previous edition of *World Facts and Figures*.

TABLE 4e. COOLEST CITIES

Rank	City and Location	Avg Temperature °F	Avg Temperature °C	Period of Record
1.	Norilsk, Russia in Asia, USSR	12.4[1]	−10.9[1]	17 yrs bef 1925
2.	Yakutsk, Russia in Asia, USSR	13.8	−10.1	1931–60
3.	Yellowknife, NWT, Canada	22.3	−5.4	1951–80
4.	Ulan-Bator, Mongolia	23.9	−4.5	1936–60
5.	Fairbanks, Alaska, USA	25.9	−3.4	1951–80
6.	Surgut, Russia in Asia, USSR	26.4	−3.1	1884–1960
7.	Chita, Russia in Asia, USSR	27.1	−2.7	1890–1919, 1924–56
8.	Nizhnevartovsk, Russia in Asia, USSR	27.3[2]	−2.6[2]	1932–60
9.	Hailar, Inner Mongolia, China	27.7	−2.4	1909–42, 1950–53
10.	Bratsk, Russia in Asia, USSR	28.0	−2.2	1957–62
11.	Ulan–Ude, Russia in Asia, USSR	28.9	−1.7	66 yrs bef 1961
12.	Angarsk, Russia in Asia, USSR	29.7	−1.3	1951–60
13.	Whitehorse, Yukon Territory, Canada	29.8	−1.2	1951–80
14.	Irkutsk, Russia in Asia, USSR	30.0	−1.1	1881–1960
15.	Yakeshi, Inner Mongolia, China	30.2[3]	−1.0[3]	1914–32, 1951–53
16.	Godthab, Greenland	30.7	−0.7	1941–70
16.	Komsomolsk–na–Amure, Russia in Asia, USSR	30.7	−0.7	1932–33, 1935–60
18.	Tomsk, Russia in Asia, USSR	30.9	−0.6	1881–1960
19.	Kemerovo, Russia in Asia, USSR	31.3	−0.4	1933–60

[1]Data for Dudinka, nr Norilsk.
[2]Data for Aleksandrovskoye, nr Nizhnevartovsk.
[3]Data for Bugt (alt Pokotu), nr Yakeshi.

For an explanation of symbols and abbreviations, see pages 16–17. (Continued)

Figure 29. Lenin Avenue in the historic Siberian city of Yakutsk, whose average daily temperature of 13.8° F (-10.1° C) is the coolest for any city recorded over a recent extended period of time. (Credit: Sovfoto, New York.)

TABLE 4e. (Continued)

Rank	City and Location	Avg Temperature		Period of Record
		°F	°C	
20.	Novosibirsk, Russia in Asia, USSR	31.8	−0.1	1930–57
21.	Blagoveshchensk, Russia in Asia, USSR	32.0	0	1881–90, 1892–1960
21.	Omsk, Russia in Asia, USSR	32.0	0	1930–60
23.	Murmansk, Russia in Europe, USSR	32.2	0.1	1931–70
24.	Kurgan, Russia in Asia, USSR	32.4[4]	0.2[4]	? yrs bef 1948
25.	Prokopyevsk, Russia in Asia, USSR	32.7[5]	0.4[5]	1925–60
25.	Syktyvkar, Russia in Europe, USSR	32.7	0.4	1888–1960
27.	Biysk, Russia in Asia, USSR	32.9	0.5	1934–60
27.	Krasnoyarsk, Russia in Asia, USSR	32.9	0.5	1931–60
27.	Petropavlovsk, Kazakhstan, USSR	32.9	0.5	62 yrs bef 1961
30.	Zlatoust, Russia in Asia, USSR	33.1	0.6	? yrs bef 1959
31.	Berezniki, Russia in Europe, USSR	33.3	0.7	1891–1954
31.	Novokuznetsk, Russia in Asia, USSR	33.3	0.7	1931–37, 1944–54
33.	Archangel, Russia in Europe, USSR	33.4	0.8	1881–1970
33.	Severodvinsk, Russia in Europe, USSR	33.4	0.8	1945–60
35.	Beian, Heilongjiang, China	33.6[6]	0.9[6]	1933–41, 1952–53
35.	Nizhniy Tagil, Russia in Asia, USSR	33.6	0.9	1881–1912, 1915
37.	Barnaul, Russia in Asia, USSR	34.0	1.1	1881–1960
38.	Tyumen, Russia in Asia, USSR	34.3	1.3	1884–1942
39.	Khabarovsk, Russia in Asia, USSR	34.5	1.4	66 yrs bef 1961
39.	Tselinograd, Kazakhstan, USSR	34.5	1.4	73 yrs bef 1961
41.	Kirov, Russia in Europe, USSR	34.8	1.5	1881–1970
42.	Kamensk–Uralskiy, Russia in Asia, USSR	34.9[7]	1.6[7]	1931–60
42.	Kustanay, Kazakhstan, USSR	34.9	1.6	1950–63
42.	Rubtsovsk, Russia in Asia, USSR	34.9	1.6	1924–60
42.	Saskatoon, Saskatchewan, Canada	34.9	1.6	1951–80
42.	Sverdlovsk, Russia in Asia, USSR	34.9	1.6	1931–60
47.	Chelyabinsk, Russia in Asia, USSR	35.2	1.8	? yrs bef 1960
47.	Perm, Russia in Europe, USSR	35.2	1.8	1921–50, 1962–69
49.	Anchorage, Alaska, USA	35.3	1.8	1951–80
50.	Pavlodar, Kazakhstan, USSR	35.4	1.9	1906–11, 1922–60
50.	Petropavlovsk–Kamchatskiy, Russia in Asia, USSR	35.4	1.9	48 yrs bef 1961
50.	Sankt Moritz, Switzerland	35.4	1.9	1961–70
53.	Joensuu, Finland	35.5	1.9	1931–60
54.	Oulu, Finland	35.6	2.0	1881–1935
55.	Izhevsk, Russia in Europe, USSR	35.8	2.1	1933–60
55.	Yuzhno–Sakhalinsk, Russia in Asia, USSR	35.8	2.1	1946–60
57.	Petrozavodsk, Russia in Europe, USSR	36.0	2.2	1949–63
57.	Regina, Saskatchewan, Canada	36.0	2.2	1951–80
57.	Winnipeg, Manitoba, Canada	36.0	2.2	1951–80
60.	Karaganda, Kazakhstan, USSR	36.1	2.3	1933–60
60.	Temirtau, Kazakhstan, USSR	36.1[8]	2.3[8]	1933–60
60.	Thunder Bay, Ontario, Canada	36.1	2.3	1951–80
60.	Yoshkar–Ola, Russia in Europe, USSR	36.1	2.3	1940–60
64.	Naberezhnyye Chelny, Russia in Europe, USSR	36.3	2.4	1948–55

[4]Data for Staro-Siderovo, nr Kurgan.
[5]Data for Kiselevsk, nr Prokopyevsk.
[6]Data for Hailun, nr Beian.
[7]Data for Sverdlovsk, nr Kamensk-Uralskiy.
[8]Data for Karaganda, nr Temirtau.

For an explanation of symbols and abbreviations, see pages 16–17.

(Continued)

TABLE 4e. (Continued)

Rank	City and Location	°F	°C	Period of Record
		Avg Temperature		
64.	Vologda, Russia in Europe, USSR	36.3	2.4	1884–1918, 1924–70
66.	Daqing, Heilongjiang, China	36.5[9]	2.5[9]	1914–43, 1952–53
66.	Kuopio, Finland	36.5	2.5	1883–1935
66.	Suihua, Heilongjiang, China	36.5[9]	2.5[9]	1914–43, 1952–53
69.	Cherepovets, Russia in Europe, USSR	36.7	2.6	1937–60
69.	Sterlitamak, Russia in Europe, USSR	36.7	2.6	? yrs bef 1950
69.	Ufa, Russia in Europe, USSR	36.7	2.6	? yrs bef 1960
72.	Kostroma, Russia in Europe, USSR	36.9	2.7	1925–60
72.	Qiqihar, Heilongjiang, China	36.9	2.7	1930–42, 1949–53
72.	Yaroslavl, Russia in Europe, USSR	36.9[10]	2.7[10]	1925–60
75.	Jyvaskyla, Finland	37.0	2.8	1931–60
75.	Mudanjiang, Heilongjiang, China	37.0	2.8	1909–43, 1949–53
77.	Cheboksary, Russia in Europe, USSR	37.2	2.9	1927–60
77.	Tromso, Norway	37.2	2.9	1931–60
79.	Orsk, Russia in Europe, USSR	37.4	3.0	1925–60
79.	Ust–Kamenogorsk, Kazakhstan, USSR	37.4	3.0	1921–22, 1926–48
81.	Edmonton, Alberta, Canada	37.6	3.1	1951–80
82.	Dzerzhinsk, Russia in Europe, USSR	37.8[11]	3.2[11]	1922–70
82.	Gorkiy, Russia in Europe, USSR	37.8	3.2	1922–70
82.	Semipalatinsk, Kazakhstan, USSR	37.8	3.2	64 yrs bef 1949
82.	Ulyanovsk, Russia in Europe, USSR	37.8	3.2	1937–54
86.	Bozeman, Montana, USA	37.9	3.3	1951–80
86.	Harbin, Heilongjiang, China	37.9	3.3	1909–42, 1949–52
86.	Ivanovo, Russia in Europe, USSR	37.9	3.3	1891–1918, 1922–48
86.	Prince George, British Columbia, Canada	37.9	3.3	1951–80
86.	Sudbury, Ontario, Canada	37.9	3.3	1951–80
86.	Vladimir, Russia in Europe, USSR	37.9	3.3	? yrs bef 1948
92.	Calgary, Alberta, Canada	38.1	3.4	1951–80
92.	Chicoutimi, Quebec, Canada	38.1	3.4	1951–80
92.	Hegang, Heilongjiang, China	38.1[12]	3.4[12]	1938–42, 1949–53
92.	Jiamusi, Heilongjiang, China	38.1	3.4	1938–42, 1949–53
92.	Jonquiere, Quebec, Canada	38.1[13]	3.4[13]	1951–80
92.	Shuangyashan, Heilongjiang, China	38.1[12]	3.4[12]	1938–42, 1949–53
92.	Umea, Sweden	38.1	3.4	1931–60
99.	Duluth, Minnesota, USA	38.2	3.4	1951–80
100.	Vaasa, Finland	38.3	3.5	1931–60
101.	Kazan, Russia in Europe, USSR	38.4	3.6	1881–1970
102.	Aktyubinsk, Kazakhstan, USSR	38.5	3.6	46 yrs bef 1961
102.	Kaluga, Russia in Europe, USSR	38.5	3.6	20 yrs bef 1912
102.	North Bay, Ontario, Canada	38.5	3.6	1951–80
105.	Saransk, Russia in Europe, USSR	38.7	3.7	1927–42, 1944–60
106.	Butte, Montana, USA	38.8	3.8	1951–80
106.	Dunhua, Jilin, China	38.8[14]	3.8[14]	1950–52
106.	Jixi, Heilongjiang, China	38.8	3.8	1949–52
106.	Kuybyshev, Russia in Europe, USSR	38.8	3.8	1935–60
106.	Tampere, Finland	38.8	3.8	1931–60

[9]Data for Anda (alt Anta), nr Daqing and Suihua.
[10]Data for Kostroma, nr Yaroslavl.
[11]Data for Gorkiy, nr Dzerzhinsk.
[12]Data for Jiamusi, nr Hegang and Shuangyashan.
[13]Data for Chicoutimi, nr Jonquiere.
[14]Data for Jiaohe (alt Chiaoho), nr Dunhua.

TABLE 4e. (Continued)

Rank	City and Location	Avg Temperature °F	Avg Temperature °C	Period of Record
111.	Grand Forks, North Dakota, USA	38.9	3.8	1951–80
112.	Kalinin, Russia in Europe, USSR	39.0	3.9	? yrs bef 1948
112.	Novgorod, Russia in Europe, USSR	39.0	3.9	70 yrs bef 1961
112.	Orenburg, Russia in Europe, USSR	39.0	3.9	1886–1960
112.	Penza, Russia in Europe, USSR	39.0	3.9	1887–1919, 1923–1960
112.	Yinchuan, Ningxia, China	39.0	3.9	1951–53, 1955
117.	Vladivostok, Russia in Asia, USSR	39.2	4.0	1917–60
118.	Smolensk, Russia in Europe, USSR	39.3	4.1	1951–70
119.	Sault Sainte Marie, Ontario, Canada	39.6	4.2	1951–80
120.	Superior, Wisconsin, USA	39.7	4.3	1951–80
120.	Tula, Russia in Europe, USSR	39.7	4.3	? yrs bef 1948
122.	Leningrad, Russia in Europe, USSR	39.8	4.3	1881–1970
122.	Vitebsk, White Russia, USSR	39.8[15]	4.3[15]	? yrs bef 1948
124.	Jilin, Jilin, China	39.9	4.4	1911–13
124.	Ryazan, Russia in Europe, USSR	39.9	4.4	1892–1915
124.	Syzran, Russia in Europe, USSR	39.9	4.4	54 yrs bef 1961
124.	Tolyatti, Russia in Europe, USSR	39.9	4.4	1938–42
124.	Uralsk, Kazakhstan, USSR	39.9	4.4	1893–1917, 1923–60
129.	Juneau, Alaska, USA	40.0	4.4	1951–80
129.	Moscow, Russia in Europe, USSR	40.0	4.4	1931–70
129.	Podolsk, Russia in Europe, USSR	40.0[16]	4.4[16]	1931–70

[15]Data for Novoye Korolevo, nr Vitebsk.
[16]Data for Moscow, nr Podolsk.
For an explanation of symbols and abbreviations, see pages 16–17.

4f. Cities with Most Precipitation

Contents

Rank.

Conventional name of city, and division and country in which located.

Average annual precipitation (i.e., rainfall plus the rain equivalent of snowfall), in inches and in millimeters.

Period of time on which the average precipitation is based.

Coverage

All cities listed in Table 2a with annual precipitation averaging at least 80 in (2032 mm).

Entries

120.

Note. More detailed climatic tables, giving temperature and precipitation data for all important cities, can be found on pp 484–578 of the previous edition of *World Facts and Figures*.

TABLE 4f. CITIES WITH MOST PRECIPITATION

Rank	City and Location	Annual Precipitation		Period of Record
		in.	mm	
1.	Buenaventura, Colombia	265.47	6743	1910–16, 1956, 1959–61
2.	Monrovia, Liberia	202.01	5131	1953–56
3.	Pago Pago, American Samoa	196.46	4990	1932–42, 1945–51
4.	Moulmein, Burma	191.02	4852	1891–1940
5.	Lae, Papua New Guinea	182.87	4645	18 yrs bef 1971
6.	Baguio, Luzon I, Philippines	180.04	4573	1910–38
7.	Sylhet, Bangladesh	175.47	4457	? yrs bef 1984
8.	Padang, Sumatra I, Indonesia	173.35	4403	1891–1940
9.	Conakry, Guinea	170.91	4341	1922–54
10.	Bogor, Java I, Indonesia	166.34	4225	1933–37
11.	Douala, Cameroon	161.77	4109	1951–60
12.	Kuching, Sarawak, Malaysia	159.45	4050	1947–64
13.	Cayenne, French Guiana	147.40	3744	1951–60
14.	Freetown, Sierra Leone	143.27	3639	1874–1959
15.	Villavicencio, Colombia	140.20	3561	6 yrs bef 1951
16.	Ambon, Ambon I, Indonesia	138.98	3530	1879–1940, 1948–50
17.	Mangalore, Karnataka, India	133.78	3398	1931–60
18.	Pontianak, Borneo I, Indonesia	131.69	3345	1879–1950
19.	Bandar Seri Begawan, Brunei	131.0	3327	5 yrs bef 1967
20.	Colon, Panama	130.75	3321	1891–1940
21.	Legaspi, Luzon I, Philippines	128.23	3257	1951–70
22.	Hilo, Hawaii, USA	128.15	3255	1951–80
23.	Calicut, Kerala, India	125.12	3178	1931–60
24.	Libreville, Gabon	122.83	3120	1951–60
25.	Jambi, Sumatra I, Indonesia	122.01	3099	1956–65
26.	Macapa, Amapa, Brazil	121.26	3080	1967
27.	Calabar, Nigeria	120.87	3070	1895–1950
28.	Cochin, Kerala, India	119.96	3047	1931–60
29.	Keelung, Taiwan	119.80	3043	1903–52
30.	Hue, Vietnam	118.78	3017	1931–44, 1947–62
31.	Suva, Fiji	115.79	2941	1951–70
32.	Apia, Samoa	113.58	2885	1941–70
33.	Coatzacoalcos, Veracruz, Mexico	113.54	2884	1921–44
34.	Minatitlan, Veracruz, Mexico	113.23	2876	1921–44
35.	Chittagong, Bangladesh	112.52	2858	1931–60
36.	Iquitos, Peru	112.01	2845	1949–70
37.	Kuala Trengganu, Peninsular Malaysia, Malaysia	111.30	2827	1924–36, 1961–70
38.	Johore Baharu, Peninsular Malaysia, Malaysia	109.49	2781	1975–78
39.	Kota Kinabalu, Sabah, Malaysia	109.21	2774	1947–63
39.	Ujung Pandang, Celebes I, Indonesia	109.21	2774	1956–65
41.	Bassein, Burma	108.98	2768	1881–1940
42.	Panaji, Goa, Daman, and Diu, India	108.94	2767	1931–60
43.	Kota Baharu, Peninsular Malaysia, Malaysia	108.70	2761	1951–70
44.	Dibrugarh, Assam, India	108.62	2759	1931–60
45.	Darjiling, West Bengal, India	108.58	2758	1931–60
46.	Banjarmasin, Borneo I, Indonesia	108.46	2755	1956–65
47.	Manado, Celebes I, Indonesia	107.95	2742	1891–1940
48.	Salatiga, Java I, Indonesia	105.87	2689	1879–1941
49.	Pakanbaru, Sumatra I, Indonesia	105.20	2672	1907–41, 1961–70
50.	Kanazawa, Honshu I, Japan	104.80	2662	1941–70

For an explanation of symbols and abbreviations, see pages 16–17.   (Continued)

Figure 30. *Port area of Buenaventura, Colombia, whose average annual rainfall of about 265.5 inches (6743 millimeters) designates it as the city with the most precipitation. (Credit: Colombia Information Service, New York.)*

TABLE 4f. (Continued)

Rank	City and Location	Annual Precipitation		Period of Record
		in.	mm	
51.	Rangoon, Burma	104.29	2649	1881–1940, 1949–60
52.	Kochi, Shikoku I, Japan	104.09	2644	1941–70
53.	Miyazaki, Kyushu I, Japan	102.13	2594	1941–70
54.	Jayapura, Irian Jaya, Indonesia	100.12	2543	34 yrs bef 1971
55.	Jember, Java I, Indonesia	99.02	2515	1887–1941
56.	Moroni, Comoros	98.94	2513	1951–52, 1955–70
57.	Penang, Peninsular Malaysia, Malaysia	98.74	2508	1961–70
58.	Kuala Lumpur, Peninsular Malaysia, Malaysia	98.52	2502	1951–70
59.	Thana, Mararashtra, India	97.52	2477	1901–50
60.	Fukui, Honshu I, Japan	97.32	2472	1948–70
61.	Naga, Luzon I, Philippines	96.50	2451	1916–38
62.	Kagoshima, Kyushu I, Japan	95.79	2433	1941–70
63.	Armenia, Colombia	95.71	2431	1946–50
64.	Shillong, Meghalaya, India	95.08	2415	1931–60
65.	Colombo, Sri Lanka	94.3	2395	1931–60
65.	Port Harcourt, Nigeria	94.3	2395	1951–60
67.	Toyama, Honshu I, Japan	94.02	2388	1941–70
68.	Rhondda, Wales, UK	93.87	2384	1916–50
69.	Palembang, Sumatra I, Indonesia	93.74	2381	1956–65
70.	Ipoh, Peninsular Malaysia, Malaysia	93.07	2364	1961–70
71.	Shizuoka, Honshu I, Japan	92.72	2355	1941–70
71.	Ulhasnagar–Kalyan, Maharashtra, India	92.72	2355	1901–50
73.	Quezon City, Luzon I, Philippines	91.62	2327	1952–55
74.	Mymensingh, Bangladesh	91.43	2322	35 yrs bef 1937
75.	Kingstown, Saint Vincent and the Grenadines	90.12	2289	1914–27
76.	Singapore, Singapore	89.49	2273	1951–70
77.	Nikko, Honshu I, Japan	89.41	2271	1944–70
78.	Cordoba, Veracruz, Mexico	89.29	2268	1921–44
79.	Valdivia, Chile	89.17	2265	? yrs bef 1981
80.	Aba, Nigeria	89.1	2263	? yrs bef 1961
81.	Cirebon, Java I, Indonesia	88.90	2258	1937
81.	Paramaribo, Suriname	88.90	2258	1931–60
83.	Balikpapan, Borneo I, Indonesia	88.62	2251	35 yrs bef 1937
84.	Porto Velho, Rondonia, Brazil	88.58	2250	? yrs bef 1975
85.	Dagupan, Luzon I, Philippines	88.46	2247	1951–70
86.	Iloilo, Panay I, Philippines	88.19	2240	1903–60
87.	Santos, Sao Paulo, Brazil	87.87	2232	1888–1941
88.	Vila, Vanuatu	87.72	2228	1954–70
89.	Georgetown, Guyana	87.44	2221	1916–22
90.	Songkhla, Thailand	86.93	2208	1931–60
91.	Belem, Para, Brazil	86.10	2187	1912–24
92.	Castries, Saint Lucia	85.98	2184	1899–1927
93.	Bacolod, Negros I, Philippines	85.55	2173	6 yrs bef 1919
94.	Agana, Guam	85.33	2167	1951–70
95.	Surakarta, Java I, Indonesia	85.24	2165	1933–37
96.	Honiara, Solomon Islands	84.96	2158	1951–70
97.	Hong Kong, Hong Kong	84.92	2157	1884–1940
98.	Dehra Dun, Uttar Pradesh, India	84.61	2149	1931–60
99.	Abidjan, Ivory Coast	84.41	2144	1941–60
100.	Tanjungkarang–Telukbetung, Sumatra I, Indonesia	83.70	2126	1879–1941

TABLE 4f. (Continued)

Rank	City and Location	Annual Precipitation		Period of Record
		in.	mm	
101.	Petropolis, Rio de Janeiro, Brazil	83.54	2122	1913–19
102.	Naha, Okinawa I, Japan	83.39	2118	1941–70
103.	Victoria, Seychelles	83.33	2117	1941–6O
104.	Orizaba, Veracruz, Mexico	83.27	2115	1921–44
105.	Cotabato, Mindanao I, Philippines	83.11	2111	1910–36
106.	Santarem, Para, Brazil	82.76	2102	1951–60
107.	Tacloban, Leyte I, Philippines	82.68	2100	1951–70
107.	Taipei, Taiwan	82.68	2100	1897–1952
109.	Numazu, Honshu I, Japan	82.44	2094	1897–1926
110.	Saipan, Pacific Islands (USA)	82.36	2092	19 yrs bef 1974
111.	Malacca, Peninsular Malaysia, Malaysia	82.17	2087	1951–70
112.	Lucena, Luzon I, Philippines	82.01	2083	1916–32
113.	Da Nang, Vietnam	81.61	2073	1931–44, 1947–62
114.	Manila, Luzon I, Philippines	81.46	2069	71 yrs bef 1961
115.	Male, Maldives	80.94	2056	4 yrs bef 1948
116.	Manizales, Colombia	80.91	2055	1942, 1944–52
117.	Pereira, Colombia	80.87	2054	1942, 1944, 1946–53
118.	Ibague, Colombia	80.83	2053	1941–47, 1949–59, 1961
119.	Medan, Sumatra I, Indonesia	80.16	2036	1879–1941
120.	Semarang, Java I, Indonesia	80.04	2033	1956–65

For an explanation of symbols and abbreviations, see pages 16–17.

4g. Cities with Least Precipitation

Contents

Rank.

Conventional name of city, and division and country in which located.

Average annual precipitation (i.e., rainfall plus the rain equivalent of snowfall), in inches and in millimeters.

Period of time on which the average precipitation is based.

Coverage

All cities listed in Table 2a with annual precipitation averaging 10 in. (254 mm) or less.

Entries

125.

Note. More detailed climatic tables, giving temperature and precipitation data for all important cities, can be found on pp 484–578 of the previous edition of *World Facts and Figures.*

TABLE 4g. CITIES WITH LEAST PRECIPITATION

Rank	City and Location	Annual Precipitation in.	mm	Period of Record
1.	Aswan, Egypt	0.02	0.5	1951–60
2.	Luxor, Egypt	0.03	0.7	1941–60
3.	Arica, Chile	0.04	1.1	? yrs bef 1981
4.	Ica, Peru	0.09	2.3	1954–60
5.	Antofagasta, Chile	0.19	4.9	? yrs bef 1981
6.	Minya, Egypt	0.20	5.1	1945–60
7.	Asyut, Egypt	0.20	5.2	1900–34, 1941–47
8.	Callao, Peru	0.47	12	9 yrs bef 1956
9.	Trujillo, Peru	0.54	14	1963–72
10.	Fayyum, Egypt	0.75	19	1928–34, 1941–47
11.	Chimbote, Peru	0.79	20	1963–72
12.	Suez, Egypt	0.87	22	1910–34, 1941–47
13.	Cairo, Egypt	1.04	26	1909–34, 1945–60
14.	Shibin al Kawm, Egypt	1.05	27	1945–47
15.	Giza, Egypt	1.10	28	1909–34
16.	Hulwan, Egypt	1.18	30	1941–60
17.	Lima, Peru	1.22	31	1931–60
17.	Zagazig, Egypt	1.22	31	23 yrs bef 1948
19.	Ismailia, Egypt	1.49	38	16 yrs bef 1961
20.	Aden, South Yemen	1.61	41	1891–1937, 1941–60
21.	Chiclayo, Peru	1.65	42	1963–72
22.	Piura, Peru	1.69	43	1963–72
23.	Tanta, Egypt	1.97	50	1927–34, 1941–47
24.	Jidda, Hejaz, Saudi Arabia	2.09	53	1951–60
25.	Shache, Xinjiang, China	2.15	54	1954–55
26.	Mansurah, Egypt	2.24	57	1927–34, 1941–47
27.	Dubayy, United Arab Emirates	2.4	61	5 yrs bef 1967
28.	Medina, Hejaz, Saudi Arabia	2.44	62	1957–60
29.	Doha, Qatar	2.48	63	1951–60
30.	Port Said, Egypt	2.59	66	1945–60
31.	Yuma, Arizona, USA	2.65	67	1951–80
32.	Mexicali, Baja California, Mexico	2.99	76	1921–44
33.	Kashi, Xinjiang, China	3.07	78	49 yrs bef 1941
34.	Manama, Bahrain	3.23	82	1901–14, 1927–60
35.	Arequipa, Peru	3.41	87	1963–72
36.	San Juan, San Juan, Argentina	3.66	93	1901–50
37.	Sukkur, Pakistan	3.70	94	1926–60
38.	Riyadh, Nejd, Saudi Arabia	3.82	97	1941–45, 1951–60
39.	Damanhur, Egypt	3.90	99	1929–34, 1941–47
40.	Muscat, Oman	3.94	100	1893–1931, 1935–59
41.	Hudaydah, North Yemen	3.98	101	? yrs bef 1971
41.	Qom, Iran	3.98	101	1940–53, 1960–62
43.	Yazd, Iran	4.06	103	19 yrs bef 1971
44.	La Serena, Chile	4.09	104	? yrs bef 1981
44.	Zahedan, Iran	4.09	104	1938–66
46.	Las Vegas, Nevada, USA	4.19	106	1951–80
47.	Kzyl–Orda, Kazakhstan, USSR	4.21	107	1881–90, 1892–1960
48.	Isfahan, Iran	4.33	110	1951–69
48.	Port Sudan, Sudan	4.33	110	1906–34, 1943–59
50.	Abadan, Iran	4.84	123	1951–69
51.	Jericho, West Bank	4.92	125	1921–34
52.	Santa Marta, Colombia	5.00	127	1940–42, 1944

For an explanation of symbols and abbreviations, see pages 16–17. (Continued)

Figure 31. Top: The Aga Khan Mausoleum at Aswan; bottom: Massive columns of the temple at Luxor. Aswan and Luxor are the cities with the least precipitation, averaging only 2 or 3 hundredths of an inch (5 or 7 tenths of a millimeter) of rain annually. (Credit: Press and Information Bureau, Embassy of the Arab Republic of Egypt, Washington.)

TABLE 4g. (Continued)

Rank	City and Location	Annual Precipitation		Period of Record
		in.	mm	
53.	Kuwait, Kuwait	5.04	128	1908–53
53.	Zarqa, Jordan	5.04	128	1923–65
55.	Djibouti, Djibouti	5.12	130	1912–14, 1939–60
56.	Palm Springs, California, USA	5.20	132	1951–80
57.	Bukhara, Uzbekistan, USSR	5.31	135	1951–60
58.	Khartoum North, Sudan	5.63	143	1913–34
59.	Bahawalpur, Pakistan	5.67	144	1926–40
59.	Bandar Abbas, Iran	5.67	144	1951–69
61.	Bakersfield, California, USA	5.72	145	1951–80
62.	Nouakchott, Mauritania	5.90	150	1930–54
63.	Las Palmas, (Canary Islands), Spain	5.98	152	1951–70
64.	Neuquen, Neuquen, Argentina	6.02	153	1941–50
65.	Baghdad, Iraq	6.14	156	1938–62
66.	Hyderabad, Pakistan	6.18	157	1931–60
67.	Basra, Iraq	6.34	161	1937–62
67.	Kerman, Iran	6.34	161	1951–69
67.	Khartoum, Sudan	6.34	161	1931–60
70.	Torreon, Coahuila, Mexico	6.50	165	1951–60
71.	Taif, Hejaz, Saudi Arabia	6.54	166	? yrs bef 1970
72.	Multan, Pakistan	6.57	167	1931–60
73.	Fergana, Uzbekistan, USSR	6.65	169	1933–60
74.	Potosi, Bolivia	6.69	170	1969
75.	Richland, Washington, USA	6.78	172	1951–80
76.	La Paz, Baja California Sur, Mexico	6.81	173	1921–44
77.	Astrakhan, Russia in Europe, USSR	6.89	175	1881–1960
78.	Shihezi, Xinjiang, China	7.05	179	1953–55
79.	Phoenix, Arizona, USA	7.11	181	1951–80
80.	Beersheba, Israel	7.20	183	1951–60
81.	Sumgait, Azerbaijan, USSR	7.28	185	1935–36, 1938–60
82.	Ciudad Juarez, Chihuahua, Mexico	7.36	187	1921–44
83.	Namangan, Uzbekistan, USSR	7.40	188	1924–60
84.	Ahwaz, Iran	7.48	190	11 yrs bef 1954
84.	Alexandria, Egypt	7.48	190	1901–34, 1945–60
86.	Reno, Nevada, USA	7.49	190	1951–80
87.	Kennewick, Washington, USA	7.55	192	1951–80
88.	Mendoza, Mendoza, Argentina	7.76	197	1901–50
88.	Sfax, Tunisia	7.76	197	1901–50
90.	El Paso, Texas, USA	7.82	199	1951–80
91.	Mesa, Arizona, USA	7.85	199	1951–80
92.	Ulan–Ude, Russia in Asia, USSR	7.95	202	66 yrs bef 1961
93.	Yakima, Washington, USA	7.98	203	1951–80
94.	Yinchuan, Ningxia, China	7.99	203	1951–53, 1955
95.	Grand Junction, Colorado, USA	8.00	203	1951–80
95.	Tempe, Arizona, USA	8.00	203	1951–80
97.	Karachi, Pakistan	8.03	204	1931–60
98.	Scottsdale, Arizona, USA	8.06	205	1941–70
99.	Albuquerque, New Mexico, USA	8.12	206	1951–80
100.	Andizhan, Uzbekistan, USSR	8.27	210	1931–57
100.	Ashkhabad, Turkmenia, USSR	8.27	210	1931–60
100.	Kandahar, Afghanistan	8.27	210	1940–44, 1958–63

TABLE 4g. (Continued)

Rank	City and Location	Annual Precipitation in.	mm	Period of Record
103.	Ciudad Obregon, Sonora, Mexico	8.31	211	1921–44
103.	Las Cruces, New Mexico, USA	8.31	211	1951–80
105.	Yakutsk, Russia in Asia, USSR	8.39	213	1931–60
106.	Chula Vista, California, USA	8.67	220	1951–80
107.	Timbuktu, Mali	8.86	225	1951–60
108.	Damascus, Syria	8.94	227	1951–70
109.	Tehran, Iran	9.02	229	1892–1960
110.	Almeria, Andalucia, Spain	9.09	231	1934–60
110.	Herat, Afghanistan	9.09	231	1900–44
112.	Urumqi, Xinjiang, China	9.17	233	22 yrs bef 1948
113.	Quetta, Pakistan	9.29	236	1881–1951
114.	San Diego, California, USA	9.32	237	1951–80
115.	Baku, Azerbaijan, USSR	9.37	238	1891–1917, 1921–60
115.	Karaj, Iran	9.37	238	1940–53
115.	Meshed, Iran	9.37	238	1951–69
118.	Riverside, California, USA	9.64	245	1951–80
119.	Roswell, New Mexico, USA	9.70	246	1951–80
120.	Kirovabad, Azerbaijan, USSR	9.76	248	47 yrs bef 1961
121.	Idaho Falls, Idaho, USA	9.77	248	1951–80
122.	Marrakesh, Morocco	9.80	249	1941–70
123.	Santa Cruz de Tenerife, (Canary Islands), Spain	9.90	251	1931–70
124.	Pavlodar, Kazakhstan, USSR	10.00	254	54 yrs bef 1964
124.	Ulan-Bator, Mongolia	10.00	254	1936–60

Note. Although exact precipitation data are unavailable, the location of the following cities (listed in Table 2a) makes it highly probable that they too should be included in this table of cities with least precipitation:

Aaiun, Western Sahara
Abu Zaby, United Arab Emirates
Dammam, Nejd, Saudi Arabia
Glendale, Arizona, USA
Hillah, Iraq
Mahalla al Kubra, Egypt
Mecca, Hejaz, Saudi Arabia
Omdurman, Sudan
Paradise, Nevada, USA
Shubra al Khaymah, Egypt

For an explanation of symbols and abbreviations, see pages 16–17.

5

COMPARISONS OF
CULTURAL FEATURES

5a. Largest Universities

Contents

Rank.

Name of university.

City, and division and country in which located.

Student enrollment (i.e., thousands of full-time and part-time students, excluding correspondence students, enrolled in the university and its affiliated institutions[1]). Wherever possible, however, the enrollment figures exclude students at branches and campuses where no graduate degrees are conferred.

Academic staff (i.e., number of full-time and part-time teachers). Teachers at branches and campuses where no graduate degrees are conferred are excluded.

Date of foundation.[2]

Coverage

100 largest universities in student enrollment.

Rounding

Enrollments are rounded to the nearest 1,000 students.

Entries

103.

---

[1]In India most universities include as affiliates numerous educational institutions of lower level, such as preparatory or other secondary schools; thus the size of these universities is usually exaggerated with respect to that of universities in other countries, where only college-level students are usually included in the enrollment statistics.

[2]See p 252 for the meaning of this date.

TABLE 5a. LARGEST UNIVERSITIES

Rank	University	Location	Students (thousands)	Teachers	Year Founded
1.	Universidad Nacional Autonoma de Mexico	Mexico, Distrito Federal, Mexico	327	27,515	1551
2.	Universite de Paris	Paris, Region Parisienne, France	289	17,560	1200
3.	Universidad de Guadalajara	Guadalajara, Jalisco, Mexico	212	7,436	1791
4.	University of Madras	Madras, Tamil Nadu, India	203		1794
5.	Instituto Politecnico Nacional (univ)	Mexico, Distrito Federal, Mexico	161	17,405	1931
6.	State University of New York	Albany, New York, USA	156	10,078	1844
	Albany campus	Albany, New York, USA	16	915	1844
	Buffalo campus	Buffalo, New York, USA	38	2,399	1846
7.	Universita degli Studi di Roma	Rome, Lazio, Italy	155	6,366	1303
8.	University of Wisconsin	Madison, Wisconsin, USA	153	7,836	1848
	Madison campus	Madison, Wisconsin, USA	44	2,269	1848
9.	University of California	Berkeley, California, USA	143	14,879	1855
	Berkeley campus	Berkeley, California, USA	30	3,800	1873
	Los Angeles campus	Los Angeles, California, USA	35	3,200	1881
9.	University of Gorakhpur	Gorakhpur, Uttar Pradesh, India	143		1933
11.	University of Calcutta	Calcutta, West Bengal, India	141		1817
12.	University of Rajasthan	Jaipur, Rajasthan, India	134		1873
13.	Universita degli Studi di Napoli	Naples, Campania, Italy	129	3,430	1224
14.	University of Bombay	Bombay, Maharashtra, India	125		1832
15.	City University of New York	New York, New York, USA	123	8,603	1847
16.	Ain Shams University	Cairo, Egypt	122	4,220	1950
17.	Madurai-Kamaraj University	Madurai, Tamil Nadu, India	119		1958
17.	University of Texas	Austin, Texas, USA	119	7,183	1881
	Austin campus	Austin, Texas, USA	48	2,337	1881
19.	Gauhati University	Gauhati, Assam, India	115		1914
19.	Kanpur University	Kanpur, Uttar Pradesh, India	115		1955
21.	Cairo University	Giza, Egypt	114	5,830	1908
22.	University of Calicut	Calicut, Kerala, India	111	4,169	1968
23.	Lalit Narayan Mithila University	Darbhanga, Bihar, India	110	1,251	1938
24.	Universidad de Buenos Aires	Buenos Aires, Distrito Federal, Argentina	105	16,600	1821
25.	University of London	London, England, UK	104	6,630	13th c
26.	University of Kerala	Trivandrum, Kerala, India	102		1937

For an explanation of symbols and abbreviations, see pages 16–17.

(Continued)

Figure 32. *Universidad Nacional Autonoma de Mexico in Mexico City, the university with the largest student enrollment. (Credit: Mexican Government Tourism Office.)*

TABLE 5a. (Continued)

Rank	University	Location	Students (thousands)	Teachers	Year Founded
26.	Utkal University	Bhubaneswar, Orissa, India	102	3,000	1943
28.	Universidad Complutense de Madrid	Madrid, Castilla la Nueva, Spain	97	8,260	1508
28.	Sampurnanand Sanskrit University	Varanasi, Uttar Pradesh, India	97		1958
30.	University of Pune	Pune, Maharashtra, India	95		1885
31.	Gujarat University	Ahmadabad, Gujarat, India	94		1949
32.	Alexandria University	Alexandria, Egypt	92	3,610	1942
33.	Al-Azhar University	Cairo, Egypt	90	3,604	970
34.	University of Delhi	Delhi, Delhi, India	89		1881
34.	Universidad Autonoma de Nuevo Leon	San Nicolas de los Garza, Nuevo Leon, Mexico	89	5,374	1826
36.	Panjab University	Chandigarh, Chandigarh, India	87		1947
37.	University of Dhaka	Dhaka, Bangladesh	84	950	1910
38.	Nihon University	Tokyo, Honshu I, Japan	81	6,016	1889
39.	Osmania University	Hyderabad, Andhra Pradesh, India	78		1887
40.	Universidad Autonoma de Puebla	Puebla, Puebla, Mexico	77	2,650	1578
41.	Bangalore University	Bangalore, Karnataka, India	75	4,415	1858
42.	Zagazig University	Zagazig, Egypt	71	3,080	1973
43.	University of Bihar	Muzaffarpur, Bihar, India	70		1952
44.	Andhra University	Waltair, Andhra Pradesh, India (nr Visakhapatnam)	69	800	1926
45.	Indiana University	Bloomington, Indiana, USA	68	3,930	1820
	Bloomington campus	Bloomington, Indiana, USA	33	1,581	1820
46.	Universite du Quebec	Quebec, Quebec, Canada	66	1,728	1968
46.	Ranchi University	Ranchi, Bihar, India	66	2,000	1899
48.	Dibrugarh University	Dibrugarh, Assam, India	65		1965
49.	University of Burdwan	Burdwan, West Bengal, India	64	2,587	1960
49.	University of the East	Manila, Luzon I, Philippines	64	1,534	1946
49.	University of Maryland	College Park, Maryland, USA	64	4,841	1807
	College Park campus	College Park, Maryland, USA	50	3,021	1856
49.	Universita degli Studi di Milano	Milan, Lombardia, Italy	64	2,210	1923
49.	Universidad del Zulia	Maracaibo, Venezuela	64	3,362	1891
54.	Universita degli Studi di Bologna	Bologna, Emilia-Romagna, Italy	63	2,560	1088?
54.	Magadh University	Bodh Gaya, Bihar, India (nr Gaya)	63	3,000	1944

TABLE 5a. (Continued)

Rank	University	Location	Students (thousands)	Teachers	Year Founded
56.	Universita degli Studi di Padova	Padua, Veneto, Italy	62	4,340	1222
57.	Kurukshetra University	Kurukshetra, Haryana, India	61	1,949	1956
58.	Universidad Central del Ecuador	Quito, Ecuador	60	2,500	1586
58.	Universidad de Guayaquil	Guayaquil, Ecuador	60	3,080	1867
60.	Guru Nanak Dev University	Amritsar, Punjab, India	59	2,712	1969
60.	University of Illinois	Urbana and Champaign, Illinois, USA	59	3,799	1867
	Urbana-Champaign campus	Urbana and Champaign, Illinois, USA	35	2,561	1867
60.	Meerut University	Meerut, Uttar Pradesh, India	59	1,942	1965
63.	Purdue University	West Lafayette, Indiana, USA	58	4,898	1865
	West Lafayette campus	West Lafayette, Indiana, USA	31	3,100	1865
64.	Universidad de Barcelona	Barcelona, Cataluna, Spain	57	4,120	1430
64.	University of Belgrade	Belgrade, Serbia, Yugoslavia	57	3,702	1808
64.	Bhagalpur University	Bhagalpur, Bihar, India	57	900	1887
67.	University of Damascus	Damascus, Syria	56	955	1903
67.	Ohio State University	Columbus, Ohio, USA	56	3,384	1870
	Columbus campus	Columbus, Ohio, USA	52	3,262	1870
69.	Awadhesh Pratap Singh University	Rewa, Madhya Pradesh, India	55		1968
69.	University of Mysore	Mysore, Karnataka, India	55		1833
71.	Ludwig-Maximilians-Universitat Munchen	Munich, Bayern, West Germany	54	10,100	1472
71.	University of Minnesota	Minneapolis, Minnesota, USA	54	6,356	1851
	Minneapolis campus	Minneapolis, Minnesota, USA	45	5,800	1851
73.	Universite d'Aix-Marseille	Aix-en-Provence and Marseilles, Provence-Cote d'Azur, France	53	3,172	1413
	Marseilles campus	Marseilles, Provence-Cote d'Azur, France	39	1,814	1854
	Aix-en-Provence campus	Aix-en-Provence, Provence-Cote d'Azur, France	14	1,358	1413
73.	University of Missouri	Columbia, Missouri, USA	53	4,520	1839
	Columbia campus	Columbia, Missouri, USA	23	2,485	1839
75.	Universidad Central de Venezuela	Caracas, Venezuela	52	6,987	1696
75.	Shivaji University	Kolhapur, Maharashtra, India	52	3,122	1962

For an explanation of symbols and abbreviations, see pages 16–17.

(Continued)

TABLE 5a. (Continued)

Rank	University	Location	Students (thousands)	Teachers	Year Founded
75.	University of Toronto	Toronto, Ontario, Canada	52	2,900	1827
78.	Freie Universitat Berlin	Berlin, West-Berlin, West Germany	51	4,340	1948
78.	Karnatak University	Hubli-Dharwar, Karnataka, India	51	3,506	1917
78.	Universidad Autonoma de Santo Domingo	Santo Domingo, Dominican Republic	51	1,178	1538
78.	Sri Venkateswara University	Tirupati, Andhra Pradesh, India	51	3,000	1954
82.	Sambalpur University	Sambalpur, Orissa, India	50	1,537	1967
83.	Bundelkhand University	Jhansi, Uttar Pradesh, India	49		1975
83.	National and Capodistrian University of Athens	Athens, Greece	49	1,738	1837
85.	Universite de Lyon	Lyons, Rhone-Alpes, France	48	2,549	1809
85.	Universidad de Puerto Rico	San Juan, Puerto Rico	48	2,996	1903
	San Juan campus	San Juan, Puerto Rico	22	1,773	1903
85.	Universidad de San Carlos de Guatemala	Guatemala, Guatemala	48	3,007	1676
85.	Universitat Wien	Vienna, Austria	48	3,995	1365
89.	Universidad de El Salvador	San Salvador, El Salvador	47	1,728	1841
89.	Rutgers University	New Brunswick, New Jersey, USA	47	1,796	1766
	New Brunswick campus	New Brunswick, New Jersey, USA	33	1,245	1766
89.	Universite de Toulouse	Toulouse, Midi-Pyrenees, France	47	1,819	1229
92.	University of Houston	Houston, Texas, USA	46	3,246	1927
93.	Universitat zu Koln	Cologne, Nordrhein-Westfalen, West Germany	45	2,070	1388
93.	Mansurah University	Mansurah, Egypt	45	1,820	1960
93.	University of Michigan	Ann Arbor, Michigan, USA	45	3,315	1817
	Ann Arbor campus	Ann Arbor, Michigan, USA	34	2,768	1837
93.	Universidad Michoacana de San Nicolas de Hidalgo	Morelia, Michoacan, Mexico	45	1,748	1541
93.	Nagpur University	Nagpur, Maharashtra, India	45	2,738	1923
98.	Agra University	Agra, Uttar Pradesh, India	44		1927
98.	Universita degli Studi di Firenze	Florence, Toscana, Italy	44	1,631	1321
98.	Louisiana State University	Baton Rouge, Louisiana, USA	44	2,899	1855
	Baton Rouge campus	Baton Rouge, Louisisna, USA	29	1,282	1869

TABLE 5a. (Continued)

Rank	University	Location	Students (thousands)	Teachers	Year Founded
98.	Universite de Montreal	Montreal, Quebec, Canada	44	1,811	1876
98.	Universidade de Sao Paulo	Sao Paulo, Sao Paulo, Brazil	44	4,461	1827
98.	Westfalische Wilhelms-Universitat Munster	Munster, Nordrhein-Westfalen, West Germany	44	2,253	1780

For an explanation of symbols and abbreviations, see pages 16–17.

5b. Largest Libraries

Contents

Rank.

Name of library.

City, and division and country in which located.

Size of collection (i.e., thousands of volumes of books and pamphlets, usually including bound volumes of periodicals).[1]

Date of foundation.[2]

Coverage

100 largest libraries in size of collection.

Rounding

Collections are rounded to the nearest 1,000 volumes.

Entries

100.

---

[1]Most of the so-called "Communist countries" include documents and miscellaneous materials in reporting the size of collection for their libraries. Thus the ranks given in Table 5b must be viewed with skepticism. In Czechoslovakia, for example, 22 large public and university libraries are officially reported to have 34,514,000 volumes, of which 21,712,000 (62.9%) are books and periodicals and 12,802,000 (37.1%) are documents and source materials,(*Statisticka Rocenka* . . . 1986, p 580). If the same proportions held for the Lenin State Library in Moscow, that library would rank second to the Library of Congress in Washington with 18,081,000 volumes. Similarly, the Saltykov-Shchedrin State Public Library in Leningrad would rank fourth in the world (behind the Library of Congress, the Lenin State Library, and the British Library in London) instead of second, with 13,523,000 volumes.

[2]The date of foundation given for libraries is preferably the year in which the library was opened on a permanent basis; that is the one since which it has been continuously operative. By "library," however, is meant the nucleus of the present book collection, not necessarily the institution under its present name.

TABLE 5b. LARGEST LIBRARIES

Rank	Library	Location	Volumes (1,000)	Year Founded
1.	V. I. Lenin State Library of the USSR	Moscow, Russia in Europe, USSR	28,745	1828
2.	M. E. Saltykov-Shchedrin State Public Library	Leningrad, Russia in Europe, USSR	21,500	1795
3.	Library of Congress	Washington, District of Columbia, USA	19,768	1800
4.	British Library	London, England, UK	14,800	1753
5.	Library for Natural Sciences of the USSR Academy of Sciences	Moscow, Russia in Europe, USSR	13,541	1934
6.	USSR Academy of Sciences Library	Leningrad, Russia in Europe, USSR	12,789	1714
7.	New York Public Library	New York, New York, USA	12,450	1854
8.	Bibliotheque Nationale	Paris, Region Parisienne, France	12,300	1368
9.	Harvard University Library	Cambridge, Massachusetts, USA	11,300	1638
10.	Yale University Library	New Haven, Connecticut, USA	11,200	1701
11.	National Library of China	Beijing, China	11,000	1910
12.	State Public Scientific-Technical Library of the USSR	Moscow, Russia in Europe, USSR	10,420	1958
13.	Bibliotheque de l'Universite de Paris	Paris, Region Parisienne, France	10,350	1624
14.	Institute of Social Sciences Library of the USSR Academy of Sciences	Moscow, Russia in Europe, USSR	10,144	1918
15.	State Public Scientific-Technical Library of the Siberian Department of the USSR Academy of Sciences	Novosibirsk, Russia in Asia, USSR	9,974	1918
16.	Academy of the Romanian Socialist Republic Library	Bucharest, Romania	8,794	1867
17.	National Diet Library	Tokyo, Honshu I, Japan	8,466	1872
18.	Karl Marx State Library of the Georgian SSR	Tbilisi, Georgia, USSR	8,000	1846
19.	Central State Library	Bucharest, Romania	7,930	1955
20.	Central Scientific Library of the Ukrainian Academy of Sciences	Kiev, Ukraine, USSR	7,756	1919
21.	Stanford University Library	Stanford, California, USA (nr Palo Alto)	7,755	1892
22.	Berkeley Campus Library of the University of California	Berkeley, California, USA	7,700	1868
23.	Deutsche Bucherei	Leipzig, East Germany	7,379	1912
24.	Los Angeles Campus Library of the University of California	Los Angeles, California, USA	7,300	1919
25.	M. V. Lomonosov Moscow State University Library	Moscow, Russia in Europe, USSR	7,200	1756
26.	Shanghai Library	Shanghai, China	7,000	1952
27.	Deutsche Staatsbibliothek	Berlin, East Germany	6,896	1661
28.	University of London Library	London, England, UK	6,800	1673
29.	Ann Arbor Campus Library of the University of Michigan	Ann Arbor, Michigan, USA	6,688	1838
30.	Urbana Campus Library of the University of Illinois	Urbana, Illinois, USA	6,616	1868
31.	Austin Campus Library of the University of Texas	Austin, Texas, USA	6,563	1883

For an explanation of symbols and abbreviations, see pages 16–17.

(Continued)

Figure 33. *V. I. Lenin State Library of the USSR in Moscow, one of the two largest in the world. Top: The old building (formerly Pashkov House, completed in 1786) and, to the right, one of six new adjoining buildings opened between 1928 and 1958; bottom: A main reading room. (Credit: Sovfoto, New York.)*

Figure 34. Library of Congress in Washington, one of the two largest in the world, showing (front left) Thomas Jefferson Building, completed in 1897, (behind it) John Adams Building (1939), and (front right) James Madison Building (1980). (Credit: US Library of Congress.)

TABLE 5b. (Continued)

Rank	Library	Location	Volumes (1,000)	Year Founded
32. A.F. Myashnikyan State Library of the Armenian SSR	Yerevan, Armenia, USSR	6,400	1832
33. University of Toronto Library	Toronto, Ontario, Canada	6,150	1827
34. Bloomington Campus Library of Indiana University	Bloomington, Indiana, USA	6,032	1824
35. Library of the Lithuanian Institute of Technical Information and Research	Vilnyus, Lithuania, USSR	6,000	1957
35. University of Oxford Library	Oxford, England, UK	6,000	1602
35. V. I. Lenin State Library of the White Russian SSR	Minsk, White Russia, USSR	6,000	1922
38. University of Chicago Library	Chicago, Illinois, USA	5,981	1891
39. Columbia University Library	New York, New York, USA	5,940	1761
40. Los Angesles County Public Library	Downey, California, USA	5,825	1912
41. Madison Campus Library of the University of Wisconsin	Madison, Wisconsin, USA	5,805	1849
42. Columbus Campus Library of Ohio State University	Columbus, Ohio, USA	5,720	1873
43. Cape Provincial Library Service	Cape Town, Cape of Good Hope, South Africa	5,652	1945
44. Helsinki University Library	Helsinki, Finland	5,500	1640
45. Nanjing Library	Nanjing, Jiangsu, China	5,400	1908
46. State Library of the Czech Socialist Republic	Prague, Bohemia, Czechoslovakia	5,355	1366?
47. Universitats- und Stadtbibliothek	Cologne, Nordrhein-Westfalen, West Germany	5,250	1602
48. University of Bucharest Library	Bucharest, Romania	5,200	1857
48. Central Library of the Chinese Academy of Sciences	Beijing, China	5,200	1951
50. Boston Public Library	Boston, Massachusetts, USA	5,189	1854
51. Scientific-Technical Library	Alma-Ata, Kazakhstan, USSR	5,150	1960
52. Los Angeles Public Library	Los Angeles, California, USA	5,107	1872
53. A. A. Zhdanov Leningrad State University Library	Leningrad, Russia in Europe, USSR	5,100	1819
54. Warsaw University Library	Warsaw, Poland	5,030	1817
55. University of Tokyo Library	Tokyo, Honshu I, Japan	5,015	1886
56. Stadt- und Universitatsbibliothek	Frankfurt am Main, Hessen, West Germany	5,010	1484
57. National Library of Scotland	Edinburgh, Scotland, UK	5,000	1682
58. Universitatsbibliothek (of Frei Universitat Berlin)	Berlin, West-Berlin, West Germany	4,930	1948
59. Bayerische Staatsbibliothek	Munich, Bayern, West Germany	4,850	1558
60. Niedersachsische Staats- und Universitatsbibliothek	Gottingen, Niedersachsen, West Germany	4,770	1734
61. Cornell University Library	Ithaca, New York, USA	4,769	1868
62. Scientific-Technical Library	Gorkiy, Russia in Europe, USSR	4,755	1934
63. Universitetsbiblioteket	Oslo, Norway	4,650	1811
64. Slovak National Library	Martin, Slovakia, Czechoslovakia	4,621	1863
65. Universitatsbibliothek	Munich, Bayern, West Germany	4,610	1473
66. Chicago Public Library	Chicago, Illinois, USA	4,588	1873
67. Wayne State University Library	Detroit, Michigan, USA	4,514	1923
68. Biblioteca Nazionale Centrale	Florence, Toscana, Italy	4,500	1747

For an explanation of symbols and abbreviations, see pages 16–17.

(Continued)

TABLE 5b. (Continued)

Rank	Library	Location	Volumes (1,000)	Year Founded
68. V. Stefanik State Scientific Library of the Ukrainian Academy of Sciences	Lvov, Ukraine, USSR	4,500	1940
70. Vilis Lacis State Library of the Latvian SSR	Riga, Latvia, USSR	4,467	1919
71. State Scientific Library- University Library	Brno, Moravia, Czechoslovakia	4,404	1770
72. Transvaal Provincial Library Service	Pretoria, Transvaal, South Africa	4,359	1943
73. Philadelphia Free Library	Philadelphia, Pennsylvania, USA	4,318	1821
74. University of Pennsylvania Library	Philadelphia, Pennsylvania, USA	4,316	1750
75. Universitatsbibliothek	Vienna, Austria	4,315	1365
76. University of Washington Library	Seattle, Washington, USA	4,292	1862
77. Ervin Szabo Municipal Library	Budapest, Hungary	4,289	1904
78. Queens Borough Public Library	New York, New York, USA	4,261	1896
79. Kyoto University Library	Kyoto, Honshu I, Japan	4,259	1897
80. Staats- und Universitatsbibliothek	Hamburg, Hamburg, West Germany	4,180	1479
81. Princeton University Library	Princeton, New Jersey, USA	4,170	1746
82. Brooklyn Public Library	New York, New York, USA	4,169	1869
83. Alisher Navoi State Library of the Uzbek SSR	Tashkent, Uzbekistan, USSR	4,157	1870
84. University of Cambridge Library	Cambridge, England, UK	4,150	1400
85. Universitatsbibliothek (of Humboldt-Universitat zu Berlin)	Berlin, East Germany	4,140	1831
86. All-Union State Library of Foreign Literature	Moscow, Russia in Europe, USSR	4,138	1921
87. National Library	Warsaw, Poland	4,131	1928
88. V. I. Lenin Kazan State University Library	Kazan, Russia in Europe, USSR	4,120	1798
89. V. G. Korolenko State Scientific Library	Kharkov, Ukraine, USSR	4,096	1886
90. Minneapolis Campus Library of the University of Minnesota	Minneapolis, Minnesota, USA	4,080	1851
91. University of North Carolina at Chapel Hill Library	Chapel Hill, North Carolina, USA	4,079	1795
92. Warsaw Public Library	Warsaw, Poland	4,040	1907
93. Central Scientific Library of the All-Union Agricultural Academy	Moscow, Russia in Europe, USSR	4,000	1930
93. Karl Marx State Public Library of the Turkmen SSR	Ashkhabad, Turkmenia, USSR	4,000	1895
93. State Library of the Lithuanian SSR	Vilnyus, Lithuania, USSR	4,000	1919
93. V. Kapsukas Vilnyus State University Library	Vilnyus, Lithuania, USSR	4,000	1570
97. Universitatsbibliothek	Heidelberg, Baden-Wurttemberg, West Germany	3,980	1386
98. Universitatsbibliothek	Bonn, Nordrhein-Westfalen, West Germany	3,930	1818
99. Birmingham Public Library	Birmingham, England, UK	3,900	1861
100. Duke University Library	Durham, North Carolina, USA	3,885	1838

For an explanation of symbols and abbreviations, see pages 16–17.

5c. Highest Buildings

Contents

Rank.

Present name of building.

City, and division and country in which located.

Year of completion.

Height above street level, in feet and meters.

Coverage

Above * * *, all buildings standing or under construction, excluding observation and television towers, with a height of at least 650 feet (198 m).

Below * * *, other well-known high buildings, including the highest in certain cities and countries.

Entries

172.

TABLE 5c. HIGHEST BUILDINGS

Rank	Building	City and Location	Year Completed[1]	Height ft	Height m
1.	Sears Tower	Chicago, Illinois, USA	1974	1454	443
2.	World Trade Center	New York, New York, USA	1972	1350[2]	411[2]
3.	Empire State	New York, New York, USA	1931	1250	381
4.	Amoco	Chicago, Illinois, USA	1973	1136	346
5.	John Hancock Center	Chicago, Illinois, USA	1967	1127	344
6.	Chrysler	New York, New York, USA	1930	1046	319
7.	Bank of China	Hong Kong, Hong Kong	UC	1028	313
8.	Texas Conmerce Tower	Houston, Texas, USA	1980	1002	305
9.	Allied Bank Plaza	Houston, Texas, USA	1982	985	300
10.	Eiffel Tower (off Tour Eiffel)[3]	Paris, Region Parisienne, France	1889	984	300
11.	Columbia Center	Seattle, Washington, USA	1984	954	291
12.	First Canadian Place	Toronto, Ontario, Canada	1976	952	290
13.	American International	New York, New York, USA	1931	950	290
14.	One Liberty Place	Philadelphia, Pennsylvania, USA	UC	945	288
15.	Interfirst Plaza	Dallas, Texas, USA	1984	939	286
16.	40 Wall Tower	New York, New York, USA	1930	927	283
17.	Overseas Union Bank Centre	Singapore, Singapore	1987	919	280
18.	Citicorp Center	New York, New York, USA	1977	914	279
19.	Transco Tower	Houston, Texas, USA	1984	899	274
20.	Scotia Place	Toronto, Ontario, Canada	1987	886	270
21.	Mellon Bank Center	Philadelphia, Pennsylvania, USA	UC	880	268

[1]UC, under construction.
[2]Two buildings of this height.
[3]Primarily an observation tower.

For an explanation of symbols and abbreviations, see pages 16–17.

(Continued)

Figure 35. *Sears Tower in Chicago (completed in 1974), the highest office building yet constructed. (Credit: Sears, Roebuck & Company.)*

Figure 36. Artist's drawing of Pacific Place, scheduled for completion in early 1990 in Hong Kong, which is beginning to rival New York and Chicago in the construction of skyscrapers. Pacific Place includes, left to right, the Shangri-la Hotel, the Conrad Hotel/Apartments, One Pacific Place, and the Marriott Hotel/The Atrium. (Credit: Swire Properties Projects, Ltd., Hong Kong.)

Figure 37. Transamerica Pyramid in San Francisco, completed in 1973, a skyscraper of unusual design. (Credit: Transamerica Corporation.)

TABLE 5c. (Continued)

Rank	Building	City and Location	Year Completed[1]	Height ft	Height m
22.	Water Tower Place	Chicago, Illinois, USA	1976	859	262
23.	First Interstate Bank	Los Angeles, California, USA	1974	858	262
24.	Tramsamerica Pyramid	San Francisco, California, USA	1973	853	260
25.	First National Bank	Chicago, Illinois, USA	1969	852	260
26.	RCA[4]	New York, New York, USA	1933	850	259
27.	United States Steel	Pittsburgh, Pennsylvania, USA	1969	841	256
28.	(Edificio) Mazuera	Bogota, Colombia		814	248
29.	IBM Tower	Atlanta, Georgia, USA	UC	813	248
29.	One Chase Manhattan Plaza	New York, New York, USA	1960	813	248
31.	MLC Centre	Sydney, New South Wales, Australia	1974	808	246
31.	Pan Am	New York, New York, USA	1961	808	246
33.	Eichner	New York, New York, USA	UC	799	244
34.	Rialto Centre	Melbourne, Victoria, Australia	UC	797	243
35.	Woolworth	New York, New York, USA	1913	792	241
36.	John Hancock Tower	Boston, Massaohusetts, USA	1970	790	241
37.	Commerce Court West	Toronto, Ontario, Canada	1971	784	239
38.	Republic Bank Center	Houston, Texas, USA	1984	780	238
38.	Singapore Treasury	Singapore, Singapore	1986	780	238
40.	Bank of America	San Francisco, California, USA	1969	778	237
41.	IDS Center	Minneapolis, Minnesota, USA	1971	775	236
41.	Three First National Plaza	Chicago, Illinois, USA	1982	775	236
43.	Norwest	Minneapolis, Minnesota, USA	UC	772	235
44.	Palace of Culture and Science (off Palac Kultury i Nauki)	Warsaw, Poland	1955	768	234
45.	Korea Insurance Company	Seoul, South Korea	1985	764	233
45.	One Penn Plaza	New York, New York, USA	1972	764	233
45.	Southeast Financial Center	Miami, Florida, USA	1985	764	233
48.	Heritage Plaza	Houston, Texas, USA	1987	762	232
49.	Tun Abdul Razak	Penang, Peninsular Malaysia, Malaysia	1985	761	232
50.	Toronto-Dominion Tower	Toronto, Ontario, Canada	1967	758	231
51.	Shangri-la Hotel	Hong Kong, Hong Kong	UC	755	230
52.	Tour Maine-Montparnasse	Paris, Region Parisienne, France	1972	751	229
53.	Crocker Center North	Los Angeles, California, USA	1982	750	229
53.	Equitable Center Tower West	New York, New York, USA	1986	750	229
53.	Exxon	New York, New York, USA	1971	750	229
53.	Prudential Tower	Boston, Massachusetts, USA	1964	750	229

[1]UC, under construction.
[4]To be renamed GE.

TABLE 5c. (Continued)

Rank	Building	City and Location	Year Completed[1]	Height ft	m
57.	InterFirst Plaza	Houston, Texas, USA	1982	744	227
58.	One Liberty Plaza	New York, New York, USA	1971	743	226
59.	Ikebokoru Tower (alt Sunshine 60)	Tokyo, Honshu I, Japan	1978	742	226
59.	Westin Stamford Hotel	Singapore, Singapore	1986	742	226
61.	Citibank	New York, New York, USA	1931	741	226
62.	World Financial Center, Tower C	New York, New York, USA	1987	739	225
63.	Security Pacific National Bank	Los Angeles, California, USA	1973	735	224
64.	One Astor Plaza	New York, New York, USA	1971	730	223
65.	1600 Smith Street	Houston, Texas, USA	1984	729	222
66.	Olympia Centre	Chicago, Illinois, USA	1984	727	222
67.	Gulf Tower	Houston, Texas, USA	1982	725	221
68.	One Mellon Bank Center	Pittsburgh, Pennsylvania, USA	1982	725	221
69.	Westin	Atlanta, Georgia, USA	1976	723	220
69.	Westin Hotel	Detroit, Michigan, USA	1977	723	220
71.	Conrad Hotel/Apartments	Hong Kong, Hong Kong	UC	722	220
72.	M. V. Lomonosov Moscow State University	Moscow, Russia, USSR	1953	720	219
73.	Metropolitan Tower	New York, New York, USA	1986	716	218
74.	One Shell Plaza	Houston, Texas, USA	1971	714	218
74.	Republic Plaza	Denver, Colorado, USA	1984	714	218
76.	First International	Dallas, Texas, USA	1973	710	216
77.	Hopewell Centre	Hong Kong, Hong Kong	1981	709	216
77.	Shinjuku Center	Tokyo, Honshu I, Japan	1979	709	216
79.	Terminal Tower	Cleveland, Ohio, USA	1930	708	216
80.	Union Carbide	New York, New York, USA	1960	707	215
81.	Mountain Bell Center	Denver, Colorado, USA	1984	706	215
82.	General Motors	New York, New York, USA	1967	705	215
83.	Petroleos Mexicanos	Mexico, Distrito Federal, Mexico	1984	702	214
84.	Blue Cross Tower	Philadelphia, Pennsylvania, USA	UC	700	213
84.	Metropolitan Life	New York, New York, USA	1909	700	213
86.	Atlantic Richfield Plaza	Los Angeles, California, USA	1971	699[2]	213[2]
87.	500 Fifth Avenue	New York, New York, USA	1930	697	212
87.	Georgia Pacific Tower	Atlanta, Georgia, USA	1981	697	212
87.	One Shell Square	New Orleans, Louisiana, USA	1972	697	212
87.	United Bank of Denver	Denver, Colorado, USA	1984	697	212
91.	IBM Plaza	Chicago, Illinois, USA	1971	695	212
92.	Four Allen Center	Houston, Texas, USA	1983	692	211
93.	Petro-Canada Tower Number 2	Calgary, Alberta, Canada	1984	689	210
93.	Shinjuku Mitsui	Tokyo, Honshu I, Japan	1974	689	210
93.	Shinjuku Nomura Tower	Tokyo, Honshu I, Japan	1978	689	210
96.	Nine West 57th Street	New York, Nev York, USA	1972	688	210
97.	Chemical Bank, New York Trust	New York, New York, USA	1964	687	209
97.	55 Water Street	New York, New York, USA	1972	687	209

[1]UC, under construction.
[2]Two buildings of this height.

For an explanation of symbols and abbreviations, see pages 16–17.

(Continued)

TABLE 5c. (Continued)

Rank	Building	City and Location	Year Completed[1]	Height ft	Height m
99.	LTV Center	Dallas, Texas, USA	1983	686	209
100.	Capital National Bank Plaza	Houston, Texas, USA	1980	685	209
101.	Chanin	New York, New York, USA	1928	680	207
102.	Gulf and Western	New York, New York, USA	1969	679	207
103.	One Houston Center	Houston, Texas, USA	1977	678	207
104.	Marine Midland	New York, New York, USA	1966	677	206
104.	Southern Bell Telephone	Atlanta, Georgia, USA	1980	677	206
106.	McGraw-Hill	New York, New York, USA	1972	674	205
107.	Lincoln	New York, New York, USA	1929	673	205
107.	One Magnificent Mile	Chicago, Illinois, USA	1984	673	205
109.	1633 Broadway	New York, New York, USA	1971	670	204
110.	Multifoods Tower	Minneapolis, Minnesota, USA	1982	668	204
111.	Bank of Oklahoma Tower	Tulsa, Oklahoma, USA	1975	667	203
112.	Bond Corporation	Perth, Western Australia, Australia		666	203
113.	Trump Tower	New York, New York, USA	1982	664	202
114.	Daley Center	Chicago, Illinois, USA	1965	662	202
114.	First City Tower	Houston, Texas, USA	1980	662	202
116.	Arco Tower	Dallas, Texas, USA	1982	660	201
116.	Overseas-Chinese Banking Corporation	Singapore, Singapore	1976	660	201
118.	Carlton Centre Tower	Johannesburg, Transvaal, South Africa	1971	656	200
118.	Shinjuku Sumitomo	Tokyo, Honshu I, Japan	1974	656	200
118.	Torre Parque Central	Caracas, Venezuela	1979	656	200
121.	599 Lexington Avenue	New York, New York, USA	1986	653	199
122.	1100 Milam	Houston, Texas, USA	1974	651	198
123.	Museum of Modern Art Tower	New York, New York, USA	1984	650	198
123.	Sohio Tower	Cleveland, Ohio, USA	1983	650	198
123.	Ukraina Hotel	Moscow, Russia, USSR	bef 1961	650	198
		***			
	Belmont Centre	Kuala Lumpur, Peninsular Malaysia, Malaysia		633	193
	Gateway Arch	Saint Louis, Missouri, USA	1965	630	192
	One Kansas City Place	Kansas City, Missouri, USA	1987	626	191
	First Wisconsin Center and Office Tower	Milwaukee, Wisconsin, USA	1973	625	190
	Waldorf-Astoria Hotel	New York, New York, USA	1931	625	190
	James A. Rhodes (alt State Office Tower)	Columbus, Ohio, USA	1973	624	190
	Place Victoria	Montreal, Quebec, Canada	1965	624	190
	Place Ville-Marie	Montreal, Quebec, Canada	1962	616	188
	Hong Kong and Shanghai Bank	Hong Kong, Hong Kong	1986	610	186
	Board of Trade	Chicago, Illinois, USA	1930	605	184
	National Westminster Bank	London, England, UK	1980	600	183
	Port of Singapore Authority	Singapore, Singapore	1986	600	183
	Marriott Hotel/The Atrium	Hong Kong, Hong Kong	UC	591	180
	One Pacific Place	Hong Kong, Hong Kong	UC	591	180

[1]UC, under construction.

TABLE 5c. (Continued)

Rank	Building	City and Location	Year Completed[1]	Height ft	Height m
	Marina City Apartments	Chicago, Illinois, USA	1962	588[2]	179[2]
	Municipal	New York, New York, USA	1913	580	177
	Post Office Tower	London, England, UK	1966	580	177
	Building of Offices	Madrid, Castilla la Nueva, Spain	1984	574	175
	Carew Tower	Cincinnati, Ohio, USA	1930	568	173
	Palacio Zarzur Kogan	Sao Paulo, Sao Paulo, Brazil	1960	558	170
	Penobscot	Detroit, Michigan, USA	1928	557	170
	Washington Monument[3]	Washington, District of Columbia, USA	1884	555	169
	Vehicle Assembly	Cape Canaveral, Florida, USA	1966	552	168
	City Hall Tower	Philadelphia, Pennsylvania, USA	1901	548	167
	Mole Antonelliana	Turin, Piemonte, Italy	1863	548	167
	University of Pittsburgh (alt Cathedral of Learning)	Pittsburgh, Pennsylvania, USA	1956	535	163
	Cathedral (off Munster)	Ulm, Baden-Wurttemberg, West Germany	1890	528	161
	International Foreign Trade	Shenzhen, Guangdong, China		525	160
	House of Seagram	New York, New York, USA	1958	525	160
	Cathedral (off Dom Sankt Peter)	Cologne, Nordrhein-Westfalen, West Germany	1880	515	157
	United Nations Secretariat	New York, New York, USA	1950	505	154
	Cathedrale Notre-Dame	Rouen, Haute-Normandie, France	1530	512	156
	Karl-Marx-Universitat Leipzig	Leipzig, East Germany	1971	502	153
	International Trade Centre	Dubayy, United Arab Emirates	1978	492	150
	CBS	New York, New York, USA	1965	491	150
	Hochhaus Platz der Republik	Frankfurt am Main, Hessen, West Germany	1973	469	143
	Tribune Tower	Chicago, Illinois, USA	1925	462	141
	Pyramid of Khufu (alt Pyramid of Cheops)	Giza, Egypt	2568 BC?	450	137
	Bangkok Bank, Ltd	Bangkok, Thailand		440	134
	Saint Peter's Basilica (off Basilica di San Pietro)	Vatican City, Vatican City	1615	435	133
	Bayer A. G.	Leverkusen, Nordrhein-Westfalen, West Germany	1962	433	132
	Pirelli	Milan, Lombardia, Italy	1960	413	126
	Hotel Oberoi Sheraton	Bombay, Maharashtra, India	1973	381	116
	Shwedagon Pagoda	Rangoon, Burma	1774	326	99
	Statue of Liberty	New York, New York, USA	1886	305	93
	Home Life Insurance	Chicago, Illinois, USA	1885	180	55
	Leaning Tower (alt Torre Pendente; off Campanile)	Pisa, Toscana, Italy	1350	179	55

[1]UC, under construction.
[2]Two buildings of this height.
[3]Primarily an observation tower.

For an explanation of symbols and abbreviations, see pages 16–17.

5d. Longest Bridges (Span)

Contents

Conventional and alternate names of bridge.

Body of water spanned, and division and country in which located.

Type of bridge.

Use to which bridge is put.

Year of completion.

Longest span, in feet and meters.

Coverage

All bridges standing or being built with spans of at least the following lengths:

  Suspension bridges—1200 ft (366 m)

  Cantilever bridges—1100 ft (335 m)

  Steel arch bridges—1000 ft (305 m)

  Cable-stayed girder bridges—900 ft (274 m)

  Continuous truss bridges—900 ft (274 m)

  Concrete arch bridges—750 ft (229 m)

  Concrete cable-stayed girder bridges—750 ft (229 m)

  Continuous plate and box girder bridges—750 ft (229 m)

Additionally, the longest span bridge is listed for each of the following types: bascule, simple truss, swing span, and vertical lift.

Entries

159.

TABLE 5d. LONGEST BRIDGES (SPAN)

Bridge	Body of Water and Location	Type[1]	Use[2]	Year Completed[3]	Span ft	Span m
Humber	Humber R, England, UK	S	H	1981	4626	1410
Verrazano-Narrows	New York B of Atlantic O, New York, USA	S	H	1964	4260	1298
Golden Gate	San Francisco B of Pacific O, California, USA	S	H	1937	4200	1280
Mackinac	Straits of Mackinac, Michigan, USA	S	H	1957	3800	1158
Bosporus II	Bosporus Strait, Turkey	S	H	UC(1988?)	3576	1090
Bosporus I	Bosporus Strait, Turkey	S	H	1973	3524	1074
George Washington	Hudson R, New Jersey-New York, USA	S	H	1931	3500	1067
25 de Abril (for Salazar)	Tagus R, Portugal	S	H;RR	1966	3323	1013
Forth Road	Forth R, Scotland, UK	S	H	1964	3300	1006
Severn	Severn R, England-Wales, UK	S	H	1966	3240	988
Onaruto	Naruto Strait, Honshu I, Japan	S	H	1985	2874	876
Tacoma Narrows II	Puget Sound of Pacific O, Washington, USA	S	H;RR	1950	2800	853
Innoshima	Innoshima Strait, Honshu I, Japan	S	H	1982	2526	770
Angostura	Orinoco R, Venezuela	S	H	1967	2336	712
Kammon	Kammon Strait, Honshu I-Kyushu I, Japan	S	H	1973	2336	712
San Francisco-Oakland Bay (alt Transbay)	San Francisco B of Pacific O, California, USA	S	H;RT	1936	2310[4]	704[4]
Bronx-Whitestone	East R, New York, USA	S	H	1939	2300	701
Pierre Laporte (for Quebec Road)	Saint Lawrence R, Quebec, Canada	S	H	1970	2190	668
Delaware Memorial I	Delaware R, Delaware-New Jersey, USA	S	H	1951	2150	655
Delaware Memorial II	Delaware R, Delaware-New Jersey, USA	S	H	1968	2150	655
Seaway Skyway	Saint Lawrence R, Canada-USA	S	H	1960	2150	655
Walt Whitman	Delware R, New Jersey-Pennsylvania, USA	S	H	1957	2000	610
Tancarville	Seine R, Haute-Normandie, France	S	H	1959	1995	608
Little Belt (off Lillebaelt)	Little Belt Strait, Denmark	S	H	1969	1969	600
Ambassador	Detroit R, Canada-USA	S	H	1929	1850	564

1B, bascule; C, cantilever; CA, concrete arch; CCSG, concrete cable-stayed girder; CPBG, continuous plate and box girder; CSG, cable-stayed girder; CT, continuous truss; S, suspension; SA, steel arch; SS, swing span; ST, simple truss; VL, vertical lift.

2H, highway; RR, railroad; RT, rapid transit.

3UC, under construction.

4Two spans of this length, and two additional spans each of 1160 ft, 354 m.

For an explanation of symbols and abbreviations, see pages 16–17.

(Continued)

Figure 38. Artist's impression of the Humber Bridge near Hull, England, a 1981 suspension bridge with the longest span ever constructed. (Credit: British Information Services.)

Figure 39. Quebec Bridge, completed across the Saint Lawrence River at Quebec in 1917 but still boasting the longest cantilever span in the world. (Credit: Quebec Office of Tourism.)

TABLE 5d. (Continued)

Bridge	Body of Water and Location	Type[1]	Use[2]	Year Completed[3]	Span ft	Span m
Quebec	Saint Lawrence R, Quebec, Canada	C	H;RR[5]	1917	1800	549
Throgs Neck	East R, New York, USA	S	H	1961	1800	549
Benjamin Franklin	Delaware R, New Jersey-Pennsylvania, USA	S	H;RT	1926	1750	533
Kvalsund	Kvalsund R, Norway	S	H	1977	1723	525
Skjomen	Skjomen Fjord of Norwegian Sea, Norway	S	H	1971	1723	525
Forth	Forth R, Scotland, UK	C	RR	1890	1710[6]	521[6]
New River Gorge	New R, West Virginia, USA	SA	H	1977	1700	518
Osaka Port	Yodo R, Honshu I, Japan	C	H	1974	1673	510
Bayonne (alt Kill van Kull)	Kill van Kull, New Jersey-New York, USA	SA	H	1931	1652	504
Sydney Harbour	Sydney Harbor of Pacific O, New South Wales, Australia	SA	H;RR	1932	1650	503
Commodore John Barry	Delaware R, New Jersey-Pennsylvania, USA	C	H	1973	1644	501
Kleve-Emmerich	Rhine R, Nordrhein-Westfalen, West Germany	S	H	1965	1640	500
Bear Mountain	Hudson R, New York, USA	S	H	1924	1632	497
Chesapeake Bay I (alt William Preston Lane Memorial I)	Chesapeake B of Atlantic O, Maryland, USA	S	H	1952	1600	488
Chesapeake Bay II (alt William Preston Lane Memorial II)	Chesapeake B of Atlantic O, Maryland, USA	S	H	1973	1600	488
Newport	Narragansett B of Atlantic O, Rhode Island, USA	S	H	1969	1600	488
Williamsburg	East River, New York, USA	S	H;RT	1903	1600	488
Brooklyn	East River, New York, USA	S	H;RT	1883	1595	486
Greater New Orleans	Mississippi R, Louisiana, USA	C	H	1958	1575	480
Lions Gate	Burrard Inlet of Strait of Georgia, British Columbia, Canada	S	H	1939	1550	472
Sotra	Vatle(straumen) Channel, Norway	S	H	1971	1535	468
Annacis Island	Fraser R, British Columbia, Canada	CSG	H	1986	1525	465

[1]B, bascule; C, cantilever; CA, concrete arch; CCSG, concrete cable-stayed girder; CPBG, continuous plate and box girder; CSG, cable-stayed girder; CT, continuous truss; S, suspension; SA, steel arch; SS, swing span; ST, simple truss; VL, vertical lift.

[2]H, highway; RR, railroad; RT, rapid transit.

[3]UC, under construction.

[5]Railroad traffic only since opening of Pierre Laporte Bridge in 1970.

[6]Two spans of this length.

For an explanation of symbols and abbreviations, see pages 16–17.

(Continued)

Figure 40. New River Gorge Bridge, opened across the New River in West Virginia, USA, in 1977, which has the longest span of any steel arch bridge. (Credit: Peggy Powell for West Virginia Department of Commerce.)

Figure 41. Annacis Island Bridge at Vancouver, which set a new record for cable-stayed bridge spans in 1986. (Credit: Ministry of Transportation and Highways, British Columbia, Canada.)

TABLE 5d. (Continued)

Bridge	Body of Water and Location	Type[1]	Use[2]	Year Completed[3]	Span ft	Span m
Yokohama-Ko-Odan	Honshu I, Japan	CSG	H	UC	1509	460
Hooghly I (alt Haora)	Hooghly R, West Bengal, India	C	H;RT	1943	1500	457
Hooghly II	Hooghly R, West Bengal, India	CSG	H	1986	1500	457
Mid-Hudson (alt Poughkeepsie)	Hudson R, New York, USA	S	H	1930	1500	457
Vincent Thomas	San Pedro B of Pacific O, California, USA	S	H	1964	1500	457
Chao Phraya	Chao Phraya R, Thailand	CSG	H	1986	1476	450
Manhattan	East R, New York, USA	S	H;RT	1909	1470	448
Angus L. MacDonald (alt Halifax Harbour)	Halifax Harbor of Atlantic O, Novia Scotia, Canada	S	H	1955	1447	441
Barrios de Luna	Luna R, Leon, Spain	CSG	H	1983	1444	440
A. Murray MacKay	Halifax Harbor of Atlantic O, Nova Scotia, Canada	S	H	1970	1400	427
San Francisco-Oakland Bay (alt Transbay)	San Francisco B of Pacific O, California, USA	C	H;RT	1936	1400	427
Triborough	East R, New York, USA	S	H	1936	1380	421
Iwaguroshima	Shikoku I, Japan	CSG	H	UC	1378	420
Shizakuishima	Shikoku I, Japan	CSG	H	UC	1378	420
Alvsborg	Gota R, Sweden	S	H	1966	1368	417
Meiko Nishi	Honshu I,Japan	CSG	H	1985	1329	405
Saint-Nazaire	Loire R, Pays de la Loire, France	CSG	H	1975	1325	404
Namhae Island	Cheju Strait, South Korea	S	H	1973	1312	400
Rande	Rande Strait, Galicia, Spain	CSG	H	1977	1312	400
Dames Point	Saint Johns R, Florida, USA	CSG	H	UC	1300	396
Aquitaine	Garonne R, Aquitaine, France	S	H	1967	1293	394
Krk Island	Adriatic Sea, Croatia,Yugoslavia	CA	H	1980	1280	390
Koln-Rodenkirchen	Rhine R, Nordrhein-Westfalen, West Germany	S	H	1955	1240	378
Baton Rouge	Mississippi R, Louisiana, USA	C	H	1969	1235	376
Astoria	Columbia R, Oregon-Washington, USA	CT	H	1966	1232	376
Fremont	Willamette R, Oregon, USA	SA	H	1973	1225	373
Hale Boggs Memorial (alt Luling)	Mississippi R, Louisiana, USA	CSG	H	1983	1222	372
Zdakov (alt Orlik)	Vltava R, Bohemia, Czechoslovakia	SA	H	1967	1214	370

For an explanation of symbols and abbreviations, see pages 16–17.

[1]B, bascule; C, cantilever; CA, concrete arch; CCSG, concrete cable-stayed girder; CPBG, continuous plate and box girder; CSG, cable-stayed girder; CT, continuous truss; S, suspension; SA, steel arch; SS, swing span; ST, simple truss; VL, vertical lift.
[2]H, highway; RR, railroad; RT, rapid transit.
[3]UC, under construction.

TABLE 5d. (Continued)

Bridge	Body of Water and Location	Type[1]	Use[2]	Year Completed[3]	Span ft	Span m
Tappan Zee (alt Nyack-Tarrytown)	Hudson R, New York, USA	C	H	1955	1212	369
Saint Johns	Willamette R, Oregon, USA	S	H	1931	1207	368
Dusseldorf-Flehe	Rhine R, Nordrhein-Westfalen, West Germany	CSG	H	1980	1205	367
Wakato	Dokai B of Korea Strait, Kyushu I, Japan	S	H	1962	1204	367
Tjorn II	Askero Fjord of Skagerrak, Sweden	CSG	H	1981	1201	366
Francis Scott Key	Patapsco R, Maryland, USA	CT	H	1976	1200	366
Longview	Columbia R, Oregon-Washington, USA	C	H	1930	1200	366
Mount Hope	Mount Hope B of Atlantic O, Rhode Island, USA	S	H	1929	1200	366
Port Mann	Fraser R, British Columbia, Canada	SA	H	1964	1200	366
Sunshine Skyway II	Tampa B, Florida, USA	CSG	H	1987	1200	366
	* * *					
Queensboro	East R, New York, USA	C	H;RT	1909	1182[7]	360[7]
Yamato	Yamato R, Honshu I, Japan	CSG	H	1982	1165	355
Duisburg-Neuenkamp	Rhine R, Nordrhein-Westfalen, West Germany	CSG	H	1970	1148	350
Thatcher Ferry	Panama Canal, Panama	SA	H	1962	1128	344
Hercilio Luz (alt Florianopolis)	Strait between Norte B and Sul B of Atlantic O, Santa Catarina, Brazil	S	H;RT	1926	1114	340
West Gate	Yarra R, Victoria, Australia	CSG	H	1977	1102	336
Carquinez I	Carquinez Strait, California, USA	C	H	1927	1100[6]	335[6]
Carquinez II	Carquinez Strait, California, USA	C	H	1958	1100[6]	335[6]
Laviolette (alt Trois-Rivieres)	Saint Lawrence R, Quebec, Canada	SA	H	1967	1100	335
Second Narrows	Burrard Inlet of Strait of Georgia, British Columbia, Canada	C	H	1960	1100	335
Jacques Cartier (alt Montreal Harbour)	Saint Lawrence R, Quebec, Canada	C	H;RR	1930	1097	334
Brazo Largo	Parana Guazu R, Entre Rios, Argentina	CSG	H;RR	1976	1083	330
Parana	Parana R, Argentina-Paraguay	S	H;RR	1987	1083	330
Runcorn-Widnes	Mersey R, England, UK	SA	H	1961	1083	330
Zarate	Parana de las Palmas R, Buenos Aires, Argentina	CSG	H;RR	1975	1083	330
Birchenough	Sabi R, Zimbabwe	SA	H	1935	1080	329
Richmond-San Rafael	San Francisco B of Pacific O, California, USA	C	H	1957	1070[6]	326[6]
Kohlbrand	Elbe R, Hamburg, West Germany	CSG	H	1974	1066	325
Oshima	Iyo Sea, Honshu I, Japan	CT	H	1976	1066	325
Cincinnati-Covington	Ohio R, Kentucky-Ohio, USA	S	H	1867[8]	1057	322
Brotonne	Seine R, Haute-Normandie, France	CCSG	H	1976	1050	320

Name	Location	Type		Year	ft	m
Knie	Rhine R, Nordrhein-Westfalen, West Germany	CSG	H	1969	1050	320
Glen Canyon	Colorado R, Arizona, USA	SA	H	1959	1028	313
Mannheim-Seckenheim	Rhine R, Baden-Wurttemberg, West Germany	CCSG	H		1011	328
Wheeling	Ohio R, Ohio-West Virginia, USA	S	H	1849[9]	1010	308
Erskine	Clyde R, Scotland, UK	CSG	H	1971	1000	305
Gladesville	Parramatta R, New South Wales, Australia	CA	H	1964	1000	305
Lewiston-Queenston	Niagara R, Canada-USA	SA	H	1962	1000	305
Bratislava	Danube R, Slovakia, Czechoslovakia	CSG	H	1972	994	303
Perrine	Snake R, Idaho, USA	SA	H	1976	993	303
Severin	Rhine R, Nordrhein-Westfalen, West Germany	CSG	H	1960	991	302
Costa e Silva (alt Rio de Janeiro-Niteroi)	Guanabara B of Atlantic O, Rio de Janeiro, Brazil	CPBG	H	1974	984	300
Kiev	Dnieper R, Ukraine, USSR	CSG	H	1975	984	300
Kuronoseto	Kurono Strait, Kyushu I, Japan	CT	H	1974	984	300
Temmon-Kyo	Misumi Strait, Kyushu I, Japan	CT	H	1966	984	300
Pasco-Kennewick	Columbia R, Washington, USA	CCSG	H	1978	981	299
Hell Gate	East R, New York, USA	SA	RR	1917	977	298
Omishima	Hakata Strait, Shikoku I, Japan	SA	H	1979	974	297
Amizade (alt Foz de Iguacu)	Parana R, Brazil-Paraguay	CA	H	1965	951	290
Deggenau	Danube R, Bayern, West Germany	CSG	H	1975	951	290
Rainbow	Niagara R, Canada-USA	SA	H	1941	950	290
Kurt Schumacher (alt Mannheim-Nord)	Rhine R, Baden-Wurttemberg—Rheinland-Pfalz, West Germany	CSG	H	1969	945	288
Wadi al Kuf Gorge	(Wadi al) Kuf R, Cyrenaica, Libya	CCSG	H	1971	925	282
Friedrich Ebert (alt Bonn-Nord)	Rhine R, Nordrhein-Westfalen, West Germany	CSG	H	1967	919	280
Leverkusen	Rhine R, Nordrhein-Westfalen, West Germany	CSG	H	1964	919	280
Tjorn I	Askero Fjord of Skagerrak, Sweden	SA	H	1960	912	278
Ravenswood	Ohio R, Ohio-West Virginia, USA	CT	H	1981	902	275
Memphis	Mississippi R, Arkansas-Tennessee, USA	SA	H	1972	900[6]	274[6]
Arrabida	Douro R, Portugal	CA	H	1963	885	270
Royal Gorge[10]	Arkansas R, Colorado, USA	S	H	1929	880	268

(Continued)

1B, bascule; C, cantilever; CA, concrete arch; CCSG, concrete cable-stayed girder; CPBG, continuous plate and box girder; CSG, cable-stayed girder; CT, continuous truss; S, suspension; SA, steel arch; SS, swing span; ST, simple truss; VL, vertical lift.
2H, highway; RR, railroad; RT, rapid transit.
3UC, under construction.
6Two spans of this length.
7A second span of 984 ft, 300 m.
8Reconstructed in 1898.
9Reconstructed in 1856.
10Height of deck above water: 1053 ft, 321 m—a record.
For an explanation of symbols and abbreviations, see pages 16–17.

TABLE 5d. (Continued)

Bridge	Body of Water and Location	Type[1]	Use[2]	Year Completed[3]	Span ft	Span m
Tiel	Rhine R, Netherlands	CCSG	H	1974	876	267
Sando	Angerman R, Sweden	CA	H	1943	866	264
Sava I	Sava R, Serbia. Yugoslavia	CPBG	H	1956	856	261
Zoo	Rhine R, Nordrhein-Westfalen, West Germany	CPBG	H	1966	850	259
Dubuque	Mississippi R Illinois-Iowa, USA	CT	H	1943	845	258
Sava II	Sava R, Serbia, Yugoslavia	CPBG	H	1970	820	250
Sibenik	Krka R, Croatia, Yugoslavia	CA	H	1967	808	246
Chaco-Corrientes	Parana R, Chaco-Corrientes Argentina	CCSG	H	1973	804	245
Auckland Horbour	Waitemata Harbor, North I, New Zealand	CPBG	H	1969	800	244
Saikai	Inoura Strait, Kyushu I, Japan	SA	H	1955	800	244
Koror-Babelthuap	(Toagel) Mid Channel, Pacific Islands (USA)	CCSG	H	1978	790	241
Hamana	Hamana Lagoon, Honshu I, Japan	CCSG	H	1976	787	240
Koblenz-Sud	Rhine R, Rheinland-Pfalz, West Germany	CPBG	H	1973	774	236
Shimonoseki	Kammon Strait, Honshu I, Japan	CCSG	H	1975	774	236
General Rafael Urdaneta	Maracaibo L. Venezuela	CCSG	H	1962	771[11]	235[11]
Grand Duchess Charlotte	Alzette R, Luxembourg	CPBG	H	1966	768	234
Fiumarella	Fiumarella R, Calabria, Italy	CA	H	1961	758	231
Bonn-Sud	Rhine R, Nordrhein-Westfalen, West Germany	CPBG	H	1971	755	230
Urado	Urado B of Pacific O, Shikoku I, Japan	CCSG	H	1972	755	230
San Mateo-Hayward II	San Francisco B of Pacific O, California, USA	CPBG	H	1967	750	229
Chester	Ohio R, Ohio-West Virginia, USA	ST	H	1976	746	227
Marine Parkway	Jamaica B of Atlantic O, New York, USA	VL	H	1937	590	180
Ferdan	Suez Canal, Egypt	SS	H;RR	1965	550	168
Pearl River	Pearl L, Louisiana-Mississippi, USA	B	H	1969	482	147

[1]B, bascule; C, cantilever; CA, concrete arch; CCSG, concrete cable-stayed girder; CPBG, continuous plate and box girder; CSG, cable-stayed girder; CT, continuous truss; S, suspension; SA, steel arch; SS, swing span; ST, simple truss; VL, vertical lift.

[2]H, highway; RR, railroad; RT, rapid transit.

[3]UC, under construction.

[11]Five spans of this length.

For an explanation of symbols and abbreviations, see pages 16–17.

5e. Longest Railroad, Highway, and Canal Tunnels

Contents

Conventional and alternate names of tunnel.

Division and country in which located.

Use to which tunnel is put.

Year of completion.

Length from portal to portal, in miles and kilometers.

Coverage

Above * * *, all railroad, highway, and canal tunnels, built or under construction, with a length of at least 4.5 mi (7.24 km).

Below * * *, other such tunnels of considerable length that are well known.

Entries

90.

TABLE 5e. LONGEST RAILROAD, HIGHWAY, AND CANAL TUNNELS

Tunnel	Location	Use[1]	Year Completed[2]	Length mi	km
Seikan (underwater)	Hokkaido I-Honshu I, Japan	RR	1988	33.46	53.85
Shimizu III	Honshu I, Japan	RR	1979	13.84	22.28
Simplon II (alt Sempione II)	Italy-Switzerland	RR	1922	12.32	19.82
Simplon I (alt Sempione I)	Italy-Switzerland	RR	1906	12.30	19.80
New Kammon (off Shin Kammon) (underwater)	Honshu I-Kyushu I, Japan	RR	1974	11.63	18.71
Apennine (off Appennino)	Emilia-Romagna— Toscana, Italy	RR	1934	11.51	18.52
Gotthard (alt Saint- Gotthard)	Switzerland	H	1980	10.14	16.32
Rokko	Honshu I, Japan	RR	1972	10.10	16.25
Furka	Switzerland	RR	1982	9.57	15.4
Gotthard (alt Saint- Gotthard)	Switzerland	RR	1882	9.32	15.00
Nakayama	Honshu I, Japan	RR		9.13	14.7
Lotschberg	Switzerland	RR	1913	9.08	14.61
Haruna	Honshu I, Japan	RR		8.95	14.4
Arlberg	Austria	H	1978	8.70	14.0
Hokuriku	Honshu I, Japan	RR	1962	8.62	13.87
Mont-Cenis (alt Frejus, Monte Cenisio)	France-Italy	RR	1871	8.49	13.66
Shimizu II	Honshu I, Japan	RR	1967	8.38	13.49

[1]C, canal; H, highway; RR, railroad.
[2]UC, under construction.

For an explanation of symbols and abbreviations, see pages 16–17.

(Continued)

Profile of Main Tunnel

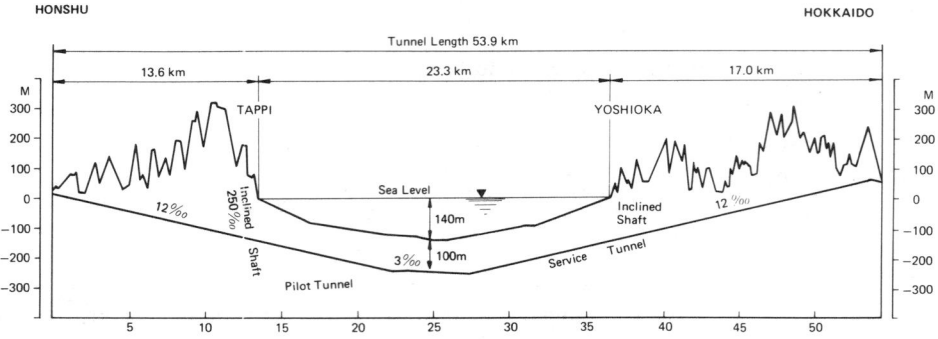

Figure 42. *Seikan Tunnel, an underwater tube connecting Honshu and Hokkaido Islands in Japan, which is two and a half times longer than any other railroad tunnel and was opened for traffic in 1988. Top: Profile of the main tunnel; bottom: Site of the Honshu Island approach. (Credit: Japanese National Railways.)*

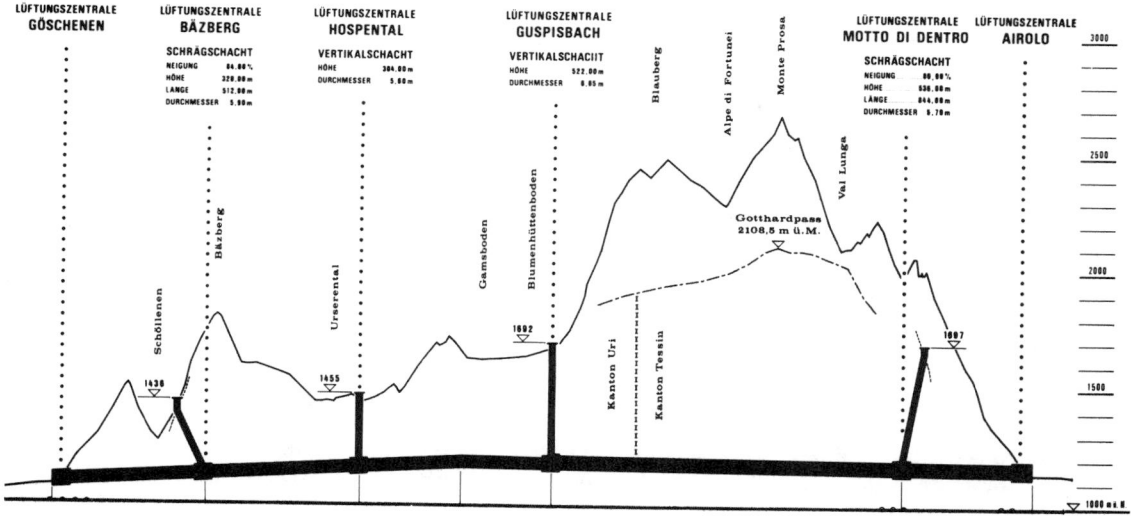

Figure 43. *Gotthard Tunnel, a transalpine bore in Switzerland, which became the longest highway tunnel when it was opened for traffic in 1980. top: Longitudinal profile of the tunnel; bottom: Site of the southern approach at Airolo. (Credit: Swiss Federal Office of Highways and Rivers.)*

TABLE 5e. (Continued)

Tunnel	Location	Use[1]	Year Completed[2]	Length mi	Length km
Aki	Shikoku I, Japan	RR	1975	8.10	13.04
Mont-Cenis (alt Frejus, Monte Cenisio)	France-Italy	H	1980	7.95	12.8
Cascade	Washington, USA	RR	1929	7.79	12.54
Mont-Blanc (alt Monte Bianco)	France-Italy	H	1965	7.25	11.67
Kubiki	Honshu I, Japan	RR	1969	7.05	11.35
Flathead	Montana, USA	RR	1970	7.0	11.27
Kan-Etsu	Honshu I, Japan	H	1984	6.77	10.90
Lierasen	Norway	RR	1973	6.65	10.7
Santa Lucia	Catania, Italy	RR	1977	6.38	10.26
Arlberg	Austria	RR	1884	6.37	10.25
Gran Sasso	Abruzzi e Molise, Italy	H	1976	6.21	10.0
Shimizu I	Honshu I, Japan	RR	1930	6.03	9.70
Moffat	Colorado, USA	RR	1928	5.97	9.61
North Kyushu	Kyushu I, Japan	RR	1974	5.97	9.60
Seelisberg	Switzerland	H	1980	5.75[3]	9.25[3]
Kvineshei	Norway	RR	1943	5.63	9.06
Bingo	Japan	RR	1974	5.54	8.92
Kaimai	North I, New Zealand	RR	1978	5.49	8.84
Rimutaka	North I, New Zealand	RR	1955	5.47	8.80
Otira	South I, New Zealand	RR	1923	5.37	8.65
Ena II	Honshu I, Japan	H	1985	5.36	8.62
Ricken	Switzerland	RR	1910	5.35	8.60
Grenchenberg	Switzerland	RR	1915	5.33	8.58
Tauern	Austria	RR	1909	5.31	8.55
Fukuoka	Kyushu I, Japan	RR	1974	5.28	8.50
Haegebostad	Norway	RR	1943	5.27	8.47
Ena I	Honshu I, Japan	H	1975	5.25	8.45
Ronco (alt Giovi)	Liguria, Italy	RR	1889	5.16	8.30
Hauenstein	Switzerland	RR	1916	5.05	8.13
Colle di Tenda (alt Col de Tende)[4]	France-Italy	RR	1900	5.03	8.10
Connaught	British Columbia, Canada	RR	1916	5.02	8.08
Karawanken (alt Karavanke)	Austria-Yugoslavia	RR	1906	4.96	7.98
Kobe	Honshu I, Japan	RR	1970	4.95	7.97
Tanna II	Honshu I, Japan	RR	1964	4.94	7.96
Somport	France-Spain	RR	1928	4.89	7.87
Tanna I	Honshu I, Japan	RR	1934	4.85	7.80
Ulriken	Norway	RR	1964	4.76	7.66
Hosaka	Honshu I, Japan	RR	1970	4.72	7.59
Hoosac	Massachusetts, USA	RR	1875	4.70	7.56
Monte Orso	Lazio, Italy	RR	1927	4.68	7.53
Lupacino	Italy	RR	1958	4.67	7.51
Castiglione	Italy	RR	1977	4.59	7.39
Vivola	Lazio, Italy	RR	1927	4.57	7.35
* * *					
Jungfrau	Switzerland	RR	1912	4.43	7.12

[1]C, canal; H, highway; RR, railroad.
[2]UC, under construction.
[3]Two parallel tubes of this length.
[4]Closed since World War II.

TABLE 5e. (Continued)

Tunnel	Location	Use[1]	Year Completed[2]	Length mi	Length km
Rove	Provence-Cote d'Azur, France	C	1927	4.42	7.11
Severn (underwater)	England-Wales, UK	RR	1886	4.36	7.01
Rokko II	Honshu I, Japan	H	1974	4.29	6.90
San Bernardino (alt Bernhardin)	Switzerland	H	1967	4.10	6.6
Tauern	Austria	H	1974	3.98	6.4
Haneda (underwater)	Honshu I, Japan	RR	1971	3.72	5.98
Grand Saint-Bernard (alt Gran San Bernardo)	Italy-Switzerland	H	1964	3.64	5.85
Felber-Tauern	Austria	H	1967	3.48	5.6
Katschberg	Austria	H	1974	3.36	5.4
Viella	Cataluna, Spain	H	1941	3.13	5.04
New Sasago (off Shin Sasago)	Honshu I, Japan	H		2.74	4.42
Kammon (underwater)	Honshu I-Kyushu I, Japan	RR	1942	2.24	3.6
Kammon (underwater)	Honshu I-Kyushu I, Japan	H	1958	2.15	3.46
Mersey (alt Queensway) (underwater)	England, UK	H	1934	2.13	3.43
Elbe (underwater)	Hamburg-Niedersachsen, West Germany	H	1973	2.06	3.32
Transandine Summit (off Cumbre)	Argentina-Chile	RR	1910	1.97	3.17
Tsuruga	Honshu I, Japan	H		1.97	3.17
Pyrenees (alt Pirineos)	France-Spain	H	1970	1.87	3.01
Sasago II	Honshu I, Japan	H	1958	1.83	2.95
Rokko I	Honshu I, Japan	H	1967	1.76	2.84
Reboucas	Rio de Janeiro, Brazil	H	1967	1.75	2.82
Brooklyn-Battery (underwater)	New York, USA	H	1950	1.73	2.78
Eisenhower Memorial	Colorado, USA	H	1971	1.70	2.74
Kuriko II	Honshu I, Japan	H	1966	1.66	2.67
Holland (underwater)	New Jersey-New York, USA	H	1927	1.62	2.61
Lincoln I (underwater)	New Jersey-New York, USA	H	1937	1.56	2.51
Lincoln III (underwater)	New Jersey-New York, USA	H	1957	1.52	2.45
Baltimore Harbor (underwater)	Maryland, USA	H	1958	1.45	2.33
Lincoln II (underwater)	New Jersey-New York, USA	H	1945	1.42	2.29

[1]C, canal; H, highway; RR, railroad.
[2]UC, under construction.

For an explanation of symbols and abbreviations, see pages 16–17.

5f. Highest Dams

Contents

Conventional and alternate names of dam.

River dammed, and division and country in which located.

Type of dam.

Year of completion.

Height of dam, excluding projections, in feet and meters.

Volume of structure, in millions of cubic yards and cubic meters.

Coverage

Above * * *, all dams in place or under construction with a height of at least 550 ft (168 m).

Below * * *, other well-known high dams.

Rounding

Volumes are rounded to the nearest 100,000 yd^3 (m^3).

Entries

84.

TABLE 5f. HIGHEST DAMS

Dam	River and Location	Type[1]	Year Completed[2]	Height ft	Height m	Volume yd³	Volume m³
Rogun	Vakhsh R, Tadzhikistan, USSR	R	UC	1099	335	98.8	75.5
Nurek	Vakhsh R, Tadzhikistan, USSR	R	1980	984	300	75.9	58.0
Grande Dixence	Dixence R, Switzerland	G	1962	935	285	7.8	6.0
Inguri	Inguri R, Georgia, USSR	CA	1980	892	272	5.2	4.0
Boruca	Grande de Terraba R, Costa Rica	R	UC	876	267	56.2	43.0
Vaiont	Vaiont R, Veneto, Italy	CA	1961	860	262	0.46	0.35
Chicoasen	Grijalva R, Chiapas, Mexico	R	1980	856	261	20.1	15.4
Tehri	Bhagirathi R, Uttar Pradesh, India	R	UC	856	261	29.8	22.7
Kishau	Tons R, Uttar Pradesh, India	R	UC	830	253	24.1	18.4
Sayano-Shushenskaya	Yenisey R, Russia, USSR	CA	1980	804	245	11.9	9.1
Guavio	Guavio R, Colombia	R	1987	797	243	23.2	17.8
Mica	Columbia R, British Columbia, Canada	R	1973	794	242	42.0	32.1
Mihoesti	Aries R, Romania		1983	792	242		
Chivor (for Esmeralda)	Bata R, Columbia	R	1975	778	237	14.1	10.8
Mauvoisin	Drance de Bagnes R, Switzerland	CA	1957	778	237	2.7	2.0
El Cajon	Humuya R, Honduras	CA	1985	768	234	2.1	1.6
Chirkey	Sulak R, Russia, USSR	CA	1978	764	233	1.8	1.4
Oroville	Feather R, California, USA	E	1968	755	230	78.0	59.6
Bhakra	Sutlej R, Himachal Pradesh, India	G	1963	742	226	5.4	4.1
Hoover (for Boulder)	Colorado R, Arizona-Nevada, USA	CA	1936	725	221	4.4	3.4
Contra	Verzasca R, Switzerland	CA	1965	722	220	0.86	0.66
Dabaklamm	Dorfer(bach) Creek, Austria	CA	UC	722	220	1.3	1.0
Mratinje	Piva R, Montenegro, Yugoslavia	G	1976	722	220	0.97	0.74
Dworshak	North Fork of Clearwater R, Idaho, USA	G	1973	717	219	6.4	4.9
Glen Canyon	Colorado R, Arizona, USA	CA	1966	709	216	4.9	3.7
Toktogul	Naryn R, Kirgizia, USSR	G	1978	705	215	4.4	3.3
Daniel Johnson	Manicouagan R, Quebec, Canada	CA	1968	702	214	2.9	2.3
Dez	Dez R, Iran	CA	1962	699	213	0.60	0.46

[1]A, arch; C concrete; E, earth; G, gravity; R, rock.
[2]UC, under construction.
[3]In millions of cubic yards and cubic meters.

For an explanation of symbols and abbreviations, see pages 16–17.

(Continued)

Figure 44. *Hydropower station at Nurek Dam on the Vakhsh River in Tadzhikistan, USSR. Although the Nurek is the highest dam already completed, an even higher one, the Rogun, is now nearing completion on the same river. (Credit: Embassy of the USSR, Washington.)*

TABLE 5f. (Continued)

Dam	River and Location	Type[1]	Year Completed[2]	Height ft	Height m	Volume yd3	Volume m3
Bakun	Rajang R, Sarawak, Malaysia	R	UC	689	210	38.5	29.4
Lower Tunguska	Lower Tunguska R, Russia, USSR	G	UC	689	210	30.1	23.0
San Roque	Agno R, Luzon I, Philippines	R	UC	689	210	56.4	43.1
Luzzone	Brenno di Luzzone R, Switzerland	CA	1963	682	208	1.7	1.3
Keban	Euphrates R, Turkey	R	1974	679	207	20.4	15.6
Almendra (alt Vallarino)	Tormes R, Leon, Spain	CA	1970	662	202	2.9	2.2
Khudoni	Inguri R, Georgia, USSR	CA	UC	659	201	1.9	1.5
Cipasang	(Ci)manuk R, Java I, Indonesia	R	UC	656	200	117.7	90.0
Karun	Karun R, Iran	CA	1975	656	200	2.1	1.6
Kolnbrein	Malta (Bach) Creek, Austria	CA	1977	656	200	2.1	1.6
Kayraktepe	Goksu R, Turkey	R	UC	653	199	22.2	17.0
Itaipu	Parana R, Brazil-Paraguay	R	1982	643	196	38.2	29.2
Altinkaya	Kizil (Irmak) R, Turkey	R	1986	640	195	3.4	2.6
New Bullard's Bar	North Yuba R, California, USA	CA	1970	637	194	2.6	2.0
Lakhwar	Yamuna R, Uttar Pradesh, India	G	1985	630	192	2.6	2.0
New Melones	Stanislaus R, California, USA	R	1979	625	190	16.0	12.2
Nan Choan	Quae Yai R, Thailand	R	UC	614	187	16.2	12.4
Kurobe Number 4	Kurobe R, Honshu I, Japan	CA	1964	610	186	1.8	1.4
Swift	Lewis R, Washington, USA	E	1958	610	186	15.4	11.8
Zillergrundl	Ziller R, Austria	CA	1986	610	186	1.8	1.4
Mossyrock	Cowlitz R, Washington, USA	CA	1968	607	185	1.3	0.97
Oymapinar	Manavgat R, Turkey	CA	1984	607	185	0.73	0.56
Ataturk	Euphrates R, Turkey	R	UC	604	184	111.2	85.0
Shasta	Sacramento R, California, USA	G	1945	602	183	8.7	6.7
W. A. C. Bennett	Peace R, British Columbia, Canada	E	1967	600	183	57.2	43.7
Dartmouth	Mitta Mitta R, Victoria, Australia	R	1979	591	180	18.4	14.1
Emosson	Barberine R, Switzerland	CA	1974	591	180	1.4	1.1
Karaj	Karaj R, Iran	CA	1964	591	180	0.98	0.75
Ozkoy	Gediz R, Turkey	R	1983	591	180	14.7	11.3

[1]A, arch; C concrete; E, earth; G, gravity; R, rock.

[2]UC, under construction.

[3]In millions of cubic yards and cubic meters.

For an explanation of symbols and abbreviations, see pages 16–17.

(Continued)

TABLE 5f. (Continued)

Dam	River and Location	Type[1]	Year Completed[2]	Height ft	Height m	Volume yd³	Volume m³
Tachien (alt Tehchi)	Tachia R, Taiwan	CA	1974	591	180	0.60	0.46
Tignes	Isere R, Rhone-Alpes, France	CA	1952	591	180	0.83	0.63
Los Leones	Los Leones R, Chile	E	1986	587	179	12.0	9.2
Takase	Takase R, Honshu I, Japan	R	1978	577	176	15.2	11.6
Hasan Ugurlu (alt Ayvacik)	Yesil (Irmak) R, Turkey	R	1981	574	175	3.0	2.3
Marun	Marun R, Iran	E	1978	574	175	9.4	7.2
Revelstoke	Columbia R, British Columbia, Canada	G	1984	574	175	1.7	1.3
Alpe Gera	Cormor R, Friuli-Venezia Giulia, Italy	G	1964	571	174	2.3	1.7
Piedra del Aquila	Limay R, Neuquen-Rio Negro, Argentina	G	UC	571	174	3.6	2.8
Don Pedro	Tuolumne R, California, USA	R	1971	568	173	16.0	12.2
Karakaya	Euphrates R, Turkey	CA	1986	568	173	2.6	2.0
Hungry Horse	South Fork of Flathead R, Montana, USA	CA	1953	564	172	3.1	2.4
Longyangxia	Huang R, Qinghai, China	CA	1987	564	172	2.3	1.7
Cabora Bassa	Zambezi R, Mozambique	CA	1974	561	171	0.67	0.51
Urra II	Sinu R, Colombia	R	UC	558	170	30.7	23.5
Idikki	Periyar R, Kerala, India	CA	1974	554	169	0.60	0.46
Charvak	Chirchik R, Uzbekistan, USSR	R	1977	551	168	28.3	21.6
Grand Coulee	Columbia R, Washington, USA	G	1942	551	168	10.6	8.1
Gura Apelor	(Riul) Mare R, Romania	R	1984	551	168	11.8	9.0
La Grande Number 2	Grande R, Quebec, Canada	R	1978	551	168	30.3	23.2

* * *

Ross	Skagit R, Washington, USA	CA	1959	540	165	0.92	0.70
Trinity	Trinity R, California, USA	E	1962	537	164	29.4	22.5
Raul Leoni (alt Guri)	Caroni R, Venezuela	R	1986	532	162	102.0	78.0
Yellowtail	Bighorn R, Montana, USA	CA	1966	525	160	1.5	1.2
Cougar	South Fork of McKenzie R, Oregon, USA	R	1964	519	158	13.0	9.9
Flaming Gorge	Green R, Utah, USA	CA	1964	502	153	0.99	0.75
Kariba	Zambezi R, Zambia-Zimbabwe	G	1959	420	128	1.3	1.0

1A, arch; C concrete; E, earth; G, gravity; R, rock.

2UC, under construction.

3In millions of cubic yards and cubic meters.

For an explanation of symbols and abbreviations, see pages 16–17.

5g. Largest Dams (Volume of Structure)

Contents

Conventional and alternate names of dam.

River dammed, and division and country in which located.

Type of dam.

Year of completion.

Volume of structure, in millions of cubic yards and cubic meters.

Height of dam, excluding projections, in feet and meters.

Coverage

All dams in place or under construction with a volume of at least 25,000,000 yd^3 (19,125,000 m^3).

Rounding

Volumes are rounded to the nearest 100,000 yd^3 (m^3).

Entries

74.

TABLE 5g. LARGEST DAMS (VOLUME OF STRUCTURE)

Dam	River and Location	Type[1]	Year Completed[2]	Volume yd³	Volume m³	Height ft	Height m
Chapeton	Parana R, Entre Rios-Santa Fe, Argentina	G	UC	387.4	296.2	115	35
Pati	Parana R, Parana, Argentina	G	UC	301.1	230.2	118	36
Tarbela	Indus R, Pakistan	R	1976	138.1	105.6	469	143
Fort Peck	Missouri R, Montana, USA	E	1937	125.6	96.0	250	76
Lower Usuma	Usuma R, Nigeria	E	UC	121.6	93.0	161	49
Cipasang	(Ci)manuk R, Java I, Indonesia	R	UC	117.7	90.0	656	200
Ataturk	Euphrates R, Turkey	R	UC	111.2	85.0	604	184
Raul Leoni (alt Guri)	Caroni R, Venezuela	R	1986	102.0	78.0	532	162
Rogun	Vakhsh R, Tadzhikistan, USSR	R	UC	98.8	75.5	1099	335
Oahe	Missouri R, South Dakota, USA	E	1960	92.0	70.3	245	75
Gardiner	South Saskatchewan R, Saskatchewan, Canada	E	1968	85.5	65.4	226	69
Mangla	Jhelum R, Pakistan	E	1967	85.5	65.4	453	138
Tucurui	Tocantins R, Para, Brazil	G	1984	84.1	64.3	305	93
Afsluitdijk	IJssel(meer) L, Netherlands	E	1932	83.0	63.4	62	19
Yacyreta-Apipe	Parana R, Argentina-Paraguay	G	UC	80.0	61.2	154	47
Oroville	Feather R, California, USA	E	1968	78.0	59.6	755	230
San Luis	San Luis Creek, California, USA	E	1967	77.9	59.6	382	116
Nurek	Vakhsh R, Tadzhikistan, USSR	R	1980	75.9	58.0	984	300
Nagajunasagar	Krishna R, Andhra Pradesh, India	E	1966	73.6	56.3	409	125
Garrison	Missouri R, North Dakota, USA	E	1956	66.5	50.8	203	62
Cochiti	Rio Grande R, New Mexico, USA	E	1975	65.7	50.2	253	77
Oosterschelde	Vense Gat Oosterschelde R, Netherlands	G	1986	65.4	50.0	164	50
Tabka (alt Thawra)	Euphrates R, Syria	E	1976	60.2	46.0	197	60
Gorkiy	Volga R, Russia, USSR	E	1955	58.0	44.3	105	32
Aswan High [off (Sadd al) Aali]	Nile R, Egypt	R	1970	57.9	44.3	364	111
W. A. C. Bennett	Peace R, British Columbia, Canada	E	1967	57.2	43.7	600	183

(Continued)

[1] A, arch; C, concrete; E, earth; G, gravity; R, rock.

[2] UC, under construction.

[3] In millions of cubic yards and cubic meters.

For an explanation of symbols and abbreviations, see pages 16–17.

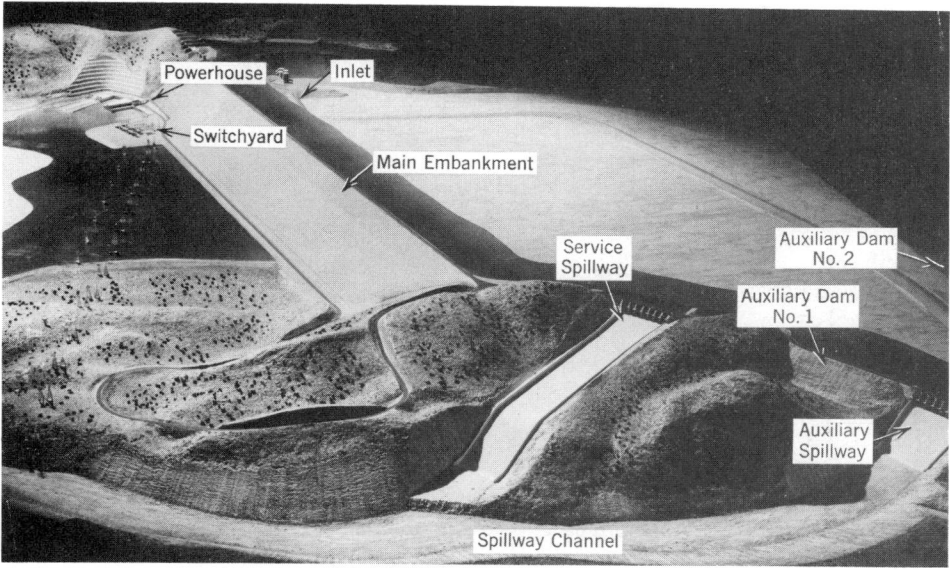

Figure 45. *Tarbela Dam on the Indus River in Pakistan, the world's largest in volume of structure. Top: Scale model of the dam; bottom: Service spillway. (Credit, respectively: Tippetts-Abbett-McCarthy-Stratton, New York; Tomas Sennett for the World Bank.)*

TABLE 5g. (Continued)

Dam	River and Location	Type[1]	Year Completed[2]	Volume		Height	
				yd³	m³	ft	m
San Roque	Agno R, Luzon I, Philippines	R	UC	56.4	43.1	689	210
Boruca	Grande de Terraba R, Costa Rica	R	UC	56.2	43.0	876	267
Kiev	Dnieper R, Ukraine, USSR	E	1964	56.0	42.8	223	68
Saratov	Volga R, Russia, USSR	E	1967	52.8	40.4	131	40
Itumbiara	Paranaiba R, Goias-Minas Gerais, Brazil	G	1980	50.8	38.8	348	106
Fort Randall	Missouri R, South Dakota, USA	E	1956	50.2	38.4	160	49
Kakhovskaya	Dnieper R, Ukraine, USSR	G	1955	46.6	35.6	121	37
Lauwerszee	Lauwers(zee) B, Netherlands	E	1969	46.5	35.6	75	23
Beas	Beas R, Himachal Pradesh, India	G	1974	46.4	35.5	436	133
Sao Felix	Tocantins R, Goias, Brazil	R	UC	44.5	34.0	525	160
Tsimlyansk	Don R, Russia, USSR	G	1952	44.3	33.9	135	41
Volga–V. I. Lenin	Volga R, Russia, USSR	G	1955	44.3	33.9	148	45
Castaic	Castaic Creek, California, USA	E	1973	44.0	33.6	410	125
Kanev	Dnieper R, Ukraine, USSR	E	1976	43.2	33.0	131	40
Jari	Jari R, Pakistan	E	1967	42.4	32.4	234	71
Mica	Columbia R, British Columbia, Canada	R	1973	42.0	32.1	794	242
Kremenchug	Dnieper R, Ukraine, USSR	G	1960	41.2	31.5	108	33
Michihuae	Limay R, Neuquen-Rio Negro, Argentina	E	UC	39.0	29.8	230	70
Bakun	Rajang R, Sarawak, Malaysia	R	UC	38.5	29.4	689	210
Itaipu	Parana R, Brazil-Paraguay	R	1982	38.2	29.2	643	196
Ludington	Michigan L, Michigan, USA	E	1973	37.7	28.8	171	52
Kama	Kama R, Russia, USSR	G	1954	36.2	27.7	121	37
Sao Simao	Paranaiba R, Goias-Minas Gerais, Brazil	R	1978	35.8	27.4	394	120
Brouwershavense Gat	Brouwershavense Gat R, Netherlands	E	1972	35.3	27.0	118	36
Ilha Solteira	Parana R, Mato Grosso do Sul-Sao Paulo, Brazil	R	1973	34.4	26.3	243	74
Volga–22nd Congress	Volga R, Russia, USSR	G	1958	33.9	25.9	154	47
Ukai	Tapti R, Gujarat, India	G	1972	33.0	25.2	266	81
Hirakud	Mahanadi R, Orissa, India	G	1956	32.8	25.1	194	59
El Majaara	(Oued) Ouerrha R, Morocco	E	UC	32.7	25.0	285	87

Emboracao	Paranaiba R, Goias-Minas Gerais, Brazil	R	1982	32.7	25.0	518	158
Kingsley	North Platte R, Nebraska, USA	E	1942	32.0	24.5	170	52
Urra II	Sinu R, Columbia	R	UC	30.7	23.5	558	170
La Grande Number 2	Grande R, Quebec, Canada	R	1978	30.3	23.2	551	168
Lower Tunguska	Lower Tunguska R, Russia, USSR	G	UC	30.1	23.0	689	210
Mosul	Tigris R, Iraq	E	1983	30.1	23.0	430	131
Tehri	Bhagirathi R, Uttar Pradesh, India	R	UC	29.8	22.7	856	261
Trinity	Trinity R, California, USA	E	1962	29.4	22.5	537	164
Warm Springs	Dry Creek, California, USA	E	1982	29.2	22.3	318	97
La Grande Number 3	Grande R, Quebec, Canada	R	1981	28.9	22.1	305	93
Dneprodzerzhinsk	Dnieper R, Ukraine, USSR	G	1964	28.8	22.0	112	34
Cerros Colorados	Neuquen R, Neuquen, Argentina	G	1972	28.3	21.6	115	35
Charvak	Chirchik R, Uzbekistan, USSR	R	1977	28.3	21.6	551	168
Agua Vermelha	Grande R, Minas Gerais-Sao Paulo, Brazil	G	1975	27.6	21.1	220	67
Maqarin	Yarmuk R, Jordan-Syria	R	1987	27.5	21.0	538	164
Navajo	San Juan R, New Mexico, USA	E	1963	26.8	20.5	402	123
Haringvliet	Haringvliet Estuary, Netherlands	E	1970	26.2	20.0	79	24
Sterkfontein	Nuwe Jaar(spruit) R, Orange Free State, South Africa	E	1986	25.9	19.8	305	93
La Grande Number 4	Grande R, Quebec, Canada	R	1984	25.2	19.3	420	128

1A, arch; C concrete; E, earth; G, gravity; R, rock.

2UC, under construction.

3In millions of cubic yards and cubic meters.

For an explanation of symbols and abbreviations, see pages 16–17.

6

GEOGRAPHIC TABLES AND COMPARISONS: SEAS

6a. Largest Seas, by Ocean

Contents

Conventional and alternate names of sea.

Surface area in thousands of square miles and square kilometers.

Greatest recorded depth of water in feet and meters.

Coverage

Above * * *, all seas (including those commonly designated as gulfs, bays, straits, and the like) that are generally recognized by oceanographic authorities and that have an area of at least 25,000 square miles (64,750 square kilometers).

Below * * *, other well-known seas.

Rounding

Depths are rounded to the nearest 10 ft (m) if above 100 ft (m).

Entries

132.

TABLE 6a. LARGEST SEAS, BY OCEAN

Sea	Surface Area		Greatest Depth	
	1,000 mi²	1,000 km²	(ft)	(m)
Pacific O, with adjacent seas	70,017	181,344	36,200	11,030
Coral Sea	1,850	4,791	29,990	9,140
South China (alt Nan) Sea	1,423	3,685	17,780	5,420
Tasman Sea	900	2,331	19,670	5,990
Bering Sea	873	2,261	15,660	4,770
Sea of Okhotsk	537	1,392	12,000	3,660
G of Alaska	512	1,327	18,570	5,660
Bellingshausen Sea	430	1,110	17,250	5,260
Amundsen Sea	400	1,036	17,060	5,200

For an explanation of symbols and abbreviations, see pages 16–17.

(Continued)

TABLE 6a. (Continued)

Sea	Surface Area		Greatest Depth	
	1,000 mi²	1,000 km²	(ft)	(m)
Arafura Sea	400	1,036	12,070	3,680
Philippine Sea	400	1,036	34,580	10,540
Sea of Japan	389	1,008	12,180	3,710
Ross Sea	371	960	14,010	4,270
East China (alt Dong, Tung) Sea	290	752	8,910	2,720
Solomon Sea	278	720	29,970	9,140
Banda Sea	268	695	24,410	7,440
Timor Sea	237	615	10,860	3,310
Celebes (alt Sulawesi) Sea	182	472	20,410	6,220
Java (alt Jawa) Sea	167	433	290	89
Sulu Sea	162	420	16,800	5,120
Yellow (alt Huang, Hwang) Sea	161	417	350	110
G of Carpentaria	120	310	290	89
Molucca (alt Maluku) Sea	119	307	13,710	4,180
G of Thailand (alt Siam)	92	239	240	73
Bismarck Sea	87	225	8,740	2,670
Makassar (alt Macassar, Makasar) Strait	75	194	8,060	2,460
Ceram (alt Seram) Sea	72	187	17,450	5,320
G of California	62	161	10,260	3,130
G of Chihli (alt Bo G, Po G)	54	140	120	36
Flores Sea	47	121	17,170	5,230
Bali Sea	46	119	5,220	1,590
G of Tonkin (alt Tongking)	45	117	270	82
Savu Sea	41	105	11,390	3,470
Tatar Strait	39	100	750	230
Korea Strait	36	94	690	210
Formosa (alt Taiwan) Strait	34	87	230	70
Bass Strait	29	75	330	100
Korea B	27	70	6,560	2,000
Halmahera Sea	26	67	6,690	2,040
Bristol B	25	65	290	88
* * *				
G of Papua	21	54	3,180	970
G of Liaodong (alt Liaotung)	15	39	160	50
G of Panama	12	30	330	100
Torres Strait	12	30	72	22
Norton Sound	11	28	89	27
Mindanao Sea	9.8	25	6,480	1,980
Bering Strait	6.0	16	140	42
Inland (alt Seto) Sea [Japan]	3.7	9.5	790	240
Puget Sound	2.0	5.2	800	250
Atlantic O, with adjacent seas	36,415	94,314	30,250	9,220
Weddell Sea	1,080	2,796	16,490	5,030
Caribbean Sea	1,063	2,754	25,200	7,680
Mediterranean Sea	969	2,510	16,900	5,150
G of Mexico	596	1,543	17,070	5,200
G of Guinea	592	1,533	20,880	6,360
Scotia Sea	347	900	26,000	7,920
Hudson B	316	819	990	300
Labrador Sea	309	800	12,480	3,800
Drake Passage	240	620	19,160	5,840
North Sea	232	600	2,380	730
Davis Strait	230	596	1,530	470

TABLE 6a. (Continued)

Sea	Surface Area		Greatest Depth	
	1,000 mi²	1,000 km²	(ft)	(m)
Black Sea	163	422	7,250	2,210
Baltic Sea	147	382	1,540	470
Tyrrhenian Sea	100	260	12,240	3,730
Foxe Basin	93	240	360	110
G of Saint Lawrence	92	238	3,270	1,000
B of Biscay	71	184	16,730	5,100
Ionian Sea	69	180	16,900	5,150
Aegean Sea	69	179	8,300	2,530
Bight of Bonny (alt Biafra)	60	155	11,230	3,420
Hudson Strait	55	142	3,090	940
Adriatic Sea	51	132	5,210	1,590
B of Campeche	49	128	9,840	3,000
G of Bothnia	45	117	950	290
Irish Sea	40	103	520	160
James B	37	96	330	100
English Channel (alt La Manche)	35	90	560	170
Foxe Channel	29	75	1,500	460
Bight of Benin	26	67	14,040	4,280

* * *

Sea	Surface Area		Greatest Depth	
Ungava B	22	57	980	300
G of Sidra (alt Sirte, Surt)	19	50	3,280	1,000
Sea of Azov	15	39	46	14
Sea of Crete (alt Candia)	15	39	6,660	2,030
G of Finland	12	30	330	100
Skagerrak	11	29	2,380	730
G of Darien	11	28	6,560	2,000
Straits of Florida	10	26	5,370	1,640
G of Honduras	10	26	6,560	2,000
Kattegat	9.8	25	410	120
G of San Jorge	9.7	25	300	90
Saint George's Channel	7.5	19	420	130
G of Riga	7.0	18	200	62
Chesapeake B	6.2	16	350	110
Strait of Magellan	5.8	15	2,000	610
G of Venezuela	5.7	15	130	40
Sea of Marmara	4.6	12	4,560	1,390
G of Gabes (alt Qabis)	4.2	11	660	200
B of Fundy	3.6	9.3	680	210
Strait of Dover	3.1	8.0	240	72
Massachusetts B	1.4	3.6	660	200
Long Island Sound	1.2	3.1	330	100
Strait of Gibraltar	0.7	1.9	3,870	1,180
Indian O, with adjacent seas	28,617	74,118	24,460	7,460
Arabian Sea	1,492	3,863	17,070	5,200
B of Bengal	839	2,172	17,250	5,260
Mozambique Channel	376	975	9,840	3,000
Andaman (alt Burma) Sea	232	602	13,690	4,170
Great Australian Bight	187	484	660	200
Red Sea	175	453	9,220	2,810
Persian G (alt G of Iran)	92	238	340	100
G of Aden	85	220	12,070	3,680

For an explanation of symbols and abbreviations, see pages 16–17.

(Continued)

TABLE 6a. (Continued)

Sea	Surface Area		Greatest Depth	
	1,000 mi²	1,000 km²	(ft)	(m)
G of Oman	70	181	12,120	3,690
Strait of Malacca	25	65	660	200
	* * *			
Strait of Hormuz	4.7	12	510	160
G of Suez	3.7	9.7	260	80
G of Aqaba	1.7	4.3	6,000	1,830
Arctic O, with adjacent seas	4,732	12,257	17,880	5,450
Barents Sea	542	1,405	1,970	600
Norwegian Sea	534	1,383	12,860	3,920
Greenland Sea	465	1,205	15,900	4,850
East Siberian Sea	361	936	510	160
Kara Sea	341	883	2,030	620
Laptev Sea	270	700	11,110	3,390
Baffin B	266	689	7,010	2,140
Chukchi (alt Chuckchee) Sea	225	582	520	160
Beaufort Sea	184	476	15,360	4,680
Denmark Strait	54	140	1,970	600
White Sea	35	90	1,080	330
Viscount Melville Sound	28	73	1,890	580
	* * *			
Amundsen G	23	60	950	290
G of Boothia	23	60	440	130
World (total for all oceans and seas)	139,781	362,033	36,200	11,030

For an explanation of symbols and abbreviations, see pages 16–17.

6b. Largest Seas, Irrespective of Ocean

Contents

Rank.

Conventional and alternate names of sea.

Ocean to which the sea is adjacent.

Surface area in thousands of square miles and square kilometers.

Coverage

50 largest seas.

Entries

50.

TABLE 6b. LARGEST SEAS, IRRESPECTIVE OF OCEAN

Rank		Ocean to Which Adjacent	Surface Area	
			1,000 mi^2	1,000 km^2
1.	Coral Sea	Pacific	1,850	4,791
2.	Arabian Sea	Indian	1,492	3,863
3.	South China (alt Nan) Sea	Pacific	1,423	3,685
4.	Weddell Sea	Atlantic	1,080	2,796
5.	Caribbean Sea	Atlantic	1,063	2,754
6.	Mediterranean Sea	Atlantic	969	2,510
7.	Tasman Sea	Pacific	900	2,331
8.	Bering Sea	Pacific	873	2,261
9.	B of Bengal	Indian	839	2,172
10.	G of Mexico	Atlantic	596	1,543
11.	G of Guinea	Atlantic	592	1,533
12.	Barents Sea	Arctic	542	1,405
13.	Sea of Okhotsk	Pacific	537	1,392
14.	Norwegian Sea	Arctic	534	1,383
15.	G of Alaska	Pacific	512	1,327
16.	Greenland Sea	Arctic	465	1,205
17.	Bellingshausen Sea	Pacific	430	1,110
18.	Amundsen Sea	Pacific	400	1,036
18.	Arafura Sea	Pacific	400	1,036
18.	Philippine Sea	Pacific	400	1,036
21.	Sea of Japan	Pacific	389	1,008
22.	Mozambique Channel	Indian	376	975
23.	Ross Sea	Pacific	371	960
24.	East Siberian Sea	Arctic	361	936
25.	Scotia Sea	Atlantic	347	900
26.	Kara Sea	Arctic	341	883
27.	Hudson B	Atlantic	316	819
28.	Labrador Sea	Atlantic	309	800
29.	East China (alt Dong, Tung) Sea	Pacific	290	752
30.	Solomon Sea	Pacific	278	720
31.	Laptev Sea	Arctic	270	700
32.	Banda Sea	Pacific	268	695
33.	Baffin B	Arctic	266	689
34.	Drake Passage	Atlantic	240	620
35.	Timor Sea	Pacific	237	615
36.	Andaman (alt Burma) Sea	Indian	232	602
37.	North Sea	Atlantic	232	600
38.	Davis Strait	Atlantic	230	596
39.	Chukchi (alt Chuckchee) Sea	Arctic	225	582
40.	Great Australian Bight	Indian	187	484
41.	Beaufort Sea	Arctic	184	476
42.	Celebes (alt Sulawesi) Sea	Pacific	182	472
43.	Red Sea	Indian	175	453
44.	Java (alt Jawa) Sea	Pacific	167	433
45.	Black Sea	Atlantic	163	422
46.	Sulu Sea	Pacific	162	420
47.	Yellow (alt Huang, Hwang) Sea	Pacific	161	417
48.	Baltic Sea	Atlantic	147	382
49.	G of Carpentaria	Pacific	120	310
50.	Molucca (alt Maluku) Sea	Pacific	119	307

For an explanation of symbols and abbreviations, see pages 16–17.

7

GEOGRAPHIC TABLES AND COMPARISONS: ISLANDS

7a. Largest Islands, by Continent

Contents

Latitude and longitude, in degrees and minutes, at center of island.

Conventional and other (alternate, former, and official) names of island.

Principal body of water adjacent to island.

Division and country in which island is located.

Surface area in thousands of square miles and square kilometers.

Highest elevation in feet and meters.

Name of largest city and its latest population, in thousands, with year of census or estimate (e).[1]

Coverage

Above * * *, all islands with an area of at least 1,000 mi² (2,590 km²).

Below * * *, other well-known islands, including the largest in certain countries.

Rounding

Areas are rounded to the nearest three significant digits.

Elevations are rounded to the nearest 10 ft (m) if above 100 ft (m).

Entries

422, as follows: Africa—35

Antarctica—4

Asia—89

Europe—85

North America—120

Oceania—64

South America—25

---

[1]On some islands the "largest city" is actually a small town or even a village. No attempt has been made to differentiate in the index, where each is identified simply as a city. When the population of this largest settlement is unknown, the population of the entire island is usually supplied.

TABLE 7a. LARGEST ISLANDS, BY CONTINENT

Latitude and Longitude	Island	Principal Body of Water	Location	Area 1,000 mi²	Area 1,000 km²	Highest Elev ft	Highest Elev m	Largest City and Its Latest Population (thousands), with Date
AFRICA								
20.00S, 47.00E	Madagascar (alt Madagaskara)	Indian O	Madagascar	227	587	9,470	2890	Antananarivo: 663 (1985e)
49.30S, 69.30E	•Kerguelen	Indian O	French Southern and Antarctic Lands	2.32	6.00	6,070	1850	Port-aux-Francais: 0.09 (1972e)
			***					
21.06S, 55.36E	Reunion (for Bourbon)	Indian O	Reunion	0.969	2.51	10,070	3070	Saint-Denis: 109 (1982)
3.30N, 8.42E	Bioko (for Fernando Po)	Bight of Bonny of G of Guinea	Equatorial Guinea	0.779	2.02	9,840	3000	Malabo: 37 (1983)
28.19N, 16.34W	Tenerife (for Teneriffe)	Atlantic O	(Canary Islands), Spain	0.745	1.93	12,200	3720	Santa Cruz de Tenerife: 194 (1985e)
20.18S, 57.35E	Mauritius [for Ile de] France]	Indian O	Mauritius	0.720	1.86	2,710	830	Port Louis: 132 (1983)
28.20N, 14.00W	Fuerteventura	Atlantic O	(Canary Islands), Spain	0.642	1.66	2,650	810	Puerto del Rosario (for Puerto de Cabras): 14 (1981)
6.10S, 39.20E	Zanzibar (alt Unguja)	Indian O	Zanzibar, Tanzania	0.640	1.66	430	130	Zanzibar: 133 (1985e)
28.00N, 15.36W	Gran Canaria (alt Grand Canary)	Atlantic O	(Canary Islands), Spain	0.592	1.53	6,400	1950	Las Palmas: 379 (1985e)
11.35S, 43.20E	Njazidja (for Grande Comore)	Mozambique Channel	Comoros	0.443	1.15	7,750	2360	Moroni: 20 (1980)
15.05N, 23.40W	Sao Tiago (alt Santiago)	Atlantic O	Cape Verde	0.384	0.994	4,570	1390	Praia: 49 (1985e)
5.10S, 39.48E	•Pemba	Indian O	Zanzibar, Tanzania	0.380	0.984	300	91	Wete: 13 (1978)

Lat, Long	Island	Water body	Country			low elev		Largest town: population (year)
15.40N, 40.05E	•Dahlac (alt Dahlak, Grand Dahlac; off Dehalak)	Red Sea	Ethiopia	0.347	0.900			
0.12N, 6.39E	Sao Tome (for Sao Thome)	G of Guinea	Sao Tome and Principe	0.330	0.854	6,640	2020	Sao Tome: 35 (1984e)
29.00N, 13.40W	Lanzarote	Atlantic O	(Canary Islands), Spain	0.302	0.782	2,200	670	Arrecife: 30 (1981)
17.05N, 25.10W	Santo Antao	Atlantic O	Cape Verde	0.302	0.782	6,490	1980	Ribeira Grande: 23 (1970)
32.44N, 17.00W	Madeira	Atlantic O	(Madeira Islands), Portugal	0.286	0.741	6,110	1860	Funchal: 44 (1981)
28.40N, 17.52W	La Palma (alt Palma)	Atlantic O	(Canary Islands), Spain	0.256	0.662	7,960	2430	Santa Cruz de la Palma: 17 (1981)
16.05N, 22.50W	Boa Vista	Atlantic O	Cape Verde	0.239	0.620	1,270	390	Sal Rei: ? [island population 3 (1980)]
33.48N, 10.54E	Djerba (off Jarbah)	G of Gabes of Mediterranean Sea	Tunisia	0.197	0.510	160	50	Houmt Souk (off Hawmat as Suq): 9 (1966)
14.55N, 24.25W	Fogo	Atlantic O	Cape Verde	0.184	0.476	9,280	2830	Sao Filipe: 4 (1980)
12.15S, 44.25E	Nzwani (for Anjouan)	Mozambique Channel	Comoros	0.164	0.424	5,170	1570	Mutsamudu: 13 (1980)
12.50S, 45.10E	Mayotte (alt Mahore)	Mozambique Channel	Mayotte	0.144	0.374	1,970	600	Mamoudzou: 12 (1985)
28.06N, 17.08W	Gomera	Atlantic O	(Canary Islands), Spain	0.136	0.353	4,880	1490	San Sebastian de la Gomera: 6 (1981)
16.35N, 24.15W	Sao Nicolau	Atlantic O	Cape Verde	0.132	0.343	4,280	1300	Ribeira Brava: ? [island population 14 (1980)]
15.15N, 23.10W	Maio (for Mayo)	Atlantic O	Cape Verde	0.104	0.269	1,430	440	Porto Ingles: ? [island population 6 (1980)]
27.45N, 18.00W	Ferro (off Hierro)	Atlantic O	(Canary Islands), Spain	0.102	0.264	4,920	1500	Valverde: 3 (1981)
16.50N, 25.00W	Sao Vicente	Atlantic O	Cape Verde	0.088	0.227	2,540	770	Mindelo: 37 (1980)
4.40S, 55.30E	Mahe	Indian O	Seychelles	0.055	0.142	2,970	905	Victoria: 25 (1982e)
1.37N, 7.25E	Principe	G of Guinea	Sao Tome and Principe	0.049	0.128	3,110	950	Santo Antonio: 2 (1970)
15.57S, 5.42W	Saint Helena	Atlantic O	Saint Helena	0.047	0.122	2,700	820	Jamestown: 2 (1976)

For an explanation of symbols and abbreviations, see pages 16–17.

(Continued)

TABLE 7a. (Continued)

| Latitude and Longitude | Island | Principal Body of Water | Location | Area | | Highest Elev | | Largest City and Its Latest Population (thousands), with Date |
				1,000 mi2	1,000 km2	ft	m	
19.42S, 63.25E	Rodrigues	Indian O	Mauritius	0.040	0.104	1,300	400	Petit Gabriel: 1.3 (1972)
37.05S, 12.17W	Tristan da Cunha	Atlantic O	Saint Helena	0.038	0.098	6,760	2060	Edinburgh: ? [island population 0.3 (1985e)]
7.57S, 14.22W	Ascension	Atlantic O	Saint Helena	0.034	0.088	2,870	870	Georgetown: ? [island population 2 (1985e)]
7.20S, 72.25E	•Diego Garcia	Indian O	British Indian Ocean Territory	0.010	0.027	low elev		none [island population 2 (1986e)]

* * *

ANTARCTICA

71.00S, 70.00W	•Alexander (for Alexander I)	Bellingshausen Sea	Antarctica	16.7	43.2	10,300	3140	uninhabited
79.30S, 49.30W	•Berkner	Weddell Sea	Antarctica	1.50	3.88	3,200	980	uninhabited
67.15S, 68.30W	•Adelaide	Bellingshausen Sea	Antarctica	1.27	3.30	10,500	3200	uninhabited
77.30S, 168.00E	•Ross	Ross Sea	Antarctica	0.888	2.30	12,450	3790	uninhabited
69.45S, 75.15W	•Charcot	Bellingshausen Sea	Antarctica	0.772	2.00	2,000	610	uninhabited

ASIA

1.00N, 114.00E	•Borneo (alt Kalimantan)	South China Sea	Brunei-Indonesia-Malaysia	285	737	13,450	4100	Banjarmasin: 424 (1983e)
0.00, 102.00E	•Sumatra (off Sumatera)	Andaman Sea	Indonesia	164	425	12,470	3800	Medan: 1805 (1983e)
36.00N, 138.00E	•Honshu (alt Hondo)	Pacific O	Japan	88.0	228	12,390	3780	Tokyo: 8354, 11,828s (1985)
2.00S, 121.00E	•Celebes (off Sulawesi)	Celebes Sea	Indonesia	67.4	174	11,340	3450	Ujung Pandang: 840 (1983e)
7.30S, 110.00E	•Java (for Dijawa; off Jawa)	Indian O	Indonesia	50.0	129	12,060	3680	Jakarta: 7873 (1985e)
15.00N, 121.00E	Luzon	Pacific O	Philippines	40.4	105	9,610	2930	Manila: 1766, 6942s (1985e)

Coordinates	Name	Sea/Ocean	Country					Principal town: population
8.00N, 125.00E	Mindanao	Pacific O	Philippines	36.5	94.6	9,690	2950	Davao: 610 (1980)
44.00N, 143.00E	•Hokkaido (for Ezo, Yezo)	Pacific O	Japan	30.1	78.0	7,510	2290	Sapporo: 1543 (1985)
51.00N, 143.00E	Sakhalin (for Karafuto, Saghalien)	Sea of Okhotsk	Russia, USSR	29.5	76.4	5,280	1610	Yuzhno-Sakhalinsk: 158 (1985e)
7.30N, 80.30E	Sri Lanka (alt Ceylon; for Serendib)	Indian O	Sri Lanka	25.2	65.3	8,280	2520	Colombo: 643 (1984e)
23.30N, 121.00E	Taiwan (alt Formosa)	Pacific O	Taiwan	13.8	35.8	13,110	4000	Taipei: 2508 (1985e)
33.00N, 131.00E	•Kyushyu (alt Kiushu)	Pacific O	Japan	13.8	35.7	5,870	1790	Kitakyushu: 1056 (1985)
19.00N, 109.30E	Hainan	South China Sea	Guangdong, China	13.1	34.0	6,160	1880	Haikou: 209 (1985e)
8.50S, 126.00E	•Timor	Timor Sea	Indonesia	10.2	26.3	9,720	2960	Kupang: 403 (1980)
1.00N, 128.00E	•Halmahera (for Djailolo; off Jailolo)	Molucca Sea	Indonesia	6.95	18.0	6,260	1910	Jailolo (for Djailolo): 3 (1971)
33.45N, 133.30E	•Shikoku	Pacific O	Japan	6.86	17.8	6,500	1980	Matsuyama: 427 (1985)
3.00S, 129.00E	•Ceram (off Seram)	Banda Sea	Indonesia	6.62	17.2	10,020	3050	Masohi (alt Amahai): 2 (1971)
8.30S, 121.00E	•Flores	Flores Sea	Indonesia	5.50	14.2	7,820	2380	Ende: 27 (1971)
79.30N, 97.00E	Oktyabrskoy Revolyutsii (alt October Revolution)	Arctic O	Russia, USSR	5.47	14.2	3,170	960	uninhabited
8.40S, 118.00E	•Sumbawa (for Soembawa)	Indian O	Indonesia	5.16	13.4	9,350	2850	Raba; 41 (1971)
12.00N, 125.00E	Samar	Pacific O	Philippines	5.05	13.1	2,790	850	Calbayog: 107 (1980)
10.00N, 123.00E	Negros	Sulu Sea	Philippines	4.90	12.7	8,090	2470	Bacolod: 262 (1980)
10.30N, 118.30E	Palawan (for Paragua)	South China Sea	Philippines	4.55	11.8	6,840	2080	Puerto Princesa: 60 (1980)
75.45N, 138.44E	Kotelnyy	Arctic O	Russia, USSR	4.50	11.7	1,230	370	
10.42N, 122.33E	Panay	Sulu Sea	Philippines	4.45	11.5	6,730	2050	Iloilo: 245 (1980)
2.15S, 106.00E	•Bangka (alt Banka)	Java Sea	Indonesia	4.37	11.3	2,310	700	Pangkalpinang: 90 (1980)

For an explanation of symbols and abbreviations, see pages 16–17.

(Continued)

TABLE 7a. (Continued)

Latitude and Longitude	Island	Principal Body of Water	Location	Area 1,000 mi²	Area 1,000 km²	Highest Elev ft	Highest Elev m	Largest City and Its Latest Population (thousands), with Date
78.40N, 102.30E	Bolshevik	Arctic O	Russia, USSR	4.35	11.3	3,070	930	uninhabited
10.00S, 120.00E	•Sumba (for Sandalwood, Soemba)	Indian O	Indonesia	4.31	11.2	4,020	1220	Waingapu (for Waingapoe): 16 (1971)
12.50N, 121.10E	Mindoro	South China Sea	Philippines	3.76	9.73	8,480	2590	Calapan: 67 (1980)
35.05N, 33.15E	Cyprus (off Kibris, Kypros)	Mediterranean Sea	Cyprus	3.57	9.25	6,410	1950	Nicosia: 217 (1982e)
80.30N, 95.00E	Komsomolets	Arctic O	Russia, USSR	3.48	9.01	2,560	780	uninhabited
3.24S, 126.40E	•Buru (for Boeroe)	Banda Sea	Indonesia	3.47	9.00	7,970	2430	Namlea: 4 (1971)
71.00N,179.30W	Wrangel (off Vrangelya)	Chukchi Sea	Russia, USSR	2.82	7.30	3,600	1100	Ushakovskiy: ?
10.50N, 124.52E	Leyte	Visayan Sea	Philippines	2.78	7.21	4,430	1350	Ormoc: 105 (1980); Tacloban: 103 (1980)
45.00N, 148.00E	Iturup (for Etorofu)	Pacific O	Russia, USSR	2.60	6.72	5,360	1630	Kurilsk: 1 (1970?)
75.00N, 149.00E	Novaya Sibir (alt New Siberia)	East Siberian Sea	Russia, USSR	2.39	6.20	250	76	Bolshoy Zimovye: ?
8.30N, 115.00E	•Bali	Indian O	Indonesia	2.17	5.62	10,310	3140	Denpasar: 261 (1980)
8.45N, 116.30E	•Lombok	Indian O	Indonesia	2.10	5.43	12,220	3730	Mataram: 69 (1980)
7.00S, 113.30E	•Madura (for Madoera)	Java Sea	Indonesia	2.04	5.29	1,550	470	Pamekasan: 56 (1971)
75.30N, 144.00E	Faddeyevskiy	Arctic O	Russia, USSR	1.93	5.00	200	61	uninhabited
2.50S, 108.00E	•Billiton (off Belitung)	Java Sea	Indonesia	1.85	4.80	1,670	510	Tanjungpandan (for Tandjoengpandan): 37 (1971)
1.05N, 97.35E	•Nias	Indian O	Indonesia	1.84	4.77	2,910	890	Gunungsitoli (for Goenoengsitoli): 9 (1971)
73.35N, 142.00E	Bolshoy Lyakhovskiy	Arctic O	Russia, USSR	1.78	4.60	890	270	

Lat/Long	Island	Sea/Ocean	Country			Area	Elev	Chief town: pop (yr)
10.23N, 123.50E	Cebu (for Zebu)	Visayan Sea	Philippines	1.71	4.42	3,320	1010	Cebu: 490 (1980)
5.00S, 122.55E	•Butung (off Buton; for Boetoeng)	Banda Sea	Indonesia	1.62	4.20	3,900	1190	Baubau (for Baoebaoe): 18 (1971)
9.50N, 124.10E	Bohol	Mindanao Sea	Philippines	1.49	3.86	2,630	800	Tagbilaran: 43 (1980)
12.30N, 54.00E	•Socotra (alt Sokotra; off Suqutra)	Indian O	South Yemen	1.40	3.63	4,930	1500	Hadiboh (for Tamrida): 3 (1960?e)
7.48S, 126.18E	•Wetar	Banda Sea	Indonesia	1.40	3.62	4,630	1410	Ilwaki: 0.2 (1971)
12.15N, 123.30E	Masbate	Visayan Sea	Philippines	1.26	3.27	2,280	700	Masbate: 53(1980)
1.20S, 98.55E	•Siberut (for Siberoet)	Indian O	Indonesia	1.22	3.17	1,330	410	Muarasiberut (for Moearasiberoet): 8 (1971)
7.36S, 131.25E	•Yamdena (for Jamdena)	Arafura Sea	Indonesia	1.10	2.86	low elev		Saumlaki: 2 (1971)
1.48S, 124.48E	•Taliabu (for Taliaboe)	Molucca Sea	Indonesia	1.10	2.85	4,330	1320	Todeli: 0.5 (1971)
6.35S, 134.20E	•Trangan	Arafura Sea	Indonesia	1.02	2.65	290	90	Rebi: 0.5 (1971)
			∗ ∗ ∗					
1.30S, 127.45E	•Obi (alt Obira)	Ceram Sea	Indonesia	0.951	2.46	5,290	1610	Wayaloar: 1 (1971)
1.20S, 123.10E	•Peleng	Molucca Sea	Indonesia	0.929	2.40	3,470	1060	Tataba: 0.5 (1971)
0.35S, 127.30E	•Bacan (for Batjan, Bachan)	Molucca Sea	Indonesia	0.913	2.36	6,930	2110	Labuha (for Laboeha): 2 (1971)
8.15S, 124.45E	•Alor (alt Ombai)	Banda Sea	Indonesia	0.900	2.33	5,790	1760	Kalabahi: 10 (1971)
19.06N, 93.48E	•Ramree (off Yanbye)	B of Bengal	Burma	0.888	2.30	3,000	910	Kyaukpyu: 7 (1953)
50.25N, 155.50E	Paramushir (for Paramushiro)	Pacific O	Russia, USSR	0.788	2.04	5,960	1820	Severo-Kurilsk. 2 (1947e)
58.50N, 164.00E	Karagin (off Karaginskiy)	Bering Sea	Russia, USSR	0.772	2.00	2,990	910	Ostrovnoy: ?
2.33N, 95.55E	•Simeulue (for Simeuloee)	Indian O	Indonesia	0.712	1.84	2,180	580	Sinabang: 7 (1971)
33.20N, 126.30E	•Cheju (for Quelpart, Saishu)	East China Sea	South Korea	0.710	1.84	6,400	1950	Cheju: 203 (1985)
2.20N, 128.25E	•Morotai	Molucca Sea	Indonesia	0.695	1.80	4,100	1250	Berebere: 0.8 (1971)

For an explanation of symbols and abbreviations, see pages 16–17.

(Continued)

TABLE 7a. (Continued)

Latitude and Longitude	Island	Principal Body of Water	Location	Area 1,000 mi2	Area 1,000 km2	Highest Elev ft	Highest Elev m	Largest City and Its Latest Population (thousands), with Date
55.00N, 137.42E	Bolshoy Shantar	Sea of Okhotsk	Russia, USSR	0.691	1.79	2,300	700	Shantar: ?
5.00S, 122.30E	•Muna (for Moena)	Banda Sea	Indonesia	0.658	1.70	1,460	440	Raha: 12 (1971)
55.00N, 166.15E	Bering (off Beringa)	Pacific O	Russia, USSR	0.641	1.66	2,460	750	Nikolskoye: 0.5 (1948e)
22.30N, 90.45E	•Dakhin Shahbazpur (for Dakshin Shabazpur)	B of Bengal	Bangladesh	0.612	1.59	low elev		Bhola: 9 (1961)
44.10W,146.00E	Kunashir (for Kunashiri)	Pacific O	Russia, USSR	0.598	1.55	5,970	1820	Yuzhno-Kurilsk (for Furukamappu): ?
12.30N, 92.50E	Middle Andaman	B of Bengal	Andaman and Nicobar, India	0.593	1.54	1,680	510	none [island population 24 (1981)]
13.45N,124.15E	Catanduanes	Philippine Sea	Philippines	0.552	1.43	2,510	760	Virac: 40 (1980)
13.15N, 92.55E	North Andaman	B of Bengal	Andaman and Nicobar, India	0.531	1.38	2,400	730	none [island population 16 (1981)]
11.45N, 92.10E	South Andaman	B of Bengal	Andaman and Nicobar, India	0.520	1.35	1,060	320	Port Blair: 50 (1981)
26.45N, 55.45E	•Qeshm (alt Qishm; for Kishm, Tawila)	Strait of Hormuz	Iran	0.515	1.33	1,310	400	Qeshm (alt Qishm; for Kishm): 7 (1976)
6.34N, 122.03E	Basilan	Celebes Sea	Philippines	0.494	1.28	3,320	1010	Isabela (alt Basilan): 50 (1980)
26.42N,128.11E	Okinawa	Pacific O	Japan	0.471	1.22	1,600	490	Naha: 304 (1985)
1.05N,104.30E	•Bintan (alt Bintang)	South China Sea	Indonesia	0.415	1.07	1,140	350	Tanjungpinang (for Tandjoengpinang): 44 (1971)
7.00N, 93.50E	Great Nicobar	Indian O	Andaman and Nicobar, India	0.403	1.04	2,100	640	none [island population 2 (1971)]
29.47N, 48.10E	Bubiyan (alt Bobian)	Persian G	Kuwait	0.333	0.863	low elev		uninhabited
38.00N,138.25E	Sado	Sea of Japan	Japan	0.331	0.857	3,850	1170	Ryotsu: 20 (1985)

(Continued)

Coordinates	Name	Sea/Ocean	Country					City
3.40S, 128.10E	•Ambon (alt Amboina)	Banda Sea	Indonesia	0.294	0.761	3,410	1040	Ambon: 209 (1980)
28.15N, 129.20E	Amami(-Oshima)	Pacific O	Japan	0.274	0.709	2,280	690	Naze (alt Nase): 50 (1985)
19.12N, 72.54E	•Salsette	Arabian Sea	Maharashtra, India	0.246	0.637	1,530	470	Bombay (in part): 2584 (1971)
26.00N, 50.30E	Bahrain (alt Bahrein; off Bahrayn)	Persian G	Bahrain	0.217	0.563	440	140	Manama: 109 (1981)
1.22N, 103.48E	Singapore (alt Singapura)	South China Sea	Singapore	0.210	0.543	580	180	Singapore: 2586 (1986e)
5.24N, 100.14E	Penang (off Pinang)	Strait of Malacca	Peninsular Malaysia, Malaysia	0.108	0.280	2,720	830	Penang: 251 (1980)
0.41N, 127.24E	•Tidore	Molucca Sea	Indonesia	0.045	0.116	5,680	1730	Soasiu (alt Tidore; for Soasioe): 1 (1971)
22.15N, 114.11E	Hong Kong (alt Xiangjiang, Hsiangchiang, Hsiangkang)	South China Sea	Hong Kong	0.029	0.075	1,800	550	Hong Kong (in part): 1184 (1981)
0.48N, 127.20E	•Ternate	Molucca Sea	Indonesia	0.025	0.065	5,630	1710	Ternate: 35 (1971)
18.59N, 72.50E	Bombay	Arabian Sea	Maharashtra, India	0.024	0.062	180	55	Bombay (in part): 3387 (1971)

EUROPE

Coordinates	Name	Sea/Ocean	Country					City
53.30N, 2.30W	•Great Britain (alt Britain)	North Sea	UK	84.4	219	4,410	1340	London: 2497, 6696s (1981)
65.00N, 18.00W	Iceland (off Island)	Atlantic O	Iceland	39.7	103	6,950	2120	Reykjavik: 89, 130s (1984e)
53.25N, 8.00W	•Ireland (alt Eire)	Atlantic O	Ireland-UK	32.5	84.1	3,410	1040	Dublin: 502, 921s (1986)
75.00N, 61.30E	Novaya Zemlya (north island)	Kara Sea	Rusia, USSR	18.9	48.9	5,080	1550	Russkaya Gavan: ?
78.45N, 16.00E	West Spits-bergen (off Vestspitsbergen)	Arctic O	Svalbard	15.3	39.5	5,630	1720	Longyearbyen: 1 (1977)
72.00N, 54.00E	Novaya Zemlya (south island)	Barents Sea	Russia, USSR	12.8	33.3	4,400	1340	Krasino: ?

For an explanation of symbols and abbreviations, see pages 16–17.

TABLE 7a. (Continued)

Latitude and Longitude	Island	Principal Body of Water	Location	Area 1,000 mi²	Area 1,000 km²	Highest Elev ft	Highest Elev m	Largest City and Its Latest Population (thousands), with Date
37.30N, 14.00E	Sicily (off Sicilia)	Mediterranean Sea	Sicilia, Italy	9.81	25.4	10,760	3280	Palermo: 716 (1985e)
40.00N, 9.00E	Sardinia (off Sardegna)	Mediterranean Sea	Sardegna, Italy	9.19	23.8	6,020	1830	Cagliari: 224 (1985e)
79.48N, 22.24E	North East Land (off Nordaustlandet)	Barents Sea	Svalbard	5.79	15.0	2,510	760	none
42.00N, 9.00E	Corsica (off Corse)	Mediterranean Sea	Corse, France	3.37	8.72	8,890	2710	Ajaccio: 54 (1982)
35.29N, 24.42E	Crete (for Candia; off Kriti)	Mediterranean Sea	Greece	3.19	8.26	8,060	2460	Iraklion: 102, 111s (1981)
55.30N, 11.45E	Zealand (off Sjaelland)	Baltic Sea	Denmark	2.71	7.02	410	130	Copenhagen: 483, 1366s (1984e)
77.45N, 22.30E	Edge	Barents Sea	Svalbard	1.94	5.03	1,900	580	none
57.15N, 9.50E	Vendsyssel-Thy[1]	Skagerrak	Denmark	1.81	4.68	450	140	Frederikshavn: 25 (1984e)
38.34N, 24.24E	Euboea (off Evvoia)	Aegean Sea	Greece	1.41	3.65	5,720	1740	Chalcis (off Khalkis): 45 (1981)
39.30N, 3.00E	Majorca (off Mallorca)	Mediterranean Sea	Baleares, Spain	1.40	3.63	4,740	1440	Palma: 316 (1985e)
70.00N, 59.30E	Vaygach	Kara Sea	Russia, USSR	1.31	3.38	560	170	
69.05N, 49.15E	Kolguyev	Barents Sea	Russia, USSR	1.24	3.20	540	170	
57.30N, 18.33E	Gotland (for Gottland)	Baltic Sea	Sweden	1.16	3.00	270	83	Visby: 20 (1984e)
55.20N, 10.30E	Fyn (for Funen)	Baltic Sea	Denmark	1.15	2.98	430	130	Odense: 137, 163s (1984e)
80.30N, 49.00E	Zemlya Georga	Barents Sea	Russia, USSR	1.12	2.90	1,360	420	uninhabited
80.45N, 46.00E	Zemlya Aleksandry	Barents Sea	Russia, USSR	1.08	2.80	1,250	380	Nagurskoye: ?
58.25N, 22.30E	Sarema (alt Saaremaa; for Osel)	Baltic Sea	Estonia, USSR	1.03	2.68	180	54	Kingisepp (for Arensburg, Kuressaare): 12 (1970)

Lat, Long	Island	Sea/Ocean	Country					Chief town
68.30N, 16.00E	Hinn(oya)	Norwegian Sea	Norway	0.849	2.20	4,150	1270	Harstad: 22 (1986e)
58.05N, 6.40W	•Lewis with Harris	Atlantic O	Scotland, UK	0.770	1.99	2,620	800	Stornoway: 9 (1981)
57.20N, 6.15W	•Skye	Sea of the Hebrides	Scotland, UK	0.643	1.67	3,310	1010	Portree: 2 (1981)

* * *

Lat, Long	Island	Sea/Ocean	Country					Chief town
39.10N, 25.50E	Lesbos (alt Mytilene; off Lesvos)	Aegean Sea	Greece	0.629	1.63	3,180	970	Mytilene (for Kastro; off Mitilini): 24 (1981)
69.20N, 17.30E	Senja (for Senjen)	Norwegian Sea	Norway	0.614	1.59	3,310	1010	Torsken: 2 (1980)
36.10N, 28.00E	Rhodes (off Rodhos)	Mediterranean Sea	Greece	0.541	1.40	3,990	1210	Rhodes: 40 (1981)
56.45N, 16.38E	Oland	Baltic Sea	Sweden	0.519	1.34	170	51	Borgholm: 11 (1985e)
54.46N, 11.30E	Lolland (for Laaland)	Baltic Sea	Denmark	0.480	1.24	98	30	Nakskov: 16 (1984e)
58.50N, 22.40E	Khiuma (alt Hiiumaa; for Dago)	Baltic Sea	Estonia, USSR	0.382	0.989	180	54	Kardla: 3 (1972e)
60.16N, 1.16W	Mainland (Shetland Islands)	Atlantic O	Scotland, UK	0.378	0.979	1,470	450	Lerwick: 7 (1981)
56.25N, 5.54W	•Mull	Atlantic O	Scotland, UK	0.367	0.951	3,180	970	Tobermory: 0.8 (1981)
54.25N, 13.24E	Rugen	Baltic Sea	East Germany	0.358	0.926	400	120	Sassnitz: 14 (1985e)
38.22N, 26.00E	Chios (off Khios)	Aegean Sea	Greece	0.325	0.842	4,260	1300	Chios (off Khios): 24, 30s (1981)
38.15N, 20.35E	Cephalonia (off Kefallinia)	Ionian Sea	Greece	0.302	0.781	5,340	1630	Argostolion: 7 (1981)
37.47N, 25.30W	Sao Miguel	Atlantic O	(Azores), Portugal	0.288	0.747	3,630	1100	Ponta Delgada: 21 (1981)
60.15N, 20.00E	Ahvenanmaa (alt Aaland, Aland)	G of Bothnia	Finland	0.285	0.738	420	130	Maarianhamina (alt Mariehamn): 10 (1984e)
53.17N, 4.22W	Anglesey (alt Ynys Mon)	Irish Sea	Wales, UK	0.266	0.689	499	152	Llangefni: 4 (1981)

[1]Usually regarded as part of the Danish mainland [i.e., Jutland (off Jylland) Peninsula], but actually an island since 1825, when Lim Fjord of the Kattegat reached the North Sea, cutting the peninsula in two.

For an explanation of symbols and abbreviations, see pages 16–17.

(Continued)

TABLE 7a. (Continued)

Latitude and Longitude	Island	Principal Body of Water	Location	Area		Highest Elev		Largest City and Its Latest Population (thousands), with Date
				1,000 mi²	1,000 km²	ft	m	
40.00N, 4.00E	Minorca (off Menorca)	Mediterranean Sea	Baleares, Spain	0.266	0.689	1,170	360	Mahon: 23 (1981)
55.48N, 6.12W	•Islay	Atlantic O	Scotland, UK	0.235	0.609	1,540	470	Bowmore: 1 (1981)
39.40N, 19.42E	Corfu (off Kerkira)	Ionian Sea	Greece	0.229	0.592	2,970	910	Corfu (off Kerkira): 34 (1981)
55.10N, 15.00E	Bornholm	Baltic Sea	Denmark	0.227	0.588	530	160	Ronne: 14 (1984e)
54.14N, 4.33W	(Isle of Man)	Irish Sea	Isle of Man	0.227	0.588	2,040	620	Douglas: 20 (1986)
39.00N, 1.25E	Ibiza (alt Iviza)	Mediterranean Sea	Baleares, Spain	0.219	0.568	1,560	470	Ibiza (alt Iviza): 25 (1981)
59.00N, 3.15W	Pomona [alt Mainland (Orkney Islands)]	Atlantic O	Scotland, UK	0.207	0.536	880	270	Kirkwall: 6 (1981)
54.48N, 11.58E	Falster	Baltic Sea	Denmark	0.198	0.514	140	44	Nykobing Falster: 19 (1984e)
39.54N, 25.21E	Lemnos (off Limnos)	Aegean Sea	Greece	0.184	0.476	1,410	430	Mirina: 4 (1981)
37.48N, 26.44E	Samos	Aegean Sea	Greece	0.184	0.476	4,700	1430	Samos (for Limin Vatheos): 6 (1981)
54.00N, 14.00E	Usedom (alt Uznam)	Baltic Sea	East Germany-Poland	0.172	0.445	200	60	Swinoujscie (for Swinemunde): 44 (1984e)
38.28N, 28.20W	Pico	Atlantic O	(Azores), Portugal	0.167	0.433	7,710	2350	Lajes do Pico: 0.8 (1981)
37.02N, 25.35E	Naxos	Aegean Sea	Greece	0.165	0.428	3,300	1010	Naxos: 4 (1981)
55.36N, 5.15W	•Arran	Firth of Clyde	Scotland, UK	0.165	0.427	2,860	870	Corrie and Brodick: 0.9 (1981)
45.05N, 14.35E	Krk (for Veglia)	Adriatic Sea	Croatia, Yugoslavia	0.158	0.408	1,870	570	Krk (for Veglia): 2 (1971)
44.40N, 14.25E	Cres (for Cherso)	Adriatic Sea	Croatia, Yugoslavia	0.156	0.404	2,130	650	Cres (for Cherso): 2 (1971)
37.52N, 20.44E	Zante (alt Zacynthus; off Zakinthos)	Ionian Sea	Greece	0.155	0.402	2,480	760	Zante (off Zakinthos): 10 (1981)

Coordinates	Island	Sea	Country					Chief town
38.43N, 27.13W	Terceira	Atlantic O	(Azores), Portugal	0.153	0.397	3,350	1020	Angra do Heroismo (alt Angra): 12 (1981)
43.19N, 16.40E	Brac (for Brazza)	Adriatic Sea	Croatia, Yugoslavia	0.153	0.395	2,550	780	Pucisce: 2 (1971)
50.40N, 1.17W	•(Isle of) Wight	English Channel	England, UK	0.147	0.381	790	240	Ryde: 24 (1981)
37.50N, 24.50E	Andros	Aegean Sea	Greece	0.147	0.380	3,310	1010	Andros: 2 (1981)
71.00N, 8.20W	Jan Mayen	Greenland Sea	Norway	0.147	0.380	7,470	2280	uninhabited
40.40N, 24.40E	Thasos	Aegean Sea	Greece	0.146	0.379	3,950	1200	Thasos (for Limin): 2 (1981)
62.08N, 7.00W	Streymoy (off Stromo)	Atlantic O	Faeroe Islands	0.144	0.373	2,590	790	Torshavn: 13 (1984e)
56.00N, 5.54W	•Jura	Sound of Jura	Scotland, UK	0.140	0.363	2,570	780	Craighouse: ? [island population 0.2 (1981)]
56.50N, 8.45E	•Mors	Lim Fjord of Kattegat	Denmark	0.140	0.363	290	89	Nykobing Mors: 9 (1984e)
38.43N, 20.38E	Leucas (for Santa Maura; off Levkas)	Ionian Sea	Greece	0.117	0.302	3,800	1160	Leucas (for Santa Maura; off Levkas): 6 (1981)
35.40N, 27.10E	Karpathos (for Scarpanto)	Mediterranean Sea	Greece	0.116	0.301	4,000	1220	Karpathos (for Pigadhia): 1 (1971)
43.07N, 16.45E	Hvar (for Lesina)	Adriatic Sea	Croatia, Yugoslavia	0.116	0.300	2,050	630	Hvar (for Lesina): 3 (1971)
36.50N, 27.10E	Kos (alt Cos; for Coo)	Aegean Sea	Greece	0.112	0.290	2,780	850	Kos (for Coo): 12 (1981)
44.30N, 15.00E	Pag (for Pago)	Adriatic Sea	Croatia, Yugoslavia	0.110	0.285	1,140	350	Pag (for Pago): 2 (1971)
55.00N, 10.50E	•Langeland	Baltic Sea	Denmark	0.110	0.284	85	26	Rudkobing: 5 (1984e)
40.10N, 25.50E	Gokceada (for Imbros, Imroz)	Aegean Sea	Turkey	0.108	0.280	1,960	600	Gokce (for Imbros, Imroz, Panagia): 5 (1980)
36.15N, 23.00E	Cythera (for Cerigo; off Kithira)	Mediterranean Sea	Greece	0.107	0.278	1,660	510	Kithira (for Kapsali): 0.3 (1981)
42.57N, 16.55E	Korcula (for Curzola)	Adriatic Sea	Croatia, Yugoslavia	0.107	0.276	1,860	570	Blato: 6 (1971)
35.53N, 14.27E	Malta	Mediterranean Sea	Malta	0.095	0.246	830	250	Sliema: 20 (1984e)
38.38N, 28.03W	Sao Jorge	Atlantic O	(Azores), Portugal	0.092	0.238	3,500	1070	Velas: 1 (1981)

For an explanation of symbols and abbreviations, see pages 16–17.

(Continued)

TABLE 7a. (Continued)

Latitude and Longitude	Island	Principal Body of Water	Location	Area 1,000 mi²	Area 1,000 km²	Highest Elev ft	Highest Elev m	Largest City and Its Latest Population (thousands), with Date
42.46N, 10.17E	•Elba	Mediterranean Sea	Toscana, Italy	0.086	0.224	3,340	1020	Portoferraio: 11 (1981)
54.28N, 11.08E	Fehmarn	Baltic Sea	Schleswig-Holstein, West Germany	0.071	0.185	89	27	Burg: 6 (1976e)
40.27N, 25.35E	Samothrace (off Samothraki)	Aegean Sea	Greece	0.069	0.178	5,250	1600	Samothrace (off Samothraki): 1 (1971)
38.34N, 28.42W	Faial (for Fayal)	Atlantic O	(Azores), Portugal	0.065	0.168	3,420	1040	Horta: 6 (1981)
49.13N, 2.07W	Jersey	English Channel	Channel Islands	0.045	0.116	450	140	Saint Helier: 25 (1981)
36.03N, 14.15E	Gozo (off Ghawdex)	Mediterranean Sea	Malta	0.026	0.067	640	190	Victoria (for Rabat): 5 (1980e)
49.27N, 2.36W	Guernsey	English Channel	Channel Islands	0.024	0.063	350	110	Saint Peter Port: 16 (1976)
40.33N, 14.13E	Capri	Tyrrhenian Sea	Campania, Italy	0.004	0.010	1,932	589	Capri: 7 (1981)
NORTH AMERICA								
73.00N, 42.00W	•Greenland (off Gronland, Kalaallit Nunaat)	Atlantic O	Greenland	823	2131	12,140	3700	Godthab: 11 (1985e)
68.00N, 70.00W	Baffin (for Baffin Land)	Baffin B	NWT, Canada	196	507	6,750	2060	Frobisher Bay: 2 (1981)
71.00N,114.00W	Victoria	Viscount Melville Sound	NWT, Canada	83.9	217	2,150	660	Cambridge Bay: 0.8 (1981)
81.00N, 80.00W	Ellesmere	Arctic O	NWT, Canada	75.8	196	8,580	2620	Grise Fiord: 0.1 (1981)
49.00N, 56.00W	Newfoundland	Atlantic O	Newfoundland, Canada	42.0	109	2,670	810	Saint John's: 96, 161s (1986)
21.30N, 80.00W	Cuba	Caribbean Sea	Cuba	40.5	105	6,480	1970	Havana: 2015 (1985e)
19.00N, 71.00W	Hispaniola (for Hayti; off Haiti, Santo Domingo)	Atlantic O	Dominican Republic-Haiti	29.2	75.6	10,420	3170	Santo Domingo: 1313 (1981)
73.15N,121.30W	Banks	Arctic O	NWT, Canada	27.0	70.0	2,400	730	Sachs Harbour: 0.2 (1981)

For an explanation of symbols and abbreviations, see pages 16–17.

(Continued)

Figure 46. Century-old houses and modern apartment blocks at Godthab, capital of Greenland, the largest island in the world and the least densely populated country. (Credit: Ministry of Foreign Affairs of Denmark.)

TABLE 7a. (Continued)

Latitude and Longitude	Island	Principal Body of Water	Location	Area 1,000 mi²	Area 1,000 km²	Highest Elev ft	Highest Elev m	Largest City and Its Latest Population (thousands), with Date
87.00N, 75.00W	Devon	Baffin B	NWT, Canada	21.3	55.2	6,300	1920	uninhabited
80.30N, 92.00W	Axel Heiberg	Arctic O	NWT, Canada	16.7	43.2	8,400	2560	uninhabited
75.15N, 110.00W	Melville	Viscount Melville Sound	NWT, Canada	16.3	42.1	3,500	1070	uninhabited
64.20N, 84.40W	Southampton	Hudson B	NWT, Canada	15.9	41.2	1,750	530	Coral Harbour: 0.4 (1981)
72.40N, 99.00W	Prince of Wales	Viscount Melville Sound	NWT, Canada	12.9	33.3	830	250	uninhabited
49.00N, 125.00W	Vancouver	Pacific O	British Columbia, Canada	12.1	31.3	7,220	2200	Victoria: 66, 256s (1986)
73.15N, 93.30W	Somerset	Lancaster Sound	NWT, Canada	9.57	24.8	1,600	490	uninhabited
76.00N, 100.30W	Bathurst	Viscount Melville Sound	NWT, Canada	6.19	16.0	1,480	450	uninhabited
76.45N, 119.30W	Prince Patrick	Arctic O	NWT, Canada	6.12	15.8	600	180	Mould Bay (weather station)
69.00N, 97.30W	King William	Queen Maud G	NWT, Canada	5.06	13.1	450	140	Gjoa Haven: 0.5 (1981)
78.30N, 104.00W	Ellef Ringnes	Arctic O	NWT, Canada	4.36	11.3	2,000	610	Isachsen (weather station)
73.13N, 78.34W	Bylot	Baffin B	NWT, Canada	4.27	11.1	6,600	2010	uninhabited
18.15N, 77.30W	Jamaica	Caribbean Sea	Jamaica	4.23	11.0	7,400	2260	Kingston: 104, 509s (1982)
46.00N, 60.30W	Cape Breten	Atlantic O	Nova Scotia, Canada	3.98	10.3	1,750	530	Sydney: 28, 119s (1986)
67.50N, 76.00W	Prince Charles	Foxe Basin	NWT, Canada	3.68	9.52	50	15	uninhabited
57.30N, 153.30W	Kodiak	Pacific O	Alaska, USA	3.67	9.51	3,400	1040	Kodiak (for Pavlovsk Gavan): 5 (1980)
18.15N, 66.45W	Puerto Rico (for Porto Rico)	Atlantic O	Puerto Rico	3.35	8.67	4,390	1340	San Juan: 425, 1081s (1980)
69.45N, 53.20W	Disco (alt Disko)	Davis Strait	Greenland	3.31	8.58	6,300	1920	Godhavn: 1 (1985e)
49.30N, 63.00W	Anticosti	G of Saint Lawrence	Quebec, Canada	3.07	7.94	620	190	Port-Menier: 0.4 (1971)
75.15N, 94.30W	Cornwallis	Barrow Strait	NWT, Canada	2.70	7.00	1,350	410	Resolute Bay: 0.2 (1981)
55.30N, 132.45W	Prince of Wales	Pacific O	Alaska, USA	2.59	6.70	3,160	960	Craig: 0.5 (1980)
53.00N, 132.00W	Graham	Pacific O	British Columbia, Canada	2.46	6.36	3,940	1200	Masset: 2 (1981)

Coordinates	Island	Water body	Location	Area (10³ mi²)	Area (10³ km²)	Elev. (ft)	Elev. (m)	Largest town
24.26N, 77.57W	Andros[1]	Great Bahama Bank	Bahamas	2.30	5.96	100	30	Nicolls Town: 3 (1980)
46.30N, 63.00W	Prince Edward	G of Saint Lawrence	Prince Edward Island, Canada	2.18	5.66	460	140	Charlottetown: 15, 45s (1981)
62.30N, 83.00W	Coats	Hudson B	NWT, Canada	2.12	5.50			uninhabited
57.50N,135.40W	Chichagof	G of Alaska	Alaska, USA	2.08	5.40	3,500	1070	Hoonah: 0.7 (1980)
78.00N, 97.00W	Amund Ringnes	Peary Channel	NWT, Canada	2.03	5.26			uninhabited
77.45N,111.00W	Mackenzie King	Hazen Strait	NWT, Canada	1.95	5.05	1,000	300	uninhabited
10.30N, 61.15W	Trinidad	Atlantic O	Trinidad and Tobago	1.86	4.83	3,080	940	Port of Spain: 58 (1980)
73.17N,106.45W	Stefansson	Viscount Melville Sound	NWT, Canada	1.72	4.46	1,120	340	uninhabited
63.30N,170.30W	Saint Lawrence	Bering Sea	Alaska, USA	1.71	4.43	2,070	630	Gambell: 0.4 (1980)
57.45N,134.25W	Admiralty	Chatham Strait	Alaska, USA	1.65	4.27	4,640	1410	Angoon: 0.5 (1980)
60.06N,166.20W	Nunivak	Bering Sea	Alaska, USA	1.62	4.21	1,670	510	Mekoryuk: 0.2 (1980)
70.45N, 26.00W	Milne Land	Greenland Sea	Greenland	1.62	4.20	6,230	1900	
54.45N,164.00W	Unimak	Pacific O	Alaska, USA	1.61	4.16	9,370	2860	False Pass: 0.07 (1980)
57.00N,135.00W	Baranof	G of Alaska	Alaska, USA	1.60	4.14	4,530	1380	Sitka: 8 (1980)
72.30N, 24.00W	•Traill	Greenland Sea	Greenland	1.60	4.14	4,520	1380	
40.50N, 73.00W	Long	Atlantic O	New York, USA	1.40	3.63	390	120	New York (in part): 4122 (1980); 4216 (1986e)
62.00N, 79.50W	Mansel	Hudson B	NWT, Canada	1.23	3.18	300	90	uninhabited
53.00N, 81.20W	Akimiski	James B of Hudson B	NWT, Canada	1.16	3.00			uninhabited
55.35N,131.20W	Revillagigedo	Behm Canal	Alaska, USA	1.14	2.97	4,590	1400	Ketchikan: 7 (1980)
56.46N,133.25W	Kupreanof	Frederick Sound	Alaska, USA	1.09	2.82	3,980	1210	Kake: 0.6 (1980)
78.30N,110.30W	Borden	Arctic O	NWT, Canada	1.08	2.80	500	150	uninhabited
45.50N, 82.20W	Manitoulin	Huron L	Ontario, Canada	1.07	2.77	1,120	340	Little Current: 2 (1981)
53.45N,167.00W	Unalaska	Pacific O	Alaska, USA	1.06	2.76	6,680	2040	Unalaska: 1 (1980)
52.45N,131.50W	Moresby	Pacific O	British Columbia, Canada	1.01	2.61	3,440	1050	Sandspit: 0.5 (1971)
			* * *					
52.55N,128.50W	Princess Royal	Princess Royal Channel	British Columbia, Canada	0.869	2.25	5,500	1680	Butedale: 0.01 (1971)
21.40N, 82.50W	Juventud [for (Isle of) Pines, Pinos]	Caribbean Sea	Cuba	0.849	2.20	1,020	310	Nueva Gerona: 34 (1984e)

[1]Actually several (unnamed) islands.

For an explanation of symbols and abbreviations, see pages 16–17.

(Continued)

TABLE 7a. (Continued)

Latitude and Longitude	Island	Principal Body of Water	Location	Area 1,000 mi²	Area 1,000 km²	Highest Elev ft	Highest Elev m	Largest City and Its Latest Population (thousands), with Date
60.40N,164.50W	Nelson	Etolin Strait	Alaska, USA	0.843	2.18	1,500	460	Toksook Bay: 0.3 (1980)
56.30N,134.05W	Kuiu	Chatham Strait	Alaska, USA	0.750	1.94	3,000	910	uninhabited
58.15N,152.35W	Afognak	Pacific O	Alaska, USA	0.721	1.87	2,550	780	uninhabited
53.15N,168.20W	Umnak	Pacific O	Alaska, USA	0.687	1.78	7,050	2150	Nikolski: 0.05 (1980)
21.05N, 73.18W	Inagua (alt Great Inagua)	Windward Passage	Bahamas	0.596	1.54	110	33	none [island population 0.9 (1980)]
53.40N,129.50W	Pitt	Principe Channel	British Columbia, Canada	0.531	1.38	3,150	960	uninhabited
26.38N, 78.25W	Grand Bahama	Northwest Providence Channel	Bahamas	0.530	1.37	34	10	Freeport: 26 (1980)
14.40N, 61.00W	Martinique	Atlantic O	Martinique	0.425	1.10	4,580	1400	Fort-de-France: 100 (1982)
53.25N,130.12W	Banks	Hecate Strait	British Columbia, Canada	0.382	0.989	1,760	540	uninhabited
26.28N, 77.05W	Abaco (alt Great Abaco)	Atlantic O	Bahamas	0.372	0.963	100	30	Coopers Town: 4 (1980)
16.10N, 61.40W	Basse-Terre	Caribbean Sea	Guadeloupe	0.364	0.943	4,870	1480	Basse-Terre: 13 (1982)
29.20N,113.25W	Angel de la Guarda	G of California	Baja California, Mexico	0.330	0.855	4,310	1320	uninhabited
52.15N,127.40W	King	Burke Channel	British Columbia, Canada	0.312	0.808	5,500	1680	uninhabited
15.25N, 61.20W	Dominica	Atlantic O	Dominica	0.290	0.751	4,750	1450	Roseau: 8 (1981)
29.00N,112.25W	Tiburon	G of California	Sonora, Mexico	0.290	0.751	4,000	1220	none
18.51N, 73.03W	Gonave	G of Gonave of Caribbean Sea	Haiti	0.270	0.700	2,480	750	Anse-a-Galet: 0.5 (1950)
13.55N, 60.59W	Saint Lucia	Atlantic O	Saint Lucia	0.238	0.616	3,140	960	Castries: 51s (1984e)
16.20N, 61.25W	Grande-Terre	Atlantic O	Guadeloupe	0.219	0.566	910	280	Les Abymes: 56, 121s (1982)
48.00N, 88.50W	(Isle) Royale	Superior L	Michigan, USA	0.210	0.544	1,310	400	none
45.30N, 73.35W	•Montreal	Saint Lawrence R	Quebec, Canada	0.201	0.521	760	230	Montreal: 1015 (1986)
7.27N, 81.45W	•Coiba	Pacific O	Panama	0.200	0.518	1,390	420	none [island population 0.8 (1980)]

(Continued)

25.10N, 76.14W	Eleuthera	Atlantic O	Bahamas	0.200	0.518	170	51	Rock Sound: 4 (1980)
20.25N, 86.55W	Cozumel	Caribbean Sea	Quintana Roo, Mexico	0.189	0.490	low elev	54	Cozumel (off San Miguel de Cozumel): 19 (1980)
23.15N, 75.07W	Long	Atlantic O	Bahamas	0.173	0.448	180	98	none [island population 3 (1980)]
48.10N,122.33W	Whidbey	Puget Sound of Pacific O	Washington, USA	0.172	0.445	320	370	Oak Harbor: 12 (1980)
12.10N, 69.00W	Curacao	Caribbean Sea	Netherlands Antilles	0.171	0.444	1,220	340	Willemstad: 100 (1980e)
13.10N, 59.33W	Barbados	Atlantic O	Barbados	0.166	0.431	1,110	63	Bridgetown: 8, 90s (1980)
24.27N, 75.30W	Cat	Atlantic O	Bahamas	0.150	0.388	210	430	none [island population 2 (1980)]
46.13N, 83.57W	Saint Joseph	Huron L	Ontario, Canada	0.141	0.365	1,400	270	Hilton Beach: 0.2 (1981)
46.02N, 83.43W	Drummond	Huron L	Michigan, USA	0.136	0.352	880	1230	none [island population 0.7 (1980)]
13.15N, 61.12W	Saint Vincent	Atlantic 0	Saint Vincent and the Grenadines	0.133	0.344	4,050	840	Kingstown: 24 (1980)
12.06N, 61.42W	Grenada	Atlantic O	Grenada	0.120	0.311	2,760		Saint George's: 7 (1981e)
29.34N, 91.52W	Marsh	G of Mexico	Louisiana, USA	0.117	0.303	5	2	uninhabited
11.15N, 60.40W	Tobago	Atlantic O	Trinidad and Tobago	0.116	0.301	1,900	580	Scarborough (for Port Louis): 6 (1980)
12.15N, 68.27W	Bonaire	Caribbean Sea	Netherlands Antilles	0.111	0.288	780	240	Kralendijk: ? [island population 10 (1984e)]
17.09N, 61.49W	Antigua	Atlantic O	Antigua and Barbuda	0.108	0.280	1,320	400	Saint John's: 36 (1983e)
44.20N, 68.18W	Mount Desert	Atlantic O	Maine, USA	0.108	0.280	1,530	470	Bar Harbor: 3 (1980)
26.50N, 97.13W	Padre	G of Mexico	Texas, USA	0.099	0.256	40	12	South Padre Island: 0.8 (1980)
45.37N, 73.43W	Jesus	Ottawa R	Quebec, Canada	0.095	0.246	160	50	Laval: 284 (1986)
41.24N, 70.32W	Martha's Vineyard	Atlantic O	Massachusetts, USA	0.093	0.241	310	94	Vineyard Haven: 2 (1980)
28.28N, 80.40W	Merritt	Banana River Lagoon	Florida, USA	0.093	0.241			Merritt Island: 31 (1980)
17.45N, 64.45W	Saint Croix	Caribbean Sea	Virgin Islands (USA)	0.084	0.218	1,160	360	Christiansted: 3 (1980)

For an explanation of symbols and abbreviations, see pages 16–17.

TABLE 7a. (Continued)

Latitude and Longitude	Island	Principal Body of Water	Location	Area 1,000 mi2	Area 1,000 km2	Highest Elev ft	Highest Elev m	Largest City and Its Latest Population (thousands), with Date
25.02N, 77.24W	New Providence	Northeast Providence Channel	Bahamas	0.080	0.207	120	37	Nassau: 135s (1980)
19.20N, 81.15W	Grand Cayman	Caribbean Sea	Cayman Islands	0.076	0.197	50	15	George Town: 4 (1979)
33.24N,118.25W	Santa Catalina	Pacific O	California, USA	0.075	0.194	2,110	640	Avalon: 2 (1980)
12.30N, 70.00W	Aruba	Caribbean Sea	Aruba	0.075	0.193	620	190	Oranjestad: 17 (1980e)
21.47N, 71.43W	Grand Caicos (alt Middle Caicos)	Atlantic O	Turks and Caicos Islands	0.073	0.189	250	76	none [island population 0.4 (1980)]
46.55N, 71.00W	(Ile d')Orleans	Saint Lawrence R	Quebec, Canada	0.072	0.186	290	89	Beaulieu: 0.8 (1976)
17.20N, 62.45W	Saint Christopher (alt Saint Kitts)	Caribbean Sea	Saint Christopher and Nevis	0.068	0.176	3,710	1130	Basseterre: 14 (1980)
17.38N, 61.48W	Barbuda	Atlantic O	Antigua and Barbuda	0.062	0.161	140	44	Codrington: 1 (1982e)
24.02N, 74.28W	San Salvador (for Watling)	Atlantic O	Bahamas	0.059	0.153	120	37	none [island population 0.7 (1980)]
15.56N, 61.16W	Marie-Galante	Atlantic O	Guadeloupe	0.058	0.149	670	200	Grand-Bourg: 6 (1982)
40.35N, 74.09W	Staten	New York B of Atlantic O	New York, USA	0.057	0.148	410	120	New York (in part): 352 (1980); 375 (1986e)
18.08N, 65.25W	Vieques (alt Crab)	Caribbean Sea	Puerto Rico	0.051	0.132	660	200	Vieques: 7 (1980)
17.10N, 62.34W	•Nevis	Caribbean Sea	Saint Christopher and Nevis	0.050	0.129	3,230	990	Charlestown: 2 (1980)
41.16N, 70.05W	Nantucket	Atlantic O	Massachusetts, USA	0.046	0.119	100	31	Nantucket: 3 (1980)
16.44N, 62.11W	Montserrat	Caribbean Sea	Montserrat	0.039	0.102	3,000	920	Plymouth: 3 (1980)
18.13N, 63.03W	Anguilla (for Snake)	Caribbean Sea	Anguilla	0.035	0.091	210	65	The Valley: ? [island population 7 (1986e)]
18.04N, 63.04W	Saint-Martin (alt Sint-Maarten)	Caribbean Sea	Guadeloupe-Netherlands Antilles	0.033	0.086	1,390	420	Philipsburg[1]: 10 (1980e)

Coordinates	Island	Body of water	Country					Largest city
18.21N, 64.55W	Saint Thomas	Atlantic O	Virgin Islands (USA)	0.028	0.073	1,550	470	Charlotte Amalie: 12 (1980)
40.47N, 73.57W	Manhattan	Hudson R	New York, USA	0.022	0.057	270	82	New York (in part): 1428 (1980); 1478 (1986e)
18.27N, 64.36W	•Tortola	Atlantic O	Virgin Islands (UK)	0.021	0.054	1,780	540	Road Town: 2 (1980)
18.20N, 64.45W	Saint John	Caribbean Sea	Virgin Islands (USA)	0.020	0.052	1,280	390	Cruz Bay: 2 (1980)
32.18N, 64.45W	Bermuda	Atlantic O	Bermuda	0.014	0.036	260	79	Hamilton: 2, 15s (1980)
OCEANIA								
5.00S,140.00E	•New Guinea (alt Irian, Papua)	Pacific O	Indonesia-Papua New Guinea	305	790	16,500	5030	Jayapura: 150 (1980); Port Moresby: 150 (1985e)
44.00S,170.00E	South (New Zealand)	Pacific O	New Zealand	58.2	151	12,350	3760	Christchurch: 168, 299s (1986)
38.00S,175.40E	North (New Zealand)	Pacific O	New Zealand	44.2	114	9,180	2800	Auckland: 149, 821s (1986)
42.00S,147.00E	Tasmania (for Van Diemen's Land)	Indian O	Tasmania, Australia	24.9	64.4	5,310	1620	Hobart: 180s (1986e)
5.40S,151.00E	New Britain (for Neupommern)	Bismarck Sea	Papua New Guinea	14.6	37.8	8,000	2440	Rabaul: 16 (1984e)
21.30S,165.30E	New Caledonia (off Nouvelle-Caledonie)	Coral Sea	New Caledonia	6.47	16.7	5,380	1640	Noumea: 60 (1983)
7.50S,138.30E	•Yos Sudarso (for Dolak, Kolepon, Frederik Hendrik)	Arafura Sea	Irian Jaya, Indonesia	4.16	10.8	low elev		Kimaam: 8 (1971)
19.30N,155.30W	Hawaii	Pacific O	Hawaii, USA	4.04	10.5	13,800	4210	Hilo: 35 (1980)
18.00S,178.00E	Viti Levu	Pacific O	Fiji	4.01	10.4	4,340	1320	Suva: 69 (1986)
6.00S,155.00E	Bougainville	Pacific O	Papua New Guinea	3.88	10.0	10,210	3110	Kieta: 3 (1980)
3.20S,152.00E	New Ireland (for Neumecklenburg)	Pacific O	Papua New Guinea	3.34	8.65	7,500	2290	Kavieng: 5 (1980)

(Continued)

[1] Netherlands Antilles.

For an explanation of symbols and abbreviations, see pages 16–17.

TABLE 7a. (Continued)

Latitude and Longitude	Island	Principal Body of Water	Location	Area 1,000 mi2	Area 1,000 km2	Highest Elev ft	Highest Elev m	Largest City and Its Latest Population (thousands), with Date
11.40S,131.00E	Melville	Timor Sea	Northern Territory, Australia	2.40	6.22	low elev		none [island population 0.6 (1981)]
9.32S,160.12E	Guadalcanal	Solomon Sea	Solomon Islands	2.17	5.63	8,030	2450	Honiara: 23 (1984e)
16.33S,179.15E	Vanua Levu	Pacific O	Fiji	2.14	5.53	3,500	1070	Lambasa (alt Labasa): 4 (1976)
15.15S,166.50E	Espiritu Santo (alt Santo; for Marina)	Coral Sea	Vanuatu	1.93	5.00	6,160	1880	Luganville (alt Santo): 5 (1979)
9.00S,161.00E	Malaita	Pacific O	Solomon Islands	1.75	4.53	4,700	1430	Auki Station: 0.9 (1970)
35.50S,137.06E	Kangaroo	Indian O	South Australia, Australia	1.68	4.35	900	270	Kingscote: 3 (1981)
8.00S,159.00E	Santa Isabel (alt Ysabel)	Pacific O	Solomon Islands	1.55	4.01	4,000	1220	Kia: 0.6 (1970)
10.36S,161.45E	San Cristobal (alt Makira, San Cristoval)	Pacific O	Solomon Islands	1.35	3.50	4,100	1250	Kirakira: 0.4 (1970)
			***					
0.14S,130.45E	•Waigeo (for Waigeoe)	Pacific O	Irian Jaya, Indonesia	1.25	3.25	3,280	1000	Tapokreng: 8 (1971)
7.00S,157.00E	Choiseul	Pacific O	Solomon Islands	1.20	3.10	3,500	1070	Sasamungga: 0.5 (1970)
16.15S,167.30E	Malekula (alt Malakula, Mallicolo)	Coral Sea	Vanuatu	0.965	2.50	2,920	890	Norsup: 2 (1979)
1.00S,136.00E	•Biak	Pacific O	Irian Jaya, Indonesia	0.950	2.46	3,390	1030	Biak: 19 (1971)
14.00S,136.40E	Groote Eylandt	G of Carpentaria of Arafura Sea	Northern Territory, Australia	0.950	2.46	520	160	none
1.45S,136.15E	•Yapen (for Japen)	Sarera B of Pacific O	Irian Jaya, Indonesia	0.940	2.43	4,910	1500	Serui (for Seroei): 14 (1971)

For an explanation of symbols and abbreviations, see pages 16–17.

(Continued)

Figure 47. *Mount Jaya (formerly Carstensz) in Irian Jaya, Indonesia (New Guinea Island), the highest mountain on an island. (Credit: Information Division, Embassy of Indonesia, Washington.)*

TABLE 7a. (Continued)

Latitude and Longitude	Island	Principal Body of Water	Location	Area 1,000 mi2	Area 1,000 km2	Highest Elev ft	Highest Elev m	Largest City and Its Latest Population (thousands), with Date
8.15S,157.30E	New Georgia	New Georgia Sound	Solomon Islands	0.900	2.33	3,300	1010	Paradise (alt Menakasapa): 0.4 (1970)
40.00S,148.00E	Flinders	Bass Strait	Tasmania, Australia	0.802	2.08	2,700	820	Whitemark: ? [island population 1 (1981)]
11.37S,130.23E	Bathurst	Timor Sea	Northern Territory, Australia	0.786	2.04	low elev		Ngulu: ? [island population 1 (1981)]
20.48N,156.20W	Maui	Pacific O	Hawaii, USA	0.729	1.89	10,030	3060	Kahului: 13 (1980)
13.36S,172.22W	Savaii	Pacific O	Samoa	0.703	1.82	6,090	1860	Safotu: 2 (1976)
1.52S,130.10E	•Misool	Ceram Sea	Irian Jaya, Indonesia	0.676	1.75	3,250	990	Misool: 4 (1971)
47.00S,167.40E	Stewart	Pacific O	New Zealand	0.674	1.75	3,210	980	Halfmoon Bay (for Oban): ? [island population 0.6 (1981)]
2.05S,147.00E	•Manus (alt Admiralty)	Pacific O	Papua New Guinea	0.633	1.64	2,360	720	Lorengau: 4 (1980)
21.30N,158.00W	Oahu	Pacific O	Hawaii, USA	0.608	1.57	4,020	1230	Honolulu: 365, 582s (1980)
22.05N,159.32W	Kauai	Pacific O	Hawaii, USA	0.553	1.43	5,170	1580	Kapaa: 4 (1980)
9.30S,150.40E	•Fergusson	Solomon Sea	Papua New Guinea	0.518	1.34	6,000	1830	Salamo: ? [island population 13 (1971)]
20.53S,167.13E	Lifou (alt Lifu)	Coral Sea	New Caledonia	0.462	1.20	200	60	none [island population 8 (1983)]
2.30S,150.15E	•New Hanover (alt Lavongai; for Neuhan-nover)	Pacific O	Papua New Guinea	0.460	1.19	2,870	870	Taskul: ? [island population 7 (1971?)]
13.55S,171.45W	Upolu	Pacific O	Samoa	0.430	1.11	3,610	1100	Apia: 33 (1981)
9.06S,152.50E	•Woodlark (alt Murua)	Solomon Sea	Papua New Guinea	0.430	1.11	1,200	370	Kulumadau: ? [island population 2 (1971)]
39.50S,144.00E	King	Bass Strait	Tasmania, Australia	0.425	1.10	700	210	Currie: 0.9 (1976)
17.37S,149.27W	Tahiti	Pacific O	French Polynesia	0.402	1.04	7,340	2240	Papeete: 23, 79s (1983)
10.00S,151.00E	•Normanby	Solomon Sea	Papua New Guinea	0.400	1.04	3,600	1100	Esaala: ? [island population 10 (1971)]

18.48S,169.05E	•Erromango (alt Eromanga)	Pacific O	Vanuatu	0.376	0.975	2,950	900	Dillon's Bay: 0.3 (1979)
17.40S,168.25E	•Efate (alt Vate)	Pacific O	Vanuatu	0.353	0.914	2,140	650	Vila: 14 (1985e)
5.15S,154.35E	•Buka	Pacific O	Papua New Guinea	0.320	0.829	1,650	500	Gagan ?: Hanahan ? [island population 32 (1971)]
11.30S,153.30E	•Tagula (alt Sudest)	Coral Sea	Papua New Guinea	0.310	0.803	3,000	910	none [island population 2 (1971)]
9.22S,150.16E	•Goodenough (for Morata)	Solomon Sea	Papua New Guinea	0.290	0.751	8,500	2590	Bolubolu: ? [island population 11 (1971)]
21.08N,157.00W	Molokai	Pacific O	Hawaii, USA	0.259	0.671	4,970	1510	Kaunakakai: 2 (1980)
21.30S,168.00E	Mare	Coral Sea	New Caledonia	0.248	0.642	490	150	none [island population 5 (1983)]
13.26N,144.43E	Guam	Pacific O	Guam	0.212	0.549	1,330	410	Tamuning: 9 (1980)
7.30N,134.36E	Babelthuap	Pacific O	Pacific Islands (USA)	0.153	0.396	700	210	Airai: 0.7 (1980)
1.52N,157.20W	•Kiritimati (alt Christmas)	Pacific O	Kiribati	0.150	0.388	25	8	none [island population 1.3 (1978)]
20.50N,156.55W	Lanai	Pacific O	Hawaii, USA	0.141	0.365	3,370	1030	Lanai City: 2 (1980)
6.55N,158.15E	Ponape	Pacific O	Pacific Islands (USA)	0.129	0.334	2,580	790	Kolonia (alt Ponape): 6 (1980)
19.02S,169.52W	Niue (for Savage)	Pacific 0	Niue	0.100	0.259	230	69	Alofi: 1 (1981)
21.10S,175.10W	Tongatapu	Pacific O	Tonga	0.099	0.257	270	82	Nukualofa: 28 (1984)
16.50S,151.25W	Raiatea	Pacific O	French Polynesia	0.092	0.238	3,390	1030	Uturoa: 3 (1977)
21.55N,160.10W	Niihau	Pacific O	Hawaii, USA	0.072	0.186	1,280	390	none [island population 0.2 (1980)]
9.45S,139.00W	Hiva-Oa	Pacific O	French Polynesia	0.058	0.150	4,130	1260	Atuona: ? [island population 1 (1977)]
14.18S,170.42W	Tutuila	Pacific O	American Samoa	0.052	0.135	2,140	650	Pago Pago: 3 (1980)
17.32S,149.50W	Moorea (for Eimeo)	Pacific O	French Polynesia	0.051	0.132	3,960	1210	Afareaitu: ? [island population 6 (1977)]
8.54S,140.06W	Nuku-Hiva	Pacific O	French Polynesia	0.046	0.120	3,860	1180	Taiohae: ? [island population 1 (1977)]
15.12N,145.45E	Saipan	Pacific O	Pacific Islands (USA)	0.046	0.119	1,550	470	Saipan: 15 (1980)

(Continued)

For an explanation of symbols and abbreviations, see pages 16–17.

TABLE 7a. (Continued)

Latitude and Longitude	Island	Principal Body of Water	Location	Area		Highest Elev		Largest City and Its Latest Population (thousands), with Date
				1,000 mi²	1,000 km²	ft	m	
SOUTH AMERICA								
54.00S, 69.00W	•Grande de Tierra del Fuego	Atlantic O	Argentina-Chile	18.7	48.4	8,090	2470	Ushuaia: 11 (1980)
1.00S, 49.30W	•Marajo	Atlantic O	Para, Brazil	18.5	48.0	66	20	Soure: 11, 16s (1980)
11.30S, 50.15W	•Bananal	Araguaia R	Goias, Brazil	7.72	20.0	590	180	Wari-Wari: ?
42.30S, 73.55W	•Chiloe	Pacific O	Chile	3.24	8.39	2,650	810	Ancud: 17 (1982)
49.20S, 74.40W	•Wellington	Trinidad G of Pacific O	Chile	2.61	6.75	3,540	1080	none
51.55S, 58.45W	•East Falkland (alt Malvina del Este)	Atlantic O	Falkland Islands	2.44	6.31	2,310	700	Stanley (alt Port Stanley): 1 (1980)
53.45S, 72.45W	•Santa Ines	Pacific O	Chile	2.12	5.50	4,390	1340	uninhabited
0.10N, 50.10W	•Caviana	Atlantic O	Para, Brazil	1.92	4.97	low elev		none
1.00S, 51.30W	•Grande de Gurupa	Amazon R	Para, Brazil	1.88	4.86	66	20	none
51.50S, 60.00W	•West Falkland (alt Malvina del Oeste)	Atlantic O	Falkland Islands	1.68	4.35	2,300	700	none [island population 0.5 (1962)]
55.15S, 69.00W	•Hoste	Pacific O	Chile	1.59	4.11	4,300	1310	none [island population 0.01 (1982)]
0.30S, 91.06W	•Isabela (alt Albemarle)	Pacific O	Ecuador[1]	1.45	3.76	5,600	1710	Villamil: 0.4 (1982)
54.15S, 36.45W	•South Georgia	Atlantic O	Falkland Islands	1.45	3.76	9,620	2930	Grytviken Harbour: 0.02 (1973e)

Coordinates	Island	Body of water	Country					Population
53.00S, 72.30W	•Riesco	Strait of Magellan	Chile	1.20	3.11	5,460	1660	none [island population 0.2 (1982)]
		* * *						
44.40S, 73.10W	•Magdalena	Moraleda Channel	Chile	0.998	2.58	5,450	1660	uninhabited
55.05S, 67.40W	•Navarino	Nassau B of Atlantic O	Chile	0.955	2.47	3,900	1190	Puerto Williams: 1 (1982)
54.10S, 71.50W	•Clarence	Strait of Magellan	Chile	0.863	2.24	3,000	910	none [island population 0.005 (1982)]
0.02S, 49.35W	•Mexiana	Atlantic O	Para, Brazil	0.592	1.53	low elev		none
2.36S, 44.14W	•Sao Luis (for Maranhao)	Atlantic O	Maranhao, Brazil	0.465	1.20	low elev		Sao Luis: 182 (1980), 564s (1985e)
0.38S, 90.23W	•Santa Cruz (alt Indefatigable)	Pacific O	Ecuador[1]	0.358	0.927	2,550	780	Puerto Ayora: 2 (1982)
11.00N, 64.00W	Margarita	Caribbean Sea	Venezuela	0.355	0.920	4,800	1460	Porlamar: 59 (1985e)
0.25S, 91.30W	•Fernandina (alt Narborough)	Pacific O	Ecuador[1]	0.253	0.655	4,500	1370	uninhabited
0.14S, 90.45W	•San Salvador (alt James, Santiago)	Pacific O	Ecuador[1]	0.199	0.515	2,970	910	uninhabited
0.50S, 89.26W	•San Cristobal (alt Chatham)	Pacific O	Ecuador[1]	0.185	0.480	2,490	760	Baquerizo Moreno: 2 (1982)
27.07S,109.22W	•Easter (alt Rapa Nui; off Pascua)	Pacific O	Chile	0.045	0.117	1,970	600	Hanga Roa: ? [island population 2 (1982)]

[1]Galapagos (off Colon) Islands.

For an explanation of symbols and abbreviations, see pages 16–17.

7b. Largest Islands, Irrespective of Continent

Contents

Rank.

Conventional and other names of island.

Continent in which located.

Surface area in thousands of square feet and square kilometers.

Coverage

50 largest islands.

Rounding

Areas are rounded to the nearest three significant digits.

Entries

50.

TABLE 7b. LARGEST ISLANDS, IRRESPECTIVE OF CONTINENT

			Area	
Rank	Island	Continent	1,000 mi^2	1,000 km^2
1.	•Greenland (off Gronland, Kalaallit Nunaat)	North America	823	2131
2.	•New Guinea (alt Irian, Papua)	Oceania	305	790
3.	•Borneo (alt Kalimantan)	Asia	285	737
4.	Madagascar (alt Madagaskara)	Africa	227	587
5.	Baffin (for Baffin Land)	North America	196	507
6.	•Sumatra (off Sumatera)	Asia	164	425
7.	•Honshu (alt Hondo)	Asia	88.0	228
8.	•Great Britain (alt Britain)	Europe	84.4	219
9.	Victoria	North America	83.9	217
10.	Ellesmere	North America	75.8	196
11.	•Celebes (off Sulawesi)	Asia	67.4	174
12.	South (New Zealand)	Oceania	58.2	151
13.	•Java (for Djawa; off Jawa)	Asia	50.0	129
14.	North (New Zealand)	Oceania	44.2	114
15.	Newfoundland	North America	42.0	109
16.	Cuba	North America	40.5	105
17.	Luzon	Asia	40.4	105
18.	Iceland (off Island)	Europe	39.7	103
19.	Mindanao	Asia	36.5	94.6
20.	•Ireland (alt Eire)	Europe	32.5	84.1
21.	•Hokkaido (for Ezo, Yezo)	Asia	30.1	78.0
22.	Sakhalin (for Karafuto, Saghalien)	Asia	29.5	76.4
23.	Hispaniola (for Hayti; off Haiti, Santo Domingo)	North America	29.2	75.6
24.	Banks	North America	27.0	70.0
25.	Sri Lanka (alt Ceylon; for Serendib)	Asia	25.2	65.3
26.	Tasmania (for Van Diemen's Land)	Oceania	24.9	64.4
27.	Devon	North America	21.3	55.2
28.	Novaya Zemlya (north island)	Europe	18.9	48.9

TABLE 7b. (Continued)

Rank	Island	Continent	Area 1,000 mi²	Area 1,000 km²
29.	•Grande de Tierra del Fuego	South America	18.7	48.4
30.	•Marajo	South America	18.5	48.0
31.	•Alexander (for Alexander I)	Antarctica	16.7	43.2
31.	Axel Heiberg	North America	16.7	43.2
33.	Melville	North America	16.3	42.1
34.	Southampton	North America	15.9	41.2
35.	West Spitsbergen (off Vestspitsbergen)	Europe	15.3	39.5
36.	New Britain (for Neupommern)	Oceania	14.6	37.8
37.	Taiwan (alt Formosa)	Asia	13.8	35.8
38.	•Kyushu (alt Kiushu)	Asia	13.8	35.7
39.	Hainan	Asia	13.1	34.0
40.	Prince of Wales	North America	12.9	33.3
41.	Novaya Zemlya (south island)	Europe	12.8	33.3
42.	Vancouver	North America	12.1	31.3
43.	•Timor	Asia	10.2	26.3
44.	Sicily (off Sicilia)	Europe	9.81	25.4
45.	Somerset	North America	9.57	24.8
46.	Sardinia (off Sardegna)	Europe	9.19	23.8
47.	•Bananal	South America	7.72	20.0
48.	•Halmahera (for Djailolo; off Jailolo)	Asia	6.95	18.0
49.	•Shikoku	Asia	6.86	17.8
50.	•Ceram (off Seram)	Asia	6.62	17.2

For an explanation of symbols and abbreviations, see pages 16–17.

7c. Largest Island in Each Country

Contents

Conventional name of country.

Conventional and other names of island.

Principal body of water adjacent to island.

Surface area in thousands of square miles and square kilometers.

Coverage

All countries with an area of at least 300 mi² (777 km²) that have or share an island
of significant size.

Rounding

Areas are rounded to the nearest three significant digits.

Entries

104.

TABLE 7c. LARGEST ISLAND IN EACH COUNTRY

Rank	Island	Continent	Area 1,000 mi2	Area 1,000 km2
Argentina	•Grande de Tierra del Fuego	Atlantic O	18.7	48.4
Australia	Tasmania (for Van Diemen's Land)	Indian O	24.9	64.4
Bahamas	Inagua (alt Great Inagua)	Windward Passage	0.596	1.54
Bangladesh	•Dakhin Shahbazpur (for Dakshin Shabazpur)	B of Bengal	0.612	1.59
Belize	•Ambergris (Cay)	Caribbean Sea	0.060	0.155
Brazil	•Marajo	Atlantic O	18.5	48.0
Brunei	•Borneo (alt Kalimantan)	South China Sea	285	737
Burma	•Ramree (off Yanbye)	B of Bengal	0.888	2.30
Canada	Baffin (for Baffin Land)	Baffin B	196	507
Cape Verde	Sao Tiago (alt Santiago)	Atlantic O	0.384	0.994
Chile	•Grande de Tierra del Fuego	Atlantic O	18.7	48.4
China	Hainan	South China Sea	13.1	34.0
Comoros	Njazidja (for Grande Comore)	Mozambique Channel	0.443	1.15
Costa Rica	Chira	G of Nicoya of Pacific O	0.020	0.052
Cuba	Cuba	Caribbean Sea	40.5	105
Cyprus	Cyprus (off Kibris, Kypros)	Mediterranean Sea	3.57	9.25
Denmark	Zealand (off Sjaelland)	Baltic Sea	2.71	7.02
Dominican Republic	Hispaniola (for Hayti; off in Dominican Republic Santo Domingo)	Atlantic O	29.2	75.6
Ecuador	•Isabela (alt Albemarle)	Pacific O	1.45	3.76
Egypt	•Tiran	Red Sea	0.030	0.070
Equatorial Guinea	Bioko (for Fernando Po)	Bight of Bonny of G of Guinea	0.779	2.02
Ethiopia	•Dahlac (alt Dahlak, Grand Dahlac; off Dehalak)	Red Sea	0.347	0.900
Faeroe Islands	Streymoy (off Stromo)	Atlantic O	0.144	0.373
Falkland Islands	•East Falkland (alt Malvina del Este)	Atlantic O	2.44	6.31
Fiji	Viti Levu	Pacific O	4.01	10.4
Finland	Ahvenanmaa (alt Aaland, Aland)	G of Bothnia	0.285	0.738
France	Corsica (off Corse)	Mediterranean Sea	3.37	8.72
French Guiana	•Cayenne	Atlantic O	0.060	0.155

For an explanation of symbols and abbreviations, see pages 16–17.

(Continued)

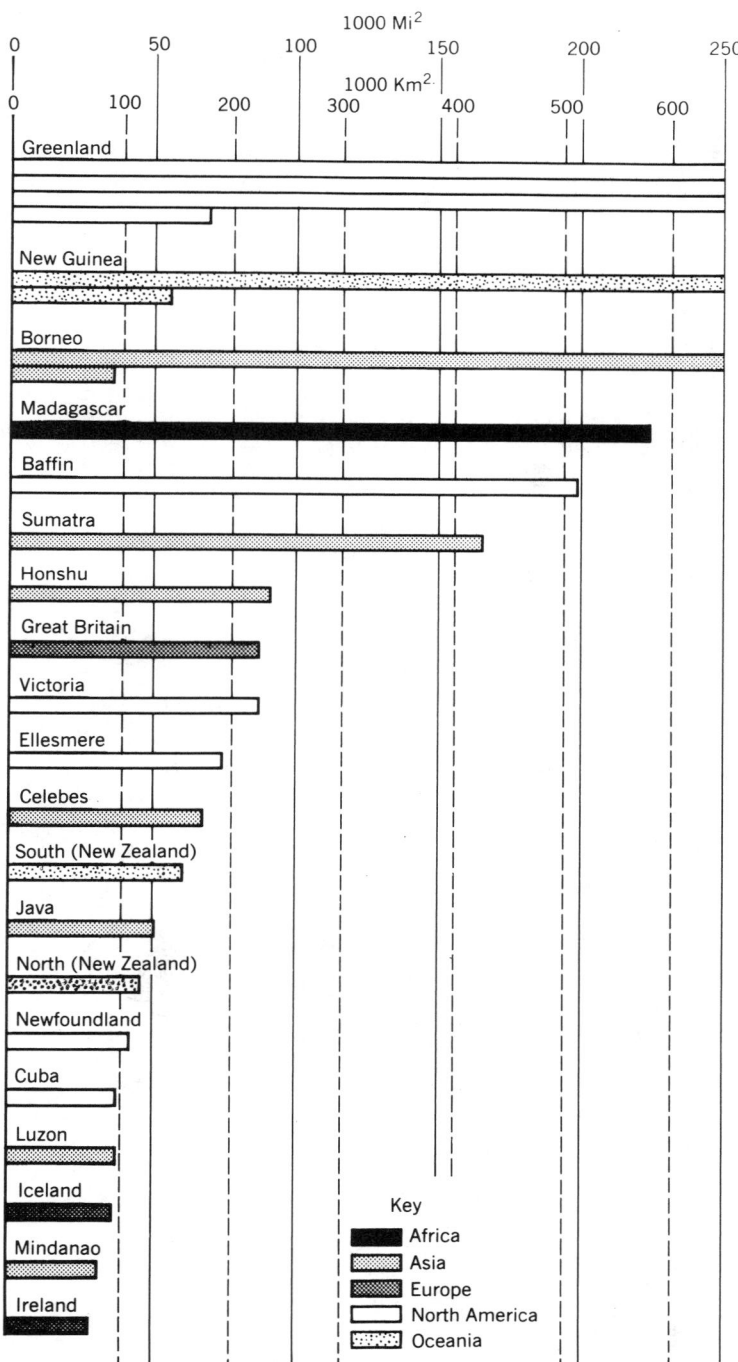

Figure 48. *Twenty largest islands.*

TABLE 7c. (Continued)

Rank	Island	Continent	Area 1,000 mi2	Area 1,000 km2
French Polynesia	Tahiti	Pacific O	0.402	1.04
French Southern and Antarctic Lands	•Kerguelen	Indian O	2.32	6.00
Germany				
East	Rugen	Baltic Sea	0.358	0.926
West	Fehmarn	Baltic Sea	0.071	0.185
Greece	Crete (for Candia; off Kriti)	Mediterranean Sea	3.19	8.26
Greenland	•Greenland (off Gronland, Kalaallit Nunaat)	Atlantic O	823	2131
Guadeloupe	Basse-Terre	Caribbean Sea	0.364	0.943
Guinea-Bissau	•Orango	Atlantic O	0.120	0.300
Haiti	Hispaniola (for Hayti; off in Haiti Haiti)	Atlantic O	29.2	75.6
Honduras	•Roatan	Caribbean Sea	0.077	0.200
Hong Kong	Lantau	South China Sea	0.055	0.142
Iceland	Iceland (off Island)	Atlantic O	39.7	103
India	Middle Andaman	Bay of Bengal	0.593	1.54
Indonesia				
in Asia	•Borneo (alt Kalimantan)	South China Sea	285	737
in Oceania (Irian Jaya)	•New Guinea (alt Irian, Papua)	Pacific O	305	790
Iran	•Qeshm (alt Qishm; for Kishm, Tawila)	Strait of Hormuz	0.515	1.33
Ireland	•Ireland (alt Eire)	Atlantic O	32.5	84.1
Italy	Sicily (off Sicilia)	Mediterranean Sea	9.81	25.4
Jamaica	Jamaica	Caribbean Sea	4.23	11.0
Japan	•Honshu (alt Hondo)	Pacific O	88.0	228
Kiribati	•Kiritimati (alt Christmas)	Pacific O	0.150	0.388
Korea				
North	•Sinmi (for Shimmi; off Shimmi)	Korea B of Yellow Sea	0.020	0.053
South	•Cheju (for Quelpart, Saishu)	East China Sea	0.710	1.84
Kuwait	Bubiyan (alt Bobian)	Persian G	0.333	0.863
Madagascar	Madagascar (alt Madagaskara)	Indian O	227	587
Malaysia	•Borneo (alt Kalimantan)	South China Sea	285	737

Martinique	Martinique	Atlantic O	0.425	1.10
Mauritius	Mauritius [for (Ile de) France]	Indian O	0.720	1.86
Mexico	Angel de la Guarda	G of California	0.330	0.855
Netherlands	•Schouwen-Duiveland	North Sea	0.086	0.222
Netherlands Antilles	Curacao	Caribbean Sea	0.171	0.444
New Caledonia	New Caledonia (off Nouvelle-Caledonie)	Coral Sea	6.47	16.7
New Zealand	South (New Zealand)	Pacific O	58.2	151
Nicaragua	•Ometepe	Nicaragua L	0.106	0.275
Norway	Hinn(oya)	Norwegian Sea	0.849	2.20
Oman	•Masirah	Arabian Sea	0.250	0.650
Pacific Islands (USA)	Babelthuap	Pacific O	0.153	0.396
Panama	•Coiba	Pacific O	0.200	0.518
Papua New Guinea	•New Guinea (alt Irian, Papua)	Pacific O	305	790
Philippines	Luzon	Pacific O	40.4	105
Portugal in Africa (Madeira Islands)	Madeira	Atlantic O	0.286	0.741
in Europe	Sao Miguel	Atlantic O	0.288	0.747
Puerto Rico	Puerto Rico (for Porto Rico)	Atlantic O	3.35	8.67
Reunion	Reunion (for Bourbon)	Indian O	0.969	2.51
Samoa	Savaii	Pacific O	0.703	1.82
Sao Tome and Principe	Sao Tome (for Sao Thome)	G of Guinea	0.330	0.854
Saudi Arabia	•Farasan al Kabir	Red Sea	0.120	0.300
Seychelles	Mahe	Indian O	0.055	0.142
Sierra Leone	•Sherbro	Atlantic O	0.260	0.670
Singapore	Singapore (alt Singapura)	South China Sea	0.210	0.543
Solomon Islands	Guadalcanal	Solomon Sea	2.17	5.63
South Africa	•Marion	Indian O	0.140	0.350
Spain in Africa (Canary Islands)	Tenerife (for Teneriffe)	Atlantic O	0.745	1.93
in Europe	Majorca (off Mallorca)	Mediterranean Sea	1.40	3.63
Sri Lanka	Sri Lanka (alt Ceylon; for Serendib)	Indian O	25.2	65.3
Svalbard	West Spitsbergen (off Vestspitsbergen)	Arctic O	15.3	39.5
Sweden	Gotland (for Gottland)	Baltic Sea	1.16	3.00

(Continued)

For an explanation of symbols and abbreviations, see pages 16–17.

TABLE 7c. (Continued)

Rank	Island	Continent	Area 1,000 mi²	Area 1,000 km²
Taiwan	Taiwan (alt Formosa)	Pacific O	13.8	35.8
Tanzania	Zanzibar (alt Unguja)	Indian O	0.640	1.66
Thailand	•Phuket (for Salang)	Andaman Sea	0.206	0.534
Tonga	Tongatapu	Pacific O	0.099	0.257
Trinidad and Tobago	Trinidad	Atlantic O	1.86	4.83
Tunisia	Djerba (off Jarbah)	G of Gabes of Mediterranean Sea	0.197	0.510
Turkey				
in Asia	Marmara	Sea of Marmara	0.045	0.117
in Europe	Gokceada (for Imbros, Imroz)	Aegean Sea	0.108	0.280
UK	•Great Britain (alt Britain)	North Sea	84.4	219
USA				
in North America	Kodiak	Pacific O	3.67	9.51
in Oceania (Hawaii)	Hawaii	Pacific O	4.04	10.5
USSR				
in Asia	Sakhalin (for Karafuto, Saghalien)	Sea of Okhotsk	29.5	76.4
in Europe	Novaya Zemlya (north island)	Kara Sea	18.9	48.9
Vanuatu	Espiritu Santo (alt Santo; for Marina)	Coral Sea	1.93	5.00
Venezuela	Margarita	Caribbean Sea	0.355	0.920
Vietnam	•Phu Quoc	G of Thailand	0.230	0.596
Yemen				
North	•Zuqar	Red Sea	0.070	0.180
South	•Socotra (alt Sokotra; off Suqutra)	Indian O	1.40	3.63
Yugoslavia	Krk (for Veglia)	Adriatic Sea	0.158	0.408

For an explanation of symbols and abbreviations, see pages 16–17.

8

GEOGRAPHIC TABLES AND COMPARISONS: RIVERS

8a. Longest Rivers, by Continent

Contents

Latitude and longitude, in degrees and minutes, at mouth of river. Conventional and other (alternate, former, and official) names of river and of its tributaries (if any) constituting the longest watercourse.

Outflow (sea, lake, river, etc) and division and country in which located.

Total length of watercourse, in miles and kilometers.

Area of drainage basin of river and all its tributaries, in thousands of square miles and square kilometers.

Average discharge rate, in thousands of cubic feet per second and in cubic meters per second. The discharge rate given is that of the main stream, preferably averaged over several recent years and measured at the gauging station registering the greatest discharge (or nearest the mouth of the river).

Coverage

Above * * *, all rivers with continuous watercourses of at least 500 miles (805 kilometers) in Africa, Asia, and South America, and 300 miles (483 kilometers) in Europe, North America, and Oceania.

Below * * *, other well-known rivers, including the longest in certain countries and border rivers of strategic importance. Also included are all nontributary rivers in the USA at least 250 miles (402 kilometers) long.

Rounding

Lengths are rounded to the nearest 10 mi (km); drainage basin areas to the nearest 1,000 mi² (km²); and average discharge rates to the nearest 1,000 cfs (100 when less than 10,000) and to the nearest 10 m³/sec (one when less than 1,000).

Entries

711, as follows: Africa—73
                    Asia—184
                    Europe—129
                    North America—219
                    Oceania—25
                    South America—81

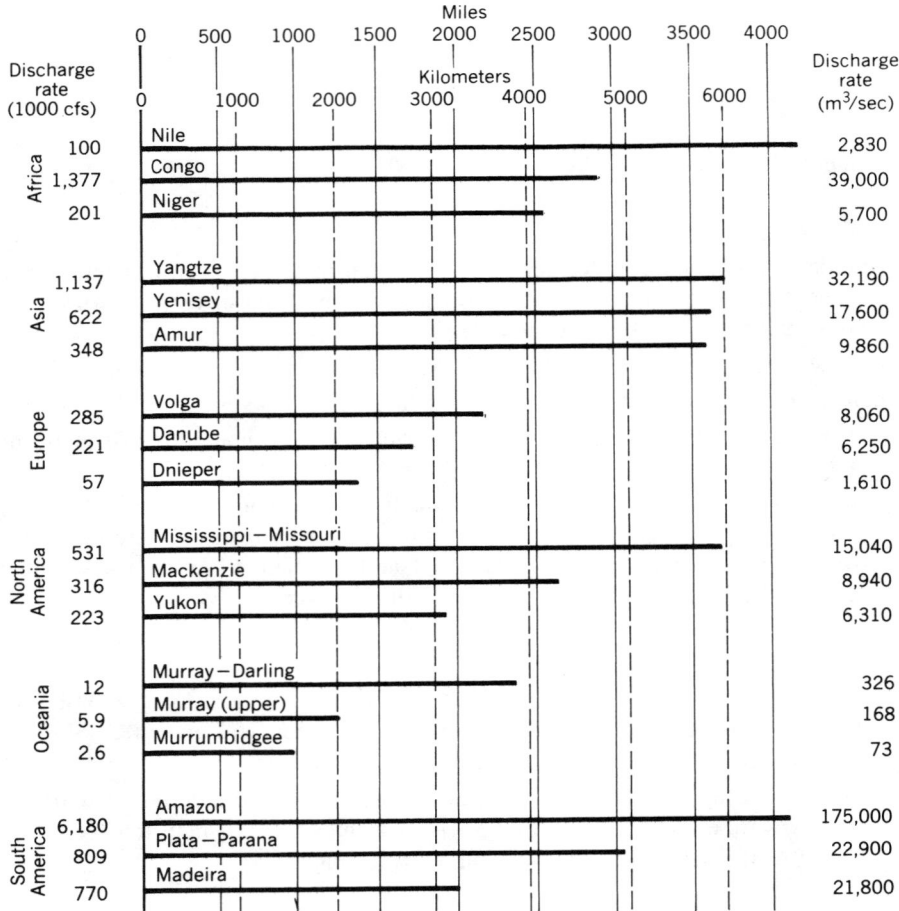

Figure 49. *Three longest rivers of each continent, showing average discharge rate of each river.*

TABLE 8a. LONGEST RIVERS, BY CONTINENT

Latitude and Longitude	River	Outflow and Location	Length		Drainage Basin		Discharge Rate	
			mi	km	1,000 mi²	1,000 km²	1,000 cfs	m³/sec
AFRICA								
31.32N, 31.51E[1]	•Nile (off Nil)-Kagera-Ruvuvu-Luvironza	Mediterranean Sea, Egypt	4140	6670	1293	3349	100	2,830
6.04S, 12.24E	Congo (alt Zaire; for Kongo)-Lualaba	Atlantic O, Angola-Zaire	2880	4630	1476	3822	1377	39,000
4.20N, 6.00E	•Niger	G of Guinea, Nigeria	2550	4100	808	2092	201	5,700
18.50S, 36.17E	•Zambezi (alt Zambesi, Zambeze)	Mozambique Channel, Mozambique	1650	2650	514	1331	250	7,070
0.30S, 17.42E	•Ubangi (alt Oubangui)-Uele-Kibali	Congo R; Congo-Zaire	1530	2460	298	773	265	7,500
28.38S, 16.27E	Orange (alt Oranje)	Atlantic O, Namibia-South Africa	1400	2250	330	855	7.6	215
3.02S, 16.57E	•Kasai (alt Cassai)	Congo R, Zaire	1200	1930	349	904	351	9,950
0.12N, 42.45E	•Shebele (alt Shabale, Shabeelle, Shibeli; for Scebeli)	Balli Swamp, Somalia	1200	1930	77	200	11	320
15.48N, 16.32W	Senegal-Bafing	Atlantic O, Mauritania-Senegal	1050	1700	170	440	29	815
18.53S, 22.24E	•Okovanggo (alt Cubango, Okavango)	Okovanggo Basin, Botswana	1000	1610	303	785	9.0	255
5.47N, 0.43E	•Volta-Black Volta (alt Volta Noire)	G of Guinea, Ghana	990	1600	154	398	42	1,180
25.12S, 33.32E	•Limpopo (alt Crocodile)	Indian O, Mozambique	990	1590	159	412	6.0	169
0.15S, 42.38E	•Juba (alt Ganana Jubba; for Giuba)-Ganale-Dorya (alt Genale)	Indian O, Somalia	970	1560	76	196	7.1	200
6.46S, 26.58E	•Luvua-Luapula-Chambezi	Lualaba R, Zaire	930	1500	97	250		
15.38N, 32.31E	•Blue Nile (off Abay, Azraq)	Nile R, Sudan	900	1450	128	331	57	1,620
0.46N, 24.16E	•Lomami	Congo R, Zaire	900	1450	42	110		
12.58N, 14.31E	•Shari (alt Chari)-Sara (alt Ouham)	Chad L, Cameroon-Chad	900	1450	270	700	43	1,230
8.00S, 39.20E	•Rufiji-Luwegu	Indian O, Tanganyika, Tanzania	870	1400	69	178	34	973

[1]For Damietta (off Dumyat) R distributary; for Nile R proper: 30.10N, 31.06E.
For an explanation of symbols and abbreviations, see pages 16–17.

(Continued)

Figure 50. Egyptian *felluka* (sailboat) on the Nile River, which, from the source of its headwaters in Burundi to its outlet into the Mediterranean Sea, forms the longest watercourse on earth. (Credit: Press and Information Bureau, Embassy of the Arab Republic of Egypt, Washington.)

TABLE 8a. (Continued)

Latitude and Longitude	River	Outflow and Location	Length		Drainage Basin		Discharge Rate	
			mi	km	1,000 mi2	1,000 km2	1,000 cfs	m³/sec
1.13S, 16.49E	•Sangha-Kadei	Congo R, Congo	870	1400	70	181	64	1,800
7.50N, 6.50E	•Benue (alt Benoue)	Niger R, Nigeria	810	1300	130	337	112	3,170
1.13N, 23.36E	•Aruwimi-Ituri	Congo R, Zaire	800	1290	45	116		
0.05N, 18.17E	•Ruki-Busira-Tshuapa	Congo R, Zaire	800	1290	67	174		
0.49S, 9.00E	•Ogooue (alt Ogowe)	G of Guinea, Gabon	750	1210	83	216	165	4,670
4.17S, 20.25E	•Sankuru-Lubilash	Kasai R, Zaire	750	1210	60	156	88	2,500
29.04S, 23.38E	•Vaal	Orange R, Cape of Good Hope, South Africa	750	1210	60	155	1.3	36
11.35N, 41.38E	Awash (alt Hawash)	Abbe L, Ethiopia	750	1200	21	55	5.7	160
13.27N, 16.37E	Gambia (alt Gambie)	Atlantic O, Gambia	700	1130	70	182		
3.14S, 17.22E	•Kwango (alt Cuango)	Kasai R, Zaire	700	1130	102	263	95	2,700
17.40N, 33.58E	•Atbarah (alt Atbara)-Takaze (off Satit, Tekeze)	Nile R, Sudan	700	1120	27	69	14	389
14.30N, 4.12W	Bani-Bagoe	Niger R, Mali	690	1110	50	130	28	796
3.01S, 16.58E	•Fimi-Lukenie	Kasai R, Zaire	660	1070	51	132		
3.22S, 17.22E	•Kwilu (alt Cuilo)	Kwango R, Zaire	650	1050	35	90	2.5	71
13.49N, 10.50W	•Bakoye-Baoule	Senegal R, Mali	620	1000	37	95		
17.47S, 25.10E	•Chobe (alt Linyanti)-Kwando (alt Cuando)	Zambezi R, Botswana-Namibia	620	1000	22	56		
15.56S, 28.55E	•Kafue	Zambezi R, Zambia	600	970	58	150		
28.31S, 20.13E	•Molopo	Orange R, Cape of Good Hope, South Africa	600	970				
9.19S, 13.08E	Cuanza	Atlantic O, Angola	600	960	60	156	29	835
12.06N, 15.02E	•Logone-Mbere	Shari R, Chad	600	960	29	76	14	403
17.20S, 11.50E	Cunene (alt Kunene)	Atlantic O, Angola-Namibia	590	940	32	83	7.6	215
3.35N, 9.38E	•Sanaga-Lom	Bight of Bonny of G of Guinea, Cameroon	570	920	52	135	77	2,190
5.02S, 21.07E	•Lulua	Kasai R, Zaire	550	890	25	65	8.5	240
9.10N, 1.15W	•White Volta (alt Volta Blanche)	Volta R, Ghana	550	890	40	105		

For an explanation of symbols and abbreviations, see pages 16–17.

(Continued)

TABLE 8a. (Continued)

Latitude and Longitude	River	Outflow and Location	Length mi	Length km	Drainage Basin 1,000 mi2	Drainage Basin 1,000 km2	Discharge Rate 1,000 cfs	Discharge Rate m3/sec
3.17N, 9.54E	•Nyong	Bight of Bonny of G of Guinea, Cameroon	530	860	10	26	4.4	125
0.43N, 18.23E	•Lulonga-Lopori	Congo R, Zaire	510	820	25	66	33	940
4.28S, 11.41E	•Kouilou-Niari	Atlantic O, Congo	510	810	22	56	12	327
5.10N, 5.00W	•Bandama	G of Guinea, Ivory Coast	500	800	23	60	2.6	73
25.46S, 32.43E	•Komati (alt Incomati)	Delagoa B of Indian O, Mozambique	500	800	18	46		
0.14S, 20.42E	•Lomela	Busira R, Zaire	500	800				
15.36S, 30.25E	•Luangwa (alt Aruangua)	Zambezi R, Zambia	500	800	56	145		
		* * *						
4.31N, 35.59E	Omo	Rudolf L, Ethiopia	470	760	26	67	5.3	151
9.22N, 31.33E	•Sobat-Baro	Nile R, Sudan	460	740	95	245	9.7	274
10.29S, 40.28E	Ruvuma (alt Rovuma)	Indian O, Mozambique-Tanzania	450	730	60	155	6.0	170
4.08N, 22.27E	•Bomu (alt Mbomou)	Ubangi R, Central African Republic–Zaire	450	720	97	250	0.6	17
2.32S, 40.31E	•Tana	Indian O, Kenya	440	710	16	42	2.5	71
5.12N, 3.44W	•Comoe (alt Komoe)	G of Guinea, Ivory Coast	430	700	29	74	5.6	158
6.29N, 2.32E	•Oueme	Porto-Novo Lagoon, Benin	430	700	15	40		
36.02N, 0.08E	•Sheliff (alt Cheliff; off Shalaf)	Mediterranean Sea, Algeria	430	700	14	35		
11.24N, 4.07E	Sokoto	Niger R, Nigeria	390	630	32	83		
21.00S, 35.02E	Sabi (alt Save)	Mozambique Channel, Mozambique	380	610	34	88		
13.31S, 40.32E	Lurio	Mozambique Channel, Mozambique	380	600	23	61	8.2	232
33.19N, 8.20W	•Oum er Rbia	Atlantic O, Morocco	370	600	13	34	4.6	130
4.58N, 6.05W	•Sassandra-Tienba	G of Guinea, Ivory Coast	370	600	19	50	11	325
17.42S, 35.19E	•Shire (alt Chire)	Zambezi R, Mozambique	370	600	50	130	21	589
11.45N, 15.35W	•Geba-Corubal (alt Koliba)	Atlantic O, Guinea-Bissau	350	560	3	8		

Lat, Long	River	Outflow / Location	mi	km	1000 mi²	1000 km²	1000 cfs	m³/sec
21.29S, 43.41E	•Mangoky	Mozambique Channel, Madagascar	350	560	19	50	16	459
29.14S, 31.30E	•Tugela	Indian O, Natal, South Africa	350	560	11	29	5.3	149
7.48N, 0.08E	•Oti	Volta R, Ghana	340	550	28	73	18	500
35.06N, 2.20W	•Moulouya	Mediterranean Sea, Morocco	320	520	21	54	1.6	44
4.22N, 7.32W	•Cavally (alt Cavalla)	Atlantic O, Ivory Coast-Liberia	320	510	12	30		
6.16N, 1.49E	Mono	Bight of Benin of G of Guinea, Benin-Togo	310	500	10	25	3.4	96
34.16N, 6.41W	•Sebou	Atlantic O, Morocco	280	450	15	39	7.1	200
8.30N, 13.15W	•Sierra Leone-Rokel	Atlantic O, Sierra Leone	270	440				
37.07N, 10.13E	•Medjerda (off Majardah)	G of Tunis of Mediterranean Sea, Tunisia	230	360	9	23	0.7	19
ASIA								
31.48N, 121.10E	Yangtze (off Chang)	East China Sea, Jiangsu, China	3720	5980	705	1827	1137	32,190
71.50N, 82.40E	Yenisey (alt Yemisei)-Angara[1]-Selenga (alt Selenge)-Ider	Yenisey G of Kara Sea, Russia, USSR	3650	5870	996	2580	622	17,600
52.56N, 141.10E	Amur (alt Heilong, Heilung)-Argun (alt Ergun, Oerhkuna)-Kerulen (alt Kolulun; off Herlen)	Tatar Strait, Russia, USSR	3590	5780	716	1855	348	9,860
66.45N, 69.30E	Ob-Irtish[2] (alt Irtish)	G of Ob of Kara Sea, Russia, USSR	3360	5410	1154	2990	438	12,400
37.32N, 118.19E	Huang (alt Hwang, Yellow)	G of Chihli of Yellow Sea, Shandong, China	3010	4840	297	771	54	1,530
72.25N, 126.40E	Lena	Laptev Sea, Russia, USSR	2730	4400	961	2490	586	16,600
10.15N, 105.55E	•Mekong (alt Khong, Lancang, Lantsang, Mekongk, Tien Giang)	South China Sea, Vietnam	2600	4180	313	811	501	14,200
61.04N, 68.52E	Ob (upper)-Katun	Ob R, Russia, USSR	1970	3180	295	765	174	4,920
46.03N, 61.00E	Syr (Darya)-Naryn-Bolshoy Naryn	Aral (Sea) L, Kazakhstan, USSR	1880	3020	85	219	26	730
65.48N, 88.04E	Lower Tunguska (off Nizhnyaya Tunguska)	Yenisey R, Russia, USSR	1860	2990	183	473	117	3,300
24.20N, 67.47E	Indus (alt Yintu)	Arabian Sea, Pakistan	1790	2880	450	1165	235	6,640
22.50N, 90.50E[3]	Brahmaputra (alt Tsangpo, Yarlung Zangbo, Yalutsangpu)	B of Bengal, Bangladesh	1770	2840	224	580	678	19,200

[1] Data for Angara-Selenga-Ider: 2120 mi, 3410 km; 401,000 mi², 1,039,000 km²; 179,000 cfs, 5,080 m³/sec.
[2] Data for Irtysh: 2640 mi, 4250 km; 634,000 mi², 1,643,000 km²; 76,000 cfs, 2,150 m³/sec.
[3] For Meghna R distributary; for Brahmaputra R proper: 24.02N, 90.59E.

For an explanation of symbols and abbreviations, see pages 16–17.

(Continued)

TABLE 8a. (Continued)

Latitude and Longitude	River	Outflow and Location	Length mi	Length km	Drainage Basin 1,000 mi²	Drainage Basin 1,000 km²	Discharge Rate 1,000 cfs	Discharge Rate m³/sec
16.31N, 97.37E	•Salween (alt Khong, Lu, Nu)	G of Martaban of Andaman Sea, Burma	1750	2820	125	324	353	10,000
41.05N, 86.40E	Tarim (alt Talimu)-Yarkant (alt Yeherhchiang; for Yarkand)	Tarim Basin, Xinjiang, China	1710	2750	173	447	5.2	146
64.24N, 126.26E	Vilyuy (alt Vilyui)	Lena R, Russia, USSR	1650	2650	175	454	52	1,470
43.40N, 59.01E	Amu (Darya) (alt Oxus)-Panj (alt Pyandzh)-Vakhan	Aral (Sea) L, Uzbekistan, USSR	1580	2540	119	309	71	2,000
21.55N, 88.05E[1]	•Ganges (alt Ganga)-Bhagirathi	B of Bengal, Bangladesh-India	1560	2510	368	952	411	11,650
69.30N, 161.00E	Kolyma (alt Kolima)-Kulu	East Siberian Sea, Russia, USSR	1560	2510	250	647	79	2,250
57.42N, 71.12E	Ishim	Irtysh R, Russia, USSR	1520	2450	68	177	1.9	5.3
29.57N, 48.34E	(Shatt al) Arab-Euphrates (off Firat, Furat)-Kara Su	Persian G, Iran-Iraq	1510	2430	427	1105	101	2,860
47.00N, 51.48E	Ural	Caspian (Sea) L, Kazakhstan, USSR	1510	2430	92	237	13	360
63.28N, 129.35E	Aldan	Lena R, Russia, USSR	1410	2270	281	729	177	5,010
73.00N, 119.55E	Olenek	Laptev Sea, Russia, USSR	1410	2270	85	219	31	820
57.43N, 83.51E	Chulym (alt Chulim)-Belyy Iyus	Ob R, Russia, USSR	1260	2020	52	134	27	773
15.50N, 95.06E	•Irrawaddy (off Iyawadi)-Nmai	Andaman Sea, Burma	1240	1990	158	409	447	12,660
59.26N, 112.34E	Vitim-Vitimkan	Lena R, Russia, USSR	1230	1980	87	225	54	1,520
70.48N, 148.54E	Indigirka-Khastakh	East Siberian Sea, Russia, USSR	1230	1970	139	360	55	1,570
22.45N, 113.37E	Zhu (alt Canton, Chu, Pearl, Yueh)-Xi (alt Hsi, Si, West)-Hongshui (alt Hungshui)-Nanpan	South China Sea, Guangdong, China	1220	1960	164	426	441	12,500
61.36N, 90.18E	Stony Tunguska (off Podkamennaya Tunguska	Yenisey R, Russia, USSR	1160	1860	93	240	60	1,690
47.42N, 132.30E	Sungari (alt Sunghua; off Songhua)	Amur R, Heilongjiang, China	1160	1860	202	524	87	2,450
31.00N, 47.25E	Tigris (off Dicle, Dijlah)	(Shatt al) Arab R, Iraq	1150	1850	145	373	44	1,250
72.55N, 106.00E	Khatanga-Kotuy	Khatanga G of Laptev Sea, Russia, USSR	1020	1640	141	364	117	3,320

(Continued)

Latitude	Longitude	River	Location						
58.10N	68.12E	Tobol	Irtysh R, Russia, USSR	1010	1630	164	426	28	802
58.06N	93.00E	Yenisey (upper)	Yenisey R, Russia, USSR	1010	1630	115	299	103	2,910
58.55N	81.32E	Ket	Ob R, Russia, USSR	1010	1620	36	94	16	445
70.51N	153.34E	Alazeya-Kadylchan	East Siberian Sea, Russia, USSR	990	1600	25	65	11	300
53.20N	121.26E	Shilka-Onon	Amur R, Russia, USSR	990	1590	80	206	19	532
25.30N	81.53E	•Yamuna (alt Jumna)-Chambal	Ganges R, Uttar Pradesh, India	950	1530	139	359	109	3,080
28.57N	70.30E	Panjnad-Sutlej	Indus R, Pakistan	940	1520	206	533	42	1,200
30.34N	114.17E	Han (Shui)	Yangtze R, Hubei, China	930	1500	67	174	33	935
71.31N	136.32E	Yana-Sartang	Laptev Sea, Russia, USSR	930	1490	92	238	6.0	170
62.38N	134.32E	Amga	Aldan R, Russia, USSR	910	1460	27	69		
17.00N	81.45E	Godavari	B of Bengal, Andhra Pradesh, India	910	1460	121	313	112	3,180
45.24N	74.08E	Ili-Tekes	Balkhash L, Kazakhstan, USSR	890	1440	54	140	17	470
60.22N	120.42E	Olekma	Lena R, Russia, USSR	890	1440	81	210	35	1,000
15.57N	80.59E	Krishna (alt Kistna)	B of Bengal, Andhra Pradesh, India	870	1400	100	259	70	1,990
67.32N	78.40E	Taz	G of Ob of Kara Sea, Russia, USSR	870	1400	58	150	32	905
57.47N	67.16E	Tavda-Lozva	Tobol R, Russia, USSR	840	1360	34	88	15	429
40.39N	122.12E	Liao	G of Liadong of Yellow Sea, Liaoning, China	840	1340	83	215	22	624
58.06N	94.01E	Taseyeva-Chuna (alt Uda)	Angara R, Russia, USSR	820	1320	49	128	26	736
26.37N	101.48E	Yalong (alt Yalung)	Yangtze R, Sichuan, China	820	1320	56	144	88	2,500
21.38N	72.36E	Narmada (alt Narbada)	G of Cambay of Arabian Sea, Gujarat, India	820	1310	36	93	46	1,290
45.00N	67.44E	Chu-Dzhuvanaryk	Sauma(kol) L, Kazakhstan, USSR	810	1300	24	62	2.1	61
50.15N	127.35E	Zeya	Amur R, Russia, USSR	770	1240	90	233	63	1,790
41.45N	35.59E	Kizil (Irmak)	Black Sea, Turkey	730	1180	30	77	4.7	133
63.28N	118.50E	Markha	Vilyuy R, Russia, USSR	730	1180	38	99	13	375
45.26N	124.39E	Nen(alt Nonni, Nun)	Sungari R, Heilongjiang, China	730	1170	94	244	25	700
29.23N	71.02E	Chenab-Chandra	Panjnad R, Pakistan	720	1160	53	138	72	2,050
59.34N	69.17E	Demyanka	Irtysh R, Russia, USSR	720	1160	13	35		
64.54N	176.13E	Anadyr (alt Anadir)	G of Anadyr of Bering Sea, Russia, USSR	710	1150	74	191	59	1,680
37.24N	60.38E	Hari (Rud) (alt Tedzhen)	Kara (Kum) Desert, Turkmenia, USSR	710	1150	27	71	0.9	24

[1]For Hooghly R distributary; for Ganges R proper: 23.22N, 90.32E.

For an explanation of symbols and abbreviations, see pages 16–17.

TABLE 8a. (Continued)

Latitude and Longitude	River	Outflow and Location	Length		Drainage Basin		Discharge Rate	
			mi	km	1,000 mi²	1,000 km²	1,000 cfs	m³/sec
20.17N, 106.34E	Red (alt Coi, Koi; off Hong, Yuan)	G of Tonkin of South China Sea, Vietnam	710	1150	46	120	138	3,900
29.26N, 113.08E	Xiang (alt Hsiang, Siang)	Dongting L, Hunan, China	710	1150	39	100	88	2,500
48.01N, 62.45E	Turgay (alt Turgai)-Karaturgay	Chelkar-Tengiz Marsh, Kazakhstan, USSR	710	1140	61	157		
50.21N 106.05E	Orhon (alt Orkhon)	Selenga R, Mongolia	700	1120	51	133	4.2	120
21.26N, 95.15E	•Chindwin	Irrawaddy R, Burma	690	1110	44	114	141	4,000
31.12N, 61.34E	•Helmand (alt Helmund, Hirmand)	Seistan Basin, Afghanistan-Iran	690	1110	143	370	10	286
68.42N, 158.36E	Omolon	Kolyma R, Russia, USSR	690	1110	44	113	25	700
60.40N, 69.46E	Konda	Irtysh R, Russia, USSR	680	1100	28	73	9.4	267
33.12N, 118.33E	Huai (alt Hwai)	Hongze L, Anhui, China	680	1090	81	210	38	1,090
54.59N, 73.22E	Om	Irtysh R, Russia, USSR	680	1090	20	53	2.2	61
63.46N, 121.35E	Tyung	Vilyuy R, Russia, USSR	680	1090	19	50	6.4	180
25.47N, 84.37E	Ghaghara (alt Gogra, Kauriala)	Ganges R, Bihar-Uttar Pradesh, India	670	1080	49	127	78	2,200
54.30N, 134.38E	Maya	Aldan R, Russia, USSR	670	1080	66	171	40	1,130
59.07N, 80.46E	Vasyugan	Ob R, Russia, USSR	670	1080	24	62	12	328
60.55N, 73.40E	Bolshoy Yugan	Ob R, Russia, USSR	660	1060	13	35	4.9	138
30.35N, 71.49E	•Ravi	Chenab R, Pakistan	660	1060			8.8	250
40.30N, 80.48E	•Hotan (alt Hotien, Khotan)-Karakax (alt Kalakashih, Kara-Kash)	Tarim R, Xinjiang, China	640	1030	17	44	4.2	120
57.12N, 66.56E	Tura	Tobol R, Russia, USSR	640	1030	31	80	6.1	174
67.31N, 77.55E	Pur-Pyakupur	G of Ob of Kara Sea, Russia, USSR	640	1020	43	112	31	872
57.43N, 95.24E	Biryusa (alt Ona)	Taseyeva R, Russia, USSR	630	1010	22	56	12	347
0.25S, 109.40E	Kapuas (alt Kapuas-Besar; for Kapoeas)	South China Sea, Borneo I, Indonesia	630	1010	39	102		
41.48N, 86.47E	Konqi [alt Konche (Darya), Kungchueh]-Kaidu [alt Kaitu, Karaxahar, Khaydyk(gol)]	Tarim Basin, Xinjiang, China	630	1010	71	184	1.3	36

61.36N, 96.30E	Chunya	Stony Tunguska R, Russia, USSR	620	1000	27	70	2.6	74
29.34N, 106.35E	Jialing (alt Chialing, Kialing)	Yangtze R, Sichuan, China	620	1000	62	160	88	2,500
37.23N, 50.11E	•Safid-Qezel Owzan	Caspian (Sea) L, Iran	620	1000	22	58	4.6	120
13.32N, 100.36E	Chao Phraya (alt Menam)-Nan	G of Thailand, Thailand	620	990	58	150	31	883
38.18N, 61.12E	Murgab (alt Morghab)	Kara (Kum) Desert, Turkmenia, USSR	610	980	18	47	1.8	52
50.30N, 69.59E	Nura	Tengiz L, Kazakhstan, USSR	610	980	23	61	0.6	18
38.57N, 117.43E	Hai-Bai (alt Pai)	G of Chihli of Yellow Sea, Hebei, China	600	970	80	208	8.3	234
45.12N, 66.36E	Sarysu-Dzaman Sarysu	Tele(kol) L, Kazakhstan, USSR	600	960	32	82	0.3	7
60.45N, 76.45E	Vakh	Ob R, Russia, USSR	600	960	30	77	18	516
59.25N, 80.04E	Tym	Ob R, Russia, USSR	590	950	12	32	6.4	182
73.08N, 113.36E	Anabar	Laptev Sea, Russia, USSR	580	940	39	100	16	442
29.43N, 107.24E	Wu	Yangtze R, Sichuan, China	570	920	34	88	53	1,500
56.36N, 66.24E	Iset-Miass	Tobol R, Russia, USSR	560	900	23	59	2.5	69
28.46N, 104.38E	•Min-Dadu (alt Tatu)	Yangtze R, Sichuan, China	560	900	52	134	107	3,040
48.28N, 135.02E	Ussuri (alt Wusuli)-Ulakhe	Amur R, China-USSR	560	900	75	193	34	953
66.30N, 87.12E	Kureyka (alt Kureika)	Yenisey R, Russia, USSR	550	890	17	45	22	634
39.20N, 119.10E	Luan	G of Chihli of Yellow Sea, Hebei, China	540	880	18	46	4.9	140
39.32N, 63.45E	Zeravshan	Kyzyl(kum) Desert, Uzbekistan, USSR	540	880	7	18	5.7	162
29.12N, 116.00E	Gan (alt Kan)-Gong (Shui) [alt Kung (Shui)]	Poyang L, Jiangxi, China	540	860	32	82	88	2,500
34.36N, 110.10E	Wei	Huang R, Shaanxi, China	540	860	24	63	7.7	219
28.58N, 111.49E	Yuan	Dongting L, Hunan, China	540	860	35	90	88	2,500
52.52N, 83.36E	Aley (alt Alei)	Ob R, Russia, USSR	530	860	8	21	1.2	34
20.19N, 86.45E	Mahanadi	B of Bengal, Orissa, India	530	860	51	132	75	2,120
52.56N, 139.38E	Amgun-Suluk	Amur R, Russia, USSR	530	850	21	55	17	488
60.22N, 120.50E	Chara	Olekma R, Russia, USSR	530	850	34	88	22	632
30.25N, 48.12E	•Karun	(Shatt al) Arab R, Iran	530	850	23	61	18	522
67.48N, 144.54E	Selennyakh-Khargy Sala	Indigirka R, Russia, USSR	530	840	14	37	6.4	180
51.19N, 106.59E	Khilok	Selenga R, Russia, USSR	520	840	18	46	3.7	105
65.10N, 115.52E	Morkoka	Markha R, Russia, USSR	520	840	13	32		
56.50N, 84.27E	Tom	Ob R, Russia, USSR	510	830	24	62	40	1,120
53.31N, 83.10E	Chumysh-Karachumysh	Ob R, Russia, USSR	510	820	9	24	5.2	146

(Continued)

For an explanation of symbols and abbreviations, see pages 16–17.

TABLE 8a. (Continued)

Latitude and Longitude	River	Outflow and Location	Length mi	Length km	Drainage Basin 1,000 mi2	Drainage Basin 1,000 km2	Discharge Rate 1,000 cfs	Discharge Rate m3/sec
68.44N, 103.42E	Moyyero (alt Moyero)	Kotuy R, Russia, USSR	510	820	12	31	92	2,600
73.50N, 87.10E	Pyasina	Kara Sea, Russia, USSR	510	820	70	182	9.1	257
41.07N, 30.39E	Sakarya	Black Sea, Turkey	510	820	21	55	30	860
64.10N, 65.28E	Severnaya Sosva-Bolshaya Sosva	Ob R, Russia, USSR	510	820	38	98		
48.57N, 104.48E	Tuul (alt Tola)	Orhon R, Mongolia	510	820	19	50		
59.08N, 135.06E	Yudoma-Nitkan	Maya R, Russia, USSR	510	820	17	44	12	342
48.54N, 93.23E	Dzavhan (alt Dzabkhan)	Ayrag L, Mongolia	500	810	27	71	2.1	60
58.44N, 81.35E	Parabel-Kenga	Ob R, Russia, USSR	500	810	10	25	3.2	90
56.42N, 74.36E	Tara	Irtysh R, Russia, USSR	500	810	7	18	1.4	41
58.48N, 130.35E	Uchur	Aldan R, Russia, USSR	500	810	44	113	46	1,300
39.55N, 124.20E	Yalu (alt Amnok)	Korea B of Yellow Sea, China-North Korea	500	810	24	63	37	1,040
21.15N, 105.20E	Black (alt Lihsien; off Da, Lixian)	Red R, Vietnam	500	800	16	41	3.8	109
62.54N, 111.06E	Chona	Vilyuy R, Russia, USSR	500	800	7	19		
25.32N, 83.10E	•Gomati (alt Gumti)	Ganges R, Uttar Pradesh, India	500	800	20	53		
1.16S, 104.05E	•Hari (for Djambi)	Berhala Strait, Sumatra I, Indonesia	500	800			53	1,500
11.09N, 78.52E	•Kaveri (alt Cauvery)	B of Bengal, Tamil Nadu, India	500	800	31	80	33	934
64.57N, 124.36E	Linde	Lena R, Russia, USSR	500	800	8	20		
60.32N, 116.14E	Nyuya	Lena R, Russia, USSR	500	800	15	38	4.1	115
48.36N, 52.30E	Uil	Aralsor L, Kazakhstan, USSR	500	800	12	31		
68.23N, 145.50E	Uyandina-Irgichyan	Indigirka R, Russia, USSR	500	800	16	41	4.5	128
		* * *						
71.54N, 102.06E	Kheta-Ayan	Khatanga R, Russia, USSR	490	780	39	100	48	1,370
25.42N, 84.52E	Son	Ganges R, Bihar, India	480	780	28	72		
39.46N, 78.15E	Kaxgar (alt Kashgar, Kashihkaerh, Kyzylsu)	Tarim R, Xinjiang, China	480	760	35	91	2.7	77
56.15N, 162.30E	Kamchatka	Bering Sea, Russia, USSR	470	760	22	56	35	992

Coordinates	Name	Location						
37.06N, 68.18E	Vakhsh-Kyzylsu	Amu (Darya) R, Tadzhikistan, USSR	470	760	15	39	24	666
23.20N, 110.05E	Yu	Xi R, Guangxi, China	470	750	34	87	63	1,780
28.41N, 112.43E	Zi (Shui) [alt Tze (Shui), Tzu (Shui)]	Dongting L, Hunan, China	470	750				
57.47N, 108.07E	Kirenga	Lena R, Russia, USSR	460	750	18	47	23	657
49.27N, 129.30E	Bureya-Pravaya Bureya	Amur R, Russia, USSR	460	740	27	71	32	918
25.34N, 86.42E	Kosi	Ganges R, Bihar, India	450	730	34	87	63	1,770
31.12N, 72.08E	Jhelum	Chenab R, Pakistan	450	720	21	55	31	883
0.35S, 117.17E	Mahakam (alt Kutai)	Makassar Strait, Borneo I, Indonesia	450	720	31	80		
38.52N, 38.48E	Murat	Euphrates R, Turkey	450	720	15	40		
21.06N, 72.41E	Tapti (alt Tapi)	G of Cambay of Arabian Sea, Gujarat, India	450	720	26	67	9.7	274
46.38N, 53.14E	Emba	Caspian (Sea) L, Kazakhstan, USSR	440	710	16	40	0.5	15
62.28N, 165.18E	Penzhina	Penzhina B of Sea of Okhotsk, Russia, USSR	440	710	28	73	24	680
35.36N, 110.42E	Fen	Huang R, Shanxi, China	430	690	15	39	1.8	51
27.05N, 79.58E	Ramganga	Ganges R, Uttar Pradesh, India	430	690	13	33	0.3	9
37.28N, 54.03E	Atrek (alt Atrak)	Caspian (Sea) L, Iran-USSR	420	670	11	27		
15.19N, 105.30E	Mun	Mekong R, Thailand	420	670	41	107	20	580
75.41N, 99.20E	Taymyra (alt Taimyra)	Kara Sea, Russia, USSR	410	660	48	124	35	988
3.32S, 114.29E	Barito (alt Dusun)	Java Sea, Borneo I, Indonesia	400	650	39	100	69	1,960
51.42N, 128.53E	Selemdzha	Zeya R, Russia, USSR	400	650	26	69	25	707
26.05N, 119.32E	Min-Jian (Xi) [alt Chien (Hsi)]	East China Sea, Fujian, China	360	580	22	56		
36.02N, 35.58E	Orontes (off Asi)	Mediterranean Sea, Turkey	350	570	9	23	2.2	62
5.42N, 118.23E	Kinabatangan	Sulu Sea, Sabah, Malaysia	350	560	23	60	12	329
2.07N, 111.12E	Rajang	South China Sea, Sarawak, Malaysia	350	560				
22.17N, 88.05E	Damodar	Hooghly R, West Bengal, India	340	540	8	22	268	7,600
6.47S, 112.33E	Solo (alt Bengawan)	Java Sea, Java I, Indonesia	340	540	6	15		
35.07N, 128.57E	Naktong (for Rakuti)	Korea Strait, South Korea	330	520	10	25	13	375
23.48N, 109.31E	Liu	Hongshui R, Guangxi, China	320	520	18	46	48	1,360
2.20S, 104.56E	•Musi (for Moesi)	Bangka Strait, Sumatra I, Indonesia	320	520	22	57	12	350

(Continued)

For an explanation of symbols and abbreviations, see pages 16–17.

TABLE 8a. (Continued)

Latitude and Longitude	River	Outflow and Location	Length mi	Length km	Drainage Basin 1,000 mi²	Drainage Basin 1,000 km²	Discharge Rate 1,000 cfs	Discharge Rate m³/sec
42.18N, 130.41E	Tumen (alt Tuman, Tumyntszyan)	Sea of Japan, North Korea-USSR	320	520	9	23	2.2	62
37.45N, 126.11E	Han (for Kan)	Yellow Sea, South Korea	320	510	10	25	17	485
30.15N, 120.15E	Fuchun (alt Tsientang)	East China Sea, Zhejiang, China	310	490	16	43	53	1,490
31.10N, 74.59E	Beas	Sutlej R, Punjab, India	290	460	10	26	18	497
23.02N, 113.31E	Dong (alt East, Tung)	Zhu R, Guangdong, China	270	440	10	25	34	957
33.55N, 72.14E	•Kabul (for Cabul)	Indus R, Pakistan	270	430	32	83	26	742
22.18N, 72.22E	Sabarmati	G of Cambay of Arabian Sea, Gujarat, India	260	420	21	55	1.4	39
37.57N, 139.04E	Shinano	Sea of Japan, Honshu I, Japan	230	370	5	12	16	448
23.02N, 112.58E	Bei (alt North, Pei)	Zhu R, Guangdong, China	220	350	15	38	53	1,500
18.22N, 121.37E	•Cagayan (alt Grande de Cagayan)	Babuyan Channel, Luzon I, Philippines	220	350	14	37	9.3	263
28.01N, 120.44E	Ou	East China Sea, Zhejiang, China	210	340	7	18	21	608
6.41N, 79.57E	Mahaweli Ganga	Indian O, Sri Lanka	210	330	4	10	8.0	226
23.41N, 116.38E	Han	South China Sea, Guangdong, China	200	320	11	29	33	922
7.07N, 124.24E	•Mindanao (alt Cotabato)-Pulangi	Moro G of Celebes Sea, Mindanao I, Philippines	200	320	6	16	12	350
35.44N, 140.51E	Tone	Pacific O, Honshu I, Japan	200	320	7	17	5.1	143
43.15N, 141.23E	Ishikari	Sea of Japan, Hokkaido I, Japan	170	270	6	14	11	315
44.53N, 141.45E	Teshio	Sea of Japan, Hokkaido I, Japan	160	260	2	6	5.6	159
31.46N, 35.33E	•Jordan (off Urdunn, Yarden)	Dead (Sea) L, Jordan-West Bank	160	250	6	16	1.3	37

EUROPE

Latitude and Longitude	River	Outflow and Location	Length mi	Length km	Drainage Basin 1,000 mi²	Drainage Basin 1,000 km²	Discharge Rate 1,000 cfs	Discharge Rate m³/sec
45.45N, 47.52E	Volga	Caspian (Sea) L, Russia, USSR	2190	3530	525	1360	285	8,060
45.20N, 29.40E	Danube (off Donau, Duna, Dunai, Dunarea, Dunav, Dunay)	Black Sea, Romania-USSR	1780	2860	315	816	221	6,250
46.30N, 32.18E	Dnieper (off Dnepr)	Black Sea, Ukraine, USSR	1370	2200	195	504	57	1,610
47.04N, 40.30E	Don	Sea of Azov of Black Sea, Russia, USSR	1160	1870	163	422	31	873

Coordinates	River	Destination						
64.32N, 40.30E	Northern Dvina (off Severnaya Dvina)-Vychegda (alt Vichegda)	White Sea, Russia, USSR	1160	1860	138	357	120	3,400
68.13N, 54.15E	Pechora (for Petchora)	Barents Sea, Russia, USSR	1120	1810	124	322	141	4,000
55.25N, 50.40E	Kama	Volga R, Russia, USSR	1120	1800	196	507	99	2,800
56.20N, 43.59E	Oka	Volga R, Russia, USSR	930	1500	95	245	46	1,300
55.54N, 53.33E	Belaya	Kama R, Russia, USSR	890	1430	55	142	30	845
39.24N, 49.19E	Kura	Caspian (Sea) L, Azerbaijan, USSR	850	1360	73	188	20	570
46.18N, 30.17E	Dniester (off Dnestr)	Black Sea, Moldavia, USSR	840	1350	28	72	10	293
51.47N, 4.10E[1]	Rhine (off Rhein, Rhin, Rijn)	North Sea, Netherlands	820	1320	97	252	88	2,490
55.36N, 51.30E	Vyatka (alt Viatka)	Kama R, Russia, USSR	820	1310	50	129	31	866
54.21N, 18.56E	Vistula (for Visla, Weichsel; off Wisla)-Bug (alt Zapadnyy Bug)	G of Danzig of Baltic Sea, Poland	750	1200	75	194	37	1,040
53.50N, 9.00E	Elbe (alt Labe)	North Sea, Niedersachsen-Schleswig-Holstein, West Germany	720	1160	56	144	25	703
50.33N, 30.32E	Desna	Dnieper R, Ukraine, USSR	700	1130	34	89	12	346
39.56N, 48.20E	Araks (alt Aras)	Kura R, Azerbaijan, USSR	670	1070	39	102	10	285
47.35N, 40.54E	Donets (alt Northern Donets; off Severnyy Donets)	Don R, Russia, USSR	650	1050	38	99	5.4	153
47.16N, 2.11W	Loire	B of Biscay, Pays de la Loire, France	630	1020	46	120	31	871
57.00N, 24.00E	Western Dvina (alt Daugava; for Duna; off Zapadnaya Dvina)	G of Riga of Baltic Sea, Latvia, USSR	630	1020	34	88	21	603
38.40N, 9.24W	Tagus (off Tajo, Tejo)	Atlantic O, Portugal	630	1010	31	81	4.5	128
59.57N, 30.20E	Neva-Volkhov-Lovat	G of Finland of Baltic Sea, Russia, USSR	620	1000	108	281	88	2,480
45.30N, 28.12E	Prut (alt Prutul; for Pruth)	Danube R, Romania-USSR	610	990	11	27	2.5	70
49.36N, 42.19E	Khoper	Don R, Russia, USSR	610	980	24	61	5.3	151
66.11N, 43.59E	Mezen	White Sea, Russia, USSR	600	970	30	78	23	642
45.15N, 20.17E	Tisza (alt Tisa, Tissa; for Theiss)	Danube R, Serbia, Yugoslavia	600	970	61	157	30	844
51.47N, 4.10E[2]	Meuse (alt Maas)	North Sea, Netherlands	590	950	19	49	9.5	269
53.32N, 14.38E	Oder (alt Odra)-Warta (for Warthe)	Baltic Sea, East Germany-Poland	590	950	46	119	20	560
55.18N, 21.23E	Neman (alt Nemunas; for Memel, Niemen)	Baltic Sea, Lithuania-Russia, USSR	580	940	38	98	20	578

(Continued)

[1] For Haringvliet Estuary distributary; for Rhine R proper: 51.52N, 6.02E.
[2] For Haringvliet Estuary distributary; for Meuse R proper: 51.49N, 5.01E.
For an explanation of symbols and abbreviations, see pages 16–17.

TABLE 8a. (Continued)

Latitude and Longitude	River	Outflow and Location	Length mi	Length km	Drainage Basin 1,000 mi2	Drainage Basin 1,000 km2	Discharge Rate 1,000 cfs	Discharge Rate m3/sec
44.50N, 20.28E	Sava (alt Save; for Sau, Szava)	Danube R, Serbia, Yugoslavia	580	940	37	96	60	1,700
54.40N, 56.00E	Ufa	Belaya R, Russia, USSR	570	920	21	53	14	390
40.43N, 0.54E	Ebro	Mediterranean Sea, Cataluna, Spain	570	910	33	85	6.1	173
45.20N, 37.22E	Kuban	Sea of Azov of Black Sea, Russia, USSR	560	910	22	58	15	425
41.08N, 8.40W	Douro (alt Duero)	Atlantic O, Portugal	560	890	38	98	11	312
56.18N, 46.24E	Vetluga	Volga R, Russia, USSR	550	890	15	39	8.2	231
56.06N, 46.00E	Sura	Volga R, Russia, USSR	520	840	26	67	7.3	207
64.08N, 41.54E	Pinega-Belaya	Northern Dvina R, Russia, USSR	510	820	16	42	13	357
43.20N, 4.50E	Rhone	Mediterranean Sea, Languedoc-Provence-Cote d'Azur, France	500	810	38	99	53	1,500
46.59N, 31.58E	Southern Bug (off Yuzhnyy Bug)	Dnieper R, Ukraine, USSR	500	810	25	64	2.9	83
44.55N, 46.32E	Kuma	Caspian (Sea) L, Russia, USSR	500	800	13	33	0.4	11
46.15N, 20.12E	Maros (alt Mures, Muresul)	Tisza R, Hungary	500	800	12	30	5.4	154
51.46N, 55.01E	Sakmara	Ural R, Russia, USSR	500	800	12	30	4.7	133
47.31N, 40.45E	Sal	Don R, Russia, USSR	500	800	8	21	0.4	12
37.14N, 7.22W	Guadiana	G of Cadiz of Atlantic O, Portugal-Spain	480	780	26	68	3.2	91
49.26N, 0.26E	Seine	English Channel, Haute-Normandie, France	480	780	30	79	9.6	272
51.10N, 30.30E	Pripet (off Pripyat)	Dnieper R, Ukraine, USSR	480	770	44	114	13	370
51.27N, 32.34E	Seym (alt Seim)	Desna R, Ukraine, USSR	460	750	11	27	3.6	103
49.35N, 42.41E	Medveditsa	Don R, Russia, USSR	460	740	13	35	2.5	71
43.43N, 24.51E	Olt (for Aluta)	Danube R, Romania	460	740	9	24	5.7	160
53.32N, 8.34E	Weser-Werra	North Sea, Niedersachsen, West Germany	460	730	18	46	12	334
57.42N, 11.52E	Gota-Klar	Kattegat, Sweden	450	720	19	50	23	640
52.35N, 14.39E	Oder (upper)	Oder R, Poland	450	720	21	54		
49.01N, 33.32E	Psel	Dnieper R, Ukraine, USSR	450	720	9	23	1.9	54

Coordinates	Name	Location						
45.33N, 18.55E	Drava (alt Drau, Drave)	Danube R, Croatia, Yugoslavia	440	710	15	40	22	611
45.24N, 28.01E	Siret (for Sereth; off Seret, Siretul)	Danube R, Romania	440	710	18	48	14	400
51.30N, 53.22E	Ilek-Zharyk	Ural R, Russia, USSR	430	700	16	41	1.3	36
59.27N, 28.02E	Narva-Velikaya	G of Finland of Baltic Sea, Estonia, USSR	430	700	22	56	15	415
56.10N, 42.58E	Klyazma	Oka R, Russia, USSR	430	690	16	42	7.1	202
52.31N, 21.05E	Vistula (upper)	Vistula R, Poland	420	680	33	85		
52.01N, 47.24E	Bolshoy Irgiz	Volga R, Russia, USSR	420	670	9	24	0.8	24
52.08N, 27.17E	Goryn	Pripet R, White Russia, USSR	410	660	11	28	3.1	88
36.47N, 6.22W	Guadalquivir	G of Cadiz of Atlantic O, Andalucia, Spain	410	660	22	57	6.4	182
54.44N, 41.53E	Moksha	Oka R, Russia, USSR	410	660	20	51	5.4	154
65.57N, 56.55E	Usa-Bolshaya Usa	Pechora R, Russia, USSR	410	660	36	94	36	1,030
45.35N, 1.03W	Gironde-Garonne (alt Garona)	B of Biscay, Aquitaine-Poitou-Charentes, France	400	650	33	85	21	590
51.57N, 30.48E	Sozh	Dnieper R, White Russia, USSR	400	650	16	42	7.3	207
43.44N, 46.33E	Terek	Caspian (Sea) L, Russia, USSR	390	620	17	43	7.9	224
44.57N, 12.04E	Po	Adriatic Sea, Veneto, Italy	380	620	29	75	54	1,540
52.33N, 30.14E	Berezina	Dnieper R, White Russia, USSR	380	610	9	24	4.5	127
59.12N, 10.57E	Glomma (off Glama)	Skagerrak, Norway	370	600	16	42	25	720
60.30N, 32.48E	Svir-Suna	Ladoga L, Russia, USSR	370	600	33	84	22	617
58.13N, 56.22E	Chusovaya	Kama R, Russia, USSR	370	590	18	48	8.0	226
53.10N, 50.04E	Samara	Volga R, Russia, USSR	370	590	18	46	1.7	47
62.48N, 42.56E	Vaga	Northern Dvina R, Russia, USSR	360	570	17	45	14	396
60.45N, 46.20E	Yug	Northern Dvina R, Russia, USSR	360	570	14	36	11	300
65.48N, 24.08E	Torne (alt Tornio)-Muonio-Konkama (alt Kongama)	G of Bothnia of Baltic Sea, Finland-Sweden	350	570	15	39	13	366
60.46N, 46.24E	Sukhona	Northern Dvina R, Russia, USSR	350	560	19	50	16	452
52.53N, 11.58E	Havel-Spree	Elbe R, East Germany	340	550	9	24	3.2	90
46.41N, 32.50E	Ingulets	Dnieper R, Ukraine, USSR	340	550	5	14	0.3	9
65.47N, 24.30E	Kemi	G of Bothnia of Baltic Sea, Finland	340	550	20	51	20	578
50.22N, 7.36E	Moselle (alt Mosel)	Rhine R, Rheinland-Pfalz, West Germany	340	550	11	28	10	292

(Continued)

For an explanation of symbols and abbreviations, see pages 16–17.

TABLE 8a. (Continued)

Latitude and Longitude	River	Outflow and Location	Length		Drainage Basin		Discharge Rate	
			mi	km	1,000 mi²	1,000 km²	1,000 cfs	m³/sec
44.43N, 21.03E	Morava (off Velika Morava)-Southern Morava (off Juzna Morava)	Danube R, Serbia, Yugoslavia	330	540	14	37	8.9	253
65.19N, 52.54E	Izhma	Pechora R, Russia, USSR	330	530	12	31	6.9	196
57.20N, 43.08E	Unzha-Kema	Volga R, Russia, USSR	330	530	11	27	6.2	176
50.00N, 8.18E	Main	Rhine R, Hessen, West Germany	330	520	10	27	3.5	100
48.49N, 2.24E	Marne	Seine R, Region Parisienne, France	330	520	5	14	3.5	98
60.38N, 17.27E	Dal	G of Bothnia of Baltic Sea, Sweden	320	520	11	29	12	333
51.31N, 39.05E	Voronezh-Polnoy Voronezh	Don R, Russia, USSR	320	520	8	22	2.5	71
48.35N, 13.28E	Inn	Danube R, Bayern, West Germany	320	510	10	26	26	735
65.36N, 44.35E	Peza-Rochuga	Mezen R, Russia, USSR	320	510	6	15	4.6	130
54.54N, 23,53E	Viliya (alt Neris; for Wilja)	Neman R, Lithuania, USSR	320	510	10	25	6.6	188
39.09N, 0.14W	Jucar	Mediterranean Sea, Valencia, Spain	310	500	8	21	2.1	60
55.05N, 38.51E	Moscow (off Moskva)	Oka R, Russia, USSR	310	500	7	18	2.3	64
40.52N, 26.12E	Maritsa (alt Evros, Meric)	Aegean Sea, Greece-Turkey	300	490	14	35		
44.18N, 0.20E	Lot	Garonne R, Aquitaine, France	300	480	4	10	4.5	128
52.26N, 20.42E	Narew (alt Narev)	Bug R, Poland	300	480	29	75	11	316
45.44N, 4.50E	Saone	Rhone R, Rhone-Alpes, France	300	480	12	30	15	424
	* * *							
45.02N, 0.35W	Dordogne	Garonne R, Aquitaine, France	290	470	9	23	10	286
63.47N, 20.16E	Ume	G of Bothnia of Baltic Sea, Sweden	290	460	10	27	16	450
48.50N, 34.05E	Vorskla	Dnieper R, Ukraine, USSR	290	460	6	15	1.1	30
58.50N, 37.11E	Mologa	Volga R, Russia, USSR	280	460	11	30	11	314
62.48N, 17.56E	Angerman	G of Bothnia of Baltic Sea, Sweden	280	450	12	32	16	448
65.35N, 22.03E	Lule	G of Bothnia of Baltic Sea, Sweden	280	450	10	25	16	444

58.25N, 31.20E	Msta	Ilmen L, Russia, USSR	280	440	9	23	5.7	161
50.45N, 21.51E	San	Vistula R, Poland	280	440	7	17	4.6	131
46.18N, 16.55E	Mur (alt Mura)	Drava R, Creatia, Yugoslavia	270	440	5	14	5.9	166
51.57N, 11.55E	Saale (alt Sachsische Saale)	Elbe R, East Germany	270	430	9	24	3.7	105
51.22N, 4.15E	Scheldt (alt Escaut, Schelde)	North Sea, Netherlands	270	430	8	20	5.5	155
48.07N, 22.20E	Somes (off Somesul, Szamos)	Tisza R, Romania	270	430	7	19	2.8	80
50.22N, 14.28E	Vltava (alt Moldau)	Elbe R, Bohemia, Czechoslovakia	270	430	11	28	5.1	145
63.58N, 38.02E	Onega	Onega B of White Sea, Russia, USSR	260	420	22	57	17	493
40.35N, 22.50E	Vardar (alt Axios, Vardaris)	G of Salonika of Aegean Sea, Greece	260	420	11	28	4.8	135
45.10N, 12.20E	Adige (for Etsch)	Adriatic Sea, Veneto, Italy	250	410	6	15	9.3	262
44.42N, 27.51E	Ialomita	Danube R, Romania	250	410	5	12	2.5	70
41.44N, 12.14E	Tiber (off Tevere)	Tyrrhenian Sea, Lazio, Italy	250	410	7	17	8.4	239
47.55N, 18.00E	Vah (for Vag, Waag)	Danube R, Slovakia, Czechoslovakia	240	390	4	11	5.6	158
52.30N, 9.55W	Shannon	Atlantic O, Ireland	230	370	6	16	7.0	198
70.30N, 28.23E	Tana	Tana Fjord of Barents Sea, Norway	220	360	6	16	6.7	190
51.25N, 3.00W	Severn	Bristol Channel, England, UK	210	340	8	21	2.2	62
53.32N, 0.08E	•Humber-Trent	North Sea, England, UK	210	330	9	23	7.0	198
38.06N, 0.38W	Segura	Mediterranean Sea, Valencia, Spain	200	320	6	16	0.2	6
51.30N, 0.45E	Thames	North Sea, England, UK	200	320	6	16	2.4	67
41.52N, 8.51W	Mino (alt Minho)	Atlantic O, Portugal-Spain	190	310	7	18	9.7	276
47.36N, 8.13E	Aare (alt Aar)	Rhine R, Switzerland	180	290	7	18	19	552
41.45N, 19.34E	Drin	Adriatic Sea, Albania	170	280	2	6	10	290
43.41N, 10.17E	•Arno	Ligurian Sea, Toscana, Italy	150	240	3	8	4.9	140
63.47N, 20.48W	•Thjorsa	Atlantic O, Iceland	140	230	3	7	14	395
56.22N, 3.21W	Tay	North Sea, Scotland, UK	120	190	2	6	5.5	156
56.29N, 10.13E	Gudena	Kattegat, Denmark	100	160	1	3	0.6	16

NORTH AMERICA

29.02N, 89.15W	Mississippi-Missouri¹-Jefferson-Beaverhead-Red Rock	G of Mexico, Louisiana, USA	3710	5970	1247	3230	531	15,040
69.15N,134.08W	Mackenzie-Slave-Peace-Finlay	Beaufort Sea, NWT, Canada	2630	4240	690	1787	316	8,940

(Continued)

¹Data for Missouri-Jefferson-Beaverhead-Red Rock: 2530 mi; 4080 km; 529,000 mi²; 1,370,000 km²; 80,900 cfs; 2,290 m³/sec.

For an explanation of symbols and abbreviations, see pages 16–17.

TABLE 8a. (Continued)

River	Latitude and Longitude	Outflow and Location	Length mi	Length km	Drainage Basin 1,000 mi²	Drainage Basin 1,000 km²	Discharge Rate 1,000 cfs	Discharge Rate m³/sec
Saint Lawrence (alt Saint-Laurent)-(Great Lakes)-Saint Louis	48.09N, 67.10W	G of Saint Lawrence, Quebec, Canada	2060[1]	3320[1]	550	1424	355	10,050
Yukon-Lewes-Teslin-Nisutlin	62.32N,163.54W	Bering Sea, Alaska, USA	1980	3180	328	850	223	6,310
Rio Grande (alt Bravo)	25.58N, 97.09W	G of Mexico, Mexico-USA	1880	3030	177	460	1.2	34
Nelson-Saskatchewan-South Saskatchewan-Bow	57.04N, 92.30W	Hudson B, Manitoba, Canada	1600	2570	437	1132	80	2,270
Arkansas	33.47N, 91.04W	Mississippi R, Arkansas, USA	1460	2350	161	417	41	1,160
Colorado	31.54N,114.57W	G of California, Baja California-Sonora, Mexico	1450	2330	247	640	1.5	42
Atchafalaya-Red	29.53N, 91.28W	G of Mexico, Louisiana, USA	1400	2260	95	246	247[2]	6,990[2]
Columbia-Snake[3]	46.15N,124.03W	Pacific O, Oregon-Washington, USA	1390	2240	258	668	194	5,490
Brazos	28.52N, 95.22W	G of Mexico, Texas, USA	1310	2110	46	120	7.7	217
Ohio-Allegheny	36.59N, 89.08W	Mississippi R, Illinois-Kentucky, USA	1310	2100	204	528	272	7,710
Churchill-Beaver	58.47N, 94.12W	Hudson B, Manitoba, Canada	1300	2100	115	298	35	996
Mississippi (upper)	38.49N, 90.07W	Mississippi R, Missouri, USA	1170	1880	172	446	102	2,900
Platte-North Platte	41.03N, 95.53W	Missouri R, Nebraska, USA	990	1590	90	233	6.4	181
Pecos	29.42N,101.22W	Rio Grande R, Texas, USA	930	1490	38	99	0.09	2
Canadian	35.27N, 95.03W	Arkansas R, Oklahoma, USA	910	1460	48	124	5.1	143
Tennessee-Holston	37.04N, 88.34W	Ohio R, Kentucky, USA	900	1450	41	106	65	1,850
Columbia (upper)	46.12N,119.02W	Columbia R, Washington, USA	890	1430	97	251	120	3,400
Colorado	28.36N, 95.59W	Matagorda B of G of Mexico, Texas, USA	860	1390	42	109	1.5	42
Fraser	49.04N,123.07W	Strait of Georgia, British Columbia, Canada	850	1370	90	233	120	3,410
North Saskatchewan	53.15N,105.05W	Saskatchewan R, Saskatchewan, Canada	800	1290	51	133	8.5	242
Ottawa (alt Outaouais)	45.25N, 74.00W	Saint Lawrence R, Quebec, Canada	790	1270	56	146	70	1,970

Coordinates	River	Outlet						
30.41N, 88.00W	Mobile-Alabama-Coosa-Etowah	Mobile B of G of Mexico, Alabama, USA	780	1260	44	113	68	1,940
35.16N, 95.31W	North Canadian	Canadian R, Oklahoma, USA	780	1260	15	39	0.6	18
58.40N,110.50W	Athabasca (alt Athabaska)	Athabasca L, Alberta, Canada	760	1230	63	163	24	681
38.11N,109.53W	Green	Colorado R, Utah, USA	730	1170	47	122	6.3	178
48.03N,106.19W	Milk	Missouri R, Montana, USA	730	1170	23	58	0.7	19
60.05N,162.25W	Kuskokwim	Kuskokwim B of Bering Sea, Alaska, USA	720	1170	49	127	41	1,160
37.09N, 88.24W	Cumberland	Ohio R, Kentucky, USA	720	1160	18	47	39	1,090
33.57N, 91.05W	White	Mississippi R, Arkansas, USA	720	1160	28	73	23	646
29.45N, 94.43W	Trinity	Galveston B of G of Mexico, Texas, USA	710	1150	18	47	7.1	202
42.52N, 97.18W	James (alt Dakota)	Missouri R, South Dakota, USA	710	1140	22	57	0.4	11
39.07N, 94.37W	Kansas (alt Kaw)-Smoky Hill	Missouri R, Kansas, USA	710	1140	61	159	7.1	200
50.24N, 96.48W	Red-Assiniboine	Winnipeg L, Manitoba, Canada	710	1140	111	287	7.7	218
36.07N, 96.30W	Cimarron	Arkansas R, Oklahoma, USA	700	1120	19	49	1.2	33
61.51N,121.18W	Liard	Mackenzie R, NWT, Canada	690	1120	108	280	83	2,350
18.24N, 92.38W	Usumacinta-Chixoy	B of Campeche of G of Mexico, Tabasco, Mexico	690	1110	40	103	61	1,730
47.58N,103.59W	Yellowstone	Missouri R, North Dakota, USA	690	1110	70	181	13	370
65.09N,151.57W	Tanana-Chisana	Yukon R, Alaska, USA	660	1060	44	115	24	674
50.37N, 96.20W	Winnipeg-English	Winnipeg L, Manitoba, Canada	650	1050	52	135	29	835
49.53N, 97.07W	Red (upper)-Otter Tail	Red R, Manitoba, Canada	640	1030	48	124	5.3	150
32.43N,114.33W	Gila	Colorado R, Arizona, USA	630	1010	58	150	0.4	11
21.36N,105.26W	Santiago (alt Grande de Santiago)-Lerma	Pacific O, Nayarit, Mexico	630	1010	48	125	13	363
34.08N, 96.36W	Washita	Red R, Oklahoma, USA	630	1010	8	21	1.4	39
52.17N, 81.31W	Albany-Cat	James B of Hudson B, Ontario, Canada	610	980	52	134	36	1,020
56.02N, 87.36W	Severn-Black Birch	Hudson B, Ontario, Canada	610	980	39	101	25	713
67.15N, 95.15W	Back (for Great Fish)	Arctic O, NWT, Canada	600	970	41	107	17	470
31.16N, 91.50W	Black-Ouachita	Red R, Louisiana, USA	600	970	18	47	18	496

1For Saint Lawrence R proper: 590 mi, 960 km.

2Inc approximately 25% of the Mississippi R flow, diverted to control flooding; the average discharge rate of the Mississippi at Vicksburg, above the point of diversion, is 579,000 cfs, 16,400 m3/sec. The average discharge rate of the Red R is 30,900 cfs, 875 m3/sec.

3Data for Snake: 1040 mi, 1670 km; 109,000 mi2, 282,000 km2; 56,600 cfs, 1,600 m3/sec.

For an explanation of symbols and abbreviations, see pages 16–17.

(Continued)

TABLE 8a. (Continued)

Latitude and Longitude	River	Outflow and Location	Length		Drainage Basin		Discharge Rate	
			mi	km	1,000 mi2	1,000 km2	1,000 cfs	m3/sec
29.59N, 93.47W	Sabine	Sabine L, Louisiana-Texas, USA	580	930	10	27	7.4	210
47.36N,102.25W	Little Missouri	Missouri R, North Dakota, USA	560	900	9	23	0.6	17
64.16N, 96.05W	Thelon	Baker L, NWT, Canada	560	900	60	155	27	757
53.50N, 79.00W	Grande (alt Fort George)	James B of Hudson B, Quebec, Canada	550	890	38	98	60	1,700
39.03N, 96.48W	Republican-Arikaree	Kansas R, Kansas, USA	550	890	25	65	0.9	24
58.30N, 68.10W	Koksoak-Caniapiscau (alt Ka-niapiskau)	Ungava B of Hudson Strait, Quebec, Canada	540	870	53	137	85	2,420
33.07N, 79.17W	Santee-Wateree-Catawba	Atlantic O, South Carolina, USA	540	870	15	39	3.4	95
53.20N, 60.20W	Churchill (for Hamilton)-Ashuanipi	Atlantic O, Newfoundland, Canada	530	860	37	96	62	1,750
40.23N, 91.25W	Des Moines	Mississippi R, Iowa-Missouri, USA	530	860	16	41	5.8	165
44.41N,101.18W	Cheyenne	Missouri R, South Dakota, USA	530	850	25	66	0.8	24
37.48N, 88.02W	Wabash	Ohio R, Illinois-Indiana, USA	530	850	33	86	28	783
67.49N,115.04W	Coppermine	Arctic O, NWT, Canada	530	840	16	40	3.6	102
29.43N, 84.58W	Apalachicola-Chattahoochee	G of Mexico, Florida, USA	520	840	20	51	29	834
64.33N,100.06W	Dubawnt	Beverly L, NWT, Canada	520	840	27	69	12	329
64.55N,157.32W	Koyukuk	Yukon R, Alaska, USA	520	840	33	84	14	411
31.08N, 87.57W	Tombigbee	Mobile R, Alabama, USA	520	840	20	52	31	878
43.42N, 99.27W	White	Missouri R, South Dakota, USA	510	820	10	27	0.5	15
49.00N,117.36W	Pend Oreille-Clark Fork	Columbia R, British Columbia, Canada	500	810	26	67	27	772
62.12N,159.43W	Innoko	Yukon R, Alaska, USA	500	800	15	39	10	289
38.35N, 91.58W	Osage-Marais des Cygnes	Missouri R, Missouri, USA	500	800	10	26	9.9	280
30.11N, 89.31W	Pearl	G of Mexico, Louisiana-Mississippi, USA	490	790				
32.22N, 90.54W	Yazoo-Tallahatchie	Mississippi R, Mississippi, USA	490	790	9	23	10	292
46.44N,105.26W	Powder	Yellowstone R, Montana, USA	490	780	13	34	0.6	17
49.15N,117.39W	Kootenay (alt Kootenai)	Columbia R, British Columbia, Canada	480	780	19	50	28	798
51.25N, 78.55W	Nottaway-Bell-Megiscane	James B of Hudson B, Quebec, Canada	480	780	25	66	37	1,040

17.55N,102.10W	Balsas	Pacific O, Guerrero-Michoacan, Mexico	480	770	43	112	16	439
52.15N, 78.32W	Eastmain	James B of Hudson B, Quebec, Canada	470	760	18	46	32	909
51.30N, 78.48W	Rupert-Temiscamie	James B of Hudson B, Quebec, Canada	470	760	17	43	31	875
15.00N, 83.10W	•Coco (alt Segovia)	Caribbean Sea, Honduras-Nicaragua	470	750	10	27	18	500
52.57N, 82.18W	Attawapiskat	James B of Hudson B, Ontario, Canada	460	750	19	50	15	411
28.27N, 96.47W	Guadalupe	San Antonio B of G of Mexico, Texas, USA	460	740	11	28	2.1	59
35.48N, 95.18W	Neosho (alt Grand)	Arkansas R, Oklahoma, USA	460	740	13	33	7.6	214
64.03N, 95.35W	Kazan	Baker L, NWT, Canada	450	730	29	74	15	413
31.20N, 81.20W	Altamaha-Ocmulgee-South	Atlantic O, Georgia, USA	450	720	14	36	14	388
46.09N,107.28W	Bighorn-Wind	Yellowstone R, Montana, USA	450	720	22	58	3.9	111
55.16N, 77.48W	Grande (Riviere) de la Baleine (alt Great Whale)	Hudson B, Quebec, Canada	450	720	17	43	19	547
66.34N,145.19W	Porcupine	Yukon R, Alaska, USA	450	720	46	120	12	337
50.56N,109.54W	Red Deer	South Saskatchewan R, Saskatchewan, Canada	450	720	18	47	2.5	70
49.39N, 99.34W	Souris	Assiniboine R, Manitoba, Canada	450	720	24	62	0.5	13
41.07N,100.41W	South Platte	Platte R, Nebraska, USA	440	710	24	63	0.4	13
39.32N, 76.04W	Susquehanna	Chesapeake B of Atlantic O, Maryland, USA	440	710	28	71	42	1,190
60.51N,115.44W	Hay	Great Slave L, NWT, Canada	440	700	19	49	3.5	100
18.36N, 92.39W	Grijalva (alt Mezcalapa)	B of Campeche of G of Mexico, Tabasco, Mexico	430	700	20	52	7.1	200
33.22N, 79.16W	Pee Dee-Yadkin	Winyah B of Atlantic O, South Carolina, USA	430	700	9	23	9.9	281
48.10N, 69.45W	Saguenay-Peribonca	Saint Lawrence R, Quebec, Canada	430	700	34	88	42	1,180
21.45N,105.30W	San Pedro (alt Mezquital)	Pacific O, Nayarit, Mexico	430	700	7	18	3.9	110
69.42N,129.01W	Anderson	Wood B of Beaufort Sea, NWT, Canada	430	690	24	62	5.7	162
38.41.N, 85.11W	Kentucky	Ohio R, Kentucky, USA	430	690	7	18	8.3	235

For an explanation of symbols and abbreviations, see pages 16–17.

(Continued)

TABLE 8a. (Continued)

Latitude and Longitude	River	Outflow and Location	Length mi	Length km	Drainage Basin 1,000 mi²	Drainage Basin 1,000 km²	Discharge Rate 1,000 cfs	Discharge Rate m³/sec
42.46N, 98.03W	Niobrara	Missouri R, Nebraska, USA	430	690	13	33	1.5	44
42.59N, 91.09W	Wisconsin	Mississippi R, Wisconsin, USA	430	690	12	31	8.7	246
42.29N, 96.27W	Big Sioux	Missouri R, Iowa-South Dakota, USA	420	680	9	23	1.0	28
51.58N, 98.04W	Dauphin-Fairford-Red Deer	Winnipeg L, Manitoba, Canada	420	680	32	83	2.2	62
38.58N, 90.28W	Illinois-Kankakee	Mississippi R, Illinois, USA	420	680	28	72	22	628
67.41N,134.32W	Peel-Ogilvie	Mackenzie R, NWT, Canada	420	680	27	71	27	768
34.37N, 90.35W	Saint Francis	Mississippi R, Arkansas, USA	420	680	8	22	5.3	149
45.51N,116.47W	Salmon	Snake R, Idaho, USA	420	680	14	36	11	323
27.37N,110.39W	Yaqui-Bavispe	G of California, Sonora, Mexico	420	680	25	66	3.8	108
45.15N, 66.04W	Saint John	B of Fundy of Atlantic O, New Brunswick, Canada	420	670	21	55	30	849
36.56N, 76.27W	James-Jackson	Chesapeake B of Atlantic O, Virginia, USA	410	670	9	23	7.5	214
41.16N, 72.20W	Connecticut	Long Island Sound of Atlantic O, Connecticut, USA	410	660	11	28	17	469
35.56N, 76.42W	Roanoke	Albemarle Sound of Atlantic O, North Carolina, USA	410	660	10	26	8.1	229
63.18N,139.24W	Stewart	Yukon R, Yukon Territory, Canada	400	640	20	51	16	451
39.15N, 75.20W	Delaware	Delaware B of Atlantic O, Delaware-New Jersey, USA	390	630	11	30	12	332
38.50N, 82.08W	Kanawha-New	Ohio R, West Virginia, USA	390	630	12	31	15	425
70.01N,126.42W	Horton	Amundsen G of Arctic O, NWT, Canada	380	620				
38.00N, 76.23W	Potomac	Chesapeake B of Atlantic O, Maryland-Virginia, USA	380	620	14	38	11	326
51.20N, 80.24W	Moose-Abitibi	James B of Hudson B, Ontario, Canada	380	610	42	109	28	793
62.47N,137.20W	Pelly	Yukon R, Yukon Territory, Canada	380	610	20	52	13	382

Name	Coordinates	Location						
Sacramento	38.03N,121.56W	Suisun B of Pacific O, California, USA	380	610	27	70	25	702
•Atoyac (alt Verde)	16.30N, 97.31W	Pacific O, Oaxaca, Mexico	370	600	7	19	3.2	90
Colville	70.27N,150.07W	Beaufort Sea, Alaska, USA	370	600	24	62		
•Conchos	29.35N,104.25W	Rio Grande R, Chihuahua, Mexico	370	590	25	64	0.8	24
Green	37.54N, 87.30W	Ohio R, Kentucky, USA	360	580	9	24	11	318
Iowa-Cedar	41.10N, 91.10W	Missouri R, Iowa, USA	360	580	13	34	7.0	198
San Juan	37.16N,110.26W	Colorado R, Utah, USA	360	580	23	60	2.5	72
Savannah-Seneca	32.02N, 80.53W	Atlantic O, Georgia-South Carolina, USA	360	580	10	26	12	343
Skeena	54.09N,130.05W	Chatham Sound of Pacific O, British Columbia, Canada	360	580	21	55	32	910
Battle	52.43N,108.15W	North Saskatchewan R, Saskatchewan, Canada	350	570	12	31	0.6	16
Sevier	39.04N,113.07W	Sevier L, Utah, USA	350	570	6	16	0.2	5
Bear	41.27N,112.15W	Great Salt L, Utah, USA	350	560	7	18	1.7	49
•Fuerte-Verde	25.54N,109.22W	G of California, Sinaloa, Mexico	350	560	14	36	6.0	171
George	58.50N, 66.10W	Ungava B of Hudson Strait, Quebec, Canada	350	560	16	42	26	740
Grand	45.40N,100.45W	Missouri R, South Dakota, USA	350	560	6	16	0.2	7
Licking	39.06N, 84.30W	Ohio R, Kentucky, USA	350	560	4	10	4.1	117
Manicouagan	49.10N, 68.15W	Saint Lawrence R, Quebec, Canada	350	560	18	46	31	871
Noatak	67.00N,162.30W	Kotzebue Sound of Chukchi Sea, Alaska, USA	350	560	13	33		
Penobscot	44.30N, 68.48W	Atlantic O, Maine, USA	350	560	10	26	12	338
Saint-Maurice	46.21N, 72.31W	Saint Lawrence R, Quebec, Canada	350	560	17	43	25	703
San Joaquin	38.04N,121.51W	Suisun B of Pacific O, California, USA	350	560	14	36	4.8	136
South Nahanni	61.03N,123.22W	Liard R, NWT, Canada	350	560	13	34	14	403
Verdigris	35.48N, 95.19W	Arkansas R, Oklahoma, USA	350	560	8	20	3.7	105
Nueces	27.50N, 97.29W	Nueces B of G of Mexico, Texas, USA	340	550	19	49	0.9	24
Pembina	54.45N,114.17W	Athabasca R, Alberta, Canada	340	550	5	13	1.3	38
Petit Mecatina (alt Little Mecatina)	50.39N, 59.29W	G of Saint Lawrence, Quebec, Canada	340	550	8	20	17	495

(Continued)

For an explanation of symbols and abbreviations, see pages 16–17.

TABLE 8a. (Continued)

Latitude and Longitude	River	Outflow and Location	Length		Drainage Basin		Discharge Rate	
			mi	km	1,000 mi²	1,000 km²	1,000 cfs	m³/sec
41.07N, 96.18W	Elkhorn	Platte R, Nebraska, USA	330	540	7	18	1.2	34
56.31N,132.24W	Stikine	Stikine Strait, Alaska, USA	330	540	20	51	55	1,550
38.25N, 87.44W	White	Wabash R, Indiana, USA	330	540	12	31	12	330
32.03N, 91.04W	Big Black	Mississippi R, Mississippi, USA	330	530	3	8	3.6	103
51.10N, 79.45W	Harricana (alt Harricanaw)	James B of Hudson B, Ontario, Canada	330	530	11	29	4.7	134
44.54N, 93.09W	Minnesota	Mississippi R, Minnesota, USA	330	530	17	44	3.6	103
33.23N,112.18W	Salt-Black	Gila R, Arizona, USA	330	530	7	18	0.9	27
33.53N, 78.01W	Cape Fear-Deep	Atlantic O, North Carolina, USA	320	520	6	16	5.8	164
59.33N,124.01W	Fort Nelson-Sikanni Chief	Liard R, British Columbia, Canada	320	520	18	47	12	334
47.01N, 96.49W	Sheyenne	Red R, North Dakota, USA	320	520	10	26	0.2	5
37.58N, 89.57W	Kaskaskia	Mississippi R, Illinois, USA	320	510	6	16	3.9	112
22.16N, 97.47W	Panuco-Santa Maria	G of Mexico, Tamaulipas-Veracruz, Mexico	320	510	25	66	19	548
67.27N,133.45W	Arctic Red	Mackenzie R, NWT, Canada	310	500	7	19	5.4	153
25.45N,102.50W	•Nazas	Mayran L, Coahuila, Mexico	310	500	14	36	3.4	95
49.05N, 68.23W	Outardes	Saint Lawrence R, Quebec, Canada	310	500	7	19	14	385
43.49N,117.02W	Owyhee	Snake R, Oregon, USA	310	500	12	31	0.4	12
50.18N, 63.48W	Romaine	G of Saint Lawrence, Quebec, Canada	310	500	6	14	11	315
40.42N, 74.01W	Hudson	New York B of Atlantic O, New Jersey-New York, USA	310	490	13	35	14	388
56.11N,117.19W	Smoky	Peace R, Alberta, Canada	310	490	21	55	13	367
50.14N,121.34W	Thompson-North Thompson	Fraser R, British Columbia, Canada	300	490	22	57	28	786
39.35N, 96.34W	Big Blue	Kansas R, Kansas, USA	300	480	10	25	2.1	61
35.53N, 84.29W	Clinch	Tennessee R, Tennessee, USA	300	480	3	9	4.6	132
58.46N, 70.05W	Feuilles (alt Leaf)	Ungava B of Hudson Strait, Quebec, Canada	300	480	16	43	21	587
39.23N, 93.06W	Grand	Missouri R, Missouri, USA	300	480	7	18	3.9	110

Coordinates	River	Location						
57.00N, 92.15W	Hayes	Hudson B, Manitoba, Canada	300	480	42	108	23	650
36.12N, 111.48W	Little Colorado	Colorado R, Arizona, USA	300	480	27	70	0.2	7
51.03N, 80.55W	Moose (upper)-Mattagami	Moose R, Ontario, Canada	300	480	25	65	15	420
30.23N, 88.37W	Pascagoula-Chickasawhay	Mississippi Sound of G of Mexico, Mississippi, USA	300	480	7	18	10	283
41.29N, 90.37W	Rock	Mississippi R, Illinois, USA	300	480	11	28	6.1	173
28.48N, 111.49W	•Sonora	G of California, Sonora, Mexico	300	480	11	29		
55.16N, 85.05W	Winisk	Hudson B, Ontario, Canada	300	470	26	67	17	484
		* * *						
44.26N, 102.18W	Belle Fourche	Cheyenne R, South Dakota, USA	290	470	8	20	0.4	10
39.59N, 118.36W	Humboldt	Humboldt L, Nevada, USA	290	470	17	44	0.2	7
41.24N, 97.19W	Loup-Middle Loup	Platte R, Nebraska, USA	290	470	15	39	0.6	18
45.18N, 100.43W	Moreau	Missouri R, South Dakota, USA	290	470	6	16	0.2	6
47.21N, 107.57W	Musselshell	Missouri R, Montana, USA	290	470	9	23	0.3	8
32.32N, 87.51W	Black Warrior	Tombigbee R, Alabama, USA	290	460	6	16	13	382
53.56N, 122.42W	Nechako	Fraser R, British Columbia, Canada	290	460	17	43	11	300
35.38N, 91.19W	Black	White R, Arkansas, USA	280	450	8	21	8.6	244
51.21N, 78.53W	Broadback	James B of Hudson B, Quebec, Canada	280	450	8	21	11	314
39.19N, 92.57W	Chariton	Missouri R, Missouri, USA	280	450	2	6	1.2	35
60.18N, 145.03W	Copper	G of Alaska, Alaska, USA	280	450	24	63	38	1,060
45.44N, 120.39W	John Day	Columbia R, Oregon, USA	280	450	8	21	2.1	59
66.54N, 160.38W	Kobuk	Kotzebue Sound of Chukchi Sea, Alaska, USA	280	450	12	31	15	425
29.58N, 93.51W	Neches	Sabine L, Texas, USA	280	450	8	21	5.2	147
35.06N, 76.29W	Neuse	Pamlico Sound of Atlantic O, North Carolina, USA	280	450	3	8	2.9	82
59.03N, 158.23W	Nushagak-Mulchatna	Bristol B of Bering Sea, Alaska, USA	280	450	14	37	23	641
31.58N, 82.32W	Oconee	Altamaha R, Georgia, USA	280	450	5	13	5.0	142
18.42N, 95.38W	Papaloapan-Tuxtepec	Alvarado Lagoon, Veracruz, Mexico	280	440	9	23	44	1,240
30.24N, 81.24W	Saint Johns	Atlantic O, Florida, USA	280	440	9	23	5.5	157
33.44N, 80.38W	Congaree-Broad	Santee R, South Carolina, USA	270	440	8	21	9.4	266

(Continued)

For an explanation of symbols and abbreviations, see pages 16–17.

TABLE 8a. (Continued)

Latitude and Longitude	River	Outflow and Location	Length mi	Length km	Drainage Basin 1,000 mi²	Drainage Basin 1,000 km²	Discharge Rate 1,000 cfs	Discharge Rate m³/sec
58.15N, 67.38W	Baleine (alt Whale)	Ungava B of Hudson Strait, Quebec, Canada	270	430	12	32	19	537
32.30N, 86.16W	Tallapoosa	Alabama R, Alabama, USA	270	430	5	12	4.9	139
45.39N,122.46W	Willamette	Columbia R, Oregon, USA	270	430	11	29	34	970
30.57N, 84.34W	Flint	Apalachicola R, Georgia, USA	260	430	8	21	7.0	197
38.40N, 91.33W	Gasconade	Missouri R, Missouri, USA	260	430	4	9	2.6	73
46.25N,105.52W	Tongue	Yellowstone R, Montana, USA	260	430	6	16	0.4	12
43.03N, 86.15W	Grand	Michigan L, Michigan, USA	260	420	5	13	3.6	102
41.17N, 91.21W	Iowa (upper)	Iowa R, Iowa, USA	260	420	4	11	2.9	81
61.15N,150.36W	Susitna	G of Alaska, Alaska, USA	260	420	19	50	49	1,400
45.38N,120.55W	Deschutes	Columbia R, Oregon, USA	250	400	11	28	5.9	166
41.33N,124.05W	Klamath	Pacific O, California, USA	250	400	12	31	18	513
31.50N, 81.03W	Ogeechee	Atlantic O, Georgia, USA	250	400	3	8	2.3	66
29.17N, 83.10W	Suwannee	G of Mexico, Florida, USA	250	400	10	26	11	301
44.06N, 77.34W	Trent-Otonabee-Irondale	Ontario L, Ontario, Canada	250	400	5	12	4.8	137
40.04N,109.40W	White	Green R, Utah, USA	250	400	5	13	0.6	18
34.06N, 98.10W	Wichita	Red R, Texas, USA	250	400	4	10	0.3	8
40.32N,108.59W	Yampa	Green R, Colorado, USA	250	400	4	10	1.6	44
45.27N, 75.40W	Gatineau	Ottawa R, Quebec, Canada	240	390	9	24	13	360
20.17N, 75.56W	Cauto	G of Guacanayabo of Caribbean Sea, Cuba	230	370	4	11		
43.58N, 69.52W	Androscoggin-Magalloway	Atlantic O, Maine, USA	220	360	4	10	6.1	174
13.14N, 88.49W	Lempa	Pacific O, El Salvador	200	320	7	18	13	377
17.32N, 88.14W	•Belize	Caribbean Sea, Belize	180	290				
19.15N, 72.47W	Artibonite	G of Gonave of Caribbean Sea, Haiti	170	280	4	10		
19.51N, 71.41W	Yaque del Norte	Atlantic O, Dominican Republic	170	280			1.7	49
46.03N, 73.08W	Richelieu	Saint Lawrence R, Quebec, Canada	110	170	9	24	13	360

OCEANIA

Coordinates	Name	Mouth / Location						
35.22S, 139.22E	Murray-Darling[1]-Culgoa-Balonne-Condamine	Indian O, South Australia, Australia	2330	3750	408	1057	12	326
34.07S, 141.55E	Murray (upper)	Murray R, New South Wales, Australia	1090	1750	103	267	5.9	168
29.56S, 146.20E	Barwon-Macintyre-Dumaresq-Severn	Darling R, New South Wales, Australia	980	1580	87	225	2.1	60
34.43S, 143.12E	Murrumbidgee	Murray R, New South Wales, Australia	980	1580	37	97	2.6	73
34.21S, 143.57E	Lachlan	Murrumbidgee R, New South Wales, Australia	920	1480	33	85	0.6	17
8.25S, 143.10E	•Fly-Strickland	G of Papua of Coral Sea, Papua New Guinea	800	1290	25	64	157	4,450
3.51S, 144.34E	•Sepik	Pacific O, Papua New Guinea	700	1130				
23.32S, 150.52E	•Fitzroy-Dawson	Pacific O, Queensland, Australia	690	1110	55	143	6.7	191
30.07S, 147.24E	Macquarie	Barwon R, New South Wales, Australia	590	950	18	47	0.9	25
30.00S, 148.07E	Namoi	Barwon R, New South Wales, Australia	530	850	17	43	0.7	21
17.36S, 140.36E	Flinders	G of Carpentaria, Queensland, Australia	520	840	42	108	0.6	16
24.52S, 113.37E	Gascoyne	Indian O, Western Australia, Australia	510	820	31	80	0.6	17
29.57S, 146.21E	•Bogan	Barwon R, New South Wales, Australia	450	720	10	26	0.07	2
19.39S, 147.30E	Burdekin	Pacific O, Queensland, Australia	440	710	51	131	10	287
1.26S, 137.53E	Mamberamo-Taritatu (for Idenburg)	Pacific O, Irian Jaya, Indonesia	420	670				
29.27S, 149.48E	Gwydir	Barwon R, New South Wales, Australia	410	670	10	26	0.9	25
15.12S, 129.43E	•Victoria	Timor Sea, Northern Territory, Australia	400	650	30	78	3.1	87
4.02S, 144.40E	•Ramu (for Ottilien)	Pacific O, Papua New Guinea	400	640				
30.12S, 147.32E	Castlereagh	Barwon R, New South Wales, Australia	340	550	7	18	0.2	5
7.07S, 138.42E	Digul (for Digoel)	Arafura Sea, Irian Jaya, Indonesia	340	540				

[1]Data for Darling-Culgoa-Balonne-Condamine: 1810 mi, 2910 km; 247,000 mi2, 640,000 km2; 7,900 cfs, 225 m3/sec.

For an explanation of symbols and abbreviations, see pages 16–17.

(Continued)

TABLE 8a. (Continued)

Latitude and Longitude	River	Outflow and Location	Length		Drainage Basin		Discharge Rate	
			mi	km	1,000 mi2	1,000 km2	1,000 cfs	m3/sec
		***						
33.30S, 151.10E	Hawkesbury	Pacific O, New South Wales, Australia	290	470	8	22	2.3	66
32.50S, 151.42E	Hunter	Pacific O, New South Wales, Australia	290	470	8	20	1.0	30
37.23S, 174.42E	Waikato	Tasman Sea, North Island, New Zealand	260	420	6	14	12	334
29.25S, 153.22E	Clarence	Pacific O, New South Wales, Australia	240	390	9	23	4.1	116
46.21S, 169.48E	Clutha-Makarora	Pacific O, South Island, New Zealand	200	320	8	22	23	651
SOUTH AMERICA								
0.10S, 49.00W	•Amazon (off Amazonas)-Ucayali-Tambo-Ene-Apurimac	Atlantic O, Amapa-Para, Brazil	4080	6570	2375	6150	6180	175,000
35.00S, 57.00W	Plata-Parana-Grande	Atlantic O, Argentina-Uruguay	3030	4880	1197	3100	809	22,900
3.22S, 58.45W	•Madeira-Mamore-Grande (alt Guapay)	Amazon R, Amazonas, Brazil	1990	3200	463	1200	770	21,800
2.37S, 65.44W	•Jurua (alt Yurua)	Amazon R, Amazonas, Brazil	1860	3000	93	240	141	4,000
3.42S, 61.28W	•Purus	Amazon R, Amazonas, Brazil	1860	3000	154	400	445	12,600
10.30S, 36.24W	Sao Francisco	Atlantic O, Alagoas-Sergipe, Brazil	1730	2780	241	623	102	2,890
1.00S, 48.30W	Para-Tocantins	Atlantic O, Para, Brazil	1710	2750	323	836	305	8,630
27.18S, 58.38W	Paraguay (alt Paraguai)	Parana R, Argentina-Paraguay	1610	2600	425	1100	155	4,400
3.08S, 64.46W	•Caqueta (alt Japura, Yapura)	Amazon R, Amazonas, Brazil	1420	2280	120	310	247	7,000
2.24S, 54.41W	•Tapajos-Juruena	Amazon R, Para, Brazil	1380	2220	179	463	212	6,000
5.21S, 48.41W	•Araguaia	Tocantins R, Para, Brazil	1370	2200	124	320	217	6,140
34.12S, 58.18W	Uruguay (alt Uruguai)-Canoas	Plata R, Argentina-Uruguay	1370	2200	119	307	194	5,500
8.37N, 62.15W	Orinoco	Atlantic O, Venezuela	1330	2140	340	880	890	25,200
1.30S, 51.53W	•Xingu	Amazon R, Para, Brazil	1300	2100	174	450	73	2,060
3.08S, 59.55W	•Negro (alt Guainia)	Amazon R, Amazonas, Brazil	1240	2000	386	1000	1236	35,000
3.07S, 67.58W	•Putumayo (alt Ica)	Amazon R, Amazonas, Brazil	1240	2000	43	112	177	5,000

(Continued)

For an explanation of symbols and abbreviations, see pages 16–17.

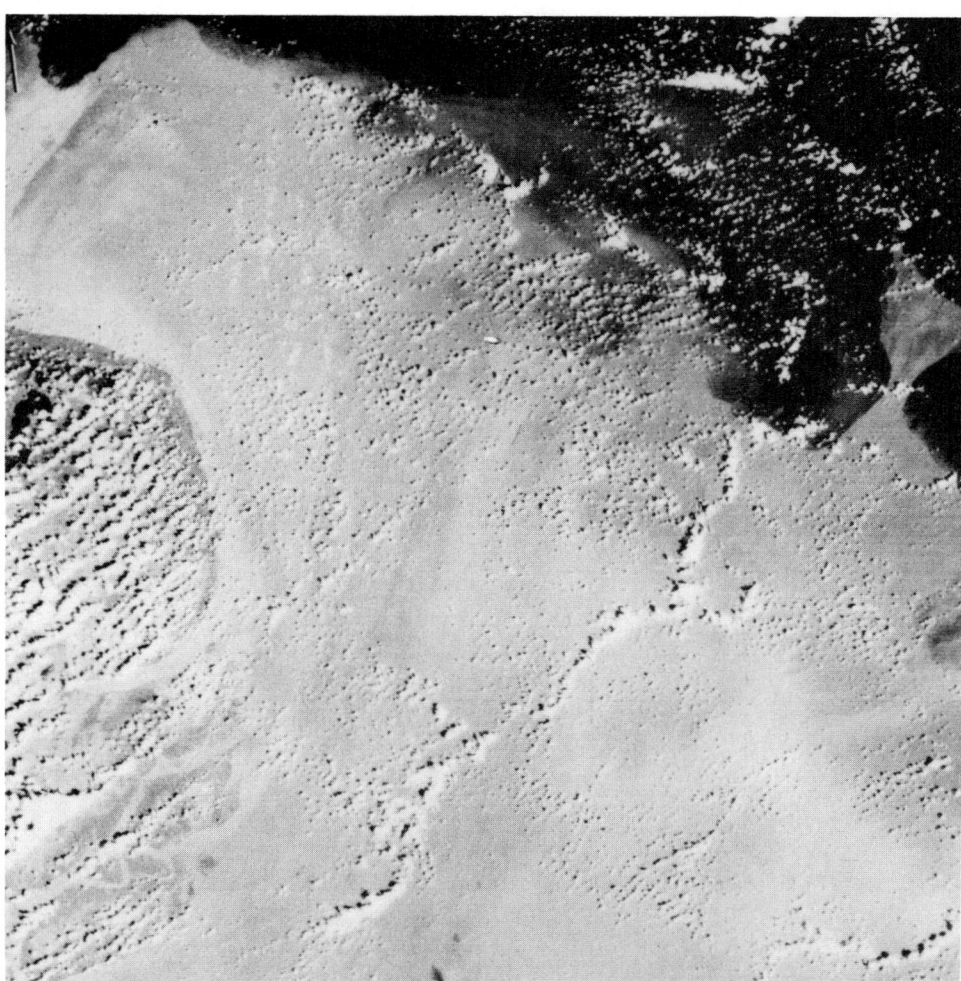

Figure 51. North Channel (Canal do Norte) mouth of the Amazon, the river with the largest drainage basin and with an average discharge rate more than four times higher than that of any other stream. This is a composite photograph from the Landsat-1 satellite taken from an altitude of 568 statute miles (914 kilometers). (Credit: US National Aeronautics and Space Administration.)

TABLE 8a. (Continued)

Latitude and Longitude	River	Outflow and Location	Length mi	Length km	Drainage Basin 1,000 mi2	Drainage Basin 1,000 km2	Discharge Rate 1,000 cfs	Discharge Rate m3/sec
11.54S, 65.01W	•Guapore (alt Itenez)	Mamore R, Bolivia-Brazil	1120	1800	232	600	71	2,000
3.00S, 41.50W	•Parnaiba	Atlantic O, Maranhao-Piaui, Brazil	1060	1700	135	350	85	2,400
11.06N, 74.51W	Magdalena	Caribbean Sea, Colombia	960	1540	100	260	283	8,000
31.42S, 60.44W	Salado (alt Salado del Norte)	Parana R, Santa Fe, Argentina	930	1500	309	800	1.3	38
1.24S, 61.51W	•Branco-Uraricoera	Negro R, Roraima, Brazil	920	1470	75	195	191	5,400
39.50S, 62.08W	Colorado-Salado-Desaguadero-Bermejo	Atlantic O, Buenos Aires, Argentina	890	1430	42	110	4.7	133
4.30S, 73.27W	Maranon	Amazon R, Peru	880	1410				
7.21S, 58.03W	•Teles Pires (alt Sao Manuel, Tres Barras)	Tapajos R, Mato Grosso-Para, Brazil	870	1400			62	1,750
8.54N, 74.28W	Cauca	Magdalena R, Colombia	840	1350	24	63	78	2,200
4.03N, 67.44W	Guaviare	Orinoco R, Colombia	840	1350				
3.55N, 67.42W	Inirida	Guaviare R, Colombia	840	1350				
25.36S, 54.36W	Iguacu (alt Iguazu; for Iguassu)	Parana R, Argentina-Brazil	820	1320	24	62	62	1,750
5.07S, 60.24W	•Aripuana-Roosevelt	Madeira R, Amazonas, Brazil	800	1290				
10.23S, 65.24W	•Beni-Madre de Dios	Madeira R, Bolivia	800	1290	27	69	82	2,310
20.07S, 51.05W	Paranaiba	Parana R, Mato Grosso do Sul-Minas Gerais, Brazil	790	1270			53	1,500
41.02S, 62.47W	Negro-Neuquen	Atlantic O, Buenos Aires-Rio Negro, Argentina	750	1210	48	125	36	1,010
1.23S, 69.25W	Apaporis	Caqueta R, Colombia	750	1200				
2.52S, 44.12W	•Itapecuru	Sao Jose B of Atlantic O, Maranhao, Brazil	750	1200	17	45		
2.43S, 66.57W	•Jutai	Amazon R, Amazonas, Brazil	750	1200	12	31	18	500
4.21S, 70.02W	Javari (alt Yacarana, Yavari)	Amazon R, Brazil-Peru	740	1180	35	91	4.2	120
5.10S, 75.32W	Huallaga	Maranon R, Peru	710	1140	37	95	124	3,500
21.37S, 41.03W	Paraiba do Sul (alt Paraiba)	Atlantic O, Rio de Janeiro, Brazil	710	1140	22	57	12	331
20.40S, 51.35W	•Tiete	Parana R, Sao Paulo, Brazil	700	1130	28	72	13	378
3.04S, 44.35W	•Mearim	Sao Marcos B of Atlantic O, Maranhao, Brazil	680	1100	39	100		
25.21S, 57.42W	Pilcomayo	Paraguay R, Paraguay	680	1100	74	192	7.0	197
15.51S, 38.53W	•Jequitinhonha	Atlantic O, Bahia, Brazil	680	1090	24	62	20	557

26.52S, 58.23W	Bermejo	Paraguay R, Chaco-Formosa, Argentina	660	1060	36	94	11	325
19.37S, 39.49W	•Doce	Atlantic O, Espirito Santo, Brazil	620	1000	32	83	34	969
3.52S, 52.37W	•Iriri	Xingu R, Para, Brazil	620	1000				
6.12N, 67.28W	Meta	Orinoco R, Colombia-Venezuela	620	1000	40	104	88	2,500
0.02N, 67.16W	•Vaupes (alt Uaupes)	Negro R, Amazonas, Brazil	620	1000	27	69		
6.58N, 58.23W	•Essequibo	Atlantic O, Guyana	600	970	50	130	77	2,190
7.37N, 66.25W	Apure-Uribante	Orinoco R, Venezuela	600	960	37	95	67	1,890
8.21N, 62.43W	Caroni	Orinoco R, Venezuela	570	920	10	25	168	4,750
38.49S, 64.57W	Colorado (upper)-Grande	Colorado R, La Pampa, Argentina	570	920				
1.29S, 48.30W	•Guama-Capim	Para R, Para, Brazil	560	900				
22.40S, 53.09W	•Paranapanema	Parana R, Parana-Sao Paulo, Brazil	560	900	22	56	12	348
		* * *						
3.35S, 64.47W	•Tefe	Amazon R, Amazonas, Brazil	560	900				
6.25N, 58.37W	•Mazaruni-Cuyuni	Essequibo R, Guyana	550	880				
3.20S, 72.40W	•Napo	Amazon R, Peru	550	880	8	21	40	1,150
10.44S, 73.45W	Urubamba	Ucayali R, Peru	540	860	14	36	12	340
6.15S, 42.52W	•Caninde	Parnaiba R, Piaui, Brazil	530	860	7	18	14	393
23.18S, 53.42W	•Ivai	Parana R, Parana, Brazil	520	860				
4.26S, 74.05W	Tigre	Maranon R, Peru	500	840	12	31	1.7	49
7.24N, 66.35W	Arauca	Orinoco R, Venezuela	500	810	24	61	45	1,280
43.20S, 65.03W	Chubut	Atlantic O, Chubut, Argentina	500	810	15	39	0.6	17
10.25S, 58.20W	•Arinos	Juruena R, Mato Grosso, Brazil	500	800				
10.58S, 66.09W	•Beni (upper)	Beni R, Bolivia	500	800	27	70	22	637
3.41S, 44.48W	•Grajau	Mearim R, Maranhao, Brazil	500	800				
1.13S, 46.06W	•Gurupi	Atlantic O, Maranhao-Para, Brazil	500	800				
11.47S, 37.32W	•Itapicuru	Atlantic O, Bahia, Brazil	500	800				
11.45S, 50.44W	•Mortes	Araguaia R, Mato Grosso, Brazil	500	800				
33.24S, 58.22W	•Negro	Uruguay R, Uruguay	500	800				
15.39S, 38.57W	•Pardo	Atlantic O, Bahia, Brazil	500	800	17	45	2.2	62
12.28S, 64.24W	•Itonamas-San Miguel	Guapore R, Bolivia	470	760				
17.13S, 44.49W	•Velhas	Sao Francisco R, Minas Gerais, Brazil	470	760				
8.17N, 76.58W	Atrato	G of Uraba of Caribbean Sea, Colombia	470	750	14	35	173	4,900

(Continued)

For an explanation of symbols and abbreviations, see pages 16–17.

TABLE 8a. (Continued)

Latitude and Longitude	River	Outflow and Location	Length		Drainage Basin		Discharge Rate	
			mi	km	1,000 mi2	1,000 km2	1,000 cfs	m3/sec
7.38N, 64.53W	Caura-Merevari	Orinoco R, Venezuela	450	720	19	50	95	2,700
5.43N, 53.58W	•Maroni (alt Marowyne)	Atlantic O, French Guiana-Suriname	420	680	24	62	66	1,850
5.55N, 55.10W	•Suriname	Atlantic O, Suriname	370	600	6	16	16	440
1.55S, 55.35W	•Trombetas	Amazon R, Para, Brazil	340	550	48	124	53	1,500
47.49S, 73.37W	Baker	G of Penas of Pacific O, Chile	270	440	10	25	21	600
6.00N, 57.04W	•Courantyne (alt Corantijn)	Atlantic O, Guyana-Suriname	270	440	26	67	71	2,000
21.26S, 70.04W	Loa	Pacific O, Chile	270	440	13	34	0.06	1.6
36.49S, 73.10W	Bio-Bio	Arauco G of Pacific O, Chile	240	380	9	24	35	1,000

For an explanation of symbols and abbreviations, see pages 16–17.

8b. Longest Rivers, Irrespective of Continent

Contents

Rank.

Conventional and other names of river and of its tributaries (if any) constituting the longest watercourse.

Outflow (sea, lake, river, etc) and division and country in which located.

Total length of watercourse, in miles and kilometers.

Coverage

50 longest rivers.

Rounding

Lengths are rounded to the nearest 10 mi (km).

Entries

50.

TABLE 8b. LONGEST RIVERS, IRRESPECTIVE OF CONTINENT

Rank	River	Outflow and Location	Length mi	Length km
1.	•Nile (off Nil)-Kagera-Ruvuvu-Luvironza	Mediterranean Sea, Egypt	4140	6670
2.	•Amazon (off Amazonas)-Ucayali-Tambo-Ene-Apurimac	Atlantic O, Amapa-Para, Brazil	4080	6570
3.	Yangtze (off Chang)	East China Sea, Jiangsu, China	3720	5980
4.	Mississippi-Missouri-Jefferson-Beaverhead-Red Rock	G of Mexico, Louisiana, USA	3710	5970
5.	Yenisey (alt Yenisei)-Angara-Selenga (alt Selenge)-Ider	Yenisey G of Kara Sea, Russia, USSR	3650	5870
6.	Amur (alt Heilong, Heilung)-Argun (alt Ergun, Oerhkuna)-Kerulen (alt Kolulun; off Herlen)	Tatar Strait, Russia, USSR	3590	5780
7.	Ob-Irtysh (alt Irtish)	G of Ob of Kara Sea, Russia, USSR	3360	5410
8.	Plata-Parana-Grande	Atlantic O, Argentina-Uruguay	3030	4880
9.	Huang (alt Hwang, Yellow)	G of Chihli of Yellow Sea, Shandong, China	3010	4840
10.	Congo (alt Zaire; for Kongo)-Lualaba	Atlantic O, Angola-Zaire	2880	4630
11.	Lena	Laptev Sea, Russia, USSR	2730	4400
12.	Mackenzie-Slave-Peace-Finlay	Beaufort Sea, NWT, Canada	2630	4240
13.	•Mekong (alt Khong, Lancang, Lantsang, Mekongk, Tien Giang)	South China Sea, Vietnam	2600	4180
14.	•Niger	G of Guinea, Nigeria	2550	4100
15.	Murray-Darling-Culgoa-Balonne-Condamine	Indian O, South Australia, Australia	2330	3750
16.	Volga	Caspian (Sea) L, Russia, USSR	2190	3530

For an explanation of symbols and abbreviations, see pages 16–17.   (Continued)

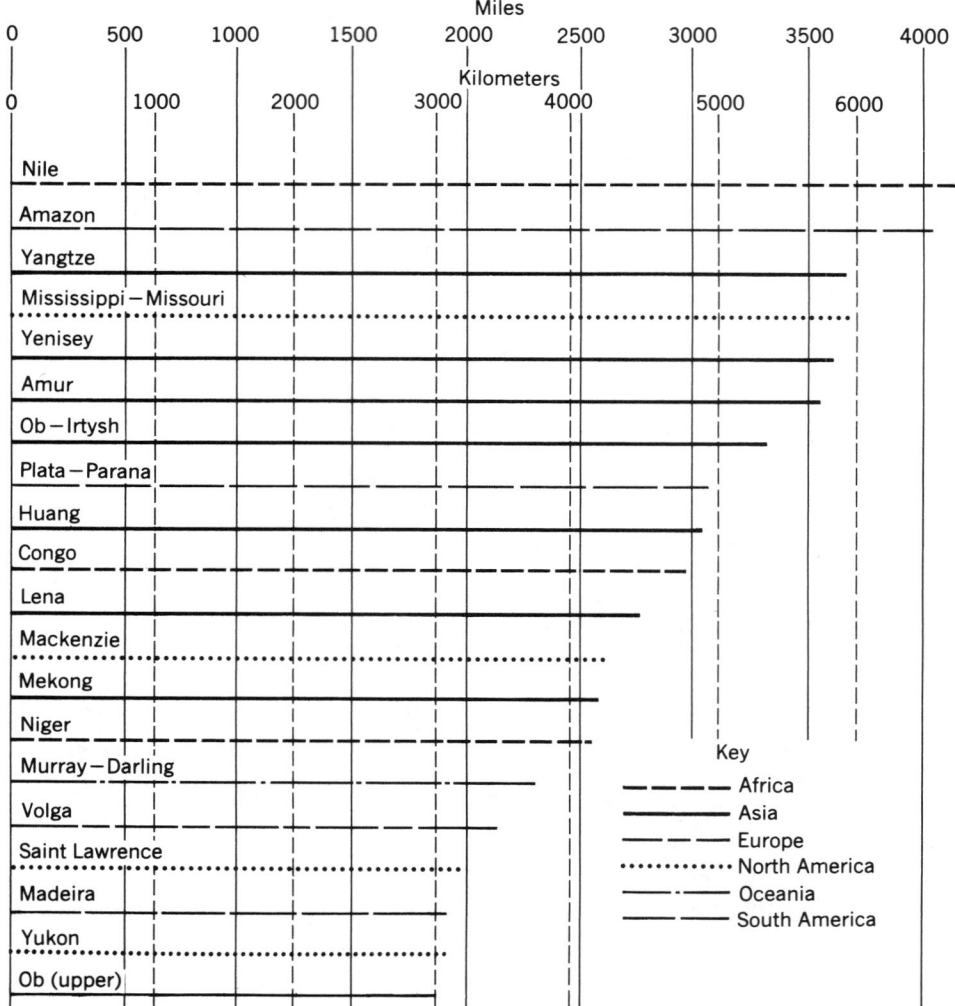

Figure 52. Twenty longest rivers.

TABLE 8b. (Continued)

Rank	River	Outflow and Location	Length	
			mi	km
17.	Saint Lawrence (alt Saint-Laurent)-(Great Lakes)-Saint Louis	G of Saint Lawrence, Quebec, Canada	2060	3320
18.	•Madeira-Mamore-Grande (alt Guapay)	Amazon R, Amazonas, Brazil	1990	3200
19.	Yukon-Lewes-Teslin-Nisutlin	Bering Sea, Alaska, USA	1980	3180
20.	Ob (upper)-Katun	Ob R, Russia, USSR	1970	3180
21.	Rio Grande (alt Bravo)	G of Mexico, Mexico-USA	1880	3030
22.	Syr (Darya)-Naryn-Bolshoy Naryn	Aral (Sea) L, Kazakhstan, USSR	1880	3020
23.	•Jurua (alt Yurua)	Amazon R, Amazonas, Brazil	1860	3000
23.	•Purus	Amazon R, Amazonas, Brazil	1860	3000
25.	Lower Tunguska (off Nizhnyaya Tunguska)	Yenisey R, Russia, USSR	1860	2990
26.	Indus (alt Yintu)	Arabian Sea, Pakistan	1790	2880
27.	Danube (off Donau, Duna, Dunaj, Dunarea, Dunav, Dunay)	Black Sea, Romania-USSR	1780	2860
28.	Brahmaputra (alt Tsangpo, Yarlung Zangbo, Yalutsangpu)	B of Bengal, Bangladesh	1770	2840
29.	•Salween (alt Khong, Lu, Nu)	G of Martaban cf Andaman Sea, Burma	1750	2820
30.	Sao Franscisco	Atlantic O, Alagoas-Sergipe, Brazil	1730	2780
31.	Para-Tocantins	Atlantic O, Para, Brazil	1710	2750
31.	Tarim (alt Talimu)-Yarkant (alt Yeherhchiang; for Yarkand)	Tarim Basin, Xinjiang, China	1710	2750
33.	Vilyuy (alt Vilyui)	Lena R, Russia, USSR	1650	2650
33.	•Zambezi (alt Zambesi, Zambeze)	Mozambique Channel, Mozambique	1650	2650
35.	Paraguay (alt Paraguai)	Parana R, Argentina-Paraguay	1610	2600
36.	Nelson-Saskatchewan-South Saskatchewan-Bow	Hudson B, Manitoba, Canada	1600	2570
37.	Amu (Darya) (alt Oxus)-Panj (alt Pyandzh)-Vakhan	Aral (Sea) L, Uzbekistan, USSR	1580	2540
38.	•Ganges (alt Ganga)-Bhagirathi	B of Bengal, Bangladesh-India	1560	2510
38.	Kolyma (alt Kolima)-Kulu	East Siberian Sea, Russia, USSR	1560	2510
40.	•Ubangi (alt Oubangui)-Uele-Kibali	Congo R, Congo-Zaire	1530	2460
41.	Ishim	Irtysh R, Russia, USSR	1520	2450
42.	(Shatt al) Arab-Euphrates (off Firat, Furat)-Kara Su	Persian G, Iran-Iraq	1510	2430
42.	Ural	Caspian (Sea) L, Kazakhstan, USSR	1510	2430
44.	Arkansas	Mississippi R, Arkansas, USA	1460	2350
45.	Colorado	G of California, Baja California-Sonora, Mexico	1450	2330
46.	•Caqueta (alt Japura, Yapura)	Amazon R, Amazonas, Brazil	1420	2280
47.	Aldan	Lena R, Russia, USSR	1410	2270
47.	Olenek	Laptev Sea, Russia, USSR	1410	2270
49.	Atchafalaya-Red	G of Mexico, Louisiana, USA	1400	2260
50.	Orange (alt Oranje)	Atlantic O, Namibia-South Africa	1400	2250

For an explanation of symbols and abbreviations, see pages 16–17.

8c. Rivers with Largest Drainage Basins

Contents

Rank.

Conventional and other names of river and of its tributaries (if any) constituting the longest watercourse.

Outflow (sea, lake, river, etc) and division and country in which located.

Area of drainage basin of river and all its tributaries, in thousands of square miles and square kilometers.

Coverage

50 rivers with the largest drainage basins.

Rounding

Drainage basin areas are rounded to the nearest 1,000 mi² (km²).

Entries

50.

TABLE 8c. RIVERS WITH LARGEST DRAINAGE BASINS

			Drainage Basin	
Rank	**River**	**Outflow and Location**	**1,000 mi²**	**1,000 km²**
1.	•Amazon (off Amazonas)-Ucayali-Tambo-Ene-Apurimac	Atlantic O, Amapa-Para, Brazil	2375	6150
2.	Congo (alt Zaire; for Kongo)-Lualaba	Atlantic O, Angola-Zaire	1476	3822
3.	•Nile (off Nil)-Kagera-Ruvuvu-Luvironza	Mediterranean Sea, Egypt	1293	3349
4.	Missisippi-Missouri-Jefferson-Beaverhead-Red Rock	G of Mexico, Louisiana, USA	1247	3230
5.	Plata-Parana-Grande	Atlantic O, Argentina-Uruguay	1197	3100
6.	Ob-Irtysh (alt Irtish)	G of Ob of Kara Sea, Russia, USSR	1154	2990
7.	Yenisey (alt Yenisei)-Angara-Selenga (alt Selenge)-Ider	Yenisey G of Kara Sea, Russia, USSR	996	2580
8.	Lena	Laptev Sea, Russia, USSR	961	2490
9.	•Niger	G of Guinea, Nigeria	808	2092
10.	Amur (alt Heilong, Heilung)-Argun (alt Ergun, Oerhkuna)-Kerulen (alt Kolulun; off Herlen)	Tatar Strait, Russia, USSR	716	1855
11.	Yangtze (off Chang)	East China Sea, Jiangsu, China	705	1827
12.	Mackenzie-Slave-Peace-Finlay	Beaufort Sea, NWT, Canada	690	1787
13.	Saint Lawrence (alt Saint-Laurent)-(Great Lakes)-Saint Louis	G of Saint Lawrence, Quebec, Canada	550	1424
14.	Volga	Caspian (Sea) L, Russia, USSR	525	1360

TABLE 8c. (Continued)

Rank	River	Outflow and Location	Drainage Basin	
			1,000 mi²	1,000 km²
15.	•Zambezi (alt Zambesi, Zambeze)	Mozambique Channel, Mozambique	514	1331
16.	•Madeira-Mamore-Grande (alt Guapay)	Amazon R, Amazonas, Brazil	463	1200
17.	Indus (alt Yintu)	Arabian Sea, Pakistan	450	1165
18.	Nelson-Saskatchewan-South Saskatchewan-Bow	Hudson B, Manitoba, Canada	437	1132
19.	(Shatt al) Arab-Euphrates (off Firat, Furat)-Kara Su	Persian G, Iran-Iraq	427	1105
20.	Paraguay (alt Paraguai)	Parana R, Argentina-Paraguay	425	1100
21.	Murray-Darling-Culgoa-Balonne-Condamine	Indian O, South Australia, Australia	408	1057
22.	•Negro (alt Guainia)	Amazon R, Amazonas, Brazil	386	1000
23.	•Ganges (alt Ganga)-Bhagirathi	B of Bengal, Bangladesh-India	368	952
24.	•Kasai (alt Cassai)	Congo R, Zaire	349	904
25.	Orinoco	Atlantic O, Venezuela	340	880
26.	Orange (alt Oranje)	Atlantic O, Namibia-South Africa	330	855
27.	Yukon-Lewes-Teslin-Nisutlin	Bering Sea, Alaska, USA	328	850
28.	Para-Tocantins	Atlantic O, Para, Brazil	323	836
29.	Danube (off Donau, Duna, Dunaj, Dunarea, Dunav, Dunay)	Black Sea, Romania-USSR	315	816
30.	•Mekong (alt Khong, Lancang, Lantsang, Mekongk, Tien Giang)	South China Sea, Vietnam	313	811
31.	Salado (alt Salado del Norte)	Parana R, Santa Fe, Argentina	309	800
32.	•Okovanggo (alt Cubango, Okavango)	Okovanggo Basin, Botswana	303	785
33.	•Ubangi (alt Oubangui)-Uele-Kibali	Congo R, Congo-Zaire	298	773
34.	Huang (alt Hwang, Yellow)	G of Chihli of Yellow Sea, Shandong, China	297	771
35.	Ob (upper)-Katun	Ob R, Russia, USSR	295	765
36.	Aldan	Lena R, Russia, USSR	281	729
37.	•Shari (alt Chari)-Sara (alt Ouham)	Chad L, Cameroon-Chad	270	700
38.	Columbia-Snake	Pacific O, Oregon-Washington, USA	258	668
39.	Kolyma (alt Kolima)-Kulu	East Siberian Sea, Russia, USSR	250	647
40.	Colorado	G of California, Baja California-Sonora, Mexico	247	640
41.	Sao Francisco	Atlantic O, Alagoas-Sergipe, Brazil	236	611
42.	•Guapore (alt Itenez)	Mamore R, Bolivia-Brazil	232	600
43.	Brahmaputra (alt Tsangpo, Yarlung Zangbo, Yalutsangpu)	B of Bengal, Bangladesh	224	580
44.	Panjnad-Sutlej	Indus R, Pakistan	206	533
45.	Ohio-Allegheny	Mississippi R, Illinois-Kentucky, USA	204	528

For an explanation of symbols and abbreviations, see pages 16–17.

(Continued)

TABLE 8c. (Continued)

Rank	River	Outflow and Location	Drainage Basin	
			1,000 mi²	1,000 km²
46.	Sungari (alt Sunghua; off Songhua)	Amur R, Heilongjiang, China	202	524
47.	Kama	Volga R, Russia, USSR	196	507
48.	Dnieper (off Dnepr)	Black Sea, Ukraine, USSR	195	504
49.	Lower Tunguska (off Nizhny-aya Tunguska)	Yenisey R, Russia, USSR	183	473
50.	•Tapajos-Juruena	Amazon R, Para, Brazil	179	463

For an explanation of symbols and abbreviations, see pages 16–17.

8d. Rivers with Highest Discharge Rates

Contents

Rank.

Conventional and other names of river and of its tributaries (if any) constituting the longest watercourse.

Outflow (sea, lake, river, etc) and division and country in which located.

Average discharge rate, in thousands of cubic feet per second and in cubic meters per second. The discharge rate given is that of the main stream, preferably averaged over several recent years and measured at the gauging station registering the greatest discharge (or nearest the mouth of the river).

Coverage

50 rivers with the highest average discharge rates.

Rounding

Discharge rates are rounded to the nearest 1,000 cfs and to the nearest 10 m³/sec.

Entries

51.

TABLE 8d. RIVERS WITH HIGHEST DISCHARGE RATES

Rank	River	Outflow and Location	Discharge Rate	
			1,000 cfs	m³/sec
1.	•Amazon (off Amazonas)-Ucayali-Tambo-Ene-Apurimac	Atlantic O, Amapa-Para, Brazil	6180	175,000
2.	Congo (alt Zaire; for Kongo)-Lualaba	Atlantic O, Angola-Zaire	1377	39,000
3.	•Negro (alt Guainia)	Amazon R, Amazonas, Brazil	1236	35,000
4.	Yangtze (off Chang)	East China Sea, Jiangsu, China	1137	32,190
5.	Orinoco	Atlantic O, Venezuela	890	25,200
6.	Plata-Parana-Grande	Atlantic O, Argentina-Uruguay	809	22,900

TABLE 8d. (Continued)

Rank	River	Outflow and Location	Discharge Rate	
			1,000 cfs	m³/sec
7.	•Madeira-Mamore-Grande (alt Guapay)	Amazon R, Amazonas, Brazil	770	21,800
8.	Brahmaputra (alt Tsangpo, Yarlung Zangbo, Yalutsangpu)	B of Bengal, Bangladesh	678	19,200
9.	Yenisey (alt Yenisei)-Angara-Selenga-(alt Selenge)-Ider	Yenisey G of Kara Sea, Russia, USSR	622	17,600
10.	Lena	Laptev Sea, Russia, USSR	586	16,600
11.	Mississippi-Missouri-Jefferson-Beaverhead-Red Rock	G of Mexico, Louisiana, USA	531	15,040
12.	•Mekong (alt Khong, Lancang, Lantsang, Mekongk, Tien Giang)	South China Sea, Vietnam	501	14,200
13.	•Irrawaddy (off Iyawadi)-Nmai	Andaman Sea, Burma	447	12,660
14.	•Purus	Amazon R, Amazonas, Brazil	445	12,600
15.	Zhu (alt Canton, Chu, Pearl, Yueh)-Xi (alt Hsi, Si, West)-Hongshui (alt Hungshui)-Nanpan	South China Sea, Guangdong, China	441	12,500
16.	Ob-Irtysh (alt Irtish)	G of Ob of Kara Sea, Russia, USSR	438	12,400
17.	•Ganges (alt Ganga)-Bhagirathi	B of Bengal, Bangladesh-India	411	11,650
18.	Saint Lawrence (alt Saint-Laurent)-(Great Lakes)-Saint Louis	G of Saint Lawrence, Quebec, Canada	355	10,050
19.	•Salween (alt Khong, Lu, Nu)	G of Martaban of Andaman Sea, Burma	353	10,000
20.	•Kasai (alt Cassai)	Congo R, Zaire	351	9,950
21.	Amur (alt Heilong, Heilung)-Argun (alt Ergun, Oerhkuna)-Kerulen (alt Kolulun; off Herlen)	Tatar Strait, Russia, USSR	348	9,860
22.	Mackenzie-Slave-Peace-Finlay	Beaufort Sea, NWT, Canada	316	8,940
23.	Para-Tocantins	Atlantic O, Para, Brazil	305	8,630
24.	Volga	Caspian (Sea) L, Russia, USSR	285	8,060
25.	Magdalena	Caribbean Sea, Colombia	283	8,000
26.	Ohio-Allegheny	Mississippi R, Illinois-Kentucky, USA	272	7,710
27.	Solo (alt Bengawan)	Java Sea, Java I, Indonesia	268	7,600
28.	•Ubangi (alt Oubangui)-Uele-Kibali	Congo R, Congo-Zaire	265	7,500
29.	•Zambezi (alt Zambesi, Zambeze)	Mozambique Channel, Mozambique	250	7,070
30.	•Caqueta (alt Japura, Yapura)	Amazon R, Amazonas, Brazil	247	7,000
31.	Atchafalaya-Red	G of Mexico, Louisiana, USA	247	6,990
32.	Indus (alt Yintu)	Arabian Sea, Pakistan	235	6,640
33.	Yukon-Lewes-Teslin-Nisutlin	Bering Sea, Alaska, USA	223	6,310
34.	Danube (off Donau, Duna, Dunaj, Dunarea, Dunav, Dunay)	Black Sea, Romania-USSR	221	6,250
35.	•Araguaia	Tocantins R, Para, Brazil	217	6,140
36.	•Tapajos-Juruena	Amazon R, Para, Brazil	212	6,000
37.	•Niger	G of Guinea, Nigeria	201	5,700
38.	Uruguay (alt Uruguai)-Canoas	Plata R, Argentina-Uruguay	194	5,500
39.	Columbia-Snake	Pacific O, Oregon-Washington, USA	194	5,490

For an explanation of symbols and abbreviations, see pages 16–17.

(Continued)

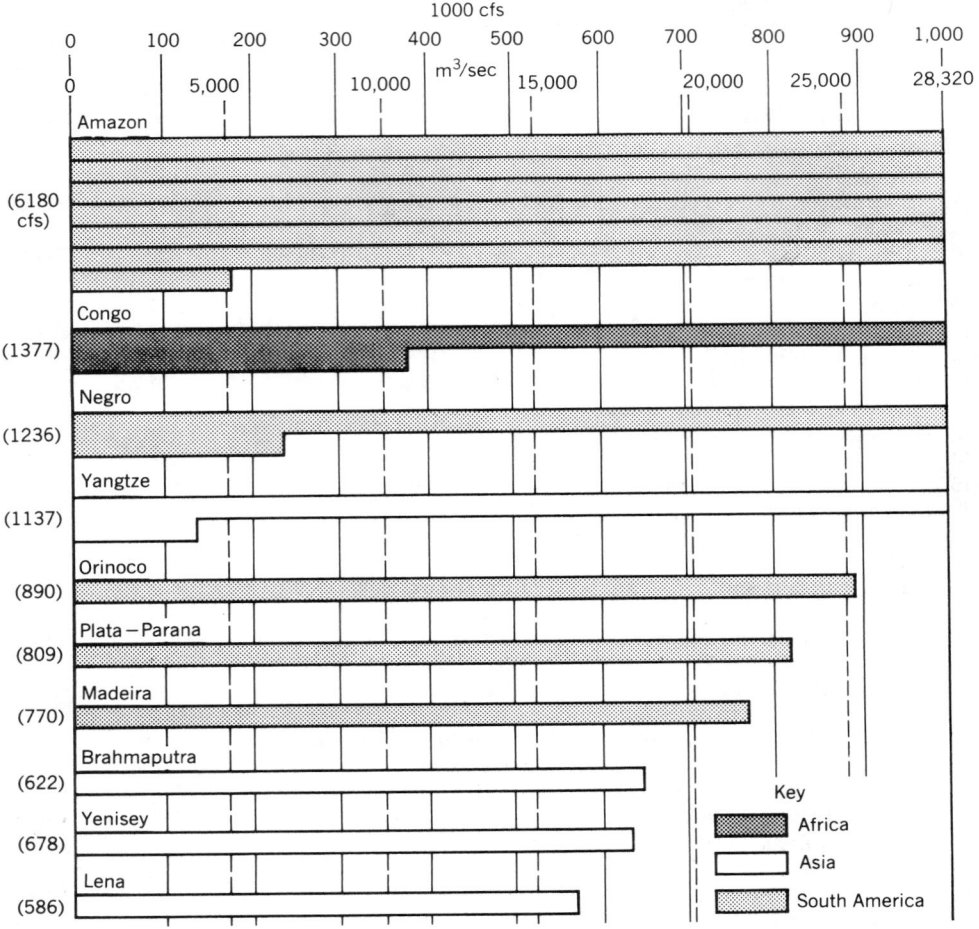

Figure 53. *Ten rivers with highest average discharge rates.*

TABLE 8d. (Continued)

Rank	River	Outflow and Location	Discharge Rate 1,000 cfs	Discharge Rate m³/sec
40.	Branco-Uraricoera	Negro R, Roraima, Brazil	191	5,400
41.	Aldan	Lena R, Russia, USSR	177	5,010
42.	•Putumayo (alt Ica)	Amazon R, Amazonas, Brazil	177	5,000
43.	Ob (upper)-Katun	Ob R, Russia, USSR	174	4,920
44.	Atrato	G of Uraba of Caribbean Sea, Colombia	173	4,900
45.	Caroni	Orinoco R, Venezuela	168	4,750
46.	•Ogooue (alt Ogowe)	G of Guinea, Gabon	165	4,670
47.	•Fly-Strickland	G of Papua of Coral Sea, Papua New Guinea	157	4,450
48.	Paraguay (alt Paraguai)	Parana R, Argentina-Paraguay	155	4,400
49.	Chindwin	Irrawaddy R, Burma	141	4,000
49.	•Jurua (alt Yurua)	Amazon R, Amazonas, Brazil	141	4,000
49.	Pechora (for Petchora)	Barents Sea, Russia, USSR	141	4,000

For an explanation of symbols and abbreviations, see pages 16–17.

8e. Longest River in Each Country

Contents

Conventional name of country.

Conventional and other names of river and of its tributaries (if any) constituting the longest watercourse.

Outflow (sea, lake, river, etc) and division and country in which located.

Total length of watercourse, in miles and kilometers.

Coverage

All countries with an area of at least 500 mi² (1,295 km²) that have a river of significant length.

Rounding

Lengths are rounded to the nearest 10 mi (km).

Entries

144.

TABLE 8e. (Continued)

Country	River	Outflow and Location	Length mi	Length km
Afghanistan	Amu (Darya) (alt Oxus)-Panj (alt Pyandzh)-Vakhan	Aral (Sea) L, Uzbekistan, USSR	1580	2540
Albania	Drin	Adriatic Sea, Albania	170	280
Algeria	•Sheliff (alt Cheliff; off Shalaf)	Mediterranean Sea, Algeria	430	700
Angola	Congo (alt Zaire; for Kongo)-Lualaba	Atlantic O, Angola-Zaire	2880	4630
Argentina	Plata-Parana-Grande	Atlantic O, Argentina-Uruguay	3030	4880
Australia	Murray-Darling-Culgoa-Balonne-Condamine	Indian O, South Australia, Australia	2330	3750
Austria	Danube (off in Austria Donau)	Black Sea, Romania-USSR	1780	2860
Bangladesh	Brahmaputra (alt Tsangpo, Yarlung Zangbo, Yalut-sangpu)	B of Bengal, Bangladesh	1770	2840
Belgium	Meuse (alt Maas)	North Sea, Netherlands	590	950
Belize	•Belize	Caribbean Sea, Belize	180	290
Benin	•Niger	G of Guinea, Nigeria	2550	4100
Bhutan	•Manas	Brahmaputra R, Assam, India	220	350
Bolivia	•Madeira-Mamore-Grande (alt Guapay)	Amazon R, Amazonas, Brazil	1990	3200
Botswana	•Zambezi (alt Zambesi, Zambeze)	Mozambique Channel, Mozambique	1650	2650
Brazil	•Amazon (off Amazonas)-Ucayali-Tambo-Ene-Apurimac	Atlantic O, Amapa-Para, Brazil	4080	6570
Brunei	•Limbang	South China Sea, Brunei-Malaysia	120	200
Bulgaria	Danube (off in Bulgaria Dunav)	Black Sea, Romania-USSR	1780	2860
Burkina Faso	•Volta-Black Volta (alt Volta Noire)	G of Guinea, Ghana	990	1600
Burma	•Mekong (alt Khong, Lancang, Lantsang, Mekongk, Tien Giang)	South China Sea, Vietnam	2600	4180
Burundi	•Nile (off Nil)-Kagera-Ruvuvu-Luvironza	Mediterranean Sea, Egypt	4140	6670
Cameroon	•Shari (alt Chari)-Sara (alt Ouham)	Chad L, Cameroon-Chad	900	1450
Canada	Mackenzie-Slave-Peace-Finlay	Beaufort Sea, NWT, Canada	2630	4240
Central African Republic	•Ubangi (alt Oubangui)-Uele-Kibali	Congo R, Congo-Zaire	1530	2460
Chad	•Shari (alt Chari)-Sara (alt Ouham)	Chad L, Cameroon-Chad	900	1450
Chile	Baker	G of Penas of Pacific O, Chile	270	440
	Loa	Pacific O, Chile	270	440
China	Yangtze (off Chang)	East China Sea, Jiangsu, China	3720	5980

TABLE 8e. (Continued)

Country	River	Outflow and Location	Length	
			mi	km
Colombia	•Amazon (off Amazonas)-Ucayali-Tambo-Ene-Apurimac	Atlantic O, Amapa-Para, Brazil	4080	6570
Congo	Congo (alt Zaire; for Kongo)-Lualaba	Atlantic O, Angola-Zaire	2880	4630
Costa Rica	•San Juan	Caribbean Sea, Costa Rica-Nicaragua	140	220
Cuba	Cauto	G of Guacanayabo of Caribbean Sea, Cuba	230	370
Cyprus	•Pedias	Mediterranean Sea, Cyprus	62	100
Czechoslovakia	Danube (off in Czechoslovakia Dunaj)	Black Sea, Romania-USSR	1780	2860
Denmark	Gudena	Kattegat, Denmark	100	160
Dominican Republic	Yaque del Norte	Atlantic O, Dominican Republic	170	280
Ecuador	•Putumayo (alt Ica)	Amazon R, Amazonas, Brazil	1240	2000
Egypt	•Nile (off Nil)-Kagera-Ruvuvu-Luvironza	Mediterranean Sea, Egypt	4140	6670
El Salvador	Lempa	Pacific O, El Salvador	200	320
Equatorial Guinea	•Benito	G of Guinea, Equatorial Guinea	200	320
Ethiopia	•Shebele (alt Shabale, Shabeelle, Shibeli; for Scebeli)	Balli Swamp, Somalia	1200	1930
Fiji	Rewa	Pacific O, Viti Levu I, Fiji	95	150
Finland	Torne (alt Tornio)-Muonio-Konkama (alt Kongama)	G of Bothnia of Baltic Sea, Finland	350	570
France	Rhine (off in France Rhin)	North Sea, Netherlands	820	1320
French Guiana	•Maroni (alt Marowyne)	Atlantic O, French Guiana-Suriname	420	680
Gabon	•Ogooue (alt Ogowe)	G of Guinea, Gabon	750	1210
Gambia	Gambia (alt Gambie)	Atlantic O, Gambia	700	1130
Germany East	Elbe (alt Labe)	North Sea, Niedersachsen-Schleswig-Holstein, West Germany	720	1160
West	Danube (off in Germany Donau)	Black Sea, Romania-USSR	1780	2860
Ghana	•Volta-Black Volta (alt Volta Noire)	G of Guinea, Ghana	990	1600
Greece	Maritsa (off in Greece Evros)	Aegean Sea, Greece-Turkey	300	490
Guatemala	Usumacinta-Chixoy	B of Campeche of G of Mexico, Tabasco, Mexico	690	1110
Guinea	•Niger	G of Guinea, Nigeria	2550	4100
Guinea-Bissau	•Geba-Corubal (alt Koliba)	Atlantic O, Guinea-Bissau	350	560
Guyana	•Essequibo	Atlantic O, Guyana	600	970
Haiti	Artibonite	G of Gonave of Caribbean Sea, Haiti	170	280

For an explanation of symbols and abbreviations, see pages 16–17.

(Continued)

TABLE 8e. (Continued)

Country	River	Outflow and Location	Length mi	Length km
Honduras	•Coco (alt Segovia)	Caribbean Sea, Honduras-Nicaragua	470	750
Hungary	Danube (off in Hungary Duna)	Black Sea, Romania-USSR	1780	2860
Iceland	•Thjorsa	Atlantic O, Iceland	140	230
India	Brahmaputra (alt Tsangpo, Yarlung Zangbo, Yalutsangpu)	B of Bengal, Bangladesh	1770	2840
Indonesia in Asia	Kapuas (alt Kapuas-Besar; for Kapoeas)	South China Sea, Borneo I, Indonesia	630	1010
in Oceania (Irian Jaya)	Mamberamo-Taritatu (for Idenburg)	Pacific O, Irian Jaya, Indonesia	420	670
Iran	(Shatt al) Arab-Euphrates (off in Iran Furat)-Kara Su	Persian G, Iran-Iraq	1510	2430
Iraq	(Shatt al) Arab-Euphrates (off in Iraq Furat)-Kara Su	Persian G, Iran-Iraq	1510	2430
Ireland	Shannon	Atlantic O, Ireland	230	370
Israel	•Jordan (off in Israel Yarden)	Dead (Sea) L, Jordan-West Bank	160	250
Italy	Po	Adriatic Sea, Veneto, Italy	380	620
Ivory Coast	•Volta-Black Volta (alt Volta Noire)	G of Guinea, Ghana	990	1600
Jamaica	Minho	Caribbean Sea, Jamaica	57	92
Japan	Shinano	Sea of Japan, Honshu I, Japan	230	370
Jordan	•Jordan (off in Jordan Urdunn)	Dead (Sea) L, Jordan-West Bank	160	250
Kampuchea	•Mekong (off in Kampuchea Mekongk)	South China Sea, Vietnam	2600	4180
Kenya	•Tana	Indian O, Kenya	440	710
Korea North	Yalu (alt Amnok)	Korea B of Yellow Sea, China-North Korea	500	810
South	Naktong (for Rakuti)	Korea Strait, South Korea	330	520
Laos	•Mekong (off in Laos Khong)	South China Sea, Vietnam	2600	4180
Lebanon	Orontes (off Asi)	Mediterranean Sea, Turkey	350	570
Lesotho	Orange (alt Oranje)	Atlantic O, Namibia-South Africa	1400	2250
Liberia	•Cavally (alt Cavalla)	Atlantic O, Ivory Coast-Liberia	320	510
Luxembourg	Moselle (alt Mosel)	Rhine R, Rheinland-Pfalz, West Germany	340	550
Madagascar	•Mangoky	Mozambique Channel, Madagascar	350	560
Malawi	•Shire (alt Chire)	Zambezi R, Mozambique	370	600
Malaysia Peninsular	•Pahang	South China Sea, Peninsular Malaysia, Malaysia	200	320
Sabah	Kinabatangan	Sulu Sea, Sabah, Malaysia	350	560
Sarawak	Rajang	South China Sea, Sarawak, Malaysia	350	560
Mali	•Niger	G of Guinea, Nigeria	2550	4100

TABLE 8e. (Continued)

Country	River	Outflow and Location	Length mi	Length km
Mauritania	Senegal-Bafing	Atlantic O, Mauritania-Senegal	1050	1700
Mexico	Rio Grande (off in Mexico Bravo)	G of Mexico, Mexico-USA	1880	3030
Mongolia	Yenisey (alt Yenisei)-Angara-Selenga (alt Selenge)-Ider	Yenisey G of Kara Sea, Russia, USSR	3650	5870
Morocco	•Oum er Rbia	Atlantic O, Morocco	370	600
Mozambique	•Zambezi (alt Zambesi, Zambeze)	Mozambique Channel, Mozambique	1650	2650
Namibia	•Zambezi (alt Zambesi, Zambeze)	Mozambique Channel, Mozambique	1650	2650
Nepal	Ghaghara (alt Gogra, Kauriala)	Ganges R, Bihar-Uttar Pradesh, India	670	1080
Netherlands	Rhine (off in Netherlands Rijn)	North Sea, Netherlands	820	1320
New Caledonia	Diahot	Coral Sea, New Caledonia	56	90
New Zealand	Waikato	Tasman Sea, North Island, New Zealand	260	420
Nicaragua	•Coco (alt Segovia)	Caribbean Sea, Honduras-Nicaragua	470	750
Niger	•Niger	G of Guinea, Nigeria	2550	4100
Nigeria	•Niger	G of Guinea, Nigeria	2550	4100
Norway	Glomma (off Glama)	Skagerrak, Norway	370	600
Pakistan	Indus (alt Yintu)	Arabian Sea, Pakistan	1790	2880
Panama	•Chepo (alt Bayano)	G of Panama of Pacific O, Panama	100	160
Papua New Guinea	•Fly-Strickland	G of Papua of Coral Sea, Papua New Guinea	800	1290
Paraguay	Plata-Parana-Grande	Atlantic O, Argentina-Uruguay	3030	4880
Peru	•Amazon (off Amazonas)-Ucayali-Tambo-Ene-Apurimac	Atlantic O, Amapa-Para, Brazil	4080	6570
Philippines	•Cagayan (alt Grande de Cagayan)	Babuyan Channel, Luzon I, Philippines	220	350
Poland	Vistula (for Visla, Weichsel; off Wisla)-Bug (alt Zapadnyy Bug)	G of Danzig of Baltic Sea, Poland	750	1200
Portugal (in Europe)	Tagus (off in Portugal Tejo)	Atlantic O, Portugal	630	1010
Puerto Rico	•Plata	Atlantic O, Puerto Rico	45	72
Romania	Danube (off in Romania Dunarea)	Black Sea, Romania-USSR	1780	2860
Rwanda	•Nile (off Nil)-Kagera-Ruvuvu-Luvironza	Mediterranean Sea, Egypt	4140	6670
Senegal	Senegal-Bafing	Atlantic O, Mauritania-Senegal	1050	1700
Sierra Leone	•Sierra Leone-Rokel	Atlantic O, Sierra Leone	270	440
Somalia	•Shebele (alt Shabale, Shabeelle, Shibeli; for Scebeli)	Balli Swamp, Somalia	1200	1930
South Africa	Orange (alt Oranje)	Atlantic O, Namibia-South Africa	1400	2250

For an explanation of symbols and abbreviations, see pages 16–17.

(Continued)

TABLE 8e. (Continued)

Country	River	Outflow and Location	Length mi	Length km
Spain (in Europe)	Tagus (off in Spain Tajo)	Atlantic O, Portugal	630	1010
Sri Lanka	Mahaweli Ganga	Indian O, Sri Lanka	210	330
Sudan	•Nile (off Nil)-Kagera-Ruvuvu-Luvironza	Mediterranean Sea, Egypt	4140	6670
Suriname	•Maroni (off in Suriname Marowyne)	Atlantic O, French Guiana-Suriname	420	680
Swaziland	•Komati (alt Incomati)	Delagoa B of Indian O, Mozambique	500	800
Sweden	Gota-Klar	Kattegat, Sweden	450	720
Switzerland	Rhine (off in Switzerland Rhein, Rhin)	North Sea, Netherlands	820	1320
Syria	(Shatt al) Arab-Euphrates (off in Syria Furat)-Kara Su	Persian G, Iran-Iraq	1510	2430
Taiwan	Choshui	Formosa Strait, Taiwan	120	190
Tanzania	•Nile (off Nil)-Kagera-Ruvuvu-Luvironza	Mediterranean Sea, Egypt	4140	6670
Thailand	•Mekong (off in Thailand Khong)	South China Sea, Vietnam	2600	4180
Togo	•Oti	Volta R, Ghana	340	550
Trinidad and Tobago	•Ortoire	Atlantic O, Trinidad I, Trinidad and Tobago	31	50
Tunisia	•Medjerda (off Majardah)	G of Tunis of Mediterranean Sea, Tunisia	230	360
Turkey				
in Asia	(Shatt al) Arab-Euphrates (off in Turkey Firat)-Kara Su	Persian G, Iran-Iraq	1510	2430
in Europe	Maritsa (off in Turkey Meric)	Aegean Sea, Greece-Turkey	300	490
Uganda	•Nile (off Nil)-Kagera-Ruvuvu-Luvironza	Mediterranean Sea, Egypt	4140	6670
UK	Severn	Bristol Channel, England, UK	210	340
Uruguay	Plata-Parana-Grande	Atlantic O, Argentina-Uruguay	3030	4880
USA				
in North America	Mississippi-Missouri-Jefferson-Beaverhead-Red Rock	G of Mexico, Louisiana, USA	3710	5970
in Oceania (Hawaii)	•Kaukonahua (Stream)	Pacific O, Oahu I, Hawaii, USA	63	100
USSR				
in Asia	Yenisey (alt Yenisei)-Angara-Selenga (alt Selenge)-Ider	Yenisey G of Kara Sea, Russia, USSR	3650	5870
in Europe	Volga	Caspian (Sea) L, Russia, USSR	2190	3530
Venezuela	Orinoco	Atlantic O, Venezuela	1330	2140
Vietnam	•Mekong (off in Vietnam Tien Giang)	South China Sea, Vietnam	2600	4180
West Bank	•Jordan (off in West Bank Urdunn)	Dead (Sea) L, Jordan-West Bank	160	250
Yugoslavia	Danube (off in Yugoslavia Dunav)	Black Sea, Romania-USSR	1780	2860

TABLE 8e. (Continued)

Country	River	Outflow and Location	Length mi	Length km
Zaire	Congo (for Kongo; off in Zaire Zaire)-Lualaba	Atlantic O, Angola-Zaire	2880	4630
Zambia	•Zambezi (alt Zambesi, Zambeze)	Mozambique Channel, Mozambique	1650	2650
Zimbabwe	•Zambezi (alt Zambesi, Zambeze)	Mozambique Channel, Mozambique	1650	2650

For an explanation of symbols and abbreviations, see pages 16–17.

9

GEOGRAPHIC TABLES AND COMPARISONS: MOUNTAINS

9a. Highest Mountains (Peaks), by Continent

Contents

Latitude and longitude of mountain peaks, in degrees and minutes.

Conventional and other (alternate, former, and official) names of peak and of massif, if any (in brackets).

Mountain range or system (unconventional names are given only for initial, italicized entry), and division and country in which located.

Elevation (i.e., altitude of summit above sea level), in feet and meters.

Year of first successful ascent.

Coverage

Above * * *, all named peaks rising to at least the following elevations:

Africa—15,000 ft (4,572 m)
Antarctica—14,000 ft (4,267 m)
Asia—25,500 ft (7,772 m)
Europe—14,800 ft (4,511 m)
North America—14,250 ft (4,343 m)
Oceania—14,000 ft (4,267 m)
South America—20,700 ft (6,309 m)

Below * * *, other well-known peaks, including the highest in certain countries and in important ranges.

Rounding

Elevations are rounded to the nearest 10 ft (m).

Entries

456, as follows: Africa—70
                    Antarctica—15
                    Asia—109
                    Europe—98
                    North America—80
                    Oceania—25
                    South America—59

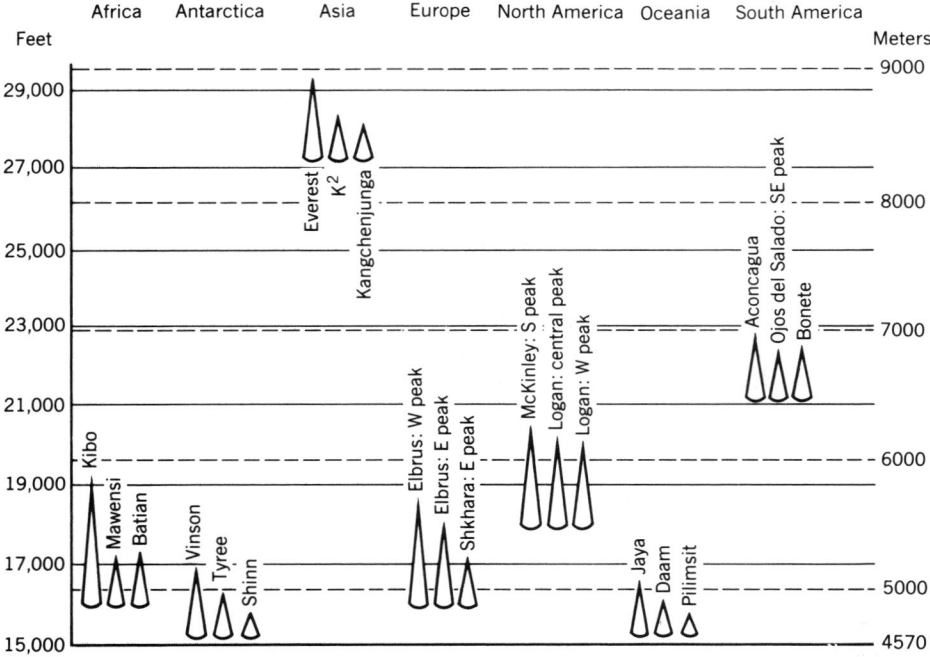

Figure 54. *Three highest mountains of each continent.*

TABLE 9a. HIGHEST MOUNTAINS (PEAKS), BY CONTINENT

Latitude and Longitude	Peak and [Massif]	Mountain Range or System	Location	Elevation ft	Elevation m	First Ascent
AFRICA						
3.04S, 37.12E	Kibo (volc¹) [Kilimanjaro]	—	Tanganyika, Tanzania	19,340	5890	1889
3.06S, 37.27E	Mawensi (volc¹) [Kilimanjaro]	—	Tanganyika, Tanzania	17,100	5210	1912
0.09S, 37.18E	Batian [Kenya]	—	Kenya	17,050	5200	1899
0.09S, 37.18E	•Nelion [Kenya]	—	Kenya	17,020	5190	1929
0.23N, 29.52E	Margherita [Stanley]	*Ruwenzori*	Uganda-Zaire	16,760	5110	1906
0.23N, 29.52E	Alexandra [Stanley]	Ruwenzori	Uganda-Zaire	16,700	5090	1906
0.23N, 29.52E	Albert [Stanley]	Ruwenzori	Zaire	16,690	5090	1932
0.23N, 29.52E	Savoia [Stanley]	Ruwenzori	Uganda	16,330	4980	1906
0.23N, 29.52E	Elena [Stanley]	Ruwenzori	Uganda	16,300	4970	1906
0.23N, 29.52E	Elizabeth [Stanley]	Ruwenzori	Uganda	16,170	4930	1953
0.23N, 29.52E	Philip [Stanley]	Ruwenzori	Uganda	16,140	4920	1954
0.23N, 29.52E	Moebius [Stanley]	Ruwenzori	Uganda	16,130	4920	1906
0.24N, 29.53E	Vittorio Emanuele [Speke]	Ruwenzori	Uganda	16,040	4890	1906
0.24N, 29.53E	Ensonga [Speke]	Ruwenzori	Uganda	15,960	4860	1926
0.22N, 29.53E	Edward [Baker]	Ruwenzori	Uganda	15,890	4840	1906
0.24N, 29.53E	Johnston [Speke]	Ruwenzori	Uganda	15,860	4830	1926
0.26N, 29.54E	Umberto [Emin]	Ruwenzori	Zaire	15,740	4800	1906
0.22N, 29.53E	Semper [Baker]	Ruwenzori	Uganda	15,730	4790	1906
0.26N, 29.54E	Kraepelin [Emin]	Ruwenzori	Zaire	15,720	4790	1932
0.26N, 29.55E	Iolanda [Gessi]	Ruwenzori	Uganda	15,470	4720	1906
0.26N, 29.55E	Bottego [Gessi]	Ruwenzori	Uganda	15,420	4700	1906
0.20N, 29.53E	Sella [Luigi di Savoia]	Ruwenzori	Uganda	15,180	4630	1906
0.22N, 29.53E	Wollaston [Baker]	Ruwenzori	Uganda	15,180	4630	1906
0.22N, 29.53E	Moore [Baker]	Ruwenzori	Uganda	15,170	4620	1906
0.20N, 29.53E	Weismann [Luigi di Savoia]	Ruwenzori	Uganda	15,160	4620	1906
0.23N, 29.52E	Great Tooth [Stanley]	Ruwenzori	Uganda	15,100	4600	1935
0.22N, 29.51E	Wasuwameso [Mugule]	Ruwenzori	Zaire	15,030	4580	
0.19N, 29.52E	Okusoma [Luigi di Savoia]	Ruwenzori	Uganda	15,020	4580	
0.24N, 29.53E	Trident [Speke]	Ruwenzori	Uganda	15,000	4570	
		* * *				

¹No known eruption.

For an explanation of symbols and abbreviations, see pages 16–17.

(Continued)

TABLE 9a. (Continued)

Latitude and Longitude	Peak and [Massif]	Mountain Range or System	Location	Elevation		First Ascent
				ft	m	
3.14S, 36.45E	•Meru (volc)	—	Tanganyika, Tanzania	14,980	4570	
13.15N, 38.24E	Ancua [Ras Dashan (off Ras Dashen)]	Semien (off Simen)	Ethiopia	14,930	4550	
13.18N, 38.21E	Lagada	Semien	Ethiopia	14,870	4530	
1.30S, 29.27E	Karisimbi (volc[1])	Virunga	Rwanda-Zaire	14,790	4510	
1.27S, 29.26E	Mikeno (volc[1])	Virunga	Zaire	14,560	4440	
	Karra	Arusi	Ethiopia	14,240	4340	
1.08N, 34.33E	Elgon	—	Kenya-Uganda	14,140	4310	1911
6.55N, 39.44E	Batu	Mendebo	Ethiopia	14,130	4310	
11.10N, 39.10E	Collo (alt Kollo)	Lasta	Ethiopia	14,110	4300	
31.03N, 7.57W	Toubkal: W peak [Toubkal]	Atlas	Morocco	13,670	4160	1923
10.45N, 37.55E	Birhan	Choke	Ethiopia	13,630	4150	
1.23S, 29.40E	Muhavura (volc[1])	Virunga	Rwanda-Uganda	13,540	4130	1900
4.12N, 9.11E	Fako (volc) [Cameroon (alt Cameroun)]	Cameroon (alt Cameroun)	Cameroon	13,350	4070	1861
0.19S, 36.37E	Lesatima	Aberdare	Kenya	13,120	4000	
28.16N, 16.38W	Teide (volc)	—	(Canary Islands), Spain[2]	12,200	3720	
19.50N, 18.30E	(Emi) Koussi (volc)	Tibesti	Chad	11,470	3490	1915
29.28S, 29.16E	Thabana Ntlenyana (alt Thabantshonyana)	Drakens(berg)	Lesotho	11,420	3480	1951
29.12S, 29.22E	•Injasuti	Drakens(berg)	Lesotho-South Africa	11,310	3450	
29.06S, 29.20E	Champagne Castle	Drakens(berg)	Lesotho-South Africa	11,080	3380	1888
3.57N, 32.54E	•Kinyeti	Imatong	Sudan	10,460	3190	
21.25N, 18.42E	•Kegueur Terbi (alt Chegor Tedi, Hessi)	Tibesti	Chad-Libya	10,330	3150	
21.05S, 55.29E	Neiges (volc)	—	Reunion	10,070	3070	
15.59S, 35.36E	Mlanje	Mlanje	Malawi	10,000	3050	
3.35N, 8.46E	Malabo (for Santa Isabel) (volc)	—	Equatorial Guinea[3]	9,840	3000	
23.18N, 5.32E	Tahat [Atakor]	Ahaggar (alt Hoggar)	Algeria	9,570	2920	1912?
14.01S, 48.58E	Maromokotro	Tsaratanana	Madagascar	9,470	2890	
14.56N, 24.21W	Cano (volc)	—	Cape Verde[4]	9,280	2830	
28.31N, 33.57E	Katrinah (alt Catherine) [Musa]	Sinai	Egypt	8,650	2640	
12.30S, 15.19E	Moco	Upanda	Angola	8,600	2620	
21.10S, 14.33E	Konigstein [Brand(berg)]	Kaokoveld	Namibia	8,550	2610	

Coordinates	Peak	Range	Country			Year
18.18S, 32.54E	Inyangani	Inyanga	Zimbabwe	8,510	2590	
11.12N, 49.30E	Faddisome [Hor Bogor]	Carcar (off Karkaar)	Somalia	8,500	2590	
19.47S, 33.09E	Binga	Chimanimani	Mozambique-Zimbabwe	7,990	2440	
35.20N, 6.40E	Chelia	Aures (off Awras)	Algeria	7,640	2330	
20.00N, 8.35E	•Greboun	Air (alt Azbine)	Niger	7,550	2300	
8.20N, 11.45E	Vogel	Banglang	Nigeria	6,700	2040	
9.13N, 11.07W	•Bintimani	Loma	Sierra Leone	6,390	1940	
32.45N, 16.56W	Ruivo de Santana	—	(Madeira Islands), Portugal[5]	6,110	1860	
25.57S, 31.11E	•Emlembe	Drakens(berg)	Swaziland	6,100	1860	
7.37N, 8.25W	Nimba	Nimba	Guinea-Ivory Coast-Liberia	5,780	1760	
35.13N, 8.41E	Shanabi (alt Chambi)	Dorsale	Tunisia	5,070	1540	

ANTARCTICA

Coordinates	Peak	Range	Country			Year
78.35S, 85.25W	—[Vinson]	Sentinel	Antarctica	16,860	5140	
78.24S, 85.55W	•Tyree	Sentinel	Antarctica	16,290	4970	1966
78.27S, 85.46W	•Shinn	Sentinel	Antarctica	15,750	4800	1967
78.23S, 86.02W	•Gardner	Sentinel	Antarctica	15,370	4690	1966
78.26S, 85.53W	•Epperly	Sentinel	Antarctica	15,100	4600	1966
84.20S, 166.19E	•Kirkpatrick	Queen Alexandra	Antarctica	14,850	4530	
83.54S, 168.23E	•Elizabeth	Queen Alexandra	Antarctica	14,700	4480	
82.51S, 161.21E	•Markham	Queen Elizabeth	Antarctica	14,290	4360	
84.04S, 167.30E	•Bell	Queen Alexandra	Antarctica	14,120	4300	
83.59S, 166.39E	•Mackellar	Queen Alexandra	Antarctica	14,100	4300	

* * *

Coordinates	Peak	Range	Country			Year
84.33S, 175.18E	•Kaplan	Hughes	Antarctica	13,880	4230	
71.23S, 63.22W	•Jackson	Gutenko	Antarctica	13,750	4190	
77.02S, 126.00W	•Sidley	Executive Committee	Antarctica	13,720	4180	
71.47S, 168.45E	•Minto	Admiralty	Antarctica	13,670	4170	
77.32S, 167.09E	•Erebus (volc)	—	Antarctica	12,450	3790	1908

[1]No known eruption.
[2]Tenerife I.
[3]Bioko I.
[4]Fogo I.
[5]Madeira I.

For an explanation of symbols and abbreviations, see pages 16–17.

(Continued)

TABLE 9a. (Continued)

Latitude and Longitude	Peak and [Massif]	Mountain Range or System	Location	Elevation ft	Elevation m	First Ascent
ASIA						
27.59N, 86.56E	Everest (alt Qomolangma, Chumulangma) [Everest]	Nepal *Himalaya*	China-Nepal	29,030	8850	1953
35.53N, 76.31E	K2 (alt Chogori, Dapsang, Godwin Austen)	*Karakoram*	Pakistan-held Kashmir	28,250	8610	1954
27.42N, 88.09E	Kangchenjunga (alt Kanchenjunga): highest peak [Kangchenjunga]	Nepal Himalaya	India-Nepal	28,170	8590	1955
27.58N, 86.56E	Lhotse (alt E1, Luozi, Lotzu) [Everest]	Nepal Himalaya	China-Nepal	27,890	8500	1956
27.41N, 88.09E	Kangchenjunga: S peak [Kangchenjunga]	Nepal Himalaya	India-Nepal	27,800	8470	
27.53N, 87.05E	Makalu I [Makalu]	Nepal Himalaya	China-Nepal	27,790	8470	1955
27.42N, 88.09E	•Kangchenjunga: W peak [Kangchenjunga]	Nepal Himalaya	India-Nepal	27,620	8420	1973
27.57N, 86.57E	•Lhotse Shar (alt Lhotse: E peak) [Everest]	Nepal Himalaya	China-Nepal	27,500	8380	1970
28.42N, 83.30E	Dhaulagiri I (alt Daulagiri I)	Nepal Himalaya	Nepal	26,810	8170	1960
28.06N, 86.39E	Cho Oyu (alt Zhuoaoyu, Choaoyu): highest peak	Nepal Himalaya	China-Nepal	26,750	8150	1954
28.33N, 84.34E	Manaslu (alt Kutang I): highest peak [Manaslu]	Nepal Himalaya	Nepal	26,660	8130	1956
35.14N, 74.35E	Nanga Parbat: highest peak	*Punjab Himalaya*	Pakistan-held Kashmir	26,660	8130	1953
28.36N, 83.49E	Annapurna I	Nepal Himalaya	Nepal–Pakistan-held Kashmir	26,500	8080	1950
35.43N, 76.42E	Gasherbrum I (alt Hidden) [Gasherbrum]	Karakoram	Pakistan-held Kashmir	26,470	8070	1958
35.49N, 76.34E	Broad: highest peak [Gasherbrum]	Karakoram	Pakistan-held Kashmir	26,400	8050	1957
35.46N, 76.39E	Gasherbrum II: highest peak [Gasherbrum]	Karakoram	Pakistan-held Kashmir	26,360	8030	1956
28.21N, 85.47E	Gosainthan (alt Shishma Pangma, Kaosengtsan; off Gaosengzan)	Nepal Himalaya	Tibet, China	26,290	8010	1964
35.49N, 76.34E	•Broad: mittel (gipfel) peak [Gasherbrum]	Karakoram	Pakistan-held Kashmir	26,250	8000	
35.46N, 76.39E	Gasherbrum III [Gasherbrum]	Karakoram	Pakistan-held Kashmir	26,090	7950	1975
28.32N, 84.07E	Annapurna II	Nepal Himalaya	Nepal	26,040	7940	1960
35.46N, 76.37E	Gasherbrum IV [Gasherbrum]	Karakoram	Pakistan-held Kashmir	26,000	7920	1958
28.06N, 86.45E	Gyachung Kang	Nepal Himalaya	China-Nepal	25,990	7920	1964

For an explanation of symbols and abbreviations, see pages 16–17.

(Continued)

Figure 55. Mount Everest (Chinese: Qomolangma) on the border of Tibet and Nepal, which exceeds all other mountain peaks in height. (Credit: Department of Tourism, Ministry of Industry and Commerce of Nepal.)

TABLE 9a. (Continued)

Latitude and Longitude	Peak and [Massif]	Mountain Range or System	Location	Elevation ft	Elevation m	First Ascent
35.14N, 74.35E	•Nanga Parbat: vor(gipfel) peak	Punjab Himalaya	Pakistan-held Kashmir	25,950	7910	
27.43N, 88.07E	Kangbachen [Kangchenjunga]	Nepal Himalaya	India-Nepal	25,930	7900	1974
28.33N, 84.34E	•Manaslu: E pinnacle [Manaslu]	Nepal Himalaya	Nepal	25,900	7900	
36.20N, 75.11E	Distaghil Sar	Karakoram	Pakistan-held Kashmir	25,870	7890	1960
27.58N, 86.53E	Nuptse (alt E2) [Everest]	Nepal Himalaya	Nepal	25,850	7880	1961
28.26N, 84.39E	Himalchuli: highest peak	Nepal Himalaya	Nepal	25,800	7860	1956
36.11N, 75.13E	•Khiangyang Kish (alt Khinyang Chhish)	Karakoram	Pakistan-held Kashmir	25,760	7850	
28.06N, 86.41E	Ngojumba Ri (alt Cho Oyu: E peak)	Nepal Himalaya	China-Nepal	25,720	7840	1965
28.30N, 84.34E	Dakura (alt Kutang II) [Manaslu]	Nepal Himalaya	Nepal	25,710	7840	
35.39N, 76.19E	Masherbrum: E peak	Karakoram	Pakistan-held Kashmir	25,660	7820	1960
30.23N, 79.58E	Nanda Devi: W peak	Kumaun Himalaya	Uttar Pradesh, India	25,650	7820	1936
35.15N, 74.35E	Nanga Parbat: N peak	Punjab Himalaya	Pakistan-held Kashmir	25,650	7820	
27.55N, 87.08E	Chomo Lonzo (alt Makalu) [Makalu]	Nepal Himalaya	China-Nepal	25,640	7820	1954
35.38N, 76.18E	Masherbrum: W peak	Karakoram	Pakistan-held Kashmir	25,610	7810	
36.09N, 74.29E	Rakaposhi	Haramosh (Ridge)	Pakistan-held Kashmir	25,550	7790	1958
36.31N, 74.31E	Batura Mustagh I (alt Hunza-Kunji I)	Karakoram	Pakistan-held Kashmir	25,540	7790	1976
35.46N, 76.39E	•Gasherbrum II: E peak [Gasherbrum]	Karakoram	Pakistan-held Kashmir	25,500	7770	
		* * *				
30.56N, 79.35E	Kamet (alt Kameite)	Zaskar	China-India	25,440	7760	1931
29.40N, 95.10E	Namcha Barwa (alt Namuchopaerhwa: off Namuzhuobaerwa)	Assam Himalaya	Tibet, China	25,440	7760	
30.26N, 81.18E	Gurla Mandhata (alt Kualamantata; off Gualamandata)	Nepal-Tibet (Watershed)	Tibet, China	25,350	7730	
36.25N, 87.25E	•Ulugh Mustagh (alt Wulukomushih; off Wulukemushi)	Kunlun	Tibet-Xinjiang, China	25,340	7720	
38.40N, 75.21E	Kungur II (alt Kungkoerh II; off Kongur II)	Mustagh Ata (alt Mussutakoate; off Muztagata)	Xinjiang, China	25,330	7720	1955
36.15N, 71.50E	•Tirich Mir: W peak	Hindu Kush	Pakistan	25,260	7700	1950
36.15N, 71.50E	•Tirich Mir: E peak	Hindu Kush	Pakistan	25,230	7690	1964
34.52N, 77.45E	•Saser Kangri I	Saser (Ridge)	Pakistan-held Kashmir	25,170	7670	

Coordinates	Name	Range	Location	Elevation (ft)	Elevation (m)	Year
29.34N, 101.53E	•Minya Konka (alt Kungka, Minyag Gangkar; off Gongga)	*Daxue* (alt Tahsueh)	Sichuan, China	24,890	7590	1932
28.14N, 90.36E	Khula Kangri I (alt Kula Gangri I; off Kula I)	Assam Himalaya	Bhutan-China	24,780	7550	
38.16N, 75.09E	•Mustagh Ata (alt Mussutakoate; off Muztagata)	Mustagh Ata	Xinjiang, China	24,760	7550	1956
28.01N, 86.54E	Changtse (alt Zhangzi, E3, Changtzu) [Everest]	Nepal Himalaya	China-Nepal	24,730	7540	
38.56N, 72.02E	Kommunizma (for Garmo, Stalina)	*Pamir-Alay* (alt Pamir-Alai)	Tadzhikistan, USSR	24,590	7490	1933
36.26N, 71.50E	•Noshaq: highest peak	Hindu Kush	Afghanistan-Pakistan	24,580	7490	1960
42.03N, 80.11E	Pobedy (alt Shengli)	*Tian* (alt Tyan, Tien)	China-USSR	24,410	7440	1956
32.46N, 81.02E	•Alung Gangri (off Aling)	Alung (off Aling)	Tibet, China	24,000	7320	
27.50N, 89.16E	Chomo Lhari (alt Zhuomolali, Chomolali)	Assam Himalaya	Bhutan-China	24,000	7310	1937
39.20N, 72.55E	Lenina (for Kaufmann)	Pamir-Alay	Kirgizia-Tadzhikistan, USSR	23,380	7130	1928
34.24N, 100.10E	Amne Machin (alt Animaching, Chishih; off Anyemaqen)	*Amne Machin* (alt Chishih; off Anyemaqen)	Qinghai, China	23,300	7100	1960
30.27N, 90.33E	•Nyenchhen Thanglha (alt Nienchingtan; off Nyainqentanglha)	*Nyenchhen Thanglha*	Tibet, China	23,250	7090	
29.56N, 84.33E	•Lombo Kangra (alt Lungpu; off Longbo)	*Kailas* (alt Kangtissu; off Gangdise)	Tibet, China	23,160	7060	
42.15N, 81.10E	Khan-Tengri	Tian	Kirgizia, USSR	22,950	6990	1931
31.04N, 81.19E	Kailas (alt Kangtissu; off Gangdise)	Kailas	Tibet, China	22,030	6710	
37.09N, 72.26E	Karla Marksa	Vakhan	Tadzhikistan, USSR	21,980	6700	1946
38.35N, 97.45E	•Shule (alt Shulenan, Sulo)	Nan	Qinghai, China	20,820	6350	
28.17N, 97.46E	Hkakabo Razi	Kumon	Burma	19,300	5880	
35.56N, 52.08E	•Damavand (alt Demavend)	*Alborz* (alt Elburz)	Iran	18,610	5670	1837
39.42N, 44.18E	Great Ararat (off Buyukagri) (volc[1])	—	Turkey	16,950	5160	1829
30.50N, 51.35E	•Dinar	*Zagros*	Iran	16,400	5000	
56.04N, 160.38E	Klyuchevskaya (volc)	Kamchatka	Russia, USSR	15,670	4770	1931
49.48N, 86.35E	Belukha: W peak	Altay (alt Altai)	Kazakhstan-Russia, USSR	15,160	4620	
38.54N, 42.48E	Suphan (volc[1])	—	Turkey	14,550	4430	1903

(Continued)

[1]No known eruption.
For an explanation of symbols and abbreviations, see pages 16–17.

TABLE 9a. (Continued)

Latitude and Longitude	Peak and [Massif]	Mountain Range or System	Location	Elevation ft	Elevation m	First Ascent
49.10N, 87.55E	Khuitun (alt Nayramdal; off Huyten) [Tavan Bogd]	Altay	Mongolia	14,350	4370	
37.30N, 44.00E	Geliasin [Resko (alt Cilo)]	*Hakkari*	Turkey	13,680	4170	
6.05N, 116.33E	Kinabalu: highest peak	*Crocker*	Sabah, Malaysia	13,450	4100	1851
23.28N, 120.57E	Yu (alt Hsinkao, Morrison)	*Central* (off Chungyang)	Taiwan	13,110	4000	1896?
38.32N, 35.28E	Erciyas (volc2)	—	Turkey	12,850	3920	
1.42S, 101.16E	Kerinci (for Indrapura, Kerintji) (volc)	*Barisan*	Sumatra I, Indonesia	12,470	3800	1877
35.22N, 138.44E	Fuji (alt Huzi) (volc)	—	Honshu I, Japan	12,390	3780	7th c?
15.20N, 43.55E	•Hadur Shuayb	*Yemen (Highlands)*	North Yemen	12,340	3760	
36.43N, 44.50E	•Algurd (alt Halgurd)	*Zagros*	Iraq	12,250	3730	
8.24S, 116.28E	Sangkariyan (for Sangkarijan) (volc) [Rinjani (for Rindjani)]	—	Lombok I, Indonesia	12,220	3730	
8.06S, 112.55E	Mahameru (volc)	*Semeru*	Java I, Indonesia	12,060	3680	1838
16.52N, 43.22E	•Razikh	*Yemen (Highlands)*	North Yemen-Saudi Arabia	11,990	3650	
51.45N, 100.20E	Munku-Sardyk	*Sayan*	Mongolia-USSR	11,450	3490	1868
3.21S, 120.01E	Rante Kombola	*Quarles*	Celebes I, Indonesia	11,340	3450	
15.04N, 107.59E	•(Ngoc) Linh	*Annamese* (off Trungphan)	Vietnam	10,500	3200	
35.40N, 138.15E	Kitadake [Shirane]	*Akaishi*	Honshu I, Japan	10,470	3190	
36.48N, 139.08E	Oku-Hotaka [Hotaka]	*Mikuni*	Honshu I, Japan	10,470	3190	
8.21S, 115.30E	Agung (volc)	—	Bali I, Indonesia	10,310	3140	
22.18N, 103.46E	Fan Si Pan	*Fan Si Pan*	Vietnam	10,310	3140	
23.13N, 57.16E	•Sham	*Akhdar*	Oman	10,190	3110	
34.18N, 36.07E	Makmel [Qurnat al Sawda]	*Lebanon* (off Lubnan)	Lebanon	10,120	3080	
8.55S, 125.30E	Tata Mailau (alt Ramelau)	—	East Timor, Indonesia	9,720	2960	
6.59N, 125.16E	Apo (volc2)	—	Mindanao I, Philippines	9,690	2950	
16.36N, 120.54E	Pulog	*Central*	Luzon I, Philippines	9,610	2930	
18.59N, 103.10E	•Bia	*Tranninh*	Laos	9,240	2820	

Coordinates	Peak	Range	Country	Elevation (ft)	Elevation (m)	Date
33.24N, 35.50E	Hermon (off Shaykh)	*Anti-Lebanon (off Sharqi)*	Lebanon-Syria	9,230	2810	
41.59N, 128.04E	•Baitou (alt Paektu, Paitou)	*Changbai (alt Changbaek, Changpai)*	China-North Korea	8,900	2710	1886
18.35N, 98.29E	Inthanon (alt Angka)	*Phi Pan Nam*	Thailand	8,450	2580	
7.00N, 80.46E	Pidurutalagala	*Piduru (Ridges)*	Sri Lanka	8,280	2520	
13.53N, 45.12E	•Thamar (off Thamir)	*Yemen (Highlands)*	South Yemen	8,240	2510	
13.15N, 123.42E	•Mayon (volc)	—	Luzon I, Philippines	7,940	2420	1938
4.38N, 102.14E	Tahan	*Cameron (Highlands)*	Peninsular Malaysia, Malaysia	7,190	2190	
34.55N, 32.52E	Khionistra (alt Olympus)	*Troodos*	Cyprus	6,410	1950	
33.22N, 126.32E	•Halla	—	South Korea[1]	6,400	1950	
12.02N, 104.10E	•Aural	*Cardamomes*	Kampuchea	5,950	1810	
29.36N, 35.24E	•Ramm	*Sharah*	Jordan	5,750	1750	
33.00N, 35.25E	•Meron (for Jarmaq, Sharqi)	*Galilee*	Israel	3,960	1210	
6.07S, 105.24E	Krakatoa (off Krakatau) (volc)	—	Rakata I, Indonesia	2,670	810	
EUROPE						
43.21N, 42.26E	Elbrus (for Elborus): W peak (volc2) [Elbrus]	*Caucasus (off Kavkaz)*	Russia, USSR	18,480	5630	1874
43.21N, 42.26E	Elbrus: E peak (volc2) [Elbrus]	Caucasus	Russia, USSR	18,360	5590	1829
43.00N, 43.06E	Shkhara: E peak	Caucasus	Georgia-Russia, USSR	17,060	5200	1888
43.03N, 43.08E	Dykh(-Tau): W peak	Caucasus	Russia, USSR	17,050	5200	1888
43.03N, 43.08E	Dykh(-Tau): E peak	Caucasus	Russia, USSR	16,900	5150	1938
43.03N, 43.13E	Koshtan(-Tau)	Caucasus	Russia, USSR	16,880	5140	1888
43.00N, 43.06E	Shkhara: W peak	Caucasus	Georgia-Russia, USSR	16,880	5140	
43.03N, 43.10E	Pushkina	Caucasus	Russia, USSR	16,730	5100	1938
43.03N, 43.03E	Dzhangi(-Tau): NW peak	Caucasus	Georgia, USSR	16,570	5050	1903
42.42N, 44.31E	Kazbek: E peak	Caucasus	Georgia, USSR	16,560	5050	1868
43.02N, 43.03E	Dzhangi(-Tau): SE peak	Caucasus	Georgia, USSR	16,520	5030	1888
43.02N, 43.02E	Katyn(-Tau)	Caucasus	Georgia-Russia, USSR	16,310	4970	1888
43.02N, 43.05E	Shota Rustaveli	Caucasus	Georgia-Russia, USSR	16,270	4960	1937
43.02N, 43.09E	Mizhirgi: W peak	Caucasus	Russia, USSR	16,170	4930	1934

1Cheju I.
2No known eruption.
For an explanation of symbols and abbreviations, see pages 16–17.

(Continued)

TABLE 9a. (Continued)

Latitude and Longitude	Peak and [Massif]	Mountain Range or System	Location	Elevation		First Ascent
				ft	m	
43.02N, 43.09E	Mizhirgi: E peak	Caucasus	Russia, USSR	16,140	4920	1889
43.04N, 43.13E	Kundyum-Mizhirgi	Caucasus	Russia, USSR	16,010	4880	1946
43.03N, 43.01E	Gestola	Caucasus	Georgia-Russia, USSR	15,930	4860	1886
43.02N, 42.58E	Tetnuld	Caucasus	Georgia, USSR	15,920	4850	1887
45.50N, 6.52E	(Mont-)Blanc (alt Bianco) [Blanc (alt Bianco)]	Alps (off Alpe, Alpen, Alpes, Alpi)	France-Italy	15,770	4810	1786
42.43N, 44.25E	Dzhimariy(-Khokh)	Caucasus	Georgia, USSR	15,680	4780	1890
43.02N, 43.04E	Adish	Caucasus	Georgia-Russia, USSR	15,570	4750	1931
43.08N, 42.40E	Ushba: SW peak	Caucasus	Georgia, USSR	15,450	4710	1903
43.08N, 42.40E	Ushba: NE peak	Caucasus	Georgia, USSR	15,400	4690	1888
43.05N, 43.13E	Ullu-Auz(-Bashi)	Caucasus	Russia, USSR	15,360	4680	1888
43.05N, 43.12E	Panoramnyy	Caucasus	Russia, USSR	15,350	4680	1946
43.02N, 43.10E	Krumkol	Caucasus	Russia, USSR	15,320	4670	1937
42.42N, 44.31E	Kazbek: W peak	Caucasus	Georgia, USSR	15,250	4650	1890
42.46N, 43.48E	Uilpata [for Aday(-Khokh)]	Caucasus	Russia, USSR	15,240	4650	1890
42.45N, 44.25E	Shau(-Khokh)	Caucasus	Georgia, USSR	15,240	4640	1936
45.56N, 7.52E	Dufour(spitze) [Rosa]	Alps	Italy-Switzerland	15,200	4630	1855
45.56N, 7.52E	Grenz(gipfel) [Rosa]	Alps	Italy-Switzerland	15,190	4630	1851
43.20N, 42.25E	Kyukyurtlyukol(-Bashi) [Elbrus]	Caucasus	Russia, USSR	15,170	4620	1936
45.56N, 7.51E	Nordend [Rosa]	Alps	Italy-Switzerland	15,130	4610	1861
43.08N, 42.59E	Tikhtengen: N peak	Caucasus	Georgia-Russia, USSR	15,130	4610	1936
43.08N, 42.59E	Tikhtengen: S peak	Caucasus	Georgia-Russia, USSR	15,130	4610	1935
42.42N, 44.28E	Mayli(-Khokh)	Caucasus	Georgia, USSR	15,100	4600	1903
42.45N, 43.47E	Dubl: N peak	Caucasus	Russia, USSR	15,030	4580	1933
45.56N, 7.52E	Zumstein(spitze) [Rosa]	Alps	Italy-Switzerland	15,000	4570	1820
45.55N, 7.52E	Signal(kuppe) [Rosa]	Alps	Italy-Switzerland	14,960	4560	1842
43.06N, 43.13E	Dumala(-Tau)	Caucasus	Russia, USSR	14,950	4560	1930
43.03N, 43.15E	Tyutyun(-Bashi)	Caucasus	Russia, USSR	14,930	4550	1933
46.06N, 7.51E	Dom [Mischabel]	Alps	Switzerland	14,910	4540	1858
42.57N, 43.11E	Aylama	Caucasus	Georgia-Russia, USSR	14,890	4540	1889
43.12N, 42.57E	Dzhaylyk(-Bashi)	Caucasus	Russia, USSR	14,890	4540	1936
45.55N, 7.50E	Lyskamm [Rosa]	Alps	Italy-Switzerland	14,890	4540	1861

Coordinates	Name	Range	Country	ft	m	Year
43.01N, 43.15E	Tyutyun(-Tau)	Caucasus	Russia, USSR	14,890	4540	1933
42.45N, 43.47E	Dubl: S peak	Caucasus	Russia, USSR	14,880	4530	1933
43.01N, 43.03E	Lakutsa	Caucasus	Georgia, USSR	14,830	4520	1931
42.47N, 43.46E	Karaugom: E peak	Caucasus	Russia, USSR	14,810	4510	1890
42.20N, 46.15E	Addala Shukhgelmeer	Caucasus	Russia, USSR	14,800	4510	1935
42.47N, 43.46E	Karaugom: W peak	Caucasus	Russia, USSR	14,800	4510	1937
42.42N, 44.29E	Spartak	Caucasus	Georgia, USSR	14,800	4510	1940
		* * *				
46.07N, 7.43E	Weiss(horn)	Alps	Switzerland	14,780	4500	1861
46.05N, 7.51E	Tasch(horn) [Mischabel]	Alps	Switzerland	14,730	4490	1862
45.58N, 7.39E	Matter(horn) [Cervino]	Alps	Italy-Switzerland	14,690	4480	1865
45.51N, 6.53E	Maudit [Blanc]	Alps	France-Italy	14,650	4470	1878
41.51N, 47.51E	Bazar-Dyuzi	Caucasus	Azerbaijan-Russia, USSR	14,550	4430	1873
46.02N, 7.37E	(Dent) Blanche	Alps	Switzerland	14,300	4360	1862
46.32N, 8.08E	Finsteraar(horn)	Alps	Switzerland	14,020	4270	1812
46.28N, 8.00E	Aletsch(horn)	Alps	Switzerland	13,760	4190	1859
46.33N, 7.58E	Jungfrau	Alps	Switzerland	13,640	4160	1811
46.33N, 8.01E	Monch	Alps	Switzerland	13,450	4100	1857
46.34N, 8.01E	Eiger	Alps	Switzerland	13,020	3970	1858
47.04N, 12.42E	Grossglockner	Alps	Austria	12,460	3800	1800
37.03N, 3.19W	Mulhacen	Nevada	Andalucia, Spain	11,410	3480	1840
42.38N, 0.40E	Aneto	Pyrenees (alt Pirineos)	Aragon, Spain	11,170	3400	1842
37.50N, 14.55E	Etna (volc)	—	Sicilia, Italy[1]	10,760	3280	
47.25N, 10.59E	Zug(spitze)	Alps	Austria-West Germany	9,720	2960	1820
42.11N, 23.34E	Musala	Rhodope (off Rodhopis, Rodopi)	Bulgaria	9,600	2920	
40.05N, 22.21E	Mytikas [Olympus (off Olimbos)]	Olympus (off Olimbos)	Greece	9,570	2920	1913
42.28N, 13.34E	Corno Grande	Apennines (off Appennino)	Abruzzi e Molise, Italy	9,560	2910	1794
41.46N, 23.24E	Vikhren	Rhodope	Bulgaria	9,560	2910	
46.23N, 13.50E	Triglav	Alps	Slovenia, Yugoslavia	9,400	2860	1778
41.44N, 20.32E	Korab	Korab	Albania-Yugoslavia	9,050	2760	
42.23N, 8.56E	Cinto	—	Corse, France[2]	8,890	2710	

(Continued)

1Sicily I.
2Corsica I.
For an explanation of symbols and abbreviations, see pages 16–17.

TABLE 9a. (Continued)

Latitude and Longitude	Peak and [Massif]	Mountain Range or System	Location	Elevation ft	Elevation m	First Ascent
49.09N, 20.05E	Gerlachovsky (alt Gerlachovka; for Stalin)	*Tatra* (off Tatry)	Slovakia, Czechoslovakia	8,710	2650	1855?
43.12N, 4.48W	Cerredo [Europa]	*Cantabrian* (off Cantabrica)	Asturias-Castilla la Vieja-Leon, Spain	8,690	2650	1892
45.36N, 24.44E	Moldoveanu	*Transylvanian Alps* (off Carpatii Meridionali)	Romania	8,340	2540	
45.35N, 24.34E	Negoiu	Transylvanian Alps	Romania	8,320	2530	1793
49.12N, 20.04E	Rysy	Tatra	Czechoslovakia-Poland	8,200	2500	1840?
61.37N, 8.17E	Galdhopiggen	*Jotunheimen*	Norway	8,100	2470	1850
61.39N, 8.33E	Glittertinden	Jotunheimen	Norway	8,090	2470	
38.32N, 22.35E	Parnassus (off Parnassos) [Parnassus]	—	Greece	8,060	2460	
42.43N, 24.55E	Botev	*Balkan* (off Stara)	Bulgaria	7,800	2380	
38.28N, 28.25W	Ponta do Pico (alt Pico) (volc)		(Azores), Portugal[1]	7,710	2350	
64.01N, 16.41W	Hvannadalshnukur	—	Iceland	6,950	2120	
67.53N, 18.31E	Kebnekaise	*Kolen*	Sweden	6,930	2110	1883
40.19N, 7.37W	Estrela	*Estrela*	Portugal	6,530	1990	
65.04N, 60.09E	Narodnaya	*Ural*	Russia, USSR	6,210	1890	
45.32N, 2.50E	Sancy	*Auvergne*	Auvergne, France	6,190	1890	
79.02N, 17.30E	Newton	—	Svalbard[2]	5,630	1720	1900
56.48N, 5.00W	(Ben) Nevis	*Grampian*	Scotland, UK	4,410	1340	
69.18N, 21.16E	Haltiatunturi (alt Reisduoddarhaldde)	*Haltia* (alt Halddia)	Finland-Norway	4,360	1330	
40.49N, 14.26E	Vesuvius (off Vesuvio) (volc)	—	Campania, Italy	4,190	1280	
50.26N, 12.57E	Fichtel(-berg)	*Erz(gebirge)*	East Germany	3,980	1210	
52.00N, 9.45W	Carrantuohill (alt Carrantual)	*Macgillicuddy's Reeks*	Ireland	3,410	1040	
47.52N, 20.01E	Kekes	*Matra*	Hungary	3,330	1010	
38.46N, 15.13E	Stromboli (volc)	—	Sicilia, Italy[3]	3,040	930	
NORTH AMERICA						
63.04N,151.00W	McKinley: S peak [McKinley]	*Alaska*	Alaska, USA	20,320	6190	1913
60.34N,140.24W	Logan: central peak [Logan]	*Saint Elias*	Yukon Territory, Canada	19,520	5950	1925
60.34N,140.25W	Logan: W peak [Logan]	*Saint Elias*	Yukon Territory, Canada	19,470	5930	1925

Coordinates	Name	Range	Location	ft	m	Year
63.04N,151.00W	McKinley: N peak [McKinley]	Alaska	Alaska, USA	19,470	5930	1910
60.34N,140.22W	Logan: E peak [Logan]	Saint Elias	Yukon Territory, Canada	19,420	5920	1957
19.02N, 97.16W	Citlaltepetl (alt Orizaba) (volc[4])	Neovolcanica	Puebla-Veracruz, Mexico	18,410	5610	1848
60.35N,140.24W	•Logan: N peak [Logan]	Saint Elias	Yukon Territory, Canada	18,270	5570	1959
60.17N,140.55W	Saint Elias	Saint Elias	Canada-USA	18,010	5490	1897
19.01N, 98.32W	Popocatepetl (volc)	Neovolcanica	Puebla, Mexico	17,930	5460	1520
62.58N,151.24W	Foraker	Alaska	Alaska, USA	17,400	5300	1934
60.35N,140.39W	•Queen [Logan]	Saint Elias	Yukon Territory, Canada	17,300	5270	1966
19.11N, 98.38W	Iztaccihuatl (alt Ixtaccihuatl)	Neovolcanica	Puebla, Mexico	17,160	5230	16th c?
61.01N,140.28W	Lucania	Saint Elias	Yukon Territory, Canada	17,150	5230	1937
60.35N,140.39W	King [Logan]	Saint Elias	Yukon Territory, Canada	16,970	5170	1952
61.06N,140.23W	Steele	Saint Elias	Yukon Territory, Canada	16,640	5070	1935
61.23N,141.45W	Bona	Saint Elias	Alaska, USA	16,500	5030	1930
61.44N,143.26W	Blackburn: highest peak	Wrangell	Alaska, USA	16,390	5000	1958
61.44N,143.26W	Blackburn: SE peak	Wrangell	Alaska, USA	16,290	4960	1912
62.13N,144.08W	Sanford	Wrangell	Alaska, USA	16,240	4950	1938
61.14N,140.30W	Wood	Saint Elias	Yukon Territory, Canada	15,880	4840	1941
60.20N,139.42W	Vancouver	Saint Elias	Canada-USA	15,700	4790	1949
61.25N,141.43W	Churchill	Saint Elias	Alaska, USA	15,640	4770	1951
61.11N,140.33W	Slaggard	Saint Elias	Yukon Territory, Canada	15,570	4750	1959
61.12N,140.30W	•McCauley (alt Macauly)	Saint Elias	Yukon Territory, Canada	15,470	4720	1959
19.06N, 99.46W	Toluca (alt Zinantecatl)	Neovolcanica	Mexico, Mexico	15,360	4680	
58.54N,137.31W	Fairweather	Saint Elias	Canada-USA	15,300	4660	1931
61.20N,141.48W	University	Saint Elias	Alaska, USA	15,030	4580	1955
60.19N,139.04W	Hubbard	Saint Elias	Canada-USA	15,010	4580	1951
61.17N,141.09W	Bear	Saint Elias	Alaska, USA	14,850	4530	1951
61.00N,140.01W	Walsh	Saint Elias	Yukon Territory, Canada	14,780	4500	1941
19.14N, 98.02W	Malinche (alt Matlalcueyetl)	Neovolcanica	Puebla-Tlaxcala, Mexico	14,640	4460	
62.57N,151.05W	Hunter	Alaska	Alaska, USA	14,570	4440	1954
60.21N,139.04W	Alverstone	Saint Elias	Canada-USA	14,530[5]	4430[5]	1951
63.06N,150.56W	Browne Tower [McKinley]	Alaska	Alaska, USA	14,530	4430	1913

1Pico I.
2West Spitsbergen I.
3Stromboli I.
4Dormant since 1687.
5Average of elevations officially given by Canada (14,500 ft, 4420 m) and USA (14,560 ft, 4440 m).
For an explanation of symbols and abbreviations, see pages 16–17.

(Continued)

TABLE 9a. (Continued)

Latitude and Longitude	Peak and [Massif]	Mountain Range or System	Location	Elevation		First Ascent
				ft	m	
36.35N,118.17W	Whitney	Sierra Nevada	California, USA	14,490	4420	1873
61.22N,141.54W	•Aello	Saint Elias	Alaska, USA	14,440	4400	1967
39.07N,106.26W	Elbert	Rocky	Colorado, USA	14,430	4400	1874
38.55N,106.19W	Harvard	Rocky	Colorado, USA	14,420	4390	1869
39.11N,106.28W	Massive	Rocky	Colorado, USA	14,420	4390	1874
46.51N,121.46W	Rainier (volc)	Cascade	Washington, USA	14,410	4390	1870
39.02N,106.28W	La Plata	Rocky	Colorado, USA	14,370	4380	1873
36.39N,118.21W	Williamson	Sierra Nevada	California, USA	14,370	4380	1884?
37.35N,105.29W	Blanca	Rocky	Colorado, USA	14,320	4360	1874
38.04N,107.28W	Uncompahgre	Rocky	Colorado, USA	14,310	4360	1874
37.59N,105.35W	Crestone	Rocky	Colorado, USA	14,290	4360	1916
39.21N,106.06W	Lincoln	Rocky	Colorado, USA	14,290	4350	1861
38.40N,106.15W	Antero	Rocky	Colorado, USA	14,270	4350	
39.38N,105.49W	Grays	Rocky	Colorado, USA	14,270	4350	1869
39.39N,105.49W	Torreys	Rocky	Colorado, USA	14,270	4350	1860?
39.01N,106.52W	Castle	Rocky	Colorado, USA	14,260	4350	bef 1875
39.35N,105.38W	Evans	Rocky	Colorado, USA	14,260	4350	
40.15N,105.37W	Longs	Rocky	Colorado, USA	14,260	4350	1868
39.24N,106.12W	Quandary	Rocky	Colorado, USA	14,260	4350	
60.37N,140.11W	McArthur [Logan]	Saint Elias	Yukon Territory, Canada	14,250	4340	1961
		***				
41.25N,122.12W	Shasta (volc)	Cascade	California, USA	14,160	4320	1854
62.00N,144.00W	Wrangell (volc)	Wrangell	Alaska, USA	14,160	4320	1908
38.50N,105.03W	Pikes (Peak)	Rocky	Colorado, USA	14,110	4300	1820
60.19N,139.00W	Kennedy	Saint Elias	Yukon Territory, Canada	13,900	4240	1965
15.02N,91.55W	Tajumulco (volc)	Madre	Guatemala	13,850	4220	
43.44N,110.48W	Grand Teton	Teton	Wyoming, USA	13,770	4200	1872
51.22N,125.14W	Waddington	Coast	British Columbia, Canada	13,100	3990	1936
53.07N,119.08W	Robson	Canadian Rocky	British Columbia, Canada	12,970	3950	1913
19.31N,103.38W	Colima (volc)	—	Jalisco, Mexico	12,590	3840	
9.29N,83.30W	Chirripo Grande	Talamanca	Costa Rica	12,530	3820	
68.50N,29.45W	Gunnbjørn	—	Greenland	12,140	3700	1935

Coordinates	Name		Location	ft	m	Year
8.48N, 82.38W	•Chiriqui (alt Baru) (volc[1])	*Central*	Panama	11,410	3480	1854
45.22N,121.42W	Hood	*Cascade*	Oregon, USA	11,240	3430	
40.29N,121.30W	Lassen (volc)	*Cascade*	California, USA	10,460	3190	1863
19.02N, 70.59W	Duarte (for Trujillo)	*Central*	Dominican Republic	10,420	3170	
18.22N, 71.59W	Selle	*Selle*	Haiti	8,790	2680	
46.12N,122.11W	•Saint Helens (volc)	*Cascade*	Washington, USA	8,400	2560	1853
13.50N, 89.38W	Santa Ana (volc)	*Apareca Lamatepeque*	El Salvador	7,730	2360	
18.03N, 76.35W	Blue (Mountain)	*Eastern*	Jamaica	7,400	2260	
13.45N, 86.23W	•Mogoton	*Dipilto*	Honduras-Nicaragua	6,910	2110	
35.46N, 82.16W	Mitchell	*Blue (Ridge) (Appalachian)*	North Carolina, USA	6,680	2040	
19.59N, 76.50W	Turquino	*Maestra*	Cuba	6,480	1970	
44.16N, 71.18W	Washington	*White (Appalachian)*	New Hampshire, USA	6,290	1920	1642
16.03N, 61.40W	Soufriere (volc)	*—*	Guadeloupe[2]	4,870	1480	
14.48N, 61.10W	Pelee (volc)	*—*	Martinique	4,580	1400	
18.10N, 66.36W	Punta	*Central*	Puerto Rico	4,390	1340	

OCEANIA

Coordinates	Name		Location	ft	m	Year
4.05S, 137.11E	Jaya (for Carstensz, Djaja, Sukarno)	*Sudirman (for Nassau)*	Irian Jaya, Indonesia	16,500	5030	1936
4.21S, 138.26E	Daam	*Jayawijaya (for Djajawidjaja, Orange)*	Irian Jaya, Indonesia	16,150	4920	

* * *

Coordinates	Name		Location	ft	m	Year
4.03S, 137.02E	Pilimsit (for Idenburg)	*Sudirman*	Irian Jaya, Indonesia	15,750	4800	1962
4.15S, 138.45E	Trikora (for Wilhelmina)	*Jayawijaya*	Irian Jaya, Indonesia	15,580	4750	1913
4.44S, 140.20E	Mandala (for Juliana)	*Jayawijaya*	Irian Jaya, Indonesia	15,420	4700	1959
5.43S, 145.03E	•Wilhelm	*Bismarck*	Papua New Guinea	15,400	4690	
4.25S, 139.56E	Wisnumurti (for Jan Pieterszoon Coen)	*Jayawijaya*	Irian Jaya, Indonesia	15,080	4590	
4.42S, 140.06E	Yamin (for Prins Hendrik)	*Jayawijaya*	Irian Jaya, Indonesia	14,860	4530	
6.07S, 144.42E	•Kubor	*Kubor*	Papua New Guinea	14,300	4360	
5.38S, 145.01E	•Herbert	*Bismarck*	Papua New Guinea	14,000	4270	

* * *

Coordinates	Name		Location	ft	m	Year
19.50N,155.28W	(Mauna) Kea: highest peak (volc[3])	*—*	Hawaii, USA[4]	13,800	4210	1824?

[1]Dormant since 1550.
[2]Basse-Terre I.
[3]No known eruption.
[4]Hawaii I.
For an explanation of symbols and abbreviations, see pages 16–17.

(Continued)

TABLE 9a. (Continued)

Latitude and Longitude	Peak and [Massif]	Mountain Range or System	Location	Elevation		First Ascent
				ft	m	
19.28N,155.36W	(Mauna) Loa (volc)	—	Hawaii, USA[1]	13,680	4170	
6.04S, 143.53E	•Giluwe	Hagen	Papua New Guinea	13,660	4160	
6.16S, 147.04E	•Bangeta	Saruwaged	Papua New Guinea	13,470	4110	
8.53S, 147.33E	•Victoria	Owen Stanley	Papua New Guinea	13,360	4070	1889
43.37S, 170.08E	Cook (alt Aorangi): highest peak	Southern Alps	South I, New Zealand	12,350	3760	1894
5.55S, 154.59E	•Balbi (volc2)	Emperor	Papua New Guinea[3]	10,210	3110	
20.43N,156.13W	Haleakala (volc)	—	Hawaii, USA[4]	10,020	3060	1828?
9.43S, 160.02E	Makarakombou	Kavo	Solomon Islands[5]	8,030	2450	
17.37S,149.28W	Orohena	—	French Polynesia[6]	7,340	2240	
36.27S, 148.16E	Kosciusko	Great Dividing	New South Wales, Australia	7,330	2230	1840?
15.20S, 166.44E	•Tabwemasana: E peak	—	Vanuatu[7]	6,160	1880	
13.35S,172.27W	•Silisili (alt Hertha)	—	Samoa[8]	6,090	1860	
20.36S, 164.46E	Panie	—	New Caledonia	5,340	1630	
17.37S, 178.01E	Tomaniivi (alt Victoria)	—	Fiji[9]	4,340	1320	
SOUTH AMERICA						
32.39S, 70.01W	Aconcagua	Andes	Mendoza, Argentina	22,840	6960	1897
27.06S, 68.32W	Ojos del Salado: SE peak (volc2)	Andes	Argentina-Chile	22,560[10]	6870[10]	1937
27.51S, 68.47W	Bonete	Andes	La Rioja, Argentina	22,550	6870	1913
27.47S, 68.51W	Pissis	Andes	Catamarca-La Rioja, Argentina	22,240	6780	1937

1Hawaii I.
2No known eruption.
3Bougainville I.
4Maui I.
5Guadalcanal I.
6Tahiti I.
7Espiritu Santo I.
8Savaii I.
9Viti Levu I.
10Average of elevations officially given by Argentina (22,540 ft, 6870 m) and Chile (22,570 ft, 6880 m).

For an explanation of symbols and abbreviations, see pages 16–17.

(Continued)

Figure 56. *Snow-covered Aconcagua, the highest mountain in the Western Hemisphere, towers above a desolate and forbidding section of the Argentinian Andes. (Credit: Organization of American States.)*

TABLE 9a. (Continued)

Latitude and Longitude	Peak and [Massif]	Mountain Range or System	Location	Elevation ft	Elevation m	First Ascent
9.07S, 77.37W	Huascaran: S peak	Blanca (Andes)	Peru	22,210	6770	1932
31.59S, 70.07W	Mercedario	Andes	San Juan, Argentina	22,210	6770	1934
24.43S, 68.33W	Llullaillaco (volc)	Andes	Argentina-Chile	22,100[1]	6730[1]	bef 1550
24.58S, 66.22W	Libertador (for Cachi: N peak) [Cachi]	Andes	Salta, Argentina	22,050	6720	1950
27.06S, 68.32W	•Ojos del Salado: NW peak (volc[2])	Andes	Argentina-Chile	22,050	6720	1937
33.22S, 69.47W	Tupungato	Andes	Argentina-Chile	21,900[3]	6670[3]	1897
27.03S, 68.27W	•Gonzalez: highest peak	Andes	Argentina-Chile	21,850	6660	
9.07S, 77.37W	Huascaran: N peak	Blanca (Andes)	Peru	21,840	6650	1908 or 1939
27.04S, 68.29W	Muerto	Andes	Argentina-Chile	21,820[4]	6650[4]	1950?
10.16S, 76.54W	Yerupaja: N peak	Huayhuash (Andes)	Peru	21,760	6630	1950
27.02S, 68.18W	Incahuasi (alt Incaguasi)	Andes	Argentina-Chile	21,700[5]	6610[5]	1859 or 1913
25.55S, 66.52W	Galan	Andes	Catamarca, Argentina	21,650	6600	
27.06S, 68.47W	Tres Cruces: central peak	Andes	Argentina-Chile	21,540[6]	6560[6]	1937
27.03S, 68.27W	•Gonzalez: N peak	Andes	Argentina-Chile	21,490	6550	1955
18.06S, 68.54W	Sajama	Occidental (Andes)	Bolivia	21,460	6540	1939
10.16S, 76.54W	•Yerupaja: S peak	Huayhuash (Andes)	Peru	21,380	6510	1958
27.16S, 68.32W	Nacimiento	Andes	Catamarca, Argentina	21,300	6490	1937
15.31S, 72.42W	Coropuna: highest peak	Occidental (Andes)	Peru	21,080	6420	1911
15.50S, 68.34W	Illampu [Sorata]	Real (Andes)	Bolivia	21,070	6420	1928
27.08S, 68.49W	Puntiagudo	Andes	Argentina-Chile	21,060[7]	6420[7]	
32.05S, 69.59W	Ramada	Andes	San Juan, Argentina	21,030	6410	1934
9.07S, 77.36W	Chopicalqui (alt Huascaran: E peak)	Blanca (Andes)	Peru	21,000	6400	1932
26.30S, 68.32W	Laudo	Andes	Catamarca, Argentina	21,000	6400	
9.32S, 77.18W	Huantsan: S peak	Blanca (Andes)	Peru	20,980	6390	1952
13.48S, 71.14W	Ausangate: highest peak	Vilcanota (Andes)	Peru	20,950	6380	1953
15.51S, 68.36W	Ancohuma [Sorata]	Real (Andes)	Bolivia	20,930	6380	1919
29.08S, 69.48W	Toro	Andes	Argentina-Chile	20,930	6380	
9.02S, 77.41W	Huandoy: central peak	Blanca (Andes)	Peru	20,850	6360	1932
9.02S, 77.41W	•Huandoy: W peak	Blanca (Andes)	Peru	20,850	6360	1954
10.17S, 76.54W	Siula: N peak	Huayhuash (Andes)	Peru	20,850	6360	1936
27.06S, 68.47W	•Tres Cruces: S peak	Andes	Argentina-Chile	20,850	6360	1937

Coordinates	Name	Range	Country	ft	m	Eruption
15.31S, 72.42W	•Coropuna: NW peak	Occidental (Andes)	Peru	20,790	6340	1952
13.48S, 71.14W	•Ausangate: E peak	Vilcanota (Andes)	Peru	20,770	6330	1952
29.56S, 69.54W	Tortolas	Andes	Argentina-Chile	20,760[8]	6330[8]	1924 or 1952
16.39S, 67.48W	Illimani: S peak	Real (Andes)	Bolivia	20,740	6320	1898
15.50S, 71.52W	Ampato: highest peak	Occidental (Andes) ***	Peru	20,700	6310	1950
16.39S, 67.48W	•Illimani: N peak	Real (Andes)	Bolivia	20,670	6300	1915
1.28S, 78.48W	•Chimborazo	Occidental (Andes)	Ecuador	20,580	6270	1880
18.10S, 69.09W	Parinacota (volc2) [Payachata]	Andes	Bolivia-Chile	20,440[9]	6230[9]	1928
18.25S, 69.08W	Guallatiri (volc)	Andes	Chile	19,880	6060	1926?
0.40S, 78.26W	•Cotopaxi (volc)	Oriental (Andes)	Ecuador	19,340	5900	1872
22.26S, 67.55W	Tocorpuri: highest peak (volc2)	Andes	Bolivia-Chile	19,140	5830	1939
16.18S, 71.24W	Misti (volc)	Occidental (Andes)	Peru	19,100	5820	1677?
3.00N, 76.00W	Huila (volc2)	Central (Andes)	Colombia	18,870	5750	1944
23.23S, 67.45W	Lascar (volc)	Andes	Chile	18,420	5610	
6.26N, 72.18W	Guican [Cocuy]	Oriental (Andes)	Colombia	18,020	5490	
4.54N, 75.18W	Ruiz (volc)	Central (Andes)	Colombia	17,680	5390	
10.48N, 73.41W	Bolivar [Horqueta]	Santa Marta	Colombia	17,390	5300	1939
10.49N, 73.41W	Colon (alt Cristobal Colon) [Horqueta]	Santa Marta	Colombia	17,390	5300	1939
8.33N, 71.03W	Bolivar (alt Columna)	Merida	Venezuela	16,430	5010	1935 or 1936
0.50N, 65.25W	Neblina	Imeri	Amazonas, Brazil	9,890	3010	
20.26S, 41.47W	Bandeira	Caparao	Espirito Santo-Minas Gerais, Brazil	9,480	2890	
31.59S, 64.59W	Champaqui	Cordoba	Cordoba, Argentina	9,460	2880	
5.12N, 60.44W	Roraima	Pacaraima	Brazil-Guyana-Venezuela	9,430	2870	1884
22.23S, 44.38W	Agulhas Negras [Itatiaia]	Mantiqueira	Minas Gerais-Rio de Janeiro, Brazil	9,140	2790	

1Average of elevations officially given by Argentina (22,060 ft, 6720 m) and Chile (22,150 ft, 6750 m).
2No known eruption.
3Average of elevations officially given by Argentina (22,310 ft, 6800 m) and Chile (21,490 ft, 6550 m).
4Average of elevations officially given by Argentina (21,460 ft, 6540 m) and Chile (22,200 ft, 6760 m).
5Average of elevations officially given by Argentina (21,720 ft, 6620 m) and Chile (21,690 ft, 6610 m).
6Average of elevations officially given by Argentina (20,850 ft, 6360 m) and Chile (22,210 ft, 6770 m).
7Average of elevations officially given by Argentina (19,360 ft, 5900 m) and Chile (22,770 ft, 6940 m).
8Average of elevations officially given by Argentina (20,740 ft, 6320 m) and Chile (20,770 ft, 6330 m).
9Average of elevations officially given by Bolivia (20,120 ft, 6130 m) and Chile (20,770 ft, 6330 m).

For an explanation of symbols and abbreviations, see pages 16–17.

9b. Highest Mountain or Elevation in Each Country

Contents

Conventional name of country.

Conventional and other names of mountain peak and of massif, if any (in brackets).

Conventional and other names of mountain range or system.

Island, if any, on which mountain is located.

Elevation (i.e.,altitude of summit aboves sea level), in feet and meters.

Coverage

All countries with an area of at least 200 mi^2 (518 km^2).

Rounding

Elevations are rounded to the nearest 10 ft (m).

Entries

188.

TABLE 9b. HIGHEST MOUNTAIN OR ELEVATION IN EACH COUNTRY

Country	Peak and [Massif]	Mountain Range or System	Island, if Any	Elevation ft	Elevation m
Afghanistan	•Noshaq: highest peak	Hindu Kush		24,580	7490
Albania	Korab	Korab		9,050	2760
Algeria	Tahat [Atakor]	Ahaggar (alt Hoggar)		9,570	2920
Andorra	•Plan del Estans	—		9,680	2950
Angola	Moco	Upanda		8,600	2620
Argentina	Aconcagua	Andes		22,840	6960
Australia	Kosciusko	Great Dividing		7,330	2230
Austria	Grossglockner	Alps (off in Austria Alpen)		12,460	3800
Bahamas	Alvernia [for Como (Hill)]	—	Cat	210	63
Bahrain	•Dukhan	—	Bahrain	440	140
Bangladesh	•Keokradong	Chittagong (Hills)		4,030	1230
Barbados	•Hillaby	—	Barbados	1,110	340
Belgium	Botrange	Ardennes		2,270	690
Belize	Victoria	Maya		3,680	1120
Benin	—[Tanekas]	Togo		2,150	650
Bhutan	Khula Kangri I (alt Kula Gangri I; off Kula I)	Assam Himalaya		24,780	7550
Bolivia	Sajama	Occidental (Andes)		21,460	6540
Botswana	•Tsodilo (Hill)	—		5,920	1810
Brazil	Neblina	Imeri		9,890	3010
Brunei	•Pagon	Crocker	Borneo	6,070	1850
Bulgaria	Musala	Rhodope (off in Bulgaria Rodopi)		9,600	2920
Burkina Faso	•Nakourou	—		2,460	750
Burma	Hkakabo Razi	Kumon		19,300	5880
Burundi	•Muhungwe	?		9,840	3000
Cameroon	Fako (volc) [Cameroon (alt Cameroun)]	Cameroon (alt Cameroun)		13,350	4070
Canada	Logan: central peak [Logan]	Saint Elias		19,520	5950
Cape Verde	Cano (volc)	—	Fogo	9,280	2830
Central African Republic	Gaou	Yade		4,660	1420
Chad	(Emi) Koussi (volc)	Tibesti		11,470	3490

For an explanation of symbols and abbreviations, see pages 16–17.

(Continued)

TABLE 9b. (Continued)

Country	Peak and [Massif]	Mountain Range or System	Island, if Any	Elevation ft	Elevation m
Chile	Ojos del Salado: SE peak (volc)	Andes		22,560	6870
China	Everest (alt Qomolangma, Chumulangma) [Everest]	Nepal Himalaya		29,030	8850
Colombia	Huila (volc)	Central (Andes)		18,870	5750
Comoros	•Kartala (alt Karthala) (volc)	—	Njazidja	7,750	2360
Congo	Berongou	?		3,280	1000
Costa Rica	Chirripo Grande	Talamanca		12,530	3820
Cuba	Turquino	Maestra	Cuba	6,480	1970
Cyprus	Khionistra (alt Olympus)	Troodos	Cyprus	6,410	1950
Czechoslovakia	Gerlachovsky (alt Gerlachovka; for Stalin)	Tatra (off Tatry)		8,710	2650
Denmark	•Ejer Bavnehoj	—		560	170
Djibouti	•Mousaalli (alt Musa Ali)	—		6,770	2060
Dominica	Diablotin (volc)	—	Dominica	4,750	1450
Dominican Republic	Duarte (for Trujillo)	Central	Hispaniola	10,420	3170
Ecuador	•Chimborazo	Occidental (Andes)		20,580	6270
Egypt	Katrinah (alt Catherine) [Musa]	Sinai		8,650	2640
El Salvador	Pital	Celaque		8,960	2730
Equatorial Guinea	Malabo (for Santa Isabel) (volc)	—	Bioko	9,840	3000
Ethiopia	Ancua [Ras Dashan (off Ras Dashen)]	Semien (off Simen)		14,930	4550
Faeroe Islands	Slaettaratindur	—	Eysteroy (off Ostero)	2,890	880
Falkland Islands	•Paget (volc)	—	South Georgia	9,620	2930
Fiji	Tomaniivi (alt Victoria)	—	Viti Levu	4,340	1320
Finland	Haltiatunturi (alt Reisduoddarhaldde)	Haltia (alt Halddia)		4,360	1330
France	(Mont-)Blanc (alt Bianco) [Blanc (alt Bianco)]	Alps (off in France Alpes)		15,770	4810
French Guiana	—[Timotakem]	Tumuc-Humac		2,620	800
French Polynesia	Orohena	—	Tahiti	7,340	2240
French Southern and Antarctic Lands	•Ross (volc)	—	Kerguelen	6,070	1850
Gabon	Iboundji	Chaillu		5,160	1570
Gambia	?	—		230	70

(Continued)

Country	Mountain	Range/location	Island	ft	m
Germany					
East	Fichtel(-berg)	Erz(gebirge)		3,980	1220
West	Zug(spitze)	Alps (off in Germany Alpen)		9,720	2960
Ghana	Afadjoto	Akwapim-Togo		2,900	890
Greece	Mytikas [Olympus (off Olimbos)]	Olympus (off Olimbos)		9,570	2920
Greenland	Gunnbjorn	—	Greenland	12,140	3700
Guadeloupe	Soufriere (volc)	—	Basse-Terre	4,870	1480
Guam	•Lamlam	—	Guam	1,330	410
Guatemala	Tajumulco (volc)	Madre		13,850	4220
Guinea	Nimba	Nimba		5,780	1760
Guinea-Bissau	?	Fouta Djallon		980	300
Guyana	Roraima	Pacaraima		9,430	2870
Haiti	Selle	Selle	Hispaniola	8,790	2680
Honduras	Las Minas	Celaque		9,400	2870
Hong Kong	Tai Mo	—		3,140	960
Hungary	Kekes	Matra		3,330	1010
Iceland	Hvannadalshnukur	—	Iceland	6,950	2120
India	Kangchenjunga (alt Kanchenjunga): highest peak [Kangchenjunga]	Nepal Himalaya		28,170	8590
Indonesia					
in Asia	Kerinci (for Indrapura, Kerintji) (volc)	Barisan	Sumatra	12,470	3800
in Oceania (Irian Jaya)	Jaya (for Carstensz, Djaja, Sukarno)	Sudirman (for Nassau)	New Guinea	16,500	5030
Iran	•Damavand (alt Demavend)	Alborz (alt Elburz)		18,610	5670
Iraq	•Algurd (alt Halgurd)	Zagros		12,250	3730
Ireland	Carrantuohill (alt Carrantual)	Macgillicuddy's Reeks	Ireland	3,410	1040
Isle of Man	Snaefell		(Isle of) Man	2,040	620
Israel	•Meron (for Jarmaq, Sharqi)	Galilee		3,960	1210
Italy	(Mont-)Blanc (alt Bianco) [Blanc (alt Bianco)]	Alps (off in Italy Alpi)		15,770	4810
Ivory Coast	Nimba	Nimba		5,780	1760
Jamaica	Blue (Mountain)	Eastern	Jamaica	7,400	2260
Japan	Fuji (alt Huzi) (volc)	—	Honshu	12,390	3780
Jordan	•Ramm	Sharah		5,750	1750
Kampuchea	•Aural	Cardamomes		5,950	1810
Kenya	Batian [Kenya]	—		17,050	5200
Kiribati	•Banaba (volc)	—	Banaba (alt Ocean)	270	81

TABLE 9b. (Continued)

Country	Peak and [Massif]	Mountain Range or System	Island, if Any	Elevation	
				ft	m
Korea					
North	•Baitou (alt Paektu, Paitou)	Changbai (alt Changbaek, Changpai)		8,900	2710
South	•Halla	—	Cheju I	6,400	1950
Kuwait	?	—		980	300
Laos	•Bia	Tranninh		9,240	2820
Lebanon	Makmel [Qurnat al Sawda]	Lebanon (off Lubnan)		10,120	3080
Lesotho	Thabana Ntlenyana (alt Thabantshonyana)	Drakens(berg)		11,420	3480
Liberia	Nimba	Nimba		5,780	1760
Libya	•Kegueur Terbi (alt Chegor Tedi, Hessi)	Tibesti		10,330	3150
Liechtenstein	Grau(spitze)	Alps (off in Liechtenstein Alpen)		8,530	2600
Luxembourg	•Burgplatz	Ardennes		1,840	560
Madagascar	Maromokotro	Tsaratanana	Madagascar	9,470	2890
Malawi	Mlanje	Mlanje		10,000	3050
Malaysia					
Peninsular	Tahan	Cameron (Highlands)		7,190	2190
Sabah	Kinabalu: highest peak	Crocker	Borneo	13,450	4100
Sarawak	Murud	Tama Abu	Borneo	7,950	2420
Mali	Hombori Tondo	Hombori		3,770	1150
Malta	—[Dingii (Cliffs)]		Malta	830	250
Martinique	Pelee (volc)	—	Martinique	4,580	1400
Mauritania	Ijill (alt Idjil)	—		3,000	910
Mauritius	Riviere Noire	—	Mauritius	2,710	830
Mexico	Citaltepetl (alt Orizaba) (volc)	Neovolcanica		18,410	5610
Mongolia	Khuitun (alt Nayramdal; off Huyten) [Tavan Bogd]	Altay (alt Altai)		14,350	4370
Morocco	Toubkal: W peak [Toubkal]	Atlas		13,670	4160
Mozambique	Binga	Chimanimani		7,990	2440
Namibia	Konigstein [Brand(berg)]	Kaokoveld		8,550	2610
Nepal	Everest (alt Qomolangma, Chumulangma) [Everest]	Nepal Himalaya		29,030	8850

(Continued)

Country	Island	Range	Peak		
Netherlands	Saba	—	•Vaalser(berg)	1,060	320
Netherlands Antilles		—	•Scenery	2,900	860
New Caledonia	New Caledonia	—	Panie	5,340	1630
New Zealand	South (New Zealand)	Southern Alps	Cook (alt Aorangi): highest peak	12,350	3760
Nicaragua		Dipilto	•Mogoton	6,910	2110
Niger		Air (alt Azbine)	•Greboun	7,550	2300
Nigeria		Banglang	Vogel	6,700	2040
Norway		Jotunheimen	Galdhopiggen	8,100	2470
Oman		Akhdar	•Sham	10,190	3110
Pacific Islands (USA)	Agrihan	—	•Agrihan (volc)	3,170	960
Pakistan		Karakoram	K^2 (alt Chogori, Dapsang, Godwin Austen)	28,250	8610
Pakistan[1]		Hindu Kush	•Tirich Mir: W peak	25,260	7700
Panama		Central	•Chiriqui (alt Baru) (volc)	11,410	3480
Papua New Guinea	New Guinea	Bismarck	•Wilhelm	15,400	4690
Paraguay		Aracanguy	—[Villa Rica]	2,790	850
Peru		Blanca (Andes)	Huascaran: S peak	22,210	6770
Philippines	Mindanao	—	Apo (volc)	9,690	2950
Poland		Tatra (off Tatry)	Rysy	8,200	2500
Portugal in Africa (Madeira Islands)	Madeira	—	Ruivo de Santana	6,110	1860
Portugal in Europe	Pico	—	Ponta do Pico (alt Pico) (volc)	7,710	2350
Puerto Rico	Puerto Rico	Central	Punta	4,390	1340
Qatar			?	320	99
Reunion	Reunion	—	Neiges (volc)	10,070	3070
Romania		Transylvanian Alps (off Carpatii Meridionali)	Moldoveanu	8,340	2540
Rwanda		Virunga	Karisimbi (volc)	14,790	4510
Saint Helena	Tristan da Cunha	—	•Tristan da Cunha (volc)	6,760	2060
Saint Lucia	Saint Lucia	—	Gimie	3,140	960
Samoa	Savaii	—	Silisili (alt Hertha)	6,090	1860
Sao Tome and Principe	Sao Tome	—	(Pico de) Sao Tome	6,640	2020
Saudi Arabia		Yemen (Highlands)	•Razikh	11,990	3650
Senegal		—	• ?	1,910	580

[1] Exc Pakistan-held Kashmir.

For an explanation of symbols and abbreviations, see pages 16–17.

TABLE 9b. (Continued)

Country	Peak and [Massif]	Mountain Range or System	Island, if Any	Elevation ft	Elevation m
Sierra Leone	•Bintimani	Loma		6,390	1940
Singapore	•(Bukit) Timah	—	Singapore	580	180
Solomon Islands	Makarakombou	Kavo	Guadalcanal	8,030	2450
Somalia	Faddisome [Hor Bogor]	Carcar (off Karkaar)		8,500	2590
South Africa	•Injasuti	Drakens(berg)		11,310	3450
Spain					
in Africa (Canary Islands)	Teide (volc)	—	Tenerife	12,200	3720
in Europe	Mulhacen	Nevada		11,410	3480
Sri Lanka	Pidurutalagala	Piduru (Ridges)	Sri Lanka	8,280	2520
Sudan	•Kinyeti	Imatong		10,460	3190
Suriname	—[Wilhelmina]	Wilhelmina		4,200	1280
Svalbard	Newton	—	West Spitsbergen	5,630	1720
Swaziland	•Emlembe	Drakens(berg)		6,100	1860
Sweden	Kebnekaise	Kolen		6,930	2110
Switzerland	Dufour(spitze) [Rosa]	Alps (off in Switzerland Alpen, Alpes, Alpi)		15,200	4630
Syria	Hermon (off Shaykh)	Anti-Lebanon (off Sharqi)		9,230	2810
Taiwan	Yu (alt Hsinkao, Morrison)	Central (off Chungyang)	Taiwan	13,110	4000
Tanzania	Kibo [Kilimanjaro] (volc)	—		19,340	5890
Thailand	Inthanon (alt Angka)	Phi Pan Nam		8,450	2580
Togo	Agou (alt Baumann)	Togo		3,240	990
Tonga	•Kao (volc)	—	Kao	3,380	1030
Trinidad and Tobago	Aripo	—	Trinidad	3,080	940

Country	Highest point	Range	Location	ft	m
Tunisia	Shanabi (alt Chambi)	Dorsale		5,070	1540
Turkey					
in Asia	Great Ararat (off Buyukagri) (volc)	—		16,950	5160
in Europe	Mahya	Istranca		3,380	1030
Uganda	Margherita [Stanley]	Ruwenzori		16,760	5110
UK	(Ben) Nevis	Grampian	Great Britain	4,410	1340
United Arab Emirates	•Adhan	Hajar al Gharbi		3,700	1130
Uruguay	•Animas	Animas		1,640	500
USA					
in North America	McKinley: S peak [McKinley]	Alaska		20,320	6190
in Oceania (Hawaii)	(Mauna) Kea: highest peak (volc)	—	Hawaii	13,800	4210
USSR					
in Asia	Kommunizma (for Garmo, Stalina)	Pamir-Alay (alt Pamir-Alai)		24,590	7490
in Europe	Elbrus (for Elborus): W peak (volc) [Elbrus]	Caucasus (off Kavkaz)		18,480	5630
Vanuatu	•Tabwemasana: E peak	—	Espiritu Santo	6,160	1880
Venezuela	Bolivar (alt Columna)	Merida		16,430	5010
Vietnam	•(Ngoc) Linh	Annamese (off Trungphan)		10,500	3200
West Bank	•Asur	—		3,330	1020
Western Sahara	?	—		2,700	820
Yemen					
North	•Hadur Shuayb	Yemen (Highlands)		12,340	3760
South	•Thamar (off Thamir)	Yemen (Highlands)		8,240	2510
Yugoslavia	Triglav	Alps (off in Yugoslavia Alpe)		9,400	2860
Zaire	Margherita [Stanley]	Ruwenzori		16,760	5110
Zambia	?	Nyika		7,400	2260
Zimbabwe	Inyangani	Inyanga		8,510	2590

For an explanation of symbols and abbreviations, see pages 16–17.

10

GEOGRAPHIC TABLES AND COMPARISONS: NATURAL LAKES

10a. Largest Natural Lakes, by Continent

Contents

Latitude and longitude, in degrees and minutes, at center of lake.
Conventional and other (alternate, former, and official) names of lake.
Division and country (or countries) in which located.
Area in square miles and square kilometers.[1]
Elevation (i.e., altitude of surface above sea level), in feet and meters.
Greatest recorded depth of water, in feet and meters.[1]

Coverage

Above * * *, all natural lakes with an area of at least 300 mi² (777 km²).
Below * * *, other well-known natural lakes, including the largest and deepest in
   certain countries.

Rounding

Areas are rounded to the nearest 10 mi² (km²) if above 100 mi² (km²).

Entries

318, as follows: Africa—28
                        Asia—73
                        Europe—63
                        North America—122
                        Oceania—13
                        South America—19

[1]When area and/or depth vary from season to season, the normal minima and maxima are shown as follows:
4,000/10,000.

TABLE 10a. LARGEST NATURAL LAKES, BY CONTINENT

Latitude and Longitude	Lake	Location	Area		Elevation		Greatest Depth	
			mi²	km²	ft	m	ft	m
AFRICA								
1.00S, 33.00E	Victoria	Kenya-Tanzania-Uganda	24,300	62,940	3,721	1134	279	85
6.00S, 29.30E	Tanganyika	Burundi-Tanzania-Zaire-Zambia	12,350	32,000	2,539	774	4825	1471
12.00S, 34.30E	Malawi (alt Niassa, Nyasa)	Malawi-Mozambique-Tanzania	8,680	22,490	1,558	475	2316	706
13.20N, 14.00E	Chad (alt Tchad)	Cameroon-Chad-Niger-Nigeria	4,000/ 10,000	10,360/ 25,900	787	240	36/13	11/4
3.30N, 36.00E	Rudolf (alt Turkana) (salt)	Ethiopia-Kenya	2,470	6,400	1,401	427	240	73
1.40N, 31.00E	Mobutu Sese Seko (for Albert)	Uganda-Zaire	2,160	5,590	2,024	617	197/ 164	60/ 50
2.00S, 18.20E	Mai-Ndombe (for Leopold II)	Zaire	900/ 3,170	2,070/ 8,210	1,116	340	39/33	12/10
11.05S, 29.45E	Bangweulu	Zambia	1,930	5,000	3,740	1140	16	5
1.30N, 33.00E	•Kyoga (alt Kioga)	Uganda	1,710	4,430	3,400	1036	26	8
9.00S, 28.45E	Mweru	Zaire-Zambia	1,680	4,350	3,025	922	10/6	3/2
12.10N, 37.20E	Tana (alt Tsana)	Ethiopia	1,390	3,600	6,037	1840	30	9
8.00S, 32.25E	Rukwa (salt)	Tanganyika, Tanzania	1,100	2,850	2,602	793	shallow	
2.00S, 29.10E	Kivu	Rwanda-Zaire	860	2,220	4,790	1460	1575	480
0.21S, 29.35E	Rutanzige (for Edward, Idi Amin Dada)	Uganda-Zaire	830	2,150	2,992	912	384	117
31.15N, 32.00E	•Manzala (off Manzilah) (salt, lag)	Egypt	530	1,360	0	0	shallow	
6.20N, 37.50E	Abaya (for Margherita)	Ethiopia	450	1,160	4,160	1268	43	13
3.40S, 35.05E	Eyasi (salt)	Tanganyika, Tanzania	410	1,050	3,379	1030		
15.12S, 35.50E	Chilwa (alt Chirua, Shirwa) (salt)	Malawi-Mozambique	400	1,040	1,805	550	shallow	
2.25S, 36.00E	Natron (salt)	Kenya-Tanzania	350	900	2,001	610		
11.10N, 41.47E	•Abbe (alt Abe; off Abhe) (salt)	Djibouti-Ethiopia	300	780	0	0		
5.15N, 3.14W	•Aby (salt, lag)	Ivory Coast	300	780	0	0		
		* * *						
16.45N, 3.54W	Faguibine	Mali	230	590			34	10

Coordinates	Name	Country						
5.50N, 37.33E	Chamo (alt Chama; for Ruspoli)	Ethiopia	210	550	4,052	1235	33	10
8.36S, 26.26E	•Upemba	Zaire	200	530	3,281	1000	11	3
0.48S, 18.03E	Tumba	Zaire	190	500	1,115	340	39/33	12/10
8.00N, 38.50E	Ziway (alt Zeway, Zwai)	Ethiopia	170	430	6,057	1846	13	4
9.29N, 38.32E	Shala	Ethiopia	160	410	5,141	1567	820	250
14.38S, 35.12E	•Malombe	Malawi	150	390	1,542	470	20	6

ASIA

Coordinates	Name	Country						
42.00N, 50.00E	Caspian (Sea) (off Kaspiy-skoye, Khazar) (salt)	Iran-USSR	146,100	378,400	−92	−28	3363	1025
45.00N, 60.00E	Aral (Sea) (off Aralskoye) (salt)	Kazakhstan-Uzbekistan, USSR	24,750	64,100	171	52	223	68
54.00N, 109.00E	Baykal (alt Baikal)	Russia, USSR	12,160	31,500	1,493	455	5712	1741
46.00N, 74.00E	Balkhash (alt Balkash) (salt)	Kazakhstan, USSR	7,070	18,300	1,112	339	85	26
13.00N, 104.00E	•(Tonle) Sap	Kampuchea	1,040/3,860	2,700/10,000			39	12
42.25N, 77.15E	Issyk(-Kul) (salt)	Kirgizia, USSR	2,420	6,280	5,279	1609	2303	702
37.40N, 45.30E	•Orumiyeh (for Rezaiyeh, Urmia) (salt)	Iran	1,500/2,300	3,880/5,960	4,183	1275	52	16
74.30N, 102.30E	Taymyr (alt Taimyr)	Russia, USSR	1,760	4,560	20	6	85	26
37.00N, 100.20E	Koko (alt Kuku, Chinghai, Tsinghai; off Qinghai) (salt)	Qinghai, China	1,720	4,460	10,489	3197	125	38
29.18N, 112.45E	Dongting (alt Tungting)	Hunan, China	1,200/2,010	3,100/5,200	36	11	33	10
38.33N, 42.46E	Van (salt)	Turkey	1,430	3,710	5,401	1646	82	25
45.00N, 132.24E	Khanka (alt Xingkai, Hsingkai)	China-USSR	1,170/1,620	3,030/4,190	223	68	35	11
29.00N, 116.25E	Poyang	Jiangxi, China	1,290	3,350	5,906	1800	66	20
50.20N, 92.45E	Uvs (alt Ubsa, Ubsu) (salt)	Mongolia	1,290	3,350	2,490	759	shallow	
33.18N, 118.41E	Hongze (alt Hungtse, Hungtze)	Anhui-Jiangsu,China	1,040	2,700	49	15	13	4
46.10N, 81.50E	Ala(kol) (salt)	Kazakhstan, USSR	1,020	2,650	1,148	350	177	54
51.00N, 100.30E	Hovsgol (alt Hobsogol, Khubsugul, Kosogol)	Mongolia	1,010	2,620	5,328	1624	807	246
30.45N, 90.30E	Nam (alt Namu, Tengri) (salt)	Tibet, China	970	2,500	15,181	4627	16	5
31.15N, 120.10E	Tai	Jiangsu-Zhejiang, China	850	2,210	39	12		

(Continued)

For an explanation of symbols and abbreviations, see pages 16–17.

Figure 57. Beach at Bandar-e Anzali on the southern shore of the Caspian Sea, which not only has the largest area of any lake on earth but holds more than three times as much water as any other lake. (Credit: Iran National Tourist Organization.)

TABLE 10a. (Continued)

Latitude and Longitude	Lake	Location	Area mi2	Area km2	Elevation ft	Elevation m	Greatest Depth ft	Greatest Depth m
54.50N, 77.30E	Chany (salt)	Russia, USSR	770	1,990	345	105	30	9
30.50N, 47.10E	•Hammar	Iraq	750	1,940			7	2
31.50N, 89.00E	•Siling (alt Chilin, Goring, Ziling) (salt)	Tibet, China	720	1,860	14,748	4495	26	8
48.00N, 92.10E	Har Us (alt Hara Usa, Khara-Us)	Mongolia	720	1,850	3,783	1153	15	4
48.00N, 84.00E	Zaysan (alt Zaisan)	Kazakhstan, USSR	690[1]	1,800[1]	1,296	395	33	10
49.00N, 117.27E	•Hulun (alt Dalai) (salt)	Inner Mongolia, China	620	1,590	4,183	1275	5	2
40.30N, 90.30E	Lop (alt Lopu, Lob) (salt)	Xinjiang, China	0/1,160	0/3,010	2,520	768	7/0	2/0
38.45N, 33.25E	Tuz (salt)	Turkey	580	1,500	3,035	925	shallow	
49.12N, 93.24E	Hyargas (alt Hirgis, Khirgis) (salt)	Mongolia	540	1,410	3,373	1028	262	80
31.00N, 86.22E	•Tangra (alt Tangkulayumu, Dangrayum) (salt)	Tibet, China	540	1,400	15,499	4724		
42.00N, 87.00E	Bosten (alt Possuteng, Baghrash, Bagrax) (salt)	Xinjiang, China	530	1,380	3,406	1038		
7.30N, 100.15E	•(Thale) Luang (alt Sap) (salt, lag)	Thailand	500	1,290	0	0	shallow	
50.24N, 68.57E	Tengiz (salt)	Kazakhstan, USSR	450	1,160	997	304	26	8
2.35N, 98.40E	Toba	Sumatra I, Indonesia	440	1,150	2,973	906	1736	529
44.55N, 82.55E	•Ebi(nur) (alt Aipi) (salt)	Xinjiang, China	410	1,070	699	213	49	15
19.45N, 85.25E	•Chilka (salt, lag)	Orissa, India	350/ 450	910/ 1,170	0	0	shallow	
31.30N, 35.30E	Dead (Sea) (off Lut, Mayyit, Melah) (salt)	Israel-Jordan-West Bank	390	1,020	−1,289	− 393	1421	433
34.35N, 117.13E	•Weishan	Jiangsu-Shandong, China	390	1,000				
31.31N, 117.33E	•Chao	Anhui,China	350	900				
14.23N, 121.15E	Bay (salt)	Luzon I, Philippines	340	890	7	2	21	6
28.35N, 90.20E	•Puma (alt Pomo, Pumuchang)	Tibet, China	340	880	16,194	4936		6

[1]This original area has been increased by damming to 2,130mi2, 5,510 km2.

For an explanation of symbols and abbreviations, see pages 16–17.

(Continued)

TABLE 10a. (Continued)

Latitude and Longitude	Lake	Location	Area mi²	Area km²	Elevation ft	Elevation m	Greatest Depth ft	Greatest Depth m
47.20N, 87.10E	•Ulungur (alt Wulunku, Pulunto, Urungu) (salt)	Xinjiang, China	320	830	1,536	468		
68.20N, 91.00E	Khantayskoye	Russia, USSR	320	820	240	73		
31.06N, 85.35E	•Tielinanmu (alt Terinam, Tiehlinanmu) (salt)	Tibet, China	310	810	15,368	4684		
29.00N, 90.40E	•Yamzho (alt Yangchoyun, Yamdrok)	Tibet,China	310	800	14,350	4374		
		* * *						
34.45N, 51.36E	•Namak (salt)	Iran	290	750	984	300	shallow	
53.15N, 73.15E	Seletyteniz (salt)	Kazakhstan, USSR	290	750	213	65	10	3
46.35N, 81.00E	Sasyk(kol) (salt)	Kazakhstan, USSR	280	740	1,139	347	15	5
53.00N, 79.36E	Kulunda (off Kulundinskoye)	Russia, USSR	280	730	322	98	16	5
69.45N, 87.45E	Pyasino	Russia, USSR	280	730	108	33	33	10
32.50N, 119.15E	•Gaobao (alt Kaoyu, Kaopao)	Anhui-Jiangsu, China	270	700				
35.15N, 136.05E	Biwa	Honshu I, Japan	270	690	285	87	314	96
31.10N, 88.15E	•Zhalin (alt Dzharing, Chalin)	Tibet, China	260	670	15,447	4708		
37.40N, 31.30E	Beysehir	Turkey	250	660	3,678	1121	30	9
34.55N, 98.00E	•Ngoring (alt Oling)	Qinghai, China	250	650	14,010	4270		
47.48N, 117.42E	Buyr (alt Buir, Peierh, Bor)	China-Mongolia	240	610	1,913	583	36	11
33.45N, 79.15E	•Pangong (alt Bangong, Pangkung) (salt)	China-Pakistan-held Kashmir	230	600	13,936	4248	142	43
2.45S, 121.32E	Towuti	Celebes I, Indonesia	220	580	961	293	463	141
34.52N, 97.30E	•Gyaring (alt Chaling, Tsaring)	Qinghai,China	220	570	14,010	4270		
48.06N, 93.12E	Har (alt Hara, Khara)	Mongolia	220	570	3,622	1104	23	7
30.40N, 81.25E	•Mapam (alt Manasalowu, Manasarowar)	Tibet, China	200	520	14,952	4557	269	82
38.02N, 30.53E	Egridir (alt Egirdir)	Turkey	180	470	3,005	916	43	13
24.50N, 102.43E	Dian (alt Tien)	Yunnan, China	150	400	6,400	1950		
39.00N, 73.30E	Kara(kul)	Tadzhikistan, USSR	150	380	12,842	3914	781	238
1.52S, 120.35E	Poso	Celebes I, Indonesia	110	280	1,700	518	1444	440
51.35N, 87.40E	Teletskoye [for Altyn(-Kol)]	Russia, USSR	86	220	1,431	436	1066	325

2.28S,	121.20E	•Matana	Celebes I, Indonesia	75	190	1,253	382	1936	590
32.48N,	35.35E	•Tiberias [alt (Sea of) Galilee; off Kinneret]	Israel	64	170	−686	− 209	157	48
38.13N,	72.50E	Sarez (off Sarezskoye)	Tadzhikistan, USSR	33	86	10,627	3239	1657	505
51.27N,	157.05E	Kurile (off Kurilskoye)	Russia, USSR	30	77	341	104	1004	306
42.45N,	141.20E	Shikotsu	Hokkaido I, Japan	30	77	814	248	1191	363
40.28N,	140.55E	Towada	Honshu I, Japan	23	59	1,312	400	1096	334
39.43N,	140.40E	Tazawa	Honshu I, Japan	10	26	817	249	1394	425
1.01S,	100.43E	•Dibaruh	Sumatra I, Indonesia	4	11	4,803	1464	1017	310

EUROPE

61.00N,	31.30E	Ladoga (off Ladozhskoye)	Russia, USSR	6,830	17,700	13	4	755	230
61.30N,	35.45E	Onega (off Onezhskoye)	Russia, USSR	3,750	9,720	108	33	417	127
58.55N,	13.30E	Vanem (alt Vaner, Vener)	Sweden	2,160	5,580	144	44	322	98
57.19N,	30.52E	Peipus (off Chudskoye)	Estonai-Russia, USSR	1,370	3,550	98	30	49	15
58.24N,	14.36E	Vattern (alt Vatter, Vetter)	Sweden	740	1,910	289	88	420	128
61.15N,	28.15E	Saimaa (alt Saima)	Finland	680	1,760	249	76	269	82
55.00N,	21.00E	•Kurisches (Haff) (off Kurskiy) (salt, lag)	Lithuania-Russia, USSR	630	1,620	0	0	33	10
40.20N,	45.20E	Sevan (for Gokcha)	Armenia, USSR	530	1,360	6,250	1905	282	86
60.15N,	37.40E	White (off Beloye)	Russia, USSR	500	1,290	371	113	66	20
52.35N,	5.30E	•IJssel(meer) [for Zuider (Zee)]	Netherlands	470	1,210	26	8	shallow	
59.30N,	17.12E	Malaren (alt Malar)	Sweden	440	1,140	1	0.3	210	64
63.40N,	34.40E	Vyg(ozero)	Russia, USSR	440	1,140	292	89	59	18
61.35N,	25.30E	Paijanne	Finland	420	1,090	256	78	305	93
69.00N,	28.00E	Inari (alt Enare)	Finland	390	1,000	374	114	197	60
65.40N,	32.00E	Top(ozero)	Russia, USSR	380	990	361	110	184	56
58.17N,	31.20E	Ilmen	Russia, USSR	380	980	59	18	33/13	10/4
53.46N,	14.14E	Oder(-Haff) [alt Szczecinski; for Stettiner (Haff)] (salt, lag)	East Germany-Poland	350	900	0	0	30	9
64.20N,	27.15E	Oulu (alt Ule)	Finland	350	900	400	122	125	38
67.30N,	33.00E	Imandra	Russia, USSR	340	880	417	127	220	67
54.20N,	19.30E	•Vistula [for Frisches (Haff); off Vislinskiy, Wislany] (salt, lag)	Poland-USSR	330	860	0	0	17	5
63.15N,	29.40E	Pielinen	Finland	330	850	308	94	161	49
63.18N,	33.45E	Seg(ozero)	Russia, USSR	310	810	394	120	318	97

(Continued)

For an explanation of symbols and abbreviations, see pages 16–17.

TABLE 10a. (Continued)

Latitude and Longitude	Lake	Location	Area mi²	Area km²	Elevation ft	Elevation m	Greatest Depth ft	Greatest Depth m
		* * *						
66.28N, 32.05E	Not(ozero)	Russia, USSR	290	740	262	80	161	49
66.05N, 30.58E	Pya(ozero)	Russia, USSR	250	660	331	101	36	11
46.50N, 17.45E	Balaton (alt Platten)	Hungary	230	590	341	104	1017	310
46.25N, 6.30E	Geneva (off Geneve, Ginevra, Leman)	France-Switzerland	220	580	1,221	372	827	252
47.35N, 9.25E	Constance [alt Boden(see), Costanza]	Austria-Switzerland-West Germany	210	540	1,299	396	59	18
59.15N, 15.45E	Hjalmaren	Sweden	190	480	72	22	243	74
63.12N, 14.18E	Storsjon i Jamtland	Sweden	180	460	958	292	102	31
54.40N, 6.25W	•Neagh	Northern Ireland, UK	150	400	49	15	10	3
44.54N, 28.57E	Razelm (alt Razim) (salt)	Romania	150	390	10	3	144	44
42.10N, 19.20E	Scutari (off Shkodres, Skadarsko) (salt)	Albania-Yugoslavia	150[1]	380[1]	20	6	1135	346
45.40N, 10.41E	•Garda	Lombardia-Trentino-Alto Adige-Veneto, Italy	140	370	213	65	1473	449
60.40N, 11.00E	Mjosa	Norway	140[2]	360[2]	397	121	938	286
41.00N, 20.45E	Ohrid (off Ohridsko, Ohrit)	Albania-Yugoslavia	120	320	2,280	695	5	1
47.50N, 16.45E	Neusiedler (alt Ferto)	Austria-Hungary	110[3]	280[3]	377	115	177	54
40.55N, 21.00E	Prespa (off Megal Prespa, Prespes, Prespansko)	Albania-Greece-Yugoslavia	110	280	2,799	853	shallow	
45.25N, 12.19E	•Venice (off Veneta) (salt, lag)	Veneto, Italy	89/	230/	0	0	725	221
66.14N, 17.30E	Hornavan	Sweden	110	280	1,394	425	502	153
46.54N, 6.53E	Neuchatel [alt Neuenburger-(see)]	Switzerland	84	220	1,408	429	1221	372
45.57N, 8.39E	Maggiore [alt Langen(see), Majeur)]	Italy-Switzerland	82	210	633	193	151	46
53.26N, 9.14W	Corrib	Ireland	66	170	29	9	1352	412
46.00N, 9.17E	•Como	Lombardia, Italy	56	150	653	199	968	295
60.02N, 10.08E	Tyrifjorden	Norway	52	130	207	63		

53.25N,	12.42E	Müritz	East Germany	45	120	203	62	108	33
47.00N,	8.28E	Lucerne (alt Lucerna, Vierwald-statter)	Switzerland	44	110	1,424	434	702	214
53.46N,	21.44E	Sniardwy (for Spirding)	Poland	44	110	381	116	75	23
47.14N,	8.42E	Zurich(see) (alt Zürigo)	Switzerland	35	90	1,332	406	469	143
56.08N,	4.38W	•Lomond	Scotland, UK	27	70	27	8	623	190
57.18N,	4.27W	•Ness	Scotland, UK	22	57	53	16	754	230
59.54N,	8.55E	Tinnsjo	Norway	21	54	623	190	1509	460
61.56N,	6.22E	Hornindals(vatnet)	Norway	20	51	174	53	1686	514
59.06N,	8.12E	Fyres(vatn)	Norway	19	50	919	280	1211	369
45.58N,	9.00E	Lugano [alt Ceresio, Luganer-(see)]	Italy-Switzerland	19	49	886	270	945	288
64.43N,	11.40E	Sals(vatnet)	Norway	19	49	52	16	1522	464
61.35N,	11.12E	Storsjoen	Norway	19	49	820	250	1014	309
46.42N,	7.44E	Thun [alt Thuner(see)]	Switzerland	19	48	1,831	558	712	217
45.44N,	5.52E	Bourget	Rhone-Alpes, France	17	45	758	231	476	145
59.42N,	7.57E	Totak	Norway	15	38	2,247	685	1004	306
59.35N,	6.45E	Suldals(vatnet)	Norway	11	29	223	68	1234	376
59.24N,	8.15E	Bandak	Norway	10	26	236	72	1066	325
56.57N,	5.43W	•Morar	Scotland, UK	10	26	31	9	1017	310
58.22N,	6.36E	Lunde(vatnet)	Norway	9	24	148	45	1030	314

NORTH AMERICA

48.00N,	88.00W	Superior	Canada-USA	31,760[4]	82,260[4]	604	184	1329	405
44.30N,	82.15W	Huron	Canada-USA	23,000[5]	59,580[5]	581	177	750	229
44.00N,	87.00W	Michigan	Illinois-Indiana-Michigan-Wisconsin, USA	22,400	58,020	581	177	935	285
66.00N,	121.00W	Great Bear	NWT, Canada	12,030	31,150	512	156	1356	413
61.30N,	114.00W	Great Slave	NWT, Canada	11,030	28,570	513	156	2015	614

(Continued)

[1] Average of areas officially given by Albania (140 mi², 370 km²) and Yugoslavia (150 mi², 390 km²).
[2] Average of areas officially given by Albania (140 mi², 370 km²) and Yugoslavia (130 mi², 350 km²).
[3] Average of areas officially given by Albania (110 mi², 280 km²) and Yugoslavia (110 mi², 270 km²).
[4] Average of areas officially given by Canada (31,700 mi², 82,100 km²) and USA (31,820 mi², 82,410 km²).
[5] Average of areas officially given by Canada (23,000 mi², 59,570 km²) and USA (23,010 mi², 59,600 km²).

For an explanation of symbols and abbreviations, see pages 16–17.

Figure 58. Lake Superior, the largest freshwater lake in the world, viewed from the rugged shore of Isle Royale, Michigan, USA, its biggest island, which has been a national park since 1931. (Credit: US National Park Service.)

TABLE 10a. (Continued)

Latitude and Longitude	Lake	Location	Area		Elevation		Greatest Depth	
			mi²	km²	ft	m	ft	m
42.15N, 81.00W	Erie	Canada-USA	9,920[1]	25,690[1]	572	174	210	64
52.00N, 97.30W	Winnipeg	Manitoba, Canada	9,420	24,390	713	217	92	28
43.45N, 78.00W	Ontario	Canada-USA	7,430[2]	19,240[2]	246	75	801	244
11.30N, 85.30W	Nicaragua (alt Cocibolca)	Nicaragua	3,170	8,200	105	32	230	70
59.05N,109.30W	Athabasca (alt Athabaska)	Alberta-Saskatchewan, Canada	3,060	7,940	700	213	407	124
57.15N,102.40W	Reindeer	Manitoba-Saskatchewan, Canada	2,570	6,650	1,106	337	720	219
66.30N, 70.40W	Nettilling	NWT, Canada[3]	2,140	5,540	95	29		
52.30N,100.00W	Winnipegosis	Manitoba, Canada	2,070	5,370	830	253	39	12
49.50N, 88.30W	Nipigon	Ontario, Canada	1,870	4,850	856	261	541	165
51.00N, 98.45W	Manitoba	Manitoba, Canada	1,800	4,660	813	248	92	28
41.10N,112.30W	•Great Salt (salt)	Utah, USA	1,700	4,400	4,200	1280	48	15
49.15N, 94.45W	Woods	Canada-USA	1,580[4]	4,100[4]	1,060	323	69	21
63.08N,101.30W	Dubawnt	NWT, Canada	1,480	3,830	774	236		
65.00N, 71.00W	Amadjuak	NWT, Canada[3]	1,200	3,120	370	113		
53.45N, 59.30W	Melville (salt)	Newfoundland, Canada	1,180	3,070	0	0	840	256
58.15N,103.20W	Wollaston	Saskatchewan, Canada	1,030	2,680	1,306	398	233	71
59.30N,155.00W	Iliamna	Alaska, USA	1,000	2,590	50	15	980	299
51.00N, 73.30W	Mistassini	Quebec, Canada	900	2,340	1,220	372	600	183
60.30N, 99.30W	Nueltin	Manitoba-NWT, Canada	880	2,280	911	278		
57.10N, 98.40W	Southern Indian	Manitoba, Canada	870	2,250	835	255	59	18
54.00N, 64.00W	Michikamau	Newfoundland, Canada	780	2,030	1,510	460	262	80
64.10N, 95.20W	Baker	NWT, Canada	730	1,890	8	2	756	230
26.57N, 80.52W	Okeechobee	Florida, USA	700	1,810	19	6	20	6
63.15N,116.55W	La Martre	NWT, Canada	690	1,780	870	265		

[1]Average of areas officially given by Canada (9910 mi², 25,670 km²) and USA (9930 mi², 25,720 km²).
[2]Average of areas officially given by Canada (7340 mi², 19,010 km²) and USA (7520 mi², 19,480 km²).
[3]Baffin I.
[4]Average of areas officially given by Canada (1680 mi², 4350 km²) and USA (1480 mi², 3850 km²).

For an explanation of symbols and abbreviations, see pages 16–17.

(Continued)

TABLE 10a. (Continued)

Latitude and Longitude	Lake	Location	Area mi²	Area km²	Elevation ft	Elevation m	Greatest Depth ft	Greatest Depth m
50.20N, 92.30W	Seul	Ontario, Canada	640	1,660	1,170	357	112	34
56.00N,124.00W	Williston	British Columbia, Canada	640	1,660	2,180	664	550	168
30.13N, 90.07W	Pontchartrain (salt, lag)	Louisiana, USA	620	1,620	0	0	15	5
18.37N, 91.33W	•Terminos (salt, lag)	Campeche, Mexico	600	1,550	0	0	shallow	
62.41N, 98.00W	Yathkyed	NWT, Canada	560	1,450	461	141		
58.35N,112.05W	Claire	Alberta, Canada	550	1,440	700	213	8	2
57.30N,106.30W	Cree	Saskatchewan, Canada	550	1,430	1,597	487	148	45
55.10N,105.00W	La Ronge	Saskatchewan, Canada	550	1,410	1,193	364	135	41
56.00N, 74.30W	Eau Claire (for Clearwater)	Quebec, Canada	530	1,380	790	241		
54.00N,100.10W	Moose	Manitoba, Canada	530	1,370	838	255		
53.20N,100.00W	Cedar	Manitoba, Canada	520	1,350	830	253		
60.20N,102.10W	Kasba	NWT, Canada	520	1,340	1,102	336		
44.35N, 73.20W	Champlain	Canada-USA	490	1,270	100	30	400	122
55.10N, 73.15W	Bienville (for Apiskigamish)	Quebec, Canada	480	1,250	1,400	427		
53.47N, 94.25W	Island	Manitoba, Canada	470	1,220	744	227		
57.56N,156.23W	Becharof	Alaska, USA	460	1,190	14	4		
55.25N,115.25W	Lesser Slave	Alberta, Canada	450	1,170	1,892	577	70	21
48.02N, 94.55W	Red	Minnesota, USA	450	1,170	1,175	358	31	9
42.28N, 82.40W	Saint Clair	Canada-USA	450[1]	1,160[1]	575	175	21	6
54.45N, 94.00W	Gods	Manitoba, Canada	440	1,150	585	178		
20.15N,103.00W	Chapala	Jalisco-Michoacan, Mexico	440	1,140	5,004	1525	42	13
15.23N, 83.55W	Caratasca (salt, lag)	Honduras	430	1,110	0	0	16	5
64.27N, 99.00W	Aberdeen	NWT, Canada	420	1,100	261	80		
45.50N, 60.50W	Bras d'Or (salt, lag)	Nova Scotia, Canada[2]	420	1,100	0	0	230	70
66.30N,113.27W	Napaktulik (for Takiyuak)	NWT, Canada	420	1,080	1,250	381		
63.55N,111.00W	MacKay	NWT, Canada	410	1,060	1,414	431		
12.21N, 86.21W	Managua (alt Xolotlan)	Nicaragua	400	1,040	120	37	262	80
48.35N, 72.05W	Saint-Jean (for Saint John)	Quebec, Canada	390	1,000	321	98	204	62
66.00N,100.00W	Garry	NWT, Canada	380	980	487	148		
33.13N,115.51W	Salton (Sea) (salt)	California, USA	370	970	−231	−70	48	15
65.40N,110.40W	Contwoyto	NWT, Canada	370	960	1,460	445		

Coordinates	Name	Location						
48.42N, 79.45W	Abitibi	Ontario-Quebec, Canada	360	930	868	265	112	34
65.04N,118.29W	Hottah	NWT, Canada	350	920	592	180		
48.42N, 93.10W	Rainy	Canada-USA	350[3]	910[3]	1,108	338		
9.05N, 82.05W	•Chiriqui (salt, lag[4])	Panama	350	900	0	0	deep	
64.05N,108.30W	Aylmer	NWT, Canada	330	850	1,230	375		
69.30N,132.00W	Eskimo North	NWT, Canada	320	840	1	0.3		
46.17N, 79.45W	Nipissing	Ontario, Canada	320	830	644	196	72	22
70.35N,153.26W	Teshekpuk	Alaska, USA	310	820	5	2		
62.40N,109.30W	Nonacho	NWT, Canada	300	780	1,047	319		
55.55N,108.44W	Peter Pond	Saskatchewan, Canada	300	780	1,382	421	79	24
59.30N,133.45W	Atlin	British Columbia-Yukon Territory, Canada	300	770	2,190	668	930	283

* * *

Coordinates	Name	Location						
54.47N, 97.22W	Cross	Manitoba, Canada	290	760	679	207		
57.30N, 75.00W	Minto	Quebec, Canada	290	760	550	168		
44.25N, 79.20W	Simcoe	Ontario, Canada	290	740	718	219	136	41
56.15N, 76.20W	Guillaume-Delisle (for Richmond G) (salt, lag)	Quebec, Canada	270	700	0	0	361	110
53.45N, 90.00W	Big Trout	Ontario, Canada	250	660	698	213		
53.52N, 98.05W	Playgreen	Manitoba, Canada	250	660	711	217		
54.46N,107.17W	Dore	Saskatchewan, Canada	250	640	1,506	459	67	20
58.38N,155.52W	Naknek	Alaska, USA	240	630	34	10		
52.45N, 66.15W	Ashuanipi	Newfoundland, Canada	230	600	1,735	529		
15.30N, 89.10W	Izabal	Guatemala	230	590	26	8		
44.00N, 88.25W	Winnebago	Wisconsin, USA	210	560	747	228	59	18
49.00N, 57.20W	Grand	Newfoundland, Canada[5]	210	540	284	87	22	7
46.14N, 93.39W	Mille Lacs	Minnesota, USA	210	540	1,249	381	360	110
47.51N,114.07W	Flathead	Montana, USA	200	510	2,892	881	43	13
18.27N, 71.39W	Enriquillo (salt)	Dominican Republic	190	500	-144	-44	220	67
39.06N,120.02W	Tahoe	California-Nevada, USA	190	500	6,229	1899	1645	501
19.55N,101.05W	Cuitzeo	Guanajuato-Michoacan, Mexico	180	460	5,975	1821	11	3

[1]Average of areas officially given by Canada (430 mi², 1110 km²) and USA (460 mi², 1190 km²).
[2]Cape Breton I.
[3]Average of areas officially given by Canada (360 mi², 940 km²) and USA (340 mi², 890 km²).
[4]Actually a bay.
[5]Newfoundland I.

For an explanation of symbols and abbreviations, see pages 16–17.

(Continued)

TABLE 10a. (Continued)

Latitude and Longitude	Lake	Location	Area mi²	Area km²	Elevation ft	Elevation m	Greatest Depth ft	Greatest Depth m
47.09N, 94.24W	Leech	Minnesota, USA	180	460	1,290	393	35	11
40.01N,119.35W	Pyramid (salt)	Nevada, USA	170	440	3,802	1159	330	101
48.10N,116.21W	Pend Oreille	Idaho, USA	150	380	2,063	629	1200	366
42.24N,121.54W	Upper Klamath	Oregon, USA	140	370	4,139	1262	45	14
40.12N,111.48W	Utah	Utah, USA	140	360	4,487	1368	16	5
44.27N,110.22W	Yellowstone	Wyoming, USA	140	350	7,733	2357	300	91
45.37N, 69.40W	Moosehead	Maine, USA	120	300	1,058	322	246	75
60.10N,150.50W	Tustumena	Alaska, USA	120	300	90	27		
41.59N,111.20W	Bear	Idaho-Utah, USA	110	280	5,943	1811	175	53
60.13N,154.22W	Clark	Alaska, USA	110	280			606	185
38.42N,118.43W	Walker (salt)	Nevada, USA	110	280	4,000	1219	1000	305
47.26N, 94.12W	Winnibigoshish	Minnesota, USA	110	280	1,300	396	25	8
53.18N,126.42W	Eutsuk	British Columbia, Canada	110	270	2,817	859	1060	323
60.18N,163.43W	Dall	Alaska, USA	100	260				
41.55N,120.25W	Goose (salt)	California-Oregon, USA	100	260	4,716	1437	24	7
52.33N,120.59W	Quesnel	British Columbia, Canada	100	260	2,380	725	1560	475
29.52N, 93.50W	Sabine (salt, lag)	Louisiana-Texas, USA	95	250	0	0	shallow	
49.31N,121.52W	Harrison	British Columbia, Canada	92	240	34	10	916	279
55.22N,125.54W	Takla	British Columbia, Canada	92	240	2,260	689	941	287
30.15N, 90.30W	Maurepas (salt, lag)	Louisiana, USA	91	240	0	0	shallow	
29.45N, 92.30W	White	Louisiana, USA	81	210	1	0.3	shallow	
43.12N, 75.54W	Oneida	New York, USA	80	210	369	112	55	17
50.03N,124.27W	Powell	British Columbia, Canada	72	190	175	53	1174	358
43.37N, 71.21W	Winnipesaukee	New Hampshire, USA	72	190	504	154	169	52
42.40N, 76.41W	Cayuga	New York, USA	67	170	382	116	435	133
45.57N, 66.02W	Grand	New Brunswick, Canada	67	170	4	1		
42.39N, 76.53W	Seneca	New York, USA	67	170	445	136	618	188
59.50N,158.50W	Nuyakuk	Alaska, USA	64	170			930	283
51.17N,124.00W	Chilko	British Columbia, Canada	61	160	3,860	1177	1200	366
47.50N,120.01W	Chelan	Washington, USA	55	140	950	290	1605	489
51.12N,119.35W	Adams	British Columbia, Canada	51	130	1,356	413	1500	457

Coordinates	Lake	Location						
14.42N, 91.12W	Atitlan	Guatemala	49	130	5,128	1563	1050	320
43.37N, 73.33W	George	New York, USA	44	110	319	97	200	61
42.56N,122.00W	Crater	Oregon, USA	21	54	6,176	1882	1932	589

OCEANIA

Coordinates	Lake	Location						
28.30S, 137.20E	Eyre (salt)	South Australia, Australia	0/2,970	0/7,690	−39	−12	4/0	1/0
31.00S, 137.50E	Torrens (salt)	South Australia, Australia	0/2,230	0/5,780	98	30	shallow	shallow
31.35S, 136.00E	Gairdner (salt)	South Australia, Australia	0/1,840	0/4,770	112	34	shallow	
30.44S, 139.48E	Frome (salt)	South Australia, Australia	0/930	0/2,410	160	49	4/0	1/0

* * *

Coordinates	Lake	Location						
38.50S, 175.56E	Taupo	North I, New Zealand	230	610	1,172	357	522	159
35.26S, 139.10E	Alexandrina (lag[1])	South Australia, Australia	220	570	0	0	15	5
45.12S, 167.48E	Te Anau	South I, New Zealand	130	340	679	207	906	276
45.05S, 168.34E	Wakatipu	South I, New Zealand	110	290	1,017	310	1240	378
44.30S, 169.08E	Wanaka	South I, New Zealand	74	190	915	279	1086	331
43.48S, 172.25E	Ellesmere (salt, lag)	South I, New Zealand	70	180	0	0	7	2
44.07S, 170.10E	Pukaki	South I, New Zealand	65	170	1,620	494		
45.30S, 167.30E	Manapouri	South I, New Zealand	55	140	607	185	1453	443
44.30S, 169.17E	Hawea	South I, New Zealand	54	140	1,132	345	1286	392

SOUTH AMERICA

Coordinates	Lake	Location						
9.40N, 71.30W	Maracaibo (salt, lag)	Venezuela	5,020	13,010	0	0	197	60
31.06S, 51.15W	•Patos (salt, lag)	Rio Grande do Sul, Brazil	3,920	10,140	0	0	15	5
15.48S, 69.24W	Titicaca	Bolivia-Peru	3,100	8,030	12,497	3809	997	304
32.45S, 52.50W	•Mirim (alt Merin) (salt, lag)	Brazil-Uruguay	1,150	2,970	0	0	33	10
46.30S, 72.00W	Buenos Aires (alt General Carrera)	Argentina-Chile	860	2,240	712	217		
30.42S, 62.36W	(Mar) Chiquita (salt)	Cordoba, Argentina	720	1,850	230	70	13/10	4/3
50.13S, 72.25W	Argentino	Santa Cruz, Argentina	550	1,410	656	200	984	300
18.45S, 67.07W	Poopo	Bolivia	520	1,340	12,094	3686	10	3
49.35S, 72.35W	Viedma	Santa Cruz, Argentina	420	1,090	820	250	10	3

(Continued)

[1]Freshwater.
For an explanation of symbols and abbreviations, see pages 16–17.

TABLE 10a. (Continued)

Latitude and Longitude	Lake	Location	Area		Elevation		Greatest Depth	
			mi2	km2	ft	m	ft	m
48.52S, 72.40W	San Martin (alt O'Higgins)	Argentina-Chile	390	1,010	656	200	558	170
45.30S, 68.48W	Colhue Huapi	Chubut, Argentina	310	800	869	265	13	4
41.08S, 72.48W	Llanquihue	Chile	310	800	171	52	1148	350
		***						
54.38S, 68.00W	Fagnano (alt Cami)	Argentina-Chile	230	590	827	252	656	200
40.58S, 71.30W	Nahuel Huapi	Neuquen-Rio Negro, Argentina	210	550	2,517	767	1437	438
48.55S, 71.15W	Cardiel	Santa Cruz, Argentina	180	460	886	270		
45.27S, 69.13W	Musters	Chubut, Argentina	170	430	889	271	328	100
40.14S, 72.24W	Ranco	Chile	150	400	230	70	262	80
10.11N, 67.45W	Valencia	Venezuela	140	370	1,332	406	131	40
39.15S, 72.06W	•Villarrica	Chile	66	170	755	230		

For an explanation of symbols and abbreviations, see pages 16–17.

10b. Largest Natural Lakes, Irrespective of Continent

Contents

Rank.

Conventional and other names of lake.

Division and country (or countries) in which located.

Area in square miles and square kilometers.

Coverage

50 largest natural lakes.

Rounding

Areas are rounded to the nearest 10 mi^2 (km^2).

Entries

51.

TABLE 10b. LARGEST NATURAL LAKES, IRRESPECTIVE OF CONTINENT

Rank	Lake	Location	Area mi^2	Area km^2
1.	Caspian (Sea) (off Kaspiyskoye, Khazar) (salt)	Iran-USSR	146,100	378,400
2.	Superior	Canada-USA	31,760	82,260
3.	Aral (Sea) (off Aralskoye) (salt)	Kazakhstan-Uzbekistan, USSR	24,750	64,100
4.	Victoria	Kenya-Tanzania-Uganda	24,300	62,940
5.	Huron	Canada-USA	23,000	59,580
6.	Michigan	Illinois-Indiana-Michigan-Wisconsin, USA	22,400	58,020
7.	Tanganyika	Burundi-Tanzania-Zaire-Zambia	12,350	32,000
8.	Baykal (alt Baikal)	Russia, USSR	12,160	31,500
9.	Great Bear	NWT, Canada	12,030	31,150
10.	Great Slave	NWT, Canada	11,030	28,570
11.	Erie	Canada-USA	9,920	25,690
12.	Winnipeg	Manitoba, Canada	9,420	24,390
13.	Malawi (alt Niassa, Nyasa)	Malawi-Mozambique-Tanzania	8,680	22,490
14.	Ontario	Canada-USA	7,430	19,240
15.	Balkhash (alt Balkash) (salt)	Kazakhstan, USSR	7,070	18,300
16.	Chad (alt Tchad)	Cameroon-Chad-Niger-Nigeria	4,000/ 10,000	10,360/ 25,900
17.	Ladoga (off Ladozhskoye)	Russia, USSR	6,830	17,700
18.	Maracaibo (salt, lag)	Venezuela	5,020	13,010
19.	•Patos (salt, lag)	Rio Grande do Sul, Brazil	3,920	10,140
20.	Onega (off Onezhskoye)	Russia, USSR	3,750	9,720
21.	Nicaragua (alt Cocibolca)	Nicaragua	3,170	8,200
22.	Titicaca	Bolivia-Peru	3,100	8,030
23.	Athabasca (alt Athabaska)	Alberta-Saskatchewan, Canada	3,060	7,940

For an explanation of symbols and abbreviations, see pages 16–17. (Continued)

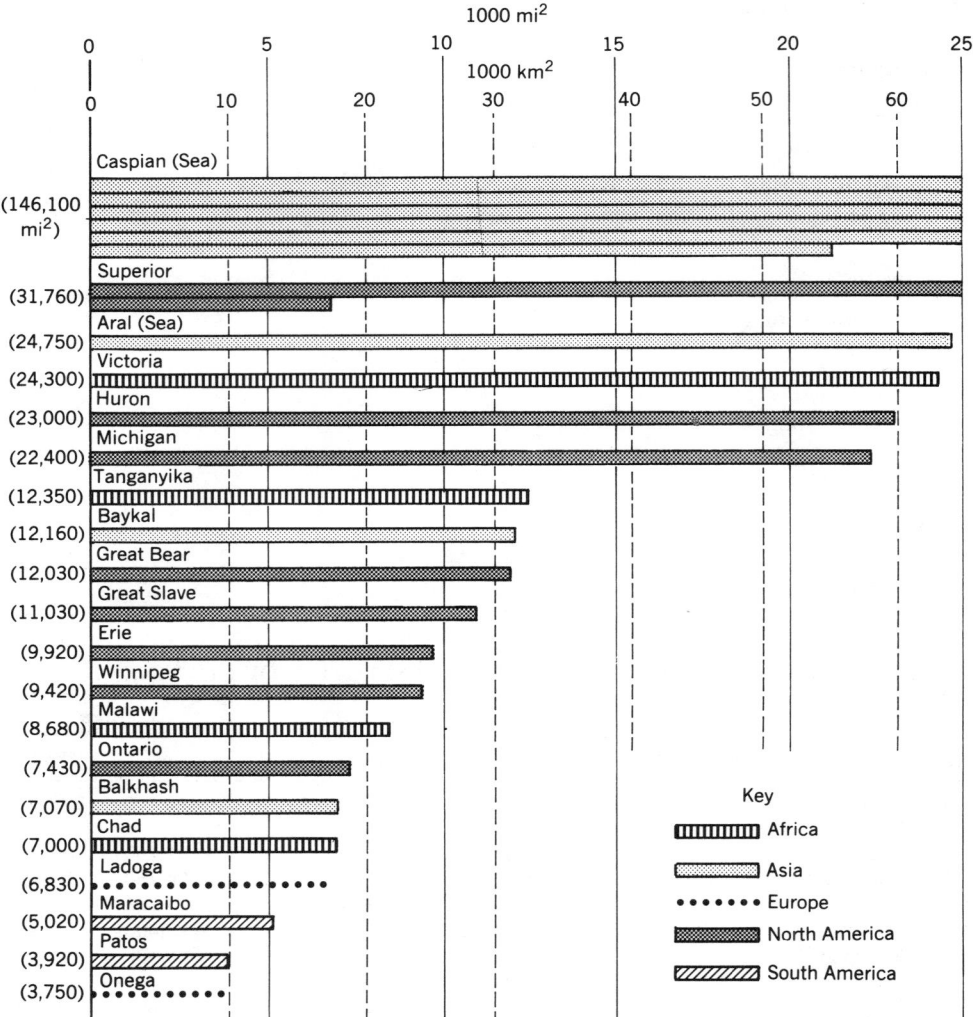

Figure 59. *Twenty largest natural lakes.*

TABLE 10b. (Continued)

Rank	Lake	Location	Area mi^2	km^2
24.	Reindeer	Manitoba-Saskatchewan, Canada	2,570	6,650
25.	Rudolf (alt Turkana)	Ethiopia-Kenya	2,470	6,400
26.	•(Tonle) Sap	Kampuchea	1,040/ 3,860	2,700/ 10,000
27.	Issyk(-Kul) (salt)	Kirgizia, USSR	2,420	6,280
28.	Mobuto Sese Seko (for Albert)	Uganda-Zaire	2,160	5,590
29.	Vanern (alt Vaner, Vener)	Sweden	2,160	5,580
30.	Nettilling	NWT, Canada	2,140	5,540
31.	Winnipegosis	Manitoba, Canada	2,070	5,370
32.	Mai-Ndombe (for Leopold II)	Zaire	900/ 3,170	2,070/ 8,210
33.	Bangweulu	Zambia	1,930	5,000
34.	•Orumiyeh (for Rezaiyeh, Urmia) (salt)	Iran	1,500/ 2,300	3,880/ 5,960
35.	Nipigon	Ontario, Canada	1,870	4,850
36.	Manitoba	Manitoba, Canada	1,800	4,660
37.	Taymyr (alt Taimyr)	Russia, USSR	1,760	4,560
38.	Koko (alt Kuku, Chinghai, Tsinghai; off Qinghai) (salt)	Qinghai, China	1,720	4,460
39.	•Kyoga (alt Kioga)	Uganda	1,710	4,430
40.	Great Salt (salt)	Utah, USA	1,700	4,400
41.	Mweru	Zaire-Zambia	1,680	4,350
42.	Dongting (alt Tungting)	Hunan, China	1,200/ 2,010	3,100/ 5,200
43.	Woods	Canada-USA	1,580	4,100
44.	Eyre (salt)	South Australia, Australia	0/2,970	0/7,690
45.	Dubawnt	NWT, Canada	1,480	3,830
46.	Van (salt)	Turkey	1,430	3,710
47.	Khanka (alt Xingkai, Hsingkai)	China-USSR	1,170/ 1,620	3,030/ 4,190
48.	Tana (alt Tsana)	Ethiopia	1,390	3,600
49.	Peipus (off Chudskoye)	Estonia-Russia, USSR	1,370	3,550
50.	Poyang	Jiangxi, China	1,290	3,350
50.	Uvs (alt Ubsa, Ubsu) (salt)	Mongolia	1,290	3,350

For an explanation of symbols and abbreviations, see pages 16–17.

10c. Deepest Natural Lakes

Contents

Rank.

Conventional and other names of lake.

Divison and country (or countries) in which located.

Greatest recorded depth of water, in feet and meters.

Coverage

52 deepest natural lakes—all natural lakes with a maximum depth of at least 1,000 feet (305 meters).

Entries

52.

TABLE 10c. DEEPEST NATURAL LAKES

Rank	Lake	Location	Greatest Depth ft	m
1.	Baykal (alt Baikal)	Russia, USSR	5712	1741
2.	Tanganyika	Burundi-Tanzania-Zaire-Zambia	4825	1471
3.	Caspian (Sea) (off Kaspiyskoye, Khazar) (salt)	Iran-USSR	3363	1025
4.	Malawi (alt Niassa, Nyasa)	Malawi-Mozambique-Tanzania	2316	706
5.	Issyk(-Kul) (salt)	Kirgizia, USSR	2303	702
6.	Great Slave	NWT, Canada	2015	614
7.	•Matana	Celebes I, Indonesia	1936	590
8.	Crater	Oregon, USA	1932	589
9.	Toba	Sumatra I, Indonesia	1736	529
10.	Hornindals(vatnet)	Norway	1686	514
11.	Sarez (off Sarezskoye)	Tadzhikistan, USSR	1657	505
12.	Tahoe	California-Nevada, USA	1645	501
13.	Chelan	Washington, USA	1605	489
14.	Kivu	Rwanda-Zaire	1575	480
15.	Quesnel	British Columbia, Canada	1560	475
16.	Sals(vatnet)	Norway	1522	464
17.	Tinnsjo	Norway	1509	460
18.	Adams	British Columbia, Canada	1500	457
19.	Mjosa	Norway	1473	449
20.	Manapouri	South I, New Zealand	1453	443
21.	Poso	Celebes I, Indonesia	1444	440
22.	Nahuel Huapi	Neuquen-Rio Negro, Argentina	1437	438
23.	Dead (Sea) (off Lut, Mayyit, Melah) (salt)	Israel-Jordan	1421	433
24.	Tazawa	Honshu I, Japan	1394	425
25.	Great Bear	NWT, Canada	1356	413
26.	•Como	Lombardia, Italy	1352	412
27.	Superior	Canada-USA	1329	405
28.	Hawea	South I, New Zealand	1286	392
29.	Wakatipu	South I, New Zealand	1240	378

For an explanation of symbols and abbreviations, see pages 16–17.   (Continued)

Figure 60. *Cape Shamanka, a picturesque spot on Lake Baykal in the southern part of Asiatic Russia, USSR. Baykal is the deepest lake and the one with the greatest volume of fresh water. (Credit: Embassy of the USSR, Washington.)*

TABLE 10c. (Continued)

Rank	Lake	Location	Greatest Depth ft	m
30.	Suldals(vatnet)	Norway	1234	376
31.	Maggiore [alt Langen(see), Majeur]	Italy-Switzerland	1221	372
32.	Fyres(vatn)	Norway	1211	369
33.	Chilko	British Columbia, Canada	1200	366
33.	Pend Oreille	Idaho, USA	1200	366
35.	Shikotsu	Hokkaido I, Japan	1191	363
36.	Powell	British Columbia, Canda	1174	358
37.	Llanquihue	Chile	1148	350
38.	•Garda	Lombardia-Trentino-Alto Adige-Veneto, Italy	1135	346
39.	Towada	Honshu I, Japan	1096	334
40.	Wanaka	South I, New Zealand	1086	331
41.	Bandak	Norway	1066	325
41.	Teletskoye [for Altyn(-Kol)]	Russia, USSR	1066	325
43.	Eutsuk	British Columbia, Canada	1060	323
44.	Atitlan	Guatemala	1050	320
45.	Lunde(vatnet)	Norway	1030	314
46.	•Dibaruh	Sumatra I, Indonesia	1017	310
46.	Geneva (off Geneve, Ginevra, Leman)	France-Switzerland	1017	310
46.	•Morar	Scotland, UK	1017	310
49.	Storsjoen	Norway	1014	309
50.	Kurile (off Kurilskoye)	Russia, USSR	1004	306
50.	Totak	Norway	1004	306
52.	Walker (salt)	Nevada, USA	1000	305

For an explanation of symbols and abbreviations, see pages 16–17.

10d. Natural Lakes with Greatest Volume of Water

Contents

Rank.

Conventional and other names of lake.

Division and country (or countries) in which located.

Average estimated depth of water, in feet and meters.

Estimated volume of water (area multiplied by average depth), in cubic miles and cubic kilometers.

Coverage

20 natural lakes with the greatest volume of water.

Entries

20.

TABLE 10d. NATURAL LAKES WITH GREATEST VOLUME OF WATER

Rank	Lake	Location	Average Depth		Volume of Water	
			ft	m	mi³	km³
1.	Caspian (Sea) (off Kaspiyskoye, Khazar) (salt)	Iran-USSR	682	208	18,882	78,707
2.	Baykal (alt Baikal)	Russia, USSR	2395	730	5,517	22,995
3.	•Tanganyika	Burundi-Tanzania-Zaire-Zambia	1877	572	4,391	18,304
4.	Superior	Canada-USA	486	148	2,921	12,174
5.	•Malawi (alt Niassa, Nyasa)	Malawi-Mozambique-Tanzania	896	273	1,473	6,140
6.	Michigan	Illinois-Indiana-Michigan-Wisconsin, USA	276	84	1,169	4,874
7.	Huron	Canada-USA	196	60	858	3,575
8.	•Victoria	Kenya-Tanzania-Uganda	131	40	604	2,518
9.	•Great Bear	NWT, Canada	238	72	542	2,258
10.	•Great Slave	NWT, Canada	203	62	425	1,771
11.	Issyk(-Kul) (salt)	Kirgizia, USSR	915	279	420	1,752
12.	Ontario	Canada-USA	262	80	369	1,539
13.	Aral (Sea) (off Aralskoye) (salt)	Kazakhstan-Uzbekistan, USSR	52	16	246	1,026
14.	Ladoga (off Ladozhskoye)	Russia, USSR	167	51	217	903
15.	•Titicaca	Bolivia-Peru	338	103	198	827
16.	Erie	Canada-USA	59	18	111	462
17.	•Hovsgol (alt Hobsogol, Khubsugul, Kosogol)	Mongolia	459	140	88	367
18.	•Kivu	Rwanda-Zaire	492	150	80	333
19.	Winnipeg	Manitoba, Canada	43	13	76	317
20.	Onega (off Onezhskoye)	Russia, USSR	95	29	68	282

For an explanation of symbols and abbreviations, see pages 16–17.

10e. Largest Natural Lake in Each Country

Contents

Conventional name of country.

Conventional and other names of lake.

Countries (if any) with which shared.

Area in square miles and square kilometers.

Coverage

All countries with an area of at least 5,000 mi² (12,950 km²) having or sharing a natural lake of significant size.

Rounding

Areas are rounded to the nearest 10 mi² (km²) if above 100 mi² (km²).

Entries

100.

TABLE 10e. LARGEST NATURAL LAKE IN EACH COUNTRY

Country	Lake	Country with Which Shared	Area	
			mi²	km²
Afghanistan	•(Ab-i-)Istada (salt)		200	520
Albania	Scutari (off in Albania Shkodres) (salt)	Yugoslavia	150	380
Algeria	•Oran (off Ouahran) (salt, lag)		120	320
Angola	•Dilolo		8	20
Argentina	Buenos Aires (alt General Carrera)	Chile	860	2,240
Australia	Eyre (salt)		0/2,970	0/7,690
Austria	Constance [off in Austria Boden(see)]	Switzerland, West Germany	210	540
Bangladesh	•Chalan (Bil)		20/150	52/390
Benin	Nokoue (salt, lag)		53	140
Bolivia	Titicaca	Peru	3,100	8,030
Botswana	•Dow		70	180
Brazil	•Patos (salt, lag)		3,920	10,140
Burma	•Indawgyi		80	210
Burundi	Tanganyika	Tanzania, Zaire, Zambia	12,350	32,000
Cameroon	Chad (alt Tchad)	Chad, Niger, Nigeria	4,000/ 10,000	10,360/ 25,900
Canada	Superior	USA	31,760	82,260
Chad	Chad (alt Tchad)	Cameroon, Niger, Nigeria	4,000/ 10,000	10,360/ 25,900
Chile	Buenos Aires (off in Chile General Carrera)	Argentina	860	2,240
China	Koko (alt Kuku, Chinghai, Tsinghai; off Qinghai) (salt)		1,720	4,460
Colombia	•Tota		23	59
Cuba	•Leche (salt, lag)		30	78
Denmark	•Arre		16	41
Djibouti	•Abbe (alt Abe; off Abhe) (salt)	Ethiopia	300	780
Dominican Republic	Enriquillo (salt)		190	500
Egypt	•Manzala (off Manzilah) (salt, lag)		530	1,360
El Salvador	Ilopango		28	72
Ethiopia	Rudolf (alt Turkana) (salt)	Kenya	2,470	6,400
Finland	Saimaa (alt Saima)		680	1,760
France	Geneva (off in France Geneve)	Switzerland	220	580
Gabon	•Onangue		90	250
Germany				
East	Oder(-Haff) [alt Szczecinski; for Stettiner (Haff)] (salt, lag)	Poland	350	900
West	Constance [off in Germany Boden(see)]	Austria, Switzer- land	210	540
Ghana	•Bosumtwi		18	48
Greece	Prespa (off in Greece Megal Prespa)	Albania, Yugoslavia	110	280
Guatemala	Izabal		230	590
Haiti	Saumatre (alt Azuel)		65	170
Honduras	Caratasca (salt, lag)		430	1,110

TABLE 10e. (Continued)

Country	Lake	Country with Which Shared	Area mi²	Area km²
Hungary	Balaton (alt Platten)		230	590
Iceland	•Thingvalla(vatn)		32	83
India	•Chilka (salt, lag)		350/ 450	910/ 1,170
Indonesia (in Asia)	Toba		440	1,150
Iran	Caspian (Sea) (off in Iran Khazar) (salt)	USSR	146,100	378,400
Iraq	•Hammar		750	1,940
Ireland	Corrib		66	170
Israel	Dead (Sea) (off in Israel Melah) (salt)	Jordan, West Bank	390	1,020
Italy	•Garda		140	370
Ivory Coast	•Aby (salt, lag)		300	780
Japan	Biwa		270	690
Jordan	Dead (Sea) (off in Jordan Lut, Mayyit) (salt)	Israel, West Bank	390	1,020
Kampuchea	•(Tonle) Sap		1,040/ 3,860	2,700/ 10,000
Kenya	Victoria	Tanzania, Uganda	24,300	62,940
Korea (North)	Kwangpo (salt, lag)		5	13
Liberia	•Fisherman's		30	78
Madagascar	•Alaotra		70	180
Malawi	Malawi (alt Niassa, Nyasa)	Mozambique, Tanzania	8,680	22,490
Malaysia	•(Tasek) Dampar		40	100
Mali	Faguibine		230	590
Mauritania	•Rkiz (alt Cayar)		60	160
Mexico	•Terminos (salt, lag)		600	1,550
Mongolia	Uvs (alt Ubsa, Ubsu) (salt)		1,290	3,350
Mozambique	Malawi (off in Mozambique Niassa)	Malawi, Tanzania	8,680	22,490
Netherlands	•IJssel(meer) [for Zuider (Zee)]		470	1,210
New Zealand	Taupo		230	610
Nicaragua	Nicaragua (alt Cocibolca)		3,170	8,200
Niger	Chad (alt Tchad)	Cameroon, Chad, Nigeria	4,000/ 10,000	10,360/ 25,900
Nigeria	Chad (alt Tchad)	Cameroon, Chad, Niger	4,000/ 10,000	10,360/ 25,900
Norway	Mjosa		140	370
Pakistan	Pangong (alt Bangong, Pangkung) (salt)	China	230	600
Pakistan[1]	•Manchhar		30/100	78/260
Panama	•Chiriqui (salt, lag[2])		350	900
Papua New Guinea	•Murray		120	300
Paraguay	•Ipoa		100	260
Peru	Titicaca	Bolivia	3,100	8,030
Philippines	Bay (salt)		340	890

[1]Exc Pakistan-held Kashmir.
[2]Actually a bay.

For an explanation of symbols and abbreviations, see pages 16–17.

(Continued)

TABLE 10e. (Continued)

Country	Lake	Country with Which Shared	Area mi²	km²
Poland	Oder(-Haff) [for Stettiner (Haff); off in Poland Szczecinski] (salt, lag)	East Germany	350	900
Romania	Razelm (alt Razim) (salt)		150	390
Rwanda	Kivu	Zaire	860	2,220
Senegal	•Guiers		60	150
South Africa	•Saint Lucia (salt, lag)		150	390
Sri Lanka	•Batticaloa (salt, lag)		46	120
Sweden	Vanern (alt Vaner, Vener)		2,160	5,580
Switzerland	Geneva (off in Switzerland Geneve, Ginevra, Leman)	France	220	580
Syria	Jabbul		58	150
Tanzania	Victoria	Kenya, Uganda	24,300	62,940
Thailand	•(Thale) Luang (alt Sap) (salt, lag)		500	1,290
Tunisia	•Bizerta (alt Bizerte; off Banzart) (salt, lag)		42	110
Turkey				
in Asia	Van (salt)		1,430	3,710
in Europe	Terkos		9	24
Uganda	Victoria	Kenya, Tanzania	24,300	62,940
UK	Neagh		150	400
Uruguay	•Mirim (off in Uruguay Merin) (salt, lag)	Brazil	1,150	2,970
USA (in North America)	Superior	Canada	31,760	82,260
USSR				
in Asia	Caspian (Sea) (off in USSR Kaspiyskoye) (salt)	Iran	146,100	378,400
in Europe	Ladoga (off Ladozhskoye)		6,830	17,700
Venezuela	Maracaibo (salt, lag)		5,020	13,010
Vietnam	•Cau Hai (salt, lag)		40	100
West Bank	Dead (Sea) (off in West Bank Lut, Mayyit) (salt)	Israel, Jordan	390	1,020
Yugoslavia	Scutari (off in Yugoslavia Skadarsko) (salt)	Albania	150	380
Zaire	Tanganyika	Burundi-Tanzania-Zambia	12,350	32,000
Zambia	Tanganyika	Burundi-Tanzania-Zaire	12,350	32,000

For an explanation of symbols and abbreviations, see pages 16–17.

11

GEOGRAPHIC TABLES AND COMPARISONS: WATERFALLS

11a. Highest Waterfalls (Individual Leaps), by Continent

Contents

Latitude and longitude, in degrees and minutes.
Conventional and other (alternate, former, and official) names of waterfall.
River, and division and country in which located.
Height of greatest individual leap, in feet and meters.

Coverage

Above ∗ ∗ ∗, all known and named waterfalls with a height of at least 300 ft (91 m).
Below ∗ ∗ ∗, other well-known waterfalls.

Entries

179, as follows: Africa—22
Asia—21
Europe—52
North America—32
Oceania—25
South America—27

TABLE 11a. HIGHEST WATERFALLS (INDIVIDUAL LEAPS), BY CONTINENT

Latitude and Longitude	Waterfall	River and Location	Height ft	Height m
AFRICA				
28.45S, 28.56E	Tugela: highest fall	Tugela R, Natal, South Africa	1350	411
10.12S, 27.27E	Kaloba (alt Lofoi)	Lofoi R, Zaire	1115	340
18.36S, 32.42E	Mtarazi	Mtarazi R, Mozambique-Zimbabwe	1000	305
18.25S, 32.47E	Pungwe	Pungwe (alt Pungoe, Pungue) R, Zimbabwe	909	277
8.36S, 31.14E	Kalambo	Kalambo R, Tanzania-Zambia	704	215
29.52S, 28.04E	Maletsunyane	Maletsunyane R, Lesotho	630	192
9.12N, 37.56E	Finchaa	Finchaa R, Ethiopia	508	155
28.35S, 20.23E	Aughrabies (alt King George's)	Orange (alt Oranje) R, Cape of Good Hope, South Africa	482	147
5.28N, 40.12E	Baratieri	Ganale-Dorya (alt Genale) R, Ethiopia	459	140
31.26S, 29.38E	Magwa	Magwa R, Cape of Good Hope, South Africa	450	137
8.51S, 31.02E	Izi (alt Chirombo)	Izi R, Zambia	440	134
0.49S, 36.46E	Kitaru	Tana R, Kenya	440	134
14.35S, 29.07E	Lunsemfwa	Lunsemfwa R, Zambia	400	122
20.21S, 57.27E	Tamarin	Tamarin R, Mauritius	400	122
31.15S, 28.57E	Tsitsa	Tsitsa R, Cape of Good Hope, South Africa	375	114
17.23S, 14.15E	Ruacana	Cunene (alt Kunene) R, Angola-Namibia	352	107
29.29S, 30.14E	Howick	Umgeni R, Natal, South Africa	311	95
17.55S, 25.51E	Victoria (alt Mosi-oa-Tunya)	Zambezi (alt Zambesi, Zambeze) R, Zambia-Zimbabwe	304	92
20.26S, 57.23E	Chamarel	Cap R, Mauritius	300	91

***

Latitude and Longitude	Waterfall	River and Location	Height ft	Height m
9.06S, 15.57E	Dianzundu (alt Duque de Braganca)	Lucala R, Angola	200	61
11.29N 37.35E	Tisissat (off Tis Isat)	Blue Nile (off Abay, Azraq) R, ˙Ethiopia	140	43
2.17N, 31.41E	Kabalega (for Murchison)	Nile (off Nil) R, Uganda	130	40
ASIA				
25.10N, 91.45E	Mawsmai	Sohryngkew R, Meghalaya, India	1148	350
6.04N, 116.29E	Kalapis	Kalapis R, Sabah, Malaysia	1100	335
25.30N, 91.40E	Thylliejlongwa	Umngi R, Meghalaya, India	997	304
14.14N, 74.50E	Gersoppa (alt Jog): highest fall	Sharavati R, Karnataka-Maharashtra, India	829	253
25.34N, 91.50E	Nohkalikai	Umtru R, Meghalaya, India	650	198
7.05N, 80.05E	Kurundu Oya	Kurundu R, Sri Lanka	620	189
6.44N, 81.02E	Diyaluma	Punagala R, Sri Lanka	560	171
1.19N, 124.54E	Tondano	Manado (alt Menado) R, Celebes I, Indonesia	492	150
45.31N, 148.53E	Ilya Muromets	? R, Iturup I, Russia, USSR	463	141
6.46N, 80.50E	Bambarakanda: lower fall	? R, Sri Lanka	461	141
35.05N, 133.41E	Kamba	Asahi R tributary, Honshu I, Japan	459	140

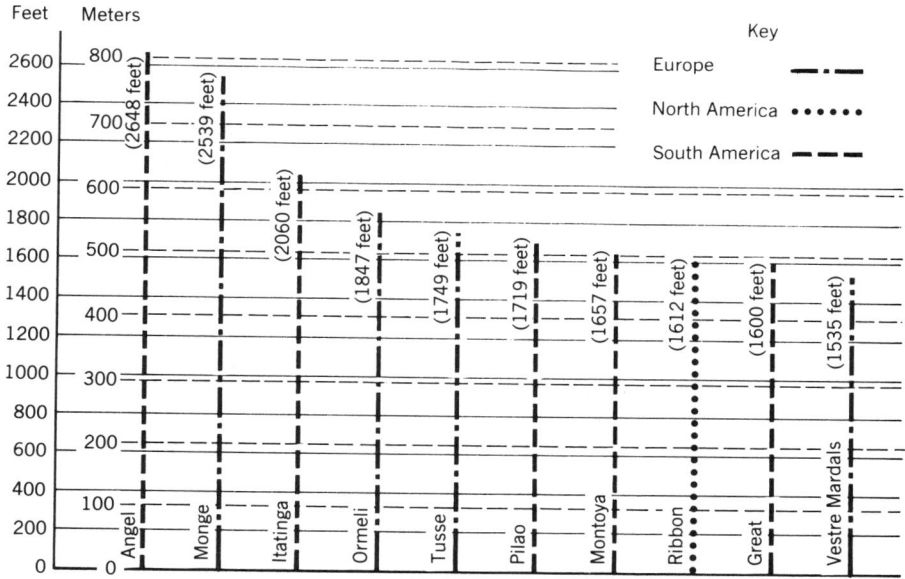

Figure 61. *Ten highest waterfalls.*

TABLE 11a. (Continued)

Latitude and Longitude	Waterfall	River and Location	Height ft	Height m
11.27N, 77.41E	Bhavani	Bhavani R, Tamil Nadu, India	450	137
33.40N,135.53E	Nachi	Nachi R, Honshu I, Japan	436	133
6.54N, 80.30E	Laksapana	? R, Sri Lanka	377	115
24.32N, 81.18E	Bihar	Bihar R, Madhya Pradesh, India	370	113
7.22N, 80.55E	Ratna Ella	Ratna R, Sri Lanka	365	111
6.38N, 80.34E	Kirinidi Ela	Kirindi R, Sri Lanka	347	106
7.04N, 80.42E	Ramboda	Panna (alt Puna) R, Sri Lanka	329	100
12.15N, 77.10E	Kaveri (alt Cauvery)	Kaveri (alt Cauvery) R, Karnataka-Tamil Nadu, India	320	98
36.44N,139.27E	Kegon	Daiya R, Honshu I, Japan	318	97

* * *

Latitude and Longitude	Waterfall	River and Location	Height ft	Height m
13.56N,105.56E	Khone	Mekong (alt Khong, Lancang, Lantsang, Mekongk, Tien Giang) R, Kampuchea-Laos	70	21

EUROPE

Latitude and Longitude	Waterfall	River and Location	Height ft	Height m
62.28N, 7.54E	Monge	Rauma R, Norway	2539	774
	Ormeli	? R, Norway	1847	563
62.05N, 6.37E	Tusse	Tussa L. Norway	1749	533
62.34N, 8.11E	Vestre Mardals (alt Western Mardals)	Eikesdals L, Norway	1535	468

For an explanation of symbols and abbreviations, see pages 16–17.

(Continued)

TABLE 11a. (Continued)

Latitude and Longitude		Waterfall	River and Location	Height	
				ft	m
42.42N,	0.00	Gavarnie: highest fall	Pau R, Midi-Pyrenees, France	1385	422
62.21N,	8.04E	Verma	Verma R, Norway	1250	381
60.50N,	7.30E	Austerbo	? R, Norway	1247	380
46.44N,	8.01E	Giessbach	Giess(bach) Creek, Switzer-land	1148	350
60.31N,	7.15E	Rembesdals: highest fall	Rembesdals L, Norway	984	300
60.29N,	7.15E	Skykkjedals: highest fall	Skykkjua R, Norway	984	300
60.07N,	6.48E	Tyssestrengene: highest fall	Tysso R, Norway	984	300
46.36N,	7.54E	Staubbach	Staub(bach) Creek, Switzer-land	980	299
62.34N,	8.11E	Austre Mardals (alt Eastern Mardals): upper fall	Eikesdals L, Norway	974	297
46.24N,	12.55E	Farina del Diavolo	? R, Friuli-Venezia Giulia, Italy	919	280
61.22N,	7.55E	Vettis: highest fall	Morkedola R, Norway	902	275
60.22N,	7.08E	Valur	Veig R, Norway	892	272
69.20N,	21.50E	Molli	Molles R, Norway	883	269
67.21N,	15.47E	Austerkrok: highest fall	Austerkrok R, Norway	843	257
46.15N,	11.15E	Stuls: highest fall	Cascata R, Trentino-Alto Adige, Italy	755	230
60.45N,	7.07E	Kjos	Flams R, Norway	738	225
62.34N,	8.11E	Austre Mardals: lower fall	Eikesdals L, Norway	722	220
		Rogaland: highest fall	? R, Norway	689	210
58.13N,	4.52W	Eas Coul Aulin	Glencoul L, Scotland, UK	658	201
61.23N,	7.26E	Feigum: highest fall	Feigum R, Norway	656	200
61.27N,	7.59E	Maradals	Maradals Glacier, Norway	656	200
61.53N,	8.21E	Aurstaupet: highest fall	Aura R, Norway	633	193
		Sote: highest fall	? R, Norway	577	176
46.05N,	10.04E	Serio: highest fall	Serio R, Lombardia, Italy	545	166
61.07N,	10.30E	Mesna	Mesna R, Norway	525	160
46.25N,	9.24E	Pianazzo	Scalcoggia R, Lombardia, Italy	525	160
60.07N,	6.46E	Skjeggedals	Tysso R, Norway	525	160
45.40N,	6.59E	Rutor: highest fall	Rutor R, Valle d'Aosta, Italy	492	150
60.26N,	7.15E	Vorings: highest fall	Bjoreia R, Norway	476	145
46.24N,	8.24E	Frua (alt Toce)	Toce R, Piemonte, Italy	470	143
		Hundkastet: highest fall	? R, Norway	459	140
47.12N,	12.10E	Krimmler: lower fall	Krimmler R, Austria	459	140
47.12N,	12.10E	Krimmler: upper fall	Krimmler R, Austria	459	140
60.44N,	6.53E	Rjoande: highest fall	Rjoand(ani) R, Norway	459	140
60.50N,	6.40E	Stalheims	Jordals R, Norway	413	126
57.16N,	5.18W	Glomach	Glomach R, Scotland, UK	370	113
67.20N,	15.40E	Fagerbakk: highest fall	Fager(bakk) Creek, Norway	367	112
41.58N,	12.48E	Tivoli: highest fall	Aniene R, Lazio, Italy	354	108
59.52N,	8.34E	Rjukan	Mane R, Norway	345	105
		Heis: highest fall	? R, Norway	328	100
47.12N,	12.10E	Krimmler: middle fall	Krimmler R, Austria	328	100
46.10N,	10.44E	Nardis	Nardis R, Trentino-Alto Adige, Italy	328	100
59.49N,	6.48E	Novle: highest fall	Stor R, Norway	328	100
41.50N,	13.29E	Zompo lo Schioppo	Romito R, Abruzzi e Molise, Italy	328	100
46.43N,	8.12E	Reichenbach	Reichen(bach) Creek, Switzerland	300	91

***

TABLE 11a. (Continued)

Latitude and Longitude	Waterfall	River and Location	Height ft	Height m
42.33N, 12.43E	Marmore: highest fall	Velino R, Umbria, Italy	295	90
47.07N, 13.08E	Gastein: lower fall	Gasteiner Ache R, Austria	280	85
47.41N, 8.37E	Rhine (off Rhein, Rhin)	Rhine (off Rhein, Rhin) R, Switzerland	69	21

NORTH AMERICA

Latitude and Longitude	Waterfall	River and Location	Height ft	Height m
37.44N,119.39W	Ribbon	Ribbon Creek, California, USA	1612	491
49.15N,125.45W	Della	Tofino Creek, British Columbia, Canada	1443	440
37.45N,119.36W	Yosemite: upper fall	Yosemite Creek, California, USA	1430	436
51.30N,116.29W	Takakkaw: highest fall	Yoho R tributary, British Columbia, Canada	1200	366
37.42N,119.40W	Silver Strand (alt Widow's Tears)	Meadow Brook, California, USA	1170	357
28.13N,108.14W	Basaseachic	(Arroyo) Basaseachic Creek, Chihuahua, Mexico	1020	311
51.33N,116.33W	Twin	Twin Falls Creek, British Columbia, Canada	900	274
52.17N,125.46W	Hunlen	Atnarko Creek, British Columbia, Canada	830	253
46.47N,121.42W	Fairy	Stevens Creek, Washington, USA	700	213
39.34N,121.17W	Feather	Fall R, California, USA	640	195
37.43N,119.39W	Bridalveil	Bridalveil Creek, California, USA	620	189
52.11N,117.03W	Panther	Nigel Creek, Alberta, Canada	600	183
37.43N,119.32W	Nevada	Merced R, California, USA	594	181
45.34N,122.06W	Multnomah: highest fall	Multnomah R, Oregon, USA	542	165
37.43N,119.36W	Sentinel: lower fall	Sentinel Creek, California, USA	500	152
51.57N,120.11W	Helmcken	Murtle R, British Columbia, Canada	450	137
49.11N,121.44W	Bridal Veil	Bridal Creek, British Columbia, Canada	400	122
37.43N,119.34W	Illilouette	Illilouette Creek, California, USA	370	113
46.47N,121.47W	Comet	Van Trump Creek, Washington, USA	320	98
37.45N,119.36W	Yosemite: lower fall	Yosemite Creek, California, USA	320	98
37.44N,119.33W	Vernal	Merced R, California, USA	317	97
44.43N,110.28W	Yellowstone: lower fall	Yellowstone R, Wyoming, USA	308	94
10.44N, 61.24W	Maracas	Caraguate R, Trinidad I, Trinidad and Tobago	300	91
46.47N,121.43W	Sluiskin	Paradise R, Washington, USA	300	91

* * *

Latitude and Longitude	Waterfall	River and Location	Height ft	Height m
61.38N,125.42W	Virginia	South Nahanni R, NWT, Canada	294	90
46.55N, 71.10W	Montmorency	Montmorency R, Quebec, Canada	273	83
47.33N,121.49W	Snoqualmie	Snoqualmie R, Washington, USA	270	82

For an explanation of symbols and abbreviations, see pages 16–17.   (Continued)

TABLE 11a. (Continued)

Latitude and Longitude	Waterfall	River and Location	Height ft	Height m
35.39N, 85.22W	Fall Creek	Fall Creek, Tennessee, USA	256	78
53.30N, 64.10W	Churchill (for Grand)	Churchill (for Hamilton) R, Newfoundland, Canada	245	75
42.33N, 76.34W	Taughannock	Taughannock Creek, New York, USA	215	66
42.36N,114.26W	Shoshone	Snake R, Idaho, USA	195	59
43.04N, 79.04W	Niagara	Niagara R, Canada-USA	186	57
OCEANIA				
21.10N,156.49W	Kahiwa	Wailau (Stream), Molokai I, Hawaii, USA	1750[1]	533[1]
21.10N,156.48W	Papalaua	Kawainui (Stream), Molokai I, Hawaii, USA	1200[1]	366[1]
8.54S,140.06W	Ahui	? R, Nuku-Hiva I, French Polynesia	1148	350
21.01N,156.37W	Honokohau	Honokohau (Stream), Maui I, Hawaii, USA	1120[1]	341[1]
30.32S,152.03E	Wollomombi: highest fall	Wollomombi R, New South Wales, Australia	1100	334
20.06N,155.36W	Hiilawe	Wailoa (Stream), Hawaii I, Hawaii, USA	1000	305
34.38S,150.34E	Belmore: three falls	Barrengarry Creek, New South Wales, Australia	984	300
	Cannabullen	Cannabullen Creek, Queensland, Australia	984	300
33.39S,150.16E	Horseshoe	Govetts Leap Creek, New South Wales, Australia	984	300
18.17S,146.03E	Wallaman (alt Stony Creek)	Stony Creek, Queensland, Australia	970	296
17.43S,145.35E	Elizabeth Grant	Tully R, Queensland, Australia	900	274
45.28S,167.10E	Helena	Helena R, South I, New Zealand	830	253
44.48S,167.44E	Sutherland: upper fall	Arthur R, South I, New Zealand	815	248
22.06N,159.40W	Waipoo: two falls	Waimea R, Kauai I, Hawaii, USA	800	244
16.50S,145.39E	Barron	Barron R, Queensland, Australia	770	235
44.48S,167.44E	Sutherland: middle fall	Arthur R, South I, New Zealand	751	229
13.55S,171.45W	Tiavi	Vaisigano R, Upolu I, Samoa	600	183
17.47S,145.35E	Tully: highest fall	Tully R, Queensland, Australia	550	168
44.40S,167.55E	Bowen	Bowen R, South I, New Zealand	520	158
44.36S,167.52E	Stirling	Stirling R, South I, New Zealand	480	146
19.51N,155.09W	Akaka	Kolekole (Stream), Hawaii I, Hawaii, USA	442	135
34.39S,150.29E	Fitzroy: highest fall	Shoalhaven R tributary, New South Wales, Australia	400	122
33.43S,150.23E	Wentworth: upper fall	Wentworth R, New South Wales, Australia	360	110

[1]Total fall.

TABLE 11a. (Continued)

Latitude and Longitude	Waterfall	River and Location	Height ft	Height m
44.48S,167.44E	Sutherland: lower fall	Arthur R, South I, New Zealand	338	103
20.09N,155.38W	Waiilikahi	Waiilikahi (Stream), Hawaii I, Hawaii, USA	320	98

SOUTH AMERICA

Latitude and Longitude	Waterfall	River and Location	Height ft	Height m
5.57N, 62.30W	Angel: upper fall	Churun R, Venezuela	2648	807
23.07S 48.36W	Itatinga	Itatinga R, Sao Paulo, Brazil	2060	628
27.12S, 49.21W	Pilao	Itajai R, Santa Catarina, Brazil	1719	524
4.00N, 62.50W	Montoya	Porah-Pi R, Venezuela	1657	505
5.46N, 61.08W	Great (alt King George VI)	Kamarang R. Guyana	1600	488
5.13N, 60.51W	Cuquenan (alt Kukenaam): highest fall	Cuquenan (alt Kukenaam) R, Guyana-Venezuela	1040	317
5.22N, 72.45W	Candelas	Cusiana R, Colombia	984	300
12.15S, 73.45W	Sewerd	Cutibireni R, Peru	877	267
5.43N, 59.38W	Tiboku (alt King Edward VIII)	Semang R, Guyana	840	256
5.09N, 59.29W	Kaieteur	Potaro R, Guyana	741	226
20.20S, 46.22W	Casca d'Anta	Sao Francisco R, Minas Gerais, Brazil	666	203
5.57N, 62.30W	Angel: lower fall	Churun R, Venezuela	564	172
4.35N, 74,18W	Tequendama	Bogota (alt Funza) R, Colombia	515	157
6.32N, 60.50W	Sakaika: highest fall	Ekreku R, Guyana	460	140
6.38N, 60.44W	Wakowaieng	Morong R, Guyana	440	134
22.31S, 43.10W	Fagundes	Piabanha R, Rio de Janeiro, Brazil	413	126
17.12S, 54.07W	Itiquira	Itiquira R, Mato Grosso, Brazil	394	120
5.25N, 59.30W	Marina: highest fall	Ipobe R, Guyana	360	110
13.02S, 58.17W	Utiariti	Saueruina (alt Papagaio) R, Mato Grosso, Brazil	350	107
2.22N, 52.40W	Manoa (alt Manaua)	Oyapock (alt Oiapoque) R, Brazil-French Guiana	345	105
5.03N, 65.41W	Quenque (alt Tencua)	Manapiare R, Venezuela	328	100

*   *   *

Latitude and Longitude	Waterfall	River and Location	Height ft	Height m
9.24S, 38.13W	Paulo Afonso	Sao Francisco R, Alagoas-Bahia, Brazil	262	80
25.41S, 54.26W	Iguacu (alt Iguazu; for Iguassu)	Iguacu (alt Iguazu; for Iguassu) R, Argentina-Brazil	230	70
24.02S, 54.16W	Sete Quedas (alt Guaira)[1]	Parana R, Brazil-Paraguay	213	65
20.18S, 49.10W	Maribondo (alt Marimbondo)	Grande R, Minas Gerais-Sao Paulo, Brazil	115	35
31.14S, 57.55W	Grande	Uruguay (alt Uruguai) R, Argentina-Uruguay	75	23
20.36S, 51.33W	Urubupunga	Prana R, Mato Grosso do Sul-Sao Paulo, Brazil	27	9

[1]The Sete Quedas waterfall was totally submerged after the completion of the Itaipu dam in 1982.

For an explanation of symbols and abbreviations, see pages 16–17.

Figure 62. *Angel Falls on the Churun River, Venezuela, the highest waterfall, which drops half a mile in a single leap. (Credit: Information Service, Embassy of Venezuela, Washington.)*

11b. Greatest Waterfalls (Volume of Water)

Contents

Rank.

Conventional and other names of waterfall.

River, and division and country in which located.

Average rate of flow, in thousands of cubic feet per second and in cubic meters per second.

Height of greatest individual leap, in feet and meters.

Coverage

All waterfalls with an average rate of flow of at least 20,000 cfs (566 m³/sec).

Rounding

Rates of flow are rounded to the nearest 1,000 cfs.

Entries

14.

TABLE 11b. GREATEST WATERFALLS (VOLUME OF WATER)

Rank	Waterfall	River and Location	Average Flow		Height	
			1,000 cfs	m³/sec	ft	m
1.	Khone	Mekong (alt Khong, Lancang, Lantsang, Mekongk, Tien Giang) R, Kampuchea-Laos	410	11,610	70	21
	Sete Quedas (alt Guaira1)	Parana R, Brazil-Paraguay	292	8,260	213	65
2.	Niagara	Niagara R, Canada-USA	206	5,830	186	57
3.	Grande	Uruguay (alt Uruguai) R, Argentina-Uruguay	159	4,500	75	23
4.	Paulo Afonso	Sao Francisco R, Alagoas-Bahia, Brazil	102	2,890	262	80
5.	Urubupunga	Parana R, Mato Grosso do Sul-Sao Paulo, Brazil	97	2,750	27	9
6.	Iguacu (alt Iguazu; for Iguassu)	Iguacu (alt Iguazu; for Iguassu) R, Argentina-Brazil	60	1,700	230	70
7.	Maribondo (alt Marimbondo)	Grande R, Minas Gerais-Sao Paulo, Brazil	53	1,500	115	35
8.	Churchill (for Grand)	Churchill (for Hamilton) R, Newfoundland, Canada	49	1,390	245	75
9.	Kabalega (for Murchison)	Nile (off Nil) R, Uganda	42	1,200	130	40
10.	Victoria (alt Mosi-oa-Tunya)	Zambezi (alt Zambesi, Zambeze) R, Zambia-Zimbabwe	38	1,090	304	92
11.	Kaveri (alt Cauvery)	Kaveri (alt Cauvery) R, Karnataka-Tamil Nadu, India	33	934	320	98
12.	Rhine (off Rhein, Rhin)	Rhine (off Rhein, Rhin) R, Switzerland	25	700	69	21
13.	Kaieteur	Potaro R, Guyana	23	650	741	226

1The Sete Quedas waterfall was totally submerged after the completion of the Itaipu dam in 1982.

For an explanation of symbols and abbreviations, see pages 16–17.

Figure 63. Aerial view of Niagara Falls on the US-Canadian border, with the Horseshoe, or Canadian, falls in the foreground and the American falls to the rear. Niagara Falls replaced the Sete Quedas, or Guaira, Falls between Brazil and Paraguay as the greatest waterfall with a height of at least 100 feet (30 meters) in 1982, when the latter falls were submerged by the new Itaipu Dam. (Credit: Embassy of Canada, Washington.)

SELECTED BIBLIOGRAPHY

Of the thousands of books and periodicals consulted in the preparation of *World Facts and Figures* (Third Edition), 258 of the most useful sources of information are listed here. For the convenience of readers who seek more detailed information on a particular subject than can be given in this book, these sources are listed alphabetically by author (by title if the authorship is anonymous) under 28 headings, as indicated below.

Encyclopedias
   Universal
   National and regional
Official statistical yearbooks
Unofficial yearbooks and almanacs
Gazetteers
   Universal
   National and regional
Atlases
Geography
   Universal
   National and regional
Demography
   Universal
   National and regional
Economy
Transportation and communications
Climate
   Universal
   National and regional
Universities
   Universal
   National and regional

Libraries
  Universal
  National and regional
Engineering structures
  Buildings
  Bridges
  Tunnels
  Dams
Physical features
  Oceans and seas
  Islands
  Rivers and lakes
  Mountains
  Waterfalls

* * *

Encyclopedias: Universal

1. *Aschehoug og Gyldendals Store Norske Leksikon.* Oslo, 1978–1981, 13 v.
2. *Bolshaya Sovetskaya Entsiklopediya*, 3rd ed. Moscow, 1969–1981, 31 v.
3. Idem, 2nd ed. Moscow, 1949–1958, 53 v.
4. *Chambers's Encyclopaedia.* Oxford, 1967, 15 v.
5. *Collier's Encyclopedia.* New York, 1987, 24 v.
6. *(New) Columbia Encyclopedia*, 4th ed. New York, 1975, 3052 pp.
7. *Diccionario Enciclopedico Salvat Universal.* Barcelona, 1969–1974, 20 v.
8. *Diccionario Enciclopedico U.T.E.H.A.* Mexico, 1950–1952, 10 v.
9. *Dizionario Enciclopedico Italiano.* Rome, 1955–1961, 12 v.
10. *Enciclopedia Italiana di Scienze, Lettere ed Arti.* Rome 1929–1939, 36 v.
11. *Enciclopedia Mirador Internacional.* Sao Paulo, 1975, 20 v.
12. *Enciclopedia Universal.* Sao Paulo, 1969, 10 v.
13. *Enciclopedia Universal Ilustrada Europeo-Americana* (short title: *Espasa*). Barcelona, 1907–1930, 70 v.
14. Idem; *Apendice.* Madrid, 1930–1933, 10 v.
15. *(New) Encyclopaedia Britannica*, 15th ed. Chicago, 1987, 31 v.
16. *Encyclopaedia Britannica*, 11th ed. New York, 1910–1911, 29 v.
17. *Encyclopedia Americana.* Danbury, Connecticut, USA, 1987, 30 v.
18. *Grand Dictionnaire Encyclopedique Larousse.* Paris, 1982–, v 1–9 (A–S).
19. *Grande Enciclopedia Portuguesa e Brasileira.* Lisbon, 1935–1958, 37 v.
20. *Grande Encyclopedie.* Paris, 1886–1902, 31 v.
21. *Grand Larousse Encyclopedique.* Paris, 1960–1964, 10 v.
22. *Gran Enciclopedia del Mundo.* Barcelona, 1961–1964, 20 v.
23. *Great Soviet Encyclopedia* [English translation of reference 2]. New York, 1973–1983, 32 v.

24. *Grosse Brockhaus.* Wiesbaden, 1977–1981, 13 v.
25. *Grote Winkler Prins*, 7th ed. Amsterdam, 1966–1975, 20 v.
26. *(Uj) Magyar Lexikon.* Budapest, 1959–1972, 7 v.
27. *Meyers Enzyklopadisches Lexikon.* Mannheim, 1971–1979, 25 v.
28. *Meyers Grosses Konversations-Lexikon.* Leipzig, 1909, 20 v.
29. *Revai Nagy Lexikona.* Budapest, 1911–1926, 19 v.
30. *Schweizer Lexikon.* Zurich, 1945–1948, 7 v.
31. *Svensk Uppslagsbok.* Malmo, 1957–1965, 32 v.
32. *Wielka Encyklopedia Powszechna PWN.* Warsaw, 1962–1969, 12 v.

Encyclopedias: National and Regional

33. *Australian Encyclopaedia*, 3rd ed. Sydney, 1977, 6 v.
34. *Diccionario Porrua*, 5th ed. Mexico, 1986, 3 v (3282 pp).
35. *Enciklopedija Jugoslavije.* Zagreb, 1955–1971, 8 v.
36. *Encyclopaedia of New Zealand.* Wellington, 1966, 3 v.
37. *Encyclopaedie van Nederlandsch-Indie*, 2nd ed. Hague, 1917–1939, 8 v.
38. *Encyclopedia Canadiana.* Toronto, 1977, 10 v.
39. *Gran Enciclopedia Argentina.* Buenos Aires, 1956–1963, 8 v.
40. *Kodansha Encyclopedia of Japan.* Tokyo, 1983, 9 v.
41. *Standard Encyclopaedia of Southern Africa.* Cape Town, 1970–1976, 12 v.

Official Statistical Yearbooks

42. Argentina, Instituto Nacional de Estadistica y Censos. *Anuario Estadistico de la Republica Argentina, 1981/1982.* Buenos Aires, 1984, 706 pp.
43. Australia, Australian Bureau of Statistics. *Year Book, Australia, 1986.* Canberra, 1986, 771 pp.
44. Austria, Statistisches Zentralamt. *Statistisches Handbuch fur die Republik Osterreich . . . 1986.* Vienna, 1986, 602 pp.
45. Bangladesh, Bureau of Statistics. *1983–84 Statistical Yearbook of Bangladesh.* Dhaka, 1984, 847 pp.
46. Belgium, Institut National de Statistique. *Annuaire Statistique de la Belgique . . . 1986.* Brussels, 1987, 796 pp.
47. Brazil, Fundacao Instituto Brasileiro de Geografia e Estatistica. *Anuario 1985 Estatistico do Brasil.* Rio de Janeiro, 1986, 759 pp.
48. Bulgaria, Tsentralno Statistichesko Upravlenie. *Statisticheski Godishnik na Narodna Republika Bulgariya, 1986.* Sofia, ND, 682 pp.
49. Canada, Statistics Canada. *Canada Year Book, 1985.* Ottawa, 1985, 894 pp.
50. China, State Statistical Bureau. *Statistical Yearbook of China, 1986.* Oxford, 1986, 761 pp.
51. Colombia, Departamento Administrativo Nacional de Estadistica. *Colombia Estadistica, 85.* Bogota, 1984, 580 pp.
52. Cuba, Comite Estatal de Estadisticas. *Anuario Estadistico de Cuba, 1985.* Havana, 1986, 650 pp.
53. Czechoslovakia, Federalni Statisticky Urad. *Statisticka Rocenka Ceskoslovenske Socialisticke Republiky, 1986.* Prague, 1986, 695 pp.

54. Denmark, Danmarks Statistik. *Statistisk Arbog, 1987.* Copenhagen, 1987, 514 pp.

55. East Germany, Staatliche Zentralverwaltung fur Statistik. *Statistisches Jahrbuch 1987 der Deutschen Demokratischen Republik.* Berlin, 1987, 424 plus 96 pp.

56. Egypt, Central Agency for Public Mobilisation and Statistics. *Statistical Year Book ...1986.* Cairo, 1986, 279 pp.

57. Finland, Tilastokeskus. *Suomen Tilastollinen Vuosikirja, 1987.* Helsinki, 1987, 557 pp.

58. France, Institut National de la Statistique et des Etudes Economiques. *Annuaire Statistique de la France, 1986.* Paris, 1986, 846 pp.

59. Greece, Ethnike Statistike Iperesia. *Statistike Epeteris tes Ellados . . . 1985.* Athens, 1986, 469 pp.

60. Hungary, Hungarian Central Statistical Office. *Statistical Yearbook, 1985.* Budapest, 1987, 415 pp.

61. India, Central Statistical Organisation. *Statistical Abstract, India, 1984.* New Delhi, 1985, 679 pp.

62. Indonesia, Biro Pusat Statistik. *Statistik Indonesia . . . 1986.* Jakarta, 1987, 627 pp.

63. Ireland, Central Statistics Office. *Ireland Statistical Abstract, 1982–1985.* Dublin, 1986, 410 pp.

64. Israel, Central Bureau of Statistics. *Statistical Abstract of Israel, 1986.* Jerusalem, 1986, 735 plus 104 pp.

65. Italy, Istituto Centrale di Statistica. *Annuario Statistico Italiano, Edizione 1986.* Rome, 1986, 731 pp.

66. Japan, Statistics Bureau. *Japan Statistical Yearbook, 1987.* Tokyo, 1987, 836 pp.

67. League of Nations. *Statistical Year-Book, 1926–1942/1944.* Geneva, 1927–1945, 17 v.

68. Mexico, Instituto Nacional de Estadistica, Geografia e Informatica. *Anuario Estadistico de los Estados Unidos Mexicanos, 1986.* Mexico, 1987, 706 pp.

69. Netherlands, Central Bureau of Statistics. *Statistical Yearbook of the Netherlands, 1986.* Hague, 1987, 425 pp.

70. New Zealand, Department of Statistics. *New Zealand Official Yearbook, 1986–87.* Wellington, 1986, 865 pp.

71. Nigeria, Federal Office of Statistics. *Annual Abstract of Statistics, 1985 Edition.* Lagos, 1985, 187 pp.

72. Norway, Statistisk Sentralbyra. *Statistisk Arbok, 1986.* Oslo, 1986, 528 pp.

73. Pakistan, Federal Bureau of Statistics. *Pakistan Statistical Yearbook, 1986.* Karachi, 1986, 592 pp.

74. Philippines, National Economic and Development Authority. *1986 Philippines Statistical Yearbook.* Manila, 1986, 711 pp.

75. Poland, Glowny Urzad Statystyczny. *Rocznik Statystyczny, 1986.* Warsaw, 1986, 630 pp.

76. Portugal, Instituto Nacional de Estatistica. *Anuario Estatistico, 1983.* Lisbon, 1985, 271 pp.

77. Romania, Directia Centrala de Statistica. *Anuarul Statistic al Republicii Socialiste Romania, 1986.* Bucharest, ND, 395 pp.

78. South Korea, National Bureau of Statistics. *Korea Statistical Yearbook, 1986.* Seoul, 1986, 602 pp.

79. Spain, Instituto Nacional de Estadistica. *Anuario Estadistico de Espana ...1986.* Madrid, ND, 889 pp.

80. Sweden, Statistiska Centralbyran. *Statistisk Arsbok for Sverige, 1987.* Stockholm, 1986, 563 pp.

81. Switzerland, Bundesamt fur Statistik. *Statistisches Jahrbuch der Schweiz, 1987/1988.* Bern, 1987, 607 pp.

82. Syria, Central Bureau of Statistics. *Statistical Abstract, 1985.* Damascus, 1985, 559 pp.

83. Taiwan, Directorate-General of Budget, Accounting & Statistics. *Statistical Yearbook of the Republic of China, 1986.* Taipei, ND, 540 pp.

84. Turkey, Devlet Istatistik Enstitusu. *Turkiye Istatistik Yilligi, 1987.* Ankara, 1988, 479 pp.

85. UK, Central Statistical Office. *Annual Abstract of Statistics . . . 1987 Edition.* London, 1987, 340 pp.

86. United Nations, Statistical Office. *Monthly Bulletin of Statistics* [monthly supplement to reference 87].

87. United Nations, Statistical Office. *Statistical Yearbook, 1948–1983/84.* New York, 1949–1986, 34 v.

88. US, Bureau of the Census. *Statistical Abstract of the United States, 1988,* 108th ed. Washington, 1987, 943 pp.

89. USSR, Tsentralnoye Statisticheskoye Upravleniye. *Narodnoye Khozyaystvo v 1985 G.* Moscow, 1986, 655 pp.

90. Venezuela, Oficina Central de Estadistica e Informatica. *Anuario Estadistico de Venezuela, 1985.* Caracas, 1986, 842 pp.

91. West Germany, Statistisches Bundesamt. *Statistisches Jahrbuch 1987 fur die Bundesrepublik Deutschland.* Wiesbaden, 1987, 788 pp.

92. Yugoslavia, Savezni Zavod za Statistiku. *Statisticki Godisnjak Jugoslavije, 1986.* Belgrade, 1986, 794 pp.

Unofficial Yearbooks and Almanacs

93. *Almanach de Gotha, 1763–1944.* Gotha, East Germany, 1763–1944, 181 v.

94. *Almanaque Abril, '88.* Sao Paulo, 1987, 770 pp.

95. *(1987) Britannica Book of the Year* [supplement to reference 15]. Chicago, 1987, 958 pp.

96. *Caribbean Year Book, 1979/80.* Toronto, 1980, 919 pp.

97. *Europa Year Book, 1959–1987.* London, 1959–1987. 57 v.

98. *Hubner's Weltstatistik . . . 1939.* Vienna, 1939, 327 pp.

99. *Information Please Almanac . . . 1988.* Boston, 1988, 976 pp.

100. *Pacific Islands Year Book,* 15th ed. Sydney, 1984, 556 pp.

101. *(1988) South American Handbook,* 64th ed. Bath, England, UK, 1987, 1341 pp.

102. *Statesman's Year Book, 1864—1987–1988.* London, 1864–1987, 124 v.

103. United Nations Educational, Scientific and Cultural Organization (UNESCO). *Statistical Yearbook . . . 1987.* Paris, 1987, various paging.

104. Whitaker, Joseph. *Almanack for the Year of Our Lord 1988,* 120th ed. London 1987, 1236 pp.

105. *World Almanac and Book of Facts, 1867–1988.* New York, 1868–1987, 120 v.

Gazetteers: Universal

106. Chisholm, George G., Ed. *Times* [of London] *Gazetteer of the World.* London, 1899, 1787 pp.

107. Clarke, J.W. *New Geographical Dictionary.* London, 1822, 2 v.

108. *Columbia Lippincott Gazetteer of the World.* New York, 1952, 2148 pp.

109. *Edinburgh Gazetteer, or Geographical Dictionary.* Edinburgh, 1822, 6 v.

110. *Gazetteer of the World, or, Dictionary of Geographical Knowledge.* Edinburgh, 1850–1856, 7 v.

111. *Harper's Statistical Gazetteer of the World.* New York, 1855, 1952 pp.

112. *Imperial Gazetteer.* Glasgow, 1855, 2 v.

113. Johnston, A. Keith. *General Dictionary of Geography.* London, 1877, 1513 pp.

114. *Kratkaya Geograficheskaya Entsiklopediya.* Moscow, 1960–1966, 5 v.

115. *Lippincott's Gazetteer of the World.* Philadelphia, 1902, 2636 pp.

116. *Lippincott's Pronouncing Gazetteer.* Philadelphia, 1855, 2182 pp.

117. Malte-Brun, [Conrad]. *Diccionario Geografico Universal.* Paris, 1828, 2 v.

118. *Ritters Geographisch-Statistisches Lexikon.* Leipzig, 1910, 2 v.

119. Vivien de Saint-Martin, [Louis], and Louis Rousselet. *Nouveau Dictionnaire de Geographie Universelle.* Paris, 1879–1895, 7 v.

120. *Webster's New Geographical Dictionary.* Springfield, Massachusetts, USA, 1984, 1376 pp.

Gazetteers: National and Regional

121. Canada, Board on Geographical Names. *Gazetteer*[s of individual provinces]. Ottawa, 1952–1962, 10 v.

122. *Diccionario Geografico de Espana.* Madrid, 1956–1961, 17 v.

123. *Dicionario Geografico Brasileiro,* 2nd ed. Porto Alegre, 1972, 619 pp.

124. *Imperial Gazetteer of India.* Oxford, 1907–1909, 26 v.

125. Papinot, E. *Historical and Geographical Dictionary of Japan.* Tokyo, 1909, 842 pp.

126. Playfair, G. M. H. *Cities and Towns of China; a Geographical Dictionary,* 2nd ed. Shanghai, 1910, 582 plus 76 pp.

127. US, Office of Geography. *Gazetteer*[s of individual countries and regions].[1] Washington, 1950–1987, 182 v.

Atlases

128. *National Geographic Atlas of the World.* Washington, 1981, 383 pp.

129. *(1985) Rand McNally Commercial Atlas & Marketing Guide,* 116th ed.[2] Chicago, 1985, 579 plus 22 pp.

130. *Rand McNally New International Atlas.* Chicago, 1980, 320 plus 232 pp.

131. *Times* [of London] *Atlas of China.* London, 1974, 145 plus 27 pp.

132. *Times* [of London] *Atlas of the World,* 7th ed. London, 1985, 123 plates plus 227 pp.

133. Touring Club Italiano. *Atlante Internazionale,* 8th ed. Milan, 1968, 173 leaves.

134. Idem; *Indice dei Nomi.* Milan, 1968, 1032 pp.

---

[1]These gazetteers, which since July 1972 have been prepared by the US Defense Mapping Agency, are continuing. The 182 volumes cited here exclude earlier editions of gazetteers that have been revised. Since two or more volumes are required for some of the gazetteers, they cover only 153 different regions or areas of the world but many more countries, for several countries are often included in a single gazetteer.

[2]This atlas is published annually, but the 1985 edition is the latest one that includes the population of foreign cities.

135. US, Geological Survey. *National Atlas of the United States of America*. Washington, 1970, 417 pp.

Geography: Universal

136. Agostini, Federico de. *Enciclopedia Geografica; Imago Mundi*. Turin, 1970–1975, 13 v.
137. *Worldmark Encyclopedia of the Nations*, 6th ed. New York, 1984, 5 v.

Geography: National and Regional

138. *Anuario Geografico Argentino*. Buenos Aires, 1941, 650 pp.
139. Arango Cano, Jesus. *Geografia Fisica y Economica de Colombia*. Bogota, 1956, 338 pp.
140. *Argentina, Suma de Geografia*. Buenos Aires, 1958–1963, 9 v.
141. Federal Writers' Project (or Writers' Program). *Alabama* [etc] *(American Guide Series)* [guidebooks to individual US states]. Various places, 1937–1949, 50 v.
142. Nugroho. *Indonesia, Facts and Figures*. Jakarta, 1967, 608 pp.
143. *(New) Official Guide: Japan*. Tokyo, 1975, 1088 pp.
144. Philippines, Bureau of Coast and Geodetic Survey. *Geographical Data of the Philippines*. Manila, 1962, 22 pp.
145. Spate, O.H.K., and A.T.A. Learmonth. *India and Pakistan*. London, 1967, 877 pp.
146. UK, Central Office of Information. *Britain 1987, an Official Handbook*. London, 1987, 468 pp.
147. Vila, Pablo. *Geografia de Venezuela*. Caracas, 1960–1965, 2 v.
148. Zaychikov, V.T., Ed. *Fizicheskaya Geografiya Kitaya*. Moscow, 1964, 739 pp.
149. Zaychikov, V.T., Ed. *Physical Geography of China* [English translation of reference 148]. Washington, 1965, 650 pp. (US Joint Publications Research Service, number 32,119).

Demography: Universal

150. *Bevolkerung der Erde* (in *Petermanns Geographische Mitteilungen*). Gotha, East Germany, 1872–1931. 14 v.
151. Chandler, Tertius, and Gerald Fox. *3000 Years of Urban Growth*. New York, 1974, 431 pp.
152. Hassel, G. *Statistische Uebersichts-Tabellen der Sammtlichen Europaischen und Einiger Aussereuropaischen Staaten*. Gottingen, 1809, 106 pp.
153. United Nations, Statistical Office. *Demographic Yearbook, 1948–1985*. New York, 1949–1987, 38 v.
154. United Nations, Statistical Office. *Population and Vital Statistics Reports* [quarterly/ supplement to reference 153].

Demography: National and Regional

155. Beloch, Karl Julius. *Bevolkerungsgeschichte Italiens*. Berlin, 1937–1961, 3 v.
156. China, State Statistical Bureau. *China Urban Statistics, 1986*. Hong Kong, 1987, 492 pp.
157. Sanchez-Albornoz, Nicolas. *Population of Latin America; a History*. Berkeley, 1974, 431 pp.

158. Ullman, Morris B. *Cities of Mainland China: 1953 and 1958*. Washington, 1961, 46 pp.

159. Yazaki, Takeo. *Social Change and the City in Japan*. Tokyo, 1968, 549 pp.

Economy

160. International Monetary Fund. *International Financial Statistics Yearbook, 1987* Washington, 1987, 744 pp.

161. United Nations, Statistical Office. *1985 Energy Statistics Yearbook*. New York, 1987, 437 pp.

162. United Nations, Statistical Office. *1985 International Trade Statistics Yearbook*. New York, 1987, 2 v, 2486 pp.

163. US, Central Intelligence Agency. *World Factbook, 1987*. Washington, 1987, 290 pp.

164. World Bank. *World Bank Atlas, 1985*. Washington, 1985, 28 pp.

Transportation and Communications

165. *Civil Aviation Statistics of the World*, 11th ed. Montreal, 1986, 174 pp.

166. International Road Federation. *World Road Statistics, 1982–1986*. Geneva, 1987, 208 pp.

167. International Telecommunication Union. *Yearbook of Common Carrier Telecommunication Statistics*, 13th ed. Geneva, 1986, 414 pp.

168. *Jane's World Railways, 1987–88*. London, 1987, 964 pp.

169. Motor Vehicle Manufacturers Association of the United States. *Motor Vehicle Facts & Figures, '87*. Detroit, 1987, 96 pp.

170. *Railway Directory & Year Book, 1987*. London, 1986, 730 pp.

171. Verband der Automobilindustrie E. V. *Tatsachen und Zahlen . . . 1986*. Frankfurt am Main, 1986, 448 pp.

Climate: Universal

172. Sokhrina, R.F., et al. *Davieniye Vezdukha i Atmosfernyye Osadki Severnogo Polushariya*. Leningrad, 1959, 473 pp.

173. UK, Meteorological Office. *Tables of Temperature, Relative Humidity and Precipitation for the World*. London, 1958, 6 v.

174. *World Survey of Climatology*. Amsterdam, 1969–1984. 15 v.

175. *World Weather Records, 1921–1970*. Washington, 1934–1981, 13 v.

Climate: National and Regional

176. Argentina, Servicio Meteorologico Nacional. *Estadisticas Climatologicas, 1901–1950*. Buenos Aires, 1958, 44 pp.

177. Argentina, Servicio Meteorologico Nacional. *Estadisticas Climatologicas, 1941–1950*. Buenos Aires, 1958, 161 pp.

178. Canada, Environment Canada. *Canada Climate Normals . . . 1951–1980*. Ottawa, 1982, v 2, 3.

179. China, Office of Climatological Research. *Chungkuo Chihou Tu (Atlas of Chinese Clima-*

tology). Washington, 1962, 582 pp. (US/Joint Publications Research Service, number 16,321).

180. Gherzi, E. *Meteorology of China.* Macao, 1951, 2 v.

181. India, Meteorological Department. *Climatological Tables of Observatories (1931–1960).* New Delhi, 1967, 470 pp.

182. Japan, Kishocho. *Climatic Table of Japan . . . 1941–1970.* Tokyo, 1972, parts, 2, 3.

183. *Klimaticheskiy Spravochnik Afriki.* Leningrad, 1962, 2 v.

184. *Klimaticheskiy Spravochnik Zarubezhnoy Azii.* Leningrad, 1974, 2 v.

185. Leningrad, Glavnaya Geofizicheskaya Observatoriya. *Klimat SSSR.* Leningrad, 1958–1963, 8 v.

186. *Spravochnik po Klimatu SSSR.* Leningrad, 1964–, 34 v.

187. UK, Meteorological Office. *Averages of Temperature for the United Kingdom, 1941–70.* London, 1976, 93 pp.

188. US, National Oceanic and Atmospheric Administration. *Climates of the States,* 3rd ed. Detroit, 1985, 2 v. 1572 pp.

189. Vivo, Jorge A. and Jose C. Gomez. *Climatologia de Mexico.* Mexico, 1946, 73 pp.

Universities: Universal

190. *International Handbook of Universities*, 10th ed. Paris, 1987, 1300 pp.

191. *Minerva; Jahrbuch der Gelehrten Welt.* Berlin, 1966–1969, 3 v.

192. *World of Learning, 1987* 37th ed. London, 1986, 1933 pp.

Universities: National and Regional

193. *American Universities and Colleges*, 12th ed. Washington, 1983, 2156 pp.

194. Association of Indian Universities. *Universities Handbook, 1985–86.* New Delhi, 1985, 1130 pp.

195. *College Handbook, 1987–88,* 25th ed. New York, 1987, 2014 pp.

196. *Commonwealth Universities Yearbook, 1987.* London, 1987, 4 v 2950 pp.

197. *Directory of Canadian Universities, 1986–1987.* Ottawa, 1986, 402 pp.

198. US, Department of Education, Center for Statistics. *Educational Directory, Colleges and Universities, 1985–86.* Washington, 1986, 259 pp.

Libraries: Universal

199. *World Guide to Libraries*, 7th ed. Munich, 1986, 1203 pp.

Libraries: National and Regional

200. *Adresar Ustrednich Knihoven Siti, Statnich Vedeckych Knihoven, Lidovych Knihoven a Vysokoskolskych Knihoven v CSR.* Prague, 1973, 307 pp.

201. *All India Educational Directory.* Chandigarh, 1972, 1262 pp.

202. *American Library Directory, 1987–88,* 40th ed. New York, 1987, 2 v, 2386 pp.

203. Beirens, Gerard. *Bibliotheekgids van Belgie.* Brussels, 1974, 9 v.

204. *Biblioteki SSSR . . . Spravochnik.* Moscow, 1973–1974, 2 v.

205. *Bibliotheek- en Documentatiegids voor Nederland, Suriname en de Nederlandse Antillen.* Hague, 1966, 442 pp.

206. Brazil, Instituto Nacional do Livro. *Guia das Bibliotecas Brasileiras.* Rio de Janeiro, 1979, 1017 pp.

207. Dayrit, Marina G., et al. *Directory of Libraries in the Philippines.* Quezon City, 1973, 131 pp.

208. France, Direction des Bibliotheques et de la Lecture Publique. *Repertoire des Bibliotheques et Organismes de Documentation.* Paris, 1971, 733 pp.

209. Giuffra, Carlos Alberto. *Guia de Bibliotecas Argentinas.* Buenos Aires, 1967, 334 pp.

210. Italy, Direzione Generale delle Academie e Biblioteche. *Annuario delle Biblioteche Italiane.* Rome, 1969–1981, 5 v.

211. *Jahrbuch der Bibliotheken, Archive und Informationseinrichtungen der Deutschen Demokratischen Republik, 1980/82,* 12th ed. Leipzig, 1984, 385 pp.

212. *Jahrbuch der Deutschen Bibliotheken . . . 1987,* 52nd ed. Wiesbaden, 1987, 642 pp.

213. Kelly, Thomas. *History of Public Libraries in Great Britain, 1845–1975.* London, 1977, 582 pp.

214. Klimowiczowa, Irena, and Ewa Suchodolska. *Informator o Bibliotekach i Osrodkach Informacji Naukowej w Polsce.* Warsaw, 1973, 557 pp.

215. *Libraries, Museums and Art Galleries Year Book, 1978–79.* Cambridge, England, UK, 1981. unp.

216. Mexico, Direccion General de Publicaciones y Bibliotecas. *Directorio de Bibliotecas de la Republica Mexicana.* Mexico, 1979, 2 v 924 pp.

217. Moldoveanu, Valeriu, et al. *Ghidul Bibliotecilor din Romania.* Bucharest, 1970, 475 pp.

218. Pretoria, State Library. *Handbook of Southern African Libraries.* Pretoria, 1970, 939 pp.

Engineering Structures: Buildings

219. Goldberger, Paul. *Skyscraper.* New York, 1981, 180 pp.

220. *Tall Office Buildings in the United States.* Washington, 1985, 114 pp.

221. Yusoff, Norzan, et al. *Tall Buildings of the World.* Bethlehem, Pennsylvania, USA, 1986, 194 pp.

Engineering Structures: Bridges

222. Gies, Joseph. *Bridges and Men.* New York, 1963, 343 pp.

223. Smith, H. Shirley. *World's Great Bridges.* New York, 1964, 250 pp.

224. Virola, Juhani. "World's Greatest Bridges," *Civil Engineering* [New York], v 38, pp 52–55, October 1968.

225. Wittfoht, Hans. *Building Bridges.* Dusseldorf, 1984, 327 pp [a revised English edition of his *Triumph der Spannweiten* (Dusseldorf, 1972, 314 pp)]

Engineering Structures: Tunnels[1]

226. Beaver, Patrick. *History of Tunnels.* London, 1972, 155 pp.

227. Pequignot, C.A. *Tunnels and Tunnelling.* London, 1963, 555 pp.

[1]The 1980 and earlier editions of *Railway Directory & Year Book* (see reference 170) include an authoritative list of the longest railroad tunnels constructed up to the date of publication.

Engineering Structures: Dams

228. International Commission on Large Dams. *World Register of Dams.* Paris, ND, 4 v.
229. *International Water Power & Dam Construction Handbook, 1987.* London, 1987, 126 pp.

Physical Features: Oceans and Seas

230. Fairbridge, Rhodes W., Ed. *Encyclopedia of Oceanography.* New York, 1966, 1021 pp.
231. Groves, Donald G., and Lee M. Hunt. *Ocean World Encyclopedia.* New York, 1980, 443 pp.
232. International Hydrographic Bureau. *Limits of Oceans and Seas* (Special Publication number 23). Monte-Carlo, Monaco, 1953, 35 pp.
233. Menard, H.W., and Stuart M. Smith, "Hypsometry of Ocean Basin Provinces," *Journal of Geophysical Research*, v 71, pp 4305–4325, 15 September 1966.

Physical Features: Islands

234. Huxley, Anthony, Ed. *Standard Encyclopedia of the World's Oceans and Islands.* New York, 1962, 383 pp.
235. US, National Ocean Survey. *America's Islands.* Rockville, Maryland, USA, 1974. 31 pp.

Physical Features: Rivers and Lakes

236. Bue, Conrad D. *Principal Lakes of the United States.* Washington, 1963, 22 pp.
237. Canada, Environment Canada. *Canadian Survey on the Water Balance of Lakes.* Ottawa, 1974, 92 pp.
238. Domanitskiy, A.P., et al. *Reki i Ozera Sovetskogo Soyuza.* Leningrad, 1971, 104 pp.
239. Grande, Jose Carlos P. "O Maior Rio do Mundo," *Boletim Geografico* [Rio de Janeiro], v 13, pp 183–192, March–April 1955.
240. Gresswell, R. Kay, and Anthony Huxley, Ed. *Standard Encyclopedia of the World's Rivers and Lakes.* New York, 1965, 384 pp.
241. Halbfass, Wilhelm. *Seen der Erde.* Gotha, East Germany, 1922, 169 pp.
242. Iseri, Kathleen T., and W.B. Langbein. *Large Rivers of the United States.* Washington, 1974, 10 pp.
243. United Nations Educational, Scientific and Cultural Organization (UNESCO). *Discharge of Selected Rivers of the World.* Paris, 1969–1985, 3 v.
244. Van der Leeden, Frits, compiler. *Water Resources of the World.* Port Washington, New York, USA, 1975, 568 pp.
245. Voskresenskiy, K.P. *Norma i Izmenchivost Godovogo Stoka Rek Sovetskogo Soyuza.* Leningrad, 1962, 546 pp.

Physical Features: Mountains

246. *Alpinistes Celebres.* Paris, 1956, 416 pp.
247. Baumgartner, Albert, et al. *Welt der Gebirge.* Luzern, 1977, 304 pp.
248. Bolinder, Anders, and G.O. Dyhrenfurth. "List of the World's Known Peaks of Over 7,400 Metres (24,280 Feet)," *Mountain World, 1964–1965* [London, 1966], pp 196–199.

249. Burrard, S.G., et al. *Sketch of the Geography and Geology of the Himalaya Mountains and Tibet.* Delhi, 1933, 359 plus 32 pp.

250. Cleare, John. *World Guide to Mountains and Moutaineering.* London, 1979, 208 pp.

251. Echevarria C., Evelio. "Survey of Andean Ascents," *American Alpine Journal,* v 13, pp 155–192, 425–452, 1962–1963.

252. Frison-Roche, Roger. *Montagnes de la Terre.* Paris, 1964, 2 v.

253. International Volcanological Association, Ed. *Catalogue of the Active Volcanoes of the World Including Solfatara Fields.* Naples, 1951–1966, 19 parts.

254. *K Vershinam Sovetskoy Zemli.* Moscow, 1949, 575 pp.

255. Noyce, Wilfrid, and Ian McMorrin. *World Atlas of Mountaineering.* London, 1969, 224 pp.

256. Smithsonian Institution. *Volcanoes of the World.* Stroudsburg, Pennsylvania, USA, 1981, 232 pp.

257. Ziak, Karl. *Mensch und die Berge; eine Weltgeschichte der Alpinismus.* Salzburg, 1981, 350 pp.

Physical Features: Waterfalls

258. Rashleigh, Edward C. *Among the Waterfalls of the World.* London, 1935, 288 pp.

INDEX

The following index lists broad subject headings as well as individual names. Alphabetizing is letter by letter in accordance with the English alphabet, without regard for spaces, punctuation marks, or foreign combination letters. For further explanation, see under "Alphabetization" in the General Explanatory Notes.

All country names given in Tables 1a through 1k, all city names, both conventional and alternate, given in Tables 2a and 2b, and the names of all cultural features given in Tables 5a through 5g are indexed. The comparative tables of Chapters 3 and 4, however, are not indexed in detail unless they contain information about countries or cities not given in Chapters 1 and 2. Tables 4d through 4g *are* indexed in detail because climatic data are not given in Chapter 2.

The same rule holds for the geographic tables and comparisons of Chapters 6 through 11. The basic tables (6a, 7a, 8a, 9a, 10a, and 11a) are indexed by both conventional and alternate names, whereas the supplemental tables (6b, 7b and 7c, and so forth) are indexed in detail only if they contain information not given in the basic tables.

Finally, it should be noted that, in the case of Table 7a, the largest settlement listed for each island is indexed (as a city) as well as the islands themselves.